THE MANAGERIAL MIND
Science and Theory in
Policy Decisions

The Managerial Mind
Science and Theory in
Policy Decisions

CHARLES E. SUMMER
Graduate School of Business Administration
University of Washington

JEREMIAH J. O'CONNELL
Centre d'Etudes Industrielles (C.E.I.)
Geneva, Switzerland

With the Collaboration of **BORIS YAVITZ**
Graduate School of Business, Columbia University

NEWMAN S. PEERY, Jr.
Simon Fraser University
and **CAROL CARLISLE SUMMER**

Third Edition · 1973
RICHARD D. IRWIN, INC. *Homewood, Illinois 60430*
IRWIN-DORSEY INTERNATIONAL *London, England WC2H 9NJ*
IRWIN-DORSEY LIMITED *Georgetown, Ontario L7G 4B3*

Third Edition

First Printing, March 1973

Second Printing, December 1973

Third Printing, June 1974

ISBN 0-256-00512-5
Library of Congress Catalog Card No. 72–86623

Printed in the United States of America

To our parents

Edgar and Emily Summer
Jerry and Mary O'Connell

PREFACE

The third edition of this book incorporates some important changes when compared with previous editions—changes which we believe will make the book more relevant to the careers of managers in the 1970s, as contrasted with earlier times when the first two editions were published.

Specifically, this is the only book, we think, which forces analysis in equal depth of the technical-economic side of management *and* the human side of management. Cases are all written with data on both of these aspects of managerial problems (managerial decisions). The readings represent both viewpoints, so that the student may gain a deeper understanding of what is going on in the case situation.

A second important innovation has to do with identification of six important problem areas which every manager must face, and in connection with which a balance of technology and human behavior must be achieved. These key issues form the themes of Parts I through VI:

The philosophy and attitudes of a managerial decision maker (Part I)

Strategic planning and organization design: What kinds of goals and objectives might balance "things" and "people"? What kind of planning process might achieve such balance? (Part II)

Financial control as it relates to human behavior (Part III)

Rational decision making (management science), utilized by expert staff men, as it relates to human behavior (Part IV)

How leadership action and organization development techniques affect *both* the technical efficiency of a firm *and* the human motivation in a firm (Part V)

The social responsibility dilemma: The responsibility for production (efficiency of technology) balanced against the responsibility for other aspects of "the good society" (Part VI)

A third innovation has to do with the second and last key issues mentioned above. This book takes the position that the social responsibility for production (production of a good or service for society "out there") is an important end in itself. It is on an equal footing with other human values, which are also noble ends in themselves: clean air, equality among men, freedom, relief from poverty, and so on. The manager as a functionary in his organization must give these often-conflicting values consideration, facing the tough dilemmas involved. It will do little good for society, for the manager's own inner competence, or for the firm, if a one-sided view of responsibility is invoked. The manager must not be "all ecology" or "all production."

It may be useful for certain professions in society to specialize in carrying the banner for one or the other viewpoint, but not the manager who plans, organizes and directs the internal parts of a productive organization. Whether he be in a position of leadership in the Chase Manhattan Bank, the Presbyterian Church, the Police Department of Tampa, or General Motors, efficiency of social production must be a major concern. We believe that many management or policy textbooks stress one viewpoint at the expense of the other.

Organizing the book in this fashion, we believe, has two advantages. For the student who takes courses in finance, management science, managerial planning, and the behavioral sciences, each of which takes its own "view of the world" without raising implications (and without revealing unintended consequences of blindly applying one of these), this kind of practice will help integrate these diverse and conflicting disciplines. It will add *relevance* to what one is learning and show how these things relate in the world of practical action.

For the teacher, on the other hand, the new organization of the book makes it easier to focus the course in policy or general management. Rather than take a large number of cases which seem random and lacking in focus, one can easily see, for example, that a particular group of cases shows how the manager must balance technology, economics, and human behavior when engaging in strategic planning, or when using management science techniques, or when trying to reconcile the need for efficient production with other human values such as racial equality or economic justice.

This book is the joint effort of two people, and its concept grew out of certain experiences that we have had in teaching, in studying the social sciences, and in working in business organizations. Some of these experiences are reported in the beginning chapter, in the form of our reflections on, and observations of, situations in which social science and operations research came into contact with the practice of management—in which scholars and applied scholars came into contact with businessmen.

At this point, we shall simply recount some of the specific settings in which these situations took place.

First we owe to the healthy churning and ferment of the doctoral program at Columbia a special debt. We were caught up in a period of change, in which the rigor of economics, plus advanced work in more practical technologies such as finance and management theory, stood in danger (it appeared at times) of being rendered technologically obsolete. There was first the addition of behavioral sciences, particularly sociology and cultural anthropology, later joined by increased emphasis on applied mathematics, in addition to what had already been a rigorous exposure to statistics. At about the same time came emphasis on the humanities and social philosophy in business administration. This confusion, painful at times, has resulted in a healthy balance in the curriculum among all of these things, and the baby (economics and the technical fields) did not get thrown out with the bath water (he is simply being updated).

Secondly, we observed in this process a healthy conflict between people of diverse disciplines which led to many of the conclusions in this book. Underlying much of the curriculum ferment, we noticed that different people, including ourselves, had vastly different ideas about what ought to go into the education of a practicing businessman, and what issues, or areas of research, should be undertaken to advance the state of the . . . (art? science?). We saw mathematicians and economists and management theorists (who have much in common with political scientists) wondering about how important human behavior, studied rigorously, is. We saw people oriented to one type of human organization philosophy wondering about the value of other types, and wondering about whether one philosophy might be more applicable at the firm level while another might be more applicable at the level of the national economic society. We also saw some who felt that practice and case work were more important in terms of both teaching time and research; while others felt that study of fundamental disciplines was more important, in these terms. Perhaps somewhere in between in this latter case, some people felt that study of technologies, usually referred to as the functional fields of business, were more important.

A third factor was our exposure to business institutions and businessmen—our employment experience, in manufacturing firms and consulting firms, as full-time employees and later as part-time consultants. At points in these experiences, we were called upon to utilize behavioral science, economics, mathematics, and the technologies, such as management theory, or capital budgeting, or marketing. The problem of making sense out of company problems, we found, led many times to admiration for theories we had learned; but on the other hand led many times to the full impact of the fact that no theory ever fits any problem in the sense of giving completely accurate predictions, or in indicating action solutions. In some cases, we found either that there were apparently no theories covering certain aspects of problems, or that those theories which gave the impression of being relevant were, in fact, useless in the particulars of the problem, in that specific situation.

A fourth and very valuable experience was working with students. An advanced seminar resulted in major changes in our thinking. For one thing, it started as an attempted application of philosophical theories and basic values to policy problems. Ernest Nagel, for example, addressed himself to the question "What is truth and what does it mean in business decisions?" The following week, students and instructor took policy cases and tried to apply what Nagel had said, in the difficult process of relating it to cases in their buzzing confusion. The late Lyman Bryson addressed himself to "What is beauty and what does it mean in business institutions or policy systems?" The following week produced cases in which these ideas were related to practice. Over the years, this approach was abandoned in favor of more formal or more empirical theories from various disciplines in the social sciences. In the sense that values and ideals *do* get mixed into social science, which Chapter 3 will explain, the initial experience in trying to apply deep, basic, "pure" values influenced us greatly when trying to make sense out of applying social science to cases.

The authors are indebted to the General Electric Advanced Management program for the opportunity to do research with cases and theories, and later to publish two volumes and use these as teaching devices in that school, working with businessmen. In the process of that research, we were groping our way with theories and cases. Lawrence Klein, from the Columbia Law School; Paul Jonas, who has degrees in economics from both Budapest and Columbia; and Samuel Gluck, a philosopher on the faculty of City College, aided in gathering concepts. That procedure went something like this: One of the authors would read the cases and then ask naïve questions of the three specialists. For example, to Klein: "Why do people obey laws (or company policies)?" Or, to Jonas: "Why is this company moving its plant from Chicago to Buffalo?" Or, to Gluck: "Why is this bank president using a committee, and letting the subordinates make this decision?"

The researchers would come back with a series of abstracts of theories and conceptual schemes. We would then try to eliminate bias in the total spread of readings by asking: Is there an important opposing point of view? Can we get an abstract which gives a different answer to the question?

This process was repeated in research in connection with the Columbia curriculum, for which we express appreciation to Dean Courtney C. Brown and Clarence C. Walton, President of Catholic University, for their support, and to the Ford Foundation for its support. This time, we had excellent help from our colleagues. Boris Yavitz gave us help in the field of engineering and operations research. Kirby Warren helped in writing cases, and lent expertise in managerial economics and financial planning. John Hutchinson wrote one of the cases in which a great deal of knowledge of manufacturing and labor relations was necessary. Fred Abrahams, of the Bureau of Applied Social Research, provided suggestions in the field of sociology.

We also acknowledge the contributions of former students in the seminar Science and Philosophy in Policy Decisions for nine of the readings, and help on research for four of the cases in this book. Messrs. Rooks, Beck, Sansone, Steindler, Rosenbaum, Stockbridge, Easton, Turko, Garrity, Worth, Sauer, and Kisch are all now practicing businessmen or teachers from San Francisco to Zurich.

In this edition we are indebted for case materials to two Wharton School colleagues, Richard Swersey and Wayne Howard, and to Messrs. Jerome Schnee, Avrel Mason, E. Gerald Hurst, and Raymond Vernon.

Professor Newman Peery of Simon Fraser University has been of great help in this edition in finding theoretical concepts to apply to the cases, in framing the questions which link theory to practice, and in otherwise using his rare blend of analytical thought and creative insight to make this a better book.

Because so much indication of how this book might be used is given in the individual case introductions, little need be said here about what the individual teacher may want to do in this respect. We do not claim to have been either exhaustive or comprehensive in selecting which theories apply to a given case. In fact, the teacher may want to take other theories, in his experience found useful, which illuminate the fundamental forces at work in any given case situation.

In most instances, the questions included in the case introduction to tie theories to the case situation are, at least in one sense, "nondirective." They ask a practical question, referring to a theory which is useful, but without indicating how a theory would indicate the answer. Thus, instead of asking, "How does the theory of individual motivation explain how people react to forceful leaders?" we ask, "From the viewpoint of motivation theory why is Mr. Johnston saying what he does, and why do you think the branch managers react the way they do?"

One can easily perceive that any teacher or student may see theories, events, or causes of problems that the authors have not included. Far from being a diversion in class or a source of confusion, this would represent a very constructive course of events. So long as the teacher bears in mind that the main goal of the instruction is clear, deep, precise thinking, and practice in relating theory to cases in action decisions —and so long as he makes this known through example in the classroom—he will not be thought of by students as conducting a confused, purposeless, nonsystematic discussion. Why? First, because the world does not come in neat formulas, and the cases are miniature representations of reality. Second, theories and conceptual schemes do not fit together—there is no universal common language or way of predicting the world between economics and psychology. The resulting class discussions will therefore tend to be highly creative and highly motivated, all the while referring to concepts and theories which have meaning to the business school student in terms of his problems in business, and at the same time have more precision and power than cases used without the benefit of theory.

The method we prefer for structuring class discussions is to divide total class time into two parts; to make an arbitrary split between (1) the time devoted to analysis and diagnosis (questions and theoretical readings are labeled that way in the case introductions), and (2) the time devoted to solutions—to managerial and policy questions. For example, if a complex case requires four class meetings, three might be devoted to the first decision-making phase and one to the second phase. While the teacher's manual will give some suggestion of the time that might be allotted to each case, the individual instructor would do well to experiment with time allocations, making his own guess as to how much effort is involved.

A second method for approaching class work is to start first with solutions or policy questions (alternative courses of action), bringing in the analytical and theoretical work as action solutions are proposed. If this plan is used, it requires much more intensive and high quality individual student study *before* class. It also requires some precision on the part of the instructor in listing advantageous and disadvantageous consequences to various alternative solutions, based on the underlying predictions from theoretical readings.

The advantage of this approach lies in the fact that less class time, and fewer numbers of class meetings, are required for rigorous analysis and solution.

As a final point from our teaching experience, we believe that the fact that no case can be solved in a discussion of limited time, with comprehensiveness and clear agreement, should be recognized clearly. The clock runs out on all case discussions, and this has educational value too. In the business world, decisions could be researched and talked about, with enormous amounts of data being gathered, and in the end someone must use judgment at some point of time to stop the decision-making process. Therefore, students and teacher alike may do well to recognize and accept this fact. Policy makers and managers need courage and a willingness to face ambiguity in their decisions, where there is no overall conceptual scheme which gives them certainty and predictability.

Finally, we express our appreciation in this edition to Carol Summer, who handled the large task of cross-referencing the manuscript's cases and readings and performed all the tasks of an editor; to Marie-Claude Pasquier for her valuable assistance in Geneva; and to the Centre d'Etudes Industrielles (C.E.I.) in Geneva for its support of our efforts.

February 1973   C. E. S.
                                                          J. J. O'C.

CONTENTS I
Plan of the Book

**Part I. PHILOSOPHY OF SCIENCE AND
PHILOSOPHY OF GENERAL MANAGEMENT**

CHAPTER 1
Theory and Practice in General Management................................. 3

The Relation between Theory and Policy Decisions. The Managerial Mind, the
Scholarly Mind, and the Applied Scholarly Mind. This Book as a Textbook. This
Book as a Practice Laboratory. This Book as a Research Document. This Book as
the Basis for Further Research. The Problematic Situation. Technology and Central
Planning in Modern Institutions. Complexity and Unintended Consequences.
The Law of Subdisciplinization. Reactions of Executives and Theorists. "Responsibility"
of the Executive. What This Book Will Not Do.

CHAPTER 2
Conceptual Schemes and Science... 21

Concepts and Abstraction. Theory and Conceptual Schemes. Physical Science
and Physical Scientists. Repetitive versus Divergent Phenomena. Operationalism
in Science. The Lesson of Physical Science for Policy Makers.

CHAPTER 3
Social Science and Applied Social Science 35

Theory Formulation in the Social Sciences: An Example from Sociology. Theory
Construction: An Example from Social Psychology. Theory Construction: An
Example from Economics and Industrial Engineering. Ceteris Paribus in Social
Science. Who Has the Final Answer for Policy Determination? Social Science and
Social Philosophy. The Value of Social Science in Policy Decisions.

Notes on the Study of Cases 48

Part II. STRATEGIC PLANNING AND ORGANIZATION DESIGN

Introduction. 49

Why Organization Structure is Important: A Means to Social Goals. Organization Design as a Function and Responsibility of Managers. Some Approaches to Design of Organizations. The "Science" of Organization. The Similarity and Diversity of Specific Company Situations. Strategic Planning as Related to All Management Functions.

Part III. FINANCIAL CONTROL, ORGANIZATION STRUCTURE AND HUMAN BEHAVIOR

Introduction. 251

Allocation of Resources: An Important Social Obligation of Managers. Financial Management as a Technique for Allocating Resources. Financial Information and Human Perception. Optimization of the Whole Company as a Source of Human Conflict. Organization of the Financial Function.

Part IV. DECISION-MAKING, MANAGEMENT SCIENCE, AND HUMAN BEHAVIOR

Introduction. 411

Origins of Management Science. Power and Limitations of Science in Management. The Philosophical Importance of Management Science. Examples of Quantitative Techniques and Managerial Problems. Managerial (Policy) Decision-Making.

Part V. LEADERSHIP AND ORGANIZATION DEVELOPMENT

Leadership as an Important Function of Management. Expedient Obligations and Social Responsibility of Leaders. Concepts and Theories of Human Behavior. Practices and Technologies of Leadership. Technology and Human Behavior: The Manager as a Mediator Between Parts of a Total System.

Part VI. RECONCILING THE RESPONSIBILITY TO PRODUCE WITH OTHER SOCIAL RESPONSIBILITIES

The Social Responsibility Dilemma: Productivity Versus Other Values. Organization Goals as Social Responsibilities. Organizational Strategies as Social Responsibilities. Organization Strategies as Threats to Society. Executive Myopia as Creator of Threatening Strategies. The Need for Reconciling; The Need for Judgment and Wisdom. Who Should Make Decisions That are "Socially Responsible"?

CONTENTS II

CASES RELATED TO DISCIPLINES AND CONCEPTS IN READINGS

Case					
3. Mississippi Valley Equipment Corporation p. 145	Technological expertise and planning Application of science for efficiency Value of quantification and models	Profit maximization The invisible hand Function of the entrepreneur Economies of scale and organization structure Effects of specialization	Necessity for roles and rational planning Sociological concepts of authority Conflict of hierarchy and free communication	Manager attitudes in strategic planning Decentralization Strategy and structure Customary law and codified law	Decisiveness, action, and innovation Informal organization Motivation to chaos or cooperation Competence, central planning Directive leadership Human needs and organization
4. National Bank of San Francisco p. 171	Technical expertise and leadership practice	Principles of specialization Economies of scale and organization structure	Limits to democratic leadership in complex organization Functions of executive in the firm Symbolic influence Sociological concepts of authority Status, role, role conflict	Organization responds to environment Leadership action and profit Conditions for participative management Pluralism as a decision process Origins of government	Executive personality Line/staff behavior Constructive conflict Conversation as a decision process Authority as a psychological phenomenon Organization Development
5. Electronics International Corporation p. 204	Decision theory and competitive bidding Risk management	Cost estimation Sealed bid competition Fixed price bidding Cost plus incentive fee bidding	The organization's needs for action-oriented roles	Unity of command Functional authority Departmentation and coordination Project management Matrix organization De jure versus de facto authority	Personal influence and organization authority Human needs Laws of perception Leadership styles

Case and Page Number	Technology, Engineering and Management Science	Economic Science and Philosophy	Sociology and Social Philosophy	Political Science, Legal Theory, Management Philosophy	Psychology, Social Psychology, Group Dynamics
Part III. FINANCIAL CONTROL, ORGANIZATION STRUCTURE AND HUMAN BEHAVIOR					
6. Norman Manufacturing Company p. 255	Engineering and the philosophy of efficiency Concept of sub-optimization	Economic innovation and the entre-preneur Profit center accounting	Dysfunctions of bureaucracy Benefits of rational planning	Philosophy of de-centralization Conflict and balance of objectives Line/staff conflict Design and use of control standards	Executive motiva-tion and behavior Psychological con-cept of authority Process of per-ception Human response to controls
7. Seaboard Chemical Corporation p. 283	The concept of cash flow Need for central planning Technical compe-tence and organization	Economics and or-ganization struc-ture The law of specialization	Dysfunctions of bureaucracy Authority versus knowledge Formal organization as behavior determinant	Fiduciary relation-ships to stock-holders Line/staff conflict Unity of command Source of manage-ment authority Motivations to civil government Concept of decen-tralization Pluralism	Structural deter-minants of perception Functional deter-minants of perception Theory of individual motivation Constructive conflict Participative management Organization Development

8. Continental Electric Company p. 309	Quantitative measurements and self-control Limitations of the average as a statistical criteria for action Power of mathematics Suboptimization	Profit center accounting Difference in profit and cash flow Cash flow as investment criterion Capital budgeting	Knowledge as power Conflict of specialist and manager Technology as cause for divergence between authority and ability The monocratic model	Results of decentralization Conflict of long- and short-term objectives Conflict of multiple objectives The right versus the ability to decide Conditions for participative leadership	Structural factors in perception Functional factors in perception Group decision making Joint setting of performance standards Motivations for lack of cooperation
9. AB Thorsten (A–C, R) p. 342	Suboptimization Learning curves Organizational determinants of technological change	Cash flow planning Economies of scale and overhead costs Investment criteria and capital budgeting Optimum size plant Balance of payments	Nationalism Multinational corporation	Decentralization pro and con Multiple firm goals Centralization pro and con Ownership and control	Executive motivation Participative management Interpersonal conflict Constructive conflict
10. Sola Chemical Company p. 387	Bounded rationality Suboptimization System size and efficiency	International Monetary System Government controls and corporate financial management	Multinational corporation Ethnocentrism, polycentrism, geocentrism	Functional authority Decentralization Controllership Headquarters/subsidiary relationships Stages of corporate internationalization Information requirements in different roles	Sources of conflict Conflict management Feedback from measurement to behavior identification

Case and Page Number	Technology, Engineering and Management Science	Economic Science and Philosophy	Sociology and Social Philosophy	Political Science, Legal Theory, Management Philosophy	Psychology, Social Psychology, Group Dynamics
Part IV. DECISION-MAKING, MANAGEMENT SCIENCE AND HUMAN BEHAVIOR					
11. Midwest Hardware Manufacturing Company p. 416	Internal generation of funds / Mathematical inventory models / Suboptimization / Balance of forces in technical system / Benefits of science and mathematics	Firm size, specialization, economies of scale / Indivisibility of units / Diminishing returns / Marginal productivity of specialist	Knowledge as power / Limits to participation in decision making / Organization structure and personality / Pressure as stimulus to group formation / Hierarchical differentiation and decision making / Role of the expert	Unity of command / Staff expert and line authority / Controls and performance standards / Central intelligence and efficiency / Democracy and scientific management / Autocratic versus democratic leadership	Response to tension and pressure / Anxiety and social support / Conflicts of interest and dialectical change / Self-confidence and participation / Personality differences of expert and manager / Unstable interaction patterns and stress
12. Lightronics, Inc. p. 448	Probability theory / Subjective and objective probabilities / Decision making rules (risk, uncertainty) / Expected monetary value criterion	Olgopolistic pricing / Premium versus penetration pricing / Market structure and competition / Incremental costs / Sunk costs		Need for consensus on objectives	Psychological limits to rationality / Dynamics of group decisions

Case					
	Quantification and clarification of objectives Decision trees				The attitude of regularity in nature
13. Sea Breeze Motel, Inc. p. 487	Rationality and the control of nature Divergent phenomena Open versus closed systems	Economics of overhead costs	The authority of knowledge The function of ignorance		
14. National Motor Parts p. 500	Quantitative standards for output Money units in engineering decisions Input-output analysis of production Models and quantification: use and limits	Performance standards and profit maximization	The paramount position of production Science and the social order Technical competence and social organization Knowledge as power Indispensability as power Legitimate and hierarchical authority	Organization adjustment to environment Philosophy of central planning Unity of command Necessity for law and order Private property as source of authority Sanction as power	Motivations to obey a rule system Psychological concept of authority Participative leadership
15. Western Office Equipment Company p. 525	Rational design of organizations Rational decision-making Information structure	Power of specialization Marginal revenues as planning devices	Types of conflict Organization Development	Strategic planning Corporate objectives Control systems Participative management Sources of authority	Motivation of staff specialists Suboptimization as human conflict Dependency

Case and Page Number	Technology, Engineering and Management Science	Economic Science and Philosophy	Sociology and Social Philosophy	Political Science, Legal Theory, Management Philosophy	Psychology, Social Psychology, Group Dynamics
Part V. LEADERSHIP AND ORGANIZATION DEVELOPMENT					
16. Lakeland Food Products Company, Inc. p. 576	Marketing science Technological necessity for formal organization	Necessity for specialization and economies of scale	Dilemmas of leadership Large organization and human competence Organization Development	Pluralism in the firm Managerial assumptions Participative management	Human needs Defense mechanism Perception The power motive The affiliative motive Executive motivation
17. Harrogate Asphalt Products, Ltd., (AR) p. 616	Synergy in organization planning		Professional management versus owner managers Role structures Social responsibility of managers Types of conflict	Strategic planning Authority structures Organization Development as management strategy	Executive values as determinants of strategy and structure Organization man Perception as source of conflict
18. Bergen Metalfabrik, A/S p. 655		Innovation as an economic process	Cultural differences and management Organization as a socio/technical system	Headquarters/subsidiary relationships Growth and organization stress	Styles of consultation Role concept Organization Development

			Intervention theory	Link pin organization form Sources of power Executive as mature autocrat	Team building Group dynamic processes Trust Openness Interpersonal communications Creativity as a psychological process
19. Shoe Corporation of Illinois p. 697	Production lot sizes Suboptimization	Market segmentation Pure competition and oligopoly Pricing policies Product strategy	Bureaucratic rigidities Sources of conflict in organizations	Strategic planning Managers as integrators Participation systems	Human needs and motives Responses to leadership
Part VI. RECONCILING THE RESPONSIBILITY TO PRODUCE WITH OTHER SOCIAL RESPONSIBILITIES					
20. Standard Oil Company (New Jersey) p. 739	Cash flow concept: allocation of scarce resources	Corporate philanthropy and profit maximization Social overhead capital	Corporation's role in social progress Corporate philanthropy and academic freedom Pluralism as a social value Legitimacy of power Conflicting claimants on the corporation	Stockholder rights Fiduciary duties of board of directors Inside versus outside directors Principle of subsidiarity Pluralism as a political process	Involvement and objectivity Executive motivation: self-interest versus altruism

Case and Page Number	Technology, Engineering and Management Science	Economic Science and Philosophy	Sociology and Social Philosophy	Political Science, Legal Theory, Management Philosophy	Psychology, Social Psychology, Group Dynamics
21. General Motors Corporation p. 768		Economies of location Cost/benefit analysis Pecuniary versus social costs Externalities Capital budgeting	Profit as governor of economic system Esthetics as social goal Constructive conflict Bargaining and compromise	Multiple goals Conflicting goals Legal responsibilities Pluralism	Executive motivations in strategic planning
22. F.A. Weber Company, Incorporated p. 799		Price system as resource allocation Circular flow of products—funds Money payments as directing mechanism for output decisions and employment decisions The invisible hand Profit maximization	Social needs and the market mechanism	Economic planning by political officials Dangers of central planning	Bias of parts versus whole
23. Polaroid Corporation p. 822		International investment Expansion and market penetration strategies Government/corporate relations	Racial justice Interdependence in a world system Institutional ethics Tactics in social protest	Due process Legitimacy of power Metrocorporate theory Participation	Conflict management

CONTENTS III

Cases and Interrelated Action Problems

*Problems of less emphasis and subsidiary issues.
** Problems of major emphasis or multiple issues of a particular problem classification.

Management of Technical Operations and Work Flow	Personnel Administration, Employee Motivation, and Organization Development	Planning Technological Change, Long-Range Planning, Capital Investment Planning	Executive Motivation, Behavior, Personal Leadership (including Line-Staff Relations)	Designing the Structure of Duties, Standards and Controls	External Relationships: Economic, Legal, Social, National-International
*	*	—	**	**	—
—	—	**	**	**	*
**	**	*	**	**	—
—	**	*	**	**	—
*	—	*	**	**	**
*	*	—	**	**	—
—	*	*	**	**	*
—	*	**	**	**	—
*	**	**	**	*	**
—	—	**	**	**	*
**	*	*	**	**	—
—	—	**	—	—	—
**	—	**	—	*	—
**	*	**	*	**	*
—	*	*	*	*	—
*	**	**	*	—	*
*	**	**	**	*	*
—	—	—	**	*	—
**	**	**	*	**	—
—	—	—	*	—	**
—	—	*	**	—	**
—	—	—	**	—	**
—	—	*	—	—	**

PART I Philosophy of Science and Philosophy of General Management

Chapter 1. THEORY AND PRACTICE IN GENERAL MANAGEMENT

THE RELATION BETWEEN THEORY AND POLICY DECISIONS

It is one of the central theses of this book that *theories* are powerful aids to decision making by general managers in policy systems of today —in large complex institutions of the second half of the 20th century. They are powerful in that they help in diagnosis and identification of managerial (action and policy) problems, in the clarification of goals which managers are attempting to reach, and in the prevention of harmful unintended consequences which managers might overlook without the use of theory. They are powerful, also, because they call attention to a wide variety of forces at work in the managerial system—technological forces, economic forces, sociological forces, political forces, and psychological forces. They prevent the executive from unknowingly making decisions which satisfy one goal while seriously compromising another, and from concentrating on good technological and economic subsystems (within the larger policy system) while doing damage to the human subsystems.[1] Conversely, they prevent him from concentrating on satisfying and harmonious human subsystems while doing damage to efficient technological and economic subsystems.[2] Finally, theories are valuable to the general manager in assembling, organizing, and allocating physical resources in the policy system, and in organizing and influencing the behavior of human beings in that system.

The second central thesis of this book is that theories have serious, sometimes even dangerous, limitations for managers who must make

---

[1] The term "human system," as we use it, refers to any frame of reference which describes or predicts how human beings will act or behave. Thus political science and legal philosophy undertake this kind of explanation as well as sociology, psychology, and small group theory. The term "technological and economic system," as we use it, refers to the sum total of all structures and dynamic events that are of a nonhuman nature. Plants, machines, flow of goods in process, inventories of goods, money inventories, cash flows, accounting systems, formal organization structures, job descriptions, and the like, fall within the meaning of this concept.

[2] This is not meant to imply that technological systems are, or are not, ends in themselves. They satisfy human needs through production of goods and services, through provision of employment, and in some cases through provision of a psychologically secure place to "belong" in a large-scale society.

3

decisions in large complex policy systems of today. Stated in a reciprocal way, *judgment* or *intuition* (often referred to as "art," as opposed to "science" of management) has a powerful place in decision making by general managers.

Any one theory, or any group of theories in a discipline, does not represent reality in the *total* policy system, and may lead the manager to suboptimize, or overemphasize, one part of the system to the exclusion of another. For example, political forces may be overlooked while economic forces are stressed or political forces may be stressed and psychological forces minimized.

It may seem a paradox that theories seemingly have contradictory effects on the decision-making mind at the same time: they prevent unintended consequences on the one hand, but they encourage such consequences on the other. The answer to this, to be more fully explained later, hinges on how theories are used—in the degree of comprehensiveness in their use, in the open-minded entertainment of diverse views, and in the judgmental courage to pick, choose, test, and modify theory in action situations. Another limitation in the use of theories is that they often do not suggest alternatives in terms of things that are operational for the executive—in terms of things he can take hold of and change in the world of action. Though theories may be operational for the scientist in terms of his controlled and measured experiments, practicing managers react to this limitation by calling them "longhair" ideas, "up in the clouds."

A third and final thesis held by the authors is that there is such a concept as "the managerial mind," or "the policy orientation," which bridges the gap between the power of science and theory on the one hand and the limitations of theory in practice on the other. This particular orientation is characterized by—

Managerial or Policy Attitudes and Methodology. These consist of a cluster of attitudes about the nature of policy systems and policy makers, and a philosophy of general management as an endeavor in life, as contrasted with scholarship (science or philosophy) or applied science.

Substantive Theory of Policy Decision and Management. This theory is of two kinds: first, recognition of the major policy issues faced by leaders in policy systems which are enduring through changing times and which are faced by leaders in all types of institutions (government, business, medical, voluntary associations), and at varying levels of hierarchy (divisions, departments, whole industries); and second, selected key disciplines and key concepts within these disciplines which are of high relevance to the major policy issues.

A tentative formulation of the first of these ideas (managerial attitudes and methodology) is presented in Chapters 1 through 3 of this book. Evidence for this concept as well as practice in its application is provided in the cases, the theoretical readings, and the case introductions. Regarding the attitudinal-methodological aspects of the managerial mind, the authors make no claim that the statements on these pages are the last word, or even that the attitudes and methodologies are in final, systematic form. Our only claim is that this is the first time these two attributes have been presented from the viewpoint of the general manager or the policy-making executive, *his problems,* and the *goals of a policy system* instead of from the viewpoint of a scholar, his problems, and the goals of scholarly schemes of thought.

THE MANAGERIAL MIND, THE SCHOLARLY MIND, AND THE APPLIED SCHOLARLY MIND

While the following ideas will be made more explicit throughout the introductory chapters, some notion of what we mean when we say "the managerial mind" or "the policy orientation" is necessary at the very outset.

These terms should not be confused with "the scientific mind" or "the philosophical mind." In briefest terms, the scientist and philosopher are engaged in thought rather than action; in understanding the environment rather than controlling it;[3] in selecting out facts for study which meet *their* problems rather than those which meet someone else's (e.g., the general manager's). They are not as much concerned with the *time* or *costs* involved in their decision-making process. Scientists and philosophers thus share common attributes on the basis of which both can be termed, on a higher level of abstraction, *scholars.*

Neither should the terms "managerial mind" and "policy orientation," as used in this book, be confused with the ideas of "the policy orientation" as used by some authors. A "general manager" or "policy maker" is not the same as a "technologist" or "practitioner." Technologists are people who are interested first and foremost in applying concepts from some particular nonhuman-oriented disciplines (physics, engineering, certain branches of economics such as material-goods-machine structures and dynamics) to the action problems of the world.

"Practitioners," on the other hand, are interested first and foremost in applying a discipline, or group of disciplines, from "human sciences" and "human philosophy" to the action problems of the world.[4]

Applied scholars (technologists and practitioners) share one common attribute with scholars (scientists and philosophers). Their life endeavor gives them a high interest value in one body of knowledge, in some branch of theory, in a limited network of conceptual schemes. Thus they pick and choose problems, pick and choose facts to study, and bring a bias to their final conclusions based upon the knowledge in their area of study.

But technologists and practititoners have another characteristic which distinguishes them from scientists and philosophers and which

---

[3] With the exception of some scholars in moral and ethical philosophy.

[4] For an idea of the orientation of applied social scientists, see Daniel Lerner and Harold D. Lasswell, *The Policy Sciences* (Stanford, Calif.: Stanford University Press, 1951); Warren G. Bennis, Kenneth D. Benne, and Robert Chin, *The Planning of Change* (New York: Holt, Rinehart & Winston, Inc., 1961); and Ronald Lippitt, Jean Watson, and Bruce Westley, *Planned Change* (New York: Harcourt, Brace & Co., 1958). For an excellent example of the clinical method of a practitioner, see Paul R. Lawrence, *The Changing of Organizational Behavior Patterns* (Boston: Harvard University, Graduate School of Business Administration, 1958).

they hold in common with general managers or policy makers—they have an interest in the problems of the world. They have an interest in choosing problems for study and selecting facts for observation which leads them to *prescriptions* for action rather than, as in the case of the scientist, description and understanding of nature.

Finally, technologists and practitioners have one other attribute which separates them from policy system and general managers. The latter begin with (1) the policy system in its totality as it exists in the buzzing confusion of the world—in an "open system," and (2) the goals of the organization. In the sense that policy makers choose problems to study which are relevant to the goals of policy systems, they close their system of thought. But in the sense that they pick and choose facts and theories, regardless from which discipline of scholarship they originate, they deal with an "open system." Technologists and practitioners start first with theories from some discipline or group of disciplines and move in the other direction. They pick problems in the total policy system which can be attacked by their disciplines and look for and deal with facts which can be fitted into theories in their area of study. In this sense, the applied scholars have a primary interest in *some* of the problems of the world. It is in this sense, too, that they deal with a system which is more "open" than the scientist's system but is more "closed" or "biased" than that of the policy maker or general executive.

THIS BOOK AS A TEXTBOOK

This book has four goals. We intend it to serve (1) as a textbook in the traditional meaning of imparting knowledge; (2) as a practice laboratory in the sense of reinforcing this knowledge with meaning and providing the active experience that develops the attitudes and methodologies of the managerial mind; (3) as a research document to show how we arrived at our concept of the managerial mind; and (4) as the basis for research in further clarification of the attitudinal and methodological aspects of the managerial mind, and in beginning the accumulation of the substantive issues and underlying concepts of most relevance to policy makers and general executives.

As a textbook, Chapters 1–3 present fundamental ideas about scholarly theories, about policy making, and about the way in which these two are related in the making of policy decisions by general managers in policy systems.

Chapter 1 presents a preliminary overview of the central relationships between theory and practice of general management, sets forth the authors' beliefs about how managerial knowledge and skill are developed, and describes the symptomatic conflicts in society that have led the authors to study the relationship of theory to policy making.

Chapter 2 presents something of the nature of concepts in general, of scientific theories in the physical sciences, and of the way such theories are generated by the scientist. Inferences are drawn as to the power of science in action problems and its limitations.

Chapter 3 presents the nature of theory in social science and social philosophy, and the way such theory is generated by the minds of social scientists. Inferences are drawn as to the power and limitations of social science in total policy systems.

THIS BOOK AS A PRACTICE LABORATORY

But knowledge, verbalized, written down, and read is not enough in the managerial orientation. It lacks two things. Reading words cannot convey real meaning in terms of being operational to the person who is to use the words. One can read a book on playing baseball, flying an airplane, or driving a car. But until this knowledge is reinforced—until one *understands* the *meaning* of terms by playing, flying, or driving, and attaches an emotional belief to the fact that *it* (the knowledge) *works* —knowledge is not operational in the sense of being able to use it. This is the pragmatic attitude. Meaning, and the pragmatic attitude, must be developed through practice.

A second thing that verbalized knowledge, read by the learner, lacks in being operational (usable) to the man of action, is skill. It is very difficult to jump back and forth from ideas and theory, on the one hand, to action problems and their solution, on the other—from the world of abstract thought to the world of reality in its buzzing confusion. The first time one plays golf it is difficult to apply the rules (words). One may "know the grip" but it "feels unusual"; you "know" the course the swing should follow, but it "doesn't connect." Only after practice, during which knowledge is tempered with intuition, and during which it is incorporated as habit, is the knowledge operational or useful.

Thus, a second goal of the book is the development of reinforced, meaningful, operational knowledge, modified by intuition and judgment, and the development of an ability or skill in applying it. The remainder of the book—cases, case introductions, and theory readings—is devoted to this second goal. In this part, the material is not a "textbook" in the traditional sense. It is not a body of orderly, verbalized ideas put down in printed words. It corresponds more closely to a laboratory in physics and chemistry. You can study concepts like "acceleration," which is measured by "foot-pounds per second per second," but when you repeat an experiment in the physics laboratory which records amounts of acceleration, you not only *understand* more deeply the meaning of the word symbol "acceleration" but you learn something about the rigorous methods required in the practice of science, and develop attitudes regarding the "proper" practice of science and the practice of experiments in the laboratory.

The case introductions help the student to use the theories (readings) in the practice of policy decision making, or synonymously, in the practice of general management. They ask questions which help to bridge the gap between theory and practice. The diagnostic and predictive questions refer the student to aspects of the practical problem which can be understood in terms of underlying theories from different disciplines; the policy questions refer him to action problems and practical solutions.

THIS BOOK AS A RESEARCH DOCUMENT

A third goal of the book is the authors' hope that it will serve as a research document. This has nothing to do with the training or education of general managers. To anyone concerned about how we arrived at the concept of the managerial mind presented in the introductory chapters, or concerned as to whether this concept is valid or true, we say, "Try it yourself; attempt to diagnose policy problems or arrive at action solutions with theories, using our readings and questions, or choices of your own. Then judge the validity of the concept in the introductory chapters."

To those more practical minded who may question the usefulness of theory in action problems, whether in the business world or the case method of instruction in business schools, we say, "Study the introductory chapters, go through the experience of merging theory and practice with the cases, and then judge the validity of managerial orientation."

To those more scientifically or technologically oriented who may question the way in which theory is limited in the practice of general management, or policy making, we say, "There is no conceptual scheme or theory which can be applied directly, and without modification, to decisions regarding total policy systems. If you wish to know how we arrive at this, and other concepts of the managerial mind, take any such schemes and try them in case situations."

THIS BOOK AS THE BASIS FOR FURTHER RESEARCH

The authors believe that the conceptual scheme which is formulated in the introductory chapters is subject to much further research.

Regarding the attitudes and methodology of the policy orientation, we believe that these are set down in a form which is of value to general managers and policy makers working in the complex and rapidly changing world of the mid-twentieth century. They are preliminary, however, in the sense that they are not formulated as precisely, nor organized as systematically, as we hope that they can be in the future.

When it comes to the substantive aspects of the policy orientation, we believe that the cataloging of major policy issues—those issues faced by all policy makers and leaders in policy systems—and the selection of key underlying theories which are of most relevance to these issues is something which can only occur slowly, over many years in the future. We have not even attempted to give *systematic* or comprehensive treatment to these two substantive types of knowledge.

What the book does do is to give a nonsystematic and highly tentative treatment in these ways:

It catalogs five major discipline groups which bear importantly on policy problems. These can be seen as the column headings of Contents II in the form of such classifications as "Technology, Engineering, and

Management Science"; "Economic Science and Philosophy"; "Sociology and Social Philosophy"; "Political Science, Legal Theory, and Management Theory"; and "Psychology, Social Psychology, and Group Dynamics."

It selects important theories and concepts within these disciplines which are of relevance to specific cases and to groups of cases. These can be seen, cross-referenced to both case situations and to major discipline fields, in the squares of the matrix in Contents II. They also can be seen in the diagnostic and predictive questions and the connected theory readings given in each case introduction.

These concepts, for example, range from the concept of "role conflict" (sociology) to that of "pluralism" (political philosophy), to "probability theory" and "expected utility criterion" (technology and management science), or "marginal productivity" (economics) and "functional versus structural factors in perception (social psychology). There are 138 abstracts in the book which include somewhat over 200 conceptual schemes or theories that are related to 23 case situations.

Finally, the very last questions in each case introduction ask the advanced student to do exactly what the authors have done: to analyze cases, picking, choosing, or discarding theories from his own experience, and conceptualizing, independently and creatively, his own idea of major policy issues and the underlying theories of most relevance and importance to these issues.

THE PROBLEMATIC SITUATION

Before any person studies a problem, strains his mind to understand it, and to put it into some meaningful order, he faces something which John Dewey has called a "problematic situation." Particularly before a human being can become interested enough to do research and devote significantly large amounts of work and thought to a subject, there must be something in the environment that is "interesting" him or "bothering" him, and/or some internal desire which prompts him to engage in such work. We suspect that it is both. This is true in the case of all of the authors of all of the theoretical readings reproduced in this book, and it is also true in the case of the authors of this book.

For several reasons, it will be helpful to the reader if we can describe the problematic situation which led to conceptualization of the managerial mind in the introductory chapters, to the compiling of the case introductions, and to the writing of the "connective tissue" between theories and cases. Such an exposition will point up the importance of having a rationale for general managers and policy makers. It will also aid in understanding the underlying reasons for controversy between businessmen and scholars over what place theory occupies in the practice of policy making. Third, an exposition of our problematic situation will help in understanding the underlying reasons for controversy between different scholars in business education as to what is the "best" way to train people for positions of leadership in the world of action.

A fourth reason for describing the situation that interests and bothers the authors, and prompts this book, has some training value to the reader. In doing so, we will be illustrating one of the most significant ideas in the relationship of theory to practice; that is, that every person who develops a theory or conceptual scheme, such as the one we develop regarding the managerial mind, selects his concepts and explains the facts on the basis of his interest in the problematic situation. This is particularly true of those whose interest is in the *social* sciences and *social* philosophy. It is less true in the physical sciences in general, and it is somewhat irrelevant in the matter of astronomy—the mother of physical science. Incidentally, problematic situations do not come in orderly form, or neatly laid out in formulae and clear outlines. They are confused, often interrelated, descriptions of problems, conflicts, and the like. They have something of the "buzzing confusion" of the world even in their verbalized form on the printed page.

We will be describing the problematic situation in symptomatic terms, that is, describing surface problems which we have seen around us, and in our own endeavors. The deeper explanation of these surface problems is to be found in Chapters 2 and 3 which deal with the inherent differences in science, philosophy, applied science, and practice; and in the inherent differences in the attitudes and methodologies of scientists, philosophers, technologists, practitioners, and policy makers.

We can bring some order out of the more chaotic situations we saw and were interested in over the last several years by viewing the problematic situation according to the outline as presented in section headings. The following discussion, including the conclusions we reach about policy systems and policy decision making, is a halfway house between the world of confusion the authors originally faced and the analytical reasons for the confusion which are pointed out in Chapters 2 and 3.

TECHNOLOGY AND CENTRAL PLANNING IN MODERN INSTITUTIONS

Beginning roughly in World War II, and continuing in an accelerated fashion from 1950 to the present time, there has been a great increase in the size of organizations and in their complexity. In that war, the United States marshalled a military establishment of over twelve million men, and the technological machines and dynamic logistic movements to fight a war on a scale never before undertaken. This was supported by an industrial organization with a degree of central planning which represented greater control of the economic sector of our nation than had ever been experienced before. The planning, the allocation of inputs and outputs of the firms of the nation, and the regulation of consumer demand resulted in an *efficient* flow of goods to the civilian sector and the military sector and in the chain of production from industry to industry. In other words, the timing of flows, the quality of flows (e.g., steel, sugar, gasoline, etc.), and the quantity of flows (how many pounds of sugar, how many tons of iron ore, how much steel, how many tanks of gasoline) were synchronized in such a way that the final output—the quantity of civilian consumption and external output of national defense—was accomplished in a quick enough time to win a war against another formidable opponent.

In this instance, the United States engaged in a form of central planning for the goal of technology efficiency, in contradiction to another goal of our culture, freedom of individual firms. If we should have another war, the input-output analysis which will be carried out in Washington with planning formulae, plus the hardware to process data (electronic computers), will dwarf any planning that we have heretofore witnessed. The economic society will be *managed* because that is the way to technological efficiency—achieving output of defense effort in a limited time— at least in the short run.

Whether or not such planning in detail results in greater technological and economic efficiency *in the long run* is a question open to debate. Political and economic philosophy in the Western world holds that in the long run loss of initiative and creativity under such planning will mean that it is less efficient. The invisible hand, whereby what is good for an independent firm pursuing its selfish interest is good for the gross national product *and* for the freedom of individuals, will eventually render inefficient such an industrial society, according to this economic science and economic philosophy. The industrial system of the Soviet Union might, in one respect, be viewed as a massive experiment in which there is rational planning of technology which is based on clearly defined national goals and planned in terms of subgoals for industrial segments down to the individual firm. Officials in that society suppose that a higher level of national technological efficiency will be reached, not through the invisible hand but through the highly visible hand of the planners in the central planning body (Gosplan), the area councils, industry councils, and the plant hierarchy—all aided by new devices for information processing and communication.

We see an attempt to raise the level of technological efficiency in western European countries such as France through industry-government cooperation in allocating materials, manpower, and outputs of various segments of the economy as they become inputs to other segments in the dynamic flows of goods. We even see many examples in the United States which attempt to regulate technological activities. These central plans—decisions—take many forms. The report of the President's Commission on the National Goals is an attempt to think through and put down in rational form a set of balanced goals—both technological and human goals—in the hope that decisions made by semiautonomous executives in suborganizations in society will be more nearly coordinated. Many of the growing number of governmental laws and regulations relative to industrial organizations are attempts to influence the flow of goods, the movement of workers, the wages of labor, the income of corporations, or similar matters. They tend toward central planning in the case of the freedom allowed to merge corporations into horizontally or vertically integrated companies, or the formal approval by such bodies as the Federal Reserve Board and the Interstate Commerce Commission to merge banks, railroads, and airlines. In other instances, they move toward central planning at the government level, but against central planning at the corporate level—trustbusting larger units which result in divesting of certain operations.

Between units in our semifree technological society, we see evidence of increasing complexity and of increasing degrees of central planning. All government contracts, for example, specify that prime contractors use Program Evaluation and Review Technique (PERT) to link together sometimes as many as a thousand separate contracting companies into a flow diagram of jobs to be accomplished (subobjectives), the time of completion of each job, the time it takes to do the job, and the quality and quantity of resources needed for each job. Each separate firm then takes its part in the overall plan and breaks this down into more detailed PERT diagrams within divisions, departments, sections, and down to individual production lines. The resulting complex total plan may contain hundreds of thousands of technological events, specifying the quantity, quality, and timing of inputs and outputs.

At the individual firm level, central planning is not new. Traditionally, the internal operation of an individual firm has not been viewed as a social democracy by practical men or by scholars, even in the United States. The free enterprise economists, stressing autonomy and freedom, were addressing themselves to freedom of the owners and managers of firms, not freedom of employees to elect their bosses, determine production runs, and the like. In fact, the economist's value of freedom disappeared in the micro or firm side of the analysis (as contrasted with the macro or social level). The executive was viewed as an expert rational planner who allocated resources and planned production runs, acting as a rational computer of supply, demand, marginal costs, marginal revenues, and then gave orders to execute these centrally and expertly reasoned decisions.

In more recent years, the traditional view of the firm has been challenged by several forces, each explained by readings in this volume. Behavioral scientists have suggested that the firm *ought* to be viewed as a social system where workers *do* determine production runs. Labor unions have worked out customs whereby pluralistic decision making, jointly practiced by labor and management, *are* a fact of reality. Some businessmen stress decentralization as a political alternative to central planning.

In spite of these views, with the advent of more and more technological specialists, the United States in the second half of the 20th century has witnessed acceleration of the trend to central planning *inside* corporations. The crude functional planners in Frederick Taylor's steel mill have been supplanted by operations researchers, market researchers, applied psychologists, computer programmers, organization analysts, research and development administrators, labor experts, or executive compensation specialists; or, and this is the epitome of rational planning, people who are given the full-time job of long-range planning at divisional levels or company levels.

To cope with the enormous complexity of operations, there is a distinct trend toward the establishment of specialists whose full-time day is spent in long-range planning, in drawing up the *substance* of plans, utilizing expertise and skill in the *methodology* of such planning.[5]

Each of these specializations, resulting in the establishment of a staff department at some organizational level, at the top or in the middle echelons of a company represents a trend toward central planning at that level. The movement toward decentralization in American companies has not stopped the trend toward central planning, in our opinion, for more than one reason. First, the march toward more and more specialization is not stopped. The specialists are lodged in another echelon of the organization which itself becomes a centrally planned unit and is by the act of decentralization enabled to grow much larger in terms of size and complexity. Second, we have observed a move to re-centralization in many of the large companies which had previously moved to decentralization. These companies apparently judge that the gradual addition of new staff departments at the top level of the company is a technological necessity.[6]

Underlying all of these tendencies toward centralization—whether at the level of national society, or at the level of interindustry groups, or at the level of internal firm operations—are several powerful factors. The increasing size, complexity, and interdependence of subparts of policy systems, facilitated by developments in science, technology, and rapid communication devices which represent part of the scientific explosion since World War II, is probably the most important factor.

The necessity for rapid change of the whole complex structures in the face of outside forces (political forces such as the U.S.S.R. and technological forces such as scientific discovery) is another important cause for the trend to centralization. It implies speed of change, which in turn implies the use of authority or power. Evidence of this cause is the willingness of the United States to plan and manage the economy through political power in Washington, when the goal of technological efficiency in national defense superseded the ideology of freedom.

A third cause, interconnected with the other two, is the rigidity and difficulty of quick change in large bureaucratic and technologically rigid structures. In the American Telephone and Telegraph Company, for example, the process of changing from the letter exchange code dialing system to an all-number code involved changing literally hundreds of thousands of pieces of technological equipment, as well as in changing the behavior and habits of thousands of people inside the company and outside (customers). This particular process of change in a technological-social pattern is now in its fourteenth year, and will be completed only after the elapse of still more time.

These trends, and the factors which produce them, are in evidence in many of the cases in this book. In the Electronics International Corporation case of government-business relations in defense contracting we see the incredibly complex exigencies of national defense prompt central-

---

[5] See Charles E. Summer, "The Future Role of the Corporate Planner," *California Management Review,* Winter 1961.

[6] *Idem.*

ized plans and decisions which may run counter to the logic of technical specialists, political experts, or military strategists.

The National Bank of San Francisco moves toward central staff planning as contrasted with planning in its branches. Sola Chemical Corporation and AB Thorsten find that central planning of a financial nature is imperative as they move to worldwide operations. Norman Manufacturing, Harrogate Asphalt, and Mississippi Valley Equipment Corporation in fact develop more central planning as a technological necessity when two corporations are merged. Continental Electric and Western Office Equipment Corporation find that powerful discoveries in finance (applied economics) and management science (applied mathematics), implemented through central staff departments, are, in the judgment of their managements, necessary changes to be made in company organization structure.

Virtually every case in the book dealing with internal operations of a company illustrates the same tendencies toward central planning, caused by technological and economic forces, and the dilemma of such planning, presented by psychological, sociological, and ideological forces. The problem exists at top company levels (e.g., in the Continental Electric Company problem of centralization-decentralization). It exists at middle management levels (e.g., in the Kansas City branch of the Mississippi Valley Equipment Corporation). And it exists at the lowest levels (e.g., the small group of sales managers in Lakeland Food Products Company).

In summary, there are powerful forces of technology and economics which result in a tendency to central planning in our society. These forces are in part created, and accentuated, by increasing size and complexity of our sociotechnological institutions. They seem to operate at the national social level (one policy system) as well as at suborganizational levels within that larger system: at the level of industries, at the level of firms, at intermediate middle-level departments, and at the lowest, small work group, level. Given such a tendency, and given the increasing availability of science and theory to understand and cope with (make policy decisions for) our complex environment, the authors began to wonder about the extent to which science and theory really are useful in policy decisions, the extent to which their use is limited or dangerous, and about some of the things general managers ought to know regarding *how* to use them. The latter, we thought, would result in some approximation to a methodology for decision making by general executives in complex policy systems.

COMPLEXITY AND UNINTENDED CONSEQUENCES

Faced with increasing complexity in the form of different specializations, with concentration-interdependence whereby everything in social dynamics and the technological dynamics seems to depend partly on everything else, with increasing size of institutions, and with an apparent tendency to central planning in practice, the authors reasoned to other points. The central planning is done by general managers who legitimize or approve recommendations and information contributions of many specialists in and outside the company. These plans, or policy decisions, are themselves becoming more complex. Unless the manager[7] has some acquaintance with the vast array of forces at work in the policy system, which theories can provide, plus some attitudes about or skill in the difficult task of *applying* these theories (jumping back and forth from theory to practice), it is likely that he will face unintended consequences after the decision is made.

The theory of unanticipated consequences arose in the behavioral sciences. It implies that the executive who looks only (or more closely) at technological, political, and economic goals of his organization is likely to find that there are some human forces at work which he overlooked and which have consequences such that his original goals are, in effect, not reached. They may be sabotaged, for example, by a hostile group or a labor union. Decisions made and passed on may cause human beings to do something that the executive wants, but also to do something that he doesn't want. In many of the cases in this book this will be seen to be true—in the operating affairs inside a company or in the governing of the affairs in a nation.

There is, however, another side to the theory of unanticipated consequences which has received little attention and which bothered the authors. As we studied the theories of the behavioral sciences and then tried to relate them to case situations and to our experience in the business world, we found that many of the things which behavioral scientists imply strongly to executives, *in themselves* would result in unanticipated and (to the executive) harmful consequences in terms of the executive's economic and technological goals. Any one conceptual scheme from social psychology, it seemed (including, for example, democratic leadership as implied executive behavior), might have serious unanticipated technological or economic consequences for the survival and growth of the organization, depending on the individual departmental, company, or national situation. It also seemed from our study of theories of small group dynamics or from our actual participation in training groups that the technological or economic variables (e.g., time) were ignored. Furthermore, various aspects of technological and economic efficiency may be adversely affected to a serious degree if one attempted to operate on such theories in large complex organizations. In this sense, the behavioral scientist is as apt to be a victim of unanticipated consequences as is the executive, the engineer, or the economist.

THE LAW OF SUBDISCIPLINIZATION

When writing articles or books for the businessman market, it is highly probable that technologists and social scientists will imply cer-

---

[7] This book is addressed to general managers who perform decision functions. Some may be heavily involved in gathering facts and reasoning; some may be involved only in putting the stamp of approval on decisions made by teamwork of a number of specialists. In either of these two cases, our conclusion is the same. This book is also addressed to a third kind of manager—the specialist who forms part of the influential leadership group. In short, at any given organizational level, there is a group of decision makers (the relatively few) whose mental efforts influence the relatively many. Political science has referred to such a system as an oligarchy. Sociology refers to the smaller group as the influentials or simply as the leaders. Management theory refers to them as executives or managers.

tain courses of action which should be taken in view of the types of more basic phenomena they study. The psychologist will imply that, though there are other important factors, human needs and motivations are most important, and therefore that such alternative decisions as participative leadership or job enlargement are the things that any intelligent businessman will seek. The political theorist will imply that, though there are other factors involved, law and order, based on what the "reasonable man" will see, obviously means that the intelligent businessman will seek a workable authority delegation system. The operations researcher, while including other important factors as assumptions or constraints on his model, gives the impression that the intelligent businessman will optimize the technological flows in his plant location or inventory system, "if other factors don't prevent this."

This kind of impression, conveyed by so-called "pure" scientists, and to a lesser but nevertheless important extent by technologists in the physical realm and practitioners in the social realm, is a phenomenon that can be called "subdisciplinization." These individuals need not necessarily become company employees, or do consulting work, or even leave the university, though each of these degrees of involvement determines how conscious and explicit they will be about the "other things" in a policy decision-making situation. In the social sciences, where values are more likely to enter scientific theory and where social science frequently merges into social philosophy, scholars frequently develop highly complex and "factual" theories, where subdisciplinization is likely to be hidden in assumptions. This will be more clearly understood and illustrated in Chapter 3.

We are not saying that this is right or wrong, good or bad. It simply exists. It is a natural thing for people who become highly interested in one view of part of the world to exaggerate the influence of this view in the total scheme of things. Read, for example, the introductions to books explaining such divergent theories as those dealing with human groups, industrial dynamics and cybernetics, capital budgeting, or management principles.

This is simply one of the outcomes of the phenomena of specialization. It is more particular than the generic term "trained incapacity" in that we are relating it to (1) the failure of scholars to be fully aware of, or clearly explicit about, the unintended consequences if executives follow their implications; and (2) those specialists in science, technology, or practice who imply to the leadership group in companies, either explicitly or implicitly, that one set of forces in the company is so important that the executive's time, attention, or analytical power should be devoted to these in great detail, in making decisions, where time is scarce in making *the decision.*

REACTIONS OF EXECUTIVES AND THEORISTS

Another factor in the problematic situation which seemed important was the feelings of two parties who, by all counts, should work together a great deal for the mutual benefit of both. Executives, both in our work contacts with them and in the Columbia Executive Program at Arden

House, express feelings ranging from admiration for the application of science, to suspicion of the actual results, to a feeling of threat that the "buzz boys will take over." We see this too, for example, in feelings of company executives toward some business school graduates when they enter employment; or, when we read in the newspapers that officials in the Defense Department have these same feelings about the greatly accelerated rate with which planners, systems men, and a wide variety of specialists, using techniques of powerful analysis, are being given decision-making responsibility.

On the other side of the fence, it is not uncommon to find people from various disciplines in science—technologists who engineer physical science or practitioners who apply social science—who are ambiguous in their feelings toward policy systems and executives who manage them. These range from the feeling that, somehow, executives can't understand the truth and importance attached to their theories, to a feeling of admiration for an executive who has the personality and physical stamina to make complex and definite decisions in the face of ambiguity. As above, there is sometimes the feeling that "uninformed people will take over" (the reverse of the feeling that buzz boys will take over).

In both cases, there is the implicit threat to the individual that the other person has something which will depreciate the life work and product of his endeavors. Consciously or unconsciously, the specialist in theory knows that there is no policy system, no real world problem or situation, in which a given theory will work. To that extent, a policy decision is threatening. Consciously or unconsciously, the executive knows that there are many things in the complex problem he faces that he may not see or understand, and that the theories may point up something that he is not knowledgeable about. To this extent, a conceptual scheme is threatening.

It has become a cliché to say that much of science has grown out of technology, and that it is in trying to solve the problems of the world that some of our most important discoveries (theories) are made, and further, that scholars can therefore reap benefit by studying policy problems and communicating with policy makers. It is also a cliché to say that many of our machines and social systems of today could never have been constructed if some scholar had not generated some theory which allowed such structures. The power of science in controlling nature, as well as the power of ideas in shaping nations and companies, is great.

We conclude that, in view of the need for interchange between ideas and people, and in view of the feelings on both sides which inhibit interchange, something might be done to adjust the latter. Thus, (1) in Chapters 1–3, we put into words some of the causes of such feelings, and (2) in the remainder of the book, we provide practice in the difficult task of using theory in the light of both its advantages and disadvantages.

"RESPONSIBILITY" OF THE EXECUTIVE

In recent years, there has been much talk to the effect that business executives either *do, don't, or should* have something which is loosely referred to as "responsibility." Many writers have addressed themselves to the thesis that executives today are responsible, while many have argued that they are not. Others have tried explicitly to say what this responsibility is: some say business executives are (should be) responsible for profits, and that everything else will fall in line; still others have expressed they are not (should not be) responsible for profits, in the absolute sense, but that they are responsible for the production of other values in society. One group holds that the philosophy of equilibrium (the invisible hand) does not work in today's complex society, nor does the philosophy of human-technological integration work inside a company. To this group, what's good for the nation is not necessarily good for General Motors (and vice versa); what's good for the company is not necessarily good for a department or subgroup (and vice versa); and what's good for the group is not necessarily what's good for the individual person (and vice versa).

Finally, another group of writers have attempted to say what the businessman owes to different groups, implying a balance or compromise between the stockholders, department heads, individual employees, suppliers, customers, and so on.

The readings in this book, we believe, are balanced in terms of presenting various points of view on this subject. In this sense, one can examine the meaning of various conceptual schemes, from the "scientific" analysis of equilibrium economics and psychology to the "philosophical" conceptual schemes of political philosophy.

Confronted with this great interest in current society on the subject of "responsibility," we wondered why the interest developed, why there should be so much talk about it. We concluded that it is partly due to the increasing size and complexity of policy systems. In smaller systems, with few human beings, and with less complex machines, the problem of balancing the needs for technological efficiency and the needs of human subparts or organizations was less formidable. Not only could the leaders in small organizations see what was going on and have time, through personal observation of facts and communication with people, to make decisions or react with enlightened wisdom, but the organizations themselves were more flexible. The lesser rigidity of technological and social systems, due to size, enabled the "long run" to be a relatively short period of time. In this way, the theories of equilibrium tended to work in practice: what was good for any part of the organization did, through the process of correction by common sense, human feeling, and wisdom, correspond roughly to the good of the whole organization, and vice versa.

In our own value system, we believe that a human being will more nearly "be responsible"—acting on his own moral and ethical values, in accordance with those values developed by his culture—if he can "be informed." He will see what is going on in the system, both in terms of human needs and in terms of the technological constructs in society, if he can comprehend what is happening. He will act responsibly if he can predict what effects his policy decisions will have "out there in the world," on other people, other groups, and on the technological systems which societies have set up in the world as institutions for the service of man.

Here is where the power of theory and conceptual schemes comes into the more value-laden *feeling* of responsibility which lies within the individual executive. We shall see that theories are the result of scholars exerting enormous amounts of time, human effort, and creativity in order to see the fundamental forces operating in nature which are not seen by other people who do not have the time, the effort, or the interest in that *particular* phenomenon. Furthermore, the theories do something which is vital in a world as enormously complex as our world is today. They produce *abstractions,* in that they simplify and reduce the world to manageable ideas which the human mind can handle. They report on *regularities,* or patterns of events over time, so that much decision-making time is saved by not dealing with masses of events and detail. In a particular sense, then, one who can apply theories to policy decisions is more informed, and therefore more responsible, in a world of increasing complexity: (1) he utilizes the distilled experience from other brains, and (2) he receives this in a form which comprehends the complexity in generalized bundles—in concepts and abstraction, and in predictable regularity. These ideas will be developed more explicitly in the following chapters.

There is another side of responsibility which must be emphasized with equal weight in comparison with our first value of keeping informed. "Informed," as used above, implies the study of, and an ability to apply, the rational conceptual schemes developed by the minds (logic) and experiments (experiences) of the social sciences, industrial engineering, and operations research. In addition, we believe that there are two other responsiblities which fall on the executive of today. One has to do with reasonableness and rationality in that part of the policy system that cannot be reduced to regularity and prediction. Working with the cases in this book, or in actual policy problems, one sees constantly that *irregularity,* or what in the next chapter Langmuir calls "divergent phenomena," is a matter which the executive must face with courage, and with a willingness to attack ambiguous problems. He must be willing to think deeply about these problems, put subjective weights on alternative solutions, and otherwise cope with the factors in a problem that cannot be put precisely into words or reduced to quantitative measurement. A second interconnected responsibility of the businessman is to deal with the fact in policy problems that rationality is not the only cause of human behavior. Feelings, sentiments, and nonrational responses are part of the executive's own behavior, as well as that of those around him (including the behavior of theorists, logicians, specialists of various kinds, and scientists). We believe that an understanding of the limitations of science and theory, and a deeper understanding which is associated with practice in relating these to policy problems, particularly in group discussion, generates these two kinds of responsibilities.

What about the more substantive attitudes of morality represented by religious and moral philosophies? So far, we have taken a position of intellectual morality about the way the executive should use his mind in the solution of problems. In regard to the former, the authors have their own convictions regarding individual human morality and regarding the kind of social structures which man creates that in turn can be judged as good or bad. However, we have not dealt with these value positions in any way except, perhaps, that they influence to some degree the selection of theoretical readings and the values of the theorists who developed the theories. We doubt that preaching a philosophy, at least in the brief pages of this book, can have any real impact on the behavior of most readers. In this belief we have been influenced by the seemingly lifeless (in terms of changing anyone's behavior, as opposed to talking) nature of speeches which say that management has a responsibility to the community, to stockholders, to employees, and the like. What the cases in this book do, in many instances, is to show precisely this problem: that people often verbalize noble ideals, but their actions tell a different story. For example, insofar as there is a discrepancy between one's *ideas* about democracy and anyone's *actions* which jeopardize democratic institutions, case practice brings to a conscious level the problem and helps one to clarify just what one's ideals are.

WHAT THIS BOOK WILL NOT DO

As a final note to this first chapter, we need to be clear about certain limitations to the present book. The attempted merger of theory and practice involves certain costs.

First, we do not believe that study of the abstracts of theoretical readings, even though in the author's original words, is a substitute for studying more deeply and comprehensively the theories of social science and technology. The study in depth of economics, operations research, finanical accounting, psychology, organization theory, and many other areas of inquiry, is a valuable thing in the world of today. Abstracts frequently cannot give the total context, or complete understanding, of the author's conceptual scheme. This does not mean, we hasten to say, that such abstracts, and practice in using them, is not valuable. One cannot be a philosopher king, nor can he or should he know everything about everything. On the other hand, it is intended that the student draw on his entire educational experience, which hopefully has been developed in considerably more power and detail than is presented in the readings in this book. Certain of the questions in case introductions are phrased to encourage this.

A second price we pay is the fact that study of theories does, in one sense, stifle the creativity and initiative of the problem solver. Just as the advocates of John Dewey's progressive education argue that injection of too much arithmetic and too little playing with clay in the first grade inhibits the growth of children, certain advocates of the pure nondirective case method have argued that injection of theories in case problems interferes with a learner's hard drive, tough thinking, and creative analysis and solution of problems. That there is truth in this viewpoint cannot be denied. Perhaps in answer we can say only what we have already said in regard to the complexity of modern institutions, and add the comment that this is the age of Sputnik and the Soviet Union, not the age of the power loom and Victorian England.

Chapter 2. CONCEPTUAL SCHEMES AND SCIENCE

In this chapter we will examine the nature of concepts, of scientific conceptual schemes or theories, and something of the nature of how these are generated by the minds of scientists. By doing this, we set the stage for understanding their power as an aid to men of action—policy makers and general executives—and for understanding their limitations in the control of policy systems.

CONCEPTS AND ABSTRACTION

A concept is an invention of the mind, a product of the imagination, which enables human beings to make sense out of the world about them. Around us at all times, in our environment, are thousands of objects and dynamic events which give stimulus to the sense organs—eyes, ears, nose, touch—in profusion. After infancy, the human being would be helpless to cope with these unless he has some means of cataloging them into terms that have meaning in dealing with day-to-day problems.

Some of these are cataloged as "good" or "bad," as to whether they satisfy or penalize a person's basic desires. These are normative or value concepts, and we label them "attitudes" or "values." Others are relatively neutral in emotional value; they simply *are*. These are descriptive concepts.

As I sit in my office, I see an object with four legs, two arms, and an upright back and I catalogue this as a "chair." The semantic symbol "chair" does not need to be spoken, since I cannot think without conceptualizing and without the power of word symbols. Somewhere along the line in our cultural development, the symbol "chair" was *conceptualized* to denote the particular constellation of characteristics of legs, back, and arms. The process which the human mind uses to conceptualize the enormous complexity of the world into ideas is known as the process of abstraction.

But the chair in my office is really a particular object—it is not exactly like any other chair in the world. It may have a solid back or a cane back. It may have a round seat or square seat. It may have round legs or square legs, or it may even have a big scratch on the back whereas the chair

21

across the hall is new and unblemished. These are particular character-istics, rather than general characteristics, similar to what scientists refer to as divergent phenomena. The point to be made here is that, in the process of abstraction, we select certain abstract characteristics, di-vorced from the total reality of hard cold facts in the world. Only in this way can we make sense out of the buzzing confusion around us. Thus, legs plus arms plus back equals chair—three abstract characteristics are cataloged into a larger concept or idea. The pigeon-hole system in the mind eliminates irrelevant details if we simply want something to sit upon and do not want other attributes. Notice that the concepts we select for thinking depend on what our problem is.

This process of abstraction can proceed to higher and higher levels of abstract concepts. I have another concept in my mind labeled "table," another labeled "bookcase," another labeled "file cabinet." If my purpose is to construct a new "building" for the business school, I know that one of the things I will have to direct my attention to is "furniture," a concept which abstracts on another characteristic or dimension. This concept eliminates, for purposes of this specific decision, the difference between divergent furniture objects (bookcases don't have arms) because the myr-iad of details are not relevant to certain decisions, and because one would literally go crazy if every detail in the environment were to be enter-tained in the mind in every thought or decision.

When we face problems of achieving our goals and subgoals in life, of building buildings, going to work in public transportation, furnishing houses, managing business corporations, deciding on what to have for dinner, getting tired of standing upright, we pick and choose concepts which are useful in understanding the world (analysis), in predicting what will happen "out there" (prediction), and what we might do to get what we want (control). Concepts are therefore powerful mechanisms for thought and action.

Value (attitudinal) abstraction is even more powerful to us in these three respects. We learn that "fire" is "bad" for sticking hands in, but "good" for cooking. We do not have to make decisions over and over about what to do around, or with, fire because we have built-in policies (values and attitudes) in the mind which enable us to react (1) in quick time, and (2) without cluttering our minds with new decisions and facts every time we face similar situations.

Finally, concepts have one other very powerful use to society and to individuals. Semantic symbols or concepts not only aid the individual person to think, predict, and in some measure control things around him; they also enable one human being to pass on *experience, learned* from prior actions, to other human beings. You may have never been bitten by a "snake," but somewhere along the line someone either told you what a snake is (described it in terms of abstract characteristics such as "long" and "round"), pointed one out to you, or showed you a picture. They then gave you a predictive statement: snakes bite; their bites cause sickness or death.

In the conceptual or semantic sense, then, concepts enable cultures to develop. They enable people to control others' behavior; they enable one person to learn and get help from the distilled experience of someone else.

Value (attitudinal) concepts, in fact, are one of the primary ways in which societies control the behavior of divergent individuals and groups. In certain societies, for example, alcoholic beverages are "bad," and this is conveyed through families to children. This is a form of "conscience control." Social pressures, and social penalties, or even the formal codification of value concepts into prohibition laws, are added means of control. But even these could not exist without the existence of concepts and the power of abstraction.

THEORY AND CONCEPTUAL SCHEMES

So far, we have used the term "concept" to denote any meaningful idea which exists in the mind and which *partially* (in the sense of selecting certain abstract characteristics) describes reality—what is "out there" in the world.

A theory is a form of conceptualization in that it (1) is more precise than the garden variety of ideas generated by common sense, (2) it was arrived at by a process of thought which is more rigorous than common sense and day-to-day action, and (3) it therefore is more likely to describe what is reality and what will happen "out there."

Let us look for a moment at the second of these. For our purposes, theories can be classified in two ways, depending on (*a*) whether they were developed for the purpose of understanding nature versus controlling nature, or (*b*) whether they were arrived at with the aid of observation or experiment[1] or with the aid of logic and reason alone. The first of these dimensions separates scientific and philosophical theories on the one hand from technological theories on the other. The second dimension separates scientific theories from philosophical theories.

PHYSICAL SCIENCE AND PHYSICAL SCIENTISTS

Scientific theory is one form of conceptualization which is aimed primarily at understanding the operation of nature, not in controlling nature. This has very important implications for policy makers because many of the ideas generated by scientists either seemingly are beyond the control of the policy maker at the time of his decision, or because they actually are beyond his control (regardless of timing), or because they are irrelevant to his problems and goals.

Additionally, scientific theories are arrived at in a very special way: through observation (or experiment), by the imagination of a hypothesis which explains why things happen, and then by a testing of that hypothesis.

In the science of astronomy, many years of patient observation of

---

[1] The phrase "with the aid of" is very important. Later discussion will show that in many scientific theories, particularly in the social sciences, the theories are not generated *by* observation and experiment alone. The scientist's values, needs, and subjective preconditioning leads him to "speculate" or to "imagine" an hypothesis, the hypothesis being a concept which exists in the mind, not solely in the facts.

"planets" (note that someone distinguished these from "stars") enabled astronomers to speculate that a planet's orbit was determined by several forces, one of which is the "gravitational force" of other planets (in addition to the gravitational force of the sun). Another factor is the size and mass of both the planet under study and the size and mass of the other heavenly bodies within the field of influence or force of the planet under study.

The following record of the observations and hypotheses that led to the discovery of Neptune serves as an example to show (1) how the scientist, with great concentration of time and effort, is able to come up with understandings of nature which laymen could not attain through common sense; (2) how *measurement* enables the scientist to prove the truth of his hypotheses; and (3) how great amounts of creative imagination, as well as brute facts and observations, are involved in the development of a theory.[2]

> 1820   *The first attempt to chart and predict the motions of the three outer planets (Uranus, Saturn, Jupiter) was developed by the French mathematician Laplace in the* Mechanique Celeste. *This theory, based on the mutual perturbations of these planets, was used by Bovard of Paris to construct highly accurate tables of their past and predicted future positions. Jupiter and Saturn moved very satisfactorily according to prediction, but the observations of Uranus showed it to move well outside the tolerable limits of error of the predictions. The outstanding difference noted between the prediction and the observation was one minute of arc (one minute equals one sixtieth of a degree which equals about one one-hundred-eightieth of the sky).*
>
> *In the light of these circumstances, mathematicians and astronomers of the time approached the problem in two different ways. First they tried to make a generality of all observations of Uranus and thus render the tables of prediction clearly erroneous. Secondly, they tried discarding all older observations, using only the most recent ones. A few years of observation showed that both these methods were inadequate to describe the deviations of Uranus from any predicted path. Past history and fact was of no avail. The question was put forth that perhaps the mass of Saturn had been miscalculated: a rapid calculation showed that the mass necessary to create the noted deviations of Uranus would have to be so enormous as to be impossible.*
>
> 1834   *An English amateur astronomer offered the solution to the problem of an ultra-Uranian planet beyond the orbit of Uranus. He offered to search for it in a general sort of way if the Royal Academy would supply estimates of its position. Sir George Airy, the respondent to this letter, doubted that the deviations were caused by such a planet, believing firmly that the deviations were caused by miscalculation of Uranus' orbit. His main support of this thesis was a calculation he presented showing the size of Uranus to be in error as well as its heliocentric longitude. Nothing was done.*

---

[2] From B. A. Gould, *Report to the Smithsonian Institution on the History of the Discovery of Neptune* (Washington, D.C.: Smithsonian Institution, 1850), *passim.*

1843   *The Royal Society of Science in Göttingen (Germany) offered a prize of fifty ducats to whomever would offer the best solution to the problem of Uranus' orbit.*

The question having now exhausted all known proofs, combined with the incentives of the prize money, it remained for an astute mathematician to work upon the only remaining hypothesis: that of the ultra-Uranian planet. In England, J. C. Adams undertook such work, and within several years was able to prove that the deviations could be fairly well represented by the gravitational effects of an unknown planet of which he then calculated the motion and orbital elements. The planet he described from his derivations is only one and a half degrees in error from the actual position of the heliocentric longitude as it is now known, and only one-half degree in error from the position along the ecliptic.

But Airy, in replying to all this information presented to him by Adams, merely inquired if the assumed perturbation would also explain the error of the radius vector of Uranus. Adams, incensed, made no reply.

Meanwhile, in France, the mathematician Leverrier had drawn the same conclusion as Adams. His investigations were more thorough, though, in that he proved by scientific demonstration and logical deduction that there was no known admissible solution to the problem except that of an ultra-Uranian planet.

1846   *At this point, both groups began searching the skies for the new planet. Airy, being convinced that it might be possible, set an assistant to sweeping the sky in the neighborhood of the area predicted by Adams. The plan required the comparison of two sweeps, of all stars noted down to the sixth magnitude, in order that the new planet might be detected by its motion. Nothing was found, after this had been carried out.*

On August 31, 1846, Leverrier wrote to the Berlin Observatory that now-famous letter stating that if they would but train their telescopes on a certain point in the sky, comparing their results over several nights, they would discover the presence of a new planet. By chance the proper chart for comparison had just been completed; the new planet was discovered two evenings later as an eight-magnitude body whose movements could be shown. The existence of the new planet was thus established.

In the above example, note how the scientists involved could not possibly have imagined the hypothesis that Neptune was out there without the concepts of "size," "mass," "heliocentric longitude," and "gravitational effects." These concepts of the mind had already been arrived at through generations of other scientists devoting all of their time, all of their energies, and all of their intellectual and creative power to the understanding of celestial movements. This was an example of deductive thinking, or reasoning from certain concepts (force, mass), to prove facts that were not known. It is the opposite of inductive thinking, or the mental process that produced the original theory of force and mass as determinants of planets' orbits. This theory, and these concepts, were formulated from observation of the facts. It is in this sense that science, being the result of efforts of many people, with different mental powers[3] than laymen, have much to offer to the latter in the solution of everyday problems.

Notice also that to the policy maker in the mid-twentieth century, there is not much usefulness in knowing that Neptune is there. Neither the President of the United States nor the Chairman of the Communist Central Committee of the U.S.S.R. is going to change its orbit. But the conceptual scheme of "mass," "size," "heliocentric longitude," and "gravitational effect"—the theory of cause and effect—is very much a policy matter. Laplace, charting Jupiter in 1820, probably did not think that President James Monroe would put a man on Jupiter, or the moon. In our century, until recently, a man on the moon was a matter for comic books and science fiction writers. Today, however, any intelligent citizen, or any president of a corporation which makes rockets, metals, or electronic equipment for the space industry, or who sells food supplies or builds houses for personnel at the missile base in Cape Kennedy, might well recognize that part Laplace had in shaping their lives, determining the products they sell, or, in the case of the space industry, determining the processes and operations which must take place in their companies.

REPETITIVE VERSUS DIVERGENT PHENOMENA

In a powerful chapter on "The Origins of Modern Science,"[4] Alfred North Whitehead, the eminent mathematician-philosopher, points out that "there can be no living science unless there is a widespread instinctive conviction in the existence of an *order of things*"—that is, scientists believe instinctively that events will repeat themselves, and that the events can be observed (in the skies, in the laboratory) as forming a repetitive pattern. This pattern is described in terms of lower order facts, and then general laws or principles are stated at higher levels of abstraction. For example, repeated observations are made and recorded, and then conceptualized into concepts such as "force," "mass," and "orbit."

Orbit is a pattern, and the forces producing it continue to operate, year in and year out. There are no "divergent" phenomena, no outside disturbances or forces which interrupt the pattern.

Yet there is a paradox here. Whitehead goes on to point out that even in the physical sciences, "nothing ever really occurs in exact detail. No two days are identical, no two winters. What has gone, has gone forever. Accordingly, the practical philosophy of mankind has been to expect broad recurrences, and to accept the details as emanating from the inscrutable womb of things beyond the ken of rationality."

In sciences such as astronomy, in which the systems are in reality (as

---

[3] The word "different" is used here rather than "superior." Viewed in one way, scientists are specialists who devote their lives to a certain pursuit. Whether this is "superior power" depends upon what one's criteria for "superior" is. For instance, if we measure superiority by the degree of complexity of problems on which a human mind works, policy decisions in policy systems can be distinctly more complex than scientific systems.

[4] Alfred North Whitehead, *Science and the Modern World,* Lowell Lectures, February, 1925 (New York: The Macmillan Co., 1925), chap. i.

well as the mind) relatively simple, with no disturbing forces, the assumption of repeated patterns seems to yield theories which are true, from year to year and century to century.

Today in the physical sciences, when we get away from astronomy, scientists are discovering that their laws are quite tentative, and that the study of change, differences in detail, and disruptions to the system or pattern are as important as recurring patterns. These divergent phenomena, as opposed to convergent phenomena (patterns), in the modern world of intellectual and cultural complexity are extremely important in the social sciences, and they are even more important in the world of policy making and managerial action. Why? Because, as we shall see later, there are many disturbances in an action system or policy system.

For the present, the following statement by the retiring president of the American Association for the Advancement of Science should help to understand the paradox to which Whitehead refers.[5] In one way, this paradox is caused by the fact that scientists, in their process of abstraction, leave out important details which, as Langmuir points out, "are important in altering the course of human history" and "profoundly affect human lives."

Up to the beginning of the present century one of the main goals of science was to discover natural laws. This was usually accomplished by making experiments under carefully controlled conditions and observing the results. Most experiments when repeated under identical conditions gave the same results.

The scientist, through his own experiments or from previous knowledge based on the work of others, usually developed some theory or explanation of the results of his experiments. In the beginning this might be a mere guess or hypothesis which he would proceed to test by new types of experiments. . . .

. . . The usefulness of the theory lies just in its ability to predict the results of future experiments. The extraordinary accomplishments of the great mathematical physicists in applying Newton's Laws to the motions of the heavenly bodies gave scientists of more than a century ago the conviction that all natural phenomena were determined by accurate relations between cause and effect. If the positions, the velocities and the masses of the heavenly bodies were given it was possible to predict with nearly unlimited accuracy the position of the bodies at any future time. The idea of causation, or a necessary relation of cause and effect, has long been embedded in the minds of men. The recognized responsibility of the criminal for his acts, the belief of the value of education and thousands of words in our language all show how implicitly we believe in cause and effect. The teachings of classical science, that is, the science up to 1900, all seem to reinforce this idea of causation for all phenomena.

*   *   *   *   *

[5] Irving Langmuir, "Science, Common Sense and Decency," *Science,* Vol. 97, No. 2505 (January 1943), pp. 1–7, reprinted from *Science* by permission. The authors are indebted to Professor Joseph Bailey of the Harvard Business School for calling attention to the importance of Langmuir's ideas in the practice of administration.

The theories or explanations which were developed in connection with the natural laws usually involved a description in terms of some kind of a model. In general, instead of thinking of the whole complex world we select only a few elements which we think to be important and concentrate our minds on these. Thus, the chemist developed the atomic theory according to which matter was made up of atoms of as many different kinds as there are chemical elements. These were thought of as small spheres, but no thought was given as to the material of which they were made. When later theories indicated that these atoms were built up of electrons and positive nuclei this made very little difference to the chemist, for he had not needed previously to consider that aspect of the model.

*   *   *   *   *

The essential characteristic of a model is that it shall resemble in certain desired features the situation that we are considering. On this basis we should recognize that practically any theory has many arbitrary features and has limitations and restrictions imposed by the simplifications that we have made in the development of the theory or the construction of our model.

Beginning with Einstein's relativity theory and Planck's quantum theory a revolution in physical thought has swept through science. Perhaps the most important aspect of this is that the scientist has ceased to believe that words or concepts can have any absolute meaning. He is not often concerned with questions of existence; he does not know what is the meaning of the question, "Does an atom really exist?" The definition of "atom" is only partly given in the dictionary. Its real meaning lies in the sum total of knowledge on this subject among scientists who have specialized in this field. No one has been authorized to make an exact definition. Furthermore, we can not be sure just what we mean even by the word "exist." Such questions are largely metaphysical and in general do not interest the modern scientist. Bridgman has pointed out that all concepts in science have value only in so far as they can be described in terms of operations or specifications. Thus it doesn't mean much to talk about length or time unless we agree upon the methods by which we are to measure length and time.

For many years, up to about 1930, the new physics based on the quantum theory seemed to be fundamentally irreconcilable with the classical physics of the previous century. Through the more recent development of the uncertainty principle, developed by Bohr and Heisenberg, this conflict has now disappeared. According to this principle it is fundamentally impossible to measure accurately both the velocity and the position of any single elementary particle. It would be possible to measure one or the other accurately but not both simultaneously. Thus it becomes impossible to predict with certainty the movement of a single particle. Therefore, Ampere's estimate of the scope of science has lost its basis.

According to the uncertainty principle, which is now thoroughly well established, the most that can be said about the future motion of any single atom or electron is that it has a definite probability of acting in any given way. Probability thus becomes a fundamental factor in every elementary process. By changing the conditions of the environment of a given atom, as, for example, by changing the force acting on it, we can change these probabilities. In many cases the probability can be made so great that a given result will be almost certain. But in many important cases the uncertainty becomes the dominating feature just as it is in the tossing of a coin.

The net result of the modern principles of physics has been to wipe out almost completely the dogma of causation.

How is it, then, that classical physics has led to such definite clean-cut laws? The simplest answer is that the classical physicist naturally chose as the subjects for his studies those fields which promised greatest success. The aim of the scientist in general was to discover natural laws. He therefore carried on his experiments in such a way as to find the natural laws, for that is what he was looking for. He was best able to accomplish this by working with phenomena which depended upon the behavior of enormous numbers of atoms rather than upon individual atoms. In this way the effects produced by individual atoms averaged out and become imperceptible. We have many familiar examples of this effect of averaging—the deaths of individual human beings can not usually be predicted but the average death rate in any age group is found to come close to expectation.

Since the discovery of the electron and the quantum and methods of detecting or even counting individual atoms, it has been possible for scientists to undertake investigations of the behavior of single atoms. Here they have found unmistakable experimental evidence that these phenomena depend upon the laws of probability and that they are just as unpredictable in detail as the next throw of the coin. If, however, we were dealing with large numbers of such atoms the behavior of the whole group would be definitely determined by the probability of the individual occurrence and therefore would appear to be governed by laws of cause and effect.

Just as there are two types of physics, classical physics and quantum physics, which have for nearly twenty-five years seemed irreconcilable, just so must we recognize two types of natural phenomena. First, those in which the behavior of the system can be determined from the average behavior of its component parts and second, those in which a single discontinuous event (which may depend upon a single quantum change) becomes magnified in its effect so that the behavior of the whole aggregate does depend upon something that started from a small beginning. The first class of phenomena I want to call convergent *phenomena, because all the fluctuating details of the individual atoms average out giving a result that converges to a definite state. The second class we may call* divergent *phenomena, where from a small beginning increasingly large effects are produced. In general then we may say that classical physics applies satisfactorily to convergent phenomena and that they conform well to the older ideas of cause and effect. The divergent phenomena on the other hand can best be understood on the basis of quantum theory of modern physics.*

$$*\quad*\quad*\quad*\quad*$$

The formation of crystals on cooling a liquid involves the formation of nuclei or crystallization centers that must originate from discrete, atomic phenomena. The spontaneous formation of these nuclei often depends upon chance.

At a camp at Lake George, in winter, I have often found that a pail of water is unfrozen in the morning after being in a room far below freezing, but it suddenly turns to slush upon being lifted from the floor.

Glycerine is commonly known as a viscous liquid, even at low temperatures. Yet if crystals are once formed they melt only at 64° F. If a minute crystal of this kind is introduced into pure glycerine at temperatures below 64° the entire liquid gradually solidifies.

During a whole winter in Schenectady I left several small bottles of glycerine outdoors and I kept the lower ends of test-tubes containing glycerine in liquid air for days, but in no case did crystals form.

My brother, A. C. Langmuir, visited a glycerine refinery in Canada which had operated for many years without ever having any experience with crystalline glycerine. But suddenly one winter, without exceptionally low temperatures, the pipes carrying the glycerine from one piece of apparatus to another froze up. The whole plant and even the dust on the ground became contaminated with nuclei and although any part of the plant could be temporarily freed from crystals by heating above 64° it was found that whenever the temperature anywhere fell below 64° crystals would begin forming. The whole plant had to be shut down for months until outdoor temperatures rose above 64°.

Here we have an example of an inherently unpredictable divergent phenomenon that profoundly affected human lives.

Every thunderstorm or tornado must start from a small beginning and at least the details of the irregular courses of such storms across the country would be modified by single quantum phenomena that acted during the initial stages. Yet small details such as the place where lightning strikes or damage occurs from a tornado may be important to a human being.

$$*\quad*\quad*\quad*\quad*$$

As the implications of the uncertainty principle, especially as applied to divergent phenomena, are more generally recognized the limitations of the idea of causality should have profound effects on our habits of thought. The science of logic itself is involved in these changes. Two of the fundamental postulates of logic are known as the law of uniformity of nature and the law of the excluded middle. The first of these laws is equivalent of the postulate of causality in nature. The second law is simply the familiar postulate that a given proposition must be either true or false. In the past these so-called laws have formed the basis of much of our reasoning. It seems to me, however, that they play no important part in the progress of modern science. The cause and effect postulate is only applicable to convergent phenomena. The second postulate in assuming that any proposition must be true or false implies that we attach absolute meanings to words or concepts. If concepts have meanings only in terms of the operations used to define them we can see that they are necessarily fuzzy. Take, for example, this statement, "Atoms are indestructible." Is this true or false? The answer depends upon what aspect of atoms is considered. To the chemist the statement is as true as it ever was. But a physicist, studying radioactive changes, recognized that some atoms undergo spontaneous disintegration or destruction. The fact is that the chemist and the physicist have no exact definition of the word "atom" and they also do not know in any absolute sense what they mean by "indestructible."

Fortunately such questions no longer occupy much of the time of scientists, who are usually concerned with more concrete problems which they endeavor to treat in common-sense ways.

It is often thought by the layman, and many of those who are working in so-called social sciences, that the field of science should be unlimited, that reason should take the place of intuition, that realism should replace emotions and that morality is of value only so far as it can be justified by analytical reasoning.

Human affairs are characterized by a complexity of a far higher order than that encountered ordinarily in the field of science.

To avoid alternating periods of depression and prosperity economists propose to change our laws. They reason that such a change would eliminate the cause of the depressions. They endeavor to develop a science of economics by which sound solutions to such problems can be reached.

I believe the field of application of science in such problems is extremely limited. A scientist has to define his problem and usually has to bring about simplified conditions for his experiments which exclude undesired factors. So the economist has to invent an "economic man" who always does the thing expected of him. No two economists would agree exactly upon the characteristics of this hypothetical man and any conclusions drawn as to his behavior are of doubtful application to actual cases involving human beings. There is no logical scientific method for determining just how one can formulate such a problem or what factors one must exclude. It really comes down to a matter of common sense or good judgment. All too often wishful thinking determines the formulation of the problem. Thus, even if scientifically logical processes are applied to the problem, the results may have no greater validity than that of the good or bad judgment involved in the original assumptions.

Some of the difficulties involved in a scientific approach to economic problems is illustrated by the following: If we wish to analyze the cause of a depression (or for example, a war) we should ask ourselves what we mean by the word "cause" in this connection. In terms of operations the usual meaning of the word cause is something as *follows: It is a common experience, in a study of convergent phenomena, that if a given set of physical conditions are brought about repeatedly at different times, the same result occurs in each case. Except in so far as it is possible to repeat the experiment and get the same result it is impossible to give a definite meaning to the word cause.*

In the case of a depression or a war, we logically need to produce, or at least to observe, a given set of possible antecedent conditions and to see whether they are always followed by depressions. Since we can not produce experimental depressions, nor have we sufficient observational data to enable us by statistical means to unravel the enormous number of factors involved, we must conclude that the word "cause" as applied to a depression has an extremely fuzzy meaning.

When we consider the nature of human affairs it is to me obvious that divergent phenomena frequently play a role of vital importance. It is true that some of our historians cynically taught most of our college students from 1925 to 1938 that wars, the rise and fall of a nation, etc., were determined by nearly cosmic causes. They tried to show that economic pressure, and power politics on the part of England or France, etc., would have brought the same result whether or not Kaiser Wilhelm or Hitler or any other individual or group of individuals had or had not acted the way they did. Germany, facing the world in a realistic way, was proved, almost scientifically, to be justified in using ruthless methods—because of the energy and other characteristics of the German people they would necessarily acquire and should acquire a place in the sun greater than that of England, which was already inevitably on the downward path.

I can see no justification whatever for such teaching that science proves that general causes (convergent phenomena) dominate in human affairs over the results of individual action (divergent phenomena). It is true that it is not possible to prove one way or the other that human affairs are determined primarily by convergent phenomena. The very existence of divergent phenomena almost precludes the possibility of such proof.

OPERATIONALISM IN SCIENCE

In Dr. Langmuir's article, he asks why it was that classical physicists could find such clean-cut laws. The answer is that "the classical physicist naturally chose as the subjects for his studies those fields which promised greatest success" (that is, chose subjects and imagined concepts of a kind that did show recurring patterns).

Today, even with quantum thinking in the natural sciences and emphasis on probability in social sciences such as economics and sociology, we must note one more characteristic of science which bears on its usefulness in the formulation of policy problems and the analysis and solution of policy decisions.

The individual scientist will not select problems to work on nor will he select concepts to investigate unless they are operational to him—unless they fit his method. The two things which determine this are (1) the concepts and events must be repetitive in observation, or reproducible in the laboratory; and (2) they must be things that can be quantified. Only in this way can the scientist test the reality of his "imagined" concepts and hypotheses. Numbers and mathematics are the one thing on which different human minds can agree. If phenomena are not repetitive in an absolute sense, they must be in the statistical sense, so that probability figures can be attached.

For example, chemists have discovered through patient experiment that "hydrogen" (note the concept) has an "atomic weight" of 1, and that oxygen has an atomic weight of 16, and that the "valence" (combining power) of hydrogen is 1 while the valence of oxygen is 2. From these, he can predict that of any amount of water (H_2O), say 200 pounds, 11% will be made up of hydrogen and 89% of oxygen. He does this by dividing the total of the molecular weight [$(2 \times 1) + (1 \times 16)$] into the atomic weights of the individual elements ($1 \div 18$). If you do not "believe" this, he can take you into the laboratory, weigh the water sample, reduce it to hydrogen and oxygen, and then weigh them under repetitive, experimental conditions.

J. W. N. Sullivan, one important philosopher of science, states that this predisposition to select out of the universe only those things that could be *measured* experimentally or observationally was due simply to a *faith* on the part of Copernicus, Kepler, and Galileo "that mathematics is the key to the universe . . . a belief which was very proper to born mathematicians . . . (which) gave the mathematical aspects of the universe a much more exalted position than they occupied in the current Aristotelian outlook. . . ."

"(Kepler's) deepest conviction was that nature is essentially mathematical, and all his scientific life was an endeavor to discover nature's hidden mathematical harmonies. Galileo, also, had no doubt that mathematics is the one true key to the universe. It was this persuasion that gave these men their criterion for selection amongst the total elements of the universe."[6]

Whitehead, on the other hand, gives a slightly different reason for the scientist's willingness to deal only with problems which can be reproduced, quantitatively, in experiment or by observation. To him it was a loss in faith, by scholars, in the dogmatic speculation of the Middle Ages, when philosophy and truth were laid down, speculatively, without reference to facts in the world. Copernicus, for example, felt a great anxiety because he knew that the Ptolemaic theory of the universe was not true. That theory, with the earth as the center, and stationary at that, was a current conceptual scheme of the mind, which explained how the stars rotated around the earth. Copernicus had "heard" that some of the great Greek philosophers had put forward the hypothesis that the earth was in motion. Copernicus then took the sun as his center of reference (he imagined a new theory or conceptual scheme) and proceeded to collect data.

It is significant that in 1973 the concept of operationalism (experi-

⁶J. W. N. Sullivan, *The Limitations of Science* (New York: New American Library Edition), pp. 128–29. Copyright, 1933, Viking Press, Inc., reprinted by permission.

ment-quantification) is important in physical science, in some social science, and in the current application of mathematics in business administration, that is, in the field of operations research. One of the better recent textbooks on operations research states:

> *The goals of individuals have been the subject of discussion and debate for many centuries. To say that happiness is the goal of the individual . . . does not solve any problem. We cannot define happiness in operational terms. Operationalism is an important concept for understanding operations research. It implies concreteness, the ability to observe, measure, and analyze. . . . We cannot treat happiness as an operational term.*[7]

Facts which are operational to the scientist and statistician in the laboratory, quantified and under controlled experimental (repetitive and abstract) conditions, are not always operational to the policy maker; or they may be relevant to his problems, but not of high relevance in terms of his goals; or they may be relevant, but uncontrollable in terms of executive action. Finally, they may be highly relevant, and controllable by the executive, but subject to overriding importance of *other* forces than explained by any one theory.[8]

THE LESSON OF PHYSICAL SCIENCE FOR POLICY MAKERS

Why have we spent time discussing the nature of science, the idea of divergent phenomena, and the idea of operationalism in science? First, because it helps the policy maker, the man of action, to recognize that the great power of creativity and the enormous amounts of time and energy expended add to the value of many scientific concepts. It also helps to see that the very bias of scientists—their preconditioning and their attitudes—is one of the factors that enable them to see things that laymen may overlook. Secondly, some of the characteristics of science, divergent phenomena, and operationalism have contradictory implications in policy systems—they put a limitation on the degree to which science can be used in policy formation. They indicate that the practicing executive must pick and choose his theories, must test them, modify them, use them, or discard them, depending on how they operate in the world of action, where experimental conditions cannot be met, where divergent phenomena are many times as important as convergent phenomena, and where everything cannot be measured by mathematics.

Finally, many social scientists, whether rightly or wrongly, try, with varying degrees of success, to adopt the methods of the physical sciences. To the extent that they do, this chapter has set the state for understanding the nature and methods of social sciences discussed in the next chapter.

---

[7] David Miller and Martin Starr, *Executive Decisions and Operations Research* (Englewood Cliffs, N.J.: Prentice-Hall, Inc., 1960).

[8] In many of the cases in the latter part of the book, one of these three limitations can be seen. For example, see the following cases: Midwest Hardware Manufacturing Company, National Motor Parts Company, and Continental Electric Company.

Chapter 3. SOCIAL SCIENCE AND APPLIED SOCIAL SCIENCE

THEORY FORMULATION IN THE SOCIAL SCIENCES: AN EXAMPLE FROM SOCIOLOGY

In the last chapter, we looked at the nature of conceptual schemes, as formulated by those scientists whose main interest is understanding non-human objects in the environment, for the purpose of explaining how one object or event causes another.

The social sciences occupy a special place in policy making by general executives. In fact, "management" has been defined by some as "getting results through human organizations."[1] Such a definition implies that the proper study of decisions by men of action—military, governmental, legal—should be based on political philosophy, or political science, or one of the so-called behavioral sciences—psychology and certain branches of sociology and anthropology.

In this chapter, we will be looking at the nature of social science, its concepts, and the way they are derived (its methods), in the hope that the reader himself, in both reading these words and working with the cases, will gain an appreciation for the value of social science, and its limitations, in the world of policy-making action.

We will begin by using an explanation of "The Theory Construction Function of Science" put forth by Ernest Greenwood.[2] The example he cites, that of Durkheim's theory of suicide, is a classic one, often used by social scientists to illustrate their methods:

---

[1] This, of course, is a conceptual idea which puts the relationships between people, and their governance or management, in the center of analysis, rather than the relationships between machines, goods, money flows, and the like. Neither is true: the policy system, as we shall see, is a very complex conglomerate of human structures and dynamics, and technological-economic structures and dynamics.

[2] From Ernest Greenwood, "The Practice of Science and the Science of Practice" presented as a University Lecture at Brandeis University, October 1959, and published as one of the Brandeis University Papers in Social Welfare by the Florence Heller Graduate School for Advanced Studies in Social Welfare, 1960. This Lecture is also abridged in *The Planning of Change,* edited by Warren Bennis, Kenneth D. Benne, and Robert Chin (New York: Holt, Rinehart & Winston, 1962). The latter is considered an excellent collection of writings from the viewpoint of the practitioner—the applied social scientist who is interested in planned change (control) in the environment rather than simply in understanding the operation of nature.

[*L*]*et me describe in more specific language the nature of the scientific activity. The end product of the collective efforts of scientists within a given discipline is a system of internally consistent propositions which describe and explain the phenomena that constitute the subject matter of that discipline. This system is called a body of theory. The function of all science is to construct theories about the what, the how, and the why of the natural world. There is some current misunderstanding regarding this function of science, many laymen believing that only philosophers theorize and that scientists "stick close to facts." I wish to dwell a bit on the theory-construction focus of science. In this connection it will prove clarifying if I were to distinguish between two levels of knowledge with which scientists are concerned. On the first level are first-order facts called* empirical generalizations; *on the second and higher level are the explanations or interpretations of these facts called* theory. *These constitute two orders of abstraction.*

Nature of Empirical Generalizations

To make clear the distinction between these two orders of abstraction, let me present you with a few examples of an empirical generalization. Thus:

a. In Western societies, Jews commit fewer suicides than Gentiles, and Catholics commit fewer suicides than Protestants.

b. American middle-class wives participate in communal health and welfare activities more than their husbands.

c. In cities key commercial facilities concentrate at point of convergence of transportation lines.

d. Juvenile delinquency rates are higher in urban census tracts with lower median monthly rentals.

An empirical generalization may be defined as a proposition about a class of units which describes the uniform recurrence of two or more factors among them. As the term empirical implies, such generalizations are derived inductively by actual observation of the class members. The procedures pursued in their derivation can be operationalized and textbooks on research methods are written to describe them; these involve scaling, sampling, controlled observation, data manipulation, application of statistical tests, et cetera. Given time and patience, there is no limit to the number of hitherto unsuspected empirical generalizations, or first-order facts, that one could discover about the social world. The body of knowledge of a science, however, consists of more than empirical generalizations.

Description versus Explanation

That shrewd critic of the sociological scene, Robert Bierstedt, in a brilliant article, entitled "A Critique of Empiricism in Sociology," puts the matter in the following form.[3] *Surveys, he states, have*

---

[3] Robert Bierstedt, "A Critique of Empiricism in Sociology," *American Sociological Review,* Vol. 14 (October 1949), pp. 584–92.

amassed an assortment of facts about bread consumption in the United States. Thus: Americans are consuming decreasing amounts of home-made and increasing amounts of factory-made bread. Most Americans perfer white to dark bread. Men consume more bread than women. Adolescents consume more bread than other age groups. Negroes consume more bread than Whites. Rural dwellers consume more bread than urban dwellers. Low income families consume more bread than high income families. This factual list might be extended without adding significantly to our comprehension of the American bread consumption phenomenon. To achieve the latter requires a formulation that will tie together these discrete generalizations and will explain their interrelationships. Such a formulation would constitute a theory of American bread consumption.

The function of social scientists is to develop theories which will explain such social phenomena as bread consumption, alcoholism, class conflict, crime, drug addiction, juvenile delinquency, marital discord, population migration, suicide, technological change, urban growth, et cetera. In constructing theory, the scientist uses empirical generalizations as building blocks.

An Example of Theory Building

I would like to present an idealized description of theory construction taken from Durkheim's work on the social aetiology of suicide. Although now over a half century old, it still remains an impeccable model of theory construction.[4] I have deliberately selected an example at a relatively simple level of theory, thereby ignoring so-called grand and all-embracing theories.

Durkheim begins his search for the societal cause of suicide by casting his net far and wide, garnering all the available facts about the problem. The data yield him a series of empirical generalizations. Careful scrutiny of Durkheim's volume reveals over three dozen such generalizations which assume a wide variety. Let me present some of them.

a. Countries predominantly Protestant in population have higher suicide rates than countries predominantly Catholic.

b. Christians have higher suicide rates than Jews.

c. Countries with high literacy rates have higher suicide rates than countries with low literacy.

d. The liberal professions as a group have a higher suicide rate than the manual occupations.

e. The unmarried have a higher suicide rate than the married.

f. The divorced have a higher suicide rate than the married.

g. The childless married have a higher suicide rate than the married with children.

h. Average size of family is inversely related to the suicide rate.

---

[4] Emile Durkheim, *Suicide. A Study in Sociology* (New York: The Free Press of Glencoe, 1951). Translation by John A Spaulding and George Simpson. Durkheim's theory of suicide presented in this paper is a highly abstracted version of the original, necessitated by space requirements. Any distortions in the theory are the responsibility of this writer.

Having extracted these empirical generalizations from the data, Durkheim next, in essence, asks the question: What common thread runs through these generalizations? What do Protestants, high literacy countries, liberal professions, the unmarried, the divorced, the childless, have in common that should make for higher suicide rates among them than in their opposite classes? At this point Durkheim begins to speculate, and his speculation bears recapitulation.

If Protestants are more prone to suicides than Catholics, religious differences must be held accountable. Protestantism permits individualism and free inquiry, while Catholicism brooks no scrutiny by the faithful. The more binding the creed, the more unified the religious group and the more attached is the individual to the group. The atmosphere permitted by Protestantism weakens the traditional beliefs that solidify the religious group. That group discipline exerts a preservative influence is borne out by the case of the Jews, a cohesive minority living in compact communities, with a low suicide rate. Attachment to a group must be a potent factor in the suicide phenomenon as indicated by the marital correlates of suicide. Note how the unmarried state encourages suicide and how the disruption of marriage by divorce and death increases its chances. Close examination of the facts reveals that even more preservative than the conjugal relationship between the spouses is the familial relationship between parents and children. In fact, the more children the better. The common thread that runs through these empirical generalizations is clear. A well-integrated group holds its members by strong bonds, preventing them from evading their social obligations by self-elimination, at the same time providing them the support to enable them to perform their obligations in the face of otherwise disabling personal stress. Where group solidarity is weak, the individual feels detached from the group and is thrown on his own feeble resources to sustain him in his personal frustrations.

This, highly condensed, is Durkheim's theory of the social cause of suicide. The theory may now be summarized into a single proposition, i.e., *a law of suicide:* Suicide is a function of the degree of group integration which provides the psychic support to group members for handling acute stress.

Nature of Theory Building

Durkheim's method epitomizes the scientific process. From a host of apparently disconnected first-order facts he theorizes to a law. He moves from the facts to an abstract proposition which interprets the interrelationship among them. Note the difference in levels of abstraction between the law and the empirical generalizations. Note how much more abstract is the proposition with which he terminates the theorizing process from the propositions with which he initiates it. Theory may thus be defined as a systematic interpretation in abstract terms of a generalizable trend that prevails within a set of varied facts, explaining the interrelationship among them. Law is the summarization of the theory in causal terms.

> *As indicated earlier, the derivation of empirical generalizations can be operationalized, but I have yet to find a textbook that will operationalize the theorizing process. The interpretive process, the development of a formulation which will account for a series of facts, is essentially a free-wheeling, speculative one. It is an inferential process whereby the inquiring mind churns the available information over and over, employing all the logical devices and bringing to bear upon it any and all kinds of relevant knowledge. The process allows for a considerable play of the imagination, and the final formulation bears the personal imprint of its formulator.*

In this example of fact gathering and speculation-theory construction in the social sciences, the policy maker might well take note of some of the characteristics of the theory itself and of its formulator, Durkheim.

First, the final law of suicide contains two concepts or variables which Durkheim "saw." By the process of abstraction, he simplified the world: "suicide," as an event or occurrence, and "group integration," which determines the suicide rate. These two concepts are, at one and the same time, products of his imagination, and representative of the underlying facts. The intermediate variables with which he reasoned (the other concepts he imagined and formulated) are "phychic support" for handling "acute stress." Thus, we get these cause-and-effect relationships: low degrees of group participation cause a feeling of lack of psychic support in the individual which cause him to be unable to handle problems of acute stress, which in turn cause him to commit suicide.

Second, to test the theory, one can reason deductively from the theory to other facts, just as in the case of the prediction that Neptune was "out there" (Chapter 2). One can look for groups with low degrees of "group integration," and without experiment, deductively predict that members of that group would have a high suicide rate; further, one can then test to see if the members of that group *in fact* have a higher suicide rate.

Third, Durkheim's central theory does not refer to any other causes of suicide. He assumes that group integration is the uniformly constant and most important cause, and that other causes are either less important, or are simply deviant, random events, not relevant to scientific study and rational explanation. He treats suicide as a repetitive, convergent phenomena (in Langmuir's term), a pattern which varies with one central cause—group integration.

Fourth, Durkheim had an interest in studying suicide. He was not interested in making automobiles, wining a war, setting the discount rate of the federal reserve banks, influencing the behavior of subordinate personnel in a factory, or explaining the rise and fall of governments.

If he were interested in a very broad range of problems and events and variables in a policy system, he could not have conceptualized in precise enough terms to produce the power of thought and the understanding of nature, which he did.

Finally, the principle itself (any principle is a statement of explanation—of cause and effect) is not "engineered"—it does not prescribe to a government official *how* to provide group integration. Only by restudying the underlying facts, as to how the various groups provided (or did not provide) integration, can the policy maker infer what they did in a practical sense to influence the suicide rate. This is an important difference in science, technology, and practice.

THEORY CONSTRUCTION: AN EXAMPLE FROM SOCIAL PSYCHOLOGY

In order to understand the use of theories in policy formulation more deeply, we need another example—one from a practitioner whose interests are nearer to the business organization. This time, we will look at a theory which explains the ways in which "organizations" have certain effects on "individual behavior" and "group behavior" and how the latter two variables reciprocally affect "organizations." This theory, that explained by Chris Argyris in *Personality and Organization,*[5] has received wide attention.

In formulating this conceptual scheme, Argyris utilizes 640 footnotes, many of which draw on empirical research in the social sciences. He draws on a breadth of experimental and observed situations—from studies of motivation in children, of personality tests in business, and of rational behavior in large bureaucracies to studies of why people join trade unions. Argyris is *primarily interested* in how large organizations affect human personality and how they affect informal group behavior. At the highest level, he is interested in what causes conflict between organizations, on the one hand, and the rank-and-file members of organizations, on the other.

With these interests, he proceeds to conceptualize meaning from a wealth of diverse facts which have "come to his attention." The overall theory and its intermediate concepts can be stated in briefest terms as follows:

1. All human beings have a capacity for "self-actualization" (growth), for developing from infancy in terms of interests, abilities, and activities. Such development satisfies needs, and it is the continuing striving for such development which gives us energy.

2. The formal organization has four characteristics: jobs are split up and specialized, there is a chain of command, everyone has only one boss, and there is a long hierarchy or pyramid of command.

3. These characteristics of formal organization severely limit the self-actualization, development, and growth of the human being.

4. Rank-and-file members of the organization, thus confronted with a block to their growth and development, either quit, become apathetic (lose their energy), or become aggressive against the organization.

5. The leaders of organizations see the rank and file behaving this

---

[5] New York: Harper & Bros., 1957. The presentation of the theory here is a highly abstracted version of Professor Argyris' book. Responsibility for abstraction is assumed by the authors. A longer version, in Professor Argyris' own words, appears as a reading in this volume. The theory is also highly controversial—see the review of Argyris' later work by Mason Haire, *Management Science,* April 1963, p. 505.

way, develop beliefs that they are lazy or hostile, and tighten up on the characteristics of formal organization (step [2]). They define jobs more minutely, stress the chain of command, and rigidify the hierarchical pyramid.

6. This causes the apathy and aggression of employees who remain in the organization to intensify: they become lethargic and devote less energy to their work; or they increase their aggression in the form of cliques to "get around" the rules; or they even form formal labor unions to fight back.

7. The vicious circle continues, with steps (5) and (6) reinforcing the conflict.

Argyris' interest in organization-personality conflict led him to conceptualize a series of cause-and-effect relationships between two highly abstract concepts: "the organization" and "personality." In order to think about these, however, his original interest dictated that he had to formulate some lower order concepts about what a "human being" is and about what an "organization" is. What did he do about these two variables? What did he see? In effect, he said, "A personality (human being) is first and foremost an organism which has an almost unlimited capacity for self-actualization and growth"; and "an organization is a construct with specialized jobs, chain of command, and a hierarchical pyramid."

The choice of these two larger abstractions, "personality" and "organization" with their lower order abstractions, "growth," "chain of command," etc., enabled him to reason the further cause-and-effect relationships pointed out above.

THEORY CONSTRUCTION: AN EXAMPLE FROM ECONOMICS AND INDUSTRIAL ENGINEERING

The founder of the discipline of economics, Adam Smith, had as his main interest exactly what the title of his famous book implies: *An Inquiry into the Nature and Causes of the Wealth of Nations.* He was interested in the national balance sheet, the assets and liabilities of a nation, and the national income and gross national product which produces the national wealth. Thus motivated in terms of interest, Smith conceptualized the first and most important cause of the productivity of a nation as the "principle of specialization"—the division of work into smaller parts which produced efficiency of the whole.[6]

This is the same "specialization" which Argyris refers to as one of the characteristics of organizations, in step (2) in the preceding section, except that the two scholars derived different meanings from it. To Adam Smith, it is the foremost cause of the productivity of an industrial system, yet to Argyris it is one of the causes of apathy or aggression in organizations. Even today, in modern economics, the principle of specialization

---

[6] The relevant argument is presented in this volume as pages 4–15 of *The Wealth of Nations.*

has important implications for creating larger organizations, for creating staff departments for central planning in organizations, and for realizing "increasing returns to scale."[7]

In the field of industrial engineering and in operations research models, there is implied a certain physical division of labor between parts of the system (including locations, such as jobs, factories, and warehouses). If this division of labor produces the greatest job output in the case of industrial engineering or the optimum balance between the inputs and outputs of an inventory system (in operations research), then the engineers or researchers tend either to ignore the motivational effects of specialization,[8] or to assume that they have less importance than the rational planning of jobs and the flow of material. In this sense, the *interests* of industrial engineers, or operations researchers, simply cause them to select certain variables which are more important in their view of the world.[9] This, incidentally, does not mean that all industrial engineers, operations researchers, and economists ignore the meaning of "specialization" as it occurs to Argyris. It simply means that they must, if they are to accomplish their principal objectives of inquiry, devote their greatest attention to their own expertise and logic, as based on what they are trying to accomplish.[10] In the process of building their models or conceptual schemes, they are exercising the prerogative of a scholar or technologist: to derive meaning from facts *as they see them.*

CETERIS PARIBUS IN SOCIAL SCIENCE

Even in the pure version of social science, such as is directed toward the understanding of nature rather than the controlling of nature through technology, and as exemplified in the Durkheim theory, the scientist sees certain important, central meanings to a wide variety of facts. Though Durkheim's theory seems the "very model of theoretic and methodologic sophistication . . . (indicating his stature) as a pure social scientist,"[11] there is no assurance that another social scientist will not one day set out to derive different meanings from different orders of facts, thus showing another important cause of suicide, and a different conceptual scheme. In this sense, even in pure varieties of social science, the

---

[7] Study particularly the Mississippi Valley Equipment Company case, plus the readings, for insight into the meaning of the term "specialization" in relation to internal organization planning.

[8] That is, in their formal models. They cover such divergent phenomena in their assumptions when they study a technological system, but these generally receive less rigorous analysis and proof than the phenomena of primary focus.

[9] For more detailed examples of these views of the world, see the following cases and their collateral readings: Midwest Hardware Manufacturing Company, National Motor Parts Company, AB Thorsten, Western Office Equipment Company, Sea Breeze Motel and Lightronics Corporation.

[10] Many students of Adam Smith, being interested in his major thesis, will not have been "interested" enough to remember his later passages which state, in a powerful way, the harmful effects of specialization on human beings. These are reproduced herein as pages 734–35 of *The Wealth of Nations.* Smith did not consider these as important as the opposite principle when he formulated economic theory.

[11] Alvin W. Gouldner, "Theoretical Requirements of the Applied Social Sciences," *American Sociological Review,* Vol. 22, No. 1 (February 1957), p. 98.

social scientist assumes *ceteris paribus,* or "other things being equal." Operations researchers and Chris Argyris, because of their choice of when to close the system—of what other things would be assumed to be equal—arrive at totally different meanings of the same phenomenon, specialization.

As one moves nearer and nearer to the control of the environment— when one becomes a technologist, or even more a policy maker—he must realize that "other things" are present in the policy system: that divergent or assumed phenomena can be of lesser importance, equal importance, or greater importance than the convergent phenomena presented by the scientist.

Economics has traditionally been concerned, in part, with control of the environment. As scholars who reason, *a priori,* from "supply" and "demand," economists assume, for example, that all men are motivated by "competition," and they are very careful to state their principles in terms of *other things being equal.* This is a signal to men of action that they are studying only parts of a policy system at any one time.

What we are saying here is that in a policy decision made by a general executive in a policy system, each theory (from each discipline) may predict a certain outcome, in absolute terms, if a given course of action (policy, decision, and strategy) is decided upon. But when many theories, from many disciplines, predict different outcomes, the *absolute* result predicted by each theory must be given a *weight* by the general executive. From the standpoint of any one individual theory, other outcomes from other theories may be weighted lower, the same, or higher, depending on the goals of the policy system as interpreted by the manager. These weights based on goals which the executive is trying to accomplish *are not necessarily the same* as the weight that a psychologist would assign to psychological outcomes based on the goals of psychologists. They are not necessarily the same as the weights an applied mathematician would assign to technological performance, such as the quantities in an inventory control and product planning system, when he expresses this system in a mathematical, operations research model.

WHO HAS THE FINAL ANSWER FOR POLICY DETERMINATION?

In philosophy of knowledge, the term "validity" means that a conceptual scheme of concepts linked together in an explanation of cause and effect is internally consistent. That is, terms are defined precisely and reasoning proceeds according to rules, either the older Aristotelian syllogistic rules or the newer rules of general semantics.

There is no such thing as this kind of "validity" in a policy decision. There may be validity in each of the separate theories, but that is because scholars used methods to simplify the world which yielded this kind of validity.

In the world of theory, "truth" (reliability) means that the conceptual schemes generated by the human mind through scientific method have been (and can be) verified by repeating the observation or by reproducing an experiment. Thus, Leverrier verified the scheme of "force, mass, heliocentric longitude, orbit" when he predicted that Neptune was there, looked through his telescope, and saw it.

One might also verify the scheme of "suicide-group integration" by observing groups in the real world. The scientist would then go out and look for groups with high or low integration and, using statistical probability, prove that the higher suicide rate could not have been caused by random factors. It therefore must have been caused by the variable or concept of group integration. In this case, the theory of group integration caused the researcher to measure group characteristics only on this scale. He closed out the rest of the world, so to speak.

In the other means of verification (experimentation), were it not for our social mores regarding experimenting with human beings, one might set up two experimental groups, controlled in the sense that (1) the two groups have different degrees of the independent variable, group integration, and (2) in all other respects, the groups are alike. By changing the degree of group integration in one group, one then would measure the difference in the suicide rates which result and subject them to tests of statistical probability. The scientist has deliberately created a factual situation "out there" which eliminates the world in its confusion and simplifies it into a controlled experiment, abstracted from the world. In one sense, then, he is creating a situation, by controlling reality, which produces the very phenomena which his imagination created in the first place. In Langmuir's sense, he is setting up a factual situation in which divergent phenomena are deliberately kept out.

Thus in both the observations and in the reproducible experiments of social science, *ceteris paribus,* other things being equal, presents a special problem. In astronomy, an observational science where the phenomena under study are literally "in a vacuum" and where other things are equal in the reality of day-to-day dynamics, conceptual schemes and reality approximate the same thing. In social science, where controlled conditions create artificial vacua or where choosing of facts to study "closes the system" and where other things in the complexity of day-to-day events are such that other things are *not* equal, theory and total reality are not necessarily the same thing. Such theories are creations of the human mind.

In answer to our question, who has the final answer for policy determination, the answer is: probably nobody. An executive may seem to question the validity and truth of theories as he evaluates them for his policy making. Not so! Because the executive has moved away from the closed system of the scholar to the open policy system, he must apply another criterion: does the theory work? No one theory fits the policy system with its multitude of interacting variables. As we have said, theories come to grips with a slice of reality, burying the remainder of reality in the *ceteris paribus* assumption. The executive recognizes that a theory may have validity and truth within the closed system of the scholar's purpose. If Durkheim's purpose is to understand suicide, there may well be validity and truth in his statement of its cause. If Argyris' purpose is to understand conflict in organizations, there may well be validity and truth in his more elaborate scheme. If the applied mathematician's purpose is to minimize the cost of holding inventory, there may also be validity and truth in his mathematical formula for the optimum lot size, based on a number of technological and economic variables. But when the executive comes to policy determination, he must eclectically draw from valid and true theories, those aspects which are relevant to *his* problems, and which aid in his analysis and his decisions.

Roethlisberger, in a book reporting on one of the most significant research projects undertaken in social science, points out that there is within sociology and anthropology today a controversy over the "historical" versus the "functional" conceptual schemes. He clearly points out that neither is true nor false, but "more or less convenient or useful for certain purposes . . . [and] its usefulness can only be decided after it has been used."[12] He then cites a rather powerful passage from a book by Thurman Arnold:

> *The eye of the artist or poet looking at the human body is different from the eye of the physician looking for pathological symptoms. Neither one has the "true" nor the "false" view of the body. The physician, however, is the better person when therapy rather than decoration is demanded.*[13]

SOCIAL SCIENCE AND SOCIAL PHILOSOPHY

The social scientist's study of *certain problems* in the environment is complicated by the fact that he cannot isolate his own emotional needs from the hypothesis he generates. In the physical sciences, an astronomer is not necessarily mad or happy when he finds Neptune in a certain orbit. He does not think this is good or bad.

In the social sciences this is not necessarily true, particularly in the study of organizations. Every social scientist has been living in organizations from birth (the family), and shall be in organizations until death (government, universities, business). As he performs the scientific operations noted in the preceding section, selection of facts to observe, interpretation of meanings, setting up of experiments, these value predispositions (positive-negative) influence the total intellectual process in each of its stages.

In this sense, social "science" has something in common with social "philosophy." Faced with limitations on the methods the astronomer uses to leave his emotions out of his observations in a pure, simplified system, the social scientist in one sense reasons *a priori,* i.e., from a combination of assumptions and facts, rather than from facts alone. He is denied the very conditions (a simple, closed system) which would have been a check on his deeper, unconscious assumptions.

Still other scholars, social philosophers, attack large social issues

---

[12] F. J. Roethlisberger, *Management and Morale* (Cambridge: Harvard University Press, 1941), p. 69.

[13] *The Symbols of Government* (New Haven: Yale University Press, 1935), p. 30.

where measurement, observation, reproducible experiment, and validation are not possible. These people reason from assumptions freely and employ logic (philosophy) rather than a combination of fact and logic (science) to explain their concepts. The individual scholar's values are even more likely to influence such theories in these cases. A good example of how different values create different conceptual schemes is to be found in the apparent contradiction between traditional management theory based on economics and political science and certain forms of management theory based on psychology.

Management theory, based primarily on economic principles such as specialization, and interested primarily in the necessity of technological coordination of the inputs and outputs between operating and staff functions, proceeds to reason out such concepts as "division of work," "delegation of authority," and "unity of command (power)." In this sense, management theory is quite akin to political philosophy. It starts with assumptions similar to John Locke's[14]—that "all men are biased" (note that it does not start with "growth") and that men need and want an "indifferent judge," with "authority," so that chaos and anarchy will not prevail (note that there is no reference to the fact that the "indifferent judge" will stifle the "growth" of men). Management theory also has some unconscious assumptions similar to engineering and operations research. That is, the importance of technological coordination in the production of goods—between the timing, quality, and quantity of work flow, with the aid of central, rational planning—is of paramount concern.

On the other hand, theories based on psychology and small group dynamics imply that, in order to liberate the largest amount of human energy and creativity in the organization, a maximum amount of participation, by group members, is a desirable type of managerial and subordinate behavior. Most of these theories do not refer to the increment of efficiency due to technological coordination by central planners, or expert staff personnel such as engineers and operations researchers, or to the time consumed in patient, "two-way communication" (one of their central concepts). Rather, such theories highlight the fact that such communication arrives at the best decisions on how to structure the business, and at the same time produce the most harmonious human system. (Note that these theories do not deliberately reason with Locke that all people need authority, or with the economists, that all people are competitive.[15] Nor do they say that anarchy would prevail without some legalized authority.)

Obviously, we could go on and on in giving examples of differences

---

[14] Reproduced herein as pages 53–54 of John Locke, *Concerning Civil Government.*

[15] Note, also, that the assumptions of scholars vary according to the nature of the institution they are studying. Classical economists were "in favor of" freedom of the firm's management to do as it wished, but they never implied that *within* the firm there should be "free enterprise." They imply quite the contrary: that the executive, either as an expert computer of economic data, or as a deterministic agent, should determine jobs and specializations, and allocate resources up to the margin. The applied economists, such as budget analysts, financial planners, and the like, imply even more explicitly that people and other resources should be managed on the basis of expert calculation of marginal revenues, cash flows, break-even charts, and the like.

in conceptual schemes, due to differences in the deeper values of the scholars who formulate them. The point to be made is that in the study of mankind as opposed to the study of nonhuman objects and phenomena, values do get into the picture in more than one way. For philosophers, who use assumptions and reasoning, the values can clearly influence what they see, both in terms of selecting assumptions from which to reason and in showing relationships. For applied social scientists, the practitioners who study large complex organizations, and particularly those who study matters of human individuality and organizational attributes, these values influence the choice of facts to observe, the way experiments are set up, and derivation of meaning from those facts.

THE VALUE OF SOCIAL SCIENCE IN POLICY DECISIONS

In this chapter we have seen some of the methods used by social scientists and social philosophers to arrive at their theories and conceptual schemes.

If there is anything which should stand out to the policy maker, to the man of action, it is the fact that social science provides an enormous pool of experience from a wide variety of people who spend their lives looking for meaning of events within their field. The very bias with which they approach their subjects, occasioned by different viewpoints or preconceptions, or, as in the Durkheim case, occasioned by their interest in a certain problem, means that they see people, organizations, and events in a light not available to laymen. To the policy maker these theories are valuable in determining managerial goals, in creatively formulating alternative courses of action, and in predicting what will happen if policy makers make decisions one way or another. Most important, *in all three* of these steps, they help to prevent a decision being made which later is discovered to have adverse unintended consequences.

For further insight into how the executive uses theory in his policy decisions, one might refer to an article by one of the authors which served as a precursor to the present volume.[16]

---

[16] Charles E. Summer, "The Managerial Mind," *Harvard Business Review,* January–February, 1959.

NOTES ON THE STUDY OF CASES

1. The diagnostic and predictive questions framed in each case introduction will help you apply theories and concepts from a certain discipline of thought (e.g., economics, psychology, political science) to the facts of the particular case situation. These concepts are valuable to help *understand* basic forces at work in the policy system (diagnosis of what is going on), and to *predict* what will happen in the system in the future. Each reading or theory abstracts from the real world certain factors into the closed system view of one discipline. No one of these disciplines can have the final truth or answer to a real world situation in its buzzing confusion. As one writer has put it, the medical doctor and the artist may both look at the human body and "see" different things. Which is *true?* The answer is that neither has the truth of the world in its entirety. Therefore, the diagnostic question helps one see reality, but only parts of reality.

2. The policy questions require the manager to deal with the whole situation—he cannot become solely an economist, a political scientist or a psychologist. The result of diagnosis and prediction, which actually reduces the amount of judgment necessary, does not eliminate the need for judgment and intuition. Since certain parts of the world cannot be reduced to science, and since "other things are not equal," judgment must still be used to fill in the factors not accounted for by readings. One must also use a second kind of judgment to put value weights on different scientific predictions because different theories might indeed predict conflicting ideal solutions.

3. In summary, the diagnostic (scientific) understanding of cases demonstrates the power of theory and concepts, if used by practicing managers. The policy-making action questions demonstrate the limitations of science and the need for judgment in the world of action. This dual need for *both* science *and* judgment has been more fully explained in the introductory chapters.

PART II Strategic Planning and Organization Design

Part II of this book is addressed to three of the most important functions of any manager: (1) designing an organization structure which will accomplish the technical goal of the enterprise, (2) adjusting this structure to eliminate conflict between human beings who must cooperate if the organization's goal is to be achieved, and (3) adapting the structure so that the individuals who fill the boxes on the organization chart will feel like contributing their efforts to excellence in their jobs.

WHY ORGANIZATION STRUCTURE IS IMPORTANT: A MEANS TO SOCIAL GOALS

Every organization must achieve some primary goals, otherwise society "out there" will not in the long run continue to support the organization. This is true of a hospital which must render quality patient care at a level of efficiency satisfactory to patients and governing boards. It is true of a public school which must render quality education at a cost that is not unduly high in the minds of the board of education or parents. It is true of a business corporation which must make certain kinds of products of a quality desired by the customer at an efficiency cost that is not unreasonable.

Each of these organizations is chartered by society to perform an economic mission: to produce some good or service which is wanted by people *outside,* and to produce at a level of efficiency that is acceptable externally. Internal efficiency, as important as it may seem, is simply a means to the larger end—social productivity.

Regardless of whether one thinks that organizations in general are "good" or "bad" (there are both kinds in the world), they are a fact of life. They exist in primitive societies when a group of men fish together and sell their fish to others. They exist in developing countries such as Iran and Ethiopia, where society needs goods and services at an economical cost. They exist in societies such as Russia, the United States, and Denmark with highly developed exchange economies, in which almost nobody can do without the goods and services produced by organized corporations, firms, hospitals, government offices, and airlines.

The primary purpose of any organization, then, is to serve certain segments of society out there beyond the organization. In an age when social responsibility of the firm (and the managers in it) is coming to be recognized as a question of vital importance, it is well to recognize at the outset that organizations *must* produce what they are chartered for, and what society wants. This is the primary goal of organizations that survive. The primary goal of a hospital is quality patient care produced efficiently. If pollution materials are a byproduct of the hospital, then the managers of the institution may have a responsibility to comply with the health standards of environmental pollution control. But the economic function of producing patient care is still the primary goal. If the primary goal of an airline is to transport passengers and freight and if society indeed wants this kind of transportation, the airline must observe noise limitation requirements, but it cannot deny as its primary specialization the transporting of passengers. Nobody wants to go to an airline pilot for treatment of the liver, and nobody wants a heart specialist piloting his airplane to Chicago.

Given this responsibility to society to produce the primary goal in a productive, efficient manner, what are the principal ways that a manager functions to do this? Stated in another way, what are the task specializations of a manger, what are his job duties?

ORGANIZATION DESIGN AS A FUNCTION AND RESPONSIBILITY OF MANAGERS

The first step in organization is clearly to assess the environment outside the organization and set goals that are in tune with the demands of society. This act of strategic planning is covered in several of the readings in Part II, and is particularly highlighted in the Yarway Corporation and Mississippi Valley Equipment Corporation. We shall see in both cases that not only is the economic function demanded by society a factor in goal setting, but also that the values of the executives in the organization—their beliefs, interests, and attitudes—influence the goal-setting process. Goals are in one sense part of the total organization structure. They determine what work, tasks, and technology are necessary to produce the goal. Given air transportation, some manager or group of managers must think out the various tasks and specializations, the various coordinating procedures or positions which connect these positions (the interrelationships between tasks and specializations). The ticket seller must be related to the baggage handler, the pilot to the scheduling manager, the food service producers to the stewardesses, and so on.

In three of the cases in Part II, the design problem involves structuring an entire firm: taking the goal of the firm as its external output to society, how should the internal parts of the firm be conceptualized and related to one another.

In two of the following cases, the design problem is one of structuring the organization of a department within a firm. In most important respects, this problem is identical with the one above. That is, the department also has its society or environment—its external world. The design problem becomes one of structuring the internal system: taking the goal of the department as its output to other departments in the firm, how should the internal parts of the department be structured in terms of (1) parts, specializations or jobs; and (2) relationships, procedures or interconnections between parts.

For example, the Weapons System Division of Electronics International Corporation and the Management Systems Division within Manco Corporation are organizational entities in themselves. The "environment" of these departments—society out there—is the corporation as a whole. It is the larger corporation which is making demands on the systems division within Manco Corporation. The "customers" are other divisions in the same company. The managers of departments are in the same position relative to their "world" as the managers of a corporation such as National Bank of San Francisco or Yarway Corporation. They must design an internal organization structure which fits the external world outside the department.

SOME APPROACHES TO DESIGN OF ORGANIZATIONS

The first purpose of this book is to expose the reader to the *reality* of organizational problems—how they look in the real world, what subproblems are faced by managers designing an organization, and what kinds of solutions managers devise to achieve the three organizational responsibilities stated in the first sentence of this introduction.

Nevertheless, there are certain theories of organization structure which have been conceptualized by practicing businessmen or scholars and which may be of use depending on the specific facts in a particular company or department.

These are interspersed as readings with the various case problems. Some are techniques of strategic planning and goal setting (particularly important as part of the organization problem of Yarway Corporation and Mississippi Valley Equipment Corporation). Others come from the field of general management theory. For example, we include guides to departmentation (how to split a large task into subparts), concepts of operating positions versus management positions, the use of line and staff coordinating positions, use of the auxiliary service departments for output to primary operating departments, and the use of decentralized (divisionalized) structures. Still other approaches have been developed more recently: the matrix form of organization which is being tried by the Electronics International Corporation, or the informal behavior of "integrators" (as opposed to line executives wielding formal authority) which is a possibility for Manco Corporation. Organization development, which views the organization as a more or less fluid, changing, and dynamic entity (rather than a structured and rationalized entity) is suggested for consideration in some of the cases, although it will be more fully covered in Part V.

THE "SCIENCE" OF ORGANIZATION

There is another kind of reading included with the cases which is of great aid to the practicing manager. The technologies of organization suggest to him various solutions to problems, or at least how to recognize a certain breed of organization when he sees it. But if he is to understand reality at an even more basic level, the manager must be able to "see" more fundamental forces at work which cause one technology (for example, matrix form of organization) to have certain results. It is one thing for a manager to be able to suggest the line-staff structure or the matrix structure as alternatives for solving a particular company's problem, but it is quite another to be able to predict what will happen if one of these structures is actually selected as the solution. What will be the effect on the quantity of output of Mississippi Valley Equipment Corporation or National Bank of San Francisco? What will be the difference in manpower and talent required? What will be the difference in the overhead cost of operating the Equipment Corporation or the Bank? These are questions to which the social science of economics is addressed.

Or, what will be the effect of one alternative structure on the feelings of loyalty and commitment of lower managers and employees? What will be the effect in terms of conflict generated between men in the organization? These are questions to which the social sciences of psychology and sociology have been addressed.

Concepts and theories from the social sciences thus serve as a checklist for the practical manager. They help him predict what will happen if he designs a formal authority position, a staff coordinator position, or a matrix organization. In all five of the cases presented in Part II we shall see that *both* economic and human factors loom large as inputs to the practical manager's brain *if* he is to choose a structure with wisdom.

THE SIMILARITY AND DIVERSITY OF SPECIFIC COMPANY SITUATIONS

No two organizational problems are ever alike in the real world. Organizations are so rich in different people, different finances, and different technologies that each problem must be studied *as it is*—not only as textbook writers in social science theorize. That is not to say theories of organization are valueless. We have already shown how both scientific type insights (basic forces) and technological type insights (suggested solutions) can be of help. But these must be used with caution, picking and choosing which are relevant. The manager must use his own brain, in effect devising a custom-made analysis of each problem (what is going on in this particular organization) and a custom-made solution (what kind of structure is best here). Included in the following section are a diverse number of organizational situations.

In the Systems Department within Manco Corporation, we see a relatively stable and mature department, in the sense that it has been furnishing a group of computer and systems services to other internal departments for some time. Its customers—the marketing department and manufacturing plants—demand very specialized services such as a system for recording and billing customer accounts, and a computer program to operate this system. Management of the department has tried departmentalizing these specialties separately, only to be confronted with problems of coordination between the specialists. Now management is trying to combine these specialties by creating "enlarged" jobs and "generalist" positions, in the hope that each man can do his own coordinating. But this solution presents still further problems. What kind of structure will maintain the necessary specialized functions, and achieve coordination between these? What kind of coordinating positions are possible to aid in this problem?

Yarway Corporation presents both similarities to and differences from Manco Corporation. Faced with growing foreign markets, and competition from giant multinational firms, what structure will enable the company efficiently to manufacture and sell its engineering equipment to electric power companies and chemical plants around the world? Should the company maintain its present trend toward geographical "generalist" operating units, or should it consider reverting to worldwide "specialist" units which report vertically to Philadelphia headquarters? Which is best to achieve good specialization of manufacturing and sales and yet also to achieve good coordination between these functions (or coordination between Europe and South America)?

National Bank of San Francisco has some of the same problems as Manco Corporation and Yarway Corporation. There are pressures from the outside world for certain goals—good banking services at reasonable costs. To meet these pressures, the question arises as to who should specialize in technical matters of physical space, bank machines, and personnel practices. Should the corporate staff insure this specialization (and coordination between branches around San Francisco), or should the "generalist" branch managers assume these responsibilities? What other kinds of specialization or coordinating devices are possible? Committees? Participative task forces? Formal authority?

These examples, plus other cases in Part II, show that there is a certain similarity between organizational problems, and that the informed manager should know how to catalogue alternative structures which he might use to solve generic type problems. They also show that the informed manager will know enough about basic economics and psychology that he can intelligently investigate vital factors when he chooses one alternative.

But the examples show further that National Bank of San Francisco is not similar to Yarway Corporation or Manco Corporation in certain equally important ways. No two organization problems are identical. There is no substitute for tailoring *both* the analysis/diagnosis of the organizational problem *and* the final decision on structure to the reality of a specific organization at a particular time.

The readings in Part II aim at helping the manager to be more *informed* as to alternative structures for organization and basic forces in the problem. Practice with the cases in Part II aims at helping the manager to be more wise in his decision making when he selects a particular structure to fit his specific company or department.

STRATEGIC PLANNING AS RELATED TO ALL MANAGEMENT FUNCTIONS

Though the paragraphs above stress management's function of strategic planning as it relates to the way another key function is performed (organization design), the manager must recognize that it is in one sense related to *all* key tasks of the manager, as explained in other sections of this book: to the task of financial planning, the task of scientific decision making, the task of leadership, and to problems of social responsibilities other than production and efficiency.

For example, the long-range planning methods suggested in the Tilles reading are applicable not only to how managers in Yarway (Part II) structure the organization of their company, but also to how managers in Western Office Equipment Company (Part IV) decide to allocate salesmen to territories, using management science techniques. Or the way managers of Shoe Corporation of Illinois (Part V) exercise personal leadership is in part determined by strategic planning of product lines. If very frequent style changes for women's shoes are required by the strategic plan, one leadership style may be called for. If stable, standard tennis shoes are to be produced over the years, another style seems appropriate. We shall see in Part VI that the strategic plans of Polaroid must include the company's racial policies, or that strategic plans for Standard Oil's future relationship with stockholders is affected by prevailing social norms regarding corporate citizenship as well as norms relating to profits and dividends.

These examples serve to highlight the fact that strategic planning (or long-range planning) is pervasive as a key function of managers. It cuts across all others. The fact that the major part titles in this book are addressed to five other key management tasks should not obscure this vital sixth task.

1. MANCO CORPORATION

Case Introduction

SYNOPSIS

During the formative years of the management systems department of a consumer specialities manufacturing and marketing company, the staff witnesses three major reorganizations. In the three years from 1963 to 1966, the organization moves from a specialization by function (systems analysts and programmers) to specialization by customer (internal operating divisions like Marketing, Finance, Manufacturing, and R.&D.). The "generalists" in management systems serve the operating divisions in project groups headed by systems project administrators. This latter position evolves from a liaison and coordination role to a formal, supervisory role with accountability for the project itself and the project personnel involved in the new, integrated, staff service.

A former specialist, who is promoted to the systems project administrator position, seems to resist the newly integrated approach. He leaves the organization, and one of his former subordinates runs into serious trouble with an important EDP system for an operating division. A systems project administrator who had not previously been involved with the faulty system nor its designer assumes responsibility for both. Arrangements are made to correct the system. The systems project administrator "is very troubled" over what to do with the system's designer in view of his superior's statement: "I'm not sure where he fits in . . . do what you have to do."

WHY THIS CASE IS INCLUDED

The brief history of the management systems department records the interplay between the individual and organization structure. It is instructive to trace the development of role demands and the relationship between such role demands and perceived roles of those involved in the case. The history of the management systems department also points to the interdependence of people, structure, and technology—no one of the factors is altered in an organizational change effort without affecting the other two. There is opportunity to explore the degree of openness in interpersonal relationships and how this affects executive decisions. Finally, the case poses the issue of due process for the white-collar or management employee—that is, the degree of protection the employee has from unilateral behavior of superiors, especially when he works for a succession of different superiors with seemingly different criteria for acceptable performance.

DIAGNOSTIC AND PREDICTIVE QUESTIONS

The readings included with this case are marked (*). The author index at the end of this book locates the other readings.

1. In an economic sense, what was Manco trying to accomplish in the 1963 reorganization of the management systems department? Keeping in mind the two concepts of specialization and coordination, trace the impact of the reorganization on the customer account computer system.

Read: *O'Connell, "Beyond Economics: Coordinomics," Part I.

2. Trace the interdependencies of people and structure during the 1963–66 period of growth and change in the management systems department of the Manco Corporation. Should top management have been able to predict the "people impact" of the structural changes and the "structure impact" of the personnel changes?

Read: *Leavitt, *Managerial Psychology,* pp. 317–25.

3. Using the social psychology conceptual schema for role development, trace the impact of the 1963 reorganization on the behavior (role performance) of the specialists in programming and the specialists in systems. What were the new role demands for each class of specialist? For the newly appointed systems project administrators?

Read: *Levinson, "Role, Personality, and Social Structure in the Organizational Setting."

4. Using the theoretical model of interpersonal relations analyze the relations between the following pairs as they are pictured and as they develop in the case: Carson-Wallace, Wallace-Roberts, Roberts-Carson, Behrens-Wallace, Behrens-Jonas, Jonas-Roberts, Carson-Jonas. Do you find perception "errors" in any of these relationships? If so, why do the individuals misperceive one another?

Read: *McGrath, *Social Psychology,* pp. 50–52.

5. Trace the development of Wallace's self-concept and Roberts' self-concept. Relate each self-concept to role performance by using the bridging construct of role concept.

Read: The readings assigned in the two previous questions.

6. After Behrens announces the departure of Wallace, Jonas asks: "Why don't you call a spade a spade?" How can you explain Behrens' behavior on this occasion? How explain Carson's behavior in his last interview with Jonas?

Read: *Carr, "Is Business Bluffing Ethical?"

7. When Wallace's job was eliminated in a reorganization of Behrens' unit, Jonas raised the issue of the "very involved system for placing

unsatisfactory performers on warning. . . ." He said: "That system's supposed to protect the employee." Does Jonas voice a legitimate concern? What are the consequences of what Jonas calls "a completely arbitrary system?" Does Roberts have due process protection?

Read: *Evan, "Organization Man and Due Process of Law."

POLICY QUESTIONS

8. From what has happened to Wallace and Roberts in the Manco Company do you find cause to revise the appraisal system? If so, what would you recommend?

9. Would you have planned or implemented the Manco reorganizations any differently? If so, how?

10. If you were Behrens, what would you do at the end of the case? If you were Carson? If you were Jonas?

11. In one sense, the systems analysts prior to the 1963 reorganization were staff integrators. They were supposed to visit the marketing division or manufacturing division client, for example, and learn his operations. They then began to design the new system for the client—coming back to the systems division and working with the specialist programmers (who were to put the new system in computer language). After the reorganization, each systems analyst was supposed to know *both* the client management system *and* programming. Both the individual systems man and the project administrator were supposed to *integrate* the client needs with the computer program.

What advise would you give the company as to improving their method of integrating? This might be advice on the organization structure (whether to revert to systems department integrators, or whether to maintain the present structure wherein every man is an integrator, or to increase the integrating activities of the project administrator).

Read: Lawrence and Lorsch, "New Management Job: The Integrator."

QUESTIONS FOR ORIGINAL STUDENT WORK IN ANALYSIS AND POLICY

12. While reflecting on case facts, what additional theories from prior education give you insights as to "what is going on" in the Manco Corporation? As to what might be predicted to happen in the future?

13. Other than the policy questions asked by the authors, what pragmatic ways can you think of to state the practical problems faced by executives in the case?

Case Text*

The Manco Corporation serves the consumer field with a broad line of high-quality specialty products. Most of the corporation's 6,000 employees work in Saginaw, Michigan, the headquarters and main plant location. Manco, with the other nine leading companies in its field, invests heavily in R.&D. and relies more on product innovation than on the protection of its numerous patents. Manco's $200 million sales volume is made up of about 75 percent domestic sales and 25 percent foreign sales. Growth over the past half-dozen years has averaged somewhat over 5 percent a year, and profit margins have stayed well in excess of 10 percent before tax.

One of the staff support groups serving the expanding and ever more sophisticated management is the management systems department. The partial organization chart of the Manco Corporation in Exhibit 1 shows the position of this department as of June 1966.

THE MANAGEMENT SYSTEMS DEPARTMENT

The 55 professional people in the management systems department serve all the operating divisions of the corporation as part of the central staff reporting to Elkin Parker, the vice president of Manco's Administrative Division, through Harold Simken, the director of administrative services.

The department is responsible for performing a broad range of internal consulting activities. The management systems department's major efforts are concentrated in the design and maintenance of computer-based information systems. Project work is also conducted in the areas of organization planning, operations research, general systems design, and standard operating procedures.

All management systems work is conducted on a project request basis. For example, the customer account system mentioned later resulted from a problem first seen by Ned O'Donnell, manager of the physical distribution department, which in turn is a part of the Sales Division of the company. O'Donnell and the vice president for sales had long wanted a method for keeping customer charge accounts more accurately, and a method for processing these with great speed. They had called the management systems department for help.

The systems department thus forms a central service unit for the whole company. The company has a rule that only if a major operating division requests assistance on its own initiative can work actually com-

---

EXHIBIT 1
Partial Manco Organization Chart (June 1966)

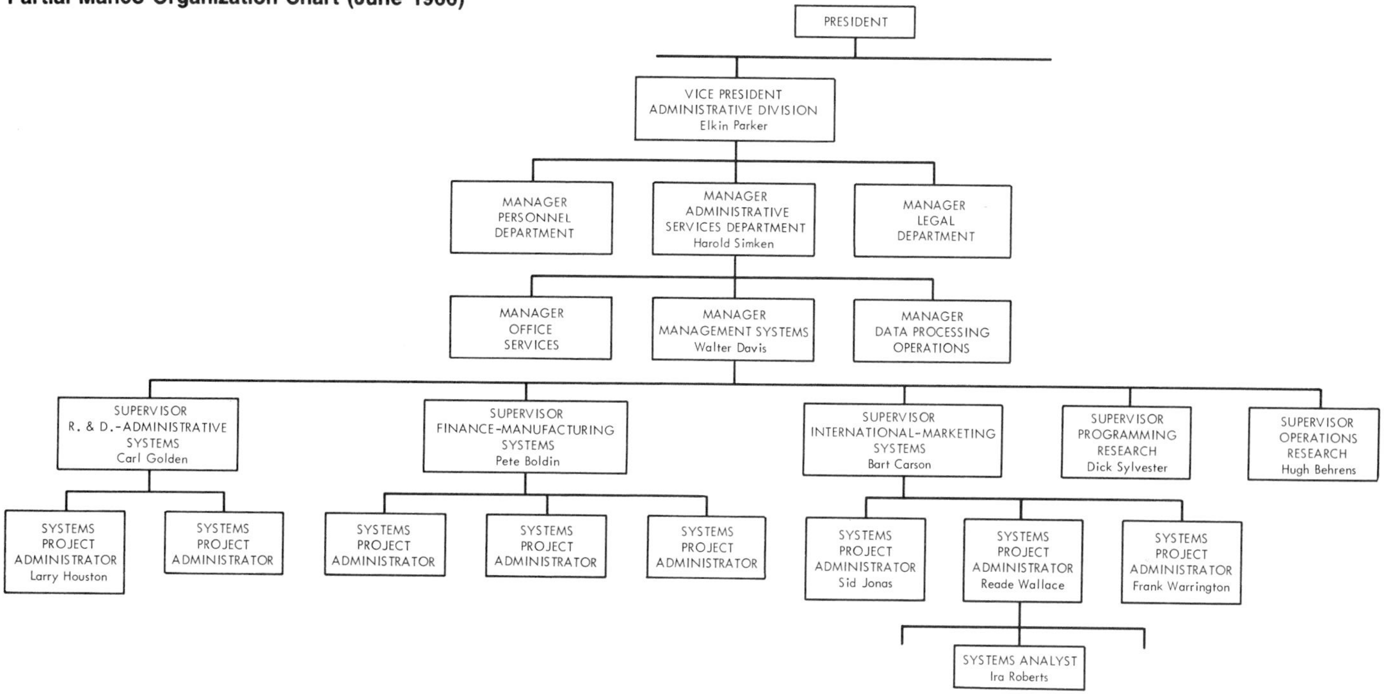
PRESIDENT
VICE PRESIDENT ADMINISTRATIVE DIVISION Elkin Parker
MANAGER PERSONNEL DEPARTMENT
MANAGER ADMINISTRATIVE SERVICES DEPARTMENT Harold Simken
MANAGER LEGAL DEPARTMENT
MANAGER OFFICE SERVICES
MANAGER MANAGEMENT SYSTEMS Walter Davis
MANAGER DATA PROCESSING OPERATIONS
SUPERVISOR R. & D.-ADMINISTRATIVE SYSTEMS Carl Golden
SUPERVISOR FINANCE-MANUFACTURING SYSTEMS Pete Boldin
SUPERVISOR INTERNATIONAL-MARKETING SYSTEMS Bart Carson
SUPERVISOR PROGRAMMING RESEARCH Dick Sylvester
SUPERVISOR OPERATIONS RESEARCH Hugh Behrens
SYSTEMS PROJECT ADMINISTRATOR Larry Houston
SYSTEMS PROJECT ADMINISTRATOR
SYSTEMS PROJECT ADMINISTRATOR
SYSTEMS PROJECT ADMINISTRATOR
SYSTEMS PROJECT ADMINISTRATOR
SYSTEMS PROJECT ADMINISTRATOR Sid Jonas
SYSTEMS PROJECT ADMINISTRATOR Reade Wallace
SYSTEMS PROJECT ADMINISTRATOR Frank Warrington
SYSTEMS ANALYST Ira Roberts

mence in the systems department. This rule is designed so that the systems analysts will assume the role of consultants to the other divisions of the company, rather than to assume the active role of managing the operating divisions either by initiating their plans, or by controlling and acting as policemen. According to Simkin, "this means that the systems department is somewhat like a small business seeking customers. We are here to perform services for the operating departments. They must feel a need for our service and, in effect, hire us to perform them. They're also in the position of not buying our services if the services don't genuinely contribute to solving their problems."

After another division requests assistance, the project request is jointly reviewed by the management systems department manager and his five unit supervisors so that a priority might be assigned to the project. The considerable project backlog has made it necessary for managers within the department to devote substantial time to identifying the most important projects.

The organization of management systems (Exhibit 1) reflects Harold Simken's and Walter Davis' strong interest in maintaining satisfactory and stable relationships with all company divisions. Three systems units—the international-marketing unit, the financial-manufacturing unit, and the R.&D.-administrative unit—form the core of the department. Each unit performs work for two company divisions on a continuing basis. The operations research and programming research units provide technical support to the three systems units. Operations research and programming research personnel often work on those systems projects which require very specialized skills, and they are frequently involved in nonproject development work.

The mix of project work and personnel within each of the three systems units is determined by the pattern of project requests made by the various Manco divisions. The potential for meaningful systems design work and the receptivity of key managers vary from division to division. These differences create demands for divergent sets of skills in the three systems units. Project requests from the Research and Development Division, for example, involve the computerized retrieval of scientific information on laboratory experiments. On the other hand, systems work for the Administrative Division primarily consists of issuing and revising standard operating procedures. As a result of these project demands the R.&D.—administrative unit has two distinct types of analysts—programmers and standard procedure specialists.

The requests made by the International and Marketing Divisions demand a still wider set of skills in the international-marketing systems unit. This unit has been involved in large-scale simulations of domestic and international distribution networks, organizational studies of the Marketing Division and several international branches, and other complex systems studies. Since these projects usually require skills different from either programming or procedure work, the international-marketing systems unit employs management scientists and organizational planning specialists, as well as programmers and systems analysts.

Within each systems unit, there are two or three systems project administrators, who handle the day-to-day administrative activities of the systems units. Each project administrator is responsible for specific departments in one or two Manco divisions. Thus, in the international-marketing systems unit, one project administrator is responsible for projects in the market research and promotion planning departments, while another supervises project work for the sales, advertising, and general promotion departments. The systems project administrator is, in essence, a working first-line supervisor. From a supervisory standpoint, the project administrators supervise client project requests, plan and schedule work loads, administer salary, and appraise performance of their subordinates. In addition, they spend approximately one third of their time actually performing some of the more complex project work.

The present management systems department was formed during a June 1963 reorganization, which combined all systems and programming activities. Prior to the reorganization, separate systems and programming sections existed. Most of the analysts believed that the reorganization was precipitated by mangement's dissatisfaction with the divided responsibility for projects, which so often called for both systems and programming work. There had been an increasing number of complaints concerning the inability of the two sections to meet deadlines for converting systems from manual to computer processing. The systems analysts believed that the programmers were at fault for not adhering to schedules. The programmers contended that the systems analysts did not appreciate the magnitude and complexity of the programming task. Because of this lack of understanding, argued the programmers, the systems analysts made unrealistic calendar commitments to the divisional managers responsible for the particular system.

The reorganization was also designed to eliminate the discontent among systems analysts and programmers over advancement opportunities. As a result of the reorganization, the positions of management systems manager and unit supervisor were upgraded to higher salary classifications. The new position of systems project administrator was created one level below the unit supervisor level. Between June 1963 and June 1966, eight former senior system analysts and senior programmers were elevated to systems project administrators.

In the spirit of the 1963 reorganization, the systems analysts working for each systems project administrator were expected to perform both systems and programming activities. Initially the interests and assignments of most analysts corresponded to their previous specialty—systems or programming. Salary increases and promotions in the new organization, however, were designed to reward the generalist—the man who was able and willing to do both systems and programming and demonstrated this in project work. The hiring and training of new employees were also geared to produce this new breed of systems analysts.

THE INTERNATIONAL-MARKETING SYSTEMS UNIT

The supervisor of the international-marketing systems unit (see Exhibit 1) is Bart Carson. Carson, who had transferred into systems from the Manufacturing Division in 1958, is generally considered by his peers to be the most experienced and talented systems supervisor. Although his (pre-1963) experience had been confined to the systems section, he has been very positive about the new integrated approach of the 1963 reorganization. Carson has made conscious efforts to give his analysts diversified exposure and gradually has begun to develop what is regarded as a well-rounded unit within the context of the new management systems job responsibilities.

One of the three systems project administrators reporting to Carson in the summer of 1966 was Reade Wallace. Carson had given Wallace responsibility for project work in the International Division and the distribution department of the Marketing Division. Wallace, who had joined the company in 1959 after obtaining his MBA degree, had been regarded as a mainstay of the pre-1963 systems section. He had specialized in organization planning, standard operating procedures, and general systems work. Wallace's associates noted that his diplomacy and tact had enabled him to establish excellent rapport with several key managers in the company, in general, and in the International Division, in particular. Harold Simken, manager of administrative services, and Walter Davis, manager of management systems, were keenly interested in generating new international project work, and they both often spoke of how much they valued Wallace's interpersonal skills.

After the 1963 reorganization but before his promotion to systems project administrator, Wallace had made it clear to Bart Carson, systems supervisor, that he had no desire to get involved in EDP or management science projects. He preferred to continue his concentration in organizational planning and general administrative systems and said so publicly. Wallace was, in fact, the only analyst after the 1963 reorganization who overtly resisted Carson's plan for development. Consequently, Wallace's promotion to systems project administrator in October 1964 had been a very controversial move. To many analysts, the promotion represented a flagrant violation of the criteria established for the systems project administrator position. Some analysts attributed the move to pressure exerted on Carson by Simken and/or Davis.

MANAGEMENT SYSTEMS DEPARTMENT EXPANDS

The management systems department experienced rapid growth between June 1963 and June 1965, expanding from a personnel complement of 30 analysts to one of 55 analysts. One source of new people was the company's management training program, a rotational program consisting of several six- to eight-week assignments in various Manco divisions.

Among the trainees in this program was Ira Roberts, a former high school teacher who had taught for four years. As he completed the program in December 1965, Roberts' record showed he had created favorable impressions throughout the company during his rotational assignments. Roberts' first permanent position was as management systems analyst in Bart Carson's international-marketing unit, reporting to

Reade Wallace. Roberts had performed poorly on the programming aptitude test administered to all prospective management systems employees. He had received a B– on the exam, lower than anyone currently in the department. The independent psychological consulting firm, which administers the test, placed Roberts in the "Not Recommended" category on the analysis accompanying his test score. Since Roberts' principal work was to be in the general systems area, Carson and Wallace agreed that Roberts' personal strengths offset his relatively weak performance on the aptitude test. Carson and Wallace planned to increase Roberts' exposure to programming at some later date.

Roberts' first assignment was to develop a small-scale system to centralize information on grants to foundations and charities made by various company departments. His second project involved procedural work with various company divisions to insure companywide compliance with new federal legislation affecting the sale of company products. After some training in network scheduling techniques, Roberts performed admirably in developing a PERT chart to plan and schedule the introduction of Manco's first product in the Australian market. Co-workers observed Roberts working yeoman's hours, and the manager of the new Australian Branch was unstinting in his praise of Roberts and his network schedule.

Roberts' performance during his first year in systems was formally appraised by Wallace in January 1967. He noted the following strengths:

1. Quick mind.
2. Ability to shoulder responsibility.
3. Works well with others.
4. Loyal and excellent attitude towards the company.
5. Documents work well and is both cost and profit conscious.

Wallace listed project planning as Roberts' major area for improvement. He rated Roberts satisfactory overall and concluded the appraisal by discussing his potential:

Roberts handles work very well and has high potential. Could develop into one of our better senior analysts with a bit more programming experience.

At the bottom of the appraisal sheet in the section entitled "Promotability," Wallace checked off "Promotable within two years." The only rating superior to this was "Promotable immediately." The appraisal was reviewed and signed by Carson, in accordance with company policy.

During the early part of 1967, the personnel department notified Roberts that several managers in the company were interested in offering him positions in their departments. These offers of employment in the public relations, distribution, and personnel departments were transmitted through the company's formal system for recruiting internal candidates. Each of these opportunities represented a promotion for Roberts. While these advancement opportunities all appeared attractive, Roberts expressed enthusiasm for his work in systems and was reluctant to leave. When he discussed the situation with Wallace and Carson, they both spoke optimistically about his future progress and their plans for him. Roberts decided to turn down the various internal opportunities and remain in management systems.

On April 1, 1967 Wallace and Carson jointly announced that Roberts had been promoted from management systems analyst to senior management systems analyst.

THE CUSTOMER ACCOUNT COMPUTER SYSTEM (CACS) PROJECT

As part of his plan to increase Roberts' programming experience, Wallace assigned him in April 1967 to a major EDP project, under the direction of another analyst. The basic purpose of this project was to create a computerized information system of all retail and wholesale accounts that distributed a major section of the product line. The system was designed to assist in processing orders during the hectic fall and winter sale periods. A secondary objective was to use the system for recording salesmen's call activities. The system was scheduled to go "on-line" in the fall of 1967.

In May 1967, the project was dealt a serious setback when the senior systems analyst leading the project resigned from the company. Wallace decided to have Roberts direct the project and assigned a new analyst to assist him. Between May and September, Roberts worked feverishly to complete the system. He worked a considerable amount of overtime each week, including six Saturdays during the summer months. Throughout this period, he assured Wallace and Carson and the mangement of the distribution department that the system would be ready to go into operation by September 1, 1967.

In the midst of Roberts' efforts on the CACS project, corporate organization changes affected the management systems department.

THE CORPORATE REORGANIZATION

In July 1967, a major corporate reorganization was announced. The objectives of the reorganization were the separation of planning activities from operations and the introduction of a strong profit center philosophy.

As a result of the reorganization, some key management changes occurred in the management systems department. Walter Davis, manager of the department, was appointed director, organization and policy planning, on the new corporate staff. Carl Golden, supervisior of the R. & D.—administrative systems unit, joined Davis' staff as manager of organization planning.

Bart Carson replaced Davis as management systems manager (see Exhibit 2). Dick Sylvester, previously supervisor, programming research, was named to direct a new management research group. The three systems units were merged into two new units, reporting to Pete Boldin and Hugh Behrens. Behrens, who has previously served as super-

EXHIBIT 2
Partial Manco Organization Chart (August 1967)

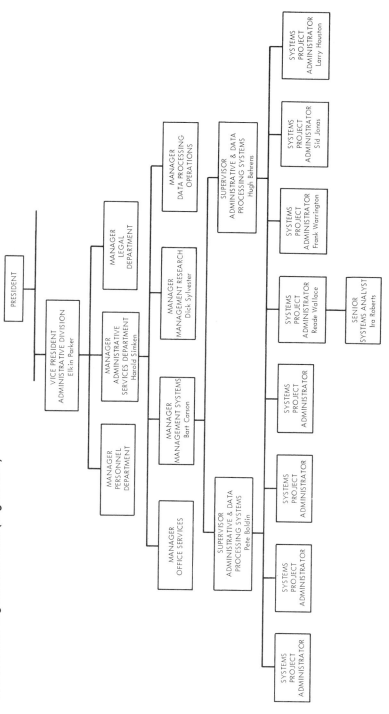

visor, operations research, assumed responsibility for Carson's international-marketing systems unit and for all R.&D. systems. The administrative systems would henceforth be designed by the new corporate staff group headed by Walter Davis and Carl Golden. Boldin retained responsibility for all financial and manufacturing systems.

THE JULY 1967–OCTOBER 1967 PERIOD

After the initial excitement generated by the announcement of management appointments, management systems activities continued with no major changes in direction. Carson and his two direct subordinates, Boldin and Behrens, conferred regularly to establish project objectives for 1968, plan the impending conversion to a 360 computer, and develop a new project control system.

Behrens' four systems project administrators (Sid Jonas, Frank Warrington, Larry Houston, and Reade Wallace) found him more conservative and less communicative than Carson, and yet by late summer they felt they had good rapport with him. Behrens started with Manco as a programmer in 1960, and had since served in various capacities in the programming section, systems section, and operations research section. He was credited with conducting the company's most successful operations research effort—a large-scale simulation of the entire Manco distribution network. His several diverse skills had enabled him to establish an excellent reputation throughout the corporation.

Behrens called informal meetings of his four systems project administrators whenever he felt it necessary to review plans or communicate information. These hour-long meetings occurred about every two weeks during the late summer and early fall.

On October 18, Behrens called a 1:30 meeting of his systems project administrators. The only unusual aspect of the scheduling was the short two-hour notice. When the group assembled, they noted that Behrens, who was typically a very calm individual, seemed upset. Warrington, Jonas, and Houston were also surprised to see that Wallace was not present. Behrens began the meeting by announcing:

> *I've called you together to tell you that our unit has been reorganized as of this afternoon. Reade Wallace's job has been eliminated and he is leaving the company today. Sid Jonas will pick up Reade's responsibilities for all systems and management science projects in International. Ira Roberts will report to you, and we'll continue to recruit for a replacement for Ira's predecessor on the CACS project. Frank will handle all EDP projects for International. Barbara Mellor and Murray Hankins [Wallace's other analysts] will report to you.*

Jonas was the first to speak after a long silence. "Does that mean that Reade was fired due to unsatisfactory performance?" "No," replied Behrens, "Reade was doing a satisfactory job, but we no longer had a position for him in our organization." Jonas reacted sharply to Behrens' answer:

*Now, how can you do a thing like that? We have a very involved
system for placing unsatisfactory performers on warning for 30 to 90
days and advising them that they will be canned if they don't shape
up. You just subverted the whole system by reorganizing him out of
a job. That system's supposed to protect the employee. Now all of the
analysts will think that this is a completely arbitrary system and the
axe can fall on them any time. We all know that Reade was deficient
in certain respects. Why don't you call a spade a spade?*

Interrupting, Behrens said:

*Hold on a minute, Sid. Some of your points are valid, but you don't
have all the facts. First of all, Wallace did get severance pay amount-
ing to over $5,000. More important, we talked to all the personnel
experts, and they said it would be in his best interest to do it this way.
The company can give him a good reference without any black marks
on his record. And, as an aside, we tried to place him elsewhere in the
company. Distribution and International were interested, but because of the budget cutbacks throughout the company, they couldn't
afford someone at his salary level. It's been my most traumatic experience since I've been with the company. What more can I say?*

Jonas was preparing to resume the verbal battle but thought better of it
and added, "I'm sorry, Hugh, but I don't agree. I'm probably unfair arguing with you over this since Reade only worked for you for three months.
It's Bart Carson who's responsible, and I plan to tell him that I think the
whole situation was handled poorly." With that the meeting was adjourned.

THE CUSTOMER ACCOUNT COMPUTER SYSTEM FAILS

Following the announcement of Wallace's departure, Jonas and Warrington met with their newly assigned analysts to review work loads and
project plans. The main topic during the first meeting between Jonas and
Roberts on October 20 was the CACS project. Roberts first explained the
system to Jonas, pointing out its objectives and major features. He explained that the system began operating in September, although a few
"bugs" still had to be ironed out. Roberts expressed confidence that the
system would be operating smoothly before too long.

The CACS project seemed to be moving toward final completion when
Jonas was called into Behrens office on Thursday, November 9. Behrens
informed Jonas that one of the scheduled computer runs for the CACS
project had produced incorrect results and Ned O'Donnell, the distribution department manager, had phoned a complaint to Bart Carson. Behrens expressed the fear that there might be some major problem with the
entire system. Jonas suggested they speak to Roberts. Behrens phoned
Roberts, requesting that he come to his office. Roberts explained that the
error in sales totals resulted from 50 duplicate records on the master file.

He had scheduled a computer printout of the master file so that the clerks in the distribution department could correct the errors. He assured Jonas and Behrens that he would take care of the problem.

The master file printout was checked by the distribution clerks on Monday, November 13, and Tuesday, November 14. On the 15th, Ned O'Donnell asked Harold Simken, manager of administrative services, to come to his office. When Simken arrived, he saw that O'Donnell had several hundred pages of a computer report on his desk. O'Donnell began to shout at Simken, "Harold, you see this printout? You know how much it's worth? This much!" And with that O'Donnell stuffed the printout in the waste basket. O'Donnell continued, "What's wrong with your damn department. If it's not one kind of mistake, it's another. Now that guy has gone and dropped all of our accounts in Northern California from the file. I can't make any sense out of this."

Simken returned to his office and asked to see Jonas, since Carson and Behrens were both out of the office. Carson was at a week-long management training session, and Hugh Behrens was attending a seminar in operations research. Simken gave Jonas a monotone hello when he entered and asked him what he was doing about the CACS situation. Jonas identified the various problems as best he could and reviewed the instructions he had given Roberts. Simken listened without comment until Jonas was through and then began to speak in a very stern voice. "Sid, I know you weren't involved in this system from the start, and you aren't responsible for these problems. But, it's yours now, and I'm holding you responsible for correcting this mess. Now, get busy on this and keep me informed of your progress."

When Behrens returned to the office the following morning, he was treated to a similar—in his words—"severe harangue," from Simken. Behrens decided to form a task force of himself, Pete Boldin, Jonas, and Roberts to conduct a comprehensive review of the system. After a three-day review, Behrens submitted a report to Carson and Simken, outlining the various technical problems and the proposed remedial action. The review had made it clear to Jonas and Behrens that Roberts did not have the technical EDP expertise to direct a project as complex as CACS. Moreover, some aspects of the system were misrepresented to marketing management in that the system was touted as a panacea for all of distribution's information problems. The cost of the system was vastly underestimated. Original estimates for development costs and annual operating costs were $14,000 to $19,000 and $8,500 to $14,000. Actual development costs exceeded $32,000, while annual operating costs zoomed to $30,000.

When Jonas and Behrens reviewed the report, Behrens began to discuss Roberts' capabilities:

> *Sid, we really gave you a personnel problem. That review convinced me that Roberts is not capable of senior analyst performance. There's no question about his technical deficiencies as far as I'm concerned. We know he wasn't a technical whiz but, if that wasn't bad enough, he did a terrible job of directing the project. There's no evidence of*

any planning. He missed every deadline, and I'm not sure he properly represented the critical status of the system to marketing or us. He probably didn't know how bad he off he really was. You better think about how you're going to use him in the future. Given the type of things we expect from you in the future, I'm not sure where he fits in.

Jonas raised some questions about the apparently poor supervision and direction which Roberts had received from Wallace. Behrens agreed that this was a consideration. Behrens' secretary interrupted to remind him of a meeting, and he abruptly ended the discussion, "Well, give it some thought, Sid, and let's discuss it in a few days."

On Wednesday, November 22, Jonas arranged a session with Carson and Behrens to discuss the Roberts situation. Jonas opened the discussion by summarizing his position for Carson:

Bart, I've given this issue considerable thought, and I'm very troubled by it. I'm not reluctant to be a so-called "tough-minded manager" and place Roberts on warning for unsatisfactory performance. The problem with this approach is that it's the easy way out because it avoids the real troubling issues. Someone in this organization has to accept responsibility for the things that were said to Roberts six months ago. We told him that his future was very bright in systems and dissuaded him from accepting other jobs in the company. In fact, we promoted him in a relatively short span of time. In retrospect, that was the wrong decision. He's better suited for less technical work, such as personnel or public relations. So far, he hasn't demonstrated that he can perform at a senior level. And, don't forget, one big reason for his poor performance was the lack of proper supervision from Wallace.

If you want me to, I'll try to compensate for our past errors by getting back to basics and developing Roberts the right way. But I can't do this if you're not willing to adjust your expectations of my group. Hugh thinks that Roberts doesn't fit into my operation. So now it seems that if I try to develop one of my less adequate subordinates, I don't meet my technical responsibilities. If I stick to the technical goals, I ship Roberts out the door.

Carson answered:

Sid, I don't want you to worry about things that were said to Roberts before he started working for you. Perhaps we were premature in promoting him. I'll accept responsibility for all of that. We expect big things of you, and you need the proper blend of skills in your group. It's very easy for Hugh and me to sit here and tell you what to do. But, if we did that, we'd impair your development as a supervisor. All I can say is do what you have to do.

Selected Readings

From

BEYOND ECONOMICS: COORDINOMICS*

By Jeremiah J. O'Connell

The word economics is taken from the two Greek words *oikos* and *nemein*. *Oikos* means "household" and *nemein* means "to manage." The root meaning of the word economics, therefore, is "to manage a household." In the economics of business enterprise we concentrated on the specialized segments or segmented departments of the corporation. Historically, the emphasis has been on efficiency within functional departments—a concentration on the area described by each of the boxes on the organization chart. Each box was a household, so to speak, to be managed in such a way that, within the confines of that functional box on the organizational chart, we achieved all the efficiencies produced by specialization and derived all the benefits from economies of scale or size. Now, in the mature business enterprise it seems we are approaching the point of diminishing returns to our efforts at managing these segmented compartments of the organization. We are at a point now where the emphasis is shifting in the quest for efficiency to inter-departmental cooperation and coordination—that is, to a concentration on managing the spaces between the boxes on the organization chart. We are at the point where there are greater returns to an investment spent on achieving coordination among the functional departments of an organization than to an investment spent on improving the operations in any one of the functional departments.

Historically, when we spoke of systems, we behaved as if the organization were a mechanical system, that is, that the whole was nothing other than and nothing different from the sum of the several, functionally specialized, parts of the organization. Systems today have come to mean something organic rather than mechanical—that is, the whole is something other than and something in addition to the sum of the functionally specialized parts. In this sense, then, we have moved beyond economics—the management of separate households—to coordinomics—the managements of the process of coordination. Economics had us focus on the compartments of the organization; coordinomics would have us focus on the spaces between the compartments in the organization. . . .

---

* Excerpt from Keynote Address at the Eighth Annual Systems Conference of the Southwest, Dallas, Texas, May 9, 1966.

From

THE VOLATILE ORGANIZATION: EVERYTHING TRIGGERS EVERYTHING ELSE*

By Harold J. Leavitt†

In this first chapter in Part IV, we have just one purpose—to encourage the reader to think about organizations not just as simple, static charts or as milling collections of people or as smoothly oiled man-machine systems but as rich, volatile, complicated but understandable systems of *tasks, structures, tools,* and *people* in states of continuous change.

Toward that purpose, consider the following example:

If, as a manager, you have a rather complicated problem, you may want to call in a consultant for help. Suppose the problem is a typically hard one: one of your larger field units is turning in much poorer results than all your forecasts had predicted.

So you call in the partner in charge of the local office of one of the reputable older consulting firms—the largest in town. They contract to take on the problem and send some people out to the unit to collect information.

When they finally come in with a report, you scan it and then turn to the recommendations. They recommend the following: (1) You need tighter controls. (2) Job relationships need to be reorganized and redefined; job descriptions need to be rewritten with greater precision (to get rid of squabbles about overlapping authority). (3) The functional form of organization they now have down there ought to be switched over to a product form. (4) In fact, that unit has grown so big that it ought to go through a partial decentralization itself, with a lot more authority given to the product managers. (5) You need a thorough methods analysis. The number of reports that are being generated now is excessive. There is wasteful duplication of effort and communication. You ought to streamline the organization's procedures. (6) And you may have to move a few people out, too. There is too much fat in the organization, and so on.

If you are a manager with a experimental turn of mind and a pocket full of money, you will decide not to act on this consultant's report yet. You decide, instead, to knock on the door of another consultant and get a second independent assessment.

You had gotten to know the first firm by now. You had found that the people in it were active in the Society for the Advancement of Management, and highly experienced in business organization. You note, with some discomfort, that this second firm professes different allegiances and displays other pedigrees. This

---

* Chapter 21, from Harold J. Leavitt, *Managerial Psychology* © 1964 by The University of Chicago Press. All rights reserved. Excerpts from pp. 317–25. Reprinted by permission.

† The author is a Professor in the Graduate School of Business, Stanford University.

second group is active in the Operations Research Society, and the Institute for Management Sciences. Its experiences in industry really are not as extensive as those of number-one firm, but it has done a lot of recent military work, and its senior people all have Ph.D's. It looks like a group of whiz kids. But they have cut their hair and they sound reasonable, so you hire them to look into the same problems.

They send their people out to the unit, and they, too, come up with a report. But their conclusions are different. Instead of recommending modifications in the *structure* of the organization, they recommend modifications in the *technical* and *analytic* methods being used. They are technologists who think technological improvement is the means to the best of all possible worlds. They want to linear program the inventory control methods being used in that division, and to automate the purchasing operation. They want to modify the information flows, so that decisions can be made at different points in the organization, and faster. And instead of job descriptions and organization charts as their tools, their pockets are full of computers and long equations. You will have to hire some hot-shot college boys if you want to carry out their recommendations; because neither you nor any of your top people can fully understand them.

But if you are *really* an experimental manager, and if your pockets are really full of gold, and if you don't satisfy easily, you call in the only other consulting firm in town. Its members are Ph.D. types, too. Their offices aren't very elaborate, either. Their affiliations are different, again. They are members of the American Psychological Association, and/or members of the consultant network of the National Training Laboratories. They are clinical or social psychological types. And they view the world from the human side. They don't carry computers in their back pockets, or write job descriptions, or draw organization charts. Their favorite tools are the meeting, the discussion, the face-to-face group, and the open-ended interview.

So you hire them and let them and take a look at your difficult unit. And they too come up with a report. But their report is different again. It argues that the solution to unit *X*'s problem lies in changing the attitudes and interrelations of the people in that unit. Morale is low, they say. Apathy is high. People are constricted and anxious, afraid to speak up or take risks. What your organization needs is more *openness,* more *participation,* more *involvement,* more *creativity.*

So their recommendation is that you work on the people end of the problem. They want you to set up a series of "laboratory" training programs, in which you take groups of your people from division *X* out to a country club for a week at a time to talk things over; to open up valid communication among themselves; to express what they really feel; and to develop much more mutual trust and confidence.

Probably you could go on experimenting, but the board members are giving you strange looks by now, and the people in unit *X* are really up in the air. So you decide to stop there and take a look at what you have. Which of the three firms' recommendations should you follow up? Since you are the manager, we'll leave it to you to answer that question.

But though we can't answer it, let's not leave it quite there. As of right now we have a situation that looks like this:

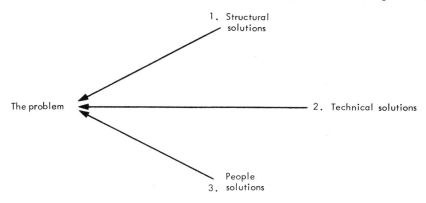

We have one group that wants to solve the problem of unit X by working on *structure,* by changing the organization chart and the locations of authority and responsibility. We have another group that's going to solve the same problems *technologically,* by improving the analytic quality of decisions and applying new techniques for controlling and processing information. And we have a third group that's going to solve the very same problems humanly, by working on persons and interpersonal relations. But there is one more important point that needs to be made here, before you decide which one of these to use. They aren't mutually exclusive. The point is that the diagram above is incomplete. Because no one of these actions will affect the way the task of division X gets done without also involving each of the other points on that chart. *Structure* and *technology* and *people* are not separable phenomena in organizations. If we hire the structurally oriented firm, and if we decentralize the unit, or if we change the present allocation of responsibilities, it will not only affect the problem but will also affect (perhaps adversely) people's attitudes and interpersonal relations. We will have to draw an arrow like this:

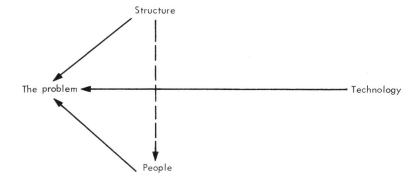

If you tighten controls, for example, some people may get angry or uncomfortable. If you switch from a functional to a product organization form, there will be new problems of interpersonal relations.

And if we play with the organization structure we will also get some effects on *technology*. The kinds of techniques that are now appropriate in a highly decentralized scheme—the accounting techniques for example—may have to be very different than those appropriate for highly centralized organizations.

And similarly, if we hire the technically oriented consulting firm, and go on to introduce the computer and new information flows, then we can darn well expect effects not only on the way the job gets done but also on structure and on people. If we can centralize information in locations where we couldn't centralize before, we will find decisions being made and responsibilities being taken in different places than they were being taken before. And while we may be talking about de-centralization, that new information system may be pushing us toward centralization. We may also find that the kinds and numbers of people we need in our new, technically sophisticated organization may be quite different from the kind and number of members we needed before. Moreover some things that were done judgmentally and thoughtfully are now pretty well programed, so that essentially they can be done by the machine—with some consequent effects on the attitudes and feelings of persons.

Finally, if we move in on the people side, hiring the human relations firm, we will encourage people to be more open and more valid in their communication, encourage people to take more responsibility, and encourage people to interact more with other members of the organization. If we do these things, let us not for a moment think that we can do them without exerting great pressure on our existing organizational structure. The authority system will change and so will the status system. And we will exert pressure on technology too. The newly freedup people may want new tools or the abolition of old ones that have been technically useful but are psychologically frustrating.

And so we end up with a diagram that looks like this:

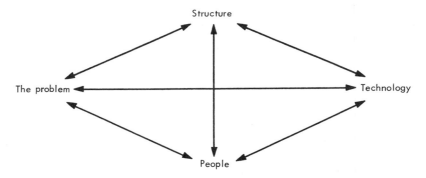

In this one everything feeds back on everything else, so that although we started out to worry only about the relationship between structure and task, or technology and task, or people and task, we must end up worrying about the effects of changes in any one on all of the others. Some of those changes may be very helpful, but some may be negative. And the manager has to somehow diagnose the secondary and tertiary effects of action in any one of these areas.

For organizations do not stand still. If we inject something into one part of the system bells begin to ring and lights begin to go on all over the system, often in places we hadn't counted on and at times we hadn't expected.

This is not to say that the complexity of the organization is so great that we can never tell what will happen when we do something. It is only to say that an organization is complex enough to make any simple structural or technical or human model inadequate. But we have made a lot of progress in understanding the complexities in the last few decades. We now know a good deal more about ways of acting on structure or people or technology; and we know somewhat more about how they are wired to one another. There is real progress in the organizational world. The three classes of consulting firms in our example should not be taken as an indication that things have gone to pot. On the contrary they are an indication of how much we have learned about organizations. And about how much we now know of ways to change or modify them.

The practitioner in each of these three realms may be oversold on his own product. He may be overly enthusiastic about all that can be done by changing structure, or technology, or people. Each may be partially and understandably blind to the perspectives of the others. But the manager need not be blind. He has lots more to work from than he did in the days when we so naïvely believed that the simple line drawing on the organization chart actually did capture the essence of our live, volatile organization.

In Summary

Organizations can be thought of as lively sets of interrelated systems designed to perform complicated tasks. We can try to manipulate at least three dimensions of those systems in order to get the performance of tasks changed or improved. We can manipulate the organization structure—which means we can manipulate the communication system or the authority and power system, or the system of work flows and processes. We can manipulate the tools and techniques used in the system—which means we can provide new and better hammers or new and better information-processing devices. And we can enter from the people side, to change bodies, or attitudes, or interpersonal relations—which means we can change the training and skills of our people, or the numbers of people involved, or the kinds of people we hire.

But we must never for a moment forget that when we tamper with any one of these three variables, structure or technology or people, we are likely to cause significant effects on the others, as well as on the task.

From

ROLE, PERSONALITY, AND SOCIAL STRUCTURE IN THE ORGANIZATIONAL SETTING*

By Daniel J. Levinson†

"SOCIAL ROLE" AS A UNITARY CONCEPT

The concept of role is related to, and must be distinguished from, the concept of social position. A position is an element of organizational autonomy, a location in social space, a category of organizational membership. A role is, so to say, an aspect of organizational physiology; it involves function, adaption, process. It is meaningful to say that a person "occupies" a social position; but it is inappropriate to say, as many do, that one occupies a role.

There are at least three specific senses in which the term "role" has been used, explicitly or implicitly, by different writers or by the same writer on different occasions.

a) Role may be defined as the *structurally given demands* (norms, expectations, taboos, responsibilities, and the like) associated with a given social position. Role is, in this sense, something outside the given individual, a set of pressures and facilitations that channel, guide, impede, support his functioning in the organization.

b) Role may be defined as the member's *orientation* or *conception* of the part he is to play in the organization. It is, so to say, his inner definition of what someone in his social position is supposed to think and do about it. Mead (1934) is probably the main source of this view of social role as an aspect of the person, and it is commonly used in analyses of occupational roles.

c) Role is commonly defined as the *actions* of the individual members—actions seen in terms of their relevance for the social structure (that is, seen in relation to the prevailing norms). In this sense, role refers to the ways in which members of a position act (with or without conscious intention) *in accord with or in violation of a given set of organizational norms*. Here, as in (*b*), role is defined as a characteristic of the actor rather than of his normative environment.

Many writers use a definition that embraces all of the above meanings without systematic distinction, and then shift, explicitly or implicitly, from one meaning to another. The following are but a few of many possible examples.[1]

---

* This abridgment from the article of the same title is reprinted by permission from *Journal of Abnormal Psychology*, Vol. 58 (1959), pp. 171–80.

† The author is Professor of Psychology at Yale University. In this article Professor Levinson adds balance to the literature on role theory by emphasis to personality as well as environmental determinants of role concept and role performance. The excerpts reproduced here do not present the richness or detail of Professor Levinson's theoretical position. Those interested in going further should consult the originial article.

[1] An argument very similar to the one made here is presented by Gross, Mason, and McEachern (1958) in a comprehensive overview and critique of role theory. They point up

*　　*　　*　　*　　*

In short, the "unitary" conception of role assumes that there is a 1:1 relationship, or at least a *high degree of congruence,* among the three role aspects noted above. In the theory of bureaucratic organization, the rationale for this assumption is somewhat as follows. The organizationally given requirements will be internalized by the members and will thus be mirrored in their role-conceptions. People will know, and will want to do, what is expected of them. The agencies of role socialization will succeed except with a deviant minority—who constitute a separate problem for study. Individual action will in turn reflect the structural norms, since the appropriate role-conceptions will have been internalized and since the sanctions system rewards normative behavior and punishes deviant behavior. Thus, it is assumed that structural norms, individual role-conceptions and individual role-performance are three isomorphic reflections of a single entity: "the" role appropriate to a given organizational position.

It is, no doubt, reasonable to expect some degree of congruence among these aspects of a social role. Certainly, every organization contains numerous mechanisms designed to further such congruence. At the same time, it is a matter of common observation that organizations vary in the degree of their integration; structural demands are often contradictory, lines of authority may be defective, disagreements occur and reverberate at and below the surface of daily operations. To assume that what the organization requires, and what its members actually think and do, comprise a single, unified whole is severely to restrict our comprehension of organizational dynamics and change.

*　　*　　*　　*　　*

ORGANIZATIONALLY GIVEN ROLE-DEMANDS

The role-demands are external to the individual whose role is being examined. They are the situational pressures that confront him as the occupant of a given structural position. They have manifold sources: in the official charter and policies of the organization; in the traditions and ideology, explicit as well as implicit, that help to define the organization's purposes and modes of operation; in the views about this position which are held by members of the position (who influence any single member) and by members of the various positions impinging upon this one; and so on.

*　　*　　*　　*　　*

In attempting to characterize the role-requirements for a given position, one must therefore guard against the assumption that they are unified and logically coherent. There may be major differences and even contradictions between official norms, as defined by charter or by administrative authority, and the "informal" norms held by various groupings within the organization. Moreover, within a given-status group, such as the top administrators, there may be several conflicting

---

the assumption of high consensus regarding role-demands and role-conceptions in traditional role theory, and present empirical evidence contradicting this assumption. Their analysis is, however, less concerned than the present one with the converging of role theory and personality theory.

viewpoints concerning long range goals, current policies, and specific role-require-ments. In short, the structural demands themselves are often multiple and disuni-fied. Few are the attempts to investigate the sources of such disunity, to acknowl-edge its frequency, or to take it into conceptual account in general structure theory.

It is important also to consider the specificity or *narrowness* with which the normative requirements are defined. Norms have an "ought" quality; they confer legitimacy and reward-value upon certain modes of action, thought and emotion, while condemning others. But there are degrees here. Normative evaluations cover a spectrum from "strongly required" through various degrees of qualitative kinds of "acceptable," to more or less stringently tabooed. Organizations differ in the width of the intermediate range on this spectrum. That is, they differ in the number and kinds of adaptation that are normatively acceptable. The wider this range—the less specific the norms—the greater is the area of personal choice for the individual. While the existence of such an intermediate range is generally acknowledged, structural analyses often proceed as though practically all norms were absolute prescriptions or proscriptions allowing few alternatives for individual action.

There are various other normative complexities to be reckoned with. A single set of role-norms may be internally contradictory. In the case of the mental hospital nurse, for example, the norm of maintaining an "orderly ward" often conflicts with the norm of encouraging self-expression in patients. The individual nurse then has a range of choice, which may be narrow or wide, in balancing these conflicting requirements. There are also ambiguities in norms, and discrepancies between those held explicitly and those that are less verbalized and perhaps less con-scious. These normative complexities permit, and may even induce, significant variations in individual role-performance.

The degree of *coherence* among the structurally defined role-requirements, the degree of *consensus with which they are held, and the degree of individual choice* they allow (the range of acceptable alternatives) are among the most significant properties of any organization. In some organizations, there is very great coherence of role-requirements and a minimum of individual choice. In most cases, however, the degree of integration within roles and among sets of roles appears to be more moderate.[2] This structural pattern is of especial interest from a sociopsychological point of view. To the extent that the requirements for a given position are ambiguous, contradictory, or otherwise "open," the individual mem-bers have greater opportunity for selection among existing norms and for creation of new norms. In this process, personality plays an important part. . . .

Role-Facilities

In addition to the demands and obligations imposed upon the individual, we must also take into account the techniques, resources, and conditions of work—the means made available to him for fulfilling his organizational functions. . . .

* * * * *

---

[2] The reduced integration reflects in part the tremendous rate of technological change, the geographical and occupational mobility, and the diversity in personality that characterize modern society. On the other hand, diversity is opposed by the standardization of culture on a mass basis and by the growth of large-scale organization itself. Trends toward increased standardization and uniformity are highlighted in Whyte's (1956) analysis.

PERSONAL ROLE-DEFINITION

Individual (and Modal) Role-Conceptions

The nature of a role-conception may perhaps be clarified by placing it in relation to an ideology. The boundary between the two is certainly not a sharp one. However, ideology refers most directly to an orientation regarding the entire organizational (or other) structure—its purposes, its modes of operation, the prevailing forms of individual and group relationships, and so on. A role-conception offers a definition and rationale for one position within the structure. If ideology portrays and rationalizes the organizational world, then role-conception delineates the specific functions, values, and manner of functioning appropriate to one position within it.

*   *   *   *   *

. . . After all, individual role-conceptions are formed only partially within the present organizational setting. The individuals' ideas about his occupational role are influenced by childhood experiences, by his values and other personality characteristics, by formal education and apprenticeship, and the like. The ideas of various potential reference groups within and outside of the organization are available through reading, informal contacts, etc. There is reason to expect, then, that the role-conceptions of individuals in a given organizational position will vary and will not always conform to official role-requirements. Both the diversities and the modal patterns must be considered in organizational analysis.

Individual (and Modal) Role-Performance

This term refers to the overt behavioral aspect of role-definition—to the more or less characteristic ways in which the individual acts as the occupant of a social position. Because role-performance involves immediately observable behavior, its description would seem to present few systematic problems. However, the formulation of adequate variables for the analysis of role-performance is in fact a major theoretical problem and one of the great stumbling blocks in empirical research.

Everyone would agree, I suppose that role-performance concerns only those aspects of the total stream of behavior that are structurally relevant. But which aspects of behavior are the important ones? And where shall the boundary be drawn between that which is structurally relevant and that which is incidental or idiosyncratic?

One's answer to these questions probably depends, above all, upon his conception of social structure. Those who conceive of social structure rather narrowly in terms of concrete work tasks and normative requirements, are inclined to take a similarly narrow view of role. In this view, role-performance is simply the fulfillment of formal role-norms, and anything else the person does is extraneous to role-performance as such. Its proponents acknowledge that there are variations in "style" of performance but regard these as incidental. What is essential to *role-performance* is the degree to which norms are met.

A more complex and inclusive conception of social structure requires correspondingly multi-dimensional delineation of role-performance. An organization has, from this viewpoint, "latent" as well as "manifest" structure; it has a many-faceted emotional climate; it tends to "demand" varied forms of interpersonal allegiance, friendship, deference, intimidation, ingratiation, rivalry, and the like. If characteristics such as these are considered intrinsic properties of social structure, then they must be included in the characterization of role-performance. My own preference is for the more inclusive view. I regard social structure as having psychological as well as other properties, and I regard as intrinsic to role-performance the varied meanings and feelings which the actor communicates to those about him. Ultimately, we must learn to characterize organizational behavior in a way that takes into account, and helps to illuminate, its functions for the individual, for the others with whom he interacts, and for the organization.

It is commonly assumed that there is great uniformity in role-performance among the members of a given position. Or, in other words, that there is *a dominant, modal pattern of role-performance corresponding to the structural requirements.* The rationale here parallels that given above for role-conceptions. However, where individual variations in patterns of role-performance have been investigated, several modal types rather than a single dominant pattern were found (Argyris, 1957; Greenblatt *et al.,* 1957).

Nor is this variability surprising, except to those who have the most simplistic conception of social life. Role-performance, like any form of human behavior, is the resultant of many forces. Some of these forces derive from the organizational matrix; for example, from role-demands and the pressures of authority, from informal group influences, and from impending sanctions. Other determinants lie within the person, as for example his role-conceptions and role-relevant personality characteristics. Except in unusual cases where all forces operate to channel behavior in the same direction, role-performance will reflect the individual's attempts at choice and compromise among diverse external and internal forces.

*   *   *   *   *

ROLE-DEFINITION, PERSONALITY, AND SOCIAL STRUCTURE

*   *   *   *   *

Clearly, individual role-conception and role-performance do not emanate, fully formed, from the depths of personality. Nor are they simply mirror images of a mold established by social structure. Elsewhere (Levinson, 1954), I have used the term "mirage" theory for the view, frequently held or implied in the psychoanalytic literature, that ideologies, role-conceptions, and behavior are mere epiphenomena or by-products of unconscious fantasies and defenses. Similarly, the term "sponge" theory characterizes the view, commonly forwarded in the sociological literature, in which man is merely a passive, mechanical absorber of the prevailing structural demands.

Our understanding of personal role-definition will remain seriously impaired as long as we fail to place it, analytically, in *both intra-personal and structural-environmental contexts.* That is to say, we must be concerned with the meaning of role-definition both for the individual personality and for the social system. A given role-definition is influenced by, and has an influence upon, the *psyche* as well as the *socius.* If we are adequately to understand the nature, the determinants, and the consequences of role-definition, we need the double perspective of personality and social structure. The use of these two reference points is, like the use of our two eyes in seeing, necessary for the achievement of depth in our social vision.

From

THE PERCEPTION OF OTHER PEOPLE*

By Joseph E. McGrath

Oliver Wendell Holmes (1809–1894) once described a famous conversation between John and Henry in which six "persons" took part: John, as John knew himself; John, as he was known to Henry; the "true" John, as he was known only to God; and the equivalent trio of Henrys.

This same basic insight into the special nature of interpersonal perception was reflected in the work of early sociologists, notably in Cooley's (1902) concept of the "looking-glass self" and in George Mead's (1934) concepts of the two selves, the "I" and the "me." Both men pointed out that the child first develops an awareness of himself as an entity separate and distinct from his environment because *other people* respond to him as a separate, autonomous object. If there were no other people, we would have no self concept. As an individual develops a concept of "self," he becomes aware of himself as an object of his own perception (Mead's "me"), as distinct from himself as the perceiver (Mead's "I"). Furthermore, his own evaluation of himself arises as a *reflection of others' evaluation of him*. Thus, argued Mead and Cooley, the very heart of the individual's personality, his own concept, arises in the first instance and develops through time by the process of social interaction with other people.

Since these early formulations, there has been much research and theory on the nature and consequences of interpersonal perceptions. One whole school of psychotherapy (see Rogers, 1942) is built upon Mead's premise that the self concept is crucial to adjustment and that self evaluation changes in response to changes in others' evaluations of oneself. On this premise, the crux of therapy is to provide the patient with a consistently warm and accepting social environment, thus providing a proper climate for him to reorient his self concept. Recently, Fiedler and his coworkers (1959) have shown that interpersonal perceptions are related to the individual's adjustment. In a large study of both military and college living groups, they found that individuals who see themselves as similar to others with whom they have close associations and who are seen as similar by those "significant others" show better personal adjustment than persons for whom this is not the case.

Newcomb (1953) points out that our perceptions of other people are closely tied to our attitudes on matters related to those people. We tend to agree with those we like and like those with whom we agree. We also tend to disagree with those we dislike and dislike those with whom we disagree. Newcomb has formalized these ideas in a theoretical model that summarizes many of the concepts in this area. Newcomb's model deals with two persons (*A* and *B*) engaged in interaction about one or more objects (*X*'s), which can be ideas, physical objects, or other people . The set of attitudes which *A* and *B* have about each other and about the

* From Chapter Five from *Social Psychology: A Brief Introduction* by Joseph E. McGrath. Copyright © 1964 by Holt, Rinehart and Winston, Inc. Reprinted by permission of Holt, Rinehart and Winston, Inc.

X's constitutes a system of interrelated parts. This set of attitudes is a system because the parts are interdependent, and when one part changes other parts are likely to show compensating changes. In fact, Newcomb postulates that there are certain states of the system (patterns of attitudes) which constitute *balanced* or *equilibrium* states. These balanced states are: mutual attraction between *A* and *B*, along with agreement about *X*'s; and mutual rejection between *A* and *B* along with disagreement about *X*'s. All other states (such as disagreement with mutual attraction) are unstable states and will tend toward one or another of the equilibrium patterns.

Underlying this "objective" system or pattern are attitudes of two "subjective" *A-B-X* systems, one for *A* and one for *B*. *A*'s subjective system includes his attitudes toward *B* and toward *X* and his *perceptions* (estimates) of *B*'s attitudes toward himself (*A*) and toward *X*. *B*'s subjective system includes the corresponding attitudes and perceptions. The same kinds of balanced states (perceived agreement with positively attractive others, and perceived disagreement with negatively attractive others) and the same tendency toward system balance hold for the subjective systems as for the objective *A-B-X* system. These systems of interpersonal relationships are shown in Figure 1.

Thus, Newcomb is saying that the famous John and Henry conversation includes two other "persons" besides the six listed by Holmes, namely: John as John believes Henry sees him; and Henry's perception of how John sees Henry. Newcomb is also postulating that these interpersonal perceptions are inter-

FIGURE 1

The objective system

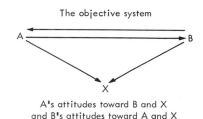

A's attitudes toward B and X
and B's attitudes toward A and X

The subjective systems

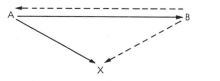

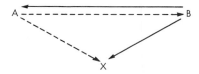

From A's point of view

From B's point of view

A's attitudes toward B and X
and A's perceptions (estimates)
of B's attitudes toward A and X

B's attitudes toward A and X
and B's perceptions (estimates)
of A's attitudes toward B and X

Diagram of Newcomb's *A-B-X* Model of Systems of Interpersonal Relationships. *A* and *B* represent two persons; *X* represents an object about which *A* and *B* are communicating or toward which *A* and *B* are co-orienting. Solid arrows represent actual attitudes of one person toward the other or toward *X*. Arrows run from holder of the attitude to target of the attitude. Broken-line arrows represent estimates by one person of the other persons' attitudes; for example, *B*————→ *X* represents *A*'s estimate of *B*'s attitude toward *X*.

dependent with John's and Henry's own attitudes about the topics of their interaction and with their perceptions of each other's attitudes. Thus, at a more general level, he postulates that interpersonal attitudes, interpersonal perceptions, and attitudes toward other objects are all interdependent with one another, tend to be compatible, and tend to change together as a system.

From

IS BUSINESS BLUFFING ETHICAL?*

By Albert Z. Carr†

A respected businessman with whom I discussed the theme of this article remarked with some heat, "You mean to say you're going to encourage men to bluff? Why, bluffing is nothing more than a form of lying! You're advising them to lie!"

I agreed that the basis of private morality is a respect for truth and that the closer a businessman comes to the truth, the more he deserves respect. At the same time, I suggested that most bluffing in business might be regarded simply as game strategy—much like bluffing in poker, which does not reflect on the morality of the bluffer.

I quoted Henry Taylor, the British statesman who pointed out that "falsehood ceases to be falsehood when it is understood on all sides that the truth is not expected to be spoken"—an exact description of bluffing in poker, diplomacy, and business. . . .

*   *   *   *   *

Pressure to Deceive

Most executives from time to time are almost compelled, in the interests of their companies or themselves, to practice some form of deception when negotiating with customers, dealers, labor unions, government officials, or even other departments of their companies. By conscious misstatements, concealment of pertinent facts, or exaggeration—in short, by bluffing—they seek to persuade others to agree with them. I think it is fair to say that if the individual executive refuses to bluff from time to time—if he feels obligated to tell the truth, the whole truth, and nothing but the truth—he is ignoring opportunities permitted under the rules and is at a heavy disadvantage in his business dealings.

But here and there a businessman is unable to reconcile himself to the bluff

---

* An abridgment of the article of the same title as it appeared in *Harvard Business Review,* Vol. XLVI, No. 1 (January–February 1968), pp. 143–53. © Harvard Business Review.

† Mr. Carr was Assistant to the Chairman of the War Production Board during World War II and later served on the White House staff and as a Special Consultant to President Truman. Among his books is *John D. Rockefeller's Secret Weapon,* a study of corporate development. This article is adapted from a chapter in his book, *Business As a Game,* published by New American Library in March 1968.

in which he plays a part. His conscience, perhaps spurred by religious idealism, troubles him. He feels guilty; he may develop an ulcer or a nervous tic. Before any executive can make profitable use of the strategy of the bluff, he needs to make sure that in bluffing he will not lose self-respect or become emotionally disturbed. If he is to reconcil personal integrity and high standards of honesty with the practical requirements of business, he must feel that his bluffs are ethically justified. The justification rests on the fact that business, as practiced by individuals as well as by corporations, has the impersonal character of a game—a game that demands both special strategy and an understanding of its special ethics.

The game is played at all levels of corporate life, from the highest to the lowest. At the very instant that a man decides to enter business he may be forced into a game situation. . . .

* * * * *

The Poker Analogy

We can learn a good deal about the nature of business by comparing it with poker. While both have a large element of chance, in the long run the winner is the man who plays with steady skill. In both games ultimate victory requires intimate knowledge of the rules, insight into the psychology of the other players, a bold front, a considerable amount of self-discipline, and the ability to respond swiftly and effectively to opportunities provided by chance.

No one expects poker to be played on the ethical principles preached in churches. In poker it is right and proper to bluff a friend out of the rewards of being dealt a good hand. A player feels no more than a slight twinge of sympathy, if that, when—with nothing better than a single ace in his hand—he strips a heavy loser, who holds a pair, of the rest of his chips. It was up to the other fellow to protect himself. In the words of an excellent poker player, former President Harry Truman, "If you can't stand the heat, stay out of the kitchen." If one shows mercy to a loser in poker, it is a personal gesture, divorced from the rules of the game.

Poker has its special ethics, and here I am not referring to rules against cheating. The man who keeps an ace up his sleeve or who marks the cards is more than unethical; he is a crook, and can be punished as such—kicked out of the game or, in the Old West, shot.

In contrast to the cheat, the unethical poker player is one who, while abiding by the letter of the rules, finds ways to put the other players at an unfair disadvantage. Perhaps he unnerves them with loud talk. Or he tries to get them drunk. Or he plays in cahoots with someone else at the table. Ethical poker players frown on such tactics.

Poker's own brand of ethics is different from the ethical ideals of civilized human relationships. The game calls for distrust of the other fellow. It ignores the claim of friendship. Cunning deception and concealment of one's strength and intentions, not kindness and openheartedness, are vital in poker. No one thinks any the worse of poker on that account. And no one should think any the worse of the game of business because its standards of right and wrong differ from the prevailing traditions of morality in our society.

* * * * *

Cast Illusions Aside

*   *   *   *   *

The illusion that business can afford to be guided by ethics as conceived in private life is often fostered by speeches and articles containing such phrases as, "It pays to be ethical," or, "Sound ethics is good business." Actually this is not an ethical position at all; it is a self-serving calculation in disguise. The speaker is really saying that in the long run a company can make more money if it does not antagonize competitors, suppliers, employees, and customers by squeezing them too hard. He is saying that oversharp policies reduce ultimate gains. That is true, but it has nothing to do with ethics. The underlying attitude is much like that in the familiar story of the shopkeeper who finds an extra $20 bill in the cash register, debates with himself the ethical problem—should he tell his partner? —and finally decides to share the money because the gesture will give him an edge over the s.o.b. the next time they quarrel.

I think it is fair to sum up the prevailing attitude of businessmen on ethics as follows:

We live in what is probably the most competitive of the world's civilized societies. Our customs encourage a high degree of aggression in the individual's striving for success. Business is our main area of competition, and it has been ritualized into a game of strategy. The basic rules of the game have been set by the government, which attempts to detect and punish business frauds. But as long as a company does not transgress the rules of the game set by law, it has the legal right to shape its strategy without reference to anything but its profits. If it takes a long-term view of its profits, it will preserve amicable relations, so far as possible, with those with whom it deals. A wise businessman will not seek advantage to the point where he generates dangerous hostility among employees, competitors, customers, government, or the public at large. But decisions in this area are, in the final test, decisions of strategy, not of ethics.

The Individual and the Game

An individual within a company often finds it difficult to adjust to the requirements of the business game. He tries to preserve his private ethical standards in situations that call for game strategy. When he is obliged to carry out company policies that challenge his conception of himself as an ethical man, he suffers.

It disturbs him when he is ordered, for instance, to deny a raise to a man who deserves it, to fire an employee of long standing, to prepare advertising that he believes to be misleading, to conceal facts that he feels customers are entitled to know, to cheapen the quality of materials used in the manufacture of an established product, to sell as new a product that he knows to be rebuilt, to exaggerate the curative powers of a medicinal preparation, or to coerce dealers.

There are some fortunate executives who, by the nature of their work and circumstances, never have to face problems of this kind. But in one form or another the ethical dilemma is felt sooner or later by most businessmen. Possibly the dilemma is most painful not when the company forces the action on the executive but when he originates it himself. . . .

*   *   *   *   *

. . . If an executive allows himself to be torn between a decision based on business considerations and one based on his private ethical code, he exposes himself to a grave psychological strain.

This is not to say that sound business strategy necessarily runs counter to ethical ideals. They may frequently coincide; and when they do, everyone is gratified. But the major tests of every move in business, as in all games of strategy, are legality and profit. A man who intends to be a winner in the business game must have a game player's attitude.

The business strategist's decisions must be as impersonal as those of a surgeon performing an operation—concentration on objective and technique, and subordinating personal feelings. . . .

*   *   *   *   *

If a man plans to take a seat in the business game, he owes it to himself to master the principles by which the game is played, including its special ethical outlook. He can then hardly fail to recognize that an occasional bluff may well be justified in terms of the game's ethics and warranted in terms of economic necessity. Once he clears his mind on this point, he is in a good position to match his strategy against that of the other players. He can then determine objectively whether a bluff in a given situation has a good chance of succeeding and can decide when and how to bluff, without a feeling of ethical transgression.

To be a winner, a man must play to win. This does not mean that he must be ruthless, cruel, harsh, or treacherous. On the contrary, the better his reputation for integrity, honesty, and decency, the better his chances of victory will be in the long run. But from time to time every businessman, like every poker player, is offered a choice between certain loss or bluffing within the legal rules of the game. If he is not resigned to losing, if he wants to rise in his company and industry, then in such a crisis he will bluff—and bluff hard.

Every now and then one meets a successful businessman who has conveniently forgotten the small or large deceptions that he practiced on his way to fortune. "God gave me my money," old John D. Rockefeller once piously told a Sunday school class. It would be a rare tycoon in our time who would risk the horse laugh with which such a remark would be greeted.

In the last third of the twentieth century even children are aware that if a man has become prosperous in business, he has sometimes departed from the strict truth in order to overcome obstacles or has practiced the more subtle deceptions of the half-truth or the misleading omission. Whatever the form of the bluff, it is an integral part of the game, and the executive who does not master its techniques is not likely to accumulate much money or power.

From

ORGANIZATION MAN AND DUE PROCESS OF LAW*

By William M. Evan†

The ideology of the "organization man," as it bears on industrial organizations, has at least two irrelated structural sources: (a) the unstructured character of the work of junior and middle managers which is conducive to the use of subjective criteria of performance appraisal, and (b) an authority structure devoid of a mechanism to insure "procedural due process of law." It is hypothesized that this ideology has largely dysfunctional consequences from the viewpoint of the individual executive, the industrial organization, and society as a whole. Two potential countervailing forces are considered: the professionalization of management and the institutionalization of norms of procedural due process. Some research implications of this analysis are noted.

*   *   *   *   *

By comparison with the unionized manual worker, whose occupational rights are protected by the grievance machinery provided by the collective bargaining agreement, the junior or middle manager is at a distinct disadvantage: lacking the right of appeal, he is at the mercy of the decisions of his immediate superior who, in his decisions regarding his subordinates, may function simultaneously as judge, jury, and prosecutor.[1] From this perspective, the organization man appears to be a member of a "new proletariat" in present-day American industry. He does not have the protection of an outside occupational organization, such as unionized employees do; nor does he have a code of professional ethics to govern his relationships with his superordinates, his peers, and his subordinates; nor does he have the protection of "colleague control," as professionals do, to counteract "hierarchical control." Since the nature of his work makes objective evaluation of performance difficult, and since he lacks the right of appeal, he is, therefore, highly motivated to fulfill his superior's expectations—even at the expense of his own ideas and wishes—in order to insure a positive appraisal and the associated rewards. However, to fulfill his superior's expectations, which are often ambiguous, he learns to avoid any actions which he suspects might displease his superior. Such actions may range from joining or not joining the Masons[2] to the choice of style of clothing. The organization man's process of adapting himself to the expectations and behavior patterns of his superior and of relinquishing, if necessary, his own preferences and judgments may be likened to the conformity patterns experi-

---

* Reprinted from *American Sociological Review,* Vol. XXVI, No. 4 (August 1961).

† The author is Professor of Sociology and Industry, Wharton School of Finance and Commerce, University of Pennsylvania.

[1] "There is no final escape from dependency if the superior is the ultimate authority, with no appeal beyond his interpretation or ruling. Unless there is some outside authority to which the subordinate can appeal, he never can be entirely safe in his dependency or quite able to develop a real independence." Mason Haire, *Psychology in Management* (New York: McGraw-Hill Book Co., 1956), p. 67.

[2] Cf. Melville Dalton, *Men Who Manage* (New York: John Wiley & Sons, Inc., 1959), pp. 178–81.

mentally observed by Sherif and Asch. Subjects faced with an ambiguous and unstructured situation—as in the case of the auto-kinetic effect—tend to adjust their statements of perceptions to one another;[3] and some subjects faced with an unambiguous and structured situation relinquish their true statement of perceptions of reality in favor of a false statement of perceptions made by others.[4]

In brief, the ideology of the organization man has at least two interrelated sources: occupational and organizational. Occupationally, the amorphous character of managerial work encourages the use of subjective criteria for evaluating performance, including a pattern of sponsorship or patronage and a concern for the organizational loyalty of subordinates. Organizationally, in the absence of norms of procedural due process of law, such as the right to appeal the decision of a superordinate, junior and middle managers are encouraged to become "conformists," developing an over-sensitivity to the expectations of superordinates in order to insure positive appraisal and corresponding rewards. Otherwise put, the ideology of organization man is an adaption to certain normless elements in the work situation of junior and middle managers.

SOME CONSEQUENCES OF THE IDEOLOGY OF THE ORGANIZATION MAN

The consequences of the ideology of the organization man are presumably—in the absence of systematic data—largely dysfunctional from the viewpoint of the individual executive as well as from the viewpoint of the industrial organization and society at large. Several illustrative and hypothetical dysfunctions will be considered.

From the standpoint of the individual executive as well as the organization, the ideology tends to inhibit original and creative effort which, by definition, departs from prevailing practices, and hence runs the risk of not being approved by a superordinate. Accordingly, the industrial organization must increasingly rely on staff specialists for new ideas rather than on line management. This entails a loss to the organization of a potential source of valuable innovations—which is not to gainsay the advantages of having staff specialists concern themselves principally with problems of innovation.

Another consequence of this ideology for the individual as well as for the organization is the paradoxical combination of high job immobility with high job insecurity. By definition, the organization man's loyalty induces him to devote his entire career to his organization. He has a "local" rather than a "cosmopolitan" orientation; in other words, his reference group in his organization rather than the occupation of management which transcends a given organization. This tends to result in a high degree of job immobility among executive personnel. From the point of view of the organization, low turnover may be highly advantageous, provided the manager's performance is judged to contribute to the organization's effectiveness. In the event that his performance is judged to interfere with the organization's attainment of its goals, the organization may transfer him to an innocuous

---

[3] Muzafer Sherif, "Group Influences upon the Formation of Norms and Attitudes," in Eleanor E. Maccoby, Theodore M. Newcomb, Eugene L. Hartley (eds.), *Readings in Social Psychology* (New York: Henry Holt & Co., 1958), pp. 219–32.

[4] Solomon E. Asch, "Effects of Group Pressure upon the Modification and Distortion of Judgments," in Maccoby, Newcomb and Hartley, *op. cit.,* pp. 174–83.

position, induce him to resign, or dismiss him.[5] In the absence of due process of law for junior and middle managers, and we might even add top managers, those who are judged undesirable for whatever reasons—relevant or irrelevant—may be discharged without an opportunity for a fair hearing.

Another consequence of the ideology which is dysfunctional for the organization is the tendency of the organization man to restrict upward communication to material which is calculated to enhance his self-image and simultaneously not threaten the superordinate in any way. On the basis of studies of experimentally created hierarchies, we would expect that organization men who are upwardly mobile—and this is presumably true of the bulk of junior and middle managers—would be strongly motivated to censor upward communication to insure positive appraisal and corresponding rewards.[6] Such action, of course, complicates the planning and coordination problems of top management.

Yet another effect of the ideology on the individual executive, related to job insecurity and the pressures for restriction of upward communication, is the tendency for discrepancies to develop between overt and covert behavior. Covert nonconformity occurs provided the probability of the discovery of such action is low. Where covert nonconformity does not occur, we may expect to find covert disbelief in the legitimacy of the authority exercised by the superior together with overt behavioral conformity. The resulting degree of cognitive dissonance, due to the discrepancy between overt conformity and covert disbelief, on the part of the organization man may be considerable. To reduce the resulting dissonance, the organization man can convince himself that his overt behavior is quite satisfactory after all, i.e., by changing his cognitions so that they are consonant with his overt behavior.[7]

The effect of the ideology of the organization man on society as a whole is probably more elusive than its effects on the individual manager and on the industrial organization, though nonetheless real. As a result of the premium put on cautious behavior calculated not to offend the preferences and expectations of a superior, the organization man may tend to transfer this behavior pattern and principle of behavior to his community life and engage in only "conformist" activity. This approach to community life lessens the chances of successfully coming to grips with new and complex social problems requiring innovative rather than "conformist" behavior. The consequences of this ideology for society as a whole may be especially marked in view of the recent efforts by corporations to encourage management to increase their participation in community affairs.

A related effect of the ideology may be observable in family values and child-rearing patterns of the organization man. The values of seeking approval from superiors, of "teamwork," and of "togetherness" may be transplanted from the corporation to the family.[8]

---

[5] Cf. Perrin Stryker, "How to Fire an Executive," *Fortune,* Vol. L (October 1954), pp. 116–17, 178–92.

[6] Cf. Harold H. Kelley, "Communication in Experimentally Created Hierarchies," *Human Relations,* Vol. IV (February 1951), pp. 39–56; Arthur R. Cohen, "Upward Communication in Experimentally Created Hierarchies," *Human Relations,* Vol. XI (February 1958), pp. 41–53.

[7] Leon Festinger, *A Theory of Cognitive Dissonance* (Evanston, Ill.: Row, Peterson & Co., 1957), pp. 1–31.

[8] Daniel R. Miller and Guy E. Swanson, *The Changing American Parent: A Study in the Detroit Area* (New York: John Wiley & Sons, Inc., 1958).

POTENTIAL COUNTERVAILING FORCES TO THE IDEOLOGY OF THE ORGANIZATION MAN

Two potential countervailing forces to the ideology of the organization man are the institutionalization of norms of procedural due process of law for corporate management and the professionalization of management.

As yet it is difficult to discern any evidence for the institutionalization of norms of due process within corporate management. It is possible, however, that such a development may be stimulated by the need for resolving conflicts between staff and line management. The high frequency of such conflicts, in the absence of unionization among staff specialists, may be conducive to the growth of norms of procedural due process. Such a development could pave the way for the extension of this institution to all corporate management.

Another source of influence favoring an extension of procedural due process is external to the corporation. There is a growing awareness of the need for restricting the powers of the corporation. In particular, it is being argued that courts and the legislatures should extend constitutional guarantees of procedural due process to the corporation[9] or that corporations should develop their own "supplementary constitutional systems."[10] The venerable doctrine of due process, which dates back at least to the Magna Carta, includes a complex of procedural safeguards against the exercise of arbitrary and unlimited power.[11] These norms seek to insure that disputes are resolved impartially and fairly. This complex of norms includes the right of all parties to a conflict to be heard, the right to confront witnesses, to cross-examine them, and to introduce evidence in one's behalf. . . . Another potential countervailing force to the ideology of the organization man is the professionalization of management. In spite of the plethora of discussions for several decades about the professionalization of management, there has been very little progress in this direction. . . .[12]

*   *   *   *   *

Either of the two potential countervailing forces to the ideology of the organization man may be conducive to the development of the other. As between these two possible developments it appears more likely that professionalization of management will be conducive to the institutionalization of norms of due process than the reverse.

Short of the institutionalization of the norms of procedural due process for junior and middle management, several other mechanisms may upon inquiry prove to have an equivalent function. The first is the institutionalization of the right of job transfer within a company. This would enable a manager, finding himself in an unsatisfactory authority relationship with his superior, to overcome this problem without suffering the consequences of adjustment to an arbitrary superior.

A related mechanism is "job rotation." To the extent that this becomes an institutionalized procedure, it affords the executive an opportunity to manifest his

---

[9] Adolph A. Berle, Jr., *The 20th Century Capitalist Revolution* (New York: Harcourt, Brace & Co., 1954), pp. 77 ff.

[10] Benjamin M. Selekman, "Power and Morality in Business," in Dan H. Fenn, Jr., *Management's Mission in a New Society* (New York: McGraw-Hill Book Co., 1959), pp. 317–19.

[11] Rodney L. Mott, *Due Process of Law* (Indianapolis, Ind.: Bobbs Merrill Co., 1926), pp. 1–29.

[12] See, for example, Henry C. Metcalf (ed.), *Business Management as a Profession* (Chicago: A. W. Shaw Co., 1927); Howard R. Bowen, "Business Management: A Profession?" *Annals of the American Academy of Political and Social Science,* Vol. 297 (January 1955), pp. 112–17.

abilities to more than one superior and in different organizational situations, which in turn increases the chances of a more objective appraisal of his talents.

A third mechanism which might be a functional substitute for the norms of due process is an increase in the opportunities for intercompany mobility. One of the major impediments to such mobility is the absence of vested pension rights. This discourages job changes because of the financial loss entailed. The vesting of pension rights for executives—such as already exists among university professors —if it should ever develop, would probably betoken a significant measure of progress toward the professionalization of management. Only an occupation with "cosmopolitan" values would encourage the institutionalization of such a practice.

2. YARWAY CORPORATION

Case Introduction

SYNOPSIS

For its first 50 years, the Yarway Corporation remained a small private firm serving the domestic power industry with a narrow range of highly engineered products. The firm entered its second half century with an old plant, old products, and aging top management. A new management team took over and launched a far-reaching renewal program. New products were developed. Penetration was achieved in new domestic and foreign markets. Through a licensee, a joint venture partner, and three foreign wholly owned subsidiaries, Yarway initiated international operations in the Far East, Latin America, Canada, and Europe. At home, Yarway spanned the North American continent with a wholly owned subsidiary on the West Coast and a new headquarters/plant complex on the East Coast. Yarway faced the 70s with a strategy of serving the worldwide power and process industries with proprietary products and services related to the flow of gasses, solids, and liquids. Yarway executives had more confidence in their strategy than they did in their organization structure for coping with the future.

WHY THIS CASE IS INCLUDED

In the Yarway case the reader can test the utility of the "principles" of classical management for the design of organization structure. At another level, the reader can test the logic of the "structure-follows-strategy" dictum of the recent management authors. At a third level, the insights of social psychology can be examined in light of the present and prospective roles of the executives within the Yarway structure. Beyond these organizational issues, the reader can examine the Yarway strategy for growing and prospering as an independent, medium-sized firm among the emerging, supergiant multinationals of the future.

DIAGNOSTIC AND PREDICTIVE QUESTIONS

The readings included with this case are marked (*). The author index at the end of this book locates the other readings.

1. Do you think Yarway is threatened by the emerging world of super-giant multinational firms? Check the force field analysis done by the Yarway top management against the arguments in the Perlmutter article. What are Yarway's chief strengths and its chief weaknesses for survival and prosperity as an independent multinational?

Read: *Perlmutter, "Super-Giant Firms in the Future."

2. Do you think Yarway's strategy for the 70s is realistic in light of market forces and Yarway's capacities?

Read: Tilles, "How to Evaluate Corporate Strategy."

3. Do you see evidence of synergy in Yarway's expansion and product development policies?

Read: Ansoff, *Corporate Strategy: An Analytical Approach for Growth and Expansion,* pp. 75–86. Pessemier, *New Product Decisions,* pp. 8–10.

4. By reference only to traditional organization theory evaluate the adequacy of Yarway's present organization structure. What is the primary basis for departmentation in Yarway? Are any of the traditional "principles" violated in Yarway's current structure?

Read: *Carzo and Yanouzas, *Formal Organizations: A Systems Approach,* pp. 24–34, 43–44, 48–49, 55–57, 65–68.

5. As Yarway has become international, has it followed the historical patterns of other U.S. firms? Are there any predictions you would make from the experiences of others for Yarway as it goes further in its internationalization?

Read: Kolde, *International Business Enterprise,* pp. 242–55, 260, 277–78. Those who wish an additional analysis of the evolving organization of multinational enterprises, consult in the library John Stoppford and Louis T. Wells, *Managing the International Enterprise* (Basic Books, 1972), Chapter 2.

6. What are the key issues in Yarway strategy that might prompt a restructuring of the firm? Is the present structure adequate to support Yarway's strategy for the 70s?

Read: *Chandler, *Strategy and Structure,* pp. 7–17, 299–300, 314–15. Or see Stoppford and Wells, *Managing the Multinational Enterprise,* Chapter 2, as cited above.

7. Examine the role of the executive vice presicent vis à vis the president in light of the conceptual schemes provided by Katz and Kahn, Levinson, and McGrath. Under what conditions is this a viable role?

Read: Katz and Kahn, *The Social Psychology of Organizations,* pp. 174–180, 182, 186–87. Levinson, "Role, Personality, and Social Structure in the Organizational Setting." McGrath, *Social Psychology,* pp. 50–52.

8. Would you expect any difficulties to arise in the management of Yarway as a private firm or in Yarway's going public because of the motivations of Mr. Yarnall as owner-manager and of his professional manager colleagues?

Read: Monsen and Downs, "A Theory of Large Managerial Firms." Cohen and Cyert, *Theory of the Firm: Resource Allocation in a Market Economy,* pp. 354–56, 361–63, 376–77, 379–80. Hampton, Summer, and Webber, *Organizational Behavior and the Practice of Management,* Chapter 10.

POLICY QUESTIONS

9. Can you recommend any strategic changes for Yarway for the next five years? Be specific in the following areas: (a) product development, (b) market development, (c) financial.

Review your responses to Questions 1–3.

10. In what way would you propose modifying the Yarway organization structure? Don't forget to take account of the people currently in top management positions. Give reasons for both the changes and the timing of the reorganization.

Review your responses to Questions 4–6.

Read: Leavitt, *Managerial Psychology,* pp. 317–25.

11. How would you allocate roles to the president and executive vice president within your proposed structure?

Review your responses to Questions 7 and 8.

QUESTIONS FOR ORIGINAL STUDENT WORK IN ANALYSIS AND POLICY

12. While reflecting on case facts, what additional theories from prior education give you insights as to "what is going on" in the Yarway Corporation? As to what might be predicted to happen in the future?

13. Other than the policy questions asked by the authors, what pragmatic ways can you think of to state the practical problems faced by executives in the case?

CASE TEXT*

1971 was a good year for Yarway and 1972 showed promise of being even better. According to Robert Yarnall, President and Chairman of the Board, "The future challenge is putting substance to the conviction that a moderate-sized, independent, company can survive and prosper in the emerging world of supergiant multinational firms. Related to this strategic issue is the current concern of our top management team that our present organization structure will not be adequate to carry the company to the next level of growth, multinational expansion, and new product development."

---

* Copyright 1973, J. J. O'Connell.

HISTORY OF THE YARWAY CORPORATION

Three enterprising men—an engineer, a salesman, and an inventor—founded the firm in 1908 in Philadelphia, Pennsylvania, to serve particularly the power industry with high-quality, proprietary, power plant equipment like valves and steam traps. The firm enjoyed steady and profitable growth until the early 50s. At that stage, sales volume had reached $4 million and the products were well established in the domestic market. Exports from the one plant in Philadelphia represented a small percentage of the total volume. The management, still with one of the founders at the top, concentrated on more in-company issues than on the market or competitive environment. Personnel administration consumed much time—job evaluation, wage and salary administration, in-plant communications, establishment of wage incentives, and negotiation of the first union contract. The late 50s were marked by progress in sales forecasting, budgeting, market research, cost control, and the establishment of a merit rating system.

As a new management team took over from the last of the founders in 1962, sales volume stood at $5.8 million but profitability had slipped. The percentage of exports had increased somewhat and some products—notably steam traps—were being manufactured and sold under license in Canada, U.K., France, and Japan. Some important product lines were growing obsolete and had entered the mature phase of the product life cycle. The single plant was now old and crowded.

The new president, D. Robert Yarnall, Jr., the 37-year-old son of one of the founders, had been with the firm since 1949 in the successive positions of personnel director, works manager, and manufacturing vice president. He began the renewal of the company by building a new management team and collaborating with them in formulating basic policies, corporate objectives, strategic guidelines for product, market, acquisitions, and financial management. Under his leadership, the new seven-man team concentrated on a two-pronged effort of running the current operations more effectively and building for the future. They inaugurated an annual planning cycle in which targets were set in five areas (profitability, sales volume, market standing, products, and corporate capability) and reviewed at the end of the year. As first priority, Yarway began renovating existing product lines and searching for new products. During the first half of the 60s, Yarway invested in an expanded training effort and started a stock option plan for executives. By 1965, the company was issuing an annual report, though it was still a private company, and could boast of a 60 percent increase in sales and a 100 percent increase in return on net worth since the succession of the new management team.

After the first decade under the new management, the company had taken on a new look. Financially (see Exhibit 1 and Appendices A and B), the company had weathered a relatively bad year in 1968 (soft market and heavy expenditures on European start-up and on product development) to show more than a 300 percent sales growth and over a 410 percent profit growth in the decade.

As is clear from Exhibit 1, penetration of new markets abroad, particularly by the replacement of European licensees with wholly owned

EXHIBIT 1
Financial Comparison (1961–1971)

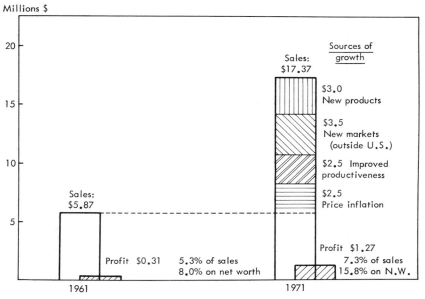

Millions $

	1961	1971
	Sales: $5.87	Sales: $17.37

Sources of growth

$3.0 New products
$3.5 New markets (outside U.S.)
$2.5 Improved productiveness
$2.5 Price inflation

Profit $0.31   5.3% of sales   8.0% on net worth

Profit $1.27   7.3% of sales   15.8% on N.W.

subsidiaries, and commercialization of new products contributed heavily to the company's growth. In facilities, replacing the one old plant in Philadelphia, Yarway in 1971 had new headquarters and plant (180,-000 square feet—one third, offices, two thirds, plant) in suburban Philadelphia, as well as new plants in its wholly owned subsidiaries in California (25,000 square feet), Canada (15,000 square feet), Great Britain (5,600 square feet), and the Netherlands (19,500 square feet). Yarway was effectively represented in Japan by Gadelius, K.K., and high priority was being given to building even stronger relationships with this exclusive agent and manufacturing licensee (steam traps). A joint venture company in Brazil had begun to make deliveries of locally manufactured Yarway steam traps in Latin America. In mid-1972, negotiations were underway for the acquisition of a small instrument company in Great Britain, a step which had been preceded by the acquisition of Kingmann White in California in 1970. The decade of renewal ended with virtually worldwide market coverage and with new and better products.

Internally, the decade of renewal witnessed the introduction of a management by objectives system for all "exempt" employees, which was tied directly to a bonus system offering significant payoff for high-quality performance on agreed targets. Those eligible for bonus in the U.S. shared, according to their performance rating and job grade, in a "pot" determined as 20 percent of pretax profits in the U.S. The bonus for someone eligible in a wholly owned subsidiary was based on the profitability of his subsidiary in a similar manner.

Another step forward within Yarway was the introduction of an integrated, computer-based, management information system. For this purpose and others, the company followed the practice of using cross-functional project teams.

In the period of growth, 232 new jobs were created, bringing the total employment in 1971 to 540. Of this number, 140 were "exempt" (professional, administrative, and sales engineers) and 400 office and plant staff (180 clerical, technicians, etc., and 220 direct and indirect labor). Average yearly pay had moved from $8,100 in 1961 to $12,400 in 1971.

MARKETS AND PRODUCT LINE

Yarway's strategic guidelines specify the following markets.

"Our product planning is directed toward serving these basic industrial markets over the entire world:

Process industries
1. Chemical
2. Petrochemical
3. Petroleum and natural gas
4. Food and beverage
5. Pulp and paper
6. Textile
7. Primary metal
8. Pharmaceuticals
9. Rubber
Electric power generation (nuclear- and fossil-fueled)

We shall be supplying the above market with specialty products and proprietary services to satisfy the following customer needs:

Instrumentation and equipment for measurement and control of process variables.

Equipment associated with process vessels, heat transfer, and distribution systems and pipelines such as steam traps, strainers, expansion joints, and specialty valves.

Particular emphasis will be given to satisfying specified customer needs that are useful in avoiding, eliminating, or minimizing environment pollution."

Exhibit 2 gives a picture of Yarway's worldwide market position in 1971.

In a number of products, Yarway competes with firms of about its own size (as in steam traps) and has the competitive advantage of better worldwide coverage. In the early stage products Yarway simultaneously encounters some larger competitors as well as a host of small, specialized producers.

The purchase decisions on virtually all the products involve multiple

EXHIBIT 2
Yarway Corporation 1971—Worldwide Market Position

Markets / Products	U.S. and Canada				EEC and EFTA		Japan and Far East		Other Areas		Sales Totals by Product Class
	Estimated Total Market (millions) $	Estimated Annual Market Growth Per-centage	Yarway Sales (mil-lions) $	Yarway Market Share Per-centage	Yarway Sales (mil-lions) $	Yarway Market Share Per-centage	Yarway Sales (mil-lions) $	Yarway Market Share Per-centage	Yarway Sales (mil-lions) $	Yarway Market Share Per-centage	(millions) $
Mature Stage											
Power Plant Products	14	0	7,9	60	0,7	7	0,7	14	0,4	7	9,7
Steam Traps	22	5	5,4	25	1,1	8	0,7	12	0,3	7	7,5
Growth Stage											
Metering Pumps	25	7	0,7	3	0,1	*	0,1	*	—	—	0,9
Specialty Con-trol Valves	50	12	1,6	3	0,1	*	—	—	—	—	1,7
Early Stage											
Specialty In-strumentation	150	10	0,2	*	—	—	—	—	—	—	0,2
Area Sales Totals			15,8		2,0		1,5		0,7		20,0†

*Negligible.
†Total here differs from those in the annual report because of the way license sales are reported in this table.

parties—consulting engineers, engineering contractors, original equipment manufacturers, and end users. To sell its specially engineered products, Yarway employs some 66 sales engineers, in the U.S., Canada, U.K., Germany, and the Netherlands. It has a network of sales agents in Japan, France, Italy, Australia, Mexico, and Western Canada, as well as an ex-

EXHIBIT 3
Typical Yarway Power Plant Products

Boiler Blow-off Valves
– purge accumulated solids from boiler water systems.

Welbond® Valves
– general purpose high pressure/high temperature valves for tight shut-off in power plant service.

Water Level Gages
– show liquid level within pressure vessels or tanks.

Remote Liquid Level Indicators – sense and transmit liquid level within a pressure vessel or tank for local or distant visual readout.

Gun-Pakt® Expansion Joints – absorb contraction and expansion in pipelines due to temperature changes.

Typical Yarway Steam Traps

Impulse® Steam Traps
– automatic valves that sense and remove heat-robbing condensate and air from steam apparatus and steam lines.

clusive distributor organization in North America for the steam trap line. Backing up the sales effort are applications engineers in the U.S., Canada, U.K., and the Netherlands. In the U.S., there are also two product managers and three assistant product managers.

Yarway products can be roughly classed in the three stages of the product life cycle: (a) mature, (b) growth, (c) early. Among the mature stage products are the valves, gages, and expansion joints used primarily in power plants and the impulse steam traps (see Exhibit 3). Leading items among the growth stage products are the metering pumps and specialty control valves (see Exhibit 4). Representative of the early stage products in the field of specialty instrumentation is the solids flow transmitter (see Exhibit 5). The technology of the mature products is essentially mechanical engineering in the context of thermodynamics. The

EXHIBIT 4
Typical Yarway Metering Pump and Specialty Control Valves

Cyclo/Phram™ Metering Pumps – inject a precisely metered volume of liquid into a process stream against a positive discharge pressure.

ARC (Auto-Recirc) Valves – maintain minimum cooling flow through centrifugal pumps to protect against overheating.

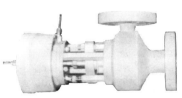

Turbo-Cascade™ Valves – control flow and dissipate energy in high pressure liquids.

Hy-Drop™ Valves – sensitively control flow in high pressure piping systems.

EXHIBIT 5
Typical Yarway Specialty Instrumentation
Solid Flows Transmitter

growth products bring the company into control technology and in the specialty instrumentation, early stage products, the technology turns to electronics and, most recently, ultrasonics in such measures as flow and density of solids, fluids, and gasses.

Yarway's "product planning guidelines" contain the following criteria for new product selection:

"1. New products should fulfill customer needs in a new and better way and serve worthwhile purposes.

2. New products should be selected to capitalize on the resources of the company.

3. New product development should be directed solely toward industrial and commercial rather than military markets.

4. New product development should be undertaken only when sound market research promises steady, profitable sales volume.

5. Products should be proprietary. This is obtained through restraints to imitation by others. Restraints include patents, specialized marketing, and engineering and manufacturing know-how (trade secrets). We consider meaningful patents as the most important restraint to imitation.

6. Products should be complete in the sense that Yarway identity is maintained. Systems in which Yarway product content represents at least 75 percent of manufacturing cost of system are also attractive opportunities.

7. Products should be aimed for specialty markets which are not likely to attract large competitors.
8. Products should have a market that is sufficiently broad that a single customer will not account for more than 10 percent sales volume.
9. Products should be such that they can be fully developed and released for full-scale marketing within three years.
10. After products are released for full-scale marketing,
    a. Development costs of the product should be returned in three years.
    b. The margin between the manufacturing cost and the selling price of the new product line must be sufficient to:
        (1) Cover costs of vigorous sales promotion and presentation, insuring that all possible purchasers shall know its advantages—and to provide necessary field service to assure user satisfaction.
        (2) Cover engineering and administrative costs to permit us to serve our customers in the future.
        (3) Return on operating profit of at least 25 percent in the third year, to provide for profit-sharing bonuses, taxes, dividends to stockholders and the capital necessary to finance future growth of Yarway Corporation.
    c. The product should achieve a sales volume in the U.S. of at least $350,000 in third year."

YARWAY CORPORATION IN THE 70S

The management team continues to refine and elaborate the strategy for the 70s, but a draft document written by the president in November 1971 sketches the outline in the spirit of the "basic policies" reviewed by the board most recently in January 1971 (see Appendix C).

"Corporate Purpose

Serve people by providing excellent products for the world's basic industries. These are the industries which must meet the steadily growing human needs for electric power, fuels, food, paper, clothing, and shipping.

Management Objectives

1. *Survival—self-determination—independence*
    a. To continue as an independent enterprise run by the present management team to their own satisfaction and to that of the stockholders and directors.
2. *Profitability*
    a. To make Yarway stock an attractive investment compared with available alternatives.
    b. To provide the capital required to finance the business.

    c. To provide extra reward opportunities for employees through profit sharing and stock ownership.
3. *Growth*
    a. To compensate for the inevitable creeping obsolescence of products, plants, practices, and people.
    b. To provide expanding opportunities for people to grow in the company.

Qualitative Goals

1. The *best* company we are capable of building—not necessarily the biggest. By this we mean an excellent company to invest in, to buy from, to work for, to sell to, and to live near.
2. An innovative company that earns its rewards in the market place by creating unique values for customers and serving them well.
3. A company that cares about the people who are affected by it.
4. A good corporate citizen—in our basic businesses and in the communities in which we function.
5. A forward looking company devoted to building tomorrow's business while succeeding in today's business.

Quantitative Goals

Earnings. Earnings per share (per year) of 12 percent of net worth (at beginning of the year).

Yield. Dividends (per year) total 4 percent of net worth (at beginning of the year).

Growth Rate. Net Worth (and earnings) per share to grow at a rate of 8 percent per year."

As the management team looked ahead, it assessed Yarway's strengths and weaknesses for surviving and prospering in the 70s. This assessment appears below under four headings: (1) external driving forces, (2) external restraining forces, (3) internal driving forces, and (4) internal restraining forces.

FORCE FIELD ANALYSIS—YARWAY CORPORATION

"External Driving Forces

1. Our markets are the world's basic industries which must meet the steadily growing human needs for power fuels, paper, food, textiles, and shipping.
2. Worldwide demand for higher quality and more sophisticated industrial equipment favors our type of new and better products.
3. Our customers (and the engineering-contractor firms serving them) are becoming increasingly internationalized in their specification and purchase of equipment.
4. Competitors in most lines do not have worldwide market coverage.

5. Growing concern for environment provides good opportunities for pollution control products.

External Restraining Forces

1. The type of customers we serve are conservative by nature in their purchase of equipment. They are slow to adopt *any* new product or supplier and the process of convincing them to do so is slow and costly. (It's nice when you are accepted, however!)
2. Engineers and buyers sometimes have nationalistic feelings which are reflected in codes, purchasing preferences, and so on.
3. The growing concern for environment may slow up the rate of construction of new plants in the power and process industries in the 70s.
4. Local competitive products are increasingly likely to appear in the market as industrialization progresses around the world.
5. The growing tendency to contract for complete systems tends to favor captive equipment suppliers under some circumstances.

Internal Driving Forces

1. Top management:
   a. Ability and willingness to manage.
   b. Commitment to achievement of excellent results and aspiration to operate effectively on a world scale.
   c. Global viewpoint and growing international experience.
   d. Understand importance of both current operations and building tomorrow's business.
2. Common purpose and mutual trust among major stockholders, board of directors, management, and employees:
   a. Basic policies.
   b. Planning guide.
   c. Management by objectives and appraisal by results with strong rewards system.
   d. Team building—task forces.
3. Continuous product innovation:
   a. Defined objectives and strategies.
   b. Search, screening, appraisal, and trial venture techniques.
   c. Patents and other proprietary values.
   d. Pipeline is filled and flowing.
4. International network established:
   a. Wholly owned marketing and manufacturing companies in U.S., Canada, EEC, and UK.
   b. Licensee in Japan with good capabilities and communications.
   c. Sales agents in most countries of the world.
5. Good well-established reputation:
   a. Founded in 1908.
   b. Well known (at least in Anglo-Saxon markets).
   c. Strong customer loyalty.

Internal Restraining Forces

1. Top management:
   a. The fact that ability and vision are limited.
   b. Some success already achieved may diminish willingness to take risks.
   c. Good international managers willing to go anywhere are hard to find.
2. Stock not publicly traded:
   a. Limits its attractiveness as currency for acquisitions.
   b. Limits visibility of the company in financial circles.
3. Polycentric rewards system:
   a. Bonuses of subsidiary managers now based on profitability of the subsidiary rather than the consolidated corporation.
4. Strategies intended to put primary emphasis on survival and profitability rather than growth of sales, for example:
   a. Commitment to be the *best*, not the *biggest*.
   b. Concentrate on *hardware* products of a *specialty* nature.
   c. Centralize control of *products* and *finances*.
5. Marketing:
   a. Sales capacity may be limited to penetrate the new customers in the worldwide process industries with the emerging control and instrumentation products."

YARWAY ORGANIZATION

Deeply involved in shaping Yarway's future are the following headquarters' executives:

D. Robert Yarnall, Jr. President and chairman of the board . . . 47 years old . . . graduated as mechanical engineer from Cornell University. . . . Previous employment with Westinghouse Electric and Leeds and Northrup, Co., director of five other companies, and numerous professional and community organizations.

Theodore B. Palmer, 3rd. Executive vice president . . . 47 years old . . . majored in economics at Princeton University . . . joined the company in 1959 in the personnel function from the Atlantic Refining Company . . . served as vice president, personnel, prior to assuming his current position in 1969.

Frank Boni. Vice president, product planning, responsible for building tomorrow's businesses and the maintaining of proprietary values . . . 45 years of age . . . mechanical engineer from University of Michigan . . . joined the company in 1962 from Griscom-Russell as director of engineering . . . served as vice president, engineering, prior to assuming his current position in 1970.

William T. Griffiths. Vice president, marketing (USA) . . . 54 years of age . . . chemical engineer from the Penn State University . . . joined the company in his present position in 1969 after serving as vice president, marketing and director of Milton Roy.

Stanley F. Myers. Vice president, manufacturing (U.S.) . . . 44 years of age . . . majored in industrial management at Antioch College . . . joined the company in 1954 after working with the American Friends

Service in India . . . performed a number of functions in manufacturing prior to assuming his present position in the mid-60s.

R. Henry Seelaus. Vice president, international operations . . . 51 years of age . . . business administration major at the Wharton School, University of Pennsylvania . . . joined the company in 1962 from Fisher and Porter where he had been vice president, finance . . . originally supervised all export activity and business outside the U.S. including creation and start up of subsidiaries in EEC, UK, and Canada . . . more recently concentrating on administration of international development activity in the Far East and Latin America.

George I. Tyndall. Vice president, finance . . . 52 years of age . . . business administration major at the Wharton School, University of Pennsylvania . . . joined the company as assistant accounting manager in 1959 from Collins and Aikman . . . became treasurer and secretary in 1960, then vice president, finance, in 1964.

Hayes H. Baker. Personnel director . . . 39 years of age . . . graduate of Wesleyan University . . . joined the company in the early 60s in the personnel function.

The board of directors is composed of two external directors: C. Graham Berwind, Jr., and Paul F. Miller, Jr.; representatives of two of the founders' families: David C. McClelland, and John S. Stoker, Jr.; two operating executives: Theodore B. Palmer, 3rd, and George I. Tyndall; and the president, D. Robert Yarnall, Jr., who also represents the third founders' family.

The current organization chart appears in Exhibit 6. The president and his three immediate colleagues work as a team in strategic matters. The president delegates day-to-day supervision of the business to the executive vice president and manages by exception but for his involve-

EXHIBIT 6
Yarway Organization Chart (mid-1972)

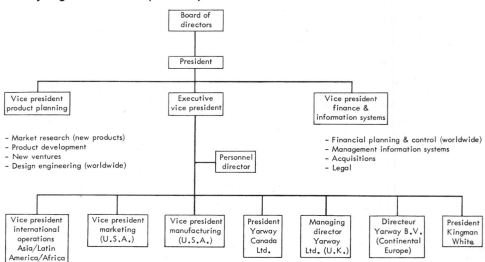

ment in overall planning and control. The six headquarters executives, excepting the president, constitute the operations team under the chairmanship of the executive vice president. The president and executive vice president express their roles respectively as focusing on creating tomorrow's business and managing today's business.

With plans in mid-1972 to add by acquisition a fifth wholly owned subsidiary, the pressure was building to restructure the company. Two issues loom as most important: first, the span of control for the executive vice president and, second, the slow pace of commercialization of new products. There was no strong sentiment for realigning the roles of the president and executive vice president. In a sense, they operated together as the chief executive's office. Together with the vice president, product planning, and the vice president, finance, they formed a corporate management team which functioned together effectively with a strong sense of common purpose and mutual trust. This arrangement had worked satisfactorily since the company abandoned its functional organization in 1969 (see Exhibit 7).

EXHIBIT 7
Yarway Organization Chart (up to September 1969)

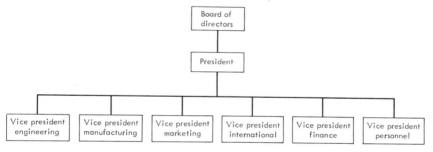

The business was growing more complex, however, as a result of the successful renewal program of recent years. Although entrepreneurial efforts were carefully focused on "engineered products for the power and process industries," they added new complexity as follows:

New types of products—metering pumps, high performance control valves, and, most recently, instrumentation for measurement of flow, density, and other process variables were added to the older steam specialty lines.

New types of customers—steam power plants (including nuclear) were still important buyers (of both new and older products) but new and different customers must also be cultivated in the chemical process and natural gas industries.

New geographic markets—the commitment to worldwide marketing of unique products had led to a good start in the major industrial markets of Europe and Japan, but much remained to be done to achieve the sort of strength enjoyed by Yarway in the North American market.

EXHIBIT 8
Geographic Organization Model

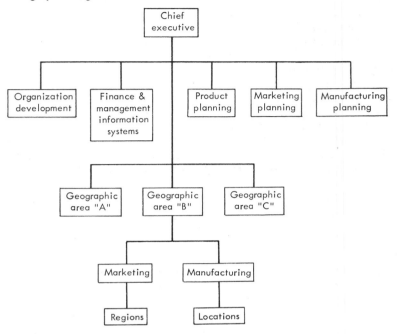

EXHIBIT 9
Geographic/Product Organization Model

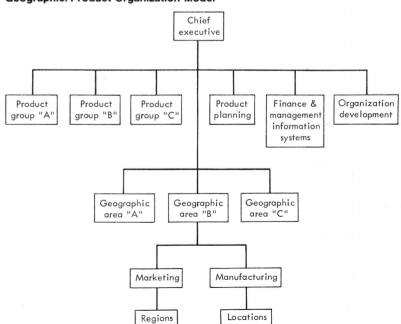

Without prejudicing the decision on the appropriate organization form for the future, the president and executive vice president agreed that the new structure should cope successfully with these complexities and facilitate the following achievements:

1. Plan each year's business and carry out the plan to meet quantitative and qualitative goals.
2. Assure that adequate resources and attention are devoted to new business development as well as the operation of more mature businesses.
3. Keep control of and enhance the proprietary values of all product lines through patents, design control, and product management.
4. Motivate key people to work for the achievement of overall goals and build allegiance to the total corporation.
5. Make best use of people's talents throughout the company and develop the human resources that will be needed in future.
6. Optimize penetration of major industrial markets around the world for each major product line, based on good knowledge of markets and competition.
7. Rationalize and coordinate manufacturing sources on a world-wide basis to assure low costs and reliable service to customers.
8. Keep control of financial commitments and facilitate access to best sources of capital consistent with fundamental objectives.
9. Provide for management of present and future acquired compa-

EXHIBIT 10
Product Organization Model

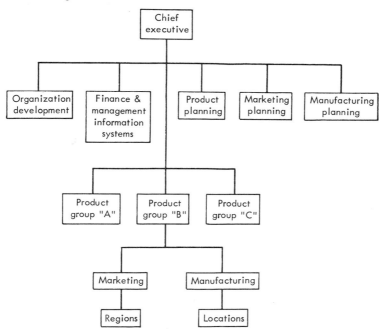

nies and of joint venture companies in Japan, Brazil, and elsewhere.

In early discussions, a number of organization forms were considered: (1) geographic model (Exhibit 8); (2) geographic-product model (Exhibit 9); (3) product model (Exhibit 10); (4) product-functional model (Exhibit 11); (5) functional model (Exhibit 12); (6) and product-geographic model (Exhibit 13).

EXHIBIT 11
Product/Functional Organization Model

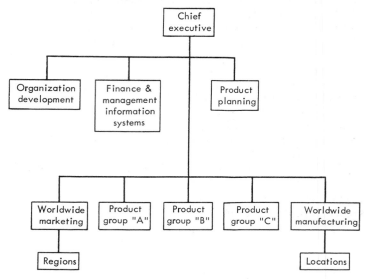

EXHIBIT 12
Functional Organization Model

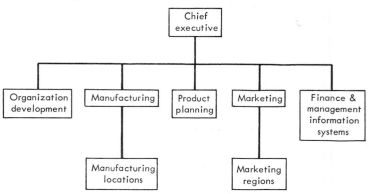

EXHIBIT 13
Product/Geographic Organization Model

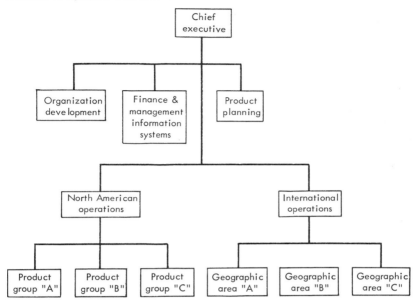

APPENDIX A

YARWAY CORPORATION—CONSOLIDATED BALANCE SHEETS

Assets

	1971	1970	1969
Current Assets:			
Cash	$ 525,585	$ 379,272	$ 410,032
Accounts receivable	3,199,345	3,415,084	2,993,499
Inventories, at lower of cost			
(first-in, first-out) or market	4,677,585	4,579,413	4,681,014
Other current assets	173,767	127,435	172,426
Total current assets	8,576,282	8,501,204	8,256,971
Property, plant and equipment, at cost:			
Land	327,151	327,151	327,151
Buildings and grounds	3,762,783	3,695,838	3,651,569
Machinery and equipment	3,669,140	3,599,356	3,458,726
	7,759,074	7,622,345	7,437,446
Less accumulated depreciation	2,898,823	2,506,305	2,084,678
Net property, plant and equipment	4,860,251	5,116,040	5,352,768
Intangible assets, at cost less			
amortization	196,020	212,624	238,012
Other assets	23,391	20,819	6,578
	$13,655,944	$13,850,687	$13,854,329

Liabilities and Shareholders' Equity

	1971	1970	1969
Current Liabilities:			
Notes payable to banks	$ 548,443	$ 1,175,546	$ 1,257,025
Accounts payable	362,052	397,724	481,845
Taxes on income	358,612	427,353	288,429
Accrued salaries, wages and bonus	954,812	871,260	638,829
Accrued pension cost	282,963	221,173	224,058
Other accrued liabilities	224,792	297,671	225,802
Long-term debt due within one year	545,453	518,750	500,000
Total current liabilities	3,277,127	3,909,477	3,615,988
Long-term debt	1,347,388	1,880,923	2,687,673
Shareholders' equity			
Common stock $1 par value; 2,000,000			
shares authorized; 661,990 issued			
(659,800 in 1970)	661,990	659,800	659,400
Capital in excess of par value	848,403	828,230	824,538
Retained earnings	7,526,090	6,579,587	6,066,730
	9,036,483	8,067,617	7,550,668
Less 350 shares (700 in 1970) of			
common stock held in treasury, at cost	5,054	7,330	—
Total shareholders' equity	9,031,429	8,060,287	7,550,668
	$13,655,944	$13,850,687	$13,854,329

APPENDIX B

YARWAY CORPORATION—11 YEAR FINANCIAL REPORT

Operations (thousands of dollars)

	1971	1970	1969	1968	1967	1966	1965	1964	1963	1962	1961
Net sales	$17,378	$16,108	$14,318	$12,829	$11,947	$11,150	$9,448	$7,738	$7,111	$6,449	$5,871
Income before taxes	2,504	1,811	1,203	721	1,308	1,885	1,628	1,193	1,045	812	781
Net income	1,277	808	492	165	675	984	816	640	485	317	316
Dividends paid	331	295	252	200	260	239	217	193	179	172	160

Financial (thousands of dollars)

	1971	1970	1969	1968	1967	1966	1965	1964	1963	1962	1961
Current assets	8,576	8,501	8,257	8,201	6,611	6,287	5,720	4,834	4,288	3,809	3,614
Current liabilities	3,277	3,909	3,616	3,738	2,325	1,750	1,503	1,080	1,000	982	868
Working capital	5,299	4,592	4,641	4,463	4,286	4,537	4,217	3,754	3,288	2,827	2,746
Fixed, intangible & other assets	5,080	5,349	5,597	5,897	6,063	2,423	2,064	1,977	1,723	1,757	1,503
Shareholders' equity (net worth)	9,031	8,060	7,551	7,283	6,877	6,421	5,663	5,062	4,534	4,202	4,023

General

	1971	1970	1969	1968	1967	1966	1965	1964	1963	1962	1961
Common shares outstanding[†]	661,640	659,100	659,400	654,650	647,900	639,340	636,290	635,220	633,220	626,440	616,560
Per share of stock:											
Net worth[*][†]	13.65	12.23	11.45	11.13	10.61	10.04	8.90	7.97	7.16	6.71	6.52
Earnings (based on average shares)[*][†]	1.93	1.23	.75	.25	1.04	1.54	1.28	1.01	.77	.51	.50
Dividends—Common shares[†] (formerly B shares)	.50	.46	.40	.32	.41	.35	.31	.27	.24	.23	.21
A shares	—	—	—	—	3.50	7.00	7.00	7.00	7.00	7.00	7.00

Ratios and Percentages

	1971	1970	1969	1968	1967	1966	1965	1964	1963	1962	1961
Current ratio	2.62	2.17	2.28	2.19	2.84	3.59	3.81	4.48	4.29	3.88	4.16
Net income to net worth (beg. of yr.)	15.8%	10.7%	6.8%	2.4%	10.5%	17.4%	16.1%	14.1%	11.5%	7.9%	8.0%
Net income to net sales	7.3%	5.0%	3.4%	1.3%	5.6%	8.8%	8.6%	8.3%	6.8%	4.9%	5.3%

[*] Restated to combine A and B common shares in prior years. A shares were exchanged for B shares in 1967 and are designated above as "common shares."

[†] Restated to reflect 10 for 1 stock distribution in 1970.

APPENDIX C

BASIC POLICIES

Preamble

Yarway Corporation recognizes the mutual opportunities and responsibilities that characterize its relationships with its customers, employees, stockholders, suppliers and surrounding communities. This recognition leads the board of directors and management to believe that it is desirable to publish the company's basic policies. They have been developed in the light of past history and of present circumstances. As new situations and changed circumstances develop, the board will review the basic policies and make appropriate additions or changes.

1. Human Values

The company should be operated to enrich the lives of all people affected by it. Every effort should be made to respect the dignity and worth of all persons. Distinctions will not be made between people because of race, religion, or national origin.

2. Integrity

All personnel should maintain at all times the company's tradition of integrity and high ethical and moral standards.

3. Opportunity

The company should provide real opportunity for each employee to develop his highest potential, and to know the satisfaction of worthwhile accomplishment in a common undertaking. All employees should be encouraged to give responsible expression to their ideas, beliefs, and convictions with the objective of advancing knowledge and understanding.

4. Performance and Rewards

All positions in the company should be staffed by employees who possess the personal qualities and the professional or trade qualifications required to achieve a high standard of performance in their work. The company will expect better-than-average performance of its employees and will reward such performance with better-than-average compensation compared with other companies in the same labor market and industry. A suitable bonus plan or plans, based on profits, sales, production or other measures of performance should be maintained to recognize and reward contributions to the company's success made by employees individually and collectively.

5. Teamwork

Management should encourage cooperation and mutual assistance between individuals and groups throughout the company. Problems should be faced promptly and squarely with emphasis on remedial and preventative action, rather than emphasis on past errors and omissions.

6. Supervision

Every employee who has responsibility for supervising the work of others should make sure that each of his subordinates understands clearly the results for which he is accountable. Furthermore, every supervisor should clearly establish each subordinate's freedom to act in achieving those results. Individuals and groups in the company should participate whenever practical in making decisions which affect them or about which they have useful knowledge or competence. It is recognized that such participation does not alter the accountability for results of the responsible supervisor, although it can often improve the quality of his decisions, gain better acceptance of them, and provide growth opportunities for his subordinates.

7. Growth

The company should grow according to plan. Growth should be in human relationships, creativeness, capability, and productiveness, as well as in sales volume and profitability. Growth should be achieved primarily by means of internal development of products and markets and secondarily by acquisition of companies or products. The rate of growth should be no faster than can be staffed by well-qualified, properly oriented, employees.

8. Company Objectives

Specific long-range company objectives should be recommended by management and approved by the board of directors in the following areas:

a. Sales volume
b. Profitability
c. Market standing
d. Products
e. Capability and productiveness

These company objectives, along with appropriate guidelines, should be incorporated in a planning guide for use by all members of management. They should be reviewed annually by management and the board of directors to keep them relevant to changing conditions.

9. Planning

Management is expected to take a long-range point of view in all of its planning. Each year management should prepare detailed budgets for the next two years and a forecast of orders by product line for each of the next five years. The budgets should include shipments and gross profit for each product line, profit and loss statements, balance sheets, and major capital expenditures. Budget preparation should be intimately related to development of marketing plans, product plans, organization development plans, and financial plans.

10. Military Business

Planned company growth should not be made dependent upon military markets.

11. Products

There should be continued development of new and improved products which meet the following conditions:

a.   New products should fulfill customer needs in a new and better way and serve worthwhile purposes.
b.   New products should be selected to capitalize on the knowledge and resources of the company.
c.   New product development should be directed solely toward industrial and commercial rather than military markets.
d.   New product development should be undertaken only when sound market research promises steady, profitable sales volume.

12. Product Quality

Yarway products should be designed, manufactured and sold to the high standards that will provide the user with dependable value in terms of performance and reliability.

13. Accounting Practices

Conservative accounting practices should be followed. The maximum allowable write-off should be taken as a charge against current operations for obsolete or slow-moving inventory, depreciation, development expense, maintenance expense, and other such items. Adequate provision should be made for funding pension commitments. All accounts will be audited regularly by a certified public accountant selected by the board of directors.

14. Contributions

Contributions in the maximum amount allowable as tax deductions should be made each year to support charitable, educational, and religious activities, either directly or through the medium of the Yarway Foundation.

15. Dividend Policy

Total dividends on all classes of stock should total 4 percent of net worth at the beginning of the year.

16. Source of New Capital

Modernization and growth should be financed primarily from undistributed profits. When debt financing is required, total debt (including current liabilities) should not exceed 75 percent of net worth.

17. Profit Goals

In order to achieve the objectives and policies outlined above, the company should have earnings per share (per year) of 12 percent of net worth at the beginning of the year.

Selected Readings

From

SUPER-GIANT FIRMS IN THE FUTURE*

By Howard V. Perlmutter†

In my discussions with political and business leaders over the past six years, I have found surprising agreement that we are moving towards a world of very large multinational firms and very small entrepreneurial firms of the "one man show" variety. The fate of the middle-size firm seems less secure. The small firm can engage in guerrilla action, gain all the advantages of smallness—speed of decision making, closeness to customer needs. The middle sized firms find it hard to get the human and financial resources, the geographical and product scope to function as world wide entities. They are targets for takeovers—with the large firm as a suitor promising world wide markets for its products.

I agree with this vision of the future. But since the prediction applies to the class of the institution called international, and not to any specific firm in existence today,

---

* Selected from an article in Winter 1968 *Wharton Quarterly,* copyright 1968 by Trustees of the University of Pennsylvania.

† The author is Professor at the Wharton School of Finance and Commerce, University of Pennsylvania.

it is perhaps more interesting to consider how the large firms will survive until 1985. Or at best, what are the competences or capacities most multinational firms, who are in existence today must develop in order to be one of the Two (or Three) Hundred who survive until 1985? For surviving, growing and remaining profitable is clearly not inevitable. It is more than likely that the list of the few will not contain only those firms which exist today.

To make some progress in this complex field, I propose to consider . . . [two] interdependent questions:

1. Why will there be very large international firms?
2. What kind of firm is most likely to become one of these super-giants? . . .

These reflections are the outcome of some rather intensive research on some of the large international firms on the world scene today, and of my collaboration with executives who share this preoccupation:

—How can I insure that our firm will be one of those which survive and grow?

—How can I attract to our firm men who believe in this long-term possibility?

By way of defining the object of our study, I consider that we do have large, internationally oriented firms today. According to *Fortune,* there are already more than 100 U.S. firms, each doing more than $600 million worth of sales, who have overseas interests. There are at least 70 or more non-U.S. firms doing a similar volume of business. But when we consider the firms of the future—of 1985—it is clear we are talking about giants, or perhaps super-giants.

Accounting for unforeseen technological breakthroughs, and managerial attrition I come out with the round number of 300 giant firms. There may be 200 or 400—but I maintain they will be distinctive because their size will place them in a separable class—with unique opportunities and problems.

Double Three Times

Many executives I know are planning to double sales every seven years. By 1985 their firms will have doubled three times. This means that the firms doing $600 million or more sales, now on *Fortune's* list, will be doing from $5 billion to $160 billion worth of sales, the latter being General Motors' sales of 1985!

Even considering that the number of employees does not grow at the same rate, the million-man firm should not be unusual. Clearly, the 300 of 1985 will be super-giants in size and power.

There are good reasons why such firms will emerge:

1. Super-giant international firms will find it easier to get capital. They will generate more earnings, and constitute less risk for bankers, financiers, and shareholders. These firms can risk sustaining larger losses and still survive. . . .

2. Super-giant international firms will be able to diversify, replace obsolescent products rapidly, and still maintain worldwide production and distribution of all their products in both developing and developed countries. They will be seen as reliable and trustworthy on the global scale.

3. Super-giant international firms can maintain a high level of research in such advanced areas as energy, food and space technology, data processing, aircraft, electronics. As an example, IBM is reputed to have invested in the neighborhood

of $5 billion over four years to develop the "hardware" for the 360 series of computers.

4. Such firms have the resources to acquire the middle-size national or regional firms and offer them worldwide markets for their products, whereas the middle-size firm simply could not afford to build up a manufacturing and marketing function worldwide.

5. Finally and very importantly, the super-giant firms can afford to hire the best specialists and managers in the world to carry out the worldwide line and staff functions in marketing and manufacturing, in research and development, in personnel, in legal matters, and in finance.

To carry out their worldwide operations, General Motors currently employs 740,000; Ford, 388,000; Siemens, 257,000; Unilever, 300,000; Philips, 244,000; ITT, 204,000; General Electric, 350,000; Royal Dutch Shell, 174,000; Fiat, 134,-000; Dunlop, 104,000.

Countervailing Forces

The second set of reasons for the emergence of the multinational super-giant comes from the absence of effective countervailing forces in the world community.

Consumers are at best unorganized. . . .

Trade unions, I am assured by union leaders, have enough difficulty at the national level managing and representing their constituents; it is hard to see how trade union organizations at the world level will for a long time constitute a serious obstacle. . . . It is much more likely to want to share in the super-giant's prosperity.

The most likely candidate to act as a countervailing force for the super-giants is the sovereign state. The weapons a nation state can muster have seemed formidable: outright nationalization, restriction of the importation of machinery and parts, price controls, limitation of remittances to foreign parent companies, legal guidance for labor policy, demands on the firm to export and to conduct research within its borders.

But I submit that any given nation state, acting alone, has limited bargaining power. When what is called "the investment climate" is considered unattractive by many firms, due to repeated threats from government, it is always possible to suggest subtly and diplomatically that other countries would seem to be better places to invest. This has had a sobering effect on the more extremist national political leaders. Nations are after all,. competing with other nations to attract human and material resources that meet worldwide standards.

Some firms have and others are developing experience in avoiding collision courses with sovereign states. They do this by spelling out their investment policies, by including in their plans a time-table to begin exporting, to do research, by specifying what training they will give to dealers, suppliers of local raw materials, etc. The super-giant firms which survive in 1985 will be those that will have found a partnership rather than a collision course, with a large number, if not most, host sovereign states. But there will be, as a political leader put it to me recently, "a reshaping of the functions of the nation state and the firm."

The next question is more difficult, and more interesting. For it concerns who will survive until 1985. The question preoccupies chief executives. Will Royal Dutch Shell be around, will General Motors and will Unilever?

I believe that it is impossible to give the names of such firms. It is likely that the very largest of firms—like General Motors, Royal Dutch Shell, Unilever—will be among those who survive. But their names may be different.

I believe it is very likely that all 1985 firms will have North American, Eastern and Western European and Asiatic divisions. The North American division may have grown from U.S. firms which have been merged with other non-U.S. firms to become more multinational. The Western European division may include companies which once were primarily French, Swiss, German, or British historically but which were acquired or taken over. The Asiatic division will no doubt have been built from a Japanese firm. The Eastern European division may have its regional headquarters in Rumania, Yugoslavia, or despite a recent setback, in Prague. The super-giant international firm will, I believe, have been built from different national origins which have been internationalized to the world scale.

Who will be around in 1985 will depend on the effectiveness with which individual firms overcome external and internal obstacles to long-term profitability, market share and survival objectives.

In my research with companies who are candidates for the 300 list, I asked senior executives to diagnose what they felt were the key driving and restraining forces, inside and outside the firms, which would account for their survival, growth and development as a world company. I found that these executives from international companies agreed concerning high priority items.

External Obstacles

*   *   *   *   *

External forces driving towards the growth of international firms which the executives most frequently cited were:

a. technological and managerial knowhow being made available in different countries;

b. demands of both international and local customers for the best product at the most reasonable price;

c. host country desire to improve its balance-of-payments;

d. finally, a general stimulus from the global competition among international firms for the human resources needed for survival and growth.

The firms which will grow to be around in 1985 are those which can influence the restraining forces and build on the driving forces in the external environment.

Internal Obstacles

The senior executives whom I interviewed also identified internal obstacles to the long-term objectives of survival, growth, and profitability. Since, there was a general consensus that a firm must have an international character, the obstacles cited are in part those which impede a given firm from becoming more genuinely international.

The following factors were cited most frequently by senior executives from both Europe-based and U.S.-based firms:

a. Mutual distrust between home-country people and foreign executives within the firm.

b. Resistance to letting foreigners into the power structure at headquarters, in key positions and on the parent board.

c. Nationalistic tendencies among staff overseas and at home.

d. Immobility of good executives. Many excellent men prefer to stay where they live—in Basle or Boston, Paris or Brussels—as executives of affiliates.

e. Problems of communication, aggravated when people do not speak the same language and have different cultural backgrounds.

The key forces driving toward long-term survival and growth were identified as follows:

a. Top management's desire to utilize human resources optimally, and not let national biases lead to waste of good ideas, products, and men.

b. Recognition that morale is lower when a company has first-class (home-country) citizens and second-class citizens—the overseas people, or the foreigners.

c. Increasing awareness and respect of good men of other than home nationality.

d. Plan for risk diversification through worldwide production and distribution systems.

e. Aim to recruit good men on a worldwide basis, not just from the home country.

f. Building a worldwide information system, manned by high-quality people who know local markets and are international in outlook.

g. Proposing to develop products and services with worldwide appeal.

h. Finally (and the factor mentioned most frequently), top management's commitment to building a truly international firm, measured in deeds, not in words.

If top management seems more comfortable investing at home, or seems to prefer working with home-country nationals only, or if the company's products are designed for home markets only, and resources are not assigned to adapt production to world markets, then there are strong doubts that the firm really seeks a world niche and will be around in 1985.

Key Factors Are Human

Thus, the key factors determining which firms will be around in 1985 are human. Survival depends on attitudes and skills in working effectively with people of other nations. The executives in my survey identified also attitudes which, if allowed to be translated into action, would make it less likely that their firm survive, grow and reach profitability objectives through 1985. These "negative" attitudes may exist at headquarters as well as in subsidiaries.

* * * * *

Capacities for Survival

Many are planning to survive to 1985 through product innovation, resource allocation of men and money, establishment of pricing levels, and meeting of performance levels and growth rates. This is hard enough in a world of rapid change. But I believe that to be alive in 1985, the international firms need to identify now what distinctive capacities it will require, so that it can improve and develop them as widely as possible in the organization starting now.

This involves a development program with three- to five-year objectives directly related to improving:

1. The capacity to work with host and home political leaders of the right, center, and left, as well as with the more permanent civil servants, with a view to defining how a partnership course can be achieved between the particular international firm and each nation state. The best men are needed for this task.

2. The capacity to acquire and effectively integrate smaller and medium-size companies in countries other than one's home base, and to energize them to function effectively as a productive part of a worldwide enterprise.

A good example of this I observed recently was the acquisition by a worldwide electronics company of a small French instrument firm. This company was a provincial, one-man, patronal, production-oriented, non-innovative and technologically obsolescent company, protected by French tariffs, and with a limited future on world markets. Within a few years after the takeover, the company was very profitable, market-oriented, run by a team of professional managers who knew how to exploit innovation and were determined to make the firm a worldwide export base for some of the most modern electronic instruments. The same employees now had access to the resources of the worldwide firm and were utilizing them to their advantage. They were becoming international, and less narrow.

Too frequently the fusion of national interests has proved unproductive, because of distrust between the acquiring group and the acquired and the resistance to rationalize the two firms. Good people have frequently left and the advantage of the acquisition seemed to be lost.

3. The capacity to develop men for international service means that the firms of 1985 will have designed challenging international careers, both attractive and humanly possible, given the problems of moving men and their families at different stages in life.

The problems of reentry are serious problems for those who accept international assignments. Only too often, they are forgotten at headquarters, with consequent loss of effectiveness of executives overseas. An obligation of the international firm is to design careers so that the president and managing directors of the future are experienced overseas, have deep first-hand knowledge of the different regions of the world.

The strategic decisions international corporations must take before 1985 must be based on experience on-the-spot rather than hearsay or visits. International careers must recruit the best men from everywhere in the world, not just the best men from the home country. Such policy requires a systematic program at the local and headquarters levels. It cannot be left to chance.

A further feature of an international career will be that professionals in such a function will feel that they are not only country experts but also meet worldwide standards of excellence. This is one guarantee of getting higher-quality recruits and building international attitudes and values in the key executives.

4. The capacity to commit to worldwide objectives personnel at headquarters, at the regional level, and in the subsidiaries, with either product or functional responsibilities. For this, a geocentrization process is required at all levels.

I believe that some kind of organizational and management development institution is needed in the firms which will survive—to develop executives inside the company, from all over the world. The experience of working together, of knowing other persons from different countries, makes a positive contribution not only to effectiveness at work but also to the creation of the international spirit. This will be a strength of the international company of the future, as it already is one of Philips, Nestle, Unilever, IBM, Royal Dutch Shell, and many others.

The international firm of the future will need to organize for the maintenance of this spirit as it becomes larger and larger, and as more product divisions are formed. Internal organizational and management development institutions are one instrument to achieve these ends.

5. The capacity to stay in direct contact with the users of company products and services everywhere in the world, and thus to know in which way each user's needs are distinctive, or similar, in each market.

This means organizing to build up the necessary market knowledge and skills for the benefit of the user, wherever he is in the world. This includes eastern Europe and the lesser developed economies. The worldwide firm must live up to a promise that each customer, in every country, will receive not just the best in the country for his money, but the fruits of knowledge and experience gathered everywhere in the world. This is the basis for determining the worldwide niche of the firm. This means further the building of a dynamic strategy, a timed sequence of decisions and resource allocations to gain and maintain worldwide markets which will number in billions, not millions, of consumers.

I suggest that the firms who improve and develop these five capacities or competences will be among the 300 who survive.

Trust within Firm

The sixth capacity, while more vague, is the most fundamental: it is to build trust and confidence among managers and experts of different nations, inside the firm.

Trust-building among nationals of European nations is not easy. There are old wounds still unhealed. The industrial concentration process underway in Europe is within nations and not across borders. This is not accident. No doubt the harmonization of laws in the European Economic Community will help, but confidence cannot be legislated. It must be built up between men. Many Europeans still say it is difficult for the vast majority of Europeans to work for persons of other European nations.

          *   *   *   *   *

I see no other route than beginning now to build international companies not companies based on U.S. or European domination of key positions.

This means that the multinational firms of the future should include Japanese international companies as such, not as satellites of a U.S. or European firm, nor as independent affiliates, nor as joint ventures with some holding company of a truly international firm, but as one part of an integrated, worldwide partnership.

          *   *   *   *   *

I feel that the efforts of European firms to build a European-wide company have been very slow. Agfa-Geveart is one of the few European "marriages." By comparison, Chrysler and General Electric have, for better or for worse, taken on such large firms as Simca and Machines Bull respectively. The difficulty of combining organizations of different nationalities is one of the most serious human problems facing Europe. As long as the level of mutual confidence and trust required to make these mergers work seems to be lacking, corporate Europeanization will continue at a slow pace.

The crucial human problems of both U.S.-owned and Europe-owned multinational firms depend as much on attitudes towards foreigners as any other factor. The final list of super-giants in 1985 will include those firms whose management has overcome the negative attitudes towards foreigners, both at headquarters and in the subsidiaries.

The man, not his passport, should be the basis for promotion.

In summary, the firm that works at building up these six capacities and competences is more likely to be around in 1985.

From

FORMAL ORGANIZATION: A SYSTEMS APPROACH*

*By Rocco Carzo, Jr.
and John N. Yanouzas†*

TRADITIONAL THEORY

It may be misleading and, according to some, unfair to label a theory "traditional," but we do it only in the sense that the ideas classified as traditional are the ones that prevailed in the early development of organizational theory and practice. Traditional organizational theory can be traced historically, for instance, to 19th-century prototype industrial, military, and ecclesiastic organizations.[1] In this section we lump the ideas of several contributors.

*   *   *   *   *

THE THEORY, IN BRIEF

As expected from the emphasis on efficiency, traditional theory prescribes an organizing process that begins with objectives. The objectives are the values that the organization seeks to achieve. Once the objectives have been determined, the next step is to determine the work necessary to achieve those objectives. For maximum efficiency, the theory specifies that the work be divided into simple tasks. Tasks are then allocated to jobs or positions, each of which requires routine and

---

* Reprinted with permission from *Formal Organization: A Systems Approach,* Richard D. Irwin and the Dorsey Press, 1967. Excerpts from pp. 24, 28–34, 48–49, 54–57, 65–68.

† Dr. Carzo is Professor at Temple University and Dr. Yanouzas is Professor at the University of Connecticut.

[1] For a philosophical speculation concerning the origin of the term "traditional organizational theory," see John M. Pfiffner and Frank P. Sherwood, *Administrative Organization* (Englewood Cliffs, N.J.: Prentice-Hall, Inc., 1960), pp. 53–54.

repetitive movements of a single worker. These jobs are grouped into administrative units to meet the need for coordination. There is only one boss at the head of each unit. Furthermore, each supervisor has a span of supervision, that is, each supervisor has limitations and therefore should have only a few subordinates reporting directly to him. Administrative units are then grouped into higher level administrative units. This grouping continues until the organization takes the shape of a pyramid with one supreme official at its apex. Authority to discharge the duties of each job is distributed to each jobholder. The means employed to discharge duties and the jurisdictional area of each official is delimited by laws or administrative regulations. Personnel assignments are made on the basis of the requirements of the job and each individual's ability to perform the tasks. Finally, the rewards given to organization members are based on job performance.

It is apparent from the above that the *work* required to achieve objectives and *efficiency* are the basis for the organizing process. The central problem, according to traditional theory, is to make sure that work gets done efficiently through a careful definition of tasks into specialized jobs and then by coordination of the jobs through a hierarchy of administrative units. Gulick emphasizes this breakdown of work as the basis for organization in the following statement:

> . . . . *Wherever many men are . . . working together the best results are secured when there is a division of work among these men. The theory of organization, therefore, has to do with the structure of co-ordination imposed upon the work-division units of enterprise. Hence, it is not possible to determine how an activity is to be organized without, at the same time, considering how the work in question is to be divided. Work division is the foundation of organization; indeed, the reason for organizing.*[2]

The concepts of traditional theory that we examine in detail in this chapter and the next are: (1) departmentation; (2) unity of command; (3) size of the supervisory unit; and (4) type and amount of authority assigned and delegated to subunits of the organization.

DEPARTMENTATION

In traditional theory, especially in the writings of Luther Gulick, four bases for grouping specialized jobs into larger specialized units or departments are provided. They are: (1) *purpose,* that is, according to an output, such as a product or service; (2) *function,* that is, according to the kind of work that must be performed; (3) *place,* that is, according to the geographical location served by the organization and/or where the work is to be done; and (4) *clientele,* that is, according to the type of persons for whom the work is done.[3] Before illustrating each of these bases for grouping specialized jobs, let us first portray specialization as the division of a large rectangle into smaller units, shown in Figure 1. This breakdown is important for the following illustrations.

---

[2] Gulick, "Notes on the Theory of Organization," *op. cit.,* p. 3.

[3] Gulick, *op. cit.,* pp. 15–30. These four bases of departmentation may be used simultaneously in one organization. Multiple departmentation is illustrated in subsequent sections.

FIGURE 1
Breakdown of a Whole Task

A_1	B_1	C_1	D_1
A_2	B_2	C_2	D_2
A_3	B_3	C_3	D_3
A_4	B_4	C_4	D_4

Purpose Departmentation

Organization on the basis of purpose involves differentiating and grouping activities according to an output of the organization, such as a service or product. This means that all of the functions required to supply a service or product, even if the activities are dissimilar, are placed in the same group or department. For instance, if the purpose of an organization is to create four products, the functions, A, B, C, and D, required for each product would be grouped in each product department. Figure 2 depicts a case in which each of four purposes (products) require four functions. Figure 3 illustrates a grouping in terms of a traditional organizational structure.

Functional Departmentation

Organization on the basis of functions requires the differentiation and grouping of similar work activities. All of the similar activities are grouped together and identified by some functional classification, such as manufacturing, engineering, marketing, teaching, financing, building, and transporting. In creating some values,

FIGURE 2
Departmentation on the Bases of Purpose or Function

	Purposes (products)			
	No. 1	No. 2	No. 3	No. 4
Functions (activities)	A_1	A_2	A_3	A_4
	B_1	B_2	B_3	B_4
	C_1	C_2	C_3	C_4
	D_1	D_2	D_3	D_4

FIGURE 3
Purpose Organization

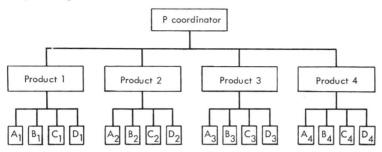

an organization may be required, for instance, to perform 16 activities: 4 similar activities under function A, 4 under function B, 4 under function C, and 4 under function D. This type of breakdown is shown in Figure 2 by reading it horizontally. In this case, the dominant type of departmentation is based on the functions that need to be performed. Figure 4 illustrates how activities would be grouped in traditional organizational structure based on functions.

*   *   *   *   *

Place Departmentation

Organization on the basis of place requires differentiation and grouping of activities according to the location where work is to be performed or an area to be served by the organization. Thus, regardless of the similarity or dissimilarity of functions and purposes, grouping is based on geographical considerations.

Place departmentation may occur in the same organization where there is purpose and functional departmentation. . . .

Figures 5 and 6 show purpose (P_1, P_2, P_3, P_4) and functional (A, B, C, D) departmentation within place organization. These illustrations do not, of course, exhaust all of the possible combinations of purpose, functional, and place departmentation.

FIGURE 4
Functional Organization

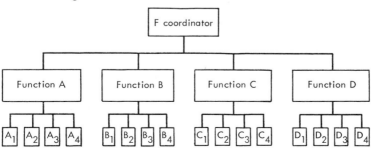

FIGURE 5
Purpose Departmentation within Place

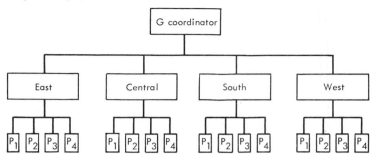

FIGURE 6
Functional Departmentation within Place

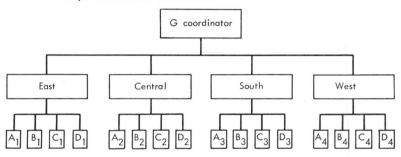

Clientele Departmentation

Organization on the basis of client involves the differentiation and grouping of activities according to the type of person or persons for whom the work is done. Client characteristics—for example, age, sex, income level, type of consumer—are the basis of departmentation. For instance, universities frequently maintain separate departments for the educational services they offer to adults and resident students. Loan departments in large banks may organize on the basis of consumer or commercial services offered to its clients. Department stores often group work on the basis of the client's sex, for instance, men's apparel versus women's apparel; or on the basis of income level, for example, bargain basements for lower income customers; or on the basis of age, for example, children's, women's, and men's clothing.

*   *   *   *   *

ADMINISTRATION IN TRADITIONAL THEORY

In this chapter, we continue the review of traditional theory, especially as it pertains to administration. Traditional theory is very specific about the administrative structure of formal organization. Its prescriptions about the chain of command, size of supervisory unit, and the dispersion of authority, seemingly leave little doubt about administration in formal organization (in Chapter 4, we indicate that there are some doubts). The underlying premise of the traditional structure is that specialized jobs can be coordinated best by one head, or one boss, that is, there shall be unity of command. This requirement that everybody in the organization reports to only one boss gives traditional structure the appearance of a pyramid with one supreme coordinating boss at the top. We will see this structure develop as the administrative concepts of traditional theory are examined in this chapter.

UNITY OF COMMAND

According to traditional theory, unity of command facilitates order because it charges one official with an area of responsibility and establishes a chain of command whereby every organization member knows to whom he reports and who reports to him. There is no confusion over who is responsible for organizational activities and over who gives orders and who carries them out. Unity of command forms the basis, therefore, for the hierarchy of authority because it defines the path of authority which extends from the top to the bottom of the formal organization. Fayol explained the importance of the unit of command in the following manner: "Should it be violated, authority is undermined, discipline is in jeopardy, order disturbed and stability threatened. . . . A body with two heads is in the social as in the animal sphere a monster, and has difficulty surviving."[4]

SPAN OF SUPERVISION

Size of Supervisory Unit. A supervisory unit is composed of a supervisor and his immediate subordinates. The size of a supervisory unit is determined by the number of subordinates reporting to the supervisor. In traditional literature, the terms "span of control," "span of management," and "span of supervision" have been used to denote size of the supervisory unit.

*   *   *   *   *.

Each supervisor according to traditional theory must manage not only individual subordinates but also the interactions among individuals and groups. Therefore, according to the theory, the number of subordinates reporting to any one supervisor should be limited to a very few. Traditional organization literature suggests that there exists an ideal number of subordinates that can be managed effectively by one superior.[5] This ideal ratio of subordinates to superior has been called the principle of "span of control" or "span of supervision" and is stated as follows:

Principle of Span of Supervision. The number of subordinates supervised directly by a single executive should be limited to a small number. No executive should supervise directly the work of more than four or, at the most, six subordinates—especially when their work is interrelated.

---

[4] Henri Fayol, *General and Industrial Management,* trans. Constance Storrs (London: Sir Isaac Pitman & Sons, Ltd., 1963), pp. 24–25.

[5] Hamilton, *op. cit.;* Graicunas, *op. cit.;* and Fayol, *op. cit.*

ORGANIZATIONAL AUTHORITY

When anyone, say a worker, is assigned to a work activity, he has an obligation to perform successfully—he has responsibility. Coincident with this responsibility, implicitly or explicitly, each worker has the authority to act or the authority to perform the activities required by the assigned work. Although we assume that authority and responsibility occur coincidently, it should be emphasized that the literature of organization theory usually treats them as if they are assigned separately. Writers on the subject stipulate that the assignment of authority should be equal to responsibility.[6] Urwick states, for example, the need for this balance as follows: "To hold a group or individual accountable for activities of any kind without assigning to him the necessary authority to discharge that responsibility is manifestly both unsatisfactory and inequitable."[7]

This same coincidence of authority and responsibility extends to the administrative levels of organization. In a superior-subordinate relationship, for example, the supervisor's authority is derived from his responsibility to coordinate the work of subordinates.

In this context, *authority* constitutes official permission to use the resources of the organization. Thus, an individual worker needs authority to use equipment or to withdraw materials from storage, the industrial foreman needs authority to command his men to do a given job, a hospital nurse needs authority to issue medicine to a patient, the surgeon needs to command the actions of an entire operating team, a baseball coach must have authority to call for the execution of a particular play, and a general manager of a baseball team needs authority to consummate a player deal.

There is another aspect to authority at the administrative level. In order to coordinate the efforts of subordinates, a superior needs to obtain their compliance to orders and commands. For this reason, administrative authority also includes official permission to use some of the possessions of the organization as inducements. Thus, a supervisor is permitted to offer rewards or to impose penalties for the purpose of gaining compliance. Included in the definition of authority, then, is the understanding that in superior-subordinate relationships, the superior has permission to invoke sanctions in order to obtain compliance from subordinates.

In the traditional literature, this authority is called "legal" or "official authority."[8] The source of this authority is not to be found in the individual, but rather it is derived from the organization.[9] It is an attribute of office or formal position. An organization member has authority because he occupies a certain position and not because of personal characteristics. In this regard, Weber states: "In the case of legal authority, obedience is owed to the legally established impersonal order. It extends to the persons exercising authority of office under it only by virtue of

---

[6] For instance, see James D. Mooney, *The Principles of Organization* (rev. ed.; New York: Harper & Row, 1939), pp. 17–23; Lyndall Urwick, *The Elements of Administration* (New York: Harper & Row, 1939), pp. 45–46; Fayol, *op. cit.,* pp. 21–22; and Taylor, *op. cit.*

[7] Urwick, *op. cit.,* p. 46.

[8] Fayol, *op. cit.,* p. 21.

[9] For a discussion summarizing the issues concerning official versus personal authority, see Harold Koontz and Cyril O'Donnell, *Principles of Management* (New York: McGraw-Hill Book Co., 1955), pp. 48–54.

the formal legality of the commands and only within the scope of authority of the office."[10]

James D. Mooney identified authority as the foundation of the first principle of organization—the coordinative principle. He labeled authority as the "supreme coordinative power" and stated that "in every form of organization, this authority must rest somewhere, else there would be no directive for any coordinated effort."[11] Locating its "resting" place in the formal organization involves defining authority according to type and amounts. Two types of authority distinguished in traditional theory are line and staff authority.

Line and Staff Authority

A relationship in which the occupant of one position can exercise direct command over the occupant of another position is called *line authority*. A superior who exercises direct command over a subordinate has line authority.

A relationship in which the occupant of one position can advise or counsel but not command the occupant of another position is called *staff authority*. A person occupying a position with staff authority does not command others, but rather his responsibility is discharged by providing information, advice, and recommendations. The principal value of staff authority is that specialized knowledge and technology can be injected into the organization to aid the incumbents of positions which have line authority.

*   *   *   *   *

Staff Concept in Business Organization

While the application of the staff concepts has a long history in military and religious organizations, not until recently has it appeared in business organizations. One of the first applications of this concept to a business organization was reported by Harrington Emerson, who applied it to the organization of the Santa Fe Railroad during the first decade of the 20th century.[12] Du Pont used the concept of general staff as early as 1908.[13]

The functional differentiation of advisory and service activities found in the military staff organization, for instance, the general staff and special staff, also exists in the organization of business staffs. On the basis of a survey study of 31 business organizations, Paul Holden, Lounsbury Fish, and Hubert Smith categorized the functions of staffs as: control, service, coordinating, and advisory.[14] The business version of staff organization appears to elaborate the task of staff units,

---

[10] A. M. Henderson and Talcott Parsons, *Max Weber: The Theory of Social and Economic Organization* (New York: Oxford University Press, Inc., 1947), p. 328.

[11] Mooney, *op. cit.,* p. 6.

[12] Harrington Emerson, *The Twelve Principles of Efficiency* (New York: Engineering Magazine Co., 1924), especially chap. ii.

[13] Ernest Dale, *Staff in Organization* (New York: McGraw-Hill Book Co., 1960), pp. 186–87. A survey of 300 business firms reported that approximately 70 percent employ staff assistance for the president. See: "Handy Men with Growing Power," *Business Week,* October 19, 1957, pp. 193–97.

[14] Paul E. Holden, Lounsbury S. Fish, and Hubert L. Smith, *Top-Management Organization and Control* (New York: McGraw-Hill Book Co., 1951), pp. 36–58.

because the control, service, and coordinative activities imply that staff units exercise some degree of authority over the line organization. Frederick Taylor's "functional management" played an important part in the development of staff specialization. Even though Taylor did not use the line-staff classification, he suggested that staff work or as he called it, "brain work" should be differentiated: "All possible brain work should be removed from the shop and centered in the planning or laying out department, leaving for the foreman and gang bosses work strictly executive in its nature."[15] Taylor's classification roughly resembles the line-staff classification. In fact, many of the activities that he removed from the "shop" and placed in the "planning department" are staff activities in modern business organizations.

The modification of the line-staff concept to serve as a basis not only for the differentiation of authority but also for the differentiation of activities, for example, control activities, service activities, and so on, complicates this seemingly simple concept.[16] The inclusion of control and service activities in the staff organization frequently requires line authority. For instance, control activities such as accounting, product inspection, and fire protection are meaningless unless some command authority is vested in them. Service activities such as purchasing and maintenance frequently are given authority that overrides the line organization. This hybrid type of authority, which has been labeled *functional authority,*[17] is really line authority limited to a specified function that can be assigned to a specialized department. This command authority is limited to the specialized function. For instance, an inspection department of a manufacturing firm may have the authority to command the production department concerning the quality characteristics of a product.

The introduction of functional authority in organization, and the tendency to perceive line and staff as types of departments, creates certain dysfunctions in organization.

AMOUNT OF ORGANIZATIONAL AUTHORITY

Another aspect of traditional theory which has received considerable attention is the delegation of authority, or as Mooney defined it "the conferring of a specified authority by a higher authority."[18] Essentially this means, even in the simplest organization, that authority must be delegated in order to get work done.

The principal issue in the delegation of authority involves the amount of authority to delegate, that is, the centralization of authority in one or a few organiza-

---

[15] Frederick W. Taylor, "Shop Management," in *Scientific Management* (New York: Harper & Row, 1947), pp. 98–99.

[16] Not only does the line-staff classification result in specialization with respect to type of authority, but it also provides a rough guide for the separation of activities into those which are directly (line) and indirectly (staff) related to the attainment of organizational goals. Ralph C. Davis argues that the department concerned with activities which are "organic" to the accomplishment are line departments, while those departments which contribute to the "secondary" and "collateral" organization goals are staff departments. See his *The Fundamentals of Top Management* (New York: Harper & Row, 1951), pp. 205–11, 337–38.

[17] See Koontz and O'Donnell, *op. cit.,* chap. viii; William H. Newman, *Administrative Action* (Englewood Cliffs, N.J.: Prentice-Hall, Inc., 1950), chap. ix; and Holden, Fish, and Smith, *op. cit.,* sec. 3.

[18] Mooney, *op. cit.,* p. 17.

tion positions as opposed to the dispersion of authority throughout most or all of the levels of the organizational hierarchy.

The early contributors to organizational theory, such as Max Weber and Frederick W. Taylor, were not unique in their concern over the issue of the dispersion of authority. The designers of the Constitution of the United States, for example, were also concerned with the problem of centralization versus decentralization. In the tableau of history this issue has acquired many different labels, for instance, autocracy versus democracy, monism versus pluralism, totalitarianism versus freedom, sectarianism versus ecumenism, federalism versus confederation, social mold versus social contract, organizationalism versus anarchy. Once the political and emotional overtones, shibboleths and labels are removed, the basic issue involves the question of how much authority to delegate, regardless of whether the institution is business, education, military, church, or government.

Centralization and Decentralization

Traditional theory prescribes that authority be equal to responsibility, that is, if a person is assigned certain duties, he *should* also have the permission to commit the resources of the organization necessary to perform the job. The authority to commit resources may range from permission to perform a simple act like drawing necessary tools from a toolroom to permission to perform a major act like an expenditure of $500,000. Thus, if authority is directly related to responsibility, the dispersion of authority throughout the organization depends upon the definition of the jobs and positions.

The dispersion of authority occurs only in terms of degree. Henri Fayol referred to the relativity of the dispersion of authority in terms of centralization and decentralization,[19] or as he suggested, "centralization . . . is always present to a greater or less extent . . . it is a matter of finding the optimum degree for the particular concern."[20] Especially in large organizations, some amount of authority must be delegated, because it may be impossible for one person to coordinate all of the organizational activities. Yet, this does not mean that authority must be delegated completely to the managers of the lower subunits. To the extent that some authority is retained by central management, there exists a degree of centralization in every organization. At a minimum, according to traditional theory, central management always retains *residual authority,* which is the authority to recall from subordinates that authority which had been previously delegated to them. Thus, the dispersion of authority among the levels of an organization cannot be dichotomized into a pattern which is entirely centralized or completely decentralized. In effect, some degree of each pattern of authority dispersion is likely to be found in every organization.

---

[19] The terms "centralization" and "decentralization" have been used to describe the geographic dispersion of organizational units, for instance, the decentralization of warehouses in Chicago, New York, and Atlanta as opposed to one central warehouse in Chicago, or the location of sales offices in London, Tokyo, and San Francisco. The use of these terms in this section of the book is limited to the dispersion of authority in the organization, for example, the decentralization of authority to several levels of an organization as opposed to the centralization of authority to one level.

[20] Fayol, *op. cit.,* p. 33. For a critical appraisal of decentralization of authority, see: John Dearden, "Mirage of Profit Decentralization," *Harvard Business Review,* Vol. 40. No. 6 (November–December, 1961), pp. 140–48.

Practitioners have found convenient ways to withhold some authority and yet permit decentralization. This is done usually by delegating operating authority and retaining policymaking authority. A rough definition of *operating authority* is the authority needed to make detailed, specific and repetitive decisions. *Policymaking authority* is confined roughly to formulating basic long-term objectives and adopting courses of action that provide general guides to operating decisions and practices. Let us turn to several examples of this practice.

Departmentation, Authority, and Size of Administrative Unit

Departmentation refers to the grouping of specialized activities into departments or subunits of an organization. The dispersion of authority and the size of the administrative unit are related to departmentation to the extent that some patterns for grouping activities facilitate decentralization and small administrative units, while others lend themselves to centralization and large administrative units. However, before we pursue these relationships, the term "administrative unit" must be defined. An *administrative unit* is an organizational unit which contains the sufficient component parts to operate autonomously. An administrative unit characteristically resembles a total organization. In other words, it is a unit which can make virtually all of the decisions and take virtually all of the actions necessary to achieve a general purpose. In a business organization, for example, this means that an administrative unit is capable of making the necessary decisions and performing the activities needed to finance, manufacture, and distribute a given product. In a military organization an administrative unit is a task force capable of making the decisions and performing all of the duties necessary in achieving a given military mission. In a hospital organization this means that an administrative unit can perform the full line of medical services needed to accomplish its goals.

Departmentation and Size of Administrative Unit. Grouping organizational components according to purpose permits smaller administrative units than departmentation on the basis of function. This result can be illustrated with a hypothetical example. Suppose that four functions, *A, B, C,* and *D* must be performed on each of four products of a business organization. Departmentation on the basis of function is shown in Figure 7. In the diagram, *S* represents supervision, *M* indicates general management, and the solid-line box encloses the administrative unit or the total organization in this case. Since the functions *A, B, C,* and *D* require coordination for each product, the coordinating authority for each product must be placed at the level of general management, *M.*

If the organizational components are grouped according to purpose (or product), the organization would be designed according to Figure 8. The administrative units indicated by broken-line boxes include all of the functions necessary to produce one product. In comparison to the functional departmentation of Figure 7, the purpose departmentation of Figure 8, requires more administrative units but each of the four units is smaller. In addition, the coordinating authority for each product is placed at a lower level of the organization, that is, at level *S* and there are fewer hierarchical levels involved in the administrative unit.

Departmentation and Dispersion of Authority. As we indicated above, departmentation by purpose or product permits the establishment of administrative units at lower levels in the organization than does departmentation by function. It was also possible to place the coordinating authority for each product at lower

FIGURE 7
Functional Departmentation and Administrative Unit

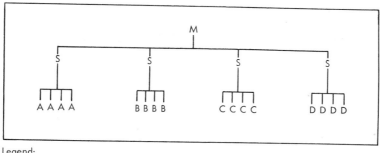

Legend:

[ ] Total organization and administrative unit

FIGURE 8
Purpose Departmentation and Administrative Unit

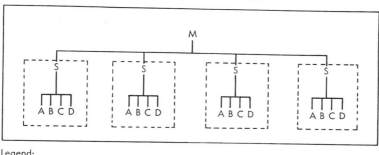

Legend:

[ ] Total organization

[- - -] Administrative unit

levels. In terms of the dispersion of authority, then, organization by product allows a greater degree of decentralization than the functional-type organization. This result may be illustrated further with more specific examples of business firms, shown in Figures 9 and 10.

In these illustrations, it is assumed that manufacturing, marketing, and finance are all the functions necessary (of course, there are others, such as personnel, engineering, and purchasing functions) to complete a product. In the purpose-type organization (Figure 10), each of the products divisions can be managed as an autonomous unit. The coordinating authority for each product can be assigned to vice presidents at level 2. The delegation of coordinating authority for each product in the functional-type organization, Figure 9, cannot be delegated below the president, level 3.

FIGURE 9
Functional-Type Organization

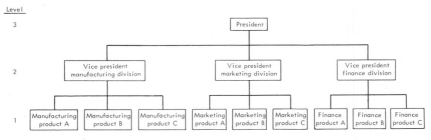

FIGURE 10
Purpose-Type Organization

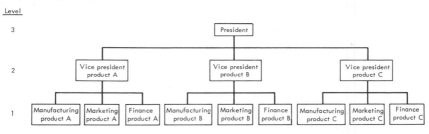

Authority and Service Activities

The delegation of authority and the arrangement of service activities are related since the assignment of work creates a responsibility which in turn, according to traditional theory, must be accompanied by authority. Service activities which may be demanded by several departments can be centralized under one service department or decentralized in each department that needs the service. For instance, if several departments within an organization have a demand for the services of an electronic computer, these services may be centralized in one department and made available to all the users, or an electronic computer installation can be placed in each of the departments. The solution to this organizational problem may be based on what is economically or technologically feasible. From the economic point of view, if each of the departments does not have a sufficient demand for the full use of a computer, this service may be centralized, because it would be uneconomical to employ a computer in each department. . . .

Authority and Span of Supervision

The dispersion of authority in any particular case is affected by the span of supervision policy adopted in an organization. The number of subordinates assigned to a superior determines, in part, the workload of the superior. In other words, if a superior has a narrow span of supervision, he can devote a considerable amount of time to each subordinate. He can supervise "closely," and retain much of the decision-making authority. Though close supervision is not a necessary consequence of a narrow span of supervision, it is at least possible to occur.

On the other hand, if a superior has a large number of subordinates, the supervisory work load may force him to delegate much of the decision-making authority and to supervise each subordinate less frequently. With a large number of subordinates, the amount of time that a superior can spend with each one of his subordinates may be severely limited. By decentralizing authority, the superior shifts some work and/or decision making to his subordinates, and thus his work load can be reduced. Worthy argues that increasing the ratio of subordinates to superior represents a method of forcing the downward delegation of authority.[21]

From

STRATEGY AND STRUCTURE*

By Alfred D. Chandler†

. . . The following set of general or theoretical propositions attempts to provide some sort of conceptual precision. Without reference to historical reality, they try to explain in fairly clear-cut, oversimplified terms how the modern, "decentralized" structure came into being.

Before developing these propositions, the term *industrial enterprise* needs to be defined. Used in a broad sense, it means here a large private, profit-oriented business firm involved in the handling of goods in some or all of the successive industrial processes from the procurement of the raw material to the sale to the ultimate customer. Transportation enterprises, utilities, or purely financial companies are not then included in this study, while those firms concerned with marketing and with the extraction of raw materials as well as those dealing with processing or manufacturing do fall within this definition. An industrial enterprise is thus a subspecies of what Werner Sombart has described as the capitalistic enterprise, which as "an independent economic organism is created over and above the individuals who constitute it. This entity appears then as the agent in each of these transactions and leads, as it were, a life of its own, which often exceeds in length that of its human members."

While the enterprise may have a life of its own, its present health and future growth surely depend on the individuals who guide its activities. Just what, then, are the functions of the executives responsible for the fortunes of the enterprise? They coordinate, appraise, and plan. They may, at the same time, do the actual buying, selling, advertising, accounting, manufacturing, engineering, or research but in the modern enterprise the execution or carrying out of these functions is usually left to such employees as salesmen, buyers, production supervisors and

---

[21] James C. Worthy, "Organizational Structure and Employee Morale," *American Sociological Review*, Vol. 15 (April 1950), pp. 109–79.

† The author is Professor of History at Johns Hopkins University.

foremen, technicians, and designers. In many cases, the executive does not even personally supervise the working force but rather administers the duties of other executives. In planning and coordinating the work of subordinate managers or supervisors, he allocates tasks and makes available the necessary equipment, materials, and other physical resources necessary to carry out the various jobs. In appraising their activities, he must decide whether the employees or subordinate managers are handling their tasks satisfactorily. If not, he can take action by changing or bringing in new physical equipment and supplies, by transferring or shifting the personnel, or by expanding or cutting down available funds. Thus, the term, *administration,* as used here, includes executive action and orders as well as the decisions taken in coordinating, appraising, and planning the work of the enterprise and in allocating its resources.

The initial proposition is, then, that administration is an identifiable activity, that it differs from the actual buying, selling, processing, or transporting of the goods, and that in the large industrial enterprise the concern of the executives is more with administration than with the performance of functional work. In a small firm, the same man or group of men buy materials, sell finished goods, and supervise manufacturing as well as coordinate, plan, and appraise these different functions. In a large company, however, administration usually becomes a specialized, full-time job. A second proposition is that the administrator must handle two types of administrative tasks when he is coordinating, appraising, and planning the activities of the enterprise. At times he must be concerned with the long-run health of his company, at other times with its smooth and efficient day-to-day operation. The first type of activity calls for concentration on long-term planning and appraisal, the second for meeting immediate problems and needs and for handling unexpected contingencies or crises. To be sure, in real life the distinction between these two types of activities or decisions is often not clear cut. Yet some decisions clearly deal very largely with defining basic goals and the course of action and procedures necessary to achieve these goals, while other decisions have more to do with the day-to-day operations carried out within the broader framework of goals, policies, and procedures.

The next few propositions deal with the content of administrative activities handled through the different types of posts or positions in the most complex administrative structures. The executives in a modern "decentralized" company carry out their administrative activities from four different types of positions. . . . Each of these types within the enterprise has a different range of administrative activities. Normally, each is on a different level of authority. At the top is a *general office.* There, general executives and staff specialists coordinate, appraise, and plan goals and policies and allocate resources for a number of quasi-autonomous, fairly self-contained divisions. Each division handles a major product line or carries on the firm's activities in one large geographical area. Each division's *central office,* in turn, administers a number of departments. Each of these departments is responsible for administration of a major function—manufacturing, selling, purchasing or producing of raw materials, engineering, research, finance, and the like. The *departmental headquarters* in its turn coordinates, appraises, and plans for a number of field units. At the lowest level, each *field unit* runs a plant or works, a branch or district sales office, a purchasing office, an engineering or research laboratory, an accounting or other financial office, and the like. The four types of administrative positions in a large multidivisional enterprise are thus: the field unit, the departmental headquarters, the division's central office, and the general office. These terms are used throughout this study to designate a specific set of administrative activities. They do not, it should be stressed, refer to an enterprise's office buildings or rooms. One office building could house executives responsible for any one of the positions or conceivably those responsible for all four. Conversely, the executives in any one of the posts could be housed in different rooms or buildings.

Only in the first, the field unit, are the managers primarily involved in carrying on or personally supervising day-to-day activities. Even here, if the volume of activity is large, they spend much of their time on administrative duties. But such duties are largely operational, carried out within the framework of policies and procedures set by departmental headquarters and the higher offices. The departmental and divisional offices may make some long-term decisions, but because their executives work within a comparable framework determined by the general office, their primary administrative activities also tend to be tactical or operational. The general office makes the broad strategic or entrepreneurial decisions as to policy and procedures and can do so largely because it has the final say in the allocation of the firm's resources—men, money, and materials—necessary to carry out these administrative decisions and actions and others made with its approval at any level.

It seems wise here to emphasize the distinction between the formulation of policies and procedures and their implementation. The formulation of policies and procedures can be defined as either strategic or tactical. *Strategic* decisions are concerned with the long-term health of the enterprise. *Tactical* decisions deal more with the day-to-day activities necessary for efficient and smooth operations. But decisions, either tactical or strategic, usually require *implementation* by an allocation or reallocation of resources—funds, equipment, or personnel. Strategic plans can be formulated from below, but normally the implementation of such proposals requires the resources which only the general office can provide. Within the broad policy lines laid down by that office and with the resources it allocates, the executives at the lower levels carry out tactical decisions.

The executives who actually allocate available resources are then the key men in any enterprise. Because of their critical role in the modern economy, they will be defined in this study as entrepreneurs. In contrast, those who coordinate, appraise, and plan within the means allocated to them will be termed managers. So *entrepreneurial* decisions and actions will refer to those which affect the allocation or reallocation of resources for the enterprise as a whole, and *operating* decisions and actions will refer to those which are carried out by using the resources already allocated.

Just because the entrepreneurs make some of the most significant decisions in the American economy, they are not all necessarily imbued with a long-term strategic outlook. In many enterprises the executives responsible for resource allocation may very well concentrate on day-to-day operational affairs, giving little or no attention to changing markets, technology, sources of supply, and other factors affecting the long-term health of their company. Their decisions may be made without forward planning or analysis but rather by meeting in an *ad hoc* way every new situation, problem, or crisis as it arises. They accept the goals of their enterprise as given or inherited. Clearly wherever entrepreneurs act like managers, wherever they concentrate on short-term activities to the exclusion or to the detriment of long-range planning, appraisal, and coordination, they have failed to carry out effectively their role in the economy as well as in their enterprise. This effectiveness should provide a useful criterion for evaluating the performance of an executive in American industry.

As already pointed out, executives in the large enterprise work in four types of offices, each with his own administrative duties, problems, and needs. The four types operate on different scales, and their officers have different business horizons. The managers in the field unit are concerned with one function—marketing, manufacturing, engineering, and so forth—in one local area. The executives in the departmental headquarters plan, administer, and coordinate the activities of one function on a broad regional and often national scale rather than just locally. Their professional activities and their outside sources of information concern men and institutions operating in the same specialized function. The divisional executives, on the other hand, deal with an industry rather than a function. They are concerned with all the functions involved in the over-all process of handling a line of products or services. Their professional horizons and contacts are determined by industry rather than functional interests. Finally, executives in the general office have to deal with several industries or one industry in several broad and different geographical regions. They set policies and procedures and allocate resources for divisions carrying out all types of functions, either in different geographical areas or in quite different product lines. Their business horizons and interests are broadened to range over national and even international economies.

While all four types of offices exist in the most complex of industrial enterprises, each can of course exist separately. An industrial enterprise can include one, two, three, or all four of these offices. Many small firms today have only a single office managing a single plant, store, laboratory, financial operation, or sales activity. Larger companies with a number of operating units carry out a single function— such as sales (wholesale or retail), manufacturing, purchasing, or engineering. Their overall administrative structure comprises a headquarters and field offices. So also today there are integrated industrial enterprises that handle several economic functions rather than just one. Finally, there are the great diversified industrial empires, carrying on different functions and producing a variety of goods and services in all parts of the globe.

Since each type of position handles a different range of administrative activities, each must have resulted from a different type of growth. Until the volume or technological complexity of an enterprise's economic activities had so grown as to demand an increasing division of labor within the firm, little time needed to be spent on administrative work. Then the resulting specialization required one or more of the firm's executives to concentrate on coordinating, appraising, and planning these specialized activities. When the enterprise expanded geographically by setting up or acquiring facilities and personnel distant from its original location, it had to create an organization at a central headquarters to administer the units in the field. When it grew by moving into new functions, a central office came to administer the departments carrying on the different functions. Such a central administrative unit proved necessary, for example, when in following the policy of vertical integration a manufacturing firm began to do its own wholesaling, procuring of supplies, and even producing raw materials. Finally, when an integrated enterprise became diversified through purchasing or creating new facilities and entered new lines of business, or when it expanded its several functional departments over a still larger geographical area, it fashioned a number of integrated divisional units administered by a general office.

The thesis that different organizational forms result from different types of growth can be stated more precisely if the planning and carrying out of such growth is considered a *strategy,* and the organization devised to administer these enlarged activities and resources, a *structure. Strategy* can be defined as the determination of the basic long-term goals and objectives of an enterprise, and the adoption of courses of action and the allocation of resources necessary for carrying out these goals. Decisions to expand the volume of activities, to set up distant plants and offices, to move into new economic functions, or become diversified along many lines of business involve the defining of new basic goals. New courses of action must be devised and resources allocated and reallocated in order to achieve these goals and to maintain and expand the firm's activities in the new areas in response to shifting demands, changing sources of supply, fluctuating economic conditions, new technological developments, and the actions of competitors. As the adoption of a new strategy may add new types of personnel and facilities, and alter the business horizons of the men responsible for the enterprise, it can have a profound effect on the form of its organization.

Structure can be defined as the design of organization through which the enterprise is administered. This design, whether formally or informally defined, has two aspects. It includes, first, the lines of authority and communication between the different administrative offices and officers and, second, the information and data that flow through these lines of communication and authority. Such lines and such data are essential to assure the effective coordination, appraisal, and planning so necessary in carrying out the basic goals and policies and in knitting together the total resources of the enterprise. These resources include financial capital; physical equipment such as plants, machinery, offices, warehouses, and other marketing and purchasing facilities, sources of raw materials, research and engineering laboratories; and, most important of all, the technical, marketing, and administrative skills of its personnel.

The thesis deduced from these several propositions is then that structure follows strategy and that the most complex type of structure is the result of the concatenation of several basic strategies. *Expansion of volume* led to the creation of an administrative office to handle one function in one local area. Growth through *geographical dispersion* brought the need for a departmental structure and headquarters to administer several local field units. The decision to expand into new types of functions called for the building of a central office and a multidepartmental structure, while the developing of new lines of products or continued growth on a national or international scale brought the formation of the multidivisional structure with a general office to administer the different divisions. For the purposes of this study, the move into new functions will be referred to as a strategy of *vertical integration* and that of the development of new products as a strategy of *diversification.*

This theoretical discussion can be carried a step further by asking two questions: (1) If structure does follow strategy, why should there be delay in developing the new organization needed to meet the administrative demands of the new strategy? (2) Why did the new strategy, which called for a change in structure, come in the first place?

There are at least two plausible answers to the first query. Either the administrative needs created by the new strategy were not positive or strong enough to require structural change, or the executives involved were unaware of the new needs. There seems to be no question that a new strategy created new administrative needs, for expansion through geographical dispersion, vertical integration, and product diversification added new resources, new activities, and an increasing number of entrepreneurial and operational actions and decisions. Nevertheless, executives could still continue to administer both the old and new activities with the same personnel, using the same channels of communication and authority and the same types of information. Such administration, however, must become increasingly inefficient. This proposition should be true for a relatively small firm whose structure consists of informal arrangements between a few executives as well as for a large one whose size and numerous administrative personnel require a more formal definition of relations between offices and officers. Since expansion created the need for new administrative offices and structures, the reasons for delays in developing the new organization rested with the executives responsible for the enterprise's long-range growth and health. Either these administrators were too involved in day-to-day tactical activities to appreciate or understand the longer-range organizational needs of their enterprises, or else their training and education failed to sharpen their perception of organizational problems or failed to develop their ability to handle them. They may also have resisted administratively desirable changes because they felt structural reorganization threatened their own personal position, their power, or most important of all, their psychological security.

In answer to the second question, changes in strategy which called for changes in structure appear to have been in response to the opportunities and needs created by changing population and changing national income and by technological innovation. Population growth, the shift from the country to the city and then to the suburb, depressions and prosperity, and the increasing pace of technological change, all created new demands or curtailed existing ones for a firm's goods or services. The prospect of a new market or the threatened loss of a current one stimulated geographical expansion, vertical integration, and product diversification. Moreover, once a firm had accumulated large resources, the need to keep its men, money, and materials steadily employed provided a constant stimulus to look for new markets by moving into new areas, by taking on new functions, or by developing new product lines. Again the awareness of the needs and opportunities created by the changing environment seems to have depended on the training and personality of individual executives and on their ability to keep their eyes on the more important entrepreneurial problems even in the midst of pressing operational needs.

The answers to the two questions can be briefly summarized by restating the general thesis. Strategic growth resulted from an awareness of the opportunities and needs—created by changing population, income, and technology—to employ existing or expanding resources more profitably. A new strategy required a new or at least refashioned structure if the enlarged enterprise was to be operated efficiently. The failure to develop a new internal structure, like the failure to respond to new external opportunities and needs, was a consequence of overconcentration on operational activities by the executives responsible for the destiny of their enterprises, or from their inability, because of past training and education and present position, to develop an entrepreneurial outlook.

One important corollary to this proposition is that growth without structural adjustment can lead only to economic inefficiency. Unless new structures are developed to meet new administrative needs which result from an expansion of a firm's activities into new areas, functions, or product lines, the technological, financial, and personnel economies of growth and size cannot be realized. Nor can the enlarged resources be employed as profitably as they otherwise might be. Without administrative offices and structure, the individual units within the enterprise (the field units, the departments, and the divisions) could undoubtedly operate as efficiently or even more so (in terms of cost per unit and volume of output per worker) as independent units than if they were part of a larger enterprise. Whenever the executives responsible for the firm fail to create the offices and structure necessary to bring together effectively the several administrative offices into a unified whole, they fail to carry out one of their basic economic roles.

The actual historical patterns of growth and organization building in the large industrial enterprise were not, of course, as clear-cut as they have been theoretically defined here. One strategy of expansion could be carried out in many ways, and often, two or three basic ways of expansion were undertaken at one and the same time. Growth might come through simultaneous building or buying of new facilities, and through purchasing or merging with other enterprises. Occasionally a firm simultaneously expanded its volume, built new facilities in geographically distant areas, moved into new functions, and developed a different type of product line. Structure, as the case studies indicate, was often slow to follow strategy, particularly in periods of rapid expansion. As a result, the distinctions between the duties of the different offices long remained confused and only vaguely defined. One executive or a small group of executives might carry out at one and the same time the functions of a general office, a central office, and a departmental headquarters. Eventually, however, most large corporations came to devise the specific units to handle a field unit, a functional department, an integrated division, or a diversified industrial empire. For this very reason, a clear-cut definition of structure and strategy and a simplified explanation or theory of the relation of one to the other should make it easier to comprehend the complex realities involved in the expansion and management of the great industrial enterprises. . . .

*   *   *   *   *

The Creative Innovation

. . . The inherent weakness in the centralized, functionally departmentalized operating company and in the loosely held, decentralized holding company became critical only when the administrative load on the senior executive officers increased to such an extent that they were unable to handle their entrepreneurial responsibilities efficiently. This situation arose when the operations of the enterprise became too complex and the problems of coordination, appraisal, and policy formulation too intricate for a small number of top officers to handle both long run, entrepreneurial, and short-run, operational administrative activities. To meet these new needs, the innovators built the multidivisional structure with a general office whose executives would concentrate on entrepreneurial activities and with autonomous, fairly self-contained operating divisions whose managers would handle operational ones.

Complexity in itself, it should be emphasized, did not assure innovation or change; some responsible administrator had to become aware of the new conditions. Furthermore, awareness had to be translated into a plan for meeting the new conditions, and then the plan had to be accepted by most of the senior executives. Since such a program dealt with the relations between persons rather than with technological or mechanical developments, the working out of the plan was more complicated than merely bringing a new product or process into effective use.

*   *   *   *   *

The Conditions for Innovation. Size, measured by volume of output, capital invested, and men employed, was clearly only one aspect of the new complexity. Growth by diversification into new lines of business and continued vertical integration in widely separated geographical areas proved more significant. . . .

*   *   *   *   *

ORGANIZATIONAL INNOVATORS

Unless structure follows strategy, inefficiency results. . . . Volume expansion, geographical dispersion, vertical integration, product diversification, and continued growth by any of these basic strategies laid an increasingly heavy load of entrepreneurial decision making on the senior executives. If they failed to re-form the lines of authority and communication and to develop information necessary for administration, the executives throughout the organization were drawn deeper and deeper into operational activities and often were working at cross purposes to and in conflict with one another.

Yet structure often failed to follow strategy. . . . A primary reason for delay was the very fact that responsible executives had become too enmeshed in operational activities. . . .

3. MISSISSIPPI VALLEY EQUIPMENT CORPORATION

Case Introduction

SYNOPSIS

A group of St. Louis bankers, who own the Valley Corporation, merge the company with another to form Mississippi Valley Equipment Corporation. J. D. Skinner, president of Mississippi Valley Equipment Corporation, takes certain actions in building the organization structure of the company and in the formulation of company-wide policies. There are problems of inventory control, sales training, finance, and personnel management—both in the corporate staff and in the Kansas City branch. T. J. Duncan, manager at Kansas City, and various staff personnel disagree on the establishment of policies in these areas.

WHY THIS CASE IS INCLUDED

The Mississippi Valley Equipment Corporation situation offers opportunity to study the rational plan of decentralization, as well as certain counter tendencies to central planning. The informal organization in the company can be studied as it relates to the formal plan. One can also see how these two types of organization influence the behavior of people, and how they may either reinforce or conflict with one another.

The technological and economic influences on organization (design and custom) can be studied along with the human influences. The case also throws light on the question as to whether there is an inherent conflict between technology and economics of organization, on the one hand, and human needs, on the other.

Finally, the case shows the place of science and rational planning in the corporate affairs of this company.

DIAGNOSTIC AND PREDICTIVE QUESTIONS

The readings included with this case are marked (*). The author index at the end of this book locates the other readings.

1. Mississippi Valley Equipment Corporation customers include the city of St. Louis which buys water system pumps, a pharmaceutical company which buys machines for its production lines that produce vitamins, and a boat manufacturer which purchases small valves to be placed in fishing boats. Do you think that the Mississippi Valley Equipment Corporation, its president, and its corporate headquarters staff are acting in the public interest?

Read: Smith, *The Wealth of Nations,* pp. 423, 508. Hayek, "The Corporation in a Democratic Society: In Whose Interest Ought It and Will It Be Run?" pp. 100–101, 104–7, 116–17. Taylor, "Principles of Scientific Management." Beard, *Public Policy and the General Welfare,* p. 148, *et. seq.*

2. What kind of interests and motivations do Skinner and his headquarters staff men have? Do you see how this might contribute to (1) the welfare of society, (2) their own attempt to use formal organization planning?

Read: Odiorne, *How Managers Make Things Happen,* pp. 4–11, 37–38, 52–53. Schumpeter, *The Theory of Economic Development,* pp. 84–94.

3. Corporate officers, using their own beliefs and values, are often important forces in the goal setting process of organizations. What influence did the previous owner have on Mississippi Valley Equipment Corporation goals? Contrast these with those of the new management.

Note: There is no reading in the literature of economics or management which adequately covers this question. The reader may draw his own conclusions, and in doing so will be drawing original hypotheses about corporate goals, what they are, who sets them, and for what reasons.

4. What two economic principles influence Skinner to design an organization structure which uses central staff specialist planners (such as Dugan and Cooper)? Why are these planning positions centralized at headquarters instead of each branch having its own staff specialists?

Read: *Summer, "Economies of Scale and Organization Structure." Marshall, *Principles of Economics,* pp. 283–85. Smith, *The Wealth of Nations,* pp. 4–15.

5. According to traditional management theory, which form of primary operating departmentation has Skinner selected and why? Why has he provided a headquarters position to perform the central purchasing "service" function? Why has he provided staff positions at headquarters?

Read: Carzo and Yanouzas, *Formal Organization: A Systems Approach,* pp. 24, 28–34, 43–44, 48–49, 54–57, 65–68.

6. Do you see how Skinner, in planning the new organization structure, is trying to relate this structure to his major strategic decisions? What, "out there in the environment," is causing him to change the strategy, and therefore the structure, of Mississippi Valley Equipment Corporation? What stage of growth is the Mississippi Valley Equipment Corporation in at present?

Read: *Dubin, "Imperatives Affecting Industrial Relations Decisions." Chandler, *Strategy and Structure,* pp. 7–17, 299–300, 314–15. *Anderson, *An Organization Appraisal,* pp. 1–2.

7. It is often said that there are two organization structures in every company—the formal structure (codified set of position descriptions and procedural rules) and the informal structure (habit patterns, customary way of doing things, "common law"). Give examples of these two structures in Mississippi Valley Equipment Corporation. Do they conflict or coincide? Which, if either, is really running the company?

Read: *Summer, "Leadership Action and the Informal Organization."

8. In addition to specialization of *parts* there is another reason why organizations are *rationally planned.* It is because the *parts* must be *related* to each other. There must not only be plugs and bulbs, but wires. How is Duncan's branch related to the rest of the company? Why might this cause Skinner to design central staff positions to figure out (plan) these relationships? Do you see why modern systems theory holds that "everything depends on everything else"?

Read: *Friedman, *Law in a Changing Society,* pp. 3–6, 22–23.

9. From a human standpoint (and the study of psychology and sociology), formal organization planning such as that being done by Skinner and the headquarters staff have certain drawbacks or dangers. What are these drawbacks? Illustrate in the case of Duncan in Kansas City.

Read: Argyris, *Personality and Organization,* pp. 27–31, 33–51, 66–67, 77–90, 95, 103–4, 123–25, 130, 137–39, 150, 153–55, 157. Blau and Scott, *Formal Organizations: A Comparative Approach,* pp. 242–51. Either Krech and Crutchfield, *Theory and Problems of Social Psychology,* pp. 81–83, 87–89, 94–96, 98, 102–3 (an advanced reading); or Leavitt, *Managerial Psychology,* pp. 27–33 (a less complicated reading). Etzioni, "Authority Structure and Organizational Effectiveness."

POLICY QUESTIONS

10. What should Skinner do about establishing the staff positions at company headquarters? Why? What, if anything, should he do in clarifying Dugan's and Cooper's position descriptions?

11. What kind of leadership pattern would be best for the president to use in the long run? In the short run?

12. In the long run, how should the informal organization in the Mississippi Valley Equipment Corporation be reconciled with the rationally planned organization? Which of these two should be changed to fit the other, or, should both be changed? Be specific about what changes should be made, in some detail.

QUESTIONS FOR ORIGINAL STUDENT WORK IN ANALYSIS AND POLICY

13. While reflecting on case facts, what additional theories from prior education give you insights as to "what is going on" in the Mississippi

Valley Equipment Corporation? As to what might be predicted to happen in the future?

14. Other than the policy questions asked by the authors, what pragmatic ways can you think of to state the practical problems faced by executives in the case?

Case Text*

BACKGROUND OF THE COMPANY

The Mississippi Valley Equipment Corporation, with headquarters in St. Louis, engages in the distribution of heavy equipment, machinery, and industrial hardware. Although it is not a "giant" corporation if measured by manufacturing company standards, its sales this year are expected by the management to exceed $17 million, thus qualifying the company as one of the largest of its kind in the nation. The present firm was formed two years ago when the owners of the Valley Corporation purchased 80 percent of the stock of Mississippi Supply Company. At that time the corporate name was changed. Today, all letterheads and nameplates on company property show the company's trademark, MVEC, enclosed in a diamond-shaped symbol.

The company acts as manufacturer's agent in the sale of approximately 11,400 items in its product line, and it purchases for its own account approximately 6,000 items. Products range in value from nuts and bolts that sell for a few cents to air and gas compressors that sell for $12,000 to $15,000 each.

Storage and sale of equipment are carried out through six branches: two in St. Louis, and one each in Houston, New Orleans, Kansas City, and Cincinnati. At every location, the company maintains extensive warehouse facilities and a sales force to call on industrial concerns that use company products.

At the time of the merger, Mississippi Supply Company, which was founded by M. J. Wheeler at the age of 28, had sales of $4 million at its St. Louis and Kansas City locations. During the last ten years of its existence, MSC increased its sales approximately 5 percent, while there was an 80 percent increase in the industry, as estimated by a trade association economist, during the same period. Mr. Wheeler states that his wife and three children all agreed that it would be wise to sell the company, since the heirs had no interest in actively entering the field. Now 70, he also says:

I will be rather frank and say that I had my hands completely full operating the St. Louis and Kansas City businesses, could not have

---

* Copyright 1973, Charles E. Summer.

worked any harder, and consciously made the decision not to try to grow to be a giant and to set the world on fire. My company has always made a good profit, and I am proud of its record. We had sales of $2 million at the time the company was sold, and our employees were well cared for. That ought to be evident by the fact that over half of the 102 people had been with me for more than 20 years.

James D. Skinner, President of MVEC, states that:

The purchase was equally good for the Valley and for Mr. Wheeler. My board employed me as president of Valley eight years ago with the specific belief that we can grow large and profitable. In its two locations, MSC sold essentially the same kinds of products as we did, but we all recognized that it had become accustomed to selling the same items to the same customers, and to carrying out its operations in warehousing, financing and shipping in the same way it always had. We knew that its sales could be increased substantially and its operating methods streamlined.

Mr. Skinner, now 49, has seen sales of the Valley Corporation increase from $12 million to $24 million in eight years before the purchase, and the combined sales of the MVEC increase from $28 million to $34 million in the two years since the merger. The owners of MVEC, five prominent St. Louis businessmen engaged in banking and real estate, believe that James Skinner is an extremely capable man for the job, and as one of them put it,

His principal qualifications are that he knows how to get the thing organized and then let it run while he sees new opportunities for sales or cost cutting. He also knows how to pick good men as lieutenants. That's all it takes.

THE KANSAS CITY BRANCH

The Kansas City Branch has been headed by T. J. (Jack) Duncan for the past 12 months. Duncan, 45 years old, had worked as operating manager of the Valley branch in St. Louis for a period of 11 years. Shortly after he became president, Mr. Skinner recognized Duncan as a good executive, and felt that he would be ideal as the man to "take hold of the Kansas City operation and make something of it."

Before the purchase, Kansas City sold industrial equipment, machinery, and construction materials to local hardware stores, builders, institutions such as office buildings and schools, and to the State Highway Department. Its profit had been "moderately good" according to Duncan.

At the time that Duncan became manager at Kansas City, Mr. Skinner spent a day in drawing up a job description (Exhibit 1) for the new position of general manager at Kansas City. He had been to Kansas City on numerous trouble-shooting trips, had spent two months there after he became president of MVEC, and appears to have considerable knowledge

EXHIBIT 1
Position Description of General Manager, Kansas City Branch

1. *The general manager is responsible for all work performed at the
    Kansas City Branch. As such, he has authority to request all per-
    sonnel to perform their specified duties.*
2. *The general manager will plan his sales, expenses, and invest-
    ment needs two times a year so that he can control his branch
    operations in order to make a profit.*
3. *The general manager will give personal attention to the two prin-
    cipal functions that make a profit for MVEC: sales and operations.
    He will draw up such policies and procedures as are required to
    produce effective selling and operating performance. He will then
    personally oversee both functions to see that his policies and
    procedures are being followed.*
4. *The general manager will, subject to the broad limits indicated
    by companywide policy, establish jobs, policies, and procedures
    in the functions of purchasing, personnel, and inventory control.*
5. *The general manager will select, hire, and compensate all person-
    nel who work in the branch.*
6. *The general manager will cooperate with representatives from the
    St. Louis office when they visit the branch seeking data and infor-
    mation for company decisions and policies.*

of operations there. Along with this he says that he knows "very much
about operations in St. Louis, and these are almost identical with Kansas
City."

Mr. Skinner feels that there are still some "rough spots to be worked
out in Kansas City."

*For example, the purchasing and personnel functions have never
been clearly defined. Both Duncan and I will get around to it one of
these days. He has been working on a set of recommendations, but we
disagree slightly on purchasing. He wants to be able to purchase all
of his own merchandise out there except (1) items which cost over
$3,000 individually, or (2) volume items in which he purchases less
than maximum quantity discount. That is, when Kansas City orders
bolts in sufficient quantity to get the discount they would not submit
through here. I'm afraid that will tend to make them carry too much
inventory out there and tie up too much money; also it cuts down on
MVEC prestige with vendors not to have our large orders handled
centrally. As a matter of fact, one of Duncan's weak spots is his inventory management—on my bimonthly visits to Kansas City I go over
the levels of inventory with his accountant for each of 400 busy items.
I don't have any exact standards to prove this, but I judge that he is
either ordering in too large quantities, or he is being too conservative
on his lead times—ordering too far ahead. I mention this each time*

to Jack but so far he only wants the two policies I mentioned a minute ago. We will have to do some long planning on this one, especially since close control of inventory is one of the ways you make money in this business. His inventory ratio to sales is less satisfactory than that of New Orleans or Cincinnati.

SPECIFIC ACTIVITIES AT KANSAS CITY

Within the last two weeks, Mr. Skinner received from J. F. Dugan, Inventory and Purchasing Manager for MVEC, a list of proposed controls that Dugan thinks should be instituted to insure that all branches keep investment and risk in inventory to a minimum. This proposal is summarized in Exhibit 2. Mr. Dugan's formal education was in mathematics and, later, in engineering. Within the last year he has attended two short courses in Operations Research and has studied the subject of mathematical techniques of inventory control in books and journals. He declares that "linear programming and other techniques will be of great help to MVEC, though it will be five years before we can hope to apply these in our company."

EXHIBIT 2
Proposed Inventory Control, Mississippi Valley Equipment Corporation

The purpose of inventory control in MVEC is to keep storage, insurance, and interests costs lower than our competitors', and to reduce the risk of damage and obsolescence.

At intervals of six months (or one year, if branches react unfavorably to more frequent checks), the branch should submit a list of all items whose value (price × quantity on hand) exceeds $250. Of the 5,000 to 6,000 items carried by the average branch, about 1,500 fall in this category. For each of these items the following information should be given:

Name of item	Code	Quantity on hand	Quantity sold in last 12 months	Lead time: for purch.

In the area of personnel management, MVEC has employed two executives to plan policies and practices for the whole company. It is felt that this will give MVEC a significant lead over its competitors through greater cooperation of employees with less turnover and less damage of stock in receiving and storage. It has confidentially been predicted that this will reduce waste and pilferage. Oliver Cooper, manager of personnel, has submitted a proposed policy manual containing approximately 45 policies and procedures, one of which states that the central office should send a personnel man to each branch once a year "for the purpose of determining, jointly with the branch manager, the salary ranges for all positions in the branch."

The selling effort at Kansas City appears to be successful. The four salesmen seem to have taken a new interest in their work with the formation of MVEC, and their sales have increased about 12 percent over the previous year since Duncan came to Kansas City. Just why this has happened, nobody is certain. Skinner is interested in finding out since he hopes to be able to apply the same incentive at other branches.

Jack Duncan gives most of the credit to Mr. Skinner.

I have a good knowledge of sales, but I've always been in operations—when I was operations manager of the Valley in St. Louis, and before that when I worked in operations both in the St. Louis Branch and in Cincinnati. I sit down with these salesmen once a month and look at their plans for the next month—new customers, routes, number of calls, items to be pushed, and so on. Mr. Skinner not only worked out the present compensation plan (which I suspect is one of our reasons for success in selling), but he also visits with salesmen here once a month and helps them go over their plans that I see two weeks later. I've gathered that "going over" is sometimes a mild way of putting it, since Mr. Skinner proceeds to lay out routes for them when he isn't satisfied with the number of customers served or the amount of territory covered. He also tells them whether salesmen in other branches are outselling them and what techniques they use. At any rate, the salesmen seem to be happy, sales are increasing, and I simply couldn't do without help in the sales area. He sometimes brings along Dick Boling, whom I knew when he was such a hot salesman in St. Louis. There's been a rumor in St. Louis that Dick will take over a new job as sales manager for the whole company and continue the kind of thing Mr. Skinner is doing.

Apparently, the salesmen are evenly divided on the value of advice from Mr. Skinner. Two indicated that Skinner was most helpful, though they had also found Duncan to be helpful. Two others said that Skinner did not know very much about territories in Missouri, Kansas, Oklahoma, and Nebraska, and that he was unreasonable because he lacked knowledge of the obstacles and hardships in certain parts of the region. "It all looked the same to him on a map."

Mr. Skinner says that, "I am wholeheartedly in favor of the decentralization idea. There is nothing that so relieves a president, and at the same time encourages people to work hard and efficiently."

At Kansas City the decentralization idea is carried out particularly in the four operating sections—receiving, handling, storing, and shipping. Duncan drew up his own job descriptions for the foremen in each section. When on visits to Kansas City, nobody from St. Louis ever sees any reason to discuss the work of these men. Duncan makes the rounds of the warehouses at least once a week in order to make suggestions for storing specific items ("We need a lower bin nearer the door for those nipples—they're a heavy moving item"), and he makes his own storage rules ("Never keep inflammable items in the east end of the building"). "Of course," says Duncan, "St. Louis specifies such things as type of equipment to be used in operations, and a methods-study man drew up handling methods for each warehouseman's job." These are provided to Duncan in manuals, but he reports that nobody from St. Louis checks to see whether the manuals are being obeyed. Duncan follows some of these instructions and ignores others.

EXPENSE AND CAPITAL BUDGETS

The only serious disagreement that Duncan has had with St. Louis is about the budget. Skinner has insisted on a procedure whereby all branch managers should submit a budget based on a certain breakdown form, supplied by St. Louis, that lists, under approximately 40 headings, all expense items in the branch. Twice a year, St. Louis furnished the branches with a forecast of total industry sales in each territory. Each manager is supposed to adjust this forecast according to his guess about the percentage of industry sales MVEC will get. With this target in mind, the branch manager then submits an estimate of the amounts of money necessary for each of the 40 expense captions (newspaper advertising, salesmen's salaries, receiving platform personnel salaries, and so on) to reach the target. In addition, there are six captions (including inventory, other working capital, and building) that show what capital investment is needed. For any capital items other than working capital, each project must be listed regardless of size.

Duncan has objected forcefully to having to present 40 expense captions every six months. He has frequently said that so long as his profits, as a percentage of sales and as a percentage of investments, are adequate, St. Louis should not even be concerned with the "numerators and denominators of this ratio—that is, if the percentages are good, why worry about whether it is as a result of increased sales, cost savings, or what?"

Skinner, on the other hand, has found three or four instances where branch managers requested either capital amounts for projects that did not pay off or expense amounts that were not needed to operate the branch. He says:

We've got to have some control beyond the profit figure, otherwise these admittedly good executives sometimes just get carried away with their own operation and can't be objective—the idea, for instance, of Duncan's requesting an extra relief man on the shipping platform is nonsense. He is under such pressure from the men that he thinks he sees the need for such. If we weren't backing him up on a number of these things he'd have to give in for sure. So we ought either to turn it down in the budget or make a rule about the use of relief men. Sure, Duncan would buck these actions, but they are for his good in the long run.

A PROBLEM IN PERSONNEL POLICY

The remainder of this case reports on a problem which arose between St. Louis management and Duncan regarding the personnel policy manual submitted by Oliver Cooper. A series of events, extending over a period of about two years, illustrates the problem.

Immediately after he was employed, Cooper was instructed to draw up a set of objectives for the personnel department and its function. He talked many hours with Skinner about this, and the two of them jointly agreed on the statement of objectives shown in Exhibit 3.

EXHIBIT 3
Objectives of the Personnel Department

1. *To draw up standard policies, procedures, and methods which will increase the efficiency of employees throughout the company.*
2. *To draw up policies that will increase the morale of employees in the branches, thus creating a more loyal work force and making MVEC a better place to work.*
3. *To instruct branch managers in the use of the policies and procedures so that they will be effective in carrying them out.*
4. *To keep the president informed of personnel practices that need improvement in specific branches.*

Cooper was then given six weeks in which to travel to all the branches, spending one week at each branch. Mr. Skinner wrote to branch managers about this visit in a memorandum (Exhibit 4).

At the completion of his trips to all branches, Cooper spent two months in St. Louis drawing up the personnel policy manual. He had collected about 200 pages of notes on what he saw happening in the branches, and had concluded that, although some branch managers did better than others in applying prudent practices, at no branch did anyone seem to give any special attention "to a balanced and systematic plan to promote better employee relations." He also did further research in publications of the Industrial Relations Research Association and of the National Industrial Conference Board. From these two sources, from information gathered at the branches, and from other research on industry practices, he isolated 45 actions he felt the branch managers should carry out.

EXHIBIT 4
Memorandum from Skinner to Duncan

To: *T. J. Duncan*
From: *James D. Skinner*
Subject: *Visit of Oliver Cooper to Kansas City*

Dear Jack:

  The purpose of this memo is to inform you of something that I imagine you will be glad to hear. As you know, the company is going great guns in tooling up for growth and for meeting the problems of a bigger and more progressive business.
  We've succeeded in getting a good man, Oliver Cooper, to help us with personnel practices. Our branch managers are all good at managing their men, but as you probably know, the bigger we get, the more we can learn about how to deal with employees to make them more responsible and more efficient. Oliver has had a lot of experience and training in personnel, and he will bring to our company an expertness that none of us have.
  I've arranged for Oliver to be in Kansas City for a week as part of an orientation program in all branches. He'll spend about three days looking around, talking to you and your men. Then he'll need about two days to collect his ideas and notes.
  I know you'll do all you can to make his stay productive.

            (s) James D. Skinner

These he grouped into six categories, which constituted the chief headings of the manual:

Employment Standards and Procedures
Compensation Practices
Employee Benefits
Disciplinary Procedures
Termination Procedures
Training Policies and Procedures.

COOPER'S FIRST VISIT

  Seven months after Skinner approved the manual and mailed it to all branches, Cooper discovered, on a trip to Kansas City, that two policies were apparently not being carried out there. These were:

1. All branch managers should hold a meeting of foremen and supervisors once a week, for the purpose of training and informing them on problems of mutual interest.
2. The branch manager should hold a meeting of all employees in

the branch once each three months to explain company employee benefits and other personnel policies.

Cooper reports as follows about what took place when he called Duncan's attention to these two policies:

Jack told me that he was glad that the subject of these two policies had come up, because he was somewhat perplexed about operating under the whole policy manual. He said that he was in close touch with his foremen and supervisors and that everyone knew enough about what was going on so that a weekly information meeting was a waste of time. He also said that a meeting of all employees every three months seemed to be a waste of time because he and his foremen could keep people informed in day-to-day conversations as problems arose. I then explained to him as best I could that, if we didn't have some system, represented by these and the other balanced policies, big and growing branches would one day let employee relations get lost in the shuffle. That seemed to make an impression on him, because at least he said it sounded reasonable.

COOPER'S SECOND VISIT

Six months after this visit, Cooper again visited Kansas City to observe what progress was being made in instituting the personnel policies suggested by headquarters. When he found that the two policies in question earlier still were not implemented, he was quite surprised. This time he spent about three hours with Duncan "during which I explained in great detail how practice in other branches pointed to the necessity of these training sessions, how recognized research in industrial relations proved that they would be valuable to him, and that Mr. Skinner would be upset when he found out that the policies weren't being followed."

On returning to St. Louis, Cooper reported to Skinner his earlier conversation with Duncan about the training matters. He told Skinner that he had spent considerable time in presenting the reasoning behind the policies and that he had, in effect, given Duncan two chances to institute them before he brought the matter up with the president.

COOPER'S THIRD CONVERSATION WITH DUNCAN

Since Jack Duncan was scheduled to be in St. Louis on a routine trip three weeks after Cooper's last visit to Kansas City, Cooper requested Mr. Skinner to have a talk with Duncan about the training situation at this time. Skinner agreed, but added that it would be a good idea if he and Cooper talked jointly to Duncan.

On the appointed morning, Skinner, Cooper, and Duncan met in Skinner's office. Skinner opened the conversation.

Skinner: Jack, I've asked Oliver and you to come in because we have a problem in getting our personnel policies into operation. Now, I'm not criticizing you personally by any means. It's just that you and I and all managers have so many urgent things on our minds that we don't have time to study and understand these policies, and to recognize the importance of putting them into effect.

Duncan: I surely know what you mean by that, Mr. Skinner. We've got our hands full meeting competition and generating sales. I'm glad, however, to take time out here to discuss more about personnel matters.

Skinner: That's right, Jack. And I do want to commend you on your sales performance out there. It's really important to us here in St. Louis. But I'm concerned because those two training policies still aren't being carried out in your branch. These things are important, too.

Duncan: I agree. Oliver and I discussed them, and close relations between management and employees is absolutely vital. Out there in Kansas City, I spend many hours a week talking not only with foremen and supervisors, but with employees, too. We have such good and frequent contacts among management that those meetings would take unnecessary time, and might even make our contacts kind of stuffy and formal.

Skinner: I would compliment you on this, too, Jack. The directors can feel fortunate in having someone like yourself out there who is capable of keeping good contact with personnel. But we believe that such things as employee benefits and work rules and various personnel practices will be ignored in the pressure of other activities. I know you must agree that when employees are aware of the benefits we give, their loyalty increases. And if they know the policies and rules, they are more likely to follow them and be good employees. What I'm really doing is proposing something that is good for you and the company. You'll find that it is going to pay off for you in the long run if you have some systematic coverage of these things in regular, periodic meetings, when there is a specific time set aside from other pressures on you and your men, a time to consider and discuss these things. Oliver, you know more about this than most of us, what do you think?

Cooper: Jack, I've seen in other companies, as they grow and become more complex, a neglect of training time and time again. Recent industry studies also show that few employees in American business are knowledgeable on just how great their employee benefits are—how much they are worth to them in dollars and cents. This isn't because there is anything wrong with management, but simply because there is no forceful and periodic indoctrination on these matters. Now I'm not trying to tell you how to run your branch out there, but only giving you information on why these policies are important. Wouldn't you agree on this?

Duncan: Yes, I agree. I certainly think, Oliver, that it's important to get this kind of message over to the employees, regardless of the specific method that we use to go about it.

Skinner: Good. I was certain that this matter didn't represent any real disagreement. We're all after the same thing—good, profitable operations and good relations with employees. Oliver, you continue to work with Jack on whatever aid you can give him out there in Kansas City with personnel problems. Either of you can call on me any time, you know, if I can be of help. Jack, we've got several other important things to cover here—sales estimates, your request for a new loading platform, and so on. With the personnel matter out of the way, let's move right ahead on sales. Oliver, did you have anything else?

Cooper: No, Mr. Skinner. Jack is going great guns on all other matters I know of. Glad I had the opportunity to get in a visit with you this time, Jack, even if it was a brief one.

Duncan: Same here, Oliver. Come on out and see us when you can let go of things here in St. Louis long enough.

FORMULATION OF A NEW TRAINING POLICY

Five months after the conversation in St. Louis, Oliver Cooper spent a day in Kansas City for the purpose of talking to Duncan about a new set of salary scales for the entire work force. This was a rather complicated project, according to both Cooper and Duncan. It involved many changes in the salary ranges for salesmen, warehousemen, clerks, foremen, and others. It was Cooper's intention to use the information he obtained from Duncan in the final preparation of ranges when he returned to St. Louis.

During this visit, the subject of training was mentioned, and Cooper found that Duncan still had not held any formal training sessions, nor did he apparently have a schedule for doing so in the future. Although Cooper was surprised, he felt that he should not pursue this matter further "in view of its past history and the fact that Jack and I had much to cover about salary ranges."

On returning to St. Louis, Cooper decided to write a new policy to be placed in the training section of the manual. This policy was approved by Mr. Skinner and was mailed out the following week to all branch managers, with instructions to insert it in the manual:

Each branch manager will submit a report to the manager of personnel each three months that shows the number of training sessions held in the branch during that quarter and a brief summary of the subjects discussed at each meeting.

Duncan later had this to say about the new policy:

Of course I'm going to follow it. Within the next three weeks we will have our first training session. I'm convinced that this isn't the way to do it, and I'm sure the sessions will be dull and unproductive. I must say that Cooper is getting pretty hard to get along with, and even Mr. Skinner is losing some of his good ways of working with branch managers. But of course this isn't a major gripe; I can get along with staff men and the president, too. But I'll tell you one thing.

*I'm going to let them run it—if they want a speech at a meeting I'll
make it. I'm going to follow the rule book from now on. I'll have to
spend more of my time setting up meetings and keeping abreast of
the directives from St. Louis, and less time wandering around the
plant talking to foremen and workers individually.*

Selected Readings

From

ECONOMIES OF SCALE AND ORGANIZATION STRUCTURE*

By Charles E. Summer

Economies of Scale in Economic Theory

Economic theory has traditionally discussed economies of larger scale firms in terms of physical efficiency (higher output with the same inputs of land, labor and capital equipment, or the same output with less inputs of land, labor and capital equipment). This theory also has discussed economies of scale in terms of monetary efficiency (higher revenue with the same costs or a given revenue with lower costs of input factors).

Using the mathematics of cost curves, or break even analyses, the principle of economies of scale stands out: with a large market to allow mass production, large and efficient machines and plants can be added (capital equipment inputs), the costs of which are spread over many units of output—thus fixed costs per unit of production become less. The long run average unit cost curves slopes downward as the *scale* (output of product units) increases. The bigger the plants added, and the larger the total company production facilities, the more efficient (less costly) is each unit of production. Presumably, the costs become less and less until the cost of coordinating the complex organization begins to rise.[1]

It has also been pointed out that the degree to which economies of scale can actually be realized in practice, is dependent on two other factors: the existence

---

* Excerpts from unpublished manuscript, copyright 1963, Charles E. Summer.

[1] This is usually assumed away by economists, simply by stating that the cost of coordinating plants begins to rise. We know from other disciplines that this phenomena may be caused by such dysfunctions as distortion of communications, or an increase in cost of passing information between many staff departments, line executives, and operating plants, in the decision-making process. Today, we would also say that, eventually, increasing costs set in because of the adverse effect of large organizations on the psychological self-actualization of individuals. This may reduce the energy and creativity released in the organization. All of these causes of increasing costs are valid, but beyond the scope of the present paper. Herein, we are interested in *economic* principles of economies of scale, as applied to organization structure, in the decreasing part of the long run cost curve.

of a mass market, large enough to warrant large plants and machines; and the fact that input units of capital equipment frequently are indivisible.

In regard to the last factor, take the case of an aircraft company that wishes to install a wind tunnel to test aircraft. These tunnels, which must be large enough to hold a complete airplane mock up, obviously will require a large capital expenditure. Suppose, hypothetically, that a small aircraft manufacturer entering the industry needs such a test device. A wind tunnel is not indivisible—the president of the XYZ company cannot say, "we are small, and our output isn't large enough to purchase a whole tunnel. So we will purchase 1/3 of a wind tunnel." He must, of course, go "whole hog or none." He may purchase the tunnel, and spread the $.5 million cost of it over a few airplanes, thus raising the fixed cost going into each unit of output, and probably pricing himself out of the market in competition with large companies, whose economies of scale are greater (fixed cost per unit are less). Or, he may decide not to enter the aircraft industry, but to produce smaller parts for large companies—in other words, he sees the laws of economies of scale as economic handwriting on the wall.[2] Only aircraft companies which have resources, and markets, to install large, complex capital equipment, can achieve a competitive long run average cost curve position which is competitive.

Economists have also concerned themselves with *size* of companies. Whole plants, rather than machines, have been viewed as the basic input units of capital equipment. Similar reasoning to the wind tunnel example, where a machine was used as the input unit, has been used to show economies of scale and its relation to size of the firm.

Economies of Scale in Organization Theory: Staff and Auxiliary Departments

Unfortunately, no literature exists which translates these principles into any realistic guides for management, when faced with the problem of adding staff and auxiliary service units to the company, or to a department of the company. It is my purpose simply to indicate along what lines such reasoning might proceed.

First, the staff or auxiliary service department should be viewed in much the same way as a machine or a plant—that is, as an input of fixed capital. If a firm's president is thinking about adding a personnel department at company headquarters, or an electronic computer service department, he is faced with the same factors as above. The market for the firm's products must be large enough to utilize the department, and spread its output over a large number of units of product. A small bank may not be able to afford a personnel manager, or an electronic computer in bookkeeping and mailing. Additionally, though there are many combinations of service and machines that might be designed for a personnel department or data processing unit, there is a limit to which the company can buy "one half of a personnel manager," or "2/3 of a memory storage unit."

There is one difference between plant scale, and staff department scale, which should be pointed out. In the case of plants, the "market size" is the number of

---

[2] In one interesting technological sense, he thereby becomes an "auxiliary department" of the larger company to which he sells. If the larger customer company gives the subcontractor advice on operations, this arrangement is similar to the decentralized company structure of General Electric, mentioned later. The difference is that in the latter case, departments of General Electric are divisions of a *legal* entity as well as a *technological* entity.

units or final product produced for customers—because the machines and plants are producing directly for shipment or service to customers. But in the case of staff and auxiliary service departments, the output of the department is an input to other *internal* company departments, instead of an input to organizations and customers *external* to the firm. In other words, the "market" or "customers" for a personnel department output are the manufacturing department, the sales department, and the central office clerical and accounting office, inside the company.

This difference has important effects on the logic which management uses to decide when to install staff and auxiliary service departments. First, it is the size of the primary operating departments (plants, sales offices, branch offices, etc.) which determines when a company can afford a staff department or auxiliary service department. Second, with the advance in specializations (in all fields from biochemistry to market research to data processing), this kind of "market," and these kinds of "economies of scale" are becoming more and more important in determining which firms survive, and what a growing company *must do,* technologically (here the word technology refers to specializations of human brains, as well as to advance in machinery).

The length of time which it takes to train and install, as a working part of the organization, a biochemist, or a corps of data systems planners and computer programmers, suggests that this kind of fixed input is even more crucial, at times, than the acquisition of plants and machines. Long run costs are not only thoroughly committed, but they are committed in large amounts to relatively fixed blocks of input resources.

The same viewpoint can be applied at lower levels in a large firm. If management of the St. Louis sales office wishes to install a personnel clerk, or the Esso Research Laboratories in Linden, New Jersey, wishes to install a training director, or a group of patent attorneys, the basic factors are the same.

Economies of Scale in Organization Theory: Line Departments

There is no clear-cut way to distinguish "line" and "staff" in organizations. Rather than get into details of a controversy, we can simply use the concept of "specialist" to denote the staff and auxiliary person, and the "general manager" notion as the line department.

Though Alfred Marshall made brief reference to the advantages of large firms in employing skilled general management,[3] he did not foresee the kind of developments in company organization which we have in the second half of the 20th century.

The same factors are relevant to economies of scale vis-à-vis line executives. A large unit today has a vast upward hierarchy of "coordinators," who devote time to planning and innovation, and whose marginal contribution to the firm's efficiency is spread over large volumes of output.

The most notable example is a company like General Electric, with 101 product divisions, each with a general manager, surrounded by staff and auxiliary service personnel—clerks, personnel people, training aids, etc. When the principle of indivisibility of people and machine prevents the duplication of a given service

---

[3] Alfred Marshall, *Principles of Economics,* Eighth edition, New York: The Macmillan Company, 1952, pp. 283–85.

department at the division level, there are group executives with their helpers at the next level up. When indivisibility sets in even at the group vice president level, then the latest in fixed human resources (executive compensation specialists, organization planners, operations research personnel, and other "departments") are available at the corporate headquarters.

Each of these levels represents a pool composed of a general executive, with whatever staff assistance is allowed by the principle of "market" size and the principle of indivisibility.

There is no doubt but that these principles become more and more important 1) in determining the future organization and destiny of growing firms, and 2) determining the gross national product which issues forth from the manufacturing companies, banks, and hospitals of the nation. Advance in science, and in information processing will assure this.

Limitations in Practice

In order to calculate when to add a staff or auxiliary service department, or when to add another level in the general management hierarchy, one would have to calculate the marginal productivity that the executive or specialist group provides to the line operating departments of the company. The marginal costs and revenues of the line departments, occasioned by adding a personnel department to advise them, would have to be calculated.

As most economics books point out, this is not possible in most situations. The data is not clearly available, nor can the marginal productivity and profits be clearly attributable to variations in the inputs of people and facilities. In spite of these limitations on quantification, and proof, the principles of market size (using the concept of market in this paper), indivisibility, and decreasing costs to scale, are, all three, useful logical tools of analysis in an age of rapidly advancing technology, and in an age of more complex organizations.

From

AN ORGANIZATION APPRAISAL*

By Richard C. Anderson

Science tells us that every living organism has within it the seeds of its own destruction. Organisms survive not alone by the strength of their parts but by a balance among those parts. The planned organization structure becomes the means for achieving this balance in the business enterprise.

The organization appraisal provides a means to measure organization efficiency and to give a picture of how well an organization unit has provided for required functions; described the relationship among those functions; and how

---

* Reprinted by permission of Richard C. Anderson (in collaboration with C. W. Barkdull), 1962 (pp. 1–2).

well it has informed each individual about his job, about what is expected of him, and about how his job relates to others. At the same time, it provides the basic information upon which to build (or rebuild) an organization structure. In the shifting tides of products and markets, the balance so essential for continued success requires that the business enterprise continually adjust its organization to meet new competitive conditions.

As product research attempts to improve the company's product line and market research to improve the company's competitive position, so organization appraisal attempts to improve the company's management capability through providing members with the most favorable working environment. Also, as in the cases of product or market research, changing conditions both inside and outside the company require continuing attention to the relationship of necessary functions and to organization structure.

The planning of organization structure is not a luxury of the giant enterprise—it is a necessity for continued profitability in all business organizations. Every manager is responsible for organization structure just as he is for budgeting, hiring of employees, maintaining financial accountability, representing the company to the public, etc. There comes a time, however, when continuing and concentrated attention should be given to organization matters just as it is given to Budgeting, Personnel, Public Relations, etc. Most companies, of course, are limited in how many specialists they can afford to employ for product research, industrial engineering, personnel recruitment, or such a new speciality as organization appraisal. At the same time, however, there is also a point beyond which the company can not afford to go in neglecting such specialized activities.

From

IMPERATIVES AFFECTING INDUSTRIAL RELATIONS DECISIONS*

By Robert Dubin†

Governing by Rules

In a large company with multiple plant operations the most obvious single consideration affecting labor relations decisions is the need for standardization and uniformity. Unquestionably, the administration of a work force of several hundred thousand, or fifty thousand, or even five thousand is a staggering job. It would be totally impracticable to attempt individualized treatment of so many workers. The almost nostalgic plea for the "clinical" approach, that is, for the setting-forth of "all the facts" in every employee problem, is hardly possible in the

---

* Reprinted by permission of the *American Journal of Sociology* (from "Decision-Making by Management in Industrial Relations"), 54:292–96 (January 1949), University of Chicago Press.

† At the time this book was written, the author was Professor of Sociology at the University of Oregon.

large-scale enterprise. This is not to say that it would not be desirable or humane to treat each worker as an individual. The emphasis is rather on the fact that administration in the big firm necessitates standardization through rules and uniform procedures as a basis for prediction of future events. Management must be in a position to predict what will be the outcome, granting a given personnel situation. Similarly, employees are provided with a basis for predicting the effect of their own action or that of management representatives in the light of the rules governing their relationship to each other.

The "reign of rules" is the administrative answer to the problems of governing in large-scale organizations. This rule-making habit is all-pervading. It takes its most obvious form in shop rules governing personal conduct and in the union agreement which sets forth the mutual rights and obligations of the contracting parties and their constituents. But job descriptions, production standards, standard procedures, wage-rate structures, and policy manuals are rule-making, too. Even a casual examination of the manuals of procedures, operating codes, standards, and specifications to be found in most any industrial or commercial firm should be convincing evidence that rule-making and enforcing for the class rather than decision-making in the individual case plays an increasing role in the functions of the executive.

There is an interesting paradox involved in the growth of governing by rule in large businesses. The goal of standardization and hence of predictability is certainly achieved. But making the rule for the class rather than the individual does two things to the individual worker. He becomes aware of his personal inability to make an individual "deal" for himself outside the company rules and procedures, except under the circumstances of a "lucky break." He tends also to view himself as part of a group of similarly situated fellow-employees who are defined by the rules as being like each other. In addition, uniform rule-making and administration of the rules makes unionism easier and, in a sense, inevitable.

From

LEADERSHIP ACTION AND THE INFORMAL ORGANIZATION*

By Charles E. Summer

In any company, there are at least two organizations which influence the behavior of people. The formal organization, often pictured in the organization manual, is a series of job descriptions showing the rational plan of how management expects people to behave. Such a manual assigns "jobs" (in management terms) or formal "roles" (in sociological terms). There is no doubt that such a formal assignment, drawing on motivations of authority (unconscious compliance based

---

* Copyright 1963, Charles E. Summer. Abstracts from unpublished manuscript. Examples are taken from W. H. Newman and C. E. Summer, *The Process of Management: Concepts, Behavior, and Practice* (Englewood Cliffs, N.J.: Prentice-Hall, Inc., 1960).

on habit, or conscious compliance based on legitimacy and reason) and power, has an important influence on what a person in the organization does.

On the other hand, there is the informal organization, based on customs that arise during the day-to-day dynamic actions of people. This organization does not come into being by a rational planning act. It rises through the reactions of people as they face day-to-day problems. In short, it evolves naturally.

It is the purpose of this paper to show how the actions of formally appointed executives give rise to the informal organization. This, of course, is a special case (superior-subordinate interaction) of the more generic concept of informal organization.

*   *   *   *   *

Almost every single action of the executive in some way influences the future actions of his subordinates. It is quite easy to see that a manager, when he writes job descriptions in the formal organization structure, expects them to influence subordinates' actions. The job description, as well as policies and other plans, are formulated to, in effect, "tell" the subordinate "this is what you are supposed to do."

However, it is not so easy to see that each little action during the day on the part of the superior is probably a more powerful determinant of employees' actions than are the written plans and organization charts.

It may be that the reason why it is difficult to see this phenomenon is that it is so obvious and simple. The executive is likely more or less unconsciously to take it for granted. It may be one of those things which is so "plain as the nose on your face" that the manager *behaves,* and acts on the spur of the moment, without being conscious of what effect each little action has on the future behavior pattern of subordinates.

*   *   *   *   *

As a first example, let us illustrate how a seemingly casual action on the part of the executive might contribute toward employee attitudes or beliefs. We know that these are in turn *one* of *the* important determinants of behavior.

C. T. Crane is manager of the Buffalo Plant of Union Paper Company, the headquarters of which is in New York. He has an organization chart which states that "the plant manager has authority over all operations and personnel in the plant." M. J. Palmer, Production Vice-President in New York, not only drew up and approved the job description for Plant Managers, but he states that he is wholeheartedly in favor of decentralizing and of autonomy at the plant level. Palmer and Crane have been working together in their present positions in a harmonious fashion for about eight years.

Because of a rather strict cost-cutting campaign instituted by the President over the past six months, Palmer recently sent one of his staff men to Buffalo "to investigate the production scheduling system." While staff men from headquarters had visited Buffalo on other subjects in the past, none had ever delved into the production scheduling system.

The visit was viewed as routine, run-of-the-mill operations by both Crane and Palmer. The production scheduling system was duly modified on recommendation of the staff man. About four months later, Palmer again asked the staff man to "go to Buffalo and see how the scheduling system is working and if there are any further changes that ought to be made."

This time, according to an interview with Crane, the latter felt "a little annoyed that New York is sending a man to make changes." Nevertheless, Crane said that little annoyances come up all the time, and it didn't make too much difference anyway.

In this actual case example (names and places have been disguised), the actions of Palmer in sending the staff man was simply one of ordinary day-to-day operating expediency. Neither man viewed the action of particular importance, yet Crane's attitudes and beliefs about both "New York headquarters" and, probably, his attitude toward Palmer, was affected in a small way. Attitudes and beliefs, after all, can be developed slowly and by small piecemeal experiences. This one little incident contributes to such attitudes and belief development.

A Series of Leadership Actions May Produce a New Job Description

Continuing the case, a study of the relationship of Palmer and Crane over the two years after that event showed that both continued to get along with one another on a friendly basis. The production control staff man in time came regularly to visit Buffalo and to work out details on the scheduling *procedures*. This also happened in two other operating problems—shipping invoices procedures, and the filing system for employee service (historical) files.

Now, we do not know whether these things are correct or incorrect. The point to be made is that, by gradual *actions* on the part of Palmer, he was changing the job description of Crane (who no longer decided on these procedures). He was also changing the *real* authority relationships. Even though Crane still, according to his job description, "had authority over all operations," Palmer's looking to the staff man for deciding on these various procedures meant that all three parties more or less unconsciously knew that he (the staff man) now has the real say-so about them.

"Personal Actions" Need Not Be Face-to-Face
Verbal Communications

Leadership is a personal process which usually involves the way an executive personally communicates and behaves with subordinates. While this is essentially true, we should at least modify that concept to include actions which a superior takes that change his subordinates' behavior without verbal communication.

In another incident which was studied in the same company as above, Crane had a minor disagreement with the New York sales manager over the level of inventories to be stored in the plant warehouse. Heretofore, Crane had carried 800,000 sheets of #2 grade book stock, but the sales manager requested him to increase this to 900,000. Both men knew that the sales manager discussed the problem with Palmer in an effort to get him to tell Crane to increase the inventory. About a year passed and Crane got no word from Palmer on this matter. The sales manager again brought up the subject with Palmer, and Palmer again did not act.

In interviewing the three parties concerned, it turned out in this case that both the sales manager and Crane *interpreted* the actions (or lack of action) by Palmer to mean that Crane was in charge of deciding on plant level inventories. All three also interpreted the sales manager's actions (or lack of action) in not appealing to the President to mean that he (the sales manager) acknowledged the authority of Palmer and Crane over plant level inventories. It is important to notice that the sales manager never *said* to the others that he knew that they had authority, nor did Palmer say to Crane that he was delegating this authority to the plant level. All that took place was a disagreement and a raising of the problem. Nobody ever enunciated a verbal solution, yet each "sensed" the communications from the sales manager and Palmer regarding the solution.

The guide to be drawn from this incident is that, granted that a superior's own behavior can change his subordinates' behavior (our first guide, above), we now see that the *superior's behavior need not even be a verbal exchange between the superior and subordinate.*

Resulting Behavior May Either Reinforce or Conflict with Formal Management Structures

*   *   *   *   *

In the last example cited, the President of Union Paper and his staff had actually written a policy three years before the event that all finished goods inventories, both in plant warehouses and in sales warehouses across the country, should be determined by the Product and Inventory Manager, Mr. Warren (a staff man assigned at the top or presidential level). The *policy* was supported by a *job description* for Warren, and *procedures* for both Crane and the sales manager to report data and information to Warren. Nevertheless, in this case, day-to-day behavior was setting up a *pattern* of customary relationships which, though not written down and official, were nevertheless part of the work structures of the company. Importantly, these new and informal policies, jobs and procedures conflicted with the rational structures on paper.

*   *   *   *   *

Dynamic Interaction: A Further Clarification

Many of us have heard the proverb from a once popular song: "It takes two to tango." Social scientists have coined the word "interaction" to denote the phenomenon of two people whose activities and communications each affect the other at the same time. This is an important concept because it shows us that leadership is not a one-way passing of orders from an executive to his subordinate. The Union Paper case above showed that when Mr. Palmer initiated some action Mr. Crane's *response* also determined whether or not leadership was actually exercised. If Crane had acted in a different way, perhaps telephoning Palmer and selling him on the idea of not sending the production control expert, there may have been a different outcome. In other words, both Palmer's and Crane's behavior *jointly* and *at the same time* determined the pattern of behavior.

The principle to be derived from these examples is that it is the *combined and concurrent day-to-day behavior of both manager and subordinate that constitutes a leadership pattern.*

Leadership as Building the Social System: A Further Clarification

In the same way that Crane, Palmer and Warren were working out a pattern (habit structure) of behavior in the Union Paper Company—there are hundreds of other people in a large company—bosses and subordinates as well as "peers" on the same level—who are *by their day-to-day actions* forming habits of behavior and more or less stable attitudes. Out of all of this comes a vast and complex network of habits which may not be written down in organization charts, procedures and policies, but which nevertheless is a *social structure that,* after it is formed, causes people to behave according to its customary "norms." A *norm,* to the sociologist, is simply an enduring (repetitive) action or an enduring belief or attitude which causes repetitive behavior. Both this social structure and the official management structures (jobs, relationships of authority and influence, standing plans such as policies) are at work as forces playing on employees and acting as determining factors in their daily action.

From one viewpoint, therefore, leadership is a process of building an informal social system through day-to-day action.

From

LAW IN A CHANGING SOCIETY*

By W. Friedman†

The controversy between those who believe that law should essentially follow, not lead, and that it should do so slowly, in response to clearly formulated social sentiment—and those who believe that the law should be a determined agent in the creation of new norms, is one of the recurrent themes of the history of legal thought. It is tellingly illustrated by the conflicting approaches of Savigny and Bentham.

For Savigny, a bitter opponent of the rationalizing and law-making tendencies, spurred by the French Revolution, law was "found," not "made." Only when popular custom in part articulated by lawyers, had fully evolved, could and should the legislature take action. Savigny particularly deprecated the trend towards the codification of law, inaugurated by the Napoleonic Codes, and spreading rapidly over the civilized world.

By contrast, Bentham, a fervent believer in the efficacy of rationally constructed reforming laws, devoted a great part of his life to the drafting of codes for a large number of countries, from Czarist Russia to the newly emergent republics of Latin America. While most of these efforts were not immediately successful, notably in his own country, whether in the field of civil law, criminal law, evidence or poor law, his philosophy became increasingly influential as the nineteenth century progressed. It was Bentham's philosophy, and that of his disciples, which turned the British Parliament—and similar institutions in other countries—into active legisla-

---

* Reprinted by permission of Stevens & Sons, Ltd., London, 1959 (pp. 3–6, 22–23).
† The late author was Professor of Law in Columbia University.

tive instruments, effecting social reforms, partly in response to, and partly in stimulation of, felt social needs. It is essentially the judge-made law that, in the countries of the common law world, has still in large measure resisted legislative—as distinct from judicial—reform, although even in the traditional fields of the common law, legislative activity is steadily increasing. In most other fields—of which electoral reform, social welfare legislation in the broadest sense, tax law and the reform of the machinery of justice are examples—the Bentham philosophy triumphed in the practice of States, as the urbanization and industrialisation of nineteenth-century Western society proceeded, and long before political and social cataclysms of the twentieth century posed a series of new challenges. . . . .

A highly urbanised and mechanized society, in which great numbers of peoples live close together and are ever more dependent upon each other's actions and the supply of necessities outside their own sphere of control, has led to an increasingly active and creative role of the conscious law-making instrumentalities of the State.

The traditional view is not without its modern defenders, especially among *laissez-faire* economists who oppose the growing role of the State in the planning and regulation of contemporary social life. Thus, Professor Hayek has restated a distinction similar to that drawn by Ehrlich by opposing the planned State to the rule of law and asserting that the former "commands people which road to take, whereas the latter only provides signposts." Even if we accept this as an adequate parable of the problem of the function of law in modern society, we need only to point to the vast number of one-way streets in modern cities to illustrate the superficiality of this distinction. No sane person would advocate the abolition of one-way streets in cities with heavy motor traffic so as to restore a measure of individual freedom of decision, with the inevitable consequence of a vastly increased rate of accidents to life and property. Such a measure would make sense only if the volume of traffic, in particular the use of motor-cars, were severely restricted, in other words, if individual freedom of property and movement were far more drastically curtailed. This might become a necessary and acceptable measure to advocate for those who accept the planning function of the law, but not for the advocates of unrestricted individual freedom.

However, the traffic problem hardly touches the core of the matter, for it may well be accepted even by the most outspoken individualists as a typical police function, and therefore properly within the regulatory function of government. The shift in public opinion and in the legislative policy of all major parties and of contemporary governments has gone much further. Conservatives and Liberals, Democrats and Republicans, Socialists and individualists, all hold the State responsible for ensuring conditions of stable and full employment through public works and relief schemes, tax policies and other instruments of public policy; it is expected by the community to provide minimum standards of living, housing, labor conditions and social insurance. While there is controversy on the degree of public controls and the socialisation of industries and public utilities, some degree of public operation or control of business is recognized by all major parties as necessary, and practiced in all modern States. In Britain, as in Australia, France, Sweden or India, not to speak of the Soviet Union, a number of important public utilities, such as electricity, forestry and transport, are run by the government or by State-controlled corporations. The Federal Government and other public authorities in the United States control a vast proportion of the generation of electric power, harbour facilities and other public utilities. Public housing programmes and social insurance schemes, farm support and other subsidy schemes have been enacted to an increasing extent.

Technical facts and a gradual change in the public philosophy thus combine to effect a drastic and organic change in the relation between lawmaking and social evolution. . . .

Public opinion on vital social issues constantly expresses itself not only through the elected representatives in the legislative assemblies, but through public discussion in press, radio, public lectures, pressure groups and, on a more sophisticated level, through scientific and professional associations, universities and a multitude of other channels.

Because of this constant interaction between the articulation of public opinion and the legislative process, the tension between the legal and the social norm can seldom be too great. It is not possible in a democratic system to impose a law on an utterly hostile community. But, a strong social ground-swell sooner or later compels legal action. Between these two extremes there is a great variety of the patterns of challenge and response. On the one hand, the law may at length, and tardily, respond to an irresistible tide of social habit or opinion. Such is the case with the gradual enlargement of divorce grounds in the great majority of non-Catholic Western countries—either through the addition of new divorce grounds (cruelty, incompatibility, etc.) or the judicial extension of existing grounds for divorce or annulment (e.g., annulment for fraud in the State of New York). The extension of legitimate divorce is a response to the increasing freedom of the movement of married women in modern Western society, a loosening of religious ties and social taboos, and the development of social habits which lead to the dissolution of a vastly increased number of marriages, with or without the sanction of law. Here the alternative for the legislator is to permit an increasing gap between legal theory and social practice to develop, or to respond to an overwhelming change in the social facts of life. . . .

We have seen that, in a democratic system of State organization, there is a great variety of interactions between social evolution and legal change. The stimulus may come from a variety of sources, some of which have been briefly surveyed. There may be the slowly growing pressure of changed patterns and norms of social life, creating an increasing gap between the facts of life and the law, to which the latter must eventually respond. There may be the sudden imperious demand of a national emergency, for a redistribution of natural resources or a new standard of social justice. There may be a far-sighted initiative of a small group of individuals, slowly moulding official opinion until the time is ripe for action. There may be a technical injustice or inconsistency of the law demanding correction. There may be a new scientific development calling for new forms of legal evidence (such as acceptance of blood-group tests for the negative proof of paternity).

The Law responds in various ways, too. The speed and manner of its response is usually proportionate to the degree of social pressure. It is also influenced by the constitutional structure. But circumstances and personalities may hasten or retard the response. In the sphere of "political law" or where a new status is created, legislative action is required. In other fields, there is a give and take between legislative and judicial remedial action in part determined by the subject-matter but in part by the changing and diverse attitudes of legislators and judges.

4. NATIONAL BANK OF
SAN FRANCISCO

Case Introduction

SYNOPSIS

The board of directors of the bank saw the need for reducing costs and achieving uniformity in certain bank operations. The president created a committee to study ways of doing this. Certain difficulties are encountered in the committee's work, in the work and morale of branch managers, and in results achieved.

WHY THIS CASE IS INCLUDED

This case offers an opportunity to see how the economics of the bank (larger-scale enterprise) affects its organization structure. In turn, one can see how organization structure affects the sociological and psychological motivations of people in the bank system, the motivation of executives, and their leadership patterns.

There is opportunity to investigate whether there is, in fact, a fundamental conflict between technology and economics, on the one hand, and the social forces in operation on the other, and to see what kinds of decision-making systems can either minimize or eliminate such conflict.

DIAGNOSTIC AND PREDICTIVE QUESTIONS

The readings included with this case are marked (*). The author index at the end of this book locates the other readings.

1. What economic and technological aims did Wellington have in mind for the bank as a total institution?

Read: Anderson, "An Organization Appraisal." Smith, *Wealth of Nations,* pp. 4–15. Summer, "Economies of Scale and Organization Structure." Hayek, "The Corporation in a Democratic Society." Coppock, *Economics of the Business Firm,* pp. 5–6, 21–22.

2. What other aims (than those in Question 1) might Wellington have in taking the actions he did in the bank? What functions do Wellington, as an executive of the bank, and Nicholson, as a headquarters staff person, serve in the bank (here view the bank as a socioeconomic system)? What functions do these executives serve in the San Francisco regional society and in the national society?

> Read: Schumpeter, *The Theory of Economic Development,* pp. 84–94. Etzioni, "Authority Structure and Organizational Effectiveness." *Barnard, *Organization and Management,* pp. 48, 85–87, 89–90, 94. *Jennings, "Business Needs Mature Autocrats." Odiorne, *How Managers Make Things Happen,* pp. 4–11, 37–38, 52–53.

3. Why did Wellington set up the particular kind of committee described in the case rather than some other kind of management organization and directive system?

> Read: *Follett, "Constructive Conflict." *Newman and Summer, *Process of Management: Concepts, Behavior, and Practice,* pp. 439–48. Eells and Walton, *Conceptual Foundations of Business,* pp. 360–63. *Montaigne, *Essais,* pp. 1031 *et seq.*

4. From the viewpoint of social psychology, why did Wellington give Simmons the title of "vice president"?

> Read: *Lippmann, *Public Opinion,* pp. 234–49.

5. What social, political, and economic forces are present in the bank organization to motivate managers and employees to carry out the desires of Wellington and the headquarters staff?

> Read: Simon *et al., Public Administration,* pp. 182, 189–200. Locke, *Concerning Civil Government,* Chapter 9. O'Donnell, "The Source of Managerial Authority."

6. What fundamental social and psychological forces are present in the National Bank system that might cause managers and employees to resist the suggestions of the systems committee and of Wellington?

> Read: *Festinger *et al.,* "Informal Social Communication." Argyris, *Personality and Organization,* pp. 27–31, 33–51, 66–67, 77–90, 95, 103–4, 123–25, 130, 137–39, 150, 153–55, 157. *Chapple and Sayles, *The Measure of Management,* pp. 37–38. Etzioni, "Authority Structure and Organizational Effectiveness."

7. What fundamental dilemmas must all executives in the bank face in trying to arrive at accurate decisions (based on accurate information transmission) while at the same time getting costs cut?

> Read: *Blau and Scott, *Formal Organizations: A Comparative Approach,* pp. 242–44, 247–51. Carr *et al., American Democracy in Theory and Practice,* pp. 214–19, Cartwright, *Public Opinion Polls and Democratic Leadership.* *Etzioni, *Comparative Analysis of Complex Organizations,* pp. 31–39, 80–82.

POLICY QUESTIONS

8. If you were the president of the bank and knew the facts presented in the case, which do you judge more important: the economies of scale

predicted by economic laws, or the morale of branch managers, predicted by sociological and psychological laws?

Review: Ideas from readings for Questions 1 and 6 above.

9. It is very unwise for a manager to choose a solution which *either* causes central staff to make the cost decision *or* causes the branch managers to make this decision. If one or the other takes over completely, there are bound to be prices paid in terms of bank efficiency, human motivation and loyalty, or both. Therefore, some means must be found to get a decision made which (1) takes advantage of the expertise and economies of the corporate staff (Question 1) and (2) maintains human motivation of branch managers (Question 6). Study the readings below, and then outline how an organization development program might be instituted in the bank to eliminate conflict and arrive at a cost control system.

Read: French, "Organization Development Objectives, Assumptions and Strategies," pp. 23–29, 32. Schein, *Process Consultation: Its Role in Organization Development,* pp. 3–9. *Montaigne, *Essais,* pp. 1031 *et seq.*

10. What, in terms of managerial objectives, organization structures, and incentives, is available to Wellington and his staff to help them solve the problem?

Read: Drucker, *The Practice of Management,* pp. 121, 128–31. Sources for Question 3 above. Shillinglaw, *Cost Accounting,* pp. 680–84, 688–89. (Additional reading, not in this volume: Arch Patton, "How to Appraise Executive Performance," *Harvard Business Review,* January–February 1960. George Strauss and Leonard Sayles, *Personnel* [Englewood Cliffs, N.J.: Prentice-Hall, Inc., 1960], chapter 28, "Incentives for Group Participation.")

QUESTIONS FOR ORIGINAL STUDENT WORK IN ANALYSIS AND POLICY

11. While reflecting on case facts, what additional theories from prior education give you insights as to "what is going on" in National Bank of San Francisco? As to what might be predicted to happen in the future?

12. Other than the policy questions asked by the authors, what pragmatic ways can you think of to state the practical problems faced by executives in the case?

Case Text*

The National Bank of San Francisco operates seven branches that receive deposits and make loans to both businesses and individual depositors. Deposits have increased from $58 million to $350 million within the past 20 years, and the directors have opened more branches as population and business activity in the Bay Area has increased.

At a meeting of the board two years ago, E. F. Wellington, president, called attention to the noticeable rate of increase in operating costs and overhead costs, and stated that he would undertake a study of ways the bank might lower, or at least hold the line on, these costs.

ORGANIZATIONAL CHANGES

Shortly thereafter, he called in James Nicholson, one of his two assistants, described the general problem of reducing costs, and told him that the bank had reached the size where it needed a man to devote his full time to operating methods and facilities. He said that he had talked this matter over with Mr. Simmons, manager of personnel, and that both of them had agreed "that you would be a fine man for this position." He also explained that Mr. Simmons would be simultaneously promoted to vice president and put in charge of all equipment purchases, the maintenance of all bank buildings, and personnel relations. "Simmons and I feel that you might have a permanent advisory committee made up of one man from each branch, and that such a group can be really effective in deciding on ways to utilize our banking buildings and equipment, and our people, more effectively. Unless you have some objection, each of the branch managers will appoint a man to meet with you regularly."

Within three months of the original reference to the subject at the directors' meeting, Simmons had been promoted to vice president, Nicholson received the title of manager of personnel and equipment planning, and all branch managers had appointed, at Wellington's request, a man to what became known as the "systems committee." At the present time, two years later, the committee appears to have taken its work seriously, as evidenced by (1) a record of regular meetings held over a period of 18 months; (2) the transcripts of those meetings and exhibits, which show that all seven men entered the discussions; (3) 17 recommendations in writing, supported by a total of 1,800 pages of research data and reasoning; (4) the fact that meetings often lasted four to five hours, extending after working hours; and (5) the statements of all seven members of the committee to the effect that they enjoyed the work, felt that

---

* Copyright 1973, Charles E. Summer.

they were accomplishing something for the bank, and had personally enjoyed being on the committee with the other members. All men have also expressed their high regard for Jim Nicholson and feel that he has done a good job.

The 17 recommendations cover such matters as salary scales, a policy on days off for personal business, a policy on central purchasing of janitorial supplies, and a recommendation that certain models of typewriter and dictating machine be adopted uniformly in all branches.

OFFICE SPACE AND FURNISHINGS

About a year ago, both Simmons and Nicholson had made inspection trips to the branches and had come to the conclusion that there was much wasted space in branch offices, and that this situation had been brought about principally because officer personnel and clerical personnel had been, over a period of years, buying equipment—such as desks, telephone stands, and extra tables—that pleased them personally but that, in many instances, was also "too large and expensive" for what the bank needed to keep up its public appearance. In addition, loan officers in some branches had succeeded in having the managers construct walls for unnecessary private offices. Nicholson had obtained the services of the bank's architect and also of systems engineers from two large equipment manufacturers; together they made a "general estimate, to be confirmed by further fact-finding" that the bank could save $40,000 a year over a 30-year period if (1) furniture were to be standardized with functional equipment that was modest in design but met the essential requirements of dignity for the branches, and if (2) henceforth, only branch managers could have private offices.

Before the meeting of the systems committee last week, Simmons expressed concern to Nicholson that his committee had not taken up these two problems. "Your committee could have done some real research on these questions. I hope that you will put them on the agenda right away and agree, let's say in six months, on standard layouts and equipment. You and I both know, for instance, that the loan officers at San Mateo and Menlo Park have entirely too much space, should not be in those large offices, and perhaps should have three standard pieces of equipment—a desk, chair, and small bookcase. There should be no telephone stands like those that were purchased there last year for $90 each."

RELATIONS WITH BRANCH MANAGERS

Branch managers have been kept informed of the committee's general work over the 18-month period. Most managers selected a loan officer (assistant manager) to represent them, and these officers made a real effort to let their managers know what was going on. Dick May, representative of the Burlingame branch, reports that he has been spending at least an hour a week with his boss telling him what the committee is doing and asking for his ideas. James Strickland of the Market Street branch says that he has been able to confer briefly with his boss about once a week on the subjects the committee is working on. Other members report that they, too, have been able to keep their managers informed, and that the latter exhibit a good deal of interest in the committee's work. In all cases except Burlingame, however, men say that their managers quite naturally do not have the time to go into the details of committee recommendations, and that they, the managers, have not been particularly aggressive or enthusiastic about putting any of those recommendations into effect.

The committee has talked about the best way to gets its recommendations adopted. Dick May claims that his manager is ready to put many of them into effect immediately and that it is up to each man to convince his own manager. All others say they believe that the president should issue the recommendations as instructions over his signature. The reason given by Strickland is typical: "We're convinced that the recommendations are best for the bank, but the managers just won't buy them. The only way to get the managers to carry them out is to have Mr. Wellington lay them out as official, and let it be known that they are going to be put into effect. Of course, they would have to be acknowledged as being drawn up by the Department of Personnel and Equipment, with some advice from our committee."

James Nicholson reported in his own weekly meeting with the president that it looked as if its is going to be "rather touchy" to get managers to accept the recommendations. Mr. Wellington thereupon stated that his own knowledge of the committee recommendations was rather sketchy, even though he had discussed them in part with Nicholson each week for a year. He therefore decided to call a meeting of all branch managers and committee members at the same time so that he and everyone concerned could be acquainted in detail with them. This meeting took place one week ago.

INFORMAL COMMENTS OF BRANCH MANAGERS

Most of the branch managers dropped in to the officers' dining room for lunch before the meeting. After the usual banter, the conversation naturally drifted onto the proposals of the systems committee.

"Sure hope my secretary likes those new typewriters. I can't spell, and if Sally left I'd be sunk."

"So what, Joe, you always talk better than you write."

"Say, I sure hated to come in here this afternoon," another manager remarked. *"Ever since Smedley Scott became president of Menlo Laboratories I've been trying to convince him to do all his banking with us. Had to break a date with him, and in my office too. If we start spending all our time buying mops our development program goes out the window."*

"How are you making out with your two [officer] trainees, Carl? I have one smart boy coming right along, but he won't be happy under the proposed salary schedule. . . ."

"The best young man we have came from the credit department

a year ago. He sure gets around. Tennis matches, hospital drives, U.N. meetings; always on the go. I thought of him when I read that proposal for days off. How do you decide when a guy like that is working? Granted his work gets behind sometimes. That's better than drawing pay for just sitting at his desk. I get a kick out of bringing a man like that along. And he is building a lot of goodwill for the bank in my area."

"Well, I kind of like that days-off rule. It would save a lot of complaints and conversation about Grandfather's weak heart."

"It might be just fine for you, Tyson, but not so good for Pete. Why not let each manager decide for himself? After all, each of us is paid to run his branch in the best interests of the bank and we wouldn't be in our present positions if we weren't doing it. What do you think, Oscar?"

"Guess I have longer service than any of the rest of you. It will be 39 years in September. But I'd say there isn't a manager who doesn't run his branch just as though it was his own business."

"And the record is not bad either. Deposits are going up and the bank is making money."

"It's making money that counts." (This from a manager of one of the slower-branches.)

"I heard from somebody about a year ago that the committee was going to study office space and equipment, and that someone figured they could save a million dollars over a period of years. But apparently they didn't get around to that."

"Don't worry. We're building a real base for the future. By the way, did you see the latest report on Zenith Radio. . . ."

Just before the meeting with the systems committee, Simmons called Jim Nicholson into his office to have a brief discussion of the recommendations. The two men read over the list of 17 final recommendations; then Nicholson explained briefly the reasons why each recommendation was made and how it would help the bank to reduce costs.

THE MEETING OF THE COMMITTEE AND BRANCH MANAGERS

The meeting started at two P.M. and was scheduled to last until five P.M., but actually ran over until six o'clock. The committee, branch managers, Wellington, and Simmons were present. Wellington opened the meeting by stating that its purpose was to study the committee recommendations and, it was hoped, to arrive at a decision on whether they should be accepted and put into effect.

In fact, however, after a reading of the 17 recommendations, the entire meeting was taken up by a discussion of the first two recommendations.

1. It is recommended that the following pay scales be adopted for clerical and nonofficer personnel in all branches. [This was followed by a list of positions and grades—the bank had had some uniformity before, but the recommendation specified absolute uniformity and also changed

some of the classifications, thus meaning, for instance, that head tellers would in the future receive more than head bookkeepers, whereas both had received the same in the past.]

2. Employees should be allowed two days per year off with pay for miscellaneous personal business, such days to be granted at the discretion of managers. Because of the possibility of abuse of this privilege, days in excess of two must be taken without pay. This limitation does not apply to sickness or death in the immediate family.

In the discussion, the branch managers found a great many points on which (*a*) they disagreed among themselves, and (*b*) they agreed among themselves but disagreed with the committee. For instance, they all agreed that uniformity was in the interest of the bank, but disagreed on many of the salary scales and classifications. On this point, they cited many instances in which one competent employee would feel hurt if the scales were arranged in the way the committee recommended.

The committee members had talked confidentially among themselves before the meeting and agreed that Jim Nicholson must be the one to present the findings and, by and large, the one to defend them. This plan was carried out, and after the meeting the president remarked to Jim that "the combined thinking of the managers, with all of their experience, made quite an impression on Simmons and me. We have confidence in you, and you know that, but I can't help but wonder if your committee really worked out the 'best' recommendation for all on this salary matter. If you had, why couldn't you convince the managers instead of raising all of the criticism?"

Yesterday, Wellington and Simmons met to consider the recommendations privately. Simmons again expressed the same idea that Wellington passed on to Nicholson, wondered out loud whether the committee should be sent back to do more research on the recommendation. Both men expressed concern that two years had elapsed since the committee was established, without any recommendation's having been accepted and put into effect.

SELECTED READINGS

From

ORGANIZATION AND MANAGEMENT*

By Chester I. Barnard†

. . . [M]atters of urgent speed, of highly technical character, of profound intellectual content, or of very complex conscious coordination, must in practice be excluded from the democratic process except in most general terms.

Moreover, a considerable capacity for abstract thought, that is, for reading, writing, and speaking is necessary. Excepting for small organizations, where decision is very closely related to concrete conditions, the democratic method is not suitable for the illiterate; but marked diversity of education and of intellectual intelligence is also not conducive to the use of this method. Wide expansion of the degrees of education, the minute specialization of knowledge and of function are unfavorable conditions.

Again, there must be such restrictions of the fields of decision or of their details that the number of decisions to be taken democratically is not large. The tediousness and slowness of the process are notorious, the difficulty of maintaining interest nearly obvious, its costliness apparent. I think it likely to be generally conceived at some later time that there is an optimum proportion of decisions in a given organization that can be made by democratic methods, or conversely by other methods. . . .

* * * * *

. . . Leaders lead. This implies activity, and suggests the obvious question "What is that they have to do?" Now, I must confess that heretofore on the few occasions when I have been asked: "What do you *do?*" I have been unable to reply intelligibly. Yet I shall attempt here to say generally what leaders do, dividing their work under four topics, which for present purposes will be sufficient. The topics I shall use are: The Determination of Objectives; The Manipulation of Means; The Control of the Instrumentality of Action; and The Stimulation of Coordinated Action.

* * * * *

. . . An obvious function of a leader is to know and say what to do, what not to do, where to go, and when to stop, with reference to the general purpose or objective of the undertaking in which he is engaged. Such a statement appears

---

* Reprinted by permission of Harvard University Press, Cambridge, Mass., 1956 (pp. 48, 85–87, 89–90, 94).

† Mr. Barnard was former President of New Jersey Bell Telephone Company.

to exhaust the ideas of many individuals as to a leader's *raison d'être*. But if they are able to observe the operations closely, it often disconcerts them to note that many things a leader tells others to do were suggested to him by the very people he leads. Unless he is very dynamic—too dynamic, full of his own ideas—or pompous or Napoleonic, this sometimes gives the impression that he is a rather stupid fellow, an arbitrary functionary, a mere channel of communication, and a filcher of ideas. In a measure this is correct. He has to be stupid enough to listen a great deal, he certainly must arbitrate to maintain order, and he has to be at times a mere center of communication. If he used only his own ideas he would be somewhat like a one-man orchestra, rather than a good conductor, who is a very high type of leader.

However, one thing should make us cautious about drawing false conclusions from this description. It is that experience has shown it to be difficult to secure leaders who are able to be properly stupid, to function arbitrarily, to be effective channels of communication, and to steal the right ideas, in such ways that they still retain followers. . . .

* * * * *

. . . [O]n the whole we may regard leadership without technical competence as increasingly exceptional, unless for the most general work. Usually leaders, even though not extraordinarily expert, appear to have an understanding of the technological or technical work which they guide, particularly in its relation to the activities and situations with which they deal. In fact, we usually assume that a leader will have considerable knowledge and experience in the specifically technical aspects of the work he directs. . . .

* * * * *

. . . *An organization is the instrumentality of action so far as leaders are concerned, and it is the indispensable instrumentality.* . . .

The primary efforts of leaders need to be directed to the maintenance and guidance of organizations as whole systems of activities. I believe this to be the most distinctive and characteristic sector of leadership behavior, but it is the least obvious and least understood. . . . [A]ny act done in such a way as to disrupt cooperation destroys the capacity of organization. Thus the leader has to guide all in such a way as to preserve organization as the instrumentality of action.

* * * * *

. . . [O]ne important kind of thing that leaders do is to induce people to convert abilities into coordinated effort, thereby maintaining an organization while simultaneously getting its work done. . . . In a broad sense this is the business of persuasion. Nor need I say that the sorts of acts or behavior by which executives "persuade" to coordinated action are innumerable. They vary from providing the example in "going over the top," or calm poise inspiring confidence, or quiet commands in tense moments, to fervid oratory, or flattery, or promises to reward in money, prestige, position, glory, or to threats and coercion. Why do they vary? Some obvious differences of combination in leaders, in followers, in organizations, in technology, in objectives, in conditions, will occur to you. . . .

* * * * *

. . . Ability to make decisions is the characteristic of leaders I think most to be noted. It depends upon a propensity or willingness to decide and a capacity to do so. . . .

* * * * *

. . . [D]ecisiveness needs to be considered in both its positive and negative aspects. Positively, decision is necessary to get the right things done at the right time and to prevent erroneous action. Negatively, failure to decide undoubtedly creates an exceedingly destructive condition in organized effort. . . .

From

BUSINESS NEEDS
MATURE AUTOCRATS*

By Eugene E. Jennings†

The democratic approach to business administration and leadership seems to have reached its apex. To some people its future is subject to much doubt. What these critics refer to as its veneer has been cracking for at least five years.

Substantial research has been devoted to seeking a pattern of management which will yield the highest production and morale. So far as the research data are concerned, evidence today is insufficient to warrant the assumption that there is a single approach to better performance. Why then, after enjoying for some 30 years a gradual and somewhat unexpected increase in acceptance, especially verbal, should the democratic approach now be subject to doubts? What kind of executives do we now need and want?

The social scientists can wait for answers to these questions but businessmen cannot. If the commonly held assumption that democratic executive procedures are most effective is being challenged, business needs to know the nature of the challenge and what kind of procedures are suggested as substitutes.

One of the most difficult things to understand is the meaning of democracy, especially in terms of the business system. A common technique is to define the opposite approach, that is, the autocratic, and base the definition of the democratic on that.

The *autocratic approach* means that group members are dependent on a single person. That person—called leader, executive, supervisor, etc.—so behaves that he makes himself the key to all group action and eventually becomes indispensable. His need to dominate is expressed by keeping the group acting as individuals and on a personal basis with him. This means usually that communication is kept to the minimum of administrative necessity except insofar as it is through him and focused upon him. Because he becomes and remains the focus of group attention, he is a firm believer in the indispensability of a good leader, such as he tries to be.

The *democratic approach* in many respects is the direct opposite. The individuals in the group, including the leader, are so closely knit that cohesion sometimes disguises who actually is running things. The leader seeks to evoke maximum

* Reprinted by permission of *Nation's Business,* Chamber of Commerce of the United States, Washington, D.C., September 1958.

† The author is a clinical psychologist and Professor in the School of Business and Public Service, Michigan State University.

participation and involvement of every member in determining group activities and objectives. He so leads the group that the result of the joint effort is not ascribable to his own virtues and superiority.

In short, the autocrat recognizes the superiority of the individual over the group, whereas the democrat recognizes the superiority of the group over himself.

There are differences of view in other regards as to how the democrat and the autocrat behave, but these definitions are generally acceptable. My own research could not find evidence that the autocratic type or democratic was superior; but criticism of the democratic, sometimes called human relations, approach which began five years ago is gaining in strength.

In 1953 Douglas McGregor of M.I.T., then president of Antioch College, warned that business was confused about human relations. He described as a major error of management the assumption that personnel administration consisted largely in dealing with human relations problems. He said that this was looking at the subject as a repair job, instead of a way to prevent the need for repairs. Since then other writers and observers have continued the attack on human relations as being essentially a tool by which management manipulates people into the desired patterns of productivity and comformity. These writers see considerable moral and intellectual degradation and degeneration as a result of the human relations exploitation approach.

Since the human relations approach has had such lofty ideals and high verbal acceptance, it is to be expected that these critics will find numerous and severe opponents. Already a defense seems to have taken shape. Some defenders, believing that the many advocates of human relations have failed to make clear just what they are talking about, have tried to relieve the misunderstanding and confusion by suggesting that the underlying theme of the human relations approach is an attempt to understand people as they really are and to accept them as such. The theme is that better understanding of the problems of people at work, of discovering ways for making work a more rewarding experience, will likely create positive benefits for all concerned.

This implies that management should so manage that the workers' purposes and the firm's purpose are mutual and complementary. Translated in the language of the critics of the manipulation-conformity thesis, this means that the unique strengths of the democratic work process can be used as positive forces for accomplishing the objective aims of the large organization: that is, making a profit.

In theory this might be logical, desirable and perhaps even necessary, but it covers up an underlying problem that may turn out to be an insurmountable contradiction. This problem is how to include in an autocratic system the democratic urges of the subordinate and inferior members of that system.

There are opposing drives here that go far deeper than changing manifest behavior to accommodate and compromise forces that are in conflict with each other.

One may question whether executives are psychologically able to allow the group to participate in decisions affecting both them and the larger organization. I have found that by and large the typical executive does not have the pscyhological capacity to integrate to this extent even if he wanted to.

Even appearing to give lip service and some degree of credence to the democratic approach in such things as decision-making and policy formulation is almost beyond the psychological capacity of most executives.

The difficulty becomes plain once we recognize what the typical executive is really like. Robert McMurry, senior partner of McMurry, Hamstra & Co., a Chicago-based personnel consulting firm, has supplied a good description. He says that most executives are likely to be hard-driving, egocentric entrepreneurs who came up in careers where they have had to keep the power in their hands. They may be veterans and victors in the give-and-take, no-quarter, in-fighting for position of power within the business. Instead of participative management, Mr. McMurry describes business as a "benevolent autocracy" wherein the top man stresses the desirability of humanistic management but remains undeniably the strong man. This diagnosis would suggest that the democratic approach is basically a result of some kind of external pressure and not a manifestation of inner conviction on the part of executives. The possibility is that the democratic approach will from here on be attacked more openly by executives themselves and repudiated by a regression to a firmer autocratic approach.

*   *   *   *   *

. . . [M]ore democracy was bound to be urged upon executives if for no other reason than that a democratic society, believing in certain dignities of the individual, will constantly exert a force to have these dignities accepted in the most inaccessible crevices. This external pressure upon management, plus the demands of large-scale organization for group decision-making, caused some degree of acceptance of the human relations approach.

Even so, this surge to group decision-making came relatively quickly. When some 69 executives of leading firms were interviewed by this writer, the general reaction was that they use group decision-making for getting acceptance of their decisions—not necessarily for getting better decisions. This reaction is in part a result of the failure of social scientists to come up with an adequate definition of what the new executive, who is bending somewhat to this pressure of democratic participation, should be.

In overthrowing previous authoritarian concepts of leadership the social scientists have failed to offer a new management pattern that is, 1, commonly agreed upon by them, 2, commonly understood by executives, and, 3, sufficiently motivating to these executives.

*   *   *   *   *

Consultants who are to some extent both observers and practitioners must offer rather arbitrary advice even though they know science will not yet affirm it. When I am placed in this role my answer has been that the type of executive needed is the polished autocrat. That is to say, the business system seems to be perfectly set up today for the individual who wants to run with the ball but who at the same time makes the team feel needed. He make decisions, he controls and dominates individually and with emphasis on personal influence but he does not arouse animosity. Historians often call him . . . a man who walks with a firm, but quiet step.

*   *   *   *   *

In presenting this model of leadership to businessmen I have had considerable concurrence that the firm but quiet type is becoming increasingly necessary. Some of the most eminent businessmen have this attribute about them.

Whether the polished, mature autocrat has replaced the crude type is still an academic question because our idealistic eyes sometimes indicate that more executives are less autocratic today than yesterday. What is a good bit of insight, although not yet supported by research, is that there must be dominance of the majority by a few and that these few must make decisions on behalf of themselves or the majority, or both, and that consultation with the majority is seldom feasible.

What is feasible is that the few appear to be humanitarian, conscientious and open minded. They generate not necessarily love or hate, but respect and a little, but not too much, fear.

They do not, however, consult any more than necessary to get acceptance. When they do it is with other power individuals who, when allied with them, will bring the advantages of their leadership.

That these polished autocrats are useful and necessary to society is attested to by the fact that they are numerously found in some our our most democratic institutions. I have found them in religious, social work agencies, and charitable organizations.

They are in educational, political, and economic organizations. They represent at best the attempt to respond as administratively as possible to the democratic urges of a mass culture.

But such a response is only possible to a degree. That degree, I believe, qualifies them to be called Mature Autocrats.

From

CONSTRUCTIVE CONFLICT*

By Mary Parker Follett†

. . . I wish to consider in this paper the most fruitful way of dealing with conflict. At the outset, I should like to ask you to agree for the moment to think of conflict as neither good nor bad; to consider it without ethical pre-judgment; to think of it not as warfare, but as the appearance of difference, difference of opinions, of interests. For that is what conflict means—difference. We shall not consider merely the differences between employer and employee, but those between managers, between the directors at the Board meetings, or wherever difference appears.

As conflict—difference—is here in the world, as we cannot avoid it, we should, I think, use it. Instead of condemning it, we should set it to work for us. Why not? What does the mechanical engineer do with friction? Of course his chief job is to eliminate friction, but it is true that he also capitalizes friction. The transmission of power by belts depends on friction between the belt and the pulley. The friction between the driving wheel of the locomotive and the track is necessary to haul the train. All polishing is done by friction. The music of the violin we get by friction. We left the savage state when we discovered fire by friction. We talk of the friction

---

* From *Dynamic Administration: The Collected Papers of Mary Parker Follett* by H. C. Metcalf and L. Urwick. Copyright © 1942. Reprinted by permission of Harper & Row, Publishers, Incorporated. (Excerpts from pp. 30–49.)

† Miss Follett was a noted industrial psychologist in Boston in the early part of this century.

of mind on mind as a good thing. So in business, too, we have to know when to try to eliminate friction and when to try to capitalize it, when to see what work we can make it do. That is what I wish to consider here, whether we can set conflict to work and make it *do* something for us.

* * * * *

There are three main ways of dealing with conflict: domination, compromise, and integration. Domination, obviously, is a victory of one side over the other. This is the easiest way of dealing with conflict, the easiest for the moment but not usually successful in the long run, as we can see from what has happened since the War.

The second way of dealing with conflict, that of compromise, we understand well, for it is the way we settle most of our controversies; each side gives up a little in order to have peace, or, to speak more accurately in order that the activity which has been interrupted by the conflict may go on. . . .

. . . Yet no one really wants to compromise, because that means a giving up of something. Is there then any other method of ending conflict? There is a way beginning now to be recognized at least, and even occasionally followed: when two desires are *integrated,* that means that a solution has been found in which both desires have found a place, that neither side has had to sacrifice anything. Let us take some very simple illustration. In the Harvard Library one day, in one of the smaller rooms, someone wanted the window open, I wanted it shut. We opened the window in the next room, where no one was sitting. This was not a compromise because there was no curtailing of desire; we both got what we really wanted. For I did not want a closed room, I simply did not want the north wind to blow directly on me; likewise the other occupant did not want that particular window open, he merely wanted more air in the room.

. . . A Dairymen's Cooperative League almost went to pieces last year on the question of precedence in unloading cans at a creamery platform. The men who came down the hill (the creamery was on a down grade) thought they should have precedence; the men who came up the hill thought they should unload first. The thinking of both sides in the controversy was thus confined within the walls of these two possibilities, and this prevented their even trying to find a way of settling the dispute which would avoid these alternatives. The solution was obviously to change the position of the platform so that both up-hillers and down-hillers could unload at the same time. But this solution was not found until they had asked the advice of a more or less professional integrator. When, however, it was pointed out to them, they were quite ready to accept it. Integration involves invention, and the clever thing is to recognize this, and not to let one's thinking stay within the boundaries of two alternatives which are mutually exclusive.

* * * * *

Some people tell me that they like what I have written on integration, but say that I am talking of what ought to be instead of what is. But indeed I am not; I am talking neither of what is, to any great extent, nor of what ought to be merely, but of what perhaps may be. This we can discover only by experiment. That is all I am urging, that we try experiments in methods of resolving differences. . . .

The key-word of psychology today is desire. If we wish to speak of conflict in the language of contemporary psychology, we might call it a moment in the interacting of desires. Thus we take from it any connotation of good or bad. Thus we shall not be afraid of conflict, but shall recognize that there is a destructive way of dealing with such moments and a constructive way. Conflict as the moment of the appearing and focusing of difference may be a sign of health, a prophecy of progress. If the Dairymen's League had not fought over the question of precedence, the improved method of unloading would not have been thought of. The conflict in this case was constructive. And this was because, instead of compromising, they sought a way of integrating. Compromise does not create, it deals with what already exists; integration creates something new, in this case a different way of unloading. And because this not only settled the controversy but was actually better technique, saved time for both the farmers and the creamery, I call this: setting friction to work, making it *do* something.

. . . What I think we should do in business organization is to try to find the machinery best suited for the normal appearing and uniting of diversity so that the difference does not stay too long crystallized, so that the pathological stage shall not be reached.

One advantage of integration over compromise I have not yet mentioned. If we get only compromise, the conflict will come up again and again in some other form, for in compromise we give up part of our desire, and because we shall not be content to rest there, sometime we shall try to get the whole of our desire. Watch industrial controversy, watch international controversy, and see how often this occurs. Only integration really stabilizes. But by stabilization I do not mean anything stationary. Nothing ever stays put. I mean only that that particular conflict is settled and the next occurs on a higher level.

*   *   *   *   *

Having suggested integration as perhaps the way which we can deal most fruitfully with conflict, with difference, we should now consider the method by which integration can be obtained. But before we do that I want to say definitely that I do not think integration is possible in all cases. When two men want to marry the same woman, there can be no integration; when two sons both want the old family home, there can usually be no integration. And there are many such cases, some of little, some of great seriousness. I do not say that there is no tragedy in life. All that I say is that if we were alive to its advantages, we could often integrate instead of compromising. . . .

*   *   *   *   *

If, then, we do not think that differing necessarily means fighting, even when two desires both claim right of way, if we think that integration is more profitable than conquering or compromising, the first step toward this consummation is *to bring the differences into the open.* We cannot hope to integrate our differences unless we know what they are. I will give some illustrations of the opposite method —evading or suppressing the issue.

I know a factory where, after the War, the employees asked for a five percent increase in wages, but it was not clear to either side whether this meant a five percent raise over present wages or over pre-War wages. Moreover, it was seen that neither side wished to know! The employees naturally preferred to think the former, the managers the latter. It was some time before both sides were willing to face the exact issue; each, unconsciously, hoped to win by keeping the whole problem hazy.

*   *   *   *   *

The first rule, then, for obtaining integration is to put your cards on the table, face the real issue, uncover the conflict, bring the whole thing into the open.

One of the most important reasons for bringing the desires of each side to a place where they can be clearly examined and valued is that evaluation often leads to *revaluation.* We progress by a revaluation of desire, but usually we do not stop to examine a desire until another is disputing right of way with it. Watch the evolution of your desires from childhood, through youth, etc. The baby has many infantile desires which are not compatible with his wish for approbation; therefore he revalues his desires. We see this all through our life. We want to do so-and-so, but we do not estimate how much this really means to us until it comes into conflict with another desire. Revaluation is the flower of comparison.

This conception of the revaluation of desire it is necessary to keep in the foreground of our thinking in dealing with conflict, for neither side ever "gives in" really, it is hopeless to expect it, but there often comes a moment when there is a simultaneous revaluation of interests on both sides and unity precipitates itself. . . .

*   *   *   *   *

. . . If the first step is to uncover the real conflict, the next is to take the demands of both sides and break them up into their constituent parts. Contemporary psychology shows how fatal it is to try to deal with conglomerates. I know a boy who wanted a college education. His father died and he had to go to work at once to support his mother. Had he then to give up his desire? No, for on analysis he found that what he wanted was not a college education, but an education, and there were still ways of his getting that. You remember the southern girl who said, "Why, I always thought damned Yankee was one word until I came north."

*   *   *   *   *

You will notice that to break up a problem into its various parts involves the *examination of symbols,* involves, that is, the careful scrutiny of the language used to see what it really means. A friend of mine wanted to go to Europe, but also she did not want to spend the money it would cost. Was there any integration? Yes, she found one. In order to understand it, let us use the method I am advocating; let us ask, what did "going to Europe" symbolize to her? In order to do that, we have to break up this whole, "going to Europe." What does "going to Europe" stand for to different people? A sea voyage, seeing beautiful places, meeting new people, a rest or change from daily duties, and a dozen other things. Now, this woman had taught for a few years after leaving college and then had gone away and led a somewhat secluded life for a good many years. "Going to Europe" was to her a symbol, not of snow mountains, or cathedrals, or pictures, but of meeting people—that was what she wanted. When she was asked to teach in a summer school of young men and women where she would meet a rather interesting staff of teachers and a rather interesting group of students, she immediately accepted. This was her integration. This was not a substitution for her wish, it was her *real* wish fulfilled.

*   *   *   *   *

We have been considering the breaking up of the whole-demand. On the other hand, one often has to do just the opposite; find the whole-demand, the real demand, which is being obscured by miscellaneous minor claims or by ineffective presentation. The man with a genius for leadership is the one who can make articulate the whole-demand, unless it is a matter of tactics deliberately to conceal it. I shall not stop to give instances of this, as I wish to have time for some consideration of a point which seems to me very important for business, both in dealings with employees and with competing firms, and that is the anticipation of demands, of difference, of conflict.

*   *   *   *   *

Finally, let us consider the chief *obstacles to integration.* It requires a high order of intelligence, keen perception and discrimination, more than all, a brilliant inventiveness: it is easier for the trade union to fight than to suggest a better way of running the factory. . . .

Another obstacle to integration is that our way of life has habituated many of us to enjoy domination. Integration seems to many a tamer affair; it leaves no "thrills" of conquest. I knew a dispute within a trade union where, by the skillful action of the chairman, a true integration was discovered and accepted, but instead of the satisfaction one might have expected from such a happy result, the evening seemed to end rather dully, flatly; there was no climax, there was no side left swelling its chest, no one had conquered, no one had "won out." It is even true that to some people defeat, as well as conquest, is more interesting than integration. That is, the person with decided fight habits feels more at home, happier, in the fight movement. Moreover, it leaves the door open for further fighting, with the possibility of conquest the next time.

Another obstacle to integration is that the matter in dispute is often theorized over instead of being taken up as a proposed activity. I think this important in business administration. Intellectual agreement does not alone bring full integration. I know one factory which deliberately provides for this by the many activities of its many sub-committees, some of which seem rather trivial unless one sees just how these activities are a contribution to that functional unity which we shall consider in a later paper.

*   *   *   *   *

A serious obstacle to integration which every businessman should consider is the language used. We have noted the necessity of making preparation in the other man, and in ourselves too, for the attitude most favorable to reconciliation. A trade unionist said to me, "Our representatives didn't manage it right. If instead of a 15 percent increase they had asked for an adjustment of wages, the management would have been more willing to listen to us; it would have put them in a different frame of mind." I don't quite see why we are not more careful about our language in business, for in most delicate situations we quite consciously choose that which will not arouse antagonism. You say to your wife at breakfast, "Let's reconsider that decision we came to last night." You do not say, "I wish to give you my criticism of the decision you made last night."

I cannot refrain from mentioning a personal experience. I went into the Edison Electric Light Company and said to a young woman at a counter. "Where shall I go to speak about my bill?" "Room D for complaints," she replied. "But I don't wish to make a complaint," I said, "I thought there was a mistake in your bill." "I think there is," I said, "but I don't wish to complain about it; it was a very natural mistake." The girl looked nonplussed, and as she was obviously speechless a man came out from behind a desk and said: "You would prefer to ask for an adjustment, wouldn't you?" and we had a chat about it.

*   *   *   *   *

I have left untouched one of the chief obstacles to integration—namely, the undue influence of leaders—the manipulation of the unscrupulous on the one hand

and the suggestibility of the crowd on the other. Moreover, even when the power of suggestion is not used deliberately, it exists in all meetings between people; the whole emotional field of human intercourse has to be taken fully into account in dealing with methods of reconciliation. I am deliberately omitting the consideration of this, not because I do not feel its importance as keenly as anyone, but because in these few papers we cannot cover everything.

Finally, perhaps the greatest of all obstacles to integration is our lack of training for it. In our college debates we try always to beat the other side. . . . Managers need it just as much. I have found, in the case of the wage boards which I have been on, that many employers . . . came to these joint conferences of employers and employees with little notion of conferring, but to push through, to force through, plans *previously* arrived at, based on *preconceived* ideas of what employees are like. It seems as if the methods of genuine conference have yet to be learned. Even if there were not the barriers of an unenlightened self-interest, of prejudice, rigidity, dogmatism, routine, there would still be required training and practice for us to master the technique of integration. A friend of mine said to me, "Open-mindedness is the whole thing, isn't it?" No, it isn't; it needs just as great a respect for your own view as for that of others, and a firm upholding of it until you are convinced. Mushy people are no more good at this than stubborn people.

From

THE PROCESS OF MANAGEMENT: CONCEPTS, BEHAVIOR, AND PRACTICE*

By William H. Newman and Charles E. Summer†

"Participation in decision-making," however, usually has a specific meaning: that when formulating a plan, a manager draws on the ideas of his subordinates and others who will be affected by the plan. . . . Normally, there is a face-to-face discussion of a problem so that a free exchange of ideas can take place. This kind of participation requires, of course, that all participants—manager and subordinates—share a belief that the final plan will be better because the ideas of two or more persons are integrated into the decision.

*　　*　　*　　*　　*

DEGREES OF PARTICIPATION

A manager dos not simply choose to use, or not to use, participation. In practice, we find varying degrees of influence by subordinates on decisions. Participa-

* William H. Newman and Charles E. Summer, *The Process of Management: Concepts, Behavior, and Practice.* © 1961. Reprinted by permission of Prentice-Hall, Inc., Englewood Cliffs, N.J. (Excerpts from pp. 439–48.)

† Professor Newman is on the Faculty of the Graduate School of Business, Columbia University; Professor Summer is on the Faculty of the Graduate School of Business, University of Washington.

tion on a specific problem may fall anywhere between two extremes: complete delegation of the problem to a subordinate or complete centralization of decision-making, whereby the manager merely announces his conclusion and tries to get subordinates to carry out the plan. The degree of participation depends on (a) who initiates ideas; (b) how completely a subordinate carries out each phase of decision-making—diagnosing, finding alternatives, estimating consequences, and making the choice; and (c) how much weight an executive attaches to the ideas he receives. . . .

*   *   *   *   *

When more than one person participates in making a decision, we often obtain these advantages: diverse knowledge, different viewpoints and biases, and complementary decision-making skills.

*   *   *   *   *

RECOGNIZING WHEN PARTICIPATION IS FEASIBLE

Participation is effective only when a manager is skillful in selecting problems that call for it and when he determines the degree of participation that is appropriate for the people who will be involved. No simple rule will tell him just when to utilize this potentially powerful technique, but we can identify several factors that will be helpful guides.

Time Available for Decision

Participation requires a suggestion by one person (say, Frank), consideration of the idea by a second person (John), and John's verbal reaction to Frank. This sequence will probably be followed by a discussion of John's ideas, further consideration by Frank, and so on. Such *interaction* takes *time.*

Time can be costly in two ways: It *may* result in a decision that comes too late for strategic effectiveness and it *always* involves an expenditure of human energies. If a crude oil pipeline breaks down, the man in charge of maintaining a flow of raw materials to the refinery served by the pipeline must act fast to arrange alternative sources of supply. At most, he has only brief consultations with other people, and he must brush aside a detailed examination of the best possible sources in making sure that the refinery can continue to operate without interruption. Participation would mean costly delays. In the following example, too, time for joint action would have meant money lost. The president of a U.S. manufacturing concern discovered on a visit to Australia that the company's sales agent was so ineffective that its reputation was suffering and new competitors were likely to enter the field. He immediately set up a new distribution arrangement while he was on the local scene without waiting to consult with his associates back home. Some toes were stepped on in the process, but everyone recognized that decisive action was more valuable in this circumstance than joint participation that would have delayed a reorganization for at least several months.

Even when there is no emergncy pressure, the time required for participation may be a serious obstacle to its use. . . .

*   *   *   *   *

Avoiding Motivational Deadlocks

A manager should think about the interests of each person he consults on a problem. The president of a chemical company, for example, was trying to decide whether the company should stop producing its own wooden boxes to pack chemicals for shipment. The Package Division of this company was large, employing 600 people—it comprised a box factory and a logging operation that cut trees to produce the boxes. In this case, the vice president in charge of the division had no experience in chemical manufacture, nor did his age and qualifications fit him for an executive position other than managing timber operations and the production of boxes and barrels. Because of the vice president's motivations and capacities, it would have been unreasonable for the president to say sincerely to this man, in effect, "Harold, we are thinking of closing up your division. I'd be greatly interested in your helping us gather facts and marshal reasons about whether this ought to be done."

Such a conflict between personal interests and company interests often arises in long-range planning. When a man has devoted his entire career to a particular product or function and has deep convictions about the importance of the activity, it may be impossible for him to think objectively and logically about a drastic curtailment of the activity or about merging it into a completely new organization structure. Once a decision has been made to move in a general direction, and a man affected by the decision has been able to reconcile himself with the inevitable, he may become a valuable participant in planning the transition. . . .

Capacity and Willingness to Contribute

A third criterion we should pay attention to when we decide whether participation is desirable deals with the characteristics of potential participants. For instance, high *mental ability* is desirable. A participant need not be exceptional in all respects, but he needs strength in at least one of the following intellectual qualities: originality, penetrating analysis, good memory, or balanced judgment. Participation for unintelligent subordinates clearly must be restricted to limited phases of simple problems.

We have already noted that some people face new problems realistically, whereas others have a habit of withdrawing from problems, dreaming rosy dreams, becoming unduly pessimistic, failing to face facts, or resorting to other defensive mechanisms. The more *realistic* a person is, the more likely he is to be a helpful participant.

Self-confidence also helps make a good participant. A man with confidence in his own ideas feels freer to express them to his boss and other senior officials, even though his views may not be in harmony with what already has been said. In contrast, a highly dependent person who typically looks to others for help in solving problems is unlikely to provide fresh ideas. Moreover, such a dependent person often gets trapped by a feeling that opposition to views of a supervisor is a sign of disloyalty. Yes-men are of little help in the process of participation.

A particular problem may be so far removed from chief interests of subordinates that they are not *willing to devote effort* to participating in its solution. . . .

*　　*　　*　　*　　*

Economic Realities

The economic facts of life may dictate a course of action, and for a manager to invite his subordinates to consider whether that action should be taken would be near chicanery. Much research is being devoted to devising electronic machines that will sort and post checks in a bank; if a machine is developed that will cut costs of these operations in half, we should not ask the clerks now performing the operation to help us decide whether to install the new equipment. We might well seek their advice on a program of transition from the existing method to the new one, but for them the adoption of a new method should simply be treated as a given premise.

*   *   *   *   *

Aid to Voluntary Cooperation

Certainly in thinking about when to use participation we should also consider how much it will develop voluntary cooperation among those who actively share in the decision-making process. The participants will have an opportunity for self-expression, an increased sense of security, and the satisfaction of being an important part of a group. Such feelings foster cooperation.

Voluntary cooperation, however, should be regarded simply as a by-product. If participation cannot be justified in terms of wiser decisions, we do not recommend its use. When participation is used merely as a motivational device, employees are led to believe that their ideas are being solicited sincerely, but in fact the soliciting executive has little or no real interest in their suggestions. Such an executive will at most half-heartedly make use of the ideas. Sooner or later, the employees will sense that what is being done under the guise of participation is an attempt to maneuver them to support management's ideas and decisions. . . .

From

ESSAIS*

By Michel de Montaigne†

THE MEETING OF MEN'S MINDS: CONVERSATION

The most fruitful and natural exercise of the mind is in the interchange between two men in serious conversation. Further, the spirit of the argument piques the

---

* Librairie Gallimard, Paris. Edition du Bibliotheque de la Pléiade, 1958. Texte établi et annoté par Albert Thibaudet (p. 1031, *et seq.*). First published in 1595.

† Montaigne, Renaissance philosopher, influenced many thinkers, including Pascal, Descartes, and even Sartre. His "earthy" philosophy is often looked down upon by the erudite. The present essay represents the focus of Montaigne's attention on the subject of active human contact, which he puts in the framework of the conversation. However, each time one interprets the word "conversation" in the text below it must be remembered that this is a poor translation of "conferer" which means argue, compare, present, measure, as well as discuss, converse. "De l'Art de Conferer," or the "Art of Conversing," is the eighth chapter of his third book of essays.

imagination and incites one to transcend one's ordinary level of thinking. Agreement is an altogether tedious feature of conversation.

Contradictions

Contradictions are the secret of intercourse between men. They should neither offend nor disturb, but arouse and "provide one with mental exercise." We flee correction when we should face it and expose ourselves to it. Facing contradiction is especially valuable when it happens during a conversation, rather than through pedagogy. But at every opposition we avoid asking ourselves if it is just, but only, how to get out of it? We must fortify our ears' tenderness against the ceremonious sound of words which soothe but say nothing. A strong association between men is based on a friendship which flatters itself not with compliments but with sharpness and vigour of verbal interchange.

Therefore, let the motto of this first part be:

"Meque enim disputari sine reprehensiene potest" (Cicero)
There can be no dispute without opposition, criticism.

Truth through Opposition

The reason that one should be attracted to rather than repelled by he who contradicts is because the cause of truth is more probably the common cause between them than between others. This kind of truth through effort is to be sought after, especially in argument, beyond the debate itself. But what difficulty to get men to admonish themselves! They have not the courage to correct others because they have not the courage to suffer themselves to be corrected; they speak always with dissimulation in each others' presence. Socrates, on the one hand, smilingly accepted and welcomed contradictions to his arguments because of the surety of his strength: this added substance to his eventual victory. On the other hand, we see that there is nothing that makes us so tenderly sensitive to contradiction as the idea of our own superiority and disdain for our adversary. The weaker is thought to be relegated to a position of always accepting with good grace our opposition which is meant to "set him right."

Healthy as it may be, all opposition must maintain order. When the argument grows confused and emotional, one attacks the form of the argument, which leads nowhere. The trouble really is that we learn to argue only that we may contradict; with everyone thus contradicting each other the danger is great of losing all sight of truth, even of destroying it.

From

PUBLIC OPINION*

By Walter Lippmann†

Because of their transcendent practical importance, no successful leader has ever been too busy to cultivate the symbols which organize his following. What privileges do within the hierarchy, symbols do for the rank and file. They conserve unity. . . . [T]hey [are] focal points where differences merge. . . . In the symbol, emotion is discharged at a common target, and the idiosyncrasy of real ideas blotted out. No wonder [the leader] hates what he calls destructive criticism. . . . Poking about, as every responsible leader suspects, tends to break the transference of emotion from the individual mind to the institutional symbol. And the first result of this is, as he rightly says, a chaos of individualism and warring sects.

       *   *   *   *   *

Because of its power to siphon emotion out of distinct ideas, the symbol is both a mechanism of solidarity, and a mechanism of exploitation. It enables people to work for a common end, but just because the few who are strategically placed must choose the concrete objectives, the symbol is also an instrument by which a few can fatten on many, deflect criticism, and seduce men into facing agony for objects they do not understand. . . .

Yet it is impossible to conclude that symbols are altogether instruments of the devil. In the realm of science and contemplation they are undoubtedly the tempter himself. But in the world of action they may be beneficent, and are sometimes a necessity. . . . [W]hen quick results are imperative, the manipulation of masses through symbols may be the only quick way of having a critical thing done. It is often more important to act than to understand. It is sometimes true that the action would fail if everyone understood it. There are many affairs which cannot wait for a referendum or endure publicity, and there are times, during war for example, when a nation, an army, and even its commanders must trust strategy to a very few minds; when two conflicting opinions, though one happens to be right, are more perilous than one opinion which is wrong. The wrong opinion may have bad results, but the two opinions may entail disaster by dissolving unity. . . .

There is here a complicated paradox arising . . . because the traditional democratic view of life is conceived, not for emergencies and dangers, but for tranquility and harmony. And so where masses of people must cooperate in an uncertain and eruptive environment, it is usually necessary to secure unity and flexibility without real consent. The symbol does that. It obscures personal intention, neutralizes discrimination, and obfuscates individual purpose. . . . The symbol is the instrument by which in the short run the masses escape from their own inertia, the inertia of indecision, or the inertia of headlong movement, and are rendered capable of being led along the zigzag of a complex situation.

The incidence of policy determines the relation between leader and following. If those whom he needs in his plans are remote from the place where the action takes place . . . the leader is likely to have a free hand. That is one great reason

---

   * Reprinted with permission of The Macmillan Company from *Public Opinion* by Walter Lippmann. Copyright 1922, 1949 by Walter Lippmann. (Excerpts from 234–49.)

   † The author is a noted writer on political and social affairs.

why governments have such a free hand in foreign affairs. . . . In foreign affairs the incidence of policy is for a very long time confined to unseen environments. . . . Where the incidence of policy is remote, all that is essential is that the program shall be verbally and emotionally connected at the start with what has become vocal in the multitude. Trusted men in a familiar role subscribing to the accepted symbols can go a very long way on their own initiative without explaining the substance of their programs.

From

INFORMAL SOCIAL COMMUNICATION*

By L. Festinger et al.

[EDITORS' NOTE: At the time this book was written, Dr. Festinger was engaged in research at the Center for Group Dynamics at the University of Michigan. In this abstract he draws an important principle of social psychology derived from research.]

The amount of change in opinion resulting from receiving a communication concerning "item X" will decrease with an increase in the degree to which the opinions and attitudes involved are anchored in other group memberships or serve important need satisfying functions for the person.

If the opinion that a person has formed on some issue is supported in some other group than the one which is at present attempting to influence him, he will be more resistant to the attempted influence. Other sources of resistance to being influenced undoubtedly come from personality factors, ego needs and the like.

From

THE MEASURE OF MANAGEMENT**

By Eliot D. Chapple and Leonard R. Sayles†

. . . In a situation requiring cooperative endeavors, whether it is a work group, employees and managers, or staff and line officials, each tries to develop a stable pattern of work, of interaction. When these stable patterns are disturbed, individu-

* Reprinted by permission of *The Psychological Review*, No. 57 (The American Psychological Association, 1950), pp. 271–82.

** Reprinted with permission of The Macmillan Company from *The Measure of Management*, by Eliot D. Chapple and Leonard R. Sayles. Copyright 1961. (Excerpts from pp. 37–38.)

† Dr. Chapple is past President of the Society of Applied Anthropology, Dr. Sayles is Professor of Business Administration, Graduate School of Business, Columbia University.

als experience stress or an uncomfortable feeling of pressure and dissatisfaction. A breakdown in the flow creates opposition as the individuals struggle to restore it. The expected responses from the individuals in the sequence prove inadequate, and new coordination problems arise. . . .

The regularities of actions and interactions disappear when this stress occurs, and erratic variation takes over. The difference is obvious between a smoothly running operation and one with a problem. Under stress, people react emotionally, and, because more than one individual is involved, the reactions usually conflict with each other. . . .

Thus, a vicious circle is established. Something happens in the work situation that causes the relationship of individuals to change or to depart from the normal pattern. This creates a stress, either of opposition or nonresponse, that is further complicated by higher levels of supervision and staff specialists whose unexpected interactions, i.e., outside the usual organization pattern, irritate the disturbed work-flow relations. People get upset; they become angry with each other and, depending on their individual characteristics, react temperamentally. These personality conflicts have direct ramifications in the work process because the emotional reactions change the pattern of contact and interaction. Joe is angry with Bill, so he does not check with him before starting a new experimental run. Consequently, a special test that should have been included in the run is left out, and the whole thing has to be done over. To complete the circle, these emotional disturbances damage the work-flow sequence, which causes additional personality stresses.

From

FORMAL ORGANIZATIONS: A COMPARATIVE APPROACH*

By Peter Blau and W. Richard Scott†

[EDITORS' NOTE: By the term "hierarchical differentiation" Blau and Scott mean, roughly, the separation of "superiors," with authority to make decisions, from "subordinates" with less authority to make decisions. Thus, in business, formal delegation of executive jobs and authority always means a differentiation in the status, power, and authority of executives from status, power, and authority of employees, or lower executives.

By the term "coordination" they mean, roughly, the setting of joint actions among people, with each assigned his part in the total action of the company or department. The opposite of this would be when everyone performs his own

---

* Reprinted by permission from Peter Blau and Richard Scott, *Formal Organizations: A Comparative Approach,* © 1962 by Chandler Publishing Company, San Francisco (pp. 242–44, 247–51).

† Messrs. Blau and Scott are Professors of Sociology at the University of Chicago and Stanford University, respectively.

actions, without regard to whether these coordinate with others' actions, or whether individual actions "add up" to the total goal of the organization.]

Dilemmas of Formal Organization

We shall review three dilemmas of formal organization: (1) coordination and communication; (2) bureaucratic discipline and professional expertness; (3) managerial planning and initiative.

Coordination and Communication. The experiments and field studies on communication and performance we have reviewed lead to the conclusion that the free flow of communication contributes to problem-solving. There are three ways in which decisions are improved by the unrestricted exchange of ideas, criticisms, and advice. First, social support relieves the anxieties engendered by decision-making. In the discussion of problems with others, their social approval of the first step taken toward a solution mitigates the anxieties that might otherwise create a blocking of associations, and it thus facilitates reaching a solution. Once consultation patterns have become established, moreover, the very knowledge that advice is readily accessible makes it less disturbing to encounter a difficult problem, and the experience of being consulted by others strengthens self-confidence; both factors lessen anxieties that impede decision-making.

Second, communication processes provide an error-correction mechanism. Different persons are guided by different frameworks in their approach to a given problem, and the differences make it easier for them to detect the mistakes and blind spots in the suggestions of one another. Although social support and error correction are in some respects opposite processes, both of them are, neverthe-less, important for problem-solving, as indicated by Pelz's finding that optimum research performance is associated with consulting some colleagues whose orien-tation differs from one's own (who challenge one's ideas) and some who share one's orientation (who support one's ideas).

Third, the competition for respect that occurs in the course of discussing prob-lems furnishes incentives for making good suggestions and for criticizing the apparently poor suggestions of others.

While the free flow of communication improves problem-solving, it impedes coordination. Unrestricted communication creates a battleground of ideas; the battle helps in selecting the only correct or best among several alternative sugges-tions, but makes it difficult to come to an agreement; and coordination always requires agreeing on *one* master-plan, even though different plans might do equally well. Processes of social communication, consequently, make the perform-ance of groups superior to that of individuals when the task is finding the best solution to a problem but inferior when the task is one of coordination.

Hierarchical differentiation is dysfunctional for decision-making because it inter-feres with the free flow of communication. Studies of experimental and work groups have shown that status differences restrict the participation of low-status members, channel a disproportionate amount of communication to high-status members, discourage criticism of the suggestions of the highs, encourage reject-ing correct suggestions of the lows, and reduce the work satisfaction of the lows and their motivation to make contributions. All these factors are detrimental to effective problem-solving. . . . But the very restriction of communication that makes hierarchical differentiation dysfunctional for problem-solving improves performance when the task is essentially one of coordination. Experiments with various communication networks show that differentiation, centralized direction, and restricted communication are necessary for efficient coordination. . . .

These conclusions point to a fundamental dilemma in formal organizations. Organizations require, of course, both effective coordination and effective problem-solving to discharge their functions. But the very mechanism through which hierarchical differentiation improves coordination—restricting and directing the flow of communications—is what impedes problem-solving. . . .

*   *   *   *   *

Managerial Planning and Initiative. The need for centralized planning and individual initiative poses a third dilemma for formal organizations—or, perhaps more correctly, a third manifestation of the basic dilemma between order and freedom. Notwithstanding the importance of free communication, freedom to follow one's best professional judgment, and conditions permitting the exercise of initiative, effective coordination in a large organization requires some centralized direction. But the assumption that managerial coordination necessitates control through a hierarchy of authority is questionable, since it can be and often is achieved by other methods, notably through various types of impersonal mechanisms of control designed by management.

The assembly line is such an impersonal mechanism through which managerial planning effects coordination of the production processes without the use of directives that are passed.down the hierarchy. As a matter of fact, the impersonal constraints exerted on operators tend to reverse the flow of demand in the hierarchy. Since the moving line makes most of the demands on workers, the role of the foreman is changed from one who primarily makes demands on workers to one who responds to their demands for help and assistance, and similar changes occur on higher levels. There is centralized direction, but it is not attained through commands transmitted down the hierarchy.

Performance records are another impersonal mechanism of control, one suitable for controlling nonmanual as well as manual tasks. The regular evaluation of employee performance on the basis of quantitative records of accomplished results exerts constraints that obviate the need for routine supervisory checking. Performance records, like the assembly line, reverse the flow of demand in the organization and cast the supervisor in the role of adviser and helper to workers rather than in the role of a person who makes continual demands on them. This evaluation system also facilitates coordination, since it centralizes the direction of operations in the hands of the higher managers who design the records.

Both performance records and assembly lines minimize reliance on hierarchical authority and discipline to control operations and, therefore, improve relations between supervisors and subordinates. . . .

*   *   *   *   *

Managerial planning of the production process and a professionalized labor force that can exercise initiative and is motivated to do so by opportunities for advancement would sharply reduce the need for hierarchical supervision and control through directives passed down the pyramid of authority. Indeed, coordination appears to be achieved frequently through centralized planning and by means of direct communication between responsible managers . . . rather than through the cumbersome process of passing messages up and down the hierarchy. But our suggestion that managerial planning interferes less with the exercise of initiative than hierarchical authority is not meant to imply that the dilemma between managerial control and initiative is resolved. The best that can be hoped for, as Bendix has suggested, is that

. . . the employees of all ranks in industry and government strike a balance between compliance and initiative, that they temper their adherence to formal rules by a judicious exercise of independent judgement and that they fit their initiative into the framework of the formal regulation.[1]

But even this best is too much to expect. For this balance is continually disrupted by the need for more order on the one hand and the need for more freedom on the other.

Dialectical Processes of Change

The conception of dilemma directs attention to the inevitability of conflict and change in organizations. . . . The innovations instituted to solve one problem often create others because effectiveness in an organization depends on many different factors, some of which are incompatible with others; hence, the dilemma. The very improvements in some conditions that further the achievement of the organization's objectives often interfere with other conditions equally important for this purpose. A by now familiar example is that hierarchical differentiation promotes coordination but simultaneously restricts the communication processes that benefit decision-making.

. . . These facts suggest that the process of organizational development is dialectical—problems appear, and while the process of solving them tends to give rise to new problems, learning has occurred which influences how the new challenges are met. Consequently, effectiveness in an organization improves as a result of accumulated experience. These dialectical processes are illustrated by the introduction of assembly-line production. This new production method raised productivity and effected centralized control and coordination without the need for hierarchical directives. However, by routinizing tasks and lowering work satisfaction, the assembly line created problems of absenteeism and turnover—problems that were particularly serious given the interdependence of operations on the assembly line. Management had succeeded in solving one set of problems, but the mechanism by which they were solved produced new problems which were quite different from those that had existed in earlier stages of mechanization. . . .

Conflicts of interest between various groups or persons in the organization are another source of dialectical change. What constitutes satisfactory adjustment for one group may be the opposite for another, since different interests serve as the criteria of adjustment. Thus, when the efforts of managers are judged by the results they achieve and they are given freedom to exercise responsibility and initiative in achieving them, conflicts between them are likely to ensue. For each manager will seek to promote the interests of his department, and his endeavors will bring him into conflict with others who have staked out the same claims. Compromises will be reached and coalitions will be formed, but since the responsibilities and interests of the managers continue to differ, new conflicts are apt to arise as changing conditions produce new challenges. . . .

---

[1] Reinhard Bendix, "Bureaucracy," *American Sociological Review,* 12 (1947), p. 503.

From

A COMPARATIVE ANALYSIS OF COMPLEX ORGANIZATIONS*

By Amitai Etzioni†

Utilitarian organizations are organizations in which remuneration is the major means of control over lower participants and calculative involvement (i.e., mild alienation to mild commitment) characterizes the orientation of the large majority of lower participants. Utilitarian organizations are commonly referred to as industries. . . . Thus, for our purposes, industries and divisions of industrial organizations can be classified into three main categories: those whose lower participants are predominantly *blue-collar* workers, such as most factories and mines; those whose lower participants are predominantly *white-collar* employees, such as offices, whether private (insurance companies and banks) or public (various governmental agencies); and those whose lower participants are *professionals,* such as research organizations, planning organizations, and law firms (these, as we will see, are normative organizations).

Statements made about one category of industry also hold, though to a lesser degree, for employees of the same type in subdivisions of other categories of organizations. Thus, statements about white-collar industries apply to office employees in factories; statements about professional organizations are also true for professional divisions in blue-collar industries, as in research and development divisions; and statements about blue-collar industries hold for janitors in a university. . . .

Remunerative power—such as the manipulation of wages, salaries, commissions, fringe benefits, working conditions, and similar rewards—constitutes the predominant source of control in blue-collar industries. These sanctions also constitute the predominant means of control in white-collar industries, but they are less pronounced there than in blue-collar industries; and they constitute an important though secondary power in professional organizations. Normative controls play a relatively limited role in blue-collar industries; an important though secondary role in white-collar industries; and they constitute the predominant means of control in professional organizations. In other words, professional organizations are not a remunerative but a normative "industry." Hence their compliance structure is examined in the subsequent chapter, with other normative organizations.

*   *   *   *   *

Remuneration is the predominant means of control of blue-collar workers. Its allocation and manipulation make these employees conform to regulations governing the required level and quality of production, the use and treatment of organizational property, tardiness, absenteeism, and the like. It may not be the central factor determining their orientation to work in general, or their choice of

---

* Reprinted with permission of the publisher from *A Comparative Analysis of Complex Organizations* by Amitai Etzioni. Copyright 1960 by The Free Press, A Corporation. (Excerpts from pp. 31–39, 80–82.)

† Dr. Etzioni is Professor of Sociology at Columbia University.

a particular line of work, but it seems to be central in affecting their orientation to particular jobs and many job-norms, and to the organization as a control structure.

It is true that other factors, including their basic values, degree of unionization, intrinsic satisfaction from work, prestige and esteem derived from it, and, to some degree, social relations on the job, also influence the job orientation and performance of workers. We suggest, however, that when the relative weight of these various factors is established, remunerative rewards and sanctions will turn out to play a more important part in control of blue-collar workers than other factors.

Some relevant material is supplied in a study of the method of control preferred by workers in an electric power company, and the method of control considered effective by their supervisors (Mann and Dent, 1954). . . .

* * * * *

Further evidence is supplied by a study of workers who chose to work on an assembly line in the automotive industry (Walker and Guest, 1952). An examination of their previous jobs indicates that by six criteria of job satisfaction, the workers were much better off on their previous job; 87.4 per cent had formerly held a job where pace was determined individually; 72 per cent had had non-repetitive jobs; about 60 per cent had had jobs requiring some skills and training; and 62.7 per cent had been entirely or partly free to determine how their jobs ought to be done (*ibid.*, pp. 34 ff.). They chose to leave these jobs and take the frustrating assembly-line jobs basically because the new jobs offered a higher and more secure income. Three quarters of the workers reported that the reasons bringing them to the new plant were primarily economic. Wage differences were about 30 per cent—$1.51 per hour compared with $1.05 (*ibid.*, p. 91).

Social scientists studying industries have emphasized that the earlier image of the worker as a rational machine, from whom greater effort can be elicited when more incentives are introduced, is not valid. By now this point is widely accepted; indeed, it seems at times to be overstressed. Students of industries should be reminded that attempts to increase the normative elements of supervision are in some cases reported to lead only to small increases in productivity; whereas in other cases they cause an increase in "morale" (i.e., job satisfaction) but none in productivity. On the other hand, reports from industry and surveys by government bureaus generally attest to the effectiveness of wage-incentive plans in increasing productivity and achieving other objectives. A government survey of 514 wage-incentive plans in the United States reported in 1945 that, under such plans, production increases averaged 38.99 per cent; unit labor costs were decreased on the average by 11.58 per cent (Viteles, 1953, p. 27). Argyris reviews a large number of studies, all supporting the same point.

* * * * *

White-collar employees are predominantly controlled by remunerative means, but less so than blue-collar workers. Normative controls, though secondary, seem to play a more important role among white-collar employees, and commitment to the organization is higher.

* * * * *

Morse's meticulous study (1953) of white-collar employees supplies information on what 742 employees "like best about working in the company" studied, and thus casts some light on the relative importance of various rewards and sanctions. Morse's findings suggest the overriding importance of remunerative rewards for white-collar employees, and support our suggestion that the compliance of lower-ranking white-collar employees is predominantly remunerative.

A study of salesgirls by Lombard (1955, esp. pp. 124–30) points out many of the phenomena usually considered typical of manual workers. He reports, for instance, that the work group restricts "output," limits competition among the girls, and enforces other norms which are in direct contrast to those supported by management.

At the same time the manipulation of esteem and prestige symbols, which as a rule has a limited effect on blue-collar workers, seems to be more effective among white-collar employees (Homans, 1953). This point is illustrated in a study of salesgirls which emphasized the role of nonremunerative "symbolic" controls. Salesgirls who made mistakes in writing out sales slips had the slips returned to them, marked with a red rubber band, to be opened and corrected in the presence of the section manager and other salesgirls. These red bands "do not result in fines or punishments of any sort, and yet the clerks feel that to get one is a disgrace" (Donovan, 1929, p. 64). Similarly, "all sorts of honors are bestowed upon the capable and efficient. . . . To be ace—the best saleswoman in your department—is a compensation enough in itself" (*ibid.,* p. 192).

* * * * *

. . . There are several reasons why organizations that have economic goals function more effectively when they employ remuneration than when they employ coercion or normative power as their predominant means of control. Production is a rational activity, which requires systematic division of labor, power, and communication, as well as a high level of coordination. It therefore requires also a highly systematic and precise control of performance. This can be attained only when sanctions and rewards can be readily measured and allocated in close relation to performance. Remunerative sanctions and rewards are the only ones that can be so applied, because money differentials are far more precisely measurable than force, prestige, or any other power differentials.

Much production requires some initiative, interest, "care," responsibility, and similar attributes of the lower participants. Engineers and personnel people frequently describe the great damage caused when workers carry out orders to the letter but ignore the spirit of the directive, in order to "get even" with a supervisor. . . .

* * * * *

The use of normative power in organizations serving economic goals may lead to highly effective performance, but in general only for work of a particularly gratifying nature, such as research and artistic performance, or for limited periods of time, particularly in crises. Thus, for example, the work of transferring the defeated British army home from Dunkirk, under the pressure of the approaching German army, was conducted by a fleet of volunteers under normative command. Similar efforts on the industrial front take place in the early stages of war.

Normative compliance can be used to conduct "services" of a dramatic nature (in the sense that they have a direct relation to ultimate values), such as fighting fires, helping flood victims, searching for lost children, or collecting money for the March of Dimes and similar causes. But production engaged in by lower participants in typical blue-collar or white-collar industries lacks such qualities. Its relation to ultimate goals is indirect; it is slow to come to fruition; the worker is segregated from the fruits; and activities are highly routinized, spread over long periods of time, and evoke little public interest. Hence production as a rule cannot rely on the moral commitments of lower participants and the normative power of organizational representatives; for example, when a relatively "dramatic" service such as searching for lost children requires continued, routinized activity, the number of volunteers and the level of normative compliance tend to decline rapidly. This is one of the reasons such activities are often delegated to permanent utilitarian organizations, such as the fire department and "professional" fund raisers. In summary, effective production of commodities and services is carried out almost exclusively by utilitarian organizations.

5. ELECTRONICS INTERNATIONAL CORPORATION

Case Introduction

SYNOPSIS

The United States Department of Defense plans a radar system to track all objects orbiting in space. In an effort to win the developmental contract for this system Electronics International Corporation attempts to influence the military to incorporate EIC concepts into the specifications for the proposed system. The Army does incorporate some EIC ideas into the specifications, but other defense contractors also appear in relatively good positions in the upcoming formal competition. Under time pressure a cross-functional task force in EIC responds to the Army Request for Quotation. Costs are estimated, the technical proposal written, and the management proposal written. Top management pares the estimated costs and decides to submit a fixed-price bid.

WHY THIS CASE IS INCLUDED

This case describes program management in action. There is opportunity to observe the interaction between the *ad hoc* program management organization and the standard, functionally departmented, organization. The *ad hoc* organizational arrangement seems to challenge the conventional wisdoms about the structural relationships and the management processes of the usual staff-line organization. The normative models of how organizations should operate may be tested against the description of how an organization does operate. The psychology of human needs and perception may be used to understand and explain the various displays of cooperative and uncooperative, defensive and aggressive, behavior of executives. This typical case of government-business—buyer-seller—relationship reveals the dynamics of this growing form of enterprise activity with its rather unique marketing practices, contract features, etc.

204

DIAGNOSTIC AND PREDICTIVE QUESTIONS

The readings included with this case are marked (*). The author index at the end of this book locates the other readings.

1. How important is the Ortrack contract to EIC and the Weapons Systems Division? By sifting case facts identify the *economic* motivation for winning the sealed bid competition.

2. How does the *de facto* organization in WDS for preparing the response to the RFQ compare to what has come to be called the "matrix" organization?

Read: *Mee "Matrix Organization"; *Cleland, "Why Project Management?" *Cleland, "Understanding Project Authority."

3. What benefits does "project management" or the matrix organization form offer in comparison with the traditional functional organization? Does the actual performance of the proposal team in WSD give evidence of these purported benefits?

Read: The readings assigned in Question 2.

4. Explain the behavior of Travers as he attempts to bring together the proposal team. Why did he appeal to Young to get cooperation from Ives?

Read: The readings assigned in Question 2.

5. Explain the behavior of Ives in the following incidents: (*a*) refusing to commit his men to the proposal team before receiving the RFQ; (*b*) removing Ransom from the proposal team; (*c*) telling Svendon not to use Ted Forbes' name in the proposed ORTRACK organization.

Read: The readings assigned in Question 2.

6. Do the management practices implied in program management jibe with the "principles" espoused and/or debated in the management literature—especially the principle of unity of command?

Read: Fayol, *General and Industrial Management,* pp. 24–25, 68–70; Taylor, "Shop Management," pp. 92–96, 98–100.

7. How can the behavior of Magnus during the cost-cutting session on October 11 be explained? What makes a man like Magnus behave differently from his colleagues? Do the various theories of human needs aid in the diagnosis?

Read: Jennings, "Business Needs Mature Autocrats," *Odiorne, *How Managers Make Things Happen,* pp. 4–11, 37–38, 52–53. Barnard, *Organizations and Management,* pp. 48, 85–87, 89–90, 94. Gellerman, *Motivation and Productivity,* pp. 109–18. Maslow, *Motivation and Personality,* pp. 80–94. Hampton, Summer, Webber, *Organizational Behavior and the Practice of Management,* Chapter 10.

8. Do the psychological theories of perception help explain why Magnus' behavior left some of his colleagues "concerned"?

Read: Leavitt, *Managerial Psychology,* pp. 27–33; Krech and Crutchfield, *Theory and Problems of Social Psychology,* pp. 81–83, 87–89, 94–96, 98, 102–3. Those who wish additional insight into the answer to this question may consult in the library, *The Image,* by Kenneth E. Boulding, University of Michigan Press, 1956, pp. 11–14.

9. How do you explain the successive levels of "paddin " in the cost estimates made in the engineering departments?

Read: Argyris, "Human Problems with Budgets."

POLICY QUESTIONS

10. Would you make any changes in the structural arrangements in the Weapons System Division for responding to future RFQ's?

Read: The readings assigned in Questions 2 and 6.

11. Would you make any changes in the manner of cost estimation procedures in drawing up future proposals? (See Question 9 and its attached readings.)

12. Would you have bid fixed price on the ORTRACK contract?

Read: Appendix 2 attached to the case and review the case facts.

13. Would the logic of decision-making techniques for risk or conflict situations be of any help in deciding between a fixed-price and a CPIF bid? (Hint: set up a two by two matrix so that both EIC and their chief competitor, Universal Electrodynamics, have a choice of strategies—FP or CPIF. Push the logic of the techniques as far as case facts will allow.)

Read: O'Connell, "Decision-Making Rules and Computational Techniques."

14. If it were your decision as an EIC executive how would you react to the extension of the proposal formulation period? Would you use the extra time to do more on the proposal? If so, what would you do? If not, why not?

QUESTIONS FOR ORIGINAL STUDENT WORK IN ANALYSIS AND POLICY

15. While reflecting on the case facts, what additional theories from prior education give you insights as to "what is going on" in the Electronics International Corporation? As to what might be predicted to happen in the future?

16. Other than the policy questions asked by the authors, what pragmatic ways can think of to state the practical problems faced by executives in the case?

Case Text*

Electronics International Corporation is a defense contractor interested in developing an orbital tracking radar system (ORTRACK) for the Department of Defense. During the current year the Weapons Systems

---

* Copyright 1973, Avrel Mason, J. J. O'Connell, and Charles E. Summer.

Division of EIC is preparing for a Request for Quotation (RFQ) on the ORTRACK system.

Company headquarters is on the East Coast of the United States, with divisions in 12 states and six foreign countries. Annual sales are $850 million, of which $300 million are in defense sales. Line operation of the company reports to the president through three group executive vice presidents responsible for consumer products, industrial products, and defense products departments (see Exhibit 1). The defense products department has three major divisions. Each of these is headed by a vice president and general manager. This case is concerned with the Weapons Systems Division (WSD).

EXHIBIT 1
Organization of Electronics International Corporation

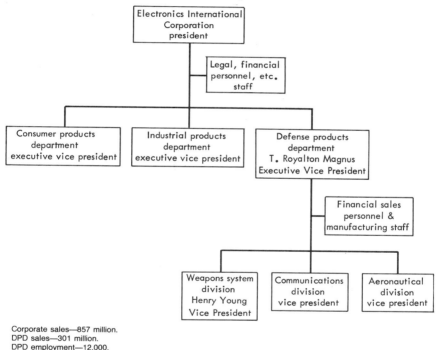

Corporate sales—857 million.
DPD sales—301 million.
DPD employment—12,000.

THE WSD ORGANIZATION

An organization chart of the WSD appears as Exhibit 2. Consisting of 2,800 people, located in Baltimore, the division is more of a "think and design" operation than it is a manufacturing one. Its output is used by the Defense Department when it subcontracts the production of weapons to still other manufacturers. For example, WSD has designed early warning radar equipment to detect potential enemy missiles or aircraft approaching the U.S.

EXHIBIT 2
Organization of Weapons System Division of EIC

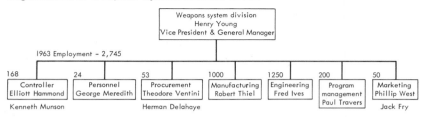

Numbers indicate size of organizational groups.

The *controller*'s function is responsible for financial accounting of all activities that go on within the WSD. He establishes rates to be quoted for various labor grades, determines overhead rates, allocates overhead to various operating departments, and establishes divisional financial plans and profit forecasts. He also has a group which assists program management in keeping track of the cost and schedule status of all WSD programs.

In the *manufacturing* organization at the time of this case, a number of medium-sized jobs were underway, but the outlook was poor for enough work to keep the 1,000-man force active over the next year.

The burden for divisional success falls on the *program management* and *engineering* departments. The chief engineer's position is looked upon as second only to that of the vice president-general manager. The engineering organization is the largest in the division.

The program management department can be thought of as a group of general contractors who are responsible for a project, and who get the work done by contracting it out to the engineering department and to such other corporate divisions and subcontractors as are needed to complete a total job. It had been found from a number of unpleasant experiences that it was undesirable for program management to report to the chief engineer. A year before this study, the group was separated from engineering to report to the general manager, in order to obtain more total management and less engineering-oriented perspective and evaluation of program status and problems. This was also appealing to the customer, who liked to think that his particular program was receiving attention directly from the general manager, and not through successive layers of supervision. Personnel comprising the program management group were generally senior men with broad interests and backgrounds, keen organizational sense, and a demonstrated capability to get things done through other people.

The *marketing* group had responsibility for actually bringing in the order, for customer contracts, and in general, handling all long-term forecasting and product planning. However, since engineering is the real product in most research and development work, marketing was virtually helpless without the detailed advice and support of both the engineering and program management departments. The marketing men tended to act as intelligence agents and door openers, operating between the customer and the engineers, who did virtually all the conceptual work and technical selling.

Exhibit 3 shows the organization of the engineering department of 1,251, including draftsmen, technicians, and model shop personnel. Seven hundred of these 1,200 are professional people, with college degrees.

ORGANIZATIONAL RELATIONSHIPS—BEFORE AND DURING A PROPOSAL

Exhibit 4 shows other parts of the Weapons System Division. This case is concerned with the interactions between the marketing, program management, and engineering departments. The *modus operandi* of completing a proposal is that a carefully chosen team of engineers is assigned to work with a market representative. The latter is supposed to know the customer, to set up meetings with him, and to gain entree to the technical and procurement personnel in the customer's organization. He is supposed to help influence all parts of the government that might affect the program.

The ORTRACK program involves many government agencies and all military services, either because they have an intelligence need for the information furnished by ORTRACK, or are going to use ORTRACK in event of a national emergency. Knowledge of existing satellite orbits, the unheralded arrival of new satellites, the disappearance of known satellites, changes in course of existing satellites, change in apparent size, changes in transmitting frequencies, and so forth, were all of vital importance from the standpoint of intelligence, deployment of ground and naval defenses, and civilian defense agencies.

Both the marketing and program management organizations (Exhibit 4) have common groups associated with strategic, range instrumentation, and tactical programs. Division of all products made by WSD into these three categories has proved to be an excellent way of focusing attention on the three different types of markets and also of coordinating the activities required between engineering, program management, and marketing in the quest for new business. It was generally agreed by those participating that since only senior personnel from each organization were assigned to large efforts, the problem of cooperation between departments was minimized. In some instances the supervisors of the various personnel working together on a program accused them of being more interested in the program than in the welfare of their own departments.

In writing proposals, the marketing department has nominal responsibility for the entire proposal effort. However, since the vast majority of the proposal is based on engineering, and the degree of engineering knowledge required is not usually available from the marketing representatives, the engineering department and program management groups are forced to shoulder the main burden of getting out the proposal, with only customer-oriented guidance, advice, and supervision from the marketing department.

EXHIBIT 3
Engineering Department Organization

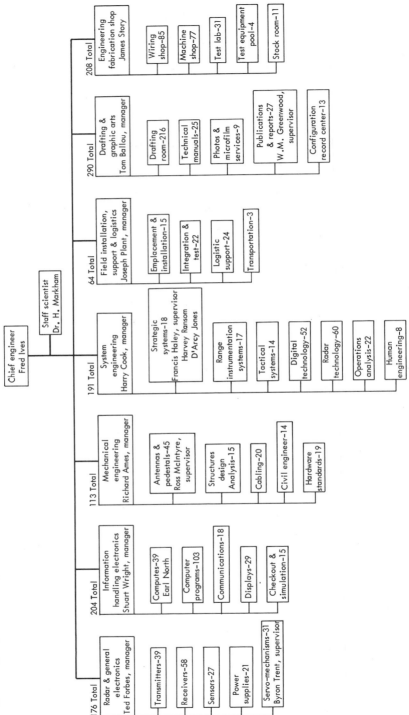

Note: Names given only for those concerned with ORTRACK Program. Numbers indicate number of personnel in each activity (1250 total).

EXHIBIT 4
Marketing and Program Management Organization of WSD

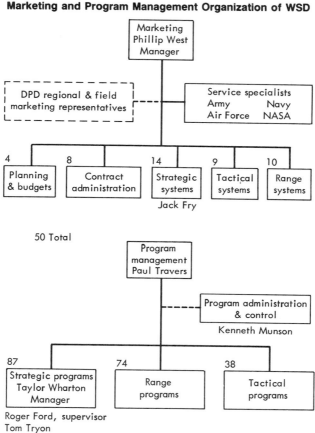

Over the years, WSD had evolved a concept that writing a proposal is a small program in itself. Indeed, for larger systems such as OR-TRACK, writing the proposal in a limited time becomes a major challenge. It is considered a job requiring the utmost in energy, technical knowledge, and organizational ability. Because a proposal requires inputs from virtually all activities, the programs are usually headed by a manager with broad capabilities, selected from the program management department. He pulls together a team which, in effect, is an organization whose sole function is to get out a winning proposal on time and within the funds allotted. To handle the many difficult organizational, procedural, and technical problems requires senior people with previous program management assigned to manage a proposal. The proposal manager is the project boss although nominally he works for the marketing department.

The proposal team is dissolved as soon as the proposal is submitted. The people assigned to carry out the design program itself are often those who helped in the proposal. This is expected to motivate people to do their best on the proposals. Both supervisory and working level groups in WSD feel that a job on a new program is desirable and that it offers opportunity to face new and creative challenges and allows opportunity for promotion.

The proposal team invariably runs out of time toward the end of the effort. Over the years it has been observed that it is almost impossible to avoid a frantic last minute rush, despite the most careful effort to schedule time for final reviews, revised editing, and so on.

Proposals are usually financed by allocation of WSD funds. Where other divisions of the corporation participate, an agreement is written allocating suitable parts of the program to them. In the event that the job is won, participating divisions win a *pro rata* share of the profit associated with their share in the program.

THE ORIGINS OF ORTRACK

WSD's radar systems had become more and more popular. EIC had achieved a national reputation for precision work in the tracking of guided missiles and satellites.

WSD had recognized several years before the eventual need for a system such as ORTRACK. In 1957, when the Russians first launched "Sputnik," the possibilities of placing in orbit satellites containing bombs which could be dropped upon command from the ground became evident. Harry Cook, present manager of systems engineering, wrote a now famous technical paper outlining the possibility of detection of satellites by a combination of high-power radars, communication, data processing links, and control centers, such that all space traffic could be detected by a number of sites placed at strategic locations around the world.

Cook approached the Air Force and the Army with this concept. Together with Jack Fry, of marketing, he made many visits to try to sell successively more refined concepts to military customers. As a result of their effort the military gathered their requirements together and focused them into a new system called ORTRACK, OR for "orbital," TRACK for "tracking." ORTRACK thus became the acronym for a system which would perform orbital tracking of *all* space objects. It would detect threats to the U.S. from changes in the orbital population.

WSD delivered to the Army an unsolicited proposal last fall, outlining a system of seven radar sensing stations.

WSD ALERTED TO EXPECT RFQ

In the spring of this year all indications from the Army were that a request for proposal would be issued to competing companies for a research program which would lead to prototype development of a sensing station data processing and control center. This phase would be followed after prototype testing by an extension of the contract for production and testing of the seven operating sites. In April, Fry sounded an alarm within WSD at a marketing staff meeting, stating that money had been approved for ORTRACK by the Department of Defense, and that it looked as though an RFQ would be forthcoming within a month or two.

Phillip West, head of marketing, personally discussed this with Cook, and decided that Fry was right. At Young's staff meeting the last week in April, West pointed out that WSD should immediately form a proposal team. It was apparent that much system analysis work remained to be done and that time was indeed running out. West got approval from the general manager, Henry Young, to treat this as the highest priority program within the division. He requested that a tentative proposal team be established and reported on at Young's next staff meeting. At that staff meeting, Fry reported that he could not get Paul Travers to name anyone from program management to manage the proposal effort. Travers replied that he recognized the importance of this program and that he had an excellent man named Roger Ford working in the strategic weapons group under Taylor Wharton. He said Ford would not be free for another month. Right now he was engaged in getting acceptance of late delivery by the customer on a piece of equipment which had been troublesome and on which the company was losing money. A penalty clause on delivery of this item made it imperative that the program not be disturbed until delivery was completed. Then Ford would be made available. Travers ended the meeting by indicating he wanted to see immediate action in formation of a proposal team. He asked Wharton to make an estimate of the cost of the proposal and report on this at Young's next staff meeting.

On May 15, at Young's staff meeting, Wharton gave a short presentation to Young's staff on an organization, a schedule, and a proposed budget for accomplishing the ORTRACK proposal. The budget was approximately $200,000 but could be less if a major subcontractor could be chosen to share the load of designing and developing the structural parts of the pedestal and antennas for the large radars required.

The controller, Elliot Hammond, questioned the wisdom of proceeding with the proposal effort at that time, in view of not having a definite indication as to when the RFQ would be issued by the Army. He pointed out the expensive gamble that was being taken by going ahead with detailed plans, without knowing fully what the RFQ would specify. The group called in Cook to express his feelings concerning what possible unforeseen requirements might be in store for them when the RFQ came in.

Cook stated that, based on contacts he and Fry had with government officials recently, there was every indication that the earlier unsolicited proposal was being used as a basis for the specification preparation. In all likelihood, the RFQ, when issued, would have their own words, specifications, and numbers in it. He stated that it was difficult to determine this accurately because the services "always clamp up tight" and are under strict instructions not to talk to prospective competitors, in order not to give one unfair advantage over the other.

Fry was called in and agreed completely with Cook that their years of doing their "homework" were paying off; that no other contractor had done nearly as much ORTRACK-oriented work as EIC; and that he was virtually certain that the specifications in the RFQ would be similar to what they had proposed earlier.

Young asked him about his certainty of dates on the RFQ, and Fry quoted Col. Bernhardt of Army Headquarters as saying that the Army "simply had to have it done and out by June, in order that competitive responses could be received, the evaluation of the competitors made, a winner chosen, and the program 'go-ahead' authorized by October of next year." Since Bernhardt was to become the officer in charge of OR-TRACK for the Army, it was agreed that Wharton should go ahead with the proposal program, bringing Ford on as soon as he could get free; that Fry would retain marketing responsibility for the job; and that Hammond was to set up a shop order that the proposal team could charge to, in the amount of $150,000. Young said the division could not afford $200,-000 for the proposal. Hammond objected to authorizing $150,000, stating that he felt a much more detailed estimate than the rough $200,000 that Wharton had prepared was desirable for an effort of this size. Before committing a full $150,000, Young requested permission to fund only $30,000, which would suffice until a more detailed cost estimate could be made. This was agreed to by all. The meeting was adjourned with the understanding that a detailed cost proposal would be available the next week.

RFQ DELAYED

At Young's May 31 staff meeting, Phillip West reported that Fry called him from Washington that morning, stating that there was going to be a delay in the RFQ. The Army internal review was taking longer than anticipated. Col. Bernhardt assured him that in all probability, the slippage would be only two weeks. But to be conservative, it might be wise to plan for up to a month. Travers reported that this was fortunate, as Wharton had reported to him that he was finding it difficult to man the team. Virtually all senior personnel were already engaged on important jobs, both within program management and within Ives' engineering department. He stated he got sympathy but no action in getting people assigned to the job. He approached Cook, manager of systems engineering, with a request that Francis Halsey personally supervise the systems engineering aspects of the proposal. Halsey had done a lot on the original unsolicited proposal. Cook said this would be impossible due to his existing commitments on other programs. He suggested Harvey Ransom for the job. Although not as experienced as Halsey, he seemed capable to represent systems engineering.

Since Ransom was available immediately, he was assigned to man the systems groups which would work under him. Ransom was known as a brilliant systems engineer with a great depth of knowledge in many technical disciplines, though somewhat mercurial in disposition. He had been known to walk off the job on one occasion; however, he had also been known to work 18-hour days for weeks on end, without being asked, if necessary in order to meet a goal in which he felt a strong personal interest. He was a key participant in the submission of the unsolicited proposal. He agreed to serve in this new role, though he suggested that he would rather spend his time on technical problems than management problems involved in organizing and running a high-pressure proposal team.

Travers said that due to lack of manpower he had not been able to get the detailed cost estimate that Hammond had asked for in the earlier meeting. However, he would have it by the next meeting and urged everyone, particularly Ives, to get good people freed up. He showed an organization chart of the proposal team to the staff. Everyone concurred on this but did not see how 50 senior engineers could be divorced from their present activities to spend two months required to turn out the proposal.

At his June 7 staff meeting, Young asked about progress on the RFQ. West had just heard from Fry. Fry had heard nothing about any further delay and said that he still expected the RFQ within two weeks. He stated that he knew that final copies of the specification were resting on the desk of the Director of Procurement, Lt. Col. Youngquest. He presumed that these were there for final review. Despite numerous attempts at contacts by Fry and Cook, as well as exploiting the full resources of the regional sales offices both at Washington and Army Headquarters, no new information could be brought to bear on either the nature of the specification or time at which the RFQ would be issued.

On June 15, West reported no new information on the proposal. He was getting skeptical that the RFQ would be out as soon as Col. Bernhardt had said. He said the delay was fortunate, because WSD still had not been able to organize effectively to do the proposal. Hammond said it was fortunate that they had not organized to do the proposal, or they would have already spent a good deal of the $150,000 originally estimated. Before WSD proceeded any further with any expenditures, they should get a firmer indication of when the RFQ would be out. He suggested curtailment of all activity.

Both West and Travers protested that all work done in the preproposal period gave them that much more chance to do a better job when the RFQ came out; they would have more homework done and would be able for once to avoid the desperate last minute climax usually associated with proposal efforts. Young agreed that effort should continue but at a low level. Travers pointed out that Wharton, despite continuing efforts over the past weeks, had been unable to get commitments for manning the proposal from Ives's engineering organization; that except for Ransom there was not a single commitment; that in general, Ives and his organization seemed to be taking the attitude that they would face up to the reality of manning the proposal team when, and if, the RFQ was issued; and that, all the cries of "wolf" had proven to be false alarms, and they were getting tired of it.

FURTHER DELAY

On June 15, Fry called from Washington saying he had heard that the RFQ would be delayed another month. The Department of Defense (Office of the Secretary for Research and Engineering) disagreed with the estimation of the orbital threat. There seemed to be dissension between the services and DOD as to what the satellite population would be in subsequent years. DOD also questioned the ability of the system to give usable information in view of possible course changes which could be made by sophisticated, self-maneuvering satellites. DOD also felt it would be cheaper and more effective to have a larger number of smaller stations equipped with lower-powered radars, deployed over a larger number of locations.

Cook said that if one looked at the economics of a large number of small stations compared to the cost of the seven large, high-power ones that WSD proposed, the odds were greatly in favor of the large stations. He pointed out that the Department of Defense was increasingly concerned over the cost of operating detection and warning sites. Concentrating the support services in several large stations represented a genuine economy, and air space orbital coverage would be about the same in either case.

With the interests in Washington strongly centered on cost effectiveness, it was agreed that this probably would be the eventual concept. Fry was ordered to keep an ear to the ground. Meanwhile, all detailed work on the preproposal effort came to a halt. Ransom was reassigned to a job in trouble, with the commitment to make himself immediately available to ORTRACK once the RFQ came in. By this time Ford became available from his previous job and was spending time studying the earlier unsolicited proposal, early marketing reports, and trying to get ready for the RFQ.

Fry, West, Ford, Wharton, and Travers all kept a close eye on what was going on with the RFQ at Army Headquarters. By this time they had briefed all personnel and all marketing activities, both within the Weapons System Division and elsewhere, to be on the alert for information on the RFQ. In particular, with regard to any intelligence which might bear upon the DOD objections to the system and any possible changes that might be forthcoming. Isolated reports were sent in from the field offices, which contributed essentially nothing to what was already known. It was concluded by Fry and West that they were closer to the situation than anyone and that they could count on little outside help in getting information.

Col. Bernhardt was embarrassed at the delay. Though he felt unable to discuss the issue, he did state that he felt he owed it to the various contractors not to keep them on the hook, for it was possible it would be another month before the RFQ was issued. He said there was still discussion going on in procurement circles, paralleling technical discussions, as to what type of contract should be issued.

Fry kept following progress by weekly contacts at Bernhardt's office. In early August, Bernhardt was called on a special assignment to the

West Coast, to be gone for three months. Fry was extremely concerned about this, as Bernhardt was the spark plug for the whole program. With him gone, Fry doubted if much action would take place until the requirement for budgeting next year's funds came up.

By this time ORTRACK was a dirty word at WSD. The word was used to denote something that was scheduled to happen and never quite did. Roger Ford stayed on the job but had no assistants. He spent his time refining his concepts of the proposal team and laying out schedules for the proposal based on various contingencies. He worked out detailed schedules in the event that a two-month, six-week, or one-month response time was given. He had discussions with the Communications Division of EIC's defense products department regarding their role in the proposal. He had a tentative agreement from their marketing manager that they would take responsibility for all communications aspects of the job, including handling any communications subcontractors who might be required.

Ford also approached a number of heavy mechanical construction firms to select a teammate for the large radar pedestal construction, which was too large to be made at WSD's electronics plant. He had established good rapport with Parker Mechanisms Company, the major manufacturer of servo-driven pedestals. They indicated an interest in teaming up with EIC, and a letter of understanding had been received stating that it was their desire to participate at their own cost in the proposal effort.

Ford discussed optimum proposal organizations with West, Fry, Wharton, Travers, Ives, Cook, Markham, Forbes, and Ames. After several rounds of refinement, an organization was evolved which was considered novel, but an improvement over the one Travers had presented at Young's May 31 meeting. Ford was unable to get any commitments for manning this organization except for himself and Ransom.

THE ORTRACK PROGRAM

August 28

Fry received a telegram from Col. Bernhardt's headquarters stating that three copies of the ORTRACK RFQ would be issued to each competitor on August 31. Fry alerted all management personnel involved in ORTRACK and told them he would go to Washington to pick up the three copies on August 31. Thus, he could review the RFQ over the weekend with Ransom and Ford so that on Monday, September 1, they would have completed an analysis of how the RFQ differed from their expectations.

August 31

Fry picked up the three copies from Lt. Col. Youngquist at 3 P.M. He delivered copies to Ransom and Ford that evening. All three spent the weekend studying the RFQ.

September 1

At 8:15 Monday morning, Ransom, Ford, and Fry reviewed their separate analyses of the RFQ. All had been distressed that a system consisting of a large number of small low-powered stations was specified. EIC's earlier analyses of the economics of the configuration were either wrong or failed to include some important considerations of DOD.

Ransom guessed that it would take 16 separate stations to get the required air space coverage, using radars with the size and power that the RFQ specified. This meant that the radar for ORTRACK would hardly resemble the giant 80-foot dish radars that WSD had been building for early warning applications and on which they had extensive prior technical, schedule, and cost knowledge. They had hoped to borrow heavily on this experience so that ORTRACK radar would be only a slightly modifed copy of a radar they had built earlier; and for which Parker Mechanisms had supplied the pedestal.

A second distressing fact was that a number of radars developed by other firms already existed which were potentially of the right size and power. The most formidable competitor of the five to whom RFQ's had been sent was Universal Electrodynamics, an industry giant which had long been working in the radar field. U.E. had won a competition, in which WSD participated, for developing a small high-frequency radar designed to exploit new technologies in signal processing and velocity resolution. Ransom stated that it appeared that the ORTRACK specification could be filled almost perfectly by that radar now completed and under test at Universal Electrodynamics.

Other requirements were similar to what had been specified in the early WSD proposal.

The RFQ called for submission of separate technical, management, and cost proposals on October 15, exactly 45 calendar days from the date of publication. Since Ford had developed his schedule for essentially a program of six weeks, he felt he had the working basis for planning the proposal. A page limitation allowed only 100 pages for the technical proposal and 75 for the management section. Detailed formats were provided for submission of cost data.

After lunch, a meeting was called in the general manager's office with all department heads, and others as required, to brief them on the content of the RFQ. Cook was stunned at the news of the small-radar requirement. He stated he would stake his professional reputation on the fact that the number of radars called for in the RFQ would cost 50 percent more than the large ones WSD had quoted earlier.

West felt that they must have missed something in their evaluation of what the customer wanted; that marketing would do its best to find out what had happened; but that meanwhile, the job must proceed, and everyone should start working.

Ives, who had remained on the fringes of previous ORTRACK planning, stated that on the basis of what he had heard that morning, he felt it would be wiser for WSD not to bid ORTRACK, since the radars represented over half of the cost of the system and since WSD was caught without an existing design of its own and would have to develop a new one, whereas Universal Electrodynamics Corporation already had a design paid for by another project. He felt WSD was virtually out of the running from a cost standpoint. Ives was overruled on this suggestion by virtually everyone present. ORTRACK was exactly the type of business that WSD had made its reputation in; it was the major procurement of the year; and no other large ones were in sight for some time. Although WSD was in an undesirable radar development position, WSD still was generally superior in the radar field to Universal Electrodynamics. In other areas WSD felt quite confident that it was superior to U.E. and might even have usable existing designs for displays, consoles, etc., that U.E. did not have. This would tend to offset their radar advantage. Travers pointed out that Parker Mechanisms had built smaller radars before; that they were already on the WSD team; and that they could be of great assistance to WSD as far as the mechanical aspects of the newer, smaller radars would be concerned.

The meeting continued until 5:30. It broke up with full agreement that WSD should proceed full speed ahead with the ORTRACK proposal. Ford was requested to pull together his "prop" team and have a full staff working by the end of the week, with the really key people assigned by the following day.

As Ransom left the meeting, he told Ford that he would not be able to start work on ORTRACK until the 5th, since he was leaving that night for Florida to brief an irate customer, General W. V. LeComte, on the performance to be expected from a small data display system that Ransom had conceived over a year ago and which was two months late on delivery schedule. He stated that it would be unheard of to cancel such a briefing, and that Ford should look to Cook to get things started.

Ford gave a copy of the RFQ to Bill Greenwood, who had been waiting all day to take it to a local printer to get 50 copies of the voluminous document made so that all personnel would have their own copy.

September 4

At 9 A.M. Ford called a kickoff meeting for all concerned with the ORTRACK job. This meeting included those whom he wanted assigned to the team, as well as most of the supervisors of the engineering department, whose people would, in one way or another, participate during the proposal effort, either as members of the proposal team or within the department working on preliminary design, costing, and scheduling of hardware items.

At the meeting, Fry pointed out the importance of this job to WSD. Ford outlined the job in detail, going through its early history, pointing out what had to be done and what the organizational concept was for getting it done, and asked for support from all concerned for what he knew would be a very busy six weeks. People left the meeting feeling generally good about the program and believing that somehow they would overcome the handicap resulting from the change in radar concept. They felt that with Ford running it, a good job would probably get done.

September 7

Travers asked Ford how the proposal was going. Ford showed him the schedule shown in Exhibit 5. He pointed out that by this date the team was to have been selected and all assignments made. However, because of Ransom's absence, and because a number of people on whom he had depended could not break free from other jobs, the proposal was only half-manned at the time. He stated he was spending all his time trying to get people assigned to the job. The 50 copies of the RFQ were delivered on the 6th and were waiting for people to come and use them.

Travers was greatly concerned at the unmanned state of the proposal organization. He called Young, requesting his urgent assistance in getting support for ORTRACK. Young called Ives, mentioning the names of some people whom Ford had told him were needed immediately on this job. Ives knew the existing assignments of several of these people and pointed out to Young that their present assignments had been planned months back; that it simply was not reasonable to expect them to drop their efforts in midstream. He said that in some cases it would take several days to phase in a substitute and that a hurried phase-in of replacement engineers would cause delays and increase the costs of existing programs. He said that Ransom had reported back from his briefing of General LeComte, that the General was furious at WSD's delay in delivering his display system as promised and had said that if WSD couldn't demonstrate a working system within the next two weeks, he would institute cancellation proceedings.

In order to preserve WSD's reputation, Ives stated that it was necessary for Ransom to stay on his present job of investigating incompatibilities between key elements of the system. He felt that two weeks was not going to see the end of the problems; that General LeComte could be convinced to stick with them. Ives stated that although Ransom should be available in from three to four weeks, this was so late into the ORTRACK effort that it would be undesirable to wait for him, and he suggested D'Arcy Jones as a substitute.

Young told Ives to get in touch with Ford and to please do whatever he could to support Ford, who had a very difficult job to do. It appeared he was getting a slow start despite energetic effort. Ives agreed to do everything he could and called Ford about Jones. Ford asked Jones to study the system over the weekend so that on Monday the 10th, he would be able to take over the systems engineering team.

Ford's problems on the technical side of the proposal were somewhat offset by good news on the management team's progress. He had been fortunate in getting Lars Svendon, another of Taylor Wharton's program management men, assigned to head the management part of the proposal. Svendon had written many management proposals, and this one appeared to be fairly straightforward. He had already sat down with those members who had been assigned to the team and outlined what

EXHIBIT 5

Schedule for ORTRACK Proposal Established August 15 by Roger Ford

		SEPTEMBER	OCTOBER
CALENDAR DATE		1 2 3 4 5 6 7 8 9 10 11 12 13 14 15 16 17 18 19 20 21 22 23 24 25 26 27 28 29 30	1 2 3 4 5 6 7 8 9 10 11 12 13 14 15
DAYS AFTER RFQ RECEIPT		1 2 3 4 5 6 7 8 9 10 11 12 13 14 15 16 17 18 19 20 21 22 23 24 25 26 27 28 29 30 31 32 33 34 35 36 37 38 39 40 41 42 43 44 45	

MANAGEMENT PROPOSAL
- RFQ REPRODUCED AND DISTRIBUTED — S
- KICK OFF MEETING — A
- PROPOSAL TEAM SELECTED — T
- ORGANIZATION CHART COMPLETE — U — (ALL ASSIGNMENTS TO TEAM MADE)
- SHOP ORDER STRUCTURE ESTABLISHED — R,S — (INDIVIDUALS NAMED FOR KEY POSITIONS – RESPONSIBILITY AND AUTHORITY ESTABLISHED)
- MGMT, INFO., & CONTROL SECTION COMPLETE — D,U — S
- FACILITY INVENTORY SECTION COMPLETE — A,N — A
- EXPERIENCE BACKGROUND SECTION COMPLETE — Y,D — T,S
- INDIVIDUAL RESUMES COMPLETE — A — U,U
- EDITING AND REWRITE — Y — R,N
- CRITICAL REVIEW — D,D
- TOP MANAGEMENT REVIEW — A,A
- PRINTING — Y,Y

TECHNICAL PROPOSAL
- RFQ REPRODUCED AND DISTRIBUTED
- KICK OFF MEETING
- PROPOSAL TEAM SELECTED — (ALL ASSIGNMENTS TO TEAM MADE)
- SYSTEM BLOCK DIAGRAM COMPLETE — (ROUGH SUBSYSTEM SPECIFICATIONS AVAILABLE)
- FINAL SUBSYSTEM SPECS AVAILABLE
- RECEIPT OF TECHNICAL DRAFTS
- EDITING AND REWRITE
- CRITICAL REVIEW
- TOP MANAGEMENT REVIEW
- PRINTING

COST PROPOSAL
- COST ESTIMATE REQUESTS SENT TO:
  - MFG. AND ENG. DEPARTMENTS
  - SUBCONTRACTORS & VENDORS
- ALL ESTIMATES RECEIVED
- PROJECT MANAGEMENT REVIEW
- V.P. COST REVIEW
- EXEC. V.P. REVIEW
- PRINTING

DELIVERY OF TOTAL PROPOSAL

he expected from each for the management proposal. He had reviewed the schedule shown in Exhibit 5 that Ford had prepared earlier, and concurred with it. He had Kenneth Munson get together all of the major proposals that had been written in the past two years, with a view toward selecting techniques and/or excerpts from the best features of each. He wanted particularly to convey to the military the unique management control concept that had evolved at WSD. This concept represented an integration of financial, cost, and schedule reporting with the majority of operations being performed automatically by computers and tabulating machines. Svendon had been instrumental in getting this system accepted at WSD and had achieved recognition in the American Management Society for his contributions to this field. He was able to report to Ford that he was on schedule with the management team and foresaw no difficulties, provided the inputs which depended on the technical proposal did not slip.

September 11

Ford reported to Travers, West, and Young that he had formed the technical part of the total team and that work was underway. The total proposal team, with various specialized subteams, is shown in Exhibit 6. Ford felt that although this was not the caliber group he had hoped for, it still represented a talented group that could do a good job.

September 12

Ford asked D'Arcy Jones if the systems block diagram would be completed on schedule on the 14th.

The systems block diagram is a schematic method of representing all the major interactions between the major components of any system. For a complex system such as ORTRACK, it takes a sheet of paper about 3 x 4 feet filled solidly with 2-inch-square blocks, each labeled for a different component in the system. All of the signal or information flow going out of, and coming into, each block is noted along appropriately coded lines drawn between blocks. It resembles a giant electrical wiring diagram for a radio. This diagram having established the performance requirements for each subteam, a specification can be written for the contents of the activity chassis to whole rows of cabinets full of electronic gear.

These specifications are then checked so that the input and output to each and every block is compatible with the output and input of related blocks throughout the whole diagram. Once the block diagram and equipment specifications have been written and checked, the major effort is concerned with further refinements.

Jones replied that due to the late start, he would be unable to complete the diagram by the 14th. He wasn't even sure he could get it out by the 18th. Ford, upon investigation, found that Jones was right, and that the whole effort was going to be slowed up by the late availability of the block

EXHIBIT 6
The "ORTRACK" Proposal Team

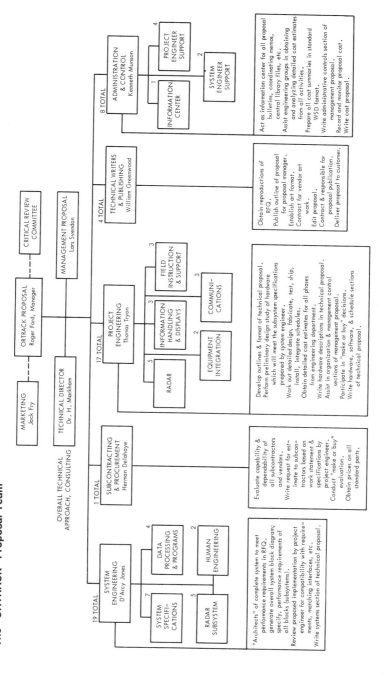

diagram. He called Cook to urge him to assist Jones in any way possible. A real bottleneck was apparent in this area. Cook authorized Jones' entire group to work over the weekend. Despite that extra time, he doubted that the block diagram would be ready by the 18th.

Ford asked Svendon whether the organization chart to be shown in the management proposal would be completed on schedule. Svendon pointed out that he had until Saturday, according to the schedule. However, he was having a difficult time getting permission from various permanent department heads to show on the ORTRACK chart their personnel whom he considered essential to ORTRACK. Previously, he and Ford had decided it would be wise to show the same people in the implementation organization chart who worked on the proposal. Many additions would be required. It was felt that the customer would react favorably to the idea of having the people who had demonstrated their knowledgeability of ORTRACK in writing the proposal assigned to the job when it was won.

Some of the line managers objected strenuously to committing their people, stating that ORTRACK was trying to gobble up the best men in every area and that the division could not afford this. For instance, Svendon wanted to show Ted Forbes as full-time manager of ORTRACK radar development; similarly Daniel Troast as full-time manager of communications, and Ross MacIntyre as manager of antennas and pedestals. Ives pointed out that with these key men spending full time on ORTRACK, their unique talents would be lost to the rest of the developments in their functional areas. The job could be done by lower-level supervision; they would have the full benefits of working under senior personnel, and this approach would not penalize all the other programs which were depending on the same level of talent.

September 17

Tom Tryon told Ford that the situation was becoming critical with regards to getting detailed design and cost estimates done on time. These depended on the availability of specifications. The system block diagram would only be in rough form by the 18th, and the specifications were barely started. Tryon and Kenneth Munson joined in saying that they had already allowed systems engineering all the time they could; that because of this, less than two weeks had been allowed for sending out RFQ's to vendors and subcontractors and for getting quotes back. This was faster than the fastest they had ever succeeded in doing this before. Tryon pointed out that in lieu of having a system block diagram, they had been in close contact with Parker Mechanisms Company and the Communications Division of DPD, as well as with Ives's functional department, but by now all preliminary groundwork and estimating that could be done had been done. Further, that work was useless until usable specifications were published that could be the basis of cost estimates from the various vendors, subcontractors, and so on.

September 20

Herman Delahaye received a telegram from Parker Mechanisms saying they had not received their RFQ yet, and that because of press of other work, they would have to take their people off the ORTRACK proposal until the RFQ arrived; that it would take them two weeks from receipt of RFQ (with specifications) to deliver firm cost estimates. They requested guidance as to whether the estimates would be expected on a CPFF, CPIF, or fixed-price basis.[1] The Army RFQ left it open to the bidders as to what contract type was proposed. Parker said they would prefer to quote CPIF, since the new radar, although similar to one they had developed before, nevertheless had some different features, so they felt it unwise to quote on a fixed-price basis.

Svendon told Ford that he had completed the organization chart, but he did not have full approval of all the names. He was worried about Ted Forbes, his proposed radar manager. He and Ford decided not to try further to obtain Ives' approval on this, since he was almost bound to say no. They felt that the best use of Forbes for the welfare of WSD was in this role, and left it for higher-level management to change, should they see fit, during the final review period. Svendon had completed a tentative shop order structure for all the hardware, by working with the project engineering people under Tryon and in Munson's group. This was done on the basis of a rough system block diagram available on the 18th.

September 21

• The system block diagram was published with specifications attached. The project organization under Tryon pounced on these, incorporated them into cost estimate requests that had already been written but were awaiting the specification to be referenced in the request.

Ford called a meeting with Young, West, Fry, Ives, Hammond, and Jones to discuss how to bid, CPIF or fixed price. Ford outlined the background WSD had in building roughly similar equipments under CPFF contracts. All but one of nine contracts in the last three years had overrun by an average of 23 percent.

Ives protested, saying that WSD was much more mature now, and would not overrun in jobs such as ORTRACK. He felt that WSD should bid CPIF to demonstrate its sincerity in meeting a target price.

West rejoined that WSD "hadn't a Chinaman's chance in hell" of winning ORTRACK on a CPIF basis. He said the customer, based on WSD'S past performance, could only conclude that WSD would overrun again and that the thought of losing 20 percent of their profit was not going to make WSD meet its cost target. West stated that the only price the customer would believe was a fixed price. This would give WSD an advantage over other competitors who also usually overran.

Ives claimed that other competitors, particularly U.E., had overrun contracts much more than WSD did and that the customer would believe

---

[1] See Appendix 2 for an explanation of the types of government contracts.

a WSD CPIF price much more than the other's CPFF or CPIF prices. He said to quote fixed price would require the addition of such large contingencies that WSD would price itself out of the competition.

Young asked, "Why are we so unsure of ourselves that we have to add large contingencies to our price?" He pointed out that WSD had built ORTRACK type equipment for many years and that if WSD could not price it accurately by now, "we'd better give up." There was a reluctant agreement that the job should be bid fixed price. Ford asked Munson to notify Parker.

September 24

By working through Saturday and Sunday, the 22nd and 23rd, Tryon's and Munson's team were able to get the cost estimate requests out to both internal and external groups.

Ford was delighted that all of the cost estimate requests had been finished over the weekend. He called Munson's boss Elliot Hammond to commend Munson for his energy and diligence. He also commended Tryon's people in a brief meeting which was designed to bring everyone up to date. At the meeting, Fry brought in some new intelligence. He had been talking with some officers from the Air Force Electronic Command. They pointed out that they had been having a good deal of trouble with natural electromagnetic radiation (aurora borealis or Northern Lights) in their northern sites, which tended to blind the radar system so that it could not see target missiles. They had sponsored a research program on means of combating this problem, which had shown that a much higher-frequency radar gave over 100 times better penetration through the electromagnetic radiation than their normal operating frequency. For future early warning work, they were going to specify higher-frequency radars.

Jones stated that this could explain the change from low- to high-frequency radars in the RFQ. He pointed out that in the original WSD proposal, the seven site locations which had been selected had been placed in such a manner that they never directly faced northward into the electromagnetic radiation zones. Accordingly, this problem was avoided in the system as proposed. With 16 stations of a shorter range, the stations had to be dispersed over a larger area and a number of the 16 were going to be forced to work against the electromagnetic environment. This being the case, it would not make sense to have both small, high-frequency and large, low-frequency radars in the same system. The smaller, high-frequency radar, utilizing techniques that had become known since the original proposal had been submitted would have better ranges than they had earlier imagined.

It was pointed out that at the higher frequency, a smaller antenna dish is desirable in order not to focus the beam too narrowly. Jones said the antenna dish size specified for the higher operating frequency resulted in a narrower radar beam than that of the large WSD radars that had been built, and that this could be the reason for the higher dynamic requirements in pedestal servo performance for the smaller radar, since the smaller beams must be moved around faster through space to cover the same volume of air as a wider beam. No one disagreed with Jones on this hypothesis.

Svendon reported that the management team was on schedule. He had completed the facility inventory and had collected résumés of people on previous teams to name final members of his organization. He felt they had done a beautiful job on the section on management information and control system. His main problem was that too much had been written to fit within the 75-page limit specified by the Army.

Ford asked Jones how he was making out with the technical team's proposal, which was limited to 100 pages. Jones said that there was a great deal of analytical background that had to go into the proposal. The systems engineering section alone would need approximately 45 pages out of the 100 to define the systems block diagram. Tryon said that he had been counting on systems not taking more than 25 pages; that it would take him at least 80 pages to describe the hardware, schedule considerations, test programs, government-furnished equipment requirements, and so on. Based on draft material he had seen, it might well total 100 pages, and he would have to edit it heavily.

September 26

At Greenwood's suggestion, Ford published a bulletin showing the exact page count allotted to every section of both the management and technical proposals. Systems engineering ended up with 35 of the 100 pages in the technical proposal. Svendon was horrified to find that the management information and control system section, of which he had been so proud, had only been allowed 10 pages. He protested that this was the real "meat" of the management prop and that at least 25 pages should be allotted to it. He reviewed with Ford the contribution of each paragraph and figure, using rough drafts. Ford agreed it was a beautiful treatment but that since WSD was bidding fixed price, "the government won't really care how we manage it, since it is our own money we are losing if we manage it poorly." Svendon disagreed, saying that the government was very concerned about management because poor management resulted in delays which in turn caused upsets in their own plans, causing additional expense. Ford overruled him, said it had to be 10 pages and patiently pointed out why he felt that way. Ford made a mental note to check on page content at the end of the week, to see how people were doing against the new targets.

Travers had succeeded in lining up a critical review team consisting of eight senior program management and engineering personnel, including two from the Communications Division. They were to receive copies of the draft material when it was submitted October 2, and were to have their criticisms back to Ford by October 5.

Young, WSD general manager, received a phone call from the president and general manager of Parker Mechanisms, Baxter Thorndyke. He protested the requirement to bid fixed price on the pedestal and antenna. He said that the dynamic servo requirements appeared too risky to them to bid fixed price; that in order to protect themselves against loss if they bid fixed price, they would have to add a large contingency to their estimate. Young told him that he expected the same professional performance from Parker Mechanisms that he expected from his own people; that WSD was going to bid fixed price without large contingencies; that if they submitted prices to the customer inflated with contingencies, they didn't stand much chance of winning the job. Young stated that his own engineers had reviewed the servo requirement and that although rigorous, they were within the state of existing technical art and shouldn't cause much uncertainty.

Thorndyke said that they had felt at first glance that they could meet the servo requirements, but that the dynamic stresses put on the antenna by high-performance servos had resulted in a requirement for much heavier antenna construction than was previously foreseen. This heavy construction in turn, made more of a load for the servos to move, so that the servo problem became increasingly harder. He said that no one had ever built such a fast response servo system for a radar set of similar size. Young asked him to do his best on price, saying that it was absolutely essential that WSD bid fixed price and that Parker bid fixed price also. Thorndyke agreed.

September 28

Tryon reported to Ford that he was getting static from everybody who received an internal ORTRACK RFQ, particularly from Ives' people who claimed that the specifications were not detailed enough for the basis of a fixed-price bid. It was true the specifications left many questions unanswered, and amendments to the specifications were being made. Tryon reported that the engineering department groups performing the detailed estimates were doing well in the data processing and display areas, but that they were floundering in the radar area, because the radars were unlike any that WSD had built before. The command and control, data processing, and display equipment was more conventional.

Tryon estimated that they would have all costs back from the vendors, the engineering department, and the Communications Division by October 5. Both Tryon and Ford realized the schedule implications of this, since estimates had to be negotiated with their originators and successive management reviews conducted prior to proposal delivery. Ford, Tryon, and Munson visited key areas in Ives' activity to determine the status of estimations, and were distressed at the lack of progress. Ives said that he, too, was disappointed; that the men were not used to bidding fixed price and were afraid of making estimating errors that could cost the company. He had trained his technical people to be conservative in their planning and this conservatism would show up in the size of their estimate.

Tryon proposed that the engineering team establish target prices for each component, which Ives' people could in turn use as a guide for detailed estimating. Tryon felt that the team had experience enough to estimate the true price for all hardware and software. If a reasonable target price for each component were placed in front of the engineers, the estimating process would be speeded up. Ives objected, saying that the engineers had to come up with prices on their own, otherwise they could not be held responsible for the work. He reminded Tryon and Ford that this particular estimating authority-responsibility controversy had gone on for years; that time-honored methods had worked out best.

Since this was an established WSD practice, Ford and Tryon agreed to leave Ives' people alone. They reemphasized the urgency of getting the estimates in by October 5. This was already five days behind their original schedule with only 10 days remaining for all the final tasks required. Ives replied he could not be expected to make up the time that the proposal team had lost by late issuance of the component specifications.

Ford reviewed the plans for work over the weekend. The entire proposal team would be working through Saturday and Sunday, the 29th and 30th. By this time most of the team effort was associated with the actual proposal writing. It appeared that the October 2 deadline would be met. An increasing irritability of all team members was evident. However, many of them had been through this experience before and, as Ford said, "it was an expected phenomenon, and everyone discounted the other fellow's sensitivity to criticism."

October 2

All draft material for management and technical teams was submitted as scheduled. However, it became evident that everyone had exceeded his allotted pages. The technical proposal was 140 pages; the management proposal 95. Ford found considerable duplication and excessive treatment variation in writing style. The critical review team asked for eight copies of the draft. Ford was reluctant to have them spend any time on what was so obviously in need of major surgery. However, recognizing the need to receive CRT comments in time for their incorporation with other rewrites, he authorized Greenwood to make the copies. Greenwood rushed the drafts to an outside printer for reproduction on a high-speed machine not available in WSD. Consternation arose when it was realized that Greenwood had the sole master copy and that until he got back from the printer, little work could be accomplished.

October 3

Draft copies were given to the critical review team and extra copies distributed among team personnel. In a staff meeting Ford chastised all concerned for their excess verbosity. He stated that a lot of thought had gone into establishing the allocation of pages and he wanted the allocation complied with, without further discussion. It was absolutely essential that the draft material be cut before the 5th. He expected those concerned to work as many hours as required to meet this deadline.

Thorndyke, president of Parker Mechanisms, called Young and said that after a sincere effort at estimating the radar pedestal and antenna on a fixed-price basis per Young's request, they simply could not do this without what appeared to be an unreasonable padding of 40 percent of engineering costs and 10 percent material cost. Thorndyke pointed out that CPIF pricing could apply only for the first prototype model. They would later be glad to quote fixed price on the 16 production units. Young asked them to quote both ways, so that WSD would have the last minute option of deciding which bid to use. Thorndyke agreed to this. They expected to be able to submit the two estimates by October 5.

When told of this call, Tryon, Munson, and Ford asked Ives to perform a quick one-day investigation of the risks involved in the equipment that Parker was bidding. Ives' servomechanisms section had done some excellent work and probably had more total servo experience than the people at Parker. Tryon felt that the opinion of Ives' group, particularly that of Bryon Trent, should be the basis of WSD's decision as to whether to use Parker's fixed price or the CPIF quote. Ives alerted Trent to the problem and proceeded immediately with three of his people to dig into it.

October 5

By Friday afternoon, Munson had received the detailed equipment estimates from Ives' engineering groups. He also had a Communications Division estimate and was promised that the Parker quote, delayed one day, would be telegraphed in on Saturday morning, the 6th. The quote from the Communications Division surprised everyone by appearing quite reasonable. However, the engineering department quotes appeared astronomical. It was apparent that fear of fixed-price contracting had resulted in considerable padding of the estimates. Whether it had been done consciously or unconsciously, Ford did not know, but he determined to find out. He made an appointment to meet with Ives on Saturday morning. Until late Friday night, Ford, Tryon, Munson, and their key hardware people worked on their own estimate of what the items to be developed by Ives' department should cost. Ford was sorry this had not been done before and that he had not insisted on establishing component cost targets for Ives' personnel.

By researching costs from other proposals, from their own records, and with considerable intuition, they arrived at what they thought was a reasonable figure for Ives' work. Their figure was 35 percent lower than the estimates of Ives' group. They agreed to put pressure on Ives to rework his estimate.

October 6

Ford, Tryon, and Munson met with Ives, Forbes, Wright, and Ames. The latter came armed with stacks of estimate notes and appeared to have been well briefed beforehand to defend the estimates. After an hour of comments as to the validity of each other's estimates, it became apparent to Ford that successive layers of supervision had reviewed the equipment estimates within Ives' department. Each level of reviewers, knowing that they would be responsible for performing the work, protected themselves against the unfamiliar fixed-price risks by padding estimates. The designers working at the subassembly level had applied a 10 percent contingency to their work. The first layer of supervision, in gathering subassembly quotes into a component quote had added another contingency, "just in case."

At Ives' staff review level, Forbes and Wright admitted that due to the uncertainty of the radar area, which embraced both Forbes' and Ames' organizations, they had added a 5 percent contingency prior to submitting the data to Ives, whose approval was required before sending it to Munson. Ford suggested they spot check the estimates from other areas for the same phenomenon. Ives protested, but finally went through Ames' notes in front of the group. In Ames' organization, too, contingencies had been added at each level of review. Ives himself, ascertaining that "cushions" had been added, decided not to add any of his own.

After this detailed look, it became apparent even to Ives, that although they might well have protected themselves by this type of estimating, they would lose the job from too high a bid. He agreed to go back and meet with his people Monday morning, to eliminate all "fat" from the estimate. He in turn requested that Tryon and Munson specify more clearly the documentation, field installation and test requirements. He had been told that each equipment designer had put in an allowance for configuration control, microfilm reproduction, and handbook rough draft writing, but that the specification invoked on the drafting and graphic arts group also requested costs for these items.

Ives also said the specifications were not clear regarding cabling responsibility and that each engineer had put in an allownace for this as well as Ames's cabling group, which had been requested to quote the cabling required for the entire system. Ives felt that more care should have been taken earlier in clarifying and eliminating duplication from the specifications. He requested this be done by Ford Monday morning, so that with one reestimating cycle, they could eliminate the duplication and the "fat" at the same time.

Ives stated that it would be impossible to call all his people to work for the remainder of the weekend. Ford had not been home before midnight for the past two and one-half weeks and decided to take off Sunday. He made sure however, that the rewrite of the technical and management proposal texts proceeded over the weekend. He established a new date of the 9th to have a final draft written for top management's review. He pointed out to all concerned that this was the date the proposals were scheduled to go to the printers.

October 8–9

·A check early in the morning did uncover some areas of overlap in the RFQ's that had been sent from the team to Ives' organization. Ives had been right about the field installation and tests. The field installation group had quoted on manning the entire site integration test phase, including site management. This duplicated design and development work that had been requested from Ives' group. This information was passed on to Ives, who was now heavily involved in expediting the recosting.

In the morning mail was a letter from Parker Mechanisms, furnishing quotes as agreed. They had neglected to telegraph their quote on the 6th as promised. Ford called Trent to see what conclusion he had reached with regard to the risk inherent in quoting the radar pedestal fixed price. Trent stated it looked like a 50–50 proposition; there was indeed some risk involved. However, rule-of-thumb performance criteria led him to believe that he could design a system meeting requirements. He stated that it should be possible to install pressure unloading valves in the hydraulic drives. This feature would decrease stresses on the antenna structure, which would permit a lighter structure, minimizing the servo, power, and response requirements that had bothered Parker.

Trent said he did not feel he should be asked to make a management decision on how Parker should bid. He would be willing to develop such a servomechanism himself and deliver it to Parker. Ford pressed Forbes, Trent's boss, for a management recommendation. Forbes felt uncomfortable about having to make a quick decision and stated that the matter really required more investigation before an intelligent decision could be made.

Time was running out, and Ford realized that if a decision were going to be made, he would have to make it personally, at the risk of criticism from the controller. Hammond would take a dim view of WSD's bidding fixed price on something that their own subcontractor only dared bid CPIF.

The afternoon and evening were spent in frantic snatches of reviewing the rewritten pieces of the proposal, and the cost estimates (now coming back considerably lower from Ives' group). By midnight, October 9th, the complete cost estimate was totaled and put into standard WSD format. The assumptions included manufacturing prototype radar in the model shop and manufacturing the 16 production models in the factory. The labor rates and overhead rates used, obtained from Hammond's office, were standard rates updated quarterly.

The Communications Division quotation was left untouched, and the Parker cost was shown at the CPIF value. Midnight also saw a completion of the final draft of the proposal which had incorporated comments of the Critical Review Board delivered on October 8th. Ford and his staff went home exhausted but with a feeling of genuine accomplishment.

October 10

Henry Young dropped into Ford's office asking when he would be able to review the proposal cost. Ford set up a meeting for 1 o'clock and requested that Young arrange with T. Royalton Magnus for a top executive review on the 11th.

In midmorning, H. Markham, the proposal technical director, who had contributed very little on the job to date, stopped in Ford's office. Markham said he had been working for the past week and a half on a new idea which should save around $2 million on each radar set. Ford called in Cook, Forbes, and Wright to hear Markham. Markham had a brilliant concept. His idea was to take the raw radar return signal from the target and to digitize it as soon as received; form the data into standard digital computer language; utilize a standard commercial type digital computer to do all the data processing. Digital-to-analogue converters in the pedestal would permit the digital computer to command the pedestal directly from the computer output for aiming at a target. This would save 12 expensive cabinets full of electronic gear on each set and would eliminate complex and risky electronic circuits in the system. The idea seemed so simple that it was remarkable that no one had thought of it before.

Forbes and Wright were enthusiastic and wanted to revise their cost estimate. Tryon asked how they could do this when no block diagram of the new system was in existence nor was a specification available. Forbes and Wright said they did not need the diagram or specification; they felt they had enough experience and knowledge of the type of equipment that would be involved to come up with good quotes without detailed estimates from their own lower levels. Ford reluctantly said that it was too late, that within half an hour he had to brief the general manager on the costs and get his approval, that one day later he was going to have to brief the executive vice president. This did not allow enough time to check out the scheme thoroughly.

Markham was incensed at this decision, saying that he had worked very hard on this concept. Ford pointed out that the Army specifically called for signal processing equipment which would be thrown out under the "Markham" concept. He felt that with adequate time the idea could be "sold" to the Army, but they had no time left. They would just have to keep it as an "ace" up their sleeve for the future. Ford secretly doubted that $2 million per set could be saved, although he felt it probably would save at least $1 million.

At 5 P.M. Ford met with Young and presented the figures, (Column 2, Table 1). Young inquired in detail as to how the estimate had been formed, what the history of the numbers were, and what risks were involved. Hammond protested (as Ford had expected) the idea of using the Parker CPIF figure in the WSD fixed-price bid. He said that Parker was more expert in the radar pedestal field than WSD, and that if they felt that a 40 percent contingency might be required to bid fixed price, "we'd better pay attention and not gamble." This whole subject was reviewed at length. Young finally agreed to keep the estimate the way it had been proposed. He pointed out that the risks associated with the Parker CPIF bid tended to be offset by the potential savings of incorporating Markham's concept, should it be permitted later by the customer.

Hammond reviewed all the markups and agreed that they were satisfactory. For the first time in anyone's knowledge, a proposal passed the vice president's review with no changes. They were scheduled to meet in Magnus' office at 1 P.M. on the 11th.

October 11

Ford found that the day before had been spent in improving the figures and artwork for both the management and technical proposals and

TABLE 1
Engineering Division Proposition Sheet   Date:

Equipment: 1 Prototype Radar Comm. Links   Proposition No:
ORTRACK System — 16 Delivery Radar 4 Display Centers
Customer: U.S. Army   Sheet *1* of *2*

All Figures in $1,000's	Column 1 Original Submission	Column 2 After Project Management Review	Column 3 After Exec. V.P. Review
Engineering — Overhead Applied *105*%			
Electrical	43,638	38,838	36,437
Mechanical	26,443	24,327	22,938
Other	1,231	1,231	1,169
Total	71,312	64,396	60,544
Support Labor — Overhead Applied *105*%			
Technician	382	382	363
Drafting	3,138	3,538	3,152
Other	1,481	1,480	1,406
Total	5,001	5,400	4,921
Model Shop — Overhead Applied *105*% MHX Applied *4.0*%			
Purchased Material	9,561	9,616	9,016
Labor	1,978	1,988	1,708
Spec. T&T	78	83	83
Total	11,617	11,687	10,807
Manufacturing (Production) — Overhead Applied *120*% MHX Applied *4.0*%			
Purchased Material	98,656	94,576	80,727
Labor	22,940	21,640	15,444
Spec. T&T	649	649	649
Mfg. Engineering	1,032	1,232	974
Total	123,277	118,097	97,794
Subcontractors — MHX Applied *4.0*%			MHX Eliminated
Parker Mechanisms	38,780	38,780	37,229
Communications Division	18,345	18,345	17,611
Total	57,125	57,125	54,840
Other Costs			
Premium Labor	160	160	158
Travel and Living	1,480	1,280	1,277
Computer Usage	985	985	985
Total	2,625	2,425	2,420
Total Proposition	270,957	259,130	231,326
Cost level			
Estimate	270,957	259,130	
Applied Research &			
Devel. @ 2.5%	6,774	6,478	
Sub Total	277,731	265,608	
General and Administrative			
Expense @ 6.8%	18,886	18,061	
Sub Total	296,617	283,669	
Profit @ 10%	29,662	28,367	
Total Sales Price	326,279	312,036	

TABLE 1 (*continued*)

		Date:
		Proposition No:
		Sheet 2 of 2

All Figures in $1,000's	Column 1 Original Submission	Column 2 After Project Management Review	Column 3 After Exec. V.P. Review
Cost Level			
Estimate		231,326	
Less: Subcontracts		54,840	
Sub Total		176,486	
Applied Research &			
Devel. @ 2.5%		4,412	
Sub Total		180,898	
General and			
Administrative			
Expense @ 6.8%		12,301	
Sub Total		193,199	
Profit @ 10%		19,320	
Sub Total		212,519	
Plus Subcontracts		54,840	
Total Sales Price		267,359	

that consequently the material had not reached the printers until that morning. Greenwood felt there would be no problem in getting the volumes printed by the 14th if he were allowed to authorize overtime for the printer. Ford asked Greenwood to send copies of the proposals to Young so he could see them before Magnus.

Ford, Munson, Young, and Hammond met with Executive Vice President Magnus and his financial staff at 1 P.M. Magnus had many years of experience in defense contracting and was noted for his memory of critical statistics, control ratios, and miscellaneous numerical operating data. Magnus inquired as to the history of the proposal, how the numbers had evolved, and asked what confidence Young and Ford had in them. Hammond replied that they looked all right except for Parker's quote and described that particular situation. Ford pointed out that the Markham concept could offset this possible liability.

Magnus pursued Markham's concept with regard to possible savings and probability of success. No one in the room could really talk knowledgeably in technical terms about the concept. However, Ford said he would guarantee that it would save at least $1 million per set. Magnus said if this were so, then the estimate should be reduced by $1 million per set in order to quote a lower price. He pointed out that some other company might have come up with the idea and had to explore it. WSD would jeopardize its competitive position substantially by not anticipating use of Markham's concept.

Hammond said if this were done it would leave no cushion to offset the liability of Parker's CPIF quote. Magnus cut him off, saying, "WSD's staff had better learn that in order to live, you have to have a job, and in order to have a job, you have to win a low bid occasionally." He likened this job to others that had been done previously in DPD, and ordered Young to take 5 percent off all remaining engineering labor, 10 percent off manufacturing labor, and 5 percent off purchased materials. He further ordered that the material handling expense (MHX) and all profit be omitted on the subcontractors, both Parker and the Communications Division. He felt that with these changes WSD had a good bid and that he was "sure Young and his boys could do the job at the stated 10 percent profit if it were won."

The group left Magnus' office in various stages of relief and concern. Hammond grumbled that he did not know how he could eliminate the MHX on the subcontractors, since a uniform application of MHX was a prerequisite to substantiating cost reimbursement. He stated that Magnus' order had put him in an impossible position. If he eliminated the MHX for the ORTRACK job, the auditors would certainly notice it and would insist that he eliminate it on all the CPFF contracts within the division. This would cause an equivalent 4 percent profit loss. If he did apply the 4 percent in spite of Magnus' instructions, it might cause WSD to lose the competition, in which case he would probably be fired.

Ford said, "unless Young tells me otherwise, I'm going to follow Magnus' instructions." He asked Munson to sit with Forbes, Wright, and Ames to get the three of them "back into" a $1 million reduction per radar set. Since this involved every type of labor and all related subsystems in software, it involved a rewrite of almost every area's cost.

The afternoon was spent revising the cost estimate to include Markham's concept and incorporate Magnus' changes. The fixed-cost figures are shown in Column 3 of Table 1.

Munson now had the job of putting the cost figures into the format required by the Army. This involved 15 pages of detailed breakdowns. A small army of administrative people was assigned, each with a few columns to correlate. The process proved more difficult than had been anticipated because the Army breakdown did not correlate the same quantities as WSD's engineering proposition sheet. The extreme detail of the Army format seemed a waste of time when one realized the manner in which some of the figures had been derived, such as the nominal $1 million cut for the Markham concept. However, there was no alternative to following the Army form. This "reformating" continued late into the night but still was not finished. Before going home, Ford called Greenwood, who was at the printers, and who stated that the management and technical forms were coming well. He requested that the project engineering staff go directly to the printers the next morning to proofread their various sections.

October 12

Munson continued his cost reformulating, and finished at noon. The pages were rushed to the printer. The project engineering staff reviewed the draft at the printers. Jones insisted on substituting seven new pages to describe the advantages of Markham's concept. (The proposal was still written on the original method of signal processing.) Markham's concept was mentioned simply as something that should be looked into in the future as an alternate method of signal processing requiring fewer parts and greater reliability. No mention was made of the fact that WSD's price was based on the Army's later approval of Markham's concept.

The printer was upset at "having all these engineers crawling around the place," but he accepted the revised text and promised delivery to Greenwood of all three volumes by noon on the 14th. Greenwood and his assistants stayed with the job over the weekend and delivered the 40 copies to Fry at his home Sunday afternoon.

October 15

Fry drove the proposals to Army Headquarters. He delivered them to Lt. Col. Youngquist, who said that it was good to see one company, at least, do something on time. He explained that all five other competitors had requested a one- or two-week extension for proposal submission, and that he had written a letter to all, including WSD, on Thursday, the 11th, granting a one-week extension. (The letter either was not delivered on time, or else it was stuck in the WSD mail room.) He asked Fry if he wanted to take the volumes back for further work during the extra week.

APPENDIX I

DESCRIPTION OF SUBDEPARTMENTS WITHIN THE ENGINEERING DEPARTMENT

Radar and General Electronics. Designs and builds transmitters, receivers and signal processors

Power Supply Group. Develops power generators for various voltages, either ac or dc, at whatever frequency is required for EIC products.

Servomechanisms Group. Theoretical design of servomechanisms for equipment designed by other departments.

Information Handling Group. Designs computers for Industrial Products Division.

Communications Group. Designs communications equipment for use in WSD products.

Displays Group. Manufactures consoles, complete with colored lights, to display the information being processed by electronic machines made by other EIC divisions. Requires knowledge of how operators of machines might act in response to various display systems.

Checkout and Simulation Group. Designs systems to test the operation of any WSD product without having an actual enemy target to test its working. Synthetic signals are inserted into the machines which can be traced through their operations.

Mechanical Engineering. Performs heavy mechanical design of auxiliary hardware required with electronic machines.

Civil Engineering Group. Designs custom buildings to house various electronic machines produced by other EIC divisions.

Systems Engineering Section. Gives theoretical and technical advise on electronic systems science and engineering to other EIC divisions.

Field Installation Section. Installs and tests equipment at sites remote from plant.

Drafting and Graphic Art. Drafts flow diagrams and equipment designs; writes technical specifications.

Configuration Records Center. Keeps master file of drawings, specifications, and block diagrams.

Engineering Fabrication Shop. Translates engineering designs for machinists, wiremen, and test technicians who build prototype electronic machines.

APPENDIX II

TYPES OF GOVERNMENT CONTRACTS

Cost Plus Fixed Fee (CPFF). The Government agrees to pay the company all costs of manufacture, however much they may be (subject to Government audit). The fixed-fee portion is the Government's way of saying "no matter how high your costs run, we will not give you more than this fixed amount of profit." These contracts have been used by the Government (1) when the item is needed so badly that costs are secondary to the emergency need, and (2) when (as in research on little known technologies) the item is so new and unknown that the company cannot possibly know the cost. No company would undertake such risk. Underbidding a CPFF job results in cost overruns which, though they may be recouped, do not allow one to profit further from additional costs or time spent on a project. Because CPFF contracts do not provide basis for competition, and because they commit the Government to unknown risks, most contracts today are not of this type.

Fixed Price. The Government agrees to pay the company a fixed price. Competitive bids from several companies are taken. The object being procured is described in minute detail as to its specifications. This is not possible in cases where the company is required to *develop* some new product outside the state of the art. For the efficient company, higher profits may be realized, since cost cutting would leave a larger margin. Competition means that contractors must be careful not to estimate either costs or profits too high.

Cost Plus Incentive Fee (CPIF). A compromise between CPFF and FP contracts. It rewards a contractor for low costs and penalizes him for high costs. For example, a contractor might receive a higher than normal fee if he completes a contract with less materials or labor cost than the original target cost estimate; or he can be rewarded if his equipment has lower maintenance requirements than the target maintenance costs.

Selected Readings

From

MATRIX ORGANIZATION*

By John F. Mee†

A matrix organizational design has evolved in the flow of aerospace technology; changing conditions have caused managers to create new relationships of established organizational concepts and principles. A matrix organization is used to establish a flexible and adaptable system of resources and procedures to achieve a series of project objectives. The accompanying figure is a conceptual framework for a matrix type of organization. It illustrates the coordinated or matrix system of relationships among the functions essential to market, finance, and produce highly specialized goods or services.

From a divisionalized organization structure has emerged a new way of thinking and working to create products dependent upon advanced research and urgency for completion. Time and technology factors forced a more efficient utilization of human talents and facilitating resources.

The traditional divisional type of organization permits a flow of work to progress among autonomous functional units of a specific division. A division manager is responsible for total programs of work involving the products of his division. In a matrix organization, the divisional manager has the same responsibility, authority, and accountability for results. Differences occur in the division of work performed as well as in the allocation of authority, responsibility, and accountability for the completion of work projects.

   * * * * *

Unless managers and operating personnel are educated and trained to work in the developing organizational designs, they can suffer frustrations, emotional disturbances, and loss of motivation. Working in an environment characterized by change as projects are started and completed is not as comfortable and secure as performing a continuing function in a more stable standardized work flow situation.

   * * * * *

---

* Reprinted from *Business Horizons,* Summer 1964.

† The author is Professor Emeritus of Management, Indiana University.

Matrix Organization (aerospace division)

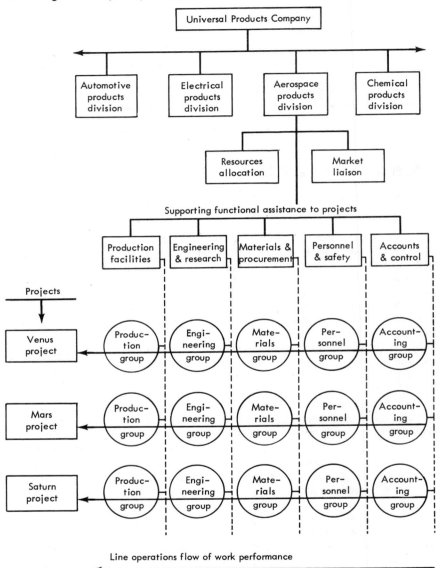

From

WHY PROJECT MANAGEMENT?*

By David I. Cleland†

The advancement of technology in all phases of industrial management since World War II has no precedent; radical changes occurring in the design and marketing of products have forced innovation in management theories and techniques. Because new products and marketing strategy often do not fit the purely functional type of organization, attention is being given to molding the organization around the task. The need for a new type of managerial surveillance is apparent as terms such as "systems management" and "project management" are heard with increasing frequency.

Traditional business organizations function mostly on a vertical basis and depend almost exclusively on a strong, inviolate superior-subordinate relationship to ensure a unified effort. Individual managers tend to identify boundaries of responsibilities and specialization. When organizations were relatively small this presented no problem since the functional manager could maintain lateral staff contact to ensure mutual support and understanding of interfunctional goals.

* * * * *

The pure functional approach cannot be applied when the task involves the coordinated effort of hundreds of organizations and people. Unique management relationships evolve in the development of a large single-purpose project that cuts across interior organizational flows of authority and responsibility, and radiates outside to independent organizations.

The traditional management theory of Henri Fayol and Fredrick Taylor is not suitable for managing large, single projects, such as those in the construction industry, or in manufacturing when a costly product requires the coordinated involvement of several organizations. A combat aircraft, for example, is developed and produced through the coordinated efforts of dozens of industrial and Department of Defense organizations.

These new purposes require a management philosophy that has no organizational or functional constraints. Project management provides this philosophy—a way of thinking that allows for radical changes in organizational theory and in the management of activities. . . .

THE PROJECT MANAGER

In a sense project management is compatible with the traditional and functional approach to management, yet it has provided a way of thinking about management of highly technical and costly products whose development and acquisition spread across several large autonomous organizations. The project manager crosses functional lines to bring together the management activities required to accomplish

* Reprinted from *Business Horizons,* Winter 1964.

† Lt. Col. Cleland is Associate Professor of Management, Department of Systems Management, Air Force Institute of Technology, Air University, Wright-Patterson Air Force Base, Ohio.

project objectives. The project manager has certain characteristics that differentiate him from the traditional manager.

1. As a manager he is concerned with accomplishing specific projects that require participation by organizations and agencies outside his direct control.

2. Since the project manager's authority cuts through superior-subordinate lines of authority, he conflicts with the functional managers who must share authority in their functional areas for the particular project.

3. As a focal point for project activities, the project manager enters into on an exception basis those matters necessary for the successful accomplishment of the project. He determines the *when* and *what* of the project activities; the functional manager, who supports many different projects in the organization, determines *how* the support will be given.

4. The project manager's task is finite; after the project is completed, the personnel directly supporting the project can be assigned to other activities.

5. The project manager oversees a high proportion of professionals; consequently he must use different management techniques than in the simple superior-subordinate relationship. His attitude regarding the traditional functions of management must necessarily be tempered by increased motivation, persuasion, and control techniques. For many professionals his leadership consists of explanations of the rationale of the effort, as well as the more obvious functions of planning, organizing, directing, and controlling.

6. His diverse and extraorganizational activities require unification and integration directed toward the objective of the project. As a unifying agent for the total management function he has no line authority to act but depends on other manifestations of authority to attain the objective. Thus the directing function is somewhat less important from the perspective of the project manager. What direction he does accomplish is through the functional managers supporting him.

7. The project manager does not normally possess any traditional line authority over the line organizations involved in creating the goods or services.

*   *   *   *   *

Authority and Responsibility

Since the project manager acts as the focal point for major decisions and considerations, he must be given a special kind of recognition with respect to his authority and responsibility in his relationships with other managers in the organization. Authority is the legal or rightful power to command, to act, and to direct. Ultimate authority derives from the society in which the organized effort exists; authority is *de jure* in the sense that it exists by rightful title. Specific delineations of the authority of an organizational position are contained in the unit's documentation, such as policy and procedure, job descriptions, and organizational charters. Not to be neglected is the *de facto* authority that can be exercised by the project manager. This authority is implied in his organizational position; it is the intrinsic and necessary power to fully discharge responsibilities inherent in the task or job. Thus an organization receiving public funds has *de facto* authority to create administrative policy stipulating how the funds will be maintained, to appoint a custodian who will assume responsibility for the safe-guarding and legal obligation of the monies, and to take other measures necessary for adequate control of the expenditure of funds within the specific conditions of authority under the grant. Other aspects of the *de facto* authority include the project manager's persuasive ability, his rapport with extraorganizational units, and his reputation in resolving opposing viewpoints intra- and extraorganizationally. Other factors influencing the degree of authority available to the project manager are:

1. Influence inherent in his rank, organizational position, or specialized knowledge
2. His status or prestige within the informal organizational relationships
3. The priority and obligation existing within the organization for the timely and efficient accomplishment of the project goals
4. The existence of a bilateral agreement with a contracting party for the completion of the project within the terms of the contract in such areas as cost, performance (quality, reliability, and technology), and schedule
5. The integrative requirements of the project manager's job in the sense that he has the sole responsibility within the organization to pull together the separate functional activities and direct them to a coordinated project goal.

The project manager's authority and responsibility flows horizontally across the vertical superior-subordinate relationships existing within the functional organizational elements. Within this environment the authority of the project manager may often come under serious questioning, particularly in cases involving the allocation of scarce resources for several projects. Generally, the project manager has no explicit authority to resolve interfunctional disputes by issuing orders to functional groups outside his office. However, since the project manager is the central point through which program information flows, and by which total project executive control is effected, he often exercises additional authority over and above that which has been specifically delegated. His superior knowledge of the relative roles and functions of the individual parts of the project places him in a logical position to become intimately involved in the major organizational decisions that might affect the outcome of his project. As the centralized and focal point through which major project decisions flow, the project manager's contribution to the decision process cannot be ignored or disparaged. The unique position of the project manager gives him superior knowledge of any subsystem or subactivity. (This superior knowledge does not exist as the single authority within the total organization, but only as the single authority with respect to a particular project.)

Organizational rank carries both explicit and implicit authority. The project manager should have sufficient executive rank to enable him to exercise a subtle and pervasive authority by virtue of his office. He should have sufficient rank (through evidence of seniority, title, status, prestige, and so on) to provide general administrative leverage in dealing with other line officials, with supporting staff personnel, and with authorities external to the parent unit. This implies a correlation between the rank of the project manager and the cost and complexity of his project. The more costly the project, the greater the degree of risk, and the more complex the internal and external organizational structures, the higher the rank of the project manager should be. Within the military services there has been a tendency to increase the authority of a project manager's position by assigning higher ranking officers to these positions. A brigadier general would be expected to exercise more influence (and thus authority) over his subordinates, his peers, and extraorganizational elements than would a lower-ranking officer.

*   *   *   *   *

The creation of the position of project manager in an organization requires careful planning to prepare existing management groups. Certain criteria are offered for delineating the authority and responsibility of project managers:

1. *The charter of the project manager should be broad enough to enable his active participation in major managerial and technical activities.* He should be given sufficient policy-making authority to integrate the functional contributions to the project goals.

2. The project manager must have the *necessary executive rank* to insure responsiveness in the parent company to his requirements and acceptance as its unquestioned agent in dealing with contractors and others.

3. His staff should be qualified to provide personal administrative and technical support. He should have sufficient authority to increase or decrease his staff as necessary throughout the life of the project. This authorization should include selective augmentation for varying periods of time from the supporting functional agencies.

4. He should participate in making technical, engineering, and functional decisions within the bounds of his project.

5. The project manager must have sufficient authority and capability to control funds, budgeting, and scheduling for the project.

From

UNDERSTANDING
PROJECT AUTHORITY*

By David I. Cleland†

. . . While early theories of management regarded authority as a gravitational force that flowed from the top down, recent theories view it as a force to be accepted voluntarily, and which moves both vertically and horizontally. The elements of participation and persuasion in the authority relationship are products of modern organizations and reflect the influence of the democratic and scientific revolution in contemporary society.

*   *   *   *   *

* Reprinted from *Business Horizons,* Spring 1967.

† Lt. Col. Cleland is an associate professor of management, department of systems management, Air Force Institute of Technology, Wright-Patterson Air Force Base. The views expressed herein are those of the author and do not necessarily reflect the views of the Air Force or the Department of Defense.

Power

Power is a concept frequently associated with authority. It is defined as the ability to unilaterally determine the behavior of others, regardless of the basis for that ability.[1] Authority provides power that is legitimately attached to the organizational position; it is delegated by job descriptions, organizational titles, standard operating procedures, and related policies.

Influence

Influence on the other hand, is authority assumed without the legitimacy of an organizational position. An individual may exercise influence in his environment simply because he has knowledge and expertise. There is little doubt that a duly appointed superior has power over his subordinates in matters involving pay, promotion, and effectiveness reports, and that this delegated power functions unilaterally, from the top down. A manager's authority however, is a result of his power and his influence combined so that subordinates, peers, and associates alike willingly accept his judgment. This combination of power and influence emphasizes both the project manager's legal rights and the personal effectiveness of his organizational position. Fayol uses this approach in defining the manager's authority as follows:

> Authority is the right to give orders and the power to exact obedience. Distinction must be made between a manager's official authority deriving from office and personal authority, compounded of intelligence, experience, moral worth, ability to lead, past services, etc. . . . personal authority is the indispensable complement of official authority.[2]

PROJECT AUTHORITY

To understand the concept of project authority, one must first understand the framework of the project environment, which points up the salient differences between the role of the project manager and the traditional functional manager. (See Figure 1.) While these differences are possibly more theoretical than actual, they do exist and they affect the manager's *modus operandi* and philosophy. Such comparison highlights a singular characteristic of the project manager—his role in managing activities that include extensive participation by organizations and agencies not under his direct (line) control.

*   *   *   *   *

A significant measure of the project manager's authority springs from his function and the style with which he performs it. Thus the project manager's authority is a combination of *de jure* and *de facto* elements in the total project environment. In this context, his authority has no organizational or functional constraints, but diffuses throughout and beyond the organization, seeking out the ideas and the people it needs to influence and control.

---

[1] For example, see James D. Thompson, "Authority and Power in 'Identical' Organizations," *American Journal of Sociology,* Vol. LX (November 1956).

[2] Henri Fayol, *General and Industrial and Industrial Management* (London: Sir Isaac Pitman & Sons, Ltd., 1949), p.21.

FIGURE 1
Comparison of Functional and Project Viewpoints

Phenomenon	*Project Viewpoint*	*Functional Viewpoint*
Line-staff organizational dichotomy	Vestiges of the hierarchal model remain, but line functions are placed in a support position. A web of authority and responsibility relationships exists.	Line functions have direct responsibility for accomplishing the objectives; the line commands, staff advises.
Scalar principle	Elements of the vertical chain exist, but prime emphasis is placed on horizontal and diagonal work flow. Important business is conducted as the legitimacy of the task requires.	The chain of authority relationships is from superior to subordinate throughout the organization. Central, crucial, and important business is conducted up and down the vertical hierarchy.
Superior-subordinate relationship	Peer to peer, manager to technical expert, associate to associate relationships are used to conduct much of the salient business.	This is the most important relationship; if kept healthy, success will follow. All important business is conducted through a pyramiding structure of superiors-subordinates.
Organizational objectives	Management of a project becomes a joint venture of many relatively independent organizations. Thus, the objective becomes multilateral.	Organizational objectives are sought by the parent unit (an assembly of suborganizations) working within its environment. The objective is unilateral.
Unity of direction	The project manager manages across functional and organizational lines to accomplish a common interorganizational objective.	The general manager acts as the head for a group of activities having the same plan.
Parity of authority and responsibility	Considerable opportunity exists for the project manager's responsibility to exceed his authority. Support people are often responsible to other managers (functional) for pay, performance reports, promotions, and so forth.	Consistent with functional management; the integrity of the superior-subordinate relationship is maintained through functional authority and advisory staff services.
Time duration	The project (and hence the organization) is finite in duration.	Tends to perpetuate itself to provide continuing facilitative support.

In its total sense, project authority is the legal and personal influence that the project manager exercises over the schedule, cost, and technical considerations of the project. Project authority exists within the legitimacy of the project; it extends horizontally, diagonally, and vertically within the parent organization and radiates to outside participating organizations. Traditional line-staff relationships are modified in the project enditional bureaucratic organization, authority relationships are based on the vertical hierarchy. The project manager, on the other hand, is concerned with the flow of work in horizontal and diagonal relationships.

*   *   *   *   *

In sum, project authority depends heavily on the personality of the project manager and how he sees his role in relation to the project environment. His authority is not necessarily weak because it is not thoroughly documented and because it functions outside the parent organization and between the participating organizations. The project manager is in a focal position in the project endeavors, which allows him to control the flow of information and to have superior knowledge of the project. The scope of power and control exercised by the project manager may be virtually independent of his legal authority.

From

HOW MANAGERS MAKE THINGS HAPPEN*

By George S. Odiorne†

Management Is Not a Passive Art

*   *   *   *   *

A manager is more than a problem solver. He's a goal setter. Without waiting for others to ask him, he envisions things that should happen, and thinks through some possible paths by which the goal can be reached. At this stage he has few, if any, people who would agree with him that the goal is possible. Because he's active in deed as well as thought, however, he converts them into action in his plan, and enlists their talents toward reaching the goal which he dreamed up. Before long he has a full scale movement afoot and people become ego-involved in his goal just as if they themselves had thought of it.

*   *   *   *·   *

Making Growth a Company Goal

. . . [A] few dominant trends seem to emerge. One of these is that *company growth* is one present day goal which seems to spur executive action and make

---

* *How Managers Make Things Happen,* George S. Odiorne. © 1961 by Prentice-Hall, Englewood Cliffs, N.J. (pp. 4–11, 37–38, 52–53).

† The author is Dean of the School of Business in the University of Utah.

things happen. This has some important implications for the company which wants to grow. It also has a great deal of relevance to the building manager—or the one who's arrived—who has talents for making things happen and seeks ample opportunity to demonstrate his prowess along these lines.

Studies by the Stanford Research Institute of several hundred companies with records of growth show that there are several traits which are common to most of them. . . .

*   *   *   *   *

Stanford's studies also showed that those companies which have growth patterns have been led by management of great moral courage in making decisions in favor of growth and sticking with them to make the growth occur. . . .

. . . [The manager has] the heavy responsibility for spurring others to overcome their own inertia. . . . He's got to be able to move projects and people off dead center and get them rolling toward his goals. He's got to generate enthusiasm for these goals so that people adopt them as their own, with the result that they generate enthusiasm on their own part for getting there. He must further instill a desire to excel and do the job fully and without mistakes or altering. To do this demands several traits in the action-getting manager which he must assiduously cultivate at the risk of failure.

1. He's going to have to maintain optimism if he's going to overcome inertia. Most managers who make things happen have ego drives that push them on personally, and unbounded optimism and confidence that others will ultimately see his vision of what's to be accomplished despite repeated defeats and failures.

2. He needs a sound knowledge of people to impel them to produce and create. He needs to know what incentives are required to get action from others, and to have some artistry in using them.

3. He needs a certain callousness in demanding high standards of performance from others who are helping him. The manager with an overdeveloped sense of sympathy and understanding of failure will usually "usurp all of the dirty jobs for himself while others stand about and marvel at his performance," as David Moore puts it.

*   *   *   *   *

Profit Requires Action

Being a successful manager in a commercial and industrial enterprise means a profit-minded one. Conversely, it's the profit-minded manager at any level who stands the best chance of moving upward. This is more than simple avarice, or single minded love of money for itself. It's largely because profit is a universal standard for measurement that is easily grasped by managers and quite clearly understood by those who judge his performance.

It's entirely possible that someday a more commonly held standard will come along, for example—service; but it must always meet the standard which profit has become—immediate, easy to calculate, universally accepted. Profit, for all the criticisms leveled against it, is the best available instrument and standard of managerial success and organizational performance. With adaptations it applies to any organization, even in Soviet Russia.

We hear a great deal of pious foolishness written and said about profit. At the annual congress of industry of the NAM each winter, solemn and quite pompous words are uttered in defense of this mysterious lubricant which causes the wheels of industry to turn. To some it becomes a divinely inspired instrument which it becomes sacrilegious to damn. This of course is not the point here.

*   *   *   *   *

Profit, then, is more than an accounting term. It's a positive creation and standard of measuring effectiveness of management action and decision making.

*   *   *   *   *

. . . Profit is the result almost wholly of the *actions of managers* who exercise initiative and leadership of a dynamic nature, and of the people who respond to this leadership to carry through toward the goals of the organization.

There is probably no company in business today which couldn't be out of business through lack of profit inside of ten years if its management attempted to conduct its affairs simply through mechanical application of administrative practice, at the expense of the more vital, personal, and human application of individual leadership.

*   *   *   *   *

. . . The most pernicious trait a manager can have when faced with obstacles is indecisiveness. Very often this is explained away as a need for mature consideration of the situation, but actually indecision is the result of the mind slipping away into inappropriate or trivial matters. He may find that ordering a new desk or settling a squabble between two secretaries is much more intriguing than writing the order, or picking up the telephone to announce the decision. The obstacle hurdler makes his decision when he can—and the sooner the better.

*   *   *   *   *

Equally vital among the qualities of the obstacle breaker is that of using people without becoming sentimentally overinvolved with their successes or failures. A survey of fifty company presidents by two graduate students at the School of Business at Michigan showed that such things as fraternal connections and other sentimental ties rated last among these executives' considerations when picking men for positions of leadership.

*   *   *   *   *

Despite his concern with meeting the needs of others and meeting the basic needs of people, the action-getter has developed a tough-mindedness. For one thing, as Chris Argyris, management researcher of Yale, has put it, he has "a high tolerance for frustration." He can plug through all sorts of red tape without blowing his top when he has to. He frequently endures the delays and runarounds of committees and clearances with spartan endurance. He is patient where such patience is the only possible way of getting the final payoff that he seeks.

This patience isn't submissiveness, however, and when the time for patience is past and more direct action is called for, the action-minded manager is willing to be ruthless. When the choice is between maintaining old relationships and getting the job done he is always ready to decide in favor of the job. Stepping on people's corns isn't his first choice, but he does it firmly if the occasion demands.

*   *   *   *   *

The action-minded manager is probably tough-minded in his relations with people, too. He's willing to stick by his people through their honest mistakes—or to chop off heads as the need arises. He assumes that men are made of tough stuff and will work hard and take heavy blows as a price of making a living and contributing to the success of the business.

He will urge on a man who is working at less than his best abilities.

He is liberal with recognition for good work, and equally liberal with a reverse kind of recognition for the people who aren't performing up to their capacities. People over their heads in their jobs find this action-minded man a fearsome figure, one who will certainly drive them to perform things they hadn't thought possible, or face up to the fact that they have no great future in the organization until they do.

He's tough-minded, too, in being willing to pay the prices for personal success. Long hours, hard work, and man-killing travel schedules are the way of life for him. He concentrates on his job with a fury and singleness of purpose that reduces other things to a lesser role. This doesn't mean he's inhuman or a dull grind. . . .

PART III Financial Control, Organization Structure, and Human Behavior

ALLOCATION OF RESOURCES: AN IMPORTANT SOCIAL OBLIGATION OF MANAGERS

One of the fundamental lessons studied in economics courses is that the job of the manager is to *allocate resources.* This phrase has unfortunately degenerated in the minds of many people either (1) to the status of a meaningless, abstract cliché, or (2) to the image of a money-motivated manager driven by desires of an efficiency expert or a scrooge with a C.P.A., green eye shade, and sharp pencil. It is even possible, as Thorsten Veblen suggested, that the manager is driven by profit and buttressed by Wall Street bankers who pressure him to forget the products he is producing and the function of those products in society.

That these things happen in poorly managed companies which do not include the public in their strategic planning, or which engage in sloppy internal financial planning, cannot be denied. However, they tend to cloud a more profound and important meaning of the verb, "to allocate resources." Namely, that in the long run those organizations are supported by society (either by legal charter or by day-to-day monetary support) which accomplish the twin goals of (1) production of a useful good or service, and (2) production of this good or service without unnecessary waste of resources. The latter is often called production with *efficiency.*

Efficiency is, therefore, a dictate of *society*, not simply a dictate of those who think like accountants, or those who are *thing*-oriented rather than *people*-oriented.

An example will help to make this concept more understandable. The Seaboard Chemical Corporation, one of the cases in Part III, is a producer of sulphuric acid. Among other fundamental forces in nature which cause this company to exist is the fact that people outside the organization want (or, as economists would say, *demand*) this product for use in drugs and medicines (Eli Lilly), in automobile tires (Goodyear), explosives (DuPont), or hospital laboratories (Roosevelt Hospital). Fixed resources within Seaboard (such as plants and machines) must be allocated so that they produce the right quality demanded outside, the proper quantities demanded, and at the right time.

The social demand for efficiency is evident by the fact that Seaboard managers will be punished by society if they buy unnecessary equipment, hire people that sit around doing nothing, or spill and ruin raw materials stored in their inventories. There are two kinds of sanctions. First, the cost of Seaboard's product will eventually prove unacceptable to those who must pay higher prices. Second, if the rumor spreads that this is a wasteful institution, public opinion (or Ralph Nader) may urge government regulation.

Efficiency is not, then, a dirty word. It can be made dirty by poor management, but efficient allocation of resources is a pragmatic social obligation of managers. An expedient thing to do. Managers will eventually be punished if they do not discharge this obligation. For those who speak in terms of ethics, efficiency may well be a social responsibility in addition. Managers who take their ethical contribution to society seriously will in effect punish themselves if they fail to strive for efficient allocation of resources.

FINANCIAL MANAGEMENT AS A TECHNIQUE FOR ALLOCATING RESOURCES

In the fields of accounting and finance, many techniques have been devised for trying to find "just the right amount" of various resources to assemble for the quantity of production demanded "out there." In theory, this represents an ideal. If it could actually be carried out in practice, the human beings in society would get what they want at the least possible cost and waste. Society as a whole would suffer the least possible waste of natural resources.

One of the most powerful technologies in finance for accomplishing this are the various methods for allocating fixed capital. In financial terms, this is "the investment decision." The methods all aim at telling a manager how to choose between alternatives. For example, Mr. North in Continental Electric Company has three possibilities for investing in projects that will improve the efficiency of the electric motors his division produces: purchase of a patent for a part of the motor, purchase of new machines for wiring motors, or paying his research department to develop new insulation materials. The student who puts himself in North's place will learn something of "how to do it"—how to choose, based on various financial techniques. The same kind of knowledge will be gained by putting oneself in the place of Ekstrom, president of a Swedish company, or Juvet, president of the Belgian company which owns the Swedish company. There, the choice is whether to invest in a plant to produce a new starch chemical, XL–4. How do these executives decide whether to build this new plant? How do they decide whether it should be located in Stockholm or in Brussels? Which decision will yield starch consumers the best quality product, produced on time, with the least cost and waste?

Another instrument for allocating resources is the budget. Executives in Norman Manufacturing Company face decisions such as how much of certain resources they must buy in order to produce and sell golf equipment, tennis raquets, and gym clothing. How much should be put into hiring advertising specialists? How much to hiring salesmen and giving them expense accounts for hotels,.meals and travel? Only if management makes the "right" decision about these matters will the company be viable competitively, discharge its responsibility to society, and survive.

A host of other financial techniques are available to managers for allocating resources efficiently. Many who study this book and who have had training in finance and accounting will see opportunity for applying their specialty to the cases. The Sola Chemical Corporation exemplifies resource allocation on worldwide operations when it must minimize the cost of taxes, and the cost of money it borrows, around the world. Seaboard Corporation happens to be concerned with how to maintain accurate records of its physical resources, and whether or not the condition of these resources is best verified by techniques of auditing.

FINANCIAL INFORMATION AND HUMAN PERCEPTION

When financial planning is done, considerable amounts of quantitative information are gathered, and this is summarized by certain methods. One of the important lessons managers might learn from the following cases is that these supposedly objective "facts" really do not give "impartial" answers to the problem of how to allocate resources. Human beings have a way of *interpreting* data differently. They see the cash flows through their own rose-colored (or dark grey) glasses.

For example, in Norman Manufacturing Company the Sporting Goods Division increases its return on investment from 14 percent to 17 percent. What does this *mean?* Is it good or bad? We shall see that one human brain interprets this as positive for the division and another human brain interprets it as negative. Or, in the Continental Electric Company, the Electric Motor Division will meet its sales target of $12,300,000. One man views this as entirely proper, another views it as not high enough. By studying these cases, one should learn once and for all that human needs, self-interests, and organizational positions all cause different men to judge financial data differently. As a former dean of the Yale Law School once said, "the law is often determined by what the judge had for breakfast."

OPTIMIZATION OF THE WHOLE COMPANY AS A SOURCE OF HUMAN CONFLICT

One of the things every manager should know is that short run technology and efficiency of a total company system often demands that some *parts* of the system must be suboptimized. They must be financially hurt in the interest of the efficient production of the firm as a whole. The question becomes "does this short run advantage outweigh the longer run effect on human initiative of those who are hurt"?

This factor has been ignored by both the financial courses in our nation's business schools and the courses in sociology and psychology. The former might be excused because they have their hands full teaching efficient allocation techniques, and have little time to explore the phenomena of technological harm to the parts of the organization, or human anxiety produced when the technical axe is wielded. The latter might be excused because they have their hands full teaching why human beings act the way they do and have little time to explore financial and economic necessities demanded by society.

But the manager must know both. The cases in Part III will show clearly for example, why a Belgian management might prevent the development of its Swedish subsidiary, and why the Swedish managers might change in their commitment to their work, their loyalty to the parent company, or both.

ORGANIZATION OF THE FINANCIAL FUNCTION

A final thing of importance to managers, which is explored in Part III cases, is the implication of financial planning (resource allocation) for the human organization structure of the firm.

Norman Manufacturing Company is faced with the problem of whether the Sporting Goods Division's *line manager* should make resource allocation decisions, whether the headquarters *staff managers* should make these decisions, or what kind of procedures might be devised to have the decisions made jointly. Seaboard Corporation is in a position of having formally assigned the decision responsibility in two places—to the Los Angeles plant manager and to the headquarters controller. Continental Electric has clearly decentralized these decisions to the Electric Motor Division, but there is evidence that the informal day-to-day behavior of headquarters line and staff officers may take over. In AB Thorsten, it is unclear where the decisions are to be made—the formal plan is that they be made in Sweden, but company politics leaves it unclear just who will make them. Finally, Sola Chemical faces the real problem of where the financial planning for its worldwide operations should take place. Should it take place at U.S. headquarters, at an area headquarters in Europe, or at the local level of, say, the individual subsidiary in France?

In each of these problems, readings on organization structure will help to raise alternative patterns of organization to be considered. In the last analysis, as with all problems which must be solved by *The Managerial Mind,* a solution must be worked out by the student which seems best for the particular company at the particular stage of its development. And the student who takes his work seriously may find a solution which is as good or better than that actually being carried out by the management in the case.

6. NORMAN MANUFACTURING COMPANY

Case Introduction

SYNOPSIS

The Norman Manufacturing Company, originally a family-owned company in the capital goods industry, has sold stock to the public and acquired a smaller company that produces sporting goods. Top management sets objectives for profit and market share for the new company, but there are problems in achieving these objectives—both technical problems from the standpoint of finance, and human problems in the form of disagreement.

WHY THIS CASE IS INCLUDED

The Norman case offers opportunity to look at the philosophy and accounting facets of decentralization, as well as the human motivations and communications patterns connected with it. Various types of authority, and the phenomena of role conflict, are studied in relation to the operation of the company system. Since the executives in the case have actually designed a decision-making procedure, this can be critically examined to see the kinds of networks that produce a workable method for deciding financial objectives, and that produce accurate appraisal of operating results.

DIAGNOSTIC AND PREDICTIVE QUESTIONS

The readings included with this case are marked (*). The author index at the end of this book locates the other readings.

1. What objectives did Norman have in mind when he decided to adopt a decentralized organization structure, dividing the company into major product divisions?

> Read: * Curtice, "General Motors Organization Philosophy and Structure."

2. Given Norman's broad philosophical objectives, what did he fail to see in the way of the economic and financial details (balance) of putting them into effect?

Read: *Shillinglaw, *Cost Accounting,* pp. 680–84, 688–89. Drucker, *The Practice of Management,* pp. 62–131.

3. Given Norman's broad philosophical objectives, what did he fail to see in the way of the psychological and sociological realities of putting them into effect?

Read: Etzioni, "Authority Structure and Organizational Effectiveness." *Newman and Summer, *The Process of Management: Concepts, Behavior, and Practice,* pp. 605–10.

4. What motivations, including those in Question 4, seem to be causing Gibbs' actions in the case? Be specific—list various of his actions throughout, and relate to various causes of behavior.

Read: Selections from Question 4. *Simon *et al., Public Administration,* pp. 182, 189–200. Etzioni, *A Comparative Analysis of Complex Organizations,* pp. 31–39, 80–82.

5. From the viewpoint of economic philosophy, what must Gibbs realize about conditions for "freedom" or "autonomy" in an organization?

Read: Clark, *Alternative to Serfdom,* pp. 4–7.

6. From the viewpoints of decision theory—suboptimization—why might not "the good of the whole Norman company" be the same as "the good of Lange division"?

Read: Miller and Starr, *Executive Decisions and Operations Research,* pp. 38–42, 45–47, 50. *Rapoport and Drews, "Mathematical Approach to Long-Range Planning."

7. What was Gibbs "ignorant" of in the case? What was Langford "ignorant" of? What implications does this have for a solution to the problem? Who, if anyone, is competent to state the "true" objectives of the Lange Division? What psychological laws cause Norman, Langford, or Gibbs to suboptimize?

Read: *Krech, and Crutchfield, *Theory and Problems of Social Psychology,* pp. 81–83, 87–89, 94–96, 98, 102–3. Merton, "Bureaucratic Structure and Personality."

8. Remembering that (profit = revenues − cost) and (rate of return on investment = revenue − cost/investment), why did Gibbs want to charge advertising and research outlays to investment? What were his ultimate goals? What were Langford's ultimate goals in wanting to charge the outlays to expense?

POLICY QUESTIONS

9. What would be the characteristics of a decision-making process which would arrive at the most accurate decisions on the objectives of the division and the most accurate way to enter outlays for advertising and research?

Read: Follett, "Constructive Conflict." Newman and Summer, *The Process of Management: Concepts, Behavior, and Practice,* pp. 439–48. *Enell and Haas, *Setting Standards for Executive Performance,* pp. 16–18, 31–32.

10. What specific process can you design for the people in this company to "apply" the insights from Question 9 to solution of their problem? Who will do what and when? (Name times, places, and people.)

11. If you were Norman and had studied the questions in this case, what would you do to put the process into action? That is, what ground rules, or insights, would you give at the first meeting with the parties concerned?

QUESTIONS FOR ORIGINAL STUDENT WORK IN ANALYSIS AND POLICY

12. While reflecting on case facts, what additional theories from prior education give you insights as to "what is going on" in Norman Manufacturing Company? As to what might be predicted to happen in the future?

13. Other than the policy questions asked by the authors, what pragmatic ways can you think of to state the practical problems faced by executives in the case?

Case Text*

The Norman Manufacturing Company produces a variety of industrial machinery and equipment, including electrical switches and relay boxes; the smaller items of coal-mining equipment; and chains, hoists, conveyers and other materials-handling products. In addition to these lines, the company has expanded, through acquisition in the past ten years, into two lines less closely connected with its original product line: the manufacture of sporting goods and of furnishings (hardware, plumbing, furniture) for pleasure yachts. At the present time, the company employs 1,650 people, and its annual sales have averaged $40 million for the past three years.

Norman Manufacturing Company originated 30 years ago as a family-owned company that specialized in manufacturing and selling chains and hoists, with a plant located in Bridgeport, Connecticut. The company has experienced rapid growth through the years. Products allied to heavy industry have been added during the past 15 years. Company headquarters were moved from Bridgeport to New York City seven years ago.

Regarding the objectives of the Company, L. D. Norman, Jr., the President, states:

> *Since my father's death 13 years ago, we have endeavored to stress even more strongly the objective of growth over the years. The public now owns 63 percent of our stock, but they, as well as our family and our management, have certain principal accomplishments in mind: to have this company grow in assets, market coverage, profitability,*

and prestige over the years; and to have it gain a national reputation for quality and service to our customers. This is the reason why we have taken on two new divisions that are not connected with our past experience. We feel that the company has a future in many product lines. Technology and consumer tastes mean you can't stand still with your same traditional products and ways of doing things.

THE LANGE DIVISION

Seven years ago, the Norman Company purchased the Lange Sporting Goods Company and established it as the Lange Division of NMC. The research bulletin of a New York investment firm, at that time, carried the following statement:

The Lange Company, with a good stable line of products, has suffered in recent years from a lack of vitality in keeping its products, production methods, and advertising up to the "zip" displayed by its competitors. We believe that Norman's record of capable and aggressive management should enable this company to show good growth over the intermediate term future.

The management of Lange had been in the hands of four members of the Lange family, all of whom retired at the time of the merger. L. D. Norman, Jr., immediately replaced them with Fred K. Gibbs as general manager of the Lange Division, and with two Norman middle management executives as controller and production superintendent respectively.

Fred Gibbs, 42, had been executive vice president of a competing sporting goods manufacturing company. After graduation from Stanford University, he held positions as production-scheduling trainee, salesman, sales manager, and marketing vice president for that company. Reference checks at the time of his employment with Norman Manufacturing Company indicated that he was well liked by his fellow executives, possessed an unusual degree of energy and drive, and had initiated many of the ideas that later, in the form of company policies, led to sales increases and the growth of his company.

L. Donald Norman, Jr., has been president of the Norman Manufacturing Company for 13 years. At age 50, he has worked for the Company 26 years, first in the plants, then as a salesman, and for 10 years as a staff man to his father, designing and supervising procedures to coordinate production, sales, shipping, and inventories. As president he has spent most of his time planning new customer strategy and sales incentive programs, and projecting financial statements to plan increases in plant investment. Together with T. M. Farish, executive vice president, and C.A. Langford, treasurer, he sits on the executive committee. This committee meets three times a week to discuss all important matters in sales, production, and finance.

At the time the Lange Division was established, the executive committee minutes show, Farish and Langford were somewhat apprehensive about the ability of Norman Company management "to take hold of this new venture and manage it successfully, since we do not have experience in consumer products."

Mr. Norman, the minutes also show, gave the committee a summary of the study he had been making of decentralization. He pointed out that such companies as General Motors and du Pont were able to grow by creating independent divisions, selecting capable men to run them, and retaining only very broad measures of performance. In this way, he said, the Norman Company could delegate virtually the entire management task "to Fred Gibbs and his team. We do not have to know much about the details of the division so long as we establish broad controls."

In the five months after the acquisition, the three top Norman officials drew up the following control points. They were careful to make clear, Norman says, that Gibbs' own performance would be measured only in terms of these controls. "Everything else—all of the details of running the division—would be left to Fred."

Rate of Return on Investment. Lange was earning an average of 14% (before taxes) on book value, and it was agreed to raise the target to 19% within five years.

Sales as a Percentage of Industry Sales. Norman judged that the Lange Company had been performing as indicated below, and new targets were set for Lange's three principal products:

Product	Present	Five-Year Target
Tennis equipment.	11%	15%
Golf bags.	8	12
Gym clothing.	10	25

Of the total dollar sales volume of Lange, averaged over the five-year period prior to acquisition, tennis equipment accounted for 40%, gym clothing for 45%, and golf bags for 15%.

In setting these figures, all three executives agreed that there was no accurate way to be "scientific" about what percentages could be reached. All recognized that the Lange Company had been, in the words of Norman, "conservative, lacking in morale, and complacent." It therefore seemed reasonable that "with a hard-hitting management and some new ideas, the targets are neither over- nor understated—they are realistic."

Gibbs at first expressed the idea that the gym clothing sales target was too high. But Langford and Norman showed him the results of their study of profits in this line compared to others. The profitability of selling gym clothing, particularly to institutions, was much higher than the other items. Gibbs, too, agreed that his target was a wise one.

OPERATING RESULTS: FIRST SIX YEARS OF OPERATION

At the time this case is written, Lange Division has been in operation for six fiscal years. Rates of return on investment and percentages of industry sales appear in Exhibits 1 and 2, respectively.

EXHIBIT 1
**Ratio of Profit (before Tax) to Investment in the Lange
Division**

Year	Method 1*	Method 2†
First....................	14%	12%
Second................	14	11
Third	15	13
Fourth.................	15	13
Fifth....................	17	16
Sixth	17	16
Present‡................	17	16

* Used by Lange Division controller, charging advertising and research to
capital investment, the lower half of the ratio.
† Used by Norman Company management, charging advertising and research
to current expense, thus decreasing the top of the ratio.
‡ First quarter adjusted.

EXHIBIT 2
Sales as a Percentage of Total Industry Sales

Year	Tennis Equipment	Golf Bags	Gym Clothing
First.....................	11%	9%	10%
Second.................	12	10	15
Third	12	9	21
Fourth..................	13	11	22
Fifth.....................	12	10	23
Sixth	12	10	22
Present (1st quarter)	12	10	21

During the first four years, the executive committee of the Norman
Company had a verbal agreement, of which they frequently reminded
themselves, that none of Norman's management should initiate inquiries about *specific* operations in Lange. Langford reports, for instance,
that when he noticed, on the expense statements furnished for the first
year, that telephone and telegraph expenses of Lange were, in his opinion, far out of line with the rest of the company, he felt that he should
not use these statements as detailed controls.

The committee also agreed that Norman should make fairly frequent
(perhaps bimonthly) visits to Lange headquarters in Providence for the
purpose of inquiring about overall sales improvement. He should also
encourage Gibbs to come to New York whenever "*he* feels the need to
discuss any matter, broad, detailed, or otherwise."

As a matter of practice, Norman, Gibbs and Langford did meet about
three times a month, at which times (*a*) they discussed overall sales
results for 10 to 20 minutes, and (*b*) they discussed and approved lump-
sum amounts of money requested by Gibbs to be budgeted for both capital
expenditures and current expenses.

At the end of the fourth year, Langford, who had been raising questions with Norman all along about the wisdom of Gibbs' expenditures, suggested that investment return and sales targets were

far less than satisfactory. We have been holding off telling him how to manage various phases of his budget too long. There is little doubt but that he has gone too fast and too far in increasing expenditures for advertising, salesmen's bonuses, and salesmen's expense accounts. Furthermore, his expenditures for employee-recreation facilities and increases in factory salaries have been unwise when we are trying to increase return on investment. The former increased the investment side of the ratio, and the latter decreased the income side.

Langford, incidentally, received expense summaries regularly—as he says, "not as control reports, but for the purpose of consolidating the figures with the rest of the company divisions for the profit and loss statement." These summaries contained 35 account captions (for excerpts of five captions, see Exhibit 3).

EXHIBIT 3
Selected Expense Captions and Amounts from Lange Division Expense Tabulation

Expense Caption	Fourth Year	Year Prior to Merger
Advertising..............	$280,000	$ 47,000
Salesmen bonuses	210,000	23,000
Salesmen expense	145,000	68,000
Factory salaries	665,000	550,000*
Employee service........	80,000	2,010

* Average salary per employee in the year prior to merger was $6,540. If this is adjusted for cost-of-living increase from that time to the fourth year, it comes out to an equivalent of $7,185. Average actual salary paid by Lange in the fourth year was $7,540.

After reviewing Langford's cost statements, the executive committee agreed that "Gibbs needs some helpful guidance." Since Langford knew more about the details of expense and capital budgets, they also agreed that he should visit Gibbs once a month to go over the 35 expense accounts and see how each progresses during the year.

Gibbs recalls that early in his fifth year at Lange, when Langford first came to Providence and told him what the executive committee had decided,

I was surprised. I guess it scared me a little right off the bat, since I had no idea they were thinking like that. The targets weren't being met, but I thought that surely they must know that things were going quite well, considering all of the things which must be done to put this division on a solid footing for the future. After my initial anxiousness and surprise, I got downright mad for a few days.

Gibbs also states that

early in the fifth year, I began to cut back on some of the spending inaugurated in the beginning. I got the salesmen together on four occasions and gave them a talk about the necessity of cutting their expense-account expenditures, and the fact that we would have to stop making some of the purely promotional calls, and concentrate on those customers that looked more like immediate prospects. I also cut the number of direct-mail promotional brochures from 12 mailings a year to six, and decided to let one man go whom we had hired as a merchandising man. He had helped, in the four years he had been with us, in designing the products for eye appeal, in creating point-of-sale displays, and in improving the eye appeal of our packages. I did not cut down on the number of salesmen employed, however.

THE QUESTION OF ADVERTISING AND RESEARCH COSTS

As early as February of the second year, Gibbs objected—in his words, "mildly"—to Norman "because of the way Langford entered on certain financial statements the money spent for advertising, the market research department, and the product research department." When the first year statement of return was prepared by Lange's own controller, Gibbs and he felt that the total of $340,000 represented an investment rather than a current operating expense. They reasoned that the increase in new products and the increase in good will or consumer acceptance would not begin to pay off for two or three years. Since return on investment is the ratio of income to investment, charging these three items to investment showed a higher performance (14 percent in the first year) than the same statement prepared by Langford (12 percent in the same year). It seemed to Gibbs that by subtracting the $340,000 from profits "was a real injustice—Tom Farish and Norman family stockholders have pretty much stayed out of my end of the business, but I don't want them to get the wrong impression. They will, from that kind of misleading figure."

Gibbs and Langford both feel that, in spite of this disagreement, the relationship of the Norman management group to Gibbs is "a pretty good one." Gibbs states that as of now,

I pretty much go along with their guidance, though it one time looked like interference. The only thing I'm still darn mad about is this way of figuring return. Norman overruled me when Langford and I had it out in front of him one time, but it's still such a hot subject that Langford and I won't bring it up any more. Why, just look at the figures for the whole period that the division has been in existence! [See Exhibit 1.]

Selected Readings

From

GENERAL MOTORS ORGANIZATION PHILOSOPHY AND STRUCTURE*

By Harlow H. Curtice†

May I first make the point that the growth of General Motors has taken place principally over the past 35 years. This period coincides with that in which the policies and business of the corporation have functioned under the existing management organization.

In my opinion there are four principal reasons for our success. These are, first, the dynamic growth of our country; second, the even more rapid growth of the automobile industry; third, our management structure; and, fourth, our approach to problems.

*   *   *   *   *

General Motors has grown faster than has the automobile industry as a whole. Quite obviously, we have made things that people wanted, and people in increasing numbers have bought them. . . .

General Motors has been able to offer greater dollar values in its products, and at the same time it has been able to operate efficiently to provide dividends for its shareholders and substantial sums for reinvestment in the business.

But, one may well ask why and how; and this brings me to what to my mind are the two fundamental reasons for the success of General Motors.

Both fall under the heading of what might be termed management philosophy. When this General Motors philosophy was formulated in the early 1920's—and I might add that the credit for its formulation largely goes to one man, Alfred P. Sloan, Jr.—it was unique as applied to industry. That it is no longer unique is in itself evidence of its soundness.

The first element of this philosophy has to do with organizational structure, the second with our approach to problems. Both, of course, concern people—in fact, can only be put into practice by people.

*   *   *   *   *

To fully appreciate the revolutionary nature of the organizational structure developed by Mr. Sloan in the early 1920's, it is necessary to appraise it in the light of conditions as they existed at that time. The business enterprise which the

---

* Reprinted by permission. From a Statement before the Subcommittee on Anti-Trust and Monopoly of the United States Senate Committee on the Judiciary, December 2, 1955 (pp. 5–12), "The Development and Growth of General Motors."

† Mr. Curtice was at one time President of General Motors Corporation.

present management took charge of in 1921 had been put together, beginning in 1908, by W. C. Durant, and it largely bore the stamp of his personality. Durant had genius as a creator and super-salesman. He was not an administrator and did not develop an effective organization. Twice under his administration the Corporation was in serious financial difficulties—first in 1910 and again in 1920.

Prior to 1921 there existed no real concept of sound management in General Motors. Operations were neither integrated nor coordinated. There was no consistent policy with respect to product programs. Frequently poor judgment was exercised in making capital expenditures and establishing production schedules. The Corporation did not have a properly developed research and engineering staff nor any sound concept of budgetary control. The central administration did not exercise adequate control over the operations of the individual divisions. There were wide variations in the competence of divisional managements. In short, the Corporation was unorganized and the individual units largely out of control.

It is not surprising, therefore, that this [Vehicle sales for 1921: G.M., 11.79%; Ford, 55.45%; all others, 32.76%] was the competitive picture in 1921 when the

CHART 1
General Motors Percent of Industry Vehicle Sales for the Year 1921

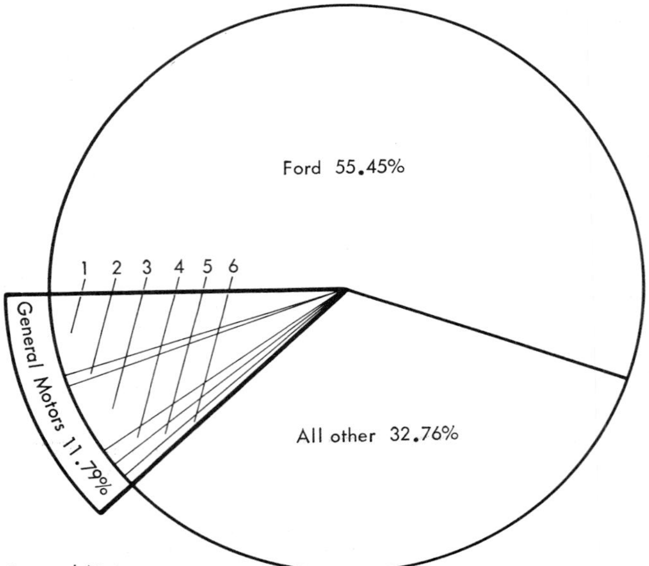

General Motors

1.	Buick	4.77%
2.	Cadillac	0.66%
3.	Chevrolet	4.04%
4.	Oldsmobile	1.13%
5.	Oakland	0.70%
6.	GMC truck and miscellaneous	0.49%
	Total	11.79%

Source: F.T.C. "Report on Motor Vehicle Industry," page 27.

management changed and Mr. Sloan began to put into effect the policies with respect to organizational structure which I will now outline.

Even before the crisis of 1920 materialized, Mr. Sloan was very conscious of the need in General Motors for a new and clearly defined concept of management philosophy. He had observed that much time was being consumed in solving detailed administrative problems and in meeting the critical situations which were constantly arising. He recognized that too great a concentration of problems upon a small number of executives limited initiative, caused delay, increased expense, reduced efficiency and retarded development.

He realized that centralization, properly established, makes possible directional control, coordination, specialization, and resulting economies. He also realized that decentralization, properly established, develops initiative and responsibility; it makes possible a proper distribution of decisions at all levels of management, including the foreman—with resulting flexibility and cooperative effort, so necessary to a large-scale enterprise. His objective was to obtain the proper balance between these two apparently conflicting principles of centralization and decentralization in order to obtain the best elements of each in the combination. He concluded that, to achieve this balance so necessary for flexibility of operation, General Motors management should be established on a foundation of centralized policy and decentralized administration.

Mr. Sloan's concept of the management of a great industrial organization, expressed in his own words as he finally evolved it, is "to divide it into as many parts as consistently as can be done, place in charge of each part the most capable executive that can be found, develop a system of coordination so that each part may strengthen and support each other part; thus not only welding all parts together in the common interests of a joint enterprise, but importantly developing ability and initiative through the instrumentalities of responsibility and ambition—developing men and giving them an opportunity to exercise their talents, both in their own interests as well as in that of the business."

In pursuance of that plan each of the various operations was established as an integral unit under a General Manager. Then, those operations which had a common relationship were grouped under a Group Executive for coordinating purposes. These Group Executives reported to the President who was the Chief Executive Officer.

To perform those functional activities that could be accomplished more effectively by one activity in the interest of the whole and to coordinate similar functional activities of the different operating units and promote their effectiveness, a General Staff, and in addition, Financial and Legal Staffs, were established to operate on a functional basis.

*   *   *   *   *

Today, General Motors has two principal committees of the Board of Directors—the Financial Policy Committee, which is concerned with the financial and legal affairs of the Corporation, and the Operations Policy Committee, which deals primarily with the operating affairs of the business.

There are two additional committees of the Board of Directors, namely, an Audit Committee and a Bonus and Salary Committee, consisting of directors who are not members of management.

*   *   *   *   *

The balance between decentralized operations, on the one hand, and coordinated control, on the other, varies according to areas. It also varies according to the temperaments and talents of executives, and the way in which they work. While the relationships of physical things are inherent in the business, it is men who establish and govern these relationships. The relationship between the Central Office Staff and the Divisional line operations may vary according to conditions and circumstances.

In summary, the organization of General Motors Corporation under the Board of Directors consists of the Financial Policy Committee and the Operations Policy Committee, supported by other committees and policy groups; staff operations; component product divisions; end product divisions; and service operations; all headed up by staff executives or general line officers who report to the Chief Executive Officer, except for the executives in charge of the financial and legal activities who report to the Chairman of the Financial Policy Committee.

*   *   *   *   *

Such a management concept provides a continuous flow of ideas and information upward and downward through the management organization, by means of reports, meetings and conferences of both staff executives and the line executives at all appropriate levels. This results in mutual education and understanding with respect to the authority, responsibility, objectives and purposes of management at all levels from the foreman to the Chief Executive Officer. It provides interpretation and understanding of policy and procedure as it is or may be established or changed. It produces an upward flow of information with respect to situations arising in operations, full knowledge of which is necessary if appropriate changes in policy or procedure are to be accomplished intelligently and promptly. It provides maximum initiative at every managerial level and at every point requiring administrative judgment, by the men closest to all the facts of the situation having full responsibility for their decisions. Finally, it makes possible accurate and prompt appraisal and evaluation of the contribution of the individual executive at every level of management, and of the contribution as well of every divisional organization and staff operation.

Although for many years this form of decentralized industrial management was identified primarily with General Motors, in more recent years decentralized management has been adopted by other large industrial companies.

The success of General Motors is the proof of the soundness of this management philosophy and its effectiveness in its application to a large industrial organization. Testifying to this has been a growing consumer preference expressed in the purchase of General Motors products.

From

COST ACCOUNTING*

By Gordon Shillinglaw†

A company is *divisionalized* whenever certain related activities are grouped together for administrative direction and control by high-level executives. Whenever this is accompanied by the delegation to division managers of the responsibility for a segment of the company's profits, then the company is said to be *decentralized.* The hallmark of the decentralized company is its subdivision into a number of smaller, relatively self-contained entities that are equipped to operate in substantially the same manner as independent firms dependent on their own profit performance for economic survival. The creation of these semiautonomous units, often referred to as *profit centers,* has three major objectives: . . .

Perhaps the most important of these is to overcome the sheer weight of the decision-making responsibility in a large corporation. With operations spread over a vast geographical area and encompassing hundreds of products and thousands of customers, central management cannot hope to be completely and continuously in direct personal contact with every segment of the company's business. To provide flexibility and adaptability to changing conditions, it has become increasingly necessary to delegate substantial powers to executives who can maintain a closer, more detailed familiarity with individual products or markets. In other words, decentralization aims to recreate in the large organization the conditions that give life and flexibility to the small company without sacrificing the advantages of size—diversification of risk, centralized financing, and specialization in the planning and advisory functions of management.

A second objective of decentralization is to bring subordinate executives into more direct contact with the ultimate profit objectives of the firm. A strictly manufacturing executive sees all problems as production problems with a cost overlay. A marketing executive focuses his attention on sales volume and distribution cost. In a centralized organization these viewpoints come together only at the top of the pyramid. Decentralization is one way of attempting to bring them together at lower levels.

Closely related to this is a third objective of decentralization, namely, to provide a more comprehensive training ground for the top managers of the future. The ranks of the top executives are continually being thinned by death and retirement, and there is a need for replacements who have been schooled in various aspects of business management and are thereby better prepared to face the major problems that can be resolved only at the top-management level. This kind of experience is best obtained at lower levels where the inevitable mistakes are likely to be smaller.

*   *   *   *   *

. . . The ideal basis for profit decentralization exists whenever a division can be relatively self-contained, with its own manufacturing and distributive facilities

---
* Reprinted by permission of Richard D. Irwin, Inc., Homewood, Ill. 1961 (pp. 680–84, 688–89).

† The author is Professor in the Graduate School of Business, Columbia University.

and relatively few transfers of product internally among divisions. In other words, decentralization is at its best whenever a division's operations come closest in scope and depth to those of separate independent companies. In these circumstances, the profit reported by each division is largely independent of operating performance in other divisions of the company, thus facilitating the interpretation of reported profits.

Unfortunately, these ideal conditions are often unattainable. Organization structure cannot be determined solely by the need for profit separability. Other factors, such as economies of common use of sales forces or facilities, may override the desirability of separating profit centers from each other. In these circumstances, the problem is to seek means of measurement and evaluation that will achieve a satisfactory compromise between conflicting objectives. Management has the task of deciding whether departures from the ideal are sufficiently serious to make profit decentralization unworkable. . . .

*   *   *   *   *

. . . No matter how it is defined, decentralization never represents a complete delegation of authority. Even in the most decentralized companies, top management retains some vestige of authority, particularly over financing and capital expenditures. In any case, divisional autonomy is limited by the need to conform to over-all company policies and by the need for co-ordination. . . .

Both at the corporate level and within each profit center there are units that are not organized on a profit responsibility basis. These are called *service centers* or *budget centers* to distinguish them from profit centers. . . . In each of these the executive in charge is responsible for costs but not for profits. . . . Within each product division there are also staff departments, such as divisional accounting or marketing research, which act in an advisory capacity to the division managers. The managers of these departments are also responsible for costs, but they generally have no direct profit responsibilities.

*   *   *   *   *

. . . Three criteria that divisional profit measures must meet stand out as especially important:

1. Divisional profit should not be increased by any action that reduces total company profit.
2. Each division's profit should be as independent as possible of performance efficiency and managerial decisions elsewhere in the company.
3. Each division's profit should reflect all items that are subject to any substantial degree of control by the division manager or his subordinates.

Four alternative concepts may be examined to see how well they fit these criteria:

1. *Variable profit,* or total revenues less total variable costs to make and sell.
2. *Controllable profit,* or variable profit less all the division's controllable fixed costs.
3. *Contribution margin,* or controllable profit less all other costs directly traceable to the division.
4. *Net profits,* or contribution margin less some share of general management and service center costs.

EXHIBIT 21–5
Four Profit Concepts Illustrated

Sales...	$760,000
Less:	
Variable costs of goods sold	$270,000
Variable divisional selling and administrative expense.	30,000
Variable profit...	$460,000
Less: Controllable divisional overhead...................	200,000
Controllable Profit	$260,000
Less: Fixed, noncontrollable divisional overhead	150,000
Contribution margin.....................................	$110,000
Less: Allocation of extradivisional fixed expenses—noncontrollable...	50,000
Net Profit before Taxes	$ 60,000

From

THE PROCESS OF MANAGEMENT: CONCEPTS, BEHAVIOR, AND PRACTICE*

By William H. Newman and Charles E. Summer †

The responses of people to standards, measurements, reports and other control devices depend, of course, on each total situation. The way a man feels toward his boss, whether he likes his work, his opportunities for self-expression, and similar factors influence his responses to controls as to other managerial actions. In the following discussion we are concerned with a narrower issue. What is there about controls per se that makes them objectionable to so many people? Why do we so often hear people say, "This is a good place to work. But I sure don't like those damn controls."

     *   *   *   *   *

One reason why people may not like a control is that they have no genuine interest in accomplishing the objective behind the control. . . .

Each of us has only a limited amount of energy, but many things he would like to do. A control, by its very nature, prods us to expend more energy in particular directions. If those directions are not so appealing to us as other things we might do, we resent the prod.

     *   *   *   *   *

---

* *The Process of Management: Concepts, Behavior and Practice,* William H. Newman and Charles E. Summer, © 1961 by Prentice-Hall, Inc., Englewood Cliffs, N.J. (pp. 605–10).

† Professor Newman is on the faculty of the Graduate School of Business, Columbia University. Professor Summer is on the Faculty of the Graduate School of Business, University of Washington.

To put this matter in terms of personal "needs," . . . if a person fails to accept certain objectives and so to include them among his needs, he is likely to find any control mechanism that pushes him toward those objectives a distinct annoyance.

*   *   *   *   *

Often a person may agree with an objective but dislike a control because he thinks the standard of performance is set too high. . . .

*   *   *   *   *

Whether a standard is considered reasonable also depends on how it is administered. Circumstances beyond the influence of a person who is being controlled may affect his actual results. Or a standard may be so tight that it can be met only half the time. . . .

A person's feeling about the unreasonableness of controls is also influenced by the total number of different controls that bear on him. Most people expect, and even welcome, some control over their activities, but as more and more aspects of their work become subject to standards, inspection, and reports, a feeling of being pressed on arises. . . .

*   *   *   *   *

Controls may increase the squabbles between departments when the people involved lack confidence in the measurements. . . .

*   *   *   *   *

Another fundamental reason why controls are unpopular is that from time to time control reports bear bad news. A person who is loath to face unpleasant facts almost always wishes the control system would vanish.

Each of us has his own personal aspirations about our work. These include both hopes and expectations. They reflect the kind of a person and the quality of worker each of us thinks he is. Now, control reports are one means of learning whether we have lived up to our own expectations. Often, we fail, and a realist accordingly adjusts the balance between expectations and facts; he may even readjust his hopes. Other persons, however, find it difficult to accept the facts of life, and so develop a sense of frustration. And since a frustrated person needs some relief, it is only natural for him to put part of the blame on the mechanism that tells him he isn't as good as he thinks he ought to be.

Furthermore, control reports may put us in an unfavorable light before our associates. To the extent that control systems measure desirable action, reports can make us appear strong or weak. . . .

The fear of unpleasant consequences can add to our aversion to controls. If an unfavorable report may lead to demotion, a cut in pay, or a bawling-out, we aren't going to feel very kindly toward the control system.

*   *   *   *   *

The response to controls depends, in part, on who tries to do the controlling. . . .

Once the social structure of a business has been established, people become sensitive about what kind of action is "legitimate.". . . Fairly strong opposition can be generated if the control pressure comes from sources employees believe are illegitimate.

*   *   *   *   *

. . . [S]ocial pressure applies to control as well as to other managerial action; . . .

*   *   *   *   *

. . . The attitudes that really count are those of associates whose friendship and respect a man wants to keep. If these persons feel that a control standard and its measurement are fair and that cooperating with management is the right thing to do, they will constitute a social force supporting that standard. Thus, there will probably be strong social support for a control over stealing money, whereas control over wasting money through unnecessary expenses will receive support only if employees feel that management administers the control reasonably and fairly. . . .

. . . [G]roup pressure becomes significant only if it is difficult to meet both company and group objectives. . . .

From

PUBLIC ADMINISTRATION*

By Herbert A. Simon, Donald W. Smithburg, and Victor A. Thompson†

From a psychological standpoint the exercise of authority involves a relationship between two or more persons. On the one side we have a person who makes proposals for the action of others. On the other side we have a person who accepts the proposals—who "obeys" them. Now a person may accept another's proposals under three different sets of circumstances:

(1) He may examine the merits of the proposal, and, on the basis of its merits become convinced that he should carry it out. We shall exclude such instances of acceptance from our notion of authority, although some writers on administration have called this the "authority of ideas."

(2) He may carry out the proposals without being fully, or even partially, convinced of its merits. In fact he may not examine the merits of the proposal at all.

(3) He may carry out the proposal even though he is convinced it is wrong— wrong either in terms of personal values or of organizational values or both.

We will treat both the second and third cases as instances of the acceptance of authority. Of course in any actual instance all three of the "pure types" of acceptance listed above may be combined in various proportions. In actual practice authority is almost always liberally admixed with persuasion. . . .

* * * * *

Because the person who accepts proposals may do so for a variety of motives, there will be seen in any organization a number of different types of authority relationship, corresponding to these different motives for acceptance. . . .

People accept the proposals of persons in whom they have great confidence.

* Reprinted from *Public Administration* by Herbert A. Simon, Donald W. Smithburg, and Victor A. Thompson, by permission of Alfred A. Knopf, Inc. Copyright 1950 by Herbert A. Simon, Donald W. Smithburg, and Victor A. Thompson. (Excerpts from pp. 182, 189–200.)

† At the time this book was written Dr. Simon was Professor of Administration at Carnegie-Mellon University; Drs. Smithburg and Thompson were Professors of Political Science at Illinois Institute of Technology.

In any organization there are some individuals who, because of past performance, general reputation, or other factors, have great influence or authority. Their proposals will often be accepted without analysis as to their wisdom. Even when the suggestions of such a person are not accepted, they will be rejected reluctantly and only because a stronger authority contradicts them.

The authority of confidence may be limited to a special area of competence in which a person has acquired a reputation. . . .

*   *   *   *   *

. . . The willingness to accept authority on the basis of confidence, both within and outside organizations, goes even one step further. Not only is the layman generally unable to judge the quality of the advice he is getting from the specialist, but he often is in no position to judge the competence of the specialist, except on the basis of certain superficial and formal criteria that give the specialist his *status.*

. . . [T]here are at least two kinds of status, which may be called *functional status* and *hierarchical status.* It is with functional status that we are concerned at the moment. A person has functional status in a particular area of knowledge when his decisions and recommendations in that area are accepted as more or less authoritative.

In the established professions, status is generally conferred on the basis of standards developed by the profession itself. The M.D. degree is conferred on the young doctor by the medical profession (acting through an "accredited" medical school). Law and engineering degrees and the certificate of the public accountant are awarded in much the same way. In other cases, job experience in a particular field confers functional status in that field. A person with long experience in a professional position in the Interstate Commerce Commission may acquire status as a transportation economist.

*   *   *   *   *

. . . Confidence can be a powerful support for hierarchical as well as for nonhierarchical authority. A subordinate will much more readily obey a command of a superior if he has confidence in the intelligence and judgment of that superior or if he believes that the superior has knowledge of the situation not available to himself.

In particular, where a problem requiring decision affects the work of several units in an organization, the superior who has hierarchical authority in the formal organization plan over all the units involved is often accepted as the person best located—because he has the "whole picture"—to make the decision. Hence, the coordinating functions that are commonly performed by those in hierarchical authority are based, in part at least, upon the authority of confidence—upon the belief of subordinates that the superior is the best informed about the situation as a whole.

*   *   *   *   *

The most generally recognized weapon of the superior is the sanction—the ability of the superior to attach pleasant or unpleasant consequences to the actions of the subordinate. . . .

*   *   *   *   *

. . . The relationship of the authority of sanctions with the organizational hierarchy can be viewed from a more general standpoint. When a person joins an organization he is accepting a system of relationships that restricts his individuality or his freedom of action. He is willing to do so because he feels that, in spite of the organizational restraints, being a member of the organization is preferable to other alternatives available to him. To continue as a member of the organization, he must continue, to some extent, to abide by the complex of procedures which constitutes the organization. Although, increasingly, the power to discharge an employee is not lodged in any specific superior (because of merit systems, central personnel offices, labor unions, etc.), nevertheless, this power resides somewhere in the organization, being, in fact, one of its working procedures. The sanctions discussed in this section are increasingly *organization* sanctions, brought into play through the working procedures of the organization, and not the special prerogatives or powers of *individual superiors*. . . .

. . . For the most part the authority of sanction rests on the behavior responses that are induced by the *possibility* that a sanction may be applied. An organization member is seldom presented with an ultimatum "to do so and so or suffer the consequences." Rather, he anticipates the consequences of continual insubordination or failure to please the person or persons who have the ability to apply sanctions to him, and this anticipation acts as a constant motivation without expressed threats from any person. . . .

*   *   *   *   *

There is another reason why employees accept the proposals of other organization members—a reason less rationalistic but probably more important than the desire to avoid the organization sanctions discussed above. People accept "legitimate" authority because they feel that they *ought* to go along with the "rules of the game."

. . . [T]hroughout their development to maturity and after, people are educated in the beliefs, values, or mores of society. They learn what they ought to do and what they ought not to do. One of the values with which they are indoctrinated is that a person should play according to the rules of the game. This ethic is acquired very early. When a child enters a ball game in the sand lot he does not expect the game to be altered at various points to suit his convenience. Rather he expects to adjust his behavior to the rules of the game. Although there may be disputes as to what the rule is on some point, once this is established, the proposition that he should abide by the rule is unquestioned.

Likewise, when people enter organizations most of them feel that they ought to abide by the rules of the game—the working procedures of the organization. These working procedures define how the work will be done; how working problems will be solved when they arise; how conflicts will be settled. They prescribe that on such and such matters the individual will accept the suggestions of this or that person or organization; secure the advice of such and such unit; clear his work with so and so; work on matters that come to him in such and such a way; etc.

The working procedures of an organization prescribe that the individual member will accept the proposals of other members in matters assigned to them. This acceptance is one of the rules of the game which he feels he should abide by. Thus, individuals in organizations also accept the authority of other persons because they think they *ought* to accept it.

*   *   *   *   *

. . . The working relationships in an organization designated by the term "hierarchy" constitute a particular organization procedure for handling the authority of legitimacy. Acceptance of the working procedures of an organization by a member includes acceptance of the obligation to go along wth the proposals of an hierarchical superior, at least within a limit of toleration—the "area of acceptance." Thus, whether the other reasons for obedience are operating or not (confidence, identification, or sanctions), organization members will feel that they ought to obey their superiors. Legitimacy is one of the most important sources of the authority of the hierarchical superior.

The feeling that hierarchical authority is legitimate is immensely strengthened by previous social conditioning. Hierarchical behavior is an institutionalized behavior that all organization members bring to the organization with them. Like the players in the Oberammergau Passion Play who begin to learn their roles in early childhood, "inferiors" obey "superiors" because they have been taught to do so from infancy, beginning with the parent-child relationship and running through almost constant experience with social and organizational hierarchies until death brings graduation from this particular social schooling. Hierarchical behavior involves an inferior-superior role-taking of persons well versed in their roles. "Inferiors" feel that they ought to obey "superiors"; "superiors" feel that they ought to be obeyed.

Our society is extremely hierarchical. Success is generally interpreted in terms of hierarchical preferment. Social position and financial rewards are closely related to hierarchical preferment, as also are education and even perhaps romantic attainment. Advancement up a hierarchy is generally considered a sign of moral worth, of good character, of good stewardship, of social responsibility, and of the possession of superior intellectual qualities.

Hierarchy receives a tremendous emphasis in nearly all organizations. This is so because hierarchy is a procedure that requires no training, no indoctrination, no special inducements. It rests also entirely on "pre-entry" training—a training so thorough that few other organization procedures can ever compete with it. Furthermore, hierarchy is a great simplification. . . .

From

MATHEMATICAL APPROACH TO LONG-RANGE PLANNING*

By Leo A. Rapoport and William P. Drews†

Almost everybody will agree that over-all optimization is desirable. At the same time, however, there still is a widespread belief that the best plan for an integrated business will be obtained by letting each of the component activities improve its own efficiency as much as possible. Another common view is that for purposes

* Reprinted by permission of the *Harvard Business Review,* May–June 1962, pp. 77–78.

† At the time this article was written the authors were Research Associates with Esso Research and Engineering Company.

of optimal planning it suffices to evaluate and screen projects or budget proposals on the basis of their individual profitability. These are serious misconceptions.

Mathematically it can be demonstrated that the maximum of a composite function generally does not correspond to the values of variables which maximize the individual components of that function. A simple graphical illustration of this situation in the context of economics appeared in a recent article by Edward G. Bennion.[1] The optimization principle has also been stated in clear terms by Peter F. Drucker:

". . . If there is one fundamental insight underlying all management science, it is that the business enterprise is a *system* of the highest order. . . .

"The whole of [such] a system is not necessarily improved if one particular function or part is improved or made more efficient. In fact, the system may well be damaged thereby, or even destroyed. In some cases the best way to strengthen the system may be to *weaken* a part—to make it *less* precise or *less* efficient. For what matters in any system is the performance of the whole. . . .

"Primary emphasis on the efficiency of parts in management science is therefore bound to do damage. It is bound to optimize precision of the tool at the expense of the health and performance of the whole.

"This is hardly a hypothetical danger. The literature abounds in actual examples —inventory controls that improve production runs and cut down working capital but fail to consider the delivery expectations of the customer and the market risks of the business; machine-loading schedules that overlook the impact of the operations of one department on the rest of the plant; forecasts that assume the company's competitors will just stand still; and so on."[2]

Admittedly, the above statements are somewhat general and, therefore, might appear as unfounded abstractions to the hardened skeptic. A simple example, however, might help to illustrate their practical importance:

In the case of our hypothetical oil company in Exhibit I, suppose that one of the refineries should find it most profitable to install a particular processing unit of Type T in order to utilize a certain low-price crude, C_t. The installation of this unit would be justified *from the refiner's viewpoint* by showing an attractive return on incremental investment. This "conventional" approach, however, may overlook the aspects of functional interdependence.

Bear in mind that the installation and efficient utilization of a processing unit of Type T would commit the producing function to a continued supply of crude, C_t. This crude, although low priced (on the outside market), may not, in fact, be the least costly to produce, nor would it necessarily remain the least costly as greater amounts of it become required in the future. Accordingly, from an over-all viewpoint, it could prove more desirable to install a different processing unit of Type S. This other unit might be more expensive to install or to operate than Type T. In compensation, however, it would permit utilization of some other crude, C_s, which in the long run might be less costly to produce than crude, C_t.

Under such conditions, it is apparent that over-all company economics could actually be improved by *weakening* the economics of one of the refineries.

---

[1] "Econometrics for Management," *Harvard Business Review*, March–April 1961, p. 100.

[2] "Thinking Ahead: Potentials of Management Science," *Harvard Business Review*, January–February 1959, p. 26.

Danger of Suboptimization

The preceding example, oversimplified as it is, highlights one of the basic shortcomings of the conventional methods of economic analysis. This shortcoming amounts to excessive "suboptimization" from the viewpoint of investment planning. . . .

From

THEORY AND PROBLEMS OF SOCIAL PSYCHOLOGY*

By David Krech and Richard S. Crutchfield†

[EDITORS' NOTE: In the passages below, the authors are discussing the mental process of *perception*. In prior pages of the chapter, they point out that the meaning a human mind derives from an event or stimuli is determined by two things: structural factors (what is "out there" in the world) and functional factors (what is "in the head" of the individual, stored in the form of needs, moods, memories of past experiences, etc.). The abstract below deals only with functional factors—how decision making is affected by the past experiences, moods, needs, attitudes, of the individual.]

TWO MAJOR DETERMINANTS OF PERCEPTION

*   *   *   *   *

Structural Factors. By *structural* factors are meant those factors deriving solely from the nature of the physical stimuli and the neural effects they evoke in the nervous system of the individual.[1] Thus, for the Gestalt psychologist, perceptual organizations are determined primarily by the physiological events occurring in the nervous system of the individual in direct reaction to the stimulation by the physical objects. Though not denying the influence, under certain conditions, of motivation and mental set, they emphasize that the sensory factors are primary in accounting for the "look of things."

To use a very simple and common example, the Gestalt psychologist would point out that our perception of the dots in Fig. 1*a* is perforce a perception of two horizontal groupings and not, say, an ungrouped collection of dots or of five vertical groupings, etc. Furthermore, they would insist that the factors which force this organization derive from the spatial relationships among the physical dots themselves as faithfully projected in the sensory region of the brain and are relatively

---

* By permission from *Theory and Problems of Social Psychology*, by David Krech and Richard S. Crutchfield. Copyright 1948. McGraw–Hill Book Company, Inc. (Excerpts from pp. 81–83, 87–89, 94–96, 98, 102–3.)

† The authors are Professors of Psychology at the University of California, Berkeley.

[1] The term *autochthonous* is frequently used by the Gestalt psychologist when referring to these factors.

FIGURE 1

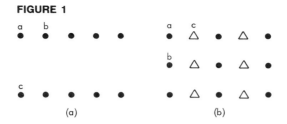

(a)   (b)

independent of our reasoning, needs, moods, past learning, etc. To repeat: Those sensory factors which are independent of the perceiving individual's needs and personality and which force certain organizations in his cognitive field are referred to as "structural factors of perception." The isolation of these factors, their careful description, and the laws of their operation have led to the formulation of the "laws of organization."

Functional Factors.   The *functional* factors of perceptual organization, on the other hand, are those which derive primarily from the needs, moods, past experience, and memory of the individual.[2] Thus, for example, in an experiment performed by Bruner and Goodman (1947), two groups of children (one a poor group from a settlement house in one of Boston's slum areas and the other a rich group from a "progressive school in the Boston area, catering to the sons and daughters of prosperous business and professional people") were asked to judge the size of various coins. The differences in the perceptions of the two groups of children were striking, with the poor group overestimating the size of the coins considerably more than did the rich group. The experimenters suggest that these results indicate the effect of need upon perception, and they formulate the following two hypotheses as possible general laws:

1. *The greater the social value of an object, the more will it be susceptible to organization by behavioral determinants.*

2. *The greater the individual need for a socially valued object, the more marked will be the operation of behavioral determinants.*

Another illustration of the operation of functional factors is found in an experiment by Levine, Chein, and Murphy (1942). In that experiment, ambiguous drawings, when presented behind a ground-glass screen to hungry college students, were more frequently perceived as food objects (ham sandwiches, salads, etc.) than when presented to college students who had just finished eating. The different perceptions of the hungry and non-hungry students could not be due to "structural" factors, since the same pictures were presented to both groups but could be due only to the differences in need or motivation of the members of the two groups.

While quantitative laws of how these "functional" factors actually operate in

---

[2] The term *functional* as applied to these factors was first suggested by Meunzinger (1942). In their treatment of these same factors, Bruner and Goodman (1947) suggest the term "behavioral determinants" which they define as ". . . those active, adaptive functions of the organism which lead to the governance and control of all higher-level functions including perception. . . ."

perception are lacking, a great deal of experimental work is available that demonstrates their pervasive influence in perception.

*   *   *   *   *

Perception Is Functionally Selective

No one perceives everything that there is "out there" to be perceived. Our mental apparatus is not an indifferent organizing machine ready to accord equal importance to all stimuli that impinge upon our sense organs. The factors that determine the specific organization of our cognitive field and select out only certain stimuli to integrate into that field are frequently at work even before we are exposed to the physical stimuli. Typically, only certain physical stimuli are "used" in making up the organized perception, while other stimuli are either not used at all or are given a very minor role. This is what is meant by saying that perception is "selective." . . . this selectivity is functional. The objects that play the major role in the organized perception, the objects that are accentuated, are usually those objects which serve some immediate purpose of the perceiving individual. . . .

. . . Let us take the simple example of two men seated at a lunchroom counter surveying the posted menu on the wall. One is very hungry; the other, only thirsty. Both are exposed to the same physical objects, yet the first will notice the hamburger and tomato-and-lettuce sandwiches, while the "tea, coffee, beer, pepsi-cola" items will be neglected or relatively so. The second man will react in the opposite manner. Ask both men to tell you what they "saw" on the menu, and the first will respond with a list of food items "and other stuff"; the second will enumerate the drink items "and other things." In one case the food items have been clearly and specifically perceived and organized against a background of nondifferential "other stuff"; in the second case the figure-ground relationships have been reversed.

Mental Set. . . . We see hundreds of men, every day, wearing different suits of clothing—suits that differ in cut, material, color, styling, number of buttons, etc. But usually all we perceive is that they are wearing clothes, and our resulting perceptual organization is not a very clear cut and differentiated one. What is the mental picture you have, for example, of the suit you saw your friend wear yesterday? But if we are on the way to a store to buy a suit, our perceptions of the clothes worn by friends and even strangers change rather remarkably. . . .

*   *   *   *   *

The Perceptual and Cognitive Properties of a Substructure Are Determined in Large Measure by the Properties of the Structure of Which It Is a Part

. . . Our mental world is a structured or organized one, and it can also be seen as broken down into hierarchies of structures. Our cognitive field does not consist of completely independent organized structures; each of our perceptions is not an experience that "lives a life of its own," as it were. Every perception is embedded in an organization of other percepts—the whole going to make up a specific "cognitive structure." . . . [W]hen we perceive a politician, our perception of that particular politician is influenced by all our other percepts involving politicians. But the major structure, politicians, may have substructures: Democratic politicians, Republican politicians, honest politicians, etc. . . .

Illustrations from Simple Visual Perception. Figure 2 is usually perceived as a simple figure of three lines meeting at a center point *O.* Each angle made by any two adjacent lines, say angle *AOC,* can be described as a substructure of the figure. That is, the perception of that angle is of an organized figure "in its own right," but it is also perceived as a part of a larger figure—the whole of Fig. 2. Each

FIGURE 2

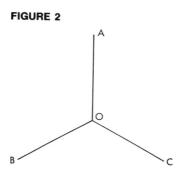

of these angles is usually perceived as an obtuse angle, *i.e.,* larger than a right angle. What would happen to our perception of angle *AOC* if we added a few lines so as to induce a change in our perception of the *whole* structure without, in any way changing the lines that make up angle *AOC*? The answer is immediately given if we look at Fig. 3. Now we perceive the substructure, angle *AOC,* as a right angle!

FIGURE 3

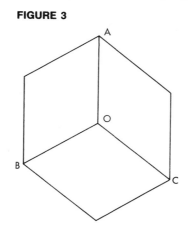

Although we have not done anything physically to angle *AOC,* it "looks" different. It looks different because the *whole* figure, of which angle *AOC* is a part, looks different.

      *   *   *   *   *

Now suppose that all you could see were angle *AOC* of Fig. 2 or only the single dot in our last illustration and you were told that a given person insisted that he perceived angle *AOC* as a right angle or that another individual perceived the dot as light gray. Would it not appear to you either that these people had defective vision or that they were inaccurate in their descriptions of their own perceptions? This would be a logical deduction if you could not see the whole of Fig. 2 of which angle *AOC* was a part. . . . We cannot understand an individual's perception, or interpretation of an event that is part of a larger organization for *him,* unless we also know what that larger organization is. . . .

* * * * *

. . . This general whole-part principle has so many ramifications in our cognitive and social life that it might be useful to reformulate it in still another way. Frequently we are forced to pay attention to new facts, facts that seem not to fit in with our existing structures or that even contradict them. At times, this results in a fairly radical reorganization of the existing major structures of our cognitive field, but frequently such a reorganization does not take place despite our perception of contradictory facts. For example, if we have a very strongly structured field in which the Jew is always penurious, we will not easily see any single Jew as a philanthropist, no matter how philanthropic his activities may be. In some way or other this disturbing Jew is "assimilated" into our rigidly structured organization. However, close analysis will reveal that such facts as these are encompassed by our original generalization. To comprehend what frequently happens when "contradictory" perceptions occur, it is useful to reformulate Proposition III in the following way: *Other things being equal, a change introduced into the psychological field will be absorbed in such a way as to produce the smallest effect on a strong structure.*

* * * * *

Objects or Events That Are Close to Each Other in Space or Time or Resemble Each Other Tend to Be Apprehended as Parts of a Common Structure

If we are to know just why certain perceptions are organized together with other perceptions to make one cognitive structure, we must have some general understanding of what determines why an individual will organize the perceptions of object *A* with that of object *B* into one common structure rather than the perception of object *A* with that of object *C*. Why, for example, do some people have a cognitive structure in which socialism and Christianity are organized together, while other people have a cognitive structure in which socialism and atheism are found together? Proposition IV attempts to indicate the major factors that determine the contents of a single structure.

Proximity and Similarity. In visual perception, experimental literature is replete with demonstrations that proximity and similarity are important organizing factors. Fig. 1*a,* which was used to illustrate the structural factors in perception, can serve to illustrate that in simple perception those objects which are close to each other in space (proximity) tend to be organized together in perception. Dot *A* is perceived as belonging to dot *B* rather than to dot *C* simply because *A* is closer to *B* than it is to *C*. A simple measurement of the physical distances among the different dots, everything else being equal, would permit us to predict, with a high degree of accuracy, which dots would be organized with which other dots. Similarly, Fig. 1*b* can be used to illustrate the principle of similarity. Here, dot *A* will be organized with dot *B* rather than with dot *C* because *A* is more similar (in shape) to *B* than it is to *C.*

From

SETTING STANDARDS FOR EXECUTIVE PERFORMANCE*

By John W. Enell and George H. Haas

[EDITORS' NOTE: At the time this article was written the authors were research associate, and director of Information Service and Surveys, respectively, both of the American Management Association. In 1960 the A.M.A. conducted a seminar on setting standards for executive performance. Fifteen corporations were represented. The abstracts below summarize certain important ideas from a 793-page transcript of the seminar proceedings.]

During the seminar, it was noted by many of the panelists that the very process of formulating standards of performance can itself be of great benefit. In almost all the companies represented in this study, supervisor and subordinate work together in drawing up standards for the subordinate's job, sometimes in conference with a staff man from the personnel department. Standards developed in this manner are usually taken seriously by the executives who have had a part in their formulation; a give-and-take discussion results in a better understanding of the nature of the job expected and also of the priorities of its various segments. This formulation-by-conference method can help, too, by giving the supervisor a better understanding of the real conditions present in the subordinate's work. The seminar participants reported that, when standards were first tried in their firms, instances were found where a supervisor and his subordinate were at the outset completely at variance in their understanding of the nature of the job under consideration. This sort of misunderstanding apparently arises at every level of management. The process of correcting these conflicting views and hammering out agreement on the nature and quality of results expected on the job is an important phase of management development.

* * * * *

Almost all the participants agreed that the executive and the subordinate must come together at some point in the process and candidly bring up—and iron out—any differences that arise. Even Robert Grover of Snap-On Tools took this point of view, despite the fact that his firm's chief standard of performance is a very detailed company-wide and departmental system of budgets. Mr. Grover remarked that the subordinate is given an opportunity to express himself when the budget for his unit is in the discussion stage. If he feels that he cannot live

* Reprinted by permission of the American Management Association, New York, Research Study No. 42, 1960 (pp. 16–18, 31–32).

within his budget or produce the amount of income required of him (provided that he is in an income-producing area), he has an adequate opportunity to make his point of view clear. Once he has agreed to his budget, he must comply with it.

. . . Mr. Daffern cited one instance in which the subordinate declared that the discussion during which standards were worked out was the only time in a long work history when he had had any really frank discussion with his boss about his responsibilities and their fulfillment. . . .

7. SEABOARD CHEMICAL CORPORATION

Case Introduction

SYNOPSIS

Auditors from the Cleveland headquarters of Seaboard Chemical Corporation visit the Los Angeles Plant, where they judge certain items in the equipment inventory to be ruined. On return to Cleveland, they advise the controller of their judgment, who in turn requests the plant manager to write off the equipment's value ($45,000) from the asset accounts, which make up the company's balance sheet. There is disagreement between various people at the plant and at headquarters as to whether the equipment is, in fact, ruined. Actions of the parties involved are described as they relate to other individuals, and to the company organization structure.

WHY THIS CASE IS INCLUDED

The Seaboard situation shows how the necessity for central planning (by experts) and the necessity for uniformity often conflict with the necessity for decision-making freedom at lower operating levels. The executive is faced with theories which prescribe different solutions to this problem; the "technology school" of management gives one answer, the "political school" gives another, and the "psychology school" gives a third.

In this case, a conflict appears between staff executives and line executives, and between parts of the organization structure (position descriptions of the executives involved). The various theories mentioned above all have some truth in them, and one must judge which ones apply to the specific situation.

DIAGNOSTIC AND PREDICTIVE QUESTIONS

The readings included with this case are marked (*). The author index at the end of this book locates the other readings.

1. From the standpoint of finance (management of cash flow), why is Mr. Turner interested in having the book figures at headquarters be an accurate "symbol" or "picture" of the assets which actually exist in the real world? Or, assuming that the physical equipment will actually be needed in the following accounting period, and that company headquarters must provide funds, why is he interested in such accuracy?

Read: *Anthony, *Management Accounting,* pp. 290–92, 306. (Remember that the equipment is part of the capital equipment inventory.)

2. From the standpoint of the company's legal position with stockholders, and the fiduciary function of controllership, why was Turner's job description written the way it was?

Read: From standard texts on accounting, or auditing, study the concept of fiduciary relationship. Or, study the job description and draw your own conclusions from case facts.

3. From the viewpoint of perception theory, and certain sociological processes, why is there disagreement between the plant personnel and the headquarters personnel in Seaboard Corporation? Why might each party rely on his own job description?

Read: *Merton, "Bureaucratic Structure and Personality." Krech and Crutchfield, *Theory and Problems of Social Psychology,* pp. 81–83, 87–89, 94–96, 98, 102–3.

4. The problem of assets might be solved partially if each plant had its own corrosion engineer to appraise assets, rather than having one corrosion engineer at headquarters who works in all three plants. Why would such an organization structure not be feasible in the Seaboard Chemical Company?

Read: Summer, "Economies of Scale and Organization Structure."

5. From the viewpoint of that management theory which stresses technological excellence, who do you predict is most capable to make the final decision in the matter of asset condition?

Read: *Taylor, "Shop Management," pp. 92–96, 98–100. Veblen, *The Engineers and the Price System,* Chapter 5. *Smith, *The Wealth of Nations,* pp. 4–15.

6. From the viewpoint of that management theory which stresses political science and "law and order," who do you predict is the most competent person (or position) to make the final decision on asset conditions?

Read: *Fayol, *General and Industrial Management,* pp. 24–25, 68–70. *O'Donnell, "The Source of Managerial Authority." *Locke, *Concerning Civil Government,* Chapter 9.

7. From the viewpoint of that management theory which stresses initiative, freedom, and autonomy of individual people, who in the whole hierarchy (from president to storehouse supervisor) is most qualified to make the decision on asset conditions?

Read: Curtice, "General Motors Organization Philosophy and Structure." McGregor, *The Human Side of Enterprise,* pp. 3–10, 47–48, 53–54.

POLICY QUESTIONS

8. Do you think any one person in the organization should decide on the condition of the equipment in the storage yard? If so, whom? If so, explain why the person you designate would have the most valid, or true, decision.

9. What specific changes would you recommend for the job descriptions of the controller and the plant manager? For any other job descriptions in the Seaboard organization?

10. Suppose answer to Question 8 is "no." What other means are available for getting a decision made which is valid or accurate?

Read: Follett, "Constructive Conflict." Eells and Walton, *Conceptual Foundations of Business,* pp. 361–63. McGregor, *The Human Side of Enterprise,* pp. 124–31, 172–75. Schein, *Process Consultation: Its Role in Organization Development,* pp. 3–9.

QUESTIONS FOR ORIGINAL STUDENT WORK IN ANALYSIS AND POLICY

11. While reflecting on case facts, what additional theories from prior education give you insights as to "what is going on" in the Seaboard Chemical Corporation? As to what might be predicted to happen in the future?

12. Other than the policy questions asked by the authors, what pragmatic ways can you think of to state the practical problems faced by executives in the case?

Case Text*

Seaboard Chemical Corporation is a producer of sulphuric acid, employing a total of 1,640 people, with headquarters in Cleveland, Ohio. Plants are operated at Cleveland; Marcus Hook, Pennsylvania; and Los Angeles. The company is one of the older firms that produce this basic chemical.

The case concerns a problem that has arisen in the work performed at the Los Angeles plant and the work performed by the controller's department in Cleveland. Excerpts from job descriptions of the Plant Manager and the Controller appear in Exhibits 1 and 2. The general duties of other people in the plant and in the controller's department are

---

* Copyright, 1973, Charles E. Summer.

EXHIBIT 1*
Position Description of Plant Manager, Los Angeles

1. The Plant Manager shall be responsible for operating the Plant profitably.
6. The Plant Manager shall attempt at all times to keep costs to a reasonable minimum, and to prevent waste of monetary and physical resources.
8. The Plant Manager's responsibility covers all operations within the plant, including direct production lines, maintenance work, and construction operations.
10. The Plant Manager shall have such authority over all personnel in the plant as is necessary to carry out the other responsibilities enumerated herein.

* Taken from page 16, Organization Manual, excerpt of certain numbered items.

EXHIBIT 2*
Position Description of Controller, Headquarters Staff

1. The Controller shall have the responsibility of conserving all assets of the Company, and of protecting them from misappropriation, abuse or other conditions prejudicial to the interests of the owning stockholders.
5. The Controller shall personally, or through his appointed representatives, make a periodic audit to determine the condition of company land, buildings, plants, warehouses and other fixed and current assets, and their accurate valuation.
8. The Controller shall gather totals of all company assets from various locations, and all company liabilities from various locations, and consolidate these into the company-wide balance sheet at the end of the year.

* Taken from page 8, Organization Manual, excerpt of certain numbered items.

mentioned later in the case. A simplified organization chart of the company appears in Exhibit 3.

It is the practice of Seaboard to do most of the construction of acid-processing units at each of its plants, rather than to farm out the construction of such machinery to outside construction firms. At each plant, a construction department, headed by a process (chemical) engineer, designs and constructs the various mixing vessels, pipe lines, agitators, and other equipment through which raw materials are converted to finished acid. Because the materials are so corrosive, some units of machinery must be replaced as often as once a year, and many others must be replaced after a useful life of one to five years. Replacement of depreciated equipment is continuous, and construction work is treated as routine, rather than as major addition to the plant.

In order to carry out the actual building and construction of processing units, each plant has a construction department, headed by a foreman. The specifications for this position state that the man who holds the job

EXHIBIT 3
Partial Organization Chart of Seaboard Chemical Corporation

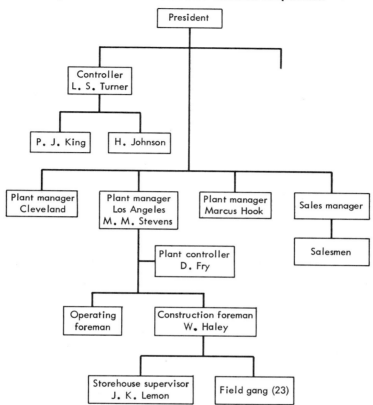

must be a graduate process (chemical) engineer, with at least five years' experience in actual construction operations. The incumbent at Los Angeles is Bill Haley. M. M. Stevens, the plant manager at Los Angeles, says that, "Haley is unusually competent in his job, having been with us for eight years. He hasn't practiced design engineering since graduation, but he knows a lot about the practical side of construction."

Haley schedules the work, and watches the progress, of 23 construction laborers. He is also responsible for the storage of materials used in construction, though this activity has been delegated to J. F. Lemon, supervisor of the storehouse department. This department operates a warehouse for storing the hundreds of parts used regularly in the construction of units. These range from pumps worth $1,200, down to nuts and bolts worth a few cents, up to large heat exchangers that may cost $20,000 or more. In addition to warehouse space, there is a storage yard adjoining the warehouse, surrounded by a steel security fence, where large equipment is maintained in open storage.

Last August, P. J. King, a CPA and financial auditor in the controller's department in Cleveland, accompanied by Harry Johnson, an engineer-auditor employed in the same department, made their yearly visit to Los Angeles for the purpose of verifying the capital equipment on hand. This procedure had been set up so that the company controller, L. S. Turner, could have an accurate consolidated picture of the company's asset accounts to put on the balance sheet at the end of the year. King and Johnson spot-check the physical equipment in the plant, compare the equipment they inspect with the accounts kept in the plant controller's office, and either verify that the dollar amount in the account represents certain physical equipment, or advise plant personnel when they are unable to locate the specific physical equipment (asset) in the warehouse that should match a monetary asset carried on the books by the controller.

In performing this spot-check and comparison, King and Johnson found in the storage yard certain items that they inspected with close scrutiny and later decided were damaged to the point where they should be physically salvaged (sold for junk or second-hand equipment) and subtracted from the assets on the books of the plant. These items, supposedly new, cost a total of $45,000. Johnson, a specialist in metals, corrosion, and condition of equipment, drafted the following memorandum to Mr. Fry, the plant controller. The memo was signed by King as well as by Johnson.

> *Our visit to Los Angeles this year has been a pleasant one, and we particularly want to thank you for the cooperation shown us by yourself and the men in your department. The only account which we believe should be adjusted is the storehouse materials account, in the amount of $45,000, and supported by the attached list. Messrs. Lemon and Haley have discussed this with us and state that the equipment is certainly in questionable condition, but that they may be able to use it in some way next year. We have, in turn, explained to them that it is in the interest of the company as a whole to have an accurate balance sheet. Only in this way can the President have the accurate information with which to run the company, and do his own planning. Since the equipment is in fact ruined, the Cleveland headquarters must provide for its replacement in next year's budget, but we cannot do this unless the accounts show the need for it. With this information, Mr. Haley said that he will go along with the decision to salvage.*

After returning to Cleveland, Johnson gave a copy of this memorandum to Mr. Turner, company controller, and explained the problem of the ruined equipment. Mr. Turner then sent a routine memorandum to Mr. Fry, the last paragraph of which read:

> *Would you therefore be kind enough to adjust the storehouse account downward in the amount of $45,000, so that when, in December, you send the totals in each account to Cleveland, the Controller here will*

have accurate figures to combine with assets of other plants for entry on the year-end balance sheet.

Fry studied the memorandum and brought up the problem with M. M. Stevens, the plant manager, at a regular Monday morning conference Stevens had set up so that he could keep abreast of financial and cost matters at the plant. Stevens had been a foreman of the blending operation for 12 years before becoming plant manager, and for the remainder of his 30 years with the company had risen from a mixer's helper up through the production operations to foreman. He had not worked in the construction department. He says, however, that, "I have watched an awful lot of construction in this plant the last 30 years, and I have a good general knowledge of the whole operation."

Stevens visited the maintenance yard along with Haley, and both men agreed that the equipment listed in the Cleveland memo was "in not too good condition." They also agreed that, "We may be able to use it next year, but we'll have to wait until then to know what shape it is in." Stevens then told Fry that an additional reason for not writing off the equipment is that, "This $45,000 will be looked at as a deduction from the profitability of this plant, and we shouldn't be blamed for it until we know definitely whether it is usable." On instruction from Stevens, Fry, on November 6th, sent the following note to Turner:

Mr. Stevens has asked me to not write off the $45,000 worth of equipment specified in your September 14 memorandum. Therefore, the asset accounts which are listed in the attached report for balance sheet purposes reflect the fact that we are still carrying this equipment on our books.

At the writing of this case, on December 15, this is where the matter stands. In effect, the company controller, Turner, has taken the information supplied by his staff men, Johnson and King, and has requested Fry, the plant controller, to write down the equipment. Fry, on the other hand, has taken the information given him by Stevens, and the information given him by Johnson and King, and written to Turner the above memo.

Selected Readings

From

MANAGEMENT ACCOUNTING*

By Robert N. Anthony†

. . . As goods are purchased or manufactured, inventory is increased; as they are sold, inventory is decreased, accounts receivables are increased, and income is earned; as the receivables are collected, cash is increased; and the cycle is completed with the use of cash to pay off the payables created when purchases were made or costs incurred. Because this cycle occurs over and over again in the course of normal operations, current assets and current liabilities are often referred to collectively as *circulating capital.*

Part of the funds tied up in current assets is supplied by vendors (accounts payable) and other short-term creditors. The remainder, which is the difference between current assets and current liabilities, and which is called working capital, must come from other, more permanent sources. These other sources must also supply the funds that are tied up in the noncurrent assets. Funds supplied for these purposes are called *permanent capital.* Changes in the sources of permanent capital and the uses to which it is put are likely to be of more than ordinary interest both to management and to outsiders since they reflect the results of the important financial decisions that have significant long-run consequences. In order to focus on these changes, we shall not bother with the recurring movement of funds among the separate current asset and current liability accounts. The necessity for tracing these separate flows can be avoided by combining all these accounts into the single item, working capital.

Basic Relationships

A balance sheet shows the net effect of funds transactions from the beginning of the business to the balance sheet date. The equities side shows the sources from which funds have been obtained, and the assets side shows the way in which these funds have been used. The balance sheet in Illustration 12–1 shows that as of the end of 1957, long-term creditors have furnished $145,000 of capital, and stockholders have furnished $394,000. Of the latter, $211,000 represents their

---

* Reprinted by permission of Richard D. Irwin, Inc., Homewood, Ill., 1960 (pp. 290–92, 306).

† The author is Professor of Business Administration, Graduate School of Business Administration, Harvard University.

ILLUSTRATION 1
Condensed Balance Sheet December 31, 1957

Assets		Equities	
Working capital	$125,000	Long-term debt	$145,000
		Capital stock	211,000
Fixed assets	414,000	Retained earnings	183,000
Total Assets	$539,000	Total Equities	$539,000

original contribution and $183,000 represents earnings that they have permitted the company to retain in the business. The total amount of funds provided is therefore $539,000, of which $125,000 is used for working capital and $414,000 is in fixed assets.

If all earnings were paid out in dividends and if replacements of fixed assets exactly equaled the annual depreciation charge, the amounts shown on Illustration 1 could remain unchanged indefinitely. Despite the fact that there would be numerous changes in the several current asset and current liability accounts, these could offset one another so that the total working capital could remain constant. Under these circumstances, the business would not need additional financing. But of course the balance sheet items do change; additional funds are provided, and these are put to use.

Consider the possible ways in which the company could obtain additional funds. For example, if it wished to buy a new plant: it could borrow, thus increasing long-term debt; it could sell more stock, thus increasing the Capital Stock account; it could wait until operations had generated funds, which would show up as an increase in Retained Earnings; it could use available cash, thus decreasing working capital; or it could sell some of its existing fixed assets, thus decreasing Fixed Assets. It follows, therefore, that *sources of funds are indicated by increases in equities and decreases in assets.*

Looking at the other side of the coin, what uses could the company make of additional funds that it acquired? It could add new fixed assets, it could add to working capital, it could pay off existing debt, or it could pay dividends to the stockholders, which decreases Retained Earnings. From these possibilities, it follows that *uses of funds are indicated by increases in assets and decreases in equities.*

In accordance with the dual-aspect principle, total sources of funds must equal total uses of funds. The following relationships therefore exist:

1. SOURCES = USES
2. INCREASES IN EQUITIES + DECREASES IN ASSETS =
   INCREASES IN ASSETS + DECREASES IN EQUITIES

These same relationships can be explained in terms of debit and credit. Increases in equities and decreases in assets are both credits; increases in assets and decreases in equities are both debits. Thus, the above equation follows from the fact that changes in debits must equal changes in credits.

*   *   *   *   *

Diagrammatic Representation of Cash Flow

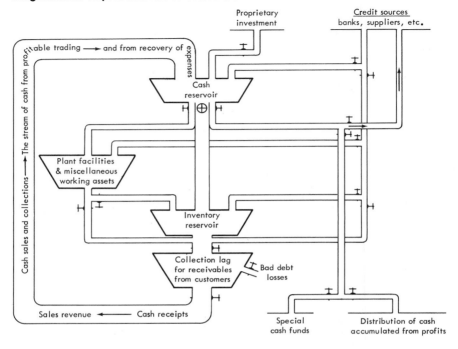

From

BUREAUCRATIC STRUCTURE
AND PERSONALITY*

By Robert K. Merton†

    . . . The chief merit of bureaucracy is its technical efficiency, with a premium placed on precision, speed, expert control, continuity, discretion, and optimal returns on input. The structure is one which approaches the complete elimination of personalized relationships and nonrational considerations (hostility, anxiety, affectual involvements, etc.). . . .

               *   *   *   *   *

    The Dysfunctions of Bureaucracy. In these bold outlines, the positive attainments and functions of bureaucratic organization are emphasized and the internal stresses and strains of such structures are almost wholly neglected. The community at large, however, evidently emphasizes the imperfections of bureaucracy, as

---

    * Reprinted by permission of *Social Forces,* Vol. XVII (1940), pp. 560–68, by permission of the author and the publisher. (Copyright, 1940, by the University of North Carolina Press.)

    † Professor Merton teaches sociology at Columbia University.

is suggested by the fact that the "horrid hybrid," bureaucrat, has become an epithet, a *Schimpfwort.* The transition to a study of the negative aspects of bureaucracy is afforded by the applications of Veblen's concept of "trained incapacity," Dewey's notion of "occupational psychosis" or Warnotte's view of "professional deformation." Trained incapacity refers to that state of affairs in which one's abilities function as inadequacies or blind spots. Actions based upon training and skills which have been successfully applied in the past may result in inappropriate responses *under changed conditions.* An inadequate flexibility in the application of skills will, in a changing milieu, result in more or less serious maladjustments. Thus, to adopt a barnyard illustration used in this connection by Burke, chickens may be readily conditioned to interpret the sound of a bell as a signal for food. The same bell may now be used to summon the "trained chickens" to their doom as they are assembled to suffer decapitation. In general, one adopts measures in keeping with his past training and, under new conditions which are not recognized as *significantly* different, the very soundness of this training may lead to the adoption of the wrong procedures. Again, in Burke's almost echolalic phrase, "people may be unfitted by being fit in an unfit fitness"; their training may become an incapacity.

Dewey's concept of occupational psychosis rests upon much the same observations. As a result of their day to day routines, people develop special preferences, antipathies, discriminations and emphases. (The term psychosis is used by Dewey to denote a "pronounced character of the mind.") These psychoses develop through demands put upon the individual by the particular organization of his occupational role.

The concepts of both Veblen and Dewey refer to a fundamental ambivalence. Any action can be considered in terms of what it attains or what it fails to attain. "A way of seeing is also a way of not seeing—a focus upon object A involves a neglect of object B." In his discussion, Weber is almost exclusively concerned with what the bureaucratic structure attains: precision, reliability, efficiency. This same structure may be examined from another perspective provided by the ambivalence. What are the limitations of the organization designed to attain these goals?

For reasons which we have already noted, the bureaucratic structure exerts a constant pressure upon the official to be "methodical, prudent, disciplined." If the bureaucracy is to operate successfully, it must attain a high degree of reliability of behavior, an unusual degree of conformity with prescribed patterns of action. Hence, the fundamental importance of discipline which may be as highly developed in a religious or economic bureaucracy as in the army. Discipline can be effective only if the ideal patterns are buttressed by strong sentiments which entail devotion to one's duties, a keen sense of the limitation of one's authority and competence, and methodical performance of routine activities. The efficacy of social structure depends ultimately upon infusing group participants with appropriate attitudes and sentiments. . . .

. . . There is a margin of safety, so to speak, in the pressure exerted by these sentiments upon the bureaucrat to conform to his patterned obligations, in much the same sense that added allowances (precautionary overestimations) are made by the engineer in designing the supports for a bridge. But this very emphasis leads to a transference of the sentiments from the *aims* of the organization onto the particular details of behavior required by the rules. Adherence to the rules, originally conceived as a means, becomes transformed into an end-in-itself; there occurs the familiar process of *displacement of goals* whereby "an instrumental value becomes a terminal value." Discipline, readily interpreted as conformance with regulations, whatever the situation, is seen not as a measure designed for specific purposes but becomes an immediate value in the life-organization of the bureaucrat. This emphasis, resulting from the displacement of the original goals, develops into rigidities and an inability to adjust readily. Formalism, even ritualism, ensues with an unchallenged insistence upon punctilious adherence to formalized procedures. This may be exaggerated to the point where primary concern with conformity to the rules interferes with the achievement of the purposes of the organization, in which case we have the familiar phenomenon of the technicism or red tape of the official. . . .

Structural Sources of Overconformity.   Such inadequacies in orientation which involve trained incapacity clearly derive from structural sources. The process may be briefly recapitulated. (1) An effective bureaucracy demands reliability of response and strict devotion to regulations. (2) Such devotion to the rules leads to their transformation into absolutes; they are no longer conceived as relative to a given set of purposes. (3) This interferes with ready adaption under special conditions not clearly envisaged by those who drew up the general rules. (4) Thus, the very elements which conduce toward efficiency in general produce inefficiency in specific instances. Full realization of the inadequacy is seldom attained by members of the group who have not divorced themselves from the "meanings" which the rules have for them. These rules in time become symbolic in cast, rather than strictly utilitarian.

Thus far, we have treated the ingrained sentiments making for rigorous discipline simply as data, as given. However, definite features of the bureaucratic structure may be seen to conduce to these sentiments. The bureaucrat's official life is planned for him in terms of a graded career, through the organizational devices of promotion by seniority, pensions, incremental salaries, *etc.,* all of which are designed to provide incentives for disciplined action and conformity to the official regulations. The official is tacitly expected to and largely does adapt his thoughts, feelings, and actions to the prospect of this career. But *these very devices* which increase the probability of conformance also lead to an over-concern with strict adherence to regulations which induces timidity, conservatism, and technicism. Displacement of sentiments from goals onto means is fostered by the tremendous symbolic significance of the means (rules).

Another feature of the bureaucratic structure tends to produce much the same result. Functionaries have the sense of a common destiny for all those who work together. They share the same interests, especially since there is relatively little competition insofar as promotion is in terms of seniority. Ingroup aggression is thus minimized and this arrangement is therefore conceived to be positively functional for the bureaucracy. However, the esprit de corps and informal social organization which typically develops in such situations often leads the personnel to defend their entrenched interests rather than to assist their clientele and elected higher officials. . . .

It would be much too facile and partly erroneous to attribute such resistance by bureaucrats simply to vested interests. Vested interests oppose any new order which either eliminates or at least makes uncertain their differential advantage deriving from the current arrangements. This is undoubtedly involved in part in bureaucratic resistance to change but another process is perhaps more significant.

As we have seen, bureaucratic officials affectively identify themselves with their way of life. They have a pride of craft which leads them to resist change in established routines; at least, those changes which are felt to be imposed by coworkers. This nonlogical pride of craft is a familiar pattern found even, to judge from Sutherland's *Professional Thief,* among pickpockets who, despite the risk, delight in mastering the prestige-bearing feat of "beating a left breech" (picking the left front trousers pocket).

. . . [T]here may ensue, in particular vocations and in particular types of organization, the *process of sanctification* (viewed as the counterpart of the process of secularization). This is to say that through sentiment-formation, emotional dependence upon bureaucratic symbols and status, and affective involvement in spheres of competence and authority, there develop prerogatives involving attitudes of moral legitimacy which are established as values in their own right, and are no longer viewed as merely technical means for expediting administration. One may note a tendency for certain bureaucratic norms, originally introduced for technical reasons, to become rigidified and sacred, although, as Durkheim would say, they are *laïque en apparence.* . . .

Primary vs. Secondary Relations. Another feature of the bureaucratic structure, the stress on depersonalization of relationships, also plays its part in the bureaucrat's trained incapacity. The personality pattern of the bureaucrat is nucleated about this norm of impersonality. Both this and the categorizing tendency, which develops from the dominant role of general, abstract rules, tend to produce conflict in the bureaucrat's contacts with the public or clientele. Since functionaries minimize personal relations and resort to categorization, the peculiarities of individual cases are often ignored. But the client who, quite understandably, is convinced of the "special features" of *his* own problem often objects to such categorical treatment. Stereotyped behavior is not adapted to the exigencies of individual problems. The impersonal treatment of affairs which are at times of great personal significance to the client gives rise to the charge of "arrogance" and "haughtiness" of the bureaucrat. . . .

Still another source of conflict with the public derives from the bureaucratic structure. The bureaucrat, in part irrespective of his position with*in* the hierarchy, acts as a representative of the power and prestige of the entire structure. In his official role he is vested with definite authority. This often leads to an actually or apparently domineering attitude, which may only be exaggerated by a discrepancy between his position within the hierarchy and his position with reference to the public. Protest and recourse to other officials on the part of the client are often ineffective or largely precluded by the previously mentioned espirt de corps which joins the officials into a more or less solidary ingroup. This source of conflict *may* be minimized in private enterprise since the client can register an effective protest by transferring his trade to another organization within the competitive system. But with the monopolistic nature of the public organization, no such alternative is possible. . . .

From

SHOP MANAGEMENT*

By Frederick Winslow Taylor†

. . . One of the most difficult works to organize is that of a large engineering establishment building miscellaneous machinery, and the writer has therefore chosen this for description.

Practically all of the shops of this class are organized upon what may be called the military plan. The orders from the general are transmitted through the colonels, majors, captains, lieutenants and noncommissioned officers to the men. In the same way the orders in industrial establishments go from the manager through superintendents, foremen of shops, assistant foremen and gang bosses to the men. In an establishment of this kind the duties of the foremen, gang bosses, etc., are so varied, and call for an amount of special information coupled with such a variety of natural ability, that only men of unusual qualities to start with, and who have had years of special training, can perform them in a satisfactory manner. . . .

*   *   *   *   *

In the writer's experience, almost all shops are under-officered. Invariably the number of leading men employed is not sufficient to do the work economically. Under the military type of organization, the foreman is held responsible for the successful running of the entire shop, and when we measure his duties by the standard of the four leading principles of management referred to above, it becomes apparent that in his case these conditions are as far as possible from being fulfilled. His duties may be briefly enumerated in the following way. He must lay out the work for the whole shop, see that each piece of work goes in the proper order to the right machine, and that the man at the machine knows just what is to be done and how he is to do it. He must see that the work is not slighted, and that it is done fast, and all the while he must look ahead a month or so, either to provide more men to do the work or more work for the men to do. He must constantly discipline the men and readjust their wages, and in addition to this must fix piece work prices and supervise the time-keeping.

The first of the four leading principles in managment calls for a clearly defined and circumscribed task. Evidently the foreman's duties are in no way clearly circumscribed. It is left each day entirely to his judgment what small part of the mass of duties before him it is most important for him to attend to, and he staggers along under this fraction of the work for which he is responsible, leaving the balance to be done in many cases as the gang bosses and workmen see fit. The second principle calls for such conditions that the daily task can always be accomplished. The conditions in his case are always such that it is impossible for him to do it all, and he never even makes a pretence of fulfilling his entire task. The third and fourth principles call for high pay in case the task is successfully done, and low pay in case of failure. The failure to realize the first two conditions, however, renders the application of the last two out of the question.

---

  * From *Scientific Management* by Frederick Winslow Taylor. Copyright © 1947. Reprinted by permission of Harper & Row, Publishers, Inc. (Excerpts from pp. 92–96, 98–100.)

  † The author was an engineer at Bethlehem Steel and became consultant for many leading industries in the first two decades of this century.

The foreman usually endeavors to lighten his burdens by delegating his duties to the various assistant foremen or gang bosses in charge of lathes, planers, milling machines, vise work, etc. Each of these men is then called upon to perform duties of almost as great variety as those of the foreman himself. The difficulty in obtaining in one man the variety of special information and the different mental and moral qualities necessary to perform all of the duties demanded of those men has been clearly summarized in the following list of the nine qualities which go to make up a well rounded man:

Brains.
Education.
Special or technical knowledge; manual dexterity or strength.
Tact.
Energy.
Grit.
Honesty.
Judgment or common sense and Good health.

Plenty of men who possess only three of the above qualities can be hired at any time for laborers' wages. Add four of these qualities together and you get a higher priced man. The man combining five of these qualities begins to be hard to find, and those with six, seven, and eight are almost impossible to get. . . .

*   *   *   *   *

It is evident, then, that the duties which the ordinary gang boss is called upon to perform would demand of him a large proportion of the nine attributes mentioned above; and if such a man could be found he should be made manager or superintendent of a works instead of gang boss. However, bearing in mind the fact that plenty of men can be had who combine four or five of these attributes, it becomes evident that the work of managment should be so subdivided that the various positions can be filled by men of this caliber, and a great part of the art of management undoubtedly lies in planning the work in this way. This can, in the judgment of the writer, be best accomplished by *abandoning the military type of organization* and introducing two broad and sweeping changes in the art of management:

(*a*) As far as possible the workmen, as well as the gang bosses and foremen, should be entirely relieved of the work of planning, and of all work which is more or less clerical in its nature. All possible brain work should be removed from the shop and centered in the planning or laying-out department, leaving for the foremen and gang bosses work strictly executive in its nature. Their duties should be to see that the operations planned and directed from the planning room are promptly carried out in the shop. Their time should be spent with the men, teaching them to think ahead, and leading and instructing them in their work.

(*b*) Throughout the whole field of management the military type of organization should be abandoned, and what may be called the "functional type" substituted in its place. "Functional management" consists in so dividing the work of management that each man from the assistant superintendent down shall have as few functions as possible to perform. If practicable the work of each man in the management should be confined to the performance of a single leading function.

Under the ordinary or military type the workmen are divided into groups. The men in each group receive their orders from one man only, the foreman or gang boss of that group. This man is the single agent through which the various functions of the management are brought into contact with the men. Certainly the most marked outward characteristic of functional mangement lies in the fact that each workman, instead of coming in direct contact with the management at one point only, namely, through his gang boss, receives his daily orders and help directly from eight different bosses, each of whom performs his own particular function. Four of these bosses are in the planning room and of these three send their orders to and receive their returns from the men, usually in writing. Four others are in the shop and personally help the men in their work, each boss helping in his own particular line or function only. Some of these bosses come in contact with each man only once or twice a day and then for a few minutes perhaps, while others are with the men all the time, and help each man frequently. The functions of one or two of these bosses require them to come in contact with each workman for so short a time each day that they can perform their particular duties perhaps for all of the men in the shop, and in their line they manage the entire shop. Other bosses are called upon to help their men so much and so often that each boss can perform his function for but a few men, and in this particular line a number of bosses are required, all performing the same function but each having his particular group of men to help. Thus the grouping of the men in the shop is entirely changed, each workman belonging to eight different groups according to the particular functional boss whom he happens to be working under at the moment.

The following is a brief description of the duties of the four types of executive functional bosses which the writer has found it profitable to use in the active work of the shop: (1) gang bosses, (2) speed bosses, (3) inspectors, and (4) repair bosses. . . .

From

THE WEALTH OF NATIONS*

By Adam Smith†

OF THE DIVISION OF LABOUR

The greatest improvement in the productive powers of labour, and the greater part of the skill, dexterity, and judgment with which it is anywhere directed, or applied, seem to have been the effects of the division of labour.

The effects of the division of labour, in the general business of society, will be more easily understood, by considering in what manner it operates in some particular manufactures. It is commonly supposed to be carried furthest in some very trifling ones; not perhaps that it really is carried further in them than in others of

* Published by Random House, Inc., in the Modern Library Series, 1937 (pp. 4–15). This citation is taken from the 1789 edition of the book.

† Adam Smith, 1723–90, Professor of Moral Philosophy at the University of Glasgow, is considered the founder of the Science of Economics.

more importance: but in those trifling manufactures which are destined to supply the small wants of but a small number of people, the whole number of workmen must necessarily be small; and those employed in every different branch of the work can often be collected into the same workhouse, and placed at once under the view of the spectator. In those great manufactures, on the contrary, which are destined to supply the great wants of the great body of the people, every different branch of the work employs so great a number of workmen, that it is impossible to collect them all into the same workhouse. We can seldom see more, at one time, than those employed in one single branch. Though in such manufactures, therefore, the work may really be divided into a much greater number of parts, than in those of a more trifling nature, the division is not near so obvious, and has accordingly been much less observed.

To take an example, therefore, from a very trifling manufacture; but one in which the division of labour has been very often taken notice of, the trade of the pin-maker; a workman not educated to this business (which the division of labour has rendered a distinct trade), nor acquainted with the use of the machinery employed in it (to the invention of which the same division of labour has probably given occasion), could scarce, perhaps, with his utmost industry, make one pin in a day, and certainly could not make twenty. But in the way in which this business is now carried on, not only the whole work is a peculiar trade, but it is divided into a number of branches, of which the greater part are likewise peculiar trades. One man draws out the wire, another straights it, a third cuts it, a fourth points it, a fifth grinds it at the top for receiving the head; to make the head requires two or three distinct operations; to put it on is a peculiar business, to whiten the pins is another; it is even a trade by itself to put them into the paper; and the important business of making a pin is, in this manner, divided into about eighteen distinct operations, which, in some manufactories, are all performed by distinct hands, though in others the same man will sometimes perform two or three of them. I have seen a small manufactory of this kind where ten men only were employed, and where some of them consequently performed two or three distinct operations. But though they were very poor, and therefore but indifferently accommodated with the necessary machinery, they could, when they exerted themselves, make among them about twelve pounds of pins in a day. There are in a pound upwards of four thousand pins of a middling size. Those ten persons, therefore, could make among them upwards of forty-eight thousand pins in a day. Each person, therefore, making a tenth part of forty-eight thousand pins, might be considered as making four thousand eight hundred pins in a day. But if they had all wrought separately and independently, and without any of them having been educated to this peculiar business, they certainly could not each of them have made twenty, perhaps not one pin in a day; that is, certainly, not the two hundred and fortieth, perhaps not the four thousand eight hundredth part of what they are at present capable of performing, in consequence of a proper division and combination of their different operations.

In every other art and manufacture, the effects of the division of labour are similar to what they are in this very trifling one; though, in many of them, the labour can neither be so much subdivided, nor reduced to so great a simplicity of operation. The division of labour, however, so far as it can be introduced, occasions, in every art, a proportionable increase of the productive powers of labour. The separation of different trades and employments from one another seems to have taken place, in consequence of this advantage. This separation too is generally carried furthest in those countries which enjoy the highest degree of industry and improvement; what is the work of one man in a rude state of society, being generally that of several in an improved one. In every improved society, the farmer is generally nothing but a farmer; the manufacturer, nothing but a manufacturer. The labour too which is necessary to produce any one complete manufacture, is almost always divided among a great number of hands. How many different trades are employed in each branch of the linen and woolen manufactures, from the growers of the flax and wool, to the bleachers and smoothers of the linen, or to the dyers and dressers of the cloth! . . .

This great increase of the quantity of work, which, in consequence of the division of labour, the same number of people are capable of performing, is owing to three different circumstances; first, to the increase of dexterity in every particular workman; secondly, to the saving of the time which is commonly lost in passing from one species of work to another; and lastly, to the invention of a great number of machines which facilitate and abridge labour, and enable one man to do the work of many.

First, the improvement of the dexterity of the workman necessarily increases the quantity of the work he can perform; and the division of labour, by reducing every man's business as some one simple operation, and by making this operation the sole employment of his life, necessarily increases very much the dexterity of the workman. A common smith, who, though accustomed to handle the hammer, has never been used to make nails, if upon some particular occasion he is obliged to attempt it, will scarce, I am assured, be able to make above two or three hundred nails in a day, and those too very bad ones. A smith who has been accustomed to make nails, but whose sole or principal business has not been that of a nailer, can seldom with his utmost diligence make more than eight hundred or a thousand nails in a day. . . .

Secondly, the advantage which is gained by saving the time commonly lost in passing from one sort of work to another, is much greater than we should at first view be apt to imagine it. It is impossible to pass very quickly from one kind of work to another, that is, carried on in a different place, and with quite familiar tools. A country weaver, who cultivates a small farm, must lose a good deal of time in passing from his loom to the field, and from the field to his loom. When the two trades can be carried on in the same workhouse, the loss of time is no doubt much less. It is even in this case, however, very considerable. A man commonly saunters a little in turning his hand from one sort of employment to another. When he first begins the new work he is seldom very keen and hearty; his mind, as they say, does not go to it, and for some time he rather trifles than applies to good purpose. . . .

Thirdly, and lastly, everybody must be sensible how much labour is facilitated and abridged by the application of proper machinery. It is unnecessary to give any example. I shall only observe, therefore, that the invention of all those machines by which labour is so much facilitated and abridged seems to have been originally owing to the division of labour. Men are much more likely to discover easier and readier methods of attaining any object, when the whole attention of their minds is directed towards that single object, than when it is dissipated among a great variety of things. But in consequence of the division of labour, the whole of every man's attention comes naturally to be directed towards some one very simple object. It is naturally to be expected, therefore, that some one or other of those who are employed in each particular branch of labour should soon find out easier and readier methods of performing their own particular work, wherever the nature of it admits of such improvement. A great part of the machines made use of in those manufactures in which labour is most subdivided, were originally the inventions of common workmen, who, being each of them employed in some very simple operation, naturally turned their thoughts towards finding out easier and readier methods of performing it. . . .

All the improvements in machinery, however, have by no means been the inventions of those who had occasion to use the machines. Many improvements have been made by the ingenuity of the makers of machines, when to make them becomes the business of peculiar trade; and some by that of those who are called philosophers or men of speculation, whose trade it is not to do any thing, but to observe every thing; and who, upon that account, are often capable of combining together the powers of the most distant and dissimilar objects. In the progress of society, philosophy or speculation becomes, like every other employment, the principal or sole trade and occupation of a particular class of citizens. Like every other employment too, it is subdivided into a great number of different branches, each of which affords occupation to a peculiar tribe or class of philosophers; and this subdivision of employment in philosophy, as well as in every other business, improves dexterity and saves time. Each individual becomes more expert in his own peculiar branch, more work is done upon the whole, and the quantity of science is considerably increased by it.

It is the great multiplication of the productions of all the different arts, in consequence of the division of labour, which occasions, in a well-governed society, that universal opulence which extends itself to the lowest ranks of the people. Every workman has a great quantity of his own work to dispose of beyond what he himself has occasion for; and every other workman being exactly in the same situation, he is enabled to exchange a great quantity of his own goods for a great quantity, or, what comes to the same thing, for the price of a great quantity of theirs. He supplies them abundantly with what they have occasion for, and they accommodate him as amply with what he has occasion for, and a general plenty diffuses itself through all the different ranks of the society.

OF THE PRINCIPLE WHICH GIVES OCCASION TO THE DIVISION OF LABOUR

This division of labour; from which so many advantages are derived, is not originally the effect of any human wisdom, which foresees and intends that general opulence to which it gives occasion. It is the necessary, though very slow and gradual, consequence of a certain propensity in human nature which has in view no such extensive utility; the propensity to truck, barter, and exchange one thing for another.

As it is by treaty, by barter, and by purchase, that we obtain from one another the greater part of those mutual good offices which we stand in need of, so it is this same trucking disposition which originally gives occasion to the division of labour. In a tribe of hunters or shepherds a particular person makes bows and arrows, for example, with more readiness and dexterity than any other. He frequently exchanges them for cattle or for venison with his companions; and he finds at last that he can in this manner get more cattle and venison, than if he himself went to the field to catch them. From a regard to his own interest, therefore, the making of bows and arrows grows to be his chief business, and he becomes a sort of armourer. Another excels in making the frames and covers of their little huts or moveable houses. He is accustomed to be of use in this way to his neighbours, who reward him in the same manner with cattle and with venison, till at last he finds it his interest to dedicate himself entirely to this employment, and to become a sort of house-carpenter. In the same manner a third becomes a smith or brazier; a fourth a tanner or dresser of hides or skins, the principal part of the clothing of savages. And thus the certainty of being able to exchange all that surplus part of the produce of his own labour, which is over and above his own consumption, for such parts of the produce of other men's labour as he may have occasion for, encourages every man to apply himself to a particular occupation, and to cultivate and bring to perfection whatever talent or genius he may possess for that particular species of business.

The difference of natural talents in different men is, in reality, much less than we are aware of; and the very different genius which appears to distinguish men of different professions, when grown up to maturity, is not upon many occasions so much the cause, as the effect of the division of labour. The difference between the most dissimilar characters, between a philosopher and a common street por- ter, for example, seems to arise not so much from nature, as from habit, custom, and education. When they came into the world, for the first six to eight years of their existence, they were, perhaps, very much alike, and neither their parents nor play-fellows could perceive any remarkable difference. About that age, or soon after, they come to be employed in very different occupations.

From

GENERAL AND INDUSTRIAL MANAGEMENT*

By Henri Fayol†

For any action whatsoever, an employee should receive orders from one su- perior only. Such is the rule of unity of command, arising from general and ever- present necessity and wielding an influence on the conduct of affairs, which to my way of thinking, is at least equal to any other principle whatsoever. Should it be violated, authority is undermined, discipline is in jeopardy, order disturbed and stability threatened. This rule seems fundamental to me and so I have given it the rank of principle. As soon as two superiors wield their authority over the same

---

* Reprinted by permission of Sir Isaac Pitman & Sons, Ltd., London, 1959 (pp. 24–25, 68–70). (This translation is published by permission of Dunod, Editeur, 92 Rue Bonaparte (VI), Paris, owners of the French copyright.) (Translated by Constance Storrs.)

† The author was Managing Director of Commentry-Fourchambault-Decazeville (French mining combine). He formed the Centre of Administrative Studies in Paris in the earliest part of the present century.

person or department, uneasiness makes itself felt and should the cause persist, the disorder increases, the malady takes on the appearance of an animal organism troubled by a foreign body, and the following consequences are to be observed: either the dual command ends in disappearance or elimination of one of the superiors and organic well-being is restored, or else the organism continues to wither away. In no case is there adaptation of the social organism to dual command.

Now dual command is extremely common and wreaks havoc in all concerns, large or small, in home and in State. The evil is all the more to be feared in that it worms its way into the social organism on the most plausible pretexts. For instance—

(a) In the hope of being better understood or gaining time or to put a stop forthwith to an undesirable practice, a superior S^2 may give orders directly to an employee E without going via the superior S^1. If this mistake is repeated there is dual command with its consequences, viz., hesitation on the part of the subordinate, irritation and dissatisfaction on the part of the superior set aside, and disorder in the work. It will be seen later that it is possible to by-pass the scalar chain when necessary, whilst avoiding the drawbacks of dual command.

(b) The desire to get away from the immediate necessity of dividing up authority as between two colleagues, two friends, two members of one family, results at times in dual command reigning at the top of a concern right from the outset. Exercising the same powers and having the same authority over the same men, the two colleagues end up inevitably with dual command and its consequences. Despite harsh lessons, instances of this sort are still numerous. New colleagues count on their mutual regard, common interest, and good sense to save them from every conflict, every serious disagreement and, save for rare exceptions, the illusion is short-lived. First an awkwardness makes itself felt, then a certain irritation and, in time, if dual command exists, even hatred. Men cannot bear dual command. A judicious assignment of duties would have reduced the danger without entirely banishing it, for between two superiors on the same footing there must always be some question ill-defined. But it is riding for a fall to set up a business organization with two superiors on equal footing without assigning duties and demarcating authority.

(c) Imperfect demarcation of departments also leads to dual command: two superiors issuing orders in a sphere which each thinks his own, constitutes dual command.

(d) Constant linking up as between different departments, natural intermeshing of functions, duties often badly defined, create an ever-present danger of dual command. If a knowledgeable superior does not put it in order, footholds are established which later upset and compromise the conduct of affairs.

In all human associations, in industry, commerce, army, home, State, dual command is a perpetual source of conflicts, very grave sometimes, which have special claim on the attention of superiors of all ranks.

*   *   *   *   *

Such is the system of organization as conceived by Taylor for running the workshops of a large mechanical engineering concern. It turns on the two following ideas—

(*a*) Need for a staff to help out shop foremen and foremen.
(*b*) Negation of the principle of unity of command.

Just as the first seems to me to be good, so the second seems unsound and dangerous.

(a) Need for a Staff to Help out Shop Foremen and Foremen

Taylor, better than anyone else, demonstrated the complexity and weight of the responsibility laid upon the men in charge of a large mechanical engineering shop. They cannot carry out their work satisfactorily unless given help. To attain his objective, Taylor devised and carried out the foregoing procedure: sundry specialists are attached to the foreman, who absolve him from having to have special knowledge at his command, and relieve him of the innumerable interruptions which would occupy too great a part of his time. This is the work of the staff. . . . Hitherto the need has been met in a variety of ways, but rarely satisfactorily. I consider that Taylor has rendered great service in drawing attention to the importance of such a mechanism and to the manner of instituting it.

(b) Negation of the Principle of Unity of Command

According to Taylor the ordinary type of organization referred to somewhat scornfully by him as "military," wherein workers receive instructions from one man only—shop foreman or gang-boss—is to be abandoned. . . . According to Taylor himself some adherents to the principle of unity of command would not abjure it even at his instance. For myself I do not think that a shop can be well run in flagrant violation of this. Nevertheless, Taylor successfully managed large-scale concerns. How, then, can this contradiction be explained? I imagine that in practice Taylor was able to reconcile functionalism with the principle of unity of command, but that is a supposition whose accuracy I am not in a position to verify. In business matters, day in and day out, from top to bottom of the scalar chain, functionalism has to be reconciled with unity of command. Considerable ability is demanded and this Taylor must have had in good measure.

I think it dangerous to allow the idea to gain ground that unity of command is unimportant and can be violated with impunity. So, until things change, let us treasure the old type of organization in which unity of command is honoured. It can, after all, be easily reconciled, as recommended by Taylor, with the assistance given to superintendents and foremen.

My reservations as regards Taylor's scientific or functional management do not prevent me from admiring the inventor of high-speed steel, the pioneer of minute and precise methods in conditions of work, the energetic and adept industrialist who, having made discoveries, shrank from no effort nor spared any pains to make them of practical application, and the tireless propagandist who meant the world to profit from his trails and experiments.

From

THE SOURCE OF
MANAGERIAL AUTHORITY*

By Cyril J. O'Donnell†

For four decades none of the writers in the management field inquired into the nature of authority, not even into its source. This is not strange, of course, when one considers that their main interest was in the specialization of enterprise tasks. But it is significant that none seemed to think that the right of managers to give orders would be questioned. Seeing all about them that business men, in fact, did give orders and that they were generally obeyed, that the state promulgated laws and that these were generally obeyed also—seeing these things, the facts seemed to point to acceptance of the idea that the right to issue orders must certainly rest with the business managers. Indeed, if the question had been put to them they probably would have agreed with Petersen and Plowman, who state that

"Under our democratic form of government the right upon which managerial authority is based has its source in the Constitution of the United States through the guaranty of private property. Since the Constitution is the creature of the people, subject to amendment and modification by the will of the people, it follows that society, through government, is the source from which authority flows to ownership and thence to management."[1]

*   *   *   *   *

First among the writers in the field of management theory to question this accepted doctrine was Chester I. Barnard, Harvard graduate, successful top manager of large-scale enterprises, and the author of *The Functions of the Executive.*[2] Apparently reading widely in the fields of philosophy and psychology, and being much impressed by the political theory of Harold Laski, Barnard postulates that a correct theory must be consistent with the facts and then proceeds to enumerate several instances wherein the members of an organization have refused to obey persons in authority. On the basis of these "facts" he states that ". . . the decision as to whether an order has authority or not lies with the persons to whom it is addressed, and does not reside in 'persons of authority' or those who issue these orders." This concept means, if anything, that the source of authority lies in the members of an organization, that they confer authority upon their superior by deigning to accept and act upon commands, that they may, if they wish, decide to accept orders seriatim, and that they may withdraw conferred authority at any time by refusing to obey the commands of their superiors.

*   *   *   *   *

---

* Reprinted by permission of the *Political Science Quarterly,* Vol. 67, No. 4 (December 1952), pp. 573–88.

† The author is Professor of Business Organization and Policy, University of California at Los Angeles.

[1] Elmore Petersen and E. Grosvenor Plowman, *Business Organization and Management* (Chicago, 1949), p. 62. This is a very restricted view of the source of authority.

[2] Cambridge, 1950. Succeeding quotations from Barnard are from his Chapter 12.

. . . Robert Tannenbaum[3] dubs as "formal" the authority of a manager when it is viewed as "originating at the top of an organization hierarchy and flowing downward therein through the process of delegation." He thinks of "informal" authority as a right conferred upon a manager by his subordinates. Thus, informal authority is equated with Barnard's complete concept. But Tannenbaum, as a practical matter, does not actually differ from Barnard because he says,

"The real source of the authority possessed by an individual lies in the acceptance of its exercise by those who are subject to it. It is the subordinates of an individual who determine the authority which he may wield. Formal authority is, in effect, nominal authority. It becomes real only when it is accepted."

In order to substantiate this conception of authority, Tannenbaum quotes approvingly from Barnard, Kardiner, Benne, and Simon. . . . And I may add that Selekman[4] simply cannot make up his mind on the subject so he says:

"It is true enough that the management executive must, directly or indirectly, obtain consent to his decisions from the men under him; the importance of such consent now receives ever-increasing recognition. Nonetheless, the manager still wields authority over his workers as of right—a right delegated to him by the owners of the business."

* * * * *

Authority is the right to command or to act. It implies the possession of the power to coerce, for obviously if there were no way to enforce an order the enterprise would become disorganized and unable to achieve its purpose. To realize how clear this is, the reader should imagine what would happen in a business if workers failed to adhere to the opening and closing hours of work; if individual players on a football team decided to engage their opposites in competition at any time; . . .

* * * * *

Now, the *order* in organized behavior implies authority—the right to command coupled with the right to coerce. Malinowski is emphatic in saying that "submission to laws as well as the power to enforce laws and rules are indispensable in human behavior."[5] Otherwise, there will only be anarchy. West is of the opinion that

"The prime requisite and firm creator of any community life is a law or order maintained by force. For human nature is such that, in all its most necessary social relationships, it is subject to the permanent threat of the self-assertive impulse, which misinterprets facts, misjudges events, and then, through consequent self-justificatory passion, breaks the social bond, unless it be externally restrained. We may claim this as adequately confirmed. Nursery studies and family life confirm it. Social and natural history confirm it. Modern psychology confirms it. And finally, our common sense tends to confirm it—for all others except ourselves, which is in itself a final confirmation. Individual, group or nation-state, we cannot judge our own cause. And if we try to do so, we shall be reduced again and again to fighting for a supposed "right" against a supposed "wrong," for one set of illusions against another."[6]

---

[3] Robert Tannenbaum, "Managerial Decision-Making," *The Journal of Business,* XXIII, 1 (January 1950).

[4] Benjamin M. Selekman, *Labor Relations and Human Relations* (New York, 1947), pp. 175–76.

[5] Bronislaw Malinowski, *Freedom and Civilization* (New York, 1944), p. 27.

[6] Ranyard West, *Conscience and Society* (London, 1942), p. 240.

*   *   *   *   *

In the case of private business enterprise the authority relationships operate in much the same way. Americans have not deprived themselves of their common-law freedom to engage in business activity. It is true that elaborate safeguards for the rights of others have been spelled out in ordinance, rule, law and constitution, but within this framework anyone can engage in business as an individual proprie-torship or on a partnership basis without special permission. Since corporations are legal persons created by law, their managers exercise authority which has reached them through the chain of delegation from the people to their constitution and thence through government to its creature. But whether a manager is operat-ing an incorporated enterprise or not, his subordinates are obliged to obey his lawful orders, as long as the employer-employee relationship exists, because the right to command issues ultimately from the collective will of the people. Neither the individual subordinate nor the trade union to which he may belong is in a position to disobey those commands. . . .

From

CONCERNING CIVIL GOVERNMENT*

By John Locke

The great and chief end, therefore, of men uniting into commonwealths, and putting themselves under government, is the preservation of their property; to which in the state of Nature there are many things wanting.

Firstly, there wants an established, settled, known law, received and allowed by common consent to be the standard of right and wrong, and the common measure to decide all controversies between them. For though the law of Nature be plain and intelligible to all rational creatures, yet men, being biased by their interest, as well as ignorant for want of study of it, are not apt to allow of it as a law binding to them in the application of it to their particular cases.

Secondly, in the state of Nature there wants a known and indifferent judge, with authority to determine all differences according to the established law. For every one in that state of being both judge and executioner of the law of Nature, men being partial to themselves, passion and revenge is very apt to carry them too far, and with too much heat in their own cases, as well as negligence and uncon-cernedness, make them too remiss in other men's.

Thirdly, in the state of Nature there often wants power to back and support the sentence when right, and to give it due execution. They who by any injustice offended will seldom fail where they are able by force to make good their injustice. Such resistance many times makes the punishment dangerous, and frequently destructive to those who attempt it.

Thus mankind, notwithstanding all the privileges of the state of Nature, being but in an ill condition while they remain in it are quickly driven into society. Hence

---

* Encyclopaedia Britannica, Inc., William Benton, Publisher, Chicago, 1952, The Great Ideas, Vol. 35 (pp. 53–54).

it comes to pass, that we seldom find any number of men live any time together in this state. The inconveniences that they are therein exposed to by the irregular and uncertain exercise of the power every man has of punishing the trangressions of others, make them take sanctuary under the established laws of government, and therein seek the preservation of their property. It is this makes them so willingly give up every one his single power of punishing to be exercised by such alone as shall be appointed to it amongst them, and by such rules as the community, or those authorised by them to that purpose, shall agree on. And in this we have the original right and rise of both the legislative and executive power as well as of the governments and societies themselves.

For in the state of Nature to omit the liberty he has of innocent delights, a man has two powers. . . .

The first power—viz., of doing whatsoever he thought fit for the preservation of himself and the rest of mankind, he gives up to be regulated by laws made by the society, so far forth as the preservation of himself and the rest of that society shall require; which laws of the society in many things confine the liberty he had by the law of Nature.

Secondly, the power of punishing he wholly gives up, and engages his natural force, which he might before employ in the execution of the law of Nature, by his own single authority, as he thought fit, to assist the executive power of the society as the law thereof shall require. For being now in a new state, wherein he is to enjoy many conveniences from the labour, assistance, and society of others in the same community, as well as protection from its whole strength, he is to part also with as much of his natural liberty, in providing for himself, as the good, prosperity, and safety of the society shall require, which is not only necessary but just, since the other members of the society do the like. . . .

. . . And so, whoever has the legislative or supreme power of any common-wealth, is bound to govern by established standing laws, promulgated and known to the people, and not by extemporary decrees, by indifferent and upright judges, who are to decide controversies by those laws; and to employ the force of the community at home only in the execution of such laws, or abroad to prevent or redress foreign injuries and secure the community from inroads and invasion. . . .

8. CONTINENTAL ELECTRIC COMPANY

Case Introduction

SYNOPSIS

The Continental Electric Company is organized by relatively autonomous product divisions for the manufacture and sale of a diverse number of electrical products. Top company management has a set of goals on which the performance of division managers is evaluated. There is a difference of opinion between top management and Mr. North, manager of the Electric Motor Division, as to whether the division has performed up to standard in the past. At the same time, Mr. North and his technical staff are faced with a choice between three investments in new technological innovation. He must recommend one of these to meet performance standards in the future. Various opinions and technical data are used to try to choose which capital investment to make.

WHY THIS CASE IS INCLUDED

This case offers opportunity to look at the philosophy of the decentralized form of organization—what advantages it *should* have for both technological excellence and human motivation. However, the details of making decentralization work, both from a financial and a human standpoint, are not so simple as the philosophy indicates.

Particularly important are conflicts between objectives at any one time, conflicts of long- versus short-run objectives, the perceptions of human beings of the "facts" they see in attaining objectives, and the problem of generalist executives who balance objectives but who also must obtain highly technical information from staff specialists.

The case offers opportunity to understand some concepts of financial management—the relation of profits, cash flows, and time—and the relation of long-term to short-run profits.

Finally, as an advanced project, this case provides opportunity to test

309

the place of "management science" or quantification in the coordination (concurrence, governance, agreement, etc.) of human beings in organizations. To what extent does quantification produce agreement? To what extent does it result in the *authority of fact* as opposed to the *authority of sentiment, authority of personal judgment,* or *authority of power?*

DIAGNOSTIC AND PREDICTIVE QUESTIONS

The readings included with this case are marked (*). The author index at the end of this book locates the other readings.

1. What has the top management tried to achieve by organizing the company by product divisions rather than by functional divisions (manufacturing, sales, etc.)? Illustrate with facts from the case as to how management expects this organization will (should) affect the actions of North and his staff, as well as the economic and technical performance of the Electric Motor Division.

Read: Curtice, "General Motors Organization Philosophy and Structure." Shillinglaw, *Cost Accounting,* pp. 680–89.

2. From the viewpoint of setting economic and financial objectives, why do Richardson and Grundy view North's performance as unsatisfactory, while North views his own performance as realistic?

Read: *Drucker, *The Practice of Management,* pp. 62–64, 66, 84–87, 121, 128–31.

3. From the two concepts of "cash flow" and "rate of return," why might Linz and Donat disagree on whether to charge the cost of the patent to current expenses or to charge it to investment?

Read: Linz' explanation of cash flow, Exhibit 3. Anthony, *Management Accounting,* pp. 290–92, 306. Also relate to Drucker, Question 2.

4. From the viewpoint of psychology—concepts of structural and functional factors in perception—what is causing the viewpoint of top management to differ from that of North in judging the quality of performance of the Motor Division?

Read: Krech and Crutchfield, *Theory and Problems of Social Psychology,* pp. 81–83, 87–89, 94–96, 98, 102–3.

5. From the viewpoint of sociology—personalities of line and technical executives, and sources of authority in organizations—what might cause friction between North and Glass if the latter's project is not accepted? If we view North as a specialist on motors and Richardson as a generalist over all products, is this also true between these two "line" executives?

Read: Thompson, *Modern Organization,* pp. 4–6, 12–13, 19–21, 61, 63–65, 77–78. *Etzioni, "Authority Structure and Organizational Effectiveness."

6. Suppose the only criterion for selecting investment projects were the total profit to the company generated over the life of the project. What advantage would this have? What limitations? Which project would be selected?

7. Suppose that the only criterion for capital investment were the

average rate of return per year from the project. What advantage would this have over the total dollar return (Question 6)? What does average rate have to do with the payback period from each project? Which project would be selected:

Study: The method for determining total profit, and average return, Exhibits 2, 4, 5.

8. Actually, Dr. Glass objected to the average rate of return as a selection criterion for investment projects. Examine his project, particularly the method of figuring the average. If you were in his shoes, why would you object? What factor does it leave out?

Read: This question has to do with the limitations of an *average* as representing a series of numbers. Look at the series of yearly profits in Exhibit 5, and see why the average figure may be misleading. For those interested, review the use of the average as a statistical measure in any introductory statistics text.

POLICY QUESTIONS

9. Which project is the best for long-run profits of Continental? Which project is best for shorter-run profits?

10. Suppose you want a criterion for selecting investment projects which would measure the worth of a project—that would select between the three taking into consideration both payback period *and* amounts. What would you use, and which project would be best?

Read: *Lewis, *Financial Controls for Management,* pp. 82–83.
*Horngren, *Accounting for Management Control,* pp. 356–63, 365–68.

11. If you were North, which project would you recommend? Would this be based on (*a*) what is best for the company as a whole? (*b*) What is best for the Motor Division? (*c*) What is best for you as an employed executive in the company? How do these differ? (Think of case facts, plus the readings in Questions 1–5.)

12. From the viewpoint of both accuracy in the decision (deciding on what is best for the technology and finance of the company) and from the viewpoint of human motivation (the morale and learning of North, his staff, and top management), what methods are available for setting the financial criteria for investments, and for selecting the right project? How would these work in this case?

Read: Newman and Summer, *The Process of Management: Concepts, Behavior, and Practice,* pp. 439–48. *McGregor, *The Human Side of Enterprise,* pp. 124–31, 172–75. Enell and Haas, *Setting Standards for Executive Performance,* pp. 16–18, 31–32.

QUESTIONS FOR ORIGINAL STUDENT WORK IN ANALYSIS AND POLICY

13. While reflecting on case facts, what additional theories from prior education give you insights as to "what is going on" in Continental Electric Company? As to what might be predicted to happen in the future?

14. Other than the policy questions asked by the authors, what pragmatic ways can you think of to state the practical problems faced by executives in the case?

Case Text*

COMPANY BACKGROUND AND ORGANIZATION

Continental Electric Company is a leading producer of a wide variety of electrical products. Organizationally, it is divided into three major product groups specializing in (1) consumer products—television sets, radios, kitchen appliances, etc.; (2) industrial products—generators, motors, transformers, and so on; and (3) military products—radar and communications equipment, missile parts, and so on.

Each of these major product groups, headed by a vice president, is in turn divided into a number of related product divisions. For example, within the consumer product group there is a lighting division which produces a wide range of lamps and bulbs. There are 16 such product divisions in the company, and each is headed by a division general manager.

Since 1950, when this organization structure was adopted, the corporate management of Continental has sought to make each of the 16 divisions a semiautonomous business. (See Exhibit 1.)

Edward M. Richardson, company president, described the philosophy of his organization's structure as follows:

> *Along with the many benefits which come with long-scale business operation one of the most serious drawbacks can be the loss of entrepreneurial drive. . . . The organization structure of Continental Electric is designed to divide our big business into sixteen little businesses. Each of my sixteen general managers thinks of himself as the president of a small business. . . .*
>
> *Each is responsible for the long-run success of his business.*
>
> *   *   *   *   *
>
> *We guide the divisions by defining their broad responsibilities, or missions, in terms of total corporate goals. Within these broad guidelines they are on their own. To be sure, division performance is evaluated regularly in terms of short- and long-range criteria.*
>
> *These criteria are:*
> 1. *Profitability:*
>   a. *Net profit before taxes: Each division computes this for corporate review just as the company as a whole computes its income statement for stockholders' review.*

* Copyright 1964 by the Graduate School of Business, Columbia University. This case was authored by E. Kirby Warren.

EXHIBIT 1
Continental Electric Company
(Relevant Portion of Organization Chart)

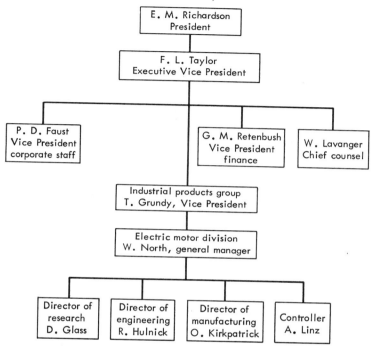

b. *Rate of return: Net income as a percent of division assets.
    Again top corporate management receives the same kind of
    figures from the divisions as the corporation must present
    to its stockholders.*
2. *Market Share: The division's percent of total industry sales.*
3. *Product Leadership: The degree to which the division main-
    tains and increases the company's reputation as a technologi-
    cal leader in the electrical products industry.*
4. *Utilization of Human Resources: A series of measures are used
    to determine the morale and effective utilization of the divi-
    sion's work force.*
5. *Corporate Citizenship: A series of measures are used to deter-
    mine whether the division is meeting its responsibilities in
    terms of local, state, and national needs.*

Mr. Richardson went on to explain that the divisions are reviewed
formally by their respective group vice presidents on a quarterly basis

and annually by the corporate review board. Chaired by Richardson, the review board is made up of the company's executive vice president, F. L. Taylor, the vice president of finance, George M. Rettenbush, and the vice president of corporate staff, Paul D. Faust. The secretary of the board is William Lavanger who is also chief counsel.

In addition to reviewing division performance, the review board also has final say on budget requests. In accord with the philosophy of decentralization, each division sets its own sales targets and develops its requests for operating funds and capital needed for more permanent divisional investments. In addition to a detailed one-year budget, the divisions also prepare three-year sales and profit forecasts which serve as a backdrop to the annual plan.

Sales targets and budget requests are reviewed by the divisions' respective group vice presidents. The group vice president does not have the authority to change the division's proposals but since he does have the authority to change divisional personnel he can exert some informal pressure if he feels that sales goals or cash requirements are out of line. However, since the success or failure of top division management is closely correlated to divisional performance, the group vice presidents tend to interfere as little as possible with division plans as long as performance is good and expectations promising.

As one group vice president put it, "The proof of who's right and who's wrong is profits. We try to let the divisions run their own show and then they stand or fall on their own decisions."

ELECTRIC MOTOR DIVISION

The Electric Motor Division produces a variety of small fractional and one-horsepower motors. Roughly 40 percent of the division's output is sold to other divisions of Continental which use small motors in their products. The remaining 60 percent is sold to outside companies some of which use the motors in products competing with Continental products.

The "sales" within the company are made at a price based on manufacturing cost plus 8 percent markup. By way of contrast, the division's profit margin on sales to outside customers has been between 12 percent and 14 percent over full cost (manufacturing plus selling and corporate overhead).

The general manager of the Electric Motor Division, William North, is 46 years old. He has been with the company for 14 years and has been manager of the Electric Motor Division for the past five years. His performance after three years in this post was regarded by Richardson as excellent.

"We were really pleased with the way Bill improved a division that had many problems in the past," Richardson said, "and we felt at that time that in a few years Bill was slated for even bigger responsibilities. Unfortunately his last two years as divisional manager have not been as successful."

In 1961 the division fell short of realizing its estimated profit level by 18 percent. Total sales were estimated at $12 million, and the profit forecast was for $1,250,000. Actual sales came to $11,860,000, but profit was only $1,025,000.

On the basis of three-quarter results it is almost certain that the Electric Motor Division sales will rise in 1962 to the $12,300,000 level which was forecast in the profit plan for 1962. In addition, it seems equally likely that the profit objective of $1,250,000 will be met. However, Thomas Grundy, group vice president of industrial products, is not overly pleased with the division's anticipated performance in 1962.

Grundy stated, "When Bill North took over the Electric Motor Division, we all saw bigger things in store for him. His performance from 1958–60 confirmed our confidence in him. However, in 1961 things seemed to turn sour, and this year it looks as though he will meet his profit forecast only by virtue of having reduced division expectations below what they should have been. While his sales and profits goals are higher than last year's results, they are not high enough. I warned him when he submitted his 1962 plan that I thought he should set his sights higher, but the bad year in 1961 must have scared him.

"Therefore, I can't get very excited about his 1962 results for even if he reaches his objectives, I feel they were too conservative to begin with. I hope Bill is willing to present a more optimistic profit outlook for his division in 1963. If he sets his goals high enough and reaches them, he may find himself promoted in 1964. If he plays it too conservatively or fails to show a better profit picture, we'll be forced to reconsider his future with Continental."

When asked whether he had informed North about his feelings, Grundy replied, "I think Bill knows where he stands. Of course, I can't promise him anything if he does a good job nor do I want to unnerve him with threats. However, if he is the kind of executive we hope he is, he should understand his position."

When questioned about his division's performance over the past two years, North made the following observations:

Our sales and profit forecasts for 1961 reflected an anticipation on our part of wide acceptance of a new half-horsepower motor designed especially for use in lawn mowers. Doug Glass, division director of research, and Ralph Hulnick, director of engineering, did a wonderful job on the design and development of the motor. Unfortunately, in order to reach projected sales targets we had to spend more than anticipated to get market acceptance. This, along with a three-week work stoppage due to a wildcat strike, pushed our operating costs above our estimates and accounted for most of the 18 percent discrepancy between projected and actual profits.

I explained this to the review board and indicated that the increased marketing expenditures would pay off in future years sales and that the stoppage was a result of a labor problem I had inherited from the previous general manager. They seemed to accept my posi-

tion, but Mr. Richardson also reminded me that "you can't run a business on tomorrow's profits or yesterday's mistakes." Somehow I don't think I got through to them.

Our 1962 profit forecast may have been lower than Tom Grundy would have liked, but I think results showed our estimates to be realistic.

DIVISION PLANS FOR 1963

In developing the 1963 profit plan for the Electric Motor Division, Mr. North is faced with a decision on three proposals for substantial capital investment put to him by his staff. Because of the size of the outlays, North feels he cannot propose more than one of these projects to corporate management.

Proposal No. 1: Purchase of a Patent on Component Part. The first proposal under consideration is one of several submitted by Ralph Hulnick, divisional director of engineering. All of Hulnick's proposals at this time have been included in the operating budget except this one, which will involve an outlay of $210,000 to acquire patent rights on a new component part. Hulnick estimates that this new component part, which would be used in the assembly of motors, would reduce manufacturing costs about $110,000 a year.

Unfortunately, the inventors of the part have tried for many years to find a way of producing it at a cost low enough to make its use economically feasible; as a result, Continental's legal department estimates that the patents have but three years of protection remaining. The inventors have recently solved the production problems, but lack the capital needed to take advantage of their discovery. They are, therefore, willing to sell their rights to Continental for $210,000.

Based on engineering estimates of cost savings, Hulnick and the division controller, Amos Linz, have prepared the figures summarized in Exhibit 2.

In submitting these estimates, Linz told Mr. North that he did not think it would be wise to propose this project to corporate management even though it showed a good rate of return.

"There is a slight chance," Linz stated, "that Donat (the corporate controller) will make us treat the $210,000 paid for the patent as a period expense thus forcing us to absorb the cost in one year. This would help the company's cash position by reducing taxable income and taxes paid next year, but it'll really knock our reported profit down for 1963."

North requested Linz to expand on this point. Linz prepared a set of tables, accompanied by explanatory notes, showing what would happen to cash flows and reported profits if the patent purchase price was treated either as a capital investment or an operating expense. These are presented in Exhibit 3.

"As you can see," Linz explained, "as long as overall corporate profits are good enough to keep the stockholders happy, Donat is probably going to insist that we expense the $210,000 since it'll almost double the available cash flow for next year. But we're not going to see a penny of this cash

EXHIBIT 2

Financial Projections for Investment in Patent (Project No. 1)

Year	Cost Savings before Taxes	Deprecia- tion*	Additional Taxable Income	Taxes†	Additional after Tax Income
1963...............	$110,000	$70,000	$40,000	$20,000	$20,000
1964...............	110,000	70,000	40,000	20,000	20,000
1965...............	110,000	70,000	40,000	20,000	20,000
					$60,000

*If the $210,000 payment for the patent is treated as a capital investment and depreciated over three years, the annual depreciation would be $70,000 ($210,000 ÷ 3 = $70,000).

†Using a 50% tax rate to simplify estimates.

Profit Summary

Total profit over life of patent = $ 60,000
Average annual profit   =   20,000
Average investment   =   105,000*

*Average capital tied up in 1963 (with annual depreciation of $70,000) = $175,000
Average capital tied up in 1964 (with annual depreciation of $70,000) = 105,000
Average capital tied up in 1965 (with annual depreciation of $70,000) =   35,000
Average capital tied up during project life   = $315,000
Average capital tied up per year, $315,000 ÷ 3 = $105,000

$$\text{Average rate of return} = \frac{\$\,20,000}{\$105,000} = 19.00\%$$

EXHIBIT 3

Purchase of Patents (Project No. 1)

Implications of Treating Purchase Price as Investment or Current Expense Alternative 1 — Capitalizing the $210,000 Expenditure (assumes the company treats the outlay as a capital expenditure and thus "writes it off" over three years)

Year	(1) Extra Cost Savings before Taxes and Depreciation	(2) Depre- ciation	(3) Taxable Income	(4) Taxes (at 50% Rate)	(5) After Tax Profit	Cash Flow; Increase or Decrease in Cash Available Col. (1)−Col. (4)
0.................	$ 0	$ 0	$ 0	$ 0	$ 0	$−210,000*
0–1..............	110,000	70,000	40,000	20,000	20,000	+ 90,000†
1–2..............	110,000	70,000	40,000	20,000	20,000	+ 90,000
2–3..............	110,000	70,000	40,000	20,000	20,000	+ 90,000
						$+ 60,000

*At point in time zero when the $210,000 is paid out, the only impact is $210,000 less in the "cash box."

†From point zero to one (calendar year 1963), an extra $110,000 is saved. The $70,000 in Col. (2) is not an actual outflow since depreciation is merely a partial delayed tax credit for the $210,000 that actually left the "cash box" earlier. Thus the company actually has an extra $110,000 it saves, minus the $20,000 in taxes it pays, or a net cash increase of $90,000 ($110,000 − $20,000 = $90,000).

EXHIBIT 3 (continued)

Alternative 2—Expensing the $210,000 expenditure (assumes entire $210,000 is charged off in 1963, and that taxable income from other division operations will be sufficient to offset losses reported from this project)

Year	Extra Cost Savings before Taxes	Expense to Purchase Patent	Taxable Income	Extra Taxes Saved or Paid	After Tax Profit	Cash Flow (Increase or Decrease in Cash Available)
0.................	$ 0	$ 0	$ 0	$ 0	$ 0	$ −210,000*
0–1............	110,000	210,000	−100,000	−50,000	−50,000	+160,000†
1–2............	110,000	0	+110,000	+55,000	+55,000	+ 55,000‡
2–3............	110,000	0	+110,000	+55,000	+55,000	+ 55,000
						$ + 60,000

*As in *Alternative Treatment 1*, at point in time zero when the $210,000 is paid out the only impact is $210,000 less in the "cash box."

† From zero to one (calendar year 1963), an extra $110,000 is saved, but if the $210,000 is treated as an expense, the division has $210,000 worth of tax credit, $110,000 of this credit is used to offset the extra income so the division "pays" no taxes on it and all $110,000 stays in the cash box.

In addition the division has $100,000 ($210,000 − $110,000 = $100,000) worth of tax credit left to apply to other division income. Thus (using a 50% tax rate) the division "pays" $50,000 less taxes on its other income and has an extra $50,000 left in the "cash box." The total effect of this first year is to have an extra $160,000 in the cash box:

$110,000 extra income
50,000 taxes saved
──────────
$160,000

‡ In years two and three, $110,000 is saved each year. There is no deduction for depreciation so $55,000 is "paid out" in extra taxes, and the division ends each year with an extra $55,000 in cash having been generated.

Comparison of Alternatives 1 and 2

Note: At the end of the three years (December 31, 1965), no matter which alternative is used, the company has a calculated net gain of $60,000.

In First Year (1963): Alternative 1 shows higher profit but lower cash available for other company uses than Alternative 2.

In Second and Third Years (1964, 1965): Alternative 1 shows lower profit, higher available cash than Alternative 2.

Summarizing Results for End of 1963

Alternative Treatment of the Expenditure	(1963) Net Profit after Taxes	1963 Cash Flow Available for Reinvestment
1. ($210,000 treated as investment)	$ +20,000	$ +90,000
2. ($210,000 treated as an expense)	$ −50,000	$ +160,000

Note: Under Alternative 2, the company will have an extra $70,000 ($160,000 − $90,000 = $70,000) working for it for a full year, which it would not have under Alternative 1. While it is true the company will recoup this $70,000 during 1964 and 1965, at least one year's income on $70,000 will be lost to the company.

until we come in with our 1964 budget. By then it's not *our* cash, but just part of the entire company's cash account, and we're but one of sixteen divisions trying to get our hands on some of it."

"In a nutshell, Bill," Linz concluded, "if we propose the patent purchase we may end up having to work just that much harder to show a good profit picture. Certainly, if they treat the $210,000 as an expense, our profits in 1964 and 1965 will be even better. But, remember Richardson's comment about not being able to run a business on next year's profits. It's the 1963 results they're going to judge us by."

North questioned this reasoning by asking, "Look Amos, don't you think that if they request us to expense the $210,000 outlay at the start of the year, they'll remember at the end of the year why our profits are a little lower?"

Linz' reply was: "Don't count on it, Bill. Don't forget this is only one of many many factors that is going to influence our divisional profits. And if we show lower profit forecasts because we expect them to treat the $210,000 as an expense, then Grundy [group vice president] will be all over us for not being more aggressive. If we come up with a more optimistic forecast and don't make it, the review board will treat any explanations on our part—as far as the $210,000 expense is concerned—as simply an alibi. If I were you I wouldn't take the chance on this one and put my money on Kirkpatrick's request."

Proposal No. 2: Purchase of New Wiring Equipment. North stated that he was not completely convinced by Amos Linz' reasoning but that he had a great deal of respect for Linz' judgment particularly in financial matters such as this. In addition, Linz has been with the company for 41 years and knows as much about company politics as anyone in the firm. Having started with the company in the accounting department as a clerk after graduation from high school, he worked his way up from the bottom. Linz is well regarded in the company, and his opinion is often sought by younger executives like North.

The project Linz advised North to include in the budget was made by Owen Kirkpatrick, director of manufacturing. Kirkpatrick has seen a piece of equipment known as the Margot-Toledo Wirer demonstrated and feels "that it could be used to automate the attachment of wire coils in the one-horsepower motors. Such automatic attachment would permit a more efficient assembly line operation, and should reduce manufacturing costs between $80,000 and $100,000 a year."

The cost of purchasing the Margot-Toledo equipment is estimated at $250,000, but Kirkpatrick stated that "even in the face of rapid changes in such automated equipment and technology, I am sure that this equipment will have at least a five-year economic life.

"I'd love to see us get that patent Ralph Hulnick's after, but if what Linz says is right and in light of my proposal's five-year life compared to the three-year life of Ralph's patent, I think we ought to put our money in the new equipment."

Working with Linz, Kirkpatrick submitted a summary of the financial estimates to North (Exhibit 4).

Proposal No. 3: Research on Insulation Materials. A third proposal under consideration has been put forth by Dr. Douglas Glass, division direc-

EXHIBIT 4
Financial Projections for Investment in New Equipment (Project no. 2)

Year	Cost Savings before Taxes	Depre-ciation*	Additional Taxable Income	Taxes†	Additional after Tax Income
1	$ 80,000	$50,000	$30,000	$15,000	$ 15,000
2	90,000	50,000	40,000	20,000	20,000
3	100,000	50,000	50,000	25,000	25,000
4	90,000	50,000	40,000	20,000	20,000
5	90,000	50,000	40,000	20,000	20,000
					$100,000

*Assuming the equipment will have a five-year economic life, depreciation will be $50,000 per year ($250,000 ÷ 5 = $50,000).
†Using a 50% tax rate to simplify estimates.

Profit Summary

Total profit $100,000
Average profit....................... 20,000
Average investment............... 125,000
Average rate of return........... $\dfrac{20,000}{125,000} = 16.00\%$

tor of research. Dr. Glass who is 42, joined the company three years ago. After having taught electrical engineering at a major eastern university for ten years, he joined the research staff of one of Continental's principal competitors where he worked for two years.

North states that he was quite happy to get Glass to join the company three years ago but soon recognized that while he had acquired the talents of a brilliant research engineer he had also taken on a strong-minded and impatient individual.

Glass explained his reasons for accepting Continental's offer as follows: "I took this job because the people I worked with on my former job should be managing a rocking chair company. They are painfully conservative, scared stiff by corporate management, and haven't listened to a new idea in ten years. I can't work in an environment like that. Things change too swiftly to sit around milking yesterday's good ideas."

Dr. Glass' largest proposal for this year's budget is the third project being considered by North. It involves embarking upon a research program designed to develop a new insulation material for use under extremely high and low temperature conditions. Success in this venture would give the division a motor which would find wide use in industry.

Dr. Glass has requested that $75,000 a year be allocated for this project for the next three years. Then if all goes well, an investment of about $100,000 will be necessary in the fourth year to begin production.

Mr. North has consulted with the group vice president of military products and the general managers of several divisions within his own group, and they are all very enthusiastic about such a breakthrough. However, none are willing to contribute to the cost of the project.

"After all," said the general manager of one division, "your division has the responsibility for updating technology in small motors. This is one of the five major criteria by which any division performance is evaluated. As much as we would like to see you come through on this project we can't see why we should subsidize you on it."

Dr. Glass, however, has taken a very strong stand for the research project.

"These other proposals are nothing but short-run cost cutting solutions to a profit problem which has long-run implications. As a division, we are dead, competitively, if we don't start moving ahead into new products and new technologies. This research cost is peanuts compared to its potential value to the company," he said, "and don't forget that product leadership is one of the goals set for us by top management."

Dr. Glass and his staff, however, are the only ones who support the project within the division. As Linz points out, "this project would take almost six years before we begin to get into the black on it. It's fine for Glass to talk about the long-run, but none of us are going to be here in the long run if we don't do something about our short-term profit picture."

Based on Glass' estimates, Linz has summarized the financial outlook for the research project in Exhibit 5.

EXHIBIT 5
Financial Projections for Research Program (Project No. 3)

Year	Added Income before Taxes	Research Cost*	Depre-ciation†	Addi-tional Taxable Income	Taxes Paid‡	Addi-tional after Tax Income
1......	$ 0	$75,000	$ 0	$—75,000	$—37,500	$—37,500
2......	0	75,000	0	—75,000	—37,500	—37,500
3......	0	75,000	0	—75,000	—37,500	—37,500
4......	50,000	0	20,000	30,000	15,000	15,000
5......	75,000	0	20,000	55,000	27,500	27,500
6......	175,000	0	20,000	155,000	77,500	77,500
7......	200,000	0	20,000	180,000	90,000	90,000
8......	200,000	0	20,000	180,000	90,000	90,000
						$187,500

* Assuming research cost will have to be treated as an expense and charged to period income.
† Assuming the $100,000 investment in the fourth year has a five-year economic life, depreciation will be $20,000 per year ($100,000 ÷ 5 = $20,000).
‡ Using 50% tax rate to simplify estimates and assuming other taxable earnings will be offset.

Profit Summary

Total profit	$187,500	
Average profit	$ 23,438	($187,500 ÷ 8 = $23,438)
Average Investment	$162,500	($225,000 + $100,000 = $325,000 $325,000 ÷ 2 = $162,500)
Average rate of return	$\dfrac{\$ 23{,}438}{\$162{,}500} = 14.42\%$	

Dr. Glass feels that the benefits from his project should go well beyond eight years, but Mr. Linz is unwilling to develop financial forecasts beyond that period. In addition, Dr. Glass feels that the use of averages to compute rate of return when comparing projects such as these is deceptive. He told North in the midst of a stormy budget meeting, "I'm no financial expert but I'm sure that all these figures Amos throws around are not true measure of these projects' value."

When Amos Linz suggested that Glass stick to his research business and not meddle with financial analysis, Glass stated that "this is the same kind of ostrich thinking" he had been forced to deal with when working for Continental's competition.

A heated exchange followed, and North thought it best to call a halt to the meeting. As Linz left he turned to North and said, "Young man, you've got a real future in this company if you use your head. Every warning I gave you about the patent proposal goes double on this research project.

"Backing the research project means sacrificing between $15,000 and $25,000 of extra profits by passing up the savings on new equipment. In addition, it sticks us with a $37,500 loss per year for the next three years. I cannot see why anyone striving for a better profit picture should want to start off by throwing away roughly $60,000 in profits a year for three years."

A summary of the financial projects for the three projects prepared by Linz for North is shown below:

Comparative Financial Projections for Three Proposals

Project	Payback Period*	Total Profit after Taxes	Average Rate of Return
No. 1 Patent....................	2 years, 4 months	$ 60,000	19.00%
No. 2 New equipment	3 years, 7 months	100,000	16.00
No. 3 Research project	6 years, 4 months	187,500	14.42

* Using cash flow (after tax income + depreciation), this is the length of time it takes to recover the cash outlays.

Selected Readings

From

THE PRACTICE OF MANAGEMENT*

By Peter F. Drucker†

Most of today's lively discussion of management by objectives is concerned with the search for the one right objective. This search is not only likely to be as unproductive as the quest for the philosopher's stone; it is certain to do harm and to misdirect.

To emphasize only profit, for instance, misdirects managers to the point where they may endanger the survival of the business. To obtain profit today they tend to undermine the future. They may push the most easily saleable product lines and slight those that are the market of tomorrow. They tend to short-change research, promotion and the other postponable investments. Above all, they shy away from any capital expenditure that may increase the invested-capital base against which profits are measured; and the result is dangerous obsolescence of equipment. In other words, they are directed into the worst practices of management.

To manage a business is to balance a variety of needs and goals. This requires judgment. The search for the one objective is essentially a search for a magic formula that will make judgment unnecessary. But the attempt to replace judgment by formula is always irrational; all that can be done is to make judgment possible by narrowing its range and the available alternatives, giving it clear focus, a sound foundation in facts and reliable measurements of the effects and validity of actions and decisions. And this, by the very nature of business enterprise, requires multiple objectives.

What should these objectives be, then? There is only one answer: *Objectives are needed in every area where performance and results directly and vitally affect the survival and prosperity of the business.* These are the areas which are affected by every management decision and which therefore have to be considered in every management decision. They decide what it means concretely to manage the business. They spell out what results the business must aim at and what is needed to work effectively toward these targets.

*   *   *   *   *

---

* From *The Practice of Management* by Peter F. Drucker. Copyright 1954 by Peter F. Drucker. Reprinted with permission of Harper & Row, Publishers, Inc. (Excerpts from pp. 62–64, 66, 84–87, 121, 128–31.)

† The author is Professor in the Graduate School of Business, New York University.

There are eight areas in which objectives of performance and results have to be set:

Market standing; innovation; productivity; physical and financial resources; profitability; manager performance and development; worker performance and attitude; public responsibility.

*   *   *   *   *

Yet, even if managing were merely the application of economics, we would have to include these three areas and would have to demand that objectives be set for them. They belong in the most purely formal economic theory of the business enterprise. For neglect of manager performance and development, worker performance and public responsibility soon results in the most practical and tangible loss of market standing, technological leadership, productivity and profit—and ultimately in the loss of business life. That they look so different from anything the economist—especially the modern economic analyst—is wont to deal with, that they do not readily submit to quantification and mathematical treatment, is the economist's bad luck; but it is no argument against their consideration.

The very reason for which economist and accountant consider these areas impractical—that they deal with principles and values rather than solely with dollars and cents—makes them central to the management of the enterprise, as tangible, as practical—and indeed as measurable—as dollars and cents.

*   *   *   *   *

"We don't care what share of the market we have, as long as our sales go up," is a fairly common comment. It sounds plausible enough; but it does not stand up under analysis. By itself, volume of sales tells little about performance, results or the future of the business. A company's sales may go up—and the company may actually be headed for rapid collapse. A company's sales may go down—and the reason may not be that its marketing is poor but that it is in a dying field and had better change fast.

A maker of oil refinery equipment reported rising sales year after year. Actually new refineries and their equipment were being supplied by the company's competitors. But because the equipment it had supplied in the past was getting old and needed repairs, sales spurted; for replacement parts for equipment of this kind have usually to be bought from the original supplier. Sooner or later, however, the original customers were going to put in new and efficient equipment rather than patch up the old and obsolescent stuff. Then almost certainly they were going to go to the competitors designing and building the new equipment. The company was thus threatened with going out of business—which is what actually happened.

*   *   *   *   *

The Time-Span of Objectives

For what time-span should objectives be set? How far ahead should we set our targets?

The nature of the business clearly has a bearing here. In certain parts of the garment business next week's clearance sale is "long-range future." It may take four years to build a big steam turbine and two more to install it; in the turbine business six years may be "immediate present" therefore. And Crown Zellerbach is forced to plant today the trees it will harvest fifty years hence.

Different areas require different time-spans. To build a marketing organization takes at least five years. Innovations in engineering and chemistry made today are unlikely to show up in marketing results and profits for five years or longer. On the other hand a sales campaign, veteran sales managers believe, must show results within six weeks or less; "Sure, there are sleepers," one of these veterans once said, "but most of them never wake up."

This means that in getting objectives management has to balance the immediate future—the next few years—against the long range: five years or longer. This balance can best be found through a "managed-expenditures budget." For practically all the decisions that affect the balance are made as decisions on what the accountant calls "managed expenditures"—those expenditures that are determined by current management decision rather than by past and irrevocable decisions (like capital charges), or by the requirements of current business (like labor and raw material costs). Today's managed expenditures are tomorrow's profit: but they may also be today's loss.

Every second-year accountancy student knows that almost any "profit" figure can be turned into a "loss" by changing the basis of depreciation charges; and the new basis can usually be made to appear as rational as the old. But few managements—including their accountants—realize how many such expenditures there are that are based, knowingly or not, on an assessment of short-range versus long-range needs, and that vitally affect both. Here is a partial list:

Depreciation charges; maintenance budgets; capital replacement, modernization and expansion costs; research budgets; expenditures on product development and design; expenditures on the management group, its compensation and rewards, its size, and on developing tomorrow's managers; cost of building and maintaining a marketing organization; promotion and advertising budgets; cost of service to the customer; personnel management, especially training expenditures.

Almost any one of these expenditures can be cut back sharply, if not eliminated; and for some time, perhaps for a long time, there will be no adverse effect. Any one of these expenditures can be increased sharply and for good reasons, with no resulting benefits visible for a long time. By cutting these expenditures immediate results can always be made to look better. By raising them immediate results can always be made to look worse.

*   *   *   *   *

Balancing the Objectives

In addition to balancing the immediate and the long-range future, management also has to balance objectives. What is more important: an expansion in markets and sales volume, or a higher rate of return? How much time, effort and energy should be expended on improving manufacturing productivity? Would the same amount of effort or money bring greater returns if invested in new-product design?

There are few things that distinguish competent from incompetent management quite as sharply as the performance in balancing objectives. Yet, there is no formula for doing the job. Each business requires its own balance—and it may require a different balance at different times. . . .

*   *   *   *   *

Any business enterprise must build a true team and weld individual efforts into a common effort. Each member of the enterprise contributes something different, but they must all contribute toward a common goal. Their efforts must all pull in the same direction, and their contributions must fit together to produce a whole—without gaps, without friction, without unnecessary duplication of effort.

Business performance therefore requires that each job be directed toward the objectives of the whole business. And in particular each manager's job must be focused on the success of the whole. . . .

*   *   *   *   *

By definition, a manager is responsible for the contribution that his component makes to the larger unit above him and eventually to the enterprise. His performance aims upward rather than downward. This means that the goals of each manager's job must be defined by the contribution he has to make to the success of the larger unit of which he is a part. The objectives of the district sales manager's job should be defined by the contribution he and his district sales force have to make to the sales department. . . .

*   *   *   *   *

This requires each manager to develop and set the objectives of his unit himself. Higher management must, of course, reserve the power to approve or disapprove these objectives. But their development is part of a manager's responsibility; indeed, it is his first responsibility. It means, too, that every manager should responsibly participate in the development of the objectives of the higher unit of which his is a part. . . . He must know and understand the ultimate business goals, what is expected of him and why, what he will be measured against and how. There must be a "meeting of minds" within the entire management of each unit. This can be achieved only when each of the contributing managers is expected to think through what the unit objectives are, is led, in other words, to participate actively and responsibly in the work of defining them. And only if his lower managers participate in this way can the higher manager know what to expect of them and can make exacting demands.

*   *   *   *   *

Self-Control through Measurements

The greatest advantage of management by objectives is perhaps that it makes it possible for a manager to control his own performance. Self-control means stronger motivation: a desire to do the best rather than just enough to get by. It means higher performance goals and broader vision. Even if management by objectives were not necessary to give the enterprise the unity of direction and effort of a management team, it would be necessary to make possible management by self-control.

So far in this book I have not talked of "control" at all; I have talked of "measurements." This was intentional. For "control" is an ambiguous word. It means the ability to direct oneself and one's work. It can also mean domination of one person by another. Objectives are the basis of "control" in the first sense; but they must never become the basis of "control" in the second, for this would defeat their purpose. Indeed, one of the major contributions of management by objectives is that it enables us to substitute management by self-control for management by domination. . . .

From

AUTHORITY STRUCTURE AND ORGANIZATIONAL EFFECTIVENESS*

By Amitai Etzioni†

. . . Managers are generally considered as those who have the major (line) authority because they direct the major goal activity. Experts deal only with means, with secondary activities. Therefore it is functional for them to have none, or only limited (staff), authority.

. . . Managers and experts may be differentiated from four points of view: (a) role structure, (b) personality, (c) background, mainly in terms of educational and occupational experience, and (d) normative orientations.

The *role* of the expert is to create and institutionalize knowledge. The role of the manager is to integrate (create or maintain) organizational systems or subsystems from the point of view of the institutional goals and needs.[1] The expert typically deals with symbols and materials (although there are many who disagree with this point of view).[2] The manager deals with people. The two role types require different *personality* types. The expert who has intensive knowledge in a limited area, tends to have a restricted perspective. The manager has extensive, though limited, knowledge of many areas, and the resulting broad perspective is essential for his role. Experts are committed to abstract ideas and therefore tend to be unrealistic, whereas managers are more practical. Managers are skilled in human relations; experts are temperamental.[3]

Managers and experts differ in *background.* Experts usually have higher educations than managers and tend to enter their first job at a later age and at higher initial salaries. They often start at relatively high positions in the hierarchy but are limited in the range of their mobility. Managers enter their first job at a younger age, with less education, and at lower positions, but they move upward faster than the experts and some of them eventually get higher than any expert.[4] Whereas many experts remain more or less restricted to the same organizational functions, the typical manager is assigned to a large variety of tasks in what is called the process of broadening.

Managers' *orientations* differ considerably from those of experts. Managers are

---

* Reprinted by permission of The Graduate School of Business and Public Administration, Cornell University, Ithaca, N.Y. (*Administrative Science Quarterly,* June 1959, pp. 45–47).

† Dr. Etzioni is Professor of Sociology in Columbia University.

[1] The roles of managers will be discussed here only with regard to the internal functions of the organization. Their roles with regard to environment will be disregarded because of space limitations.

[2] Experts can be arranged in a continuum from the less to the more skilled in human relations. Chemists, for instance, are on the average less skilled from this point of view than labor relations experts. See L. E. Danielson, "Management's Relations with Engineers and Scientists," *Proceedings of Industrial Relations Research Association,* Tenth Annual Meeting, 1957, pp. 314–321.

[3] See Robert Dubin, *Human Relations in Administration* (New York, 1951), pp. 113–138.

[4] For a comparison, see M. Dalton, "Conflicts between Staff and Line Managerial Officers," *American Sociological Review,* 15 (1950), 342–351; and C. A. Myers and J. G. Turnbull, Line and Staff in Industrial Relations, *Harvard Business Review,* 34 (July–Aug. 1956), 113–124.

more committed or loyal to their specific organization than are experts.[5] Experts are often primarily oriented toward their professional reference and membership groups. While managers are often committed to the organization's particular goals, experts are committed to the scientific and professional ethos regardless of the particular needs and goals of their institution.[6]

Obviously though there is a high correlation among these four variables, they are not inevitably associated. Two major mechanisms explain how the correlation is maintained. First of all there is *selective recruitment.* People with managerial personalities and background are recruited to managerial roles, and those with the personalities and education of experts tend to enter staff positions. The second mechanism is *role adaptation.* People who enter roles which are initially incompatible with their personalities often adjust to their new roles. . . .

From

FINANCIAL CONTROLS FOR MANAGEMENT*

By Ralph B. Lewis†

The Theory of Investment and Return

From the standpoint of pure theory, there is only one true method (for determining rate of return on an investment). This is the investor's method. It is also called the discount method, or present value method. All the money that is to be laid out prior to the start of operations is measured. This includes payments for plant, property and equipment and working capital as well as expenditures for research and development and other preparatory expenses. On the other hand, all of the money to be returned as profit or depreciation, i.e., cash throw-off, is likewise projected, perhaps for as long as fifteen or twenty years. The date for the start of operations is the significant key to the calculation, because this is the date used in computing present value. A number of probable rates are selected. Then using a financial table one converts all of the outlays and returns into present values: And that interest rate at which the present value of the outlays offsets the present value of the return is the true rate of return.

---

[5] For a case study which brings out this point, see A. H. Stanton and M. S. Schwartz, *The Mental Hospital* (New York, 1954).

[6] A. W. Gouldner, Cosmopolitans and Locals: Toward an Analysis of Latent Social Roles, *Administrative Science Quarterly,* 2 (1957), 444–480.

* *Financial Controls for Management* by Ralph B. Lewis, © by Prentice-Hall, Inc., Englewood Cliffs, N.J., 1961 (pp. 82–83).

† The author is head of management services for Author Young & Co., Certified Public Accountants.

From

ACCOUNTING FOR
MANAGEMENT CONTROL*

By Charles T. Horngren†

DEFINITION OF CAPITAL BUDGETING

Capital budgeting is long-term planning for making and financing proposed capital outlays. Most expenditures for plant, equipment, and other long-lived assets affect operations over a series of years. They are large permanent commitments that influence long-run flexibility and earning power. Decisions in this area are among the most difficult, primarily because the future to be foreseen is distant and hard to perceive. Because the unknowable factors are many, it is imperative that all the knowable factors be collected and properly measured before a decision is reached.

The problem of measuring the potential profit of long-range investments has been receiving increased attention by management accountants. This trend is likely to grow as industrial mechanization and automation grow.

The profitability of a business decision depends on two vital factors: (1) future net increases in cash inflows or net savings in cash outflows; and (2) required investment. Thus, a chance to receive an annual return of $5,000 on a bond or stock can be judged only in relationship to how much money need be committed to obtain the $5,000. If the required capital is $10,000, the $5,000 (50 per cent) return may be extremely appealing. If the required investment is $1 million, the $5,000 (½ per cent) return probably will be unappealing. Depending on risk and available alternatives, individuals and corporate investors usually have some notion of a minimum rate of return that would make various projects desirable investments.

The quantitative approach to management problem-solving is, generally, to estimate the effect of the alternatives on cash flows in relation to the required investments. Thus, all projects whose rate of return exceeds the minimum rate of return would be desirable, and vice versa. A project which promises a return of 25 per cent would ordinarily be more desirable than one which promises a return of 12 per cent. The problem of choosing the minimum acceptable rate of return (more a problem of finance than of accounting) is extremely complex. . . .

There are several different ways of approaching the capital budgeting decision. Although we shall discuss: (a) discounted cash flow; (b) payback; and (c) the unadjusted rate of return, we shall concentrate on discounted cash flow because it is conceptually superior to the others.

* Charles T. Horngren, *Accounting for Management Control: An Introduction,* © 1965, excerpts from pp. 356–63, 365–68. Reprinted by permission of Prentice-Hall, Inc., Englewood Cliffs, N.J.

† The Author is Professor of Accounting at the Graduate School of Business, Stanford University.

DISCOUNTED CASH FLOW

Time Value of Money

The old adage that a bird in the hand is worth two in the bush is applicable to the management of money. A dollar in the hand today is worth more than a dollar to be received (or spent) five years from today. This is because the use of money has a cost (interest), just as the use of a building or an automobile may have a cost (rent). *Because the discounted-cash-flow method explicitly and automatically weighs the time value of money, it is the best method to use for long-range decisions.*

Another major aspect of the cash-flow method is its focus on *cash* inflows and outflows rather than on *net income* as computed in the conventional accounting sense. . . .

There are two main variations of the discounted-cash-flow method: (a) time-adjusted rate of return; and (b) net present value. . . .

The following example will be used to illustrate the concepts:

Example 1

A manager is contemplating the rearrangement of assembly line facilities. Because of rapid technological changes in the industry, he is using a four-year planning horizon as a basis for deciding whether to invest in the facilities for rearrangement, which should result in cash operating savings of $2,000 per year. In other words, the useful life of this project is four years, after which the facilities will be abandoned or rearranged again.

Required:

1. If the plant rearrangement will cost $6,074 now, that is the time-adjusted rate of return on the project?
2. If the minimum desired rate of return is 10 per cent, and the planned rearrangement will cost $6,074, what is the project's net present value? How much more would the manager be willing to invest and still earn 10 per cent on the project?

Requirement 1 deals with the time-adjusted rate of return, which we shall consider first.

Time-adjusted Rate of Return

The time-adjusted rate of return has been defined as "the maximum rate of interest that could be paid for the capital employed over the life of an investment without loss on the project."[1] This rate corresponds to the effective rate of interest so widely computed for bonds purchased or sold at discounts or premiums. Alternatively, the rate of return can be defined as the discount rate that makes the present value of a project equal to the cost of the project.

---

[1] *Return on Capital as a Guide to Managerial Decisions,* National Association Accountants, Research Report No. 35 (New York, December, 1959), p. 57.

The cash flows relating to our rearrangement problem are shown in Exhibit 14–2. The discounted cash flow analysis of these cash flows is shown in Exhibit 14–3. The exhibit shows that $6,074 is the present value, at a rate of return of 12 per cent, of a four-year stream of inflows of $2,000 in cash. Twelve per cent is the rate that equates the amount invested ($6,074) with the present value of the cash inflows ($2,000 per year for four years). In other words, *if* money were

EXHIBIT 14-2

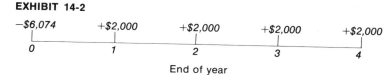

End of year

EXHIBIT 14-3
Two Proofs of Time-adjusted Rate of Return

Original investment, $6,074
Useful life, 4 years
Annual cash inflow from operations, $2,000
Rate of return (selected by trial-and-error methods), 12 per cent

Approach 1: Discounting Each Year's Cash Inflow Separately*

	Present Value of $1, Discounted at 12%	Total Present Value	Sketch of Cash Flows 0 1 2 3 4
End of Year Cash flows:			
Annual savings	.893	$ 1,786	$2,000
	.797	1,594	$2,000
	.712	1,424	$2,000
	.636	1,272	$2,000
Present value of future inflows		$ 6,074‡	
Initial outlay	1.000	(6,074)	$(6,074)
Net present value (the zero difference proves that the rate of return is 12 per cent)		$ 0	

Approach 2: Using Annuity Table†

Annual savings	3.037	$ 6,074	$2,000 $2,000 $2,000 $2,000
Initial outlay	1.000	(6,074)	$(6,074)
Net present value		$ 0	

*Present values from Table 1, Appendix II to Chapter 14 (p. 378).
‡Present values of annuity from Table 2, Appendix II to Chapter 14 (p. 380).
†Sum is really $6,076, but is rounded.

borrowed at an effective interest rate of 12 per cent, the cash inflow produced by the project would exactly repay the hypothetical loan plus the interest over the four years. If the cost of capital (minimum desired rate of return on the capital) is less than 12 per cent, the project will be desirable. If the cost of capital exceeds 12 per cent, the cash inflow will be insufficient to pay the interest and repay the principal of the hypothetical loan. Therefore, 12 per cent is the time-adjusted rate of return for this project.

*   *   *   *   *

Explanation of Compound Interest

The time-adjusted rate of return is computed on the basis of the cash in use from period to period, rather than on the original investment. Exhibit 14-4 shows that the return is 12 per cent of the cash invested during the year. After 12 per cent of the cash invested is deducted, the remainder is the recovery of the original investment. Over the four years the cash inflow equals the recovery of the original investment plus annual interest, at the rate of 12 per cent of the unrecovered capital.

Depreciation and Discounted Cash Flow

Students are often mystified by the apparent exclusion of depreciation from discounted-cash-flow computations. A common homework error is to deduct depreciation. This is a misunderstanding of one of the basic ideas involved in the concept of the time-adjusted rate of return. Discounted-cash-flow techniques and tables *automatically* provide for recoupment of the principal. Therefore, *it is unnecessary to deduct depreciation from operating cash inflows before consulting present value tables.*

In Exhibit 14-4, at the end of Year 1, the $2,000 cash inflow represents a 12 per cent ($729) return on the $6,074 unrecovered investment at the beginning of Year 1 *plus* a $1,271 recovery of principal. The latter is similar to the depreciation provision in conventional accounting.

This difficult point warrants another illustration. Assume that a company is considering investing in a project with a two-year life and no residual value. Cash

EXHIBIT 14-4
Rationale of Time-adjusted Rate of Return

Note. Same data as in Exhibit 14-3: Original investment, $6,074; Useful life, 4 years; Annual cash inflow from operations $2,000; Rate of return, 12 per cent. Unrecovered investment at the beginning of each year earns interest for the whole year. Annual cash inflows are received at the end of each year.

Year	(a) Unrecovered Investment at Beginning of Year	(b) Annual Cash Inflow	(c) Return: 12% per Year (a) × 12%	(d) Amount of Investment Recovered at End of Year (b) − (c)	(e) Unrecovered Investment at End of Year (a) − (d)
1	$6,074	$2,000	$729	$1,271	$4,803
2	4,803	2,000	576	1,424	3,379
3	3,379	2,000	405	1,595	1,784
4	1,784	2,000	216*	1,784	0

* Rounded.

inflow will be equal payments of $4,000 at the end of each of the two years. How much would the company be willing to invest to earn a time-adjusted rate of return of 8 per cent? A quick glance at the table for either the present value of $1 or the present value of an ordinary annuity of $1.00 will reveal:

Present Value of $4,000 at end of Year 1: $4,000 × .926 = $3,704
Present Value of $4,000 at end of Year 2: $4,000 × .857 = 3,428 $7,132

Present Value of annuity of $4,000 for 2 years at 8 per cent: $4,000 × 1.783 = $7,132

The following is an analysis of the computations that are automatically considered in the construction of present value tables.

Year	Investment at Beginning of Year	Operating Cash Inflow	Return. @ 8% per Year	Amount of Investment Received at End of Year	Unrecovered Investment at End of Year
1	$7,132	$4,000	.08 × $7,132 = $571	$4,000 − $571 = $3,429	$7,132− $3,429 = $3,703
2	3,703	4,000	.08 × $3,703 = $297	$4,000 − $297 = $3,703	$3,703 − $3,703 = 0

A study of the above calculations will demonstrate that discounted-cash-flow techniques and tables have, built into them, the provisions for recovery of investment.

Net Present Value

Another type of discounted-cash-flow approach may be called the net present value method. Computing the exact time-adjusted rate of return entails trial-and-error and, sometimes, cumbersome hand calculations and interpolations within a compound interest table. In contrast, the net present value method assumes some minimum desired rate of return. All expected future cash flows are discounted to the present, using this minimum desired rate. If the result is positive, the project is desirable, and vice versa.

Requirement (2) of Example 1 (p. 358) will be used to demonstrate the net present value approach. The problem assumes that the rearrangement will cost $6,074. Exhibit 14–5 shows a net present value of $264, so the investment is desirable. The manager would be able to invest $264 more, or a total of $6,338 (i.e., $6,074 + $264), and still earn 10 per cent on the project.

The higher the minimum desired rate of return, the less the manager would be willing to invest in this project. At a rate of 16 per cent, the net present value would be $−478 (i.e., $2,000 × 2.798 = $5,596, which is $478 less than the required investment of $6,074). (Present value factor, 2,798 is taken from Table 2, p. 380.) When the desired rate of return is 16 per cent, rather than 10 per cent, the project is undesirable at a price of $6,074.

*   *   *   *   *

Solution

A difficult part of long-range decision making is the structuring of the data. We want to see the effects of each alternative on future cash flows. The focus here is on bona fide *cash* transactions, not on opportunity costs. . . .

EXHIBIT 14-5
Net Present Value Technique

Original investment, $6,074; Useful life, 4 years; Annual cash inflow from opera-tions, $2,000; Minimum desired rate of return, 10 per cent

Approach 1: Discounting Each Year's Cash Inflow Separately*

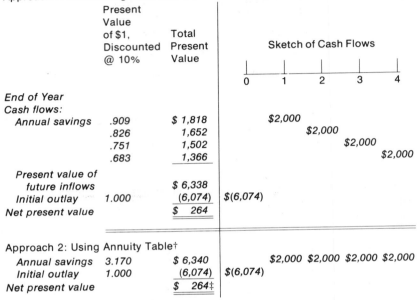

	Present Value of $1, Discounted @ 10%	Total Present Value
End of Year		
Cash flows:		
Annual savings	.909	$ 1,818
	.826	1,652
	.751	1,502
	.683	1,366
Present value of future inflows		$ 6,338
Initial outlay	1.000	(6,074)
Net present value		$ 264

Sketch of Cash Flows: $2,000 (year 1), $2,000 (year 2), $2,000 (year 3), $2,000 (year 4); $(6,074) at 0.

Approach 2: Using Annuity Table†

Annual savings	3.170	$ 6,340
Initial outlay	1.000	(6,074)
Net present value		$ 264‡

$(6,074); $2,000 $2,000 $2,000 $2,000

*Present values from Table 1, Appendix II to Chapter 14, p. 378.
†Present annuity values from Table 2, p. 380.
‡Rounded.

The following steps are likely to be the clearest:

Step 1. Arrange the relevant cash flows by project, so that a sharp distinction is made between total project flows and incremental flows. The incremental flows are merely algebraic differences between two alternatives. (There are *always* at least two alternatives. One is the *status quo,* the alternative of doing nothing.) Exhibit 14–6 shows how the cash flows for *each* alternative are sketched.

Step 2. Discount the expected cash flows and choose the project with the least cost or the greatest benefit. Both the total project approach and the incremental approach are illustrated in Exhibit 14–6. Which approach you use is a matter of preference. However, to develop confidence in this area, you should work with both at the start. In this example, the $8,425 net difference in favor of replacement is the ultimate result under either approach.

Analysis of Typical Items under Discounted Cash Flow

1. Future Disposal Values. The disposal value at the date of termination of a project is an increase in the cash inflow in the year of disposal. Errors in

EXHIBIT 14-6

Total Project versus Incremental Approach to Net Present Value (data from Example 2)

End of Year	Present Value Discount Factor, @ 14%	Total Present Value	Sketch of Cash Flows 0	1	2	3	4	5
Total Project Approach								
A. Replace								
Recurring cash operating costs, using an annuity table*	3.433	$(102,990)		($30,000)	($30,000)	($30,000)	($30,000)	($30,000)
Disposal value, end of Year 5	.519	1,557						3,000
Initial required investment	1.000	(31,000)	($31,000)					
Present value of net cash outflows		$(132,433)						
B. Keep								
Recurring cash operating costs, using an annuity table*	3.433	$(137,320)		($40,000)	($40,000)	($40,000)	($40,000)	($40,000)
Overhaul, end of Year 2	.769	(7,690)			(10,000)			
Disposal value, end of Year 5	.519	4,152						8,000
Present value of net cash outflows		$(140,858)						
Difference in favor of replacement		$ 8,425						
Incremental Approach								
A–B Analysis Confined to Differences								
Recurring cash operating savings, using an annuity table*	3.433	$ 34,330		$10,000	$10,000	$10,000	$10,000	$10,000
Overhaul avoided end of Year 2	.769	7,690			$10,000			
Difference in disposal values, end of Year 5	.519	(2,595)						(5,000)
Incremental initial investment	1.000	(31,000)	($31,000)					
Net present value of replacement		$ 8,425						

*Table 2, p. 380.

forecasting disposal value are usually not crucial because the present value is usually small.

2. Current Disposal Values and Required Investment. There are a number of correct ways to analyze this item, all of which will have the same ultimate effect on the decision. . . . Generally, the required investment is most easily measured by offsetting the disposal value of the old assets against the gross cost of the new assets.

3. Book Value and Depreciation. Depreciation is a phenomenon of accrual accounting that entails an allocation of cost, not a specific cash outlay. Depreciation and book value are ignored in discounted-cash-flow approaches for the reasons mentioned earlier in this chapter.

4. Income Taxes. In practice, comparison between alternatives is best made after considering tax effects, because the tax impact may alter the picture. . . .

5. Overhead Analysis. In relevant cost analysis, only the overhead that will differ between alternatives is pertinent. There is need for careful study of the fixed overhead under the available alternatives. In practice, this is an extremely difficult phase of cost analysis, because it is difficult to relate the individual costs to any single project.

6. Unequal Lives. Where projects have unequal lives, comparisons may be made either over the useful life of the longer-lived project or over the useful life of the shorter-lived project. For our purposes, let us estimate what the residual values will be at the end of the longer-lived project. We must also assume a reinvestment at the end of the shorter-lived project. This makes sense primarily because the decision maker should extend his time horizon as far as possible. If he is considering a longer-lived project, he should give serious consideration to what would be done in the time interval between the termination dates of the shorter-lived and longer-lived projects.

*   *   *   *   *

[7.] The General Guide to Capital Budgeting Decisions. The following decision rule, subject to the cautionary words just stated, should guide the selection of projects: The net present value method should be used, and *any* project that has a positive net present value should be undertaken. When the projects are mutually exclusive, so that the acceptance of one automatically entails the rejection of the other (e.g., buying Dodge or Ford trucks) the project which maximizes wealth measured in net present value in dollars should be undertaken.

OTHER APPROACHES TO ANALYZING LONG-RANGE DECISIONS

*   *   *   *   *

Payback Method

Payback, or *payout,* or *payoff,* is the measure of the time it will take to recoup in the form of cash inflow from operations, the initial dollars invested. Assume that $12,000 is spent for a machine with a an estimated useful life of eight years. Annual savings of $4,000 in *cash* outflow are expected from operations. Depreciation is ignored. The payback calculations follow:

$$P = \frac{I}{O} = \frac{\$12,000}{\$4,000} = 3 \text{ years} \tag{1}$$

Where P is the payback time; I is the initial incremental amount invested; and O is the uniform annual incremental cash inflow from operations.

The payback method, by itself, does not measure profitability; it measures how quickly investment dollars may be recouped. This is its major weakness, because a shorter payback time does not necessarily mean that one project is preferable to another.

For instance, assume that an alternative to the $12,000 machine is a $10,000 machine whose operation will also result in a reduction of $4,000 annually in cash outflow. Then

$$P_1 = \frac{\$12,000}{\$4,000} = 3.0 \text{ years}$$

$$P_2 = \frac{\$10,000}{\$4,000} = 2.5 \text{ years}$$

The payback criterion indicates that the $10,000 machine is more desirable. However, one fact about the $10,000 machine has been purposely withheld. Its useful life is only 2.5 years. Ignoring the impact of compound interest for the moment, the $10,000 machine results in zero benefit, while the $12,000 machine generates cash inflows for five years beyond its payback period.

The main objective in investing is profit, not the recapturing of the initial outlay. If a company wants to recover its outlay fast, it need not spend in the first place. Then no waiting time is necessary; the payback time is zero.

From

THE HUMAN SIDE OF ENTERPRISE*

By Douglas McGregor†

Participation is one of the most misunderstood ideas that have emerged from the field of human relations. It is praised by some, condemned by others, and used with considerable success by still others. The differences in point of view between its proponents and its critics are about as great as those between the leaders of Iron Curtain countries and those of the Free World when they use the term "democracy."

Some proponents of participation give the impression that it is a magic formula which will eliminate conflict and disagreement and come pretty close to solving all of management's problems. These enthusiasts appear to believe that people yearn to participate, much as children of a generation or two ago yearned for Castoria. They give the impression that it is a formula which can be applied by any manager regardless of his skill, that virtually no preparation is necessary for

* By permission from *The Human Side of Enterprise,* by Douglas McGregor. Copyright 1960. McGraw-Hill Book Company, Inc. (Excerpts from 124–31, 172–75.)

† The late author was Professor in the School of Industrial Management at the Massachusetts Institute of Technology.

its use, and that it can spring full-blown into existence and transform industrial relationships overnight.

Some critics of participation, on the other hand, see it as a form of managerial abdication. It is a dangerous idea that will undermine management prerogatives and almost certainly get out of control. It is a concept which for them fits the pattern of "soft" management exclusively. It wastes time, lowers efficiency, and weakens management's effectiveness.

A third group of managers view participation as a useful term in their bag of managerial tricks. It is for them a manipulative device for getting people to do what they want, under conditions which delude the "participators" into thinking that they have had a voice in decision making. The idea is to handle them so skillfully that they come up with the answer which the manager had in the first place, but believing it was their own. This is a way of "making people feel important" which these managers are quick to emphasize as a significant motivational tool of management. (It is important to note the distinction between making people *feel* important and *making* people important.)

Naturally, there are severe critics of this manipulative approach to participation, and they tend to conceive of all participation as taking this form.

A fourth group of managers makes successful use of participation, but they don't think of it as a panacea or magic formula. They do not share either the unrestrained enthusiasm of the faddists or the fears of the critics. They would flatly refuse to employ participation as a manipulative sales device.

Among all of these these groups is a rather general but tacit agreement—incorrect, I believe—that participation applies to groups and not to individuals. None of them appears to view it as having any relationship to delegation. After all, it has a different name! Many of the strong proponents of delegation have no use whatever for participation.

In the light of all this it is not surprising that a fair number of thoughtful managers view this whole subject with some skepticism.

The effective use of participation is a consequence of a managerial point of view which includes confidence in the potentialities of subordinates, awareness of management's dependency downwards, and a desire to avoid some of the negative consequences of emphasis on personal authority. . . .

It is perhaps most useful to consider participation in terms of a range of managerial actions. At one end of the range the exercise of authority in the decision-making process is almost complete and participation is negligible. At the other end of the range the exercise of authority is relatively small and participation is maximum. There is no implication that more participation is better than less. The degree of participation which will be suitable depends upon a variety of factors, including the problem or issue, the attitudes and past experience of the subordinates, the manager's skill, and the point of view alluded to above.

        *   *   *   *   *

. . . Participation is not confined to the relationship between a first-line supervisor and his workers. It can occur between a president and his executive committee. Moreover, since there are many managerial decisions which affect a single subordinate, it is equally applicable to the individual or to the group. The kind of participation which will be utilized will vary depending upon the level of the organization as well as upon the other factors mentioned above.

        *   *   *   *   *

Since one of the major purposes of the use of participation is to encourage the growth of subordinates and their ability to accept responsibility, the superior will be concerned to pick appropriate problems or issues for discussion and decision. These will be matters of some significance to subordinates; otherwise they will see little point in their involvement. . . .

Of course, there are some risks connected with the use of participation. All significant managerial activities involve risk, and this is no exception. The usual fear is that if employees are given an opportunity to influence decisions affecting them, they will soon want to participate in matters which should be none of their concern. Managements who express this fear most acutely tend to have a very narrow conception of the issues which should concern employees. If management's concern is with the growth of employees and their increasing ability to undertake responsibility, there will of course be an expectation that employees will become involved in an increasing range of decision-making activities.

* * * * *

In any event, there are now so many instances of the successful use of participation which has not in any discernible way weakened management's ability to manage that I can see little basis for anxiety over the issue of management prerogatives. The only conclusion I would draw is that the managements who are primarily concerned to protect their power and authority had better leave the whole matter alone.

. . . In view of the interdependence characteristic of industrial organizations there is reason for modifying the typical unilateral nature of the decision-making process. Participation, used judiciously, and in many different ways, depending upon the circumstances, offers help along these lines. It is a process which differs very little from delegation in its essential character. In fact, participation is a special case of delegation in which the subordinate gains greater control, greater freedom of choice, with respect to his own responsibility. The term participation is usually applied to the subordinate's greater influence over matters within the sphere of his superior's responsibilities. When these matters affect him and his job—when interdependence is involved—it seems reasonable that he should have the opportunity to exert some influence. . . .

Participation . . . offers substantial opportunities for ego satisfaction for the subordinate and thus can affect motivation toward organizational objectives. It is an aid to achieving integration. In the first place, the subordinate can discover the satisfaction that comes from tackling problems and finding successful solutions for them. This is by no means a minor form of satisfaction. It is one of the reasons that the whole do-it-yourself movement has grown to such proportions in recent years. Beyond this there is a greater sense of independence and of achieving some control over one's destiny. Finally, there are the satisfactions that come by way of recognition from peers and superiors for having made a worth-while contribution to the solution of an organizational problem. At lower levels of the organization, where the opportunities for satisfactions like these are distinctly limited, participation in departmental problem solving may have considerable significance in demonstrating to people how they can satisfy their own needs best by working toward organizational objectives.

Viewed thus, participation is not a panacea, a manipulative device, a gimmick, or a threat. Used wisely, and with understanding, it is a natural concomitant of management by integration and self-control.

*   *   *   *   *

In order to create a climate of mutual confidence surrounding staff-line relationships within which collaboration in achieving organizational objectives will become possible, several requirements must be met:

1. The inadequacy of the conventional principles of unity of command and of equality of authority and responsibility must be recognized. Not only are these principles unrealistic in the modern industrial corporation, they are the source of many of the difficulties we are trying to correct. . . .

2. The primary task of any staff group is that of providing specialized help to *all levels* of management, not just to the level at which the group reports.

3. The proper role of the staff member is that of the professional vis-à-vis his clients. The genuinely competent professional recognizes (*a*) that help is always defined by the recipient and (*b*) that he can neither fulfill his responsibilities to the organization nor maintain proper ethical standards of conduct if he is placed in a position which involves conflicting obligations to his managerial "clients."

4. The central principle of managerial control is the principle of self-control. This principle severely limits *both* staff and line use of data and information collected for control purposes as well as the so-called coordinative activities of staff groups. If the principle of self-control is violated, the staff inevitably becomes involved in conflicting obligations, and in addition is required to occupy the incompatible roles of professional helper and policeman.

It may seem impractical to attempt to create a climate of staff-line relationships within the organization similar to that which characterizes effective professional-client relationships in private practice, yet this is essentially what is required. . . .

We are now in a position to consider a couple of interesting questions about the staff-line relationship. First, where is the issue of who exercises authority over whom?

With the approach suggested above, the traditional principles which define the role of staff evaporate. The professional-client relationship is an interdependent one in which neither typically exercises authority over the other although there is influence in both directions. The managerial client is dependent on the specialized knowledge and skill of the professional, but if he attempts to get the help he needs by authoritative methods he will defeat his purposes. It is not possible to obtain by command the imaginative, creative effort which distinguishes the competent professional from the glorified clerk. The manager who perceives staff members as flunkies to carry out his orders will never obtain *professional* staff help. On the other hand, the manager who perceives himself as a client utilizing the knowledge and skill of professional specialists will not attempt to achieve this purpose by relying on his authority over them.

The professional, in turn, is dependent upon his clients. Unless they accept and use his help, he has no value to the organization and therefore there is no reason for employing him. If, however, he attempts to impose "help" authoritatively (whether directly or by accepting assignments of control and coordinative responsibilities from his superiors), he places himself in the role of policeman, which is completely incompatible with the professional role.

There is, in fact, no solution to the problem of staff-line relationships in authoritative terms which will achieve organizational objectives adequately. Waste of human resources, friction and antagonism, elaborate and costly protective mechanisms, and lower commitment to organizational objectives are the inescapable consequences of the traditional conception of the relationship.

Second, what has happened to the distinction between line and staff? It has become evident as a result of our examination of line management's task in the preceding chapters of this volume that the most appropriate roles of the manager vis-à-vis his subordinates are those of teacher, professional helper, colleague, consultant. Only to a limited degree will he assume the role of authoritative boss. The line manager who seeks to operate within the context of Theory Y will establish relationships with his subordinates, his superiors, and his colleagues which are much like those of the professional vis-à-vis his clients. He will become more like a professional staff member (although in general rather than specialized ways) and less like a traditional line manager.

The various functions within the organization differ in many ways (in the number of other functions with which they are related, for example), but not particularly in terms of the traditional line-staff distinction. All managers, whether line or staff, have responsibilities for collaborating with other members of the organization in achieving organizational objectives. Each is concerned with (1) making his own resources of knowledge, skill, and experience available to others; (2) obtaining help from others in fulfilling his own responsibilities; and (3) controlling his own job. Each has *both* line and staff responsibilities.

One consequence of this approach is the greater significance which the managerial *team* acquires at each level of organization. Much of the manager's work—be he line or staff—requires his collaboration with other managers in a relationship where personal authority and power must be subordinated to the requirements of the *task* if the organizational objectives are to be achieved. Effective collaboration of this kind is hindered, not helped, by the traditional distinctions between line and staff. The goal is to utilize the contributions of all the available human resources in reaching the best decisions or problem solutions or action strategies.

The modern industrial organization is a vast complex of interdependent relationships, up, down, across, and even "diagonally." In fact, the interdependence is so great that only collaborative team efforts can make the system work effectively. It is probable that one day we shall begin to draw organization charts as a series of linked groups rather than as a hierarchical structure of individual "reporting" relationships. . . .

9. AB THORSTEN (A-C, R)

Case Introduction

SYNOPSIS

The President of AB Thorsten, Swedish subsidiary of a large Belgian company, proposes to build a plant in Sweden for the production of XL-4, a chemical used in the paper industry. He uses modern methods of financial management (and management science) to forecast results over seven years. The investment was approved by the Thorsten board. Later, opposition to the investment develops in the headquarters of the parent company in Belgium. The Belgian corporate staff use methods similar to those used in Sweden and arrive at the decision that XL-4 should be produced in Belgium and exported to Sweden. There follows a series of moves between Belgian and Swedish managements which shows that they (1) disagree on basic technical and financial matters and (2) tend to become involved in "personal" and "national interests" kinds of conflict, in addition to conflict over rational financial matters. The president of the worldwide Belgian multinational company must decide where the plant is to be built, or how to get others to make this decision.

WHY THIS CASE IS INCLUDED

The case offers opportunity to see how basic technical-economic factors can often be the root of human conflict within any system. In this case the subsystem company happens to be across a national boundary, which magnifies such technical conflicts. The Swedish subsidiary management conflicts with the Belgian management not only because of a basic economic conflict which occurs within any complex company, but also, superimposed on this is the national culture factor: the large (parent) company is in Belgium and the smaller (subsidiary) company is in Sweden. The way "identification" and "loyalty" are affected by economic factors is also evident.

342

One can also see in clear perspective the dilemma in choosing a centralized organization structure versus a decentralized structure, including the advantageous and disadvantageous outcomes that result regardless of which solution is chosen. The final decision represents a trade-off decision process—how much human motivation and learning factors trade off against financial efficiency factors.

As a byproduct, one might learn some substantive long-range planning techniques for capital budgeting and strategic resource allocation problems, some theories of multinational company loyalty, and some theories for motivation of managers.

DIAGNOSTIC AND PREDICTIVE QUESTIONS

The readings included with this case are marked (*). The author index at the end of this book locates the other readings.

1. Notice that both Ekstrom (Sweden) and Bols (vice president, finance, Belgium) used a number of decision-making tools to help them evaluate the consequences of a particular alternative (whether to produce in Sweden or Belgium). Why did they approach the decision in this way?

Read: Horngren, *Accounting for Management Control,* pp. 356–363, 365–368. Those who wish additional insight into the answer to this question may consult in the library, *The Systems Approach,* by C. West Churchman, Dell Publishing Company, 1968, pp. 3–5.

2. The techniques used (in Question 1) show that, from the Roget S.A. point of view, it is preferable to prevent the Swedish subsidiary from maximizing its own growth or its own internal efficiency. Why is this necessary if one accepts that Roget is *the* system to be studied (that it is the most important system for analysis or action)?

Read: *Starr, *Management: A Modern Approach,* pp. 673–676. *Richmond, *Operations Research for Management Decisions,* pp. 16–20.

3. From a systems point of view, there is a conflict between the "scientific truth" discovered by Bols in Belgium and the "scientific truth" discovered by Ekstrom. Both have analyzed and quantified the question of where to build an XL-4 plant, yet each came up with different answers. Is there not one correct answer which some qualified expert could discover which would be "true" or "right"?

Read: Simon, *The New Science of Management Decisions,* pp. 15–18, 40–49.

4. Do you see why the technical conflict between the Roget production system and the Thorsten production system might be one important cause of the later human conflict between the two managements of these companies? Explain.

5. Assuming away for the moment any personal or empire building motives on the part of either Belgian or Swedish managers, why is there a technological-economic reason for centralizing the investment location in Brussels? That is, why should the Roget headquarters staff decide where plants should be built?

Review readings for Questions 2 and 3 above.

6. Some economists might view Ekstrom or Bols as entrepreneurial types, motivated by certain factors peculiar to men who build businesses. What would be causing them to make the arguments they make? Use quotations to show your reasoning.

Read: Schumpeter, *The Theory of Economic Development,* pp. 84–94.

7. Read Juvet's statement at the beginning of the case starting with "another thing we achieve in the new organization. . . ." Do you see why he hopes for a *decentralized* organization structure? Look at the statements of Ekstrom in the case. What motivates him to develop XL-4 and devote so much energy to his plan?

Read: Maslow, "A Theory of Human Motivation," pp. 80–94. *Simon, *Administrative Behavior* (2nd ed.), pp. 110–116, 118–119. Those who wish additional insight into the answer to this question may consult in the library, *Exchange and Power in Social Life,* by Peter M. Blau, John Wiley and Sons, Inc., 1967, pp. 22–24.

8. What about the morale and motivation of Bols and Lavanchy at Roget headquarters?

Review the readings in Question 7 above. Show how they apply to the Belgian executives as well as to Ekstrom and his management.

9. What are the organizational identifications of Ekstrom and Bols-Lavanchy? Explain how these cause the men to behave as they do regarding the plant location decision.

Read: *March and Simon, *Organizations,* pp. 65–66, 70–77.

10. What special organizational identifications (loyalties) do Ekstrom and Bols have by virtue of the fact that Roget S.A. is a *multinational firm?*

Read: *Perlmutter, "The Tortuous Evolution of the Multinational Corporation," pp. 10–14.

11. What kind of conflict situation resulted from the proposals of Ekstrom and Bols? Is the conflict a win-lose situation, or does it result from perceptual differences? Can the situation be viewed as constructive conflict?

Read: Leavitt, *Managerial Psychology,* pp. 27–33. Follett, "Constructive Conflict," pp. 30–49. Litterer, "Conflict in Organization: A Re-examination," pp. 178–186.

12. Is there logic in Ekstrom's statement, "if you can manufacture it for us in Sweden until we learn . . ."? Do you see how AB Thorsten might be thought of as an "underdeveloped company" just as the Congo can be thought of as an "underdeveloped nation"? If the decision is to manufacture in Belgium, how is the Roget top management governing the economic development of: (1) Thorsten, (2) Sweden as a nation, and (3) the world as a whole?

POLICY QUESTIONS

13. One alternative for M. Juvet to consider for solving his plant location is to decentralize—allowing Thorsten and other worldwide subsidiaries to build plants when *they* think necessary. List the advantages of

this alternative. The readings of Questions 1 through 12 above will help in seeing these advantages.

14. One organization structure which is similar to decentralization is the "profit center" form of organization. What are the basic requirements if this form is to be successful? What would Juvet have to adjust in the present practices of the two companies to make Thorsten a true profit center?

Read: *Anthony, "Note on Responsibility Centers." See readings for Questions 7 through 11 above.

15. Do you see a possibility of an arrangement under which "everybody wins," similar to Mary Parker Follett's "integration," rather than "compromise"?

See the reading in Question 11 for the concept of integration. Hint: possibility in setting the transfer price—the price at which Belgium would sell to Sweden.

16. Another alternative for Juvet would be to centralize the plant location decision in Brussels. What advantages and disadvantages would result from such a decision?

See readings for Questions 1 through 3 above.

17. Assume you *are* M. Juvet, an informed manager who has studied all facets of this case. What would you do regarding the Thorsten proposal and the Bols counterproposal?

18. Do you think that M. Juvet should make an economically reasonable decision about XL-4, a politically reasonable decision, or both?

Read: *Diesing, *Reason in Society: Five Types of Reason and Their Social Conditions,* pp. 20–21, 56, 170–71, 177–78, 198–99, 227–28, 231–32.

QUESTIONS FOR ORIGINAL STUDENT WORK IN ANALYSIS AND POLICY

19. While reflecting on case facts, what additional theories from prior education give you insights as to "what is going on" in AB Thorsten? As to what might be predicted to happen in the future?

20. Other than the policy questions asked by the authors, what pragmatic ways can you think of to state the practical problems faced by executives in the case?

Case Text*

This case deals with an investment proposal made by Anders Ekstrom, president of AB Thorsten, a firm engaged in the production and sale of chemicals, with headquarters in Stockholm, Sweden. This proposal was made to the management of Roget S.A., in Brussels, Belgium. AB Thorsten is a 100-percent owned subsidiary of Roget S.A.

SUMMARY OF OPERATIONS: ROGET S.A.

Roget S.A. is one of the largest industrial companies in Belgium. Founded 40 years ago, the company originally produced a line of simple products for sale in Belgium. Today it has expanded to produce 208 complex chemical products in 21 factories.

Mr. André Juvet, president of Roget, states that the organization of the company (Exhibit 1) is the result of careful planning:

> *Until five years ago, we were organized with one large manufacturing division here in Belgium, and one large sales division. One department of the sales division was devoted to export sales. However, exports grew so fast, and domestic markets became so complex, that we created three main product divisions, each with its own manufacturing plants and sales organizations. In addition, we have created foreign subsidiaries to take over the business in certain areas. For example, in Industrial Chemicals we have two subsidiaries—one in the U.K. and one in Sweden which serves all Scandinavia. At the same time, the domestic department of the Industrial Chemicals Division exports to the rest of Europe. The U.K. and Sweden account for 9 percent and 5 percent of sales in that division, but 14 percent added to total sales is very important.*
>
> *Another thing we achieve in the new organization is individual profit responsibility of all executives at all levels. Mr. Gillot is responsible for profits for all industrial chemicals, Mr. Lambert is responsible for profits from domestic operations (manufacturing and sales) and export sales to countries where we do not have subsidiaries or factories, and Mr. Ekstrom is responsible for profits in Scandinavia.*
>
> *This, together with a policy of promotion from within, helps*

---

* This case was authored by Charles E. Summer and Gordon Shillinglaw. Names of people and places have been disguised. Copyright 1969 by Institute pour l'Etude des Méthodes de Direction de l'Enterprise (IMEDE), Lausanne, Switzerland.

The letters "AB" and "S.A." are the equivalent designations in Sweden and Belgium of "Corp." or "Inc." in the U.S. and "Ltd." in the U.K.

The designation (A-C,R) indicates that this case is a revised version of Cases A, B, and C.

stimulate managers in Roget to a degree not enjoyed by some of our competitors. It also helps to keep men in an industry where experience is of great importance. Most of our executives have been in the starch chemicals business all of their lives. It is a complex business, and we feel that it takes many years to learn it.

We have developed certain policies—rules of the game—which govern relationships with our subsidiary company presidents. These are intended to maintain efficiency of the whole Roget complex, while at the same time to give subsidiary managers autonomy to run their own businesses. For example a subsidiary manager can determine what existing Roget products he wants to sell in his part of the world market. Export Sales will quote him the same price as they quote agents in all countries. He is free to bargain, and if he doesn't like the price he needn't sell the product. Second, we encourage subsidiaries to propose to division management in Brussels the development of new products. If these are judged feasible we manufacture them in Belgium for supply to world markets. Third, the subsidiary president can build his own manufacturing plants if he can justify the investment in his own market.

EXHIBIT 1
Organization Chart
Roget S.A.

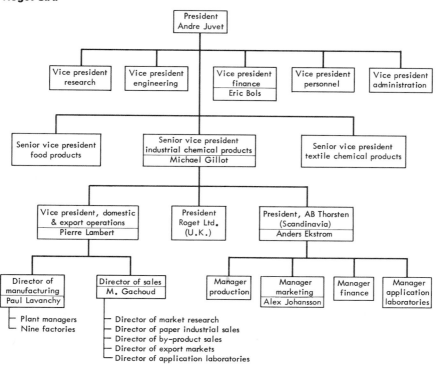

COMPANY BACKGROUND: AB THORSTEN

AB Thorsten was purchased by Roget S.A. eight years ago. Since that time the same four men have constituted Thorsten's board of directors: Ekstrom; Mr. Michael Gillot, senior vice president in charge of Roget's Industrial Chemical Products Division; Mr. Ingve Norgren, a Swedish banker; and Mr. Ove Svensen, a Stockholm industrialist. Swedish corporation law requires any company incorporated in Sweden to have Swedish directors, and the Roget management felt fortunate in finding two men as prominent as Norgren and Svensen to serve on the Thorsten board.

During the first four years of Roget's ownership, Thorsten's sales fluctuated between Skr. 5 and 7 million, but hit a low at the end of that period.[1] The board of AB Thorsten decided at that time that the company was in serious trouble, and that the only alternative to selling the company was to hire a totally different management to overhaul and streamline the entire company operation.

On advice of the Swedish directors, Mr. Anders Ekstrom, a 38-year-old graduate of the Royal Institute of Technology, was hired. He had had 16 years of experience in production engineering for a large machinery company, as marketing manager of a British subsidiary in Sweden, and as division manager responsible for profits in a large paper company. Ekstrom states his experience:

> *My experience with the paper company was particularly valuable to me. It was the European subsidiary of a large U.S. firm. Before I worked there, I knew very little of modern financial methods and strategic planning methods. In fact, the American business schools have been teaching these things for at least 15 years, but our educational system in Europe does not include but one or two places where this kind of thing is learned. The company I worked for sent over from time to time men who attended Wharton, Columbia, and Harvard. I said to myself, these are the kinds of things I need to be successful, and they are the kinds Sweden needs to operate our industry with maximum productivity. Sure enough, they have been invaluable to me and to Thorsten. A few men in Roget know them, but even there such methods are relatively unknown among managers. With all of its other faults, we owe the U.S. a debt of gratitude for teaching European executives such things. One day, everyone here will know these methods, and we will be competitive or even superior to the U.S. in management. I am proud to have learned such management techniques and they give me confidence in managing Thorsten—for the benefit of the company and for the benefit of Sweden's productive capacity.*

Ekstrom has been president of AB Thorsten for the past four years. In that time, sales have increased to Skr. 20 million and profits have

---

[1] To avoid confusion, all monetary figures in this case series are stated in Swedish kroner, even though some of the actual transactions are made in Belgian francs.

reached levels that Roget's management finds highly satisfactory. Both Ekstrom and Norgren (a director) attribute this performance to: (a) an increase in industrial activity in Scandinavia; (b) changes in production methods, marketing strategy, and organization structure made by Ekstrom; (c) the hiring of competent staff; and (d) Ekstrom's own ambition and hard work. To these reasons the case writer also adds Ekstrom's knowledge of modern planning techniques—rather sophisticated market research methods, financial planning by use of discounted cash flows and incremental analysis, and, as Ekstrom puts it, "all those things my former company had learned from the American companies."

Ekstrom says that at the time he joined Thorsten, he knew it was a risk. "I like the challenge of building a company. If I do a good job here I will have the confidence of Norgren and Svenson as well as of the Roget management in Brussels. Deep down inside, succeeding in this situation will teach me things that will make me more competent as a top executive. So I chose this job even though I had at the time (and still have) offers from other companies."

INITIAL PROPOSAL FOR MANUFACTURE OF XL-4

Two years ago, Ekstrom informed the Thorsten board of directors that he proposed to study the feasibility of constructing a factory in Sweden for the manufacture of XL-4, a product used in paper converting. He explained that he and his customer engineers had discovered a new way of helping large paper mills convert their machines at little cost so that they could use XL-4 instead of competitors' products. Large paper mill customers would be able to realize dramatic savings in material handling and storage costs and to shorten drying time substantially. In his judgment, Thorsten could develop a market in Sweden almost as big as Roget's present worldwide market for XL-4. XL-4 was then being produced in Roget's Domestic Division at the rate of 600 tons a year, but none of this was going to Sweden.

Ekstrom outlines his position:

> At that meeting Mr. Gillot and the other directors seemed enthusiastic. Gillot said, "Of course—go ahead with your study and when you have a proposed plan, with the final return on investment, send it in and we will consider it thoroughly."
>
> During the next six months, we did the analysis. My market research department estimated the total potential in Sweden at 800 tons of XL-4 per year. We interviewed important customers and conducted trials in the factories of three big companies which proved that with the introduction of our machine designs the large cost saving would indeed materialize. We determined that if we could sell the product for Skr. 1,850 per ton, we could capture one half of the market within a three-year period, or 400 tons a year.
>
> At the same time, I called the head of the Corporate Engineering Division in Brussels (see Exhibit 1) asking his help in designing a plant to produce 400 tons per year, and in estimating the cost of the

investment. This is a routine thing. The central staff divisions are advisory and always comply with requests for help. He assigned a project manager and four other engineers to work on the design of factory and machinery, and to estimate the cost. At the same time I assigned three men from my staff to work on the project. In three months this joint task group reported that the necessary plant could be built for Skr. 700,000.

All of this we summarized in a pro forma calculation (Exhibits 2 through 5). This calcualtion, together with a complete written explanation, was mailed 18 months ago to Mr. Gillot. I felt rather excited, as did most of my staff. We all know that introduction of new products is one of the keys to continued growth and profitability. The yield of this investment (15 percent) was well above the minimum 8 percent established as a guideline for new investment by the Roget vice president of finance. We also knew that it was a good analysis, done by modern tools of management. In the covering letter, I asked that it be put on the agenda for the next board meeting.

The minutes of the next board meeting held in Stockholm three weeks later show on the agenda, "A Proposal for Investment in Sweden," to be presented by Mr. Ekstrom, using a series of charts (Exhibits 2 through 5). The minutes also quote his remarks as he explained the proposal to other directors:

You will see from the summary table (Exhibit 2) that this project is profitable. On an initial outlay of Skr. 700,000 for equipment and Skr. 56,000 for working capital, we get a rate of return of 15 percent and a present value of Skr. 246,000.

Let me explain some of the figures underlying this summary table. My second chart (Exhibit 3) summarizes the operating cash flows that we expect to get from the XL-4 project. The sales forecast for the first seven years is shown in Column 2. The forecast was not extended beyond seven years because our engineers estimate that the technology of starch manufacture will improve gradually, so that major plant renovations will become economical at about the end of the seventh year. Actually, we see no reason why this particular product, XL-4, will decline in demand after seven years.

The estimated variable cost of Skr. 1,000 per ton shown in Column 3 is our estimate of the full operating cost of manufacturing XL-4 in Sweden, including out-of-pocket fixed costs such as plant management salaries, but excluding depreciation.

As Column 4 shows, we feel certain that we can enter the market initially with a selling price of Skr. 2,000 a ton, but full market penetration will require a price reduction to Skr. 1,850 at the beginning of the second year.

The variable profit resulting from these figures is shown in Columns 5 and 6. Column 7 then lists the market development and promotion expenditures that are needed to launch the product and achieve the forecasted sales levels. Column 8 contains the net operat-

EXHIBIT 2
AB Thorsten — Proposal for Manufacture of XL-4 in Sweden —
Financial Summary (all figures in Skr.)

Year	Description	After-Tax Cash Flows*	Present Value at 8%
0	Equipment...............................	−700,000	
	Working capital........................	− 56,000	
	Total	−756,000	−756,000
1	Cash operating profit.................	+105,000	
	Working capital........................	− 2,000	
	Total	+103,000	+ 95,000
2	Cash operating profit.................	+160,000	
	Working capital........................	− 7,000	
	Total	+153,000	+131,000
3	Cash operating profit.................	+215,000	+171,000
4	Cash operating profit.................	+215,000	+158,000
5	Cash operating profit.................	+215,000	+146,000
6	Cash operating profit.................	+145,000	+ 91,000
7	Cash operating profit.................	+145,000	
	Recovery value of equipment and working capital (Exhibit 5)........	+215,000	
	Total	+360,000	+210,000
	Grand Total.....................	+650,000	+246,000

*From Exhibits 3, 4, and 5

Net present value ....Skr. 246,000
Payback period (before tax)..........4 years
Internal rate of return.......................15%

ing cash flows before tax, based on figures in the preceding columns. This is the amount which this project will contribute to profit of Thorsten and our parent company.

The cost of the plant can be written off for tax purposes over a five-year period, at the rate of 20 percent of original cost each year. Subtracting this amount from the before-tax cash flow would yield the taxable income (column not shown in the table). The tax in Column 10 is then subtracted from the before-tax cash flow to yield the after-tax cash flow in Column 11. This is the final profit after taxes which the project would make for both Thorsten and Roget.

A proposal of this kind also requires some investment in working capital. My third chart (Exhibit 4) summarizes our estimates on this element. We'll need about Skr. 80,000 to start with, but some of this can be deducted immediately from our income taxes. Swedish law permits us to deduct 60 percent of the cost of inventories from taxable

EXHIBIT 3

AB Thorsten—Estimated Operating Cash Flows from Manufacture and Sales of XL-4 in Sweden

1	2	3	4	5	6	7	8	9	10	11
Year	Sales (in Tons)	Various Costs per Ton	Sales Price per Ton	Various Profit Margin per Ton 4 − 3	Total Various Profit Margin 2 × 5	Promotion Costs	Profit Contributions 6 − 7	Tax Depreciation	Tax 50% of (8 − 9)	Net Cash Flow after Tax 8 − 10
		(Skr. per ton)					(figures in thousands of Skr.)			
1	200	1,000	2,000	1,000	200	130	70	140	(35)	105
2	300	1,000	1,850	850	255	75	180	140	20	160
3	400	1,000	1,850	850	350	50	290	140	75	215
4	400	1,000	1,850	850	340	50	290	140	75	215
5	400	1,000	1,850	850	340	50	290	140	75	215
6	400	1,000	1,850	850	340	50	290	–	145	145
7	400	1,000	1,850	850	340	50	290	–	145	145
Total	2,500				2,155	455	1,700	700	500	1,200

EXHIBIT 4

AB Thorsten—Estimated Working Capital Required for Manufacture and Sale of XL-4 in Sweden (Skr. 000)*

	1	2	3	4	5	6
		Other Current Assets less		Change from	Tax Credit (30% of	Net Funds
	Inventory at Cost	Current Lia-bilities	Working Capital 1 + 2	Previous Year	Change in 1)	Required 4 − 5
Year 0............	80	0	80	+80	24	56
Year 1............	90	−5	85	+ 5	3	2
Year 2............	100	−5	95	+10	3	7
Year 3 and later	100	−5	95	0	0	0
Total........	100	−5	95	95	30	65

*These figures are in addition to the estimated equipment cost of Skr. 700,000.

income. For this reason, we can get an immediate reduction of Skr. 24,000 in the taxes we have to pay on our other income in Sweden. This is shown in Column 5. The net investment in working capital is thus only Skr. 56,000, the figure we show in Column 6.

We'll need small additional amounts of working capital in the next two years, and these amounts are also shown in Column 6. Altogether, our working capital requirements will add up to Skr. 65,000 by the end of our second full year of operations.

Now let's look at one last chart (Exhibit 5). Seven years is a very conservative estimate of the life of the product. If we limit the analysis to seven years, we'll be overlooking the value of our assets at the end of that time. At the very worst, the plant itself should be worth Skr. 300,000 after seven years. We'd have to pay tax on that, of course, because the plant would be fully depreciated, but this would still leave us with Skr. 150,000 for the plant.

The working capital should be fully recoverable, too. After paying

EXHIBIT 5

AB Thorsten—Estimated End-of-Life Value of Swedish Assets

Plant...Skr.300,000			
Less tax on gain if sold at this price	150,000		
Net value of plant..		Skr.150,000	
Working capital...Skr. 95,000			
Less payment of deferred tax on special inventory reserves...............................	30,000		
Net value of working capital		65,000	
Net Value of Swedish Assets After 7 Years..		Skr.215,000	
Present Value (Skr.215,000 discounted for 7 years at 8%)..		Skr.134,000	

the deferred tax on inventories, we'd still get Skr. 65,000 back on that. The total value at the end of seven years would thus be Skr. 215,000.

Mr. Ekstrom ended this opening presentation by saying, "Gentlemen, it seems clear from these figures that we can justify this investment in Sweden on the basis of sales to the Swedish market. The group vice president for finance has laid down the policy that any new investment should yield at least 8 percent. This particular proposal shows a return of 15 percent. My management and I strongly recommend this project." (The Thorsten vice presidents for production, sales, and finance had been called into the board meeting to be present when this proposal was made.)

Ekstrom told the case writer that while he was making this proposal he was sure that it would be accepted.

Gillot said that it seemed to him to be a clear case. He asked interesting questions, mainly about the longer term likelihood that we could see more than 400 tons a year, and about how we would get the money. I explained that we in Sweden were very firm in our judgment that we would reach 400 tons a year even before one year, but felt constrained to show a conservative estimate of a three-year transition period. We also showed him how we could finance any expansion by borrowing in Sweden. That is, if Roget would furnish the initial capital, and if our 400 tons were reached quickly, any further expansion would easily be lent by banks. The two Swedish directors confirmed this. The board voted unanimously to construct the plant.

DISAGREEMENT BETWEEN PARENT AND SUBSIDIARY

About a week later, Gillot telephoned Ekstrom. "Since my return to Brussels I have been through some additional discussions with the production and marketing people here in the domestic department. They think the engineering design and plant cost is accurate, but that you are too optimistic on your sales forecast. It looks like you will have to justify this more."

I pushed him to set up a meeting the following week, Ekstrom says. This meeting was attended by myself and my marketing and production directors, from Sweden, and four people from Belgium—Gillot, Lavanchy (director of manufacturing), Gachoud (director of sales), and Lambert (vice president for domestic and export).

That was one of the worst meetings of my life. It lasted all day. Gachoud said that they had sales experience from other countries and that in his judgment the market potential and our share were too optimistic. Then Lavanchy said that the production of this product is complicated, and that he had difficulties producing it in Belgium, even with trained workers who have long experience. I told him I only

*needed five trained production workers and that he could send me
two men for two months to train Swedes to do the job. I impressed
on him that if you can manufacture it in Belgium you can manufacture it for us in Sweden until we learn if you don't have confidence
in Swedish technology.*

*At 6 P.M. everyone was tired. Lambert had backed up his two pro-
duction and sales officials all day, repeating their arguments. Gillot
seemed to me to just sit there and listen, occasionally asking questions. I cannot understand why he didn't back me up. He seemed so
easy to get along with at the prior board meeting in Stockholm—and
he seemed decisive. Not so at this meeting. He seemed distant, indeci-
sive, and an ineffective executive.*

*He stopped the meeting without a solution, and said that he hoped
all concerned would do more investigation of this subject. He vaguely
referred to the fact that he would think about it himself and let us
know when another meeting would be held.*

OBJECTION FROM A SWEDISH DIRECTOR

Ekstrom states that he returned to Stockholm and reported the meeting to his own staff, and to the two Swedish members of his board. "They,
like I, were really disgusted. Here we were operating with initiative and
with excellent financial techniques. Roget management had often made
talks in which they emphasized the necessity for decentralized profit
responsibilities, authority, and initiative on the part of foreign subsidiary
presidents. One of my men told me that they seem to talk decentralization and act like tin gods at the same time."

Mr. Norgren, the Swedish banker on Thorsten's board, expressed surprise:

*"I considered this carefully. It is sound business for AB Thorsten,
and XL-4 will help to build one more growth company in the Swedish
economy. Somehow, the management in Brussels has failed to study
this, or they don't wish the Swedish subsidiary to produce it. I have
today dictated a letter to Mr. Gillot telling him that I don't know why
the project is rejected, that Roget has a right to its own reasons, but
that I am prepared to resign as a director. It is not that I am angry,
or that I have a right to dictate decisions for the whole worldwide
Roget S.A. It is simply that, if I spend my time studying policy decisions, and those decisions do not serve the right function for the
business, then it is a waste of time to continue.*

Finally, Ekstrom states, "while I certainly wouldn't bring these matters out in a meeting, I think those Belgian production and Sales people
simply want to build the empire and make the money in Roget Belgium.
They don't care about Thorsten and Sweden. That's a smooth way to
operate. We have the ideas and initiative, and they take them and get the
payoff."

FURTHER STUDY

After Mr. Gillot received Norgren's letter, he contacted Messrs. Lavanchy, Gachoud, and Bols (vice president, finance, Roget corporate staff). He told them that the Swedish XL-4 project had become a matter of key importance for the whole Roget group, because of its implications for company profits, and for the morale and autonomy of the subsidiary management. He asked them to study the matter and report their recommendations in one month. Meanwhile, he wrote Ekstrom, "Various members of the corporate headquarters are studying the proposal. You will hear from me within about six weeks regarding my final decision."

REPORT OF ROGET'S DIRECTOR OF MANUFACTURING

A month after he was asked to study the XL-4 project, Lavanchy gave Gillot a memorandum explaining his reasons for opposing the proposal:

> *At your request, I have reexamined thoroughly all of the cost figures that bear on the XL-4 proposal. I find that manufacture of this product in Sweden would be highly uneconomical, for two reasons: (1) overhead costs would be higher; and (2) variable costs would be greater.*
>
> *As to the first, we can produce XL-4 in Belgium with less overhead cost. Suppose that Thorsten does sell 400 tons a year so that our total worldwide sales rise to 1,000 tons. We can produce the whole 1,000 tons in Belgium with essentially the same capital investment we have now. If we produce 1,000 tons, our fixed costs will decrease by Skr. 120 a ton.[2] That means Skr. 72,000 in savings on production for domestic and export to countries other than Sweden (600 tons a year), and Skr. 120,000 for worldwide production including Sweden (1,000 tons).*
>
> *Second, we could save on variable costs. If we were to produce the extra 400 tons in Belgium, the total production of 1,000 tons a year would give us longer production runs, lower setup costs, and larger raw material purchases, thus allowing mass purchasing and material handling and lower purchase prices. My accounting department has studied this and concludes that our average variable costs will decrease from Skr. 950 a ton to Skr. 930 (Exhibit 6). This Skr. 20 per ton difference means a savings of Skr. 12,000 on Belgian domestic production or Skr. 20,000 for total on worldwide production, assuming that Sweden takes 400 tons a year.*
>
> *Taxes on these added profits are about the same in Belgium as in Sweden—about 50 percent of taxable income.*
>
> *In conclusion, that plant should not be built. Ekstrom is a bright young man, but he does not know the adhesives business. He would be head over heels in costly production mistakes from the very beginning. I recommend that you inform the Thorsten management that*

---

[2] Total fixed cost in Belgium is the equivalent of Skr. 180,000 a year. Divided by 600, this equals Skr. 300 a ton. If it were spread over 1,000 tons, the average fixed cost would be Skr. 180.

EXHIBIT 6

Roget S.A.—Estimated Variable Cost of Manufacturing XL-4 in Belgium for Shipment to Sweden

Variable costs per ton:		
Manufacturing	Skr.	930
Shipping from Belgium to Sweden		50
Swedish import duty		400
Total variable cost per ton	Skr.	1,380
Total Variable Cost, 400 tons to Sweden		Skr.552,000

it is in the company's interest, and therefore it is Roget policy, that he must buy from Belgium.

REPORT OF VICE PRESIDENT, FINANCE TO THE PRESIDENT OF ROGET S.A.

The same day, Eric Bols, chief financial officer for Roget corporate headquarters, sent the following memorandum to Mr. Juvet, president of Roget S.A., with copies to Gillot, Lavanchy, and Ekstrom.

Dear Mr. Juvet:

I am sending you herewith a complete economic study of the two alternatives which have been raised for producing XL-4 within the Roget group. The Swedish management has proposed constructing a plant in Sweden, while Messrs. Lavanchy and Lambert on our Belgian staff have proposed producing here in Belgium.

I have talked with Michael Gillot. We both agree that this kind of matter must be resolved by highest authority, since any precedent set would also apply to the food group and the textile group. Industrial chemicals is not the only group within the company which has such location problems.

After thorough analysis by the most advanced financial methods, it is clear that Roget, S.A., will benefit substantially by producing total world demand for XL-4 in Belgium, including the 400 tons per year which Swedish management estimates it will need over the next seven years. Exhibit 12 shows this. Not only will the Roget group of companies gain Skr. 16,000 (the difference between Skr. 246,000 produced in Sweden and Skr. 263,000 produced in Belgium). The really important factor is that in Belgium we would have to furnish only Skr. 72,000 in initial capital funds, while in Sweden it cost Skr. 764,-000 to build the plant.

The importance of this factor can be demonstrated. Notice from Exhibit (12) that the internal rate of return on invested capital is 60 percent in Belgium because of the low initial investment, while the same rate of return in Sweden is only 15 percent because of the high initial investment.

Stated in another way, Sweden is asking us to invest Skr. 692,000 more *than necessary (their required initial investment less ours). If this amount were invested even in Eurodollar bank certificates, which have averaged 6 percent over the last ten years, it would have grown to Skr. 1,040,491 after seven years. This shows the opportunity cost of committing needless money in Sweden. Such money is, in effect, wasted, because the internal rate of return is so much lower in Sweden.*

Another way to see the importance of initial capital is to look at the payback period. It would take the group four years to get its money back in Sweden but only two and one-half years in Belgium.

Exhibit 7 is the next most revealing logic. It summarizes all of the funds, flowing into the Roget group, and flowing out of the Roget group, that would result if we produced in Belgium. Exhibits 8 through 10 are constructed exactly as Mr. Ekstrom performed his analysis, and provide the subsidiary figures that are summarized in Exhibit 7. Exhibit 8 shows operating profits, 9 the working capital required, 10 the salvage value of assets at the end of seven years, and 11 the salvage value of Belgium assets. You already have from Paul Lavanchy the variable cost of manufacture and shipping [Exhibit 6], which are incorporated into Exhibit 8.

Finally, I must call attention to my position as compared with that

EXHIBIT 7
Roget S.A. — Proposal for Manufacture of XL-4 in Belgium for Export to Sweden and Other World Wide Markets (all figures in Skr.)

Year	Description	After-Tax Cash Flows*	Present Value at 8%
0	Working capital	− 54,000	− 54,000
1	Cash operating profit	+ 3,000	
	Working capital	− 10,000	
	Total	− 7,000	− 6,000
2	Cash operating profit	+ 39,000	
	Working capital	− 10,000	
		+ 29,000	+ 25,000
3	Cash operating profit	+ 75,000	+ 60,000
4	Cash operating profit	+ 75,000	+ 55,000
5	Cash operating profit	+ 75,000	+ 51,000
6	Cash operating profit	+ 75,000	+ 47,000
7	Cash operating profit	+ 75,000	
	Recovery value of working capital	+ 70,000	
	Total	+145,000	+ 85,000
	Projected grand total		+263,000

*From Exhibits 8, 9, 10, and 11

Net present value to the corporation	Skr.263,000
Payback period	$2\frac{1}{2}$ years
Internal rate of return	60%

EXHIBIT 8

Roget S.A.—Estimated Operating Cash Flows from Manufacture of XL-4 in Belgium for Shipment to Sweden

1	2	3	4	5	6	7	8	9	10	11	12
Year	Sales in Tons	Variable Costs per Ton	Sales Price per Ton	Variable Profit Margin per Ton 4 − 3	Direct Variable Profit Margin 2 × 5	Promotion Costs	Savings on Variable Costs for Other Markets (600 × 20)	Cash Profit Contribution 6 − 7 + 8	Tax 50% of 9	Net Cash Flow After Tax 9 − 10	Present Value at 8%
		⟵(Skr. per ton)⟶			⟵(Figures in thousands of Skr.)⟶						
1	200	1,380	2,000	620	124	130	12	6	3	3	3
2	300	1,380	1,850	470	141	75	12	78	39	39	33
3	400	1,380	1,850	470	188	50	12	150	75	75	60
4	400	1,380	1,850	470	188	50	12	150	75	75	55
5	400	1,380	1,850	470	188	50	12	150	75	75	51
6	400	1,380	1,850	470	188	50	12	150	75	75	47
7	400	1,380	1,850	470	188	50	12	150	75	75	44
Total	2,500				1,205	455	84	834	417	417	293

Note: Savings on fixed costs for Sweden and other markets not included because these costs are not incremental for the decision to produce in Belgium as compared with not to produce here. There will be no change in cash flow in or cash flow out since Roget already has the fixed plant capacity. For the same reason, there is no column for depreciation costs.

*of Mr. Lavanchy. He and I are agreed on the most important issue—
that it would be much more profitable to manufacture in Belgium.
But we differ on one point. He stresses that we would save Skr. 120,000
per year on fixed costs if we manufacture total production here, because our existing plant would produce 400 tons more per year, thus
lowering cost per ton and depreciation charges per ton. This is not
correct. The plant is already built here. There would be no actual*

EXHIBIT 9
**Roget S.A.—Estimated Working Capital Required for Manufacture of XL-4 in Belgium for
Sale in Sweden (Skr. 000)**

	1	2	3	4	5	6
				Change	Tax Credit	Net
		Other Current	Working	from	(30% of	Funds
	Inventory	Assets less	Capital	Previous	change	Required
	at Cost	Current Liabilities	1 + 2	Year	in 1)	4 − 5
Year 0...........50		10	60	+60	6*	54
Year 1...........55		15	70	+10	0	10
Year 2...........60		20	80	+10	0	10
Year 3						
and later.....60		20	80	0	0	0
Total 60		20	80	80	6	74

*Based on finished goods inventory of Skr. 20,000 in Sweden.

EXHIBIT 10
**Roget S.A.—Present Value of Working
Capital Required to Manufacture XL-4 in
Belgium**

Year	Net New Funds Required*	Present Value at 8%
0 ....Skr. 54,000		Skr. 54,000
1 10,000		9,000
2 10,000		9,000
Skr. 74,000		Skr. 72,000

*Rounded to nearest (000), including inventory and
other current assets less current liabilities, and after deduction of Belgian taxes.

EXHIBIT 11
Estimated End-of-Life Value of Belgian Assets

Working capital...Skr. 80,000
Less Belgium tax on liquidating inventory......... 10,000
Net funds realized, end of 7 years....................Skr. 70,000
Present value (70,000 Discount at 8%)............. 42,000

Note: End-of-Life value of fixed plant not included because these funds
would be the same whether or not ROGET manufactures XL-4 for Sweden. Such
increase in funds would occur if we did not increase production—and therefore
are not incremental to the proposed alternative.

EXHIBIT 12

Roget S.A.—Comparison of Economic Gains between Two Alternative Projects for Manufacture of XL-4

	Made in Belgium	*Made in Sweden*
Present value of investment (Exhibit 10)	Skr. −764,000	Skr. − 72,000
Present value of operating profit (Exhibit 8)	+876,000	+293,000
Present value of residual sale of assets (Exhibit 11)	+134,000	+ 42,000
Final economic gain	Skr. 246,000	Skr. 263,000
Payback period	4 years	2½ years
Internal rate of return	15%	60%
Final decision for economic and financial reasons	Manufacture in Belgium	

money costs one way or the other for our plant under either of three alternatives: produce in Belgium, produce in Sweden, or simply not produce additional XL-4 at all. You will notice, therefore, that I do not include any depreciation cost in Exhibit 8.

I hope that this analysis is of help to you in formulating a companywide policy on construction of manufacturing plants around the world. It seems to me that it should be the policy of Roget S.A. to construct plants whenever and wherever the group as a whole will gain most benefits, taking into consideration worldwide supply and demand, rather than supply and demand in one country or one part of the group. That is, we should produce at the point where the cost of production is lowest.

We in finance have the highest respect for the Swedish management. Mr. Ekstrom, particularly, is an outstanding manager with great financial expertise himself. In this case, he has simply not had the complete information for our total group. I trust that he will understand that this is not a personal rejection, but one that is for the good of the group as a whole—the parent company and Thorsten's sister companies in other countries.

Sincerely yours,
Eric Bols, Vice President, Finance.

COMMENT BY M. LAVANCHY

Later, M. Lavanchy, director of manufacturing, in Brussels, sent a memorandum to Messrs. Gillot and Bols regarding fixed costs in the XL-4 project:

I am still certain that if a plant costing Bfr. 100,000 produces 100,-000 pairs of shoes, that is one franc in fixed cost for each pair. If you double the production from the same plant to 200,000 pairs of shoes, that is only one-half franc for each pair in fixed costs.

I, too, am opposed to manufacturing in Sweden. I simply think that

Eric Bols' figure of Skr. 263,000 of profits generated by our production of 1,000 tons of XL-4 should be increased by a total of Skr. 120,000 per year or Skr. 840,000 savings over the seven year period. That makes it even more essential that we produce in Belgium.

POSITION OF M. JUVET

As of the present time, M. Juvet states that he is "quite concerned about the XL-4 affair. It has been dragging on for a number of months now and all parties are entitled to a clear and firm decision. I also recognize that Roget S.A. is becoming a large multinational firm and that we must deal with many of this same kind of decision over the years. In fact, just the other day our food company in the United Kingdom sent in an objection to our building one frozen food plant in Holland which would supply all of the U.K., Holland, Belgium and Scandinavia. About the same time, our senior vice president for food products was approached by his director of manufacturing who suggested that we either build the central frozen food plant in Belgium, or that we build an additional plant in Belgium to supply our domestic Benelux market."

Selected Readings

From

MANAGEMENT: A MODERN APPROACH*

By Martin K. Starr†

There is a natural compulsiveness to push analysis toward segmentation on the finest possible scale if a deterministic philosophy prevails. But organizational parameters lose their meaning at fine scale. Only *systems methods* can dictate how fine the analysis should be and this decision must be based on hypotheses for synthesis that *precede* analysis.

By the mid-twentieth century, large systems began to preempt the analyst's interest. This trend appears in the analysis of production systems, financial analysis, market studies, and industrial relations. Yet the precedents, apparatus, and background for detail had been previously set, and management's use of computer systems emphasized what "had been" rather than what was "likely to be." Accounting detail was one major focus. Use of many *independent* measures in great detail and refinement continues to be in style. The issues that are raised by the concept of independence are not unlike those of analytic electrocardiograph

---

* From *Management: A Modern Approach* by Martin K. Starr, © 1971 by Harcourt Brace Jovanovich, Inc., and reprinted with their permission. Excerpts from pp. 673–676.

† The author is a Professor in the Graduate School of Business, Columbia University.

methods, which have been monitoring an increasing number of control points as medical technology has improved. But synthesis is required to relate these measures. A synergistic result usually occurs when such synthesis is achieved. In general, the interrelatedness of information monitored at adjacent control points requires a theory of related combinations. When such theory exists, we can begin to study what is happening at each of several control points, not in isolation from one another, but with an awareness of the simultaneity of systems measures.

Management has been properly concerned with little systems because these process *I/O*'s are fundamental units of organization. But the most important issue is how to assemble and assess larger systems configurations composed of these simple units. Analysis of basic process modules is used by the manager to *explain* what is going on in terms that are *organically* and *organizationally* separable. He is readily able to think about a particular job, a specific machine, or a given function. The manager expects that the detailed analysis will be followed by suggestions for improvement *in the little subsystem*. For example, he increases the servicing capacity of a unit, changes the load on the subsystem or the rate of demand for specific transformations. When the *improved* subsystems are reassembled into the body of the *total* system, the expectation is that *overall* improvement will result.

But, as we have had occasion to indicate before, integration does not follow so easily. The subsystem improvements may actually backfire and (in the short or long run) result in a real decrease of the total system's performance. Some systems are more characteristically prone to this effect than others. As a rule, *the higher the management area involved, the less likely it is that subsystem analysis can provide overall systems improvement.* We can readily appreciate why Eero Saarinen said, in 1960, "We should stop thinking of our individual buildings—always look at the next larger thing." Or, on a behavioral level, we have a statement by Mary Parker Follett:

> Thus we see that . . . unintegrated difference is pathological, difference itself is not pathological. . . . what I think we should do in business organization is to try to find the machinery best suited for the normal appearing and uniting of diversity so that the difference does not stay too long crystalized, so that the pathological stage shall not be reached.[1]

Motivations for Smaller Systems. . . . A major force for subsystem planning is the *unwillingness to let others interfere* when planning one's own domain. Also, by enlarging the system, *many new and dominant restrictions arise* that can severely alter what would have been done without such constraints. Consequently, by ignoring the additional restrictions of large systems, the *degrees of freedom* for planning are substantially greater.

*   *   *   *   *

One large systems approach is for management to require communication between subsystem managers to facilitate coordination. A second approach is to specify a policy broad enough to cover all the segmented systems. . . . Management policies might be formulated in terms of inventory restrictions, capital expenditures, and operating budget constraints. All such policies can play a major role in the attempt to coordinate activities without establishing the communication

[1] Mary Parker Follett, "Constructive Conflict from Dynamic Administration," from H. C. Metcalf and L. Urwick, eds., *The Collected Papers of Mary Parker Follett* (New York: Harper & Row, 1941), p. 4.

required for large systems planning. Invoking tradition is another way to achieve coordination. It may be a suspect policy, but it is not necessarily a bad one, for, while it is short of a rational policy, it can help to unify and homogenize the system. The notion of coordination achieved through policy controls can be expanded to include constraints with respect to cash liquidity, payback periods, types of personnel, vendors, and product line. All tend to produce a controllable uniformity, but this only approximates the gains of coordinated activities.

The fact that the policy approach is less desirable than active coordination does not mean that coordination can always be used. Frequently, the big system is so big that the cost of attempting to actively treat it would be prohibitive. Often, there is insufficient information about the interactions that bind the big system together. In one sense or another, the parts of the system may speak different languages. Many times, top management alone has sufficient *authority* to spread across all of the components, but its information is so poor that it is not even aware of the existence of small, informal groups. Both law and social dictum often prohibit the communication that is essential to large systems planning. These physical and economic realities of the situation must be considered, no matter what the preference for coordination achieved through consensus.

Moving to the Larger System.   As a rule, *one should deal with the biggest system that is physically feasible and that maximizes net benefit.* Perhaps the net benefit changes with the system size, as illustrated in Figure 1. The reason that,

FIGURE 1
Relations of Net Benefit to System Size

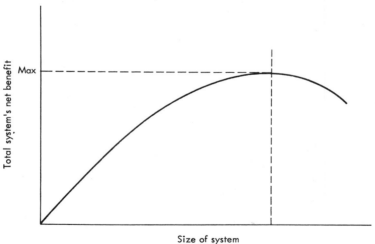

Size of system

in general, there is a falling off of net benefit after some system's size is achieved is that the costs of communication rise and the ability to set beneficial overall policies falls. On the other hand, there are gains in net benefits to be made by increasing the size of the system because the sum of a number of individually optimized subsystems $\leq$ the overall optimum of the sum of these subsystems. In other words,

$$\text{Best } 1 + \text{Best } 2 + \ldots + \text{Best } n \leq \text{Best } (1 + 2 + \ldots n)$$

At some point, these forces balance to produce an optimal value. Various systems exist in which the equality would hold in the equation above. In such cases, the subsystems are sufficiently independent of one another to be studied and improved without consideration for the other subsystems. But, for the most part, such sufficiently independent systems occur only at low levels in the management hierarchy.

. . . *Natural* and nonintentional conflict will result from following, with honesty and singleminded purpose, one design in ignorance of the others. So a strong coordinator with sufficient authority is needed if the big system is to be treated optimally. Directing, judging, and coordinating are all vital aspects of managing a large system. Everything we have been talking about comes together here. Leadership runs like a thread throughout the aggregation. To achieve large system *synthesis* we must first bring together intuition, knowledge of the behavioral sciences, and quantitative methods. Second, we must relate planning and policy to the objectives of the organization and to managerial ability to control. And, third, we must tie together the lines that cross functional area boundaries. Responsible managers cannot tolerate arbitrary compartmentalization, which creates the illusion that separate marketing, finance, and production decisions can combine to enhance the achievement of organizational objectives. Unequivocally, they cannot.

From

OPERATIONS RESEARCH FOR MANAGEMENT DECISIONS*

By Samuel B. Richmond†

The Objectives of Decision.   Typically in a management science model, the output of the model is some measure of effectiveness somehow selected and defined. We shall see that the specification of this objective function is one of the most difficult problems in the construction of these models in the real world.

. . . Our view of decision making is that it is a rational information-using process—not an emotional process. Thus, whenever anyone makes a wrong decision or has difficulty in making a decision, these difficulties can be attributable to either:

1. *Inadequate information;* incorrect or incomplete information about the various possible alternative courses of action and about their implications with respect to the ultimate outcome; or
2. *Inadequately specified objectives;* failure to specify which outcomes are more desirable than others.

---

* Samuel B. Richmond, *Operations Research for Management Decisions.* Copyright © 1968, The Ronald Press Company. (Excerpts from pp. 16–20.)

† The author is a Professor in the Graduate School of Business, Columbia University.

Often there are conflictng objectives, and the decision maker must resolve the conflict. He must, as we shall see below, emerge with a single objective function. . . .

Value measurement is one of the most vexing problems facing the social scientist today. The current attempts to peer into the human mind and to analyze and quantify subjective value systems, and to describe and explore valuation systems which may be generally applicable to a range of individuals will receive only brief treatment here. This is due not to the lack of importance of the problem, but rather to the complexity of the subject matter, and the inadequacy of the present state of knowledge. In this volume, we shall be dealing primarily with business problems, where, hopefully, the various conflicting objectives can be expressed in comparable, usually monetary, terms.

*   *   *   *   *

The typical manufacturing company provides an excellent illustration of *internal conflict,* i.e. of conflicting goals among its various functions. The sales manager typically wants a wide product line with large inventories so that all customers may be served, and served rapidly. The production manager wants a restricted product line and long production runs to minimize production costs. The finance manager wants small inventories and short production runs to minimize production costs. The finance manager wants a small inventories and short production runs to minimize financing costs. The company president, who must make company-wide decisions about the product line and inventory levels must look beyond the individual departmental preferences, because what is best for the company as a whole is probably not the best for any individual department as considered alone. The company-wide optimal course of action is probably some kind of a middle course between the preferences of the individual departments.

Optimizing on individual departments or on individual phases of a system is referred to as *suboptimization,* and it typically does not yield the best system-wide policy. It is the function of each higher level executive to consider a larger system and broader horizons than his subordinates. It is almost a truism that every decision involves suboptimization, when it is regarded from the vantage point of a larger system. The sales department suboptimizes with respect to the firm, the firm suboptimizes with respect to the industry, the industry suboptimizes with respect to the national economy, and the nation suboptimizes with respect to the world.

Nevertheless, it is not yet feasible to optimize on the universe, and, for any real decision, the decision maker must identify the scope of his real-world system, determine his objectives and how to measure them, and then choose his optimal course of action within that framework. The identification and measurement of the true objective function is often the most difficult aspect of a decision problem.

*   *   *   *   *

. . . We shall at the outset make the assumption that decision makers act rationally according to our definition, and we define a *rational decision* as the selection of that course of action which, in the light of the available information, yields the optimal expected value of the objective function. . . .

Thus, the result that emerges from our analysis is the course of action that the decision maker *should* accept, not necessarily the one he *does* accept. "Should" here refers to what he would do if he knew all of the implications of his action, and if he behaved *rationally.* It is possible of course, as we have seen, that at some higher level of analysis there may be counterindications that render our solution wrong and impossible to implement; in which case, the problem to which we are addressing ourselves is the wrong problem, or our information is inadequate. It is futile and absurd to bother with seeking information and performing analyses toward the choice of a course of action unless the selected course of action can and will be implemented.

*   *   *   *   *

. . . The rational decision for the production manager does not coincide with the rational decision for the marketing manager, and neither of their decisions may coincide with the rational decision for their superior, who must resolve both the production and marketing objectives. He must know the "cost" in sales and profits of a smaller than optimal product line, and he must set this off against the potential production-cost savings. One of the most important aspects of a management hierarchy is that, as we have seen, at each level the executive must work with larger systems and encompass broader horizons than those of his subordinates.

As we shall view it, the decision-making process consists of:

1. *Consideration of a set of alternatives,* which may be either qualitative or quantitative. The latter in turn may be either discrete or continuous.
2. *Selection of the best alternative in order to achieve a goal or objective,* which may be viewed as optimizing (minimizing or maximizing, as the case may be) some objective function such as profits, sales, costs, or any of many other possibilities.

What is involved in this simple phrase "best alternative"? First, we *must have access to* this best alternative. That is, it must be included among those being considered. This may involve what is often called *creativity.* That is, someone must conceive of a possible course of action before it can be eligible or available for consideration.

Second, the selected alternative must be "best" according to the appropriate *value system,* taking into account the possibility of conflicting goals and suboptimization.

After the problem of assessment of the objective of the decision has been satisfactorily met, in spite of our attempts to approach the decision-making process in this rational orderly way, we may still fail to select what may seem to be the best alternative because we are unwilling to seek the best alternative; and this may well be a conscious policy; that is, the decision may not be sufficiently important to warrant costly analysis or delay. What this really means is that, at a higher level, optimization dictates the acceptance of a less-than-optimal solution here, because the cost of seeking the optimal exceeds its potential value.

In this connection, the term *satisficing,* originally introduced by Herbert Simon, has been used to describe the process whereby a decision maker does not seek an optimal course of action so much as one which *satisfies* him, i.e., one which *suffices.* This has been referred to as a characterization of the decision-making process which is basically different from the optimization concept. For example, under the optimization concept, an executive with a sum of money to invest would be pictured as seeking out all the available alternative investment possibilities, evaluating them, and then choosing the one which gives the highest return—if that is his objective. On the other hand, the "satisficing" concept suggests that men do not act in this way, and that the executive is more likely to have some concept of the minimum rate that is considered an acceptable return. He then systematically considers alternatives until he finds one that gives him this minimum, or better, and the search, stops at this point, whether or not the chosen investment is in fact the best of all possible courses of action. While "satisficing" may seem to characterize much of decision making in the real world, it is doubtless that in many situations, the policy of "satisficing," so-called at a lower-level, is actually the optimum as determined by a higher-level optimization decision encompassing a larger system. That is, the investor described above may invest when he finds an opportunity which meets only his minimum requirements, if this procedure is optimal in terms of the cost of further search, the cost of delay, and the anticipated possible improvement in the return. The decision maker is, in fact, optimizing in selecting, at the margin, the optimal of the two courses of action available to him; i.e., he may "accept," or he may "search further."

From

ADMINISTRATIVE BEHAVIOR*

By Herbert A. Simon†

THE EQUILIBRIUM OF THE ORGANIZATION

*   *   *   *   *

Inducements

The clue to the participation of individuals in organization lies in . . . regarding the organized group as a system in equilibrium. Individuals are willing to accept organization membership when their activity in the organization contributes, directly or indirectly to their own personal goals. The contribution is direct if the goals set for the organization have direct personal value for the individual—church membership is a typical example of this. The contribution is indirect if the organization offers personal rewards—monetary or other—to the individual in return for his willingness to contribute his activity to the organization. Employment in a business concern is a typical example of this. Sometimes these personal rewards are directly related to the size and growth of the organization—as in the case of the stockholders of a business; sometimes, not very directly—as in the case of most wage earners. . . .

*   *   *   *   *

The members of an organization, then, contribute to the organization in return for inducements that the organization offers them. The contributions of one group are the source of the inducements that the organization offers others. If the sum

* Reprinted with permission of the Macmillan Company from *Administrative Behavior* (Second Edition), by Herbert A. Simon. Copyright © 1957, by Herbert A. Simon. (Excerpts from pp. 110–116, 118–119.)

† The author is a Professor of Industrial Administration at Carnegie-Mellon University.

of the contributions is sufficient, in quantity and kind, to supply the necessary quantity and kinds of inducements, the organization survives and grows; otherwise it shrinks and ultimately disappears unless an equilibrium is reached.[1]

Types of Organization Participants

Organization members may be classified in other ways than in terms of the inducements they receive for their participation. They may be classified in terms of the types of contributions they make to the organization: specific services (a supplier of material); money or other neutral services that may be employed as incentives (customers); and time and effort (employees).

Still a third method of classification would distinguish those who control the organization—that is, have a right to fix the terms on which the others will be permitted to participate in it—from the remaining participants. The various possible combinations of inducements, contributions, and control arrangements make for a considerable variety of organizational forms, and this variety must be taken into consideration in the succeeding discussion.

Organization Goals as Inducements

* * * * *

. . . In return for this product the customers are willing to offer money, which provides a principal inducement for the employees and entrepreneurs to participate in the group. The relation of customers to the organization is distinguished not only by the type of inducement they receive, but also by the fact that it is based on a contract or bargain for a specific product without, ordinarily, any assumption of permanence or continuity in the relationship.

* * * * *

Adaptation of the Organization Objective. The organization objective is by no means a static thing. In order to survive, the organization must have an objective that appeals to its customers,[2] so that they will make the contributions necessary to sustain it. Hence, organization objectives are constantly adapted to conform to the changing values of customers, or to secure new groups of customers in place of customers who have dropped away. The organization may also undertake special activities to induce acceptance of its objectives by customers—advertising, missionary work, and propaganda of all sorts.

* * * * *

The modification of the organization objective usually represents a compromise of the interests of several groups of potential participants, in order to secure their joint cooperation where each group individually is unable to attain its own objectives unaided. Hence the organization objective will seldom coincide exactly with the personal objectives of even those participants whose interest in the organization lies in its attainment of its goal. The crucial issue for any such individual is whether the organization objective is sufficiently close to his personal goal to make him choose to participate in the group rather than try to attain his goal by himself or in some other group. As will be seen, this process of compromise takes place,

---

[1] This idea of an equilibrium is due to C. I. Barnard. See his *The Functions of the Executive* (Cambridge: Harvard University Press, 1938), pp. 56–59 and chaps. xi and xvi.

[2] The word "customer" is used in a generic sense here to refer to any individual—customer, legislator, or volunteer—for whom the organization objective has personal value.

whether the controlling group of the organization is itself directly interested in the organization objective, or whether the inducement it receives from the organization is of some other type.

Loyalty of Employees to Organization Objective.   Although the organization objective is of greatest importance in relation to the behavior of those participants who have been called "customers," almost all the members of an organization become imbued, to a greater or lesser degree, with the organization aim, and are influenced by it in their behavior. . . .

It is one component, and a very important one, of organizational loyalty. If the objective has any appearance of usefulness, the organization members, whose attention is continually directed to it by their everyday work, will acquire an appreciation of its importance and value (often an exaggerated appreciation), and the attainment of the value will come, to that extent, to have personal value for them. . . .

Incentives for Employee Participation

To an employee of a non-volunteer organization the most obvious personal incentive that the organization offers is a salary or wage. It is a peculiar and important characteristic of his relation with the organization that, in return for this inducement, he offers the organization not a specific service but his undifferentiated time and effort. He places this time and effort at the disposal of those directing the organization, to be used as they see fit. Thus, both the customer relation (in the commercial organization) and the employee relation originate in contract, but in contracts of very different sorts. The employment contract results in the creation of a continuing authority relation between the organization and the employee.

How can this be? Why does the employee sign a blank check, so to speak, in entering upon his employment? First, from the viewpoint of the organization, nothing would be gained by offering an inducement to the employee unless the latter's behavior could be brought into the system of organization behavior through his acceptance of its authority. Second, from the viewpoint of the employee, the precise activities with which his time of employment is occupied may, within certain limits, be a matter of relative indifference to him. If the orders transmitted to him by the organization remain within these limits of acceptance, he will permit his behavior to be guided by them.

What determines the breadth of the area of acceptance within which the employee will accept the authority of the organization? It certainly depends on the nature and magnitude of the incentives the organization offers. In additon to the salary he receives, he may value the status and prestige that his position in the organization gives him, and he may value his relations with the working group of which he is part. In setting his task, the organization must take into consideration the effect that its orders may have upon the employee's realization of these values. . . .

*   *   *   *   *

Organization Equilibrium and Efficiency

The basic value criteria that will be employed in making decisions and choices among alternatives in an organization will be selected for the organization primarily by the controlling group—the group that has the power to set the terms of membership for all the participants. If the group that holds the legal control fails to exercise this power, then, of course, it will devolve on individuals further down the administrative hierarchy.

Whatever group exercises the power of determining the basic criteria will attempt to secure through the organization its own personal values—whether these be identified with the organization objective, with the conservation objectives, with profits or what not. But their power of control does not in any sense imply that the control group exercises as unlimited option to direct the organization in any path it desires, for the power will continue to exist only so long as the controlling group is able to offer sufficient incentives to retain the contributions of the other participants to the organization. No matter what the personal objectives of the control group, their decisions will be heavily influenced by the fact that they can attain their objectives through the organization only if they can maintain a positive balance of contributions over inducements, or at least an equilibrium between the two.

From

ORGANIZATIONS*

By James G. March and Herbert A. Simon†

Individual Goals

. . . Humans, in contrast to machines, evaluate their own positions in relation to the value of others and come to accept others' goals as their own. In addition, individual members of an organization come to it with a prior structure of preferences—a personality, if you like—on the basis of which they make decisions while in the organization. Thus, individual goals are not "given" for the organization, but can be varied both through recruitment procedures and through organizational practices.

There are four principal available targets for identification: (1) organizations external to the focal organization (i.e., extraorganizational identification); (2) the focal organization itself (organizational identification), (3) the work activities involved in the job (task identification); and (4) subgroups within the focal organization (subgroup identification). . . .

However, when we state a proposition about extraorganizational identifications, we cannot draw inferences about motivation to produce until we identify the factors influencing the perception of group goals. Some of these factors are indicated later in this section.

The stronger the individual's identification with a group, the more likely that his goals will conform to his perception of group norms. . . .

* From *Organizations* by J. G. March and H. A. Simon. Copyright © 1958 by John Wiley & Sons, Inc. Reprinted by permission. Excerpts pp. 65–66, 70–77.

† Dr. March is Professor of Political Science at the University of California at Irvine and Dr. Simon is Professor of Industrial Administration at Carnegie-Mellon University.

We propose five basic hypotheses:

1. The greater the *perceived prestige of the group,* the stronger the propensity of an individual to identify with it, and vice versa.

2. The greater the *extent to which goals are perceived as shared* among members of a group, the stronger the propensity of the individual to identify with the group; and vice versa.

3. The more *frequent the interaction* between an individual and the member of a group, the stronger the propensity of the individual to identify with the group; and vice versa.

4. The greater the *number of individual needs satisfied in the group,* the stronger the propensity of the individual to identify with the group; and vice versa.

5. The less the *amount of competition* between the members of a group and an individual, the stronger the propensity of the individual to identify with the group; and vice versa.

These propositions, along with a pair of others relating interaction to perceived goal-sharing and to the number of needs satisfied within the group form the basic framework within which more specific propositions can be developed. That framework is portrayed in Figure 1.

*   *   *   *   *

Identification with Extraorganizational Groups (e.g., professional associations, community groups, family groups, trade unions). In the case of *professional associations* we predict that the greater the degree of professionalization of the individual's job, the greater his identification with a professional group. Implicit in the definition of "professionalization" are the major variables through

FIGURE 1
Basic Factors Affecting Group Identification

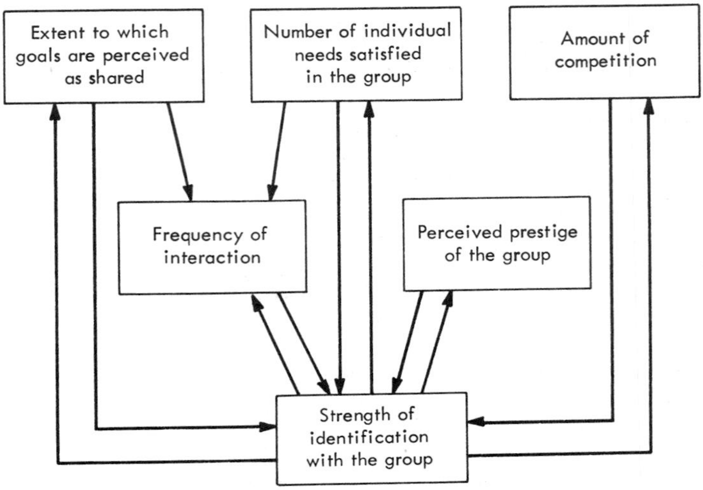

which the prediction is realized. Professionalization implies specific formal training and thus substantial homogeneity of background. It implies formal regulation of job performance and thus similarity in positions. To the extent that a job is professionalized, techniques and standards of performance are defined by the other members of the profession. Since reference to this group and its standards is indispensable in performing a professionalized job, the group's influence on action permeates a wide class of job situations. Since there is a need to be like other members of the profession in a number of attributes, there is a tendency to extend this need to other attributes and thus to identify with the group (R. C. Davis, 1954; Moore and Renck, 1955).

With respect to *community groups,* extent of exposure appears to be of critical importance for identification. Exposure is reflected in such factors as length of residence; hence, the longer the length of residence in a community, the greater the individual's identification with community groups (Hoppock, 1935). . . .

On the other hand, an organization like the foreign service, in which assignment to foreign communities is often relatively extended and identification with them largely dysfunctional, uses extended vacations to bring about periodic "re-Americanization." The longer the residence, the greater the breadth and frequency of nonorganizational community contacts. Interaction results in identification.

*   *   *   *   *

The *family* forms a third significant type of extraorganizational group. Families often have attitudes about what jobs are appropriate for their members, and those attitudes affect the orientation of individuals to their work. Similarly, family attitudes toward performance on the job are important determinants of individual performance preferences. The greater the residential mobility of the individual, the weaker his identification with family groups. Residential mobility breaks down contact with the extended family and tends to limit frequent interaction to the marital family unit (Masuoka, 1940).

*   *   *   *   *

Identification with the Organization.   The second important type of group with which members tend to identify is the organization itself. We consider a few of the major predictions about the intensity of organizational identification.

*   *   *   *   *

We are asserting that apart from self-selection the length of time served itself results in increased identification. The mechanisms involved are those previously cited: the longer an individual remains in an organization, the more his interactions occur within the organization, the more his needs are satisfied within the organization, and, therefore, the more he identifies with the organization.

The greater the vertical mobility within an organization, the stronger the identification of the individual with the organization (Stone, 1952a). Expectations of vertical mobility create expectations of interaction as well as felt similarities between subordinates and superiors. . . .

There is some evidence that supervisory practices affect organizational identification. In particular, it appears that the more supervisors facilitate the satisfaction of personal goals by individual members of the organization, the stronger the latter's identification with the organization (Comrey, Pfiffner, and Beem, 1952; Katz, Maccoby, Gurin, and Floor, 1951). To particularize further, the more general the supervision, the stronger the tendency of subordinates to identify with the organization; the more participation in making policy decisions, the stronger the tendency of subordinates to identify with the organization; the more supervisors are employee- rather than production-oriented, the stronger the tendency of subordinates to identify with the organization.

Finally, although specific evidence is sparse, we include a hypothesis relating organizational identification with factors that make the organization attractive to the individual. We have already argued that an individual is more likely to identify with an organization in which he has considerable interaction than one in which interaction is limited, that he is more likely to identify with an organization that he perceives as accepting him than one he perceives as rejecting him, that he is more likely to identify with an organization that permits him to satisfy personal goals than with one that frustrates the satisfaction of personal goals. Now we are arguing that an individual is more likely to identify with an organization that he perceives as high in prestige than one he perceives as low (Willerman and Swanson, 1953). Among other things, identification is a means of gaining personal status. As we will see below, prestige may adhere to subunits rather than to the organization as a whole, and thereby encourage subgroup identification rather than organizational identification. But under many conditions identification with the organization as a whole will be a function of generalized prestige.

The more the organization produces a distinguishable product, the stronger the identification of members with it. The greater the number of high status occupations and/or individuals in the organization, the stronger the identification of individual participants with it. The larger the organization, the stronger the identification of individual participants with it. (Note that we have already specified other factors, such as breadth of interaction, that operate in an opposite direction for the large organization.) The faster the growth of the organization, the stronger the identification of individual participants with it (Payne, 1954).

*   *   *   *   *

Identification with Subgroups. When we turn to subgroup identification, many of the same types of propositions can be made. For example, with slight modifications, propositions similar to those just outlined can be used to related the prestige characteristics of subgroups in the organization to the propensity of the individual worker to identify with the subgroup. In addition, the organization provides a standard—productivity—by which the prestige of subunits can be judged, and this standard also becomes a factor in identification. The more productive the subgroup in the organization, the stronger the identification of individual participants with the subgroup (Katz, Maccoby, Gurin, and Floor, 1951). Subgroup identification also depends on interaction and need-satisfaction. Consequently, those groups that facilitate interaction and satisfaction of personal goals will show greater cohesiveness than other groups. . . .

*   *   *   *   *

Identification with the Task Group. Task identification, the last of the four major forms of identification considered here, is probably more properly thought of as identification with the class of individuals performing the same task. Of course, the task group may be either a subgroup or an extraorganizational group, depending on the nature of the task, but at least in some cases task identification appears to be a phenomenon of sufficient importance to warrant independent treatment.

First, all factors causing identification with an extraorganizational professional group apply equally to task identification. The relevant propositions will not be repeated here.

In addition, characteristics of the job, length of service in the organization, and organizational mobility affect task identification. The more a particular task is perceived as a training rather than as a terminal job, the weaker the identification with it. Thus low-level tasks in an organization do not induce identification where they are perceived as stepping-stones to higher-level positions, but they do induce task identification where mobility is not anticipated. . . .

The characteristics of the job influence task identification primarily through another mechanism previously discussed. Individuals seek to satisfy personal needs through the medium of the job. When job characteristics permit such satisfactions we predict a strong task identification. Clearly, therefore, to make general predictions one must assume a certain amount of commonality of needs within the culture from which a given organization draws its members. Some characteristics of a task have rather clear implications for a success-oriented culture like our own. Thus, the more a given task reflects a high level of technical skill, the stronger the identification of the individual participant with the task (R. C. Davis, 1954). The more a given task reflects individual autonomy in making decisions, the stronger the identification with the task. The more a given task requires the use of a number of different programs rather than a single one, the stronger the identification with the task (Morse, 1953).

From

THE TORTUOUS EVOLUTION OF THE MULTINATIONAL CORPORATION*

By Howard V. Perlmutter†

Two hypotheses seem to be forming in the minds of executives from international firms that make the extent of their firm's multinationality of real interest. The first hypothesis is that the degree of multinationality of an enterprise is positively related to the firm's long-term viability. The "multinational" category makes sense for executives if it means a quality of decision making which leads to survival, growth and profitability in our evolving world economy.

The second hypothesis stems from the proposition that the multinational corporation is a new kind of institution—a new type of industrial social architecture particularly suitable for the latter third of the twentieth century. This type of institution could make a valuable contribution to world order and conceivably exercise a constructive impact on the nation-state. Some executives want to understand how to create an institution whose presence is considered legitimate and valuable

* Reprinted with permission from *The Columbia Journal of World Business,* January–February 1969. Excerpts from pp. 10–14, 16–18. Copyright © 1969 by The Trustees of Columbia University in the City of New York.

† The author is a Professor in the Wharton School, University of Pennsylvania.

in each nation-state. They want to prove that the greater the degree of multinationality of a firm, the greater its total constructive impact will be on host and home nation-states as well as other institutions. Since multinational firms may produce a significant proportion of the world's GNP, both hypotheses justify a more precise analysis of the varieties and degrees of multinationality.[1] However, the confirming evidence is limited.

State of Mind

* * * * *

Three primary attitudes among international executives toward building a multinational enterprise are identifiable. These attitudes can be inferred from the assumptions upon which key product, functional and geographical decisions were made.

These states of mind or attitudes may be described as ethnocentric (or home-country oriented), polycentric (or host-country oriented) and geocentric (or world-oriented).[2] While they never appear in pure form, they are clearly distinguishable. There is some degree of ethnocentricity, polycentricity or geocentricity in all firms, but management's analysis does not usually correlate with public pronouncements about the firm's multinationality.

Home Country Attitudes

The ethnocentric attitude can be found in companies of any nationality with extensive overseas holdings. The attitude, revealed in executive actions and experienced by foreign subsidiary managers, is: "We, the home nationals of X company, are superior to, more trustworthy and more reliable than any foreigners in headquarters or subsidiaries. We will be willing to build facilities in your country if you acknowledge our inherent superiority and accept our methods and conditions for doing the job."

Of course, such attitudes are never so crudely expressed, but they often determine how a certain type of "multinational" firm is designed. Table 1 illustrates how ethnocentric attitudes are expressed in determining the managerial process at home and overseas. For example, the ethnocentric executive is more apt to say: "Let us manufacture the simple products overseas. Those foreign nationals are not yet ready or reliable. We should manufacture the complex products in our country and keep the secrets among our trusted home-country nationals."

* * * * *

Ethnocentric attitudes are revealed in the communication process where "advice," "counsel," and directives flow from headquarters to the subsidiary in a steady stream, bearing this message: "This works at home; therefore, it must work in your country."

Executives in both headquarters and affiliates express the national identity of the firm by associating the company with the nationality of the headquarters: this is "a Swedish company," "a Swiss company," "an American company," depending on the location of headquarters. "You have to accept the fact that the only

---

[1] H. V. Perlmutter, "Super-Giant Firms in the Future," *Wharton Quarterly,* Winter 1968.

[2] H. V. Perlmutter, "Three Conceptions of a World Enterprise," *Révue Economique et Sociale,* May 1965.

TABLE 1
Three Types of Headquarters Orientation Toward Subsidiaries in an International Enterprise

Organization Design	Ethnocentric	Polycentric	Geocentric
Complexity of organization	Complex in home country, simple in subsidiaries	Varied and independent	Increasingly complex and interdependent
Authority; decision making	High in headquarters	Relatively low in headquarters	Aim for a collaborative approach between headquarters and subsidiaries
Evaluation and control	Home standards applied for persons and performance	Determined locally	Find standards which are universal and local
Rewards and punishments; incentives	High in headquarters low in subsidiaries	Wide variation; can be high or low rewards for subsidiary performance	International and local executives rewarded for reaching local and worldwide objectives
Communication; information flow	High volume to subsidiaries orders, commands, advice	Little to and from headquarters Little between subsidiaries	Both ways and between subsidiaries. Heads of subsidiaries part of management team
Identification	Nationality of owner	Nationality of host country	Truly international company but identifying with national interests
Perpetuation (recruiting, staffing, development)	Recruit and develop people of home country for key positions everywhere in the world	Develop people of local nationality for key positions in their own country	Develop best men everywhere in the world for key positions everywhere in the world

way to reach a senior post in our firm," an English executive in a U.S. firm said, "is to take out an American passport."

Crucial to the ethnocentric concept is the current policy that men of the home nationality are recruited and trained for key positions everywhere in the world. Foreigners feel like "second-class" citizens.

There is no international firm today whose executives will say that ethnocentrism is absent in their company. In the firms whose multinational investment began a decade ago, one is more likely to hear, "We are still in a transitional stage from our ethnocentric era. The traces are still around! But we are making progress."

Host Country Orientation

Polycentric firms are those which, by experience or by the inclination of a top executive (usually one of the founders), begin with the assumption the host-country cultures are different and that foreigners are difficult to understand. Local people know what is best for them, and the part of the firm which is located in the host country should be as "local in identity" as possible. The senior executives at headquarters believe that their multinational enterprise can be held together by good financial controls. A polycentric firm, literally, is a loosely connected group with quasi-independent subsidiaries as centers—more akin to a confederation.

European multinational firms tend to follow this pattern, using a top local executive who is strong and trustworthy, of the "right" family and who has an intimate understanding of the workings of the host government. This policy seems to have worked until the advent of the Common Market.

Executives in the headquarters of such a company are apt to say: "Let the Romans do it their way. We really don't understand what is going on there, but we have to have confidence in them. As long as they earn a profit, we want to remain in the background." They assume that since people are different in each country, standards for performance, incentives and training methods must be different. Local environmental factors are given greater weight (See Table 1).

Many executives mistakenly equate polycentrism with multinationalism. This is evidenced in the legalistic definition of a multinational enterprise as a cluster of corporations of diverse nationality joined together by ties of common ownership. It is not accident that many senior executives in headquarters take pride in the absence of non-nationals in their subsidiaries, especially people from the head office. The implication is clearly that each subsidiary is a distinct national entity, since it is incorporated in a different sovereign state. Lonely senior executives in the subsidiaries of polycentric companies complain that: "The home office never tells us anything."

Polycentrism is not the ultimate form of multinationalism. It is a landmark on a highway. Polycentrism is encouraged by local marketing managers who contend that: "Headquarters will never understand us, our people, our consumer needs, our laws, our distribution, etc. . . ."

Headquarters takes pride in the fact that few outsiders know that the firm is foreign-owned. "We want to be a good local company. How many Americans know that Shell and Lever Brothers are foreign-owned?"

But the polycentric personnel policy is also revealed in the fact that no local manager can seriously aspire to a senior position at headquarters. "You know the French are so provincial; it is better to keep them in France. Uproot them and you are in trouble," a senior executive says to justify the paucity of non-Americans at headquarters.

*   *   *   *   *

A World-Oriented Concept

The third attitude which is beginning to emerge at an accelerating rate is geocentrism. Senior executives with this orientation do not equate superiority with nationality. Within legal and political limits, they seek the best men, regardless of nationality , to solve the company's problems anywhere in the world. The senior executives attempt to build an organization in which the subsidiary is not only a good citizen of the host nation but is a leading exporter from this nation in the international community and contributes such benefits as (1) an increasing supply of hard currency, (2) new skills and (3) a knowledge of advanced technology. Geocentrism is summed up in a Unilever board chairman's statement of objectives: "We want to Unileverize our Indians and Indianize our Unileverans."

The ultimate goal of geocentrism is a worldwide approach in both headquarters and subsidiaries. The firm's subsidiaries are thus neither satellites nor independent city states, but parts of a whole whose focus is on worldwide objectives as well as local objectives, each part making its unique contribution with its unique competence. Geocentrism is expressed by function, product and geography. The question asked in headquarters and the subsidiaries is: "Where in the world shall we raise money, build our plant, conduct R&D, get and launch new ideas to serve our present and future customers?"

This conception of geocentrism involves a collaborative effort between subsidiaries and headquarters to establish universal standards and permissible local variations, to make key allocational decisions on new products, new plants, new laboratories. The international management team includes the affiliate heads.

Subsidiary managers must ask: "Where in the world can I get the help to serve my customers best in this country?" "Where in the world can I export products developed in this country—products which meet worldwide standards as opposed to purely local standards?"

Geocentrism, furthermore, requires a reward system for subsidiary managers which motivates them to work for worldwide objectives, not just to defend country objectives. In firms where geocentrism prevails, it is not uncommon to hear a subsidiary manager say, "While I am paid to defend our interests in this country and to get the best resources for this affiliate, I must still ask myself the question 'Where in the world (instead of where in my country) should we build this plant?' " This approach is still rare today.

In contrast to the ethnocentric and polycentric patterns, communication is encouraged among subsidiaries in geocentric-oriented firms. "It is your duty to help us solve problems anywhere in the world," one chief executive continually reminds the heads of his company's affiliates. (See Table 1.)

The geocentric firm identifies with local company needs. "We aim to be not just a good local company but the best local company in terms of the quality of management and the worldwide (not local) standards we establish in domestic and export production." "If we were only as good as local companies, we would deserve to be nationalized."

The geocentric personnel policy is based on the belief that we should bring in the best man in the world regardless of his nationality. His passport should not be the criterion for promotion.

*   *   *   *   *

Costs, Risks, Payoffs

What conclusions will executives from multinational firms draw from the balance sheet of advantages and disadvantages of maintaining one's present state of ethnocentrism, polycentrism or geocentrism? Not too surprisingly, the costs and risks of ethnocentrism are seen to out-balance the payoffs in the long run. The costs of ethnocentrism are ineffective planning because of a lack of good feedback, the departure of the best men in the subsidiaries, fewer innovations, and an inability to build a high calibre local organization. The risks are political and social repercussions and a less flexible response to local changes.

The payoffs of ethnocentrism are real enough in the short term, they say. Organization is simpler. There is a higher rate of communication of know-how from headquarters to new markets. There is more control over appointments to senior posts in subsidiaries.

Polycentrism's costs are waste due to duplication, to decisions to make products for local use but which could be universal, and to inefficient use of home-country experience. The risks include an excessive regard for local traditions and local growth at the expense of global growth. The main advantages are an intensive exploitation of local markets, better sales since local management is often better informed, more local initiative for new products, more host-government support, and good local managers with high morale.

Geocentrism's costs are largely related to communication and travel expenses, educational costs at all levels, time spent in decision-making because consensus seeking among more people is required, and an international headquarters bureaucracy. Risks include those due to too wide a distribution of power, personnel problems and those of re-entry of international executives. The payoffs are a more powerful total company throughout, a better quality of products and service, worldwide utilization of best resources, improvement of local company management, a greater sense of commitment to worldwide objectives, and last, but not least, more profit.

*   *   *   *   *

A Geocentric Man—?

The geocentric enterprise depends on having an adequate supply of men who are geocentrically oriented. It would be a mistake to underestimate the human stresses which a geocentric career creates. Moving where the company needs an executive involves major adjustments for families, wives and children. The sacrifices are often great and, for some families, outweigh the rewards forthcoming —at least in personal terms. Many executives find it difficult to learn new languages and overcome their cultural superiority complexes, national pride and discomfort with foreigners. Furthermore, international careers can be hazardous when ethnocentrism prevails at headquarters. "It is easy to get lost in the world of the subsidiaries and to be 'out of sight, out of mind' when promotions come up at headquarters," as one executive expressed it following a visit to headquarters after five years overseas. To his disappointment, he knew few senior executives. And fewer knew him!

The economic rewards, the challenge of new countries, the personal and professional development that comes from working in a variety of countries and cultures are surely incentives, but companies have not solved by any means the human costs of international mobility to executives and their families.

A firm's multinationality may be judged by the pervasiveness with which executives think geocentrically—by function, marketing, finance, production, R&D, etc., by product division and by country. The takeoff to geocentrism may begin with executives in one function, say marketing, seeking to find a truly worldwide product line. Only when this worldwide attitude extends throughout the firm, in headquarters and subsidiaries, can executives feel that it is becoming genuinely geocentric.

From

NOTE ON RESPONSIBILITY CENTERS*

By Robert N. Anthony†

All organizations, except the tiniest, are made up of smaller organizational units. In a large organization there is a hierarchy of such units, for example, divisions, departments within divisions, sections within departments. If an organizational unit is headed by a supervisor who is responsible for the activities of the unit, then we call the unit a responsibility center.

Every organization has at least one goal, and most organizations have several. The organization exists for the purpose of accomplishing its goal or goals. The work done by each responsibility center presumably contributes, or at least is supposed to contribute, to the attainment of the goal, or goals, of the organization of which it is a part. We take as our central premise that a management control system should be structured in such a way that when heads of responsibility centers are motivated to act in their own perceived best interests they also are acting in the best interests of the whole organization, insofar as this is feasible. We call this premise goal congruence; that is, there should be as much congruence as possible between the goals of the head of each responsibility center and the overall goals of the organization. We recognize that perfect congruence of individual interests and organizational interests is not possible. A more practical statement of the premise, therefore, is that the system should *minimize* the amount of conflict between the goals of heads of responsibility centers and the goals of the whole organization. To the extent that the management control system in-

* Reprinted by permission of Richard D. Irwin, Inc., Homewood, Ill., 1965. From *Management Control Systems: Cases and Readings,* by Robert N. Anthony, John Dearden, and Richard F. Vancil. Excerpts from p. 165. This reading was adapted from James S. Hekimian, Introduction to *Management Control in Life Insurance Branch Offices* (Harvard Business School Division of Research), 1965.

† The author is a Professor at the Graduate School of Business Administration, Harvard University.

duces people to act in a way that does not contribute to the goals of the organization, the system is said to be *dysfunctional.*

From

REASON IN SOCIETY: FIVE TYPES OF REASON AND THEIR SOCIAL CONDITIONS*

By Paul Diesing†

Whenever there are other economic units with differing valuations, the value of one's resources can be increased by exchanging resources of lesser value to oneself for those of greater value to oneself. Exchange should continue until the demand for resources is approximately equalized throughout the economy. At this point resources will have been distributed to the units where they are most highly valued, and so allocated within those units as to effect a maximum goal achievement.

From this consideration of the logic of an economy it is plain that we are dealing with rationality. An economy which operates in the way I have indicated is a functionally rational one, because it effects a maximum goal achievement, and this is the commonly accepted mark of economic rationality. . . . Maximum goal achievement is possible to the extent that (1) the ends of economic units are comparable and measurable on a single scale, (2) there are no limits on the assignability and use of means, (3) economic units are integrated enough to engage in rational allocation and exchange, and (4) information about the supply and demand prices of other economic units is available. In other words, a rational economy simply has the characteristics essential to any economy, and has them to an extreme degree.

The rationality of an economy is sometimes expressed in the language of perfect competition. A perfectly competitive economy is the most rational one, it is argued, because in such an economy all factors will be allocated to their most economical use through the continual occurrence of allocation and exchange. Anything which reduces the extent of competition in an economy reduces its functional rationality. Therefore social policy should be devoted to the aim of increasing competition as far as possible, since in this way the economy will be made as rational as possible.

The idea of competition, as used in this argument, is a corollary of the idea of alternativeness or substitutability of ends. Ends which are alternative are inevitably in competition with each other for common means. Each mean that is allocated to one end is lost to all the others, and ends must therefore bid against each other

* Reprinted by permission of the University of Illinois Press, Urbana, Ill., 1962. Excerpts from pp. 20–21, 56, 170–71, 177–78, 198–99, 227–28, 231–32.

† The author is a Professor of Philosophy. He has taught at the University of Illinois and the University of Chicago.

to get means allocated to themselves. Whichever end can promise the highest return from use of a given mean should be assigned that mean, to achieve the goal of maximum utility.

*   *   *   *   *

In summary, economizing is the allocation of scarce common means to alternative ends in such a way that the ends are maximized. It is reasonable to maximize ends when they are unlimited, that is when means are scarce, because that is what it means to have an unlimited end. Economizing is made necessary and possible by cultural conditions which make ends alternative and which provide media of comparison for them. The cumulative production of these conditions is economic progress, so that the spread of economizing is a result of economic progress.

The exactness and accuracy of economic judgments are also increased by economic progress. Three degrees of exactness and accuracy can be distinguished, depending on whether neither ends nor means have an established market price, or means only have a price, or both ends and means are priced. Variations of exactness are also possible within each degree, so that the three degrees are actually parts of a continuum ranging from nearly arbitrary judgments to judgments of machinelike precision. The vaguest and most inaccurate judgments occur in dealings with semi-economic factors at the fringes of the economy, while the most exact and accurate judgments occur at the heart of the economy where markets and subsidiary techniques are well developed.

*   *   *   *   *

. . . If the determinants of thought are properly structured, thinking can be rational, but if they are improperly structured, thinking is irrational. I shall use the term "decision-making structure" to refer to the set of sociocultural determinants of practical thought, since decisions are its product. Not all the determinants of thought are included, but only those which can be controlled and structured.

. . . Decision-making structures occur in both individuals and groups; we shall be concerned primarily with group structures, though what is said about groups will apply to individuals as well. Political rationality is the rationality of decision-making structures.

I call this type of rationality "political" because politics is concerned with decisions and how they are made. The politics of a country or group is the process by which the group decides on its own activity and on the part to be played in that activity by members. The political structure of a group is the organization of forces which determines how its decisions are made, that is, its decision-making structure. Political science is the study of decision-making structures.

Politics is also concerned with the carrying out of public decisions and the achieving of a group's goals, but this activity embodies only technical and economic rationality and so does not concern us here. . . .

*   *   *   *   *

Decision-Making Structures

A decision-making structure is composed in the first place of discussion relationships—talking and listening, asking questions and answering them, suggesting courses of action and accepting them. . . .

A decision-making structure is composed, second, of a set of beliefs and values, more or less held in common by participating members. These define the kind of ideas that can be seriously considered during discussion and decision. Beliefs about the world, about man and society, determine the kind of factual propositions that are acceptable to the group, as well as the kinds of evidence or support that make them acceptable. Values determine the goals that are acceptable within the group, the possible desires, needs, external pressures, obligations, and so forth, that can be considered in selecting a goal or goals, and the ranking of goals, desires, needs, and obligations. Legal-moral norms define available and proscribed means, methods of combining ends, techniques of relating means to ends, and guides to selecting means. Beliefs and values, in short, determine the general content and order of the universe in which discussion and decision takes place, while the roles define the participants and their manner of participation.

*   *   *   *   *

Functional Rationality

*   *   *   *   *

Any decision-making structure must have two characteristics to exist at all. First, it must make possible the presentation of a plurality of facts, values, norms, and action alternatives. At least two of each one of these is necessary, otherwise no decision is possible because there are no alternatives to decide about. This characteristic will be called "differentiation" in the ensuing account, following Bales's terminology in his experiments on role differentiation in decision-making groups (Parsons and Bales, 1955, chap. 5). Second, it must make possible a unified resolution which incorporates at least some of the presented material. This characteristic will be called "unification" in the ensuing account.

Consider, for an example, a small group of men with the common purpose of moving some heavy piece of furniture. Immediately they will differentiate their tasks by each stationing himself at a different spot around the furniture, selected by reference to the other spots. This differentiation, though originally undertaken as a technical division of labor, also creates a decision structure. All during the moving there will be a constant series of decisions, to turn, avoid an obstacle, slow down, and so forth, to which members contribute by virtue of their specialized positions. The decision structure exists because there is a unifying purpose, to move the furniture, and different roles from which a variety of perceptions and suggestions are contributed.

*   *   *   *   *

The general requirements for a functionally rational decision structure have now been stated. A functionally rational structure is one which yields adequate decisions for complex situations with some regularity; but only structures which embody the two characteristics of differentiation and unification to a considerable degree will regularly yield adequate decisions. Therefore only such structures are functionally rational. . . .

*   *   *   *   *

Political Decisions

The type of decision which I shall call "political" is that which is concerned with the preservation and improvement of decision structures. All decisions occur within a decision structure of some sort, but political decisions in addition have decision structures as their special subject matter.

Political decisions are ordinarily made by the central authority of a decision structure. . . . The central role is the one that is most closely involved with the whole structure. Any changes anywhere in the structure affect the center; improvements of any sort simplify the tasks assigned to the central role and structural deterioration complicates them, as I shall show. Because of this actual identity of fate, it is easy for persons playing a central role to identify themselves with the structure and to develop a personal concern for its improvement.

I do not mean to say that persons in central roles make nothing but political decisions. The main concern of a person in a central role may often be the achievement of group or personal aims, with the preservation of the decision structure a secondary issue. This is particularly true in comparatively rational structures, which present few structural problems to the person in the central role. Nor is it the case that only central persons make political decisions. Anybody participating in a structure can concern himself with the rationality of the structure in addition to other matters. But political decisions are made more frequently by those in central roles than by those in peripheral roles, because the condition of the structure affects the central role more directly. . . .

The central role differs from other roles both in content and, usually, in timing of activities. In formal organizations where the central role is a leadership role, the leader is the one who has the final word in a decision process. Subordinates do the preliminary work of gathering information, making predictions, drawing up initial proposals, evaluating, criticizing, and modifying them; then the leader makes the final decision, and the process is completed. . . .

*   *   *   *   *

Scope of Political Decisions

Political decisions are necessary whenever an organization, or society, or person is faced with a political problem; that is, whenever there is a deficiency in its decision structure. The deficiency may be some form of narrowness, in that the structure is not receptive to an adequate range of facts, or that it is not able to break away from well-known formulas in its estimates of problems and suggestions for action, or that it is insufficiently self-critical and slow to admit error, or that its procedures are excessively rigid and thus shut out novelty. The deficiency may be some form of indecisiveness or internal conflict, in that decisions are excessively difficult to achieve, or that they are nullified or changed by concealed internal opposition, or that the system "changes its mind" too readily after reaching a decision.

The symptom of a political deficiency is the existence of numerous and increasing nonpolitical problems for the organization: Since the function of a decision structure is to deal with problems, any deficiency in functioning leads to an accumulation of unsolved problems. Also the way in which the problems accumulate points to the specific kind of deficiency. If the accumulating problems are apparent to the outsider but not to the decision structure, the deficiency exists in the information receptors; if the problems are recognized but solutions are late and erratic in appearing, the difficulty is one of indecisiveness; if solutions consistently fail, the deficiency is one of inventiveness; if erroneous courses of action are not readily changed, the deficiency is one of self-criticism; and so on. Sometimes political deficiencies can be discovered directly, by studying the internal workings of the structure and comparing it with similar structures, but the easiest way to locate deficiencies is to work back from the results.

Though a political problem is always accompanied by numerous nonpolitical problems, the political problem is always basic and prior to all the others. Sometimes one of the other problems has a temporal priority in the sense that if something is not done about it within two weeks the organization will go out of existence. This may be the case with threatened bankruptcy, or with a violent internal dispute which is about to force crucial members out of the organization. These are emergencies, to be settled by whatever temporary expedient will succeed. But nothing is basically solved until the political problems of an organization are solved. The reason is that without a well-functioning control system the organization, or society or person, is unable to deal with its other problems in a continuing fashion. They may be temporarily solved by outside help or some emergency action, but they are sure to reappear and get worse unless the organization is politically sound. Conversely, once the decision structure has been put into working order, the organization can be expected to take care of its other problems as they come up.

This means that any suggested course of action must be evaluated first by its effects on the political structure. A course of action which corrects economic or social deficiencies but increases political difficulties must be rejected, while an action which contributes to political improvement is desirable even if it is not entirely sound from an economic or social standpoint. It sometimes happens that political and nonpolitical problems can be solved together, but if this is not possible, the political problem must receive primary attention.

*   *   *   *   *

. . . Political rationality is the fundamental kind of reason, because it deals with the preservation and improvement of decision structures, and decision structures are the source of all decisions. Unless a decision structure exists, no reasoning and no decisions are possible; and the more rational a decision structure is, the more rational are the decisions it produces. There can be no conflict between political rationality and any other kind of rationality, because the solution of political problems makes possible an attack on any other problem, while a serious political deficiency can prevent or undo all other problem solving.

10. SOLA CHEMICAL COMPANY

Case Introduction

SYNOPSIS

In the post World War II period, Sola Chemical Company began diversifying and expanding into foreign markets through export operations. At the beginning of that period, the only foreign manufacturing was done in a virtually wholly owned Canadian subsidiary and in a joint venture in France. Foreign expansion progressed at a rate faster than in the U.S., so that by 1970 manufacturing facilities were located in 15 different countries. For tax and other financial reasons, Sola established a pattern of export holding companies in Delaware, Switzerland, Curacao, and Luxembourg. From the early 60s, all the foreign operations were managed through an international division whose treasurer and controller coordinated the foreign financial decisions with their headquarters' counterparts and the controllers in each of the foreign subsidiaries. By 1970, however, decision making for foreign operations had become so complex that a new decentralized organizational arrangement was suggested by consultants. At this point, a dispute develops involving the international treasurer and the consultant over the most effective ways to achieve corporate financial objectives through the coordinated efforts of financial executives at three levels: headquarters, area, and subsidiary.

WHY THIS CASE IS INCLUDED

The Sola Chemical Company case presents a classic view of the stages of internalization for the multinational firm. The history follows the pattern for U.S. multinationals documented by the Harvard studies of the multinational firm. The reader can study the dynamics of internationalization in which the firm organizes differently for the growing complexity at each stage. In the narrower context of the finance function, there is opportunity to study the conflict of objectives at different organization levels and how the organization of the finance function influences the achievement of different objectives. The reader can explore different modes of conflict management as well as the ways to make functional authority work effectively.

DIAGNOSTIC AND PREDICTIVE QUESTIONS

The readings included with this case are marked (*). The author index at the end of this book locates the other readings.

1. Trace the changing pattern of organization design in Sola from the post War War II era to 1970. Does the pattern make sense in light of the theory and practice cited in the readings?

Read: Kolde, *International Business Enterprise,* pp. 242–55, 260, 277–78.

(For those desiring a more extended discussion of evolving organization structure of a multinational corporation, see John Stoppford and Louis T. Wells, *Managing the International Enterprise* (Basic Books, 1972), Chapter 2. Not included in this volume.)

2. Why has the consultant proposed changing Sola's organization structure at this stage of the firm's development? Could Sola have predicted the need for organizational change in advance?

Read: See readings for question 1 above.

Miller and Starr, *Executive Decisions and Operations Research,* pp. 38–42, 45–47, 50. Starr, *Management: A Modern Approach,* pp. 673–76. Simon, *The New Science of Management Decision,* pp. 15–18, 40–48.

3. What forces in the environment are influencing the international financial management function, its activities, and its position in the organization?

Read: *Watts, "Strategies for Financial Risk in Multinational Operations," pp. 15–22.

4. What financial decisions were made at which levels of Sola and in which position (treasurer or controller) prior to the proposed 1970 organizational change?

Suggestion: Present your answer in a matrix form with different decisions on one axis and positions at different levels on the other axis. As you fill in a cell, indicate whether the decision authority is independent autonomy, decision after consultation, or decision only after concurrence by some other person.

5. In what way does the organization proposed by the consultants modify the financial decision pattern identified in decision 4?

6. If the proposed organization were adopted, how would you classify the change in the Perlmutter typology of ethnocentric, polycentric, and geocentric organization designs?

Read: Perlmutter, "The Tortuous Evolution of the Multinational Corporation."

7. Why do the consultants see such divergent information needs for the performance of the treasurer's and controller's function in Sola?

Read: *Vernon, *Manager in the International Economy,* pp. 233–36. Anthony, *Management Control Systems: Cases and Readings,* p. 165.Jerome, *Executive Control—the Catalyst,* pp. 31–34.

8. What alternative patterns might Sola have chosen for organizing the financial function?

Note: One may answer this question by using common sense and analysis of case facts. Or, a clear treatment of international financial organization within a company may be found in both of the following sources. "Financing Foreign Subsidiaries of U.S.-Controlled Multinational Enterprises," by Robert Stobaugh, *Journal of International Business Studies* (Summer 1970), pp. 43–49. *International Financial Management,* by David B. Zenoff and Jack Zwick, Prentice-Hall, Inc., 1969, pp. 453–460.

9. In Sola, there has been conflict between the treasurer and the controller positions and there are forecasts of conflicts across hierarchy levels in the proposed organization. Why does such conflict arise?

Read: Litterer, "Conflict in Organization: A Reexamination."Diesing, *Reason in Society: Five Types of Reason and their Social Conditions,* pp. 20–21, 56, 170–71, 177–78, 198–99, 227–28, 231–32. March and Simon, *Organizations,* pp. 65–66, 70–77.

POLICY QUESTIONS

10. How would you structure the financial function in Sola? Review the readings and your answers to Questions 3, 7, and 8.

11. After reviewing your responses to Questions 4 and 5, specify which financial decisions should be made at which levels of Sola and in what positions (treasurer or controller). Be sure as you fill in each cell of the matrix you indicate whether the decision authority is independent autonomy, decision after consultation, or decision only after concurrence by some other person.

12. What kind of arrangements beyond the structural adjustments and the job descriptions (specifying decision competence for each position) would you make to manage the conflict within the financial function worldwide at Sola.

Review the readings and your answer to Question 9 then read Richmond, *Operations Research for Management Decisions,* pp. 16–20. Follett, "Constructive Conflict."

QUESTIONS FOR ORIGINAL STUDENT WORK IN ANALYSIS AND POLICY

13. While reflecting on case facts, what additional theories from prior education give you insights as to "what is going on" in the Sola Company? As to what might be predicted to happen in the future?

14. Other than the policy questions asked by the authors, what pragmatic ways can you think of to state the practical problems faced by executives in the case?

Case Text*

ORGANIZING THE INTERNATIONAL FINANCE FUNCTION

The year was 1970. The subject before Sola Chemical's board of directors was a set of proposals by Multinational Consultants, Inc., recommending a drastic overhaul in the organization of Sola's overseas business. The board had already agreed, albeit a bit uncertainly, that the International Division would have to be abolished and that its responsibilities for overseas production and overseas marketing would have to be distributed among some new regional division. Now the question was: What to do about the finance and control functions for which the International Division had been responsible?

Origins

Ever since World War II, Sola had been doing what came naturally in the expansion of its foreign business. In the years just after the war, Sola thought of itself as one of five or six companies that made up the leadership in the industrial and agricultural chemicals industry in the United States. At that time, a company with annual sales of $150 million could claim a leadership position. Besides, sales of the company at that time were reasonably well concentrated in only four main product groups. From the perspective of 1970, after nearly 25 years of growth and of diversification into new products and new markets, operations in the immediate postwar period seemed extraordinarily neat and tidy.

In the first years after the war, the foreign business of Sola was a limited affair. Mainly it consisted of the sales that a small export department could drum up in Western Europe and Latin America, relying largely on commission merchants, wholesalers, and industrial buyers in those areas. From time to time, Sola would discover that one of its newer products had taken hold in some country, generally at a time five or six years after it had found a market in the United States. After a few years of expansion in any foreign market, however, the attractiveness of the particular line in the area would generally fall away as quietly as it had appeared.

---

* This case, Sola Chemical Company, ICR 544, was prepared by Professor Raymond Vernon of the Harvard University Graduate School of Business Administration as the basis for classroom discussion and not to illustrate either effective or ineffective handling of an administrative situation.

Apart from the seemingly episodic and sporadic lines of business of this sort, Sola's main "foreign" commitment in the years up to World War II was a manufacturing subsidiary in Canada, a subsidiary that Sola had set up in the late 20s in response to a sharp increase in Canada's industrial tariffs. Except for a few shares nominally held by Canadian directors, this subsidiary was wholly owned by Sola. When the Imperial Preference tariff system was established in 1932, the Sola management had congratulated itself on its foresight in establishing a subsidiary inside the Commonwealth so that it could meet British competitors such as Imperial Chemical Industries on equal terms. From Sola management's viewpoint, however, the Canadian subsidiary could hardly be called "foreign." Situated not far from Windsor, Ontario, it was close enough to Sola's midwest headquarters to be run like any other branch plant. The product policies and marketing policies of Sola seemed to apply about as well to the Canadian plant as any other. True, there were some occasional crises of an unfamiliar sort, as when the Canadians tinkered with the value of their currency in relation to the U.S. dollar, or when they set up unfamiliar provisions in relation to the taxation of profits. But an occasional consultation with the company's bankers and tax attorneys was generally sufficient to deal with crises of this sort.

Quite different from Sola's relationship to its Canadian subsidiary in the years immediately after World War II were its ties to a French subsidiary which had been set up at about the same time. Unlike the Canadian subsidiary, only 53 percent of the equity of this company was owned by Sola, the rest being in the hands of Cie. Chimie Tricolor, a leading French manufacturer whose product lines fell largely within two of Sola's four product groups. Nobody at Sola could quite recall how this particular liaison had first developed. But there was an impression that Sola had been confronted with an ultimatum by the French chemical industry at one point in the 20s: either she must invite a French business interest to join her in the creation of a French manufacturing subsidiary or she must risk losing a lucrative market that was being supplied by exports from the United States. There was some recollection among Sola's oldtimers that the ultimatum had been backed up by hints from the French ministry of industry that the threats might not prove hollow. In any event, whatever the origins of the French partnership might be the subsidiary had grown away from Sola over the years. By the late 40s it was thought of as almost an independent entity, operating under the stewardship of the French partner and negotiating with Sola for product information and technology very much on an arm's-length basis.

So much for the situation at the beginning of the postwar era.

Between that time and 1970, the foreign business of Sola had expanded at an astonishing rate, considerably faster than the business in the United States. And as the foreign business grew, not only the policies and strategies but even the very structure of Sola was greatly affected. Step by step, additional locations had been selected for the establishment of new manufacturing subsidiaries: the United Kingdom in 1952; Germany in 1955; Mexico in 1956; Brazil in 1960; Italy in 1962; Australia in

1965; and so on, until Sola's manufacturing facilities covered 15 different countries. At the same time, operations in Canada had been considerably expanded, covering more of Sola's product lines. In each of these cases, Sola had preferred to go it alone, without local partners. And after a nasty confrontation or two with the French partners over the management of the French facility, a friendly divorce had been arranged, leaving Sola with a wholly owned manufacturing facility in France in lieu of the old partnership.

Although Sola had not set up more than a portion of the U.S. product line in any one country, the total number of products manufactured overseas was widening every year. In fact, there were even three or four cases in which the U.S. plants had suspended operations on an old staple item, assigning what was left of the business to one of the foreign facilities where the product still seemed to command a market. When that happened, the foreign facility took over Sola's third country markets as well.

While the manufacturing subsidiaries were spreading over the globe, Sola was setting up other units to facilitate the handling of its foreign business. Sola had discovered very early the tax advantages of a western hemisphere trade corporation and had set up a company in Delaware to qualify under the U.S. tax code. A corporation could qualify if it derived practically all its income from trade or business (as distinguished from investment), and confined its business to the Western hemisphere outside the United States. The profits of such a corporation were taxed at a rate 14 percentage points less than the standard U.S. rate. To exploit this advantage, U.S. Sola billed its exports to western hemisphere countries from the United States through its western hemisphere trade corporation. As a rule, such exports were billed out by U.S. Sola to the trade corporation at the lowest possible appropriate figure, which Sola calculated in accordance with a formula that included an 8 percent mark-up over cost. This formula had the effect of placing most of the profit on such sales in the trade corporation.

Other arrangements to minimize taxes had been made as well. Back in 1958, before the Revenue Act of 1962 had restricted the use of foreign-based holding companies as "tax havens"—that is, as vehicles for postponing the payment of U.S. taxes on foreign income—Sola's treasurer and tax attorney had pushed through the establishment of a Swiss holding company. U.S. Sola owned Sola-Switzerland, which in turn held nominal ownership over Sola's subsidiaries outside the United States. In those days, Sola-Switzerland could perform all kinds of useful services for U.S. Sola. For one thing, like the western hemisphere trade corporation, it could act as an intermediary in export sales from the U.S. When Sola-Switzerland was used as an intermediary, the tax benefits to U.S. Sola were rather different than those associated with the use of the western hemisphere company. Sola-Switzerland's profits were subject to normal tax rates once they got into the U.S. tax jurisdiction. But that did not occur until the profits were declared to U.S. Sola in the form of dividends. Meanwhile, Sola-Switzerland could shuttle the cash generated by export profits to any point in the Sola system that required it.

Sola-Switzerland's cash flow could be built up not only by exports but also by the dividends, royalties, interest and fees generated in the Sola subsidiaries that Sola-Switzerland nominally owned. As long as Swiss law did not tax the income of the Swiss holding company and as long as a U.S. law did not classify the funds as taxable in the United States, Sola-Switzerland was a highly useful mechanism.

That particular arrangement had deferred quite a lot of tax payments for a few years. Subsidiaries could declare dividends and could pay interest, agency fees, administrative charges, and royalties to the holding company without subjecting the income to U.S. taxation; the U.S. tax bite would come only when the income moved upstream as dividends to the U.S. parent. Though the U.S. system of tax credits on foreign-earned income ensured that the income would not be taxed twice when it finally appeared on the U.S. parent's books, still there was something to be gained at times from deferring the U.S. tax. The tax advantage was especially important when the subsidiary's payments to its parent had not been taxed locally because they represented expenses to the subsidiary, or when the subsidiary's income had been taxed at rates well below those in the United States. In those situations, when the payments finally were received as dividends in the United States, some U.S. taxes would be due.

When the Internal Revenue Code was amended in 1962 to restrict the use of tax haven companies, many of the tax advantages involved in the maintenance of such a company disappeared. The provisions that expose the income of such tax haven companies to U.S. taxation are exceedingly complex. But Sola's Swiss holding company clearly fell within its terms. It was controlled by U.S. Sola, and it derived more than 70 percent of its income from the dividends, interest, royalties and other fees received from Sola's operating subsidiaries located in third countries. Accordingly, the income of Sola-Switzerland was fully taxable under U.S. law just as if it had been paid directly to U.S. Sola itself.

One tax advantage associated with foreign holding companies still remained, however. Loath to discourage exports from the U.S. in any way, Congress had exempted from the new provisions such income as the tax haven companies were garnering from their role in the handling of U.S. exports. As long as a spread could exist between the price at which U.S. Sola invoiced its goods for export and the price at which the goods were invoiced for import in the foreign country of destination, there were still tax advantages in assigning the spread to an intermediate company located in a tax-free area.

Despite the fact that Sola-Switzerland had lost much of its original purpose, there was some hesitation about liquidating the Swiss company. It would entail the transfer of the equity of many underlying operating subsidiaries, the transfer of the Swiss company's claims to the long-term and short-term debt of some of the operating subsidiaries, and the shift of the Swiss company's title in patents and trade names abroad that were being licensed to the subsidiaries. Numerous contractual ties between the Swiss company and the subsidiaries also would have to be dissolved, such as the right of the Swiss company to receive payment for administrative and technical services and for sales agency services. All these rearrangements were bound to generate administrative and legal problems in a number of different countries, where the increasing curiosity and sophistication of the regulatory authorities could be counted on to stir up difficulties.

Accordingly, Sola decided to leave the Swiss holding company in existence and to create several other intermediate companies besides. One would be a Luxembourg company, set up to capture some of the profits on U.S. exports, which still were entitled to tax deferral treatment. Another enterprise would be set up to segregate the income generated by subsidiaries in advanced countries. Under the 1962 law, income originating in subsidiaries in the less-developed areas, unlike income from the advanced countries, could still be kept beyond the reach of U.S. tax collectors to the extent that it was reinvested in less-developed areas. Accordingly, a holding company was set up in Curacao to own Sola's subsidiaries in less-developed areas and to receive the income of such subsidiaries for routing to destinations where the income was needed. Curacao's virtue as a holding company headquarters consisted *inter alia* of its willingness to leave such income virtually untaxed as it passed through the holding company on its way to a new destination.

As if this complex cluster of intermediate companies was not enough, Sola decided in 1966 that another intermediate structure would be useful, namely, a holding company created under the laws of Delaware to act as Sola's *alter ego* in floating bond issues in the European market.

Well before 1966, it was clear to U.S. Sola that its European subsidiaries' voracious appetite would have to be fed by more borrowing from abroad. Sola itself was under a handicap when raising money in Europe, because U.S. internal revenue requirements obliged it to withhold 30 percent of interest or dividend payments to nonresident recipients. That provision placed a heavy handicap on the securities of U.S. issuers in Europe. Sola's Swiss holding company had been used two or three times before as the nominal borrower of dollar-denominated funds from European sources. Operating under the umbrella of a guarantee from U.S. Sola, the Swiss holding company had been able to borrow medium-term money at reasonable rates from private European sources. Though the interest costs had run a little higher than they would have in the United States, these flotations had saved the bother of registration with the Securities and Exchange Commission, the problem of qualification under the "blue sky" laws of the state regulatory agencies, and so on; the difference in costs, therefore, was not as great as the interest rates indicated. At the same time, Sola had developed some excellent European banking ties that might be in a position to help out in the event that the U.S. government really clamped down on the export of capital from the United States. As early as 1958 or 1959, that contingency had become something to worry about, as U.S. officials began to express their misgivings over the condition of the U.S. balance of payments.

By 1965, contingency had turned to reality. "Voluntary" controls had been imposed over the outflow of funds from the United States to subsidiaries in Europe. Although the controls were very loose and left many different ways in which Sola could arrange for the generation of cash flows in its overseas subsidiaries, Sola tried to respond to the spirit of the regulations by raising a larger proportion of its needed funds outside the United States.

One possible step to that end was to continue using the Swiss holding company, as it had been used in the past, to borrow from European sources. But Sola was not eager to expand the use of the Swiss holding company, now that it had lost most of its usefulness as a tax haven. True, such a holding company still had some advantages that U.S. Sola did not share, such as the fact that its payments of dividend and interest to non-U.S. recipients were not subject to the reporting and withholding requirements of U.S. tax law. But the use of such a company also had some disadvantages, when compared with a Delaware company, such as the fact that losses if any could not be consolidated in U.S. Sola's income tax return in the United States.

The upshot was that Sola decided in 1966 to create a second Delaware holding company, with functions carefully designed to retain the advantages of a Swiss holding company as a financing intermediary while avoiding some of its disabilities. The main purpose of the second Delaware holding company was to borrow funds outside the United States with the guarantee of U.S. Sola and to lend those funds to Sola's foreign subsidiaries. As long as the new holding company confined itself to this sort of operation, its only significant income—namely, interest payments from the subsidiaries—was regarded as of foreign origin. Since 80 percent or more of its income was of foreign origin, the Delaware company, like the Swiss company, was not required to withhold any sums in connection with interest payments to non-U.S. recipients. Such profits as the Delaware company might have were within the reach of the U.S. and Delaware tax jurisdiction. But profits were likely to be trivial, given the purpose of the company. Besides, Delaware tax provisions were traditionally benign in such matters, and U.S. tax provisions, ever since the adoption of the 1962 amendments, made only small distinctions between the profits of domestic holding companies and those of foreign holding companies of U.S. taxpayers.

The creation of the Delaware finance company proved to be a very wise step indeed. On January 1, 1968, the so-called "voluntary" program of capital export controls became mandatory. At the same time, the program was tightened up so that the various alternative means of transferring funds abroad became more restricted. Under the new program, Sola's right to transfer funds abroad was tied to its historical record of investment in the years just prior to 1968. Investment for that base period was defined as capital transfers in cash or in kind made to foreign subsidiaries plus profits retained in the subsidiaries during the period. Once that base figure was calculated, its application was differently defined for different groups of countries. Subsidiaries in the less developed countries, the "Schedule A" countries, were allowed to continue receiving investment from U.S. Sola at their old levels, even a little higher. Then there was a "Schedule B" group, which the U.S. regulators thought of as being especially dependent on U.S. capital flows—the oil countries, the

United Kingdom, Japan, and a few other areas. Added investments from the U.S. in these areas was cut down but not eliminated; capital flows to these areas were restricted to 65 percent of the base period. Canada, originally in this group, was exempted from the regulations altogether.

The real problem for Sola, therefore, was the European subsidiaries, that is, the subsidiaries located in "Schedule C" countries. These were cut back drastically. At first, added investment from U.S. Sola could only take place through retained earnings. And even the retained earnings could not be used under the rules if this meant a retention rate higher than base period rates or if it meant an investment rate higher than 35 percent of the base period.

If it had not been for the fact that borrowings outside the United States were exempted from the restrictions, Sola would have been in real trouble at first. That exemption carried the company through 1968. And in 1969 and 1970, the restrictions came to be somewhat eased. But the experience impressed on the minds of Sola's management more than ever the need to have an intimate knowledge of the world's sources of capital and to have the flexibility in organization to use the sources as needed. This heightened recognition centered attention on just how decisions were taken on such matters inside the organization.

The Financial Organization

As Sola expanded its overseas operations the legal instrumentalities and national environments that concerned it increased rapidly in number. From World War II until 1970, therefore, there was a constant need to restructure the internal organization and procedures that were responsible for formulating and executing financial policies and for controlling financial operations. That restructuring was tied in intimately, of course, with other changes in Sola's organization, including changes in the marketing and production systems associated with a growing overseas operation.

In the early 1960's, the foreign business had grown to such proportions that it was thought advisable to create an international division. The first executive in charge of that division, an aggressive and ambitious manager, decided that one of his major needs was to pull together the haphazard structure which up to that time had been formulating financial policy for the foreign areas. With the approval of Sola's top management, therefore, a new structure was created. Some of the essential elements of the organization tying together the financial function at that stage are suggested by the diagram in Exhibit 1.

A word or two of elaboration is needed in order to relate Sola's structure in the early 60s, portrayed in Exhibit 1, to financial decisions as taken at that time.

Major investment decisions, such as decisions to create a new foreign subsidiary or substantially to increase its capitalization, were generally recommended in the first instance by the international manager to Sola's president; he, in turn, usually sought the advice of his board of directors, as well as the advice of many other sources.

EXHIBIT 1
Sola Chemical Company
Financial Offices in the Structure of Sola Company, 1962

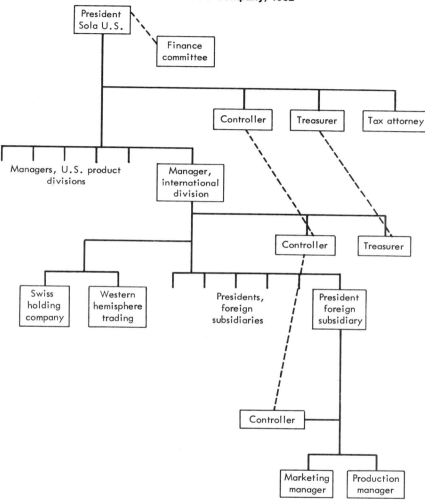

Major policies aimed at reducing taxes on overseas operations were usually initiated by the international treasurer, discussed with U.S. Sola's treasurer and tax attorney, then cleared with the finance committee.

Policies with regard to borrowing by foreign subsidiaries were no problem. Apart from accounts payable and accrued liabilities and except for a rare local loan initiated by the international treasurer, such transactions did not arise. Subsidiaries were not authorized to borrow; indeed they were not thought of as managing their own cash flow. Funds were channelled to the subsidiaries by the international treasurer as needed.

Before 1965 these funds had come mainly from the parent or the Swiss holding company, in the form of short-term dollar debt. Later on, after the Delaware company was formed and had begun to raise dollars through the sale of Eurobonds, it became the principal creditor for Sola's foreign subsidiaries.

Apart from decisions on whether and how to provide the subsidiaries with their working capital needs, the other major area of financial operating policy was how to withdraw funds from a subsidiary that held surplus cash. In this case, the main problem was viewed as minimizing the tax burden associated with withdrawal, and the main policy variable was the choice between dividends, royalties, interest and management fees. That choice was made by the tax attorney, on the basis of data provided by the international treasurer.

The international controller, as Exhibit 1 suggests, bore a somewhat different relation to the organization than the treasurer. Unlike the treasurer, the controller had representatives in each of the subsidiaries. This difference reflected the fact that the treasurer saw his function as that of managing the money flows of the system, whereas the controller saw his function as that of monitoring the performance of its various parts. The first function, so it seemed, could be performed well enough from the bridge of the enterprise, whereas the second function required getting down into the various holds below.

Proposals for Reorganization

As a rule, the international treasurer's problems were not the sort of subject that got discussed very much among Sola's directors. When a major investment abroad was involved, that of course was fairly well explored. But the discussion mostly involved questions of strategy, rather than financing and cash flow problems. These were left pretty much for the finance committee and the treasurer's office to worry about. As far as the finance committee was concerned, that group was free to admit that its ability to second-guess the treasurer's office on overseas' financing was quite limited. The subject was just too specialized, it appeared. So the international treasurer proved to be performing a vital function.

Fortunately for Sola Chemical, it had filled that post very well indeed. Milray Thaler had been international treasurer ever since 1958 when the post was first created. He had come out of the old export department, seasoned by years of selling in a world of inconvertible currencies. He had learned all about the ways in which blocked currencies could be turned into usable cash, and ways in which avoidable taxes could be avoided. As international treasurer, he ran a tight organization. He kept close touch with the problems of every subsidiary, especially their problems of cash flow. As far as he could see, the foreign subsidiaries had been well provided for, without having to worry about money and credit questions for which they were hardly equipped. And as far as taxes were concerned, the foreign side of Sola had done marvelously well in avoiding the avoidable.

Despite that fact, by 1970, the financial organization was showing certain signs of strain. By that time, Thaler's unflagging efforts to hold down taxes and to generate money where it was most needed had made a shambles of the periodic profit and loss statements of the subsidiaries. The U.S. system of controls over the export of funds to subsidiaries had increased the complexities of financing. The objective of holding down the total tax bill was now constrained by restrictions on the outflow of capital from the United States. The importance of distinguishing between the treatment of subsidiaries in different countries also was increasing. The differences between less-developed countries and advanced countries, and between countries in Schedules A, B, and C, were important. Added wrinkles, such as Canada's special status under the U.S. capital export control program, had to be kept in mind. The difficulties were heightened further by the fact that some countries, especially the United States and Germany, were beginning to take seriously their various fiscal provisions relating to the international pricing of goods and services. Provisions such as Section 482 of the U.S. Internal Revenue Code, authorizing the tax authorities to use arm's-length prices in interaffiliate transactions, were beginning to be applied seriously. Thaler's consultations with the tax people and his demands on Sola's treasurer were constantly rising in number and urgency.

In addition, Thaler's difficulties with the controller's area seemed on the increase. The more strenuous the efforts of the treasurer, the more difficult the problem of the controller. If the reported profit and loss statements of the manufacturing subsidiaries could be taken at face value, most of them were operating at practically no profit; the only exception was the subsidiary in Canada. What actually was happening depends on what the word "actually" meant. Profits were appearing in the western hemisphere trading company, in the Swiss holding company, in the Swiss holding company in Luxembourg and in Curacao. Whether these profits were "actual" or not depended on what one thought of the validity of the prices charged for products traded among the affiliates, as well as the royalty charges and administrative fees. Sometimes there was a basis for testing these prices and fees against analogous arm's-length transactions. But more often, the goods or services involved were sufficiently distinctive so that no independent arm's-length standard could readily be found, assuming an effort were made to find one.

On top of this problem was the fact that Sola's subsidiaries in Europe, facing the elimination of trade barriers in the EEC and EFTA, found themselves competing in one another's territory with similar product lines. Here and there, the problem had been reduced by the timely intervention of the international manager. Once or twice, where specialty items were involved, the subsidiaries had agreed to allocate production tasks between them without bothering to involve the international office. In situations of that sort, the transfer price was fixed according to the bargaining strength of the subsidiaries and the transaction was recorded as if it were undertaken with an outside vendor. But as the number of subsidiaries and the number of product lines kept rising, this *ad hoc* approach was beginning to prove inadequate.

For the controllers in the local subsidiaries, all these problems presented growing headaches. The performance reports were beginning to make less and less sense, unless adjusted in various ways. Adjustments, however, required the refereeing role of the international controller when it involved a decision affecting the relative performance of two foreign subsidiaries, and it required the involvement of U.S. Sola's controller when the decision affected the U.S. company's reported performance. As a result of the accumulation of decision rules arising out of these adjudications, controllers' reports were beginning to bear less and less relation to the financial statements.

With these considerations and others in mind, Multinational Consultants, Inc., a prominent international consulting firm, was called in to advise on the reorganization of Sola's foreign business. After studying the operations of the company for a number of months, Multinational Consultants produced a voluminous report covering the problems of the foreign side of Sola's business. Among other things, it had a number of observations regarding the operation of the financial function, observations that boiled down to three propositions:

1.   The treasurer's function had become much too complex and diffuse to be managed effectively from the center. Opportunities were being missed and errors committed. Among the errors cited, for instance, was the failure of the international treasurer to develop a systematic policy toward the threat of currency fluctuations. The opportunities missed as a result of the absence of such a policy were not the sort that were necessarily visible in Sola's financial statements. But once in a while, missed opportunities could be detected. One of these was the failure to hedge against a sterling devaluation in 1967, when the likelihood of the devaluation seemed extraordinarily high; this alleged oversight was said to have cost the company $350,000 in translation losses. Other opportunities overlooked, according to MCI, were those inherent in the possibilities for borrowing in local markets. The tight cash flow controls from headquarters, MCI guessed, reduced the likelihood that such opportunities were being recognized and exploited.
2.   The treasurer was much too preoccupied with tax savings and too little concerned with reducing the cost of funds.
3.   The financial data essential for the use of the treasurer's office was markedly different from the data needed for the performance of the controller's function, more so than in the case of complex operations within the United States proper. This difference was due to the fact that the units of Sola were in so many different jurisdictions with different rules covering taxation, access to capital, and so on. Essentially, the controller would be obliged to develop a separate score card, gauging the performance of profit centers on the basis of data that were compiled primarily for control purposes.

As a first step toward achieving the needed shifts in direction, Multinational Consultants, Inc., proposed a number of major organizational changes. It was proposed that the international division should be broken up into several foreign area divisions, each of which would have status on a par with a U.S. product division. The international treasurer and the international controller would be moved upstairs into the offices of Sola's treasurer and controller respectively. A new layer of treasurers, controllers, and tax attorneys would be created at the area division level.

Under the new system, the lowest control center on the foreign side would be a given product line in a given area. Where more than one subsidiary in an area was involved in the product, the control center would combine the activities in the product of all such subsidiaries. Presumably, the treasurer could not ignore the performance of the subsidiary, since that performance would affect its tax liability. But for the controller's needs, an area-product approach to performance would be taken. Exhibit 2 indicates how the financial offices would sit in the revised Sola structure after reorganization.

Practically everyone on the foreign side of the Sola organization reacted to the proposals with some degree of hostility or reserve. The international manager saw himself as risking a major demotion: Either he would be moved upstairs into the staff of the Sola's president, or would be placed at the head of the "Europe and Africa" area. In either case, his status would be a notch lower. Of all the officers reacting to the change, however, it was Milray Thaler, the international treasurer, who felt most threatened.

Thaler was furious at the report of Multinational Consultants. A few days after it had been circulated in Sola, Thaler produced a 26-page reply, refuting the report point by point. Some of the extracts from his rebuttal were especially provocative.

*   *   *   *   *

2. Of course, the international side of the treasurer's function is growing more complicated. Governments get smarter every day. Regulations get more complicated. With Section 482 on one side and OFDI on the other, it is not easy to do business abroad. But what kind of an answer is MCI offering us? To set up a treasurer in every area, so one area doesn't know what the other is doing? Who will tell German-Sola to stop trying to make a record for itself by gouging Argentine-Sola with its high invoice prices for petrochemicals? And who will stop the subsidiaries from always trying to build up their equity, instead of building up accounts payable? Much better to give me a few more high-level assistants who have had a little experience with such complicated matters so that we can stay on top of such problems.

3. Maybe production and marketing need some decentralizing at the regional level. After all, the users of industrial chemicals in Nairobi are not exactly the same types you find in Hamburg or Rio. But the management of money is another matter; that should be centralized. Money is money once you get it out of the clutches of a country and make it convertible. A dollar out of Peru is a dollar out of Turkey, and it ought to be managed that way.

*   *   *   *   *

5. How would a regional treasurer know how to use the Curacao or Luxembourg companies, or why? Today, if Sola-Switzerland needs

EXHIBIT 2
Financial Offices in Proposed Reorganization of Sola Company, 1970

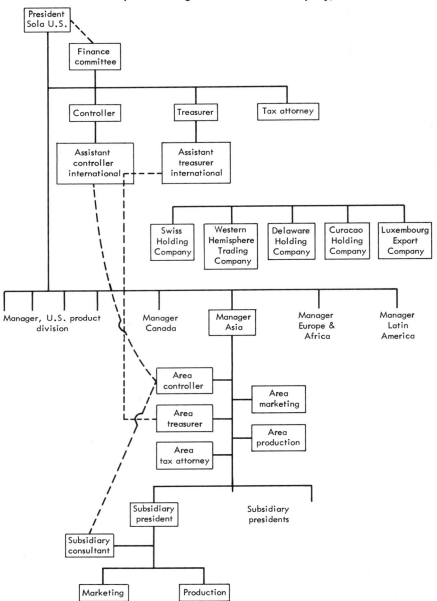

to pay a dividend to U.S. Sola, I can easily drum up the money by way of Curacao. I can do it because I know just what to expect in Curacao and I know how to compare it with Berne's cash flow prospects.

* * * * *

14. That famous $350,000 translation loss from the devaluation of sterling is getting a little ridiculous. Translation losses are not money, they are bookkeeping. They mean nothing to Sola's cash flow. Tax payments are a different matter. There is where real money can be saved. If I were to worry about every currency that might devalue tomorrow, I would eat up the time of the company and the office chasing paper butterflies.

15. Once the controller starts making up his own score card and the treasurer makes up a separate one, it will be impossible to know where we stand. The controller has everything he needs, without the headaches of a special set of books, if he gets copies of the treasurer's instructions to the subsidiaries. If he wants to adjust his records because of these instructions, so that the effect of tax transactions and cash flow transactions are cancelled out, it is easy enough for him to do it.

16. Above all, once you start putting the profit centers in the regional offices, you are a dead duck. Europe is not yet a country. Neither is Latin America. The authorities in the central banks and in the national tax administrations are not about to give up their powers and go away. These are the offices you have to keep your eye on if you are going to survive in the international business.

Selected Readings

From

STRATEGIES FOR FINANCIAL RISK IN MULTINATIONAL OPERATIONS*

By John H. Watts III†

The chief financial officer of an international company will face a number of strategic problems and choices in the 1970s, particularly those generally associated with monetary uncertainties.

* Reprinted with permission from the *Columbia Journal of World Business,* September-October, 1971. Excerpts from pp. 15–22. Copyright © 1971 by The Trustees of Columbia University in the City of New York.

† Mr. Watts is a Deputy Manager with Brown Brothers Harriman & Company, New York.

In the mid-Sixties, and indeed since World War II, monetary uncertainty meant to bankers and businessmen one main question: "Will such-and-such currency devalue?" And, if the currency in question were the pound sterling, the next question was: "Will the monetary system come tumbling down, bringing the world's economy with it?" The past three and a half years, however, have brought a lot of painful but instructive experience. Four major currencies have changed parities, and two have floated free of fixed parities. By forcing all but one of these changes the private market has proved itself more than a match for even combined official resources. The U.S. dollar has also been forced to a new relationship with gold, though this "failure," in the form of the two-tiered market, has proved surprisingly helpful.

These parity adjustments have been accompanied by an accelerating array of controls. The United States has initiated, and reinforced, comprehensive controls on lending, investing and repatriating foreign funds. Each major European country, as well as Japan, has from time to time placed new controls on access to currency markets, portfolio and direct investments, and borrowing. The most recent major examples have been a proscription against the use by U.K. Companies of the short- to medium-term Eurodollar market and a variety of interest rate and borrowing restrictions adopted by West Germany. The nuisance value of these controls has probably been more than equalled by losses from profitable projects foregone and by costs of more expensive financing. As a result, the evaluation by international companies of this past third of a decade has been clear—capital and exchange controls are worse than the parity changes. Attention, therefore, has turned to controls which apparently threaten earnings per share more than does devaluation.

$$* \quad * \quad * \quad * \quad *$$

The International Monetary System: New Rules in Sight?

The foreign exchange market is in effect the international monetary system. It is by far the largest financial market in the world, with annual turnover in trillions of dollars or their equivalent, and though operated by banks, it primarily serves the needs of international corporations. Its rules, especially those for official intervention to support prices, are set by international agreements and customs and are centered in the International Monetary Fund (IMF).

One key strategic uncertainty then is whether these rules will last. Can we count on established parities at all? . . . Students of international financial history point out that the international markets we prize today are not really novel but represent another set of arrangements in a long drama of expansion and contraction of international credit and investment.

The Eurodollar Market

$$* \quad * \quad * \quad * \quad *$$

Since the Eurodollar system can, and to at least some extent does, create credit, it has the potential to continue growing at several times the rate of various nations' domestic money supplies. The Eurodollar pool is too large and too potent for central bankers to allow it to remain uncontrolled, particularly since its use by large corporations within their countries integrates it with the money system they are charged to control. What further forms might such controls take?

Will the Eurobond market remain viable? Will those borrowings be refundable in that market? Will the Euroequities market become more important? What other instruments, such as commercial paper, may be sold and traded internationally?

Financial Institutions and International Corporations

Perhaps the greatest recent changes in the financial environment for international firms have occurred in the financial institutions themselves. Now that, in the summer of 1971, the number of foreign banks in London has passed the 200 mark, with many of the past half-decade's important newcomers being consortia composed of several institutions, the age of integrated international banking can truly be said to have begun. A recent analysis of the consortia phenomenon points out that most of their financing is done in syndicates with other consortia, thus extending multilateralism to international finance in a way that may well represent a historic turning point in world finance.[1]

The variety of nationalities, types, sizes and abilities of consortia members has been without precedent. . . .

What role will each of this multitude of new entities play vis-à-vis the international corporation? Will operating firms choose between financial houses, on the basis of the latter's special strengths, for each major financing? Or will the wider range of capabilities of the consortia mean that the more traditional relationship between major companies and their "lead" banks, and chief underwriters, will survive internationally?

*   *   *   *   *

What are likely outcomes in these major areas of risk and uncertainty? First, it seems likely that the IMF monetary arrangements will survive. But substantial changes will be necessary. The central difficulty today is that the monetary rules were designed when the basic international process was trade, and the main monetary problem was competitive devaluation. Now the dominant process is international investment and production, and the main problem is to accommodate the accompanying flows of capital. Therefore, the currency mechanism must have more adaptive capacity for absorbing these investment flows.

*   *   *   *   *

More important, however, is that there is now much greater sophistication in big firms about foreign currency exposure. They have learned how to make accounting choices, to think ahead about tax treatment, to manage their discretionary liquidity and to plan for public reporting of book losses and gains in such manner that the portions of their overseas assets which would have been considered in the 1960s to be "exposed" to parity change have been substantially reduced.

The Future of the U.S. Dollar

The dollar will remain dominant for private trade invoicing and other real transactions, for short-term borrowing and investments, and for official intervention. There may well be some competition from pooled European currencies for reserve use on the Continent and eventually for use in official intervention on the exchange

---

[1] Michael von Clemm, "The Rise of Consortium Banking," *Harvard Business Review,* May–June 1971.

market. Other currencies, such as the mark and yen, may be important for long-term borrowings. But it should continue to be a dollar world, more or less in spite of the U.S. payments position, because the liquidity of dollar markets and the broad spectrum of alternative uses and needs for dollars simply cannot be matched by any other currency or combinations of monies.

*   *   *   *   *

A Common European Currency?

The United Kingdom will probably join the EEC, although the ratification may be a closer squeak than is now generally believed. A common European currency should eventually evolve. . . .

In the developing countries there will be increasing pressures on international companies as these countries strive to use what political and economic strength they have to get the greatest benefits they can from world capital flows as well as better treatment in commodity prices. LDCs might, for example, try to hold future SDR allocations hostage in order to get some linkage between SDR creation and aid flows. On the corporate level, problems will arise from toughening policies regarding use of local banks, foreign control, dividend repatriation and other familiar issues. When, as Sol Linowitz has observed, OAS studies refer to the foreign private investment "problem," there has been a basic change in the weather.

Corporate Financial Strategy

*   *   *   *   *

. . . [T]here is the problem of what might be called "diminishing returns to additional assistant treasurers." This arises because, on the one hand, international companies increasingly are decentralizing operating control of their various enterprises yet retaining the financial initiative and control at headquarters. On the other hand, as these foreign operations mature and encompass marketing and distribution functions, their need for comprehensive financial support can exceed the ability of the headquarters staff to provide it.

A similar expansion in demands on the corporate treasurer's function has occurred domestically during the past two decades. Much more active financial management has developed in at least fourteen areas (See box). In the main, the skills have been built up by adding to the corporate financial staff—adding Assistant Treasurers—and in many cases the profit contribution of the "in-house" skill has been dramatic.

The dilemma for a truly international company is that demands for financial specialization are multiplied by the numbers of countries in which there are significant operations. Evaluating a pension fund or mobilizing cash for investment, for example, will present different problems in different countries. While overlaps and similarities do exist, in principle a company active in, say, ten separate countries could write 140 different job descriptions to cover the fourteen treasurer's functions in each country. The potential profit contribution from developing skill in any of these functions abroad is for most firms far less than it is in its parent-country operations. It simply is not economical to build a staff with detailed knowledge of how several countries' economic and political trends, laws, customs and institutional arrangements affect the variety of finanical problems facing operations in those countries.

**The Corporate Treasurer's Office:
Major Multinational Functions**

Cash Control and Mobilization
Collection and Payments Systems
Short-term Investment Management
Long-term Borrowing
Bank Borrowing and Bank Relations
Trade Financing
Commercial Paper, Other Notes Issues
Pension Surveillance and Control
Insurance Programs
Tax and Regulatory Planning and Compliance
Investor Relations—Financial Market Relations
Financial Projections and Source Planning
Foreign Exchange, Foreign Asset Risk Management
Credit Evaluations, Other Financial Analyses (e.g. Mergers)

In the present international business environment and with these specific problems, what strategies should be followed? Three strategies already underlying the financial operations of a few sophisticated international firms should be particularly useful in this decade.

First, financial officers should expect and plan for change in financial markets, anticipating controls and setting up in advance routines for managing potential "currency risks. . . ." The most important elements in this work are not the technical trade-offs between the cost of one type of cover or another, but rather policy decisions in accounting and tax choices. For example, should one attempt to hedge at all? If so, should one double-hedge so that after-tax gains match non-deductible losses? Where on the spectrum of accounting choice should a company choose to set its exposure definitions, between the highly conservative "net current asset" approach, or the other extreme in which only net financial assets are considered to be exposed? At what level of potential risk is it appropriate for a company to spend resources in trying to manage currency exposures? How much is it willing to pay for cover in the forward market before it chooses to self-insure? How should the currency risk program be staffed and organized? These issues are at the heart of any good program. It seems imperative that these policy determinations and consequent decision rules be set down ahead of crises. Decisions taken at the peak of currency crises have often been bad and costly.

A second useful strategy is to plan to obtain additional financial sources for each major foreign operation. Since many signs point to the likelihood of increased capital controls, financing flexibility should be a byword in any modern multinational operation. For example, it would seem useful to develop the company's name in the local bond market and to learn the mechanism for a medium-term borrowing. The limits of custom in the use of commercial bank lines should be known, and local instruments such as bankers' acceptances or commercial paper should be explored. Consideration should be given to setting up one or a variety of international financing corporations to tap the different markets. To achieve this greater flexibility, competent staff as well as good information should be centered at the right location. For example, a financial surveillance, information and control office in major financial markets such as London, or on the Continent or in the Far East will become increasingly useful to international companies.

A third strategy, for handling the problem of "diminishing returns" from an increased corporate financial staff, is to make explicit and careful use of expertise available in international financial institutions. . . .

From

MANAGER IN THE INTERNATIONAL ECONOMY*

By Raymond Vernon†

One of the oldest clichés in designing and operating a system of control is that each system must be tailored to its own special purposes. The obvious good sense of this principle, however, is still often honored in the breach.

The Problem in General

The systems of control that are applied to the units of a multinational enterprise typically are launched as an outgrowth of the systems that have been operating inside the U.S. parent organization. To a considerable extent, the extension of the U.S. system to other parts of the enterprise is necessary. When measuring the effectiveness with which money and manpower are being used in various parts of a large organization, standards of measurement that are common to all parts of the organization are required. Otherwise, it will not be possible to compare performance of the various parts.

Difficulties begin to appear, however, when the purpose of the control system is to measure the relative performance of management in different economic environments. This sort of difficulty, it is true, is not altogether unknown to enterprises inside the United States. Managers performing similar jobs in different regions of the country often confront somewhat different business environments; so do managers operating in the same geographical area, when their operations are in different lines of production or marketing. The need to adjust measures of control to suit different circumstances, therefore, is fairly common.

When monitoring performance among different national economies, however, the problem of adjusting measures of control to local circumstances can be expected to increase by some large order of magnitude. Accustomed relationships, generated on the basis of norms in the home country, may prove wholly irrelevant.

---

* Raymond Vernon, *Manager in the International Economy* (revised edition) © 1972. Reprinted by permission of Prentice-Hall, Inc., Englewood Cliffs, N.J. (Excerpts from pp. 233–36.)

† The author is Professor at the Graduate School of Business Administration, Harvard University.

In the control of production, for instance, measures of downtime, absenteeism, materials spoilage, warehouse pilferage, and reject rates vary enormously from one area to the next. In the control of marketing activities, measures of sales productivity, returns and allowances, and similar guides are highly sensitive to national environments. In the control of finance, standards such as collection rates, cash float, and balance sheet relationships can be drastically different from accustomed norms, reflecting different institutions, different rates of inflation, and different habits of operation.

Perhaps the largest problem of all, however, is that of devising a set of measures that appropriately reflect performance as measured against the strategic purposes of the enterprise. Recall that the purposes of establishing a subsidiary in another country, . . . may be such that they cannot be well reflected in the profit and loss statement. The main objective in creating a subsidiary, for instance, may be to reduce the risk of the multinational enterprise as a whole, or to generate knowledge to be exploited by the enterprise as a whole, or for some other purpose external to the subsidiary. Measuring success or failure by the subsidiary's income accounts in this case would not be responsive to its purpose. The appropriate measures would have to be found outside the subsidiary's profit and loss statement.

The Measure of Profit

The reported profit of an enterprise, however, serves many different purposes. Sometimes the purpose is to gauge the performance of a manager, sometimes to estimate the yield on financial resources, sometimes to formulate a proposed buying or selling price for the enterprise itself. Whatever the purpose of the profit figure, a number of problems commonly are encountered in the calculation. . . . Because the object of any subsidiary is to add to the well-being of the multinational enterprise as a whole, it is often desirable to create relationships among the affiliated units affecting their reported profit that would not willingly be assumed by them if they were independent entities.

. . . [In] typical transactions among affiliates, . . . the terms of payment may be decided on the basis of what appears good for the system as a whole, not necessarily for any entity that is a part of the system. For instance, foreign subsidiaries are commonly capitalized with a heavier use of debt and a lesser use of equity than would be likely in the home country of the parent. There are various reasons for the tendency. One has to do with reducing taxable income. When a parent receives funds from a subsidiary representing the repayment of a debt, the parent may not be required to report that repayment to his tax authorities at home as if it were income; if the same funds were received as dividends, the tax treatment would be different. Besides, when a subsidiary pays interest on a debt, this can normally be taken as a cost by the subsidiary that reduces its taxable profit in the host country; but that is not the case when dividends are paid to the parent.

Another reason why debt is sometimes preferred over equity as a means of financing subsidiaries has to do with the right of the subsidiary to remit funds to the parent. Countries that license the remission of funds tend to be more liberal in licensing the repayment of debt than in licensing the payment of dividends or the redemption of equity. The financial structure of the subsidiary, therefore, reflects the interest of the system, not that of the subsidiary alone. Once these facts are clear, of course, the usual measures for gauging profit levels, such as "return-on-investment" rates, can be appropriately adjusted.

Another group of problems, however, stems out of the transfer pricing issue. The prices at which affiliates in a multinational enterprise transfer goods and services among themselves is, of course, determined by many factors, including the tax implications of the choice. Sensitivity to tax considerations is particularly acute when the price assigned to some product or service has no arm's length yardstick and must unavoidably be arbitrary. For instance, the charges are bound to be arbitrary when they represent payment for the administrative services provided by the parent, for access to the parent's information network, or for the use of the parent's trademark and trade name.

Once these prices have been fixed in response to the interests of the system, however, they affect the recorded profit of the subsidiary; sometimes, indeed, the effect is quite powerful. Filtering out these effects for some control purposes, such as the purpose of measuring the quality of local management, turns out to be an exceedingly complex affair in large organizations. There are times, indeed, when the only solution is to maintain a separate set of records for the purpose. In any event, even if so drastic a solution proves unnecessary, extensive adjustments will be needed.

PART IV Decision Making, Management Science, and Human Behavior

ORIGINS OF MANAGEMENT SCIENCE

In the last 15 to 20 years, one approach to managerial decision making has arisen which has been variously called "operations research," "management science," or "quantitative methods." Courses under one or more of these labels now occupy an important place in the curriculum of schools of administration. At the time this book is written, the field of management science is characterized principally by a certain set of policy-type problems which apply mathematics and statistics or which apply the logic of the payoff matrix. The problems of finance and accounting already covered in Part III also use numbers and quantities. That one group of problems and techniques has come to be called "finance" and another group of problems has come to be called "operations research/ management science" is partly a result of historical accident. Finance and accounting were developed by those interested in planning and recording investment decisions of the type already seen in AB Thorsten or Continental Electric Company; or in planning and recording the current operating expense budget of the type seen in Norman Manufacturing Company.

The origins of management science courses is well known. The British Government, in World War II, needed fast solutions to a number of action problems it faced in defending the British Isles. It called upon a group of academic men from several disciplines. Not only mathematicians, but also sociologists and other specialists were asked to apply the fundamental *phenomena* from their particular fields, and to apply the *methods* of science, to practical managerial problems. In the United States, the U.S. Government established a similar effort, among other places, at the Johns Hopkins University.

In its early usage, "operations research" meant "research into operating problems." It carried a heavy bias toward looking at operating problems first, and then seeing what content or methods from various sciences might be applicable to those problems. It also meant drawing on a variety of physical and social sciences. In these two respects, the early meanings of management science were not unlike the approach used throughout all six parts of the present volume.

But shortly after its inception, management science took on a somewhat different meaning, both to its practitioners and to curriculum builders in schools of administration. It became dominated by mathematics and quantification. We have already seen in the introductory chapters that quantification has been *one* of the key attributes of science, and that this has certain powerful advantages for controlling nature. Today's management science departments in schools of administration mostly offer courses which specialize in applied mathematics. The Institute of Management Sciences is composed primarily of staff men in industry and professors in universities who are specialists in mathematical techniques.

POWER AND LIMITATIONS OF SCIENCE IN MANAGEMENT

In an age of larger and more complex organizations, it seems vital that most managers must have some knowledge and skill in solving those kinds of problems that lend themselves to mathematical decision making. Readers will recognize as they study the whole book that (1) management science of the mathematical variety is only *one* of the ways in which to use the various physical and social sciences in management, and that (2) it is perhaps more accurate to say "use of *science in management*" than it is to imply that there is such a thing as one *science of management.* Management, or policy (action) decision making is a *profession* which draws on many scientific disciplines. It puts emphasis on policy decisions first, and science as a technique second. It requires the attitudes of a professional who recognizes both the powers and limitations of science, who recognizes that different sciences can actually prescribe conflicting action solutions to him, and who has skill in balancing and reconciling such conflicts. Carrying through the theme set for *The Managerial Mind* in the introductory chapters, it will be the purposes of Part IV:

1. To examine a range of mathematical and statistical techniques that are used by managers in action (policy) problems.
2. To examine a sample of the problem areas which lend themselves to such techniques.
3. To show the advantages of such techniques as well as their limitations in practice. Particularly, human behavior, the subject of psychology and sociology, often determines when mathematical rationality will work and when it will not.
4. To develop the attitude that managerial decision making almost always involves a trade-off (compromise, balance) between rational factors of management science, on the one hand, and human factors, on the other.
5. To gain some skill, through case practice, in tailoring a professional decision to the particular operations of a certain firm and its specific people; in effect, making the above trade-offs.

6. To show how decision techniques from mathematics operate as one factor which determines the organization *structure* of the enterprise.

THE PHILOSOPHICAL IMPORTANCE OF MANAGEMENT SCIENCE

Before studying more about managerial use of mathematical techniques, the manager has a right to ask, "Why are these techniques ultimately important—why are they *good*?" This is a philosophical question. A question of what is good in life.

One importance has to do with the dictates of society outside the firm. We shall not repeat here the material from the introductions to Parts II and III. The argument is similar in the case of managerial uses of all rational sciences, and particularly similar to use of financial techniques in Part III. In summary, society depends on (1) the production of goods and services and (2) at an acceptable level of efficiency. The manager who does not operate his organization with these two goals in mind might suffer two kinds of penalties. First, he may in fact find that society "out there" no longer supports him and the organization in legal charter terms, in terms of public attitudes, or in terms of day-to-day monetary payments. In the last analysis, nobody wants to waste the natural resources of society when efficient ways exist to get the same products with less waste of manpower and raw materials. In addition, those who have ethical beliefs about the responsibilities of managers to society will penalize themselves if they run sloppy organizations that are wasteful. Managers must, as is pointed out in Part VI, observe social dicta about the good life *other than* efficiency and production, but this does not mean that they can at the same time abrogate the latter responsibilities.

EXAMPLES OF QUANTITATIVE TECHNIQUES AND MANAGERIAL PROBLEMS

One of the earliest mathematical techniques applied to work in organizations is that of work measurement. It does not employ as sophisticated techniques of mathematics as "the new management science." In fact, it is the product of an earlier movement called "scientific management." But the traditional nature of this set of techniques should not cloud the fact that work measurement is widely used through the world in the 70s. In terms of manufacturing applications, hardly a factory can be found in the developed countries of Europe, Japan, Russia, and the U.S. which does not make some use of such techniques. In developing countries such as India, this trend is likewise noticeable.

The extension of such techniques to nonmanufacturing enterprise continues to progress. The Family Service Association of America, for example, has been in effect told by some Community Chest charity boards across the nation that their social case workers are not efficient when compared to other agencies such as workers in the poverty program or the Boy Scouts. Many who disperse funds for charity have intimated that unless the family counseling agencies use some form of work measurement to show how much actual service is rendered for the money spent, they may get less funds: funds will be put to a use where the public gets more efficient social service. The Metropolitan Life Insurance Company, along with other companies in the industry, has consistently applied work measurement to paper work as contrasted with physical production in a factory. And the Czechoslovakian Government quite recently has sponsored research to apply the concept to many types of endeavor in order to help raise the gross national product.

Study of the National Motor Parts case will enable one who has not been exposed to this technique to see how it is supposed to operate in practice, and how it does in fact operate.

The more glamorous techniques developed recently are used in other cases in Part IV. The owner of the Sea Breeze Motel experiments with probability theory in order to see how many reservations he must take. Because many customers make reservations and then do not show up, he tries to predict how many "no shows" there will be so that he can decide how many reservations to take. Neither the motel owner nor society wins if scarce resources are invested in empty rooms.

In Midwest Hardware Manufacturing Company, the managers struggle with a particular type of problem faced by managers in various kinds of business—the inventory problem, as it is referred to in operations research literature. They use probabilities and formulas to tell them how much of their resources to tie up in finished goods inventories and inventories of raw materials and semifinished products kept on hand.

In Western Office Equipment Company, the top management is concerned with determining just the right number of salesmen to employ in order to sell the most office equipment at the least cost in human manpower. They want to know how many salesmen are required in Salt Lake City, San Francisco, Vancouver, and Seattle. A management science staff specialist, recently graduated from a school of administration, takes on the job of applying marginal economics to this problem. Since the amount of resources required in every branch depends in part on that in every other branch, he must have a notion of systems analysis if he is to be successful.

In Lightronics, Inc., one can see how the management uses some more sophisticated logic devices (along with quantification devices) to decide what price to charge for a new fire alarm system it is about to produce, and whether or not to build one kind of factory or another. A decision tree, a technique to help the manager arrange his logic, may be used. The concept of bounded rationality, under which the manager tries to make a "reasonable" decision without spending his life searching for precise proof which may be nonexistent, is also of use. Finally, one sees that different men in the company have different attitudes toward "numbers." Their decision criteria based on these attitudes is a source of human conflict.

MANAGERIAL (POLICY) DECISION MAKING

Sometimes the application of mathematical techniques, and the logic of the pay-off matrix, are called "decision making." This is a perfectly acceptable usage of the term provided that one recognizes that this is a *particular kind* of decision making. As one professor of English literature once said in a curriculum committee meeting at Columbia University, "I don't understand how you can call this operations research course simply decision making in general. I, too, am teaching decision making. Students who gain profound insights about human nature through study of literature can make wiser decisions in the future."

Decision making by use of quantitative techniques is a form of decision making which attempts to reduce the factors in a decision to rational alternatives (strategies, courses of action), to isolate those variables which can be measured, and to manipulate numbers so that the weight of the various factors indicate which alternative to choose. In order to comply with the second of these steps, most administrative applications measure more "thing" factors than they do "people" factors. In order to comply with the third step, most applications reduce all factors in a decision to costs or revenues, or both.

Thus, management science tends to have in common with the older scientific management, the goal of technological efficiency. That this is a worthy goal has already been established.

But this book is addressed to policy formulation, or managerial decision making in a broader sense. While it is hoped that an important byproduct of studying Part IV will be *knowledge* of valuable mathematical tools, it is also hoped that another byproduct will be *knowledge* of some valuable concepts (nonquantifiable) about human behavior, politics in organizations, and ways of coordinating organizations.

If these are byproducts, then what is the principal product? It is skill, ability, and judgment of the individual human brain in making sense of both at once, in thinking through the whole problem. It is seeing how "things" are related to "people," when mathematical techniques will work and when they will not, how quantified rational facts must be traded off against nonquantifiable human nature and organizational politics. These, together with the relevant knowledge of techniques and theories, are equally important in *The Managerial Mind.*

11. MIDWEST HARDWARE MANUFACTURING COMPANY

Case Introduction

SYNOPSIS

Recently, Midwest Hardware Manufacturing Company was in the midst of a substantial expansion program designed to increase its capacity to meet the steadily increasing demand for its products. Midwest's management was determined to finance the expansion with internally generated funds, and was therefore seeking all possible means to maximize its allocation of the cash available. A survey of current inventory control practices indicates that a large amount of funds can be released from the inventory account for more productive allocation elsewhere. Also, a revamped method of ordering component parts for assembly would bring significant savings in operating expenses. A mathematical model is used to compute optimum inventory levels and optimum purchase lot sizes.

In connection with this program, the new inventory control system was adopted and implemented. Some three months later, when the new system is evaluated by Midwest's management, results appear quite disappointing. Predicted benefits have not been realized, and some unforeseen problems have arisen. Management must decide whether the new system should be continued, modified, or abandoned.

WHY THIS CASE IS INCLUDED

Midwest's concern over the short supply of working capital—concentrating on internally generated cash as the source of funds—and the best use of such funds—allocation to inventory, receivables, fixed assets, and so on—highlights the influence of economic and financial matters on policy making. Not only does the adequacy of the sources of funds set parameters, or boundaries, around the alternatives open to management, but the same factor also acts as a stimulant and pressure to plan carefully and design effective policies for the allocation of funds.

Analyzing the use of the mathematical model for inventory control has value of itself, but this case raises the larger issue of the benefits and limitations of scientific rationality (operations research techniques) in business policy formulation. Science is pitted against "judgment." The utilization of techniques of scientific rationality affects the relationships among people and even alters organization structure. the unshared expertise of the specialist further complicates the traditional line-staff conflicts. The issue of the desirability and feasibility of subordinate participation in management decisions and action is also raised. Finally, the case offers the opportunity to examine the economic theory relating to the use of overhead departments in various size enterprises (here considering the new inventory system comparable to the introduction of a service department or overhead unit).

DIAGNOSTIC AND PREDICTIVE QUESTIONS

The readings included with this case are marked (*). The author index at the end of this book locates the other readings.

1. In what way has the short supply of funds affected the policy making of Midwest's management? Recall from the case that Mr. Gilbert, the president, pointed to the strain on working capital caused by recent expansion moves. Relate this concern to Maxon's comment: "I've always felt that we have far too much cash tied up in inventories of components awaiting assembly."

Read: Anthony, *Management Accounting,* pp. 290–92, 306.

2. Why did Maxon have more confidence in "hard thinking and close calculating" than in "flying by the seat of our pants"?

Read: *Lieber and Lieber, *The Education of T. C. Mits,* pp. 44–49.

3. What are the advantages of Maxon's "science" as compared to Iverson's "judgment"?

Read: *Taylor, "Principles of Scientific Management." Barber, *Science and the Social Order,* pp. 7–8, 12–13, 18, 21.

4. What assumptions are inherent in the inventory control model adopted by Maxon? Are all such assumptions justified by conditions in Midwest's plant? How closely would you expect Maxon's model to predict the savings to be achieved by the new system?

(A close examination of the data and formulae in the exhibits should permit an evaluation of Maxon's use of the inventory control model. More detailed discussion of the techniques used by Maxon, if required, may be found in: David Miller and M. K. Starr, *Executive Decisions and Operations Research* (Englewood Cliffs, N.J.: Prentice-Hall, Inc., 1960), Chapter 10.

5. Was Hennessey right in claiming that operations research techniques are only feasible for use in large corporations?

Read: *Marshall, *Principles of Economics,* pp. 283–85. Summer, "Economies of Scale and Organization Structure."

6. In modifying its inventory controls the management of Midwest went through at least six phases: *(a)* search for ways of increasing the available working capital, *(b)* investigation of the Iverson inventory control system, *(c)* computation of optimum stock levels and reorder quanti-

ties, *(d)* explanation of the new system and training of personnel, *(e)* implementation and administration of the new system during shakedown period, *(f)* evaluation of results. To what extent did all the interested parties participate in this process as a whole? What advantages—if any—could be gained by having subordinate participation in each phase of the process? Are there reasons which would make participation impossible or undesirable in specific phases?

   Read: McGregor, *Human Side of Enterprise,* pp. 124–30. Newman and Summer, *The Process of Management: Concepts, Behavior, and Practice,* pp. 439–48. Odiorne, *How Managers Make Things Happen,* pp. 5–11, 37–38, 52–53. Jennings, "Business Needs Mature Autocrats." *Taylor, "Testimony before the Special House Committee Investigating the Taylor and Other Systems," pp. 211–13, 215–17.

   7. Was Maxon's role in the entire process one of a line manager or a staff specialist? What should his role have been? It has been said that knowledge is power. (Francis Bacon, 1561–1626, *Religious Meditations —Of Heresies:* "Nam et ipsa scientia potestas est." Knowledge itself is power.) Does this in any way dictate what role Maxon, as an expert in operations research, will necessarily play in the organization?

   Read: *Hobbes, *Leviathan.* *Lasswell and Kaplan, *Power and Society,* pp. 157–59. Thompson, *Modern Organization,* pp. 4–6, 12–13, 19–21, 61, 63–65, 77–78. Carr *et al., American Democracy in Theory and Practice,* pp. 214–19. Etzioni, "Authority Structure and Organizational Effectiveness."

   8. In setting objective and fixed standards for inventory ordering and evaluating compliance with the new procedures, should Maxon have expected Iverson to welcome the new system or resist it?

   Read: *Argyris, "Human Problems with Budgets." Newman and Summer, *Process of Management: Concepts, Behavior, and Practice,* pp. 605–10.

   9. As the implementation of the new system evolved, should Mr. Gilbert have been able to predict that Iverson would feel he was "the guy in the middle" between Hennessey and Maxon? If so, should he have insisted that Iverson take orders from one superior only?

   Read: Fayol, *General and Industrial Management,* pp. 24–25, 68–70. Taylor, "Shop Management," pp. 92–96, 98–100. McGregor, *The Human Side of Enterprise,* pp. 124–31, 172–75.

   10. Reasoning from the logic of the scientific inventory method and its use in Midwest, why didn't Maxon's new system produce the results hoped for? Recall that at the executive committee's last meeting Hennessey stated he could see many practical difficulties which Maxon's figures did not show (e.g., low morale, quality deterioration, component C stamping costs, etc.).

   Read: *Buffa, *Modern Production Management,* pp. 442–43, 450–51, 471. Miller and Starr, *Executive Decisions and Operations Research,* pp. 38–42, 45–47, 50. Lindblom, "The Science of 'Muddling Through.' "

   11. In studying the formalization, rationalization, or bureaucratiza-

tion of organizations, sociologists have developed the notion of the dysfunctions of bureaucracy—unforeseen and undesirable consequences resulting from efforts to formalize procedures, rules, structure, and so on. Would a knowledge of this notion have helped Gilbert anticipate such things as the hoarding of parts by the foremen and the interdepartment "wars"? Would it have helped him to design preventive policies?

Read: Merton, "Bureaucratic Structure and Personality."

POLICY QUESTIONS

12. Knowing Midwest's need for more working capital, what other ways seem feasible for dealing with the problem—other than Maxon's effort to release cash from inventories and cut operating costs? (See Question 1 and its readings.)

13. Could you have done anything with the operations research technique itself to make the Maxon inventory model conform better to the concrete circumstances of the Midwest situation? (See Questions 4 and 10 with their attached readings.)

14. If you had been Gilbert, the president, would you have directed Maxon's efforts any differently? Why? Or, why not? (See Questions 6, 7, 8, 9, and 11 with their attached readings.) As president, would you have encouraged more participation of subordinates in the design and implementation of the new system? In which—if any—of the six phases of the process (identified in Question 6) would you have desired more participation?

15. Had you been Maxon, would you have handled your relationship with Iverson any differently? Why? Or, why not? (See Questions 6 and 8 and their attached readings.)

16. What should Gilbert do now about the inventory control system?

QUESTIONS FOR ORIGINAL STUDENT WORK IN ANALYSIS AND POLICY

17. While reflecting on case facts, what additional theories from prior education give you insights as to "what is going on" in Midwest Hardware Manufacturing Company? As to what might be predicted to happen in the future?

18. Other than the policy questions asked by the authors, what pragmatic ways can you think of to state the practical problems faced by executives in the case?

Case Text*

THE COMPANY AND ITS PRODUCTS

Midwest Hardware is an old-line, well-known manufacturer of hardware, plumbing supplies, spigots, valves, and other construction accessories for residential and industrial use. The assembly, finishing, and testing of its products comprise the bulk of the company's manufacturing operations. Only a small portion of the components are manufactured by Midwest itself, the majority being purchased from a relatively few near-by suppliers, most of whom are located in the same city as Midwest's plant. Almost every supplier of components had been doing business with Midwest for many years, and relations have generally been close and satisfactory between the company and its suppliers.

Annual sales volume has been fairly stable at around $28 million for the past seven years, and the work force has averaged some 300 employees. Thomas Gilbert, Jr., Midwest's president, believes that, although the company has not grown much in the past few years, it has established an outstanding reputation for quality and dependability of its products. To support his claim that the company is among the leaders in its field, he cites the fact that Midwest currently has a full year's backlog of orders on many of its products. Mr. Gilbert has recently initiated an expansion program, designed to increase manufacturing capacity by additions to plant space, machinery, and equipment. This expansion program was spurred by a rising level of regional construction activity and by market surveys forecasting a doubling of the demand for Midwest's products within the next eight years.

At the monthly meeting of the executive committee in April, Mr. Gilbert reviewed the progress of the expansion program to date, and concluded with the comment that growth was indeed exciting and satisfying, but its resultant strain on working capital was becoming evident. The balance of the meeting was devoted to discussion of working capital needs and conservation. John Wm. Maxon, the company's controller, emphasized the importance of conserving internally generated cash funds by minimizing the use of scarce cash on nonessentials. "As a prime example of what I mean," Maxon stated, "I've always felt that we have far too much cash tied up in inventories of components awaiting assembly. A whole battery of new techniques have been developed in so-called Operations Research, designed to minimize inventory costs; yet we're

---

still flying by the seat of our pants when it comes to our inventories. I firmly believe that some hard thinking and close calculating can yield pretty impressive savings in this area."

Joseph Hennessey, vice president–production, agreed that some savings might be achievable, but pointed out that production personnel had neither the time nor the mathematical backgrounds to apply O. R. methods to inventory problems. It was then agreed that Maxon would undertake an investigation of Midwest's present inventory controls and then present any recommendations he may have at the next meeting.

PRESENT METHOD OF COMPONENT INVENTORY CONTROLS

All component inventories in the plant are under the control of Peter Iverson, head foreman in charge of assembly, manufacturing, and receiving. Iverson initiates all orders for components—whether manufactured in the plant or purchased outside—and has been doing so for many years. He relies primarily on frequent inspections of inventories on hand, observations of "how things stood in each department," and periodic checks with his foremen and their requirements. Whenever Iverson judges the time is ripe, he enters a buy or make order for the needed component. Over the years Iverson has established a standard order size, in terms of number of units, for each component used.

Thus order quantities are held constant for each item, while the frequency of placing orders will vary with the rate at which components are taken into production. Since output rates and product mixes have historically been quite stable, there has been a high degree of constancy in the frequency of orders for each major component. The ordering procedure followed by Iverson is, in effect, a variant of the traditional "two bin" system, under which inventories are physically divided between two separate bins or storage areas. As one bin is exhausted, a standard-size lot order is placed, while withdrawals are continued from the second bin. Iverson believes that operating results confirm the soundness of his inventory control system: "There may be some talk about me playing it extra-safe, but Mr. Hennessey or anybody else will tell you that we've *never* been out of stock on any part we needed in all the years I've been in charge of the inventory."

ANALYSIS OF PRESENT CONTROL SYSTEM

At the May meeting of the executive committee (consisting of the president and all the department heads), Maxon was ready to present the findings of his investigation of Iverson's present component inventory controls. He reported that he had a detailed analysis of the components needed for a typical Midwest product—a gas furnace control unit— referred to as "GFC-5" on the company's product line lists.

The GFC-5 unit is assembled from five components (labeled A through E in all exhibits), of which four were purchased, and one was manufactured by Midwest. Exhibit 1 presents a simplified product flow chart for the GFC-5 superimposed on an organization chart identifying relevant supervisory personnel. Also shown is the monthly requirement of each

EXHIBIT 1
Midwest Hardware Manufacturing Company—Product Flow and Relevant Organization Chart

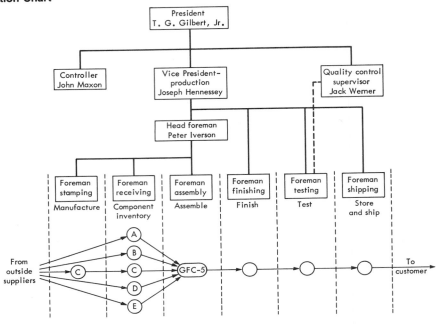

component for meeting current output levels of 5,000 GFC-5 units per month (see Exhibit 2).

Maxon distributed copies of his analysis sheets to all participants in the meeting (reproduced on Exhibits 3 and 4).

Referring to Exhibit 3, the analysis of Iverson's present practices, Maxon explained that he had calculated—from accounting records—the average value of inventories Iverson had been carrying for each GFC-5 component. (These are presented in Column 6.) He next computed the average value of the "circulating" inventory (Column 5), based on the assumptions graphed in Exhibit 4. Maxon explained that circulating inventory was derived by dividing the order lot size typically used by Iverson (Column 3) by two, thereby getting the average inventory of each component needed to meet the monthly requirements of the assembly operation. He then multiplied these units of circulating inventory (Column 5). By subtracting average circulating inventory from total inventory, he then arrived at the average value of "safety stocks" presently being carried (Column 7).

"Exhibit 3 tells us," said Maxon, "that we've had an average of $33,450

(Column 6) tied up in components for the GFC-5, and that of this amount an average of $13,155 (Column 7) was never circulated into production, but was tied up permanently as a safety cushion against a possible run-out. Safety stocks are in effect equivalent to an insurance premium

EXHIBIT 2

Midwest Hardware Manufacturing Company—Monthly Component Requirement for 5,000 Units of GFC-5 per Month

Component	Number Needed for Each GFC-5	Net Monthly Requirement	Monthly Requirement Including Allowance for Rejects, Waste	Unit Cost	Make or Buy
A 1	5,000	5,000	$9.50	B
B 1	5,000	5,000	4.00	B
C 2	10,000	10,900	1.75	M
D 4	20,000	22,000	.23	B
E 1	5,000	5,000	.95	B

EXHIBIT 3

Midwest Hardware Manufacturing Company—Components for GFC-5 Present Inventory Levels and Ordering Practices

Component	(1) Monthly Requirement in Units (D)	(2) Unit Cost (P)	(3) Order Lot Size in Units (Z)	(4) Number of Orders per Month $\left(\dfrac{D}{Z}\right)$	(5) Average Value of Circulating Inventory $\left(\dfrac{\dot{Z}}{2} \times P\right)$	(6) Average Value of Inventory Actually Carried from Accounting Records	(7) Average Value of "Safety Stock" (Col. 6 − Col. 5)
A	5,000	$9.50	1,900	2.63	$ 9,025	$14,728	$ 5,703
B	5,000	4.00	1,800	2.78	3,600	6,802	3,202
C 10,900	1.75	5,000	2.18	4,375	6,985	2,610
D 22,000	.23	8,000	2.75	920	1,612	692
E	5,000	.95	5,000	1.00	2,375	3,323	948
					$20,295	$33,450	$13,155

against runouts, and it's my contention that we're paying a high premium to cover an almost negligible risk. Quantitative analysis tells us that in setting up levels of safety stocks we must balance the cost of carrying this stock against the *cost* and *probability* of a runout on any component. The cost of running out of any component is usually tough to estimate, since it requires placing a value on the cost of missed sales and production downtime. In our case, I think it's reasonable to place this cost at close to zero. With a year's backlog of orders we're not liable to lose *any* sales, and with our flexible assembly schedules there's no reason for any downtime due to missing parts. We can easily switch assembly to other products until the missing parts come in. Furthermore the *probability* of running out, in our case, is just about negligible. Our suppliers

EXHIBIT 4
Midwest Hardware Manufacturing Company Schematic Diagram of Inventory Model

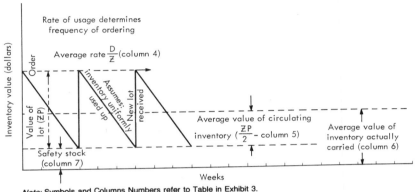

Note: Symbols and Columns Numbers refer to Table in Exhibit 3.

are highly reliable; they are very close to us and will do their darndest to deliver right on time. We could, theoretically, get by with no safety stocks whatsoever, but I'd say a stock of one or two days' production would be ample."

PROPOSED CONTROL SYSTEM

Maxon proceeded to outline the proposed inventory control system he had developed, as tabulated in Exhibit 5. By comparing Exhibits 3 and 5, he pointed out that his analytical approach to the problem achieved significant reductions in the levels of both "circulating" (Column 5 versus Column 12) and "safety" (Column 7 versus Column 13) stocks, so that the total component inventory for the GFC-5, carried by Midwest, was reduced in value from an average of $33,450 to $19,291 (Column 6 versus Column 14).

Safety stocks were reduced to a level representing one to two days' production for the reasons cited by Maxon in criticizing the present system. Circulating inventories were reduced by the application of a computing technique which establishes optimum order lot sizes for each component. By balancing the cost of placing and receiving an order against the cost of carrying the parts in inventory, this technique establishes the size of lots to be ordered so as to minimize total inventory costs.

"After quite a bit of digging around," said Maxon, "we've calculated that it costs us $11 to place a purchase order, inspect, receive, and store it in place. In the illustration worked out in Exhibit 5 we have used the symbol C_1 to indicate these ordering costs. On the other hand, we figure that it costs us 19 cents a year for every dollar we have tied up in inventory—this is based on our cost of capital of 12 percent, plus an additional 7 percent representing insurance, space charges, loss, waste, etc. In the illustration worked out in Exhibit 5 we have used the symbol C_2 to indicate these carrying costs. We use both these values, for the C_1 and C_2 factors, in the equations we set up to determine optimum lot size. Any of you who are interested in the methods used can follow the example in Exhibit 5.

EXHIBIT 5
Midwest Hardware Manufacturing Company—Components for GFC-5 optimal inventory levels and lot sizes—as proposed by Controller's office

Components	(8) Monthly Requirement in Units (D)	(9) Unit Cost (P)	(10) Optimal Order Lot Size in Units (Z)	(11) Number of Orders per Month $\left(\dfrac{D}{Z}\right)$	(12) Average Value of Circulating Inventory $\left(\dfrac{Z}{2} \times P\right)$	(13) Average Value of "Safety Stock" (1–2 Day's Production)	(14) Average Value of Inventory to Be Carried (Col. 12 + Col. 13)
A	5,000	$9.50	860*	5.81	$ 4,085	$3,800	$ 7,885
B	5,000	4.00	1,300	3.85	2,600	1,600	4,200
C	10,900	1.75	2,900	3.76	2,537	1,225	3,762
D	22,000	.23	11,500	1.91	1,322	460	1,782
E	5,000	.95	2,700	1.85	1,282	380	1,662
					$11,826	$7,465	$19,291

*Illustration of method of determining optimal order lot size

Component A

$$\text{Optimum Lot Size } Z = \sqrt{\frac{2DC_1}{PC_2}}$$

where: C_1 = cost of ordering, receiving, inspecting, etc. = $11.00 per order;
    C_2 = .016 since cost of carrying inventory = 19% of its value per year, or

$$\frac{.19}{12} = .016 \text{ per month.}$$

For Component A:

$$Z_A = \sqrt{\frac{2 \times 5.000 \times 11}{9.50 \times .016}} = \sqrt{723,684} = 851 \text{ units}$$

Rounding off: $Z_A = 860$ units—inserted in Row A, Column 10, above. In similar fashion, optimal lot sizes are calculated for components B, C, D, and E.

"Now let me show you that the proposed inventory control system will yield a number of significant benefits, both immediate and long-run.

"Initially, we should have a significant amount of cash released from

EXHIBIT 6
Midwest Hardware Manufacturing Company—Comparison of Order and Carrying Costs of "Circulating" Component inventories—present and proposed methods

$$\text{Total inventory costs, } TC = \underbrace{\frac{DC_1}{Z}}_{\substack{\text{Total ordering} \\ \text{cost per month}}} + \underbrace{\frac{ZC_2}{2}}_{\substack{\text{Total carrying} \\ \text{cost per month}}}$$

$$\text{where } C_1 = \$11.00 \\ C_2 = .016 \left.\right\} \text{ see Exhibit 5}$$

Present Method

Component	(15) Order Cost $\frac{D}{Z} \times 11.00$ (Col. 4) × (C₁)	(16) Carrying Cost $\frac{ZP}{2} \times .016$ (Col. 5) × (C₂)	(17) Total Cost (per Month) (15 + 16)
A......	$ 28.93	$144.40	$173.33
B	30.58	57.60	88.18
C	23.98	70.00	93.98
D	30.25	14.72	44.97
E........	11.00	38.00	49.00
	$124.74	$324.72	$449.46

Proposed Method

Component	(18) Order Cost $\frac{D}{Z} \times 11.00$ (Col. 11) × (C₁)	(19) Carrying Cost $\frac{ZP}{2} \times .016$ (Col. 12) × (C₂)	(20) Total Cost (per Month) (18 + 19)	(21) Saving in Total Cost (per Month) (17 − 20)
A......	$ 63.91	$ 65.36	$129.27	$44.06
B	42.35	41.60	83.95	4.23
C	41.36	40.59	81.95	12.03
D	21.01	21.15	42.16	2.81
E........	20.35	20.51	40.86	8.14
	$188.98	$189.21	$378.19	$71.27

inventory to help us in our problems with working capital. Just by reducing the average value of the GFC-5 inventories from the present $33,450 (Column 6) to the proposed $19,291 level (Column 14), we will immediately release some $14,000 of sorely needed cash. This is about 42 percent of the cash we now have tied up in GFC-5 components. If a like percentage can be drawn out of all our inventories, I would guess we're talking about something in the order of $100,000 added to our working capital. That ain't hay in any league.

"We can also put dollar and cents signs on savings on ordering and carrying costs. The proposed system will allow us to cut our operating expenses. First, Exhibit 6 compares the order and carrying costs of the *circulating component inventories* under the present system run by Iverson and our proposed system. Again, we use the GFC-5 components as our example. Monthly savings in costs of this type amount to $71.27 (Column 21). Second, Exhibit 7 compares the carrying costs of the *safety stocks* under the present Iverson system and our proposed system. Annual savings here amount to $1,018.10 (Column 26). Exhibit 8 summarizes these two aspects of the savings on operating expenses. Notice that the total annual saving is in excess of $1,900 for the GFC-5 components alone (Column 29). Assuming comparable results in all our other products, I'd guess at annual savings of over $15,000—certainly an attractive piece of change to pick up without any extra work, effort or investment on our part. It's simply a byproduct of using scientific methods to determine the proper inventory levels and reorder quantities."

In response to Mr. Gilbert's concern that suppliers may raise their unit prices as a result of the reduced order sizes, Maxon replied that he had already checked out several of the key suppliers. "They'll go along with us, and will hold their prices even on smaller individual orders as long as our annual purchases run at about the same volume we've been giving

EXHIBIT 7

Midwest Hardware Manufacturing Company—Comparison of Carrying Costs of "Safety Stocks" (present and proposed methods)

Present Method		Proposed Method		
(22) Average Value of "Safety Stock" (See Col. 7)	(23) Annual Carrying Cost of "Safety Stock" $(13,155 \times C_2)$	(24) Average Value of "Safety Stock" (See Col. 13)	(25) Annual Carrying Cost of "Safety Stock" $(7,465 \times C_2)$	(26) Annual Savings $(23 - 25)$
$13,155	$2,499.45	$7,465	$1,418.35	$1,081.10

them. They're just as anxious as we are to see us expand our sales volume, and just as quickly as possible."

EXHIBIT 8

Midwest Hardware Manufacturing Company — Summary of Annual Savings in Operating Costs by Using the Proposed System Instead of the Present System

(27) Annual Savings in Ordering and Carrying Costs of the Circulating Component Inventories (Col. 21 × 12 Months)	(28) Annual Savings in Carrying Costs of "Safety Stocks" (Col. 26)	(29) Total Annual Savings in Operating Costs under Proposed System (Col. 27 + Col. 28)
$855.24	$1,081.10	$1,936.34

Maxon's proposals were discussed at some length, and it was unanimously agreed that he should proceed to implement his suggestions as rapidly as possible. Hennessey again questioned the competence of his production personnel and their ability to devote the necessary time needed to install the new system. He did not foresee any problems, however, in their operating with the system once installed. "That means, John," said Hennessey to Maxon, "that it'll be up to you to get the thing going and do all the necessary missionary work. I'll certainly tell my boys to cooperate with you fully." Maxon was quite agreeable to undertaking the task and stated he would proceed as rapidly as possible.

IMPLEMENTATION OF NEW SYSTEM

By early June, Maxon had completed his calculations for all major components used by Midwest, and had prepared a set of procedure outlines and guide sheets for implementation of the new ordering system. On June 4 he called a meeting of all foremen and inventory clerks at which Joe Hennessey was also present. Maxon outlined Midwest's urgent need for working capital in its current expansion program. He then proceeded to explain the importance of establishing optimum order lot sizes and minimal safety stock levels. Maxon distributed the same exhibit sheets he had used in his presentation at the executive committee meetings, although his explanations were given on a more elementary level. "Don't worry too much about the formulas and tables," he suggested, "the most important thing you should note is the savings the company is going to get out of this new system. I know it'll mean writing up more orders per month than you've been dong so far, but the cost of this extra work is all allowed for in the calculations we've made and, as you see, we come out well ahead of the game."

Hennessey initiated the discussion of Maxon's presentation by stating that he too was anxious to achieve any possible savings, and that as far as he could see Maxon's ideas appeared to make good sense. "You fellows will be dealing with this new system, and you're familiar with our inventory problems," he told the group, "so let's hear your reactions to Mr. Maxon's proposals." In the discussion that followed most foremen felt they were not qualified to evaluate the mathematical computations involved and, with various degrees of reservation, agreed that the new system deserved a trial. Pointing out that Iverson would be in charge of the system, when installed, Hennessey asked for any suggestons he might have. "For a guy who had trouble with high school math" Iverson replied, "I can't claim that I understand all the figures. It doesn't seem to me that I've been loading up too heavy on parts, but I guess I could've been. I guess I was just naturally more concerned with the smooth running of the shop than with the theoretical costs involved." Iverson, after pointing out that he couldn't really tell how things would work out from just looking at tables of figures, agreed he would do his best to adapt to the new system.

Maxon spent the next two weeks distributing lists of proposed inventory levels and reorder lot sizes for all major components to the foremen and clerks involved. He devoted as much time as he could to explaining the lists and procedures to Iverson, and overseeing the ordering of any specific components which happened to come up during his visits with Iverson. While Maxon was devoting much of his time to the inventory system installation, he found that some of his other duties were being unavoidably neglected. He was, therefore, quite relieved when, towards the end of June, he felt that Iverson and the other foremen were acquiring the necessary familiarity and competence in the new system and could be safely left to their own devices. Before returning to a full-time pursuit of his controller's duties, Maxon set up a monthly summary form to be maintained by Iverson's chief clerk. The form was designed to show monthly average inventory levels and reorder quantities, by components, from which Maxon could compute actual reductions and savings for comparison with the newly set standards. Maxon felt that it would probably take three to four months for the new procedures to "shake down." Accordingly, he informed Mr. Gilbert that he would be ready to present the results of his drive on component inventories at the October meeting of the executive committee.

During the "shakedown" period, Mason made it his business to pay Iverson a visit or two a month and to ask how things were coming along. Iverson reported that he was doing his best to follow the new inventory procedures whenever his day-to-day production problems permitted it. He made a few attempts to point out some of those production problems, which seemed to be increasing in recent weeks. Maxon, conscious of his limited competence in production problems, and careful not to overstep his functional authority, suggested that Iverson discuss his manufacturing problems with Hennessey, "one of the best production men in our industry." After one of Maxon's visits, Iverson turned to his stamping foreman and said: "Boy, am I the guy in the middle! Hennessey tells me my troubles all come from this inventory system and to see Maxon, and Maxon tells me to go see Hennessey. One way or another I'm as busy as a one-armed paperhanger."

THE NEW SYSTEM REVIEWED

At the October meeting of the executive committee Mr. Gilbert called on John Maxon to present his scheduled evaluation of the new inventory procedures installed in June. Maxon reported that he was most disappointed in the results to date. His summary records showed that some reduction in inventory levels was indeed achieved, but that it was a long way from the goals he had established. Using the GFC-5 components again as a typical example, Maxon reported that average inventory levels were reduced by only about $5,000, as against the goal of $14,000 computed in his original presentations. Monthly total costs of ordering and carrying inventories showed an almost negligible reduction, well below the $1,900 annual rate predicted. The reasons for this disappointing performance, Maxon pointed out, were quite self-evident from his summary records. Iverson had only cut back his "safety stocks" by some $3,500 (instead of the proposed $5,690), and had adopted the recommended optimum order lot size in only 40 percent of his reordering. "The solution is as obvious as the cause of the failure," claimed Maxon. "Iverson is just not competent to be in charge of a system which requires some understanding of mathematical techniques and at least some appreciation of costs. Sure, Iverson can understand a price-tag of $9.50 on each 'A' component he orders, but he just has no idea of how much it costs us to have it lying around. If we're ever going to succeed in putting some of the modern mathematical techiques to work for us, we've got to have people who understand what it's all about. It is my recommendation that we pull Iverson off the inventory control job and put in some bright kid who's had some accounting or record-keeping experience. This inventory thing isn't the only modernization in plant methods that we're going to have, so we might as well face the issue and put in some people who can move with the times."

Hennessey strongly objected to Maxon's analysis of the situation. Iverson, he pointed out, was a top-notch foreman who knew his job and had demonstrated his ability to perform it for many years. The fault was not in Iverson's handling of the system, but in the system itself. "Now that we've had a few month's experience with it," Hennessey stated, "I can see many practical problems which John's figures didn't show."

"In the first place, since John's system was put in we've had several runouts on components needed for assembly. Now I know that we can theoretically switch assembly jobs around so as not to run into any downtime, but in practice my people aren't used to being shifted around without notice. They just didn't expect runouts, and as a result this switching around gets them upset and rattled. I've even noticed some secret hoarding of parts by foremen—something we've never had before. In addition every time we get hit by a runout, I find myself in the middle of interdepartmental wars. The assembly department blames ordering and receiving for disrupting their work schedules, ordering blames assembly for late requisitioning, and the shipping room—with the sales department on their neck—scream blue murder at everybody in the place when they have no finished units to ship. These frictions and hassles are really knocking down morale.

"Now in the past few weeks I've also had Jack Werner (quality control supervisor) almost constantly on my back. He's complaining bitterly about a tremendous increase in the percent rejects we're turning out. Even though I know Jack's a real nut on quality, his figures really shook me up. I started checking up and I can see the reason for these figures. Aside from the effect of the disturbances on my people, I find that Iverson just isn't giving sufficient supervision to his departments. He's constantly chasing around with his inventory and ordering problems, putting out brush fires and trying to keep the peace; so he just isn't there when he's needed.

"Another thing that's causing trouble is John's lot size for Component 'C' which we turn out in our stamping department. We used to order 5,000 units at a time, which meant scheduling about two runs of it a month. (Actually an average of 2.18 per month, see Exhibit 3, Column 4.) Now John wants it ordered in 2,900-unit lots. This means we've got to set up the job four times a month—twice as often as before—and that's double the trouble and expense. Maybe we're saving some money in 'C' inventories under the new system, but we're sure throwing it away in the stamping department.

"As far as I'm concerned, this whole trial run convinces me that we're saving pennies and throwing away dollars. I can't show you any neat figures of how much runouts, frictions, quality troubles, and disruptions are costing us in dollars and cents, but I'm convinced it's well over anything John can save us in inventory costs. I'm for going to some simpler and more practical inventory ordering system. The fancy stuff is probably good for the real big companies, with their computers and experts, but just doesn't work in an outfit our size."

Mr. Gilbert believed that the arguments presented should be studied in detail by him before making a decision on the inventory procedures to be followed. He did not feel it was worthwhile to take up the entire executive committee's time with further discussion of the issue, and accordingly set up a meeting with Maxon and Hennessey at his office for the following day. He suggested they give the matter further thought and bring whatever additional data they could develop in support of their position.

Turning to Maxon, the president remarked with a smile, "Just don't show me too much with high-level differential equations which you know I can't handle."

Upon returning to his office, Hennessey told Iverson, who was waiting for him, "I really let them have it, Pete. Maxon was trying to nail you with it, but I wasn't having any. You know, after this whole hassle, I believe there's something to cleaning up and formalizing our inventory systems. We don't need any fancy accountng stuff, but I think we can improve on what we had. Let's you and I get together Monday to work something out."

Selected Readings

From

THE EDUCATION OF T. C. MITS*

By Hugh Gray Lieber and Lillian R. Lieber

. . . Algebra is more GENERAL

than Arithmetic.
But perhaps you will say that
this is not much of a difference—
since in Arithmetic
we also have general rules,
but they are given in WORDS,
instead of in LETTERS as in (1).
Thus in Arithmetic we would say:
"To find the area of any rectangle
 multiply its altitude by its base,"
whereas in Algebra we say:
$$A = ab,$$
but, after all, you may feel that
this is merely a matter of
a convenient shorthand
rather than anything radically new.
Now the fact is that
it is not merely a question of
a convenient shorthand,
but
by writing formulas in this
very convenient symbolism—
especially when a formula is
much more complicated than
the one given above—

---

* Reprinted from *The Education of T. C. Mits* by Hugh Gray Lieber and Lilliam R. Lieber. By permission of W. W. Norton & Co., Inc. Copyright 1942, 1944 by H. G. L. R. Lieber. (Excerpts from pp. 44–49.)

we are able to tell
AT A GLANCE
many interesting facts
which would be very difficult to
dig out from a complicated
statement in words.
And, furthermore,
when we learn to handle
the formulas,
we find that
we are able to solve problems
almost automatically
which would otherwise require
a great deal of hard thinking.
Just as,
when we learn to drive a car
we are able to "go places"
easily and pleasantly
instead of walking to them
with a great deal of effort.
And so you will see that
the more Mathematics we know
the EASIER life becomes,
for it is a TOOL with which
we can accomplish things
that we could not do at all
with our bare hands.
Thus Mathematics helps
our brains and hands and feet,
and can make
a race of supermen out of us.
Perhaps you will say:
"But I like to walk,
  I don't want to ride all the time.
  and I like to talk,
  I don't want to use
  abstract symbols all the time."
To which the answer is:
By all means enjoy yourself by
walking and talking,
but when you have a hard job to do,
be sure to avail yourself
of all possible tools,
for otherwise
you may find it impossible
to do it at all.
        *   *   *   *   *
In fact

the trouble with the world today
is not that
we have too much Mathematics,
but that we do not yet have enough. . . .

    *   *   *   *   *

No doubt someone will say:
"But the war-makers
  DO use modern machinery which
  IS based on Mathematics.
  Science is really to blame for
  the success of Hitler,
  and therefore
  it cannot possibly guide us to
  the good life."
Now we hope to show here
that this is not so—
that Science and Mathematics can
not only protect us from
floods and lightning and disease
and other physical dangers,
but have within them
a PHILOSOPHY which
can protect us from
the errors of our own
loose thinking.
And thus they can be
a veritable defense against
ALL evil— . . .
The Moral: Streamline your mind
        with
        Mathematics.

From

PRINCIPLES OF
SCIENTIFIC MANAGEMENT*

By Frederick Winslow Taylor†

President Roosevelt, in his address to the Governors at the White House, prophetically remarked that "The conservation of our national resources is only preliminary to the larger question of national efficiency."

The whole country at once recognized the importance of conserving our material resources and a large movement has been started which will be effective in accomplishing this object. As yet, however, we have but vaguely appreciated the importance of the "larger question of increasing our national efficiency."

We can see our forests vanishing, our water-powers going to waste, our soil being carried by floods into the sea; and the end of our coal and our iron is in sight. But our larger wastes of human effort, which go on every day through such of our acts as are blundering, ill-directed, or inefficient, and which Mr. Roosevelt refers to as a lack of "national efficiency," are less visible, less tangible, and are but vaguely appreciated.

We can see and feel the waste of material things. Awkward, inefficient, or ill-directed movements of men, however, leave nothing visible or tangible behind them. Their appreciation calls for an act of memory, an effort of the imagination. And for this reason, even though our daily loss from this source is greater than from our waste of material things, the one has stirred us deeply, while the other has moved us but little.

As yet there has been no public agitation for "greater national efficiency," no meetings have been called to consider how this is to be brought about. And still there are signs that the need for greater efficiency is widely felt.

The search for better, for more competent men, from the presidents of our great companies down to our household servants, was never more vigorous than it is now. And more than ever before is the demand for competent men in excess of the supply.

$$* \quad * \quad * \quad * \quad *$$

In the past the man has been first; in the future the system must be first. This in no sense, however, implies that great men are not needed. On the contrary the first object of any good system must be that of developing first-class men; and under systematic management the best man rises to the top more certainly and more rapidly than ever before.

This paper has been written:

First. To point out, through a series of simple illustrations, the great loss which the whole country is suffering through inefficiency in almost all of our daily acts.

Second. To try to convince the reader that the remedy for this inefficiency lies in systematic management, rather than in searching for some unusual or extraordinary man.

---

* From *Scientific Management* by Frederick Winslow Taylor. Copyright © 1947. Reprinted by permission of Harper & Row, Publishers, Inc. (Excerpts from pp. 5–8, 40–41.)

† The author was an engineer at Bethlehem Steel and became consultant for many leading industries in the first two decades of this century.

Third. To prove that the best management is a true science, resting upon clearly defined laws, rules and principles, as a foundation. And further to show that the fundamental principles of scientific management are applicable to all kinds of human activities, from our simplest individual acts to the work of our great corporations, which call for the most elaborate cooperation. And, briefly, through a series of illustrations, to convince the reader that whenever these principles are correctly applied, results must follow which are truly astounding.

This paper was originally prepared for presentation to The American Society of Mechanical Engineers. The illustrations chosen are such as, it is believed, will especially appeal to engineers and to managers of industrial and manufacturing establishments, and also quite as much to all of the men who are working in these establishments. It is hoped, however, that it will be clear to other readers that the same principles can be applied with equal force to all social activities: to the management of our homes; the management of our farms; the management of the business of our tradesmen, large and small; of our churches, our philanthropic institutions, our universities, and our governmental departments.

*   *   *   *   *

The first illustration is that of handling pig iron, and this work is chosen because it is typical of perhaps the crudest and most elementray form of labor which is performed by man. The work is done by men with no other implements than their hands. The pig iron handler stoops down, picks up a pig weighing about 92 lbs., walks for a few feet or yards and then drops it on to the ground or upon a pile. This work is so crude and elementary in its nature that the writer firmly believes that it would be possible to train an intelligent gorilla so as to become a more efficient pig-iron handler than any man can be. Yet it will be shown that the science of handling pig iron is so great and amounts to so much that it is impossible for the man who is best suited to this type of work to understand the principles of this science, or even to work in accordance with these principles without the aid of a man better educated than he is. And the further illustrations to be given will make it clear that in almost all of the mechanic arts the science which underlies each workman's act is so great and amounts to so much that the workman who is best suited actually to do the work is incapable (either through lack of education or through insufficient mental capacity) of understanding this science. This is announced as a general principle. . . .

From

PRINCIPLES OF ECONOMICS*

By Alfred Marshall†

§ 3. Next, with regard to the economy of skill. Everything that has been said with regard to the advantages which a large establishment has in being able to afford highly specialized machinery applies equally with regard to highly specialized skill. It can contrive to keep each of its employees constantly engaged in the most difficult work of which he is capable, and yet so to narrow the range of his work that he can attain that facility and excellence which come from long-continued practice. But enough has already been said on the advantage of division of labour: and we may pass to an important though indirect advantage which a manufacturer derives from having a great many men in his employment. IV, xi, 3. Advantages of a large factory as regards specialized skill,

The large manufacturer has a much better chance than a small one has, of getting hold of men with exceptional natural abilities, to do the most difficult part of his work—that on which the reputation of his establishment chiefly depends. This is occasionally important as regards mere handiwork in trades which require much taste and originality, as for instance that of a house decorator, and in those which require exceptionally fine workmanship, as for instance that of a manufacturer of delicate mechanism.[1] But in most businesses its chief importance lies in the facilities which it gives to the employer for the selection of able and tried men, men whom he trusts and who trust him, to be his foremen and heads of departments. We are thus brought to the central problem of the modern organization of industry, viz. that which relates to the advantages and disadvantages of the subdivision of the work of business management. the selection of leading men, etc.

§ 4. The head of a large business can reserve all his strength for the broadest and most fundamental problems of his trade: he must indeed assure himself that his managers, clerks and foremen are the right men for their work, and are doing their work well; but beyond this he need not trouble himself much about details. He can keep his mind fresh and clear for thinking out the most difficult and vital problems of his business; for studying the broader movements of the markets, the IV, xi, 4. The subdivision of the work of business management: advantages of the large manufacturer;

---

* Reprinted with permission of The Macmillan Company from *Principles of Economics* by Alfred Marshall. Copyright The Royal Economic Society 1961. (Excerpts from pp. 283–85.)

† The author was Professor of Economics at Cambridge University. This book was first published in 1890.

[1] Thus Boulton writing in 1770 when he had 700 or 800 persons employed as metallic artists and workers in tortoiseshell, stones, glass, and enamel, says:—"I have trained up many, and am training up more, plain country lads into good workmen; and wherever I find indications of skill and ability, I encourage them. I have likewise established correspondence with almost every mercantile town in Europe, and am thus regularly supplied with orders for the grosser articles in common demand, by which I am enabled to employ such a number of hands as to provide me with an ample choice of artists for the finer branches of work: and I am thus encouraged to erect and employ a more extensive apparatus than it would be prudent to employ for the production of the finer articles only." Smiles' *Life of Boulton,* p. 128.

yet undeveloped results of current events at home and abroad; and for contriving how to improve the organization of the internal and external relations of his business.

For much of this work the small employer has not the time if he has the ability; he cannot take so broad a survey of his trade, or look so far ahead; he must often be content to follow the lead of others. And he must spend much of his time on work that is below him; for if he is to succeed at all, his mind must be in some respects of a high quality, and must have a good deal of originating and organizing force; and yet he must do much routine work.

those of the small manufacturer. On the other hand the small employer has advantages of his own. The master's eye is everywhere; there is no shirking by his foremen or workmen, no divided responsibility, no sending half-understood messages backwards and forwards from one department to another. He saves much of the book-keeping, and nearly all of the cumbrous system of checks that are necessary in the business of a large firm; and the gain from this source is of very great importance in trades which use the more valuable metals and other expensive materials.

And though he must always remain at a great disadvantage in getting information and in making experiments, yet in this matter the general course of progress is on his side. For External economies are constantly growing in importance relatively to Internal in all matters of Trade-knowledge: newspapers, and trade and technical publications of all kinds are perpetually scouting for him and bringing him much of the knowledge he wants—knowledge which a little while ago would have been beyond the reach of anyone who could not afford to have well-paid agents in many distant places. Again, it is to his interest also that the secrecy of business is on the whole diminishing, and that the most important improvements in method seldom remain secret for long after they have passed from the experimental stage. It is to his advantage that changes in manufacture depend less on mere rules of thumb and more on broad developments of scientific principle; and that many of these are made by students in the pursuit of knowledge for its own sake, and are promptly published in the general interest. Although therefore the small manufacturer can seldom be in the front of the race of progress, he need not be far from it, if he has the time and the ability for availing himself of the modern facilities for obtaining knowledge. But it is true that he must be exceptionally strong if he can do this without neglecting the minor but necessary details of the business. . . .

IV, xi, 5.

From

TESTIMONY BEFORE THE SPECIAL HOUSE COMMITTEE INVESTIGATING THE TAYLOR AND OTHER SYSTEMS*

By Frederick Winslow Taylor†

The Chairman. Is it not the purpose of all production to add to the comfort and well-being of mankind?

Mr. Taylor. It is.

The Chairman. If by any system of production you increase the discomfort of mankind, have you not thereby destroyed the very purposes of your production?

Mr. Taylor. That depends entirely upon the amount of discomfort which the workman had before. If a man had not been working faithfully, if he had spent one-half of his time in idleness, I do not look upon it as anything of a misfortune to that man that he is brought to spend his working time in useful effort instead of in useless exertion.

The Chairman. Do you think that the comparatively small number of employees should have the power to determine absolutely for the comparatively large number of employees what constitutes comfort for them?

Mr. Taylor. I certainly do not think it ought to be in the power of any outside man to say what shall constitute the comfort of his fellow man. Every person should be free to decide what is for his own comfort, and I think in this country, so far as I know, that is true.

The Chairman. Would not the fact that industry is to be directed by scientific management—by one central intelligence—and that the question of whether the workmen are comfortable or uncomfortable is to be determined by that central intelligence, place in the hands of the employers the power to determine what constitutes comfort for the employees?

Mr. Taylor. Mr. Chairman, I must again state that under scientific management those men who are in the management, such as, for instance, the superintendent, the foremen, the president of the company, have far, far less arbitrary power than is now possessed by the corresponding men who are occupying those positions in the older types of management. I must again state that under scientific management the officers of the company, those on the management side, are quite as much subject to the same laws as are the workmen. As I have again and again stated, our great difficulty in the introduction of scientific management has been to get those on the management side to obey these laws and to do the share which it becomes their duty to do in the actual work of the establishment in cooperating with the workmen, so that I hope that I may be able to make myself clear that under scientific management arbitrary power, arbitrary dictation, ceases; and that every single subject, large and small, becomes the question for scientific investigation, for reduction to law, and that the workmen have quite as large a share in the

---

* From *Scientific Management* by Frederick Winslow Taylor. Copyright © 1947. Reprinted by permission of Harper & Row, Publishers, Inc. (Excerpts from pp. 211–13, 215–17.)

† The author was an engineer at Bethlehem Steel and became consultant for many leading industries in the first two decades of this century.

development of these laws and in subsequently carrying them out as the management have.

The Chairman. Is not the management the final arbiter in the determining of those questions under scientific management?

Mr. Taylor. In most cases the laws and the formulas and the facts of scientific management, which are vital both to the workmen and the management, have been developed during years preceding the one in which the work is going on. And that being the case, neither the management nor the workmen have any final arbitrary dictum as to those laws. The laws of scientific management are somewhat analogous to the laws of this country. We are all working under certain laws that were not enacted by the present Congress or the present President of the United States, and which have not been interpreted by the present courts, and yet the President of the United States and all the citizens of the United States are alike working under those laws. Now, under scientific management there have gradually grown up a code of laws which are accepted by both as just and fair. What I want to make clear is that the old arbitrary way of having a dictator, who was at the head of the company, decide everything with his dictum, and having his word final, has ceased to exist.

* * * * *

The Chairman. When your scientific management has gathered together its information, its formulas, and formulated its rules and regulations, systematized its work, etc., giving its direction to the workman, and the workman fails to obey these formulas that are laid down for him, is there any method in scientific management to discipline the workman?

Mr. Taylor. There certainly is, Mr. Chairman; and any system of whatever nature under which there is no such thing as discipline is, I think I can say, pretty nearly worthless. Under scientific management the discipline is at the very minimum, but out of kindness to the workman, out of personal kindness to him, in my judgment, it is the duty of those who are in the management to use all the arts of persuasion first to get the workman to conform to the rules, and after that has been done, then to gradually increase the severity of the language until, practically, before you are through, the powers of the English language have been exhausted in an effort to make the man do what he ought to do. And if that fails, then in the interest of the workman some more severe type of discipline should be resorted to.

The Chairman. Having gathered together all your information, and built up your formulas and introduced your scientific management, if the management violates its formulas, what method is there in scientific management to discipline the management for its violation of its principles?

Mr. Taylor. I am very glad that you asked that question. Just the moment that any of our men in the planning room does not attend to his end of the business, just the moment one of the teachers or one of the functional foremen does not attend to his duties, or do whatever he ought to do in the way of serving the workmen—I say serving advisedly, because if there is anything that is characteristic of scientific management it is the fact that the men who were formerly called bosses under the old type of management, under scientific management become the servants of the workmen. It is their duty to wait on the workmen and help them in all kinds of ways, and just let a boss fall down in any one thing and not do his duty, and a howl goes right straight up. The workman comes to the planning room and raises a great big howl because the foreman has not done his duty. I tell you that those in the management are disciplined quite as severely as the workmen are. Scientific management is a true democracy.

The Chairman. Suppose that it is the man higher up that violates these formulas? As I understand your testimony before this committee, no scientific management can exist until there has been an entire change of mind on the part of the management as well as on the part of the workmen?

Mr. Taylor. Yes, sir.

The Chairman. And that this change must take place in the point of view, in the mind of the employer and the employee.

Mr. Taylor. Yes, sir.

From

LEVIATHAN (CHAPTER X, OF POWER, WORTH, DIGNITY, HONOUR, AND WORTHINESS)

By Thomas Hobbes†

The power of a man, to take it universally, is his present means to obtain some future apparent good, and is either original or instrumental.

Natural power is the eminence of the faculties of body, or mind; as extraordinary strength, form, prudence, arts, eloquence, liberality, nobility. *Instrumental* are those powers which, acquired by these, or by fortune, are means and instruments to acquire more; as riches, reputation, friends, and the secret working of God, which men call good luck. For the nature of power is, in this point, like to fame, increasing as it proceeds; or like the motion of heavy bodies, which, the further they go, make still the more haste.

The greatest of human powers is that which is compounded of the powers of most men, united by consent, in one person, natural or civil, that has the use of all their powers depending on his will; such as is the power of a Commonwealth: or depending on the wills of each particular; such as is the power of a faction, or of diverse factions leagued. Therefore to have servants is power; to have friends is power: for they are strengths united.

Also, riches joined with liberality is power; because it procureth friends and servants: without liberality, not so; because in this case they defend not, but expose men to envy, as a prey.

Reputation of power is power; because it draweth with it the adherence of those that need protection.

So is reputation of love of a man's country, called *popularity,* for the same reason.

Also, what quality soever maketh a man beloved or feared of many, or the

---

† Thomas Hobbes, 1588–1679, made significant contributions to political science through *Leviathan,* his major work.

reputation of such quality, is power; because it is a means to have the assistance and service of many.

Good success is power; because it maketh reputation of wisdom or good fortune, which makes men either fear him or rely on him.

Affability of men already in power is increase of power; because it gaineth love.

Reputation of prudence in the conduct of peace or war is power; because to prudent men we commit the government of ourselves more willingly than to others.

Nobility is power, not in all places, but only in those Commonwealths where it has privileges; for in such privileges consisteth their power.

Eloquence is power; because it is seeming prudence.

Form is power; because being a promise of good, it recommendeth men to the favour of women and strangers.

The sciences are small powers; because not eminent, and therefore, not acknowledged in any man; nor are at all, but in a few, and in them, but of a few things. For science is of that nature, as none can understand it to be, but such as in a good measure have attained it.

Arts of public use, as fortification, making of engines, and other instruments of war, because they confer to defence and victory, are power; and though the true mother of them be science, namely, the mathematics; yet, because they are brought into the light by the hand of the artificer, they be esteemed (the midwife passing with the vulgar for the mother) as his issue.

From

POWER AND SOCIETY*

By Harold D. Lasswell and Abraham Kaplan†

. . . The circulation of a leadership varies inversely with the disparity between its skills and those of the rank and file.

This is one of Michels' basic theses, elaborated throughout his study of *Political Parties:* "the leader's principal source of power is found in his indispensability." Every organization rests on a division of labor, and hence specialization. And to the degree that distinctive skills are involved the specialist becomes indispensable. The leader is such a specialist.

"The leaders cannot be replaced at a moment's notice, since all the other members of the party [or other group] are absorbed in their everyday occupations and are strangers to the bureaucratic mechanism. This special competence, this expert knowledge, which the leader acquires in matters inaccessible, or almost inaccessible to the mass, gives him a security of tenure . . . (1915, 84)."

What is fundamental is that the possession of certain values is a requisite of leadership, and that these values are nontransferable. (Leadership resting on a

* Reprinted by permission of the Yale University Press, New Haven, Conn., 1950 (pp. 157–59).

† Harold D. Lasswell is Professor of Law and Political Science, Yale Law School. Abraham Kaplan, philosopher, teaches at the University of Michigan.

transferable value could be replaced by effecting the transfer.) Skill is the most striking of the nontransferable values; but there are others as well. Thus prestige is an important requisite of leadership not readily transferable. Hence stability of leadership will also vary with the disparity in the respect accorded the leaders and the rank and file. And the same will be true with regard to personal characteristics (for instance, prowess) on which leadership in a given case might be based.

As a consequence, the major threat to the leadership is provided, not by the rank and file itself, but by potential rivals for leadership with the requisite skills and other qualities.

"Whenever the power of the leaders is seriously threatened, it is in most cases because a new leader or a new group of leaders is on the point of becoming dominant, and is inculcating views opposed to those of the old rulers of the party. . . . It is not the masses which have devoured the leaders: the chiefs have devoured one another with the aid of the masses (1915, 164–5)."

As a further consequence of the skill conditions, a leaderhip is rarely completely replaced by its rivals. In criticism of Pareto's "theory of the circulation of elites" Michels points out that "in most cases there is not a simple replacement of one group of élites by another, but a continuous process of intermixture, the old elements incessantly attracting, absorbing, and assimilating the new" (1915, 378). The rival leaderships are indispensable to one another as well as to the group. The new leadership cannot dispense altogether with the skills and experience of the old, nor can the old better maintain its favorable power position than by extending to rivals a restricted share in their own power. Hence

"very rarely does the struggle between the old leaders and the new end in the complete defeat of the former. The result of the process is not so much a 'circulation des élites' as a 'reunion des élites,' an amalgam, that is to say, of the two elements (1915, 177)."

Throughout even the most revolutionary changes a stable administration core remains, which is the more prominent the more specialized are the skills it possesses.

From

HUMAN PROBLEMS WITH BUDGETS*

By Chris Argyris†

[Professor Argyris speaks here specifically about financial budgets, but his remarks are applicable to operations research control techniques.]

* Reprinted by permission of *Harvard Business Review,* Vol. XXXI, No. 1 (January–February 1953), pp. 97–110.

† The author is a Professor in the Graduate School of Business Administration, Harvard University.

Budgets are accounting techniques designed to control costs through *people.* As such their impact is felt by everyone in the organization. They are continuously being brought into the picture when anyone is trying to determine, plan, and implement an organizational policy or practice. Moreover, budgets frequently serve as a basis for rewarding and penalizing those in the organization. Failure to meet the budget in many plants invites much punishment; success, much reward.

* * * * *

One of the most common of the factory supervisors' assumptions about budgets is that they can be used as a pressure device to increase production efficiency. Finance people also admit to the attitude that budgets help "keep employees on the ball" by raising their goals and increasing their motivation. The problem of the effects of pressure applied through budgets seems to be at the core of the budget problem.

* * * * *

. . . Being concrete, . . . budgets seem to serve as a medium through which the total effects of management pressure are best expressed. . . .

* * * * *

It is not difficult to see what happens. Tension begins to mount. People become uneasy and suspicious. They increase the informal pressure to keep production at the new level. . . .

* * * * *

. . . We know, from psychological research, that people can stand only a certain amount of pressure. After that point is passed, it becomes intolerable to an individual. We also know that one method people use to reduce the effect of the pressure (assuming that the employees cannot reduce the pressure itself) is to join groups, which help absorb much of the pressure and thus relieve the individual personally.

* * * * *

Gradually, therefore, the individuals become a group because in so doing they are able to satisfy their need to (a) reduce the pressure on each individual; (b) get rid of tension; (c) feel more secure by belonging to a group which can counteract the pressure. . . .

* * * * *

But what about the supervisor, particularly the front-line supervisor or foreman? Strong pressures also converge upon him. How does he protect himself from these pressures?

He cannot join a group against management, as his work force does. For one thing, he probably has at least partially identified himself with management. For another, he may be trying to advance in the hierarchy. Naturally, he would not help his chances for advancement if he joined an antimanagement group.

The evidence obtained from our study seems to indicate that the line supervisor cannot pass all the pressure he feels along to his workers. Time and time again factory supervisors stated that passing the pressure down would only create conflict and trouble, which in turn would lead to a decrease in production.

The question thus arises: Where does the pressure go? How do the supervisors relieve themselves of at least some of it? There is evidence to suggest at least three ways in which pressure is handled by the supervisors:

1. *Interdepartmental strife*—Some foremen seek release from pressure by continuously trying to blame others for the troubles that exist. . . .

2. *Staff versus factory strife*—Foremen also try to diminish pressure by blaming the budget people, production-control people, and salesmen for their problems.

3. *"Internalizing" pressure*—Many supervisors who do not complain about the pressure have in reality "internalized" it, and, in a sense, made it a part of themselves. Such damming up of pressure can affect supervisors in at least two different ways:

a. Supervisor A is quiet, relatively nonemotional, seldom expresses his negative feelings to anyone, but at the same time he works excessively. He can be found at his desk long after the others have gone home. He often draws the comment, "That guy works himself to death."

b. Supervisor B is nervous, always running around "checking up" on all his employees. He usually talks fast, gives one the impression that he is "selling" himself and his job when interviewed. He is forever picking up the phone, barking commands, and requesting prompt action.

* * * * *

. . . Constant tension leads to frustration. A person who has become frustrated no longer operates as effectively as he used to. He finds that he tends to forget things he used to remember. Work that he once did with pleasure he now delegates to someone else. He is not able to make decisions as fast as previously. Now he finds he has to take a walk or get a cup of coffee—anything to "get away from it all."

* * * * *

. . . Extreme application to work or extreme aggression become "natural" —part of the "human nature" of the supervisor. His consequent attempts to alleviate some of the factors causing the tension may lead to quick, ill-conceived, confused, or violent action.

Withdrawal, apathy, indifference are other results of such stresses and strains. Rumors begin to fly; mistrust, suspicion, and intolerance grow fast. In short, conflict, tension, and unhappiness become the key characteristics of the supervisor's life.

* * * * *

Our interviewers suggested that the budget people perceive their role as being "the watchdog of the company." They are always trying to improve the situation in the plant. As one finance supervisor said, "*Always* there is room to make it better." . . .

In other words, the success of the finance men derives from finding errors, weaknesses, and faults that exist in the plant. But when they discover such conditions, in effect they also are singling out a "guilty party" and implicitly, at least, placing him in failure. Naturally, any comment that "things aren't going along as well as they could in your department" tends to make the particular foreman feel he is deficient.

* * * * *

The way in which foremen's shortcomings are reported also is important.

Let us assume that a finance man discovers an error in a particular foreman's department. How is this error reported? Does the finance man go directly to the factory foreman? In the plants studied the answer, usually, is no.

The finance man cannot take the "shortest" route between the foreman and himself. For one reason, it may be a violation of policy for staff personnel to go directly to line personnel. Even more important (from a human point of view), the finance man achieves his success when *his boss* knows he is finding errors. But his boss would never know how good a job he is doing unless he brought attention to it. . . .

*   *   *   *   *

But how about factory people? The answer seems evident. In such a situation, the foreman experiences the negative feelings not only of being wrong but also of knowing that his superiors know it, and that he has placed them in an undesirable position.

Finally, to add insult to injury, the entire incident is made permanent and exhibited to the plant officials by being placed in some budget report which is to be, or has been, circulated through many top channels.

From

MODERN PRODUCTION MANAGEMENT*

By Elwood S. Buffa†

In a sense, inventories make possible a rational production system. Without them we could not achieve smooth production flow, obtain reasonable utilization of machines, reasonable material handling costs, or expect to give reasonable service to customers on hundreds of items regarded as "stock" items. At each stage of both manufacturing and distribution, inventories serve the vital function of *decoupling* the various operations in the sequence beginning with raw materials, extending through all of the manufacturing operations and into finished goods storage, and thence to warehouses and retail stores. Between each pair of activities in this sequence, inventories make the required operations enough independent of each other that low cost operations can be carried out. Thus, when raw materials are ordered, a supply is ordered that is large enough to justify the out-of-pocket cost of putting through the order and transporting it to the plant. When production orders to manufacture parts and products are released, we try to make them big enough to justify the cost of writing the orders and setting up machines to perform the required operations. Otherwise, order writing and setup costs could easily become prohibitive. Running parts through the system in lots also tends to reduce handling costs because parts can be handled in groups. . . .

*   *   *   *   *

Unfortunately, the inventory question is not a one-sided one, which is precisely why inventories are a problem in the operation of a production system. If there were not an optimal level to shoot for, there would be no problem. Anyone could follow the simple rule: "Make inventories as big as possible." Inventories require that invested capital be tied up, and, therefore, there is an appropriate opportunity cost associated with their value. Not only that, they require valuable space and absorb insurance and taxation charges. . . .

Thus, we have one set of costs that are fixed by the purchase or production

---

* Reprinted by permission of John M. Wiley, New York, 1961 (pp. 442–43, 450–51, 471).

† The author is Professor of Production Management, University of California, Los Angeles.

order size and another set of costs which increase with the level of inventory. The first set of costs exert a pressure toward large purchase and production lots to reduce unit order writing and setup costs to a reasonable level. The second set of costs exerts a pressure toward small lots in order to maintain inventory costs at reasonable levels. . . .

*   *   *   *   *

We have been discussing inventory controls as if they could be set up independently of the production system, inferring criteria, or measures of effectiveness, that do not reflect the effect of inventories on production programs and on the control of general levels of production. This independence is unrealistic because there are interactions between these problems. Inventory policy must fit in with schedules to produce a *combined* minimum cost of operation rather than a minimum for inventories alone. . . .

*   *   *   *   *

Production and inventory control are one subject, because any partitioning of the problems in this area that does not consider both will likely result in a suboptimum solution. The development of economic lot sizes is a good example of this. This concept holds in the narrower sense, but when interactions with production fluctuations are taken into account, other basic schemes of control may exhibit superior overall cost characteristics. There may be other interactions. For example, how does the length of a production run affect learning time and therefore, labor cost? Perhaps this effect is insignificant for some situations, but it is known to be important in many others. Do lot size formulations account for this effect? What other interactions are not accounted for? We are witnessing some of the difficulties in attempting mathematical solutions to problems of restricted definition.

12. LIGHTRONICS, INC.

Case Introduction

SYNOPSIS

Lightronics, Inc., is a 12-year-old high technology producer of solid state light control devices for the home and industrial construction sectors. Eighty-five percent of its $11 million sales volume comes from this segment of its product line. The company is considering the manufacture and sale of a new product, a home fire alarm device using photoelectric principles. The company must decide whether to produce in an automated or nonautomated manufacturing operation and at what price the new device should be sold to the three market segments.

WHY THIS CASE IS INCLUDED

As the Lightronics management team struggles to make a rational decision on manufacturing alternative and price, the lesson strikes home of the need for consensus on decision criteria. The use of scientific methods clearly precipitates more rigorous management thinking. The case permits testing of the applicability of decision theory to relatively complex management decisions. The reader can manipulate the data, using various decision making techniques, to test the power of the formal approach versus the judgmental approach. The classic conflict over the use of subjective probabilities in unique management decisions also appears in the case.

DIAGNOSTIC AND PREDICTIVE QUESTIONS

The readings included with this case are marked (*). The author index at the end of this book locates the other readings.

1. What assumptions about competitive behavior does the Lightronics management seem to be making in its pricing decision? Are they realistic? What are the factors which limit Lightronics' discretion in price setting?

Read: Stonier and Hague, *A Textbook of Economy Theory,* pp. 123–26, 162–64, 182–83, 189, 197–99, 201, 204–5, 208.

2. What line of economic and/or marketing reasoning would lead Lightronics to favor a relatively high price (premium pricing) for the new device? A relatively low price (penetration pricing)?

Read: Beckman and Davidson, *Marketing,* pp. 689–91.

3. What is meant by probability? What is an objective probability? What is a subjective probability? What functions do probabilities serve in decision making? Do subjective probabilities serve as well as objective probabilities in decision making? Any distinctions or exceptions? Is it appropriate to use subjective probabilities in the Lightronics decision-making process?

Read: *Morris, *Management Science in Action,* pp. 265–68, 272–78, 280.

4. Has Fred Embury used the appropriate procedure for computing the probabilities of the selling each of the four independent markets (see Exhibit 2)?

Read: *Springer, Herlihy, Mall, and Beggs, *Probabilistic Models,* p. 14.

5. Does the decision-tree approach in part III of Exhibit 3 adequately represent the decision options available to Lightronics? Is the "tree" full enough? Should it be compressed?

Read: *McCreary, "How to Grow a Decision Tree."

6. There seems to be some uneasiness about estimated figures in the case. Do you think Embury has incorporated relevant cost in his calculations? Are there other relevant costs which should have been included?

Note: If a more detailed accounting approach is desired, consult in the library a text on managerial economics. For example, Joel Dean, *Managerial Economics,* Prentice-Hall, Inc., 1951, pp. 257–271. Dean discusses "outlay costs" as those that involve an actual financial expenditure and appear on traditional accounting records now or in the future. He discusses "opportunity costs" as those which take away from profits of *alternative* ventures that are sacrificed or foregone. For example, if a company uses its limited buildings, cash, or machines for a project under consideration, they cannot use them to make a certain profit if devoted to other opportunities. Since they are never recorded as such in the conventional *accounting records* one might overlook them. They are valid costs in managerial investment decisions because these decisions always involve putting resources in one place versus putting them in alternative opportunities. Dean also stresses that both short-run and long-run costs must be included, and that only incremental costs that are incurred by the particular project under consideration should be included (not "sunk costs" that are not altered by deciding in favor of a specific project).

One may also consult Horngren, *Accounting for Management Control,* pp. 356–363, 365–368, and the methods used by executives in the AB Thorsten case.

7. Does the fact that Embury's suggested approach omits some relevant considerations invalidate the use of such a systematic process?

Read: *Lindblom, "The Science of 'Muddling Through.'" Miller and Starr, *Executive Decisions and Operations Research,* pp. 38–42, 45–47, 50.

8. What benefits would you predict from the formal and scientific approach proposed by Embury rather than "seat of the pants" managerial judgment in the decision process? Do you see evidence of any of these benefits so far in Lightronics?

Read: Lieber and Lieber, *The Education of T. C. Mits,* pp. 44–49. Barber, *Science and The Social Order,* pp. 7–8, 12–13, 18, 21. Additional insight into the power of science in decision making, and the value of quantitative-analytical thought processes, may be found in the library in *Design for Decision,* by Irwin D. Bross, The Macmillan Company, 1953, pp. 29, 38–41, 85–87, 92–94, 102–6, 108–9, 128–29, 255–57.

9. List alongside the names of each of the case characters (excluding the president) the decision criterion each proposes.

10. Given each man's decision criterion identified in Question 7, employ the appropriate decision technique to give the preferred manufacturing/price strategy for each man. Hint: the technique for Becker is maximax; Dalworth implies the use of maximin, and so forth.

Read: *O'Connell, "Decision Making Rules and Computational Techniques."

*Springer, Herlihy, Mall, Beggs, *Statistical Inference,* pp. 297–99.

POLICY QUESTIONS

11. Just on economic or marketing management issues alone, are there enough cogent arguments to favor either premium or penetration pricing without going through the mathematical decision-making procedures? If so, which one do you favor? Why?

Review your responses to Question 1 and 2.

12. Which decision criterion would you use if you were Mr. Adams? Why?

Review Question 9.

13. Which decision-making technique would you use if you were Mr. Adams? Do you favor the expected value approach or the decision making under uncertainty approach?

Review Question 10.

14. All things considered, which manufacturing alternative and which price would you choose as Mr. Adams?

QUESTIONS FOR ORIGINAL STUDENT WORK IN ANALYSIS AND POLICY

15. While reflecting on case facts, what additional theories from prior education give you insights as to "what is going on" in the Lightronics Company? As to what might be predicted to happen in the future?

16. Other than the policy questions asked by the authors, what prag-

matic ways can you think of to state the practical problems faced by executives in the case?

Case Text*

Lightronics, Inc. is a small company specializing in control devices which are for the most part related to home and industrial lighting. It was founded 12 years ago by two young engineers with one idea, namely, a solid-state variable voltage wall switch to be used for the variable control of lights in the home. At the outset, the "Rheolite" was much more reliable than the wirewound devices which it was replacing and represented a very early application of inexpensive solid-state devices for simple home use. As the first such device on the market, it initially commanded a premium price. Large companies soon followed Lightronics into the market forcing it to cut its price to be competitive. In spite of this, the product and the company remained profitable. Because its device was reliable, less expensive, and no worse looking than the offerings of competitive manufacturers, the company was able to maintain a healthy share of the market in the face of large and heavily advertised competition. The device, because of its deserved reputation for reliability, was and is especially popular with building contractors and building supply distributors, despite its lack of advertised name.

The company has added several products to its line, many of which are variations on its "bread and butter" product. For example, it has introduced a line of decorator devices which have the same works but a variety of styles of wall plates and knobs. Lightronics has also introduced variable control devices for table lamps, which are not installed in the place of a wall switch but sit on the table some distance away from the lamp being controlled. The line even includes large industrial models for use in factories, auditoriums, and other public buildings. Additionally, Lightronics has developed and marketed other types of electronic devices not directly related to lighting except by the channels of distribution, such as control panels for total electrical homes, burglar alarms, and some other smaller devices. However, the solid state rheostat and its variants still account for nearly 85 percent of the current annual sales of $11 million.

The company has maintained a very good technical staff under Vice President Charles Becker, who is one of the two founders of the firm. Mr. Becker showed real inventiveness when he was an undergraduate in one of the best engineering schools in the country. It was as a candidate for a Ph.D. in the new hybrid field of electro-mechanical engineering that he developed the idea for the Rheolite. The tinkerer in him won out over

---

* Copyright 1973 by J. J. O'Connell and E. G. Hurst.

the theoretician, and he quit the program to help found Lightronics. He still owns a large share of the company, but he likes to be in charge of research, push products through development into production, and generally to do trouble shooting in the company. He and his staff pride themselves on being ahead of the market, in particular the large companies. They see this as a singular competitive advantage. They have a variety of ideas currently in various stages of research and development, which make use of the latest technology in new and innovative ways related to their general product field.

The other founder of the company is Robert Adams, who has been president for the entire 12 years of its existence. He was a classmate of Becker's in school, and while he is not the brilliant engineer that Becker is, he has a wide variety of interests and an easy-going personality which serve him well in his role as president of a high technology company. Lightronics survived the infant mortality period which plagues companies founded by engineers when their initial capital runs out, largely through the efforts of Adams in raising more capital. While he was required to give away some equity in order to obtain enough capital to get production up to a survival level, he was able to retain a fairly large interest in the company. He, Becker, and a few other key employees still have a controlling interest among them. Adams regards the company as strong in engineering but a bit too weak in marketing. He has recently taken steps to correct this by hiring Harry Gorsage as manager of marketing from one of the large aerospace electronics firms. Gorsage had only a few contacts in the home hardware market, but he has had a wealth of experience in all phases of the electronics industry since its inception. Though his income was significantly cut, he came to Lightronics for a fairly low salary plus options, because he got tired of the "rat race," as he called it.

Production is also quite strong, once a production line has been set up for a new product. However, excessive time and money have sometimes been consumed in getting a newly developed product into production partly because production engineering is done by the research and development staff. Becker has recently appointed one of his most promising young engineers, George Franklin, to the newly created job of manager of production engineering. With so many new products to come off the drawing board, Becker decided he could no longer do that job himself on a part-time basis.

Production is headed by Edward Dalworth, who was hired to "moonlight" as a machinist when the company was still in Becker's garage, became the first foreman when the production line was started, and finally became manager of the entire plant. Dalworth knows how to get the best out of his production people, and over the years has even picked up some other skills, such as a knowledge of accounting and inventory control, to help him manage the plant. Production consists almost exclusively of assembly of purchased piece parts. The parts are either standard parts bought off the shelf, or, as in the case of the plates and knobs, bought in such large quantities that they are custom made for Lightronics. The only machine shop in the plant is in research and development, where it is used for building prototypes of new designs. The typical assembly line has 6 to 14 stations, with the piece parts brought as needed by workers to the correct assembly stations. Much manual work is required on all products, although some special assembly jigs have been installed on several of the high-volume lines to speed the flow and reduce labor cost.

NEW PRODUCT OPPORTUNITY

The company is currently considering the production and marketing of a product recently developed and released by Becker's group. It is a home fire alarm, which senses smoke photoelectrically and then rings a bell. By making some changes in one of the small unused Rheolite assembly lines, Lightronics has built a pilot assembly line for the new product, with which it has been producing samples for the market. To date, it has spent approximately $80,000 for both product development and retooling the old line. The company expects to market the product in the same channels as the current bulk of its product line. For this reason, Harry Gorsage believes that there is no need for extensive additional advertising effort, since the current salesmen can carry the new product on their calls. His newly appointed manager of market research, Ira Heinberg, a recent M.B.A. with an Operations Research major, has discovered that competition in the field is very sparse. Most of the fire alarm systems on the market are not for home use, and are usually linked to some sort of extinguishing device, such as a sprinkling system. Their price ranges from several hundred to several thousand dollars, and none of their manufacturers seems inclined to go into the home market for the time being. The other devices work mostly with heat sensing rather than smoke sensing elements, and it seems now to be impossible to manufacture an adequate heat sensing device in a home version for under $100. Of course, if the new fire alarm is successful, Lightronics expects that other manufacturers will follow it into the market. However, the executives expect that their share will remain reasonably secure, as it has been for their previous products, and for largely the same reasons.

Lightronics hopes to enter the market with a device which retails for somewhere between $100 and $160. Material costs, if there were no losses, would run $20 per unit. On the pilot line they are currently experiencing a 50 percent scrap rate, which makes the effective material costs $30 per unit. George Franklin expects that the material costs for the unit will go to the ideal plus 10 percent overall, or $22 per unit. Labor costs are currently $40 per unit. This figure will improve, the amount of improvement depending on which manufacturing alternative is chosen.

MANUFACTURING ALTERNATIVES

At this point, the firm faces two separate but definitely related decisions on the fire alarm. The first of these is the choice of manufacturing alternative. One obvious choice is to use no manufacturing facility at all, that is, never to go into the business. This would involve selling the little inventory which has been built up and leaving the pilot line as is for other later pilot uses. The workers currently on the line could be transferred to other lines for a small retraining cost. This transfer could include a $15,000 supervisor, since Lightronics is soon going to have to hire another foreman for another location in the plant. It is not known whether there would be a net loss or gain in closing the pilot line, but the amount involved in either case would not be large.

Another manufacturing choice is to make the current pilot line permanent. This would involve designing and purchasing some special jigs and other fixtures at a total cost of $50,000. It would reduce the unit labor cost to $35, and would complete the reduction of the material cost to $22 per unit. No additional personnel of any sort would be required. The maximum annual volume with this line would be 3,500 units.

The third manufacturing alternative is to construct a new highly automated assembly line for the fire alarm. The current estimated cost for this new assembly line is $600,000. It would also reduce the unit material cost to $22, and cut the labor cost approximately in half. Current estimates put the labor cost on the automated line somewhere between $16 and $20 per unit. The estimated annual volume capacity of the new line is highly uncertain. Depending on the eventual speed of the automatic portion of the assembly, to which the remainder of the line must be adjusted, this annual volume could range anywhere between 20,000 and 30,000 units. An additional full-time manufacturing engineer at an annual cost of $25,000 would be required, in addition to the supervisor currently employed on the pilot line. For both the second and third alternatives, the expected lifetime of the equipment for amortization purpose is taken to be five years.

PRICING ALTERNATIVES

The second major decision facing Lightronics is the pricing decision for the new product. Ira Heinberg has identified three distinct markets in which the product can be sold. The size of each of these markets is fairly well known to the firm from past experience, as is their propensity to move together in new product purchasing decision. Heinberg has told the manager of planning, Fred Embury, that he can assume that each of the three market segments has a fixed average annual volume. The problem is to know whether each of these markets can be entered. After much badgering from Embury, an M.B.A. who has helped with production and inventory control as well as planning in his three years with the company, Gorsage and Heinberg have come up with the probabilities of getting a foothold in each of the three markets as a function of the three prices which Lightronics is considering. These markets and the probability of selling in each of them is given in Exhibit 1.

The luxury home building market is assumed assured for any of the three prices given. The large building contractors are less sure, but the probability of selling them goes up as the price goes down. The retail hardware distributors, while representing the largest market, are also the least certain in terms of penetration.

EXHIBIT 1
Probabilities of Success in Selling Market Segments

	Market Size (units)	Price (70% of list)		
		$70	$90	$110
Luxury Home Contractors	3000	1.0	1.0	1.0
Large Building Contractors	5000	0.9	0.6	0.3
Retail Hardware Distributors	10000	0.6	0.2	0

Unfortunately, as much as Adams would wish it otherwise, Harry Gorsage has assured him that differential pricing in the three markets is not possible, because of their close ties to each other, as well as the lack of any feasible sort of product differentiation. For example, putting a fancier cover on the alarm for the luxury home market will not help, since the device is installed out of sight. When Heinberg assured him that the three markets could be considered independent, Embury pointed out that computing the probabilities for each of the four possible total market sizes[1] is just a simple matter of multiplying the correct probabilities together. When asked to show how this could be done, Embury produced Exhibit 2.

Adams called a meeting of his staff in order to make the decisions required to get the fire alarm into production. For this meeting, Embury developed tables (Exhibit 3) which showed:

1. Cost assumptions for both the nonautomated and the automated manufacturing alternatives.
2. Payoff (net profit before tax) matrices for each manufacturing alternative, given each price strategy and each market.
3. Expected value of the annual return of each price strategy, given each of the manufacturing alternatives.

No decision was reached at the meeting, but everyone present suggested different bases on which the decision ought to be made. After a considerable amount of discussion, the following positions emerged:

George Franklin (manager of production engineering) said:

I like Fred Embury's expected value numbers, because they give us a way of making the decision based on the average of what might happen. We are going to be making a lot of decisions just like this in the near future, and if we always use this criterion we'll come out better

---

[1] (a) Luxury home contractors alone (assured at any price) 3,000 units; (b) luxury home contractors plus large building contractors 8,000 units; (c) luxury home contractors plus retail hardware distributors 13,000 units; (d) luxury home contractors plus large building contractors plus retail hardware distributors 18,000 units. If the plant capacity is not sufficient to meet demand, the stockout means lost sales for Lightronics.

EXHIBIT 2
Probabilities of Selling Each of the Independent Markets (and Only Each) at the Three Price Levels

Prices \ Markets	3,000	8,000	13,000	18,000
$70	$1.0 - .9 = .1$ P* of not selling 5,000 $1.0 - .6 = .4$ P* of not selling 10,000 .04	.9 P* of selling 5,000 $1.0 - .6 = .4$ P* of not selling 10,000 .36	.6 P* of selling 10,000 $1.0 - .9 = .1$ P* of not selling 5,000 .06	.9 P* of selling 5,000 .6 P* of selling 10,000 .54
$90	$1.0 - .6 = .4$ P* of not selling 5,000 $1.0 - .2 = .8$ P* of not selling 10,000 .32	.6 P* of selling 5,000 $1.0 - .2 = .8$ P* of not selling 10,000 .48	.2 P* of selling 10,000 $1.0 - .6 = .4$ P* of not selling 5,000 .08	.6 P* of selling 5,000 .2 P* of selling 10,000 .12
$110	$1.0 - .3 = .7$ P* of not selling 5,000 $1.0 - 0 = 1.0$ P* of not selling 10,000 .7	.3 P* of selling 5,000 $1.0 - 0 = 1.0$ P* of not selling 10,000 .3	0 P* of selling 10,000 $1.0 - .3 = .7$ P* of not selling 5,000 0	.3 P* of selling 5,000 0 P* of selling 10,000 0

*Probability

on average over the long run. The only thing that worries me is the figures on production capacity and labor costs on the new line. Fred has used the middle values in his calculations, but those figures are by no means certain. In engineering, we always check the effect of the tolerances of components on the "figure of merit" for the overall design. It seems like we ought to be able to do the same thing in making business decisions. For example, Fred's figures used $18 per unit for the labor costs on the automatic line. This means that for the highest possible volume the annual labor cost figures could be off as much as $36,000 in either direction. Of course, the effect on expected values will be somewhat different. But, I'd be interested in seeing how the

EXHIBIT 3
Summary Tables Produced by Fred Embury

Part I.   Cost Assumptions

A. Using nonautomated manufacturing alternative

Variable Costs per Unit		Annual Fixed Costs	
Labor:	$35	Plant plus equipment:	$10,000
Material:	$22	Indirect labor:	$15,000
	$57		$25,000

B. Using automated manufacturing alternative

Variable Costs per Unit		Annual Fixed Costs	
Labor:	$18	Plant plus equipment:	$120,000
Material:	$22	Indirect labor:	$ 40,000
	$40		$160,000

Part II.   Payoff Matrices

A. Using nonautomated manufacturing alternative (capacity is 3,500 units/year)

Market Price	3,000	3,500
$70	$14,000	$20,000
$90	$74,000	$90,500
$110	$134,000	$160,000

B.   Using automated manufacturing alternative

Market Price	3,000	8,000	13,000	18,000
$70	$−70,000	$80,000	$230,000	$380,000
$90	$−10,000	$240,000	$490,000	$740,000
$110	$50,000	$400,000	No sales expected	No sales expected

Exhibit 3 (*continued*)

Part III.   Expected Value of Annual Return

Manufacturing Alternative	Price	Market	Net Return	Probabilities	Expected Value	(Total)
		3,000	14,000	.04	560	
		3,500	20,500	.96	19,680	
	70		Beyond capacity			20,240
		3,000	74,000	.32	23,680	
		3,500	90,500	.68	61,540	
Nonautomated	90		Beyond capacity			85,220
		3,000	134,000	.7	93,800	
		3,500	160,500	.3	48,150	
	110		Beyond capacity			141,950
		3,000	−70,000	.04	−2,800	
		8,000	80,000	.36	28,800	
	70	13,000	230,000	.06	13,800	
		18,000	380,000	.54	205,200	
						245,000
		3,000	−10,000	.32	−3,200	
Automated	90	8,000	240,000	.48	115,200	
		13,000	490,000	.08	39,200	
		18,000	740,000	.12	88,800	
						240,000
		3,000	50,000	.7	35,000	
		8,000	400,000	.3	120,000	
	110	13,000				
		18,000	No sales expected			155,000

possible changes in this figure and the other one about which we're uncertain, including the market probabilities, would affect the decision we would make.

Edward Dalworth (plant manager) said:

It's easy to talk about taking the average value, but we could go broke before we got any project to come in at average or better. Remember the story about the man six feet tall who drowned crossing the stream whose average depth was only four feet. What I think we ought to do is get as close as we can to guaranteeing that this product can pay for itself. That is, we ought to be as sure as possible that we can cover the annual fixed costs of any project we undertake, before we go looking at any sort of exotic averages.

Donald Cohen (controller) said:

I like Ed's idea of guarding against losing money, but I don't think we need to be as extreme about it as he suggests. What is of course critical from the stockholder's point of view is not that we can take one project or another with a high net return, but that we invest their money as well as we can. We have a lot of new products coming down the road soon, and it would be undesirable to have money tied up in a product that is not producing a very good return on investment and thereby miss a chance at another even better product opportunity. I think we ought to make the decision based on incremental return to incremental investment, somehow taking into account Ed's desire to guard against loss. I read somewhere about something called utility theory, which allows you to compute the different relative desirabilities of profit and loss. Isn't there some way we can construct a utility curve for Lightronics in terms of return on investment?

Harry Gorsage (manager of marketing) said:

It's a heck of a lot easier to get market share early than it is later once everybody gets into the market. Since this is pretty much a virgin market, I say we should get into it with both feet, by building up our sales volume now. Later, if necessary, we can raise the price, but the key thing initially is to get the jump on the competition in sales and therefore in market share.

Ira Heinberg (manager of market research) said:

I helped Harry develop those probability figures for the market in each of the three channels, but I have some doubts about them. What I'd really like to do is get more information about the market by doing some more market research. Whether we do that or not, I think we ought to pick the alternative which minimizes the total spread in return on sales. How can we plan on anything with the possible figures running all over the map?

Charley Becker (vice president of research and development) said:

I agree with Ira that the probability figures look a little shaky, since he and Harry more or less pulled them out of the air, but I don't think any amount of market research is going to cure the problem. We've got a good product here, and we have a good record of producing good products, and I'm as sure of this one as I have been of all our previous successes. I say that we ought to pick that combination of plant size and price which will give us the maximum return if everything goes well. I may be an incurable optimist, particularly where it concerns the products we develop, but I think everything is going to go well. Look at our track record in the past.

Fred Embury (manager of planning) said:

We're farther away from a decision now than we were when we came into the room. I thought I had a pretty good set of figures worked up which would allow us to make the decision with no fuss or bother. Now I find out that everybody wants something different. There are different measures of performance floating around, like net return, return on investment, return on sales, and so forth. There are also different ways of using them: maximum expected value, minimum risk, even maximum maximum! I think I could recommend every possible alternative if I took all your desires seriously. I suppose I ought to try it, just to see the variety of decisions we could come up with.

Adams called the meeting to a halt for the day, since it seemed to be getting nowhere fast. He suggested that Fred Embury work up all the figures suggested by each person's position, and said they would reconvene the meeting tomorrow in order to make the final decision.

EXHIBIT 4
Simplified Organization Chart
Lightronics, Inc.

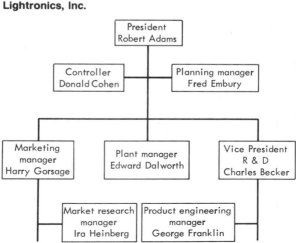

Selected Readings

From

MANAGEMENT SCIENCE IN ACTION*

By William T. Morris†

For our purposes it will suffice to consider three rough types of interpretations of the term "probability," although there are more.[1]

1. *Relative Frequency.* The probability of an event *A* is the limit of the relative frequency with which *A* is observed when an experiment is repeated an indefinitely large number of times. This is ordinarily what is meant when it is asserted that the probability of heads when a fair coin is flipped is one half. It is an unhandy kind of an operational definition since the notion of a limit is quite imaginary. In practice, however, we are perfectly willing to make an induction from a large number of replications as to what would happen in the limit. The class of all possible experiments or instances is called a reference class, and the occurrences of the event *A* form a subclass of the reference class. Sometimes the reference class is finite (the number of customers now served by the firm) and the probability of an event (sales of $1,000 or more to a customer) can in principle be learned by examining every member of the reference class. The trouble comes, as we shall see, not when we want to make statements about large or infinite reference classes but when decision making requires something be said about very small reference classes containing perhaps one or two members.

2. *Personalistic or Subjective.* The probability of the event *A* in this view is a measure of a person's "degree of belief" in the statement, "The outcome of the experiment will be *A*." It measures his confidence in the assertion or his conviction of its truth. This interpretation is itself the subject of considerable confusion. We will shortly explore more carefully its meaning and the ways in which it may be made operational. Personalistic or subjective probabilities are not, in spite of their name, products of unbounded flights of whim and fancy. The interpretation is appealing because of the possibility of dealing with a manager's confidence in assertions like, "Our chief competitor is coming out with a new model this year." Managers having feelings of certainty or uncertainty about such assertions, and

---

* Reprinted by permission of Richard D. Irwin, Inc., Homewood, Ill., 1963 (pp. 265–68, 272–78, 280).

† The author is Professor of Industrial Engineering, The Ohio State University.

[1] L. J. Savage, *The Foundation of Statistics* (New York: John Wiley & Sons, Inc., 1954), pp. 56–57; R. Duncan Luce and Howard Raiffa, *Games and Decisions* (New York: John Wiley & Sons, Inc., 1957); Robert Schlaifer, *Probability and Statistics for Business Decisions* (New York: McGraw-Hill Book Co., Inc., 1959); and Harry V. Roberts, "The New Business Statistics," *Journal of Business,* Jan. 1960.

these feelings can in no useful way be dealt with by means of the relative frequency interpretation.

3. *Everyday Language.* This is not really an interpretation of probability, but a category into which are placed all the known and unknown, vague and precise, consistent or inconsistent, meanings which attach to the term "probability" in ordinary conversation. What do managers mean when they talk about probability in discussing their decisions? What is a businessman's notion of "running a calculated risk?" Do these meanings have any useful relationship to the interpretations already mentioned?

There is ample evidence that many of the difficulties which arise between adviser and manager are in some way related to a divergence between meanings assigned to words in everyday language and the operational interpretations made of them by management science.

*   .*   *   *   *

Here, all at once, are a considerable variety of misunderstandings about what the "laws of probability" promise. The more common of these difficulties include the following:

1. "The probability of this coin coming up heads *on its next flip* is one half." Here is a problem which troubles not only the manager but the analyst as well. A businessman faces the same predicament when he tries to relate the evidence, "One half of all new business enterprises fail during their first two years" to a decision about investing in one particular new enterprise.

In the case of the coin, it is clear the next flip will come up either heads or tails. The number "one half" has no direct meaning in description of what will happen on a particular flip. We do not know what the coin will do, except to say it will land on one side or the other. The relative-frequency interpretation may hold that one half is the number approached by the long-run ratio of heads to flips, if the experiment is repeated an indefinitely large number of times. The personalistic interpretation may suggest that one half is a number which somehow measures a person's degree of belief in the truth of the statement, "The next flip of this coin will result in heads." These ideas may turn out to be useful in decision making, but not because of anything they assert about what will actually happen on a given flip. More of this later.

2. Mistaken beliefs based on "the law of averages" are popular. What does this law promise about things that will happen in the long run? "If a coin has come up heads ten times in a row, it is almost sure to come up tails on the eleventh flip." Flips of a coin are independent events, with each outcome quite unrelated to what has happened in the past. The coin, after all, cannot remember. To some extent this may parallel the thought behind such remarks as, "The law of averages requires that this decision be right because the last two (or ten, or twenty) have been wrong."

The law of averages is not at all the kind of imperative seemingly assumed by such statements. Poisson called it a "law," and thus led many astray. Its originator, Bernoulli, was careful to call it a "theorem." It promises nothing in the short run, and not what is commonly supposed in the long run. One version of it roughly stated says, "As the number of flips grows larger, the *probability* that the observed relative frequency of heads will differ from one half by more than a specified amount, grows smaller. As the number of flips approaches infinity, this probability approaches zero."

3. The common decision maker's remark, "We took a calculated risk," is seemingly meant most often as an ex post facto rationalization of a decision rather than as a description of what was done. In the majority of cases nothing resembling the calculating of a risk was carried on. Perhaps at the time the decision was made it was recognized that things might not turn out well. Actually calculating the risk is, as has been noted, the chief contribution of management science.

How little use is made of any of the statistical evidence which is widely available and potentially relevant to decisions. Vast amounts of data exist which decision makers might translate into probabilities, both in their business and personal choices, but they are little used, at least in any explicit fashion. It may even be argued that the probabilities thus derived are not relevant—say, for example, the use of a mortality table by a man buying insurance—but the reasons that support such an argument are not well known.

4. Continued interest and belief in the possibility of gambling systems suggest further this irrationality and inability to calculate the risk in reasonable ways. Hunches, which experiments in extrasensory perception suggest are not to be sneered at, are one thing, but a system which will improve one's chances in a straight gambling game is not to be found. Most are based on false impressions of the nature of independent events and the law of averages. Gamblers may feel they are challenging fate in order to conquer it, or that fate will somehow be especially kind to them, but if this happens it is not a result of their own calculations.

5. Sampling, the process of drawing inferences about a population on the basis of evidence from a sample, is a particularly difficult concept for many to accept. The *theory* of sampling is, of course, a deductive result of the theory of probability. It may be that management's difficulties with sampling are natural ones for those who often deal only with the end products of the process. It may be that the self-confidence of experienced executives manifests itself in a contempt for statistics, especially when the results disagree with their own views.

*   *   *   *   *

Relative-frequency probability is thus sometimes called "objective probability" to contrast it with the subjective or personalistic interpretation. "Objective" here may give the impression of a method of making probability operational which does not depend *in any way* on a person's state of mind but reflects some fact to which all must agree. Carefully examined, "Objective probability" is not so objective as all that, since in practice it requires a number of judgments which different people may well make in different ways.

*   *   *   *   *

The data used to obtain probabilities represent nearly always a sample of the population to which the probabilities are intended to refer. Thus, probabilities are usually based upon inferences. As has been seen, judgment is involved in making such inductions. Perhaps all that can ultimately be said about objective probabilities is that the data upon which they are based and the judgments involved in their production are (or can be) made explicit for all to see and question. This is not the case with personalistic or subjective probabilities.

The more troublesome shortcoming of this interpretation is that it provides no way of dealing with one-time events or situations which are repeated only a small number of times. Unfortunately, it is the case that many business decisions, especially those of great consequence, are not what can be usefully or reasonably viewed as repeatable situations. A "repeatable" event means that it can be classed with other events into a reference class in a way which is informative and of some use for decision-making purposes. Thus a strict relative-frequency interpretation leaves one without guidance except in the long run. It makes no logical sense to talk about the probabilities of outcomes in a one-time decision.

This, however, has not prevented people from doing so. Probabilities are used widely in decisions without regard to the number of times the decision is to be repeated. Various arguments have been used to justify this, although in actual practice the necessity for justification is hardly ever appreciated.

1. Although the decision situation is not, in the view of the decision maker, to be repeated, he stipulates an imaginary problem in which it is to be repeated many times. He then uses the probabilities which would be useful guides to action for the imaginary problem in exactly the same way for the real problem. This is supposed to "explain" the use of probabilities in the one-time case.

2. The decision maker stipulates that what he is doing is illogical but goes ahead anyway on the premise that being a little bit illogical does only a little bit of harm.

3. The probabilities are redefined so as to be regarded as measures of "degree of belief" in truth of propositions and are thus somehow relevant without regard to the repeatability of the situation. More of this shortly.

4. The decision maker proposes to use probabilities in all decisions, thus taking advantage of long-run effects in the reference class of all decisions rather than in a more restricted reference class.

* * * * *

In two general situations the relative-frequency position may lead to a model which does not reflect all the evidence available to and used by a manager. Ordinarily an experienced manager will have a large amount of accumulated information or background data which is not duplicated by the explicit evidence obtained by the staff. In a simple case, suppose a sample of a lot of a product is inspected and the resulting inference is that the lot is of acceptable quality. Suppose, however, that a manager has some information to the effect that the supplier was having a good deal of trouble with his process at the time the lot was produced. He might decide, and wisely so, to hold off on acceptance of the lot until a much larger sample can be inspected. . . .

The second case is that in which no relative-frequency data at all are available, and the evidence is solely that which the decision maker himself stipulates. Suppose a new and radically different product is to be launched and no test marketing is to be made. Clearly, the decision must be based on experience which cannot be made explicit in the staff analysis. If the staff operates without any stipulation from the manager it can only view the volume of sales for the new product as a matter of uncertainty. The manager himself may be quite unwilling to take this view, and thus he calls up from this memory all the experience he feels is relevant.

The net effect of a strict relative-frequency interpretation is to restrict staff work to those situations in which relative-frequency evidence is available, or to exclude from explicit consideration by the staff any evidence not of a statistical nature. . . .

* * * * *

It is clear that, in many important decisions, relative-frequency evidence alone will not seem to the manager a sufficient basis for choice. He will indeed add to and modify this evidence, a process loosely called judgment. To what extent should one try to reflect these judgments or applications of experience explicitly in the analysis of a decision? To put it another way, if one is really serious about the involvement of the manager in the staff analysis, why not reflect the executive's rich background and experience, together with his ability to guess at the future, directly in the model of the decision? . . .

* * * * *

To transform a manager's beliefs into personalistic probabilities and to integrate them with other evidence in the analysis would doubtless be a considerable task. What would be the advantages of doing this? It would provide one way of explicitly involving the decision maker in the work of the staff. It would help the manager impart to the staff in a careful manner some aspects of his own estimates of the decision situation. It would show the manager that his own thinking was expressly included in the model. Thus the resulting recommendations would be consistent with his beliefs, and indeed partly of his own creation. It would provide a possible means of taking advantage of both the manager's rich background of experience and the data obtained by the staff. If the practice became well developed and generally accepted, it might offer the staff a wider field of operation, including decision problems on which relative-frequency evidence was not available. It might exploit the usefulness of the staff in connection with decisions at higher management levels. It would permit the adviser to extend in a consistent fashion the choice processes of the manager. . . .

Not the least benefit of this program would be to make these probabilities explicit so they could be checked for consistency, criticized by others, and revised as new experience is obtained. . . .

* * * * *

The case in favor of subjective probabilities may include arguments such as the following:

1. All probabilities are to some extent subjective, and thus nothing new in principle is being proposed.

2. Different people, in situations where relative-frequency evidence may eventually be obtained, may have quite different subjective probabilities, but these get modified through further experience. With the aid of the staff, this modification may take place in accordance with Bayes' theorem. If this happens, then in the long run all the different subjective probabilities will converge to the relative-frequency probabilities. The effects of the initial a priori probabilities are soon washed away by the accumulation of evidence.

3. It is foolish to waste the experience of decision makers, especially when little other evidence is available. Here is a way to use and to extend it by deducing useful consequences from it.

4. It is assumed, by those who favor this approach, that reasonable men having similar experience will not differ greatly in their personalistic probabilities. This assumption may indeed be true.

From

PROBABILISTIC MODELS*

By C. H. Springer, R. E. Herlihy, R. T. Mall, and R. I. Beggs

Events A, B	Addition rules Probability that either A or B occur P(A+B) = P(A or B)	Multiplication Rules Probability that <u>both</u> A <u>and</u> B occur P(A·B) = P(A and B)
Mutually exclusive Events cannot both occur together	P(A) + P(B)	0
Conditionally dependent The occurrence of one event changes the probability of the occurrence of another event	P(A) + P(B) − P(A) · P(B|A) = P(A) + P(B) − P(B) · P(A|B)	P(A)·P(B|A) = P(B)·P(A|B)
Independent Occurrence of events are not influenced by one another	P(A)+P(B)−P(A)·P(B)	P(A)·P(B)

From

HOW TO GROW A DECISION TREE**

By Edward A. McCreary

The business schools, and a handful of bellwether companies, have a new device for long-range planning. Called a Decision Tree, this simple mathematical tool enables the planner to consider various courses of action, assign financial results to them, modify these results by their probability, and then make compari-

---

sons. It is the use of odds that distinguishes decision trees from conventional business decision-making and which sometimes produces a surprising result: the best business decision is not necessarily to prepare for the most likely event.

The clearest way to explain this is through an example. In this instance, a commonplace business decision is reduced to a decision tree:

In the winter of 1967, Emperor Products Corporation, a medium-size electronics component manufacturer, had four semiautomatic assembly machines operating at full capacity for one of its products. Sales demand for this product was rising, and company officers were trying to decide whether to expand current production by installing a fifth production unit or putting its employees on overtime. Emperor's director of marketing backed the production vice president's bid for new equipment because, as he said: "I've been talking with key customers and the way things are going I'm confident we can get 20 percent more sales by fall."

The company treasurer, however, was less ebullient: "Maybe . . . I say, maybe . . . we can get a 20 percent sales increase. But with present tax and inventory prospects we have to look at the other side of the coin. Sales may go up, but there is also a good chance that we face a sales drop."

Over the course of the next week, after back-and-forth discussion on sales prospects, Emperor's president asked his treasurer, marketing director and their staffs to quantify and agree upon a joint estimate. The two groups agreed that while there was a 60 percent likelihood that sales would increase 20 percent, there was also a 40 percent chance that sales might drop by as much as 5 percent.

During this period, the company president had called for figures on the possible dollar consequences, over the next year, of the two decision alternatives: overtime v. new equipment; and of the two possible events, sales increase v. a sales decline. Moreover, since Emperor's growth had already strained its working capital, he asked for the figures in terms of net cash flow to the company. The figures he got were as follows:

New Equipment Alternative		Overtime Alternative
(Net Cash Flow)		
Event: 20 Percent		
Sales Rise	+$460,000	+$440,000
Event: 5 Percent		
Sales Drop	+$340,000	+$380,000

Obviously, in the event things went well and sales rose, the decision to install new equipment showed the greatest payout. But a sales decrease, if new equipment had been bought, would be more painful to the company than the elimination of overtime. The probabilities of the various events somehow had to be taken into account, so the president drew up the simple decision tree shown . . . [in Exhibit 1].

At the present moment in time the company was at the square box, or decision node of a two-branched action fork. It could install new equipment or go to overtime. After it made either of these decisions the company would, sometime in the fall of the year, find itself in a circled event node of a two branched *event* fork

EXHIBIT 1

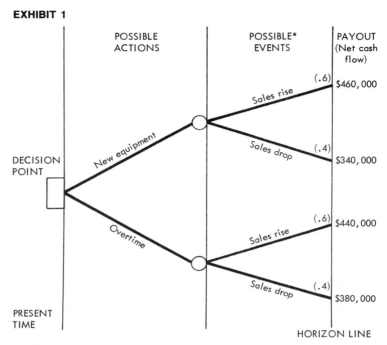

* Probabilities in brackets

which would see sales either rise (60 percent probability) or drop (40 percent probability). The 12-month payment for each possible action-event branch was as illustrated.

To determine whether the new equipment or the overtime decision branch offered the better composite value of payout-as-modified-by-probability, the president did the following:

Starting at the horizon line or top of the decision tree, he multiplied each event branch "value" at the horizon line by the probability for this event. For example in the new equipment half of the diagram he multiplied the high sales probability (.60) by the payout for this event ($460,000) to get a composite figure of $276,000. Multiplying the lower sales probability (.40) times the payout for this event ($340,-000), he got a figure of $136,000. He then added these two figures to get a total composite figure, a combined "value" at the event fork of $412,000.

Using the same technique for the overtime half of the diagram, he determined that the composite "value" of the high sales branch was $264,000, that the "value" of the low sales event which was $152,000, and that the final probability-modified "value" for the overtime event fork was $416,000.

With this information he could simplify the decision diagram. He erased the event branches and end values at the horizon line. This left the two action branches (new equipment v. overtime) and the two combined "values" of $412,-000 and $416,000 respectively. The decision diagram now looked as follows:

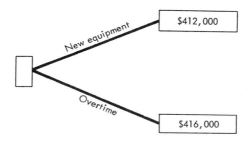

One glance at this simplified decision tree and the company president knew, considering the odds, that the best choice was overtime. It offered the highest total odds-modified value. The best decision, apparently, was to prepare for the less probable event. To complete the process the president erased the lower valued action branch which he now knew he did not wish to take, and his final decision diagram looked as follows:

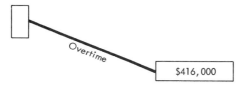

Later, in going through these numbers in order to try to explain their logic to his marketing director, treasurer and manufacturing vice president, the president noted, "Now I recognize that the $412,000 odds-modified 'value' for new equipment is something of an imaginary figure, but I'm not worried about that; I need it to compare with a similarly imaginary 'value' for the overtime alternative. Since the way the odds modify the payouts gives the overtime alternative the greater value ($416,000), I'm convinced that we should play it safe and stay with overtime. Later on, if our prospects look good, we can always add more equipment."

However, the company treasurer decided that it might be worthwhile taking that second look immediately, and extended the decision tree another year forward. After conferring with the marketing director, the treasurer decided he could safely assume that long-term trends for the component in question were excellent and that even if sales did drop 5 percent in 1967 and early 1968, the odds were 8-in-10 that sales would increase 20 percent in 1968 and 1969. The odds were 2-in-10 that sales would increase by at least 10 percent in 1968. Moreover, if sales rose in 1967, as hoped, the odds were 50–50 that they would further increase by either 20 percent or 10 percent in 1968.

With these probabilities in mind, the treasurer then drew up an extended two-year decision diagram of possible actions, events and payouts that looked as illustrated . . . [in Exhibit 2].

EXHIBIT 2

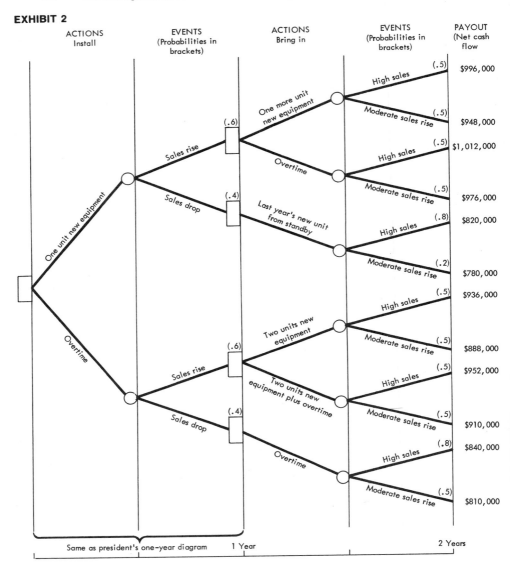

After he had "rolled back" (i.e., simplified) his new decision diagram from the 12 points at its horizon line down to one basic decision point and preferred action branch, the treasurer, a bit embarrassed but also somewhat proud of himself, dropped in on the president.

"I was wrong," he said. "On a short-term basis it seemed best to go to overtime, but over the longer term we would be smarter to get that new equipment into production. Long-term growth is probably going to make up for any drops in volume that we might meet this spring."

Smiling as he pulled out his own extended two-year decision diagram, which showed the same conclusion, the president said, "Let's go tell Harry down in Production.". . .

The above decision situations were simple enough so that, given the background information at each stage, most (but not all) executives would intuitively have made the decisions chosen by Emperor's management. What the decision trees did, however, was make abundantly clear what would have been debatable —and debated—in most companies.

*   *   *   *   *

Exponents and developers of decision trees do note, however, that the internal logic of decision diagrams is sometimes difficult to get across to veteran managers. This, because, as one businessman student remarks, "Handling decision diagrams is a bit like learning parallel skiing: you have to override some deeply inlaid intuitions and instincts to make things click." The comparison is apt, for in parallel skiing a man, already on a steep mountainside, must lean far forward to bring his weight to the tips of his skis; only then will weight come off the backs of his skis to permit him control and maneuverability. A neophyte skier may accept all this intellectually, but on a steep slope every instinct yells for him to pull back.

Among businessmen, interestingly enough, it is often precision-prone mathematicians and engineers rather than sales and general managers who balk at the probability-logic of a decision tree. Their qualms, which tend to take the form of a sharp distrust of the composite "values" and related events at an event fork, have (within their limitations) a certain logical consistency.

The best way to illustrate the "logical" objections to decision trees and how they can be overcome is by a suitably altered case study:

As part of an overall decision study involving research and development possibilities, the Pythagoras Parts Company of New York determined that for one particular $1,000,000 investment in a new process and product the company stood a 70 percent chance of developing high sales over a period of time and net cash flow of $4,000,000. However, there was also a 30 percent chance of relatively low sales and a negative cash flow of (—) $1,000,000. Project managers were anxious to get a yes or no on this decision, a diagram which looked as follows:

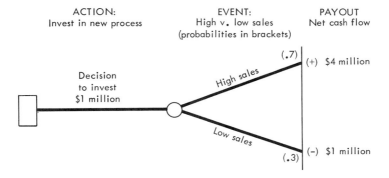

Via backwards induction, company analysts illustrated that the composite value of each event branch was: .70 × $4,000,000 = $2.8 million, and .30 × (—) $1,-

000,000 = (—) $0.3 million. With these totals they determined a composite value of $2.5 million for the event node (see diagram . . . [below].)

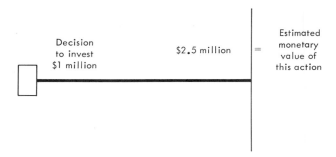

This was the first time some of the company executives had ever been presented with decision diagrams, and at this point in the presentation a number of executives began to balk.

"I agree that the odds are 70–30 for success or failure," one of them admitted, "but those are before-the-fact odds. In real life we won't get 70 percent success and 30 percent failure and some compromise average return. Once we get to making that product we are going to find sales bring in either plus $4,000,000 or we are out $1,000,000. We will either make money or lose it; there just won't be any in-between value like your $2.5 million."

On this note the meeting ended. A decision on the project was postponed.

The next week, however, another development led Pythagoras managers to review decision values in a new light. A representative of Heisenberg Investments, Inc., a venture capital group, called on Pythagoras management. Heisenberg had heard of the new process from a Pythagoras director. The investment company "might" be interested in buying out the new process.

After a number of exploratory meetings, the senior Heisenberg representative began serious negotiations by announcing, "We agree that the odds on this project are 70 percent profitable and 30 percent unprofitable. We also recognize that your company is a bit tight on cash and dubious about taking a million-dollar gamble that might not pay off.

"Well, we can convert this situation from a gamble to a sure thing for you. We are willing to buy the process. In other words, we will take over the gamble. The question is, how much must we pay?"

Bargaining then got under way. Gradually, as the Heisenberg offer rose from a $2 million starting point, the once purely "abstract" $2.5 million composite value of Pythagoras' previous decision diagrams began to get very real. There was an in-between value after all, and not the strictly win-or-lose situation seen by one of the Pythagoras executives. In fact, when offered a sure $2.5 million, the Pythagoras people found they were just about willing to give up the 70 percent chance at (+) $4,000,000 and 30 percent chance at (—) $1,000,000. They now saw $2.5 million as the *value* of being in a position to take the 70–30 gamble for $4,000,000 and (—) $1,000,000 respectively.

Once a decision-maker can accept that position values at the nodes of a decision diagram are logical and meaningful, he can readily make use of decision trees. Any further difficulties will no longer be those of philosophy but of detail— though there may be plenty of these. Decision trees, while simple in essence, can get complex in application.

Take, for instance, any of the event forks in the Emperor Products illustration . . . [above]. In actuality, both at the action and the sales-event forks there might be a great many different possible actions and a whole spectrum of possible sales rises or drops after each possible different action. What we showed as simple event forks would be more accurately portrayed as event fans which make for a very complex, multiple-branched decision tree. Fortunately, under analysis some of the values of a given event fan can turn out to be much more likely to occur than others. In fact, there are times when event fans can be effectively treated as a single branch or as relatively simple two- or three-branch forks.

Such a rationalizing of event fans, of course, makes a decision tree more manageable. One of the main difficulties in analyzing decision trees is that even with simple two and three or four branch forks the trees can, as one analyst put it, "get so bushy they are hairy."

But there are useful techniques for thinning down bushy trees. Some involve simple common sense. For example, in a situation such as Emperor's the managers automatically eliminated two possible actions: do nothing, and raise price. In that case competitive factors and the possible entry of newcomers to the field would label both these alternatives, though possible, patently unrewarding. Then, too, for purposes of comparison between alternative branches, there are techniques for thinning a fork in a tree from, say, five down to a simpler two branches. With careful staff work it is usually possible to shape and trim a decision tree down to its principal branches before bringing it up for top management consideration.

The really difficult and vital element in the construction of a decision tree is the making of assumptions and setting of probabilities from which the "magic" numbers in a decision tree are developed. When decision trees are first introduced many managers go through strenuous verbal and mental contortions to avoid being pinned down to hard number estimates. When they do assign probability values to estimates, managers tend to be inconsistent; in dealing with related multiple events they often assign individual values that total more than 100 percent. Finally, with different managers involved in developing a given valuation of the probabilities of an event, it takes time and careful analysis to reach mutual agreement.

Moreover, the complexities that underlie even one simple-seeming probability number can be extensive. In some cases, an estimated probability may be the computer-simulated resultant of the interactions of four, five and more variables, plus a number of economic indices and a string of basic assumptions.

A reassuring aspect of decision trees, however, is that they are as easily adaptable to fairly rough calculations worked out by pencil and a hand calculator as to highly refined ones. And, as further reassurance, even at their most highly refined, decision tree numbers make no pretense of developing specific point values. They are intended only as a measure of the *relative* virtues of alternate action-event paths and of the various points on these paths.

Men with some exposure to a variety of decision diagram applications, such as Vatter of Harvard and Collins of Arthur D. Little, agree that within any one company there is an indeterminate band of applications where decision trees can be of value but outside of which they approach redundancy. For instance, if the decision problem is a relatively simple one in which the executives involved are well-practiced and which they can virtually handle in their heads, the use of decision trees, even as an introductory device, might be uneconomical. But there are many marketing, pricing, research investment, new venture and acquisition decisions whose complexity and implications for the company warrant the use of decision trees.

The decision diagrams also have useful side effects. Since most upper-level middle managers are both responsible for budgets and accountable to bosses, they tend to play a conservative game—and with good reason. If they run risks that pay off, fine. But one failure that generates losses can ruin or retard a career. The result, in most concerns, is a clustering of decisions at the lower payout, lower risk end of the spectrum. In other words, the company's best strategy and an individual manager's best strategy do not necessarily coincide.

If, however, the same manager makes a formal, decision tree analysis of the investment and gets agreement from above as to the relative risks and rewards of the project, he will be in a position to make the investment with much less likelihood of career suicide in the event of losses.

There is some danger in that managers, mesmerized by the logic of the numbers they see, may take the decision tree as an answer machine rather than carefully investigating the assumptions upon which the diagram's numbers are based. But valuating the risks versus rewards for decision trees finds the balance well in their favor.

From

THE SCIENCE OF "MUDDLING THROUGH"*

By Charles E. Lindblom

Suppose an administrator is given responsibility for formulating policy with respect to inflation. He might start by trying to list all related values in order of importance, e.g., full employment, reasonable business profit, protection of small savings, prevention of a stock market crash. Then all possible policy outcomes could be rated as more or less efficient in attaining a maximum of these values. This would of course require a prodigious inquiry into values held by members of society and an equally prodigious set of calculations on how much of each value is equal to how much of each other value. He could then proceed to outline all possible policy alternatives. In a third step, he would undertake systematic comparison of his multitude of alternatives to determine which attains the greatest amount of values.

* Reprinted by permission of *Public Administration Review*, Vol. XIX, No. 2 (Spring 1959), quarterly journal of the *American Society for Public Administration*, 6042 Kimbark Avenue, Chicago 37, Ill.

In comparing policies, he would take advantage of any theory available that generalized about classes of policies. In considering inflation, for example, he would compare all policies in the light of the theory of prices. Since no alternatives are beyond his investigation, he would consider strict central control and the abolition of all prices and markets on the one hand and elimination of all public controls with reliance completely on the free market on the other, both in the light of whatever theoretical generalizations he could find on such hypothetical economies.

Finally, he would try to make the choice that would in fact maximize his values.

An alternative line of attack would be to set as his principal objective, either explicitly or without conscious thought, the relatively simple goal of keeping prices level. This objective might be compromised or complicated by only a few other goals, such as full employment. He would in fact disregard most other social values as beyond his present interest, and he would for the moment not even attempt to rank the few values that he regarded as immediately relevant. Were he pressed, he would quickly admit that he was ignoring many related values and many possible important consequences of his policies.

As a second step, he would outline those relatively few policy alternatives that occurred to him. He would then compare them. In comparing his limited number of alternatives, most of them familiar from past controversies, he would not ordinarily find a body of theory precise enough to carry him through a comparison of their respective consequences. Instead he would rely heavily on the record of past experience with small policy steps to predict the consequences of similar steps extended into the future.

Moreover, he would find that the policy alternatives combined objectives or values in different ways. For example, one policy might offer price level stability at the cost of some risk of unemployment; another might offer less price stability but also less risk of unemployment. Hence, the next step in his approach—the final selection—would combine into one the choice among values and the choice among instruments for reaching values. It would not, as in the first method of policy-making, approximate a more mechanical process of choosing the means that best satisfied goals that were previously clarified and ranked. Because practitioners of the second approach expect to achieve their goals only partially, they would expect to repeat endlessly the sequence just described, as conditions and aspirations changed and as accuracy of prediction improved.

By Root or By Branch

For complex problems, the first of these two approaches is of course impossible. Although such an approach can be described, it cannot be practiced except for relatively simple problems and even then only in a somewhat modified form. It assumes intellectual capacities and sources of information that men simply do not possess, and it is even more absurd as an approach to policy when the time and money that can be allocated to a policy problem is limited, as is always the case. . . .

Curiously, however, the literatures of decision-making, policy formulation, planning, and public administration formalize the first approach rather than the second, leaving public administrators who handle complex decisions in the position of practicing what few preach. For emphasis I run some risk of overstatement. True enough, the literature is well aware of limits on man's capacities and of the inevitability that policies will be approached in some such style as the second. But attempts to formalize rational policy formulation—to lay out explicitly the necessary steps in the process—usually describe the first approach and not the second.[1]

The common tendency to describe policy formulation even for complex problems as though it followed the first approach has been strengthened by the attention given to, and successes enjoyed by, operations research, statistical decision theory, and systems analysis. The hallmarks of these procedures, typical of the first approach, are clarity of objective, explicitness of evaluation, a high degree of comprehensiveness of overview, and, wherever possible, quantification of values for mathematical analysis. But these advanced procedures remain largely the appropriate techniques of relatively small-scale problem-solving where the total number of variables to be considered is small and value problems restricted. Charles Hitch, head of the Economics Division of RAND Corporation, one of the leading centers for application of these techniques, has written:

"I would make the empirical generalization from my experience at RAND and elsewhere that operations research is the art of sub-optimizing, i.e., of solving some lower-level problems, and that difficulties increase and our special competence diminishes by an order of magnitude with every level of decision making we attempt to ascend. The sort of simple explicit model which operations researchers are so proficient in using can certainly reflect most of the significant factors influencing traffic control on the George Washington Bridge, but the proportion of the relevant reality which we can represent by any such model or models in studying, say, a major foreign-policy decision, appears to be almost trivial."[2]

Accordingly, I propose in this paper to clarify and formalize the second method, much neglected in the literature. This might be described as the method of successive limited comparisons. I will contrast it with the first approach, which might be called the rational-comprehensive method.[3] More impressionistically and briefly —and therefore generally used in this article—they could be characterized as the branch method and root method, the former continually building out from the current situation, step-by-step and by small degrees; the latter starting from funda-

---

[1] James G. March and Herbert A. Simon similarly characterize the literature. They also take some important steps, as have Simon's recent articles, to describe a less heroic model of policy-making. See *Organizations* (John Wiley and Sons, 1958), p. 137.

[2] "Operations Research and National Planning—A Dissent," *5 Operations Research 718* (October, 1957). Hitch's dissent is from particular points made in the article to which his paper is a reply; his claim that operations research is for low-level problems is widely accepted.

For examples of the kind of problems to which operations research is applied, see C. W. Churchman, R. L. Ackoff and E. L. Arnoff, *Introduction to Operations Research* (John Wiley and Sons, 1957); and J. F. McCloskey and J. M. Coppinger (eds.), *Operations Research for Management,* Vol. II (The Johns Hopkins Press, 1956).

[3] I am assuming that administrators often make policy and advise in the making of policy and am treating decision-making and policy-making as synonymous for purposes of this paper.

mentals anew each time, building on the past only as experience is embodied in a theory, and always prepared to start completely from the ground up.

Let us put the characteristics of the two methods side by side in simplest terms.

Rational-Comprehensive (Root)	Successive Limited Comparisons (Branch)
1a. Clarification of values or objectives distinct from and usually prerequisite to empirical analysis of alternative policies.	1b. Selection of value goals and empirical analysis of the needed action are not distinct from one another but are closely intertwined.
2a. Policy-formulation is therefore approached through means-end analysis: First the ends are isolated, then the means to achieve them are sought.	2b. Since means and ends are not distinct, means-end analysis is often inappropriate or limited.
3a. The test of a "good" policy is that it can be shown to be the most appropriate means to desired ends.	3b. The test of a "good" policy is typically that various analysts find themselves directly agreeing on a policy (without their agreeing that it is the most appropriate means to an agreed objective).
4a. Analysis is comprehensive; every important relevant factor is taken into account.	4b. Analysis is drastically limited: i) Important possible outcomes are neglected. ii) Important alternative potential policies are neglected. iii) Important affected values are neglected.
5a. Theory is often heavily relied upon.	5b. A succession of comparisons greatly reduces or eliminates reliance on theory.

Assuming that the root method is familiar and understandable, we proceed directly to clarification of its alternative by contrast. In explaining the second, we shall be describing how most administrators do in fact approach complex questions, for the root method, the "best" way as a blueprint or model, is in fact not workable for complex policy questions, and administrators are forced to use the method of successive limited comparisons.

Intertwining Evaluation and Empirical Analysis (1b)

The quickest way to understand how values are handled in the method of successive limited comparisons is to see how the root method often breaks down in *its* handling of values or objectives. The idea that values should be clarified, and in advance of the examination of alternative policies, is appealing. But what happens when we attempt it for complex social problems? The first difficulty is that on many critical values or objectives, citizens disagree, congressmen disagree, and public administrators disagree. Even where a fairly specific objective is prescribed for the administrator, there remains considerable room for disagreement on sub-objectives. . . .

Administrators cannot escape these conflicts by ascertaining the majority's preference, for preferences have not been registered on most issues; indeed, there often *are* no preferences in the absence of public discussion sufficient to bring an issue to the attention of the electorate. Furthermore, there is a question of whether intensity of feeling should be considered as well as the number of persons preferring each alternative. By the impossibility of doing otherwise, administrators often are reduced to deciding policy without clarifying objectives first.

Even when an administrator resolves to follow his own values as a criterion for decisions, he often will not know how to rank them when they conflict with one another, as they usually do. Suppose, for example, that an administrator must relocate tenants, living in tenements scheduled for destruction. One objective is to empty the buildings fairly promptly, another is to find suitable accommodation for persons displaced, another is to avoid friction with residents in other areas in which a large influx would be unwelcome, another is to deal with all concerned through persuasion if possible, and so on.

How does one state even to himself the relative importance of these partially conflicting values? A simple ranking of them is not enough; one needs ideally to know how much of one value is worth sacrificing for some of another value. The answer is that typically the administrator chooses—and must choose—directly among policies in which these values are combined in different ways. He cannot first clarify his values and then choose among policies.

A more subtle third point underlies both the first two. Social objectives do not always have the same relative values. One objective may be highly prized in one circumstance, another in another circumstance. If, for example, an administrator values highly both the dispatch with which his agency can carry through its projects *and* good public relations, it matters little which of the two possibly conflicting values he favors in some abstract or general sense. Policy questions arise in forms which put to administrators such a question as: Given the degree to which we are or are not already achieving the values of dispatch and the values of good public relations, is it worth sacrificing a little speed for a happier clientele, or is it better to risk offending the clientele so that we can get on with our work? The answer to such a question varies with circumstances.

The value problem is, as the example shows, always a problem of adjustments at a margin. But there is no practicable way to state marginal objectives or values except in terms of particular policies. That one value is preferred to another in one decision situation does not mean that it will be preferred in another decision situation in which it can be had only at great sacrifice of another value. Attempts to rank or order values in general and abstract terms so that they do not shift from decision to decision end up by ignoring the relevant marginal preferences. The significance of this third point thus goes very far. Even if all administrators had at hand an agreed set of values, objectives, and constraints, and an agreed ranking of these values, objectives, and constraints, their marginal values in actual choice situations would be impossible to formulate.

Unable consequently to formulate the relevant values first and then choose among policies to achieve them, administrators must choose directly among alternative policies that offer different marginal combinations of values. Somewhat paradoxically, the only practicable way to disclose one's relevant marginal values even to oneself is to describe the policy one chooses to achieve them. Except roughly and vaguely, I know of no way to describe—or even to understand—what my relative evaluations are for, say, freedom and security, speed and accuracy in governmental decisions, or low taxes and better schools than to describe my preferences among specific policy choices that might be made between the alternatives in each of the pairs.

In summary, two aspects of the process by which values are actually handled can be distinguished. The first is clear: evaluation and empirical analysis are intertwined; that is, one chooses among values and among policies at one and the same time. Put a little more elaborately, one simultaneously chooses a policy to attain certain objectives and chooses the objectives themselves. The second aspect is related but distinct: the administrator focuses his attention on marginal or incremental values. Whether he is aware of it or not, he does not find general formulations of objectives very helpful and in fact makes specific marginal or incremental comparisons. Two policies, X and Y, confront him. Both promise him the same degree of attainment of objectives a, b, c, d, and e. But X promises him somewhat more of f than does Y, while Y promises him somewhat more of g than does X. In choosing between them, he is in fact offered the alternative of a marginal or incremental amount of f at the expense of a marginal or incremental amount of g. The only values that are relevant to his choice are these increments by which the two policies differ; and, when he finally chooses between the two marginal values, he does so by making a choice between policies.[4]

As to whether the attempt to clarify objectives in advance of policy selection is more or less rational than the close intertwining of marginal evaluation and empirical analysis, the principal difference established is that for complex problems the first is impossible and irrelevant, and the second is both possible and relevant. The second is possible because the administrator need not try to analyze any values except the values by which alternative policies differ and need not be concerned with them except as they differ marginally. His need for information on values or objectives is drastically reduced as compared with the root method; and his capacity for grasping, comprehending, and relating values to one another is not strained beyond the breaking point.

[EDITORS' NOTE: Article proceeds to discuss the remaining four points 2b–5b listed above.]

---

[4] The line of argument is, of course, an extension of the theory of market choice, especially the theory of consumer choice, to public policy choices.

From

DECISION MAKING RULES AND COMPUTATIONAL TECHNIQUES*

By J. J. O'Connell

Certain rules and techniques have become standardized for making decisions under conditions of uncertainty, risk, and conflict. The following is a brief synthesis of those rules and techniques. No effort is made to: (a) define all terms, (b) explain the complete reasoning of the steps, (c) point out the underlying assumptions, or (d) enumerate the benefits and limitations of each application. The reader will profit by attempting to infer these points from our cookbook presentation of the techniques. Help in this task and more advanced treatments can be found in the sources cited in each section below.

I. Decision Making under Uncertainty

I.1. Maximin

Situation: A will get various profit amounts depending on what strategy he uses (A_1 or A_2) and depending on which state of nature (B_1 or B_2) exists when A acts. A has no idea whether he will face B_1 or B_2.

Technique: Identify the minimum payoff for each of A's strategies (in each row). Pick the maximum of these minima.

Payoff Matrix		Minimum Payoffs	Maximum of Minima	Choose
	B_1 B_2			
A_1	23 35	23		
A_2	34 26	26	26	26 (i.e., Strategy A_2)

Rule: A should choose the strategy in which he gets the higher of the minimum payoffs open to him.

I.2. Coefficient of Optimism

Situation: Same as I.1.

Technique: Identify the maximum payoff for each of A's strategies. Identify the minimum payoff for each of A's strategies. Weight the maxima and minima by coefficients which express how optimistic you are (expect the best) relative to your pessimism (expect the worst). Sum the products in each row to get the expected value in each row.

---

* Unpublished manuscript, 1963.

Payoff Matrix		Maximum Payoffs	Minimum Payoffs	Coefficient of Optimism
	B_1 B_2			
A_1	23 35	35	23	Inclined to
A_2	34 26	34	26	expect maximum
				payoff 6 times
				out of 10.

Expected Value Table $\qquad\qquad\qquad$ *Choose*

$35 \times .6 + 23 \times .4 = 30.2$

$34 \times .6 + 26 \times .4 = 30.8$ $\qquad\qquad$ 30.8 (i.e., Strategy A_2)

Rule: A should choose the strategy with the highest expected value.

I.3. Minimax (Regret)

Situation: Same as I.1.

Technique: Subtract the highest payoff given each possible outcome from each other payoff for that outcome (subtract the highest number in each column from each number in that column). Identify the maximum "regret" for each of A's strategies. Pick the minimum of these maxima.

Payoff Matrix		Regret Matrix		Maximum Regrets	Minimum of Maxima	Choose
	B_1 B_2		B_1 B_2			
A_1	23 35	A_1	11 0	11		
A_2	34 26	A_2	0 9	9	9	Strategy A_2

Rule: A should choose the strategy in which he suffers the lesser of the maximum "regrets" he faces.

I.4. Laplace Criterion

Situation: Same as I.1.

Technique: Assign equal probabilities to each state of nature, thereby weighting each payoff equally. Sum the products in each row to get the expected values of each row.

Payoff Matrix		Probabilities		(.5) (.5)
	B_1 B_2			B_1 B_2
A_1	23 35	That B_1 will occur $= .5$	A_1	23 35
A_2	34 26	That B_2 will occur $= .5$	A_2	34 26

Expected Value Table $\qquad\qquad\qquad$ *Choose*

$23 \times .5 + 35 \times .5 = 29.0$

$34 \times .5 + 26 \times .5 = 30.0$ $\qquad\qquad$ 30.0 (i.e., Strategy A_2)

Rule: A should choose the strategy with the highest expected value.

[Editors' Note: See David W. Miller and Martin K. Starr, *Executive Decisions and Operations Research* (Englewood Cliffs, N.J.: Prentice-Hall, Inc., 1960), pp. 85–94; William J. Baumol, *Economic Theory and Operations Analysis* (Englewood Cliffs, N.J.: Prentice-Hall, Inc., 1961), pp. 368–75.]

II. Decision Making under Risk

Situation: A will get various profit amounts depending on what strategy he uses and depending on what state of nature exists when he acts. Using additional information A has about himself and about the possible states of nature, A can make some estimate how likely B_1 is to occur compared to the chances of B_2's occurring.

Technique: Assign probabilities to each state of nature which represent A's judgment about the chances of B_1 or B_2 happening. The probabilities serve as weights for the payoffs in each column. Sum the products in each row to get the expected payoff for each row.

Payoff Matrix		*Subjective Probabilities*		(.4)	(.6)
B_1	B_2			B_1	B_2
A_1 23	35	That B_1 will occur = .4		A_1 23	35
A_2 34	26	That B_2 will occur = .6		A_2 34	26

Expected Value Table   *Choose*

$23 \times .4 + 35 \times .6 = 30.2$ 30.2 (i.e., Strategy A_1)

$34 \times .4 + 26 \times .6 = 29.2$

Rule: A should choose the strategy with the highest expected value.

[Editors' Note: See Miller and Starr, *op. cit.,* pp. 82–85; Morris, *Management Science in Action* (see author index).]

III. Decision Making under Conflict (Game Theory)

Situation: A will get various profit amounts depending on what strategy he uses and depending on what strategy B uses. In this situation, the profit A gains will be a loss for B—a two-person, zero sum game. In contrast to the above situations, A here has an intelligent adversary for the first time.

Technique: Identify the minimum payoff for each of A's strategies. Pick the maximum of these minima.

Identify the maximum loss for each of B's alternatives. Pick the minimum of these maxima.

Payoff Matrix		*A's Minimum Payoffs*	*Maximum of Minima*	*A Will Choose*
B_1	B_2			
A_1 23	35	23		
A_2 34	26	26	26	26 (i.e., Strategy A_2)

B's Maximum Losses		*Minimum of Maxima*	*B will Choose*
B_1	34	34	34 (i.e., Strategy B_1)
B_2	35		

Rule: A should choose the strategy in which he gets the higher of the minimum payoffs open to him. B should choose the strategy in which he suffers the lower of the maximum losses facing him.

Note: B can figure out that A's most rational strategy is A_2. If B were 100%

certain A would use strategy A_2, B then would himself prefer strategy B_2, so that he would lose 26 instead of 34.

A can figure out that B's most rational strategy is B_1. If A were 100% certain B would use strategy B_1, A would stick with his most rational strategy, A_2. Of course, if A thought B would switch to strategy B_2, then A might be tempted to switch to strategy A_1, so that he would gain 35 instead of 34.

A could certainly "ride" with his most rational strategy, A_2, which assures him at least the better of the minimum profits, 26. On the other hand, A could use what is called a "mixed strategy."

Situation: Both opponents have figured their own most rational strategies (and each is aware of the other's) but the "game" is still indeterminate—further gamesmanship could benefit either party.

Technique: A could judge that he might outsmart B by employing a random strategy. He could use a method which made it equally probable that he would employ A_1 or A_2.[1] To see if this is a better strategy than the "most rational" one figured above, A would set equal weights to each payoff in each of his strategies. He then can determine the expected value in the two cases: B uses B_1, B uses B_2.

Apply the appropriate weights to the payoffs in each column. In each case, sum the products to get the expected value of each column.

Payoff Matrix

	B_1	B_2
A_1	23	35
A_2	34	26

Expected Value Table

B_1	B_2
23 × .50	35 × .50
34 × .50	26 × .50
28.5	30.5

Rule: Since both 28.5 and 30.5 are better than the 26 which A is willing to settle for in his most rational strategy, it will "pay" A to do some gambling. A should flip a coin. If heads, strategy A_1; if tails, strategy A_2.

[Editors' Note: See Miller and Starr, *op. cit.,* pp. 94–98; Baumol, *op. cit.,* pp. 348–66; John McDonald, *Strategy in Poker, Business and War* (New York: W. W. Norton & Co., Inc., 1950), especially pp. 50–83.]

From

UTILITY THEORY*

By C. H. Springer, R. E. Herlihy, R. T. Mall, and R. I. Beggs

Van: . . . Economists long ago invented a concept called *utility* to treat the question of individual predisposition toward risk.

---

[1] Techniques are available for determining the probabilities from the values in the payoff matrix. See the Baumol reference cited below.

* Reprinted with permission from *Statistical Inference,* Richard D. Irwin, Inc., Homewood, Ill., 1966 (pp. 297–99).

Dick: Well, how does this utility concept work, Van?

Van: Utility is a measure of the *value* or usefulness of something—money usually—to an individual. It recognizes, for instance, that a dollar is worth a lot more to the man who hasn't had a square meal in a week than it is to the guy who's already made his first million. Here, let me give you a more personal example. We all have fire insurance on our houses. We probably would have it even if the bank holding our mortgages didn't require it. Why? Because we couldn't afford the loss if our house did burn down.

Tom: What's this to do with utility, Van?

Van: Just this. What do you think are the chances of your house being totally destroyed by fire within a year?

Tom: Oh, I don't know. Probably less than one in a thousand.

Van: I would guess your house is worth about $20,000. Right? If there were one out of a thousand chances of losing your house, the expected loss is only $20. Then why are you willing to pay about $100 for fire insurance each year? I'll tell you. Because $100 has less utility for you than a .001 chance of losing $20,000.

Tom: O.K. I get the point. I can't afford the loss, so I'm willing to pay more than the expected loss. That's how the insurance companies make their money, I guess. A $20,000 loss doesn't have the same impact on them.

Harry: But how do we measure utility, Van? It seems to me that to use it, you'd have to be able to convert the payoffs from dollars to the usefulness of those dollars.

Van: There are several schemes for making the conversion. Let's look first at a picture which relates utility to dollars.

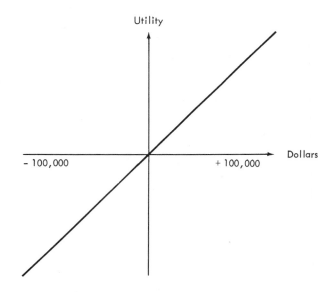

This particular graph indicates that the 100,000th dollar we earn is just as useful to us as the first dollar, because the curve goes up—that is, the utility increases— the same amount for a dollar change regardless of the amount involved. And going the other direction the 100,000th dollar we lose doesn't hurt any more than the first dollar we lose. If this linear relationship between utility and dollars were true, then dollars would be exactly equivalent to utility and there would be no point in introducing the concept of utility into the problem in the first place.

Harry: The fact of the matter is that it *does* hurt more than 10 times as much to lose $100,000 than it would to lose $10,000. Maybe we better go a little further into this utility thing, Van.

Van: The utility function for most of us average folks looks something like this.

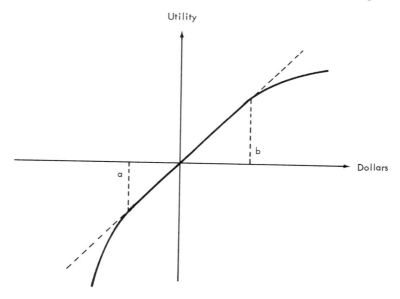

Within a range between *a* and *b* utility is about equivalent to dollars. But beyond that range, we get cautious about how much we might lose and the more we get, the less difference another dollar makes. Of course, most of our decisions involve sums in between our own personal *a* and *b* values, so utility theory never gets involved. But back to the graph. You can assign any scale to the utility axes, you choose. The unit of measure is arbitrary. The only important thing is the relative value of utility at different points on the curve.

Just for illustration, suppose the utility function for . . . [your] company looks something like this.

Harry: If I understand what you're saying, Van, that might not be too far from the way our curve would actually look.

Van: With this curve, we can convert the payoff dollars to utilities and then compute the *expected utility* in the same way we computed the expected payoff. . . .

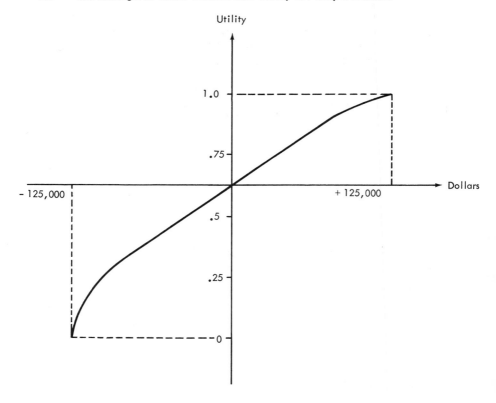

13. SEA BREEZE MOTEL, INC.

Case Introduction

SYNOPSIS

A graduate of a university program in hotel administration builds a new motel on Cape Cod. During the first season's operation, there is a considerable problem of "no-shows"—people who make reservations and then do not honor them. This often results in loss of revenues. In order to overcome this problem, the owner of the motel employs a consultant in operations research who recommends an optimum strategy, that of taking 12 reservations for a ten-room facility. During the second season's operation, the motel operates under this strategy. However, in the judgment of the owner, the formula or model is not working, and he wonders whether to use it in the third season.

WHY THIS CASE IS INCLUDED

The Sea Breeze case enables one to see both the power of scientific approaches in the practice of management and the limitations of this approach. It forces the policy maker to decide whether a management science approach will be utilized in the formulation of firm policy or whether he will place more reliance on judgment or intuition.

DIAGNOSTIC AND PREDICTIVE QUESTIONS

The readings included with this case are marked (*). The author index at the end of this book locates the other readings.

1. From the viewpoint of economics, why is it so important to Heenan to have the rooms filled to capacity at all times?

Prepare: Using your own analytical ability, think about the fixed costs such as investment in buildings and furnishings. Convert these costs to a formula that will yield fixed cost per unit of output.

2. Why did Heenan "decide right then and there that there must be a way for me to solve the problem more reliably than just by guessing"? Why did Imhoff have inner self-confidence that he could solve the problem by mathematics or "management science"?

Read: Barber, *Science and the Social Order,* pp. 7–8, 12–13, 18, 21. Also, the concept of "convergent phenomena" and the section on "physical science" in Chapter 2 of *The Managerial Mind.* Not included in this volume, but an excellent source for understanding of the nature of science as uncovering an orderliness in dynamic events is Alfred N. Whitehead, *Science and the Modern World* (New York: Macmillan Co., 1925; now available in paperback by Mentor), Chapter 1.

3. Why do you think that Heenan "obeyed" Imhoff—or, in what sense did Imhoff have "authority" over Heenan? The same question might be asked as to why the journal article had "authority" or "influence" over Heenan.

Read: *General Electric Co., *Professional Management in General Electric.* *Moore and Tumin, "Specialists and the Ignorance of Non-Specialists." Simon, Smithburg, and Thompson, *Public Administration,* pp. 182, 189–200.

4. Why didn't the facts of the real world correspond to the mathematical prediction—that is, why did the motel units fill less than predicted in June and more than predicted in July? Why did Heenan consider Shields as part of the "model" which didn't work?

Read: Chapter 2 of *The Managerial Mind,* and the section on Ceteris Paribus in Chapter 3.

POLICY QUESTIONS

5. If you were in Heenan's place, what would you do about the reservation policy in the coming season?

QUESTIONS FOR ORIGINAL STUDENT WORK IN ANALYSIS AND POLICY

6. While reflecting on case facts, what additional theories from prior education give you insights as to "what is going on" in the Sea Breeze Motel, Inc.? As to what might be predicted to happen in the future?

7. Other than the policy questions asked by the authors, what pragmatic ways can you think of to state the practical problems faced by executives in the case?

Case Text*

Since his graduation from the Cornell University School of Hotel Administration, Dave Heenan had been the owner-manager of the Sea Breeze Motel in Harwichport, Massachusetts, on Cape Cod. With funds furnished from an administered inheritance, Heenan initiated the construction of the lavish, ten-suite complex in the late autumn three years ago.

An early completion date of the following March 23 further enabled Heenan to solicit customers for the oncoming season—beginning June 1 and terminating September 10. Heenan intended to supplement his seasonal earnings at Sea Breeze by assisting his cousin in the management of the Royal Palms Hotel during the winter months.

Since the rate per suite was set at $40 a day, and because the motel has only 10 units, Heenan sought to segment the motel's market to upper-income families and to make his accommodations conducive to repeat trade over the years. Although competition on the Cape was fierce for this type of clientele, Heenan initiated measures to appeal to the appropriate market.

First, Heenan—with the assistance of experienced classmates and friends of his father—sought out and received the highest possible rating, "AAA," from the Certification Board of the New England Hotel and Motel Association (NEHMA). Knowledgeable persons in the hotel-motel industry had pointed out to Heenan that the possession and maintenance of "AAA" would be probably the most important factor in attracting desirable occupants.

In addition, Heenan embarked on a promotional campaign designed to attract wealthy vacationers. By advertising in the travel sections of the *Boston Globe,* the *Christian Science Monitor,* and appropriate national and regional media and by personally selling a carefully selected group of travel agents, Heenan felt that he had made significant headway in promoting the Sea Breeze image.

However, upon returning to Harwichport in May two years ago Heenan soon became aware that full-season occupancy of individual customers would be most difficult to achieve in the early stages of operations. The majority of early reservations received were for various periods ranging from three nights to two months. Moreover, the average duration appeared to be somewhere between one to two weeks. With this in mind, Heenan readied the Sea Breeze for the reception of its first guest in June.

While he considered the first summer's operations as favorable for the most part, Heenan realized that if his existing facilities were to be expanded annually, greater revenues and/or reduced operating costs would have to be generated. What bothered Heenan most was the so-called "no-show" problem. In a significant number of instances, people who had previously reserved a specific Sea Breeze suite neither arrived to fill their reservations nor notified management in advance of their cancellations.

Initially, Heenan thought about establishing a minimum advance deposit to protect against "no-show" losses, but he soon dropped the idea after recognizing that such a requirement would foster a host of inhibitory effects in the minds of potential upper-income occupants. As a result, Heenan adopted a policy of holding reservations until 3 P.M. of the specified day to protect against possible losses. This arbitrary deadline, he thought, would best afford sufficient customer convenience while, at the same time, hopefully enable management ample time within which to rent the rooms of canceled reservations. But in practice over a period of weeks, marked customer irritation was voiced by those unable to reach Harwichport by early afternoon, and since it was extremely difficult to rent "no-show" rooms late in the day, it soon became evident that such a policy was unwise. Nevertheless, feeling that "no-shows" were making serious inroads on the motel's profitability, Heenan saw no other course of action but to retain the 3 P.M. deadline.

It was not until Heenan's attendance at the annual assembly of hotelmen in the late fall of the same year, that a workable solution to the "no-show" dilemma seemed imminent. Originated some years ago to serve the dual role of congregating hotel executives and informing them of updated managerial methods and techniques, the assembly provided a forum for the discussion—formally and informally—of a wide variety of operational problems.

In his association with other managers, Heenan found that an ever increasing percentage of hotelmen minimized the risk of "no-shows" with a procedure of accepting more reservations than the number of rooms available. The strategy is directed at placing the motel in the optimal position of receiving sufficient reservations to fill available rooms after "no-show" reservations are deducted. Moreover, the motel's calculated demand for rooms, based on the "estimated valid" reservations (those remaining after the elimination of an estimated percentage of "no-shows"), is equated to the fixed supply of rooms.

In practice, there are costs associated with the adoption of such a strategy. For example, if the demand for rooms is underestimated, there will result vacant rooms with a consequential loss of rental revenues. Or, if the demand for rooms is overstated, there will no doubt be a loss of those highly dissatisfied customers who are rejected lodging in spite of their reservations.

Bob Fuller, manager of the Pine Manor Lodge in Lake Placid, New York, and one of Heenan's most respected classmates from Cornell, suggested that Heenan should make use of some modern operations research techniques for solving the "no-show" problem. He explained that, in operations research terms, the proprietor of a motel might adopt various "strategies" or alternatives of action. These strategies, in the last analysis, are different numbers of reservations the proprietor might wish to accept. For example, given the fixed number of ten suites at Sea Breeze, Heenan might have one strategy of accepting 11 reservations, a second strategy of accepting 12 reservations, or a third strategy of accepting 13 reservations. In Heenan's later calculations, when he drew up a decision matrix (Table 2), these strategies were listed down the left column as row headings.

Fuller went on to explain that the other critical determinant of what he should do about "no-shows" were various "states of nature" that he might encounter—things over which he has little control. "You can control the number of reservations, through your strategy, but you cannot control what all of those customers will do—whether they will cancel or simply not show up. Therefore, why not view the actual number of customers which in fact arrive as various states of nature, and then calculate which strategy will yield the least cost to Sea Breeze due to "no-show" customers."

Fuller also recommended that Heenan read an article entitled "Decision Theory Applications to the No-Show Problem" in a recent edition of a hotel trade publication. After reading this article, Heenan said, "I decided right then and there that there must be a way for me to solve this problem more reliably than just by guessing. I got in touch with a large consulting firm in Boston, and they referred me to Jim Imhoff, an individual who does operations-research-type consulting. The big firm frankly said my project was not as large or complex as they generally take on."

Heenan arranged to return from Florida in the spring a year ago, and he arranged with Imhoff to come to Harwichport to gather data from his records. This Imhoff did, and according to Heenan, "We worked well together. Jim kept asking questions and I would supply what I could. I even enlisted the help of three other motels out here to furnish data, in return for which we agreed to let them read the report." Imhoff's memorandum to Heenan appears as Exhibit 1.

EXHIBIT 1

Mr. David Heenan
Sea Breeze Motel
Harwichport, Massachusetts

Dear Dave:

I know that you are anxious to receive this final report, so that you can proceed with accepting reservations for the summer season. I have enjoyed working on this project, and hope that you will feel free to call on me again if you have further questions. I have discussed the problem with my partner before coming to the final conclusion.

The purpose of this report is to give you our final recommendation as to how many reservations you should accept, and to explain how we arrived at this figure. Let me, therefore, begin with this recommendation:

EXHIBIT 1 (*continued*)

Sea Breeze Motel should accept 12 reservations for the existing ten-suite facility, if optimum season profit is to be realized.

I know that you have been referring to this final figure as "the magic number." Here it is. But I should like to explain how we arrived at this so that it won't seem like magic. Rather, it is an orderly attempt to gather concrete factual information and then to use certain mathematical techniques to arrive at costs, revenues, and final profit. I'm fully aware that you know much of what we're doing from our past conversations. However, let me devote the rest of this report to summarizing the steps we went through.

Essentially, two different cost figures had to be determined: (a) the cost of a vacant room (given a "no-show"); and (b) the cost of the anticipated lifetime loss of a good customer if he is denied admission, even with a reservation (because of an overstated demand estimate). The former statistic was easily derived; it was simply the daily loss of revenues of a single vacant suite, or $40. However, to determine the latter expense, we had to analyze the financial record of the past season. Initially required was the average customer stay at Sea Breeze, which was found to be ten days. At the set rate of $40 per day, we calculated that some $400 in rentals were generated during this period. Furthermore, desirous of a 10 percent profit return on gross rentals, we calculated a net profit of $40 for any base period.

To project the expected lifetime customer value, it was necessary to determine the probability of one's returning to Sea Breeze in the following year. Although the infancy stage of your operations did not provide available historical information, files of the NEHMA revealed that approximately an 80 percent probability of return could be anticipated for motels comparable to the Sea Breeze. Stated otherwise, the probability that a guest will return for n *years is* $(0.80)^n$—*or Lifetime value of a customer = (Net profit base) + (Pr. return next year)*

$$(\text{Net profit base}) + \ldots + (\text{Pr. return } {}^n \text{ years}) \cdot (\text{Net profit})$$

'For Sea Breeze then—

$$\text{Lifetime value} = \$40 + (0.80) \cdot (40) + (0.64) \cdot (40) + \ldots$$
$$+ (0.80)^n \cdot (40) = \underline{\$200}$$

In summary, the expected lifetime revenue stream at Sea Breeze for the average customer was found to be $200. However, recognizing the present value of money, we discounted the above statistic (by 10 percent yearly) in order to establish the true present worth to the motel.

$$\text{Lifetime value adjusted} = \$40 + \frac{(0.80) \cdot (40)}{1.10} + \frac{(0.64)\,(40)}{1.21} +$$
$$\ldots \frac{(0.80)^n\,(40)}{(1.10)^n} = \underline{\$90.09}$$

Moreover, Sea Breeze would probably lose the entire $90.09 for any

EXHIBIT 1 (*continued*)

customer who, despite a reservation, has been turned away for his vacation stay.

To calculate the probabilities of the requisite states of nature, we first determined the probability of a "no-show" and then the total number of reservations. You were able to obtain "no-show" statistics over a five-year period from three comparable motels on Cape Cod. These records indicated that 25 percent of all reservations were of a "no-show" variety. Given the total number of reservations, we utilized the binomial probability distribution to calculate probabilities of the various numbers of "no-shows."

For R (reservations), the probability of n ("no-shows") is:

$$\frac{R\ (R-1)\ (R-2)\ ....\ (R-n+1)}{n\ (n-1)\ (n-2)\ ....\ (2)\qquad (11)}\quad (0.25)^n(0.75)^{R-n}$$

For example, given ten suites, we considered how many reservations over ten you might best be advised to accept. If 11 reservations were taken, the probability of one "no-show" (the optimal solution) could be determined as follows:

$$\text{Pr. 1 no-show} = \frac{11}{1}(0.25)^1(0.75)^{10} = 0.1459 = 15\%$$

Simply stated, there is roughly a 15 percent chance that if one "extra" reservation were accepted, the two ever present costs—loss of rentals and loss of lifetime customer value—would be erased.

Proceeding in this manner, we computed the probabilities of "no-shows" under various acceptance strategies, letting R equal the number of reservations:

TABLE 1
Probability

"No-Shows"	R = 11	R = 12	R = 13
0......................	0.0422	0.0317	0.0238
1......................	0.1549	0.1267	0.1029
2......................	0.2581	0.2323	0.2059
3......................	0.2581	0.2581	0.2517
4......................	0.1721	0.1936	0.2097
5......................	0.0803	0.1032	0.1258
6......................	0.0268	0.0401	0.0559
7......................	0.0064	0.0115	0.1186
8......................	0.0011	0.0024	0.0047
9......................	0.0001	0.0004	0.0009
			0.0001
	1.000	1.000	1.000

Finally, having computed the probabilities of the various states of nature (the number of "no-shows," over which you have no control),

EXHIBIT 1 (*continued*)

TABLE 2

"No-Shows"	0	1	2	3	4	5	6	7	8	9	Expected Cost US $
Probability strategy: $R = 11$	0.0422 $ 90.09	0.1549 0	0.2581 $40	0.2581 $80	0.1721 $120	0.0803 $160	0.0268 $200	0.0064 $240	0.0011 $280	0.0001 $320	$75.75
Probability strategy: $R = 12$	0.0317 $180.18	0.1267 $ 90.09	0.2323 $ 0	0.2581 $40	0.1936 $ 80	0.1032 $120	0.0401 $160	0.0115 $200	0.0024 $240	0.0004 $280	$63.69
Probability strategy: $R = 13$	0.0238 $270.27	0.1029 $180.18	0.2059 $90.09	0.2517 $ 0	0.2097 $ 40	0.1258 $ 80	0.0559 $120	0.0186 $160	0.0047 $200	0.0009 $240	$73.66

Note: If there are zero "no-shows" with one reservation too many, the cost is the lifetime value of a customer ($90.09).

EXHIBIT 1 *(concluded)*

and the necessary costs we calculated the resultant payoffs. By utilizing the matrix in Table 2 which blends the costs and probabilities of selected reservation strategies, we found that the minimum expected cost—hence, the optimal solution—was attained when R = 12.

By adopting a policy of accepting 12 reservations for ten rooms, the Sea Breeze would follow the safest and surest possible course of action. In short, the least cost (over time) of such a policy would be $63.69 as compared with the more costly strategies of R = 11 and R = 13.

According to the recommendation, the Sea Breeze Motel should accept 12 reservations for any given period, so long as the facility contains ten suites. Imhoff explained over the telephone, after Heenan had received the report, that no solution "will allow you to eat your cake and have it, too. You can't have completely satisfied every single customer and at the same time satisfied your desire for every dollar of profit. But 12 reservations will give the best balance—the optimum profit."

Assured that this policy would remedy the "no-show" predicament at Sea Breeze, Heenan announced his intention of accepting 12 reservations for ten suites during single time intervals of the oncoming seasons. For the first few weeks of the motel's operations last season, Heenan was pleased with the relative effectiveness of his newly stated reservations program. It was true that customers were turned away on some occasions because of overacceptance, while on others, vacant rooms resulted because of underestimated "no-shows." However, Heenan believed that these costs would be exceeded by the additional revenues gained in reserving the two extra suites.

During the remaining months of last season, however, a series of incidents occurred which caused considerable trouble, in Heenan's words, "for the smooth operations of Sea Breeze Motel, and for its reputation."

In July, Cape Cod was plagued with an unusually bad weather situation. Fog, haze, and below normal temperatures resulted in a decreased tourist business for the entire area and in a high rate of cancellations and "no-shows" for Sea Breeze. Given ten motel units, and 31 days in July, the motel would be fully occupied if the management received payment for 310 unit/days. However, for the month as a whole, paying guests occupied units only for 186 unit/days. This is the equivalent of having six units occupied for the 31-day period, instead of the full ten units. On inspection of his records, Heenan found that almost exactly half of these unoccupied unit/days were accounted for by "no-shows"—in other words, of the four units remaining unoccupied throughout July, two of these could be traced to occasions when people did not cancel their reservations. On numerous occasions, because of the quality of his property, Heenan had the opportunity of renting to tourists who, defying the weather, stopped in between 10 A.M. and 2 P.M. to see if they could stay overnight. Believing in his reservation system, he turned these potential guests away.

Just the opposite happened in August. Instead of having many cancellations and "no-shows," the Sea Breeze found that everyone seemed to want to carry through his vacation plans. Even though Table 1 in Imhoff's report indicates that there is only a 3 percent chance that there will be no "no-shows" if 12 reservations are accepted, there were in fact nine days on which reservation guests arrived for all 12 reservations.

One additional event in August troubled Heenan a great deal. On the weekend of August 14th, one of those nine times when all 12 reservations appeared for actual occupancy, a particularly important guest was refused his room. Mr. Foster Shields, Executive Secretary of the New England Motel Managers Association, arrived with a reservation made in May. He arrived just before the latest reservation hold time (3 P.M.). The desk clerk apologized for the error in bookings, and offered to help him obtain suitable accommodations elsewhere.

Shields later wrote to Heenan and informed him that the committee on certifications could lower his rating from "Triple A" to a lower category, possibly "BCC." Heenan knew that with the luxury nature of his property, such an action would seriously impair the image of his motel, and he knew that loss of qualitative status is reported in trade journals which are read widely by travel agencies.

On closing the Sea Breeze and going to Florida last fall, Heenan took with him the day-by-day records of the season. He wanted to study the records and compare them with the Imhoff report, to see what to do about a reservation policy for the motel in the coming season.

As of the time this case is written, early this year, Heenan states:

I have got to decide whether to try to operate under this system this year, whether to junk the whole thing and accept only ten reservations to match my facilities, or whether to hire Jim Imhoff again to see if he can work the bugs out of the system. Somehow I know that the thing can be solved better than just by guessing—I had faith in what Bob Fuller said, what I read in the journal, and what Jim Imhoff can do as a man with knowledge I don't have. At the same time, I think I fell between the chairs last summer. I alienated guests in August too much, I lost too much profits in July, and that problem with Shields is a sticky one. Incidentally, I did visit with Shields personally and things are temporarily OK. He is thoroughly pleased with everything he knows or has seen regarding Sea Breeze. That's the one thing that saves us. I showed him all of the calculations and tried to explain what I'm trying to do—to match a really excellent facility with good management. I don't think he understood what I was talking about but he agreed to let me inform him this month (March) what I intend to do regarding customer satisfaction through a good reservation system. One thing is certain: I've got to decide what to do about reservations for this season; this is a better year for tourist and vacation expenditures than ever.

Selected Readings

From

MEASURING*

By Professional Management in General Electric

Of the four elements of the work of a professional manager, the element of measuring has been given too little inventive attention. Conversely, this is an area in which rapid advances will be made if the area is given the attention which it deserves. The feed-back of adequate measurements into the other areas of a manager's work closes the cycle and makes dynamic progressive achievement possible. What would a sailor on the high seas do without a compass? How can a manager make wise decisions if he does not have adequate, timely facts about the working situation? The more completely, accurately, and promptly he can be kept informed, the wiser and surer his decisions can be.

*   *   *   *   *

The work of managing inherently involves exercising judgment as a basis for making decisions. Judgment, which is in essence appraisal, is in turn a function of the facts and information on which it is based. It is the manager's task, in a business enterprise, or component, to make decisions as occasion requires, and on the best information available at the time. If only qualitative appraisal, rooted in general experience or beliefs, is feasible, it is still essential to weigh and to decide. But the professional manager's job is to function through the authority of knowledge rather than of rank. Hence, the more he can "measure," the more he can ask sound, balanced, objective, and persuasive questions and when appropriate, make decisions of corresponding clarity and acceptability. As a manager develops professional skill, the advantages of seeking "measured facts" in more and more areas is increasingly realized. With modern knowledge of mathematics and statistics, and with modern tools and machines or computers to apply them, the opportunities to "measure" increasingly more complex situations are simultaneously enhanced. Hence, the areas can be minimized where reliance is on opinion and qualitative judgment alone because the appraisal factors can be stated and worded in terms which are more and more measurable.

*   *   *   *   *

In *The New York Times* for January 31, 1954, Secretary of the Treasury George M. Humphrey is quoted as saying, "There are no hard decisions, just insufficient facts. When you have the facts, the decisions come easy."

---

* By permission from *Professional Management in General Electric,* Book Three, *The Work of a Professional Manager,* copyright 1954 by the General Electric Company. (Excerpts from pp. 109–10; 142–43.)

The scientific method involves analysis and synthesis that are directed toward the simplification of concepts and the statement of generalizations or principles. The situations in which we find ourselves tend to become unmanageable, unless the simplification process keeps pace with the rapidly growing volume and complexity of observed facts. The first four chapters of this book give an orderly arrangement of the ideas that appear pertinent and of significant importance in the WORK OF A PROFESSIONAL MANAGER. By the very arrangement of these ideas, simplification of concept is achieved.

Zay Jefferies has observed that if the simplification processes keep pace with the complicating processes, "individuals with a given ability can expect to go forward indefinitely without becoming casualties of their own complexity."

The true search of the people of the world is for order, not chaos. Managing should be the science of bringing the kind of order which nature exhibits all about us; and of doing so by applying a process of rational organization to the relationships in which men associate. This is our deep need. As individuals we show little or no more capacity or ability or emotional steadiness than the able men among our forebears. Yet, unfolding science brings new complexities, and it is the manager's job to match them with patterns of simplicity, which will win the comprehension and the acceptance of the individual men whose work is being managed. . . .

From

SPECIALISTS AND THE IGNORANCE OF NON-SPECIALISTS *

By Wilbert E. Moore and Melvin M. Tumin†

The function of ignorance that is most obvious, particularly to the cynical, is its role in preserving social differentials. However, a purely cynical view is likely to overlook the extent to which the continuity of any social structure depends on differential access to knowledge in general, and, *a fortiori,* to specialized knowledge of various kinds. In many instances, of course, the counterpart of ignorance on the part of the outsider is *secrecy* on the part of the possessor of knowledge. Some of the outstanding examples of this general function of ignorance are summarized in the following paragraphs.

The Specialist and the Consumer. Ignorance on the part of a consumer of specialized services (for example, medical or legal advice) helps to preserve the privileged position of a specialized dispenser of these services. This is in some measure a by-product of the division of labor, and theoretically the same persons may occupy super-ordinate or subordinate positions as one or another service or skill is demanded. However, there are both theoretical and empirical bases for

* By permission from "Some Social Functions of Ignorance," *American Sociological Review,* Vol. 14 (December 1949), pp. 788–89. Copyright by the American Sociological Society.

† The authors are Professors of Sociology at the University of Denver and Princeton University respectively.

concluding that some persons whose skills are both scarce and functionally important will occupy a generalized superior position.[1] Although that status is not solely the product of the ignorance of others, in concrete instances it is partially maintained by such ignorance.

One evidence of the function of ignorance of as a preservative of privileged position lies in the situation where the consumer acquires, through continuous exposure to the services of the specialist, a sense of his own ability to deal with his problems, and thus to dispense with the services of the specialist (*e.g.,* when we learn how to treat common colds, simple fevers, and bruises, and where we learn how to send stern notes concerning contractual obligations). Thus the range of situations in which the special services are believed to be required is altered from the original position.

On the other hand, the specialist commonly develops devices to protect himself against this sort of attrition. A common device is that of specialized and possibly esoteric vocabulary, or the use of instruments and techniques not intrinsically required for the solution but seemingly so.

However, the central point remains that real or presumed differential knowledge and skills are inherently necessary to maintain mutually satisfactory relationships between specialist and consumer. . . .

---

[1] Kingsley Davis and Wilbert E. Moore, "Some Principles of Stratification," *American Sociological Review,* Vol. 10 (April 1945), pp. 242–49.

14. NATIONAL MOTOR PARTS COMPANY

Case Introduction

SYNOPSIS

The corporate director of industrial engineering of National Motor Parts Company proposes a general audit and research study of jobs to insure that changes over time have not reduced accuracy of standards of output for workers. The audit is approved by the executive vice president. The proposal is explained to division managers of industrial engineering, who in turn present it to division general managers for approval.

In the Metal Parts Division, the manager of industrial engineering explains the project to plant supervisors of industrial engineering, who present it to plant managers for approval. At one plant, a study of the lock pin job operation results in a new standard for the position, and for Sullivan, the incumbent in the job. The plant manager instructs Bauer, Sullivan's foreman, to relay the new standard to Sullivan.

Sullivan files a grievance with Andrews, his union steward. Leach, the plant manager, prepares to take action with Ed Lillian, head of the local union.

WHY THIS CASE IS INCLUDED

This case offers opportunity to see how rational planning of objectives and jobs in the company, based on technology and economics, conflicts with the desires of individual workers, and with the power structure of the union.

The relationship of scientific planning, in the form of quantification and research, done by specialists, to both the process of influence and to the authority process in the company can be studied.

Finally, the issues of management rights in United States society, versus the functions and rights of labor unions, stands out as a prominent issue.

DIAGNOSTIC AND PREDICTIVE QUESTIONS

The readings included with this case are marked (*). The author index at the end of this book locates the other readings.

1. From the viewpoint of technology and economics, why did King propose the general audit? Why did the industrial engineers at two lower levels approve it? Why did management approve it?

Read: *Martin's Memorandum, "Standards on Lock Pin Operation," Exhibit 2 in case. *Galbraith, *The Affluent Society,* pp. 121–24, 126. Those who wish additional insight into why efficiency, and prevention of waste, is an integral part of the engineer's job and responsibility, may consult in the library the "Foreword to *Shop Management,*" in *Scientific Management,* by Frederick Taylor, Harper & Row, Publishers, Inc., 1947, pp. 5–10. (Optional, not in this volume: J. D. Black and A. G. Black, *Production Organization* [New York: Henry Holt & Co., Inc., 1939]. This is an advanced reading in economic theory. Or, one may simply think of the inputs of physical resources, including man-hours, in relation to the output of products. This is the physical or technological relationship. This relationship of cost of inputs to value of output is the economic equivalent.).

2. From the viewpoint of science and decision theory, why did management propose the audit in the form of a quantitative, industrial engineering, approach?

Read: *Moroney, *Facts from Figures,* pp. 460–63. Anderson, An Organization Appraisal, pp. 1–2. *Barber, *Science and the Social Order,* pp. 7–8, 12–13, 18, 21. *Beard, *Public Policy and the General Welfare,* pp. 148 *et seq.* *Veblen, *The Engineers and the Price System,* Chapter 5.

3. From the viewpoint of political science and management theory, why did the industrial engineers at each level do the intellectual investigation of the decision and then recommend it to the line executives (try drawing a diagram of who did what in this decision process). Later, why did Carter, the division manager, Leach, the plant manager, and Bauer, the foreman, accept the proposals and carry out the audit?

Read: Hobbes, *Leviathan,* Chapter 10. O'Donnell, "The Source of Managerial Authority." Fayol, *General and Industrial Management,* pp. 24–25, 68–70. Locke, *Concerning Civil Government,* Chapter 9.

4. From the viewpoint of sociology, answer the same questions as immediately above.

Read: *Thompson, *Modern Organization,* pp. 4–6, 12–13, 19–21, 61, 63–65, 77–78. Lasswell and Kaplan, *Power and Society,* pp. 157–59. Simon *et al., Public Administration,* pp. 182, 189–200. *Drucker, *The Future of Industrial Man,* pp. 32–38.

5. Why do you think Glen Carter, general manager of the division, raised the issue of the right of a plant manager to manage the plant?

Read: Citations for Question 3. O'Donnell, "The Source of Managerial Authority."

(Optional, not in this volume: Montesquieu, *The Spirit of Laws,* Book I, Section 2, "Of the Laws of Nature," Section 3, "Of Positive Laws.")

POLICY QUESTIONS

6. Are the concepts of "pluralism," "constructive conflict," or "participation" applicable in this situation? Why might they work (or not work)?

Read: Newman and Summer, *The Process of Management: Concepts, Behavior, and Practice,* pp. 439–48. McGregor, *The Human Side of Enterprise,* pp. 124–31, 172–75.

(Optional: Eells and Walton, *Conceptual Foundations of Business,* pp. 361–63. Follett, "Constructive Conflict.")

7. If you were the plant manager, what line of action would you pursue with the head of the local union, Ed Lillian? Outline the steps you would take, and list carefully your reasons.

QUESTIONS FOR ORIGINAL STUDENT WORK IN ANALYSIS AND POLICY

8. While reflecting on case facts, what additional theories from prior education give you insights as to "what is going on" in National Motor Parts Company? As to what might be predicted to happen in the future?

9. Other than the policy questions asked by the authors, what pragmatic ways can you think of to state the practical problems faced by executives in the case?

Case Text*

The National Motor Parts Company is one of the five largest firms in the basic auto parts industry. It has nine operating divisions and a total work force of over 80,000 employees. Its extensive staff organization provides specialized skills at the corporate, divisional, and plant level. At each of these levels, the cost accounting and industrial engineering groups exert a considerable amount of interest over the development and execution of corporate policy. Though individual divisions are operationally autonomous, division officials generally follow the policy suggestions made by the cost accounting and industrial engineering staffs. A partial organization chart is shown in Exhibit 1.

One program recently advocated by Phil King, corporate director of industrial engineering, was a review of work standards on all jobs which

---

* Copyright 1973 by the Graduate School of Business, Columbia University. This case was authored by John Hutchinson.

EXHIBIT 1

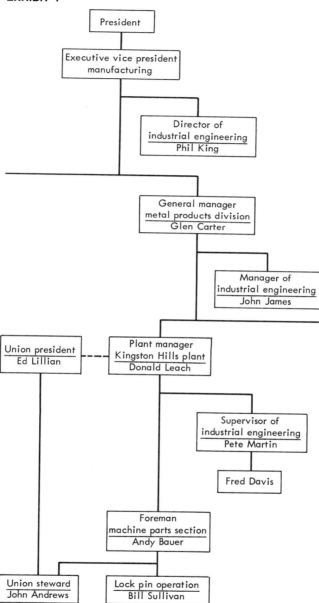

had not been checked or audited within the previous two years. King's request arose from the fact that he had seen several instances of what appeared to him to be goldbricking during a tour of plants in several of National's operating divisions. Upon his return to the central office, Mr. King met with two of his staff engineers, and after careful deliberation, an audit plan was drawn up. This plan was subsequently approved by the executive vice president in charge of manufacturing operations.

The basic plan suggested by King used a technique known as work sampling to check on the idle time present in individual job standards. In essence, the approach taken relied on the fact that a series of short, random observations, if taken often enough over an appropriate time period, could give an accurate picture of the operations performed in each job. The work sampling results would be used to determine which jobs were not requiring the employees to work for an entire day to meet their stated output standards. By the same token, those jobs which were demandng a full day's work to meet existing standards would also be recognized. Though work sampling was to be used to identify standards which were loose (i.e., standards which did not require a full day's work to meet standard output requirements for that day), King's proposal included the further suggestion that looseness, when detected, should be checked in detail by the use of stopwatch time study and a thorough motion study of the job in question.

To launch his program, Mr. King held a series of meetings with the heads of divisional industrial engineering groups. Though objections were raised about the cost and time considerations inherent in the proposal, the division engineering managers agreed that the plan was technically sound and agreed to put it into effect as soon as possible.

One of the more receptive listeners to Mr. King's standards audit procedure was John James, manager of industrial engineering in National's Metal Products Division. This division employs 21,000 people in five plants. James, who holds degrees in both industrial engineering and mathematics, thought that King's plan was both technically sound and eminently practical. He returned to division headquarters in Kingston, Michigan, and drew up procedures to utilize the plan in the Metal Products Division's five plants.

Within a month after the corporate staff meeting, James offered his own version of the audit plan to Glenn Carter, the division manager. Carter, who had come to respect James' technical ability and practical know-how, accepted the plan readily and agreed to present it at the next weekly meeting of his plant managers. Carter suggested that he should merely outline the plan to his plant managers and that James should be available to fill in details and to answer questions.

In the subsequent meeting, each of the plant managers agreed that such an audit was sound, and each, in turn, suggested that James contact the heads of their plant industrial engineering departments to explain the details of his plan. Three plant managers who had formerly been in charge of industrial engineering groups in the National hierarchy offered to provide additional clerical and engineering help on a temporary basis in order to get the program moving quickly.

After gaining the support of Mr. Carter and the five plant managers, James met with the heads of industrial engineering in each of the division's five plants. Though the familiar objections were raised about the time and cost of such a program, all five men stated that the audit procedure was practical and they agreed to put it into effect immediately. Within this group, the plan was embraced most enthusiastically by Pete Martin, the industrial engineer in charge of the Kingston Hills plant.

The Kingston Hills plant shared the same plot of land as the headquarters of the Metal Products Division. It employed more than 5,000 workers and was generally considered to be the most modern and most efficient of the division's plants. Donald Leach, the plant manager, was one of the three men in the division who rose to his present position from a supervisory job in the industrial engineering hierarchy. Leach's plant was equipped with the latest advances in automated equipment, and it was, according to division records, the most profitable plant in the division. Leach prided himself on his ability to attract and retain good managerial talent and he was particularly proud of the work done by Pete Martin in developing new methods of work and in adapting mathematical techniques and procedures to fit the needs of the operations at the Kingston Hills plant. Thus, when Martin suggested the adoption of an audit program, Leach agreed readily and offered Martin additional clerical help to work on the details of setting up the program.

Pete Martin went to work on the program immediately, and within a week the first audit reports were completed. After one month, audits had been completed on seventeen operations. Sixteen of these audits indicated that very little idle time was evident in the operations studied, but the audit performed on one job, the production of a tiny metal lock pin used in automatic transmission units, seemed to show an unusual amount of idle time. The job in question was performed by Bill Sullivan, an experienced long-service employee. Sullivan set up, tended, and performed certain minor maintenance tasks on an automatic screw machine. Because the products he worked on were varied, the original standards had been measured quite carefully.[1] Since the time when the original standards were set, changes had occurred which caused the standards to become loose. Materials changes, changes in tolerance limits on the various machined parts, the time and methods used to set up the various runs, the actual length of machine runs, and the adoption of a more standardized parts line had all occurred in recent years; and since several of these changes had apparently not been reflected in adjustments in the affected output standards, it was a rare day when Sullivan failed to obtain his expected or standard output.

The looseness of Sullivan's standards was no revelation to several of his immediate co-workers. One worker, for example, when conversing with Pete Martin about the audit, stated, "If your audit doesn't pick up that soft touch Sullivan's got, you'd better toss the whole thing down the drain." Few of the workers were bitter about Sullivan's "gravy train" job,

---

[1] Sullivan's standard at this time was .33734 minutes per piece, or approximately 180 units of output per hour. This is shown in Table 1 in Martin's memo (Exhibit 2).

however, since the looseness of his standards gave him no wage advantages over his fellow workers. In other National plants where payment was tied directly to output through the use of incentive payment plans, the relative looseness of standards had frequently caused bitter disputes because of the wage inequities it generated. In the Kingston Hills Plant, the failure of management to detect a loose standard meant that workers accrued leisure time benefits, not higher wages. Though workers objected to such "unfair" work loads, no grievance had ever been filed to ask management to correct such inequities.

The second phase of the audit procedure entailed a review of Sullivan's job by Fred Davis, one of Martin's most competent engineers. In this study, Davis compared the previously set standard (Table 1 in Martin's memo) with the newly calculated time required to perform the operation under changed conditions (Table 2 in the memo). This, in turn showed a tentative idle time of hours per shift.[2] Davis's stopwatch time study of the screw machine operation confirmed the results of the initial audit, and a detailed methods study of the job turned up substantial changes in the original working conditions including changes in materials and methods of operation. Mr. Leach, when confronted with this information by Martin and Davis, ordered them to take steps to correct what he believed was an inequity in the basic work load structure.

After several weeks of study, Davis devised a plan where, with certain layout changes and some methods improvements, Sullivan would operate not one, but two machines. Davis' methods study showed that the time allowances were adequate enough to allow Sullivan to complete the requirements of the revised job if he worked a full eight-hour day. Davis showed his plan to Pete Martin, and together they presented it to Mr. Leach. Leach approved the plan and directed the purchasing department to acquire another automatic screw machine. He thereupon called in Andy Bauer, Sullivan's immediate supervisor, and informed him that Sullivan should be told of the impending change.[3] Bauer, who had worked with Mr. Davis on the methods study, agreed to tell Sullivan that management intended to exercise its contractual right "to make changes in methods, equipment, materials and conditions of work in order to obtain greater efficiency and to adjust existing work standards to reflect such changes." The labor contract further stated that "in case of such methods change only those elements of the standard will be changed which are affected by the change in methods, etc." One other section of the contract spelled out the fact that "standards will be set on the basis of fairness and equity and that they shall be consistent with the quality of workmanship, efficiency of operation, and reasonable working capacities of normal operations." In the National Motors contract, as in most

---

[2] Though a four-hour idle time may seem to be so high as to be almost unbelievable, engineering studies performed elsewhere in National Motors uncovered similar looseness. Experts in the industrial engineering field concede that this situation can arise in even the best-managed plants.

[3] The new standard called for a time of .1664 minutes per piece, or approximately 360 units per hour.

others in the basic auto industry, the resolution of work standards disputes can be solved only by dealings between management and the labor union. Arbitration is specifically prohibited as a means of settling disputes over work standards.

Two months later, the new machine was installed at the workplace along with several minor changes in layout and work flow. Foreman Bauer instructed Sullivan in his new duties, and Sullivan, though he was unhappy about the new layout, started to work with the two machines. During the day, John Andrews, the union steward, stopped by to check on the new job.[4] Sullivan complained violently that he was the victim of a "speedup." Andrews, after listening to the details of the shift from one to two machines, suggested that Sullivan file a grievance.

That evening Sullivan wrote a grievance and, shortly before starting work the next morning, turned it over to John Andrews. Andrews, following the normal procedure for processing such grievances, presented it to Andy Bauer for discussion and possible solution. Because of the technical nature of the grievance, Bauer called upon Pete Martin and Fred Davis to explain the nature of the change to Andrews. When Martin and Davis showed their detail methods studies to Andrews, he stated, "What your guys have done here is to blow up a big smoke screen to hide the fact that you're pulling a speedup on Sullivan's job." The net result of the meeting was that the grievance, still unsettled, moved to the second step in grievance procedure. This step involved discussion between the head of the local union, Ed Lillian, and Donald Leach, the plant manager.

Mr. Leach, when presented with Bill Sullivan's grievance, immediately called Pete Martin into his office to discuss the problem. Together they reviewed the methods study and the subsequent standards revisions. The approaches and the figures shown by Martin seemed correct and reasonable to Mr. Leach, and he believed that the contractual clause allowing him to "make changes in methods equipment, materials, and conditions of work in order to obtain greater efficiency and to adjust existing work standards to reflect such changes" justified the introduction of the second machine. He stated, "It's my duty to my work force to maintain an efficient operation so that the job security of all the workers will be protected." Leach also said, "The only way we can continue to grow and prosper and provide steady employment for our workers is to push for more efficiency in all of our plant activities." In his upcoming meeting with Ed Lillian, Leach planned to use this reasoning as the basis for his insistence on the introduction of the second machine. He also intended to allow Lillian to review any and all of the data used as the basis for changes made on the disputed job.

Ed Lillian, on the other hand, expected to rely on John Andrews to present the union side of the dispute. Lillian told Andrews that he would

---

[4] One of the main duties of a union steward is to represent the worker in presenting grievances to management. He is usually elected to this office by fellow workers. Stewards hold regular jobs in the plants where they perform their duties, and they receive no extra pay for their union activities.

support him fully if the company's actions were in violation of the labor contract.

The feelings of the parties prior to the grievance meeting are summarized below:

> *Bill Sullivan: All of a sudden I'm expected to turn out three thousand pieces per day where I used to have to do fourteen hundred.[5] If this isn't a speedup I don't know what the hell it is. I've got rights and I expect the union to protect them.*
>
> *John Andrews: The company hasn't done a thing to change methods here. They've just come in and made changes to correct their mistakes from the past. Their actions violate the fairness and equity clauses relating to revisions of work standards which exist in the labor contract.*
>
> *Pete Martin: We've made good studies of Sullivan's job and we know that the lock pin standard is loose. It's not unfair to ask him to put in a fair day's work in order to earn a fair day's pay.*
>
> *Ed Lillian: Even though Don Leach is sometimes tough in his dealings with us, he's been fair and consistent. On this issue, however, I'm not sure he's really right.*
>
> *Donald Leach: I believe that I'm both contractually and economically correct when I take the stand that the second machine should be maintained on this operation. After all, if we don't have efficiency in this plant the workers won't have any job security.*
>
> *Glenn Carter: The real issue here is whether or not managers have the right to run their own plants. If we have to subsidize inefficiency in our operations we won't be in business very long.*

The grievance meeting scheduled to resolve this dispute was affected by at least two other factors:

1. Strikes over production standards are legal during the life of the labor contract. Though other issues (wages, hours, working conditions, etc.) could be grieved, no strikes could be called legally on these matters until the existing contract expired.

2. Though one more step remained in the division's grievance procedure, Mr. Carter had written a note to Ed Lillian which stated that he "would not, under any circumstances, alter the stand taken by Mr. Leach in the plant level negotiations." Since the dispute cannot be arbitrated, the parties are faced with the problem of devising some other strategy to solve (or to "win") the disagreement.

In a front-page editorial on the day before the grievance meeting, the local *Kingston Daily Record* asks the disputants to act with "caution and care." The *Record's* editorial recalls that "the steel industry in 1959 and 1960 became embroiled in a similar issue which evolved into a strike lasting six months."

---

[5] In actuality Sullivan was required to turn out 1,440 pieces per day before the audit. After the methods change and subsequent standards revision, Sullivan's quota rose to 2,880 (Exhibit 2).

EXHIBIT 2

To: *Andy Bauer, Foreman, Machined Parts Section*
From: *Peter Martin, Plant Industrial Engineer*
Subject: *Standards on lock pin operation performed by William Sullivan, Clock No. 45716*

In response to your request during our recent standards grievance meeting with Bill Sullivan and John Andrews, I have described both the general procedure for setting machine standards and the specific calculations performed to set a standard on Sullivan's lock pin operation. Though you may feel that some parts of the explanation are overly detailed, I have included them so that your records on this matter will be complete and accurate.

A production standard for a machine operation is determined by measuring two things: (1) the time used by the operator to complete a unit of output, and (2) the machine time needed to produce each unit. The operator's time might consist of the following items: setting up the necessary tooling, jigs, and fixtures to produce the part, feeding materials into the machine, inspection activities, some minor maintenance activities such as oiling the machine and keeping it clean, and other factors which could vary widely depending upon the nature of the job and/or the equipment in use. Machine time represents the time when the machine is performing some operation on the unit being produced.

A simple addition of the operator's time and the machine time rarely produces an accurate work standard, however, since workers can perform certain of their activities during the run time of the machine. It is also true that machines don't always operate perfectly, so it may be necessary to determine an allowance to compensate for such a contingency (commonly called a "downtime allowance") in the final standard. Such complicating factors make a rather knotty problem out of what seems to be at first glance nothing more than a simple job of measurement.

Take for example the standard on Bill Sullivan's job at National Motors. Sullivan was, prior to the industrial engineering audit, operating one machine. When a machine is operated by one man, a good deal of overlap generally occurs between operator time and machine run time. In order to illustrate the setting of a work standard on this operation, we would first determine which of the operator's activities can be performed during the machine's run time. We would then have to adjust the total elapsed time observed during our study of the lock pin operation to reflect such overlap. If we can grasp the relationship between operator time and machine time on a one machine job, we can, if we so desire, expand the concept to illustrate the methods used to measure standards on more complicated multimachine operations.

The first step in setting a standard is to identify the unit by which we intend to measure output. Sullivan's machine is turning out a

EXHIBIT 2 (*continued*)

metal part called a lock pin. The lock pin then is the unit of output which our standard is based.

The next task we face is to thoroughly analyze the job, to determine a standard method of performing the job, and to measure the various elements of this standard operating method. One procedure used to determine the most efficient way to do the job involves the use of a flow chart. Flow charts trace the path of materials and men as they relate to the machines needed to make the product under observation. Another attack uses detailed studies of the motions made by the operator in setting up and running a machine. This latter approach may be performed in very detailed fashion and may even utilize motion pictures of the operation to enable the industrial engineer to study the most refined and intricate motion patterns practiced by the operator.

Though a number of methods are used to set work standards, stopwatch time study is used most widely. In time study a trained observer records the time taken to manufacture (say) a lock pin. He then rates these observed times to reflect a so-called "normal" output expectation on the job. A normal or average rating is generally assigned a value of 100 percent. A below-average performance or less-than-normal performance is given a less than 100 percent rating, while a better-than-average operator would be rated in excess of the 100 percent (normal) rating. The rating factor multiplied by the observed time yields the normal time for performing the portion of the job under observation.

If, for example, a rating of 110 percent was given to a time value of .2000 (two tenths of a minute), the "normal" time to perform this task would be .2200 (1.10 × .2000). This shows us how a faster than normal man's time (.2000) would be adjusted to reflect the pace expected of an average operator (.2200). If a rating of 90 percent was placed on an observed time of .2444 for the same task, the normal time for the operation would be (still) .22 (.90 × .2444). It is no accident that both of these normal (.22) times are identical. If the rating process is done correctly, the observed times multiplied by the rating will always yield an identical normal time. *Since human errors invariably crop up in the rating procedure, there is always some variance in so-called normal times. Skilled industrial engineers, however, claim that such variance will not exceed the "true normal" by more than ± 5 percent. Though the veracity of this claim is often disputed, the rating process is still the most common method of evaluating the elapsed times recorded during a stopwatch time study.*

Once the times are recorded and rated, adjustments must be made to reflect the number of times each element occurs during the production of one lock pin. Setup time, for example, occurs only once per production run, but each run may result in thousands of lock pins. The setup time must then be spread out or prorated over the total production of lock pins. This adjustment occurs in the final standard as a setup time per unit allowance. Similar adjustments are made for

EXHIBIT 2 (*continued***)**

all other items which occur more or less frequently than the cycle needed to produce one lock pin.

As a final step in the standard setting procedure, allowances are added for personal time, delay beyond the control of the operator, and, in some cases, for fatigue. Where particularly unusual job conditions exist, other allowances are sometimes added to the standard. As you know, many of the allowances in use in our plant are set by collective bargaining rather than by work measurement.

The actual calculations of the original standard on the basic lock pin portion of Bill Sullivan's job appear in Table 1. The .33734 minutes per unit figure means that the standard time allowed to produce one lock pin is approximately one third of a minute. Thus a standard output of three lock pins per minute, or one hundred eighty lock pins per hour, is expected. If we could assume an eight-hour workday for Sullivan, his daily output quota on this standard would be 1,440 units.

To illustrate how standards can become loose, we can take Bill Sullivan's job as a prime example. Let us first assume that the setup operation became easier for Bill as he developed skill. Then, longer production runs were planned and changes were made in the materials used to manufacture the lock pin. Now let us assume that Bill performs his inspection operations during the run time of the machine and also manages to cut his oiling and cleanup time in half.

The big item to consider is the machine run time. Suppose now that the new materials allow a more rapid machining cycle and that the machines on the job, after an initial break in period, operate faster and with less down time than the same machines measured in the original job time study.

The new time study by Fred Davis detected the changes described above, and the time study summary sheet in Table 2 shows the results of Davis's study.

The .1664 minutes per unit figure means that the standard time allowed to produce one lock pin is approximately one sixth of a minute. This rate of six per minute calls for an hourly quota of 360 units. Again assuming an eight-hour day, Sullivan's new standard output requirement would be 2,880 units per day.

The problems of undetected methods changes are quite common, although they are usually not as obvious as they appear to be in this case. Though the numerical calculations shown above are quite simple, the problems they illustrate are not.

I hope that this memo answers the questions you raised last week. If I can be of any further help, do not hesitate to call me. By the way, I am now in 408 Engineering but my extension number is still 4193.

P.M.

EXHIBIT 2 (*continued*)

TABLE 1

Column 1	Column 2 Average Time*	Column 3 Rating	(Col. 3 × Col. 2) Column 4 Leveled Time	Column 5 Occurrence per Cycle	Column 6 External Time	(Col. 4 × Col. 5) Column 7 Internal Time
1. Set up machine to run lock nuts†	12.00	100 (1.00)	12.00	1/2000	.00600	
2. Feed first metal bar into machine, run initial pieces, inspect, adjust tooling‡	10.00	90 (.90)	9.00	1/2000	.00450	
3. Remove old bar end, feed new bar	4.00	90 (.90)	3.60	1/270	.01333	
4. Inspection. Sampling basis at end of each run‖	12.00	80 (.80)	9.60	1/2000	.00480	
5. Oiling and machine cleaning	31.90	100 (1.00)	31.90	1/6000	.00532	
6. Get metal bar into position to feed into machine as needed	1.35	100 (1.00)	1.35	1/270		.00500
7. Clear chips from machine	5.50	80 (.80)	4.40	1/135		.03259
8. Remove pieces from drop pans, place in slots in special tray holder	20.25	100 (1.00)	20.25	1/135		.15000
9. Sharpen spare tools for next run	20.00	100 (1.00)	20.00	1/2000		.01000
Total normal time (manual) per unit					.03395	.19759
Add allowances (10% allowance for rest and delay taken from local labor contract)					.00339	
Total standard time (manual) per unit					.03734	
Machine Time (actual) per unit§					.30000	
Standard Cycle time per unit					.33734	

*All times recorded in decimal minutes, i.e., 20 is two tenths of a minute.
†Average production run per setup—2,000 units.
‡Standard metal bars of a particular hardness are specified for this product by the general foreman.
§Based on average run time for varying grades of materials utilized. Also contains allowances for unavoidable down time.
‖Based on tolerances specified by general foreman acting under the direction of the statistical quality control group.

EXHIBIT 2 (*concluded*)

TABLE 2

Column 1	Column 2 Average Time	Column 3 Rating	Column 4 (Col. 3 × Col. 2) Leveled Time	Column 5 Occurrence per Cycle	Column 6 (Col. 4 × Col. 5) External Time	Column 7 (Col. 4 × Col. 5) Internal Time
1. Set up machine to run lock nuts*	10.00	100	10.00	1/6000	.00167	
2. Feed first metal bar into machine, run initial pieces, inspect, adjust tooling†	10.00	80	8.00	1/6000	.00133	
3. Remove old bar end, feed new bar	2.50	100	2.50	1/270	.00926	
4. Inspection. Sampling basis during each run§	1.35	100	1.35	1/270		.00500
5. Oiling and machine cleaning	15.90	100	15.90	1/6000	.00265	
6. Get metal bar into position to feed into machine as needed	1.35	100	1.35	1/270		.00500
7. Clear chips from machine	4.05	100	4.05	1/135		.03000
8. Remove pieces from drop pans and dump into metal tote boxes	1.35	100	1.35	1/270		.00500
9. Sharpen spare tools	10.00	100	10.00	1/2000		.00500
Total normal time (manual) per unit					.01491	.05000
Add allowances (10% allowance for rest and delay taken from local labor contract)					.00149	.00500
Total standard time (manual) per unit					.01640	.05500
Machine Time (actual) per unit‡					.15000	
Standard Cycle time per unit					.16640	

*Average production run per setup—6,000 units.
†Standard metal bars of a particular hardness are specified for this product by the general foreman.
‡Based on average run time for varying grades of materials utilized. Also contains unavoidable down time allowances.
§Based on tolerances and procedures specified by the statistical quality control group.

Selected Readings

From

THE AFFLUENT SOCIETY*

By John Kenneth Galbraith†

THE PARAMOUNT POSITION OF PRODUCTION

In the autumn of 1954, during the Congressional elections of that year, the Republicans replied to Democratic attacks on their stewardship by arguing that this was the second best year in history. It was not, in all respects, a happy defense. Many promptly said that second best was not good enough—certainly not for Americans. But no person in either party showed the slightest disposition to challenge the standard by which it is decided that one year is better than another. Nor was it felt that any explanation was required. . . .

Second best could mean only one thing—that the production of goods was the second highest in history. There had been a year in which production was higher and which hence was better. In fact in 1954 the Gross National Product was $360.5 billion; the year before it had been $364.5. This measure of achievement was acceptable to all. It is a relief on occasion to find a conclusion that is above faction, indeed above debate. On the importance of production there is no difference between Republicans and Democrats, right and left, white or colored, Catholic or Protestant. It is common ground for the general secretary of the Communist Party, the Chairman of Americans for Democratic Action, the President of the United States Chamber of Commerce, and the President of the National Association of Manufacturers.

*   *   *   *   *

. . . Yet production remains central to our thoughts. There is no tendency to take it, like sun and water, for granted; on the contrary, it continues to measure the quality and progess of our civilization.

Our preoccupation with production is in fact, the culminating consequence of powerful historical and psychological forces—forces which only by an act of will we can hope to escape. Productivity, as we have seen, has enabled us to avoid or finesse the tensions anciently associated with inequality and its inconvenient remedies. It has become central to our strivings to reduce insecurity. And as we shall observe in the next chapters its importance is buttressed by a highly dubious

---

* Reprinted by permission of Houghton Mifflin Co., Boston, Mass., 1958 (Chapter 9, pp. 121–24, 126).

† The author is Professor of Economics at Harvard University.

but widely accepted psychology of want; by an equally dubious but equally accepted interpretation of national interest; and by powerful vested interest. . . .

*   *   *   *   *

Thus even in the conventional wisdom no one questions the importance of technological advance for increasing the production (and also multiplying the products) from the available resources. These gains are regularly viewed with great and even extravagant pride. Improvements in technology do not come by accident. They are the result of investment in highly organized scientific and engineering knowledge and skills. Yet we do very little to increase the volume of this investment, except perhaps where some objective of military urgency is involved. Rather we accept whatever investment is currently being made and applaud the outcome.

The investment almost certainly could be much greater and far more rational. Even on the most superficial view, the scientific and engineering resources by which modern technology is advanced are most unevenly distributed between industries. In industries where firms are few and comparatively large—oil, metallurgy, automobiles, chemicals, rubber, heavy engineering—the investment in technological advance is considerable. The research and developmental work on which this advance depends is well financed and comprehensive. But in many industries where the firms are numerous and small—coal mining, home construction, clothing manufacture, the natural-fiber textile industry, the service industries—the investment in innovation is negligible. No firm is large enough to afford it on an appreciable scale; there is real question as to whether it is worth while for such firms. . . .

From

FACTS FROM FIGURES*

By M. J. Moroney†

A very little consideration shows that there is scarcely a hole or corner of modern life which could not find some application, however simple, for statistical theory and show a profit as a result. It has something to offer the man who specializes in any of the branches of management in industry. It offers assistance to the man responsible for purchasing and goods inward inspection. In the hands of the cost accountant or the time and motion study man it acts as a hone to sharpen traditional tools. . . .

Consider, for a moment, some of the fields where the techniques may be applied. There is a scope and often real necessity for them in leather tanning, in the paper-making mill, and in the preparation of pharmaceutical products. It is applied in glass technology, in rubber technology, and in the manifold branches

---

* Reprinted by permission of Penguin Books, Ltd., Baltimore, Md., 1953 (pp. 460–63).

† The author is a Fellow of the Association of Incorporated Statisticians, and of the Royal Statistical Society.

of applied chemistry and metallurgy on which we so much depend for the comforts of modern civilization. We find it in steel works, in agricultural research, and in the textiles industry. . . . Mathematical principles spread out in ever widening circles of practical application; diverse techniques developed in varying fields by practical men are unified and strengthened by the mathematicians.

At bottom it boils down to this: wherever anything is measured numerically, wherever there is an attempt, however rough, to assess anything in the form of numbers, even by the simple process of counting, then there begins to arise the necessity for making judgements as to the significance of the data and the necessity for traffic rules by which the flow of information may proceed smoothly and purposefully. In a word, there is the need for statistics. The application of scientific method to every phase of industry (which is a phenomenon of rapidly growing proportions) inevitably has brought about an increase in measurement of every kind. It is widely accepted now that, even if in the present state of knowledge and in the hurlyburly of production we are able to measure what we are dealing with only roughly, it is far better to make some rough measurement than no measurement at all. . . .

*   *   *   *   *

If you are young, then I say: Learn something about statistics as soon as you can. Don't dismiss it through ignorance or because it calls for thought. Don't pass into eternity without having examined these techniques and thought about the possibilty of application in your field of work, because very likely you will find it an excellent substitute for your lack of experience in some directions. It will curb your over-enthusiasm. If you are older and already crowned with the laurels of success, see to it that those under your wing who look to you for advice are encouraged to look into this subject. . . .

From

SCIENCE AND THE SOCIAL ORDER*

By Bernard Barber†

The Nature of Science: The Place of Rationality in Human Society

Man has always dreamed of, but never actually lived in a Garden of Eden. It is of the essence of the human condition that man lives not in a compliant but in a resistant environment, an environment which he must constantly make an effort to control, if he cannot wholly master it. Man's physical and social situations are ever setting tasks for him in which he must somehow efficiently adapt means to ends. For if it is inherent in man's situation to have to expend "effort" to cope

* Reprinted with permission of the publisher from *Science and the Social Order* by Bernard Barber. Copyright 1952 by The Free Press, A Corporation. (Excerpts from pp. 7–8, 12–13, 18, 21.)

† At the time this book was published the author was Professor of Sociology in Barnard College, Columbia University.

with the environment, it is also in his nature to have a limited amount of energy for this general effort. Man everywhere and at all times, therefore, has had to make at least some of this effort efficiently and economically.

In his need to economize energy, in his need to adapt means to ends efficiently, man has always had the indispensable aid of his power of rationality and of some knowledge about his environment. . . . Here it is enough to recognize the universality of human rationality, to examine its characteristics somewhat more closely, and to show its connection with science. For this is the essential point from which our whole investigation starts: that the germ of science in human society lies in man's aboriginal and unceasing attempt to understand and control the world in which he lives by the use of rational thought and activity. I take it that Professor Percy Bridgman, the Nobel Prize physicist, was making much the same point when he said, "I like to say there is no scientific method as such, but rather only the free and utmost use of intelligence." We shall see, of course, how rationality and intelligence must be disciplined before they become the highly developed science we are familiar with, but it is essential to understand first this prime human source of science.

$$* \quad * \quad * \quad * \quad *$$

President Conant of Harvard, who is himself a chemist, has recently described the essential functions for all science of those highly generalized and systematic sets of ideas which . . . are the heart of highly developed modern science. He calls these ideas "conceptual schemes." It is with the nature of conceptual schemes and their relations with such matters as experimentation, mathematics, and "common sense" that we now wish to deal.

$$* \quad * \quad * \quad * \quad *$$

. . . Modern science has been remarkably successful in defining and isolating "concrete" systems of phenomena which correspond precisely to the abstract systems of ideas which compose its conceptual schemes. As Professor H. Levy has indicated, this isolation of systems is highly important for science. Once a system is isolated by controlled variation of one part, the effect on other parts of the system can be ascertained. In this fashion, experimentation, as we call this procedure of controlled variation which compares like and unlike cases, discloses the effect of the several variables in the conceptual scheme.

$$* \quad * \quad * \quad * \quad *$$

Perhaps we can now see very clearly the sense in which highly developed science based on conceptual schemes of great generality is essentially a dynamic enterprise. The endless making of improved conceptual schemes introduces a dynamic element into the very center of scientific activity. In this way, human rationality takes on the unending power to move heaven and earth, for sooner or later changes in conceptual schemes issue in changes in everyday life and everyday technology. Veblen has said that "the outcome of any serious research can only be to make two questions grow where one question grew before." This is a characteristic of science, this is a dynamic quality it has, that modern man must not only learn about, but learn to live with. For this is the source of the unending social consequences of science. . . .

From

PUBLIC POLICY AND THE GENERAL WELFARE*

By Charles A. Beard†

"Every enterprise in the Great Society itself, as well as the Great Society itself, rests upon administration. Industry on a large scale depends upon organization—upon the management of large numbers of employees of different crafts and arts and the disposition of material goods. In some industries, the administration organization is national and even international in its range. Thousands, hundreds of thousands, of men and women must be brought together and distributed among various departments of production. They must be graded in a vast economic hierarchy, with skilled engineers and managers at the top and the simple day laborers at the bottom. They must be assigned specific and appropriate tasks in the operation of the organization. They must be directed, controlled."

"The state in the Great Society, like the private corporation, also rests upon administration."

From

THE ENGINEERS AND THE PRICE SYSTEM**

By Thorstein Veblen††

. . . [T]he country's industrial system . . . is a comprehensive and balanced scheme of technological administration. Industry of this modern sort—mechanical, specialised, standardised, running to quantity production, drawn on a large scale —is highly productive; provided always that the necessary conditions of productive industry are of a well-defined technical character, and they are growing more and more exacting with every farther advance in the industrial arts. . . . [T]he mechanical technology is impersonal and dispassionate, and its end is very simply to serve human needs, without fear or favor or respect of persons, prerogatives, or politics. It makes up an industrial system of an unexampled character—a mechanically balanced and interlocking system of work to be done, the prime requisite of whose working is a painstaking and intelligent co-ordination of the proc-

---

* Charles A. Beard, *Public Policy and the General Welfare*, copyright © 1941, Holt, Rinehart & Winston, Inc. Reprinted by permission. (Excerpts from pp. 148 *et seq.*)

† Mr. Beard is a prominent historian of the twentieth century.

** Reprinted from Thorstein Veblen, *The Engineers and the Price System* (New York: The Viking Press, 1921), Chapter 5.

†† The author was a prominent Professor of Economics at Chicago, California, and Columbia Universities, writing in the early decades of the twentieth century.

esses at work, and an equally painstaking allocation of mechanical power and materials. The foundation and driving force of it all is a massive body of technological knowledge, of a highly impersonal and altogether unbusinesslike nature, running in close contact with the material sciences, on which it draws freely at every turn—exactingly specialised, endlessly detailed, reaching out into all domains of empirical fact.

Such is the system of productive work which has grown out of the Industrial Revolution, and on the full and free run of which the material welfare of all of the civilised peoples now depends from day to day. Any defect or hindrance in its technical administration, any intrusion or nontechnical considerations, any failure or obstruction at any point, unavoidably results in a disproportionate set-back to the balanced whole and brings a disproportionate burden of privation on all these peoples whose productive industry has come within the sweep of the system.

It follows that those gifted, trained, and experienced technicians who now are in possession of the requisite technological information and experience are the first and instantly indispensable factor in the everyday work of carrying on the country's productive industry. They now constitute the General Staff of the industrial system, in fact; whatever law and custom may formally say in protest. The "captains of industry" may still vaingloriously claim that distinction, and law and custom still countenance their claim; but the captains have no technological value, in fact.

From

MODERN ORGANIZATION*

By Victor A. Thompson†

As the bureaucratic form has developed, associated as it is with the advance of specialization, the most stubborn problem has proved to be the securing of cooperation among individual specialists. . . .

   *   *   *   *   *

Modern bureaucracy is an adaptation of older organizational forms, altered to meet the needs of specialization. Modern specialization is grafted onto it, but old traces of the past remain. Along with technological specialization we find survivals of Genghis Khan and aboriginal war chiefs. We find the latest in science and technology associated with the autocratic, monistic, hierarchical organization of a simpler time. We find, in short, specialization and hierarchy together.

   *   *   *   *   *

. . . [M]odern bureaucracy attempts to fit specialization into the older hierarchical framework. The fitting is more and more difficult. There is a growing gap between the right to decide, which is authority, and the power to do, which is

* Reprinted from *Modern Organization* by Victor A. Thompson, by permission of Alfred A. Knopf, Inc. Copyright 1961. (Excerpts from pp. 4–6, 12–13, 19–21, 61, 63–65, 77–78.)

† The author is Professor and Chairman of the Department of Political and Social Science, Illinois Institute of Technology.

specialized ability. This gap is growing because technological change, with resulting increase in specialization, occurs at a faster rate than the change in cultural definitions of hierarchical roles. This situation produces tensions and strains the willingness to cooperate. Much bureaucratic behavior can be understood as a reaction to these tensions. In short, *the most symptomatic characteristic of modern bureaucracy is the growing imbalance between ability and authority.* . . .

*   *   *   *   *

. . . In an earlier period organizations could depend much more on the "line of command." The superior could tell others what to do because he could master the knowledge and techniques necessary to do so intelligently. As science and technology developed, the superior lost to experts the *ability* to command in one field after another, but he retained the *right* as part of his role.

*   *   *   *   *

Internally, the bureaucratic organization is a complex structure of technical interdependence superimposed upon a strict hierarchy of authority. The entire structure is characterized by a *preoccupation with the monistic ideal.* The hierarchical institution is monocratic. It is a system of superior and subordinate role-relationships in which the superior is the *only* source of legitimate influence upon the subordinate. Everyone in the organization finds himself in such a relationship. Since this was the original organizational relationship, it has dominated organizational theory and practice and still does so. This exclusive emphasis on hierarchy has produced our prevailing organizational theory and informed management practice. We shall refer to this theory as the monistic or monocratic conception of organization. Although conditions are undoubtedly changing, it is our prevailing organizational ideal. . . .

*   *   *   *   *

Under the influence of the primitive monistic ideal, modern organizations are modeled more on the parent-child relationship than on the adult relationships of specialist equals and colleagues. Attempts to maintain the legitimacy of the ideal leads to a great deal of hypocrisy and pretense and to the creation of myths, such as "the ignorance of the masses," "the indispensability of leadership," and "the magical power of fear."[1] Since a monocratic institution cannot admit the legitimacy of conflicts, the legitimacy of divergent goals and interests, much effort is spent securing the appearance of consensus and agreement—securing a "smooth-running organization." The modern organization wants converts as much as it wants workers. It is concerned with the thoughts of its members as well as their actions, and with the thoughts of its public about the thoughts and actions of its members. Consequently, it is concerned with its members' total lives, with what they think and do away from work as well as at work.

Preoccupation with hierarchy governs the distribution of rewards by modern organizations. Ranks of deference correspond to ranks of authority, and deference is manifested by the bestowal of good things. Success within our society means, for the most part, progression up an organizational hierarchy. Modern organizations, consequently, face a growing problem of rewarding specialists. To be socially regarded as successful, specialists must give up their technical fields and enter a hierarchy. Many do, leaving us with growing shortages of many kinds of technically trained people. . . .

---

[1] Peter Blau, *The Dynamics of Bureaucracy* (Chicago: University of Chicago Press; 1955), p. 219.

*   *   *   *   *

Hierarchical relations overemphasize the veto and underemphasize approval of innovation. Since there is no appeal from the superior's decision, a veto usually ends the matter. However, an approval will often have to go to the next higher level where it is again subject to a veto. A hierarchical system, therefore, always favors the status quo. . . .

*   *   *   *   *

The superior has the right to deference from his subordinates. What makes this right significant is that it is one-way. The superior has a right to be somewhat insensitive as to subordinates' personal needs.[2] The ranking of roles with regard to the amount of deference due them is what we mean by the "status system."[3] Although specialties are also status ranked, by far the most visible and virile ranking in organization is ranking according to hierarchical position. . . .

*   *   *   *   *

These roles and the corresponding status systems are simply incompatible with democratic egalitarianism. People are always grateful when a person in a superordinate position exercises his rights with humanitarian restraint. "He's a regular guy." They do not feel that they have a right to expect this.

*   *   *   *   *

The monistic concept is unable to account for specialization. More specifically, it cannot account for the delegation of nonhierarchical authority. The existence of such authority is consequently denied or hidden by fictions, such as, for example, "The staff only advises; it does not command." Furthermore, the monistic concept asserts that *hierarchical authority* is created by delegation from above. . . . Only nonhierarchical authority is created by delegation from above.

The monistic concept, since it is based entirely upon the institution of hierarchy and completely ignores the fact of specialization, naturally confuses rights with abilities: for example, the right to make decisions with the ability to do so. This confusion of rights with abilities results in the popular journalistic presentation of the actions of organizations, including states, as the actions of their top officials. It also encourages elitist interpretations of society, one of the latest of which is *The Power Elite,* by C. Wright Mills.[4]

Hierarchical roles began to develop at times and under conditions when it was credible to think of the chief as the most capable person. Under these circumstances, vast rights became associated with the role. Belief in the unusual powers, or charisma, of persons who perform such roles has continued in the form of the status system. Although specialization has enormously changed the circumstances of organized action, modern organization theory and, to a considerable

---

[2] Wilbert E. Moore, *Industrial Relations and the Social Order,* rev. ed. (New York: The Macmillan Company 1951), pp. 183–184. He says this insensitivity of superiors to the needs of subordinates is the cause of much trouble in organizations. Harold Leavitt says superiors generally resist the introduction of objective performance standards because they interfere with the superiors' right to dominate the situation, to command respect, to rule the roost. (Harold J. Leavitt, *Managerial Psychology,* Chicago: University of Chicago Press, 1958, p. 261.)

[3] The term "status system" is not entirely adequate. "Status" is a social position. Positions are ranked according to the amount of deference due them—according to their prestige. Here we are really concerned with the "prestige system"; however, the term "status system" has been used so much in place of such terms as "prestige system" that we feel it will communicate more.

[4] New York: Oxford University Press, Inc., 1957. [Mills'] "elite" consists, by definition, of the top two or three persons in big-business, political, and military hierarchies. He says that if the line were lowered, the "elite" could be defined away (p. 18).

extent, practice is fixated on the system of hierarchical roles.[5] The fact and implications of specialization are hardly recognized in organization theory. The forcing of specialization into the hierarchical framework gives us our characteristic form of organization, bureaucracy. As we shall see in the following chapters much of the behavior within bureaucracy derives from tensions generated by the conflict between specialization and hierarchy. The cultural definitions which comprise hierarchy change much more slowly than do the facts of specialization. This resistance to further rationalization of organized activity performs no particular instrumental function.[6] It is more in the nature of a "cultural lag." This lag in modification of the roles is undoubtedly reinforced by vested interests in the old role definitions because of their intimate relation to the distributive system. The lag is also reinforced by mechanisms supportive of the status system. Incompatibilities between hierarchical claims to dominance, on the one hand, and on the other, the cultural norms of autonomy, independence, and equality may be softened by charismatic overevaluations of superordinates and by the other mechanisms discussed above. Romanticism comes to the rescue of an unsatisfactory reality.

From

THE FUTURE OF INDUSTRIAL MAN*

By Peter F. Drucker†

Legitimate power stems from the same basic belief of society regarding man's nature and fulfillment on which the individual's social status and function rest. Indeed, legitimate power can be defined as rulership which finds its justification in the basic ethos of the society. In every society there are many powers which have nothing to do with such a basic principle and institutions which in no way

---

[5] Even the departmentalists, the "Gulick school," were concerned only with arranging jobs for purposes of supervision. The jobs—specialization—were taken for granted.

[6] Among those who have argued that the extreme deference ranking (status) aspect of these roles performs no organizational functon are Moore: *op. cit.,* p. 138; Carl Drefuss: *Occupation and Ideology of the Salaried Employee,* trans. Ernst E. Warbling trans. (New York: Columbia University Press; 1938), pp. 1–18; Henri De Man: *Joy in Work,* trans. Eden and Cedar Paul (London: George Allen and Unwin, Ltd., 1929), pp. 200–204. Barnard argues that *status* aids in communication, but he really means *positions* and *roles* rather than prestige ranking. His point that status, as the principal motivation in organizations, is an extremely important part of the incentive system, while true, proves too much. If status is to function as an incentive, it must be available to all. The skewed distribution of status causes it to act as an anti-incentive; it reduces solidarity, hence motivation to cooperate. Barnard himself points this out. (Chester Barnard, "Functions and Pathology of Status Systems in Formal Organizations," in William Foote Whyte, ed. *Industry and Society,* New York: McGraw-Hill Book Company, 1946). See also, Moore, *op. cit.,* p. 184; Peter Drucker: *The New Society: The Anatomy of the Industrial Order* (New York: Harper & Brothers, 1950), pp. 92–95.

† The author is Professor of Management at New York University.

are either designed or devoted to its fulfillment. In other words, there are always a great many "unfree" institutions in a free society, a great many inequalities in an equal society, and a great many sinners among the saints. But as long as that decisive social power which we call rulership is based upon the claim of freedom equality or saintliness, and is exercised through institutions which are designed toward the fulfillment of these ideal purposes, society can function as a free, equal or saintly society. For its institutional structure is one of legitimate power.

This does not mean that it is immaterial whether non-decisive powers and institutions of a society are in contradiction to its basic principles. On the contrary, the most serious problems of politics arise from such conflicts. And a society may well feel that a non-decisive institution or power relationship is in such blatant contrast to its basic beliefs as to endanger social life in spite of its non-decisive character. The best case in point is that of the American Civil War when the chattel-slavery of the South was felt to endanger the whole structure of a free society. Yet the decisive power of ante-bellum America was undoubtedly legitimate power deriving its claim from the principle of freedom, and exercised through institutions designed and devoted to the realization of freedom. American society did thus function as a free society. It was indeed only because it functioned as such that it felt slavery as a threat.

What is the decisive power, and the decisive institutional organization in any society cannot be determined by statistical analysis.

Nothing could be more futile than to measure a society by counting noses, quoting tax receipts or comparing income levels. Decisive is a political, and that means a purely qualitative, term. The English landed gentry comprised never more than a small fraction of the population; furthermore, after the rise of the merchants and manufacturers it had only a very modest share of the national wealth and income. Nevertheless, down to our times it held the decisive social power. Its institutions were the decisive institutions of English society. Its beliefs were the basis for social life; its standards the representative standards; its way of life the social pattern. And its personality ideal, the gentleman, remained the ideal type of all society. Its power was not only decisive; it was legitimate power.

Equally, laws and constitutions will rarely, if ever, tell us where the decisive power lies. In other words, rulership is not identical with political government. Rulership is a social, political government largely a legal category. The Prussian Army between 1870 and 1914 was, for instance, hardly as much as mentioned in the Imperial German Constitution; yet it undoubtedly held decisive power and probably legitimately. The government was actually subordinated to the army, in spite of a civilian and usually antimilitaristic Parliament.

*   *   *   *   *

Finally, it should be understood that legitimacy is a purely functional concept. There is no absolute legitimacy. Power can be legitimate only in relation to a basic social belief. What constitutes "legitimacy" is a question that must be answered in terms of a given society and its given political beliefs. Legitimate is a power when it is justified by an ethical or metaphysical principle that has been accepted by the society. Whether this principle is good or bad ethically, true or false metaphysically, has nothing to do with legitimacy which is as indifferent ethically and metaphysically as any other formal criterion. Legitimate power is socially functioning power; but why it functions and to what purpose is a question entirely outside and before legitimacy.

Failure to understand this was responsible for the confusion which made "legitimism" the name of a political creed in the early nineteenth century. The European reactionaries of 1815 were, of course, absolutely within their rights when they taught that no society could be *good* except under an absolute monarch; to have an opinion on what is desirable or just as basis of a society is not only a right, it is a duty, of man. But they were simply confusing ethical choice with functional analysis, when they said no society could *function* unless it had an absolute monarch. And they were probably wrong when they proclaimed the dogma that only absolute monarchy were *legitimate*. . . .

The functional analysis as to what is legitimate power does not in any way prejudge the ethical question of the individual's right or duty to resist what he considers pernicious power. Whether it is better that society perish than that justice perish is a question outside and before functional analysis. The same man who maintains most vigorously that society can function only under a legitimate power may well decide that society is less of a value than certain individual rights or beliefs. But he cannot decide, as the Legitimists did, that his values and beliefs *are* the socially accepted values and beliefs because they *ought* to be.

Illegitimate power is a power which does not derive its claim from the basic beliefs of the society. Accordingly, there is no possibility to decide whether the ruler wielding the power is exercising it in comformity with the purpose of power or not; for there is no special purpose. Illegitimate power cannot be controlled; it is by its nature uncontrollable. It cannot be made responsible since there is no criterion of responsibility, no socially accepted final authority for its justification. And what is unjustifiable cannot be responsible.

For the same reason, it cannot be limited. To limit the exercise of power is to fix the lines beyond which power ceases to be legitimate; that is, ceases to realize the basic social purpose. And if power is not legitimate to begin with, there are no limits beyond which it ceases to be legitimate.

No illegitimate ruler can possibly be a good or wise ruler. Illegitimate power invariably corrupts; for it can be only "might," never authority. It cannot be a controlled, limited, responsible, or rationally determinable power. And it has been an axiom of politics—ever since Tacitus in his history of the Roman emperors gave us one case study after another—that no human being, however good, wise or judicious, can wield uncontrolled, irresponsible, unlimited or rationally not determinable power without becoming very soon arbitrary, cruel, inhuman and capricious—in other words, a tyrant.

For all these reasons a society in which the socially decisive power is illegitimate power cannot function as a society. It can only be held together by sheer brute force—tyranny, slavery, civil war. Of course, force is the ultimate safeguard of every power; but in a functioning society it is not more than a desperate remedy for exceptional and rare diseases. In a functioning society power is exercised as authority, and *authority is the rule of right over might.* But only a legitimate power can have authority and can expect and command that social self-discipline which alone makes organized institutional life possible. Illegitimate power, even if wielded by the best and the wisest, can never depend upon anything but the submission to force. On that basis a functioning, institutional organization of social life cannot be built. Even the best tyrant is still a tyrant.

15. WESTERN OFFICE EQUIPMENT COMPANY

Case Introduction

SYNOPSIS

The company manufactures and sells office equipment through four regional offices in the western portion of the United States. Charles Porter, the president, applies a number of up-to-date management techniques in order to promote economic success for the company. Particularly, he employs corporate staff men specializing in management science applications to plan a new management control system. In allocating manpower (sales force) between Vancouver, Salt Lake City, San Francisco, and Los Angeles, policies and decision rules are developed to guide top managers and regional managers in deciding both where to locate new salesmen and how many to hire in each locality. The top management is faced with what seem to be powerful advantages of the system but also with serious disadvantages. Some of the latter seem to be technical dangers of the system. Others appear in the form of human conflict between corporate headquarters and geographic division managers.

WHY THIS CASE IS INCLUDED

The case offers opportunity to see and understand, in a real-life action situation:

1. The place of objectives in long-range or strategic planning; the need for goals, the need for balance between conflicting goals, and the conflict between long- and short-run goals.
2. A decision-making process among top managers of a company: president, corporate staff, and division line managers.
3. The advantages and disadvantages of management science as a technique of corporate management, and as an integral part of a

525

management control system. Specifically, marginal analysis and quantification applied to setting of decision rules.
   4. Both the technological and human factors which cause conflict between executives in a larger system (the company) and a smaller component system (its branches).
   5. The advantages of more sophisticated methods of management to society, as well as to an individual company.

Finally, the case offers opportunity to take a managerial viewpoint, and to construct better methods of using management science. In this pursuit, judgment between a number of diverse variables must be used. There is no final "scientific" way of solving such judgmental problems.

DIAGNOSTIC AND PREDICTIVE QUESTIONS

The readings included with this case are marked (*). The author index at the end of the book locates the other readings.
   1. From the viewpoint of management theory and strategic planning, of what importance in the future success of Western Office Equipment Company is Porter's statement that "we redefined the objectives of the company to include growth in four districts: Salt Lake, San Francisco, Vancouver, and Los Angeles," and his redefinition of how much manpower is required in each location?
   Read: Tilles, "How To Evaluate Corporate Strategy." Drucker, *The Practice of Management,* pp. 62–64, 66, 84–87, 121, 128–31.
   2. Why is the creation of the new position of manager of operations analysis an important matter in designing the organization structure of Western Office Equipment Company?
   Read: Smith, *The Wealth of Nations,* pp. 4–15. *Simon, *The New Science of Management Decisions,* pp. 15–18, 40–49.
   3. Why is Porter's search for "some guiding standards that can be applied over the years, to tell us when to hire salesmen and where to put them," an effective managerial way of thinking?
   Read: Tilles, "How to Evaluate Corporate Strategy." *Jerome, *Executive Control—the Catalyst,* pp. 31–34. Dubin, "Imperatives Affecting Industrial Relations Decisions," pp. 292–96.
   4. Olson approached the problem of "how many salesmen" by first finding the marginal revenues generated by each additional salesman, then finding the cost or worth of each salesman to the company. From the viewpoint of microeconomics, why did he do it this way?
   Read: *McGuire, *Theories of Business Behavior,* pp. 56–57. (Those wishing a more thorough description of how microeconomics approaches resource allocation may consult any economics textbook for marginal analysis techniques. For example, read William J. Baumol, *Economic Theory and Operations Analysis,* Prentice-Hall, Inc., 1961, pp. 2–24, 30–34. Not included in this volume.)
   5. Consider the methods used by Olson in arriving at the $133,333 control standard. Then look at the four action decisions he states, begin-

ning "(1) reduce the sales force in Salt Lake from. . . ." Why might Olson and Porter have high motivation to install these action recommendations? Recall especially Porter's opening statement at the meeting of district managers.

Read: Barber, *Science and the Social Order,* pp. 7–8, 12–13, 18, 21. Rapoport and Drews, "Mathematical Approach to Long-Range Planning," pp. 77–78. Gellerman, *Motivation and Productivity,* pp. 109–18.

6. If scientific methods (in this case economics) yield action decisions that Porter and Olson believe in (Question 5), and if the efficiency of this company is in the interest of society, why do Ralph Hudson in Salt Lake and James Fulmer in San Francisco not "see the light"? Can they not share in the enthusiasm for an efficient Western Office Equipment Company through the power of science and rational decision making?

Read: *Miller and Starr, *Executive Decisions and Operations Research,* pp. 38–42, 45–47, 50. Newman and Summer, *The Process of Management: Concepts, Behavior, and Practice,* pp. 605–10. *Maslow, "A Theory of Human Motivation," pp. 80–94.

7. Read carefully Porter's explanation of how the districts might grow in the future by having the manufacturing plants lower their costs to 60 percent of sales (or 60 cents of every sales dollar), instead of the present 70 percent. Do you see another reason which might add to Fulmer's and Hudson's frustration in trying to have their own districts grow in total sales or total number of salesmen employed?

Read: Leavitt, "The Volatile Organization: Everything Depends on Everything Else." Newman and Summer, *The Process of Management: Concepts, Behavior, and Practice,* pp. 605–10. Those who wish additional insight into the answer to this question may consult in the library, *Managerial Psychology* by Harold J. Leavitt, University of Chicago Press, 2d. ed., 1964, pp. 16–21, 24–26. Leavitt discusses the concept of dependency of one individual on another individual or organization, and the resultant frustration this might cause.

8. Get clearly in your own mind how this company situation involves a conflict (1) between headquarters and subsidiary district managements and (2) between those responsible for direct selling and those in other parts of the company such as manufacturing. In what sense can this be considered a "win-lose" or "zero-sum" conflict? What are the attributes of this kind of conflict, and what are the implications for whether or not the conflict can be resolved?

Read: *Litterer, "Conflict in Organization: A Re-Examination."

POLICY QUESTIONS

9. At least in theory, there is a way for Porter to think about achieving an efficient company and achieving good morale on the part of all company personnel at the same time. What kind of ideal or theoretical approaches are available? Why did they not work when Olson visited with the district managers to get their consent?

Read: Follett, "Constructive Conflict." Newman and Summer, *The Process of Management: Concepts, Behavior, and Practice,* pp. 439–48. Argyris, *Personality and Organization,* pp. 27–31, 33–51, 66–67, 77–90, 95, 103–4, 123–25, 130, 137–39, 150, 153–55, 157.

10. Another approach is what some people call a more courageous, forceful decisiveness on the part of Porter or Roberts as they exercise the leadership function. What would Porter do under this kind of theory?

Read: Jennings, "Business Needs Mature Autocrats." Odiorne, *How Managers Make Things Happen,* pp. 4–11, 37–38, 52–53. O'Donnell, "The Source of Managerial Authority," pp. 573–88.

11. One modern means of dealing with the cost problem *and* the morale of district managers would be what is called *organization development.* What would Porter do if he used this approach?

Read: *French, "Organization Development Objectives, Assumptions and Strategies." Leavitt, "The Volatile Organization: Everything Triggers Everything Else."

12. Considering all factors suggested in the above questions, what would you do if you were president of Western Office Equipment Company?

Read: Beard, *Public Policy and the General Welfare,* pp. 148 *et seq.*

QUESTIONS FOR ORIGINAL STUDENT WORK IN ANALYSIS AND POLICY

13. While reflecting on case facts, what additional theories from prior education give you insights as to "what is going on" in Western Office Equipment Company? As to what might be predicted to happen in the future?

14. Other than the policy questions asked by the authors, what pragmatic ways can you think of to state the practical problems faced by executives in the case?

Case Text*

Western Office Equipment Manufacturing Company was founded in Salt Lake City, Utah, for the purpose of making and selling steel utility shelving used in offices and warehouses. Today it is still a family-owned company, though with the retirement of the founder six years ago, a professional manager, Charles F. Porter, was employed as president. The company still makes its original line of steel shelving but has added a diverse line of medium-priced desks, chairs, bookcases, and other small

---

* Copyright 1973 by Charles E. Summer.

furniture. Porter says, "We have never tried to compete with high-quality manufacturers—our customers are medium and smaller companies who want serviceable furniture at a good price." Current sales volume is $3,830,000.

MODERNIZATION UNDER MR. PORTER'S DIRECTION

Since he assumed the presidency, Charles Porter has, in the words of one member of the founding family,

> . . . *Measured up to our expectations. Before he came to our headquarters in Salt Lake City, the company was successful mostly by trial and error. We had developed a good line of products, and our salesmen were good. We were selling in Salt Lake, San Francisco, and Vancouver. Those places were chosen somewhat by accident. The founder was originally from Seattle, worked for an eastern competitor and knew those districts well. He had fifteen salesmen when he retired, all reporting to Mr. Roberts, the marketing vice-president here in Salt Lake. Several years ago, we entered Los Angeles on a very modest basis because we hired an excellent salesman who knew customers and the market there. Today, Porter has organized the fifteen company salesmen into four district offices, with one of the senior men serving as district manager. He has also added new products to the line, set up accounting and profit controls, and enabled us to compete as we never have before with companies that are much larger than ours. In short, our objective is to grow, and Porter is the man we depend on for that.*

ALLOCATION OF SELLING EFFORT

Among other ways of improving the company, the effective allocation of salesmen to territories has been one of Porter's concerns.

> *After I joined the firm [Porter said], there were many things to do. I did not have time to look into the matter of selling effectiveness. Sam Roberts, the marketing vice-president, and I looked at the statistics on selling as the company began to grow. We set the policy that the company should add salesmen to a district as long as the average sales per salesman in the district did not fall below $250,000.*

The current allocation of salesmen by district, the average sales per salesman, and the total sales volume are shown in Exhibit 1. Porter continued:

> *We have fifteen salesmen—six in San Francisco, four each in Salt Lake City and Vancouver, and one in Los Angeles. Several months ago, we redefined the objectives of the company to include growth in four districts. Salt Lake City handles Nevada, Wyoming, Colorado, Idaho, and Montana. San Francisco handles central California; and Vancouver handles British Columbia, Washington, and Oregon. The*

EXHIBIT 1

Current Annual Sales Volume* and Salesmen Distribution by District, Western Office Equipment Manufacturing Company

District	Number of Salesmen	Total Sales Volume	Average Sales Volume per Salesman
Salt Lake City	4	$ 1,060	$ 265
Los Angeles	1	250	250
San Francisco	6	1,500	250
Vancouver	4	1,020	255
Totals†	15	$ 3,830	

* All amounts given in thousands of dollars.
† Average sales per salesman for the company as a whole: 3,830/15 = 255.3, or $255,-300.

really important decision has been to enter the Los Angeles market on a full-scale basis.

John Olson has been with us as manager of operations analysis for three years. He specialized in finance and operations research at Stanford and has done very much to analyze our plant facilities by using modern quantitative methods. I have asked him to analyze the selling effort with this objective in mind: How can we allocate salesmen in districts so that (1) we get the most sales from our total sales force, and (2) we employ the least number of salesmen to achieve this volume? In other words, I wanted him to establish some standard that will tell us how many men to hire and where to put them to get the most volume. The company is growing more complex, and we need some guide that can be applied over the years—I do not want rule-of-thumb assignment on the basis of who a particular salesman is. Decisions have to be made for the business as a whole, and over a period of years.

OLSON'S ANALYSIS AND RECOMMENDATIONS

John Olson spent the first month of his analysis visiting with district managers in the four districts. In each case he explained to them that his purpose was to forecast statistics on potential sales in the district under differing manpower assumptions. For example, he would ask the San Francisco manager to study with him market-potential figures from trade associations, statistics on number and types of businesses in the district, and other materials that he had worked up and brought with him. Then he asked the manager to use his own knowledge of territories, distances between customers, severity of competition by other companies, and other information. Finally, he and the manager jointly discussed both the territory characteristics and the market-research data.

Olson described the results: ◾

In each case, we arrived at the estimates in Exhibit 2. Look at San Francisco. You will see that if Western employs only one salesman,

EXHIBIT 2
Potential Sales Volume* by District, in Relation to Number of Salesmen, Western Office Equipment Manufacturing Company

Number of Salesmen	Salt Lake City			Los Angeles			San Francisco			Vancouver		
	Total Sales	Aver-age Sales	Marginal Incre-ment	Total Sales	Aver-age Sales	Marginal Incre-ment	Total Sales	Aver-age Sales	Marginal Incre-ment	Total Sales	Aver-age Sales	Marginal Incre-ment
1	$ 450	$450	$450	$ 250†	$250	$250	$ 400	$400	$400	$ 350	$350	$350
2	850	425	400	480	240	230	750	375	350	650	325	300
3	960	320	110	690	230	210	1,050	350	300	900	300	250
4	1,060†	265	100	860	215	170	1,300	325	250	1,020†	255	120
5	1,150	230	90	1,000	200	140	1,430	286	130	1,100	220	80
6	1,200	200	50	1,110	185	110	1,500†	250	70	1,140	190	40

*All amounts given in thousands of dollars.
†Denotes current sales volume.

we would sell $400,000. If two, $750,000; if five, $1,430,000. The incremental amount sold by each salesman decreases as you add salesmen in a district because the first salesman gets the best customers, the shortest distances to cover, and other advantages. With only one salesman, we would skim the cream off the market. Each time we add another salesman, we either take less desirable customers or raise the cost of reaching customers, or both. In fact, you can see in the column marked "marginal" the incremental amount of sales volume generated by adding one more salesman in each territory.

Notice, too, that the amount that can be sold by each salesman varies by district. The first salesman in San Francisco will sell $400,-000, but the first one in Los Angeles will sell only $250,000. These inter-district differences are caused by various factors—there may be more competition in one market than in another, or the distance between cities and customers may be greater and so the result will be fewer calls per day.

Once having determined these figures, the next step was to discover a way of measuring what a salesman is worth to the company. In financial terms, what is his contribution to the company profit picture? It costs the company an average of $40,000 a year to support a salesman. From the records, I found that this does not vary much by districts. At a conference between myself, Sam Roberts, and the district managers, we compared figures on salesmen's performance and agreed that for our company and our line of products there is very little difference in salesmen's capabilities. We have some differences, but salesmen are very similar in output.

Given this $40,000 cost, what does the salesman produce in profit contribution? Well, we very carefully got accounting figures to show that the total cost of delivering products to customers (except the cost of salesmen) was 70 percent of sales. This means that the salesman is adding 30 percent of sales as his part of the contribution to profits. Now here is the important point. We will break even if a salesman sells $133,333 worth of merchandise. Thirty percent of $133,333 is $40,000. If the salesman sells just that, he pays (in revenues) for himself. Anything beyond that is a contribution to profits. Stated in reverse, if his sales fall below $133,333, he is paid more than he contributes.

This is known as incremental analysis. In economics we learn that any resource may be evaluated this way. That is, a company should add additional units of any resource up to the point where marginal cost exceeds marginal revenue.

Now to apply this to Western's sales force, we must look at the marginal column for each district (see Exhibit 2). In the Salt Lake district, the second salesman will add $400,000 to sales, but the third will add only $110,000. Or in Los Angeles, the third salesman will add $210,000.

The incremental analysis shows that the company should take the following actions, based on the standard of $133,333:

(1) Reduce the sales force in Salt Lake district from the present four salesmen to two.

(2) Increase the sales force in Los Angeles district from one man to five.

(3) Decrease the number of salesmen in San Francisco from six to four.

(4) Decrease the salesmen in Vancouver district from four to three.

You will also notice that the total sales force comes out to be fourteen, instead of the present fifteen. The reason is that there is nowhere we can put a fifteenth salesman that he will produce the standard sales volume to break even.

Other managerial decisions are also solved by applying this standard. For example, here are the new sales volume quotas compared to the old sales performance figures for each district.

	Current Volume (000)	Planned Volume (000)
Salt Lake district	$1,060	$ 850
Los Angeles district	250	1,000
San Francisco district	1,500	1,300
Vancouver district	1,020	900
Total for company	$3,830	$4,050

Finally, we can convert all of the analysis to total profits for Western.

Sales with new allocation	$4,050,000
Sales volume at present	3,830,000
Increase in sales volume	$ 220,000
Profit margin (multiply)	.30
Additional profit	$ 66,000

TOP MANAGEMENT APPROVAL

John Olson kept Charles Porter informed throughout his analysis, giving reasoning identical with that presented to the case writer. At the conclusion, using easel charts, he presented the complete report to Porter and the board of directors. At that time, one board member said that it looked to him as if one could not draw conclusions about what a salesman could sell until he knew the specific salesman. "Some salesmen simply are better than others." Porter answered that while there will be deviations, a company cannot plan its structure of divisions, including where offices will be located and the size of the sales force, on the basis of one salesman's characteristics. "If he leaves the company, we would have no logical and rational plan."

Porter questioned Olson on how the division managers would receive the new plan and standard. He specifically wanted to know if Olson had obtained their agreement. Olson replied:

> *I have their complete agreement that our company must plan where to add salesmen on an economic basis. All managers agreed that, for the sake of our competitive position, we must do this. Also, in my meetings with division managers they each helped to draw up the amounts that would be sold by each additional salesman in their regions. In other words, the marginal and total sales figures in Exhibit 2 are their estimates as much as mine.*

The board, noting that both the added $66,000 of profits and the expansion into the more profitable market of Los Angeles (from $250,000 sales to $1,000,000) were consistent with the company's growth goal, approved the new plan. On recommendation of Porter, it set a target of three years for transfer of salesmen and buildup to the new district quotas.

Porter then made an implementation plan. He stated that he

> *knew that there would be considerable upset among the salesmen and the district managers. In consultation with Sam Roberts, we decided to transfer two men each from Salt Lake and San Francisco to Los Angeles. One of the salesmen in Vancouver will have to be terminated. We decided on him because he only has two years to go until retirement.*
>
> *Nevertheless, there are times in managing a business when you have to take steps that aren't too popular. It may cause some anxiety in our company temporarily, but five years from now everyone will be operating on the new plan as if it were always that way.*

REACTIONS OF FIELD PERSONNEL

A meeting of district managers was held at the Fairmont Hotel in San Francisco to explain the new financial and selling plan. Porter thought it best not to mail the plan in advance, but simply to explain all of the details on a face-to-face basis. "I thought it necessary to explain the whole thing at once. Only in this way could we get a meaningful understanding of it. If we mailed it in advance, the managers may have focused on only one part or aspect of the whole plan."

Porter opened the meeting by calling attention to the goal of the company to grow, using the most modern management and selling methods available.

> *I'm sure that each of you want our company to use our resources to produce the best products at lowest cost to the customer. In this way, we will always be able to stay efficient and come out ahead of competition. For this reason, I know you will want to understand thoroughly a new plan for district realignment—one that is based on the markets "out there"—that takes best advantage of where the customers are whom we can serve in the most efficient way. I'm sure, too,*

that you are interested in the fact that we have set as our goal our company becoming a leading supplier in the Rocky Mountain and West Coast states. We will no longer simply put our efforts into districts as they have grown up, often somewhat by accident, over the years.

Later, John Olson gave a complete summary of the reasoning behind the new moves, as well as a summary of his analytical methods. At the conclusion, Porter stated that there was plenty of time for questions. "I certainly want you district managers to feel free to question John or me, so that you can satisfy yourself that you know what we are doing and why."

Robert Perry, the manager-salesman from Los Angeles, stated that he had been waiting for months for the go-ahead signal to expand sales there. "The market is there just waiting to be sold. Within three years we will show those larger national firms how to sell."

Ralph Hudson asked Olson why it made sense to transfer two of his salesmen, thus decreasing his sales force by 50 percent, when his four salesmen were averaging $265,000 sales each,

You and I both agree [Olson said] that salesmen who are doing above $133,000 are making money for the company. The average salesman in the Salt Lake district is not only doing over that, but our average salesman is selling more than that of any other district. It just doesn't seem logical, from the company's viewpoint, to cut down from over $1,000,000 sales to $850,000. Why, I would be giving away customers to competition.

Porter clarified at length the reasoning that Olson had reported in the case. "But I don't think we really got across. Ralph said that he of course would be willing to do what is best for the company, but the tone of his voice and the relative lack of enthusiasm seemed negative."

James Fulmer said that he had just recently started new sales training programs in San Francisco and instituted a new kind of advertising at the same cost as his previous campaigns.

In this way, I will eventually get those fifth and sixth salesmen up above $133,000 in production. It may take a couple of years, but I can do it. I believe that you should leave the six salesmen in San Francisco. In fact, though your production forecasts are correct, and I helped draw them up, I had no idea you would draw these kinds of conclusions for them.

Both Hudson and Fulmer questioned how their districts could grow if the company were actually cutting out salesmen and lowering the sales targets, which implied cutting out customers.

Porter explained:

Actually, I see three ways. First you can make better use of sales training and promotion campaigns to raise the marginal sales of each

salesman. These are examples of ingenious new methods that can be invented within your own districts. When that contribution level goes above $133,000 you can bet that Olson and I will be quick to add salesmen.

The other method of growth is a little harder to explain. You see, in a complex business, one part actually depends on another part. One of the factors we have used in the standard is the cost of goods sold (excluding cost of supporting a salesman). That is today 70 percent. It is determined by efficiency in our manufacturing plants as well as efficiency in the central office overhead. In short, all of the cost elements in the profit-and-loss statement. Now in the long run, if we strive for efficiency here to the point where, say, our cost of goods sold is 60 percent, and if we keep our price and volume to the customer the same, the salesmen's contribution will go up to 40 percent of sales instead of 30 percent. That would immediately lower our salesmen's break-even point to $100,000 ($40,000 divided by .40). You can see that, right at the present, the two added salesmen in Salt Lake would be justified, as would six in Los Angeles, five in San Francisco, and four in Vancouver.

The same kind of effect would exist if we passed this new efficiency on to the customer in the form of lower price. Our volume would increase, the selling contribution would go up (and the break-even point down). Manufacturing contribution would go down.

Balancing a complex business like ours is a difficult matter. I'm saying that your contribution depends in part on how efficient our plants and headquarters are. We will work on these other operations as hard as we can. When their efficiency raises the contribution of the salesmen you can bet we will be quick to grow in each and every territory. But in the meantime, it is sometimes necessary to actually hurt one part of the business (for example, the Salt Lake or San Francisco selling branches) to increase overall efficiency. In the long run, it will pay off.

At this point in the meeting, all three managers (with the exception of Robert Perry from Los Angeles) asked a wide variety of questions, most of which, according to Olson, were actually phrased as arguments against the plan. For example, "You don't think you can transfer both Dolan and Franklin to Los Angeles, do you?" Or "Why can't you keep our customers in Vancouver and cut your manufacturing costs now, instead of hurting us in the market place?"

The meeting adjourned at seven in the evening, two hours later than planned. Porter described the results of the meeting.

I told them that in view of their objections, we would declare a temporary suspension of the plan. That we would have another meeting in sixty days to discuss it again. I have a lot of faith in Olson's abilities and am certain in my own mind that the plan is good for the company's growth objectives. Right now, I am wondering what to do, and how to get the plan into effect with the support of the district managers. Their own good work is, of course, vital to a company like ours.

EXHIBIT 3
Organization Chart Western Office Equipment Company

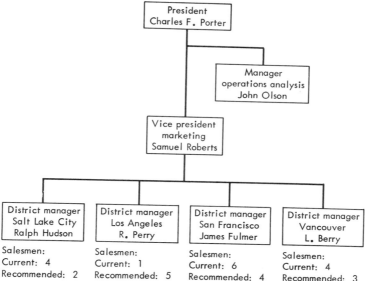

District manager Salt Lake City Ralph Hudson	**District manager** Los Angeles R. Perry	**District manager** San Francisco James Fulmer	**District manager** Vancouver L. Berry
Salesmen: Current: 4 Recommended: 2	Salesmen: Current: 1 Recommended: 5	Salesmen: Current: 6 Recommended: 4	Salesmen: Current: 4 Recommended: 3

Selected Readings

From

THE NEW SCIENCE OF MANAGEMENT DECISION*

By Herbert A. Simon†

NEW TECHNIQUES FOR PROGRAMMED DECISION MAKING

*   *   *   *   *

Along with some mathematical tools, which I shall discuss presently, operations research brought into management decision making a point of view called the systems approach. The systems approach is no easier to define than operations research for it is a set of attitudes and a frame of mind rather than a definite and

---

* Abridgment of pp. 69–73 and 98–107 in *The Shape of Automation: For Men and Management* by Herbert A. Simon. Copyright © 1960 by School of Commerce, Accounts, and Finance, New York University. Reprinted by permission of Harper & Row, Publishers, Inc.

† The author is a Professor in the Graduate School of Industrial Administration, Carnegie-Mellon University.

explicit theory. At its vaguest, it means looking at the whole problem—again, hardly a novel idea, and not always a very helpful one. Somewhat more concretely, it means designing the components of a system and making individual decisions within it in the light of the implication of these decisions for the system as a whole.[1] We now know a *little* about how this might be done:

1. Economic analysis has something to say about rational behavior in complex systems of interacting elements, and particularly about the conditions under which the choices that are optimal for subsystems will or will not be optimal for a system as a whole. Economic analysis also has a great deal to say about the price system as a possible mechanism for decentralizing decision making.[2]

2. Mathematical techniques have been developed and adapted by engineers and economists for analysing the dynamic behavior of complex systems. Under the labels of servomechanism theory and cybernetics, such techniques underwent rapid development at about the time of World War II. They have considerable usefulness in the design of dynamic systems.[3]

*   *   *   *   *

THE MATHEMATICAL TOOLS

*   *   *   *   *

Whatever the specific mathematical tool, the general recipe for using it in management decision making is something like this:[4]

1. Construct a *mathematical model* that satisfies the conditions of the tool to be used and which, at the same time, mirrors the important factors in the management situation to be analysed.

2. Define the *criterion function*, the measure that is to be used for comparing the relative merits of various possible courses of action.

3. Obtain *empirical estimates* of the numerical parameters in the model that specify the particular, concrete situation to which it is to be applied.

4. Carry through the mathematical process of finding the course of action which, for the specified parameter values, maximizes the criterion function.

In any decision-making situation where we apply this recipe successfully, we have, in fact, constructed a *program* for the organization's decisions. We have either annexed some decisions that had been judgmental to the area of programmed decision making,[5] or we have replaced a rule-of-thumb program with a more sophisticated program that guarantees us optimal decisions—optimal, that is, within the framework of the mathematical model.

But certain conditions must be satisfied in order to apply this recipe to a class

---

[1] See C. West Churchman, Russell L. Ackoff, and E. Leonard Arnoff, *Introduction to Operations Research* (New York: John Wiley & Sons, Inc., 1957), pp. 109–11.

[2] See Tjalling C. Koopmans, ed., *Activity Analysis of Production and Allocation* (New York: John Wiley & Sons, Inc., 1951).

[3] The word cybernetics was first used by Norbert Wiener in *Cybernetics* (New York: John Wiley & Sons, Inc., 1948), p. 19. A good exposition of these techniques may be found in Arnold Tustin, *The Mechanism of Economic Systems* (Cambridge: Harvard University Press, 1953).

[4] See Churchman, *et al., op. cit.,* chap. v.

[5] Thus, operations research, in addition to providing techniques for programmed decisions, also expands their boundaries.

of decision problems. First, it must be possible to define mathematical variables that represent the important aspects of the situation. In particular, a quantitative criterion function must be defined. If the problem area is so hopelessly qualitative that it cannot be described even approximately in terms of such variables, the approach fails. Second, the model will call for certain parameters of its structure to be estimated before it can be applied in a particular situation. Hence, it is necessary that there be ways of making actual numerical estimates of these parameters—of sufficient accuracy for the practical task at hand. Third, the specification of the model must fit the mathematical tools to be used. If certain kinds of nonlinearities are absolutely crucial to an accurate description of the situation, linear programming simply won't work—it is a tool adapted to mathematical systems that are, in a certain sense, linear. Fourth, the problem must be small enough that the calculations can be carried out in reasonable time and at a reasonable cost.

Some relatively simple management problems—for example, many problems of factory scheduling—turn out to be far too large for even such a powerful tool as linear programming. It is easy for the operations research enthusiast to underestimate the stringency of these conditions. This leads to an ailment that might be called mathematician's aphasia. The victim abstracts the original problem until the mathematical intractabilities have been removed (and all semblance to reality lost), solves the new simplified problem, and then pretends that this was the problem he wanted to solve all along. He expects the manager to be so dazzled by the beauty of the mathematical results that he will not remember that his practical operating problem has not been handled.

It is just as easy for the traditionalist to overestimate the stringency of the conditions. For the operations research approach to work, nothing has to be exact—it just has to be close enough to give better results than could be obtained by common sense without the mathematics. Furthermore, it is dangerous to assume that something is essentially qualitative and not reducible to mathematical form until an applied mathematician has had a try at it. . . .

*   *   *   *   *

SOME FUNDAMENTALS OF ORGANIZATIONAL DESIGN

An organization can be pictured as a three-layered cake. In the bottom layer, we have the basic work processes—in the case of a manufacturing organization, the processes that procure raw materials, manufacture the physical product, warehouse it, and ship it. In the middle layer, we have the programmed decision-making processes, the processes that govern the day-to-day operation of the manufacturing and distribution system. In the top layer, we have the nonprogrammed decision-making processes, the processes that are required to design and redesign the entire system, to provide it with its basic goals and objectives, and to monitor its performance.

*   *   *   *   *

The Hierarchical Structure of Organizations[6]

Large organizations are almost universally hierarchical in structure. That is to say, they are divided into units which are subdivided into smaller units, which are,

---

[6] The speculations of the following paragraphs are products of my joint work over recent years with Allen Newell.

in turn, subdivided, and so on. They are also generally hierarchical in imposing on this system of successive partitionings a pyramidal authority structure. However, for the moment, I should like to consider the departmentalization rather than the authority structure.

Hierarchical subdivision is not a characteristic that is peculiar to human organizations. It is common to virtually all complex systems of which we have knowledge.

*   *   *   *   *

The complex systems of chemistry and physics reveal the same picture of wheels within wheels within wheels. A protein molecule—one of the organismic building blocks—is constructed out of simpler structures, the amino acids. The simplest molecules are composed of atoms, the atoms of so-called elementary particles. Even in cosmological structures, we find the same hierarchical pattern: galaxies, planetary systems, stars, and planets.

The near universality of hierarchy in the composition of complex systems suggests that there is something fundamental in this structural principle that goes beyond the peculiarities of human organization. I can suggest at least two reasons why complex systems should generally be hierarchical:

1. *Among possible systems of a given size and complexity, hierarchical systems, composed of subsystems, are the most likely to appear through evolutionary processes.* A metaphor will show why this is so. Suppose we have two watchmakers, each of whom is assembling watches of ten thousand parts. The watchmakers are interrupted, from time to time by the telephone, and have to put down their work. Now watchmaker A finds that whenever he lays down a partially completed watch, it falls apart again, and when he returns to it, he has to start reassembling it from the beginning. Watchmaker B, however, has designed his watches in such a way that each watch is composed of ten subassemblies of one thousand parts each, the subassemblies being themselves stable components. The major subassemblies are composed, in turn, of ten stable subassemblies of one hundred parts each, and so on. Clearly, if interruptions are at all frequent, watchmaker B will assemble a great many watches before watchmaker A is able to complete a single one.

2. *Among systems of a given size and complexity, hierarchical systems require much less information transmission among their parts than do other types of systems.* As was pointed out many years ago, as the number of members of an organization grows, the number of *pairs* of members grows with the square (and the number of possible subsets of members even more rapidly). If each member, in order to act effectively, has to know in detail what each other member is doing, the total amount of information that has to be transmitted in the organization will grow at least proportionately with the square of its size. If the organization is subdivided into units, it may be possible to arrange matters so that an individual needs detailed information only about the behavior of individuals in his own unit, and aggregative summary information about average behavior in other units. If this is so, and if the organization continues to subdivide into suborganizations by cell division as it grows in size, keeping the size of the lowest level subdivisions constant, the total amount of information that has to be transmitted will grow only slightly more than proportionately with size.

These two statements are, of course, only the grossest sorts of generalization. They would have to be modified in detail before they could be applied to specific organizational situations. They do provide, however, strong reasons for believing that almost any system of sufficient complexity would have to have the rooms-within-rooms structure that we observe in actual human organizations. The reasons for hierarchy go far beyond the need for unity of command or other considerations relating to authority.

The conclusion I draw from this analysis is that the automation of decision making, irrespective of how far it goes and in what directions it proceeds, is unlikely to obliterate the basically hierarchical structure of organizations. The decision-making process will still call for departmentalization and sub-departmentalization of responsibilities. . . .

*　　*　　*　　*　　*

The organizations of the future, then, will be hierarchies, no matter what the exact division of labor between men and computers. This is not to say that there will be no important differences between present and future organizations. Two points, in particular, will have to be reexamined at each stage of automation:

1. What are the optimal sizes of the building blocks in the hierarchy? Will they become larger or smaller? This is the question of centralization and decentralization.

2. What will be the relations among the building blocks? In particular, how far will traditional authority and accountability relations persist, and how far will they be modified? What will be the effect of automation upon subgoal formation and subgoal identification?

Size of the Building Blocks: Centralization and Decentralization

One of the major contemporary issues in organization design is the question of how centralized or decentralized the decision-making process will be—how much of the decision making should be done by the executives of the larger units, and how much should be delegated to lower levels. But centralizing and decentralizing are not genuine alternatives for organizing. The question is not whether we shall decentralize, but how far we shall decentralize. What we seek, again, is a golden mean: we want to find the proper level in the organization hierarchy—neither too high nor too low—for each important class of decisions.

Over the past twenty or more years there has been a movement toward decentralization in large American business organizations. This movement has probably been a sound development, but it does *not* signify that more decentralization is at all times and under all circumstances a good thing. It signifies that at a particular time in history, many American firms, which had experienced almost continuous long-term growth and diversification, discovered that they could operate more effectively if they brought together all the activities relating to individual products or groups of similar products and decentralized a great deal of decision making to the departments handling these products or product groups. At the very time this process was taking place there were many cross-currents of centralization in the same companies—centralization, for example, of industrial relations activities. There is no contradiction here. Different decisions need to be made in different organizational locations, and the best location for a class of decisions may change as circumstances change.

There are usually two pressures toward greater decentralization in a business organization. First, it may help bring the profit motive to bear on a larger group of executives by allowing profit goals to be established for individual subdivisions of the company. Second, it may simplify the decision-making process by separating out groups of related activities—production, engineering, marketing, and finance for particular products—and allowing decisions to be taken on these matters within the relevant organizational subdivisions. Advantages can be realized in either of these ways only if the units to which decision is delegated are natural subdivisions—if, in fact, the actions taken in one of them do not affect in too much detail or too strongly what happens in the others. Hierarchy always implies intrinsically some measure of decentralization. It always involves a balancing of the cost savings through direct local action against the losses through ignoring indirect consequences for the whole organization.

Organizational form, I said earlier, must be a joint function of the characteristics of humans and their tools and the nature of the task environment. When one or the other of these changes significantly, we may expect concurrent modifications to be required in organizational structure—for example, in the amount of centralization or decentralization that is desirable.

When the cable and the wireless were added to the world's techniques of communication, the organization of every nation's foreign office changed. The ambassador and minister who had exercised broad, discretionary decision-making functions in the previous decentralized system, were now brought under much closer central control. The balance between the costs in time and money of communication with the center, and the advantages of coordination by the center had been radically altered.

The automation of important parts of business data-processing and decision-making activity, and the trend toward a much higher degree of structuring and programming of even the nonautomated part will radically alter the balance of advantage between centralization and decentralization. The main issue is not the economies of scale—not the question of whether a given data-processing job can better be done by one large computer at a central location or a number of smaller ones, geographically or departmentally decentralized. Rather, the main issue is how we shall take advantage of the greater analytic capacity, the larger ability to take into account the interrelations of things, that the new developments in decision making give us. A second issue is how we shall deal with the technological fact that the processing of information within a coordinated computing system is orders of magnitude faster than the input-output rates at which we can communicate from one such system to another, particularly where human links are involved.

*   *   *   *   *

The mismatch . . . between the kinds of records that humans produce readily and read readily and the kinds that automatic devices produce and read readily is a second technological factor pushing in the direction of centralization. Since processing steps in an automated data-processing system are executed in a thousandth or even millionth of a second, the whole system must be organized on a flow basis with infrequent intervention from outside. Intervention will take more and more the form of designing the system itself—programming—and less and less the form of participating in its minute-by-minute operation. Moreover, the parts of the system must mesh. Hence, the design of decision-making and data-processing systems will tend to be a relatively centralized function. It will be a little like ship design. There is no use in one group of experts producing the design for the hull, another the design for the power plant, a third the plans for the passenger quarters, and so on, unless great pains are taken at each step to see that all these parts will fit into a seaworthy ship.

It may be objected that the question of motivation has been overlooked in this whole discussion. If decision making is centralized how can the middle-level executive be induced to work hard and effectively? First, we should observe that the principle of decentralized profit-and-loss accounting has never been carried much below the level of product-group departments and cannot, in fact, be applied successfully to fragmented segments of highly interdependent activities. Second, we may question whether the conditions under which middle-management has in the past exercised its decision-making prerogatives were actually good conditions from a motivational standpoint.

Most existing decentralized organization structures have at least three weaknesses in motivating middle-management executives effectively. First, they encourage the formation of and loyalty to subgoals that are only partly parallel with the goals of the organization. Second, they require so much nonprogrammed problem solving in a setting of confusion that they do not provide the satisfactions which, we argued earlier, are valued by the true professional. Third, they realize none of the advantages, which by hindsight we find we have often gained in factory automation, of substituting machine-paced (or better, system-paced) for man-paced operation of the system.

. . . We can summarize the present discussion by saying that the new developments in decision making will tend to induce more centralization in decision-making activities at middle-management levels.

From

EXECUTIVE CONTROL—
THE CATALYST*

By William Travers Jerome, III†

KINDS OF CONTROL

The word "control" has the serious shortcoming of having different meanings in different contexts. Most of these meanings are negative ones that connote such things as faultfinding or obedience by subordinates to instructions emanating from superiors. That "control" should evoke these meanings is unfortunate. . . . Control in any broad management sense bespeaks a planned rather than haphazard approach by a society to the employment of both its human and material resources. Control represents those forces that make it possible for any organized activity, whether public or private, to function purposefully. . . .

Control in its broad or managerial sense . . . can be quite appropriately defined

* From *Executive Control—The Catalyst* by Wm. Travers Jerome III. Copyright © 1961 by John Wiley & Sons, Inc. Reprinted by permission. Excerpts pp. 31 34.

† The author was for many years Dean of the Business School at Syracuse University.

as "the presence in a business of that force which guides it to a predetermined objective by means of predetermined policies and decisions."[1] By "force" presumably is meant (1) management's conviction of the importance of continuous and systematic planning and (2) availability of the skills necessary to perform the planning (i.e., controlling) properly. . . .

Those with engineering backgrounds . . . seem to regard modern systems of managerial control as "strikingly similar to simple servomechanisms of the electromechanical type." Since electromechanical control systems are designed to maintain a level of performance (e.g., temperature) between predetermined limits, it is assumed that "preventiveness is the essential attribute of a control system. . . . The existence of a control system is justified by its ability to enforce its norms. Precision in the determination of norms is of elemental importance in industrial control."[2] Such a concept of control is highly appropriate for machines or some shop operations. It is far too rigid and uncompromising a concept, however, for the world of people.

For a proper perspective of the meaning of control, it is important to recognize that a whole host of important but relatively mundane controls lie outside of management's customary scope and concern. These other kinds of control help to set a precise pattern of rules and procedures, not unlike those of . . . servomechanisms, . . . to expedite the handling of a firm's routine operations. This particular pattern is known in the accounting trade as the "system of internal control.". . . It should prove both interesting and suggestive simply to classify controls on the basis of the *use* to which a given control is put. The following classification might result:

1. *Controls used to standardize performance* in order to increase efficiency and to lower costs. Included might be time and motion studies, inspections, written procedures, or production schedules.

2. *Controls used to safeguard company assets* from theft, wastage, or misuse. Such controls typically would emphasize division of responsibilities, separation of operational, custodial, and accounting activities, and an adequate system of authorization and record keeping.

3. *Controls used to standardize quality* in order to meet the specifications of either customers or company engineers. Blueprints, inspection, and statistical quality controls would typify the measures employed to preserve the integrity of the product (or service) marketed by the company.

4. *Controls designed to set limits within which delegated authority can be exercised without further top management approval.* Organization and procedure manuals, policy directives, and internal audits would help to spell out the limits within which subordinates have a free hand.

5. *Controls used to measure on-the-job performance.* Typical of such controls would be special reports, output per hour or per employee, internal audits, and perhaps budgets or standard costs.

6. *Controls used for planning and programming operations.* Such controls would include sales and production forecasts, budgets, various cost standards, and standards of work measurement.

---

[1] "The Planning and Control Concept," *The Controller,* September, 1954, p. 403.

[2] J. V. McKenna, "The Basic Theory of Managerial Control," *Mechanical Engineering,* vol. 77, no. 8, August, 1955, pp. 180 ff.

7. *Controls necessary to allow top management to keep the firm's various plans and programs in balance.* Typical of such controls would be a master budget, policy manuals, organization manuals, and such organization techniques as committees and the use of outside consultants. The overriding need for such controls would be to provide the necessary capital for . . . operations and to maximize profits.

8. *Controls designed to motivate individuals within* a firm to contribute their best efforts. Such controls necessarily would involve ways of recognizing achievement through such things as promotions, awards for suggestions, or some form of profit sharing. . . .

Certain similarities and dissimilarities in these techniques at once appear. For example, there is a preventional or compliance aspect characteristic of the controls in groupings 1 through 3. This grouping consists of the controls used to standardize performance, to safeguard assets, and to insure quality. These controls are really in the nature of directives or procedures that must be followed. Compliance with these is not left to the discretion of anyone using them. Instead, the effectiveness of performance will be judged primarily by the degree of compliance attained.

The second grouping, on the other hand, consists of controls that are intended to provide some elements of latitude to those who are affected by them. They are useful in helping to set the goals, to plan the work, to appraise the performance, and to set the tone for the firm's activity. These controls consist of the remainder of the items on the preceding list. These are the controls designed to set limits for delegated authority, to set norms against which performance can be measured, to facilitate company planning, to keep overall company balance in the interest of optimizing company objectives, and to motivate action.

This "control" classification is striking primarily in the way a number of these controls appear to belong appropriately in either of these two major groupings. Standard costs or budgets, for example, can be used to compel compliance. Thus, they provide the means for management to set the desired level of performance expected of subordinates. Variance of actual from anticipated performance is the signal built into these techniques for flagging possible investigation of the reasons for deviations.

Standard costs, and particularly budgets, are also the principal techniques for reflecting a firm's plans. They provide a method for a given level of management to gauge its own performance. These uses are constructive as they encourage both self-evaluation and the forward look.

Control techniques such as budgets that are interchangeable between the two groupings provide ample room for misunderstanding. When budgets are regarded as "planning," it is questionable whether they should be used to compel compliance. Thus, the score envisioned by a golfer on the first tee is not the same as what he intends to set for his bets! Or, as a further example, when internal auditing is sold to lower levels of management on constructive grounds, its compliance or policeman's role must be exercised with considerable restraint.

There is a second significant thing about the preceding classification. All these control techniques, except for those in the final classification, have one thing in common: each can measure performance.

In other words, each of the controls listed serves as a norm or standard of conduct. Against this standard, actual performance can be compared. Unless such comparison is made, the standards have limited value.

Another way to say this is that "control" is not something intrinsic to a given technique any more than "measurement" is inherent in a given yardstick. "Control" comes from the conscious use of such devices to influence action. This influence (or control) may be in terms of either or both: (1) the thought, the analysis, the planning, and the cooperative effort that go into constructing particular norms or yardsticks, and (2) the corrective action taken when a comparison of results with the projected performance indicates the need.

Controls governing routine and repetitive operations stress compliance, as mentioned earlier. Their primary function, therefore, is to serve in the area of internal control.

Management controls, on the other hand, serve both as a measure of performance and as conditioners of the firm's working environment. The attitudes of planning and of self-evaluation are particularly powerful influences in a firm, for they are among the key forces that contribute to decisive and continuous progress. This capability of any given executive control to motivate constructive action is by all odds its most important characteristic. This contrasts with the compliance or command feature of other types of control.

From

EXECUTIVE DECISIONS AND OPERATIONS RESEARCH*

By David W. Miller and Martin K. Starr†

Goals of the Role

People play many roles. Each role can be associated with its own objectives. Individuals simplify their decision problems by establishing for themselves these multiple objectives instead of just one basic objective. Most people, for example, will establish some kind of objective for themselves in the area of their professional activities. They will usually have other objectives relating to their interpersonal relationships; e.g., father, husband, son. They will also have objectives regarding their relationship to society as a whole, e.g., political activity or public-spirited work. They will often have some objectives regarding their leisure activities. And, of course, we can continue and obtain quite a catalogue of the different areas in which people are likely to set themselves some kind of objectives. It appears that most people handle their decision problems in a particular field of activity by ignoring the objectives of other fields of activity. Thus, a business executive will solve his decision problems in business—for example, what position he will accept—in terms of his professional objective.

Even within a single field of activity an individual has many different roles. An

* *Executive Decisions and Operations Research,* David W. Miller and Martin K. Starr © 1961 by Prentice-Hall, Inc., Englewood Cliffs, N.J. (pp. 38–42, 45–47, 50).

† The authors are professors at the Columbia University Graduate School of Business.

executive reports to his boss and in turn has people reporting to him. His position in the organization determines the extent of his responsibility and the importance of decisions he must make. The goal of the executive is strongly tied to the complex image he has of his role. Although no two executives have the same situations, the similarity of goals which they share as a group causes us to speak about executive goals. However, similarity should not blind us to the differences. In the same way, for convenience, we group employee goals, ownership goals, salesmen's goals, and so on. There is a certain relevant pattern of goal-seeking within each of these groups. It is hardly necessary to expand on what these might be. On the other hand, it is an observable fact that sometimes there is a conflict between the objectives of several groups to which the individual belongs.

Suboptimization

. . . Whenever there is no conflict between objectives, the individual can proceed to solve his decision problems separately. As long as the action taken to achieve either objective is independent of the other, he can do this. However, when objectives are dependent, the optimization of one can result in a lower degree of attainment for all the others. This condition is known as *suboptimization*. For example, an executive may decide to take a new position on the basis of his professional objectives. The new job, however, entails extremely long hours and much traveling. Assume that the new job is optimal in terms of the executive's professional objective. The fact that the time he can now spend with his family is sharply reduced may have such adverse effects that he will find that his optimization in terms of one objective has produced a result which is very much less than optimal in terms of all his objectives.

The same notion of suboptimization is involved in the effects on the decision problem of the fact that we lead our lives through time and that we have only very imperfect ability to foresee the future. This means that any decision problem can be solved only in terms of the knowledge and situation obtaining currently. But the action chosen may, and probably will, have effects on the decision-maker's situation for a considerable period in the future. An optimal action at one time may, therefore, turn out to have been a very inferior suboptimization in terms of a longer period of time.

*   *   *   *   *

It is quite clear that we can never really achieve optimization. Over time, unexpected events can change what had appeared to be an optimal decision into an inferior decision. There is almost no reversibility in decision systems. Generally speaking, by the time we find out that a decision was not a good one, we cannot return to the state which prevailed before the decision had been made. Consequently, decision systems should provide the best possible predictions of future expectations. And in addition, decision systems should not commit us to irrevocable action for very long periods of time. And so we reach the conclusion that a *sequential decision process* permits maximum flexibility with respect to both objectives and actions.

Bounded Rationality

. . . We have been using the word "optimum," and some other forms of the same word, rather loosely. In fact, it is important to note that people rarely make a prolonged effort to achieve the optimum action in any realistic decision problem facing them. To paraphrase John Maurice Clark, people simply don't have such an irrational passion for dispassionate rationality. Furthermore, there are good reasons why they shouldn't. All of the reasons have reference to the exorbitant complexity of any realistic decision problem. Three main aspects of this complexity should be noted.

First, consider the point just made, that an optimum decision made at one point in time is only suboptimum in terms of subsequent times. . . .

. . . Second, there are an enormous number of possible choices of action (strategies, as we have called them) and any attempt to obtain information on all of them would be self-defeating.

. . . Third, there are virtually innumerable factors outside the control of the decision-maker (we call them states of nature) which may affect the outcome of his decision.

. . . The net effect of these limitations on human decision-making procedures has been observed and neatly summarized by Herbert Simon in his "principle of bounded rationality." According to this principle human beings seldom make any effort to find the optimum action in a decision problem. Instead, they select a number of possible outcomes of their available strategies which would be good enough. Then they select a strategy (choose an action) that is likely to achieve one of the good-enough outcomes. Thus, the executive looking for a new job makes no effort to discover all possible jobs from which he can then select the best (optimum) one. Instead, he decides what he wants from a job in terms of his various objectives. Then he searches for a job that will provide him with the things he wants, e.g., a certain income, satisfactory working conditions, chances for advancement. He does not try to find that one job somewhere in the world which might give him the optimum. The principle of bounded rationality is a neat way to describe the actual procedure of human beings involved in the decision problems of life, and it succinctly reminds us not to assume any irrational extremes of rationality.

*   *   *   *   *

Organizational Problems of Suboptimization

. . . Under what conditions does suboptimization arise in business? Of course we can answer that it arises whenever an action has an effect on several different objectives simultaneously. But this is merely to state the same thing in different words. In fact, there is no general answer to this question. The best that can be done in any specific decision problem is to utilize intuition, experience, and all available methodology to endeavor to see whether actions intended for one purpose have any probable effects on other objectives. If they do then it follows that the problem is one that involves a possible conflict of objectives and it must be handled with this fact in mind.

It should be explicitly noted that no genuine problem of a conflict of objectives can be reconciled by expressing all the possible outcomes in terms of the utility measure for one of the objectives. Now, it is fortunate that many decision problems of business can be framed in terms such that the possible outcomes can be measured in dollars. But it is by no means the case that all business objectives can be expressed in dollars. If, to take an instance, workers' attitudes could be measured in dollars, then it would follow that all possible outcomes in the area of workers' attitudes could be expressed in dollars. The total objective need only be stated as the maximization of profit. We would not require a special description of workers' attitudes. No such easy solution to the problem of conflicting objectives is usually available. . . .

Looking at the bright side, there are a great number of important decision problems that do not involve any conflict of objectives. For any one of these we can attempt to optimize with no fear of difficulties arising from suboptimization. In particular, we can state that, at the minimum, a business must attempt to optimize its situation with regard to each specific objective as long as it does not affect adversely its situation with regard to any other objective. This construction is a variant of an idea introduced in a different context by the Italian economist and sociologist, Vilfredo Pareto. Pareto was concerned with the problem of what should govern the actions of society if it is assumed that the utilities of the various individuals composing the society cannot be compared. By utility we mean the subjective value that each individual subscribes for the various goods and services available. Under these circumstances society cannot act to achieve the greatest total utility because this idea has no meaning for the stated conditions. Pareto suggested that society should then try to achieve at least an optimum such that each individual had the maximum utility possible without subtracting anything from anyone else's utility. In other words, if society can act so as to increase one individual's total utility without taking anything away from anyone else, then it should do so. A condition where this has been accomplished is known as *Paretian optimality.*

The problem with which Pareto was dealing arises because there is no common standard of measure of value between individuals. And this is precisely analogous to the problem of multiple objectives with which we are dealing. Our problem arises because there is no common measure of value for the various objectives. If there were one common measure we could formulate one objective rather than several. Therefore we can state, along with Pareto, that any business should always attempt to achieve a condition of Paretian optimality with regard to its various objectives.

*　　*　　*　　*　　*

Business organizations are subject to still another kind of suboptimization problem. Whereas a real person is a unit that is more or less indecomposable, the fictitious person of the business corporation is usually made up of a number of different departments or divisions. The successful functioning of the business demands the integration of the efforts of the various departments that compose it. The achievement of any of the business objectives requires that the various departments should each achieve some departmental objectives. But, by the very nature of things, departments are likely to have considerable autonomy and it can happen that the objectives they set are not in accord with the over-all business objectives. It can also happen that the actions of one department have an effect on the situation of other departments such that an optimal strategy for one department in terms of its own objectives deleteriously affects other departments and, hence, the entire business. Both of these kinds of situations represent other variants of the suboptimization problem.

*　　*　　*　　*　　*

. . . We can now look at illustrations of suboptimization where two parts of the company are in conflict with each other. For example, a division's objective of achieving the best possible profitability record may lead it to purchase parts from competitors rather than from another division of the same company. This may lower the profitability of the division that normally supplies parts. As another aspect of the inventory problem, a sales manager's objective of getting the largest possible sales may lead him to want a large inventory so that all orders can be promptly filled. This might be in conflict with the controller's objective of tying up a minimum of capital in inventory. Which one is in the best interests of the business? As a final example, a production department uses less steel by cutting down on the upper limit of the tolerances to which it machines a part. This results in a higher number of rejects of the finished assembly and an eventual complete redesign of the product with no appreciable gain in quality.

All of these examples serve to demonstrate the crucial importance of the suboptimization problem. Once again we could raise the question: When does this kind of problem arise? And once again, there is no general answer. Being aware of the problem we must rely on common and uncommon sense to help us to discover which particular decision may exemplify it. Fortunately, the majority of the forms of this kind of suboptimization problem involve objectives that can be expressed in quantitative form, so many of these problems can be resolved by methods which we will be discussing at length below. Thus, for example, the problem of inventory size and the conflicting interests of the sales manager and the controller can generally be resolved by expressing all the costs in dollars and solving the decision problem in terms of the over-all business objective of minimizing costs. This simple statement may make it seem easy. It isn't, as we know from the problem of the small-plant manager. How can we express the loss of dignity which he experiences as a result of being out of stock more often than he would like? Similarly, how do we represent the loss of customer goodwill that results from being out of inventory on an item that the customer wants immediately? Nonetheless, despite some difficulties, these kinds of problems can often be satisfactorily resolved.

From

A THEORY OF HUMAN MOTIVATION*

By A. H. Maslow†

THE BASIC NEEDS

The Physiological Needs

The needs that are usually taken as the starting point for motivation theory are the so-called physiological drives. Two recent lines of research make it necessary to revise our customary notions about these needs: first, the development of the

* From pp. 80–94 from *Motivation and Personality,* 2d. ed. by A. H. Maslow. Copyright 1954 by Harper & Row Publishers, Inc. Reprinted by permission of Harper & Row Publishers Inc.

† The author was Professor of Psychology at Brandeis University.

concept of homeostasis, and second, the finding that appetites (preferential choices among foods) are a fairly efficient indication of actual needs or lacks in the body.

Homeostasis refers to the body's automatic efforts to maintain a constant, normal state of the blood stream. Cannon . . . has described this process for (1) the water content of the blood, (2) salt content, (3) sugar content, (4) protein content, (5) fat content, (6) calcium content, (7) oxygen content, (8) constant hydrogen-ion level (acid-base balance), and (9) constant temperature of the blood. Obviously this list can be extended to include other minerals, the hormones, vitamins, etc.

Young . . . has summarized the work on appetite in its relation to body needs. If the body lacks some chemical, the individual will tend (in an imperfect way) to develop a specific appetite or partial hunger for that food element.

Thus it seems impossible as well as useless to make any list of fundamental physiological needs, for they can come to almost any number one might wish, depending on the degree of specificity of description. We cannot identify all physiological needs as homeostatic. That sexual desire, sleepiness, sheer activity, and maternal behavior in animals are homeostatic has not yet been demonstrated. Furthermore, this list would not include the various sensory pleasure (tastes, smells, tickling, stroking), which are probably physiological and which may become the goals of motivated behavior.

*   *   *   *   *

Undoubtedly these physiological needs are the most prepotent of all needs. What this means specifically is that in the human being who is missing everything in life in an extreme fashion, it is most likely that the major motivation would be the physiological needs rather than any others. A person who is lacking food, safety, love, and esteem would most probably hunger for food more strongly than for anything else.

If all the needs are unsatisfied, and the organism is then dominated by the physiological needs, all other needs may become simply nonexistent or be pushed into the background. It is then fair to characterize the whole organism by saying simply that it is hungry, for consciousness is almost completely preëmpted by hunger. All capacities are put into the service of hunger-satisfaction, and the organization of these capacities is almost entirely determined by the one purpose of satisfying hunger. The receptors and effectors, the intelligence, memory, habits, all may now be defined simply as hunger-gratifying tools. Capacities that are not useful for this purpose lie dormant, or are pushed into the background. The urge to write poetry, the desire to acquire an automobile, the interest in American history, the desire for a new pair of shoes are, in the extreme case, forgotten or become of secondary importance. . . .

Another peculiar characteristic of the human organism when it is dominated by a certain need is that the whole philosophy of the future tends also to change. For our chronically and extremely hungry man, Utopia can be defined simply as a place where there is plenty of food. He tends to think that, if only he is guaranteed food for the rest of his life, he will be perfectly happy and will never want anything more. Life itself tends to be defined in terms of eating. Anything else will be defined as unimportant. Freedom, love, community feeling, respect, philosophy, may all be waved aside as fripperies that are useless, since they fail to fill the stomach. Such a man may fairly be said to live by bread alone.

. . . It is quite true that man lives by bread alone—when there is no bread. But what happens to man's desires when there *is* plenty of bread and when his belly is chronically filled?

At once other (and higher) needs emerge and these, rather than physiological hungers, dominate the organism. And when these in turn are satisfied, again new (and still higher) needs emerge, and so on. This is what we mean by saying that the basic human needs are organized into a hierarchy of relative prepotency.

One main implication of this phrasing is that gratification becomes as important a concept as deprivation in motivation theory, for it releases the organism from the domination of a relatively more physiological need, permitting thereby the emergence of other more social goals. The physiological needs, along with their partial goals, when chronically gratified cease to exist as active determinants or organizers of behavior. They now exist only in a potential fashion in the sense that they may emerge again to dominate the organism if they are thwarted. But a want that is satisfied is no longer a want. The organism is dominated and its behavior organized only by unsatisfied needs. If hunger is satisfied, it becomes unimportant in the current dynamics of the individual.

This statement is somewhat qualified by a hypothesis to be discussed more fully later, namely, that it is precisely those individuals in whom a certain need has always been satisfied who are best equipped to tolerate deprivation of that need in the future, and that furthermore, those who have been deprived in the past will react differently to current satisfactions than the one who has never been deprived.

The Safety Needs

If the physiological needs are relatively well gratified, there then emerges a new set of needs, which we may categorize roughly as the safety needs. All that has been said of the physiological needs is equally true, although in less degree, of these desires. The organism may equally well be wholly dominated by them. They may serve as the almost exclusive organizers of behavior, recruiting all the capacities of the organism in their service, and we may then fairly describe the whole organism as a safety-seeking mechanism. Again we may say of the receptors, the effectors, of the intellect, and of the other capacities that they are primarily safety-seeking tools. Again, as in the hungry man, we find that the dominating goal is a strong determinant not only of his current world outlook and philosophy but also of his philosophy of the future. Practically everything looks less important than safety (even sometimes the physiological needs, which being satisfied are now underestimated). A man in this state, if it is extreme enough and chronic enough, may be characterized as living almost for safety alone.

*   *   *   *   *

Another indication of the child's need for safety is his preference for some kind of undisrupted routine or rhythm. He seems to want a predictable, orderly world. For instance, injustice, unfairness, or inconsistency in the parents seems to make a child feel anxious and unsafe. This attitude may be not so much because of the injustice *per se* or any particular pains involved, but rather because this treatment threatens to make the world look unreliable, or unsafe, or unpredictable. Young children seem to thrive better under a system that has at least a skeletal outline of rigidity, in which there is a schedule of a kind, some sort of routine, something that can be counted upon, not only for the present but also far into the future. Child psychologists, teachers, and psychotherapists have found that permissiveness within limits, rather than unrestricted permissiveness is preferred as well as *needed* by children. Perhaps one could express this more accurately by saying that the child needs an organized world rather than an unorganized or unstructured one.

*   *   *   *   *

Confronting the average child with new, unfamiliar, strange, unmanageable stimuli or situations will too frequently elicit the danger or terror reaction, as for example, getting lost or even being separated from the parents for a short time, being confronted with new faces, new situations, or new tasks, the sight of strange, unfamiliar, or uncontrollable objects, illness, or death. Particularly at such times, the child's frantic clinging to his parents is eloquent testimony to their role as protectors (quite apart from their roles as food givers and love givers).

From these and similar observations, we may generalize and say that the average child in our society generally prefers a safe, orderly, predictable, organized world, which he can count on, and in which unexpected, unmanageable, or other dangerous things do not happen, and in which, in any case, he has all-powerful parents who protect and shield him from harm. . . .

That these reactions may so easily be observed in children is in a way a proof of the fact that children in our society feel too unsafe (or, in a word, are badly brought up). Children who are reared in an unthreatening, loving family do *not* ordinarily react as we have described above. In such children the danger reactions are apt to come mostly to objects or situations that adults too would consider dangerous.

The healthy, normal, fortunate adult in our culture is largely satisfied in his safety needs. The peaceful, smoothly running, good society ordinarily makes its members feel safe enough from wild animals, extremes of temperature, criminal assault, murder, tyranny, etc. Therefore, in a very real sense, he no longer has any safety needs as active motivators. Just as a sated man no longer feels hungry, a safe man no longer feels endangered. . . .

*   *   *   *   *

The Belongingness and Love Needs

If both the physiological and the safety needs are fairly well gratified, there will emerge the love and affection and belongingness needs, and the whole cycle already described will repeat itself with this new center. Now the person will feel keenly, as never before, the absence of friends, or a sweetheart, or a wife, or children. He will hunger for affectionate relations with people in general, namely, for a place in his group, and he will strive with great intensity to achieve this goal. He will want to attain such a place more than anything else in the world and may even forget that once, when he was hungry, he sneered at love as unreal or unnecessary or unimportant.

In our society the thwarting of these needs is the most commonly found core in cases of maladjustment and more severe psychopathology. Love and affection, as well as their possible expression in sexuality, are generally looked upon with ambivalence and are customarily hedged about with many restrictions and inhibitions. Practically all theorists of psychopathology have stressed thwarting of the love needs as basic in the picture of maladjustment. Many clinical studies have therefore been made of this need, and we know more about it perhaps than any of the other needs except the physiological ones. Suttie . . . has written an excellent analysis of our "taboo on tenderness."

One thing that must be stressed at this point is that love is not synonymous with sex. Sex may be studied as a purely physiological need. Ordinarily sexual behavior is multidetermined, that is to say, determined not only by sexual but also by other needs, chief among which are the love and affection needs. Also not to be overlooked is the fact that the love needs involve both giving *and* receiving love. . . .

The Esteem Needs

All people in our society (with a few pathological exceptions) have a need or desire for a stable, firmly based, usually high evaluation of themselves, for self-respect, or self-esteem, and for the esteem of others. These needs may therefore be classified into two subsidiary sets. These are, first, the desire for strength, for achievement, for adequacy, for mastery and competence, for confidence in the face of the world, and for independence and freedom.[1] Second, we have what we may call the desire for reputation or prestige (defining it as repect or esteem from other people), status, dominance, recognition, attention, importance, or appreciation. These needs have been relatively stressed by Alfred Adler and his followers, and have been relatively neglected by Freud. More and more today, however, there is appearing widespread appreciation of their central importance, among psychoanalysts as well as among clinical psychologists.

Satisfaction of the self-esteem need leads to feelings of self-confidence, worth, strength, capability, and adequacy, of being useful and necessary in the world. But thwarting of these needs produces feelings of inferiority, of weakness, and of helplessness. These feelings in turn give rise to either basic discouragement or else compensatory or neurotic trends. An appreciation of the necessity of basic self-confidence and an understanding of how helpless people are without it can be easily gained from a study of severe traumatic neurosis . . .

From the theologians' discussion of pride and *hubris,* from the Frommian theories about the self-perception of untruth to one's own nature, from the Rogerian work with self, from essayists like Ayn Rand . . . , and from other sources as well, we have been learning more and more of the dangers of basing self-esteem on the opinions of others rather than on real capacity, competence, and adequacy to the task. The most stable and therefore most healthy self-esteem is based on *deserved* respect from others rather than on external fame or celebrity and unwarranted adulation.

The Need for Self-Actualization

Even if all these needs are satisfied, we may still often (if not always) expect that a new discontent and restlessness will soon develop, unless the individual

---

[1] Whether or not this particular desire is universal we do not know. The crucial question, especially important today, is, Will men who are enslaved and dominated inevitably feel dissatisfied and rebellious? We may assume on the basis of commonly known clinical data that a man who has known true freedom (not paid for by giving up safety and security but rather built on the basis of adequate safety and security) will not willingly or easily allow his freedom to be taken away from him. But we do not know that this is true for the person born into slavery.

is doing what he is fitted for. A musician must make music, an artist must paint, a poet must write, if he is to be ultimately at peace with himself. What a man *can* be, he *must* be. This need we may call self-actualization. . . .

This term, first coined by Kurt Goldstein . . . , is being used in this book in a much more specific and limited fashion. It refers to man's desire for self-fulfillment, namely, to the tendency for him to become actualized in what he is potentially. This tendency might be phrased as the desire to become more and more what one is, to become everything that one is capable of becoming.

The specific form that these needs will take will of course vary greatly from person to person. In one individual it may take the form of the desire to be an ideal mother, in other it may be expressed athletically, and in still another it may be expressed painting pictures or in inventions.[2]

The clear emergence of these needs usually rests upon prior satisfaction of the physiological, safety, love, and esteem needs.

The Preconditions for the Basic Need Satisfactions

There are certain conditions that are immediate prerequisites for the basic need satisfactions. Danger to these is reacted to as if it were direct danger to the basic needs themselves. Such conditions as freedom to speak, freedom to do what one wishes so long as no harm is done to others, freedom to express oneself, freedom to investigate and seek for information, freedom to defend oneself, justice, fairness, honesty, orderliness in the group are examples of such preconditions for basic need satisfactions. Thwarting in these freedoms will be reacted to with a threat or emergency response. These conditions are not ends in themselves but they are *almost* so since they are so closely related to the basic needs, which are apparently the only ends in themselves. These conditions are defended because without them the basic satisfactions are quite impossible, or at least, severely endangered.

If we remember that the cognitive capacities (perceptual, intellectual, learning) are a set of adjustive tools, which have, among other functions, that of satisfaction of our basic needs, then it is clear that any danger to them, any deprivation or blocking of their free use, must also be indirectly threatening to the basic needs themselves. Such a statement is a partial solution of the general problems of curiosity, the search for knowledge, truth, and wisdom, and the ever-persistent urge to solve the cosmic mysteries.

We must therefore introduce another hypothesis and speak of degrees of closeness to the basic needs, for we have already pointed out that *any* conscious desires (partial goals) are more or less important as they are more or less close to the basic needs. The same statement may be made for various behavior acts. An act is psychologically important if it contributes directly to satisfaction of basic needs. The less directly it so contributes, or the weaker this contribution is, the less important this act must be conceived to be from the point of view of dynamic

---

[2] Clearly creative behavior, like painting, is like any other behavior in having multiple determinants. It may be seen in innately creative people whether they are satisfied or not, happy or unhappy, hungry or sated. Also it is clear that creative activity may be compensatory, ameliorative, or purely economic. It is my impression (from informal experiments) that it is possible to distinguish the artistic and intellectual products of basically satisfied people from those of basically unsatisfied people by inspection alone. In any case, here too we must distinguish, in a dynamic fashion, the overt behavior itself from its various motivations or purposes.

psychology. A similar statement may be made for the various defense or coping mechanisms. Some are directly related to the protection or attainment of the basic needs, others are only weakly and distantly related. Indeed, if we wished, we could speak of more basic and less basic defense mechanisms, and then affirm that danger to the more basic defenses is more threatening than danger to less basic defenses (always remembering that this is so only because of their relationship to the basic needs).

The Desires to Know and to Understand

The main reason we know little about the cognitive impulses, their dynamics, or their pathology, is that they are not important in the clinic, and certainly not in the clinic dominated by medical-therapeutic tradition, i.e., getting rid of disease. The florid, exciting, and mysterious symptoms found in the classical neuroses are lacking here. Cognitive psychopathology is pale, subtle, and easily overlooked, or defined as normal. It does not cry for help. As a consequence we find nothing on the subject in the writings of the great inventors of psychotherapy and psychody-namics, Freud, Adler, Jung, etc. Nor has anyone yet made any systematic attempts at constructing cognitive psychotherapies.

Schilder is the only psychoanalyst I know in whose writings curiosity and under-standing are seen dynamically. Among the academic psychologists Murphy, Wer-theimer, and Asch . . . have treated the problem. So far, we have mentioned the cognitive needs only in passing. Acquiring knowledge and systematizing the uni-verse have been considered as, in part, techniques for the achievement of basic safety in the world, or for the intelligent man, expressions of self-actualization. Also freedom of inquiry and expression have been discussed as preconditions of satis-factions of the basic needs. Useful though these formulations may be, they do not constitute definitive answers to the questions as to the motivational role of curi-osity, learning, philosophizing, experimenting, etc. They are at best no more than partial answers. . . .

From

CONFLICT IN ORGANIZATION: A RE-EXAMINATION*

By Joseph A. Litterer†

FUNCTIONS AND VARIABLES

*   *   *   *   *

While doubtless some forms and certain degrees of conflict are dysfunctional or "unhealthy," other types, to certain degrees, are useful. The questions then are

---

* Reprinted with permission from the *Academy of Management Journal,* Vol. 9, No. 3 (September 1966), excerpts from pp. 179–83.

† The author is Professor in the School of Business, University of Massachusetts.

how much conflict is functional and where are the limits beyond which it becomes dysfunctional. The problem before us is therefore much more complex than previously. At one time the ideal amount of conflict was zero and the common decision was "eliminate it." Now the questions are what are the limits within which conflict is useful and how does one manage conflict.

. . . Our approach instead will be from the point of view of examining what conflict is and identifying the organizational elements that produce it. If we are to manage conflict within reasonable boundaries, it is to these elements that we have to look to find the levers and handles with which to do the job.

Functions of Conflict

. . . Perhaps one of the most important functions cited by a number of investigators[1] is that conflict initiates a search for some way to resolve or ameliorate the conflict and therefore leads to *innovation* and *change*. It should be noted at the same time that conflict not only leads to a search for change but it also makes change more acceptable, even desirable.

Closely related with the above is the observation that a conflict energizes people to activity, sometimes just to reduce the conflict and its concurrent displeasures, at other times because the conflict gives a zest to certain activities.

Conflict with an organization can be an essential portion of a cybernetic system. It often occurs at the point at which some other systems within the organization are functioning inadequately and therefore calls attention to these problem areas and generates a search for solutions or improvements. Conflict often leads to shifts or reallocations of existing or future rewards or resources, thereby fundamentally changing important aspects of the organization. Budget allocation and union-management conflicts are among many widely recognized.

*   *   *   *   *

Definition of Conflict

*   *   *   *   *

Our definition of conflict, . . . is that conflict is a *type of behavior which occurs* when two or more parties are in opposition or in battle *as a result* of a perceived relative deprivation from the activities of or interacting with another person or group.

FOUR CONFLICT SITUATIONS

The organizational causes of conflict are numerous. The particular organizational elements which lead to conflict do not bring this result about directly. Instead they create conditions which affect the perception and motivation of organizational members in such a way that conflict results. There are then a set of intervening variables which transform structural forms into behavioral outputs. The many organizational structures which produce conflict seem to feed four principal types of intervening variables or organizational situations. . . .

---

[1] Melville Dalton, *Men Who Manage* (New York: John Wiley and Sons, 1959); Peter Blau and William R. Scott, *Formal Organizations* (San Francisco: Chandler Publishing Company, 1962); James G. March and Herbert A. Simon, *Organizations* (New York, John Wiley and Sons, 1959).

Win-Lose Situations

This intervening variable develops when two people or two units have goals which cannot exist simultaneously. Surprisingly, organizations set up many circumstances which lead to this condition. This is commonly witnessed in inspection situations. The inspector is hired to find errors but errors are someone else's output. Therefore every time the inspector finds an error justifying his position's existence and opening the opportunity for praise and reward, someone else is losing. The latter's output is shown to be inadequate and his rewards are endangered. . . .

Inspection is one type of win-lose situation. There are others not so obvious, however. Not long ago a major airline was faced with considerable conflict between two of its managers at a western city. Upon investigation it was found that the Sales Manager, in order to increase his sales volume, wanted to provide certain services for customers. These, however, would be provided by the employees and from the budgets of the Ramp and Services Manager. There was considerable effort to decentralize and promote as much autonomy for individual managers as possible and handsome bonus systems were set up on certain standards of individual managerial performance. If the Sales Manager could increase his sales he would have many advantages. Conversely, if the Ramp Services Manager could keep his costs down he too would have many rewards coming to him. Hence the problem, and the conflict; the Sales Manager could not get his bonus unless the Ramp Services Manager were to forego some of his own. This condition, although not always clearly recognized, exists in many organizations where reward systems are based upon individual performances which are not independent but are very much interdependent.

Competition over Means Utilization

In this area, conflict occurs not over goals which may be similar, but stems from the fact that there are differing ideas as to what means are appropriate or who will have the means. French has shown that conflicts over the means to goal accomplishment are more disruptive of group cohesiveness than conflicts over differing goals.[2]

Another common source of conflict involves shared dependence on limited resources and scheduling problems.[3] Those that center on budgetary decisions, allocation of capital resources and the efforts made by certain departments to assure themselves that adequate supplies of scarce personnel are provided by the personnel department are recognized and common.

Scheduling problems are often not as clearly recognized and are perhaps more common. A common situation is cited by Whyte in a plant where a group of women workers was asked to participate in establishing new work norms.[4] As might be expected from previous studies, the standards they established were actually above those the industrial engineering department would have provided. However,

---

[2] John R. P. French, Jr., "The Disruption and Cohesion of Groups," *The Journal of Abnormal and Social Psychology*, Vol. 36 (1941), pp. 361–377.

[3] March and Simon, *op. cit.,* p. 122.

[4] William Foote Whyte, *Money and Motivation* (New York: Harper & Brothers, 1955).

worker-set performance standards 30–50 percent over engineering standards, instead of being a satisfactory situation, created numerous problems. The department following this one faced an avalanche of material which created considerable pressure. Departments preceding this one were placed under considerable pressure to produce more. Employees in these and other departments hearing of the high earnings in the initial department complained about inequities. The engineering department felt humiliated at having so badly misjudged workable standards. Management at several levels, seeing all these events, felt that somehow things were out of control and that their position was being eroded.

Status Incongruency

As often neglected but extremely pervasive influence on behavior stems from the fact that people want to know where they stand relative to others, that is, what their status is. This might not be too much of an issue if there were but one standard for evaluating a person. But actually there are numerous status hierarchies and one's position is never the same on them all. Further, it is often changing.

One set of status problems in industry arises from the impact of changing technology. Men who entered companies years ago and rose slowly through the ranks often feel that seniority and age justify fairly high status positions. However, they may find themselves superseded by younger men moved into higher level positions because their more recent technical training better fits them to cope with modern business problems. Working for someone younger than themselves and with less seniority, these men feel their status has been eroded and often accept this with little grace.

* * * * *

Perceptual Differences

It has long been recognized that people who look at things differently often come into conflict. In organizations, people see things differently for a variety of reasons, among them locational factors. It is frequently observed that people in different functional departments will tend to have different views of what is good for the company and how things are to be done. The classic conflicts between marketing and production over such things as delivery times, quality and lengths of production runs are well known. People in these departments not only perform different types of work but also interact with different publics. Marketing people interact most frequently with people outside the company, customers and competitors; those in manufacturing interact mostly with other departments within the company or with the union. These differences in systemic linkages and activities lead to differences in perception of considerable magnitude.[5]

Hierarchal location also has an impact. The problems seen by the first line supervisor, faced with the enormous pressures of day-to-day operations, are quite different from those of the managers two and tree levels above whose time perspectives are greater and whose pressures take a different form and come from different quarters. . . .

---

[5] See for example, DeWitt C. dearborn and Herbert A. Simon, "Selective Perception: A Note on Departmental Identification of Executives," *Sociometry, Vol.* 21 (1958) pp. 140–144.

From

ORGANIZATION DEVELOPMENT OBJECTIVES, ASSUMPTIONS AND STRATEGIES*

By Wendell French†

Organization development refers to a long-range effort to improve an organization's problem solving capabilities and its ability to cope with changes in its external environment with the help of external or internal behavioral-scientist consultants, or change agents, as they are sometimes called.

*   *   *   *   *

Objectives of Typical OD Programs.   Although the specific interpersonal and task objectives of organization development programs will vary according to each diagnosis of organizational problems, a number of objectives typically emerge. These objectives reflect problems which are very common in organizations.

1. To increase the level of trust and support among organizational members.
2. To increase the incidence of confrontation of organizational problems, both within groups and among groups, in contrast to "sweeping problems under the rug."
3. To create an environment in which authority of assigned role is augmented by authority based on knowledge and skill.
4. To increase the openness of communications laterally, vertically, and diagonally.
5. To increase the level of personal enthusiasm and satisfaction in the organization.
6. To find synergistic solutions[1] to problems with greater frequency. (Synergistic solutions are creative solutions in which 2 + 2 equals more than 4, and through which all parties gain more through cooperation than through conflict.)
7. To increase the level of self and group responsibility in planning and implementation.[2]

*   *   *   *   *

Relevancy to Different Technologies and Organization Subunits.   Research by Joan Woodward[3] suggests that organization development efforts might

---

*© 1969 by The Regents of the University of California. Reprinted from *California Management Review*, Vol. XII, No. 2, pp. 23–29, 32, by permission of The Regents.

† The author is a Professor in the Graduate School of Business of the University of Washington.

[1] Cattell defines synergy as "the sum total of the energy which a group can command." Daniel Katz and Robert L. Kahn, *The Social Psychology of Organizations* (New York: John Wiley and Sons, 1966), p. 33.

[2] For a similar statement of objectives, see "What is OD?" *NTL Institute: News and Reports from NTL Institute for Applied Behavioral Science,* II (June 1968), 1–2. Whether OD programs increase the overall level of authority in contrast to redistributing authority is a debatable point. My hypothesis is that both a redistribution and an overall increase occur.

[3] Joan Woodward, *Industrial Organiztion: Theory and Practice* (London: Oxford University Press, 1965).

be more relevant to certain kinds of technologies and organizational levels, and perhaps to certain workforce characteristics, than to others. For example, OD efforts may be more appropriate for an organization devoted to phototype manufacturing than for an automobile assembly plant. However, experiments in an organization like Texas Instruments suggest that some manufacturing efforts which appear to be inherently mechanistic may lend themselves to a more participative, open management style than is often assumed possible.[4]

However, assuming the constraints of a fairly narrow job structure at the rank-and-file level, organization development efforts may inherently be more productive and relevant at the managerial levels of the organization. Certainly OD efforts are most effective when they start at the top. Research and development units—particularly those involving a high degree of interdependency and joint creativity among group members—also appear to be appropriate for organization development activities, if group members are currently experiencing problems in communicating or interpersonal relationships.

Basic assumptions.   Some of the basic assumptions about people which underlie organization development programs are similar to "Theory Y" assumptions[5] and will be repeated only briefly here. However, some of the assumptions about groups and total systems will be treated more extensively. The following assumptions appear to underlie organization development efforts.[6]

About People

Most individuals have drives toward personal growth and development, and these are most likely to be actualized in an environment which is both supportive and challenging.

Most people desire to make, and are capable of making, a much higher level of contribution to the attainment of organization goals than most organizational environments will permit.

About People in Groups

Most people wish to be accepted and to interact cooperatively with at least one small reference group, and usually with more than one group, e.g., the work group, the family group.

One of the most psychologically relevant reference groups for most people is the work group, including peers and the superior.

Most people are capable of greatly increasing their effectiveness in helping their reference groups solve problems and in working effectively together.

For a group to optimize its effectiveness, the formal leader cannot perform all of the leadership functions in all circumstances at all times, and all group members must assist each other with effective leadership and member behavior.

---

[4] See M. Scott Myers, "Every Employee a Manager," *California Management Review,* X (Spring 1968), 9–20.

[5] See Douglas McGregor, *The Human Side of Enterprise* (New York: McGraw-Hill Book Company, 1960), pp. 47–48.

[6] In addition to influence from the writings of McGregor, Likert, Argyris, and others, this discussion has been influenced by "Some Assumptions About Change in Organizations," in notebook "Program for Specialists in Organization Training and Development," NTL Institute for Applied Behavioral Science, 1967; and by staff members who participated in that program.

About People in Organizational Systems

Organizations tend to be characterized by overlapping, interdependent work groups, and the "linking pin" function of supervisors and other needs to be understood and facilitated.[7]

What happens in the broader organization affects the small work group and vice versa.

What happens to one subsystem (social, technological, or administrative) will affect and be influenced by other parts of the system.

The culture in most organizations tends to suppress the expression of feelings which people have about each other and about where they and their organizations are heading.

Suppressed feelings adversely affect problem solving, personal growth, and job satisfaction.

The level of interpersonal trust, support, and cooperation is much lower in most organizations than is either necessary or desirable.

"Win-lose" strategies between people and groups, while realistic and appropriate in some situations, are not optimal in the long run to the solution of most organizational problems.

Synergistic solutions can be achieved with a much higher frequency than is actually the case in most organizations.

Viewing feelings as data important to the organization tends to open up many avenues for improved goal setting, leadership, communications, problem solving, intergroup collaboration, and morale.

Improved performance stemming from organization development efforts needs to be sustained by appropriate changes in the appraisal, compensation, training, staffing, and task-specialization—in short, in the total personnel system.

Value and Belief Systems of Behavioral Scientist-Change Agents. While scientific inquiry, ideally, is value-free, the applications of science are not value-free. Applied behavioral scientist-organization development consultants tend to subscribe to a comparable set of values, although we should avoid the trap of assuming that they constitute a completely homogenous group. They do not.

One value to which many behavioral scientist-change agents tend to give high priority, is that the needs and aspirations of human beings are the reasons for organized effort in society. They tend, therefore, to be developmental in their outlook and concerned with the long-range opportunities for the personal growth of people in organizations.

A second value is that work and life can become richer and more meaningful, and organized effort more effective and enjoyable, if feelings and sentiments are permitted to be a more legitimate part of the culture. A third value is a commitment to an action role, along with a commitment to research, in an effort to improve the effectiveness of organizations.[8] A fourth value—or perhaps a belief—is that

---

[7] For a discussion of the "linking pin" concept, see Rensis Likert, *New Patterns of Management* (New York: McGraw-Hill Book Company, 1961).

[8] Warren G. Bennis sees three major approaches to planned organizational change, with the behavioral scientists associated with each all having "a deep concern with applying social science knowledge to create more viable social systems; a commitment to action, as well as to research . . . and a belief that improved interpersonal and group relationships will ultimately lead to better organizational performance." Bennis, "A New Role for the Behavioral Sciences: Effecting Organizational Change," *Administrative Science Quarterly*, VIII (Sept. 1963), 157–158; and Herbert A. Shepard, "An Action Research Model," in *An Action Research Program for Organization Improvement*, pp. 31–35.

improved competency in interpersonal and intergroup relationship will result in more effective organizations.[9] A fifth value is that behavioral science research and an examination of behavioral science assumptions and values are relevant and important in considering organizational effectiveness. While many change agents are perhaps overly action-oriented in terms of the utilization of their time, nevertheless, as a group they are paying more and more attention to research and to the examination of ideas.[10]

The value placed on research and inquiry raises the question as to whether the assumptions stated earlier are values, theory, or "facts." In my judgment, a substantial body of knowledge, including research on leadership, suggests that there is considerable evidence for these assumptions. However, to conclude that these assumptions are facts, laws or principles would be to contradict the value placed by behavioral scientists on continuous research and inquiry. Thus, I feel that they should be considered theoretical statements which are based on provisional data.

This also raises the paradox that the belief that people are important tends to result in their being important. The belief that people can grow and develop in terms of personal and organizational competency tends to produce this result. Thus, values and beliefs tend to be self-fulfilling, and the question becomes "What do you choose to want to believe?" While this position can become Pollyannaish in the sense of not seeing the real world, nevertheless, behavioral scientist-change agents, at least this one, tend to place a value on optimism. It is a kind of optimism that says people can do a better job of goal setting and facing up to and solving problems, not an optimism that says the number of problems is diminishing.

It should be added that it is important that the values and beliefs of each behavioral science-change agent be made visible both to himself and to the client. In the first place, neither can learn to adequately trust the other without such exposure—a hidden agenda handicaps both trust building and mutual learning. Second, and perhaps more pragmatically, organizational change efforts tend to fail if a prescription is applied unilaterally and without proper diagnosis.

Strategy in Organization Development: An Action Research Model. A frequent strategy in organization development programs is based on what behavioral scientists refer to as an "action research model." This model involves extensive collaboration between the consultant (whether an external or an internal change agent) and the client group, data gathering, data discussion, and planning. While descriptions of this model vary in detail and terminology from author to author, the dynamics are essentially the same.[11]

Figure 1 summarizes some of the essential phases of the action research model, using an emerging organization development program as an example. The key aspects of the model are diagnosis, data gathering, feedback to the client group, data discussion and work by the client group, action planning, and action.

[9] Bennis, "A New Role for the Behavioral Sciences," 158.

[10] For a discussion of some of the problems and dilemmas in behavioral science research, see Chris Argyris, "Creating Effective Relationships in Organizations," in Richard N. Adams and Jack J. Preiss, eds., *Human Organization Research* (Homewood, Ill.: The Dorsey Press, 1960), pp. 109–123; and Barbara A. Benedict, *et al.,* "The Clinical Experimental Approach to Assessing Organizational Change Efforts," *Journal of Applied Behavioral Science* (Nov. 1967), 347–380.

[11] For further discussion of action research, see Edgar H. Schein and Warren G. Bennis, *Personal and Organizational Change Through Group Methods* (New York: John Wiley and Sons, 1966), pp. 272–274.

FIGURE 1
An Action Research Model for Organization Development

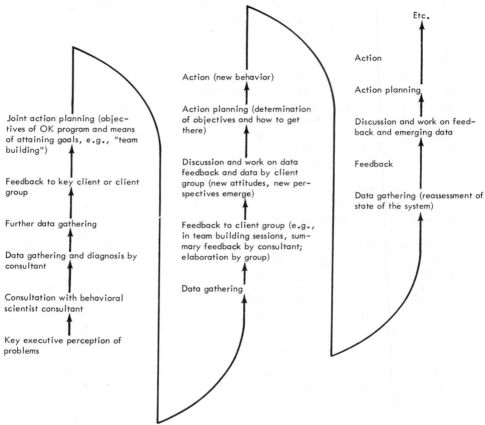

The sequence tends to be cyclical, with the focus on new or advanced problems as the client group learns to work more effectively together. Action research should also be considered a process, since, as William Foote Whyte says, it involves ". . . a continuous gathering and analysis of human relations research data and the feeding of the findings into the organization in such a manner as to change behavior."[12] (Feedback we will define as nonjudgmental observations of behavior.)

Ideally, initial objectives and strategies of organization development efforts stem from a careful diagnosis of such matters as interpersonal and intergroup problems, decision-making processes, and communication flow which are currently being experienced by the client organization. . . .

This initial diagnosis, which focuses on the expressed needs of the client is

[12] William Foote Whyte and Edith Lentz Hamilton, *Action Research for Management* (Homewood, Ill.: Richard D. Irwin, 1964), p.2.

extremely critical. . . . In the absence of a skilled diagnosis, the behavioral scientist-change agent would be imposing a set of assumptions and a set of objectives which may be hopelessly out of joint with either the current problems of the people in the organization or their willingness to learn new modes of behavior. In this regard, it is extremely important that the consultant hear and understand what the client is trying to tell him. This requires a high order of skill.[13]

Interviews are frequently used for data gathering in OD work for both initial diagnosis and subsequent planning sessions, since personal contact is important for building a cooperative relationship between the consultant and the client group. . . .

Data gathering typically goes through several phases. The first phase is related to diagnosing the state of the system and to making plans for organizational change. This phase may utilize a series of interviews between the consultant and the key client, or between a few key executives and the consultant. Subsequent phases focus on problems specific to the top executive team and to subordinate teams. (See Fig. 2.)

FIGURE 2
Organization Development Phases in a Hypothetical Organization

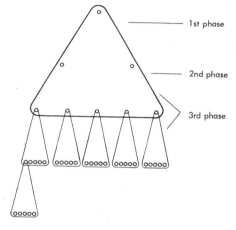

1st phase. Data gathering, feedback, and diagnosis–consultant and top executive only.

2nd phase. Data gathering, feedback, and revised diagnosis–consultant and two or more key staff or line people.

3rd phase. Data gathering and feedback to total top executive team in "team-building" laboratory, with or without key subordinates from level below.

4th and additional phases. Data gathering and team-building sessions with 2nd or 3rd level teams.
Subsequent phases. Data gathering, feedback, and interface problem–solving sessions across groups.
Simultaneous phases. Several managers may attend "stranger" T-Groups; courses in the management development program may supplement this learning.

*   *   *   *   *

Laboratory Training and Organization Development. Since organization development programs have largely emerged from T-group experience, theory, and research, and since laboratory training in one form or another tends to be an integral part of most such programs, it is important to focus on laboratory training per se. As stated earlier, OD programs grew out of a perceived need to relate laboratory training to the problems of ongoing organizations and a recognition that optimum results could only occur if major parts of the total social system of an organization were involved.

---

[13] For further discussion of organization diagnosis, see Richard Beckhard, "An Organization Improvement Program in a Decentralised Organization," *Journal of Applied Behavioral Science*, II (Jan.–March 1966), 3–4, "OD as a Process," in *What's Wrong with Work?*, pp. 12–13.

*   *   *   *   *

Ordinarily, laboratory training sessions have certain objectives in common. The following list, by two internationally known behavioral scientists,[14] is probably highly consistent with the objectives of most programs:

Self Objectives

Increased awareness of own feelings and reactions, and own impact on others.

Increased awareness of feelings and reactions of others, and their impact on self.

Increased awareness of dynamics of group action.

Changed attitudes toward self, others, and groups, i.e., more respect for, tolerance for, and faith in self, others, and groups.

Increased interpersonal competence, i.e., skill in handling interpersonal and group relationships toward more productive and satisfying relationships.

Role Objectives

Increased awareness of own organizational role, organizational dynamics, dynamics of larger social systems, and dynamics of the change process in self, small groups, and organizations.

Changed attitudes toward own role, role of others, and organizational relationships, i.e., more respect for and willingness to deal with others with whom one is interdependent, greater willingness to achieve collaborative relationships with others based on mutual trust.

Increased interpersonal competence in handling organizational role relationships with superiors, peers, and subordinates.

Organizational Objectives

Increased awareness of, changed attitudes toward, and increased interpersonal competence about specific organizational problems existing in groups or units which are interdependent.

Organizational improvement through the training of relationships or groups rather than isolated individuals.

Over the years, experimentation with different laboratory designs has led to diverse criteria for the selection of laboratory participants. Probably a majority of NTL-IABS human relations laboratories are "stranger groups," i.e., involving participants who come from different organizations and who are not likely to have met earlier. However, as indicated by the organizational objectives above, the incidence of special labs designed to increase the effectiveness of persons already working together appears to be growing. Thus terms like "cousin labs," i.e., labs involving people from the same organization but not the same subunit, and "family labs" or "team-building" sessions, i.e., involving a manager and all of his subordinates, are becoming familiar. Participants in labs designed for organizational members not of the same unit may be selected from the same rank level ("horizontal slice") or selected so as to constitute a heterogeneous grouping by rank ("diagonal slice"). Further, NTL-IABS is now encouraging at least two mem-

---

[14] Schein and Bennis, p. 37.

bers from the same organization to attend NTL Management Work Conferences and Key Executive Conferences in order to maximize the impact of the learning in the back-home situation.[15]

*   *   *   *   *

Summary Comments.   Organization development efforts have emerged through attempts to apply laboratory training values and assumptions to total systems. Such efforts are organic in the sense that they emerge from and are guided by the problems being experienced by the people in the organization. The key to their viability (in contrast to becoming a passing fad) lies in an authentic focus on problems and concerns of the members of the organization and in their confrontation of issues and problems.

Organization development is based on assumptions and values similar to "Theory Y" assumptions and values but includes additional assumptions about total systems and the nature of the client-consultant relationship. Intervention strategies of the behavioral scientist-change agent tend to be based on an action-research model and tend to be focused more on helping the people in an organization learn to solve problems rather than on prescriptions of how things should be done differently.

Laboratory training (or "sensitivity training") or modification of T-group seminars typically are a part of the organizational change efforts, but the extent and format of such training will depend upon the evolving needs of the organization. Team-building seminars involving a superior and subordinates are being utilized more and more as a way of changing social system rapidly and avoiding the cultural-distance problems which frequently emerge when individuals return from stranger labs. However, stranger labs can play a key role in change efforts when they are used as part of a broader organization development effort.

Research has indicated that sensitivity training generally produces positive results in terms of changed behavior on the job, but has not demonstrated the link between behavior changes and improved performance. Maximum benefits are probably derived from laboratory training when the organizational culture supports and reinforces the use of new skills in ongoing team situations.

Successful organization development efforts require skillful behavioral scientist interventions, a systems view, and top management support and involvement. In addition, changes stemming from organization development must be linked to changes in the total personnel subsystem. The viability of organization development efforts lies in the degree to which they accurately reflect the aspirations and concerns of the participating members.

In conclusion, successful organization development tends to be a total system effort; a process of planned change—not a program with a temporary quality; and aimed at developing the organization's internal resources for effective change in the future.

---

[15] For further discussion of group composition in laboratory training, see Schein and Bennis, pp. 63–69. NTL-LABS now include the Center for Organization Studies, the Center for the Development of Educational Leadership, the Center for Community Affairs, and the Center for International Training to serve a wide range of client populations and groups.

From

THEORIES OF BUSINESS BEHAVIOR*

By Joseph W. McGuire†

The Maximizations of Profits and "Rationality"

The economic theory of the firm does not merely postulate profits as the goal of the business concern. It states explicitly that the goal is maximum profits, and that entrepreneurs will try to move toward this objective in a rational manner.

Rationality, in the economic theory of the firm, implicitly assumes no action will be undertaken by the business enterprise that will move it away from its goal of maximum profits. Furthermore, it assumes that the decision maker, faced with two or more alternatives that will result in various outcomes, will invariably select the alternative that will tend to move the firm to (or closer to) profit maximization. In order to accomplish changes in the proper direction, and to insure that their magnitudes will be neither too large nor too small, it is customary for economists to postulate that decisions be made on the basis of marginal values. In the economic theory of the firm, then, rational action is normally understood to mean action wherein the pertinent variables are weighed at the margin, and changes are in the direction of increasing net profits. The logic of the economic entrepreneur is thus based upon marginal analysis, which is a process for finding a maximum.

Marginal functions may be defined generally as the first derivative of any continuous function, dy/dx, where $y = f(x)$. If we state that profits are $\pi = pg - C$, let us see how they may be maximized through the use of marginal analysis. Total costs include both variable costs, which change with changes in output, and fixed costs, which continue at the same level (at least in the short run) independent of output changes. We can write the total cost formula, then, as $C = f(q) + k$, where (q) represents items of output produced per unit of time and k is fixed costs. The marginal cost of production, then, is $dc/dg = f'(q)$, the derivative of costs (c) with respect to the quantity (q), or, less formally, the incremental change in C which occurs with a change in output. Marginal revenue is the change in revenue which accompanies changes in sales, so that $dr/dq = f'(pq)$. It is usually assumed, furthermore, that the revenue and cost functions are continuous, and that their derivatives exist at any point. We know that it is necessary, if profit is to be at a maximum, that $d\pi/dq = 0$. We can write this also as:

$$\frac{d\pi}{dq} = \frac{dr}{dq} - \frac{dc}{dq} = 0$$

It is evident, then, that when profits are at a maximum, $dr/dq = dc/dq$, or, in other words, that marginal costs equal marginal revenue. Finally, in order to insure that

---

* Jospeh W. McGuire, *Theories of Business Behavior,* © 1964, pp. 56–57. Reprinted by permission of Prentice-Hall, Inc., Englewood Cliffs, N.J.

† The author is Vice President of the University of California.

profits are maximized and not minimized when $d\pi/dq = 0$, we must meet the sufficient condition for a maximum, which is that $d^2\pi/dq^2 < 0$ so that

$$\frac{d^2r}{dq^2} - \frac{d^2c}{dq^2} < 0 \text{ and } \frac{d^2r}{dq^2} < \frac{d^2c}{dq^2}$$

Profits are maximized in the economic theory of the firm, therefore, when marginal costs are equal to marginal revenues, and when, at the point of intersection of the two marginal curves, the marginal cost function cuts the marginal revenue function from below. Entrepreneurs, when making their output decisions, weigh the expected costs of producing additonal units of output against the expected revenues from the sale of these additional items. If the additional revenues (marginal revenues) are larger than the additional (marginal) costs of production, output will be expanded and simultaneously (as the sufficient condition above requires) total revenues will expand more than total costs. Production will continue to expand as long as $R_m > C_m$. Additional production will not be contemplated if $C_m > R_m$, for at such an output position net revenues would be reduced by additional production.

PART V Leadership and Organization Development

LEADERSHIP AS AN IMPORTANT FUNCTION OF MANAGEMENT

In previous parts of the book, we see that managers are concerned with certain key tasks which they perform. These tasks are important functions in the organization if the organization goals are to be achieved. They are functions in the sense that the heart has a certain function if the physical body is to achieve its purposes: walking, talking, or thinking. Part II examined the tasks of strategic planning and organization design. Part III centered on the allocation of resources (principally fixed resources) through financial planning and control. Part IV turned to allocation of resources (principally day-to-day operating manpower and materials) by use of management science.

In each of these tasks and functions, it was our purpose not only to understand something of the specific tasks (e.g., organization design or scientific decision making), but also more importantly to see how that task related to other organizational tasks with which the manager must cope: financial control was related to the way he designs the organization structure; decision making was related to human behavior.

In Part V, we will be changing the center of attention. Instead of centering on *things*, such as organization goals and operating technology, with subsidiary and allied interest in how this relates to *people*, we shall center on the people side of the managerial system and ask how human behavior is affected by technology or how human behavior affects technology.

The particular kind of human behavior we are interested in is leadership. This concept has meant many things to many people. It has been studied by historians (does history make the man, or does the man make history?), sociologists (charismatic versus legal leaders), small group sociologists (is there such a thing as one leader, or is leadership shared? and is authoritarian or democratic leadership more effective?), and political scientists (are monarchies, oligarchies, or democracies best?).

For our purposes, organizational or managerial leadership is the sum total of the day-to-day actions of a man as he attempts to influence others in ways that help the organization achieve its goal, and that help the manager to know when to change organizational goals, internal operations, or policies. Leadership may be exercised by anyone in the organization who is interested in doing this—from the bottom of the pyramid to the top. In fact, the concept allows a subordinate in the hierarchy to become a leader in relation to his boss. But throughout all ages, the function of leadership and the task itself has been recognizably present in the relatively few who are most interested and most successful in this kind of behavior. In organizations from the Catholic Church to the Chase Manhattan Bank or the Black Panthers, this means the managers.

EXPEDIENT OBLIGATIONS AND SOCIAL RESPONSIBILITY OF LEADERS

It is one of the central theses of this book that the manager who is able to think through the *reality* of action problems (to diagnose what is going on in the technical system and the people system) in some depth, who knows some of the managerial techniques for coping with his organizational world, and who is skilled in using his own brain to apply both of these kinds of knowledge, will be more successful with people *and* things.

Only managers who are informed and skilled can discharge either their expedient obligations or their ethical responsibilities. For example, it is the man who can understand the motivations of people in the Shoe Corporation of Illinois, understand the technology of making shoes, is acquainted with techniques or authority, integrative behavior, or organization development methods, who can use his mind best to cope in day-to-day relations with others. He also has a higher probability of being respected by others as one who is able to cope. He is "obliged" through necessity of expediency to use what knowledge he can to make informed judgments. Otherwise the organization will not be as successful and his own actions "won't work" as well. Either there will be defective technology and efficiency, or there will be messy human relations, or both. And for those who feel ethical responsibilities to operate an excellent shoe company for society, or to operate an organization in which human beings are treated with dignity, such informed judgments and actions are the surest way to fulfill them.

CONCEPTS AND THEORIES OF HUMAN BEHAVIOR

The readings in Part V include a number of concepts and theories from the behavioral sciences that aid the manager in understanding the human system. Sociologists have devoted much time and research to the concept of *roles,* the recurring (habitual) actions of an individual, interrelated with the repetitive (habitual) action of others so that one can predict what will happen between the people playing the roles. The concept is (not surprisingly) roughly analogous to the various roles in a theatre performance or a movie. The roles in an organization, *together,* form the social system of the company. Understanding of the role of the company president in British Commercial Investments, Ltd., in relation to the role of the general manager of its subsidiary, Harrogate Asphalt

Products, Ltd., will help the student to understand why these men act the way they do, and enable him to see possibilities for a more productive leadership pattern.

Psychologists have contributed much to the understanding of basic human needs, as well as to the understanding of the games people play (in the form of defense mechanisms) in organizations. These insights may well enable one, as president of The Lakeland Food Products Company, to understand better why one of the sales vice presidents leads the sales managers in one way but seems to lose out in another way to another leader who behaves in a different fashion.

In the four cases in Part V, one may also see how different managerial values and attitudes affect how one manager acts differently from another . . . some may be motivated to do a good job for the company, others may be motivated to do a good job for themselves, and still others may seek power, prestige, or simply companionship on the job.

In most of the cases in Part V we see some form of human conflict. Perhaps this is not so unusual, since organized life implies that one person must be somehow related to other people around him. Nature seems to make each human being different from each other human being, and in order for people to arrive at a concurrence about any joint undertaking, a process of conflict and conflict resolution is always present. One question is—what kinds of conflict are positive (helping people learn to work together) and what kinds are negative (destructive to learning). Allied to this is another question: What kinds of leadership action promote positive conflicts and eliminate negative conflicts? As we study conflict between sales vice president and market planning manager in The Lakeland Food Products Company, between conglomerate president and local company president in Harrogate Asphalt Products, Ltd., or between product designers versus product producers in Shoe Corporation of Illinois, we will want to distinguish between different kinds of conflict and their causes, as well as between alternative leadership actions that might be used in the specific situation. Readings interspersed with these cases will help to identify such things as causes of conflict and actions for conflict resolution.

PRACTICES AND TECHNOLOGIES OF LEADERSHIP

It is one thing to see in theory how human beings behave in organizations. It is a somewhat different thing to see the details—the concrete facts—of how managers in the cases behave in their day-to-day dealings with others. We can see group participation as the style of Mr. Saunders in The Lakeland Food Products Company, and the task-oriented and technical leadership of his adversary, Mr. Proctor. Mr. Lampton in Harrogate Asphalt Products, Ltd., seems to use a combination of strategic competence and authority. Executives in Bergen Metalfabrik, A/S strive to use team building techniques with the aid of an organization development consultant. They temporarily turn over at least part of the leadership to organization development consultants, who use team building techniques. To see the practices of these men in action helps one to learn a deeper and more concrete meaning for leadership styles like "participation," "team building," or "technical competence."

But another form of knowledge is supplied by the readings in Part V. Technologies such as decentralization, team building, forced-field analysis, integrative behavior by line managers, brilliant technical performance, or organization development through consultants, are things with which every manager should be acquainted. These, together with the concepts of authority from Part II, offer informed alternatives for the manager who must perform the leadership function.

TECHNOLOGY AND HUMAN BEHAVIOR: THE MANAGER AS A MEDIATOR BETWEEN PARTS OF A TOTAL SYSTEM

Two of the cases in Part V offer a somewhat rare opportunity to study in depth of detail the leader as a mediator between the external economic demands of society, on the one hand, and the firm's internal system on the other. If the internal system is in turn composed of a subsystem of things (technology, finance, job structure) and a subsystem of people (human motivations, attitudes, and behavior), then the manager's job becomes one of *mediating* between three kinds of systems: the production and efficiency demands of society, the technology within the firm necessary to meet these, and the human beings within the firm who must ultimately be satisfied enough to actually carry out their part of the work.

For example, we shall see that the managers in Shoe Corporation of Illinois are confronted by dictates in terms of the style of shoes to be produced, and in terms of the cost of shoes to the public. These external demands have something to do with the way shoes must be designed and produced inside—the machines, the flows of work between people and the work to be done by various people and departments. At the same time, the designers of shoes have their own ideas about good design, about how to deal with the production plant, and about the kind of work life they want to lead during their work day. The management of this company must somehow strive to build a system that performs excellently in producing shoes for the feet of society, excellently in the machines and jobs required to do this, and excellently in terms of human satisfaction and dignity. In this sense, the cases in Part V become a merger between strategic planning, leadership, and human behavior.

This managerial function of mediating between subsystems will be expanded further in Part VI. Up to that point, we are interested in the function of mediating between three subsystems: external economic demands, internal technical/financial necessities, and internal human necessities. Part VI cases will inject a fourth subsystem, external noneconomic demands of society other than economic production. Society today is more than ever aware that firms must "produce" their economic product without harmful consequences to health, freedom, esthetic tastes, or other values which go to make up the good life or human dignity.

The job of the manager as a mediator, then, becomes a complex balancing of factors which must be taken into account in wise and just policy decisions. It is not an easy task. In some ways it means dealing with the world in its buzzing confusion, or making decisions for a can of worms. As we approach this kind of decision making and this kind of day-to-day leadership action, practice with cases, in which the human brain must conceptualize each particular situation differently and then judge the right course of action, becomes the principal learning mechanism for managerial competence. Theories and concepts from management literature will help the manager in being more informed, but they cannot, in themselves, develop the skills of a mediator.

16. LAKELAND FOOD PRODUCTS COMPANY, INC.

Case Introduction

SYNOPSIS

The president of this company asks the vice president for marketing to interview a younger man, William Proctor, for an important job in the Marketing Division, that of market planning director. Both president and vice president are instrumental in his taking the position. During the first year of Proctor's tenure, the case describes his actions and beliefs, as well as his technical competence. These competences, beliefs, and actions are contrasted with those of other executives in the Marketing Division. The vice president for marketing resigns, giving as his reasons the improvement of his career and a desire to satisfy certain family obligations.

WHY THIS CASE IS INCLUDED

Lakeland Food Products offers an opportunity to see two types of leadership patterns contrasted, together with the practical reasons each executive uses for behaving in his own way. Thus, insights may be gained into the important question, "What motivates an executive?" In the sense that the two executive styles are conflicting, one can also see both the advantages and disadvantages of the two styles. At certain points in the case, we can observe the feelings and attitudes of subordinates as they develop in response to different leader styles. Finally, the difference between overt behavior or "game playing" on the one hand, and true inner feelings, comes to light in the behavior of both individual top executives and a group of lower executives.

DIAGNOSTIC AND PREDICTIVE QUESTIONS

The readings included with this case are marked (*). The author index at the end of this book locates the other readings.

1. Why did Paul Brown "just shut up" when Proctor presented his plan to the first meeting? Why did attendance at staff meetings drop off later? Why, when Saunders asked about the value of staff meetings, did some managers seem indifferent as to advantages and disadvantages? Why did Brown and Davidson at one of the later meetings look at the floor or out the window?

Read: *Argyris, *Personality and Organization,* pp. 27–157 (sections on Defense Mechanisms and Individual Adaptation). McGregor, *The Human Side of Enterprise,* pp. 124–31, 172–75.

2. Summarize Saunders' system for staff meetings as he describes it in the case—who does what and why. Add a summary of his theory of executive behavior or leadership style. Why did he believe in this theory of management or leadership?

Read: *Gellerman, *Motivation and Productivity,* pp. 109–18 (section on The Affiliation Motive). *McGregor, *The Human Side of Enterprise,* pp. 3, 6–10, 47–48, 53–54. Also utilize the readings from Question 1.

3. What two motivations might have caused Saunders to feel conflicted or frustrated *(a)* when he "felt uncomfortable at having Proctor start work in this position," *(b)* when he "felt uneasy passing Proctor's office in the first two weeks," and *(c)* when he "felt awkward in starting the meeting" on a different agenda than the important problem raised by Proctor? Why *didn't* Proctor feel frustrated when he "had to speak up and let Brown know he was wrong?"

Read: *Gellerman, *Motivation and Productivity,* pp. 109–18 (sections on The Power Motive and The Affiliation Motive).

4. Why did Proctor think about the advertising plan over the weekend and call Saunders on Sunday afternoon?

Read: Hampton, Summer, and Webber, *Organizational Behavior and the Practice of Management,* Chapter 10. (Select which parts of the reading apply to this question.) *John Wiley & Sons, Advertisement for *Science in Marketing,* 1965.

5. Summarize Proctor's system of staff meetings—who does what and when. Why did he believe in this system of group action and this form of executive behavior? Summarize Williams' system for divisionwide meetings—who does what and why. Why did he believe in this system of group action and this form of executive behavior?

Read: Utilize readings for Question 4. Smith, *The Wealth of Nations,* pp. 4–15. *Carr *et al.,* *American Democracy in Theory and Practice,* pp. 214–19. *Cartwright. *Public Opinion Polls and Democratic Leadership,* pp. 23–32.

6. As one reason for division meetings, Williams believes that the salesmen and sales managers would "feel important as an individual by being personally invited to company headquarters." Cite reasoning as to why this might be true. Then cite reasoning why this might be false.

Preparation: Use your own analytical ability here. Or, if you are familiar with status motivation versus motivation through acting out one's own talents and abilities (personal motivation), you may want to use a more technical basis for answering.

7. Describe in factual terms any difference you see in the way in which Saunders behaves with his subordinates and the way in which he behaves with his superior, Williams. Explain the apparent contradiction.

> Preparation: Think deeply about what the most fundamental difference in his two action patterns were. If you watched him, what differences could you *see?* Then ask *why,* in terms of his attitudes, feelings, or other motivations, he differed. You might also separate these motivations into *(a)* those "from within" Saunders and *(b)* those "out there in the situation."

8. Why did Williams interpret Saunders' resignation in the way he did?

> Read: *Leavitt, *Managerial Psychology,* pp. 27–33. Readings from Questions 4 and 5 will help make the Leavitt reading more practically applicable to the case.

POLICY QUESTIONS

9. If you were the president of Lakeland, and had diagnosed the basic factors in the situation (Questions 1–8), how would you have handled Saunders and Proctor to keep this problem from occurring?

> Read: Newman and Summer, *The Process of Management,* pp. 439–48. Mary Parker Follett, "Constructive Conflict."

10. Suppose the President of Lakeland wanted to use an *organization development* or *process consultation* technique to deal with the problem in the sales department (i.e., sometime before Saunders resigned). What steps would the president take? What kind of work might the consultant do and what would be his goals? Be as specific as possible using names, situations, and facts from the actual case.

> Read: French, "Organization Development Objectives, Assumptions and Strategies." Schein, *Process Consultation: Its Role in Organization Development,* pp. 3–9.

11. (Role-Playing Question). One student who understands the motivations of Saunders should assume his role and play it as much like the Saunders in the case as possible. Another student who believes he understands the problem should assume the role of an "enlightened" Williams—that is, a Williams who *formerly* acted exactly as in the case, but who now understands the kinds of basic insights developed in the readings, individual reflection on these, and class discussion of the diagnosis.

The setting is in Williams' office, on Monday morning after Saunders has resigned the previous Friday. Williams has called Saunders in to ask him to reconsider.

Even though the role-play is short, the rest of the class should act as observers. Williams might give the class a short explanation of *what specifically* he expects to achieve with Saunders (Saunders should leave the room during this explanation). Then, after the instructor cuts off the role-play, the class might discuss how Williams performed. In this discussion, stick to objective reporting. Ask yourselves, "What did Williams *do* and *say,* and what effect did this have on Saunders?"

If time allows, Saunders should be held "constant" (the same student plays Saunders) while two or more Williams players try additional role-plays.

QUESTIONS FOR ORIGINAL STUDENT WORK IN ANALYSIS AND POLICY

12. While reflecting on case facts, what additional theories from prior education give you insights as to "what is going on" in the Lakeland Food Products Company, Inc.? As to what might be predicted to happen in the future?

13. Other than the policy questions asked by the authors, what pragmatic ways can you think of to state the practical problems faced by executives in the case?

Case Text*

Lakeland Food Products Company, Inc., produces and markets a broad variety of food products for ultimate sale through smaller grocery stores and large regional chain food stores. With net profits of $18 million in the latest year, the company is considerably smaller than the largest companies in the industry, such as General Foods Corporation, but it has been able to achieve a continuous growth rate by specializing in certain product lines such as spices, mayonnaise and salad dressings, frozen vegetables, and frozen meats. Furthermore, the company management has deliberately limited its market to one large region of the United States. In this way, according to A. F. Williams, Lakeland's president:

We can more thoroughly saturate the area with direct sales effort, and concentrate our advertising and sales promotion. I have often been asked how we can compete successfully with the giants. The answer is specialty products—we don't try to cover the whole field—and a relatively limited market, in which our brand name can become known, and in which our large sales force can work much more closely with wholesalers and large regional chain operations.

A partial organization chart of Lakeland Company appears as Exhibit 1. Reporting to A. F. Williams, the president, are five principal officers of the company: R. L. Jacobs, vice president for procurement; M. M. Healey, vice president for manufacturing and processing; J. D. Saunders, sales vice president; F. R. Preston, financial vice president; and L. D. Whitcomb, vice president for employee and public relations.

This case concerns a situation which Mr. Williams describes as one

---

EXHIBIT 1
Organization Chart Lakeland Food Products Company, Inc.

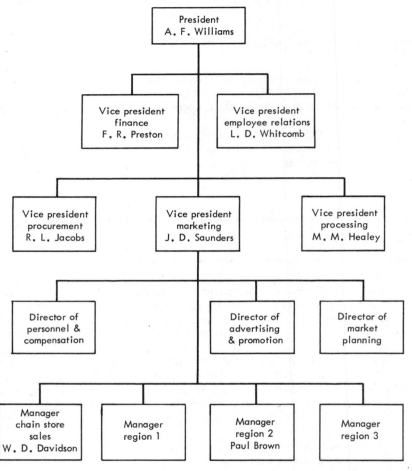

of the most pressing problems confronting him at the present time. As Williams puts it,

> *I am extremely concerned about a conversation I had with Jim Saunders, our vice president for sales. Saunders came into my office about a week ago and in a very pleasant way informed me that he thought he owed it to himself to try to improve his own career and horizons and that he had accepted a job with a large regional food chain in California. He said that there were some personal problems involved, in the way of aged parents in California, who needed caring for.*
>
> *He also said that Bill Proctor, his director of market planning, was*

fully capable of taking over the leadership of our marketing division.
I just can't account for Saunders' rather sudden decision, other
than the fact that some men do have family problems, and I guess
some people also make rather sudden and major decisions about their
careers. He and I have always had a close and rather personal working
relationship, but this decision was a bolt out of the blue.

Saunders has been with the company for 23 years, having joined
us when he first got out of college. He started as a salesman, went
through a usual training period under one of the regional managers,
and achieved a really excellent record. I can remember getting to
know him about five years after he joined the company, when I was
assistant to the vice president for procurement. I had some contact
with him over the years, and, of course, as we both got promoted up
the ladder I had more and more contact. He eventually became man-
ager of Region One, general sales manager for the whole company,
and 10 years ago, I appointed him, with board approval, to be vice
president for sales. In my opinion, Jim Saunders today knows more
about the problems of field selling, and more details of who our cus-
tomers are and why they buy from us, than anyone else in the com-
pany. He is a virtual storehouse of information—and he has the atti-
tude of a salesman. That is, he is always asking, "What does this mean
to the customer—what does he want, and how can we best get our
story over to him?"

The remainder of this case describes the relationships between Williams, Saunders, and Proctor, starting at a point of time 12 months ago
when Proctor was made director of market planning.

W. D. (Bill) Proctor joined Lakeland eight years ago, at the age of 28.
He had received his Bachelor's degree in engineering at M.I.T., spent
three years as a junior staff officer in planning and logistics in the military, and then obtained an M.B.A. degree from the Columbia University
Graduate School of Business.

Proctor's first job had been assistant to R. L. Jacobs, vice president of
the Procurement Division. Although most of Proctor's time with the company has been spent in procurement, he has, from time to time, and
before joining the sales department, spent time on leave with the manager of chain store sales and the vice president for finance. In both instances, these executives had heard of his applications of systems analysis to procurement and asked to have him assigned to them on
temporary leave. Over these years, Saunders had seen Proctor frequently
in the office, at company functions, and in other casual encounters, but
he did not know him well. He appeared to Saunders to be a very capable
young executive, always on the move.

Twelve months ago, Williams called Saunders and asked him to talk
with Proctor. "I want to know what you think of him, as it occurred to
me that he might be a good man for that opening we have in market
planning." Saunders later told Williams, "I judge Bill Proctor to be very
bright, and probably very competent. He seems to have some good ideas
about market planning, even though he does not know too much about

what we are doing. He also seems to know procurement well, and one specialized aspect of our planning of chain store volume."

Williams seemed to Saunders to be pleased with this reply, answering, "We have had excellent results with his work in procurement and even in helping to plan the product lines in chain store sales. Of course, we have had some joking around the office about his 'McNamara System,' but it has paid off."

Saunders later told the case writer that, at the time of the above conversation, he actually felt a little uncomfortable at the thought of having Proctor start work in the capacity of market planning director. Nevertheless, he decided that the Marketing Division certainly could use a person with talent, and he therefore agreed to his having the position.

As an indoctrination period, Proctor asked for two weeks to read the files of market planning which existed at the time he took the position. Particularly, he wanted to study the way in which sales territories, quotas for territories by product, and advertising were correlated in company policies in all three areas. He also wanted to read the salesmen's reports on market demand predictions.

During these two weeks, Saunders states that he felt rather uneasy as he passed Proctor's office each day. At the end of the period, he asked Proctor if he thought that the reports gave a clear picture of the Marketing Division's activities. "The files and reports are really excellent," Proctor answered with obvious sincerity. Saunders recalls that he was surprised that he felt relief at this point and that he felt almost jovial when he said goodnight to Proctor that evening.

The following Sunday, Proctor called Saunders at his home. He said that he had been studying the sales figures for each of 20 important products in Region Three, together with advertising expenditures for these products. He further seemed to Saunders to be

> . . . *very enthusiastic about his conclusions, if not downright excited. I could tell that he felt very much like telling me about a discovery that he thought was important. I remember thinking that he must be oblivious to the fact that I might be engaged in a relaxing time with the family by the pool. As he talked rather quickly about what he was doing, I exhibited some interest and told him that we could discuss it at our biweekly staff meeting on Wednesday, which is attended by our three regional sales managers, the manager of chain sales, and the three staff directors of personnel, advertising, and market planning.*

Saunders takes much pride in the way these meetings are conducted and the way major marketing policies are made in Lakeland. He believes that each of his line managers, as well as his three staff directors, has much to contribute in the way of creativity and experience, but that one man usually should take the lead in developing facts, data and a recommendation. According to Saunders:

> *In this way, the man with the most interest in a subject gets a crack at developing the original recommendation in a clear, timesaving*

format, for our discussions. At the same time, the whole group gets a crack at creatively bringing to bear their experience regarding alternative ways to solve the policy problem. After talking it through, if any one or more men have serious reservations, the originator of the recommendation should take the initiative to work with the dissenting persons after the meeting, until either both men agree on the original recommendation, or until both agree on a change or modification. In this way, the group of top sales executives always reach a consensus which is best for the company—each man understands the decision, and is prepared to carry it out.

The following Wednesday, Saunders started the meeting by bringing up a matter of change in the company's sales compensation policy. He felt somewhat awkward because he knew "that Proctor was champing at the bit to start with his own proposal, and because . . . well . . . I wanted to let him know he wasn't running the show."

Although all executives at the meeting believed that the sales force had high morale—"favorable attitudes toward the company, its products, and top managers"—all were aware that some competing companies in the food business had recently changed their compensation methods. This resulted in some suggestions from a number of salesmen to the effect that Lakeland is out-of-date, but an apparently sincere attitude on their part that they know the company will make a new policy if they supply the facts. Prior to the meeting, Ivar Sorensen, director of personnel and compensation, and the man most interested in this problem, presented a plan which he believed would be perceived as fair to the salesmen, yet which would direct their attention to the most profitable product lines and cost the company less than any alternative plan that would attain the same objectives.

At the Wednesday meeting, two of the regional managers began by saying that their reservations to Sorensen's original plan had been thoroughly discussed and that they were now prepared to make the final consensus to the plan. As Paul Brown, the manager of Region Two, put it,

. . . to try to arrive at a balance between cost to the company in salaries, maximum motivation of salesmen to spend time on the most profitable items (while not ignoring other items completely), and the general feeling of fairness in the minds of salesmen, is a tough proposition. I don't think anyone at the meeting here believes we have the ideal Utopian plan, but it is the best policy we can formulate. This present recommendation is it as far as I'm concerned.

Other members of management followed with similar statements, except for Proctor:

Although I had never studied this plan, I knew from statistics on product line mix, volume by territory, and a variety of compensation methods I've picked up in business school and in marketing journals, that this plan Sorensen recommended was just plain mediocre. I just

couldn't sit there and see a bunch of men accept it when Paul Brown said it's the best they could do, without letting him know that he was wrong.

Proctor asked Saunders if he might get up to an easel in the room and list some of the important statistics and factors that bear on Lakeland's compensation policy. First, he took Sorensen's proposed policy and asked for clarification on the reasoning behind it. Most members of the meeting entered into this discussion in rather lively fashion but, according to Paul Brown,

After about 20 minutes, it seemed to most of us that Bill was not trying to understand our proposal at all—he seemed as if he were disagreeing with it. When this happened, I for one just shut up. I felt that we were being cross-examined. Never in our staff meetings have we had to feel that way, since everyone from Jim Saunders on down uses an offhand, calm tone of voice in asking questions of each other—it's just by intuition that we know that the other man's purpose is to understand what we are proposing, before he equally calmly points out deficiencies. Certainly, no one jumps fast to another tactic, that of proposing a competitive decision, until all us have understood what we're talking about. Bill Proctor, however, was different. His tone and demeanor told us otherwise—it came through loud and clear that he was attacking Sorensen's proposal and my conclusion of consensus. And then, he moved on to present his own plan, after we all shut up.

Regarding Proctor's participation in the meeting, Jim Saunders had this to say:

I could hardly believe my ears. In spite of the fact that Bill Proctor could not possibly have prepared before the meeting on this particular subject, it was almost as if he had written out and memorized a carefully worded analysis of sales compensation. After questioning the other managers about Sorensen's proposal, he first presented a five-point proposal for a new compensation policy. Then he said he wanted to take up each of these subproposals and cite facts to prove that they were the most logical route for the company to follow. Although my stomach was beginning to get upset, I forced myself to listen—I kept feeling embarrassed at having him lecture Brown, Sorensen, and the other managers, each of whom have had great success in their work with the company. To my utter astonishment, he turned out to have a proposal that I admired and which, sure enough, was superior to Sorensen's. I suggested that we take his proposal under advisement, with each manager studying it after the meeting. All agree that he has the answer. At the next meeting, at least Bill will have the satisfaction of hearing me (and Paul Brown) report a consensus.

Saunders reports that in ensuing meetings over a period of eight months, the subject of biweekly staff meetings was brought up by W. D.

Davidson, manager of chain store sales. Davidson noted that attendance was becoming lax, "because many of us are under such heavy pressure of work—training of new salesmen, emergency calls from very important customers, or sudden demands for new advertising strategies." (These were reasons which were submitted by managers in memos to Davidson, as secretary of the meetings.) In a discussion on this point, other managers seemed to Saunders rather indifferent, without much to say about the advantages or disadvantages of holding these meetings. Proctor was very clear on this point. He stated that meetings are very expensive and time-consuming if one multiplies the salaries of the eight top marketing managers of Lakeland times the one-half day of conferences.

> *This represents 8 man-days a month or 96 man-days a year. But there is a logic to the meetings. If they are done right, we can accomplish an awful lot. I am in favor of meetings if their purpose is to inform each other of the progress we are making on our individual projects. In giving a half day, we can accomplish twice as much if reports are clearly stated, with declarative sentence headings stating the problem and the recommendations. Then, under each heading there should be various subheadings, equally clear, with facts under them to show the logic. In this way, the whole report adds up to a logical argument with precision and clarity. I remember learning in one of my case-writing courses back in business school that this is a practical, staff-report type of application of Aristotelian logic. I didn't appreciate it at the time, but I've discovered that there is no other way to so clearly convey a complex problem: The Problem and its Causes, Facts Which Bear on the Problem, Alternative Solutions, and Final Recommendations. Incidentally, it is necessary that one think of all possible alternative solutions, but it is a waste of time to write this in the report. When we have a roomful of busy executives, they don't have time to study through all of the alternatives that we* aren't *going to use—their time should be spent only on the one that we* are *going to make use of.*

Saunders also noted that during Proctor's presentations at meetings over the next few months, Paul Brown and Davidson would often look at the floor, fidget, look out of the window, or even sometimes give out a nervous "ha-ha" when Proctor was making a particularly strong point.

Five weeks ago, A. F. Williams suggested a special meeting, at company headquarters, for all sales personnel from the whole company, in order to give them a sense of feeling a part of one large organization and to bring them up-to-date on some of the recent things the company is doing in the way of studies of consumer motivation, changes in sales compensation policies, systems analysis for the flow of products to the various markets, and linear programming as used to plan new warehouse facilities, capital investment, and location. In past years, it had been Williams' firm belief that such meetings, held about once a year for each of the three major company divisions, would have a very good effect on employee performance. He felt that their effect was threefold: employees at all levels would *(a)* get a better understanding of the facts of company operations, including what the policies are and why they were decided that way, *(b)* feel a part of the total organization, with an *esprit de corps* based on knowledge that if all worked together as a team, the organization could achieve a degree of excellence through its men and leadership, and *(c)* feel important as an individual, by being invited personally to company headquarters.

At this particular meeting, Williams explained to Saunders:

The theme should be exposition of what the company is doing in forward-looking management terms, such as the application of systems analysis, mathematical programming, and advertising research. In view of the nature of the subjects, and from what I can see of Proctor's sharp and clear presentations on his feet, I think that you are really fortunate in having, this year, Bill Proctor to give the results of his work. The morale of people in the field will be raised considerably when they see what a really fine job the company is doing to insure that we are as good as anybody—including the national chains—when it comes to a hard-hitting management team and a streamlined method of carrying out our operations.

When this suggestion was made, according to Saunders:

I felt just about like that first staff meeting Bill attended. I know for sure that Williams is right, and that some of our headquarters personnel are doing impressive things, including Bill Proctor. But at the same time, I'm dead sure in my own mind that Bill is having a really bad effect on the teamwork among managers in the Marketing Division, and that this is going to have adverse effects on major marketing policy decisions in the long run. I also wonder how long those regional managers are going to sit there and carry out policies with the old hard-hitting spirit that the company has now.

Selected Readings

From

PERSONALITY AND ORGANIZATION*

By Chris Argyris†

THE HUMAN PERSONALITY

The Source of Psychological Energy Is in the Needs

The energy that most researchers postulate is pictured as being located in the need systems of the personality.

People behave. They love, hate, eat, cry, fight, work, strike, study, shop, go to the movies, play bridge, bring up children, go to church. The psychological energy to behave in all these ways comes from the need systems that exist in our personalities. . . .

The energy in every need system is always ready to release itself, to bubble over. But so long as the boundary of the need system is strong enough, the energy will not release itself. When the energy bubbles over, the need system is in action. Need systems that are quiet and not in action are inert needs or potential active needs. This is similar to the pressure in a boiler. So long as the pressure does not become too great, the boiler will not burst.

*   *   *   *   *

Let us ask, "So what?"

What is the advantage of saying that people have needs in tension in relation to goals? Why go all through this fuss? To answer the question let us imagine that there are two foremen. Mr. A. is hard-working, does an exceptional job, and is up for promotion. Mr. B., on the other hand, is slow, is lax on the job, has many problems which he does not seem to care about, and is being considered for a demotion.

Common sense answers to why these two foremen behave the way they do usually go like this:

"Well, that's human nature."

"I guess Mr. B. just doesn't give a damn."

"Mr. A. is really loyal to our company. Looks like Mr. B. isn't."

"Mr. A.'s attitudes are better; that's why he works harder."

"Maybe B. has been having some 'off days.' "

---
* From *Personality and Organization* by Chris Argyris. Copyright © 1957 by Chris Argyris. Reprinted by permission of Harper & Row, Publishers, Inc. (Excerpts from pp. 27–31, 33–51, 66–67, 77–90, 95, 103–4, 123–25, 130, 137–39, 150, 153–55, 157.)

† Dr. Argyris is Professor of Business Administration at Harvard University.

Tackling the same question by using the scheme above, we would have to say:
"Mr. A. has a need in tension which is directed at certain goals. He needs to be hard-working."

"Mr. B. had a need in tension which is also directed at a certain goal. He needs to be slow."

Examining both sets of answers, we note that the practical set jumps immediately to such vague, high-sounding conclusions as "human nature," "doesn't give a damn," "loyalty." None of these conclusions provides a jumping-off point for constructive action. Every one of them immediately implies there is something wrong with Mr. B.

The second list, on the other hand, jumps to questions. It forces the person to find out more facts. For example, "What need is in tension?" "At what goal is it directed?" "Why does Mr. A. have a certain need and why does Mr. B. have a different need in action?" The second list points out one of the most important rules in trying to understand human behavior. The real causes of human behavior are rarely found in the observable behavior. It is important to ask, "What is behind this behavior that we see?"

The second list does not immediately classify someone as "bad" and someone as "good.". . . Therefore, the second list is more useful, in that it does not automatically condemn Mr. B., or praise Mr. A. . . . Probably one of the greatest weaknesses in trying to understand others is the immediate attempt at labeling them "good" or "bad." Once this is done, it is impossible to think objectively about a person.

*   *   *   *   *

PERSONALITY HAS ABILITIES

Bordering the needs, and in most cases evolving from them, are the abilities. Abilities are the tools, so to speak, with which a person expresses and fulfills his needs. Abilities are the communications systems for the needs to express themselves. Once the energy bubbles over from the needs, it goes "through" the appropriate ability designed to express the need. . . .

Interests are usually a product of a fusion of several needs. This fusion usually comes about at an early age and is unconscious. Interests, therefore, are indicators of the kinds of needs people have. For example, a person with a strong need to be independent, to achieve, and to know things, might make a good scientist.

The skills that are given to us by inheritance are such skills as finger dexterity and other manual and manipulative skills. Few abilities are inherited. The majority of the more important abilities are learned and developed in interaction with others. This is especially true for such abilities as leadership. There are no born leaders. The personality of a leader is developed, probably during early home life and by the situations in which this personality finds appropriate expression.

Abilities, in summary, function between needs and the environment, thus providing the line of communication for needs. . . .

*   *   *   *   *

DEFENSE MECHANISMS MAINTAIN SELF AGAINST THREAT

Generally speaking, there are at least two ways to reduce feelings of threat. One is to change the self so that it becomes congruent with whatever is causing the difficulty. This involves "accepting" the fact that one is "wrong." It involves admitting the limitations associated with the difficulty will not arise again. The second approach is to defend the self by somehow denying or destroying (consciously or unconsciously) what is threatening and clinging to the present self concept. This behavior is called a defense reaction. . . .

A defensive reaction may create difficulty if it happens that the individual instead of the situation in the environment, is "wrong." A defense reaction reduces the awareness of threat but never affects that which is causing the threat. For example, let us say that supervisor A is threatened because he "knows" his boss does not think that he (supervisor A) is doing a good job. Let us assume that he defends his self by placing the blame on the boss. This will not in any way stop the boss from feeling the way he does about supervisor A. Soon the supervisor will have to justify his defensive reactions to himself. He may do this by saying that the boss is "out to get him." Each of these defenses is a distortion which in turn will require further justification and further defense. After some time supervisor A has built up deep layers of defense, all of which will have to be uncovered if he is to understand the cause. . . .

. . . All individuals have a set of defenses. This set of defenses is not to be viewed as necessarily being "bad" or "good." It is best to view them as simply the individual's way of defending himself from threat. . . .

*   *   *   *   *

Defense Mechanisms

1. Aggression. One of the common results of regression is aggression. Aggression means trying to injure or hurt the person, group, object that is acting as the barrier or as the cause of conflict. By the words "injure" and "hurt" we include all types of injuries, including social and psychological injury, such as name-calling insults, and cheating.

2. Guilt. If the "block" is due to the limitations of one's own personality, (e.g., the individual who desires to become a supervisor but does not have a good enough record), then the aggression can be turned toward the self. The person usually feels guilt, criticizes himself, or may even go so far as to hurt himself. Guilt is, therefore, aggression from ourselves to ourselves.

3. Continuation. Sometimes the conflict is not resolved but the person continues to live by making another choice which is "second best." For example, a student who becomes a businessman but still wishes he could have gone to medical school is in a sense continuing his conflict.

4. Discriminatory Decision. At times, a conflict is resolved by sitting down and writing the reasons for and the reasons against doing something. We try to make a list of the reasons and then pick out (discriminate) the best one. This mechanism almost always occurs on a conscious level. In general, it may be used when the personality is healthy and the conflict is not strong. For example, an executive, in order to choose between foreman A and foreman B for a new promotion, may sit down, list the "goods" and "bads" of each foreman, and then pick (discriminate) one.

5. Denial. An easy course to follow when threatened is simply to remain unaware of the facts which could create one side of a conflict. . . . Actually, what happens under denial is that the employees do not allow what has just been said to penetrate into their consciousness. . . . ([It] is a different thing from deliberate pretense, in which the individual knows something but decides to make believe that he does not.)

* * * * *

One resultant of defense mechanisms is that they make it difficult to differentiate between an individual's underlying motivations and the skin-surface ones. We observe Mr. A. and Mr. B. while we interview them for a job. Mr. A. talks so much that we cannot speak. Mr. B. hardly says a word. These two bits of behavior at the immediately observed "manifest" level seem to be different. But on the "latent" or deeper level—the level to which we must learn to go—both people may really have the same self-concept and, as a result, may feel insecure and fear unknown situations. But they make up for their fear in different ways. Mr. B. adapts by doing little talking. Mr. A. adapts by talking so much that no one else is able to say a word.

Or it may be that the personalities of supervisor A., who "works himself to death," and supervisor B. who "hardly lifts a finger," are basically similar. Both may feel they are not competent. One works hard and overcompensates for limitations he senses in himself. The other does very little for fear of doing something wrong.

The practical implications are that a clear distinction between "manifest" and "latent" must be made if we want to predict how individual supervisors, for example, will react to frustration, conflict, and anxiety. The same is true if changes are to be made.

If the changes made satisfy only manifest behavior, then the underlying latent reasons will not be satisfied. We can predict that the complaining will continue but probably shift to another area. It is similar to taking an aspirin to relieve migraine headaches. The headache will be relieved but not cured.

Ball parks, athletic teams, company picnics, and company lectures are programs that fulfill the skin-surface or manifest needs of the workers. Company newspapers, slogan schemes, and pep talks are also in the same category. . . . The employees, not truly satisfied and therefore still requiring need fulfillment, ask for more. Soon management begins to feel that the quality of the employees is going down. "All the employees want is more. How much do they expect us to give them?" According to this analysis, the management trains the workers to focus on material satisfactions (e.g., ball teams, pictures in the newspaper, and so on), and then complains when the workers want more. . . .

* * * * *

GROWTH MEANS AN INCREASE IN PARTS AND IN OUR "PRIVATE WORLD"

Most personality theories are in agreement that as the individual matures, he not only acquires more parts (i.e., more needs, abilities), but he also deepens many of them. As these parts are acquired, they are also integrated with the already existing parts of the personality. Every part which is added must be added so that the balance (organization) is not upset. Simultaneously with the personality growth of the individual is the expansion of the individual's private world or environment. Every time a new part is created "in" his personality, a new part is also experienced in his own private world. The world of experience is called "private" because it can never include the total objective world. It is impossible for the individual to experience everything, no matter how long he lives. . . .

Most personality theories state that the personality becomes complete, organized, and integrated only when it interacts with other people, ideas, and social organizations. Growth cannot occur if the person exists alone. He must interact with others in order to understand himself and thereby develop. Thus, we cannot understand ourselves unless we understand others, and we cannot understand others unless we understand ourselves.

To summarize man, in his need-fulfilling, goal directed behavior is to some extent: "like all other men, like some other men, like no other men."

*   *   *   *   *

BASIC SELF—ACTUALIZATION TRENDS OF THE HUMAN PERSONALITY

Since the human personality is a developing organism, one way to become more precise is to define the basic growth or development trends "inherent" in it (so long as it remains in the same culture). One can then logically assume that, at any given moment in time, the human personality is a developing organism, one will be predisposed to find expression for these developmental trends. Such an assumption implies another, namely, that there are basic development trends characteristic of a relatively large majority of the population being considered. . . .

It is assumed that human beings in our culture:

1. Tend to develop from a state of passivity as infants to a state of increasing activity as adults. . . .

2. Tend to develop from a state of dependence upon others as infants to a state of relative independence as adults. Relative independence is the ability to "stand on one's own two feet" and simultaneously to acknowledge healthy dependencies. . . .

3. Tend to develop from being capable of behaving only in a few ways as an infant to being capable of behaving in many different ways as an adult.

4. Tend to develop from having erratic, casual, shallow, quickly-dropped interests as an infant to having deeper interests as an adult. The mature state is characterized by an endless series of challenges, where the reward comes from doing something for its own sake. The tendency is to analyze and study phenomena in their full-blown wholeness, complexity, and depth.

5. Tend to develop from having a short time perspective (i.e., the present largely determines behavior) as an infant to a much longer time perspective as an adult (i.e., where the behavior is more affected by the past and the future). . . .

6. Tend to develop from being in a subordinate position in the family and society as an infant to aspiring to occupy an equal and/or superordinate position relative to their peers.

7. Tend to develop from a lack of awareness of self as an infant to an awareness of and control over self as an adult. The adult who tends to experience adequate and successful control over his own behavior tends to develop a sense of integrity (Erikson) and feelings of self-worth. Bakke shows that one of the most important needs of workers is to enlarge those areas of their lives in which their own decisions determine the outcome of their efforts.

*   *   *   *   *

THE FORMAL ORGANIZATION

Basic Incongruency between the Needs of a Mature Personality and the Requirements of Formal Organization

Bringing together the evidence regarding the impact of the formal organizational principles upon the individual, it is concluded that there are some basic *incongruencies between the growth trends of a healthy personality and the requirements of the formal organization.* If the principles of formal organization are used as ideally defined, employees will tend to work in an environment where (1) they are provided minimal control over their workaday world, (2) they are expected to be passive, dependent, and subordinate, (3) they are expected to have a short time perspective, (4) they are induced to perfect and value the frequent use of a few skin-surface shallow abilities and, (5) they are expected to produce under conditions leading to psychological failure.

All these characteristics are incongruent to the ones human beings are postulated to desire. They are much more congruent with the needs of infants in our culture. *In effect, therefore, organizations are willing to pay high wages and provide adequate seniority if mature adults will, for eight hours a day, behave in a less than mature manner!*

If the analysis is correct, this inevitable incongruency increases as (1) the employees are of increasing maturity, (2) as the formal structure (based upon the above principles) is made more clear-cut and logically tight for maximum formal organizational effectiveness, (3) as one goes down the line of command, and (4) as the jobs become more and more mechanized (i.e., take on assembly line characteristics). . . .

It is not difficult to see why some students of organization suggest that immature and even mentally retarded individuals would probably make excellent employees.

*   *   *   *   *

INDIVIDUAL AND GROUP ADAPTATION

The Individual Adapts

If the formal organization is defined by the use of such "organization" principles as task specialization, unity of direction, chain of command, and span of control, and if these principles are used correctly, the employees will work in situations in which they tend to be dependent, subordinate, and passive toward the leader. They will tend to use few of their abilities (probably none of which are important ones for the individual anyway). The degree of passivity, dependence, and submissiveness tends to increase for those employees as one goes down the line of command and as the work takes on more of the mass production characteristics. As a result, it is hypothesized that the formal organization creates in a healthy individual feelings of failure and frustration, short time perspective, and conflict. . . .

An employee experiencing frustration, failure, conflict and short time perspective may behave in any one or a combination of the following ways:

a. He may leave the organization. (But where else can he go? Most other companies are organized in the same way.)

b. He may work hard to climb the ladder and become the president. (But how many can become presidents?)

c. He may defend his self-concept and adapt through the use of defense mechanisms.

d. He may "pressure" himself to stay and, in spite of the conflict simultaneously adapt as much as possible by lowering his work standards and becoming apathetic and uninterested.

e. This apathy and disinterest may lead him to place more value on material rewards and to depreciate the value of human or nonmaterial rewards.

f. Although not directly inferable from the above, the employee may teach his children not to expect satisfaction on the job: to expect rather to earn good wages and "live" outside the plant (the same lesson the formal organizational experts are teaching him). This hypothesis is based on the known property of human beings of evaluating life in terms of their own self-concept . . . If the employee's self-concept includes as "good" activities, goldbricking, learning the ropes, and quota restricting, then these will tend to be passed on to his children through the process of acculturation. . . .

The Use of Defense Mechanisms. The third mode of adaptation, the use of defense mechanisms, is perhaps the least explored. As we have seen . . . in a defense reaction the individual distorts or denies the "facts" in order that he may live in some sort of equilibrium with himself and his environment. Systematic research is so meager in this area that our illustrations are mostly abstracted anecdotal accounts obtained from field research. We present a few:

a. To rationalize the fact that they are not accomplishing what they know the company requires. For example (one operator to another) "Take it easy—don't work too hard; this outfit has plenty of dough. They don't need whatever you give them by breaking your ass." Or, "I know the company doesn't want me to work too fast; I can get all worn out." (typist-secretary). Or (piece rate employee), "Well, they don't need those extra pieces until Monday anyway. Why should I knock myself out?"

b. To project their feelings upon others. They may blame them and ignore their own part in the problem.

For example (foreman), "it's those goddamned budgets. If I didn't have those on my neck, I'd have no problem—absolutely none." Or (an order department clerk), "Have you ever tried to keep the sales orders straight with the self-centered thickheads we have for salesmen? All they think of is themselves." Or (a production manager), "The basic problem we have is that everything we produce is custom-made. We ain't got no long runs like most other plants. We have to be careful of every order." Or (a piece-rate worker), "To hell with it," he said, "let the day man run 'em. He likes 'em. He turned in nine dollars today."

"You've got time to make another dollar yourself," I said. "To hell with that job!" Gus exclaimed. "I'm not going to bust my neck any more on it. Let the day man run it."

Another example is found in a recent study of a hospital with reports that the nurses partially adapt to their own inability to be what they believe is an effective administrator by projecting their limitations upon the administrative staff of the hospital. As one nurse describes it: "If you ask me, administration doesn't even know we exist. If they did, they would get busy and solve the many annoying administrative difficulties we have. Just take scheduling. They haven't been able to solve that at O.R. (Operating room) or X-ray or the chemical laboratories. If you want to help us nurses, please go upstairs and make administrators out of them."

*   *   *   *   *

c. To be ambivalent. "I cannot make up my mind. I like the job—yet I don't. I like the company—yet I'd leave. I don't know what it is, except I know it ain't the boss or the pay" (a clerk-typist). "I run hot and cold about this outfit."

"I can't seem to make up my mind if I should stay or ask for a transfer" (tool and die maker).

Researcher: "What kinds of things do you like and dislike about the company?" Worker: "I like the pay; I like the management—I think they're trying to be fair. But I don't like not being my own boss. I want to be my own boss, I guess. Here you got to be on a schedule. You're always working under pressure for someone else."

d. To escape from reality. An increasingly used defense against nonsatisfying work is for the individual to detach himself from his work. For example, a group of adolescent girls learned to use certain semi-automatic bookkeeping equipment. "Without advance notice," as one girl put it, "you suddenly realize you can work and at the same time think of a million other things. You know what I mean, daydream. You feel free."

e. To develop psychosomatic illnesses. Another type of defensive mechanism which has hardly been studied is the one by which the individual transforms a psychological problem into a physiological one. On the top management level, ulcers is a well-known psychosomatic disease. On the employee level, there is increasing evidence that employees are developing dubious backaches, headaches, and run-down feelings, to adapt to anxieties they tend to experience on the job.

Individual Apathy and Noninvolvement.   Apathy, lack of interest, and noninvolvement are types of defense mechanisms that may be becoming so popular that they require special emphasis. The basis of these defenses, we have pointed out, is the continuous frustration, conflict and failure an employee experiences.

Let us picture an employee whom we may call Dick. He works on an assembly line and finds that he cannot obtain minimal personality expression on his job. He is frustrated. From the studies of frustration it is hypothesized that Dick will tend to regress to a more childlike state. He will not be as "mature" as he was before he was frustrated. This "primitivation" (regression) of his personality may cause him (1) to leave the situation, (2) to try to change the work situation constructively or destructively, (3) to accept (internalize) the tension and "hang on," i.e., keep working.

*   *   *   *   *

Group Adaptation

The individual adapts to the impact of the organization by any one or some combination of: (1) leaving the organization, (2) climbing the organizational ladder,

(3) using defensive mechanisms, and (4) becoming apathetic and disinterested. These are all adaptive mechanisms and therefore need fulfilling. People will want to maintain these adaptive behaviors.

In order to guarantee their existence, the individual seeks group sanctions. The informal work groups are "organized" to perpetuate these adaptive processes (to reward those employees who follow the informal codes and to penalize those who do not). The individual adaptive acts now become sanctioned by the group, and therefore feed back to reinforce the continuance of the individual need-fulfilling adaptive behavior. . . .

*   *   *   *   *

Formalizing Small Groups (Trade Unions)

Up to now we note that the individual adapts on the psychological level and on the small informal group level. The latter are initially created to sanction and therefore perpetuate those activities that the work group on any level of the organization finds need-fulfilling.

However, if the company decides to disband the informal activities, in the final analysis they could be defended by the employees only by threatening to do harm to the productive process (e.g., strike, slow down). Such measures are not easily used and the psychological and financial costs on both sides are high.

Management's formal power is basically derived by making the employees dependent on management for their rewards, directions, positions, and so forth. It follows logically from the above that one way for the employees to reduce their dependence is to take away some of the management's formal authority and place it within their own control. According to Coleman this is an important basis for the rise of trade unions. As McGregor states, "And to the extent to which unions have attempted to place restrictions upon management's authority reflects not only a desire for power, but a conscious attempt to reduce the dependence of the workers upon their bosses.". . .

In order to create trade unions, the employees must reach outside the organization into the political world, where their power and managements (due to our political system) is, man for man, equal. Once trade unions come to existence, the employees can sanction many of their informal activities through the formal power residing in the union as an organization.

*   *   *   *   *

MANAGEMENT'S REACTION AND ITS IMPACT UPON THE EMPLOYEES

We have been primarily concerned with the employees' adaptation to the formal organizational structure, such as decreases in production and identification with the organization; increases in waste, errors, absenteeism, sickness, apathy, disinterest in work, and increase in importance of material (financial) aspects of work. These are all understandable and predictable ways for relatively healthy employees to adapt to the conflict, frustration, and failure they experience as a result of the formal organization. . . .

Management's Dominant Assumptions

The top administrators, however, tend to diagnose the problems in another way. They observe their employees while at work and they conclude: (1) The employees are lazy. (2) The employees are uninterested and apathetic. (3) The employees are money crazy. (4) The employees create errors and waste.

Management blames the employees and "sees" the disloyalty, disinterest, and goldbricking as being "in" and caused by the employees. It follows logically for management, that if any changes are to occur the employees must be changed. Thus management initiates programs to "change peoples' attitudes," to "sell them free enterprise," to "make people more interested in the company."

The basic action policy that management tends to define to solve the above "problems" actually stems from the logics of the formal organization and formal leadership already discussed . . .

*   *   *   *   *

Stronger "Dynamic" Leadership and Its Impact upon the Employees

An important pillar of most management policy is to develop competent executives who among other things: (1) are able to "needle," "drive," "sell," "push," "pressure," "persuade," "urge," "coerce," "win" employees to increase productivity, loyalty, and interest for the organization and for their job; (2) are able to get all the facts, weigh them correctly, and make effective decisions; (3) know clearly management's objectives, policies, and practices; (4) communicate these policies and practices clearly to the employees; and (5) evaluate the performance of the employee strictly and honestly according to these policies and practices.

There is ample evidence to illustrate management's use of pressure-oriented leadership.

Summarizing the characteristics found in most of the research, one may conclude that the autocratic, directive leader places the followers in a situation where they tend to be (1) passive, dependent, subordinate, and submissive; (2) centered toward the organization's and the leader's needs rather than the needs of all the followers; (3) competing with each other for the leader's favor; (4) confronted with a short time perspective; and (5) experiencing psychological failure.

We must conclude that the *impact of directive leadership upon the subordinates is similar to that which the formal* organization *has upon the subordinate. Pressure-oriented directive* leadership *"compounds the felony" that the formal organization* commits every *minute every hour of the day and every day of the year.* Authoritarian leadership *reinforces and perpetuates* the "damage" created *by the organizational structure.* The adaptive activities . . . are also caused by directive leadership. Directive leadership helps to reinforce, in the employees' minds, the necessity for the same adaptive activities that this leadership is originally designed to decrease.

Tighter Management Controls and Their Impact upon the Employees

The second policy decision made by many managers to combat reduced productivity is careful definition, inspection, and evaluation of the quality and quantity of every employee's performance. This leads us to the field of management controls.

Management controls are becoming increasingly important in the eyes of top management. Management control is seen as a fundamental process in all organization. . . .

* * * * *

Management controls are not only necessary and inevitable if the traditional formal organizational structure is to be maintained, but they also become increasingly important as the formal organization becomes larger and more decentralized. Management decision making would suffer if management controls were abandoned.

* * * * *

As a result of the pressure, tension, and general mistrust of management controls, employees tend to unite against management.

Psychological research shows that people can stand only a certain amount of pressure and tension, after which it becomes intolerable. One method people use to reduce the effect of the pressure (assuming that the employees cannot reduce the pressure itself) is to join groups, which help absorb much of the pressure and thus relieve the individual personally. Gradually, therefore, the individuals become a group because in so doing they are able to satisfy their need to (1) reduce the pressure on each individual; (2) get rid of tension; (3) feel more secure by belonging to a group which can counteract the pressure. In short, new cohesive groups developed to *combat* management pressure. In a sense, the people had learned that they could be happier if they combined against it. This result is predicted . . . [above] as a "natural" consequence of the employees' adapting to the dependence and submissiveness that they experience.

* * * * *

The impact of management controls is similar to that which the formal organization and directive leadership have upon the subordinates. Management controls feed back upon and give support to directive leadership as both "compound the felony" committed by the formal organization every hour of the day and every day of the year. . . .

The "Human Relations Fad" and Its Impact upon the Employees

The third response by management to the problems of inadequate productivity and employee apathy is the let's-be-human approach. If directive leadership and tight management controls do not succeed, perhaps helping the workers to identify with their jobs and the company might succeed.

How did the human relations fad begin? The growth of trade unionism brought to light much of the discontent the employees had been feeling for years, and placed much of the blame on poor management. A second important stimulus was the research by Mayo, Roethlisberger and Dickson, who presented concrete evidence showing that productivity and human relations were intimately tied up. Poor human relations, wrote the authors, creates low production (e.g., rate-setting and goldbricking which leads to worse human relations which in turn leads to lower production. A key to the solution, Mayo suggests, is to help the employees feel that they belong to a small primary work group. If people could be helped to feel they belong, he suggested, human relations would be better. Both of these events had a strong impact upon management, many of whom still did not fully accept trade unionism. Third, many executives were beginning to develop a sense of social responsibility.

A difficulty with Mayo and other "human realtors" is that they observed employees goldbricking, rate-setting, expressing low feelings of identification, apathy, and disinterest and they conclude, like management, that this is "bad." It may be bad from management's point of view, but as our analysis suggests, it may also be adaptive as long as relatively mature workers are working in a difficult work situation.

Management picked up the message and for the next fifteen to twenty years there existed a great interest in human relations.

*   *   *   *   *

To summarize, research shows that under democratic conditions people do tend to feel that they are part of a team and respected. However, this does not mean this will tend to be the case if a supervisor tries to be pseudo democratic or democratic under autocratic conditions. We must not forget that the formal structure of most organizations and the management controls are fundamentally autocratic. The small groups experiments from which the use of "democratic leadership" seems to have arisen never coped with these two factors.

*   *   *   *   *

Research suggests that telling a worker he is an important part of the company, when through actual experience he sees he is a very minor part (thanks to task specialization) with little responsibility (thanks to chain of command, directive leadership, and management controls) may only increase the employees' dissatisfaction with management. As one worker concluded, "Who are they kidding, us or themselves?" To emphasize to an assembly line worker that he should feel proud of the four bolts that he puts into the right rear end of a car may be viewed as an insult by the worker who is a "whole" human being (although it allays management's anxieties about employee apathy). As one employee remarked, "It's ironic—damn. It hurts to know that four bolts are important. What a hell of a life." . . .

From

MOTIVATION AND PRODUCTIVITY*

By Saul W. Gellerman†

The Classical Theories

*   *   *   *   *

Alfred Adler, a one-time collaborator of Freud's who later broke with him to establish his own school of thought, has also had an important influence on our

---

* Reprinted by permission of the American Management Association, New York. Copyright 1963. (Excerpts from pp. 109–18.)

† The author, formerly a Staff Specialist in Behavioral Sciences for International Business Machines Corporation, is now a consultant on organization matters.

understanding of work motivation. Adler is not as well known as Freud, even among professionals; in fact, many of his ideas have become accepted today without having his name attached to them. Unlike Freud, who stressed the pleasure-seeking and life-sustaining motives, Adler placed a great deal of emphasis on the power motive. By "power" he meant the ability to require others to behave in ways that suited one's purposes. An infant actually has a great deal of power over others. As any parent can testify, a baby can cause a considerable commotion among all the adults within earshot with the merest yelp.

According to Adler, this ability to manipulate other people is inherently pleasurable. Not only does the child have a hard time unlearning it, but he may also spend a good deal of his adult life trying to recapture that blissful condition of having other people do as he wills. However, Adler did not consider the child to be merely a miniature dictator. He recognized, first of all, that power was not sought for its own sake so much as it was a refuge from the utter helplessness of childhood. Adults are the child's lifeline, and it is a life-and-death matter to the child that the adults in his world be reliable; therefore, the power motive acquires an urgency which it never quite loses even though it eventually becomes unnecessary. It is especially strong in an older child or in an adult who feels handicapped in some way in his ability to win the respect and attention of others. Such people may go to considerable lengths to command attention, thereby overcoming whatever real or imagined weakness it was that had disturbed them in the first place. In describing this process, Adler introduced two well-known terms to psychology: inferiority complex (underlying fears of inadequacy or handicap which need not necessarily have a basis in fact) and *compensation* (the tendency to exert extreme efforts to achieve the goals which the "inferiority" would ordinarily deny).

Second, Adler recognized that power was not the only way to solve the problem of helplessness. In time the growing child realizes that cooperativeness wins a more permanent assurance of safety for him than power ever could, and at considerably less cost in terms of watchfulness and fear of retaliation. If the child's development proceeds normally and does not encounter too much tension, the power motive gradually transforms itself into a desire to perfect his relationships with others—that is, to make these relationships more confident, open, and helpful. Thus the mature adult would be able to move among others freely, without fear or suspicion. On the other hand, if the process were stunted somewhere along the line, perhaps by too many disappointing contacts with untrustworthy adults, the power motive would not only persist but would actually become stronger. The adult who had grown up in this way would be on guard, rarely willing to reveal very much of his plans or feelings and continually on the lookout for an advantage that would secure his position in what seemed a treacherous world.

*   *   *   *   *

THE COMPETENCE MOTIVE: ROBERT W. WHITE

*   *   *   *   *

. . . White notes that the original Freudian theory, for all its complexity, is still a little too simple to account for all the facets of human behavior. Specifically, the individual is more than just a vehicle for a set of instincts; he is also an active observer and sharer of his environment. For White, one of the mainsprings of human motivation is an interest in getting to know what the world is like and in learning to get what one wants from it. Whereas Freud stressed the life-preserving and comfort-seeking instincts and Adler, going a step further, stressed the drive for power over others, White notes that people also want to understand and manipulate their physical environment (and, later on, their social environment too). In the broadest sense, they like to be able to make things happen—to create events rather than merely to await them passively.

White calls this desire for mastery "the competence motive." It can be seen even in very young infants, he believes, in the form of random fingering of objects, poking around, and feeling whatever is in reach. Later on it takes the form of exploring, tinkering, taking things apart, putting them together, and the like. As a result of years of learning his way around his own small world, learning what its possibilities are and how to exploit them, the young boy develops a certain assurance that he can handle himself equally well in the larger world he will enter as an adult. Whether his sense of competence is strong or weak depends on the balance of successes and failures the boy has experienced in his pint-sized forays into the world around him. If successes have predominated, he will probably come to regard life as a fairly promising venture where a little common sense and persistence can take him a long way. On the other hand, if the failures have outweighed the successes, the boy may regard life as a hazardous game at best, one in which running risks is likely to lead to nothing but another fiasco, so that it makes more sense simply to wait for circumstances to come along and have their will with him than to try to influence them.

Because the individual can hardly avoid some kind of transactions with his environment every day, the ledger of successes and failures is altered constantly. Consequently, one's fate is never entirely sealed. There is always the possibility that a particularly fortunate set of experiences will come along to bolster a timid ego, or contrariwise an unfortunate set may knock the props out from under an overly confident one. While the emerging personality may be pretty well jelled in a number of important respects by age five, this is not true of the sense of competence: It can get off to a bad start and still develop strongly as the result of later successes.

But there is, alas, a limit to this. After a time the sense of competence is also likely to reach a sort of plateau from which it may vary somewhat but not (ordinarily) a great deal. This is because after a while the sense of competence begins to affect the likelihood of a given experience's turning into a success or a failure. The more venturesome spirits will be out trying to win things or change things, and by brushing aside obstacles and persisting toward their goals they tip the scales of chance in their favor. Meeker individuals will venture less and therefore gain less and will perhaps shrink a little too readily from obstacles. Thus the sense of competence gradually becomes a sort of self-fulfilling prophecy: The individual seldom achieves more than he expects because he does not try to achieve more than he thinks he can.

*   *   *   *   *

In adults the competence motive is very likely to express itself as a desire for job mastery and professional growth. It may therefore have a great deal to do with Herzberg's finding that the most lasting satisfactions of accountants and engineers are derived from solving difficult technical problems. The need for a suitable outlet for this motive, in a civilized society that has had most of the elemental challenges engineered out of it, may even underlie the growing tendency for people to identify themselves with their professions rather than with a particular employer or the region or group in which they were born and raised.

This job can be one of the few remaining arenas in which a man can match his skills against the environment in a contest that is neither absurdly easy nor prohibitively difficult. Where such a contest is possible, the competence motive may be exercised and considerable rewards may be enjoyed. But, where it is impossible, as in most routinized or oversupervised jobs, a strong competence motive leads only to frustration, while a weak one merely encourages resignation and dependency.

Further, the sense of competence probably plays a key role in effecting job success, especially in those jobs where initiative or innovation is essential. A man who trusts his own ability to influence his environment will actually try to influence it more often and more boldly than someone who is inclined to let the environment influence him. Can it be, then, that the games and horseplay of seven- and eight-year-olds have something to do with events in the executive suite thirty years later? White's theory suggests that they may. . . .

THE AFFILIATION MOTIVE: STANLEY SCHACHTER

Psychologists have been attacking the problem of human motivation from more than one angle. In addition to studying the ways in which assurance and daring evolve out of a basic sense of competence, they have turned their attention to the question of what makes some people such strikingly social creatures and why others seem to be able to spend most of their time quite happily by themselves. That most people like to be in other people's company is obvious enough, but it also seems to be true that this liking is stronger in some than in others and stronger under certain kinds of circumstances.

A promising beginning toward understanding this urge to be sociable has been made by Stanley Schachter of the University of Minnesota. . . .

*   *   *   *   *

The importance of affiliative needs is clear. . . . Yet the existence of an affiliation motive has been more or less taken for granted, so that when Schachter first began to direct serious scientific attention to it, he could find little in the way of previous research or even theorizing to guide him. It was generally assumed that affiliation could be either a means to an end or an end in itself. That is, people might seek the company of others in order to gain some kind of impersonal reward which the others meted out, such as money, favors, or protection. Or they might socialize simply because they enjoyed it. It was with this latter kind of affiliation that Schachter concerned himself: the desire to be with other people regardless of whether anything but company was apparently gained thereby.

Some previous research had touched on the question in a way. Psychologists had found that when something happens which contradicts a strongly held belief, the "believers" will tend to seek each other out with great urgency. They then go through an exicted process of comparing notes, speculating about the event, and seeking explanations. Eventually some sort of consensus emerges from all this discussion, and most of the people will quickly associate themselves with it. Whether the new ideas fit the facts any better than the old ones did, or indeed whether they are very different from the old ones at all, does not seem to matter particularly. What *does* seem to matter is that one's beliefs are squared with everyone else's. There seems, in other words, to be a great deal of relief when one's thinking is shared by many others, almost as if this agreement confirmed the "rightness" and therefore the safety of one's own ideas.

*   *   *   *   *

For Schachter, the most important element in the pattern was the reassuring effect of sharing an opinion. Apparently this kind of sharing provided a feeling that the world was understood and that therefore life was not really so dangerous after all. Evidently something more than just company was being provided by this particular form of affiliation. Socializing, in this instance, served to make life *seem* a little more manageable, a little less inexplicable, even though the shared ideas themselves might be utterly without foundation. (This probably helps to explain the unpopularity of most new ideas: They suddenly make the world seem unfamiliar!) If the pattern is not particularly rational, that does not make it any less human.

So one motive for affiliation can be the opportunity to have one's beliefs confirmed. But Schachter found himself wondering whether the discomfort of uncertainty was the only form of discomfort that would lead to affiliation or whether it was just a special case of a broader class of anxieties that would make people want to get together. To answer the question he devised an ingenious, though somewhat diabolical, series of experiments. The subjects in these experiments were those unsung heroes (heroines in this case) of most psychological research: the college sophomores who, in return for volunteering to be subjects for an experiment, are excused from a lab report.

Schachter's technique was to produce a mild state of fright by implying that his subjects would have to endure a certain amount of pain during the experiment. They endured nothing of the kind, of course; Schachter was deliberately trying to create a rather upset frame of mind. Once he had gotten his subjects sufficiently perturbed, Schachter told them that they would have to wait for further developments and gave them an opportunity to do so either alone or together. Most of them chose togetherness, despite the fact that they were strangers. At this point Schachter confessed his trick, apologized, and explained the experiment to his much-relieved subjects. He had proved his point: Misery definitely does love company.

*   *   *   *   *

The informal work group is a way of adapting to a humiliating lack of competence in the face of a mechanized organization. The group provides some degree of reassurance: Everyone else is equally "beaten" by the system; therefore, it is less of a reflection on each individual to be beaten. Viewed in this light, the informal work group is not necessarily due to "natural" gregariousness; it may also be a defensive reaction and a symptom of deep distress.

*   *   *   *   *

Affiliation, then, can be a simple expression of good fellowship or the symptom of a drastic loss of self-respect. (It can also be many other things: a voluntary stratagem for increasing the likelihood of obtaining certain advantages, for example.) . . .

From

THE HUMAN SIDE OF ENTERPRISE*

By Douglas McGregor†

[EDITORS' NOTE: In the abstract below, the author is stating some fundamental principles of human motivation.

In other chapters, McGregor points out that in the practice of management, many executives believe that many employees inherently dislike to work, that they therefore must be controlled and directed by reward and punishment to get them to put forth efforts for the organization, and that they prefer to be directed, because they have relatively little ambition.

From a psychological standpoint, however, McGregor says that employment, wages, working conditions and benefits, which control people by the "carrot and stick" method, are really the causes of indolence, passivity, and unwillingness to accept responsibility. Thus it is not the natural motivations of employees but management methods which cause these reactions.

There is thus a vicious circle: management believes people are behaving in a certain way; then management "manages" in a certain way; people in fact act to confirm the original misconception.

As a way out, McGregor suggests creation of jobs and work which satisfy social needs ("the need for the fairest possible break"; ". . . needs for belonging, association, friendship . . . for self esteem, autonomy, competence . . . recognition, respect of one's fellows . . . and for self fulfillment, that is, for realizing one's own potential for continued self-development").

This abstract gives in the author's own words the kinds of motivations that would be produced if the management and the work organization provide these things.]

There are some other reasons why management has been relatively slow to utilize social science knowledge. Two of these are specially important. The first is that every manager quite naturally considers himself his own social scientist. His personal experience with people from childhood on has been so rich that he feels little real need to turn elsewhere for knowledge of human behavior. . . .

* * * * *

Every managerial act rests on assumptions, generalizations, and hypotheses—that is to say, on theory. Our assumptions are frequently implicit, sometimes quite unconscious, often conflicting; nevertheless, they determine our predictions that if we do *a, b* will occur. Theory and practice are inseparable.

* * * * *

It is possible to have more or less adequate theoretical assumptions; it is not possible to reach a managerial decision or take a managerial action uninfluenced by assumptions, whether adequate or not. The insistence on being practical really means, "Let's accept *my* theoretical assumptions without argument or test." The common practice of proceeding without explicit examination of theoretical assumptions leads, at times, to remarkable inconsistencies in managerial behavior.

* * * * *

---

† The late author was a Professor in the School of Industrial Management at the Massachusetts Institute of Technology.

Another common way of denying the importance of theory to managerial behavior is to insist that management is an art. This also precludes critical examination of the theoretical assumptions underlying managerial actions by placing reliance on intuitions and feelings, which are by definition not subject to question. The issue is not whether management is a science. It is not. Its purposes are different. Science is concerned with the advancement of knowledge; management, like any profession, is concerned with the achievement of practical objectives. The issue is whether management can utilize scientific knowledge in the achievement of those objectives. To insist that management is an art is frequently no more than a denial of the relevance of systematic, tested knowledge to practice. So long as the manager fails to question the validity of his personal assumptions, he is unlikely to avail himself of what is available in science. . . .

An equally important reason for management's failure to make effective use of current social science knowledge has to do with a misconception concerning the nature of control in the field of human behavior. In engineering, control consists in adjustment to natural law. It does not mean making nature do our bidding. We do not, for example, dig channels in the expectation that water will flow uphill; we do not use kerosene to put out a fire. In designing an internal combustion engine we recognize and adjust to the fact that gases expand when heated; we do not attempt to make them behave otherwise. With respect to physical phenomena, control involves the selection of means which are *appropriate* to the nature of the phenomena with which we are concerned.

In the human field the situation is the same, but we often dig channels to make water flow uphill. Many of our attempts to control behavior, far from representing selective adaptations, are in direct violation of human nature. They consist in trying to make people behave as we wish without concern for natural law. . . .

*   *   *   *   *

Another fallacy is often revealed in managerial attempts to control human behavior. When we fail to achieve the results we desire, we tend to seek the cause everywhere but where it usually lies: in our choice of inappropriate methods of control. The engineer does not blame water for flowing downhill rather than up, nor gases for expanding rather than contracting when heated. However, when people respond to managerial decisions in undesired ways, the normal response is to blame them. . . .

*   *   *   *   *

There have been few dramatic break-throughs in social science theory like those which have occurred in the physical sciences during the past half century. Nevertheless, the accumulation of knowledge about human behavior in many specialized fields has made possible the formulation of a number of generalizations. . . . Some of these assumptions . . . are as follows:

1. *The expenditure of physical and mental effort in work is as natural as play or rest.* The average human being does not inherently dislike work. Depending upon controllable conditions, work may be a source of satisfaction (and will be voluntarily performed) or a source of punishment (and will be avoided if possible).

2. *External control and the threat of punishment are not the only means for bringing about effort toward organizational objectives. Man will exercise self-direction and self-control in the service of objectives to which he is committed.*

3. *Commitment to objectives is a function of the rewards associated with their*

*achievements.*The most significant of such rewards, e.g., the satisfaction of ego and self-actualization needs, can be direct products of effort directed toward organizational objectives.

4. *The average human being learns, under proper conditions, not only to accept but to seek responsibility.* Avoidance of responsibility, lack of ambition, and emphasis on security are generally consequences of experience, not inherent human characteristics.

5. *The capacity to exercise a relatively high degree of imagination, ingenuity, and creativity in the solution of organizational problems is widely, not narrowly, distributed in the population.*

6. *Under the conditions of modern industrial life, the intellectual potentialities of the average human being are only partially utilized.*

*   *   *   *   *

In the physical sciences there are many theoretical phenomena which cannot be achieved in practice. Absolute zero and a perfect vacuum are examples. Others, such as nuclear power, jet aircraft, and human space flight, are recognized theoretically to be possible long before they become feasible. This fact does not make theory less useful. . . .

Similarly, in the management of the human resources of industry, the assumptions and theories about human nature at any given time limit innovation. . . . Assumptions like those [above] open up a range of possibilities for new managerial policies and practices. . . .

From

ADVERTISEMENT FOR SCIENCE IN MARKETING (1965)

By John Wiley & Sons, Inc.

This new text offers
their objective and
lucid appraisals of . .

SCIENCE IN
MARKETING*

Edited by GEORGE SCHWARTZ, *Assistant Professor of Marketing, College of Business Administration, University of Rochester.*

Nineteen authorities on marketing science are represented in this fascinating analysis of what is known and what still needs to be learned about marketing. It will give your students an understanding of what is meant by the *realistic assessment of information* — and will show them how to determine whether or not such information constitutes *knowledge*.

SCIENCE IN MARKETING begins with a general consideration of the nature, goals, and usefulness of marketing science. Next, students are given a close look at specific aspects of marketing. The discussion of such topics as pricing, personal selling, and product development is organized around two questions: 1) What empirically validated descriptive, predictive, and control knowledge is currently available? and 2) What research studies should be undertaken to secure new knowledge?

An entire chapter is devoted to the evaluation of the utility and limitations of operations research in marketing, and another to the strengths and weaknesses of stochastic brand switching models.

SCIENCE IN MARKETING also includes an examination of the relationship of ethics to marketing science. The text concludes with an overview assessment of the state of marketing knowledge and suggestions for future research.

This is a volume in the Wiley Marketing Series, *Advisory Editor*: WILLIAM LAZER, Michigan State University.

The Contents . . .

Nature and Goals of Marketing Science.
Marketing Science: Significance to the Professor of Marketing.
Marketing Science: Usefulness to the Consumer.
Development of Marketing Thought: A Brief History.
The Marketing Concept.
Consumer Behavior: Some Psychological Aspects.
Consumer Behavior: Disbursements and Welfare.
Product Development.
Research in Personal Selling.
Pricing. Trading Areas.
Marketing Channels: Analytical Systems and Approaches.
The Concept of the Marketing Mix.
Comparative Marketing and Economic Development.
Operations Research and Marketing Science.
Stochastic Models of Brand Switching.
Ethics and Science in Marketing.
Marketing Science: Past, Present, and Future Development. Index.

The Contributors . . .

JULES BACKMAN, New York University.
ROBERT BARTELS, The Ohio State University.
WARREN J. BILKEY, University of Notre Dame.
NEIL H. BORDEN, Harvard University.
JAC L. GOLDSTUCKER, De Paul University.
JOHN U. FARLEY, Carnegie Institute of Technology.
DAVID HAMILTON, University of New Mexico.
JAMES G. HAUK, Syracuse University.
EUGENE J. KELLEY, The Pennsylvania State University.
ROBERT LEROY KING, University of South Carolina.
ALFRED A. KUEHN, Carnegie Institute of Technology.
WILLIAM LAZER, Michigan State University.
ROBERT W. LITTLE, University of Washington.
BERT C. McCAMMON, Jr., Indiana University.
JOSEPH W. NEWMAN, Stanford University.
ROBERT W. PRATT, Jr., General Electric Company.
GEORGE SCHWARTZ, University of Rochester.
STANLEY J. SHAPIRO, formerly of the University of Pennsylvania;
   currently with Canadian Advertising Agency, Ltd., Montreal.
JOHN B. STEWART, University of Richmond.

1965.   **512 pages**   **$9.95.**

From

AMERICAN DEMOCRACY IN THEORY AND PRACTICE*

By Robert Carr, Marver Bernstein, and Donald Morrison†

The higly technological character of American civilization makes it possible through the mass-circulation newspaper and magazine and the magic of radio and television, to bring essential information concerning social problems to every citizen and thereby to encourage the formation of intelligent public opinion. At the same time, it renders the problems themselves so complex and difficult that there arises a question concerning the ability of even an educated and informed citizenry to think about these problems intelligently and rationally. For example, two of the greatest issues of our time—finding satisfactory systems for the social control of atomic energy and space weapons and satellites—are made almost impossibly difficult. . . . The machine age is placing a strain upon the democratic process in this respect. It is clear that if the democratic system is to survive, increasing attention must be paid to such a basic point as bringing essential information concerning the social problems of a technological age to the people so that the process of forming public opinion may be carried forward.

*   *   *   *   *

Mention of dissemination of information by the government raises the issue whether public officers in a democracy should try to influence public opinion or should only be influenced by it. Public officers in a democracy must show a high sensitivity to public opinion. But it is also clear that they must often provide strong leadership as public opinion takes shape on a difficult issue. For example, where the President possesses expert information concerning such matters as the international situation or economic trends within the country, which information in his judgment seems to necessitate the following of particular policies, he must do his best to shape a favorable public opinion in support of these policies.

From

PUBLIC OPINION POLLS AND DEMOCRATIC LEADERSHIP**

By Dorwin Cartwright††

The great potentialities of sample surveys in serving both the legislative and administrative branches of the Government are now well established. Through an

---

* Robert Carr, Marver Bernstein, Donald Morrison, *American Democracy in Theory and Practice,* copyright © 1960 (Third Edition), Holt, Rinehart & Winston, Inc. Reprinted by permission. (Excerpts from pp. 214–19.)

† At the time this book was written Mr. Carr was President of Oberlin College; Mr. Bernstein was a Professor of Politics at Princeton University; and Mr. Morrison was former Provost and Professor of Government at Dartmouth College.

** Reprinted by permission of the *Journal of Social Issues,* Vol. II, No. 2 (1946), pp. 23–32.

†† The author is Research Coordinator, Research Center for Group Dynamics, University of Michigan.

extremely rapid growth of the science of sampling it has become possible to obtain relatively quickly and with moderate expense an accurate miniature of the total population. . . .

The Founding Fathers, not knowing of the science of sampling, could, of course, make no provision for public opinion research in the democratic process of government. Their method for keeping control in the hands of the people was that of assuring free elections in which *leaders* were chosen to represent the people. . . . The democratic control, and the very essence of democracy, lay in the fact that elected leaders would have to stand before the people periodically for re-election: In the years that have followed, this control has proved to be quite limited; on many issues the will of the people has been but weakly exercised.

. . . Had the founders of our government foreseen the tremendous growth of bureaucracy which has taken place since their day and had they been able to imagine the intimate way in which the executive agencies would come to touch the lives of all our citizens, it is possible that they would have devised some more direct method of control over this branch of government. Had they known of public opinion research, they might have made provision in the Constitution for its regular use.

Pressure groups constitute a most impressive symptom of the illness of our democratic functioning. . . . Techniques of lobbying have become so highly developed that persons with a professional reputation in the field are avidly sought by groups able to pay well to have their wishes felt in Washington.

Against such a barrage the conscientious public servant has little defense. . . .

Looking at the government through the eyes of those who shape policies, there is need to keep in touch with the public for yet another reason. It is not enough to know whether or not the public is in favor of some broadly defined program; let us say, inflation control. Even though its objectives receive overwhelming approval, a program may fail because its detailed operation does not correctly take into account the "human element" inherent in any public action. . . .

*   *   *   *   *

What do we want of our leaders in a democracy? What should they do for us? Certainly they should represent the will of the majority; . . . But they should do more. We want men who will lead as well as follow the public will; we want experts who know more about the subject than anyone else; we want men of vision who can invent new solutions to our problems. No doubt a poll of the American people would reveal support of each of these propositions. If the public really accepts these functions of the leader, however, it then follows that leaders should by no means always abide by the results of the polls. There are certain circumstances under which they are obligated to disregard them.

PUBLIC INFORMATION AND THE EXPERT

Although the educational level of this country is high and media of information reach every segment of the population daily, popular knowledge of public affairs is meager. . . . For instance, at the height of discussion of the Little Steel Formula, April, 1945, only 52 per cent of those approached by Gallup interviewers asserted that they had heard of it, and only 30 per cent could give a reasonably accurate indication of what it was intended to do. It has been found on several occasions that less than half of the population can give correctly such items of information as the number of years for which a member of the House of Representatives is elected. Perhaps more revealing is the finding of the *Fortune* poll in August, 1944, that 46 per cent of the population thought that John L. Lewis was president of the C.I.O. while nearly one per cent mentioned Eric Johnston and another Beardsley Ruml. . . .

. . . The kind of government established by our Constitution did not envision going to the public for the solution of the thousands of problems which arise each year. It was intended that these problems would be solved by leaders and experts selected by the people. Public opinion polls which go to the people and ask them to choose among specific proposals for the solution of these detailed problems actually force many people to make pronouncements upon matters about which they know little. To expect government leaders to follow these choices as a mandate from the people is to substitute mediocrity for expertness.

* * * * *

. . . Modern government has become so extensive and so complicated that even experts must specialize on certain types of problems. The danger of applying public opinion polls to these areas lies in the fact that people can be induced to express an opinion in a poll on matters about which they know little. . . .

* * * * *

Social progress, like technological progress, depends upon the widespread adoption of new procedures which have been developed by a relatively small number of people. As much as we might wish it, the average man is neither an inventor nor an innovator. . . .

In another way the inventor differs from the rest of us. He is a restless soul who is never satisfied with the present condition of things. He is constantly looking for improvements, for better procedures. But only when our needs are seriously thwarted do we common mortals search out new practices. If the horse will get us where we want to go, we are happy—until the automobile leaves us in its dust. We are quick to adopt a new and better creation after we have seen it work, but we are slow to perceive its need and to invent it.

* * * * *

. . . In the guise of being democratic and of giving the average man a greater voice in social affairs, public opinion research can be used to impede progress through misplacing the function of invention in our society. By asking the public to invent solutions to social problems and by interpreting the absence of new solutions as a desire for the *status quo,* public opinion polls are sometimes employed to bring pressure to bear against innovation and change.

* * * * *

From this discussion it would be incorrect to conclude that public opinion research can make no contribution to invention and progress in government. On the contrary, it is just this area of public life where it can be of the greatest assistance. Properly designed and executed research on public needs can give social inventors goals to aim at. . . . Sample surveys can be very useful in determining whether a program that is sound from an economics point-of-view will be at all satisfactory when the "human element" is considered.

From

MANAGERIAL PSYCHOLOGY*

By Harold J. Leavitt†

The Perceptual World

Most of us recognize that the world-as-we-see-it is not necessarily the same as the world-as-it-"really"-is. Our answer depends on what we heard, not on what was really said. The housewife buys what she likes best, not what is best. Whether we feel hot or cold depends on us, not on the thermometer. The same job may look like a good job to one of us and a sloppy job to another.

To specify the problem, consider the line drawing in Figure 1. This is a picture

FIGURE 1
Wife or Mother-in-Law?

of a woman. Here are some questions about it: (1) How old is the woman at the time of the picture? (2) Does she have any outstanding physical characteristics? (3) Is she "reasonably attractive" or "downright ugly"?

---

* From Harold J. Leavitt, *Managerial Psychology* © 1964 by The University of Chicago Press. All rights reserved. Excerpts from pp. 27–33. Reprinted by permission.

† The author is Professor of Psychology at Stanford University.

Show the picture to ten other people. Do they all see the same thing? If some think she looks between twenty and thirty, does anyone think she's over fifty? If some think she's over fifty, does anyone think she's between twenty and thirty? How does one account for the conflicts? Are the differences simply differences in taste? Or in standards of beauty? Or is each person distorting the "real" world in a different way?

This old psychology-textbook picture is intentionally ambiguous. It can be seen either as an ugly old hag with a long and crooked nose and toothless mouth or as a reasonably attractive young girl with head turned away so that one can barely see one eyelash and part of a nose. More importantly, the picture will be based on the "facts" as they are seen by the viewer, which may be different from the "facts" seen by another viewer.

Incidentally, if the reader still sees only one of the two figures, he is getting a good feeling of what a "need" is. The tension or discomfort that one feels when he thinks he is missing something others can see or when he feels he hasn't quite closed a gap in his knowledge—that is a need. And it will probably be difficult to concentrate on reading further until he satisfies that unsatisfied need by finding the second face in the picture.

The Influence of Our Needs on Our Perceptions

The hag picture is another demonstration of a commonplace observation, i.e., that people see things differently, that the world is what we make it, that everyone wears his own rose-colored glasses. But consider some additional questions: Whence the rose-colored glasses? Are the glasses always rose-colored? That is, does one always see what he wants to see, or does he see what he is afraid he will see, or both?

These questions are important because the primary issue of "human relations" is to consider ways in which individuals can affect the behavior of other individuals. If it is true that people behave on the basis of the perceived world, then changing behavior in a predetermined direction can be made easier by understanding the individual's present perception of the world. For if there is any common human-relations mistake made by industrial superiors in their relations with subordinates, it is the mistake of assuming that the "real" world is all that counts, that everyone works for the same goals, that the facts speak for themselves.

But if people do act on their perceptions, different people perceive things differently. How, then, is the manager, for example, to know what to expect? What determines how particular people will perceive particular things?

The answer has already been given in the preceding chapters. People's perceptions are determined by their needs. Like the mirrors at amusement parks, we distort the world in relation to our own tensions. Children from poorer homes, when asked to draw a quarter, draw a bigger than actual one. Industrial employees, when asked to describe the people they work with, talk more about their bosses (the people more important to their needs) than about their peers or subordinates, and so on.

But the problem is more complicated than that. People may perceive what is important to their needs, but does this mean people see what they want to see, or what they are afraid to see? Both wishes and fears are important to one's needs. The answer seems to be that we perceive both, but according to certain rules.

We magnify a compliment from higher up in the organization but we also magnify a word of disapproval. We dream of blondes, but we also have nightmares. And sometimes we just don't pay attention at all to things that are quite relevant. We forget dentist's appointments; we oversleep when we have examinations coming up; we manage to forget to clean the basement or to call on this particular customer.

Selective Perception

What, then are the rules of selective perception? The best answer we can give is this one: If one re-examines his memories of the past, he may find that his recall of positive, satisfying things is better than his recall of negative, unpleasant things. He may find it easier to wake early to go fishing than to get to a dentist's appointment. He may look forward, in fact, to doing pleasant, satisfying jobs but may evade mildly disturbing and unpleasant jobs. One senior executive recently commented to the author that the biggest problem he encounters with young management people is their tendency to avoid the little unpleasant decisions—like disciplining people or digging through boring and repetitive records or writing unpleasant letters. This executive felt that his younger men would be far more effective if they could learn to deal as promptly with these uncomfortable little decisions as they did with the big ones.

But we can see some sense in this selective remembering if we look for it. There are some advantages to a person in being blind to unpleasantness, even if such blindness cuts down his working effectiveness. Ignoring the unpleasant may represent more than "laziness." It may be a sensible defensive device, psychologically speaking. Thus, most people are able to ignore soft background conversation while working. In effect they are psychologically deaf to a potentially distracting part of the real world. And this defense helps them to concentrate on their work. Similarly, most people manage to ignore the threat of the hydrogen bomb and to go on eating and sleeping as though this dangerous part of the real world were not here. It can even be shown experimentally that words with unpleasant connotations tend to be recognized more slowly when exposed for very brief intervals than words with pleasant connotations.

The strange part of this defensive process, however, is that in order *not* to hear the distracting music or *not* to see the unpleasant words one must first hear and see them. One has to see the word, recognize that it is unpleasant, and reject it almost simultaneously, so that one can say, "No. I didn't see what that word was." Hence the label "defense" attached to this phenomenon—defense against the entry of preselected things mildly disturbing to one's equilibrium. So two of our rules of selective perception become: (1) see what promises to help satisfy needs, and (2) ignore mildly disturbing things.

Suppose, though, that while one is successfully ignoring background talk someone back there starts to shout; or, while one is successfully ignoring the H-bomb, an H-bomb falls on London. At those points, when the unpleasantness becomes intense and dangerous, people stop defending and begin attacking. They stop ignoring the irritation and start directing all their attention to it. This reversal seems to happen suddenly, at some specific threshold. The distant irritation increases to a point at which it becomes so real, so imminent, and so threatening that we reverse our course, discard the blindfold, and preoccupy ourselves completely with the thing previously ignored.

This is the third rule: Pay attention to things that are really dangerous. The whole picture now begins to look like this: *People perceive what they think will help satisfy needs; ignore what is disturbing; and again perceive disturbances that persist and increase.*

This is yet a fourth step in this process. What can happen when perceived threats become even more intense and imminent? When the soldier in combat watches his buddies die around him? That one we shall consider later, in the chapter on conflict.

This process may not seem entirely logical to an outside observer, but it is quite reasonable psychologically. For this kind of self-imposed psychological blindness helps the person to maintain his equilibrium while moving toward his objectives. An organism lacking this ability to fend off minor threats might well find itself torn apart in its attempt to deal simultaneously with all of them. Or, at least, an individual unable to ignore unpleasant realities might spend so much of his energy dealing with them that he would make little progress toward his major goals. For once a person has learned to perceive a multitude of threats and dangers in his world he needs a system of defense against them. One should add, however, that some individuals may see relatively few things as dangerous and therefore have little need for defense, while for others the world holds dangers at every turn.

In the preceding chapter we suggested that a person who has encountered a relatively helpful world is likely to perceive more of his environment as potentially helpful. If, however, the world has been mostly frustrating, then more of it, and especially new things in it, will be seen as potentially dangerous. Being dangerous, they must be fended off. But, paradoxically, to be fended off they must first be seen. So to protect himself from more insecurity, the insecure person must first see the things that will provoke insecurity and then manage to deny to himself that he has seen them.

17. HARROGATE ASPHALT PRODUCTS LTD. (AR)

Case Introduction

SYNOPSIS

British Commercial Investments, Ltd. (BCI), is an industrial holding company with headquarters in London. With 16 subsidiary companies which engage in a wide variety of industrial activities, the parent company is in the process of changing its philosophy from that of an investment banker, buying stocks in companies, to that of a conglomerate which takes active interest in managing the companies it buys.

Based on recommendations of a BCI staff analyst (who later becomes president of BCI), BCI acquires Harrogate Asphalt Products Company—a company located some distance from London, and which has a record of successful performance.

Soon after the acquisition, it became apparent that Mr. Lampton, BCI executive representative on Harrogate's board, disagreed markedly with Mr. Denham, the president of Harrogate. Denham, who had been relatively autonomous in operating the company, became increasingly subject to control by headquarters. The case describes the actions of both men as they attempt to operate the subsidiary company.

WHY THIS CASE IS INCLUDED

This case offers an opportunity to view some of the management problems centering around the acquisition of a subsidiary. The reader can see how differences in policy, management practices, and personality variables all provide special strains on both the holding company executives as well as subsidiary management personnel. Questions of policy evaluation, conflict on both the individual and the total company level, and organization structure are raised. In this last area, the structural questions center on decisions concerning whether or not to merge two subsidiary organizations, the type of interaction between the headquar-

616

ters company and the subsidiary, and the role of the boards of directors for subsidiary organizations. All of these questions should be of special interest given the current merger movement and trends toward industrial centralization.

DIAGNOSTIC AND PREDICTIVE QUESTIONS

The readings included with this case are marked (*). The author index at the end of this book locates the other readings.

1. Seymour Tilles defines a strategy as a set of goals and major policies. As such, a strategy determines how a corporation relates to its environment. What are the strategies of BCI and Harrogate Asphalt Products, Ltd., as expressed by Mr. Lampton and Mr. Denham? Are they internally consistent? Using the framework provided by Tilles, evaluate the strategy of the corporation from the perspective of both BCI and Harrogate.

Read: *Tilles, "How to Evaluate Corporate Strategy."

2. The strategy of an organization also determines what kind of synergy can be exploited. In order to utilize the effects of synergy, management selects activities that are mutually reinforcing so that the output of the total system is greater than the sum of the outputs of the activities taken singly. What are the prospects for synergy resulting from the planned merger between Harrogate and the Trowbridge Company? Are there other potential sources of synergy suggested in the case?

Read: *Ansoff, *Corporate Strategy: An Analytical Approach to Business Policy For Growth and Expansion*, pp. 76–86.

3. Some theories of business behavior suggest that there is a considerable difference in the organization, structure, and behavior of owner- and manager-controlled firms. What changes in ownership and control occurred in this case? What changes in strategy relating to staffing, diversification, and management is BCI trying to bring about in Harrogate?

Read: *Monsen and Downs, "A Theory of Large Managerial Firms."
*Cohen and Cyert, *Theory of the Firm: Resource Allocation in a Market Economy*, pp. 354–56, 361–63, 376–77, 379–80.

4. Initially the role of the managing director of Harrogate was defined by Stanley, Denham, and the organizational "culture" of an independent Harrogate. After the merger, a new organizational "culture" was established under corporation law such that the role definition of the managing director was strongly influenced by BCI top management.

Look closely at the behavior of all parties in the case. Then try to write a few sentences which describe: (a) the new role of Lampton in the BCI-Harrogate organization, (b) the new role of Sample in this organization, and (c) the new role of Denham in the BCI-Harrogate organization.

Read: *Katz and Kahn, *The Social Psychology of Organizations*, pp. 174–80, 182, 186–87. Levinson, "Role, Personality, and Social Structure in the Organizational Setting."

5. Why did Lampton feel that he must shift from a passive role of investment banker to the more active role of a professional manager? Do you think this change was beneficial to the company and to society?

Read: Friedman, "A Friedman Doctrine: The Social Responsibility of Business is to Increase its Profits." Eells and Walton, *Conceptual Foundations of Business,* pp. 185–87, 149–67, 458, 468–75. *Schumpeter, *The Theory of Economic Development,* pp. 84–94.

6. What do the role expectations established by BCI management for the BCI nominee director do to the authority structure of subsidiary corporations? Is the change of authority legitimate? On what grounds?

Read: Drucker, *The Future of Industrial Man,* pp. 32–38. Etzioni, "Authority Structure and Organizational Effectiveness." O'Donnell, "The Source of Managerial Authority"; see also readings for Question 5 above.

7. Why did Mr. Lampton refuse to discuss issues on an informal basis with Mr. Denham? What do you think was Mr. Lampton's objective for insisting that these issues be brought before a formal meeting of the board of directors?

Read: *Hampton, Summer, and Webber, *Organizational Behavior and the Practice of Management,* Chapter 10. Evan, "Organization Man and Due Process of Law." Hayek, "The Corporation in a Democratic Society: In Whose Interest Ought It and Will It Be Run."

8. What changes in motivation might be expected for Mr. Lampton, Mr. Denham, and Mr. Sample as a result of the changed authority structure and evolving status and roles of these three men as discussed in the case?

Read: Maslow, *Motivation and Personality,* pp. 80–94. Argyris, *Personality and Organization,* pp. 27–31, 33–51, 66–67, 77–90, 95, 103–4, 123–25, 130, 137–39, 150, 153–55, 157. Gellerman, *Motivation and Productivity.*

9. Mr. Lampton stated that he was against the authoritarian approach of Mr. Denham. Did he mean by this statement that he favored the participative approach to management?

Read: McGregor, *The Human Side of Enterprise,* pp. 124–31, 172–75.

10. What is Lampton's perception of a *policy decision* in a large corporation located in current British or American society? How might this explain his "doubt that Denham ever made real policy decisions?" Didn't Denham discontinue unprofitable operations, make labor saving technical improvements ahead of his competitors, and otherwise operate a profitable company?

Read: Leavitt, *Managerial Psychology,* pp. 27–33.

11. How might Lampton's concept of "policy decisions" contribute to conflict between himself and Denham? What other sources of conflict can be found in the case?

Read: Litterer, "Conflict in Organizations."

POLICY QUESTIONS

12. Assume that you are a member of the planning staff of BCI headquarters. Outline the rationale as well as a recommendation relation to (a) the approval or disapproval of the Harrogate-Trowbridge merger, (b)

if you recommend approval, how would you go about "merging" the management of these two subsidiaries.

(See Questions 1, 2, and 3 above.)

13. Analyze and evaluate the consistency of the BCI policy as it relates to (a) the role of the BCI nominee director on subsidiary boards, (b) the requirement for "in-depth" staffing at the subsidiary level, and (c) the initiation of merger decisions at the BCI headquarters level.

(See Questions 4 and 5 above.)

14. Assume that you are a management analyst reporting directly to the President of BCI. Analyze the decision-making structure of BCI and Harrogate and prepare a letter for the president indicating a summary of the results and any recommendations that you may feel necessary.

Read: Curtice, "General Motors Organization Philosophy and Structure," pp. 5–12. Shillinglaw, *Cost Accounting*, pp. 680–84, 688–89.

15. Assume that you are a consultant to Mr. Lampton in this case. What advice would you give him concerning his relationships with Mr. Denham and for other managing directors of subsidiaries in the future? Outline a number of possible approaches to the problem as you see it in this particular case and deduce the likely consequences of each before making a final suggestion to Mr. Lampton.

(See Questions 6 through 11 above.) One additional approach would be to suggest that Lampton secure the services of a consultant in organization development. See Schein, *Process Consultation: Its Role in Organization Development*, pp. 3–9.

QUESTIONS FOR ORIGINAL STUDENT WORK IN ANALYSIS AND POLICY

16. While reflecting on case facts, what additional theories from prior education give you insights as to "what is going on" in Harrogate Asphalt Products, Ltd? As to what might be predicted to happen in the future?

17. Other than the policy questions asked by the authors, what pragmatic ways can you think of to state the practical problems faced by executives in the case?

Case Text*

COMPANY BACKGROUND

This case concerns the financial and managerial relationships between two companies: British Commercial Investments, Ltd. (BCI), an industrial holding company located in London, and Harrogate Asphalt Products, Ltd., located in Frampton, a small town in Yorkshire near Harrogate.

BCI, Ltd., started life as the Pentiling Rubber Plantations, Ltd., a Malayan rubber company. The directors decided to diversify out of the politically risky area of their operations, and acquired a number of small- to medium-sized private companies, mainly in the United Kingdom. Twelve years ago, the last of Pentiling's rubber plantations was disposed of and the company was renamed British Commercial Investments, Ltd. The BCI group now comprises some 16 subsidiary companies, with operations ranging from the manufacture of oil drilling equipment to electrical components and from special steel fabrication to the construction of agricultural buildings.

Mr. Henry Lampton, the managing director of BCI, described the group's progress as follows:

> *Our subsequent growth, due partly to the acquisition of new subsidiaries and partly to internal expansion has been pretty satisfactory. Our gross tangible assets have increased in the last seven years from £9,000,000 to £31,000,000, and our pretax profits from £900,000 to £3,400,000. This large growth has caused us to institute increasingly elaborate systems for forecasting financial requirements and planning to meet them. We have instituted what we call the BCI Three-Year-Forecast, which involves much forward thinking in detail. This kind of planning is accepted as essential in modern company planning, but even if it wasn't, something very similar would be needed to ensure the continued strength of BCI.*
>
> *Furthermore, our present investment effort is directed mainly toward internal expansion by existing subsidiaries, and the acquisition of no new subsidiaries, unless they complement technologically those we already have. These two efforts—growth from within and acquisition of related companies, are what will produce the kind of profit we are interested in.*
>
> *We have been trying recently to provide additional help to our*

---

subsidiary companies. In today's world, we do not think that they can expand to their full potential, without some help from central advisory services provided by BCI central staffs. Until very recently, however, we were rather diffident about providing these services to give specialized advice in particular fields; it would be fatal to try to force them on unwilling subsidiary managements. But recently, the success of our operations-research group, the welcome accorded to the monthly economic bulletins of our chief economist, and the demand for the services of our BCI Marketing Advisor, all attest the need felt by subsidiary managers. Only in the last three weeks, Mr. J. F. Roberts has joined our staff as computer adviser and has begun to familiarize himself with existing EDP Installations and projects. We have been too slow in recognizing the part that EDP techniques will play in the future. We hope to provide companies individually too small to justify their own EDP units with access to facilities, and to reduce costs for all by organizing a coordinated network available on a BCI-wide basis.

It is, however, a part of our philosophy that our subsidiaries should be of a size that they can support their own local functional staff of a high caliber. We are not suffering under the delusion that we can operate a large central-services team capable of resolving the local problems of such a diverse organization. Our advisory staff is used as catalysts.

Finally, I would like to say something about the services rendered to subsidiary operating companies by our BCI nominee director. We like to think that the personalities, experience and sometimes wider contacts that our directors have, are an important source of help to managements of BCI subsidiary companies.

In an interview with Mr. E. M. Jackson, another executive of BCI, the case writer was told that

BCI maintains a [nonexecutive] director on the board of each of its subsidiaries, usually as chairman. Although nonexecutive, the BCI nominee normally visits each of his two or three companies about once a week, or twice every three weeks. The CBI nominee typically has had considerable industrial experience before joining our organization, either with a firm of accountants or management consultants, or with some other industrial corporation in an executive capacity. Many of them have university education, and have also attended advanced management programs such as the Administrative Staff College at Henley, Harvard Business School, Stanford Business School, or IMEDE in Lausanne.

After this statement by Jackson, Lampton continued.

The position of a BCI nominee director involves a rather heavy responsibility. We are not bankers, interested only in the financial aspects of the business. We are not there to take a normal dividend

and let it go at that. In some financial holding companies, the local managements have the idea that they are entirely self-sufficient, except for dividends. At the same time, the directors nominated by the parent company to the boards of those subsidiaries create the impression that they are banker types—somewhat superior to getting into real operating problems. I personally believe that, in some such holding companies, the headquarters managers are being supine—they sit there with talent that could add to operations, but they make no contribution. Specifically, I am certain that in this day of complex technology and society, the director has a moral responsibility to help his managers in subsidiary companies—to encourage them to do planning for the future, to aid them in selecting and staffing their operations, and to give advice in areas where the director has talent or knowledge.

I can give you one example. In June, one year ago, BCI acquired the L.M. Trowbridge Company from the Trowbridge family. This company specializes in construction projects using asphalt products—parking lots, tennis courts, large industrial asphalt areas. It is to the benefit of everyone—BCI, Harrogate (which produces asphalt materials) and Trowbridge managers, and employees of both companies—to merge the operations of the two companies [Harrogate and Trowbridge]. In this way, both will be more profitable, enjoy more growth, and stand a much better chance of survival in the British economy. This autumn we are going to form a company to hold both Harrogate and Trowbridge, in the interest of better all round operations. The move was, inevitably, initiated by the BCI nominee chairman; the managers of Harrogate and Trowbridge don't have the same chance of standing back and taking an overall view of their operations. Without our BCI man, the merger would never have come about.

This shows how far we have moved from our position when BCI was still mainly involved in Malayan plantations and when our United Kingdom subsidiaries were regarded merely as diversified investments to be bought and sold; managerial responsibilities rested wholly with the underlying unit. Gradually we have come to acknowledge that this is an untenable position, and have taken on full responsibility for the underlying units, while allowing them a very wide degree of local autonomy in the main areas of their businesses.

THE ACQUISITION OF HARROGATE

Seven years ago, Mr. Jack Stanley, a man of 82, approached a member of BCI management in London, with the idea that BCI might be interested in acquiring Harrogate Asphalt Products, Ltd., as part of the BCI group. Lampton, now managing director of BCI, was then 31 years old, lived in Birmingham, and was the BCI Midlands representative. He was assigned the job of doing a management evaluation of the Harrogate Company for possible acquisition.

Excerpts from Lampton's management and operating appraisal appear as Exhibit 1. It will be seen from that exhibit that his general conclusion was that Harrogate represented an excellent investment. He based this on a thorough analysis of finances, management, marketing, production, and raw material procurement. He also found that the Harrogate management had sold the less profitable coal business 14 years ago, concentrated on the more profitable asphalt operations, introduced a revolutionary technological process 11 years ago, and expanded production and sales.

THE FIRST FIVE YEARS OF OPERATION

As of the time this case is written, BCI has owned Harrogate Asphalt for seven years. During the first year, the board of directors of Harrogate consisted of Jack Stanley, Paul Denham, and Gerald Kemp, a full-time executive in BCI who was assigned as the parent company representative. More information on these men appears in Exhibit 1.

During those years, Henry Lampton was serving as BCI representative in the Midlands and as nominee director of two BCI subsidiaries located near Birmingham. Nevertheless, Lampton recalls certain things which he knew went on during the first five years:

> *In that period, the new equipment installed from Mason and Grant gave Harrogate an overwhelming competitive advantage in a business mainly served by fairly small companies, with the result that profits, sales, and return on new capital increased dramatically. Here is a company whose return on net worth was among the highest of any BCI company. Nevertheless, in my judgement, there were definite signs of trouble. Stanley died at the end of the second year. This left the BCI director and Paul Denham. About a year later, these two directors recommended as the third director Roger Sample, a young man who was hired by Denham six years ago (in the second year of our ownership). I'll have more to say about him later, but I acknowledged Roger from the first time I met him to be a capable chap, though his experience in Harrogate was limited.*
>
> *The Board meetings of those days consisted of a rather formal, cut-and-dried reporting of figures, once a month.*

The case writer, at this point, asked, "Was Paul Denham making the policy decisions?" Mr. Lampton responded:

> *If there were any policy decisions being made—though I doubt there were.*
>
> *Also, in about the second year, Harrogate suddenly found itself with a strike on its hands. Denham was at loggerheads with the union[1] and he was at a loss as to what to do. The BCI director had to go up there and deal with the union, and a settlement was reached. As I recall, Denham simply gave up and said that he could not deal with them.*

---

[1] In Lampton's appraisal report (Exhibit 1) it is shown that there was no union at the time of acquisition of Harrogate.

Also, Denham operated by turning up at eight in the morning, opening the mail, then sitting in the sales (internal) office for two hours, returning to his own office where he would incarcerate himself and merely look at figures of past performance. He rarely went to see customers off site, or saw customers when they came in.

OPERATIONS IN THE PAST TWO YEARS

About two and a half years ago, while some other changes were being made in BCI organization, Lampton, at age 35, returned from Birmingham to the BCI London head office as a director of BCI; at the same time he was also assigned to the board of Harrogate. The remainder of this case covers the past two years of his relationships with the latter company. Incidentally, Lampton, just recently, was named managing director of BCI Industries. Lampton described his experience with Harrogate:

I arrived on the scene of this highly successful company (60 percent on net worth is remarkable by any criteria) full of youthful bounce, and asking why they don't look at the situation in the building-products industries for growth, I knew that the company was doing no real forward planning, and that with the addition of a lot of hard work along this line the company could do much better. I also had a certain amount of goodwill and ambition—and the knowledge that I would have a delicate time with Paul Denham.

But I soon found that it was an unusual company. I saw a managing director making £15,000 a year, but no other men of responsibility. His four top men, including Roger Sample, were making £3,000 or under. This came as a surprise—here was an outstandingly successful company, profit wise (£600,000), with no staff in depth. In fact, in addition to Roger Sample, the only talent I could see was a good production assistant who had just given notice of his termination.

I'm going to give you a number of facts about what happened during those two years, but first let me say that I am not adverse to local autonomy—I believe it is best—but not for one local autocrat. Let me also say that my relationship with Denham was a good relationship, personally speaking, but when I tried to bring some things up for improvement, around the board table (I had instituted more frequent board meetings, and insisted that we discuss company policy problems, rather than just review figures of past performance), he did not want to discuss them. Instead, he would say, "This is not a matter for formal board—why don't you come around to my office and let's talk about it informally." Nevertheless, I thought that all three board members (including Sample) should be in on important matters, and that there should be formal board meetings where responsible action could be taken.

Let me give you an example. Our operators in the plant were getting very high piece-rates, but it was physically very hard work, 58 hours a week, and two one-and-a-half week holidays that had to be split, one and a half weeks in summer and one and half in winter:

anyone absent without a doctor's note got instant dismissal. When Denham asked me not to bring this up in the board, but to come to his office, I said, "No! This is a board matter." I could see that these conditions would mean trouble, and Roger Sample was telling me— not as a moral issue at all, but as a practical issue—we couldn't keep things this way. For my own part, I regarded it as a practical issue and a moral issue. In a way, we were blackmailing the workers with high pay and not providing opportunity for recreation. They were spending money in considerable amounts in gambling and drinking (this seemed to be a problem in the town). So I proposed that we allow them to take their two one-and-a-half-week holidays together, thus affording more of a real holiday and rest away from the job.

As I persisted in placing this matter before the board, Denham finally said, "I don't want any part of this discussion. If you want to make board policy, do it." Notice that he wasn't saying, "I am the managing director, I will think and be responsible about this." Instead, he was abdicating the managing directorship to us.

I mentioned Roger Sample. Denham had hired him five years ago from a local construction firm, and he subsequently became production manager. Although he had rather narrow experience working locally up there in Yorkshire, he is a man of talent. He knew I thought highly of him, but he was reticent with me at first, because he didn't know what kind of game I was playing. He did not have much confidence in pushing his ideas, because when Denham resisted, he did not know if I would back him. Gradually, however, we established a relationship of trust. It came about through situations like the following. On my side, I could see great need for looking beyond the narrow confines of present products and processes. The company needed market research and research on new technology. On Roger's side, he had been reading magazines of the industry and had become aware of some new processes that were being developed in Sweden. He wanted to go there to investigate, but had been forbidden by the managing director. Later, I raised this at the board table, but Denham's reaction was, "Don't let's meddle outside the company now. We have a system that is producing high profit." Why he took this attitude I don't know. I suspect that the real trouble lay in the fact that Denham had been outgrown by the company he managed, and he was afraid that anything new might put him still further out of his depth. Harrogate's very success was against him.

Some time later, the accountant for the plant quit. I think it was because he was mistreated by Denham. At this point, I tried to get Denham to go out and find a really topflight managerial accountant —one who could think and plan rather than simply be an audit clerk. As things proceeded, I could see that Denham just wasn't capable of doing this, so I persuaded him that we should go out and hire an outside firm of consultants to do the recruiting. The consultants presented four candidates for our approval. I was party to interviewing them. We rejected two immediately, and there were two left in my opinion, who were suitable. About this time, I left to attend the 13-

week Advanced Management Program of Harvard University in the United States. When I returned, I found to my amazement that he had rejected both of them and instead hired a local accountant at £1,800 a year, rather than the £4,000-man I had envisaged.

About this time I recognized that Paul Denham was a man who was going to reject any sort of idea, and any sort of talent, that he was not familiar with. I was utterly disenchanted with what he was doing. When I got back from Harvard, Paul Denham also recognized that I was a chap who was going to stick to his guns. I could see trouble ahead and was determined to do something about it, even though the company's profit record continued to be outstanding.

The last remark reminded the case writer of something said by E. M. Jackson, another BCI executive, who read the first draft of this case at the request of Mr. Lampton. Mr. Jackson said that, during the Harrogate affair,

Lampton knew that Denham must go and yet he was very conscious that the company's success was in some measure due to the tremendous pace that Denham set for the company in earlier years. Indeed, the competitive edge that Harrogate had gained came largely from the fact that the company utilized its machines so intensively—the credit for which, at any rate initially, was Denham's.

Mr. Lampton continued:

At the second Board meeting after I returned, Roger Sample brought up a subject that I had encouraged him to study (I had encouraged him to look at all facets of the business). Our office staff had very high turnover. The staff was working on Saturday mornings, but there was no need, no work, for this. When Roger proposed that Saturday morning hours be eliminated, Paul again said he wanted no part of it. He wasn't even fighting it. I suspect it was because he knew it was going to be put into effect anyway.

At any rate, I was intent on pursuing this to some sort of conclusion. The meeting became heated and intense. Denham said, "Hell, why do we waste our time on these matters—go out and find out what the order position is and lets get down to work." At this point, and in front of Roger, I blew my top. "This is real business," I said, "and if we don't pursue it we have a real crisis."

After this incident, which took place about a year ago, Lampton came back to London and wrote to Denham the letter that appears as Exhibit 3, and that requests Denham to come to London for a meeting. "I felt that it was stupid to keep this up," Lampton said, " and that we must resolve it somehow. Anyway, Denham had not once been to London in the six years we owned the company. I always invited him to the annual dinner we hold for subsidiary managing directors, but he always accepted and then sent a last minute excuse. The night before the meeting was to take place here at head office, Paul Denham telephoned to say that he was not feeling well."

EXHIBIT 1
Excerpts from a Financial and Managerial Appraisal of Harrogate Asphalt Products, Ltd., by Henry Lampton

This appraisal was written by Henry Lampton seven years ago, shortly before the acquisition of Harrogate. All quoted material in this exhibit is from the Lampton appraisal; all other comments are those of the case writer.

Directors and Personnel

P. Denham: Age 48, Managing Director and Secretary, Salary £4,000-plus. Mr. Denham has spent the last 25 years with Mr. Stanley and has grown up with the business. Originally, he was responsible for the coal distribution concern (sold eight years ago), but has been the prime mover in the expansion of Harrogate materials over the past ten years.

As will be appreciated later in the report, despite the rapid growth of this company, it is still relatively easy to administer and Denham has a tight personal control over it.

He has a very pleasant personality. He is a strict disciplinarian and is respected for it. As the company is in a rural area and there is a very low labor turnover, Denham regards the employees with Edwardian paternalism.

He has three sons at public school, the eldest (at 16) works in the company during vacations. Denham hopes one of the three will join him in the business later.

His remuneration has risen rapidly and it is intended that in future he should have a basic salary of £4,000 per annum and a commission of 2½ percent on all net profits over £100,000 per annum.

P. Jenkins: Age 35, Works Manager, Salary £1,600. He has spent all his life in the asphalt product industry and joined Harrogate 18 months ago from Dackman products of Nottingham. Denham has a high regard for his technical ability, but believes he is rather weak and immature in his handling of employees (this may well be because Denham himself is "ever present").

He appeared to be rather shy, but showed great enthusiasm when explaining production methods and new developments.

K. Warren: Age 32, Transport Manager, Salary £1,600. Most of the day-to-day problems in this company are not concerned with production, but rather with transport of finished goods. Until recently this has been done entirely with hired vehicles, and Warren has been responsible for handling this. To deal with 60 or 70 hired vehicles requires considerable tact, patience, humor, planning ability, and downright strength. Warren appears to have these qualities in full. He was in the Royal Navy prior to joining Harrogate some five years ago.

J. Nixon: Age 45, Sales and Production Planning Manager, Salary £1,700. Nixon was not met, but from the way Denham referred to him he was a weak member of the management team. He evidently does his work well enough in a pedestrian way, but has not much strength of personality or many ideas."

*   *   *   *   *

Jenkins, Warren, and Nixon are regarded by Stanley and Denham as future board members, but it would appear that Warren is the only one who is likely to grow to sufficient stature.

Outside Staff

In this section, Mr. Lampton pointed out that the workers in the plant earn very good wages compared to general conditions in British industry. The wages are exceptionally high in relation to the surrounding agricultural area. Wages of between £30 and £40 per week were due to the fact that when the new revolutionary production machinery was purchased 11 years ago, neither the manufacturer of the machinery nor the Harrogate management knew that it would be so productive. Piece-rates were established based on what the machines were estimated to produce, but these were "grossly wrong."

The company (in the event wisely) did not change these rates, but reserved the undisputed right to trim all production units to a bare minimum of labor. As the company has constantly expanded, no surplus labor has been laid off, but merely transferred to new units.
Needless to say, at these rates competition for jobs at Harrogate is very high. There was an intensely "brisk" air about the whole place. It is nonunion labour. There is no pension scheme. Hours worked are long (normally 07:30 to 18:30) and annual holidays are split, a week in the summer and another in the winter. The work is arduous, and in the winter, conditions are not good by the very nature of the business. As the rates are all fixed by team output there is no room for individual slacking. Relations with management appear to be good. Total labour force has risen rapidly in the past year to around 100.

Finance and Operations

After presenting a profit and sales summary (Exhibit 2), Mr. Lampton, among others, made the following points:

(1) The increase in gross profits has been due primarily to the introduction of new manufacturing equipment.
(2) The productivity of labor could be still further reduced if one operation were not necessary. "Through the engineering firm of Mason and Grant, secret experiments are taking place with a mechanism that must be changed only once daily, instead of once with each batch of product. This would mean that each large machine could be filled

automatically, cutting out one man's work on each of the five lines (at £1,500-plus per annum per line)." Mr. Lampton also made the point that "the finished product is a very strong and high quality job. Harrogate's products withstood the British Standard tests to a very satisfactory degree."

(3) In the area of purchasing and supply logistics, Harrogate has a favorable location for securing raw materials economically. Because production is increasing very rapidly (75 percent in the past year), one of the company's principal raw material suppliers suggested to Denham that a subsidiary transport company could be set up to pick up raw materials, rather than have them shipped by the vendor. This subsidiary company has been set up with Stanley and Denham as directors. A significant cost saving in raw materials has been achieved. The company has its own electricity substation. "Overall, there is a no problem with ragard to raw materials."

(4) In storage, and in distribution, Harrogate is regarded "as an excellent call" because large amounts of finished product can be handled and loaded in a short time. Use of modern materials handling equipment (the company owns, for example, 40 fork lift trucks and 20,000 pallets) has made this possible. Also, the company has bought five flat lorries and intends over the years to build up to its own fleet. However, management indicates that they will still use contractors for uneconomic trips and in emergency.

EXHIBIT 2
Selected Financial and Operating Results, Harrogate Asphalt Products, Ltd.

Years Ago	Sales*	Profits before Taxes*
14	£ 31,000	n.a.
13	55,000	£ 22,000
12	83,000	28,000
11	110,000	39,000
10	178,000	62,000
9	224,000	87,000
8	361,000	136,000
7	520,000	150,000
6	867,000	260,000
5	1,053,000	310,000
4	1,096,000	300,000
3	1,638,000	450,000
2	1,922,000	595,000
1	2,050,000	600,000
Present	2,500,000	750,000 (estimated)

* Figures are rounded to nearest £1,000.

Current Progress and Future Prospects

In this section, Mr. Lampton pointed out that productive capacity has increased significantly. He cites the month of June in each of the last four years, showing that production, in tons, had progressed from 5,600 in the first year, to 8,000, 10,000, and 17,700 in the successive three years. A new production line, together with machines, has been set up in the last three months (adding 950 tons to usage of raw materials). Sales the last ten months have increased to £452,400 as compared with £301,900 in the same period last year.

The reason for the company's success is probably due to its geographical position (both for raw materials and markets), the fact that it invested early in revolutionary production machinery (outside engineers reckon that Harrogate has more of this machinery than anyone else, but Denham has no proof of this), very efficient management (mainly by Denham) and because it is supplying a material in increasing demand over the past decade.

The future looks good. This is a first-class company and should prove an excellent investment for BCI.

EXHIBIT 3
Letter from Lampton to Denham

Mr. Paul Denham, Managing Director
Harrogate Asphalt Products, Ltd.
Frampton, Yorkshire

Dear Paul,

I have given myself some cooling time since our last meeting to consider its implications. I believe that it is most important that you and I meet away from Harrogate to discuss both the future of the business and the way in which you and I can operate together constructively for its good.

Could you come to see me and have lunch on Tuesday 2nd August, Thursday 4th, or Friday 5th. At the moment I have these days free from outside appointments.

Yours,
Henry Lampton

Selected Readings

From

HOW TO EVALUATE CORPORATE STRATEGY*

By Seymour Tilles†

DYNAMIC CONCEPT

A strategy is a set of goals and major policies. The definition is as simple as that. But while the notion of a strategy is extremely easy to grasp, working out an agreed-upon statement for a given company can be a fundamental contribution to the organization's future success.

In order to develop such a statement, managers must be able to identify precisely what is meant by a goal and what is meant by a major policy. Otherwise, the process of strategy determination may degenerate into what it so often becomes—the solemn recording of platitudes, useless for either the clarification of direction or the achievement of consensus.

Identifying Goals

Corporate goals are an indication of what the company as a whole is trying to *achieve* and to *become*. Both parts—the achieving and the becoming—are important for a full understanding of what a company hopes to attain. . . .

*   *   *   *   *

Achieving. In order to state what a company expects to achieve, it is important to state what it hopes to do with respect to its environment.

*   *   *   *   *

Becoming. If you ask young men what they want to accomplish by the time they are 40, the answers you get fall into two distinct categories. There are those—the great majority—who will respond in terms of what they want to *have*. This is especially true of graduate students of business administration. There are some men, however, who will answer in terms of the kind of men they hope to *be*. These are the only ones who have a clear idea of where they are going.

---

* From "How to Evaluate Corporate Strategy," *Harvard Business Review* (July-August, 1963), excerpts from pp. 112–116, 118, 120–21. Reprinted by permission. © 1963 by the President and Fellows of Harvard College; all rights reserved.

† At the time this article was published, the author was on the faculty of the Graduate School of Business Administration, Harvard University. He has been a consultant to the United Nations as well as to business.

The same is true of companies. For far too many companies, what little thinking goes on about the future is done primarily in money terms. There is nothing wrong with financial planning. Most companies should do more of it. But there is a basic fallacy in confusing a financial plan with thinking about the kind of company you want yours to become. It is like saying, "When I'm 40, I'm going to be *rich.*" It leaves too many basic questions unanswered. Rich in what way? Rich doing what?

The other major fallacy in stating what you want to become is to say it only in terms of a product. The number of companies who have got themselves into trouble by falling in love with a particular product is distressingly great.[1] Perhaps the saddest examples are those giants of American industry who defined their future in terms of continuing to be the major suppliers of steam locomotives to the nation's railroads. In fact, these companies were so wedded to this concept of their future that they formed a cartel in order to keep General Motors out of the steam locomotive business. When the diesel locomotive proved its superiority to steam, these companies all but disappeared.

The lesson of these experiences is that a key element of setting goals is the ability to see them in terms of more than a single dimension. Both money and product policy are part of a statement of objectives; but it is essential that these be viewed as the concrete expressions of a more abstract set of goals—the satisfaction of the needs of significant groups which cooperate to ensure the company's continued existence.

*   *   *   *   *

Role of Policy

A policy says something about *how* goals will be attained. It is what statisticians would call a "decision rule," and what systems engineers would call a "standing plan." It tells people what they should and should not do in order to contribute to achievement of corporate goals.

A policy should be more than just a platitude. It should be a helpful guide to making strategy explicit, and providing direction to subordinates. Consequently, the more definite it is, the more helpful it can be. "We will provide our stockholders with a fair return," is a policy no one could possibly disagree with—or be helped by. What *is* a fair return? This is the type of question that must be answered before the company's intentions become clear.

The job of management is not merely the preparation of valid policies for a standard set of activities; it is the much more challenging one of first deciding what activities are so strategically significant that explicit decision-rules in that area are mandatory. No standard set of policies can be considered major for all companies. Each company is a unique situation. It must decide for itself which aspects of corporate life are most relevant to its own aspirations and work out policy statements for them. . . .

*   *   *   *   *

Need to Be Explicit

The first thing to be said about corporate strategy is that having one is a step forward. Any strategy, once made explicit, can quickly be evaluated and improved.

---

[1] See Theodore Levitt, "Marketing Myopia," HBR July–August 1960, p. 45.

But if no attempt is ever made to commit it to paper, there is always the danger that the strategy is either incomplete or misunderstood.

Many successful companies are not aware of the strategy that underlies their success. It is quite possible for a company to achieve initial success without real awareness of its causes. However, it is much more difficult to successfully *branch out into new ventures* without a precise appreciation of their strategic significance. This is why many established companies fail miserably when they attempt a program of corporate acquisition, product diversification, or market expansion.

Another reason for making strategy explicit is the assistance it provides for delegation and for coordination. To an ever-increasing extent, management is a team activity, whereby groups of executives contribute to corporate success. Making strategy explicit makes it far easier for each executive to appreciate what the over-all goals are, and what his own contribution to them must be.

MAKING AN EVALUATION

Is your strategy right for you? There are six criteria on which you base an answer. These are:

1. Internal consistency.
2. Consistency with the environment.
3. Appropriateness in the light of available resources.
4. Satisfactory degree of risk.
5. Appropriate time horizon.
6. Workability.

*   *   *   *   *

1. *Is the Strategy Internally Consistent?* Internal consistency refers to the cumulative impact of individual policies on corporate goals. In a well-worked-out strategy, each policy fits into an integrated pattern. It should be judged not only in terms of itself, but also in terms of how it relates to other policies which the company has established and to the goals it is pursuing.

*   *   *   *   *

2. *Is the Strategy Consistent with the Environment?* Consistency with the environment has both a static and a dynamic aspect. In a static sense, it implies judging the efficacy of policies with respect to the environment as it exists *now.* In a dynamic sense, it means judging the efficacy of policies with respect to the environment *as it appears to be changing.* One purpose of a viable strategy is to ensure the long-run success of an organization. Since the environment of a company is constantly changing, ensuring success over the long run means that management must constantly be assessing the degree to which policies previously established are consistent with the environment as it exists now; and whether current policies take into account the environment as it will be in the future. In one sense, therefore, establishing a strategy is like aiming at a moving target: you have to be concerned not only with present position but also with the speed and direction of movement.

*   *   *   *   *

3. *Is the Strategy Appropriate in View of the Available Resources?* Resources are those things that a company *is* or *has* and that help it to achieve its corporate objectives. Included are money, competence, and facilities; but these by no means complete the list. In companies selling consumer goods, for example, the major resource may be the name of the product. In any case, there are two basic issues which management must decide in relating strategy and resources. These are:

What are our critical resources?
Is the proposed strategy appropriate for available resources?

Let us look now at what is meant by a "critical resource" and at how the criterion of a resource utilization can be used as a basis for evaluating strategy. . . .

The essential strategic attribute of resources is that they represent action potential. Taken together, a company's resources represent its capacity to respond to threats and opportunities that may be perceived in the environment. In other words, resources are the bundle of chips that the company has to play with in the serious game of business.

From an action-potential point of view, a resource may be critical in two senses: (1) as the factor limiting the achievement of corporate goals; and (2) as that which the company will exploit as the basis for its strategy. Thus, critical resources are both what the company has most of and what it has least of.

The three resources most frequently identified as critical are money, competence, and physical facilities. . . .

* * * * *

Achieving the Right Balance

One of the most difficult issues in strategy determination is that of achieving a balance between strategic goals and available resources. This requires a set of necessarily empirical, but critical, estimates of the total resources required to achieve particular objectives, the rate at which they will have to be committed, and the likelihood that they will be available. The most common errors are either to fail to make these estimates at all or to be excessively optimistic about them.

* * * * *

Another place where optimistic estimates of resources frequently cause problems is in small businesses. Surveys of the causes of small-business failure reveal that a most frequent cause of bankruptcy is inadequate resources to weather either the early period of establishment or unforeseen downturns in business conditions.

It is apparent from the preceding discussion that a critical strategic decision involves deciding: (1) how much of the company's resources to commit to opportunities currently perceived, and (2) how much to keep uncommitted as a reserve against the appearance of unanticipated demands. This decision is closely related to two other criteria for the evaluation of strategy: risk and timing. . . .

4. *Does the Strategy Involve an Acceptable Degree of Risk?*

* * * * *

. . . Our concern here is not with these quantitative aspects but with the identification of some qualitative factors which may serve as a rough basis for evaluating the degree of risk inherent in a strategy. These factors are:

1. The amount of resources (on which the strategy is based) whose continued existence or value is not assured.

2. The length of the time periods to which resources are committed.

3. The proportion of resources committed to a single venture.

*   *   *   *   *

5. *Does the Strategy Have an Appropriate Time Horizon?* A significant part of every strategy is the time horizon on which it is based. A viable strategy not only reveals what goals are to be accomplished; it says something about *when* the aims are to be achieved.

Goals, like resources, have time-based utility. A new product developed, a plant put on steam, a degree of market penetration, become significant strategic objectives only if accomplished by a certain time. Delay may deprive them of all strategic significance. . . .

In choosing an appropriate time horizon, we must pay careful attention to the goals being pursued, and to the particular organization involved. Goals must be established far enough in advance to allow the organization to adjust to them. Organizations, like ships, cannot be "spun on a dime." Consequently, the larger the organization, the further its strategic time horizon must extend, since its adjustment time is longer. . . .

*   *   *   *   *

If a strategy cannot be evaluated by results alone, there are some other indications that may be used to assess its contribution to corporate progress:

The degree of consensus which exists among executives concerning corporate goals and policies.

The extent to which major areas of managerial choice are identified in advance, while there is still time to explore a variety of alternatives.

The extent to which resource requirements are discovered well before the last minute, necessitating neither crash programs of cost reduction nor the elimination of planned programs. The widespread popularity of the meat-axe approach to cost reduction is a clear indication of the frequent failure of corporate strategic planning.

From

CORPORATE STRATEGY: AN ANALYTICAL APPROACH TO BUSINESS POLICY FOR GROWTH AND EXPANSION*

By H. Igor Ansoff†

SYNERGY AND CAPABILITY PROFILES

. . . In this chapter we begin to explore *synergy,* which is one of the major components of the firm's product-market strategy. It is concerned with the desired

---

* From *Growth Strategy: An Analytical Approach to Business Policy for Growth and Expansion,* by H. Igor Ansoff. Copyright © 1965 McGraw-Hill Book Inc. Used with permission of McGraw-Hill Book Company.

† The author is Dean of the School of Business at Vanderbilt University.

characteristics of fit between the firm and its new product-market entries. In business literature it is frequently described as the "2 + 2 = 5" effect to denote the fact that the firm seeks a product-market posture with a combined performance that is greater than the sum of its parts.

*   *   *   *   *

. . . We shall derive a method for qualitative estimation of joint effects. In the process it will be shown that measurement of synergy is similar in many ways to what is frequently called "evaluation of strengths and weaknesses." In synergy, *joint* effects are measured between two product-markets; in strength and weakness evaluation, the firm's competences are rated relative to some desired performance level. The former contributes to the decision to make a new entry; the latter, to the decision to exploit certain strengths or to remedy certain deficiencies within the firm. Thus the difference is largely one of viewpoint.

*   *   *   *   *

Concept of Synergy

. . . Each product-market makes a contribution to the overall profitability of the firm. Each product brings in annual sales of S dollars. Operating costs of O dollars are incurred for labor, materials, overhead, administration, and depreciation. To develop the product, to provide facilities and equipment, and to set up a distribution network, an investment of I dollars must be made in product development, tooling, buildings, machinery, inventories, etc.

The annual rate of return, ROI, on product P_1 can be written in the form

$$\text{ROI} = \frac{S_1 - O_1}{I_1}$$

Expressed in words, the formula states that the return on investment from a product can be obtained by dividing the difference between operating revenues and costs during a period by the average investment which is needed to support the product. A similar expression can be written for all products in the product line: $P_1, P_2, \ldots, P_n$.

If all the products are unrelated in any way, the total sales of the firm will be

$$S_T = S_1 + S_2 + \cdots + S_n$$

And similarly for operating costs and investment

$$O_T = O_1 + \cdots + O_n$$
$$I_T = I_1 + I_2 + \cdots + I_n$$

The return on the investment for the firm as a whole will be

$$(\text{ROI})_T = \frac{S_T - O_T}{I_T}$$

This condition obtains whenever the revenues, the operating costs, and the investments are unrelated. Therefore, their totals can be obtained through simple summations. In practice this is very nearly true in an investment firm which holds unrelated securities, or in a holding company in which there is no interaction among the operating units. A picture of the total profitability is obtained through a simple consolidation of the individual statements.

In a majority of firms, advantages of scale exist under which a large firm with the same total sales as a number of small firms can operate at a cost which is lower than the sum of the operating costs for the separate enterprises. The investment in a large firm can be similarly lower than a simple sum of the respective investments. Using symbols, this is equivalent to saying that for

$$S_s = S_T$$

we have

$$O_s \leq O_T$$
$$I_s \leq I_T$$

where subscript s denotes the respective quantities for an integrated firm and subscript t, the sum for independent enterprises.[1] As a result, the potential return on investment for an integrated firm is higher than the composite return which would be obtained if the same dollar volumes for its respective products were produced by a number of independent firms:

$$(\text{ROI})_s > (\text{ROI})_T$$

A similar argument can, of course, be made by keeping the total investment fixed. In this case

$$S_s \geq S_T$$
$$O_s \leq O_T$$
$$I_s = I_T$$

For a given level of investment, a firm with a complete product line can usually realize the advantages of higher total revenues and/or lower operating costs than competing independent firms.

The consequences of this joint effect are clearly very far-reaching. A firm which takes care to select its products and markets so as to optimize the effect has great flexibility in choosing its competitive stance. It can gain a larger share of the market by lowering prices, it can choose to make a larger investment in research and development than its competitors, or it can maximize its ROI and attract growth capital to the firm. All this can be done while remaining fully competitive with firms whose product-markets are not as carefully chosen.

Types of Synergy

This effect which can produce a combined return on the firm's resources greater than the sum of its parts is frequently referred to as "2 + 2 = 5." We shall call this effect *synergy.* . . . One way to classify the several types of synergy is in terms of the components of the ROI formula:

1. *Sales Synergy.* This can occur when products use common distribution channels, common sales administration, or common warehousing. Opportunity for tie-in sales offered by a complete line of related products increases the productivity of a sales force. Common advertising, sales promotion, past reputation can all have a multiple payoff for the same dollar spent.

2. *Operating Synergy.* This is the result of higher utilization of facilities and personnel, spreading of overhead, advantages of common learning curves, and large lot purchasing.

---

[1] The symbol $\leq$ means less than or equal to; the symbol $\geq$ means greater than or equal to.

3. *Investment Synergy.* This can result from joint use of plant, common raw materials inventories, carryover of research and development from one product to another, common tooling, common machinery.

4. *Management Synergy.* Although not immediately apparent from the formula, this type is an important contributor to the total effect. As will be shown below, management in different types of industry faces different strategic, organizational, and operating problems. If upon entering a new industry management finds the new problems to be similar to the ones it has encountered in the past, it is in a position to provide forceful and effective guidance to the newly acquired venture. Since competent top-level management is a scarce commodity, very positive enhancement of performance can result in the combined enterprise. Thus synergy will be strong.

If, on the other hand, the problems in the acquired area are new and unfamiliar, not only will positive synergy be low, but there is a distinct danger of a negative effect of top-management decisions. For example, management of a firm in the defense industry would be at an actual disadvantage if it attempts, without prior experience, to assume responsibility for pricing and advertising decisions in a higher competitive consumer area, such as the cigarette or the automobile industry.

This example points to the fact that management synergy, as well as the other types, can be negative as well as positive. An attempt at joint use of a facility which is not suited for manufacturing of a new product (e.g., use of airframe factories for consumer aluminum products), or of an organization which is not set up to perform a new function (e.g., use of a consumer sales organization to sell to industrial customers) can result in total profitability which is *lower* than the combined profitability of two independent operations.

Table 1 demonstrates the possibility of negative synergy through a comparison of competences in the principal functional areas found in typical firms in different industry groups. For purposes of comparison we are assuming that a firm in one of the groups shown in the first column diversifies into an industry group shown in the first line.

It is seen that the best carryover of functional competence will occur in general management, where many practices and skills in accounting, finance, industrial relations, and public relations are common among industries. However, even here the differences in the competitive environment and in basic resource allocation problems have led us to give unequal ratings to different pairs of industrial areas. In manufacturing and marketing where organizational forms, cost controls, and individual skills become more specified, greater differences in synergy appear among the groups. The differences become so great between space defense and consumer groups as to create potentially negative synergy.

It should be noted that the above table describes *potential* (rather than actual) synergy. Whether the indicated joint effects will, in fact, materialize depends on the manner in which the new acquisition is integrated into the parent organization. . . .

Startup Synergy and Operating Synergy

As discussed above, the synergistic effect can be measured in either of two ways: by estimating the cost economics to the firm from a joint operation for a

TABLE 1
Functional Synergy between Industry Groups

	New Industry			
Diversifying Industry	Functional Capability	Defense-Space	Producers	Consumers
Defense-Space	GM R&D Mfg. Mkt.	High High High High	High Moderate Low Low	Moderate Low Negative Negative
Producers	GM R&D Mfg. Mkt.	High Moderate Low Low	High High High High	Moderate Low Low Low
Consumers	GM R&D Mfg. Mkt.	Moderate Low Negative Negative	Moderate Low Low Low	High High High High

Legend
  GM—general management
  R&D—research and development
  Mfg.—manufacturing
  Mkt.—marketing

*This table is from H. I. Ansoff and J. F. Weston, "Merger Objectives and Organization Structure," *Review of Economics and Business*, August, 1963, pp. 49–58.

given level or revenue, or by estimating the increase in net revenue for a given level of investment. In this section we shall take the first approach and discuss the nature of synergy through analysis of cost economies and diseconomies.

Acquisition of a new product-market area goes through two successive phases, startup and operating. In addition to identifiable physical costs, such as the costs of facilities and inventories, the costs associated with startup include the highly intangible costs of learning a new kind of business: setting up a new organization, establishing new rules and procedures, hiring new skills and competences, paying for mistakes in developing organizational relationships and for early bad decisions made in unfamiliar business environment, and costs of gaining customer acceptance. Although these are one-time costs, most of them are not capitalized, but charged to operating expense during the startup period. They are difficult to pinpoint, since many of them are not identified (no firm is likely to have a special account labeled "management blunders made in startup"), but are evident only indirectly through substandard operating efficiencies.[2] During the period in which they are incurred they put the firm at a disadvantage with respect to the established competitors in the field, since the latter no longer incur any of these costs.

Whether the firm will, in fact, have to incur these startup costs depends on how

---

[2] This is one major reason for the difficulty encountered in determining marginal cash flows for new product-market entries.

well its skills and resources are matched to the requirements of the new product-market area. If the required new capabilities are very different from those of the firm, then, as discussed earlier, cost diseconomies may result in any of the major functional areas. Thus startup in new business can have potentially negative as well as positive synergy; a firm with positive synergy will have a competitive advantage over a firm which lacks it.

*   *   *   *   *

. . . During the startup phase, synergy can occur in two forms: in the form of dollar savings to the firm thanks to the existence of competences appropriate to the new line of business, and in the form of time savings in becoming fully competitive.

The second category of costs incurred in a new entry is the costs of a going concern: the operating costs and the investment required to support the operation. Here two basic effects operate to produce synergy. One is the advantage of scale—many operations will produce at a lower unit cost when the total volume is increased. For example, purchasing in large quantities offers the advantage of discounts; production in large quantities makes possible more efficient methods and procedures and hence lower direct costs. Many other well-known examples can be given.

A more subtle effect in synergy is a distribution of the burden of overhead expenses over a number of products. This arises from the fact that most overhead functions require a certain minimum level of effort for a wide range of business volume. If volume can be added through a type of diversification which makes use of the existing overhead services, economies will be effected in both the new and the old business. For example, a sales management and administration function must be staffed regardless of whether the firm has one product or a full line; the same research must be conducted regardless of whether it supports one or many products (so long as the products are all based on the same technology).

If top-management talent in a firm is not fully utilized in running the present business, and if its training and experience are relevant, it can provide the most critical ingredient to the new operation. Unfortunately, this potentially strongest component of synergy is also most difficult to measure. Many diversification histories can be cited in which an erroneous estimate was made, either through failure to realize that top management was already fully committed and that new responsibilities resulted in a thin spread of talent or through failure to realize that new business called for different types of talent and experience and that synergy, in fact, did not exist.

From

A THEORY OF LARGE MANAGERIAL FIRMS*

By R. Joseph Monsen, Jr., and Anthony Downs†

. . . In most of the largest and most significant modern firms, ownership and management are functions carried out by two entirely separate groups of people. Even management itself is really a combination of functions carried out by different groups. Thus the entity normally referred to as *the firm* has in fact become a number of different subentities. The people in each of these subgroups within the firm are still primarily motivated by self-interest. However, their changed relationship to the firm as a whole has changed the way in which their self-interest leads them to behave regarding the firm's profits. Therefore, our theory is really nothing more than the application of the self-interest axiom in traditional theory to a new type of firm: one in which ownership is separate from management; and management itself consists of a bureaucratic hierarchy containing several layers.

Our two central hypotheses can be stated as follows:

1. *Owners desire to have each firm managed so that it provides a steady income from dividends and gradual appreciation of the market price of the stock.*
2. *Managers act so as to maximize their own lifetime incomes.*

Since these two hypotheses are the foundations of our whole analysis, we will examine each in detail.

*   *   *   *   *

Summary

1. We have proposed a modified theory of the firm to explain the behavior of large, diffused-ownership firms, which we refer to as *large managerial* firms. This theory assumes that ownership and management are essentially separate, and that each such firm is so large that its management hierarchy contains at least three types of managers: top, middle, and lower. We postulate that both owners and managers act in their own self-interest by pursuing the following goals:

a) *Owners* are basically *satisficers* who desire uninterrupted dividends and a steady rise in the price of the firm's stock. Their remoteness from the firm's actual affairs makes it impossible for them to press for profit-maximizing behavior.

b) *Managers* are "economic men" who *desire to maximize their own lifetime incomes* (which includes both monetary and non-monetary elements), principally by obtaining rapid promotions as a result of pleasing their superiors in the firm.

---

* R. Joseph Monsen and Anthony Downs, "A Theory of Large Managerial Firms." Reprinted with permission from the *Journal of Political Economy,* © by The University of Chicago Press, 1965. (vol. LXXIII, no. 3, June 1965. Excerpts from pp. 224–25; 236; 231–35.)

† R. Joseph Monsen, Jr., is a Professor in the Graduate School of Business at the University of Washington. Anthony Downs is a noted author and consultant in economics, political science, and urban development.

2. The behavior of large managerial firms deviates from the profit maximization posited by the traditional theory of the firm for the following reasons:

a) The large size of such firms requires them to develop *bureaucratic management* structures which cannot be perfectly controlled by the men in charge of them. In particular, these structures tend to (i) provide biased information to top management which reflects its own desires and ideas too strongly and (ii) only partially carry out the orders issued by top management. These tendencies cause systematic deviations from whatever goals the organization is ostensibly pursuing. They exist in large owner-managed firms as well as large managerial firms, since they result from sheer size. In essence, such deviations are caused by divergences of goals *within* management; that is, between middle and lower management on the one hand and top management on the other. These goal divergences are able to influence the firm's behavior because large size both compels top managers to delegate authority to their subordinates and prevents them from checking up completely on how that authority is used. This behavior of the firm which is not optimal from the viewpoint of the top man can be caused *either* by size alone (technical inefficiency) or by a combination of size and divergent goals (technical plus motivational inefficiency).

b) The separation of ownership and management limits owners to being satisficers instead of maximizers; hence managers aim at achieving steady growth of earnings plus gradually rising stock prices instead of maximum profits. As a result, large managerial firms are more cautious; spend less on "crash" research programs; experience less variability of profits; have larger expense accounts; evidence more conciliation in dealings with government, unions, and the public; and probably grow more slowly than they would if they sought to maximize profits. In essence, these outcomes result from the divergence of goals *between* owners and top management set forth in paragraph 1 above. The size and structure of the firm both compel owners to delegate authority to top management and prevent them from checking up fully on its performance or imposing their own goals upon top management.

IMPLICATIONS OF THE THEORY REGARDING BEHAVIOR OF MANAGEMENT

Now that we have set forth our basic theory and examined the bureaucratic context of managerial decision-making, we will explore the theory's implications regarding the behavior of managers at various levels within the firm.

A. Top-Management Behavior

Top Management's Promotional Strategy. The best way for top management to maximize its own lifetime income is to "keep the stockholders happy." This normally involves three basic policies:

a) Carefully screening all information which is forwarded to stockholders or the public at large so that it reflects an outstanding management performance. . . .
b) Directing the firm toward achievement of constant or slightly rising dividends

plus steadily increasing stock prices. However, top management need only attain a "satisfactory" rate of stock-price growth, not a "maximum" one.

c) Maintaining a "public image" of competence by avoiding controversy and criticism. Public criticism of the firm or controversy about its policies tends to contradict this "image" and raise doubts in the minds of the stockholders about the wisdom of retaining the existing top management.

*   *   *   *   *

Thus the attention of management is focused on stock *prices* rather than *earnings* (profits), which are viewed as means to obtain higher stock prices rather than as ends in themselves. Therefore, if top management must choose between (a) maximizing profits over a given period by accepting fluctuating earnings, or (b) achieving total profits by maintaining steadily rising annual earnings, it will normally choose the latter. Therefore, diffused-ownership firms will experience less *variability of earnings* than firms which try to maximize profits.

. . . Other implications of our hypothesis and forecasts consistent with it concerning top management behavior are as follows:

a) Research and development expenditures are more likely to be budgeted for steady yearly growth than for "crash" expansion of promising innovations.

b) Diffused-ownership firms will exhibit a strong predilection for diversification of products, especially through merger, as a means of reducing risks taken on any one product or line of products. Since diversification through merger tends to reduce the rate of return on capital, owner-managers would be less likely to adopt such policies.

c) Financing rapid expansion through additional stock offerings is less likely to be used by top management in diffused-ownership firms than by owner-managers. In many cases, the original owners of a firm which expands rapidly use sales of common stock to "buy themselves out" of the corporation, thus capitalizing on their original ownership interest. Managers whose only stock comes from stock options are more likely to adopt internal financing, bank borrowing, or bond issues for such financing so as not to dilute their own interests. . . .

d) Top management will be much more sensitive to public, union, and government criticism than owner-managers would be. Hence top managers will be more conciliatory in their public dealings than might be required for profit maximization.

e) Top managers will use their roles in the firm to enhance their own personal prestige and stature. As a result, they will contribute to local causes and participate in community affairs more than they should from a purely profit-maximizing point of view.

f) In order to stabilize future profits, avoid controversy, and prevent adverse publicity, top management may make concessions to labor unions more readily than owner-managers would. . . .

g) Expense accounts are likely to be more extravagant in managerial firms than they would be if managers really maximized returns to owners. . . .

h) Managerial firms are likely to respond more slowly to declines in profits than they would if they really pursued profit maximization. Since managers wish to preserve their personal prerogatives (such as large expense accounts) and do not suffer directly from lower profits, they will be willing to "ride out" a sudden decline in profits without cutting back expenditures in the hope that it will be temporary. In contrast, true profit maximizers would exhibit no such inertia but would immediately alter their existing behavior patterns. However, if lower profits continue, even managerial firms will adjust their behavior so as to avoid having lower yearly earnings cause any decline in stock prices (if possible).

B. Middle-Management Behavior

1. *The Organizational Setting.* Middle managers are those operating executives under top management who are responsible for carrying out various specialized tasks within the firm. Middle managers are normally paid for their performance primarily by salaries and bonuses and secondarily by expense accounts and other untaxed perquisites.

2. *Middle Management's Promotional Strategy.* The best way for middle managers to maximize their lifetime incomes is to increase the size of those incomes by being promoted to higher-paying positions within the firm or in other firms. Since their promotions are determined by the recommendations of their superiors, their efforts to obtain promotion consist essentially of doing whatever will most please and impress their superiors, regardless of the effects of their actions upon the profits of the firm.

*   *   *   *   *

C. Lower-Management Behavior

1. *The Organizational Setting.* Lower managers are those supervisory personnel at the foreman or comparable level who have direct authority over production or lowest-level clerical personnel. They are normally paid for their performance by salaries and bonuses. Their salaries are partly based on seniority and longevity in the firm, and their bonuses are based on achieving production or quality goals. Normally, lower managers have little expectation of being promoted in middle or top management because the educational standards for those higher echelons are beyond their capabilities.

2. *Lower Management's Promotional Strategy.* The best way for lower managers to maximize their lifetime incomes is to seek promotions up to the highest attainable lower-management level and then to hold on to what they have achieved. Often their performances can be accurately measured objectively by means of production quotas, quality checks, costs accounting, etc. Thus the efforts of lower management are more intensively directed at meeting objective performance criteria than is the case with middle and top management.

3. *Implications of Lower-Management Behavior.* Lower managers are risk-avoiders of a high order. Their aim is primarily to retain their present positions by meeting quotas and avoiding gross errors. In this echelon are the classic bureaucrats who never violate the rules and fear to "stick their necks out." As with middle management, the result is undoubtedly a lower level of creativity, innovation, and risk-taking than would occur in a firm perfectly organized to maximize profits.

From

THEORY OF THE FIRM: RESOURCE ALLOCATION IN A MARKET ECONOMY*

By Kalman J. Cohen and Richard M. Cyert†

New Considerations in the Theory of the Firm

I. A MANAGERIAL DISCRETION MODEL

A. Rationale for the Managers' Utility Function

Williamson has developed a model of business behavior which focuses on the self-interest-seeking behavior of corporate managers.[1] This emphasis is reasonable once we acknowledge that the modern corporate enterprise is a complex organization far different from the traditional economic notion of a single entrepreneur running his own small firm.

One of the striking attributes of the typical large firm in the American economy is the separation of the ownership and the management functions which has become increasingly prevalent.[2] The owners of the firm, i.e., the stockholders, generally have little interest in, and even less direct knowledge of the day-to-day operations of the firm. It is the owners, however, who have contributed the capital with which the firm operates and who receive the dividends which are paid by the firm. The actual power of the stockholders to influence the firm's plans and operations resides in the board of directors, who are elected by stockholder vote. In practice, however, because of the widespread custom of voting by means of proxies, which are generally solicited by management, the board tends to be a self-perpetuating group, over which the stockholders individually—and even sometimes collectively—exert little power.

The top management of the firm is appointed by, and responsible to the board of directors. In many firms, however, top management is represented by membership on the board of directors and may play a dominant role on the board. Even where the board is predominantly made up of outside directors, top management usually possesses a great deal of freedom of action if the results of the firm's operations are satisfactory.

---

* Kalman J. Cohen and Richard M. Cyert, *Theory of the Firm: Resource Allocation in a Market Economy* © 1965. Pp. 354–56; 361–63; 376–77; 379–80. Reprinted by permission.

† The authors are on the faculty of the Graduate School of Industrial Administration, Carnegie-Mellon University.

[1] O. E. Williamson, "A Model of Rational Managerial Behavior," in Richard M. Cyert and James G. March, *A Behavioral Theory of the Firm* (Englewood Cliffs, N.J. Prentice-Hall, Inc., 1963), chap. 9. A more extensive development of this model is contained in Oliver E. Williamson, *The Economics of Discretionary Behavior: Managerial Objectives in a Theory of the Firm* (Englewood Cliffs, N.J.: Prentice-Hall, Inc., 1964).

[2] See A. G. Papandreou, "Some Basic Problems in the Theory of the Firm," in *A Survey of Contemporary Economics*, ed. B. G. Haley (Homewood, Ill.: Richard D. Irwin, 1952), Vol. 2, pp. 197–200; R. A. Gordon, *Business Leadership in the Large Corporation* (Berkeley: University of California Press, 1961), chaps. 2, 8; A. A. Berle, Jr., and G. C. Means, *The Modern Corporation and Private Property* (New York: Macmillan, 1932.)

This separation of ownership and management functions permits the managers of a firm to pursue their own self-interest, subject only to their being able to maintain effective control over the firm. In particular, if profits at any time are at an acceptable level, if the firm shows a reasonable rate of growth over time, and if sufficient dividends are paid to keep the stockholders happy, then the managers are fairly certain of retaining their power.

What might the management group's self-interest depend upon? As is the case in the traditional theory of household behavior, we can postulate a utility function which incorporates those goals in which management is interested. We can regard the managers' utility as dependent primarily upon

1. The salaries (and other forms of monetary compensation, such as bonuses, stock options, etc.) which the managers receive from the firm.

2. The number and quality of staff personnel who report to the managers.

3. The extent to which the managers are able to direct the investment of the firm's resources.

4. The type and amount of perquisites (such as expense accounts, lavishly furnished offices, chauffeur-driven limousines, etc.) which the managers receive from the firm and which are beyond the amount strictly necessary for the firm's operations.

There can be little disagreement that salaries are a major factor affecting the well being of managers, since monetary compensation from their jobs provides them the means for financing their private life expenditures. Money alone, however, is not the entire reward which a manager obtains from his job.

The staff personnel commanded by managers are important both as a mark of status and as a measure of power.

Discretionary spending for investments is primarily important because it represents in tangible form the command over resources which a manager possesses. By directing the flow of new investment, the manager is able to exert an influence on the future development of the firm. The larger the amount of discretionary investment spending the manager controls, the more easily can he further his own personal interests (and pet projects).

The perquisites of management represent a form of economic rent that the managers obtain from the firm. If management's perquisites go beyond the amount strictly necessary for efficient and effective operations of the firm, the extra perquisites are a return to management's privileged (and sheltered) position.

Williamson argues that there is a close relationship between the size of staff reporting to a manager and the level of monetary compensation that the manager receives. Therefore Williamson simplifies his formal model without distorting its realism by using a single variable, dollar expenditures on staff, in place of separate salary and staff variables.

Williamson treats the nonessential management perquisites, which are beyond the level required for effective operations of the firm, as "management slack"; management slack becomes part of the firm's cost function. This distinction focuses attention on that portion of managerial perquisites which functions as economic rent.

The concept of discretionary spending for investments is not intended to include those investments which are strictly necessary on the basis of economic considerations. The expenditures on those investments which are essential for a firm's survival (such as periodic replacement of equipment) are regarded as part of the minimum required profits which a firm must generate for the managers to retain effective control of the firm.

$$*\quad*\quad*\quad*\quad*$$

. . . We can state that a utility-maximizing firm has higher staff expenditures and more management slack than a profit-maximizing firm. No general statement can be made about the relative output levels for the two firms.

If we examine the comparative static properties of Williamson's model, we can find additional ways in which its implications differ from the profit maximizing model. In particular, let us consider how changes in demand (represented by shifts in ϵ), change in the profits tax rate, t, and changes in a lump sum tax (which we shall denote by $\bar{T}$) affect the optimal values of X, S, and ρ. Since the mathematical manipulations involved in deriving these results are both lengthy and fairly complicated, we shall merely present the results which Williamson has obtained. Table 1 shows the direction in which each of the decision variables changes as a result of an increase in any one parameter. Thus, for example, Table 1 indicates that $\delta X/\delta\epsilon > 0$, $\delta S/\delta\bar{T} < 0$, etc.

The import of these comparative static results for Williamson's model is best seen by contrasting them with the corresponding results for the profit-maximizing model. The latter are presented in Table 2.

A first major difference between these two models is that the profit-maximizing firm always reports the entire amount of actual profits. In Williamson's model the fraction of actual profits reported is generally less than unity, and this fraction itself changes in response to parameter changes.

The responses of firms to tax changes under the two models are also strikingly different. The output behavior of a profit-maximizing firm is not affected by changes in either the corporate profits tax rate or in a lump sum tax. This is to be expected, since the firm which is maximizing profits must necessarily also be maximizing any fraction of these profits (such as profits remaining after taxes). In Wil-

TABLE 1

Responses to Displacements from Equilibrium for Williamson's Model

Variable	Parameter		
	ϵ	t	$\bar{T}$
X	+	+	−
S	+	+	−
ρ	−	−	+

Source: O. E. Williamson. "A Model of Rational Managerial Behavior," in Richard M. Cyert and James G. March, *A Behavioral Theory of the Firm* (Englewood Cliffs, N. J.: Prentice-Hall, Inc., 1963), table 9.1, p. 248.

TABLE 2

Responses to Displacements from Equilibrium for the Profit-Maximizing Model

Variable	Parameter		
	ϵ	t	$\bar{T}$
X	+	0	0
S	+	0	0

Source: O. E. Williamson. "A Model of Rational Managerial Behavior," in Richard M. Cyert and James G. March, *A Behavioral Theory of the Firm* (Englewood Cliffs, N.J.: Prentice-Hall, Inc., 1963), table 9.2, p. 248.

liamson's model, on the other hand, all the decision variables of the firm are affected by changes in either tax rates or in lump sum taxes. Increases in the profits tax rate, t, will cause the utility-maximizing firm to increase both its output and its staff expenditures and to decrease the fraction of actual profits which are reported; increases in a lump sum tax, T, cause just the opposite types of changes in the decision variables.

The output and staff expenditures responses of these two models are the same for an increase in demand. Management slack is never supposed to exist for the profit-maximizing firm. For the utility-maximizing firm, however, there is both an absolute and a relative increase in management slack as the environment becomes more favorable (i.e., when there is an increased demand for the firm's products). Just the opposite takes place in a hostile environment: a decline in demand leads both to an absolute and a relative reduction in the amount of management slack. When it is realized that management slack includes such items as travel, office improvements, expense accounts, executive yachts and limousines, etc., causal empiricism suggests that this aspect of Williamson's model is realistic.

An increase in the corporate profits tax rate can be regarded as a higher penalty imposed on reported profits. That the utility-maximizing firm responds to an increase in this penalty by shifting away from reported profits and obtaining a larger proportion of its satisfaction from higher staff expenditures and increased management slack, seems eminently reasonable. Increases in advertising expenditures, customer services, public relations activities, etc., as well as general increases in managerial perquisites, usually accompany a rise in the profits tax rate. A profit-maximizing firm would not respond in this way to changes in the tax rate; its optimum combination of factors is unaffected by changes in the percentage of profits retained after payment of corporate taxes.

A profit-maximizing firm cannot avoid a lump sum tax except by going out of business. As long as such a tax does not force the firm to suspend its operations, it does not affect the firm's behavior. The Williamson-type of firm, however, is not maximizing profits, and thus it has some latitude to modify its behavior in order partially to compensate for any increases in a lump sum tax. In Williamson's model, a firm will generate a minimum required amount of after-tax profits. An increase in the lump sum tax thus raises the necessary amount of before-tax profits which this firm must generate. Hence the utility-maximizing firm must modify some of its decisions to generate more reported profits before taxes. Thus expenditures on staff and management slack will decrease in response to the imposition of a lump sum tax. (The decrease in output which also accompanies the imposition of a lump sum tax follows because, with lower staff expenditures, the demand curve is shifted downward.) Since a lump sum tax is effectively a fixed cost, Williamson's model predicts that changes in fixed costs will affect the short-run decisions of the firm, a different result than implied by the short-run profit-maximizing model of the firm.

The frequently observed phenomenon of a newly appointed executive achieving striking cost reductions by cutting down on managerial perquisites and by removing "excess" staff is consistent with Williamson's model. The manager who is trying to reduce cost can be interpreted as having a low preference for staff expenditures, relative to other components of his utility function. Since some of the staff expenditures in Williamson's model are devoted to management's utility maximization, rather than to profit maximization, any marked change in management taste will be accompanied by significant changes in staff.

* * * * *

III. A REVENUE-MAXIMIZATION MODEL

Baumol has proposed another variant of a maximization model in which it is assumed that firms attempt to maximize total revenues rather than profits or the value of a utility function.[3] Profits are not ignored altogether in Baumol's model, however, since a minimum profits level is imposed as a constraint.

A. Rationale for the Revenue-Maximization Hypothesis

Several reasons are presented to justify the revenue-maximization hypothesis. Some are based on a casual type of empiricism:

> Surely it is common experience that, when one asks an executive, "How's business?" he will answer that his *sales* have been increasing (or decreasing), and talk about his profit only as an after-thought, if at all. And I am told the requirements for acceptance to membership in the Young Presidents Organization (an honorific society) are that the applicant be under 40 years of age and president of a company whose annual volume is over a million dollars. Presumably it makes no difference if this firm is in imminent danger of bankruptcy. . . .
> Almost every time I have come across a case of conflict between profits and sales the businessmen with whom I worked left little doubt as to where their hearts lay. . . . a program which explicitly proposes any cut in sales volume, whatever the profit considerations, is likely to meet a cold reception.

Other evidence cited by Baumol essentially suggests that short-run revenue maximization may be consistent with the long-run profit maximization. Baumol states, however, that revenue maximization, rather than profit maximization, can be regarded as the long-run goal of the management in many oligopoly firms.[4]

The minimum acceptable level of profits which serves as a constraint on a firm's attempts to maximize its revenues is not regarded as purely arbitrary. Baumol feels that this constraint is determined by the capital market:

> The typical oligopolistic firm, while large in the market for its own product, is relatively small in the capital market. This means that, in obtaining capital by the issue of stocks, it must be prepared to meet competitive pricing conditions—the yield on its stocks will be determined by the forces of competition. . . . The firm which hopes to have more securities to sell in the future, and wishes to pay what it may consider proper regard to the interests of its current stockholders, must take this into consideration. Its minimum earnings must supply funds sufficient to pay dividends, and to reinvest in such amounts that the combination of dividend receipts and stock price rises can remunerate stockholders adequately. If this is so, each company's minimum rate of profits is set competitively in terms of the current market value of its securities.[5]

*   *   *   *   *

---

[3] William J. Baumol, *Business Behavior, Value and Growth* (New York: The Macmillan Company, 1959), chaps. 6–8.

[4] Ibid, p. 52. "I believe that sales maximization is management's objective in the long run as well as in the short."

[5] Ibid., pp. 50–51.

C. Comparisons with Other Models

It is useful to contrast the decisions of a revenue-maximizing firm with the decisions stemming from a utility-maximizing model and from a profit-maximizing model. . . . A revenue-maximizing firm produces at an output level where its marginal revenue is less than its marginal cost—in other words, the firm is giving up some profits in order to increase its revenues. . . . This is not true for the other model.

We saw . . . that the profit-maximizing firm carries staff expenditures only to the point where the marginal revenue generated by the last dollar spent on staff equals its marginal cost (which is $1). Both a Williamson type firm and a Baumol-type firm carry staff expenditures beyond the profit-maximizing point. . . . However, the basic determinants of staff expenditures differ in these two models. . . . The Baumol-type firm is essentially neutral with regard to expenditures on staff or on production, each being judged solely in terms of its relative contributions to the revenue criterion. In Williamson's model, on the other hand, the managers display a positive preference toward staff expenditures. . . .

Comparative static properties which indicate the ways in which a firm in Baumol's model modifies its output and staff decisions in response to changes in demand, the corporate profits tax rate, and a lump sum tax can be derived. These are presented in Table 3.

A comparison of Tables 1, 2, and 3 reveals that Baumol's model yields the same qualitative predictions as Williamson's model and the traditional model about the ways in which changes in demand will affect output and staff expenditures. The qualitative effects of a lump sum tax on output and staff are the same in Baumol's and in Williamson's model; but these are different effects than the traditional theory implies. The corporate tax rate is the one parameter for which distinctly different qualitative predictions arise in all three models. When the corporate tax rate is raised, Baumol's firms reduce their output and staff expenditures (i.e., reduce revenues because of the more stringent profits constraint, which is phrased in after-tax terms); Williamson's firms increase their output and staff expenditures (because on an after-tax basis, staff expenditures—to which output will optimally adjust—are now relatively cheaper, compared to investment spending); profit-maximizing firms do not change their behavior (since the same output and staff decisions which maximize profits will also maximize any proportion of profits).

TABLE 3
Responses to Displacements from Equilibrium for Baumol's Model

Variable	Parameter		
	ϵ	t	$\bar{T}$
X	+	−	−
S	+	−	−

Source: Oliver E. Williamson, *The Economics of Discretionary Behavior: Managerial Objectives in a Theory of the Firm* (Englewood Cliffs, N.J.: Prentice-Hall, Inc., 1964), table 4, p. 80.

From
THE SOCIAL PSYCHOLOGY
OF ORGANIZATION*

By Daniel Katz and Robert L. Kahn†

THE TAKING OF ORGANIZATIONAL ROLES

*   *   *   *   *

Definition of Role Behavior

Generically, role behavior refers to the recurring actions of an individual, appropriately interrelated with the repetitive activities of others so as to yield a predictable outcome. The set of interdependent behaviors comprise a social system or subsystem, a stable collective pattern in which people play their parts.

When we abstract some of the essential persisting features from the specific acts comprising role behavior we speak of roles. For example, we can speak of the role of the quarterback on a football team in general terms of play selection without specifying the particular signals he barks to his teammates or the specific plays with which they respond. This general description applies to roles both within and outside formal organizations. . . . In formal organizations many of the functionally specific behaviors comprising the system are specified in written and coded presentations. Moreover, in formal organizations the roles people play are more a function of the social setting than of their own personality characteristics. The basic criterion, then, for studying role behavior is to identify the relevant social system or subsystem and locate the recurring events which fit together in converting some input into an output. This can be done by ascertaining the role expectations of a given set of related offices, since such expectations are one of the main elements in maintaining the role system and inducing the required role behavior.

The Process of Role-Sending

All members of a person's role set depend upon his performance in some fashion; they are rewarded by it, judged in terms of it, or require it in order to perform their own tasks. Because they have a stake in his performance they develop beliefs and attitudes about what he should and should not do as part of his role. The prescriptions and proscriptions held by members of a role set are designated *role expectations,* in the aggregate they help to define his role, the behaviors which are expected of him. The role expectations held for a certain person by a member of his role set will reflect that member's conception of the person's office and of his abilities. The content of these expectations may include preferences with respect to specific acts and personal characteristics or styles; they may deal with what the person should do, what kind of person he should be, what he should think or believe, and how he should relate to others. Role expecta-

---

* From *The Social Psychology of Organizations* by D. Katz and R. L. Kahn. Copyright ©
1966 by John Wiley & Sons, Inc. Reprinted by permission. Excerpts pp. 174–80, 182, 186–87.

† The authors are Professors of Psychology at The University of Michigan.

tions are by no means restricted to the job description as it might be given by the head of the organization or prepared by some specialist in personnel, although these individuals are likely to be influential members of the role sets of many persons in the organization.

The mention of influence raises additional issues of definition and theory. Role expectations for any given office and its occupant exist in the minds of members of his role set and represent standards in terms of which they evaluate his performance. The expectations do not remain in the minds of members of the role set, however. They tend to be communicated in many ways; sometimes as direct instructions, as when a supervisor describes to a subordinate the requirements of his job; sometimes less directly, as when a colleague expresses admiration or disappointment in some behavior. The crucial point (for our theoretical view) is that the activities which define a role are maintained through the expectations of members of the role set, and that these expectations are communicated or "sent" to the focal person.[1] In referring to role expectations as sent, we are following the formulation of Rommetveit (1954). He refers to members of a role set as role senders, and to their communicated expectations as the *sent role.*

The numerous acts which make up the process of role-sending are not merely informational. They are attempts at influence, directed at the focal person and intended to bring about conformity to the expectations of the senders. Some of these influence attempts (for example, those from superiors) may be directed toward the accomplishment of formally specified responsibilities and objectives of office.

Others (perhaps from peers or subordinates) may be directed toward making life easier or more pleasant for the senders themselves, in ways which contravene official requirements.

Thus each individual in an organization acts in relation to and in response to the expectations of the members of his role set, not because those expectations constitute some mentalistic field of forces but because they are expressed in explicit behavioral ways. . . .

. . . Every attempt at influence implies consequences for compliance or non-compliance. In organizations, as we have seen, these commonly take the form of sanctions—gratifications or deprivations which a role sender might arrange for the focal person, depending on his having conformed to the sender's expectation or not. The concept of legitimacy, and its acceptance by organizational members, makes the actual use of such sanctions infrequent. Members obey because the source and substance of the command are legitimate. The availability and visibility of sanctions are important, however, whether or not they are used or even threatened. The strengthening or role-sending with the possibility of sanctions is the major basis for gaining compliance with the requirements of formal organization.

*   *   *   *   *

The Received Role

To understand the response of any member of an organization to the complex pattern of role-sending addressed specifically to him, we must regard the organization from the vantage point of his office. When we do so, we see that the members

---

[1] The term *focal person* will be used to refer to any individual whose role or office is under consideration.

of his role set and the influential pressures which they direct to him are part of his objective environment. To consider his compliance with or deviation from his sent role, however, takes us immediately beyond the objective organization and environment. Each individual responds to the organization in terms of his percep- tions of it, which may differ in various ways from the actual organization. In the immediate sense, the individual responds not to the objective organization in his objective social environment but to that representation of it which is in his psycho- logical environment.

The objective organization and the psychological organization of a person may or may not be congruent, depending on his ability and opportunity to perceive organizational reality. Thus for each person in an organization there is not only a sent role, consisting of the influential and communicative acts of the members of his role set, there is also a *received role,* consisting of his perceptions and cognitions of what was sent. How closely the received role corresponds to the sent role is an empirical question for each focal person and set of role senders, and will depend upon properties of the senders, the focal person, the substantive content of the sent expectations, the clarity of the communication, and the like.

It is the sent role by means of which the organization communicates to each of its members the do's and don'ts associated with his office. It is the received role, however, which is the immediate influence on his behavior and the immediate source of his motivation for role performance. Each sent expectation can be regarded as arousing in the focal person a motivational force of some magnitude and direction. This is not to say that these motivational role forces are identical in magnitude and direction with the sent influence attempts that evoked them. When sent-role expectations are seen by the focal person as illegitimate or coer- cive, they may arouse strong resistance forces which lead to outcomes different from or even opposite to the expected behavior. It is such processes, repeated for many persons over long periods of time, that produce the persistent component of unintended effects in organizational behavior. Pressures to increase production sometimes result in slowdowns. Moreover, every person is subject to a variety of psychological forces in addition to those stimulated by pressures from his role set in the work situation. Role-sendings are thus only a partial determinant of his behavior on the job.

Additional and important sources of influence in role-taking are the objective, impersonal properties of the situation itself. In some situations the taking of roles may be aided by the nature of the task and the previous experience of the in- dividual with respect to similar tasks. The soldier in combat seeks cover when under fire not so much because of the expectations of members of his role set as because of the demands of the situation. The man on the assembly line tightens the belt on the passing car both because he has been told that it is his job and because the structuring of his work situation is a constant reminder of what he is supposed to do. People can be conditioned to play their roles by cues other than those of the communicated expectations from other system members. Never- theless, in most organizations, role behavior is largely dependent upon role send- ing.

In addition to the motivational forces aroused by sent expectations and other cues, there are important internal sources of motivation for role performance. For example, there is the intrinsic satisfaction derived from the content of the role. The concert pianist has many motives which lead him to give performances; one of them is probably the intrinsic psychological return from exercising a hard-won and valued skill. But there is, in addition to intrinsic satisfaction in expressing valued abilities, another kind of "own force" important in the motivation of role behavior. In a sense each person is a "self-sender," that is a role sender to himself. He too has a conception of his office and a set of attitudes and beliefs about what he should and should not do while in that position. He has some awareness of what behaviors will fulfill his responsibilities, lead to the accomplishment of organizational objectives, or further his own interests. He may even have had a major part in determining the formal responsibilities of his office, especially if he occupies a line or staff position well up in the hierarchy.

Moreover, some of the persisting motives of the individual are likely to include the sector of organizational behavior. Through a long process of socialization and formal training within the organization and in the larger culture of which it and he are parts, he has acquired a set of values and expectations about his own behavior and abilities, about the nature of human organizations and the conditions for membership in them. In short, as Miller (1962), Dai (1955), and others have observed, the person has an occupational self-identity and is motivated to behave in ways which affirm and enhance the valued attributes of that identity. He comes to the job in a state of what we have previously referred to as role-readiness, a state which includes the acceptance of legitimate authority and compliance with its requests, a compliance which for many people extends to acts which they do not understand and which may violate many of their own values. . . .

Multiple Roles and Multiple Activities.   An organization is a complex arrangement of many collective cycles of behavior, some of which intersect, others of which are tangential to one another, while still others are connected only indirectly. In other words, the organization is made up of many subsystems. The common treatment of *role* and *office* tends to oversimplify this complexity by neglecting the fact that one office can be located in a number of such role subsystems and that one individual can be involved in many organizational subsystems.

Let us examine more closely the meaning and implications of these assertions. The basic unit of organizational life is the *molar unit of behavior,* the behavioral cycle. This is what we mean by *an activity:* a recurring behavior sequence which has organizational relevance, is held in the form of role expectations by some members of the role set, and which affords some sense of closure on completion. For example, taking four bolts out of a barrel and using them to fasten the left rear fender of an automobile to the body is an activity on the assembly line.

A *role consists of one or more recurrent activities* out of a total pattern of interdependent activities which in combination produce the organizational output. Role, unless otherwise qualified, will refer to a set of such activities within a single subsystem of the organization and within a single office.

An *office is a point (location) in organizational space* defined by one or more roles (and thereby one or more activities) intended for performance by a single individual. It locates the individual in relation to his fellows with respect to the job to be done and the giving and taking of orders.

The simplest organizational arrangement occurs when one activity defines role and office. Thus, the job of assembly-line operator No. 23 might consist of the one activity described in the previous example, bolting on the left rear fender. That activity defines the role, and the office is merely the point in organizational space associated with that role and activity.

The situation can become more complex in any of several ways:

Multiple activities may be defined into a single role.
Multiple roles may be defined into a single office.
Multiple offices may be held by a single person.

*   *   *   *   *

The Role Episode

Our description of role-sending and role-receiving has been based on four concepts: *role expectations,* which are evaluative standards applied to the behavior of any person who occupies a given organizational office or position; *sent role,* which consists of communications stemming from role expectations and sent by members of the role set as attempts to influence the focal person; *received role,* which is the focal person's perception of the role-sendings addressed to him, including those he "sends" to himself; and *role behavior,* which is the response of the focal person to the complex of information and influence he has received.

These four concepts can be thought of as constituting a sequence or role episode. The first two, role expectations and sent role, have to do with the motivations, cognitions, and behavior of the members of the role set; the latter two, received role and role behavior,. have to do with the cognitions, motivations, and behavior of· the focal person. A model of the role episode is presented in Figure 1.

FIGURE 1
A Model of the Role Episode

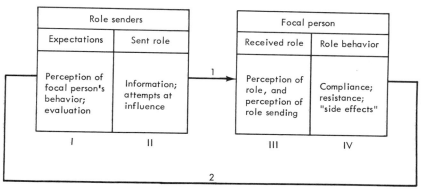

These three additional classes of variables—organizational, personality, and interpersonal—can be conveniently represented in an enlargement and extension of Figure 1. That figure presented a causal sequence: role expectations (I) lead to a role-sending (II), which leads to received role (III), which leads to behavior in response to the role as received (IV). That figure and the sequence it represents also forms the core of Figure 2.

The circles in Figure 2 represent not the momentary events of the role episode, but enduring states of the organization, the person, and the interpersonal relations between focal person and role senders. Such enduring properties are for the most

FIGURE 2
A Theoretical Model of Factors Involved in the Taking of Organizational Roles

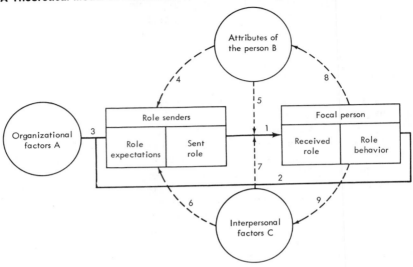

part abstractions and generalizations based upon recurrent events and behaviors. For example, characterizing a relationship as supportive means simply that the parties to the relationship have behaved in a supportive manner toward one another on a sufficient number of occasions so that we feel justified in inferring supportiveness as a quality of the relationship. Such repetitions and patterns of events provide the basis and context within which each new occurrence can best be understood.

To a considerable extent the role expectations held by the members of a role set—the prescriptions and proscriptions associated with a particular office—are determined by the broader organizational context. The technology of the organization, the structure of its subsystems, its formal policies, and its rewards and penalties dictate in large degree the content of a given office. What the occupant of that office is supposed to do, with and for whom, is given by these and other properties of the organization itself. Although human beings are doing the "supposing" and rewarding, the structural properties of organization are sufficiently stable so that they can be treated as independent of the particular persons in the role set. For such properties as size, number of echelons, and rate of growth, the justifiable abstraction of organizational properties from individual behavior is even more obvious.

From

THE THEORY OF
ECONOMIC DEVELOPMENT*

By Joseph A. Schumpeter†

[EDITOR'S NOTE: In the passages below, Schumpeter describes the function of an "executive" or "manager" in society—whether he be the owner-entrepreneur, or an "employee manager." Schumpeter's book, which is considered by many a milestone in economic theory, took as its task to study *economic development* or *change* in the economy, as opposed to traditional equilibrium analysis. By "development," he means new combinations of resources—introduction of new goods, new methods of production, opening of new markets, conquest of new supplies of materials, or carrying out of the new organization of any industry.

One of his main theses is that "it is the producer who as a rule initiates economic change, and consumers (and presumably employees) are educated by him if necessary." This is in direct contrast to the study of equilibrium, where theories hold that it is the consumer wants which are the moving force, and executives respond to these forces, acting as a mechanical computer of supply and demand.

One of the prime and fundamental causes of change, to Schumpeter, are the actions of the "relatively few" men of action—executives—whose motivations are still deeper causes. Thus the argument: If change and innovations occur, it is the executive who produces them, not the "followers," or the "customers," or the "employees."]

This is so because all knowledge and habit once acquired becomes as firmly rooted in ourselves as a railway embankment in the earth. It does not require to be continually renewed and consciously reproduced. . . . It is normally transmitted almost without friction by inheritance, teaching, upbringing, pressure of environment. Everything we think, feel, or do often enough becomes automatic and our conscious life is unburdened of it. . . . And from this it follows also for economic life that every step outside the boundary of routine has difficulties and involves a new element. It is this element that constitutes the phenomenon of leadership.
. . . First, outside these accustomed channels the individual is without those data for his decisions and those rules of conduct which are usually very accurately known to him within them. Of course he must still foresee and estimate on the basis of his experience. But many things must remain uncertain, still others are only ascertainable within wide limits, some can perhaps only be "guessed." In particular this is true of those data which the individual strives to alter and of those which he wants to create. . . . Carrying out a new plan and acting according to a customary one are things as different as making a road and walking along it.

---

* Reprinted by permission of Harvard University Press, Cambridge, Mass., 1934 (Vol. XLVI, Harvard Economic Studies), pp. 84–94.
† The author is late Professor of Economics at Harvard University.

. . . As military action must be taken in a given strategic position even if all the data potentially procurable are not available, so also in economic life action must be taken without working out all the details of what is to be done. Here the success of everything depends upon intuition, the capacity of seeing things in a way which afterwards proves to be true. . . . The more accurately, however, we learn to know the natural and social world, the more perfect our control of facts becomes; and the greater the extent, with time and progressive rationalisation, within which things can be simply calculated, and indeed quickly and reliably calculated, the more the significance of this function decreases. Therefore the importance of the entrepreneur type must diminish just as the importance of the military commander has already diminished. . . .

. . . [T]he second lies in the psyche of the businessman himself. It is not only objectively more difficult to do something new than what is familiar and tested by experience, but the individual feels reluctance to it and would do so even if the objective difficulties did not exist. . . . In the breast of one who wishes to do something new, the forces of habit rise up and bear witness against the embryonic project. A new and another kind of effort of will is therefore necessary. . . . This mental freedom presupposes a great surplus force over the everyday demand and is something peculiar and by nature rare.

The third point consists in the reaction of the social environment against one who wishes to do something new. This reaction may manifest itself first of all in the existence of legal or political impediments. But neglecting this, any deviating conduct by a member of a social group is condemned, though in greatly varying degrees according as the social group is used to such conduct or not. Even a deviation from social custom in such things as dress or manners arouses opposition, and of course all the more so in the graver cases. . . . Even mere astonishment at the deviation, even merely noticing it, exercises a pressure on the individual. . . .

There is leadership *only* for these reasons—leadership, that is, as a special kind of function and in contrast to a mere difference in rank. . . . The facts alluded to create a boundary beyond which the majority of people do not function promptly by themselves and require help from a minority. If social life had in all respects the relative immutability of, for example, the astronomical world, or if mutable this mutability were yet incapable of being influenced by human action, or finally if capable of being so influenced this type of action were yet equally open to everyone, then there would be no special function of leadership as distinguished from routine work.

. . . Our three points characterise the nature of the *function* as well as the *conduct* or behavior which constitutes the leader type. It is no part of his function to "find" or to "create" new possibilities. They are always present, abundantly accumulated by all sorts of people. Often they are also generally known and being discussed by scientific or literary writers. In other cases, there is nothing to discover about them, because they are quite obvious. To take an example from political life, it was not at all difficult to see how the social and political conditions of France at the time of Louis XVI could have been improved so as to avoid a breakdown of the *ancien régime.* Plenty of people as a matter of fact did see it. But nobody was in a position to *do* it. Now, it is this "doing the thing," without which possibilities are dead, of which the leader's function consists. . . . It is, therefore, more by will than by intellect that the leaders fulfil their function more by "authority," "personal weight," and so forth than by original ideas.

* * * * *

The entrepreneurial kind of leadership . . . consists in fulfilling a very special task which only in rare cases appeals to the imagination of the public. . . . "Personal weight" is, to be sure, not without importance. Yet the personality of the capitalistic entrepreneur need not, and generally does not, answer to the idea most of us have of what a "leader" looks like, so much so that there is some difficulty in realizing that he comes within the sociological category of leader at all. He "leads" the means of production into new channels. But this he does, not by convincing people of the desirability of carrying out his plan or by creating confidence in his leading in the manner of a political leader—the only man he has to convince or to impress is the banker who is to finance him—but by buying them or their services, and then using them as he sees fit. He also leads in the sense that he draws other producers in his branch after him. But as they are his competitors, who first reduce and then annihilate his profit, this is, as it were, leadership against one's own will. Finally, he renders a service, the full appreciation of which takes a specialist's knowledge of the case. It is not so easily understood by the public at large as a politician's successful speech or a general's victory in the field, not to insist on the fact that he seems to act—and often harshly—in his individual interest alone. . . .

We shall finally try to round off our picture of the entrepreneur in the same manner in which we always . . . try to understand human behavior, viz. by analysing the characteristic motives of his conduct. . . .

* * * * *

First of all, there is the dream and the will to found a private kingdom, usually, though not necessarily, also a dynasty. The modern world really does not know any such positions, but what may be attained by industrial or commercial success is still the nearest approach to medieval lordship possible to modern man. Its fascination is specially strong for people who have no other chance of achieving social distinction. The sensation of power and independence loses nothing by the fact that both are largely illusions. . . .

Then there is the will to conquer: the impulse to fight, to prove oneself superior to others, to succeed for the sake, not of the fruits of success, but of success itself. From this aspect, economic action becomes akin to sport—there are financial races, or rather boxing-matches. . . .

Finally, there is the joy of creating, of getting things done, or simply of exercising one's energy and ingenuity. This is akin to a ubiquitous motive, but nowhere else does it stand out as an independent factor of behavior with anything like the clearness with which it obtrudes itself in our case. Our type seeks out difficulties, changes in order to change, delights in ventures. This group of motives is the most distinctly antihedonist of the three.

Only with the first groups of motives is private property as the result of entrepreneurial activity an essential factor in making it operative. With the other two it is not. . . .

From

ORGANIZATIONAL BEHAVIOR AND THE PRACTICE OF MANAGEMENT*

By David Hampton, Charles Summer, and Ross Webber†

THE MOTIVATION OF EXECUTIVES TO POLITICAL ACTION

The motivations which cause executives to design technological systems, to convert them to systems of authority, and (in some cases) to engage in strategic actions intended to influence others can be further analyzed into (1) the value (attitude) of technological necessity, (2) the desire to be head of an organization, (3) the competitive urge and the will to conquer, (4) the urge to creative action, (5) the need for symmetry as a means of security, and (6) the pragmatic position—"it works." Each of these will be discussed separately.

The Attitude of Technological Necessity

Technological necessity was discussed in Chapter 7. Without being repetitious, let us recall that phenomenon.[1] We start with the fact that in industrially developed societies, specialization has progressed to a profound degree. Man and his family are dependent on the roundabout production process for almost everything they require in the form of material needs. The days of the nearly sufficient Vermont farm are gone forever, and one of society's great unwritten mores is what Galbraith has called "the paramount position of production." Whether in the United States or in Soviet Russia, the society has provided both "ethical" and "monetary" institutions which reward the executive when his organizational system is efficient, and which punish him when it is inefficient. Granted that there are sometimes other motivations which operate to prevent him from striving for *maximum* organizational efficiency, there are nevertheless powerful material and non-material pressures which cause him to put a high value on organizational efficiency.

This means, among other things, that the internal technological system of the firm or department—the rational division of this system into parts (specializations) and the rational relating of one of these parts to others (planning the input-output system)—must be (1) designed (an act of rule formulation) and that (2) it must be cloaked with the symbols of authority and legitimacy.

In addition to this social belief in production and prevention of waste, together with rewards and penalties which cause executives to *learn* this value, there is undoubtedly the factor of training and education of the man himself. Stated simply, if one goes to business school or engineering school and learns finance, operations research, marketing, or any of the sub-fields of administration, this stored

---

* Excerpts from *Organizational Behavior and the Practice of Management* by Charles E. Sumner, David R. Hampton and Ross A. Webber. Copyright © 1968 by Scott, Foresman and Company. Reprinted by permission.

† The authors are Professors of Organization and Management at San Diego State University, the University of Washington, and the University of Pennsylvania, respectively.

[1] The description of the technological system in Chapter 7 of *Organizational Behavior and the Practice of Management,* including the powerful statements of Veblen, Friedman, and Beard, gives added emphasis to the necessity for both technological planning and political action.

knowledge with its symbolic representation is a form of "invested capital" in one's own life and career. It represents one's functional importance in society—his repertoire of actions that help him cope with life in an industrial and economic world. This commitment no doubt reinforces the original social value attached to planning and implementing an efficient, "well run," "high quality" organization.

The Desire to Be Head of an Organization

Some people, particularly those who rise to high positions in organizations, have found that the way to get what they want and to be secure in getting it in the future, is to rely on getting into positions of status and power. This is where we get the familiar phrase "empire building." Schumpeter, the great sociologist-economist, characterized the entrepreneur this way:

> "In the breast of one who wishes to do something new . . . there is the dream and the will to found a private kingdom. . . . The modern world really does not know any such positions, but what may be attained by industrial or commercial success is still the nearest approach to medieval lordship possible to modern man. Its fascination is specially strong for people who have no other way of achieving social distinction. The sensation of power and independence loses nothing by the fact that both are largely illusions."[2]

Of course, this motivation comes to different people in degrees. In moderation, it is functional for the individual executive and functional for the organization. Running throughout much of the more accepted management literature is an implication that the executive has a degree of this motivation. When Chester Barnard . . . gives us the principles of cooperative action, we can see at least his self-confidence in creating a system for large numbers of people to live in and to follow in their behavior. This same might be said of Fayol's explanation of discipline and unity of command, of the casual way in which Newman lays out the purposes of standing policies and procedures, and of the tone in which Cordiner presents General Electric's vast philosophy for governing the behavior of 281,000 employees. Even Wilfred Brown, head of Glacier Metal Company in England, who brought industrial psychologists from Tavistock into his company, shows a high degree of self-confidence in his role as the most important single person responsible for instituting a specific "new order" for governing behavior within the firm.

In extreme cases, this desire to achieve a position of status and power can be dysfunctional for both the executive and for the organization. In literature, we have the "King Lear" syndrome, in which the desire for keeping one's status and prerogatives was so strong that decisions made by the King were finally unworkable with resulting disintegration of his own personality and rebellion by his subjects. Or, we need look only to Hitler in Germany to see the results of one imbued with maintaining personal office and power—resulting in organizational decisions which would not work.

A number of modern sociologists have cited cases where executives so focused on the rule system and the prerogatives of office, that they almost ignore changing needs of customers, of technology, or of other *facts* which should be considered in dynamic decision-making. . . .

---

[2] Joseph A. Schumpeter, *Theory of Economic Development* (Cambridge, Mass.: Harvard University Press, 1934), pp. 84–94.

Competition and the Will to Conquer

But Schumpeter gives us another set of motivations, which have some verification in subsequent studies in clinical psychology:

> "Then there is the will to conquer: the impulse to fight, to prove oneself superior to others, to succeed for the sake, not of the fruits of success, but of success itself. From this aspect, economic action becomes akin to sport—there are financial races, or rather boxing matches . . ."[3]

This motivation, too, comes parceled to differing executives in differing degrees. And here, too, moderation may well be functional for both the organization and the individual executive.

We recall from Gellerman's summary of "The Power Motive" as conceptualized by the psychoanalyst, Adler . . . , that all men may have some of this type of motivation. And in economics, the very essence of "free enterprise" has been the competitive instinct. Too little of this motivation may result in one's being a follower but not a leader, and too much may result in pathological or dysfunctional outcomes. . . . Bennis and Shepard . . . clearly [show] that, in their orientations toward authority, some people tend to have formed habitual behavior patterns of dependency, others of counter-dependency, and still others of "independency."

In extreme cases, we should not discount the possibility that the *executive* can be the one who plays Berne's deadly game, "Now I've Got You You Son of a Bitch.". . . If he plays for the rules *per se*, without regard for the reality of decisions, and if his primary motivational repertoire consists of the one strategy to check up on people, to "place the blame," this seems the proper diagnosis.

The Urge to Creative Action

A third executive motivation often cited in the literature is aptly put by Schumpeter:

> "[In addition to the dream of a private kingdom, and the will to conquer] there is the joy of creating, of getting things done, or simply of exercising one's energy and ingenuity. . . . Our [executive] type seeks out difficulties, changes in order to change, delights in ventures."[4]

Schumpeter goes on to explain that there *would be no leaders* if there were not some people who possess certain mental characteristics which enable them to get outside of their routine way of living in the organization. There are three reasons why, for many human beings, it is difficult to create new things and get things done. First, there is great risk—mental risk—in doing something new, in which the outcome is unknown. Action must be taken without working out all of the details, and success depends partly upon *Intuition.* Therefore, there is a lack of objective information "out there." Secondly, even if there were not objective insecurity out there, there is subjective insecurity for the human mind to do something new. "In the breast of one who wishes to do something new, the forces of

---

[3] *Idem.*
[4] *Idem.*

habit rise up to bear witness against the embryonic project. A new and *another kind* of effort of will is necessary. This mental freedom presupposes a great surplus force over the everyday demand and is something peculiar and by nature rare."[5] Thirdly, even if one can overcome the two obstacles above, there is a reaction of the social environment against one who wishes to do something new. For all of these reasons, we take the position in the present chapter that the men who actually engage in political action—who actively make rules, and who engage in dynamic action to get them instituted—are motivated in part by these kinds of feelings. Remembering the Maslow theory of human motivation. . . , we see that such men are engaging in a kind of self-fulfillment—and they have found a way of life to do this, that of political action.

At a number of points in this book, we have seen that there is another kind of executive who relies on the existing rules to achieve security and status, who "goes by the book," who is satisfied by the feeling of importance of office and title, and whose mental reactions are similar to the less innovating individual described above. That there are such executives cannot be denied. They are motivated by the two first of Schumpeter's forces (empire ruling and the will to conquer), but not especially by the third.

Symmetry as a Means to Security

Mental security—"peace of mind"—results in part when a person lives in an orderly world, in which "everything is in its place," and in which there are few unexpected events. If you expect that your class will begin at 10 o'clock and that there will be an examination on Chapters 3–7 in the book, think what it does to your feelings of security if the professor shows up at 10:30, or if he gives the examination on Chapters 5–8!

This kind of motivation operates for both general (line) executives and for specialist (staff) executives. In the former case, sociologists have pointed out that many executives have "a demand for control," and that this causes them to make rules for uniformity, or standards for measuring results. Given the necessity for technological coordination, the executive is much more secure if he can predict what people will do in the organization, and if he has uniform standards and policies so that all parts and people don't have to be viewed individually. Through-out the readings by Barnard . . . , Newman, Cordiner, and Brown, we see the need expressed in orderly procedures, policies and standards.

In the case of staff specialist executives, this need is expressed in the desire to formulate business operations on the basis of certain *known* bodies of knowl-edge. The finance specialist is much more secure in his thinking if he has tools of marginal analysis or discounted cash flow to apply to investment decisions or pricing problems. The marketing specialist's mind is much more at ease if there are known ways of predicting consumer motivation or of choosing advertising media. And the Operations Research specialist, through use of formulas for inven-tory control, can do his work much more securely than if he had to face entirely new projects, without models for approaching them. This kind of motivation is clear . . . when staff men are sometimes given "functional authority."

Thus, both general executives and specialist executives have an additional

---

[5] *Idem.*

reason for formulating standing plans and rules, and for instituting them in organizations. Such rules enable them to pursue their careers, and use their minds, and with less mental strain and frustration than if there were no systems, rules, and order.

The Pragmatic Position—"It Works"

A final reason why executives engage in political action is that all human beings need law and order in an interdependent organization, and the executive recognizes either explicitly or intuitively that he *can* take such action.

This has already been explained . . . on more than one level analysis. Lock's philosophical explanation of human passion, Presthus' emphasis on reduction of anxiety among peers, and Gouldner's explanation of how rule systems reduce anxiety between superiors and subordinates all confirm that the executive can, if he does so wisely, govern human behavior through formulation of systems of law and order.

The many other studies in this book which show that people react to authority systems in ways which are dysfunctional should, however, serve as a warning. The phrase "if he does so wisely" is an important one. Later in this chapter, we will examine how the technological rule system is converted to legitimate law and order.

DESIGNING THE TECHNOLOGICAL SYSTEM

It may seem odd that in a chapter on political action, we begin with a section called "Designing the Technological System." Does this not sound like engineering or economics instead of politics? The answer lies in the fact that the technological system—the organizational output goals, the system of working parts, and the input-output relationships between them—are at one and the same time the technical work operations to be performed by each part of the organization, and the rules of human conduct which the part (person, department) should follow. . . .

18. BERGEN METALFABRIK, A/S

Case Introduction

SYNOPSIS

A medium-sized Norwegian manufacturing company experiences difficulty in building relationships between headquarters and the newly merged international subsidiaries in Sweden, Denmark, Germany, Italy, and Switzerland. The director of human resources uncovers uneasiness in both headquarters and subsidiaries and decides, with the president, to engage a consultant to assist with a team-building activity during the first top management meeting planned for early 1972 in Sweden. The consultant recommends using an organization development technique called "force field analysis." While the meeting is being planned, the company acquires another major division. The management team from the new division joins the other managers for the team-building exercise during the top management meeting. In work groups with representation from headquarters, divisional, and subsidiary levels a diagnosis of the headquarters-subsidiary relationship is performed and recommendations for remedial action are presented. The consultant leaves the top management meeting ambivalent over the results.

WHY THIS CASE IS INCLUDED

Though the field of organization development is now over a decade old, few cases exist which document blow by blow, as it were, the organization development process. In the Bergen Metalfabrik case the readers can examine an organization's need for change and analyze the decision process which led to responding to the need with a particular form of consulting intervention. The organization development consulting style and the organization development technique of "force field analysis," can be observed in action. The reader can test his own ideas for change against the consultant's in light of the immediate and the likely future results of the organization development activity.

DIAGNOSTIC AND PREDICTIVE QUESTIONS

The readings included with this case are marked (*). The author index at the end of this book locates the other readings.

1. Why is it not surprising that Bergen Metalfabrik experiences some difficulties in headquarters-subsidiary relationship at this stage of its history?

2. What was Nils Guren communicating to Vince Matthews in his September 3rd letter when he asks advice on an *"organization development* project"?

Read: French, "Organization Development Objectives, Assumptions, and Strategies."

3. Is it clear that Nils Guren and Vince Matthews adapt and behave according to the values and assumptions of organization development?

Read: French, "Organization Development Objectives, Assumptions, and Strategies."

4. Describe the consulting style of Vince Matthews. What other styles might he have used? Did his style fit the circumstances at Bergen Metalfabrick?

Read: *Schein, *Process Consultation: Its Role in Organization Development,* pp. 4–9. *Kolb and Frohman, "An Organization Development Approach to Consulting."

5. Why did not the plenary session work as smoothly as Vince Matthews had hoped? What accounts for what the planning director calls "shallowness"?

Read: McGrath, *Social Psychology,* pp. 50–53. Carr, "Is Business Bluffing Ethical?"

6. Why did Vince Matthews want to see the president before the exercise?

Read: Levinson, "Role, Personality, and Social Structure in the Organizational Setting."

7. The president has been described as an entrepreneur and has led an aggressive growth drive in the past seven years. Did the organization development approach suit his personal style?

Read: Odiorne, *How Managers Make Things Happen,* pp. 4–11, 37–38, 52–53. Jennings, "Business Needs Mature Autocrats."

8. Do you see any evidence of change in Bergen Metalfabrik as you review the output of the group work? What do you predict will happen in headquarters-subsidiary relationships in the coming year? What are the bases of your prediction?

POLICY QUESTIONS

9. Would you have done anything differently if you were Nils Guren? Vince Matthews? The president?

10. What should Vince Matthews suggest at the end of the case?

11. If you were the president, what would you do now that the exercise is over?

QUESTIONS FOR ORIGINAL STUDENT WORK IN ANALYSIS AND POLICY

12. While reflecting on case facts, what additional theories from prior education give you insights as to "what is going on" in Bergen Metalfabrik? As to what might be predicated to happen in the future?

13. Other than the policy questions asked by the authors, what pragmatic ways can you think of to state the practical problems faced by executives in the case?

Case Text*

On September 10, Dr. Vincent Matthews received a letter from a Norwegian Director of human resources he had met some seven months earlier in a management development seminar.

> *Bergen Metalfabrik, A/S*
> *Bergen, Norway*
> *3 September 1971*

Dr. Vincent Matthews
Paris, France

Dear Vince:

> *May I ask your advice on someone to help us with an organization development project on headquarters-subsidiary relationships next January? We have heard good things about Edward Carey in Switzerland and Fred Post in Belgium. How about Peter Williams in England? How about your own availability? Could you recommend any other first class organization development consultants in Europe? Many thanks for your big help!*

> *Regards,*
> *Nils Guren*
> *Director of Human Resources*

Vincent Matthews recalled that Nils Guren worked for a 60-year-old medium-sized, Norwegian, family-owned firm which had recently gone multinational by acquiring several subsidiaries throughout Europe. Annual growth in the firm exceeded 10 percent but integration of the newly-

---

merged units had not yet been accomplished. The president and majority owner of the firm showed an entrepreneurial flair, but not until recently had there been concentration on the internal management of the emerging multinational enterprise. Nils Guren had joined the firm as director of human resources, just a year and a half ago after several years as training officer for an employers' federation and lecturer in psychology at the university. Vincent Matthews remembered Nils Guren as a probing and well-informed professional. The prospect of working with him on the headquarters-subsidiary organization development project was attractive to Vincent Matthews so he responded as follows:

Paris, France
13 September 1971

Mr. Nils Guren
Director of Human Resources
Bergen Metalfabrik, A/S
Bergen, Norway

Dear Nils:
Thank you very much for your letter of September 3, 1971.
You sound like you are planning an exciting meeting for your company on the topic of "headquarter-subsidiary relations." The organization development approach is most appropriate for this kind of task. I agree with you that the consultant you use must be first class.
I know Edward Carey very well. We have worked together in the States prior to coming here and we have worked here together in the recent past. He operates very well with executive groups and has the age and experience to be perfectly credible in such a sensitive task. I am not sure, however, Edward has direct experience in such an organization development approach but I have every confidence he could package it well.
I also know Fred Post from having worked with him on our research on teaching methods this past year. He is younger than Edward but he has already cumulated much experience with executives in his short career. He is formally trained by NTL† and knows the organization development material singularly well. If your group would accept his relative youth, he would be qualified to do the job.
I am sorry to say that I do not know Peter Williams first hand so I will not comment on his capacity.
There are two other men in Belgium who could do the job well. Pierre Lefol is French but has very good English. He too is NTL† trained and has done organization development work with client firms, in France especially. He has the age and experience to be immediately credible.
Wayne Burke is another good prospect. We worked together in the States for several years prior to his coming to Europe. He is first class.

† National Training Laboratories.

He has done such things for companies here and in the States and if he has time could perform very well.

The other English-speaking trainers I know in Europe do not have sufficient European exposure for me to recommend them at this time. It would be inappropriate to use a North American who is not yet culturally sensitized.

I have done such organization development work both here and in the States. I am particularly fascinated by the relationship issue between such units as headquarters-subsidiaries or information Operations Research staff and company client groups. It is in these contexts where I have done my work.

Do not feel any obligation to give me first priority because you have written to me but simply be advised that I think I could do the job and might be able to fit it into my schedule if the timing is right. There is one week in January which is impossible for me (16–21 January).

I hope you have in hand the six book series on organization development from Addison-Wesley. The authors included are Blake-Mouton, Lawrence-Lorsch, Walton, Bennis, Schein, and Beckhard.

You should also have in hand the book by Gordon Lippit entitled Organization Renewal *(Appleton Century Crofts, 1969). Finally, you will want to consult the new book by Chris Argyris,* Intervention Theory and Method *(Addison-Wesley, 1970).*

I hope these comments are useful to you in your planning.

> *Sincerely,*
> *Vincent Matthews*

On September, Vincent Matthews received the following telex from Nils:

Att: Vince Matthews　　　　24 Sept. 71
Thanks for good news. Would be pleased work with you. Next step could be discussion between us in Paris. Do you have time in near future? Regards
Nils Guren—Bergen

An exchange of telexes led to a meeting in Vincent Matthew's office in Paris on October 8th. The meeting lasted some five hours. Vincent Matthews' notes summarize the main points discussed.

Notes of 8 October Meeting with Nils Guren

1. Nils outlined the organization with the warning that positions and people are shifting rapidly.

Just about 5,000 were employed in Bergen Metalfabrik in 1971, two thirds in Division A where 75 percent of the sales were generated. Consolidated sales volume in 1970 had been almost 50 million. The product lines from Divisions A and B have many common engineering and pro-

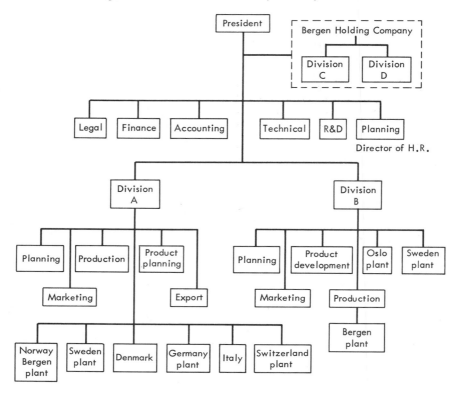

duction characteristics but serve different customer needs through different distribution systems.

The Bergen Holding Company comprised two product divisions unrelated to Division A or B products in technology, market or any other way. The president and his family held majority ownership in the holding company and operated it virtually independently of Bergen Metalfabrik. In 1970, the holding company had sales of $10 million.

The newest of the subsidiaries in Division A was the small sales company in Italy which had just been added a month ago. The German subsidiary had been added less than a year ago as had the minority interest in the Swiss company. The Danish and Swedish subsidiaries both had been part of Bergen Metalfabrik for over ten years but each started as a profit center just last year when the company was divisionalized.

2. The concern for improving the headquarters-subsidiary relationship started with the director of human resources but the president gave the project highest priority. Nils Guren had picked up many—often emotional—comments from managers in the subsidiaries concerning the unsatisfactory relations with headquarters. The subsidiary managers often did not know what headquarters wanted and found report requests

from headquarters to be burdensome. Headquarters was seen to be unresponsible to the subsidiaries' requests for technical and marketing help. Similarly, headquarters executives cited cases of poor communications and unresponsiveness from the subsidiaries.

3. About 40 executives (19 from headquarters and 21 from various subsidiaries) would be brought to neutral territory in Ronneby Brunn, Sweden, for a two and one-half day top management meeting on January 13–14, 1972. One full day of that meeting was to be committed to the organization development project. The rest of the time would be devoted to corporate planning activities.

4. Under Nils Guren's aegis, Bergen Metalfabrik had begun experimenting with organization development by beginning managerial grid seminars. Only 30 executives had participated in phase one seminars, some in public sessions, some in a special pilot session within the company. A full-scale managerial grid program would probably be launched within a year as soon as the appropriate materials were translated into Norwegian. However, neither this program nor the other educational efforts within Bergen Metalfabrik seemed adequate to cope with the headquarters-subsidiary issue. Prompt and specific action was thought desirable and necessary. The full-scale introduction of the corporate planning system would be retarded if remedial action were not taken to improve headquarters-subsidiary relationships.

5. Three proposed approaches were discussed for the organization development exercise during the January top management meeting.

    a. Small groups would work on various phases of the strategy formulation process (surveying the environment for threats and opportunities, analyzing the firm's strengths and weaknesses, objective setting, etc.) The groups would be mixed representation of headquarters and subsidiary personnel. As deemed desirable we could provide process feedback on the group meetings and/ or sessions on team building.

    b. Homogeneous small groups could begin a social perception audit by describing (each from its own perspective) the relationship between headquarters and subsidiaries. Each group would also predict the description to be given by the other group. In plenary session the descriptions and predictions would be shared and discussed. Disagreements would be revealed and misunderstandings straightened out. Critical road blocks for the relationship would be identified so that mixed small groups could design action plans to improve the relationship.

    c. Mixed small groups could engage in a force field analysis whose dependent variable would be "head quarters-subsidiary cooperation." Each group would list the forces conducive to cooperation and the forces standing in the way of cooperation. The results would be displayed in plenary session and the highest priority items on each list identified for attention in an action plan to be designed in the small groups.

6. The strategy planning exercise was rejected because it was too indirect and because it was thought premature to involve this group in so

sensitive an exercise at this stage of dramatic change in the company.

The social perception audit was rejected because it was too confrontive and uncontrollable. The more reticent Scandinavians might be threatened by the assignment.

The force field analysis was selected because of the balance built right into the force field exercise. A man could risk being negative because he could recoup quickly by adding a positive item. Nils Guren saw benefit in each man being able to manage his own risks even if this meant some of the deeper data never were revealed. In the long run, he insisted, more good would be done by taking small controlled steps than by forcing emotional confrontation.

7. Nils Guren asked Vince Matthews to make a concrete proposal and design the instrument and send the completed program plan and force field instrument to Nils Guren:

> *Paris, France*
> *4 November 1971*

Mr. Nils Guren
Director of Human Resources
Bergen Metalfabrik, A/S
Bergen, Norway

Dear Nils:

I am sorry for the delay in getting back to you. I hope you find the enclosed documents satisfactory. It would help if you or one of your colleagues would pretest the force field analysis instrument and let me see the results.

Also, of course, feel free to alter the instrument to give better examples or explanation. Does the organization development program plan seem to make sense?

I am in Malmö on the second and third of December just in case we should get together either there or in Copenhagen.

Hoping to hear from you soon, I am,

> *Sincerely,*
> *Vincent Matthews*

Encl.: Organization development program schedule and force field analysis instrument

Organization Development Program Plan

Activity	Time
I. *Introduction*—Vince Matthews will describe the exercise and the forms and respond to questions.	15 minutes 1:30–1:45
II. *Individual exercise*—Each executive will fill in the force field analysis.	60 minutes 1:45–2:45

III. *Small group discussion*—Six-man groups will discuss the individual data with the purpose of developing a group consensus. They record their consensus on flip chart pages.

120 minutes
3:15–5:15

IV. *Plenary discussion*—All the participants gather to hear the reports from group representatives. The separate group lists are combined to one master list.

Then the items are ranked—at least the top three forces in each of the four categories.

120 minutes
7:00–9:00

V. *Small group discussion*—Newly mixed groups (different than in step III) of six men each take the ranked master list of forces and design action plans (suggestions) to reinforce driving forces and remove or mitigate restraining forces. Suggestions are recorded on flip charts.

90 minutes
9:00–10:30

VI. *Plenary discussion*—All participants gather to hear the individual group reports.
The president presides and responds in two ways:
  A. Where possible he supports good ideas.
  B. In most cases he refers the suggestions to a follow-up project team (made up of both headquarters and subsidiary representatives) for further study.
The project team will be asked to submit a progress report by April 1st to all participants.

90 minutes
10:30–12:00

FORCE FIELD ANALYSIS ON HEADQUARTERS/ SUBSIDIARY COOPERATION

Instructions

Please record on the following pages your views on the forces influencing the relationships between Bergen headquarters and subsidiaries. We will be describing the *present* situation.

Certain forces (*driving forces*) will be helping or facilitating the effectiveness of communication and coordination in the relationship. Some of these *driving forces* will be external to the company and others will be internal to the company. Examples of each appear on the pages that follow.

Other forces (*restraining forces*) will be hindering or blocking the effectiveness of communication and coordination in the relationship. Again, some of these *restraining forces* will be external to the company and others will be internal to the company.

In some cases, a particular force may be both driving and restraining when viewed from different perspectives.

After individually filling in the force field analysis, we will discuss the data in small groups and then in a plenary session.

The exercise may be visualized as follows:

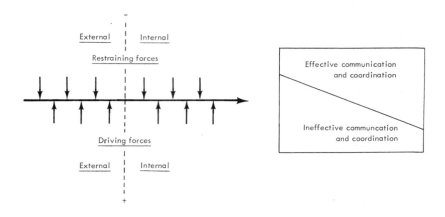

Name_____

External Driving Forces

Example: The economics of TELEX communication has reduced the cost of frequent communication.

1. _____
   _____
   _____
   _____

2. _____
   _____
   _____
   _____

3. _____
   _____
   _____
   _____

4. _____
   _____
   _____
   _____

5. _____
   _____
   _____
   _____

Internal Driving Forces

Example: People in headquarters and the subsidiaries are getting to know one another better.

1. _____

2. _____

3. _____

4. _____

5. _____

External Restraining Forces

Example: Physical separation prevents timely interaction on urgent matters.

1. _____

2. _____

3. _____

4. _____

_____
_____
5. _____
_____
_____
_____

Internal Restraining Forces

Example: Reporting forms and procedures have not yet been fully standardized.

1. _____
_____
_____
_____

2. _____
_____
_____
_____

3. _____
_____
_____
_____

4. _____
_____
_____
_____

5. _____
_____
_____
_____

Nils Guren responded by inviting Vince Matthews for a three-hour meeting in a Copenhagen hotel on December 2nd to review the program and examine the pretest results of the force field instrument.

Notes of 2 December Meeting with Nils Guren

1. Bergen Metalfabrik recently purchased a company in Norway almost the size of Division A, which roughly coincides with the product line of Division C of the Bergen holding company. Plans are not complete, but it is likely that the new company will not be fully integrated into Bergen Metalfabrik. Rather it and Division C will probably be run independently except for the sharing of some headquarters' administrative services. In any event, since the new unit "Norco" has a profit center

structure like Division A, Norco executives will participate in the top management meeting, including the headquarters-subsidiary exercise.

2. The group at Ronneby Brunn will now have 55 members, many of whom will be meeting one another for the first time. The group will be composed as follows:

Headquarters	9
Division A	
Division level...............	8
Subsidiary level	13
Division B	11
Division C + Norco	
Division level...............	10
Subsidiary level	4

3. Since Division B really has no subsidiaries, that 11-man group will do is own force field analysis on intradivisional communications. They will not report back during the plenary session but will rather observe and add comments where appropriate. Their reporting and action planning will be handled within their divisional meeting on Saturday, January 15, by Nils Guren. This group will work in Norwegian.

4. Simultaneous interpretation will be used at Ronneby Brunn because many headquarters people speak only Norwegian and many subsidiary people speak no Norwegian.

5. The exercise will be renamed "Analysis of Factors Influencing Headquarters-Subsidiary Cooperation." Nils found some resistance to the physical or engineering analogy in the term "force field analysis." For the same reason, the diagram will be omitted from the instrument.

6. Rather than just ask for five "issues" under each of the four headings in the instrument, we decided to ask for issues plus specific examples. Nils thought the more specific data would help in preparing the action plan.

7. The president preferred that Vince Matthews chair the final session and that the division general managers from Division A and Norco join him on a panel to respond to the action program suggestions. Nils reported that the president would be more comfortable with this arrangement. There is no disagreement with proposed procedure to submit the action program suggestions to a project team which will report back by early spring to the whole top management group.

8. Vince Matthews expressed some uneasiness to Nils Guren that he had had no chance to meet the president to discuss the organization development exercise with him. Nils said he knew the president well enough to sense that he understood the risks and potential payoffs of the exercise and that he was fully committed to it. Since it was inconvenient to arrange a meeting prior to going to Ronneby Brunn, it was agreed that Vince would lunch with the president on the first day of the meeting and that they could continue discussions while the groups were working on the analysis.

Vince Matthews left the Copenhagen meeting somewhat unsettled because of the significant changes in group composition and because of the awkwardness of having parallel but different exercises going with Division A and Division C plus Norco and Division B. On the plane to Sweden, he reviewed the pretest results which Nils had given him. Those results are summarized in Appendix A. He found many of the comments superficial but he thought the group work at Ronneby Brunn would produce better analytic work.

Vince Matthews had no further contact with Nils Guren until he arrived at Ronneby Brunn on the evening of 12 January. They set right to work to make the assignments to six groups, taking care to have representation of all three levels in each group—headquarters, divisions, and subsidiary. For the first set of groups, there was no crossing of divisional lines. In the second set of groups, for the action programming phase, mixed groups were composed of Division A and Norco personnel. Care was taken not to have direct superior-subordinate pairs in the same group where possible. Reporters were appointed for each group without regard to status in the group hierarchy. The Division B group stayed the same throughout. The rest of the evening was spent in arranging logistics for the conference room, a large rectangular room permitting four seats on either side of a center isle in each of seven rows.

The morning session on Thursday began by the president's remarks in Norwegian. Vince Matthews listened to the English interpretation and made the following notes.

Notes on President's Remarks—13 January

1. We are in the midst of a drive for internationality. Multinationality is a conscious objective.
2. Our problems, particularly in Division A and Norco, arise because of lack of contact and poor information flow between headquarters and subsidiaries. We will work on this later in our meeting.
3. It is no surprise that we have some problems since we have grown tenfold in seven years.
4. We want to improve communications so we can have bigger units and more cooperation.
5. In our newly enlarged group we plan to look for synergies in centrally managed activities rather than leave all decisions to the divisional level.
   a. We will coordinate finance to permit economies.
   b. We will standardize personnel policies to permit faster career movement, to encourage early responsibility for young managers, and to facilitate our programs of promoting from within and intercountry transfer.
   c. We will standardize in our management techniques, management system, and in our information system.
6. Being Norwegian by origin presents some problems:
   a. Language barrier.
   b. Geographically far from the center of activities.
   c. Underdeveloped capital market.

At some future time we could control the company from some other location.

7. There are good points in being from a small country:
   a. Ease of contacting the highest government officials.
   b. Being Scandinavian allows trade with the Comecon countries.
8. Our objectives for the future are:
   a. Continued quantitative growth.
   b. Vertical integration.
   c. An extended product range.

As Vince Matthews listened to the interpreter, he became uneasy with the artificial block to the communication represented by the earphones and the interpreter's evident difficulty in catching the full message with its business jargon. He feared that he grasped only two thirds of what the president said. In light of the forthcoming headquarters-subsidiary exercise, he wondered how the group received the president's assertion, of impending centralization of a number of management decisions and policies. He hoped for some feedback when the president threw the floor open for questions and discussion but only one man rose to ask a question about company prospects in light of the newly enlarged common market. After a period of silence, the president handed the meeting over to the planning director who began a description of the new planning system. Vince Matthews decided it was best to write out the remarks he was to make after lunch to guarantee that the interpreter could prepare for accurate translation into Norwegian.

Vince Matthews' Introductory Remarks

I. *Introduction*
   A. Nothing unusual about working on headquarters-subsidiary relationship. A concern for all firms at some stage depending on:
      1. Rate of growth.
      2. Type of growth.
         a. Internal expansion.
         b. Expansion by acquisition.
      3. Degree of multinationality.
      4. Complexity of product line.
      The time is right now for Bergen + Norco to focus on headquarters-subsidiary relationship because of the:
      1. Fast growth.
      2. Expansion by acquisition.
      3. Recent multinationality.
      4. Growing complexity of product lines.
   B. Focus not so much on problem solving but opportunity seizing. What we do here is a direct support for the growth objectives announced this morning. The men in this room are undoubtedly *smart* as individuals. We approach our task as a group to see if we cannot become *wise*.

      1. A smart man is a man who can get himself out of all sorts of problems.

      2. A wise man never gets into the problems in the first place. As a group, we will try to do maintenance on the relationship between headquarters and subsidiaries, but we will try to be wise enough to do *preventive* maintenance.

    C. This part of the top management meeting is a minor theme. The major theme focuses on *doing the right things.* In our part, we focus on *doing things right.* Obviously, it matters little how well we do things if we do the wrong things. The two themes are related, but, clearly, priority must go to planning the right growth strategies. When that's done, our organization development effort is in the right focus.

II. *What we are going to do:*

    A. Describe the present relationship between headquarters and subsidiaries.

    B. Analyze why the relationship is the way it is . . . what factors support good communications and coordination and what factors stand in the way of good communications and coordination.

    C. Search for opportunities to improve the relationship in the future.

III. *How we are going to proceed:*

    A. We will work in the next 24 hours as individuals, in small groups, and in this plenary meeting.

    B. We will document our progress at each step.

(Vincent Matthews then went on to explain the instrument and the time schedule.)

It had been impossible for Vince Matthews to lunch with the president, but they met with Nils Guren and the division general managers from Division A and Norco while the rest of the group was doing the first phase of the analysis. The man representing Norco was in transition to the position of director of corporate planning. His successor at Norco was too new to the company to be anything more than an observer. The new planning director began the meeting by predicting the groups would not focus on relations with headquarters but rather on relations with the plants or the divisional administration. The president concurred in this prediction. While no one expressed any concern over the outcome, all showed enthusiasm and curiosity over what would be said. Vince Matthews outlined the role of the panel which was to receive the action plan suggestions in the last session. The panel was to be supportive rather than evaluative and was to indicate actions already under way or contemplated on the issues raised. All agreed that the project team, which was to be appointed to coordinate and "package" the action suggestions into specific action programs, should report to the appropriate unit—headquarters or division—and issue a progress report to the whole top management group prior to June 1, 1972. Names were selected for the six-man project team, representative of each level in both Division A and Norco. For logistical ease, the project team was to meet in Bergen under the lead of Nils Guren, even though this meant that only two non-Norwegians would be on the team. Throughout this meeting, Vince Matthews frequently felt left out when discussion and side comments occurred in Norwegian.

When the six groups began discussing the analyses done individually, Nils Guren and Vince Matthews circulated the syndicate rooms. Only one group experienced definitional problems and had to be encouraged to relax the formalities and get on with the task. Lively and rather full participation characterized each group. One of the Scandinavian languages, rather than English, seemed most frequently used in the discussions. One group asked if they could meet in the sauna. Nils gave the okay but the group never left its meeting room.

After dinner, each group reporter summarized the group consensus, using flip chart graphics. Vince Matthews taped the flip chart sheets to the wall after each spoke. Clarifying questions were invited but only one was raised. Aside from two or three bursts of laughter the room was rather silent. During the presentations, the president and planning director whispered to one another frequently in the front row.

When all the flip chart sheets were displayed, Vince Matthews asked the group to pick the top three priority items in each of the four categories: external driving factors, internal driving factors, external restraining factors, internal restraining factors. He indicated the items should be controllable by Bergen/Norco and issues on which the group could design action recommendations. The selected items would be typed overnight and distributed to the second set of work groups for action programming in the morning.

Vince Matthews asked the group to begin by chosing the high priority external driving factors. No response. Long pause. Vince Matthews suggested an item which seemed common to several groups. No response. Finally, one man offered a suggestion. Vince Matthews asked if the group concurred. No response. So it proceeded through the second of the lists of driving factors. Four men made all the contributions from the floor and, except for occasional *Sotte voce* remarks by the president and planning director like "that's not important," the room was quiet. Since it was the hour designated for finishing the two more lists that remained for discussion, Vince Matthews called a five-minute stretch break. Nils Guren encouraged numbers of the group to gather around the displayed lists so they could prepare suggestions for the next priority items. Nils took Vince aside and said the lists were not visible from the back of the room. He thought this accounted for the lack of participation.

After the break, Vince Matthews began by summarizing the next list prior to asking for suggestions. The response came somewhat more quickly but five or six men remained the only contributors. In 45 minutes, the priority list was finished and the group broke up.

Nils took Vince to the bar for a drink. Vince admitted he was frustrated and disappointed but Nils tried to lift his spirits by attributing the lack of participation to the technological problem of visibility and the fatigue of the group. Vince insisted the exercise design packed too much into the evening session and prevented him from being of more help to the group. He could not digest the 200 or more items reported by the work groups in a way that would facilitate the task of drawing up the priority list. They agreed they could do no more prior to the morning session so they merely gave the list to the typist for reproduction.

Priority List of Driving and Restraining Factors

I. Internal restraining factors
   A. Information problems (quantity and quality)
      1. Slow and inaccurate reporting
      2. Not enough information inside and between functions
      3. Lack of sufficient information from the top level
   B. Delayed and unqualified feedback
   C. Inventory of corporate human resources
   D. Conflict of interests
   E. Integration of new subsidiaries
II. External restraining forces
   A. Language training
   B. Different quality demands
III. Internal driving forces
   A. Standardization
   B. Exchange of know-how (technical)
   C. Common principles for planning and reporting
IV. External driving forces
   A. Image of the group
   B. Availability of data processing
   C. Standardization

At nine in the morning, the groups began developing action plans to reinforce the driving factors and remove or mitigate the restraining forces. Each group was encouraged to select items from the list to concentrate on rather than attempt to respond to all 13 items. Again, the small group discussions seemed lively and the plenary session began with much buzzing in the room. Frequently, as each group reporter summarized his group's recommendations, laughing and random comments spread through the room. The president and planning director whispered frequently in their position at the panel table with the Division B managing director and Vince Matthews. With redundancies removed, the suggestions appear in outline form below:

1. *Standardized information:*
   a. Produce manual of policies on finance, distribution, guarantees, technical changes, reporting procedures, and simplified price list.
   b. Assure that all technical drawings at least are in English.
   c. Compile a frequently updated directory of headquarters' personnel, including organization chart for reference.

   d. Translate all information from headquarters or divisions into the local language of the subsidiary.

   e. Set specific time limit for responding to telexes.

   f. Standardize currency units for all reports.

   g. Use more visuals in all reports.

2. *Information from headquarters and divisions:*

   a. Reports comparing subsidiary performance should be issued quarterly to all subsidiaries by division.

   b. Announcements of major business decisions or appointments should be made at the same time to all company units before public dissemination.

   c. Divisions should work out procedures to prevent delayed and/or unqualified feedback to subsidiary inquiries especially concerning product development and quality control.

   d. Headquarters should require from subsidiaries no more information than the subsidiaries find useful in managing their own units.

   e. Employ management by objectives in such a way that discussed and agreed objectives are the basis for follow-up and corrective action.

3. *Information meetings:*

   a. Managers and controllers across units should meet regularly to discuss relative standing of the units.

   b. Functional meetings should be held twice a year to avoid the commander-troop mentality.

4. *Inventory of corporate human resources:*

The director of human resources should prepare a computerized file of Bergen/Norco managers and specialists, showing alternative personnel for each position. Include profile data and current project memberships. Include as well outside potential human resources. Issue a human resources policy.

5. *Conflict of interest:*

Make a top-level decision to resolve the conflict of interest among subsidiaries in Norco.

6. *Integration of new subsidiaries:*

   a. The director of planning should head a project team to develop a merger integration plan.

   b. There should be a checklist of problems arising in merger integration after the recent experience in Italy.

7. *Language training:*

The company should institute language course using appropriate technology and possibly rewarding managers who demonstrate increased language facility in English.

8. *Management information system:*

   a. A project team should develop a better sales forecasting system and factory planning and control system.

   b. Headquarters and subsidiary EDP practices should be studied and unified.

   c. Study the feasibility of centralizing EDP for the whole group via data lines.

9. *Image of the group:*
   a. Get more publicity in trade papers, radio, television, and international trade fairs.
   b. Have technical papers presented at professional meeting by Bergen/Norco personnel.
   c. Improve relations with bankers and major customers by stressing the quality of products and the quality of our people.

After the presentations were completed, the president called for a break in order for the panel to prepare its response. The three panelists agreed on a division of labor depending on whether the suggestion was more relevant to headquarters or one of the two divisions. When the group was reconvened, the president began by expressing thanks for the suggestions and committing the company to appropriate action. He announced some immediate responsible action like calling the people concerned with the conflict of interest case to a luncheon meeting. He also agreed to the formation of a number of the project teams recommended and promised immediate action on such items as the new corporate directory.

The other two panelists continued in the same spirit by committing their organizations to action or by underlining relevant work already in progress. Vincent Matthews announced the coordinating project team membership and explained its mandate of digesting the recommendations with all the back up data from the exercise and constructing a composite action plan for submission to the relevant company units. A progress report from the coordinating project team was promised to the whole top management group before 1 June.

Before closing the meeting for lunch, Vince Matthews gave the group the following feedback on its performance in the exercise:

> *What more could a consultant ask from such an exercise than that change has already begun. From what I have observed the Bergen/Norco group is well on its way not only to do the right things but also to do things right.*
>
> *How was the performance in the exercise? The quality of small group work was excellent. Everyone seemed active and involved. The groups were productive.*
>
> *The quality of analysis varied from group to group but overall coverage was wide-ranging and rather deep in some places. One is left with the feeling, however, that some things have been unsaid.*
>
> *The work in the plenary session was rather unproductive. Many in the room remained passive. Why? Altogether we were too large a group for this kind of task especially given the geography of this room where each individual saw more backs than faces. Last evening we tried too much. Aside from the difficulty of seeing the flip chart displays, we attempted to comprehend some 200 lines of data without prior preparation. The group could not do the processing quickly enough nor could I significantly help the group in its efforts. Any outside observer would comment that few people took risks during these plenary sessions. I would not consider that unusual since you*

did not know one another very well. One does not know the magnitude of risk one is taking in a group unless familiarity with colleagues allows a prediction of their likely response. Finally, the technology of simultaneous interpretation made the setting overly formal. Many people had to use second or third languages to discuss very important matters. In those circumstances, you are to be congratulated for doing so well.

For myself, I am frustrated that my language limitations prevented me from getting as fully involved in the exercise as is my custom. I am grateful, however, for your gracious hospitality and generous cooperation.

As the meeting adjourned, the planning director leaned over to Vince Matthews and asked: "Do such groups always stay on the surface? I do not think they got down to the real issues. They were too general and philosophical." Vince Matthews started to respond but the president interrupted: "How did the panel do?" Vince Matthews had only time to say: "Couldn't have been better" before the president pumped his hand, saying "thanks, and good-bye!"

Nils Guren came up with apologies for not having formally thanked Vince Matthews in front of the group. He expressed his own thanks and his conviction that the exercise went well. There was little time to talk further since Nils had to prepare for his own presentation after lunch and Vince had to catch a plane to Paris. They parted with the agreement to sit down soon and analyze the experience.

As Vince Matthews took the taxi to the airport, he tried to sort out his mixed feelings. The performance of the panel was immensely better than he could have hoped and yet he had to grant the planning director's assertion that the analysis and recommendations were somewhat superficial and unresponsive to the specific mission of the exercise. Vince could not predict very well the outcome of the coordinating project team nor the follow-up of headquarters or divisions. He wondered if the exercise could not have been better designed, or more radically, if something different should not have been done from the beginning or at least from the point at which the character of the top management meeting changed with the addition of Norco.

APPENDIX A

PRETEST RESULTS OF THE FORCE FIELD ANALYSIS (H1 AND H2 ARE HEADQUARTER'S MANAGERS AND S1 AND S2 ARE SUBSIDIARY'S MANAGERS)

External Driving Forces

H1 Standardization in technical specifications in today's Europe.

H1 The threat from large multinational companies motivates smaller ones to unite and "communicate."

H1 Development in the field of transportation.

H2 The rapid and good traffic connections between different countries (flights).

H2 The telephone connections have been better and better during last two to three years (especially Italy).

H2 Development of dictating machines in connection with phone calls.

S1 Automatic telephone network in Europe equals faster contact today.

S2 Automatic dialing telephones inside some part of group area.

S2 Generally rising level of English language knowledge all over in Europe.

S2 Transportation improving, air freight and container transportation.

S2 Lowering customs plus passport plus barriers.

S2 All businessmen are reading the same magazines today.

External Restraining Forces

H1 Language difficulties.

H1 Lack of common European standard.

H1 Lack of trained "internationalists."

H1 Growing isolationism (problems in financing, currency transfer, etc.).

H2 Geographic distances.

H2 Patriotism.

H2 Different technical development.

H2 Different laws in different countries.

Internal Driving Forces

H1 Basically a common language (in Scandinavia).

H1 Valuable exchange of know-how.

H1 Necessity to acquire export outlets in order to grow to a level sufficient for survival.

H2 Uniform information systems in different functions (budgeting, reporting, etc.).

H2 Personal contacts.

H2 Policy group meetings (we have had only two).

H2 Exchange of personnel between group companies especially between Norway and other countries.

H2 Norwegian employees in group companies.

S1 Willingness to solve common problems.

S1 Personal ambition.

S2 Some personal contacts are forming.

Internal Restraining Forces

H1 Differences in standards.

H1 Factory almost totally Norwegian speaking.

H1 Nationalistic pride.

H1 Lack of skill in operating in present scale.

H2 Lack of knowledge of group companies. We are not information minded.

H2 Bad knowledge of main languages.

H2 Lack of knowledge about organization (who is who).

H2 Low educational level in some of local companies.

H2 There does not exist any internal education within the corporation.

H2 Nonhuman climate, especially in Norway.

S1 Language barrier. English supposed to be the official language which is "foreign" to everyone. From the international point of view, still the best choice. Terminology has to be straightened out.

S1 Lack of knowledge of the other end of the communication line. More personal contact wanted. By the same token, better information regarding systems and organization wanted.

S1 National feelings among employees might affect the communication negatively. The multinational idea not always accepted. The feeling of the multinational group does not really exist at the headquarters either.

S1 Starting up of new projects is often formed via questionnaires which do not have the full explanation of background and aim of the project. First reaction: negative.

S2 Lack of personal contacts between headquarters and subsidiaries.

S2 Not very often given "why's" for different policies.

S2 The need to sell a product which you do not know fully and are not able to believe in fully.

S2 Difficult to give promises when others are depending on you.

S2 Organization divided into profit centers, therefore corporate views are forgotten now and then.

S2 Language barrier: Norwegian language.

S2 Poor planning: we are not accustomed to function as a whole—plans have to be made upon loose promises . . . lack of education and experience.

S2 Over-emphasis upon economics and forgetting all other things . . . results are demanded without giving needed resources, facilities, etc.

S2 Long line and many links between the factory and customer and much buck-passing.

S2 Bias of wanting all solutions used within corporation to be of Norwegian origin.

S2 Exaggerated fright to tell things when they are negative . . . lack of correct information . . . lack of feedback, planning, and time table.

Selected Readings

From

PROCESS CONSULTATION: ITS ROLE IN ORGANIZATION DEVELOPMENT*

By Edgar H. Schein†

INTRODUCTION

This book is about a special kind of consultation which I am calling *Process Consultation* (P-C)–what it is, and what role it plays in organizational development (OD).

*   *   *   *   *

Process consultation, . . . involves the manager and the consultant in a period of *joint* diagnosis. The process consultant is willing to come into an organization without a clear mission or clear need, because of an underlying assumption that most organizations could probably be more effective than they are if they could identify what processes (work flow, interpersonal relations, communications, inter-group relations, etc.) need improvement. A closely related assumption is that no organizational form is perfect, that every organizational form has strengths and weaknesses. The process consultant would urge any manager with whom he is working not to leap into an action program, particularly if it involves any kind of changes in organizational structure, until the organization itself has done a thorough diagnosis and assessment of the strengths and weaknesses of the present structure.

The importance of *joint* diagnosis derives from the fact that the consultant can seldom learn enough about the organization to really know what a better course of action would be for that *particular group* of people with their *particular* sets of traditions, styles and personalities. However, the consultant can help the manager to become a sufficiently good diagnostician himself, and can provide enough alternatives, to enable the manager to solve the problem. This last point highlights another assumption underlying P-C: problems will stay solved longer and be solved more effectively if the organization solves its own problems; the consultant has a role in teaching diagnostic and problem-solving skills but he should not work on the actual concrete problem himself.

*   *   *   *   *

---

* Edgar H. Schein, *Process Consultation: Its Role in Organization Development,* 1969, Addison-Wesley, Reading, Mass. Excerpts from pp. 3, 5–7, 9.

† Dr. Schein is a Professor of Industrial Psychology at The Massachusetts Institute of Technology.

Process consultation . . . focuses on joint diagnosis and the passing on to the client of diagnostic skills. The consultant may recognize early in his work what some of the problems are in the organization and how they might be solved. He does not advance them prematurely, however, for two reasons. One, he may be wrong and may damage his relationship with the client by a hasty diagnosis which turns out to be wrong. Two, he recognizes that even if he is right, the client is likely to be defensive, to not listen to the diagnosis, to misunderstand what the consultant is saying, and to argue with it.

It is a key assumption underlying P-C that the client must learn to see the problem himself, to share in the diagnosis, and to be actively *involved* in generating a remedy. The process consultant may play a key role in helping to sharpen the diagnosis and in providing alternative remedies which may not have occurred to the client. But he encourages the client to make the ultimate decision as to what remedy to apply. Again, the consultant does this on the assumption that if he teaches the client to diagnose and remedy situations, problems will be solved more permanently and the client will be able to solve new problems as they arise.

It should be emphasized that the process consultant may or may not be expert in solving the particular problem which is uncovered. The important point in P-C is that such expertise is less relevant than are the skills of involving the client in self-diagnosis and helping him to find a remedy which fits his particular situation and his unique set of needs. The process consultant must be an expert in how to diagnose and how to develop a helping relationship. He does not need to be an expert on production, marketing, finance, and the like. . . .

P-C is a set of activities on the part of the consultant which help the client to perceive, understand, and act upon process events which occur in the client's environment.

The process consultant seeks to give the client "insight" into what is going on around him, within him, and between him and other people. The events to be observed and learned from are primarily the various human actions which occur in the normal flow of work, in the conduct of meetings, and in formal or informal encounters between members of the organization. Of particular relevance are the client's own actions and their impact on other people.

It should be noted that this definition brings in several new concepts and assumptions, relating in general to what one looks for in making one's *diagnosis*. The important elements to study in an organization are the human processes which occur. A good diagnosis of an organizational problem may go beyond an analysis of such processes but it cannot afford to ignore them. By implication, the process consultant is primarily an expert on processes at the individual, interpersonal, and intergroup levels. His expertise may go beyond these areas, but it must at the minimum include them. Improvement in organizational effectiveness will occur through effective problem finding in the human process area, which in turn will depend upon the ability of managers to learn diagnostic skills through exposure to P-C.

I am not contending that focusing on human processes is the *only* path to increasing organizational effectiveness. Obviously there is room in most organizations for improved production, financial, marketing, and other processes. I am arguing, however, that the various functions which make up an organization are always mediated by the interactions of people, so that the organization can never escape its human process. . . . As long as organizations are networks of people, there will be processes occurring between them. Therefore, it is obvious that the better understood and better diagnosed these processes are, the greater will be the chances of finding solutions to technical problems which will be accepted and used by the members of the organization.

From

AN ORGANIZATION DEVELOPMENT APPROACH TO CONSULTING*

By David A. Kolb and Alan L. Frohman†

The model for planned change presented below will be most appropriate if the consultant's interventions in the client system are placed in the context of a total organizational development program. Here, organizational development refers not to the content of the consultant intervention but to the manner in which it is carried out. More specifically, an intervention is an organizational development intervention if:

1. It is not undertaken as an isolated event but rather with consideration for its impact on the organization as a total system. That is, it is part of a total plan for organization improvement.[1]

2. It is directed not only at solving the organization's immediate problem but also at improving the organization's ability to anticipate and solve similar problems. The result is an increase in the ecological wisdom of the organization through improvement of its ability to survive and grow in its environment.

While there may be some consulting relationships for which this organizational development approach is not appropriate, it is our observation that much of the dissatisfaction with consulting interventions arises from a failure to deal with these two issues.

Model for Planned Change

*   *   *   *   *

The model focuses on two central issues which are highly interrelated. One concerns the relationship between client and consultant. To whom in the client

---

* From "An Organizational Development Approach to Consulting" by David A. Kolb and Alan L. Frohman, *Sloan Management Review*, pp. 51–64. © 1970 by the Industrial Management Review Association; all rights reserved.

† Dr. Kolb is Professor of Industrial Psychology and Management at The Massachusetts Institute of Technology. Dr. Frohman is a consultant with Pugh-Roberts, Associates.

[1] Beckhard, *Organization Development: Strategies and Models.* Reading, Mass., Addison-Wesley, 1969, p. 100. Beckhard defines organization development as "an effort (1) *planned*, (2) *organization-wide*, and (3) *managed from the top*, to (4) increase *organization effectiveness* and *health* through (5) *planned interventions* in the organization's 'processes', using *behavioral-science* knowledge."

organization does the consultant relate? Who influences whom? How open will the client and the consultant be with each other? The second concerns the nature of the work. How is the problem defined? What solutions are considered? It is typically the second issue that receives the most attention from consultants even though relationship factors also strongly affect the course and outcome of consulting work. These two issues can be considered within the framework of a dynamic, seven-stage model of the planned change process: scouting, entry, diagnosis, planning, action, evaluation, and termination (see Figure 1). These stages are by

FIGURE 1
Process of Planned Change

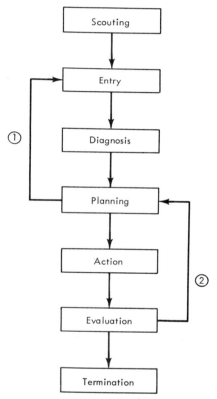

no means clear cut in practice. They may occur sequentially or simultaneously. However, the articulation of each stage provides a convenient way for the consultant to conceptualize and recognize the stages in his practice.

In the figure, the arrows connecting the stages illustrate the general developmental nature of the model. The first feedback loop, from planning to entry, defines the need for continuing renegotiation with the client in the light of diagnosis and planning activities. The second loop, from evaluation to planning, defines the need for using the evaluations of previous actions to modify planning activities. The central issues in the consulting process and their implications are summarized below for each stage in the change process. Successful intervention in the client system and implementation of change is directly related to the successful resolution of these issues.

Scouting. In the scouting phase, neither the client nor the consultant has committed himself to working with the other. Each is free to explore the potential relationship in order to obtain some preliminary data about the other. The client system is searching for resources and solutions to its problems. An invitation to a consultant to work with the client is based on the client's perception that the consultant can help in some way.

The consultant is also scouting his own interests, values, and priorities in order to decide whether this client system is one with which he wants to work. Often the first scouting goal is to answer the question: What about their perception of the problem and myself led them to contact me? An investigation of the client's actions prior to calling the consultant can be helpful here. . . .

In making his decision, the consultant may want to look at the following characteristics of the client system: (1) major resources, (2) major limitations, (3) important social and cultural norms and values, (4) major subsystems within the overall system (departments, divisions, subsidiaries), (5) gross interrelationships among major subsystems, (6) attitudes toward change, authority, outsiders, (7) relationship between client system and other systems in its environment (competitors, neighbors, regulating agencies), and (8) motivation of the client system to improve itself. In assessing these characteristics there is, of course, some danger of stereotyping the client as a result of insufficient evidence. Detailed assessment in most cases will have to wait until the diagnosis stage.

The most important result of this preliminary assessment is the choice of a formal entry point in the client system. In choosing an appropriate one, the interrelationships among the various units of the system are especially important. The acceptance and implementation of change most often requires that the recognized power structure of the system be used to establish the change. If one's initial contacts are with the deviant members of the organization, they may be very willing to accept a change for the system. But they are also likely to have little influence with the established authorities in the system.

    * * * * *

Entry. Once the entry point has been selected, the consultant and the client system, through the entry representative, begin to negotiate a contract. In its use here, the word "contract" implies more than a legal document agreed upon at the outset of the project.[2] The contract will define if and how the succeeding stages of the planned change process will be carried out. The emphasis is on a continuing process of sharing the expectations of the consultant and the client system and agreeing on the contributions to be made by both parties. Mark Frohman has listed 10 areas in which agreement over expectations is important in order to develop an effective working relationship.[3] (1) the consultant's and the client's goals for the project, (2) broad definition of the problem (to be redefined as the relationship progresses), (3) relationship of the problem to the overall system, (4) client re-

---

[2] E. Schein, *Process Consultation: Its Role in Organization Development.* Reading, Mass., Addison-Wesley, 1969.

[3] M. Frohman, "Conceptualizing a Helping Relationship," Ann Arbor, Institute for Social Research Center for Research on Utilization of Scientific Knowledge, 1968 (mimeo).

sources and abilities applicable to the problem, (5) consultant resources and abilities applicable to the problem, (6) broad mode of approach to the problem, (7) nature of the consultant/client relationship, (8) expected benefits for the client, (9) expect benefits for the consultant, and (10) ability of one party to influence the other.

Perhaps the most important issue in the negotiation process is power—gaining the influence necessary to work effectively in the client system. The four primary sources of power are: (1) legitimately constituted authority in the system, (2) expert power (the prestige of the consultant or the compelling logic of a solution, for example), (3) coercive power, and (4) trust-based power (the informal influence that flows from collaborative problem definition and solution). While in most cases all four types of power are used, trust-based power is particularly critical to the success of those planned change efforts where the system's formal power structure is the cause of the problem to be solved.

*   *   *   *   *

As the planned change process progresses and new information is gathered, it may be necessary to renegotiate the contract (see Figure 1). For example, the nature of the problem may change, the resources needed for its solution may increase or decrease, the consultant's particular expertise may become more or less relevant to the client system. As the diagnosis and planning stages proceed, the entry point into the client system may have to shift or expand to include those parts of the system which are affected by and/or responsible for the problem.

Diagnosis.   The diagnostic phase focuses on four elements: the client's felt problem, the client's goals, the client's resources, and the consultant's resources. Starting the diagnosis with the client's felt problem means something more than simply copying his words. It involves appreciating the client system's culture and language, seeiang events the way the client see them. This empathy on the part of the consultant facilitates his ability to meet the client's needs and insures the client's involvement in the diagnostic process.

The first step in defining the specific problem to be attacked is to identify the subpart(s) of the system where the problem is located and the interrelationships between the subpart and the other parts of the system. This is necessary in order to anticipate the effect of a change in one part of the system on other aspects of the system's functioning. If more and/or different problems are identified as the diagnosis progresses, the client and consultant can assign priorities and focus attention on the most important problem or the problem which must be solved before other problems can be attacked.

The second step is to define the goals of the client system. What is the desired state toward which the client is striving? If goals are operationally defined, they can give direction to a meaningful, lasting solution of the problem and can place the problem in the context of the organization's total development.

The third and fourth elements assessed in the diagnostic processes are the client's and the consultant's resources for improving the situation. One particularly important variable to consider is motivation and readiness for change on the part of both the client system and the consultant. Is the client system really committed to solution of the problem? Are the key individuals responsible for implementing the change committed? What are the consultant's motives—prestige, genuine desire to help, scientific experimentation? The consultant should look especially for resources internal to the client system which can be developed and utilized to solve the problem. In this way the development of internal resources is accelerated and dependency on the consultant is reduced.

*   *   *   *   *

Planning. The creation of plans for change should proceed cooperatively with the client to insure that the plans are appropriate to his needs, and that he will understand them and be committed to their execution. The first planning step is to define the specific behavioral objectives to be achieved by the change. . . . The formulation of specific objectives also makes the evaluation task easier.

Once clear-cut objectives have been established, alternative solutions or change strategies can be generated. Later, when choosing among the alternatives, an attempt should be made to simulate the consequences of each action plan. This can be done simply by thinking through the implications of each change strategy, or by using more sophisticated simulation methods.

Each alternative can be classified on two dimensions: the source of power used to implement the intervention (formal power, expert power, coercive power, and trust-based power) and the organizational subsystem to which the intervention is addressed. The six organizational subsystems are . . .—

1. The People Subsystem . . .

*   *   *   *   *

2. The Authority Subsystem . . .

*   *   *   *   *

3. The Information Subsystem . . .

*   *   *   *   *

4. The Task Subsystem . . .

*   *   *   *   *

5. The Policy/Culture Subsystem . . .

*   *   *   *   *

6. The Environmental Subsystem . . .

*   *   *   *   *

The four sources of power and the six organizational subsystems can be combined to form a check-list to be used by the consultant when planning or executing any action intervention. The primary purpose of the check-list is to remind the consultant that a change in one subsystem will affect other organizational subsystems. The list can be useful for selecting the best leverage point and for identifying the other subsystems most likely to be affected by the intervention.

*   *   *   *   *

The check list can also be useful for identifying the sources of power available for bringing about change and for determining which source, or combination of sources, is the most appropriate for the type of intervention planned. Certain combinations may not be enough to implement even the most optimal plan. . . .

Action. In the action phase, the best change strategy developed in the planning phase is implemented. If the work of the previous four phases has been done well, the action plan should proceed smoothly. Hitches or problems can usually be traced to unresolved issues in the early phases: a failure to diagnose the system adequately, a failure to anticipate all the consequences of the action in the planning phase. If these errors are not so great as to disrupt the total change effort, they can become useful "critical incidents" for learning about the client system.

*   *   *   *   *

Evaluation. The tradition in the scientific evaluation of change projects has been to separate the evaluation phase from the action phase. To insure unbiased results, an independent researcher is often hired to evaluate the change efforts. While this approach has some benefit from the standpoint of scientific objectivity, it has some cost in terms of the effective implementation of change. It should be clear from our model that we see the evaluation phase as an integrated part of the change process.

*   *   *   *   *

To decrease the dependency on the consultant and develop within the client system the ability to use the information generated for self-analysis, the client should monitor the progress of the action phase and evaluate the data himself. The results of the evaluation stage determine whether the change project moves to the termination stage or returns to the planning stage for further action planning and perhaps to the entry stage for further contract negotiation with the client.

Termination. The consultant-client relationship is by definition temporary. Yet most consulting relationships are conceived to bring about some permanent or far-reaching improvement in the client system's functioning. The issue of termination must therefore be given attention throughout the relationship. In the initial entry contract, the conditions of termination should be discussed and a tentative agreement reached. These conditions should be continually open for renegotiation and become clearer as the relationship progresses.

*   *   *   *   *

On the Developmental Nature of the Consulting Process

In closing, we would like to share some of our speculations about the developmental regularity of the seven stages outlined above. Following Erikson's child developmental model,[4] Figure 2 depicts a developmental matrix. The vertical axis defines the seven stages of the consulting processs in developmental order; the horizontal axis designates the actual behavior of the consultant. The white boxes represent the "normal" developmental path of a consulting relationship as outlined in the paper. On this path, the consultant resolves the issues of the scouting stage before proceeding to the issues of the entry stage; he then resolves these issues before confronting diagnosis issues, and so on.

Horizontal movement in the matrix represents a fixation—a failure to resolve the issues of one stage before proceeding to the next. The consultant represented by arrow 1, for example, has not resolved the scouting issue of selecting an appropriate entry point. Thus, he is forced in the entry stage to continue his search for a point of entry under the pretext of negotiating a contract. Vertical movement in the matrix represents arrested development—a failure to confront the issues of the next stage. Consultant 2, for example, may see an entry point, but for some reason he is reluctant to press forward toward a contract with the client. Perhaps the most common case of arrested development occurs in the action-evaluation stages (consultant 2'). In this case, the consultant, for a complex set of reasons, cannot bring himself to evaluate his actions and so continues these actions with his client.

---

[4] See E. Erikson, *Childhood and Society.* New York, Norton, 1950.

FIGURE 2
Developmental Model of Consultation Process

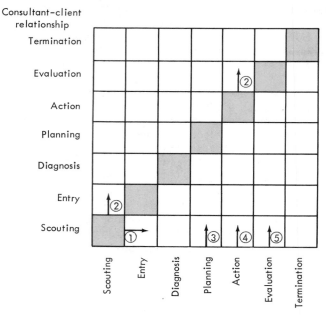

Consultant behavior

Another typical consulting strategy can be examined in this matrix. Some consultants—the planner (arrow 3) the action specialist (arrow 4), and the evaluator (arrow 5), for example—see themselves as specialists. These inexperienced consultants may choose to ignore the fact that their speciality is but one part of the client system's problem solving process. The result is a plan that is not seen by the people with the power to implement it (scouting is ignored) or a plan that has no commitment from the people who are to carry it out (entry issues are ignored) or a plan that is inappropriate for the client (diagnosis is ignored). Similar problems can be identified in evaluation studies. The action specialist, however, can cause the most difficulty.

Consultants can become so committed to their particular "bag," be it sensitivity training, achievement motivation, or information systems, that they become salesmen for their "product" rather than consultants whose commitment is to organizational development. It is often these salesmen who most lament the organization's resistance to change.

The consultant-client relationship, like any human relationship, can never be reduced to a set of mechanistic rules. We believe, however, that consulting relationships can be improved and organizational changes better implemented if consultant and client attend to the issues and problems raised in each of the seven developmental stages. This model provides no pat answers, but it will hopefully supply some guideposts along the often confusing and difficult path to organization improvement.

19. SHOE CORPORATION OF ILLINOIS

Case Introduction

SYNOPSIS

The Shoe Corporation of Illinois (SCI) is a small shoe manufacturing firm which specializes in low-priced shoes that are copied from leading fashion designers of New York and Europe. Its flexibility gives it a competitive advantage over larger producers in the shoe industry and enables S.C.I. to fill a niche in the industry. However, its flexibility also gives rise to problems of integration between production, sales, and design. The introduction of new models requires special handling and is disruptive for production. This results in some problems between the styling manager and production. New styles also require special practices on the part of salesmen who have established informal integrative practices with Freeman, the statistician, to process new orders. These informal arrangements deviate from formal company procedures. Flynn, the S.C.I. designer, recommended that S.C.I. introduce original designs but this recommendation was disapproved by the president. Flynn persisted in his idea and has worked secretly with Freeman to introduce two original models which yielded very different results.

WHY THIS CASE IS INCLUDED

This case provides an opportunity to analyze two problems frequently facing organizations: the problem of integration and the problem of motivation as it relates to broader questions of corporate policy. Firms operating in a turbulent environment must be highly flexible if they are to survive. Such flexibility presents problems of integration which are manifested in numerous technical problems as well as the human problems of organizational conflict. The latter type of problems bring into focus a number of structural alternatives which an organizational policy maker can consider.

It is often recognized that an organization needs to provide an opportunity for individual growth if individuals are to remain highly motivated. This case can be used to illustrate that questions of individual growth can have far reaching implications for corporate policy and especially for marketing policy as is the case here. A change in marketing policy can involve a requirement for changes in organizational structure, investments, long-range commitments, and ultimate questions of corporate identity. These issues get to the heart of corporate policy and must be carefully considered before a change is entertained.

Diagnostic and Predictive Questions

The readings included with this case are marked (*). The author index at the end of this book locates the other readings.

1. Based on the information available in the case, what kind of market structure would you say is present in the shoe industry? What type of competition seems to characterize this industry?

> Read: *Stonier and Hague, *A Textbook of Economic Theory,* pp. 123–26, 162–64, 182–83, 189, 197–99, 204–5, 208. Those wishing additional information on market structure may consult in the library, *Managerial Economics,* by Joel Dean, 1951, Prentice-Hall, Inc., pp. 329–335.

2. Why are larger competitors able to undercut the prices of the Shoe Corporation of Illinois (S.C.I.) on "stable" shoes? What would S.C.I. probably have to do to become competitive on these product lines?

> Note: This question may be approached by common sense. Imagine that Shoe Corporation of Illinois has $625,000 invested in certain shoe machinery which produces 12,000 pairs of shoes a year. This machinery depreciates $62,500 per year until it wears out in ten years. What is the fixed cost per unit of shoes? Now suppose that a much larger company sells 500,000 pairs and invests $15,000,000 in machines which will wear out in ten years. The depreciation per year is $1,-500,000. What is the fixed unit cost per pair of shoes?
>
> Another approach to this question might be more technical and precise application of microeconomic theory. Study the long-run price curves in any economics text. For example, Milton H. Spencer and Louis Siegelman, *Managerial Economics: Decision Making and Forward Planning,* Richard D. Irwin, Inc., Homewood, Illinois, 1959, pp. 242–48, 202–12.

3. Corporate strategy is often based upon some advantage a particular corporation has relative to other firms in the industry. Sometimes a firm seeks to identify itself in a niche based upon some unique advantage which can serve as a basis of specialization that a firm enjoys more than its competitors. Alternatively, a firm can develop competitive strength which is more broadly based due to economies of scale or diversification schemes. What approaches seem to be used by Brown Shoe and by S.C.I.? Evaluate the corporate strategy of S.C.I. based upon its compatibility with the structure of the industry and upon the criteria offered by Tilles.

> Read: Readings for Questions 1 and 2 above. Tilles, "How to Evaluate Corporate Strategy."

4. Marketing strategy is an important policy area for many business organizations. What is the basis of the marketing strategy used by S.C.I.? Does the introduction of original designs by Mr. Flynn suggest any major changes in that market policy?

Read: Pessemier, *New Product Decisions*, pp. 8–10. *Beckman and Davidson, *Marketing*, pp. 689–91. (For those who want a more thorough discussion consult Alfred R. Oxenfeldt, *Executive Action in Marketing*, Wadsworth Publishing Company, Inc., 1966, pp. 332–339. Not included in this volume.)

5. Total production costs can be decreased up to a point by increasing the quantity of a product produced per production run. Such a procedure reduces the scheduling changes and influences the costs of the inventory system because lot size is directly related to setup costs per unit produced. What would be the likely effect on total inventory costs of minimizing production costs through using "optimum" production quantities?

Note: Optimum production quantities means roughly "just the right quantity of output," taking into account various factors which cause the cost of a pair of shoes to increase. There are many such factors, such as handling and storage costs, capital cost of shoes standing in inventory, and costs that depend on the lot size of an item produced— the setup costs. These include clerical cost of preparing these customer orders and converting them to production schedules, down time of machines while changing from one style to another, and so on. For some aid in answering this question, see Elwood Buffa, *Modern Production Management*, pp. 442–43, 450–51, 471 (in this volume), or "Basic Inventory Models," by the same author in his *Production-Inventory Systems: Planning and Control*, Richard D. Irwin, Inc., Homewood, Illinois, 1968, pp. 49–58.

6. In addition to inventory costs being inversely related to total setup costs of production, sales revenue might be similarly related to production costs. What is the likely effect of the special treatment afforded "pilot runs" on production costs? What is the likely effect of this special handling on sales revenue?

Read: Rapoport and Drews, "Mathematical Approach to Long Range Planning."

7. Bureaucracies are often characterized by a high reliance on rules, written procedures, precise job descriptions, and an organizational hierarchy. It is sometimes argued that these characteristics encourage efficiency at the expense of innovation and flexibility. Would you classify S.C.I. as a bureaucracy? Why do you think Ferguson is insisting that salesmen send new orders to him instead of to Freeman?

Read: Thompson, *Modern Organizations*, pp. 4–6, 12–13, 19–21, 63–65, 77–78. Merton, "Bureaucratic Structure and Personality."

8. What are the possible explanations for Flynn's recommendation and subsequent action to promote shoes designed by S.C.I.? What might explain Freeman's cooperation with Flynn and Freeman's special interest in new designs? Is there any conflict between the motivational factors influencing these two men and the broader interests of S.C.I.?

Read: Maslow, *Motivation and Personality*, pp. 80–94. Argyris, *Per-*

sonality and Organization, pp. 27–31, 33–51, 66–67, 77–90, 95, 103–4, 123–25, 130, 137–39, 150, 153–55, 157. Gellerman, *Motivation and Productivity,* pp. 108–18.

9. What do you think is the cause of the problems between Lawson and Robbins? Are the causes of these problems different from those which resulted in problems among Ferguson, Freeman, and the salesmen?

Read: Litterer, "Conflict in Organization: A Re-Examination." *Seiler, "Diagnosing Interdepartmental Conflict." *Lawrence and Lorsch, "New Management Job: The Integrator."

POLICY QUESTIONS

10. Assume that you are a consultant hired by Allison to review and evaluate S.C.I. corporate policy. You are asked to specifically look at marketing policy. Write a letter to the president summarizing the advantages and disadvantages of introducing original designs and recommend the marketing policy you feel is most appropriate.

Read: See readings for Questions 1 through 4 above.

11. One approach to avoid some of the adverse effects of a bureaucratic organization is through the use of participative management. To what extent does S.C.I. use participative management? What are the effects of the use of participative management on the authority structure of S.C.I.? Is this causing other problems?

Read: McGregor, *The Human Side of Enterprise,* pp. 124–31, 172–75.

12. What should Allison do to insure that his managers remain highly motivated? In order to answer this question, see if you can use path goal analysis to outline the action to motivate Flynn, Ferguson, Freeman, and Robbins.

Read: Readings for Questions 8 above. *Evans, "Leadership and Motivation: A Core Concept."

13. How would the establishment of an "integrator" position in the organization structure of S.C.I. help solve the various technical problems? How might it solve the various human problems?

Read: See readings for Question 9 above.

QUESTIONS FOR ORIGINAL STUDENT WORK
IN ANALYSIS AND POLICY

14. While reflecting on case facts, what additional theories from prior education give you insights as to "what is going on" in S.C.I.? As to what might be predicted to happen in the future?

15. Other than the policy questions asked by the authors, what pragmatic ways can you think of to state the practical problems faced by executives in the case?

Case Text*

Shoe Corporation of Illinois produces a line of women's shoes that sell in the lower-price market, for $11.95 to $13.95 per pair. Profits averaged 25¢ to 30¢ per pair ten years ago, but, according to the president and the controller, labor and materials costs have risen so much in the intervening period that profits today average only 15¢ to 20¢ per pair.

Production at both of the company's plants totals 12,500 pairs per day. The two factories are located within a radius of 60 miles of Chicago: one at Centerville, which produces 4,500 pairs per day, and the other at Meadowvale, which produces 8,000 pairs per day. Company headquarters is located in a building adjacent to the Centerville plant.

It is difficult to give an accurate picture of the number of items in the company's product line. Shoes change in style perhaps more rapidly than any other style product, including garments. This is so chiefly because it is possible to change production processes quickly, and because historically, each company, in attempting to get ahead of competitors, gradually made style changes ever more frequently. At present, including both major and minor style changes, S.C.I. offers between 100 and 120 different products to customers each year.

A partial organization chart, showing the departments involved in this case, appears in Exhibit 1.

COMPETITIVE STRUCTURE OF THE INDUSTRY

Very large general shoe houses, such as International and Brown, carry a line of ladies shoes and are able to undercut prices charged by Shoe Corporation of Illinois, principally because of the policy in the big companies of producing large numbers of "stable" shoes, such as the plain pump and the loafer. They do not attempt to change styles as rapidly as their smaller competitors. Thus, without constant changes in production processes and sales presentations, they are able to keep costs substantially lower.

Charles F. Allison, the president of Shoe Corporation of Illinois, feels that the only way for a small independent company to be competitive is to change styles frequently, taking advantage of the flexibility of a small organization to create designs that appeal to customers. Thus, demand can be created, and a price set high enough, to make a profit. Allison, indicidentally, appears to have an artistic talent in styling, and a record of successful judgments in approving high-volume styles over the years.

Regarding Illinois' differences from its large competitors, Allison says:

---
* Copyright 1973 by Charles E. Summer. Names and places have been disguised.

EXHIBIT 1
Partial Organization Chart of Shoe Corporation of Illinois

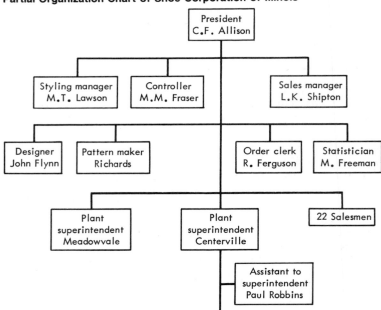

"You see, Brown and International Shoe Company both produce hundreds of thousands of the same pair of shoes. They store them in inventory at their factories. Their customers, the large wholesalers and retailers, simply know their line and send in orders. They do not have to change styles nearly as often as we do. Sometimes I wish we could do that, too. It makes for a much more stable and orderly system. There is also less friction between people inside the company. The salesmen always know what they're selling, the production people know what is expected of them. The plant personnel are not shook up so often by someone coming in one morning and tampering with their machine lines or their schedules. The styling people are not shook up so often by the plant saying 'we can't do your new style the way you want it'."

MAJOR STYLE CHANGES

The decision about whether to put a certain style into production requires information from a number of different people. Here is what typically happens in the company. It may be helpful to follow the organization chart in tracing the procedure.

M. T. Lawson, the style manager, and his designer, John Flynn, originate most of the ideas about shape, size of heel, use of flat sole or heels, and findings (the term used for ornaments attached to, but not part of, the shoes—bows, straps, and so forth). They get their ideas principally from reading style and trade magazines or by copying a top-flight designer. Lawson corresponds with publications and friends in large stores in New York, Rome, and Paris in order to obtain by air mail pictures and samples of up-to-the-minute style innovations.

When Lawson decides on a design, he takes a sketch to Allison, who either approves or disapproves it. If Allison approves, he (Allison) then passes the sketch on to Shipton, the sales manager, to find out what lasts (widths) should be chosen. Shipton, in turn, simply forwards the design to Martin Freeman, a statistician in the sales department, who maintains summary information on customer demand for colors and lasts.

To compile this information, Freeman visits salesmen twice a year to get their opinions on the colors and lasts that are selling best, and he keeps records of shipments by color and by last. For these needs, he simply totals data that is sent to him by the shipping foreman in each of the two plants.

When Freeman has decided on the lasts and colors, he sends Allison a form that lists the colors and lasts in which the shoe should be produced. Allison, if he approves this list, forwards the information to Lawson, who passes it on to Richards, an expert pattern maker. Richards makes a paper pattern and constructs a prototype in leather and paper, sends this to Lawson, who in turn approves or disapproves it. He forwards any approved prototype to Allison. Allison, if he too approves, notifies Lawson, who takes the prototype to Paul Robbins, assistant to the superintendent of the Centerville plant. Only this plant produces small quantities of new or experimental shoe styles. Such production is referred to as a "pilot run" by executives at the plant.

Robbins then literally carries the prototype through the six production departments of the plant—from cutting to finish—discussing it with each foreman, who in turn works with men on the machines in having a sample lot of several thousand pairs made.

When the finished lot is delivered by the finishing foreman to the shipping foreman (because of the importance of styling, Allison has directed that each foreman personally deliver styling goods in process to the foreman of the next department), the latter holds the inventory in storage and sends one pair each to Allison and Lawson. If they approve of the finished product, Allison instructs the shipping foreman to mail samples to each of the company's 22 salesmen throughout the country. Salesmen have instructions to take the samples immediately (within one week) to at least ten customers. Orders for already established shoes are normally sent to Ralph Ferguson, a clerk in Shipton's office, who records them and forwards them to the plant superintendents for production. In the case of first orders on new styles, however, salesmen have found by experience that Martin Freeman has a greater interest in the success of new "trials," so they rush orders to him, air mail, and he in turn places the first orders for a new style in the interoffice mail to plant superintendents. He then sends a duplicate of the order, mailed in by the salesmen, to Ferguson for entering in his statistical record of all orders received by the company.

Three weeks after the salesmen receive samples, Allison requires Ralph Ferguson to give him a tabulation of orders. At that time, he decides whether the salesmen should push the item and the superintendents should produce large quantities, or whether he will tell them that although existing orders will be produced, the item will be discontinued in a short time.

The procedures outlined here have, according to Allison:

> . . . *worked reasonably well. The average time from when Lawson decides on a design until we notify the Centerville plant to produce the pilot run is two weeks to a month. Of course, if we could speed that up, it would make the company just that much more secure in staying in the game against the big companies, and in taking sales away from our competitors. There seems to be endless bickering among people around here involved in the styling phase of the business. That's to be expected when you have to move fast—there isn't much time to stop and observe all of the social amenities. I have never thought that a formal organization chart would be good in this company—we've worked out a customary system here that functions well.*

M. T. Lawson, manager of styling, says that within his department all work seems to get out in minimum time, he also states that both Flynn and Richards are good employees, and skilled in their work. He mentioned that Flynn had been in to see him twice in the last year:

> . . . *to inquire about his (Flynn's) future in the company. He is 33 years old, and has three children. I know that he is eager to make money, and I assured him that over the years we can raise him right along from the $15,000 we are now paying. Actually, he has learned a lot about shoe styles since we hired him from the design department of a fabric company six years ago.*

John Flynn revealed that:

> *I was actually becoming dissatisfied with this job. All shoe companies copy styles—it's generally accepted practice within the industry. But I've picked up a real feel for designs, and several times I've suggested that the company make all its own original styles. We could make S.C.I. a style leader and also increase our volume. When I ask Lawson about this, he says it takes too much time for the designer to create originals—that we have all we can handle to do research in trade*

magazines and maintain contracts feeding us the results of experts. Besides, he says, our styles are standing the test of the market place.

"PROJECTS X AND Y"

Flynn also said that he and Martin Freeman had frequently talked about the styling problem. They felt that:

Allison is really a great president, and the company surely would be lost without him. However, we've seen times when he lost a lot of money on bad judgments in styles. Not many times—perhaps six or seven times in the last 18 months. Also, he is, of course, extremely busy as president of the corporation. He must look after everything from financing from the banks to bargaining with the union. The result is that he is sometimes unavailable to do his styling approvals for several days, or even two weeks. In a business like this, that kind of delay can cost money. It also makes him slightly edgy. It tends, at times when he has many other things to do, to make him look quickly at the styles we submit, or the prototypes Richards makes, or even the finished shoes that are sent for approval by the shipping foreman. Sometimes I worry that he makes two kinds of errors. He simply rubber stamps what we've done, in which sending them to him is simply a waste of time. At other times he makes snap judgments of his own, overruling those of us who have spent so much time and expertise on the shoe. We do think he has good judgment, but he himself has said at times that he wishes he had more time to concentrate on styling and approval of prototypes and final products.

Flynn further explained (and this was corroborated by Freeman) that the two had worked out two plans, which they referred to as "project X" and "project Y." In the first, Flynn created an original design that was not copied from existing styles. Freeman then gave special attention to color and last research for the shoe and recommended a color line that didn't exactly fit past records on consumer purchases—but one he and Flynn thought would provide "great consumer appeal." This design and color recommendation were accepted by Lawson and Allison; the shoe went into production and was one of the three top sellers during the calendar year. The latter two men did not know that the shoe was styled in a different way from the usual procedure.

The result of a second, similar project (Y) was put into production the next year, but this time sales were discontinued after three weeks.

PROBLEM BETWEEN LAWSON AND ROBBINS

Frequently, perhaps ten to twelve times a year, disagreement arises between Mel Lawson, manager of styling, and Paul Robbins, assistant to the superintendent of the Centerville plant. Robbins says that:

The styling people don't understand what it means to produce a shoe in the quantities that we do, and to make the changes in production that we have to. They dream up a style quickly, out of thin air. They do not realize that we have a lot of machines that have to be adjusted, and that some things they dream up take much longer on certain machines than others, thus creating a bottleneck in the production line. If they put a bow or strap in one position rather than others, it may mean we have to keep people idle on later machines while there is a pile-up on the sewing machines on which this complicated little operation is performed. This costs the plant money. Furthermore, there are times when they get the prototype here late, and the foremen and I either have to work overtime or the trial run won't get through in time to have new production runs on new styles, to take the plant capacity liberated by our stopping production on old styles. Lawson doesn't know much about production and sales and the whole company. I think all he does is to bring shoes down here to the plant sort of like a messenger boy. Why should he be so hard to get along with? He isn't getting paid any more than I am, and my position in the plant is just as important as his.

Lawson, in turn says that he has a difficult time getting along with Robbins:

There are many times when Robbins is just unreasonable. I take prototypes to him five or six times a month, and other minor style changes to him six or eight times. I tell him every time that we have problems in getting these ready, but he knows only about the plant, and telling him doesn't seem to do any good. When we first joined the company, we got along all right, but he has gotten harder and harder to get along with.

CERTAIN OTHER PROBLEMS THAT HAVE ARISEN

Ralph Ferguson, the clerk in the sales department who receives orders from salesmen and forwards totals for production schedules to the two plant superintendents, has complained that the salesmen and Freeman are bypassing him in their practice of sending experimental shoe orders to Freeman. He insists that his job description (one of only two written descriptions in the company) gives him responsibility for receiving *all* orders throughout the company and for maintaining historical statistics on shipments.

Both the salesmen and Freeman, on the other hand, say that before they started the new practice (that is, when Ferguson still received the experimental shoe orders), there were at least eight or ten instances a year when these were delayed from one to three days on Ferguson's desk. They report that Ferguson just wasn't interested in new styles, so the salesmen "just started sending them to Freeman." Ferguson acknowledged that there were times of short delay, but there were good reasons for them:

They (salesmen and Freeman) are so interested in new designs, colors, and lasts, that they can't understand the importance of a systematic handling of the whole *order procedure, including both old and new shoe styles. There must be accuracy. Sure, I give some priority to experimental orders, but sometimes when rush orders for existing company products are piling up, and when there's a lot of planning I have to do to allocate production between Centerville and Meadow-vale, I decide which comes first—processing of these, or processing the experimental shoe orders. Shipton is my boss, not the salesmen or Freeman. I'm going to insist that these orders come to me.*

Selected Readings

From

A TEXTBOOK OF ECONOMIC THEORY*

By Alfred W. Stonier and Douglas C. Hague†

PURE AND PERFECT COMPETITION

. . . We spoke in Chapter V of *pure competition* where demand for the product of the individual firm was infinitely elastic, so that the firm could sell all it wished at the existing market price, but was unable to alter the price by its own actions. . . . There are three fundamental prerequisites for the existence of pure competition between producers. These are as follows:

(a) Large Numbers

The first condition for pure competition in an industry is that there must be a large number of firms in the industry. This is essential, because only when there are many firms in an industry can each firm be sure that any action on its own part will have no noticeable effects on the price and output of the whole industry. . . .

(b) Homogeneous Products

Second, each of the firms in a "purely" competitive industry must be making a product which is accepted by customers as being identical, or *homogeneous,* with that made by all other producers in the industry. . . .

*　　*　　*　　*　　*

* Reprinted with permission from Alfred W. Stonier and Douglas C. Hague, *A Textbook of Economic Theory,* 1953, John Wiley & Sons, Inc. (pp. 123–26, 162–64, 182–83, 189, 197–99, 201, 204–5, 208).

† A. W. Stonier is Senior Lecturer in Political Economy, University College, London. D. C. Hague is Newton Chambers Professor of Economics in the University of Sheffield.

It is probably worth pointing out here that we have so far assumed, and shall continue to assume until further notice, that there is always pure competition *between buyers*. We have taken it for granted that the total number of buyers is very large, and that each one takes so small a proportion of the total sales of any good that no one buyer can alter the price of a good by his own actions. Buyers must therefore take prices as given. . . .

(c) Free Entry

The third fundamental condition which must be fulfilled if there is to be pure competition in an industry is that anyone who wishes to enter the industry must be allowed to do so. . . .

*   *   *   *   *

These three conditions, large numbers of firms, homogeneous products and free entry, between them ensure that there is pure competition in the sense that there is competition which is completely free from any monopoly elements. . . . One can, however, distinguish also between pure competition, which we have just defined, and "perfect" competition—a concept frequently used by economists. For there to be "perfect" competition, it is necessary to make some additional assumptions. In particular, it is necessary to assume that there is perfect knowledge on the part of all buyers and of all sellers about conditions in the market. In addition it is usual to assume complete mobility of factors of production between industries. It is also convenient when discussing perfect competition to make the assumption that all producers work sufficiently close to each other for there to be no transport costs. . . .

*   *   *   *   *

[IMPERFECT COMPETITION]

. . . We turn now . . . to a study of . . . imperfect competition. . . .

We shall continue to assume that there is perfect competition *between buyers*. . . . We shall also continue to assume that each consumer is "rational," . . .

So far as the individual firm is concerned we shall continue to assume that the sole aim of its entrepreneur is to earn maximum profits. . . . When competition is imperfect, there are no longer sufficient firms in the industry for a change in the output of any one of them to have a negligible effect on the output of the industry as a whole. . . .

*   *   *   *   *

. . . We shall discuss these various narrower types of imperfect competition in turn. . . .

Monopoly

Strictly interpreted, a "monopolist" is the sole producer of his product, and the distinction between the firm and the industry, both producing the same product, so important in perfect competition, goes. The firm of the monopolist is not only a firm, it is an industry. It is the only firm producing the product in question. . . .

*   *   *   *   *

Monopolistic Competition

         *   *   *   *   *

In the real world, . . . imperfect competition does not usually mean only one producer who has no closely related goods competing with his own—as we suggest when we talk of a monopolist. The great majority of imperfectly competitive producers in the real world produce goods which are very similar to those made by their rivals. It follows that such producers must always be very concerned about the way in which the actions of these rivals affect their own profits. This kind of situation is dealt with in economic theory by the analysis of what is called *monopolistic competition. . . .*

It is reasonable to suppose that in these circumstances the shape of the firm's average revenue curve will be determined not only by the tastes and whims of consumers, but also by the price-output decisions of rival producers. The problems of monopolistic competition are therefore more complicated than those of perfect competition. In perfect competition there is at any rate only one homogeneous commodity. In monopolistic competition there is differentiation of products. Products are not homogeneous, as in perfect competition, but neither are they only remote substitutes, as in monopoly. What this really means is that in monopolistic competition there are various "monopolists" competing with each other. These competing "monopolists" do not produce identical goods. Neither do they produce goods which are completely different. Product differentiation means that products are different in some ways, but not altogether so. "Branding," the use of attractive packets and wrappers, and the use of trade-marks and of trade-names will be the most usual methods by which products are differentiated, even if physically they are identical, or almost so. In addition, of course, it will be possible to make slight improvements or alterations in the physical constitution of a product to persuade consumers that it is rather superior to other similar products.

         *   *   *   *   *

. . . [T]he more closely competitive substitutes there are, the more elastic the demand for the product of any one firm in the "group" will be.

         *   *   *   *   *

Oligopoly

. . . Oligopoly . . . occurs where there are only a few sellers. It differs both from monopoly, where there is only one seller, and from perfect and monopolistic competition, where there are many. . . .

The simplest case of oligopoly occurs when there are only two sellers and is known as *duopoly*. Duopoly analysis raises all the fundamental problems of oligopoly.

         *   *   *   *   *

Oligopoly Without Product Differentiation

. . . The important feature of duopoly, with or without product differentiation, is that the individual producer has to consider very carefully what the indirect effects of his own decision to change price or output will be. Since, in duopoly without product differentiation, there are only two producers of identical goods, any price or output change by the first producer is bound to affect the second, whose reactions will in turn change the position of the first, and so on. The individual producer therefore has to acknowledge that he may change the whole situation in which he is producing in this indirect way if he changes his own price-output policy.

*   *   *   *   *

. . . Both firms are producing identical goods. So, if we continue to assume (as we must) that consumers are indifferent which producer they patronize when prices are the same for each firm's good, we cannot say how many consumers will go to A except on some assumption about what B's price is. . . . It will be a matter of pure accident whether *individual* consumers go to A or to B.

*   *   *   *   *

Oligopoly with Product Differentiation

Where there is oligopoly *with* product differentiation in any market, not only is the number of firms small but their products are also differentiated. . . .

. . . [I]n oligopoly *with* product differentiation the fact that products are somewhat different means that it may be possible for one producer to raise or lower his price without needing to fear either the loss of all his customers on the one hand, or an immediate response by his rival on the other.

In such a situation it is possible for consumers to be attached more or less firmly to one product rather than the other. So, the assumption that the producers will share the market equally, which we could make for duopoly without product differentiation, need no longer hold. . . .

*   *   *   *   *

A Classification of Market Situations

	Type of Market Situation	
Number of Firms	*Homogeneous Products*	*Differentiated Products*
Many firms	Perfect competition	Monopolistic competition
Few firms	Oligopoly without product differentiation	Oligopoly with product differentiation
One Firm	Monopoly	————

From

MARKETING*

By Theodore N. Beckman and William R. Davidson†

Low-Price Policies. Some vendors follow a policy of underselling competitors. A notable historical example is the famous R. H. Macy & Company department store in New York. Over a number of generations, its policy has been to sell at less than the shopped price for comparable items. More recently, this policy has been used by various discount houses, especially Masters, Inc., and E. J. Korvette, Inc., both of which operate a number of establishments in eastern markets, and Polk Bros. of Chicago. This price policy is by no means confined to the field of retailing. In the wholesaling of goods, arrangements are frequently made whereby the vendor agrees to supply his customers with merchandise at or below the lowest price quoted by competitors, thus following the policy of "meet or beat" competitors' prices.

There are some manufacturers who believe in and follow a low or lowest price policy. In some cases a low-price policy may be a relatively temporary expedient to meet conditions in an unsettled market. For example, the St. Joseph Lead Co. attracted considerable attention in 1960 with a policy announcement that it would discount any competitive posted price for zinc by one-half cent per pound.[1] This policy was adopted when prices for the commodity were very unsettled, and all suppliers were making special concessions of one form or another to customers. Buyers were uncertain about alternative costs available to them. Hence the policy announcement of this major supplier was a means of communicating to the trade that a customer could not likely do better by buying elsewhere. When market conditions become more settled in early 1961, and discounting of base selling prices diminished, St. Joseph rescinded its lowest price policy and reverted to its previous policy of selling at the market level.

A low-price policy, pursued on a continuing basis, is likely to succeed in markets in which there are considerable latent demands at lower prices, and the manufacturers most likely to do so are those with a relatively high physical efficiency. Such a policy tends to widen the market and to give the seller the opportunity of utilizing his facilities to best advantage. A bold and imaginative policy of low or greatly reduced prices can sometimes reach such broader bases of potential demand involving new applications that the low price becomes in itself a product innovation. This has been aptly illustrated as follows:[2]

"A new synthetic fiber, for example, may be so costly and high priced that it is used only for surgical and other very limited purposes. By dropping the price in anticipation of reduced costs, the hosiery and fine apparel markets may be reached; still further down the price scale, the rug, carpet, and industrial markets may be tapped."

---

* Theodore N. Beckman and William R. Davidson, *Marketing,* Seventh Edition. Copyright © 1962, The Ronald Press Company. (Excerpts from pp. 689–91.)

† The authors are both Professors of Marketing at Ohio State University.

[1] "Zinc Breathes Easier—and Hopes," *Business Week,* January 28, 1961, p. 103.

[2] Clare E. Griffin, "When Is Price Reduction Profitable?" *Harvard Business Review,* September–October, 1960, p. 129.

There are definite limits, however, to what may be deemed desirably low prices for any period of time. Unless the reduction is a matter of competitive necessity, no businessman can be expected to reduce his prices materially in the face of a belief that he would not be compensated by sufficient increases in sales volume and satisfactory profitability on the basis of cost and revenue factors applying to the larger volume marketed. Assuming a homogeneous product, the price of the product may be constant at a given time and no firm may be able to sell above the ruling price. No lower price, therefore, need be quoted in order to get the business. In fact, a further lowering of price may bring retaliatory action from competitors or at best may result in a permanent lowering of prices by all of them. In any event, when the basic policy is to sell at relatively low prices this is assigning to pricing a major and an offensive role in the marketing mix.

* * * * *

Selling at Relatively High Prices. Some firms find it possible to market products at a relatively high price. This is not ordinarily practical on a sustained basis unless there is a strong degree of market control. Such control may be achieved by significant differentiation in the physical attributes or the functioning of products which are protected by patents or which are manufactured according to complex or secret processes that are difficult to duplicate. In some cases significant differentiation may exist as a result of unusually successful promotional effort which has created an exceptional favorable enterprise or brand image. If the product is a complicated durable good, either consumer or business equipment, differentiation may exist in the form of an outstanding reputation for installation or maintenance service, which may be more important to the user than initial cost.

Selling at a relatively high price level may also be a temporary expedient under certain conditions. For example, a firm brings out a product which is entirely new in its class in some distinctive way, but feels that competitors will follow with similar product modifications after some period of time. The decision may be to price at a relatively high level initially, to recover product research, developmental, and promotional costs as quickly as possible, before it becomes necessary to meet intensive competition. As another example, relatively high price levels are sometimes established on new products or substantial product modifications in order "to try the market." The firm may be totally lacking in information about the nature of elasticity of demand. If it must actually experiment, it is much easier to start with a price that is too high and lower it later, if necessary, than to do the opposite.

When a firm decides to sell at relatively high prices, the assumption is that price is not a very important factor in getting or retaining business. The role of price in the marketing mix is nearly a negative one, having been subordinated almost completely to product development, advertising, or other ingredients. There remains, nevertheless the major management problem about deciding just what specific price to establish.

From

DIAGNOSING INTERDEPARTMENTAL CONFLICT*

By John A. Seiler †

"Purchasing and production are always at each other's throats. I don't know why they can't get along better."

"If the way research and engineering work together were typical for all departments in our company, our executive vice president would be out of a job. Somehow those guys are able to work out their disagreements."

"Sales and production just refuse to deal with each other. Every time a decision is needed, someone higher up has to do a lot of handholding or head-knocking. Why won't they bargain?"

*   *   *   *   *

TRADITIONAL EXPLANATIONS

Why are some interdepartmental relationships successful and others not? Managers typically find themselves advancing one or the other of these explanations:

One popular opinion is the "personality clash" theory, which holds that stubborn prejudices and differences in ingrained personal styles (none of which are actuated by organizational influences) are behind nonproductive relations. As compelling as this explanation often seems to be, it fails to account for the fact that we seldom, if ever, encounter a group composed of people with identical or even closely similar personalities. . . .

Another view holds that failure in interdepartmental relations is the result of "conflicting ideas." This theory asserts that nonproductive relations occur between groups whose respective memberships are so different in terms of skills, training, job activities, personal aspirations, and so on that they cannot possibly find a common area in which to communicate. While this explanation seems to apply to some nonproductive relations, it is not unheard of to find an advanced research group which works quite effectively with a nontechnical, highly consumer-oriented sales group. Seemingly, at least, groups can differ on many counts without a breakdown occurring in their relations. Furthermore, it is not unusual to find groups with remarkably similar points of view which seem to go out of their way to make trouble for each other. Something in addition to different points of view must be playing a part in forming the character of these relationships.

A third popular explanation for nonproductivity puts the blame on competition between groups for authority, power, and influence. Breakdowns occur because

* From "Diagnosing Interdepartmental Conflict," *Harvard Business Review,* Vol. 41, No. 5 (September–October 1963), excerpts from pp. 121–25, 128–32. Reprinted by permission. © 1963 by the President and Fellows of Harvard College; all rights reserved.

† The author is on the faculty of the Graduate School of Business Administration, Harvard University.

each department operates from an entrenched position which, if compromised, will bring the group nothing but defeat and loss of influence. Many nonproductive relationships seem to display characteristics of this kind. But if this theory is to be sufficient unto itself, the only productive relationship would be one in which either or both of the groups had no desire or opportunity for influence over the other. Under these conditions, passivity would seem to be a requirement for productivity. Yet the most highly productive relations appear to take place between aggressive, confident, and high-achievement departments. Apparently other determinants, in addition to competition for prestige and power, must be operating to make interdepartmental relations successful or unsuccessful.

*   *   *   *   *

BALANCE OF ENERGY

Fundamental to understanding why some relationships are productive and others less so is a recognition that people have limited energies. When a multitude of demands are made on us, we naturally assign priorities to them. If the demands for organizationally productive work take second place to other demands, then the organization loses out. Demands on departments can also be viewed in this way. If a department's energies are consumed by plottings of defense and attack, little time will be left for devotion to more fruitful business. Consequently, departments, too, must assign priorities to demands on their energy.

*   *   *   *   *

Group Control

The setting of priorities by groups is not much different. Groups are, after all, only interdependent individuals who keep their group membership because it is valuable to them. The uniqueness of a group, that which makes it more than the simple addition of its members' wishes and actions, lies in its ability to motivate member behavior toward goals which are attractive to the entire group but which are not attainable by any member alone. Primary among these goals, of course, and basic to group life in general, is the satisfaction of a person's need to belong to something. But groups provide more than simple social satisfaction to their members. They also provide protection from other groups and individuals. They contain power which can be used to gain liberties, self-respect, and prestige for their members. In return for these benefits, the member submits to group discipline.

When a group's existence is threatened by such changes as a formal reorganization which will disperse its members, by rumors of layoff or firing, or by technical change disrupting the relationships among members, the full energy of the group is mobilized. There is a tightening of member discipline, particularly centering on the activities most likely to thwart any alarming changes. On such occasions, the only "work" done is that which protects the group from jeopardy. On the other hand, when groups do not fear for their survival, but see before them a challenging opportunity to work together toward an end of positive value to the group, all their energies become absorbed by the project they are working on.

Energies freed from defense will seek outlets in activities which strengthen the group's ability to survive in the long run and which add zest to the life of its members. If the work formally available to the group is dull and lacking in challenge (or if other obstacles such as restrictive supervisory actions or lack of member skills get in the way), activity is likely to be predominantly social in character. If the work is challenging, and obstacles are not present to hinder its meeting the challenge, the group is likely to find its formal assignment a satisfying outlet for the application of its energy.[1]

Productive Focus on Task

Company A developed and manufactured ethical pharmaceuticals. The activities required to transform a product idea into a marketable item were performed in sequence by subunits of the research, engineering, and production departments. An idea would first take form in a research department test tube. It would then be evaluated by research chemists and chemical engineers in the pilot plant. Next, new process equipment would be designed by mechanical engineers and job designs laid out around the equipment by industrial engineers. Actual plant construction and placement of equipment were accomplished by construction engineers, and, finally, production responsibility was assumed by production chemists. The members of these formal units agreed that research had the highest prestige of all the work groups and that the relative prestige of the other units declined in the order in which each became actively involved in the new product sequence.

* * * * *

Company A had an outstanding reputation for important production innovations and rapid development of ideas into mass-production items. Nevertheless, there was frequent argument among research, engineering, and production as to who should take responsibility for the product at what point in the development sequence. Engineering wanted control at the pilot plant. Production wanted control from the time the product entered its physical domain. Research wanted control, as one of its members put it, "until the actual factory yield reaches the theoretical yield."

* * * * *

The physical, mental, and emotional energies of these departments appeared to be devoted to the work at hand to a very high degree. While not absent from their relationships, conflicts took the form of tension between the inherently opposing values of quality and economy. The result was a competitive balance between the extremes of both. Why was conflict not destructive in this situation? There are basically three reasons:

(1) Each of the three departments represented a social unit in which members could find not only satisfaction for their needs to belong, but also job interest, promotion opportunity, and so on. No one of these departments suffered from internal fragmentation.

(2) At each point of significant interdepartmental contact, the members of the interacting groups agreed on certain important ideas as to how work should be accomplished. Wherever technical interdependence required intergroup contact,

---

[1] The cases cited in this article have been taken from the case and project research files of the Harvard Business School and are reproduced by permission of the President and Fellows of Harvard College.

the groups tended to view each other and their common work with a markedly similar appreciation.

(3) The hierarchy of authority among the departments was identical to the informally agreed-upon prestige hierarchy among these departments. This hierarchy was determined by the technical work limits set by one department for another, and by the initiation of activity by one department for another. The work done by research, for example, limited what the chemical engineers could work on but, at the same time, was the impetus which set the chemical engineers to work on each new product. The same was true of relationships down through the development sequence.

Very simply, then, a man (or a group) told another what to do and when to do it, he did so as a member of a group of superior prestige, as agreed on by both groups. We might say that the orders which passed from one group to another were "legitimate," since most workers feel that it is legitimate in our society for a person of higher prestige to direct the activities of someone with less prestige, while it is illegitimate for the opposite to occur.

*   *   *   *   *

The three elements—*internal social stability, external value sharing* and *legitimate authority hierarchy*—comprise a triumvirate of measures which indicate the extent to which departmental energy will tend to be freed for productive work. These factors can be thought of as miniumum requirements for interdepartmental effectiveness. For, in their absence, it is highly unlikely that either intrinsically interesting work or encouragement from supervision will achieve much in the way of productivity increases.

*   *   *   *   *

VARYING VIEWPOINTS

In each of these four cases, the forces siphoning energy away from productive work have been of a particular kind. In each instance, relationships within groups were at least socially satisfactory. . . . The work of the various groups was intrinsically interesting to group members. Supervision was relatively permissive in allowing group members to "complicate" their lives about the work itself. Obviously, these elements are not always present in organized situations. Equally obvious from our cases is the fact that these elements, by themselves, do not result in effective interdepartmental relations, though they may be considered to contribute to such relations if other conditions are also met.

Focal Points

What the above cases focus on are the troubles caused by differences in point of view and legitimacy of authority. What these cases teach about group conflicts arising from these two trouble sources is just as true for our understanding of the interrelationships of individuals, for intergroup problems are only special cases of interpersonal issues. The only difference between them is the complexity of dealing with the problem, since the individual persons in our cases are representatives of social groups. Thus, their behavior cannot be modified by actions which are based on the assumption that groups respond exactly as do individuals. In short, the causes of conflict are similar, but the remedies are different.

What happens when groups suffer from authority and viewpoint conflicts is summarized in Exhibit I. Like any diagram dealing with a limited number of factors, Exhibit I runs the danger of implying that these cause-and-effect tendencies represent all that need be known about interdepartmental relations. Such an implication, were it intended, would, of course, be fatuous. Research in the area of interdepartmental problems has scarcely begun. Furthermore, we have already noted that other factors can be expected to intervene and render the exhibit's hypotheses, as they should be called, inoperative. Three of these factors have been emphasized—group cohesion, job interest, and supervisory practices.

Once we allow for these mitigating factors, however, we will find it useful to conceive of interdepartmental relations as though they were subject to the dominant influences cited in the diagram. The manager can make this concept more

EXHIBIT I
Dominant Influences in Interdepartmental Relations

	Where points of view are closely allied	Where points of view are in conflict
Where authority* is consistent with prestige differences	We will tend to find...	We will tend to find...
	...Collaboration and productive conflict	...Energies absorbed by efforts to force points of view on other groups. Relations will be formal and often arbitrated by outsiders.
Where authority is inconsistent with prestige differences	We will tend to find...	We will tend to find...
	...Energies devoted to regaining a "proper" authority relationship. Relations will usually be distant and between low hierarchical levels of the two groups (e.g., messenger).	...Energies initially expended on forcing points of view and righting authority relations, but the task will be so patently fruitless that the groups will break off contact rather than expose themselves to further threat.

* As indicated by work flow.

relevant personally if he reviews his own observations of interdepartmental conflict to see how they compare with the kind of analysis described here.

PLAN FOR ACTION

While the primary purpose of this article has been to explain certain types of interdepartmental problems, the question inevitably arises, "Suppose some sense can be made of interdepartmental difficulties by this kind of thinking; what then do we do with this understanding, even if it does prove to be acccurate? How would we go about applying it to lessen interdepartmental conflicts in our company?" Let's look at some action ideas which stem from what has already been said.

Stop, Look, & Listen

As frustrating as it might seem, the first suggestion is to stop to see if action is required and, if it is, whether it is feasible. It often may be wise to heed the admonishment (in reverse of the usual form), "Don't just do something, stand there!" The basis for this wisdom lies in the fact that formal organizations often display some of the characteristics of a biological organism, particularly insofar as the latter has some capacity to heal itself. The administrator, if this contention be true, may find the role of the modern physician attractive. He attempts to control the environment so that natural healing processes can take place unhindered within the human body. . . .

*   *   *   *   *

Types of Resolution

Our cases (and there are unlimited examples like them) have shown that some interdepartmental difficulties go beyond the capacity of the groups to resolve them at anything but a survival level, if that. That level may well be, and often is, intolerable for the organization as a whole. Let us look at the two alternative types of resolution.

First are the resolutions which arise in response to conflicts of authority. In such cases the work flow designed into the organization (e.g., the passage of blueprints from production engineering to production) violates the notions of the organization's members as to who legitimately should, by right of superior prestige, tell whom what to do. Although such problems are not restricted to particular hierarchical levels of the organization, they do tend to become more intense wherever prestige relations are ambiguous or under threat. The higher one goes in many organizations, the more these conditions tend to apply. There are several ways of resolving such problems:

(1) An obvious solution is to take whatever steps are available to reduce prestige ambiguity and threat. For example if . . . management had realized how pertinent production's resentment at being rated "second class" was to the interdepartmental problems in which it was involved, investigation might have produced ways of clarifying production's status and of enriching its participation in important decisions. . . .

(2) Another step in reducing the amount of nonproductivity in illegitimate authority relations is to reorganize subunits of the organization in such a way that authority and prestige become consistent. . . .

*   *   *   *   *

This crucial aspect of conflict resolution—receptivity to change—brings us to the second major strategy for helping departmental energies engage in constructive action instead of working against members of another department. This strategy involves what might be called intergroup counseling, therapy, or training. Conflicts in points of view are susceptible only to this strategy, short of complete personnel turnover in one or the other of the warring departments. And, because authority illegitimacy must inevitably engender conflict of viewpoint, it too can be mitigated, if only partially, by intergroup training. Several aspects of this strategy are worthy of attention, though the subject is a difficult and complex one.

Some studies show that intergroup conflict resolution hinges on a particular type of training which seeks an integration of viewpoints by making warring groups realize they are dependent on one another.[2] Such a strategy tends to work more readily when both groups fear some external threat to both of them. This idea is

---

[2] See *Intergroup Relations and Leadership*, edited by Muzafer Sherif (New York, John Wiley & Sons, Inc., 1962).

not greatly different from the idea contained in the observation that members of families may fight viciously with one another but when an outsider attacks one of the family, the family abandons its differences to fight together against the intruder. It seems obvious from the analysis presented in this article, however that this strategy is operable only when prestige-authority issues are not present.

A number of researchers, teachers, and managers have begun to explore more direct methods for reducing point-of-view conflict. Some have pointed out that bringing group representatives together to explore their differences is usually doomed to failure since representatives, if they are to remain such, must be loyal to their respective groups.[3] Simple measures to increase contact also appear fruitless, because negative stereotypes end up simply becoming reinforced by the contact.

Other measures have proved more effective. Although they vary in form, almost all of these contain the following basic element: *the groups in conflict must be brought together as totalities under special conditions.*[4] The goal of all of these conditions is to reduce individual and group anxieties sufficiently so that a point of view can not only be made explicit but can be heard by those who do not share it. This procedure requires not only considerable candor between groups, but also candor within each group and within the individual himself. Naturally, sessions in which such training is supposed to take place can be extremely threatening and should be mediated by an external agent to keep threat within manageable bounds and help guide the groups into explorative rather than recriminative behavior.[5]

*   *   *   *   *

Such a pursuit, carried on openly and sincerely, cannot help but raise issues of interdepartmental ambiguity, illegitimacy, and conflicting points of view to a level where they can be re-examined and dealt with. An easy process? No. But as "old wives' tales" have told us, no remedy is without pain.

From

NEW MANAGEMENT JOB: THE INTEGRATOR*

By Paul R. Lawrence and Jay W. Lorsch†

What will be new and unique about organizational structures and management practices of business enterprises that are their industries' competitive leaders a

---

[3] See Robert Blake and Jane S. Mouton, *Group Dynamics—Key to Decision Making* (Houston, Texas, Gulf Publishing Co., 1961).

[4] See Herbert R. Shepard and Robert R. Blake, "Changing Behavior Through Cognitive Change," *Human Organization,* Summer 1962, p. 88.

[5] See Chris Argyris, *Interpersonal Competence and Organizational Effectiveness* (Homewood, Illinois, The Dorsey Press, Inc. and Richard D. Irwin, Inc., 1962).

* From "New Management Job: The Integrator," *Harvard Busines Review,* Vol. 45, No. 6 (November–December, 1967), pp. 142–51 (excerpts). Reprinted by permission. © 1967 by The President and Fellows of Harvard College; all rights reserved.

† The authors are on the faculty of the Graduate School of Business Administration, Harvard University.

decade from now? Because of the rapid rate of market and technological change, with the accompanying strains and stresses on existing organizational forms, managers are becoming increasingly concerned with the difficulty of reconciling the need for specialization with the need for integration of effort.

*   *   *   *   *

. . . [W]e first need to define what we mean by the term *integration*. As used in this article, integration is the achievement of unity of effort among the major functional specialists in a business. The integrator's role involves handling the nonroutine, unprogrammed problems that arise among the traditional functions as each strives to do its own job. It involves resolving interdepartmental conflicts and facilitating decisions, including not only such major decisions as large capital investment but also the thousands of smaller ones regarding product features, quality standards, output, cost targets, schedules, and so on. Our definition reads much like the customary job description of any company general manager or divisional manager who has "line" authority over all the major functional departments.

Although the need for organizational integration is not new, the traditional method of using the "shared boss" as the integrator is rapidly breaking down, and a radically new approach is becoming necessary. The increasingly dynamic nature of many organizational environments is making the integrating job so important and so complex that it cannot be handled by a single general manager, no matter how capable he may be.

*   *   *   *   *

SURVEY FINDINGS

To this point in the discussion, we have demonstrated that integrative roles are needed and are being developed in many companies. In fact, our study of ten organizations in three distinctly different industries—plastics, consumer foods, and containers—provides dramatic evidence of the importance of effective integration in any industry. This is because our research reveals a close correlation between the effectiveness of integration among functional departments and company growth and profits. However, separate integrating roles or departments are not the solution for all organizations. While formal integrative roles are highly important in R&D-intensive industries, such as plastics and consumer food products, in a comparatively stable industry, such as containers, integration can be achieved through the management hierarchy.

The important point is that in the future more organizations will be operating in rapid changing environments, and the problem of managers will be to make certain that this integrative function is effectively carried out. In order to to do this, they will need to learn how to select, train, organize, supervise, and control these new integrators.

Organization Structure

Two questions arise when we think of designing the structure of the organization to facilitate the work of integrators:

1. *Is it better to establish a formal integration department, or simply to set up integrating positions independent of one another?*

2. If individual integrating positions are set up, how should they be related to the larger structure?

In considering these issues it should first be pointed out that if an organization needs integrators at all, it is preferable to legitimize these roles by formal titles and missions rather than to leave them in an informal status. We derive the primary evidence on this point from an intensive study of an electronics company, where the limitations of using informal integrators are clearly revealed.[1] This research demonstrates that the effectiveness of the informal integrators is severely circumscribed when it comes to dealing with difficult interdepartmental relationships. Consider:

☐ In this organization the boundaries between the production and engineering departments were not well established, and there was intense competition and conflict between these two groups. The informal integrators were unable to achieve effective collaboration, at least in part because their roles were not clearly defined. Therefore, their integrative attempts were often seen as inappropriate infringements on the domains of other departments.

For example, an engineering supervisor, whose own inclinations and interests led him to play a coordinating role between the two departments, was frequently rebuffed by the production personnel because he was seen as intruding into their activities. Without a clearly defined role, his integration efforts were limited to exchanging information across the interface of the two departments.

These data indicate that the more intense the problem of interdepartmental collaboration is, the more need there is for the integrative roles to be formally identified so that such activities are seen as legitimate.

The question of whether to establish independent integrative roles or to create a formal department is illuminated to a considerable extent by our data. Consider:

☐ In the plastics industry, which has the fastest rate of technical change of the three industries we studied, the basic departments (production, sales, and research) are the most highly specialized and differentiated. Five of the six plastics companies studied, including the one with the best integration record, have what could be called "full-scale integrating departments," although they are not formally labeled as such. (See *Exhibit I* for suggested structural solutions to the integration problem.)

☐ In the consumer foods industry, which has both a medium rate of technical change and a medium degree of difference between basic departments, one of the two companies studied uses a full-scale "integrating department"; the other— with the better integration record—simply utilizes a set of scattered integration roles.

☐ The container industry has the most stable technology, and thus only slight differences are perceptible between basic departments. In this industry the company with the best integration record has no formal integrators of any kind; it relies entirely on its regular line organization to do the coordinating. By contrast, a second container company, employing a full-fledged integrating department, has experienced considerable integrating difficulties. This suggests not only that the department is redundant, but that it actually impedes the coordination process.

All of this evidence indicates that the elaborateness of the integrating function

---

[1] Unpublished study conducted by John Seiler and Robert Katz for the Division of Research, Harvard Business School.

EXHIBIT I
Structural Solutions to the Organizational Integration Problem

Stable and homogeneous environment

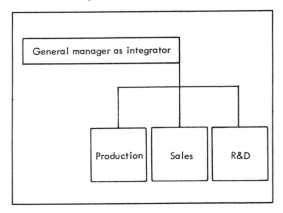

Semidynamic and heterogeneous environment

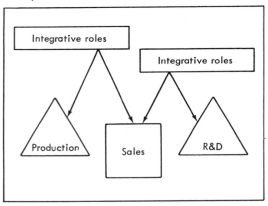

Highly dynamic and heterogeneous environment

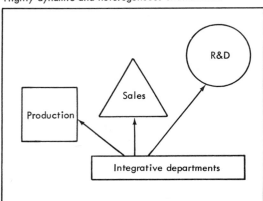

should vary both with the complexity of the problems and with the size of the gap that specialization creates between the basic departments. Moreover, management should keep in mind that it is possible to get too many integrators into the act as well as too few.

BEHAVIOR CHARACTERISTICS

Our research enables us to identify four important characteristics about the behavior of effective integrators, as well as the organizational practices that contribute to their effectiveness:

1. Integrators need to be seen as contributing to important decisions on the basis of their competence and knowledge, rather than on their positional authority.
2. Integrators must have balanced orientations and behavior patterns.
3. Integrators need to feel they are being rewarded for their total product responsibility, not solely on the basis of their performance as individuals.
4. Integrators must have a capacity for resolving interdepartmental conflicts and disputes.

*　*　*　*　*

Decision Contribution

Although this integrator, like many of his colleagues, complains that he does not have formal authority over the other groups with whom he works, our measures of actual influence on decisions in the organizations studied indicate that all integrators, except for those in the less well-integrated container company, have a larger voice in interdepartmental decisions than their peers in functional departments. And their influence is essential in industries requiring highly specialized and well-integrated organizations, where the integrator must often initiate activities for managers in other departments.

Personal Competence. There is another important factor related to influence that distinguishes the integrators in effective organizations from those in less effective ones. In the more effective, the integrators are influential because of their knowledge and expertise, while in less effective organizations they are influential only because of the formal authority of their positions.

*　*　*　*　*

These and similar comments indicate that the managers in effectively integrated organizations view the integrators as persons who have knowledge of and expertise in solving organizational problems. This personal competence appears to be the foundation on which their large voice in interdepartmental decisions rests.

Positional Power. In the organizations that were having difficulty in achieving integration, the tone of the functional managers' commentaries on the influence of the integrators was quite different.

*　*　*　*　*

Comments . . . suggest that the integrators in organizations having integration problems were influential only because of the formal authority given to them by the top management and because of their proximity to top management. Other responses stressed that generally the integrators in these companies were considered less knowledgeable about industry conditions. Moreover, the specialist managers frequently volunteered disparaging remarks about the integrators' abilities and knowledge.

Other Factors. In planning for these integrating positions, attention must be given to placing them at levels in the organization where the incumbents will have ready access to the knowledge and information relevant to decisions. In the well-integrated organizations we studied, for example, this level was usually at the middle of the management hierarchy. Since these organizations were in dynamic, rapidly changing industries where knowledge was complex and uncertain, only those middle managers with specific problem experience had been able to master the required knowledge.

If the integrator selected has had prior work experience in two or more of the several functional departments, the specialist managers will regard him as competent because of the knowledge that his experience has provided. While persons with these ideal qualifications may be extremely scarce, it is important to recognize the necessity to fill these crucial positions. One common failing of the less well-integrated organizations is their tendency to assign young managers lacking sufficient experience in all facets of the business to these positions. Although this may provide a useful learning experience for the young managers, our evidence suggests that it really does not lead to effective integration.

Balanced Orientation

The second important characteristic of effective integrators is that their orientations and ways of thinking strike a good balance between the extremes of the members of the specialized departments whose efforts they are integrating. For instance, our study shows that:

☐ Research scientists think about long-term projects and issues and about solutions to scientific and technical problems.

☐ Production managers and engineers, on the other hand, are concerned with shorter term problems, especially those that relate to an efficient and timely plant operation.

☐ Sales personnel are also concerned with shorter term issues, but for them the important problems are those that deal with the market—that is, how to meet sales objectives, what to do about competitors' product changes, what characteristics a new product must have to meet the needs of customers, and so forth.

These differences in ways of thinking are, of course, part of what makes it difficult for these groups to collaborate effectively.

The fact that the effective integrators have balanced orientations means that they share more ways of thinking and more behavior patterns with the functional managers than those managers normally do with each other. In a sense, effective integrators speak the language of each of the specialist groups, and thus they are able to work at resolving interdepartmental conflicts. When integrators do not have balanced orientations, their ability to facilitate joint decision making between functional managers suffers. . . .

*   *   *   *   *

Our research also reveals that effective integrators tend to use an interpersonal style of behavior that falls between the two characteristic behavior orientations of specialized departments. At one extreme, sales personnel are most concerned with maintaining sound personal relationships with their colleagues in other departments. At the other extreme, production managers (and research scientists to a lesser extent) are primarily concerned with getting on with the job, even if this causes the disruption of some established relationships. Our evidence indicates that, to be effective, an integrator needs to think and act in ways which evenly balance the highly social and the highly task-oriented behavior patterns of the units he is attempting to link.

Our research further reveals that entire integrating departments are much more effective when they are intermediate in their degree of structure in relation to the specialized departments they are linking. To analyze the formalization of structure, we examined the degree to which formal rules are utilized, the average span of control, the frequency and specificity of both departmental and individual performance reviews, and the number of levels in the hierarchy.

We found, for example, that most of the formally integrated companies were in an industry where specialized departments had to develop distinctly different organizational practices to perform their respective tasks. Thus, at one extreme, the production units needed highly formalized organizational practices to perform their more routinized tasks. At the other extreme, researchers with problem-solving tasks were more effective in units that had less formalized structures. Between these extremes, the sales personnel operated most effectively with intermediate organizational practices.

When the integrators worked within an intermediate structure, they developed behavior patterns not too unlike those of the different specialists they were linking, and thus they were able to work effectively with all of them.

While our data on the need for intermediate orientations and structures are drawn from a study of integrators attempting to link research, sales, and production units, the same conclusions would seem to hold for integrators linking other functional units.

Performance Recognition

The third important characteristic of effective integrators is the basis on which they see themselves being evaluated and rewarded. For example, in organizations where the integrators were highly effective, they reported that the most important basis for their superior's evaluation was the overall performance of the products on which they were working. Where the integrators were less effective, the superior's evaluation was more on the basis of their individual performance.

This indicates that if integrators are to perform effectively in coordinating the many facets of complex decisions, they need to feel they are being evaluated and rewarded for the total results of their efforts. When they feel they are judged only on the basis of their performance as individuals, they may become so concerned with making decisions to please their superiors or to avoid rocking the boat that they will easily overlook what is desirable from the point of view of their total product responsibility.

Conflict Resolution

The final characteristic of effective integrators is the mode of behavior they utilize to resolve interdepartmental conflict. It seems inevitable that such conflicts will arise in any complex organization from time to time. So, rather than being concerned with the essentially impossible goal of preventing conflict, we are more interested in finding ways for integrators and their colleagues to handle it. Our analysis identifies three modes of behavior for resolving conflict.

Confrontation Technique. The first method, *confrontation,* involves placing all relevant facts before the disputants and then discussing the basis of disagreement until some alternative is found that provides the best solution for the total organization. Confrontation often involves extended discussion. . . .

$$* \qquad * \qquad * \qquad * \qquad *$$

Smoothing Approach. The second technique for dealing with conflict, *smoothing,* essentially emphasizes the maintenance of friendly relations and avoids conflict as a danger that could disrupt these relations. Managers using this approach are, in effect, indicating anxiety about facing the consequences of their conflicting points of view. Such action, they feel, might not only threaten their continuing friendly relations, but even their jobs. So they smooth over their differences, perhaps by using superficial banter and kidding, and thus sidestep conflict. . . .

Forcing Method. The final approach, *forcing,* entails the straightforward use of power in resolving conflict. The disputing parties bring to bear whatever power or influence they have to achieve a resolution favoring their own point of view. This mode of behavior often results in a "win-lose" struggle. Unfortunately, it is often the objectives of the total organization that suffer the greatest loss. . . . Our data indicate that there is a close relationship between the effectiveness of integration in an organization and the reliance of its members on confrontation as a way to resolve interdepartmental conflict.

While confrontation showed up as a common mode of resolving conflict in all of the ten organizations we studied, the integrators and functional managers in the six most effectively integrated organizations did significantly more confronting of conflict than their counterparts in the four less well-integrated organizations. Similarly, the managers and integrators in the two organizations that had achieved a medium degree of integration were confronting conflict more often than the managers in the least effectively integrated organizations.

There is one other point worth considering: in the highly integrated organizations, we also found that the functional managers were using more forcing, and/or less smoothing, behavior than their counterparts in the less effective organizations. This suggests that, while confrontation of conflict must be the primary basis for resolving interdepartmental issues, it is also important to have a backup mode of some forcing behavior to ensure that the issue will at least be addressed and discussed, and not avoided.

$$* \qquad * \qquad * \qquad * \qquad *$$

Preferred Styles

In addition to measuring the integrators' motives, their preferred behavioral styles were investigated, with certain interesting results:

□ Effective integrators prefer to take significantly more initiative and leadership; they are aggressive, confident, persuasive, and verbally fluent. In contrast, less effective integrators are retiring, inhibited, and silent, and they avoid situations that involve tension and decisions.

☐ Effective integrators seek status to a greater extent; they are ambitious, active, forceful, effective in communication, and have personal scope and breadth of interests. Less effective integrators are restricted in outlook and interests, and are uneasy and awkward in new or unfamiliar social situations.

☐ Effective integrators have significantly more social poise; they are more clever, enthusiastic, imaginative, spontaneous, and talkative. Less effective integrators are more deliberate, moderate, and patient.

☐ Effective integrators prefer more flexible ways of acting; they are adventurous, humorous, and assertive. Less effective integrators are more industrious, guarded, methodical, and rigid.

* * * * *

While American industry still needs many types of organizations, as the trend continues for more and more industries to be characterized by rapid rates of technological and market change, more organizations will be like the R&D-intensive firms described here. These firms will require both high differentiation between specialist managers in functional units and tight integration among these units. Although differentiation and integration are essentially antagonistic, effective integrators can help organizations obtain both and thus contribute to economic success. . . .

From

LEADERSHIP AND MOTIVATION: A CORE CONCEPT*

By Martin G. Evans†

The question of whether a leader's behavior has an impact upon the job satisfaction and performance of the subordinate has been subjected to considerable empirical exploration. This, however, has been on a broad front rather than in any great depth. There has been a great deal of replication of Fleishman's[1] original finding that supervisory *initiation of structure* and *consideration* have an impact upon worker behavior and satisfaction. Originally it was found that satisfaction was positively related to consideration, while performance was positively related to initiation of structure. However, even in this early study, differences appeared between different types of work groups—the results were stronger for those foremen in production departments than for those in non-production departments. Additional work in the area has added to the confusion. A variety of studies has shown little consistency in the strength or even direction of the relationships observed.

---

* Reprinted by permission of *Academy of Management Journal,* Vol. 13, No. 1 (March 1970). Excerpts from pp. 91–97, 99–100.

† The author is on the business faculty at the University of Toronto.

[1] E. A. Fleishman, E. F. Harris and H. E. Burtt, *Leadership and Supervision in Industry* (Columbus, Ohio: Bureau of Educational Research, Ohio State University, 1955).

Among the few studies that have attempted to go below the surface of the observed relationships to try to discover the conditions under which either positive or negative relationships are observed is that of Fiedler.[2] This has been a significant contribution. However, his use of a model of leadership which implies that the consideration and initiation of structure styles are the two extremes of a single continuum rather than being two orthogonal continua may have restricted its utility. Nevertheless, he found that the relationship between employee performance and supervisory behavior was moderated by aspects of the "favorableness" of the situation for the supervisor. Highly favorable situations were characterized by:

a. High formal power of the supervisor
b. High degree of liking for the supervisor by the work group
c. Highly structured task

Highly unfavorable situations were characterized by:

a. Low formal power of the supervisor
b. Dislike of the supervisor by the work group
c. Unstructured task

Fiedler found that in highly favorable and in highly unfavorable situations the more task-oriented (initiating structure) the supervisor then the more effective were the subordinates. Only in moderately favorable/unfavorable situations was the relationship reversed so that the more person-oriented (considerate) the supervisor the more effective the subordinates. This research has defined one set of external conditions that influence the nature of the relationship between leader and follower.

*   *   *   *   *

A Working Theory of Motivation

[One] . . . strand in motivation theory concerns the interrelationship between the action or behavior of the individual and his goal attainment and need satisfaction. This has been called the *Path-goal* approach to motivation. As a basic premise, the assumption is made that the individual is basically goal directed; in other words, that he will actively strive to engage in actions that he perceives as leading to his important goals. This is a simplification of the actual state of affairs; for the individual presumably has a set of goals (see above), all of which may be of importance to him, so that his choice of actions will be such as to satisfice this set of goals. However, this does not alter the basis whereby action decisions are made; i.e., the actions taken by the individual will be consistent with his perception of their instrumentality for goal attainment.

At this point we should emphasize that our initial concern is with the individual's *perception* of whether or not a particular activity helps or hurts him in the attainment of the goal. Such a perception may or may not be based upon the reality of the situation; nevertheless, the action decisions of the individual will be based

---

[2] F. E. Fiedler, "Engineer the Job to Fit the Manager," *Harvard Business Review* (1965), 43, 5, pp. 115–122.

upon these perceptions of path-goal instrumentality. We may, therefore, introduce the core concept of *Path-Goal Instrumentality* which is defined as the degree to which the individual perceives that a given path will lead to a particular goal.[3] We are now in a position to make some predictions about an individual's motivation to engage in specific behavior. This will be a function of the instrumentality of the behavior for his goals; and the relationship will be stronger for the more important goals of the individual. This can be summarized:

1. Motivation to engage in specific behavior =

$$f \ (\sum^{goals} \ \begin{array}{l} \text{(Behavior's perceived Instrumentality for goal} \times \\ \text{Goal importance)} \end{array}$$

The actual frequency with which paths are followed by the individual will be a function not only of the individual's motivation to follow it, but also of the constraints on him in his choice of behavior (such as: his ability, the nature of the task, etc).[4]

2. Frequency with which a path is followed =

   f (Motivation to follow paths/ability, freedom, etc.)

This can be taken one step further; the extent to which a path is followed will, in combination with the acual path-goal instrumentality, affect the degree to which an individual's goals are attained. In other words, by frequently taking paths which actually lead to an individual's goals there is a strong likelihood that these goals will be attained; more formally:

3. Degree of Goal Attainment =

$$f \ (\sum^{paths} \ \text{(Path Frequency} \times \text{Actual Path Instrumentality)}$$

We suggested earlier that perceived path-goal instrumentality (which is the basis for a choice of paths) might or might not be based upon actual situations. In the ongoing organization, it is to be expected that as a result of experience, people will develop realistic perceptions of the path-goal instrumentalities; though we should be aware that both organizational and individual factors may inhibit the process of verification.[5]

The first strand of motivation theory helped us to understand the kinds of needs and goals that are relevant for motivating individual behavior. This second strand in motivation theory provides us with the relationship between action and goal attainment. This indeed sheds some light on the thorny problem of the relationship between job satisfaction and job performance.[6] In Figure 1, this is outlined dia-

---

[3] This position has been outlined most recently (with slightly different terminology) in V. H. Vroom, *Work and Motivation* (New York: Wiley, 1964).

[4] A multiplicative relationship has been suggested by Vroom, *op. cit.*, for the moderating effect of ability: Frequency of behavior = f (Motivation × Ability).

[5] For example organizational complexity, organizational change, and managerial policies on secrecy may contribute to creating ambiguity in an individual's role requirments and hence in his perception of path-goal instrumentalities, R. L. Kahn, M. Wolfe, R. P. Quinn, J. D. Snoek, and R. A. Rosenthal, *Organizational Stress: Studies in Role Conflict and Ambiguity* (New York: Wiley, 1964); while central individual beliefs about whether the environment is essentially random in its rewards or whether such rewards are contingent upon behavior will distort the individual's perception of actual path-goal instrumentalities, J. B. Rotter, "Generalized Expectancies for Internal Versus External Control of Reinforcements," *Psychological Monographs* (1966), 80, 1 whole number 609.

[6] L. W. Porter and E. E. Lawler, "What Job Attitudes Tell About Motivation," *Harvard Business Review* (1969), 46, 1, pp. 118–126.

FIGURE 1
Motivation Model

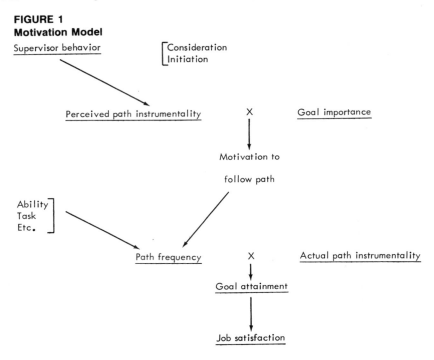

grammatically. First, the path-goal instrumentality, in conjunction with goal importance, determines the level of motivation to follow a given path; second, this motivation level, in conjunction with environmental factors, determines the actual frequency with which a path is followed; third, path frequency, in conjunction with path-goal instrumentality, determines the level of goal attainment, which is a partial measure of job satisfaction. We can, therefore, see that the individual will choose a level of performance that is perceived as instrumental for the attainment of his goals. If the individual sees low performance leading to his goals, then he will be a low performer; if he sees high performance as leading to his goals, then he will be a high performer; if he is able to choose paths that lead to his goals, then he will be satisfied; if he is unable to do so, then he will be dissatisfied.

Articulation Between Supervisory Behavior and the Motivation Model

If the outline presented above is an accurate description of the motivational patterns in human behavior then the concept of *perceived path-goal instrumentality* becomes a crucial point at which influence can be exerted on the individual. To be sure, there are a variety of factors that can affect path-goal instrumentalities, but, in certain conditions, the behavior of the supervisor can be one of the most potent. In this section, we shall consider aspects of the supervisor's behavior that impinge upon the subordinate's perceptions of the instrumentalities of his paths for his goal attainments.

Fleishman and his associates identify two major components of supervisory behavior *(initiation of structure and consideration)* that seem to result in different patterns of subordinate behavior (in terms of both job performance and job satisfaction). These are defined as:

Consideration which includes behavior indicating mutual trust, respect and a certain rapport between the supervisor and his group. This does not mean that this dimension reflects a superficial "pat-on-the-back," "first name calling" kind of human relations behavior. This dimension appears to emphasize a deeper concern for group members' needs and includes such behavior as allowing subordinates more participation in decision-making and encouraging more two-way communication.

Initiation of Structure which includes behavior in which the supervisor organizes and defines group activities and his relation to the group. Thus, he defines the role he expects each member to assume, assigns tasks, plans ahead, establishes ways of getting things done, and pushes for production. This dimension seems to emphasize overt attempts to achieve organizational goals.[7]

Path instrumentality is the subordinate's expectation that a specific goal will be attained by following a specific path; so that, in trying to effect path-goal instrumentality, it would appear that there are three aspects involved:[8]

1. The subordinate must perceive that it will be possible for him to attain his goals. In other words, he must envisage a situation in which there exists a supply of rewards and punishments. In most formal organization situations, the supervisor is one of the sources of such a supply. It would appear that the level of *consideration* exhibited by the supervisor would affect the abundance of this source and also the appropriateness of the reward to the individual. In other words, the highly considerate supervisor is going to have a larger range of rewards (he will offer rewards in all need areas—pay, security, promotion, social and esteem) than his less considerate colleague (who will be locked in on pay and security as rewards). He is also going to ensure that these rewards are distributed selectively to his subordinates in accordance with their individual desires, while the less considerate supervisor will not make such sophisticated discriminations among his subordinates.

2. The individual must see that his rewards and punishments (whether from an abundant and sophisticated source, or from a meagre and simplistic one) are coming to him as the result of his specific behavior. In other words, there must be a perceived connection between his behavior and the rewards or punishments that he receives. It is here that *initiation of structure* by the supervisor has its impact. The supervisor who is high on initiation indicates to the subordinate the kinds of paths that he (the supervisor) wants followed and links his reward behavior to a successful following of the path. The supervisor who is low on this dimension

[7] E. A. Fleishmann and E. F. Harris, "Patterns of Leadership Behavior Related to Employee Grievances and Turnover," *Personnel Psychology* (1962), 15, 43–56.

[8] This section is based upon my recent paper: M. G. Evans, "The Effects of Supervisory Behavior on the Path-Goal Relationship," *Organizational Behavior and Human Performance* (1970, 5, in press).

does not indicate which paths should be followed and distributes his rewards without reference to the successful following of a path.

3. Implied in this is a third way in which supervisory behavior affects the strength of the path of instrumentality. Through his initiation of structure, the supervisor indicates those paths or activities that he thinks are appropriate to the role of the subordinate. It may be that the type of path that the superior deems appropriate is a function of the supervisor's *consideration*. This last impact is going to be very much a function of the path: presumably all supervisors see good performance as an appropriate activity for workers; whereas only those with high consideration might see "helping fellow workers" as an appropriate activity.

*   *   *   *   *

Implications for Management

For a management that wishes to bring about changes in the organization so as to improve worker motivation, performance, and satisfaction, and wishes to do so through the changing of leadership behavior, the initial strategy depends upon whether the two conditions are met; i.e., that a strong relationship exists between supervisory behavior and the Path-goal instrumentalities *and* a strong relationship exists between Path-goal instrumentalities and behavior and satisfaction.

If both conditions are met, then a relatively simple strategy will suffice. Any change in leadership behavior should have direct consequences for Path-goal instrumentalities and hence on worker performance and satisfaction.

If the first condition is not met (there is no relationship between leadership behavior and Path-goal Instrumentalities), the organization must investigate other aspects of the system, explore to see what variables have an impact on Path-goal Instrumentalities or inhibit the effect of supervisory behavior on Path-goal Instrumentalities—such things as the formal reward and penalty system or the nature of the work group might have this sort of impact. The organization may then decide that one of these variables is salient and that changes in this can bring about greater worker motivation; or it may decide that supervisory behavior is still salient and undertake to bring about two changes.

a. create the conditions for a strong relationship to exist between supervisory behavior and Path-goal instrumentalities by change of the other inhibiting organizational variables, and

b. if necessary, bring about changes in supervisory behavior with resulting changes in worker motivation.

If the second condition is not met, the organization must be examined to find out what factors inhibit the appearance of this relationship. Here such variables as individual ability, the nature of the task, etc. are likely to be crucial. The procedure is then to undertake such changes as to strengthen the relationship in the second condition prior to undertaking any changes in leadership behavior.

PART VI Reconciling the Responsibility to Produce with Other Social Responsibilities

THE SOCIAL RESPONSIBILITY DILEMMA: PRODUCTIVITY VERSUS OTHER VALUES

In almost all of the cases in this book we see that managing, leading, or governing organizations is neither a simple nor an easy task. There are almost inevitable choices that must be made between ultimate values—things one believes in and wants to achieve because they are good in themselves.

The cases in Part VI illustrate these kinds of choices as they must be made between the firm's ideal economic and technical system (its goals and substrategies) on the one hand, and certain ideals that are noneconomic in nature on the other. The good life is seen to be composed not only of goods and services that serve society, but also of education of people, an esthetic environment, the prevention of poverty, the preservation of human dignity, and many other *values, ideals,* or *ethical ends.*

This idea is not new in this book. Already we have considered many times implications for human dignity as they apply to human beings inside the firm. The characteristic that sets off Part VI cases from the others is that they deal with actions of a total organization as they impinge on groups outside the firm, or on society as a whole.

Standard Oil Company of New Jersey (and its managers) is trying to balance the value of efficient oil production with attention and costs directed toward better education in the United States. General Motors Corporation is confronted with public demand for quality automobile transportation and at the same time with demands not to spoil the beauty or historic interest of Grand Army Plaza. The president of F. A. Weber Company, Inc., is bothered by an economic system that can produce high quality dog food while many human beings are living in poverty. Polaroid management is concerned with eliminating racial discrimination and poverty but is faced with charges that it is itself aiding discrimination.

That these kinds of dilemmas are not unusual is also pointed up in one of the readings in Part VI. Turvey, A British economist, cites cases where management of a fish company must produce food efficiently and immediately but in doing so may endanger the permanent supply of this natural resource. The management of an airline must provide transportation cheaply but the noise it produces disturbs people who live by airports. The management of a brickyard must provide cheap materials for sheltering mankind but smoke from its factory may cause cattle in the area to become sick.

ORGANIZATIONAL GOALS AS SOCIAL RESPONSIBILITIES

As pointed out in the introduction to Part II, almost any organization has as its principal goal—the one which must be met satisfactorily if the organization is to survive—the *production* of some good or service. A hospital must produce patient care. A bank must produce loans and offer deposit service. An airline must provide transportation.

One side of the social responsibility dilemma is the *demand* from society "out there" for production. In other words, in all societies at all times, there has been demand that organizations specialize in producing things for other human beings.

In discharging this responsibility, however, the first question which arises is whether or not the good or service is in itself "good" in the ethical sense. Opium, fire arms, cigarettes, atomic bombs, whiskey, devices for a motorist to detect police radar speed zones, contraceptives, and many other things are well-known controversial items of production. This is the kind of question faced by the president of F. A. Weber Company, Inc., one of the cases which follow. Mr. Weber wonders if the production of dog food is "good" in a society where many human beings live in poverty.

In answering such a question, we shall see that the informed manager must look rather deeply at "what is going on." He needs to know *how* monetary resources are allocated by society to a dog food company, *why* the system allocates resources that way, and some of the advantages and disadvantages of allocating them in a different way. He can understand the latter by studying some comparative economic systems—how it is done in the United States, in France, in Scandinavia, or in Russia.

A second type of question involves a trade-off between organization goals that are "good," on the one hand, and the unintended consequences that producing these has on *other* social values which make up the good life for humanity, on the other. Given the fact that medicine for the sick is a worthy end, does the production strategy necessary to produce this involve negative effects on air we breathe, water we drink, or the health of employees on the production line?

ORGANIZATIONAL STRATEGIES AS SOCIAL RESPONSIBILITIES

A strategy is the series of substeps an organization must go through to achieve its goal. These strategies vary enormously from organization to organization. They reflect the operations necessary to produce a particular "something." For example, in the Lakeland Food Products Company (Part V), we saw that in order to produce mayonnaise and spices for society to eat, the marketing function was a subgoal or strategy. That is, somebody had to actually sell the products. The selling methods taken together represent the sales strategy. In addition, somebody had to give attention to paying the salesmen, to figuring out compensation methods. This was the sales compensation strategy. Someone else had to decide on advertising methods—the promotion strategy.

Notice that there is a hierarchy of objectives and strategies here. Or, as some theories state, there is a means-end chain of higher objectives related to lower-order strategies. The advertising, selling, and compensation strategies become a means to the marketing strategy. The marketing strategy plus the manufacturing strategy (operations) plus the finance strategy (operations and actions) all equal the goal of producing food of a certain type.

Here is where the dilemma of the second type enters. The manager must play an important part in planning the operating technology (the strategic means) by which the social product is produced. At the same time, many times the "unintended consequences" (as the sociologists call them) are totally unthought of, or the "externalities and side effects" (as the economists call them) may be thought of but weighted lower than the value of strategic production operations.

Of particular importance is a certain characteristic of all strategies which is necessary in all organizations to some degree. Society demands, as Parts III and IV indicated, at least reasonable efficiency. No society will tolerate either the unreasonable waste of effort and materials, or the unreasonable cost to ultimate consumers, of a product that is produced with waste. It was this value itself which was one factor that impelled the financial planners, management scientists, and general managers in Parts III and IV cases to concentrate on efficiency. Lakeland demanded that the compensation and advertising strategies avoid excessive costs, so that it is possible to have the mayonnaise eaten by human beings. National Bank of San Francisco must keep its costs of typewriters, office space, and furniture to within a reasonable minimum; otherwise the public cannot borrow funds to build housing and shelter.

It has already been pointed out that it is true of *any* organization that it must be reasonably efficient. A militant revolutionary group cannot succeed or survive if it does not use its guns and printing presses efficiently. Its propaganda strategies and operating strategies, means to the organization's goals, must be, to some extent, rationally planned. No police force can survive if the strategies of vice control, traffic control, or school safety are not performed with cost and waste in mind. Roosevelt Hospital's efficiency in nursing strategies, surgical strategies, and emergency care strategies are as important to the hospital's success as Polaroid's strategies for manufacturing and selling sunglasses and film around the world are to the company's success.

ORGANIZATION STRATEGIES AS THREATS TO SOCIETY

Scholars in many different disciplines have searched for a natural harmony in nature. They have sought to find a way out of the seeming hardships and conflicts that plague the world.

In economics, we have the theory of the unseen hand. One of the readings in Part VI explains this hand. The theory is that what is good for General Motors Corporation is good for the nation. Good cheap automobiles mean employment of workers, want-satisfying transportation for citizens, and prosperity for the nation. The same theory can be found in international economics. Free trade, with every nation doing what it can and wants, is good for the world.

We must be very careful to judge this kind of argument. It must not be rejected out of hand. There is truth in it. But the rub comes often in the *means—the strategies*—which must be employed to pursue this theory in reality. These strategies may indeed make for more employment, lower costs, or higher-quality products *in the long run,* as economists long postulated in their natural harmony theory. *But,* as Lord Keynes said, *in the long run we're all dead.* He meant by this that strategies are short run means to long-run harmony. If you make all decisions on long-run harmony theories, you just may do some things in the short run that are not so nice.

Organizations, pressured by resource scarcity on the one hand and by demands from society to be efficient on the other, pursue manufacturing policies, sales and distribution policies, and financial (including accounting and management science) policies which themselves might have harmful unintended consequences for the good life.

This may be due to two factors. The demands from society, and groups within society, are real. The reading by Friedman (a prominent economist) and Rostow (dean of a leading law school) eloquently point out that there are powerful forces of law and public demand that pressure policy makers in organizations to devise technologically efficient strategies.

EXECUTIVE MYOPIA AS CREATOR OF THREATENING STRATEGIES

A second cause of strategic decisions that threaten society unreasonably lies in either the motivation or the knowledge deficiency of the executive himself. At the very outset we must recognize that leaders and executives, even when they are motivated by a desire to "run things," are not necessarily "bad" because of this. There are many organizations whose leaders include in their thinking either a knowledge of or a "feel" for what they are doing, and how it affects both the technical side of society and the human side of society.

At the same time, a number of readings in this book show that the manager's own values affect his decisions, in addition to any responsibility he may feel for satisfying the organization's need for efficient strategies. If the executive is one who overemphasizes his own need for power, for example, at the expense of other groups in society, and at the expense of the *organization's* success, the formulation of strategies will certainly run afoul of social justice.

THE NEED FOR RECONCILING; THE NEED FOR JUDGMENT AND WISDOM

From what has been said about organization goals, strategies, and policy making so far, it it clear that somebody somewhere in society must do some very clear thinking, or decision making, as it is called in more scholarly terms. This thinking must be directed toward how to reconcile the good of society's production (and its elaborated strategies) with the good of society's other human values.

This requires a certain kind of decision making. The brains which do it must be informed enough that they know the effects of their decisions on "the whole system." This probably means education, with theories from science and philosophy to help in understanding. But it also, as is so well pointed out by the Turvey reading, requires an element of fairness and justice. There shall probably never be a scientific way of measuring the social good that can make decisions of this kind without the aid of wisdom and judgment.

Given the dilemma, and the need for reconciling diverse social ends in strategic decision making, the next question which arises is *who* should make these kinds of decisions?

WHO SHOULD MAKE DECISIONS THAT ARE "SOCIALLY RESPONSIBLE"?

This question is one on which the reader must make up his own mind. At various points in the study of the following cases and readings, different authors take different approaches to an answer.

In the case of Standard Oil's charity contribution dilemma and of Frank Weber's dog food versus poverty dilemma, three brilliant legal and economic philosophers believe that a free market mechanism, on balance, is the best solution. They argue that the human beings who are managers will be forced, by the system pressures, so to speak, to be socially responsible. It is interesting to probe deeply as to what they mean by the social good, and to see how they recognize the disadvantages of such a system but put heavy weights on its advantages.

In Polaroid's racial discrimination dilemma, and in U.S. Steel's pricing-inflation dilemma, there is opportunity to examine the theories of those writers who believe that government planners are the ones who are most likely to exercise informed wisdom in this type of decision making.

Those cases also examine the possibility of pluralism, constructive conflict, or due process. This approach holds that no one person or group is sufficiently free from bias. One man or one group would always be doing "his thing," and not enough of "society's thing." To correct this kind of biased thinking, according to this approach, we must depend on people straightening out each other. It is not a serene and orderly world; it is a world of conflicting opinions and conflict resolution.

Finally, there are those who believe in conscience control by informed and wise managers in organizations. According to this approach, individual executives and managers will not only (1) be informed of how the system works and how human beings behave, but will also (2) be buttressed by new beliefs in society about the function of managers, and (3) use their own brains to judge the wisdom and justice of a particular operating strategy. Presumably, the latter would include interacting with other groups pluralistically in order to keep the manager's brain clear, and not let it become myopic to the viewpoint of others.

Regardless of which of these approaches turns out to be the principal one, all managers should know what it means to think deeply about the matter of social justice and social good, and to face the tough dilemmas of life which threaten it. That is the purpose of this entire book, and the most specific purpose of Part VI.

20. STANDARD OIL COMPANY (NEW JERSEY)

Case Introduction

SYNOPSIS

A stockholder of Standard Oil Company objects to management's policy of annually granting the equivalent of 1½ cents a share to philanthropic and educational institutions. At the annual meeting a shareholder attempts to force management to commit corporate earnings only to those projects which *directly* further the company's quest for profits or to distribute the earnings to the owners.

WHY THIS CASE IS INCLUDED

The stockholder challenge raises the question: Who are the legitimate claimants on the corporation? In this context one can bring to bear the conflicting views of economic philosophers concerning the objectives of the corporation and the theories of political philosophers concerning the role of voluntary organizations in society. The stated motivations of the corporate managers can be examined to see how they jibe with these conceptual schemes. There is opportunity, too, to see how the very composition of the board of directors may affect corporate policy. Finally, corporate philanthropy raises the issue of the legitimacy of power among subgovernmental units of society.

DIAGNOSTIC AND PREDICTIVE QUESTIONS

The readings included with this case are marked (*). The author index at the end of this book locates the other readings.

1. Where did the $8.3 million, which Standard Oil allocated in the past five years to educational aid, come from? Where might these funds have been allocated had they not been donated to educational institutions?

Read: Anthony, *Management Accounting,* pp. 290–92, 306.

2. Mrs. Alice V. Gordon, the stockholder challenging Standard Oil's philanthropy, contended: "Your company is supposedly run solely for the stockholders' benefit." What is Mr. Rathbone's (Standard Oil president) view on this point? From the standpoint of economic philosophy, should the corporation be run *solely* for the stockholder's benefit?

Read: *Eells and Walton, *Conceptual Foundations of Business,* pp. 185–87, 149–67, 458–75. *Rostow, "To Whom and for What Ends Is Corporate Management Responsible?" Hayek, "The Corporation in a Democratic Society: In Whose Interest Ought It and Will It Be Run?" *Berle, *The 20th Century Capitalistic Revolution,* pp. 164–69, 171–73, 182–88.

3. Concentrating now on the motivations involved in the allocation of $8.3 million, recall that Mrs. Gordon said: "It (Standard Oil) is not an *eleemosynary* institution. Many stockholders undoubtedly feel that *charity* begins at home." (Emphasis added.) What was the motivation for Standard Oil's gifts to education? Was it charity, as Mrs. Gordon implied? Was it economic self-interest—the hope of a monetary return usually expected of corporate investments? Was it compliance with an informally imposed "tax" obligation (". . . the public has come to expect it of corporations")? Some other motivation, or some mixture of motivations?

Read: *A. P. Smith Manufacturing Company* v. *Barlow et al.* *Glover, *The Attack on Big Business,* pp. 328, 330–35. *Smith, *Wealth of Nations,* pp. 423, 508.

4. From the viewpoint of political philosophy what is the role of the corporation in the social system? Do you find a consciousness of this role definition in the statements of Standard Oil's directors and president, Mr. Rathbone? In what way, if any, should this role definition affect corporate policy?

Read: *Clark, *Alternative to Serfdom,* pp. 4–7. *O'Connell, "Social Overhead Capital and the Principle of Subsidiarity." Eells and Walton, *Conceptual Foundations of Business,* pp. 360–63.

5. In matters like the one presently before the annual meeting, what are the advantages and disadvantages of having all full-time, inside directors? Recall that such is the composition of Standard Oil's board. Answer the question from the viewpoint of corporate management, the individual shareholder, and the public.

Read: *Brown and Smith, *The Director Looks at His Job,* pp. 38–39, 77–78, 81–83, 85–86, 89, 91–93.

(Additional reading, not in this volume: Peter F. Drucker, *The Practice of Management* [New York: Harper & Bros., 1954], pp. 161–81.)

6. "Allowing corporations to give one fifth of all voluntary support to higher education is putting further power into the hands of corporate managers, who are in effect responsible to no one, instead of into the hands of a duly elected (and controlled) representative body." Comment. Do corporations in fact gain power through their philanthropy? If so, is this legitimate power?

Read: Drucker, *The Future of Industrial Man,* pp. 32–38.

POLICY QUESTIONS

7. If you were Mr. Rathbone, Standard Oil's president, how would you justify corporate gifts to education to the stockholders? (See Questions 2, 3, 4, and their attached readings.)

8. Again, as Standard Oil's president, what steps, if any, would you take to allay the fears of those who suspect that control will follow contribution—that the party holding the purse strings will manipulate educational institutions or stifle academic freedom? (See Question 6.)

9. If you were a director of Standard Oil, would you vote to continue the educational aid? Do you think it would make a difference in your opinion if you were an outside instead of an inside director? (See Question 5.)

10. If you were a stockholder, how would you have voted on Mrs. Gordon's proposal at the annual meeting?

QUESTIONS FOR ORIGINAL STUDENT WORK IN ANALYSIS AND POLICY

11. While reflecting on case facts, what additional theories from prior education give you insights as to "what is going on" in the Standard Oil Company? As to what might be predicted to happen in the future?

12. Other than the policy questions asked by the authors, what pragmatic ways can you think of to state the practical problems faced by executives in the case?

Case Text*

As the Standard Oil Company (New Jersey) prepared for its annual meeting on May 24, 1961, Mrs. Alice V. Gordon, a stockholder, challenged management's policy on philanthropic and educational contributions. Mrs. Gordon proposed an amendment to the corporation bylaws: "No corporate funds of this corporation shall be given away to any charitable, educational, or similar organization except for purposes in direct furtherance of the business interests of this corporation." The proxy statement of April 4, 1961 appraised all the stockholders of the proposed resolution which was to be discussed and voted on in the forthcoming annual meeting.

COMPANY PROFILE

The Standard Oil Company of New Jersey is a holding company for a worldwide complex of affiliates engaged in the exploration, production,

---

* Copyright 1973 by Charles E. Summer and J. J. O'Connell.

refining, transportation, and marketing of petroleum products. The parent and affiliate companies, which together employ some 145,000 people, generate about 35 percent of the consolidated earnings in the United States. Almost 60 percent of the remainder is earned in other Western Hemisphere operations. In terms of assets—almost $10 billion—Standard Oil of New Jersey ranks first in the industry, almost triple the size of the next largest integrated petroleum company. The company's 680,000 shareholders have recently been receiving an annual per share cash dividend of $2.25.

Year	Gross Operating Income	Net Income
1955	6,272,440,655	709,309,992
1956	7,126,855,410	808,534,919
1957	7,830,250,000	805,178,000
1958	7,543,571,000	562,475,000
1959	7,910,659,000	629,778,000
1960	8,034,735,000	688,573,000
1961	8,437,722,000	758,083,000

Source: Moodys.

CONTRIBUTIONS BY STANDARD OIL COMPANY

Mr. M. J. Rathbone, president of Standard Oil, states that the annual after-tax cost of the philanthropic and educational contributions made by the entire company since 1955 amount to 1½ cents per share. By far the largest proportion of this amount is directed toward education.

In 1955 Standard Oil of New Jersey created the ESSO Education Foundation to coordinate and administer grants to education made by the parent company and its domestic affiliates. Some 429 private colleges have benefited from the foundation's program since 1955.

Esso Education Foundation Statement of Grants

	1956–61	Number of Grants
Unrestricted	$3,783,500	1,390
National Fund for Medical Education	415,000	5
United Negro College Fund	225,000	5
Total Unrestricted	$4,423,500	1,400
Capital	1,159,000	139
Scientific research	828,715	129
Miscellaneous	495,044	61
Subtotal	$6,906,259	1,729
Special three-year science program	1,464,568	210
Total	$8,370,827	1,939

Source: Standard Oil public statements.

STOCKHOLDER OPPOSITION TO COMPANY CONTRIBUTIONS

Mrs. Alice V. Gordon felt that corporate contributions were inimical to her stockholder rights unless such gifts directly furthered the business interests of the Standard Oil Company. She presented her reasons in the April 4 proxy statement as follows:

> *Your directors are giving millions of dollars of your corporation's money to charity. This seems wrong. Your company is supposedly run solely for the stockholders' benefit. It is not an eleemosynary institution. Many stockholders undoubtedly feel that charity begins at home. Others who can afford donations are certainly entitled to choose their own beneficiaries. The current practice is especially reprehensible when as here nearly ten million have been given since 1955 to educational institutions many of which now teach socialism and ridicule business men, savers and investors, as recently explained in the well-documented best-seller "Keynes at Harvard."*

CORPORATE DIRECTORS' DEFENSE OF CONTRIBUTIONS POLICY

In the same proxy statement Standard Oil's directors appealed to the stockholders to vote against Mrs. Gordon's proposal. They defended the long-standing corporate policy on contributions in the following words:

> *By requiring that a "direct" benefit be shown in order to validate a particular philanthropic or educational contribution, this proposed by-law would unduly restrict the management in the normal discharge of its responsibilities and deprive it of an effective tool in furthering corporate and shareholder interests.*
>
> *As a responsible corporate citizen, any company of Jersey's stature must give financial support to philanthropic and educational institutions that rely on private sources for support. Such participation has become an integral part of the discharge of a corporation's business and civic responsibilities and, as such, has been encouraged by our tax laws, sustained by our courts and legislatures, and widely endorsed by the public at large. In the directors' judgment, such contributions further the interests of the shareholders and are extremely important if the company is to enjoy and retain the good will of the public which is so essential to the company's prosperity. Quite clearly, the benefits arising from such contributions, although of real and substantial value, cannot be measured in dollars and cents.*
>
> *Corporate contributions are as much the responsibility of management, and receive the same careful consideration from management, as any other legitimate and necessary business expenditure. The amount of such contributions by Jersey is believed by the directors to be reasonable by any standard. In each of the last five years, the total after-tax cost to the company and its domestic and foreign affiliates of supporting educational and philanthropic objectives has amounted to about 1½ cents per share. In management's opinion, the*

benefits derived and to be derived, although not necessarily "direct," fully justify this expenditure.

DISCUSSION AT THE ANNUAL MEETING

At the annual meeting of the Standard Oil Company in Boston, Massachusetts, on May 24, 1961, Mr. Watson Washburn represented Mrs. Alice V. Gordon. Before the assembled shareholders Mr. Washburn expanded on the arguments supporting the proposed amendment to the corporation bylaws.

> *. . . undoubtedly the directors are tremendously busy running the affairs of this gigantic enterprise we're all interested in. They apparently don't have enough time—and I'm very glad of it for the sake of the profits of the company—to spend their energies investigating hundreds of charities to see whether they are charities to which you stockholders would want to have your money given, assuming that the directors should give your money away to anyone over the objection of even a single stockholder.*
>
> *Actually your company has made unrestricted grants to 429 different educational institutions in this country in the last five years. By merely inspecting the list one could say that some of them were not the kind of college where they encourage companies like ours and stockholders like ours. For example, among the men's colleges Harvard, Yale, and Princeton have been the beneficiaries of the company's donations; and among the women's colleges, Smith, Vassar, and Sarah Lawrence. Those are just examples of places where, on the whole, left-wing doctrines are taught in the economics departments.*
>
> *[To support his point about economic doctrines, Mr. Washburn then read from and commented critically on the writings of Stuart Chase, with specific reference to an article by Mr. Chase which appeared in the Spring 1961 issue of* The Lamp, *a Standard Oil Company magazine.]*

Mr. M. J. Rathbone, Standard Oil's president, answered Mr. Washburn, giving the company's rationale for its contributions and the selection of beneficiaries:

> *When you're a good corporate citizen, it is often necessary to give support to private institutions from which no direct dollars-and-cents benefit—hospitals, community service organizations, the Red Cross, colleges, universities, and so on. If good citizens, corporate and individual alike, did not support these institutions, they would have to turn to the government for support—and that, certainly, is not the way to advance the cause of free enterprise.*
>
> *As to the merits of giving to one institution, or one type of institution, over another, the possibilities for discussion are infinite. As we normally do in such a situation, we call upon a competent staff to gather information, to study the various facets of the problem, to*

appraise and analyze the facts, to evaluate the direct and indirect benefit to the company and its shareholders, and to make recommendations to the board. Your directors are then in a position to make a sound decision, and I assure you that in every instance the shareholders' interests are paramount.

Certainly I take no exception with Mr. Washburn or his principal, Mrs. Gordon, with respect to the undesirability of supporting anything unsound and improper, We try not to do that. We know that the group of our people studying these matters is capable, competent, and objective. I would be the first to agree that there is hardly a college or a university in the United States in which some of the faculty do not hold and express views which are contrary to what we, sitting as your board, might think was right and proper.

And yet this goes to the heart of the Bill of Rights. We have freedoms in this country which few other countries have to the same extent, and these freedoms must be protected. If we reserve judgment to any small group of people as to what's right and what's wrong, without the ability of expression, we have lost something we can't afford to lose. In effect, we have to take a bit of the bitter with the sweet.

An exchange of questions and comments followed between Mr. Rathbone and stockholders for and against Mrs. Gordon's proposal. The chairman then declared voting on the resolution in order. Ballots were distributed; voting proceeded.

Selected Readings

From

TO WHOM AND FOR WHAT ENDS IS CORPORATE MANAGEMENT RESPONSIBLE?*

By Eugene V. Rostow†

From the point of view of legal and economic orthodoxy, the New Capitalism is all bewildering balderdash. The law books have always said that the board of directors owes a single-minded duty of unswerving loyalty to the stockholders, and

---

* Reprinted by permission of Harvard University Press, Cambridge, Mass., 1960 (in Edward S. Mason, *The Corporation in Modern Society,* pp. 63–65, 68–71).

† E. V. Rostow is Sterling Professor of Law and Public Affairs at Yale University.

only to the stockholders. The economist has demonstrated with all the apparent precision of plane geometry and the calculus that the quest for maximum revenue in a competitive market leads to a system of prices, and an allocation of resources and rewards, superior to any alternative, in its contributions to the economic welfare of the community as a whole. To the orthodox mind, it is therefore unsettling, to say the least, to have the respected head of the Standard Oil Company of New Jersey equating the management's duty to stockholders with its obligation to employees, customers, suppliers, and the public at large.

*   *   *   *   *

[W]hat does the "new" concept of corporate responsibility imply? Does it mean that the management of a great corporation should not bargain very hard in negotiations over wages or the prices paid to suppliers? Does it mean that a statesman-like and well-run company should charge less for its product than the market would bear, less than the prices which would maximize its short-term revenues, or what it conceives to be its long-term profits? Should it regard its residual profits, not as "belonging to" its stockholders in some ultimate sense, but as a pool of funds to be devoted in considerable part to the public interest, as the directors conceive it—to hospitals, parks, and charities in the neighborhood of its plants; to the local symphony or the art museum; to scholarships for the children of employees, or to other forms of support for the educational system of the nation at large? If what is good for the country is good for General Motors, as is indeed the case, does this view of managerial responsibility set any limit upon the directors' discretion in spending corporate funds for what they decide is the public good?

*   *   *   *   *

If, as is widely thought, the essence of corporate statesmanship is to seek less than maximum profits, postwar experience is eloquent evidence that such statesmanship leads to serious malfunctioning of the economy as a whole. . . .

*   *   *   *   *

This kind of policy, in either of its aspects, records a failure of the market as the chief instrument for guiding the allocation of capital and labor. If long continued, policies of self-restraint may result in a serious distortion in the pattern of resource use. . . .

*   *   *   *   *

The political and legal aspects of corporate statesmanship present vistas which are quite as disturbing as its economics. The endocratic corporations are accepted as powerful and effective instruments for carrying on the business of society. If their directors begin to act as if they really were general trustees for the public at large, they may well imperil their present freedom. Corporations are not accepted in public opinion as institutions through which society makes its educational policy, its foreign policy, or its political policy. Programs which would give reality to the idea of spending corporate funds to advance the general welfare, as the directors visualize it, will sooner or later invite the critical attention of legislators, governors, and presidents, who consider that they have been elected by the people to advance the general welfare, and know more about it than the directors of endocratic corporations. As Professor Ben W. Lewis has recently said, commenting on the thesis that "the corporation, almost against its will, has been compelled to assume in appreciable part the role of conscience-carrier of twentieth century American society":

"It is not going to happen; if it did happen it would not work; and if it did work it would still be intolerable to free men. I am willing to dream, perhaps selfishly, of a society of selfless men. Certainly, if those who direct our corporate concentrates are to be free from regulation either by competition or government, I can only hope that they will be conscientious, responsible, and kindly men; and I am prepared to be grateful if this proves to be the case. But I shall still be uneasy and a little ashamed, with others who are ashamed, to be living my economic life within the limits set by the gracious bounty of the precious few. If we are to have rulers, let them be men of good will; but above all, let us join in choosing our rulers—and in ruling them."[1]

The responsibility of corporate directors requires redefinition. It may give us a warm and comfortable feeling to say that the director is a trustee for the community, rather than for his stockholders; that he is a semipublic official, or a quasi-public official, or some other kind of hyphenated public officer. It would be more constructive, however, to seek redefinition in another sense: to restate the law of corporate trusteeship in terms which take full account of the social advances of this century, but which direct the directors more sharply to concentrate their efforts on discharging their historic economic duties to their stockholders. The economic job of directors and management is quite difficult enough to absorb the full time of first-rate minds, in an economy of changing technology, significant general instability, and considerable competition, both from rival firms in the same industry and from those which steadily offer rival products.

*   *   *   *   *

. . . Is "the long-run economic interest of stockholders" any more meaningful as a standard to guide the deliberation of directors, or the decisions of courts or other public bodies reviewing what the directors have done, than "the interests of the enterprise as a whole," or "the interests of the community?" . . .

*   *   *   *   *

. . . As an abstract statement of the social duty of business enterprise in the middle of the twentieth century, I believe the "rule" I have suggested—that of long-term profit maximization—conforms more concretely than any alternative both to the image of preferred reality for business behavior in public opinion, at this state in the evolution of our legal and economic order, and to the ends business enterprise is expected to fulfill as part of the nation's system of law for governing the economy.

*   *   *   *   *

. . . [A] clear acceptance of profit maximization as a legal principle might well do something, perhaps a good deal, to order the pattern of corporate policy. Legal rules are not always fully self-enforcing, of course. But they do exert an influence, even though procedures of enforcement are not comprehensive. Adequate means for surveillance and accounting can and should be developed, to minimize abuses of corporate power. The more important problem, however, is the orientation of legitimate business policy: should it be essentially economic in purpose, or should it become an ambiguous amalgam of economic and non-economic themes? I, for one, conclude that a clear cut economic directive should help directors to discriminate more effectively among competing claims upon them, in carrying out their public trusteeship for the economic system as a whole.

---

[1] "Economics by Admonition," *American Economic Review,* Supplement, 49: 384, 395 (1959).

From

CONCEPTUAL FOUNDATIONS OF BUSINESS*

By Richard Eells and Clarence Walton†

"Property" is the word we use to describe land, tangible objects, and certain intangible legal rights, with specific reference to the ownership thereof. "Private property" is property the ownership of which is vested, more or less, in individuals or groups other than public governments. The commonest form of group ownership today is the business corporation.

Historically, "ownership" has meant possession *and* the right, enforceable by legal process, to possess, control, and use the particular item of property and its products. . . . One of the great law teachers of the early part of this century defined property as follows: "A true property may, therefore, be shortly defined as possession coupled with the unlimited right of possession. If these two elements are vested in different persons there is a divided ownership."[1]

* * * * *

. . . It is easy to demonstrate that property, especially that which is productive, has rarely if ever in our Western civilization been entirely free from the claims of the polity.

* * * * *

The varieties of claimants on the corporation—and hence upon the resources controlled by managerial decision makers—can best be understood in another way: through a study of the art of governance within the corporate constellation and through a consideration of the roles of *direct* and *indirect* claimants and contributors to the wealth and welfare of the organization.

DIRECT CLAIMANTS ON THE CORPORATION

Security Holders

Those who supply the capital represented by the capital stock, the corporate bonds, and the notes with maturities in excess of a year are potent contributors to the corporate enterprise. The contributors of capital thus fall into several categories of senior and junior security holders. Their respective "stakes" in the venture are variously defined by law and custom, and their claims on the corporate usufruct vary accordingly.

* * * * *

The property of a corporation is owned by the *persona ficta* and not, either in law or in fact, by the "share owners." The corporate "person" acts through its

---

* Reprinted by permission of Richard D. Irwin, Inc., Homewood, Ill., 1961 (pp. 185–87, 149–67, 458, 468–75).

† Dr. Walton is President of Catholic University of America. Dr. Eells is a noted author and consultant to business.

[1] James Barr Ames, "The Disseisin of Chattels," in Association of American Law Schools (ed.), *Select Essays in Anglo-American Legal History* (Boston: Little, Brown & Co., 1909), Vol. III, p. 563.

board of directors, as a collective body, and it is they alone who may determine how the property is used, how earnings are calculated, and how net earnings are distributed. Although they must act within the boundaries of legally set norms, their discretionary area for decision making is wide. . . .

*   *   *   *   *

If, as the more adamant traditionalists[2] argue, the common stockholders alone have a legitimate claim on the earnings of a company, it is obvious that the structure of authority in most corporations does not guarantee such a result. On the contrary, what we have is a business institution in which the directors tend to act as "trustees for the institution and not merely as attorneys for the stock-holder" and in which "the management of large corporations is largely unaccountable to the stockholders.[3] This is not to say that management bears no responsibility to stockholders, but that the line of accountability does not run to the "ultimate owners" directly. And it is often said that managerial responsibility ought not to run either directly *or* indirectly to the share owners *alone*.

*   *   *   *   *

The contrary view is that this amounts to establishing an authoritarian status for a managerial elite "who from their *own* ethical standards will 'assign' income shares."[4] It is one thing to say that the risk-bearing stockholder has little function; it is quite another to say that he deserves little respect. When the demands of other claimants are given equal weight, it is argued, the nature of corporate enterprise is radically altered and the foundations of capitalism are threatened.

The issue thus joined is certain to become one of the most difficult for strategic decision makers of the future, in the fields both of business and of public policy.

Employees

Employees as a group are clearly direct claimants on the corporate enterprise because they are direct contributors to it and are contractually related to the firm. Like the contributors of risk capital, they invest something they own. Their investment is comparable in that they expect a return on it from the fruits of the venture.

Dividends have been called "the wages of capital." . . . In much the same way, people invest the best part of their lives in some established and promising companies at a rate of return—in the form of wages and salaries—that may seem modest enough at the start but is acceptable in anticipation of other benefits.

Nor are these benefits only the expected wage and salary benefits and advances over the years; the anticipated income includes those "fringe benefits" that increasingly go along with the job, plus some benefits that nowhere appear in the formal employment contracts. Association with certain companies yields "psychic income." Prestige, a sense of security, the feeling that one works for a "good corporate citizen" in a laudable field of endeavor, satisfaction in work that contributes to one's skills and enlightenment about some aspect of nature or society—these are some of the considerations that attract the necessary human

---

[2] Louis O. Kelso and Mortimer J. Adler, *The Capitalist Manifesto* (New York: Random House, 1958). See Eells, *The Meaning of Modern Business,* pp. 77–94.

[3] George B. Hurff, *Social Aspects of Enterprise in the Large Corporation* (Philadelphia: University of Pennsylvania Press, 1950), pp. 96 ff.

[4] David McCord Wright, "The Modern Corporation—Twenty Years After," *University of Chicago Law Review,* Vol. XIX (Summer, 1952), pp. 663 ff.

resources to the organization, just as the anticipated growth and earnings prospects of a company attract capital resources.

*   *   *   *   *

There is . . . a competition for the loyalty and solidarity of employees between firm and union. Insofar as an employee's loyalties are polarized toward the outside organization, his place in the constellation of corporate interests moves toward the periphery of that constellation.

The corporate executive of the future will have to recast the theory of the firm to account for this trend. The implications are many. One, or course, has to do with the whole area of "human relations," or the restoration of organic unity in the enterprise as a human association, and not merely an aggregation of capital in the accounting sense of that term. . . .

*   *   *   *   *

Customers

According to Peter F. Drucker, "there is only one valid definition of business purpose: to create a customer." It follows that "any business enterprise has two—and only two—basic functions: marketing and innovation." This is in line with the doctrine of customer sovereignty: "King Customer" must be placed above all.

Here some distinctions are in order. Does one mean that the general public is the legitimate determiner of corporate policy? Or is something else meant—for example, the meeting and creating of "demands" for salable products and services, regardless of the "public interest" as expressed by representatives of the general public? Obviously not all products of profitable enterprise are "good" products, and some salable services are proscribed by law and morals. Customers and consumers are not necessarily identical groups, nor can either be designated, without careful qualification, as a direct contributor-claimant in any corporate constellation of interests.

A corporation's customers are the main source of its business income; but it is one thing to center the goals of the business on supplying demand and quite another to proliferate corporate objectives so as to meet all the ideal requirements of a hypothetical consumer public.

*   *   *   *   *

Suppliers

The sources of supply for the large corporation as a going concern are extremely diverse. In the widest sense, suppliers include all contributors of material, financial, and human resources. Supply refers also to certain social costs, that are not accounted for in the entrepreneurial outlays but instead are shifted to and borne by third persons and the community as a whole.[5]

Here we are concerned with those direct contributor-claimant suppliers outside

---

[5] K. William Kapp, *The Social Costs of Private Enterprise* (Cambridge: Harvard University Press, 1950). He includes cost resulting from the impairment of the human factor of production; depletion and destruction of animal resources; depletion of energy resources; soil erosion, soil depletion, and deforestation; and social costs of air and water pollution, of technological change, of unemployment and idle resources, and of distribution and transportation.

the firm whose goods and services are reflected directly in entrepreneurial outlays, except for taxes. . . .

*   *   *   *   *

INDIRECT CLAIMANTS ON THE CORPORATION

*   *   *   *   *

Competitors

A competitive firm has no obligation, strictly speaking, toward competitors; its obligation, if any, is to the competitive system and to the norms that organized society establishes for competitive conduct. All responsible business executives recognize that, quite aside from their legal obligations to obey antitrust laws, there is a moral obligation to competitors that arises independently of the rules of law. Some of this nonlegal obligation has its roots in "enlightened self-interest" to the extent that competition is regarded as "the life of trade," or as a stimulant to innovation and *esprit de corps* in the organization, and so on. . . .

*   *   *   *   *

Local Communities

The most immediate peripheral group of interests that vitally concern a corporation is the local community—or rather the numerous local communities—in which it operates as a going concern. The contributions of these communities are many, and so are their claims on the businesses located there.

*   *   *   *   *

The claimant community specifies its own requirements: regular employment, good working conditions, fair play, satisfying work, local purchase of a reasonable part of the firm's supply of goods and services, the maintenance of a plant worthy of a good neighbor, and interest in and support of the local government and of local charitable and cultural projects.

The General Public and Governments

The contributions of the general public have been alluded to earlier with reference to the "social costs of private enterprise." As a taxpayer, the corporation is clearly a direct contributor to public governments as claimants on the fruits of the enterprise. . . .

*   *   *   *   *

"Social Responsibilities"

*   *   *   *   *

But what are the major or minor types of responsibility? As to the ultimate owners, is it a "fair return" on their investment or all the net profits in any year? As to customers, is it a "fair" price for products or all that the traffic will bear? (Or is it a "good" product and constant innovation to provide more and better new products?) As to employees, is it a "fair" wage and good working conditions or status, with all the overtones of security and the dimensions of the good life? As to others in the business community—competitors, suppliers—is it the minimal standard of conduct in a hard and competitive drive for profits or behavior in accordance with some ideal code? As to the public and governments, is it a shrewd avoidance of infractions of the law and the building of stout barriers against any encroachment of government on business, or a common pursuit of the general welfare through some form of mixed economy?

The question of the "social responsibilities" of the modern corporation thus turns out to be no simple issue but a large bundle of issues. It cannot be reduced to the single relationship between corporation and society, for the referents in these ambiguous terms are unclear. . . .

*   *   *   *   *

Interrelationships and the Balancing of Interests

If we concede that there is an accountability that goes with wealth and power, then the logic of responsibility for those who hold it is easy to establish. The corporation is a center of wealth and power, and it has, therefore, responsibilities to those most dependent upon it. These are its stockholders, its employees, and its customers. But its employees, its customers, and its stockholders are also the community. Therefore, it has a social as well as an economic responsibility.

To assess the nature of this responsibility is one of the functions of management. . . .

*   *   *   *   *

THE MIDDLE GROUND

The large business corporation is here to stay. It is an indispensable instrument for getting done some of the things that people want done. It is neither the exclusive instrument of one class of interests nor an indiscriminate roster of "social" interests. Like other large organizations, the corporation must be tempered to the times, and as a viable instrument it must adapt to the changing requirements of our free, complex, and interdependent society.

The impossibility of direct owner management of large-scale private enterprise calls for professional management by persons whose relationship to the owners is difficult to define. Is it a fiduciary relationship, one of agency, or perhaps one of representation?

*   *   *   *   *

To resist the many new claims made on the corporation is to assume an eminently respectable traditional position grounded on the logic of property. But to be rational is not necessarily to be reasonable. Reasonable regard for the interests of society is a practical necessity.

From

THE 20TH CENTURY CAPITALISTIC REVOLUTION*

By Adolf A. Berle†

Now planning all or any fragment of an economy has enormous implications. This is why any "planned economy" has been feared in America; why economy planned by the state has usually been bitterly fought; why emergence of planning power immediately raises doubts and wonders in the minds of the constituency affected. Naturally, any plan (if it is not a naked power-grab) must be a plan for something, and affects or limits people. Planning, however limited in scope, means planning for some kind of a community, or at least some aspect of a community, deemed by some group to be desirable. Capacity to plan, united with power to give effect to the plan, is perhaps the highest trust granted to statesmen. Its devolution has forced into the hands of many businessmen a complex of problems far beyond their chosen fields, problems of overpassing those of producing oil or electrical supplies, of manufacturing steel or motor cars, as the case may be. It may have been naive public relations for an officer of General Motors, proposed for confirmation as Secretary of Defense in the Cabinet of the United States, to. say that what was good for General Motors was good for the country, and what was good for the country was good for General Motors; but he could have adduced an impressive array of statistical fact to back up his statement.

For the fact seems to be that the really great corporation managements have reached a position for the first time in their history in which they must consciously take account of philosophical considerations. They must consider the kind of a community in which they have faith, and which they will serve, and which they intend to help to construct and maintain. In a word, they must consider at least in its more elementary phases the ancient problem of the "good life," and how their operations in the community can be adapted to affording or fostering it. They may endeavor to give their views exact statement, or they may merely proceed on undisclosed premises; but, explicitly or implicitly, the premises are there.

Businessmen charged with commercial enterprise are not accustomed to this sort of thinking. As a rule, they reject the idea that this is part of their function. Most corporation executives are acutely aware of the fact that foresight is extremely difficult. Many believe quite frankly, and not without justification, that community welfare is as likely to be developed soundly by hazard as by plan.

The greatest leaders in the corporate field take a contrary view. They forcefully argue that corporations are always citizens of the community in which they operate, while large ones necessarily play a mighty part in the life of their time. It is not possible for them, these men state, to carry on great corporate businesses apart from the main context of American life. If private business and businessmen

---

* From *The 20th Century Capitalistic Revolution*, copyright, 1954, by Adolf A. Berle, Jr. Reprinted by permission of Harcourt, Brace & World, Inc. (Abstracts from pp. 164–69, 171–73, 182–88.)

† At the time this book was published the author was Professsor Emeritus of Law at Columbia Law School, a corporate lawyer, corporate director, and government official.

do not assume community responsibilities, government must step in and American life will become increasingly statist. In consequence, they have urged that corporations must share the burdens of supporting the non-governmental philanthropic and educational institutions which have played so stately a role in the development of twentieth-century America. Mr. Irving Olds, at the time Chairman of the Board of Directors of U.S. Steel Company, made a brilliant and moving address at Yale University, insisting that corporations must contribute to the general educational facilities of the country, such as universities and graduate schools, and that the duties of big business overpass their traditional power to make gifts to those minor or local charities incident to plant and sales operations. He was forcefully supported by Mr. Frank Abrams, Chairman of the Board of Standard Oil Company of New Jersey. Both corporations gave emphatic proof of assent by voting substantial gifts to liberal arts colleges. Twenty-nine states have already passed statutes authorizing corporations, both presently existing and subsequently organized to make contributions to philanthropy and education. . . . For practical purposes, the state has authorized corporations to withhold from their shareholders a portion of their profits, channeling it to schools, colleges, hospitals, research, and other good causes.

Twenty years ago, the writer had a controversy with the late Professor E. Merrick Dodd, of Harvard Law School, the writer holding that corporate powers were powers in trust for shareholders while Professor Dodd argued that these powers were held in trust for the entire community. The argument has been settled (at least for the time being) squarely in favor of Professor Dodd's contention.

*   *   *   *   *

Growing consciousness of the power thus achieved and its implications has excited a very considerable discussion in the corporate world. Directors, especially those of the largest and most responsible companies, are acutely aware of the problems thus raised. A division of opinion is reported in these circles. One group believes it necessary to pick up the load and tackle the immense responsibilities foreshadowed as did Mr. Olds and Mr. Abrams. Another group takes the view that this is not their affair, that they are not equipped to meet it, and that they should find ways of avoiding so great a burden. After all, a board of directors is chosen primarily for its ability in running a particular business. It cannot properly or effectively enter into a whole series of extraneous problems extending all the way from methods of administering individual justice to community development, community organization and community values. This school of thought believes that teachers, scholars, philosophers, and possibly politicians and governments, have to wrestle with these questions: boards of directors cannot. Both views are expressed with honesty and great sincerity.

Corporations still have, perhaps, some range of choice: they can either take an extended view of their responsibility, or a limited one. Yet the choice is probably less free than would appear. Power has laws of its own. One of them is that when one group having power declines or abdicates it, some other directing group immediately picks it up; and this appears constant throughout history. The choice of corporate managements is not whether so great a power shall cease to exist; they can merely determine whether they will serve as the nuclei of its organization or pass it over to someone else, probably the modern state. The present current of thinking and insistence that private rather than governmental decisions are soundest for the community are clearly forcing the largest corporations toward a greater rather than a lesser acceptance of the responsibility that goes with power.

Men squarely facing this problem, in small or in large application, now find themselves, with some surprise, in the realm of philosophy. They have not, it is true, been assigned the job of sketching an Utopia; they only have to take—indeed, can only take—one step at a time. But they can hardly avoid determining the direction of the steps, and the aggregate of their steps in the second half of the twentieth century must necessarily go far toward determining the framework of the American community of the twenty-first. Some sort of hypothesis, however hazy, as to what that community should be, should do, and should look like, seems implicit in this situation.

*   *   *   *   *

. . . [T]he corporation, almost against its will, has been compelled to assume in appreciable part the role of conscience-carrier of twentieth-century American society. Unlike other great groups which have attempted a major part in this task, the modern corporation has done so without intent to dominate and without clearly defined doctrine. . . .

. . . [O]ut of the common denominator of the decision-making machinery, some sort of consensus of mind is emerging, by compulsion as it were, which for good or ill is acting surprisingly like a collective soul. Great organizations energizing this sort of causative apparatus have their frightening side. When Mary Wollstone-craft Shelley's hero, Frankenstein, endowed his synthetic robot with a human heart, the monster which before had been a useful mechanical servant suddenly became an uncontrollable force. Our ancestors feared that corporations had no conscience. We are treated to the colder, more modern fear that, perhaps, they do.

Certain safeguards do exist. Perhaps during the next hitch in this twentieth-century drama they will be sufficient. The great difference between the American corporate system and any socialist system lies in the fact that in America there are a few hundred powerful units, each of which has a limited capacity to disagree with its fellow giants and to do something different. . . .

. . . The reality—a "conscience" in business organizations which do control many men—need be neither impractical nor dangerous once the business community has learned to honor difference and deviation as well as agreement and conformity. Happily in America there have always been the men who will not "go along." We have reason to hope there will be enough disagreement so that the nuclei of power and of social organization will not only agree, but differ as well.

There is also still another and greater hope. Even within the pressures which organizations exact—even in spite of the necessity that men in great enterprises shall work as a team—the individuals themselves are invariably influenced by certain great philosophical premises. These, in our system, are not derived from within business organization. They come from schools and from teachers; from universities and philosophers; from men of deep human instinct who are, by occasional miracle, saints. . . .

*   *   *   *   *

. . . There is fair historical ground to anticipate that moral and intellectual leadership will appear capable of balancing our Frankenstein creations. Men working in that range are measurably steeled to resist normal pressures and often free from normal fears. They frequently have a rough time on the way. It is no accident that some of the greatest saints in the Christian Calendar were non-conformist deviants in their time; but they still grasp the future with their conceptions.

These, I think, are the real builders of any "City of God" Americans would come to accept. Corporations cannot make them. But they may protect and maintain them. Corporate managements, like others, knowingly or unknowingly, are constrained to work within a frame of surrounding conceptions which in time impose themselves. The price of failure to understand and observe them is decay of the corporation itself. . . .

From

A. P. SMITH MANUFACTURING COMPANY V. BARLOW ET AL.*

[EDITORS' NOTE: A. P. Smith Manufacturing Company appropriated $1,500 as a gift to Princeton University. Stockholders objected on the grounds that such gift-giving was an *ultra vires* act—outside the chartered powers of the company. Below are excerpts from statements made in the case by business executives, a college President, and one of the Supreme Court judges.]

Mr. Hubert F. O'Brien, the president of the company, testified that he considered the contribution to be a sound investment, that the public expects corporations to aid philanthropic and benevolent institutions, that they obtain good will in the community by so doing, and that their charitable donations create favorable environment for their business operations. In addition, he expressed the thought that in contributing to liberal arts institutions, corporations were furthering their self-interest in assuring the free flow of properly trained personnel for administrative and other corporate employment. Mr. Frank W. Abrams, chairman of the board of the Standard Oil Company of New Jersey, testified that corporations are expected to acknowledge their public responsibilities in support of the essential elements of our free enterprise system. He indicated that it was not "good business" to disappoint "this reasonable and justified public expectation," nor was it good business for corporations "to take substantial benefits from their membership in the economic community while avoiding the normally accepted obligations of citizenship in the social community." Mr. Irving S. Olds, former chairman of the board of the United States Steel Corporation, pointed out that corporations have a self-interest in the maintenance of liberal education as the bulwark of good government. He stated that "Capitalism and free enterprise owe their survival in no small degree to the existence of our private, independent universities" and that if American business does not aid in their maintenance, it is not "properly protecting the long-range interest of its stockholders, its employees and its customers." Similarly, Dr. Harold W. Dobbs, President of Princeton University, suggested that if private institutions of higher learning were replaced by governmental institutions our society would be vastly different and private enterprise in other fields would fade out rather promptly.

---

* Reprinted from 98 *Atlantic Reporter,* 2nd Series, New Jersey Supreme Court 1953 (pp. 582–83, 586, 590).

Further on he stated that "democratic society will not long endure if it does not nourish within itself strong centers of nongovernmental fountains of knowledge, opinons of all sorts not governmentally or politically originated. If the time comes when all these centers are absorbed into government, then freedom as we know it, I submit, is at an end."

*   *   *   *   *

[Judge Jacobs:]

*   *   *   *   *

During the first world war corporations loaned their personnel and contributed substantial corporate funds in order to insure survival; during the depression of the '30's they made contributions to alleviate the desperate hardships of the millions of unemployed; and during the second world war they again contributed to insure survival. They now recognize that we are faced with other, though nonetheless vicious, threats from abroad which must be withstood without impairing the vigor of our democratic institutions at home and that otherwise victory will be pyrrhic indeed. More and more they have come to recognize that their salvation rests upon sound economic and social environment which in turn rests in no insignificant part upon free and vigorous nongovernmental institutions of learning. It seems to us that just as the conditions prevailing when corporations were originally created required that they serve public as well as private interests, modern conditions require that corporations acknowledge and discharge social as well as private responsibilities as members of the communities within which they operate.

From

THE ATTACK ON BIG BUSINESS*

By John Desmond Glover†

. . . It is surprising and ironical, that, to judge by what businessmen often *say,* one would think that they, too, agree that the nature of business corporations is exactly and precisely what critics say it is; namely, that the corporation has no other purpose, and recognizes no other criterion of decision except profits, and that it pursues these profits just as single-mindedly and irresponsibly as it can.

*   *   *   *   *

For one thing, it is probable that some objectives of corporate policy and some of the considerations which actually enter decisions are so much *taken for granted* that, in all its dealing with suppliers, customers, employees, and others, "the company" will endeavor to be generous, honest, sincere, and responsible. Yet it sometimes seems difficult for people to talk about things like this—to concede, for instance, that one of the major objectives of the company *is* to be a *good*

---

* Reprinted by permission of the Graduate School of Business Administration, Harvard University, Division of Research, Cambridge, Mass., 1954 (pp. 328, 330–35).

† The author is Professor of Business Administration, Graduate School of Business Administration, Harvard University.

company. Perhaps it is because that is entirely taken for granted. Perhaps it is because, in our culture, people are sometimes "ashamed" or embarrassed to talk of such things. . . .

Another factor which may account for the curiously narrow concept of the purposes and values of the large corporation that often seems to come through to the public may be that business enterprise has, as yet, no systematic rationalization that takes into account these other "taken-for-granted" factors. The only systematic rationalization we have is that which stemmed out of a materialistic, mechanistic philosophy. Possibly, these ideas have been buried themselves so deeply in our thinking that many people, when they come to rationalize about business, have only these traditional concepts with which to think and to talk about it. . . .

. . . [I]t is probably that these two considerations account for the fact that in their talk and in their rationalizations, businessmen sometimes do *sound* just like the stereotype cast up for them by the critics. Some businessmen seem emotionally as well as intellectually unable to admit that they do govern their actions by something more than economic expediency and that they are, in fact, at least no less responsible and less good citizens than others in the community. . . .

. . . For many purposes of the law, the business corporation is conceived to be the very same bloodless, heartless, opportunistic, selfishly calculating entity depicted by its critics. . . .

This stark concept of the corporation shows up nowhere more clearly than in decisions in suits concerning the power of corporations to make contributions and in decisions as to what are "ordinary and necessary" business expenses.

A leading case in this field is the English case of *Hutton* v. *West Cork Railway Company.* In this case, a company *in liquidation* had voluntarily made additional severance payments to employees who were being discharged and who had been paid their regular wages in full. In the stockholders' suit over this matter, the judge accepted the argument that the stockholders of the company could receive no benefit in return from these additional payments. That is, they could receive no pecuniary return. He therefore ruled that the directors exceeded their powers in making such terminal payments.

Revealing the concept of the corporation as a chilled entity quite unresponsive to feelings of warmth, obligation, or responsibility, the judge held that the directors exceeded their powers in making these payments, because they were not *businesslike,* but *charitable.* He laid down the rule that, "Charity has no business to sit at boards of directors *qua* charity."

*   *   *   *   *

The judge, if he had had a different concept of business and of the corporation, might have viewed these payments simply as a warm act flowing from a feeling of obligation—the kind of act that people individually and in corporate bodies engage in every day in the normal carrying on of business. Had he had such a concept, the judge might well have held that making such payments was well "within the ordinary scope of the company's business." He did accept the idea, however, that since there was no pecuniary return to the stockholders, the act was not an act of *business,* but—and the categorical contrast is a deeply invidious one—an act of "charity."

*   *   *   *   *

. . . [A] seemingly charitable act can be justified if it can be shown that it was *really* motivated only by the ulterior intent of furthering the corporation's own interest in a calculated way. For that *is* in accord with the assumed nature of the corporation, which is to direct all its actions to furthering its own interests.

*   *   *   *   *

In other words, the test of an act, as to whether it is the sort of thing a corporation might ordinarily and necessarily do in carrying on its business, is whether the motivation is *purely mercenary.*

In the inverted morality of corporations—as laid down for them by the law—any act in which there enters a thought of charity or philanthropy, or any imponderable feelings of business responsibility and obligation, is not the kind of thing corporations can be expected ordinarily to do. The reason, of course, is that the corporation is conceived to be single-purposed and irresponsible. The norm of corporate behavior is what such an entity as this might do—not what a normal group of people might do.

This concept of the business corporation in law, and the rule which flows from it, results in corporation lawyers cooking up, for formal resolutions to be adopted by boards of directors, the most far-fetched kinds of reasons to rationalize as calculating acts for gain what were simply normal acts of people trying to exercise ordinary judgment. In fact, the rule *drives* lawyers to insist upon the invention of elaborate ulterior reasons for decisions which are actually made on the basis of ordinary, common-sense judgments. Corporations are compelled, for the record, to malign their own motives.

From

THE WEALTH OF NATIONS*

By Adam Smith†

. . . [E]very individual necessarily labours to render the annual revenue of the society as great as he can. He generally, indeed, neither intends to promote the public interest, nor knows how much he is promoting it. By preferring the support of domestic to that of foreign industry, he intends only his own security; and by directing that industry in such a manner as its produce may be of the greatest value, he intends only his own gain, and he is in this, as in many other cases, led by an invisible hand to promote an end which was no part of his intention. Nor is it always the worse for the society that it was no part of it. By pursuing his own interest he frequently promotes that of the society more effectually than when he really intends to promote it. I have never known much good done by those who affected to trade for the public good. It is an affectation, indeed, not very common among merchants, and very few words need be employed in dissuading them from it.

*   *   *   *   *

. . . The natural effort of every individual to better his own condition, when suffered to exert itself with freedom and security, is so powerful a principle, that

---

* Published by Random House Inc., in the Modern Library Series, 1937 (pp. 423, 508).

† Adam Smith (1723–90) is generally considered to be the father of classical economic theory, an archenemy of mercantilism and a proponent of laissez-faire capitalism.

it is alone, and without any assistance, not only capable of carrying on the society to wealth and prosperity, but of surmounting a hundred impertinent obstructions with which the folly of human laws too often incumbers its operations; though the effect of these obstructions is always more or less either to encroach upon its freedom, or to diminish its security. . . .

From

ALTERNATIVE TO SERFDOM*

By John Maurice Clark†

[EDITORS' NOTE: This articulate spokesman of the free enterprise system sounds a clarion of warning to self-interest—"the price of freedom is its responsible exercise." He scores exclusive reliance on the market mechanism to equitably maintain the balance within our social system. Mutuality of interest demands a new dimension of intelligent interaction.]

So, if this series of talks has a single keynote, it is the principle that the price of freedom is its responsible exercise. This has always been true; irresponsible self-interest would have wrecked our system long ago if it had been pushed to the utmost limits that some theories contemplated. But today the need is vastly greater and more immediate. New and greater private powers call for new and greater responsibilities, and the disaster that waits on failure is more immediate and more complete.

The responsibility in question works in two directions. Whenever man acts as an individual, he is responsible to his group or his community; and when he acts on behalf of his group, he is responsible to the members of the group he represents; and on behalf of the group he is responsible to his community—to the whole society or to some larger constituent group of which the first group is a member. This two-way relationship extends from the smallest groups to the largest one of which we are accustomed to thinking—the nation. The nation is recognizing long-neglected responsibilities to its individual members, and in addition is wrestling with its responsibilities to the world community that is struggling to be born, and that must be born if the world is to go on living.

Groups are numerous and varied, and every individual is a member of many. Our job of social salvation lies in reworking the relations of these groups and of the individuals within them. And there is much to be done. The democratic state has not found its place, nor how to do its job, in the new world. Instead of being the organ of a unified society, with its functions and powers arising rather naturally from the constitution of the society it represents, it is groping desperately, precisely

* Reprinted from *Alternative to Serfdom,* by John Maurice Clark, by permission of Alfred A. Knopf, Inc. Copyright 1948 by The Regents of the University of Michigan. (Excerpts from pp. 4–7.)

† The late author was Professor of Economics at Columbia University.

because it has no organized society back of it in respect of most things—only when the country is attacked overtly, by force of arms and by a foreign power. More dangerous threats to our social constitution, from within, do not unify, but divide us.

Economically, we are not a community. The market has had such marvelous organizing powers that it has deluded many of us, for some hundred and seventy years; into thinking that it could do all that was needed to organize an economic community on a basis oi consent as embodied in the act of free exchange. But it has been growingly evident for many years that this was expecting from it something beyond its powers, great as these were. We have gradually discovered—though many have not admitted it—that markets can organize material interests only, and not all of these, and that this is not enough to constitute a society. Some of us learned this many years ago, from Charles H. Cooley; today the lesson is being driven home again, with freshly urgent emphasis, by Karl Polanyi. Things the market pseudo-society has wrecked are hopefully turned over to the state, a too vast and impersonal mechansim whose constitution does not correspond too well to the economic realities.

Between the individual and government, or markets, stand great organized groups; farm federations, business corporations, and labor unions. And these are the crux of the present dilemma. In a simple economy without such groups, irresponsible self-interest is—almost—a possible organizing principle in the strictly material realm. It would merely mean the exploitation of the weak by the strong, the incapable by the capable. But organize society into groups, and irresponsible self-interest can both corrupt the groups and shatter the society.

Why does a state need an organized community back of it, to the constitution of which its own constitution corresponds? Because otherwise the alternative is coercion or chaos. If the community is itself well knit, it can call on the state to do various things that the state can best do; but coercion will be needed only to keep recalcitrant minorities within bounds. But if within the society there is a "state of nature" that approximates a state of war, then the state either will fail to maintain tolerable order, or will do it at the cost of general and indiscriminate coercion, and either way personal liberty is lost.

And at present the economic groups into which we are organized are too near this condition, groups are too large, too sophisticated, too consciously and rationally purposeful, to organize themselves into a community of the "natural" sort of which anthropologists tell us, as found, for example, in the South Sea Islands before white civilization submerged them. The organizing of these warring groups must be done by the most deliberate kind of action associated with the theory of the "social contract." In fact, we seem to be in a stage of human development to which some form of "social contract" theory may, for the first time, be applicable on the scale of a "great society." But not for the whole job of organizing a community. There must be an underlying feeling of a common bond, if only the danger of mutual annihilation, to furnish a basis for a willingness to recognize mutual rights and responsibilities. And so we come back to our central theme.

This calls for an adventure in reconstruction, for which no happy outcome can be guaranteed. The world is in the grip of a mightly struggle. On one side are forces driving toward chaos and anarchy, political, social, economic, and moral. On the other side are forces of centralized control. Between them stand the forces and men who are trying desperately to salvage a workable basis for a humane and ordered community, in which some effective degree of freedom and democracy may be kept alive, without wrecking society by their undisciplined exercise and disruptive excesses. There is no point in asking, in the Year of Atomic Energy II, for a world safe for freedom and democracy. Society is condemned to live dangerously—of that much we can be sure. Our fighting chance depends on developing the capacity for generous and constructive thinking and acting, beneath the sword of Damocles.

From

SOCIAL OVERHEAD CAPITAL AND THE PRINCIPLE OF SUBSIDIARITY*

By J. J. O'Connell

Colleges and universities face a 100% increase in enrollment in the next decade. We are on the verge of tearing down the "distance curtain" with a satellite communications system to simultaneously unite all men with sight and sound. Expanded life expectancy and shorter work hours open vistas of the "good life" for millions and hold out vast leisure time markets if we can overcome the choking effects of megopolis and provide recreational and cultural facilities. Cancer, heart diseases, and the common cold have yet to be conquered by medical science.

In all these and in innumerable other areas our nation faces the challenges of growth and progress. Who foots the bill? Who should invest in these basic areas? Can we step back and get guides to policy by examining some conceptual schemes from economics and political philosophy?

Our title borrows one concept from economics and one from political philosophy. The first is descriptive (what is) of one part of our economic system. The second is prescriptive (what should be) about one phase of our political system. Neither system exists by itself, so we put the two concepts together to throw some light on policy-making in the politico-economic system.

Jargon need not prevent us from getting a handle on an illusive segment of economic reality and on a powerful conceptualization of political experience. We first examine these two ideas separately and then combine them to see if they help us understand better how our politico-economic system does (or should) work.

Social Overhead Capital

The concept of social overhead capital (hereafter abbreviated SOC) is used mostly by economists who deal with economic development. Broadly speaking, SOC is the substrata of assets and institutions necessary for growth and stability— the underpinnings of a country. The "assets" share the nature of fixed assets in that they are not consumed in use (though they may depreciate)—a dam, for

---

instance. The "institutions" are formalized and relatively permanent behavior pat-terns—the jury system, for example. Obviously, a nation's stock of SOC grows and changes in composition at different stages of development. The SOC of U.S.A.—1963 is vastly different from the SOC of U.S.A.—1776, and just as differ-ent from the SOC of present-day Haiti. It is not easy to define the concept so that it will include the stock of both the mature and the underdeveloped nations. We will build on the attempts at definition made by economists speaking in the context of emerging nations in order to clarify our notion of the stock of SOC of U.S.A.—1963.

One author[1] defines SOC "as comprising those basic services without which primary, secondary, and tertiary productive activities cannot function." While we find Hirshman's definition too confining, his list of distinguishing characteristics is more meaningful, especially when supplemented by W. W. Rostow's similar list.[2] Generally speaking, SOC includes those assets and institutions which (1) support a wide range of economic activities and (2) cannot be imported in the normal sense. The investments called for by such assets and institutions (3) tend to be sizable, indivisible, lump sums, and (4) the payoff period is usually very long. (5)The capital-output ratio (dollars invested divided by dollars realized) is generally large, and (6) the returns more likely benefit the community at large directly than the investors. Pedantically rigid application of these criteria would serve no purpose. We find sufficient reason to include the following in the fund of SOC of the U.S.A.—1963: physical assets like harbors, airports, highways, railroads, dams, munitions and armaments, national forests, satellites, air raid sirens, gas transmis-sion lines, reservoirs, etc.; assets representing institutions (figuratively, the part for the whole) like police revolvers, postal trucks, judges' gavels, legislators' benches, blackboards, etc.; intangible assets like (a) the accumulated knowledge and skill of doctors, managers, scientists, lathe operators, generals, teachers, composers, judges, etc., (b) the physical and mental health of the population, (c) the mobility, and (d) even the sense of security and wellbeing of the citizenry. Are these not the underpinnings of our growing and stable country?

Our listing prompts three observations. First, not all SOC is government owned nor the product of government investment alone. Second, some items of SOC seem difficult to express in our customary dollar terms. However, reduction to dollar valuation may not be impossible if we follow the logic of the corporation and value the asset in terms of the money outlay necessary to secure it. Note that some costs will have to be opportunity costs (the foregone earnings of a doctor during medical school, for instance). Note, too, that there is danger of double counting in valuing something like a fund of knowledge of an individual and in registering the cost of a school building. Such quantification is hazardous and far from perfec-tion.

Third, the quantification of returns generated by SOC raises even more difficul-ties than the quantification of the costs of such assets. Each case has its peculiar difficulties, so a general treatment here is impossible. We can give an example, though, which indicates economists are making progress in this complex area. Men like Professors Gary S. Becker and Jacob Mincer of Columbia University have

---

[1] Hirshman, Albert O., *The Strategy of Economic Development,* New Haven: The Univer-sity Press, 1958, p. 83.

[2] Rostow, W. W., *The Stages of Economic Growth,* Cambridge: The University Press, 1961, pp. 24–25.

been working on projects to figure the rate of return on educational investments. In one study Professor Mincer determined a 12.7% return on the total cost of medical specialization by measuring the returns in dollar income differentials of specialists and general practitioners.[3] Of course, such estimates do not include any quantification of what the incremental education did for the man himself or of what societal satisfactions were derived from the extra education. These attempts may be crude but it is hard to deny that they are steps in the right direction.

Our final point about SOC concerns the investors in such assets. A consideration of the examples we have cited will reveal that, while government is the largest investor, groups and individuals too invest in SOC. The policy question of prime importance is: who *should* invest in SOC? Approaches to an answer must wait until we discuss the principle of subsidiarity.

Principle of Subsidiarity

Stated simply, the principle of subsidiarity prescribes that in any system each function be performed by the lowest competent and willing level in the system's hierarchy. In speaking of the structure of the state, political philosophers reason that a higher level does not exist to swallow up or supersede the lower level but to supplement and extend it. Such reasoning is based on a view of man with rights pre-existing the state. Man as a person transcends the state, yet the individual needs the state. Living in an organized society is natural to man. Such a concept of man and the state dictates that the relationship of the parts, or the building blocks of society be viewed as an organic unity. The individual, the family, voluntary organizations, and the state form a hierarchical arrangement that is organic—in the moral sense. That is, a necessary mutuality of purpose binds the building blocks together without causing the parts to lose independent identity as cells do in a biological entity. On the other side, the organic unity avoids the trap of the atomistic view of society which exaggerates the independence of the parts so that all that remains is a mere juxtaposition of self-serving units.[4]

Given the organic unity in society, the ends of society are best achieved when the individuals, the families, voluntary organizations, and the state severally contribute a pyramid of efforts toward the common good. The principle of subsidiarity offers a guide to order these contributions so that the system as a whole maintains its balanced existence. To repeat: in any system each function should be performed by the lowest competent and willing level in the system's hierarchy.

We have sketched elliptically how the principle is deductively derived—reasoning from premise to conclusion. History shouts empirical verification in every era. Economic statism is lampooned in Adam Smith's diatribe against 18th century mercantilism. Hitler's Germany provides dramatic evidence of a system's deterioration because of state usurpation of virtually all societal functions. Witness the parody of proper order in company unions and industrial paternalism. Agricultural difficulties in China are commentary enough on a communal system which does violence to the family. We should not forget either that the lower level can usurp a higher level's function, as when churches over-stepped their competence and entered the political sphere.

---

[3] Mincer, Jacob, "On-the-Job Training: Costs, Returns, and Some Implications," *Journal of Political Economy*, Oct., 1962, p. 65. (This entire *Journal* Supplement is pertinent to our subject.)

[4] Fagothey, Austin, *Right and Reason*, St. Louis: C. V. Mosby, 1959, pp. 379–95.

Who Should Invest in Social Overhead Capital?

Because of the nature of SOC (described best by the six characteristics listed above) we tend to start and end with the question: who *can* invest in SOC? We reduce the issue to a financial question, jerk a thumb skyward, and say: "Let George do it!" By juxtaposing SOC with the principle of subsidiary, the burden of our message is that a concern for the perversion of societal order should be added to the financial criteria in feasibility studies on SOC projects. A prior consideration of who *should* invest in SOC will hopefully affect the decision about who *can* invest in SOC by adding some cogency to the development of creative approachs by subgovernmental units.

A social critic inclined to sounding jeremiads might prophesy that units of society, whose functions are passed to the next higher level by default, will atrophy so that they no longer can do what they once could do, should have done, but did not do.

From

THE DIRECTOR LOOKS AT HIS JOB*

By Courtney C. Brown and E. Everett Smith (eds.)†

[EDITORS' NOTE: The material in this abstract is drawn from a symposium in which the participants were directors of leading American corporations.]

A director may be either "inside," in the sense of having come up through the company and of being identified with its management, or "outside," in the sense of a person who has been unconnected with the business and has no operating familiarity with it. Directors may also be part-time or full-time, depending on whether they devote the whole of their attention to their director's job or only some portion of their time.

*　　*　　*　　*　　*

The Inside Full-Time Director. Such a person is exemplified in the board of Standard Oil Company (New Jersey) and by the executive committee of the du Pont board. In these and other such cases men who have spent years in the service of the company, having occupied responsible operating positions, have been made directors. But, in contrast to the inside part-time director, they have been released from all operating responsibilities. . . .

*　　*　　*　　*　　*

—The board in a sense is legally conceived, isn't it, to protect the stockholders' interest? It is a representative of the stockholder, if you will.

—Yes.

—There's the implication there that there might be a difference between the

---

* Reproduced by permission of Columbia University Press, New York, 1957 (pp. 38–39, 77–78, 81–83, 85–86, 89, 91–93).

† Courtney C. Brown is Dean Emeritus of the Graduate School of Business, Columbia University. E. Everett Smith is Director, McKinsey and Company.

interest of the management and that of the stockholder, and the board is there to see that it's properly cared for. The implication of the inside board . . . is that there is no distinction between the interest of the management and that of the stockholder.

—I don't follow your conclusion that there is no difference in interest; obviously there is an adverse interest any way you look at it—by adverse I don't mean hostile interest.

—No.

—The more management takes for itself the less there is available for stockholders. So there is that basic conflict of interest.

—Is the inside full-time board as likely to be as perceptive to the political requirements of a corporation as some of the outside people might?

*   *   *   *   *

—. . . [T]he reason we have outside auditors is because even honest and capable accounting executives recognize the need for an independent check on their judgment; and isn't there a need for some kind of external check, and isn't it likely to be welcomed even by capable people?

—Well, are you going to get that through an outside part-time director?

—As one possibility, not the only one.

—I think that you'd get it a lot better through education of full-time directors.

*   *   *   *   *

—As between the strong board, which is a full-time payroll board concerned only with this company, and the board of the kind I described for our company, we prefer the latter on the premise of the danger of getting ingrown—it seems to us to be too real the other way, the danger of overcentralizing too great the other way. Men who have come to a full-time board position through talent and ability as strong executives inside the company carry that symbolism in front of the people in the organization into their new full-time directorate job; they are executives inside the company. We do not think that brings the independence on their part, or the capacity for taking an objective view on their part, or the relationship with the people still in the executive and operating setup, on the other hand, that you can and should get.

*   *   *   *   *

—. . . I don't think there's the slightest doubt in my mind that a great many shareholders have a feeling of satisfaction when they see the names of some very prominent people on their board of directors. I have a feeling also that they place a great deal more confidence in the contribution the big name people make to the company than is justified. But they certainly have a feeling of satisfaction about it; they would like to see, oh, President Eisenhower on the board. It just makes them feel good to have those kinds of people.

—I think the general run of stockholders rather favor outside part-time boards of directors. Not only because they're used to it but I think they're more comfortable about the operation of the company. . . .

*   *   *   *   *

—. . . Let's assume that there is a gradual diminution in the share of the market which a company is getting, or a part of a company. It goes on for let's say five years. Now how do you, with an internal board, a full-time board, measure that decline in participation of market, and how quickly can an inside board do something about it, rather than an outside board?

—I think I can answer that with a great deal of assurance. I think that our board would be much more sensitive to the development of that kind of a situation than the outside or part-time director would be. I'm positive of that, because we look at the thing all the time, we live with it all the time.

I'm also sure that we would be able to evaluate the basic factors, the reasons that are behind that decline, much more quickly and much more readily than part-time directors would, and institute some kind of action, if action is indicated, much more readily than a person who is not close to the business.

* * * * *

—. . . I think one of the things that might be argued in favor of getting, in this case, outside directors into the picture, rather than those that are being brought up through the ranks of the company, is the fact that you will put on the board a completely new viewpoint, because they haven't got a heritage or any background of tradition or preceptorship that has been drilled into them through many years of association with the organization.

So I think that is one of the arguments for at least a leavening of that type of addition to a full-time board.

* * * * *

In summary, the philosophy behind the advocacy of the full-time director is that the meaningful discharge of a director's responsibilities requires a more extensive knowledge of corporate operations than can be acquired through part-time contact. Especially in the large corporation, some of the panel felt, directing is a full-time job, requiring substantial work on the part of individual directors between board meetings, to understand the full range of the business' affairs. Moreover, if the one overriding function of the board is to select the management and to continue to evaluate it, this requires a more continuous contact with management than is possible through even monthly board meetings. Appraisal of management must include more than simple inspection of results as they appear in certain operating statements, if costly mistakes are to be avoided.

The responsibility of the board is a group responsibility, and it is difficult to make this operationally meaningful when the members of the board assemble only briefly and at intervals. Moreover, the danger of a board's becoming ingrown through too much reliance on home-grown talent is reduced when its members can be released from all operational responsibilities, even if they come from the inside (that is, have been brought up through the ranks). Finally, the fear that inside board members will subordinate independent judgment to the will of the chief executive is partly removed since any who have come up through the ranks shed their administrative or executive functions upon assuming the directorial function. Their job specifications change in a more complete and thorough way than is possible when they continue to serve dual functions.

There are, however, serious practical problems in the full-time arrangement. The questions of cost and availability of personnel were raised. . . .

. . . The inside-outside blueprint had evoked a favorable response because it emphasized the independent character of the board and appeared to sharpen the distinction between the functions of the board and those of management. At the same time, the conception of a full-time board had the attractive quality of providing a knowledgeable group in whose judgment management might have greater confidence, on whom it might rely to a greater extent because of its familiarity with the firm's operations, even though the actual organizational arrangements might tend to blur somewhat the lines dividing directional from management functions.

21. GENERAL MOTORS CORPORATION

Case Introduction

SYNOPSIS

The management of General Motors announces plans for joining with a London-based investment trust to construct a modern office building at Fifth Avenue and Fifty-Ninth Street in New York City. This particular area, known as Grand Army Plaza, is characterized by more unique architecture, expensive shops, and, in general, more esthetic surroundings than almost anywhere in Manhattan. The building is opposed by certain groups for a variety of reasons (e.g., that it would destroy an architectural landmark) and supported by others—architects and urban planners. The company management is faced with the problem of whether to proceed with the building or take some other course of action.

WHY THIS CASE IS INCLUDED

In putting himself in the place of a top executive in General Motors, the student can become acquainted with two or three *decision methods* which might help the brain make more reasonable or rational decisions in the kind of problem that is part economic in nature and part "social" or "esthetic" in nature. Two kinds of cost-benefit analysis might be used, as well as the technique of opportunity costs and the technique of discounting future returns. The inclusion of nonquantitative factors and social values in a cost benefit table is another important decision technique which might be used.

Whether the decisions in a company represent the will of the "impersonal" corporation, or the will of executives themselves, is another important insight to be gained from the case.

Finally, the issue of managerial responsibility is explored. Should managers be responsible primarily for profits (as the traditional philosophy of economics holds), or should they be responsible for other social values outside the corporation at the same time?

768

DIAGNOSTIC AND PREDICTIVE QUESTIONS

The readings included with this case are marked (*). The author index at the end of this book locates the other readings.

1. Why do you think General Motors' top management chose the cite at Fifth Avenue and Fifty-Ninth Street for the new building? What benefits did they have in mind?

Read: *Friedman, "A Friedman Doctrine—The Social Responsibility of Business Is to Increase Its Profits."

2. If General Motors could invest its money in more facilities for making automobiles, or in some other business venture, and realize 8 percent return after taxes from this alternative venture, what would be the cost over the next ten years of capital tied up in the land and building? Remember that General Motors would probably put up 50 percent of the capital.

Read: *Bierman and Smidt, *The Capital Budgeting Decision,* pp. 112–13.

3. If the real estate man quoted in the case is correct, what would be the incremental cost to General Motors in yearly rental of floor space per year over the next ten years? (Recall the opportunity cost reading above.)

4. Assume that the Savoy Corporation will make a profit of $2 before taxes on each of the 750,000 square feet rented to the public (tenants other than General Motors). Assume further that General Motors' profit after taxes from this source would be $.50 per foot. What profit will General Motors derive over the next ten years by going into the real estate business?

5. One financial investment planning device used by large businesses, government bureaus, or hospitals is cost-benefit analysis. In this method, a company considers a total project, listing the total costs they will incur and the total benefits they will derive. Combine the answers to Questions 1 to 4 for the next ten-year period.

6. Why were the "save the landmarks" committee concerned about the new building? Weren't there "thousands" of other landmarks available?

Read: *Turvey, "Side Effects of Resource Use. *"America's Everyday Dreariness." *Leopold, "Landscape Esthetics."

7. From the standpoint of the president of General Motors, what is the ethical responsibility of a corporate management? Is the building fulfilling this responsibility or not?

Read: *Friedman (Question 1 above). *Turvey (Question 6 above). Berle, "The Corporation in a Democratic Society." Clark, *Alternative to Serfdom,* pp. 4–7. Drucker, *The Future of Industrial Man,* pp. 32–38.

POLICY QUESTIONS

8. Considering the high cost ($33–40 million) of land for the new building, what alternatives are there for General Motors management to attain their objectives?

Note: Those who wish a discussion of business moving to the suburbs may see "When Companies Go Suburban," *Business Week,* December 12, 1970, pp. 58–60.

9. Draw a line down the middle of a sheet of paper. Label the left side "costs to General Motors and its' management" and the right side "benefits to General Motors and its' management." Utilize the answers from Question 5 to start your listing. This will approximate the costs and benefits to the corporation. Then expand the cost-benefit analysis to include benefits or costs to society (Questions 6 and 7) as added factors. View the effect on General Motor's management's own ethical standards (Question 8). Arrive at a total summary judgment as to whether you, as president of the corporation, would proceed with the new building.

Note: Cost-benefit analysis has been used as a means of judging proposals for public or semipublic investment projects. According to the authorities referred to below, it is "a practical way of assessing the desirability of projects where it is important to take a long view (looking at repercussions in the further, as well as the nearer future) and a wide view (in the sense of allowing for side effects of many kinds on persons, industries, regions)." Those who wish may read of the method in P. K. Else and M. Howe, "Cost-Benefit Analysis and the Withdrawal of Railway Services," *Journal of Transport Economics and Policy,* Vol. 1, No. 2 (May 1969). (Not included in this volume.)

10. Can the conflict between General Motors management and the other parties be viewed as a constructive conflict—one in which everyone might win? If so, list the *real* objectives of the management and the *real* objectives of the other groups. Address a letter to the General Motors president recommending how he might proceed to work out a solution which is "constructive" for both sides.

Read: Follett, "Constructive Conflict."

QUESTIONS FOR ORIGINAL STUDENT WORK IN ANALYSIS AND POLICY

11. While reflecting on case facts, what additional theories from prior education give you insights as to "what is going on" in General Motors Corporation? As to what might be predicted to happen in the future?

12. Other than the policy questions asked by the authors, what pragmatic ways can you think of to state the practical problems faced by executives in the case?

Case Text*

On August 20, 1964, British Commercial Property Investments, Ltd., a subsidiary of a large London investment trust, announced that one of its properties, the Savoy Plaza Hotel, on Fifth Avenue and 59th Street in New York City, would be razed to make way for a 40-story office building. It was later announced that British Commercial had formed a subsidiary corporation, the Savoy Fifth Avenue Corporation, with General Motors Corporation. Each parent company owns 50 percent of Savoy Fifth Avenue. The latter company's principal business is to own the land and construct a new building on the hotel site. General Motors will also be the principal tenant, occupying about 750,000 square feet out of a total floor space of 1.5 million square feet. The new building will be named the General Motors Building.

According to *The New York Times,* no estimate of the cost of the new building was given by any of the principals. However, one official of the London company said that it would probably be comparable in cost to the recently constructed Pan American Building. That building, the *Times* went on, is generally regarded as having a total cost of $100 million.

In an interview with the case writer at the time this case was being written (March 1965), an executive of one of the largest real estate firms in New York stated:

A prime, 80,000-square-foot block similar to the Savoy location would sell at a price somewhere between $33 million and $40 million. These are prices for blocks termed "best available," of which there are no more than three in the city, one of which GM bought. After all, Fifth and Park Avenues are prime, with Madison and Lexington Avenues a close second, in terms of prestige desirability. GM is simply willing to pay much more in investment and in rental for this prestige location. I estimate that the space in the new building will rent between $6.50 and $8.50 a square foot, whereas rent in the area of their old building would be somewhere around $4.50 a square foot.

General Motors' net income for 1964 amounted to $1.7 billion.

THE GRAND ARMY PLAZA AREA

One of the unique features of Manhattan Island is that a walk of a few blocks can transport a person from one entirely different atmosphere to

---

* Copyright 1973 by Charles E. Summer.

another. The ten-minute walk from the present General Motors Building at Broadway and 57th Street, to the Grand Army Plaza at Fifth Avenue and 59th Street is an example. The first location is characterized by heavy, fast-moving traffic, many trucks, automobile dealer displays, and neon advertisements. On the other hand, the second location is vastly different. No commercial trucks are allowed on Fifth Avenue. The pedestrians are expensively dressed, and the buildings house either luxury hotels (the Plaza, the St. Regis, the Pierre) or New York's most sophisticated stores (Bergdorf Goodman, Bonwit Teller, Van Cleef & Arpels, Tiffany & Co., and Cartier). Limousines line the side streets, waiting for owners to return from shopping, or from lunch in elegant hotels or restaurants.

Across the Grand Army Plaza from the Plaza Hotel is the 1,000-room Savoy Plaza Hotel. The two photographs in Exhibit 1 show the front of the Savoy as viewed looking east across Fifth Avenue, through the trees and past the Pulitzer Fountain located in Grand Army Plaza. The hotel was built in the 20s from plans by the architects McKim, Mead, and White, generally accepted as the leading firm of the era. Particularly well known and one of the best know architects in the nation was Stanford White, who was later murdered while dining at the roof restaurant of Madison Square Garden.

VARIOUS REACTIONS TO THE MOVE

Shortly after the announcement of the building in August, there was considerable attention given to the project from a number of different people and groups.

The Fifth Avenue Association, composed of executives of stores and hotels located on Fifth Avenue, immediately retained a panel of architects who, it was hoped, would be given a voice in the plans for the building. Walter Hoving, chairman of Tiffany and Company, said that the project could not help hurting the area, while Andrew Goodman, chairman of Bergdorf Goodman, said, "It will bring a lot of purchasing power into the area and should increase the value of our property. These views are presented in Exhibit 2.

The New York Times itself, in an editorial, expressed "fear of a dismaying new plunge . . . toward architectural mediocrity," and held that "the tragedy, of course, is that New York, unlike Paris or Washington, has no review rights on its main avenues or plazas" (Exhibit 3). Arnold D. Kates, vice president of the Park Association of New York, responded in a letter to the editor that he was pleased with the editorial, that he hoped that the parties concerned would heed its admonitions, and that, if not, "this will arouse the Park Association of New York and the civic agencies with which it cooperates."

Later on, in January and February of 1965, a group of socially prominent New York women formed a committee which threatened a boycott of General Motors products unless the building project was abandoned. The activities of this committee are reported in Exhibits 4 and 5.

EXHIBIT 1
SAVOY PLAZA HOTEL

Looking north on Fifth Avenue. To the left is entrance to Bergdorf Goodman.

View of entrance taken from front door of Plaza Hotel at lunchtime. Fountain at right is in the Grand Army Plaza (park).

Prominent architects of the current era also joined in the public controversy. On September 2, Robert Weinberg warned that "if the area's solid core of hotel, restaurant, and distinguished shopping character is breached, the resulting change in the nature of the open space we call the Plaza may affect New York's prestige more than the facade of a single building." Mr. Weinberg went on to say that the selection of a "name" architect is not enough to insure good design—that unless the *owners* "adopt a publicly announced policy" of esthetics, and unless the architect is "backed up by the owners," there is danger of damage to the area (Exhibit 6). Joseph Watterson, editor of the *Journal of the American Institute of Architects,* went one step further. He wrote the *Times* on October 3 that government review or control is necessary if the esthetic values of the city are to be maintained (Exhibit 7).

One architect, William Lescaze, wrote to the *Times* on September 17 in support of the new building:

> . . . since when do we not welcome new and fresh sources of invest-
> ment, and fresh adventures in building and design? I fail to see why
> the Fifth Avenue Association should become so disturbed that a new
> and modern building would be built on that site. In my opinion, this
> may very well be good not only for our Fifth Avenue, but also for our
> whole city. We cannot assume that the British-Canadian sponsors are
> motivated solely by the revenue and profit factors.

Throughout this period, the General Motors Corporation offered no public comment on its reasons for moving the headquarters to this site, or on the opposition appearing in the press. Statements were made, however, by Mrs. Cecilla Benatter, secretary-treasurer of the Savoy Fifth Avenue Corporation, wholly owned subsidiary of British Commercial (Canada), Ltd. Mrs. Benattar stated in the August 21 *Times* that no architect had been engaged but that "we are going to build a really beautiful building. The whole aim of ourselves and of General Motors is to achieve excellence."

On December 16, however, the public relations firm of Wolcott & Associates, representing Savoy Fifth Avenue Corporation, released an announcement stating that Edward Stone and Emery Roth & Sons had been appointed architects for the building. This release, commenting on Mr. Stone's qualifications, appears as Exhibit 8. On January 27, the *Times* reported that General Motors had filed plans with the New York City Department of Buildings for permission to build the building under existing zoning laws. Sometime after, Wolcott & Associates released the preliminary sketch of the building appearing as Exhibit 9.

On February 4, the officers and Architectural Committee members of the Fifth Avenue Association were invited to view preliminary designs and models of the building in the office of Edward Durell Stone, one of the principal architects. These officers and committee members gave their endorsement to the building, stating that they had not previously known of the unique way in which architect Stone was to design the plaza in front of the building. "[This plaza] will provide a delightful promenade for sightseers and shoppers."

Apparently concerned about the "tougher job of preserving landmarks in big cities as realty values climb," *The Wall Street Journal* surveyed the national situation (Exhibit 10). "Unless the landmarks advocates can find new uses for old buildings, the wrecking is likely to continue. Already about 2,500 of the 10,000 structures (in the United States) recorded since the 1930's in the Government's Historic American Buildings survey have been torn down."

EXHIBIT 2
Merchants Scan Savoy Plaza Plan (Panel of architects named to urge that new building uphold 5th Ave. Dignity)

By Thomas Buckley

The Fifth Avenue Association urged yesterday that the 40-story office building that will replace the Savoy Plaza Hotel "conform to the character and dignity" of the area.

Frank E. Conant, president of the association, appointed a committee of three architects to confer with the company that plans to build the skyscraper and with the General Motors Corporation which will be the principal tenant.

*   *   *   *   *

Although an official of the Canadian concern said that "a really beautiful building" would be erected on the site, real estate leaders here said they doubted that it would be economically possible to construct a showplace such as the Seagram Building or Lever House.

However, at least one leading merchant, Andrew Goodman, chairman of Bergdorf Goodman, said he favored the project.

"It will bring a lot of purchasing power into the area," he said, "and should increase the value of our own property."

Walter Hoving, the chairman of Tiffany & Co., said demolition of the Savoy Plaza could not help hurting the area, which for many years has been noted for fine shops and hotels, and he expressed doubt that it would increase trade.

"I view with a certain amount of sadness the reduction of high-grade residential facilities," he said.

*   *   *   *   *

Looking across the street at the 33-story gray-brick and limestone Savoy Plaza, a Good Humor man tending his wagon at the edge of Central Park said, "I can think of at least 1,000 buildings they could tear down before they tear down that one."

Paul Wilson, driver of one of the carriages that stand along the plaza, said: "It'll spoil the area. This whole section is strictly like the Riviera, cities in Europe, where you've got fine hotels and stores, but no office buildings."

Mr. Wilson, a slender, elegant figure with a hairline mustache, neatly brushed topper and black silk jacket, went on: "Now you've got shops in the Savoy. It's a pleasure. Jewels, perfume, flowers at Max Schling's. So along comes an office building and what've you got? A bank on the street floor?"

Source: From *The New York Times*, August 22, 1964.

EXHIBIT 3
Down with the Savoy Plaza

The news that New York is to have another blockbuster like the Pan Am Building and that it is to be built on the city's most urbane and gracious midtown plaza stirs fear of a dismaying new plunge in the city's unrelenting postwar movement toward architectural mediocrity.

A large British investment trust plans to raze the Savoy Plaza Hotel and erect a metropolitan headquarters for General Motors on the site. "It promises to be," in the trust's words, "one of the most important construction projects of its kind in the world." It also promises to be a concrete threat to one of the city's few genuine claims to urban elegance—the handsome open square at Fifty-ninth Street and Fifth Avenue, at the foot of Central Park, where General Sherman rides confidently toward the tasteful luxuries of Bergdorf Goodman and the last of the grand hotels surround a landscaped fountain offering the waters of Abundance to grateful New Yorkers.

Not that the new building can't be a good one, or a suitable one in its setting. Seagram has proved that corporate palaces may be splendid additions to the city's theme. General Motors, when it built for itself in Michigan, had the late Eero Saarinen design a commercial complex acclaimed as an "industrial Versailles."

On this critical, central New York site anything but the best will spell catastrophe. This will be the first sizeable breach by large commercial construction of a rare area of Old World style and distinction; there is too much danger it could be the beginning of the end.

The tragedy, of course, is that New York, unlike Paris or Washington, has no review rights on its main avenues or plazas. It is now up to the conscience, capabilities and sense of public responsibility of a group of private investors with no direct ties to New York to make or mar the city's face. New York needs no more cut-rate monuments like Pan Am. If the results of this gigantic undertaking are of less than landmark quality it will be an urban disaster.

Source: An Editorial from *The New York Times,* August 24, 1964.

EXHIBIT 4
Women Score G.M. on Building Plan
(group threatens a boycott if
'tombstone' is erected on
site of Savoy Plaza
landmark ruin feared
Fannie Hurst and daughter
of Alfred E. Smith among
supporters of move)

By Thomas W. Ennis

A group of socially prominent New York women are threatening to organize a nationwide boycott of General Motors cars and home appliances.

EXHIBIT 4 (continued)

They say they would do so if the company proceeded with plans to participate in the construction of a 48-story skyscraper on the site of the Savoy Plaza Hotel. The hotel occupies the blockfront on Fifth Avenue between 58th and 59th Streets opposite the Grand Army Plaza at Central Park.

Some of the women own General Motors stock and it is understood that they will put pressure on other women shareholders in the giant industrial concern to join the boycott.

The women have formed a committee called Save our Landmarks! —Save the Plaza Square. The committee, which is still in formation, has about 32 members. Several men have joined it.

Fannie Hurst, the novelist, is honorary chairman of the committee. The chairman and spokesman is Mrs. Helen M. Clark, a lawyer active in New York civic affairs. Among the committee members listed in the Social Register is Mrs. John A. Warner, the former Emily Smith, daughter of the late Gov. Alfred E. Smith.

*   *   *   *   *

In an interview yesterday Mrs. Clark, a middle-aged woman with soft, cultivated, yet firm, voice, said if General Motors was "only interested in the dollar sign at the expense of ruining our landmarks . . . we are not interested in buying their cars." The boycott, she declared, would be concentrated on. General Motors automobiles, the company's principal product, but would include its several lines of home appliances.

"We don't care," Mrs. Clark said, "if General Motors wants to put up another tombstone; that's all right, but don't build on the Grand Army Plaza."

*   *   *   *   *

"The Plaza Square," she declared, "is an internationally known landmark, and is the ony part of New York where visitors, particularly from abroad, wish to stay." Other luxury hotels in the vicinity of the Savoy Plaza are the Pierre, the Sherry-Netherland and the Plaza.

*   *   *   *   *

Her indignation increased when she recalled that the Federal Government had contributed $12 million to the United Arab Republic last October to help save the 3,000-year-old Abu Simbel temples in Egypt. The temples, on the banks of the Nile, were threatened by the construction on the Aswan High Dam.

*   *   *   *   *

A General Motors spokesman said yesterday the company's officials would refrain from comment "at this time." A spokesman for Savoy Fifth Avenue seemed surprised at the committee's opposition, remarking that the Savoy Plaza was not an "architectural gem" and that the company did not know the committee was in existence.

*   *   *   *   *

One member of the committee that proposes a General Motors boycott is Mrs. Frederick E. C. Roelker, secretary of the group. She said

EXHIBIT 4 (concluded)

the committee was formed because its members "got tired of seeing office buildings going up one after the other, every pretty spot in the city deteriorate and the human element disappear."

Mrs. Roelker is the wife of a retired lawyer.

Other members of the committee are Miss Rosalie Armistead Higgins, Mrs. Raymond Seabrook, Mrs. Albert Bostwick, Mrs. Louis J. de G. de Milhau, Mrs. C. Hendry Mellon, Mrs. Cutting Wilmerding, Mrs. James McVickar, Mrs. George Harris, Mrs. Harold T. Pulsifer, Mrs. R. B. Montgomery, Mrs. George McMurtry, Mrs. Nathaniel Hill, Miss Jane Ashley, Mrs. William Morris and Mrs. Edward Wineapple.

Source: From *The New York Times*, January 20, 1965.

EXHIBIT 5
Staunch Defenders of the Savoy Plaza

By Ann Geracimos

The battle to prevent General Motors from putting up an office building on the site of the Savoy Plaza Hotel continues over telephones and behind locked doors.

The chief protagonist is a stocky, gray-haired lawyer named Mrs. Helen M. Clark, chairman of Save Our Landmarks!—Save the Plaza Square committee. She vows a struggle to the death before one of the world's largest corporations begins demolition of the hotel— scheduled the day after the World's Fair closes.

Committee members, she says, number in "the hundreds" and come from all parts of the country. Petitions are now in circulation, and boycotts and picketing are planned.

Like David before Goliath, Mrs. Clark is undaunted by the size of her foe. She has fought giants before. "Anything can be stopped," she says.

"I hear they are quite worried," she confided to well-wishers last week. G.M. hired a public relations agency specially to handle her group, she said.

GM Owns Half

The public relations man in question, Harry Corlson, of Wolcott & Associates, said he was hired by the Savoy Fifth Avenue Corp. last August, five months before Mrs. Clark's committee formed. G.M. owns 50 percent of the Savoy Fifth Avenue Corp., which is putting up the 48-story building designed by Edward Durell Stone, in co-operation with Emery Roth & Sons, on Fifth Ave., between 58th and 59th Sts., opposite the Plaza Hotel. The officers and architectural committee of the Fifth Ave. Assn., to which Mr. Stone belongs, have heartily endorsed the preliminary design.

Mrs. Clark wouldn't qualify her strength or say what is the largest

EXHIBIT 5 (*continued*)

number of shares owned by any one member. (The boycott plan includes giving up G.M. stock.) The petitons read: "We, the Undersigned, Support the Preservation of Our Landmarks." Nowhere is mention made of General Motors.

Neither side has spoken directly to the other. G.M. recently issued a statement from Mr. Stone pleading for "patience and forebearance."

"Fifth Avenue has always been a nostalgic, esthetic battleground," the statement reads. "When the old gothic Vanderbilt Mansions between 57th and 58th gave way to commercial structures, when the old Waldorf-Astoria was replaced by the Empire State Building, and when Rockefeller Center went up, the hue and cry was heard across the land."

To Be Prepared

The statement was prepared "just to be ready for any inquiry," according to Mr. Carlson. "There's no reason to get people stirred up. There always are a handful of cranky shareholders who write in and ask when something happens." General Motors has nearly 1.2 million shares outstanding. Recently announced the largest profits ever made by a U.S. company in a year.

Mrs. Clark doesn't intend to argue the building's design, only its location on the Grand Army Plaza.

"The area is more or less a residential center for people from all over the world," she said. "Now they're trying to make it commercial. I don't care if they want to put it some place else." She suggested a site on 110th St. and Fifth Ave.

Mr. Carlson, who refers to the committee as "Fannie Hurst's group," said he would consider inviting them to view a seven-foot model when it is ready, in about a month's time. Miss Hurst is honorary chairman of the committee.

Miss Hurst, who says she is "utterly free of the delights of General Motors ownership," admits their effort is like "attempting to fight the Grand Canyon."

But, "if we let such things go on, we will have no past," she tells interview audiences. "I don't consider the Savoy Plaza the most beautiful building, but it is a lively and healthy monument of what we have been."

It appears there are people from as far away as California and Quebec whose stomachs turn upside down at the thought of a general office building with a ground-floor automobile showroom, replacing the elegant Savoy, the somber Madison Hotel, Lanvin perfume displays, Mayflower Coffee House and a host of little businesses.

A woman in Orlando, Fla., said she would sell her 400 shares of G.M. stock because she doesn't approve of "greedy buildings." An owner of three automobile outlets in California pledged to stop selling G.M. cars. A woman with 200 shares said she would sell these and cancel the family's order for a G.M. car.

EXHIBIT 5 (*concluded*)

Mrs. Clark's office is a third-floor suite in the Greybar Building, at 420 Lexington Ave., with rooms for a receptionist, secretary and the lawyers who work for her.

Prominent on the coffee table in the large conference room was a copy of FACT magazine headlined, "American Cars Are Deathtraps." A tiny room with a portable bar contained a carton of paperback books about the Krebiozen drug case. She is a counsel for cancer patients in the government's case againt Dr. Andrew Ivy, the inventor of Krebiozen.

Source: From the *New York Herald-Tribune*, February 17, 1965.

EXHIBIT 6
Letter from Robert C. Weinberg to *The New York Times* September 2, 1964

To the Editor:

There are two things to be added to the excellent editiorial that appeared in The Times of Aug. 24 regarding the proposal to replace the Savoy Plaza by an office building.

First, if such a building must be built, the selection of a "name" architect is not enough to insure good design. The owners must adopt a publicly announced policy program which would establish that the design will measure up esthetically to the standards so well set forth by The Times, and the architect will be backed up by the owner when he produces such a design. With these assurances of quality no "name" architect is necessary.

Secondly, an important consideration which The Times's editorial did not cover: if the area's solid core of hotel, restaurant and distinguished shopping character is breached, the resulting change in the nature of the open space we call the Plaza may affect New York's prestige more than the facade of a single building.

The Plaza as a space has for generations been the city's most famous center of fashion and glamour, like the Place Vendome in Paris. Its nature stems from the people who use it and what goes on there as much as from the design of the structures that surround it. Populating its sidewalks with thousands of office workers will obliterate the atmosphere that has made it, during the past century, New York's true center of swank.

Unfortunately, neither the Planning Commission nor the Landmarks Commission—the latter not yet officially with powers—is in a position to take action in such a matter, much less enforce any decision. Without official restraining powers in New York, esthetic controls of open spaces as well as of buildings rest in the pressure of public opinion.

The future of the Plaza area may be favorably affected by convincing the new owners they should adopt a combination of the two considerations I have outlined. They must be persuaded not to retain a name architect as a mere empty gesture, and also to announce at the

EXHIBIT 6 (*continued*)

outset that, to maintain the present characteristic usage of the great open space on which their building will face, no ground floor space will be leased to—much less designed for—banks, airlines or other occupancies creating dead sidewalk activity, especially at night.

Frontage on the Plaza must be specifically developed for restaurants, cafes and specialty shops, perhaps with arcaded sidewalks. Ultraluxury hotel suites could occupy certain parts of the new building, entering from Fifth Avenue, while access to the office spaces would be firmly restricted to Madison Avenue or the side streets. In this way New Yorkers and the building investors could actually have their cake and eat it, too.

EXHIBIT 7
Letter from Joseph Watterson, Editior of the *Journal of the F.A.I.A.* to *The New York Times*, October 3, 1964

To the Editor:

Robert C. Weinberg in his letter published Sept. 21 made some important points regarding the disaster that is threatening the Plaza area.

He is right when he says that a "name" architect is not necessary to insure good design for the building proposed for the site of the Savoy Plaza. However, the architect must be a "good" architect— whatever that means.

I can tell you what it means to me: It means an architect, big name or unknown, who is sensitive to the spirit of the place.

The Plaza has a very special character which stands alone now in the entire area of New York City, and Mr. Weinberg defines it very well. The Plaza is the one spot in the city where elan and true sophistication have survived, and the unsophisticated love it! The new building must preserve the flavor that now exists in this little enclave.

When the building housing Bergdorf Goodman's was built years ago, many of us groaned, for surely it could not equal the quality of the great French Renaissance mansion which stood on the site. It didn't, but in scale and character it turned out all right. When the Savoy Plaza was built, we groaned again—despite its name architects. But it too turned out all right. Now what? It must turn out all right!

Quality, character, scale, atmosphere—these are the most important attributes of urban architecture. Their adherence to prevailing standards of "good design" is secondary. The quality of urban neighborhoods depends more upon the neighborly sympathy and harmony of its buildings than upon their pronouncement of a new breakthrough in architectural design. Possibly we've had enough of that for a while.

There is one great step that must be taken by all cities sooner or later, and the sooner they face it the less damage they will have to undo later. This idea is not my own, for it is put forth in "Pittsburgh Perceived," a study of the visual possibilities of that city prepared last

EXHIBIT 7 (*continued*)

year by Patrick Horsbrugh, at the behest of the City Planning Commission.

This is it: Within certain areas—all the downtown portion of the city, at least—no building permit should be issued until the owner and the architect of the property involved have appeared with their designs before a responsible commission and convinced them that the proposed building would be an asset to and an enhancement of its environment, not just economically, but visually.

New York, and all cities, have taken too many steps backward because any building newer than the one it replaced was considered better.

It is inescapable that old buildings must be torn down, sometimes. But it is inexcusable that what replaces them should be poorer architecture. If a new building is not better in every way than the one it is replacing it has no justification whatever.

So the improvement of the neighborhood should be demonstrated before the building permit is granted. The future amenity of New York and all cities will depend upon control over the quality of the design of its buildings and the spaces which they enclose.

EXHIBIT 8

From: Wolcott & Associates, Inc.
777 Third Avenue
New York, New York 10017
Contact: Harry Carlson
PLaza 5–5530
For: Savoy Fifth Avenue Corporation

FOR RELEASE
Wednesday, Dec. 16, 1964

New York, Dec. 16—The appointment of Edward Durell Stone and Emery Roth & Sons as associated architects for the 48-story Fifth Avenue office building in which General Motors Corporation will be a major tenant was announced today by Savoy Fifth Avenue Corporation.

The new General Motors Building will occupy the entire city block from Fifth to Madison Avenues and between 58th and 59th Streets. It will contain in excess of 1,500,000 square feet of space.

The site is now occupied by the 33-story Savoy Plaza Hotel, the 15-story Madison Hotel and the four-story Emmet Arcade Building. Demolition is scheduled to begin the latter part of 1965. Construction of the new building is expected to be completed in 1968.

The white tower of the new structure, which will rise from a low, landscaped podium, will be placed almost 100 feet back from the Fifth Avenue building line, the architects revealed in releasing design plans for the building.

EXHIBIT 8 (*continued*)

"In effect, this will create additional park-like space, with sunken courtyards and gardens," they said. "Naturally, we wish to bring more beauty, not less, to the neighborhood."

Mr. Stone, considered by many as the foremost living American architect, said he has set out "to create a building that will salute the skyline and enhance one of New York's finest neighborhoods."

"We have sought the quality of permanence and have designed for the future as well as the present and the past. That is to say, we have also considered that in its particular location, this building should harmonize with the neighboring buildings which are primarily built of masonry."

A typical office floor in the new building will contain approximately 32,000 square feet. The main landscaped plaza on Fifth Avenue plus one facing Madison Avenue will cover an area in excess of one-half acre.

Shops will be located in arcades around the perimeter of the sunken plaza and at street level along portions of the 58th and 59th Street frontages.

Parking facilities for tenants will be provided in an underground garage.

Mr. Stone has designed buildings of architectural distinction throughout the world, including the United States Embassy in New Delhi and the United States Pavilion at the Brussels World's Fair. In the United States, his designs include those for the Stanford Medical Center in Palo Alto, California, the State University of New York in Albany, the National Geographic Building and the John Fitzgerald Kennedy Center for the Performing Arts, both in Washington, D.C.

In New York City, he has designed the Museum of Modern Art, the Huntington Hartford Gallery of Modern Art, and is one of the architects on the proposed Civic Center in lower Manhattan.

Emery Roth & Sons is headed by brothers Richard and Julian Roth, sons of the firm's founder. Since World War II their firm has been very active in Manhattan and has been responsible for numerous office buildings, including The Chemcial New York Trust Company Building, The Burroughs Building, and The Sperry Rand Building. They were recently awarded the Fifth Avenue Association prize for The Bankers Trust Company Building and the Regency Hotel.

Completion of the new building will enable General Motors to consolidate all of its present operations in New York City in a single location. It is expected that General Motors will occupy about one-half of the new building.

General Motors currently employs approximately 3,300 persons headquartered in midtown Manhattan, most of whom are in the 25-story General Motors Building at 1775 Broadway.

EXHIBIT 9
Photograph of Sketch of Proposed General Motors Building

EXHIBIT 10
Preserving Landmarks
It Becomes Tougher Job in Big Cities as Realty Values Climb
By Laurence G. O'Donnell

New York—How can American cities preserve historically impor-
tant buildings in the face of mounting economic pressures for op-
timum usage of land and space?

Here in the nation's largest city, an emotionally charged campaign
to save worthy old buildings seems on the verge of a significant vic-
tory: The chances are New York soon will become the 70th city in the
nation to pass legislation aimed at preserving its landmarks. Yet talk
to proponents of such legislation and they give the impression of
being at the door of defeat. The difficulties they cite are common to
most other cities and point up the problem of saving old buildings
even when nearly everyone agrees it's a good idea.

No one expects the New York City bill to totally halt the wrecking
boom that is removing many of Manhattan's landmarks. Advocates
of preservation already are fretting privately that the bill, like those
in most other cities, will have "no teeth"—that is, it probably won't
empower a city landmarks commission to buy buildings it deems
worthy of saving or to prevent permanently their destruction.

At best, leaders of the preservation movement hope the New York
bill will do what most others do: Buy time by delaying demolition or
alteration while city officials or others work behind the scenes to save
the landmarks with private funds.

Economic Justifications

In fact, there is a growing awareness among experts in the field of
saving old buildings that victories are scored only when arguments
of economics, not aesthetics, are brought to bear. "In areas where
preservation has been spectacular, it has been done by private
money," mainly putting deteriorating residential property back into
use, says an official of the National Trust for Historic Preservation,
a Washington, D.C., clearinghouse for such movements.

In cities such as Charleston, S.C., New Orleans and San Juan, resto-
ration efforts have received a push from business interests eager to
promote historic districts as tourist attractions. "In a sense," says one
landmarks authority, "for the drive to be successful there has to be
an economic justification. Aesthetic reasons unfortunately aren't
enough."

But in many major cities, and here in New York City in particular,
the economic justifications are becoming increasingly hard to come
by. In Manhattan, skyscraper builders long since have used up all the
prime sites so they've triggered a wrecking boom in their search for
new places to build. A few weeks ago, the Bowery Savings Bank paid
$5 million an acre for an old bus terminal site on which it plans to
place a 48-story skyscraper.

EXHIBIT 10 (*continued*)

"Now anything under 12 stories in the center of Manhattan is going to be torn down because of the value of the real estate under it," enthuses one wrecker. "In other words, taller buildings are replacing smaller ones because of the land value."

For the last year and a half, architects, historians and other citizens have been protesting that increasingly these smaller buildings include structures the city ought to save. When wreckers arrived at Pennsylvania Station in mid-1963, they were greeted by pickets who argued the 54-year-old superstructure with its ornate, high-ceiling waiting room and columned facade should be preserved.

The pickets lost the Penn Station battle. Many of its columns now lie discarded in a New Jersey swamp. And wreckers are busy preparing the site for a sports arena and office building slated to rise over the underground tracks and waiting rooms.

But the Penn Station defeat fueled a campaign that has been on the front pages of New York newspapers ever since. The movement has gained wide support. During a seven-hour public hearing recently on proposed landmarks legislation, 84 speakers argued in favor while only five, mainly representing real estate and building interests, opposed the bill.

Yet many advocates realize that despite lopsided support for the bill city councilmen were paying careful attention to the objections of builders and property owners. A spokesman for one industry group was asked to submit suggested legislation that would meet these objections.

As in many other cities, New York counts heavily on real estate taxes to pay the mounting costs of the services its taxpayers demand. Bigger buildings raise assessments and produce increased revenues, so the city has a vital stake in continuing the building boom.

In a city like New York where prime building sites are scarce, the cost squeeze on the city raises the question of whether the city can afford to save its landmarks. "I certainly think this is something we have to consider," says David Ross, majority leader on New York's City Council. He believes the city could be hurt by a landmarks bill that stifles improvements and shrinks the amount of building sites.

"We would assume most people agree landmarks ought to be preserved," says Mr. Ross. "The problem is how you do it. We will have to see to it that the bill is good and sound, considering aesthetics, economics and city finances."

The city council's special committee on codes is now at work hammering out a bill. Some officials are already bristling about the pressure to produce some sort of bill that the landmarks campaign has engendered.

Off the Tax Rolls

They also view as a mixed blessing one result the campaign recently brought about. Two Park Avenue mansions, considered to be

EXHIBIT 10 (*concluded*)

"among the finest in the country of their period and type," were saved from demolition after wreckers had already started their work. A granddaughter of John D. Rockefeller, Jr., paid an estimated $2 million to buy the buildings and now reportedly plans to give them to the city for cultural use. One city offical observes the proposed gift, besides giving the city two buildings it hadn't sought, will remove valuable property from the tax rolls.

Advocates of preservation are sensitive to such criticism. Recently one group of socially prominent New York women decided to take their fight to the doorstep of the builder rather than to city hall. The builder happened to be General Motors Corp.

The women said they would organize a campaign to boycott General Motors products—including presumably its Cadillacs—if the auto giant and its British partner went ahead with plans to tear down the stately 33-story Savoy Plaza hotel and replace it with a 48-story "tombstone," housing General Motors headquarters here. The skyscraper, they suggested, would besmirch the quaint plaza onto which the hotel now faces.

Whether such tactics will dent the auto giant's plans seems doubtful. In fact, unless landmarks advocates can find new uses for old buildings, the wrecking boom is likely to continue unabated. Already about 2,500 of the 10,000 structures recorded since the 1930s in the Government's Historic American Buildings Survey have been torn down, mainly to make way for new buildings.

Ironically, as cities get older, and passing time produces more landmarks, the pressures will increase to remove them. Growing slums, the cost of city services and spiraling urban land costs—all these factors are conspiring against preserving buildings that help new generations retain their ties with the past.

"Our best chance," according to one veteran in the landmarks field, "is by making these buildings useful and continuing them on the tax rolls. Buildings saved as museums are the hardest to justify." Despite the trend toward more landmarks legislation, he adds, the job of actually saving old buildings is getting tougher.

Source: From *The Wall Street Journal,* March 11, 1965.

Selected Readings

From

A FRIEDMAN DOCTRINE: THE SOCIAL RESPONSIBILITY OF BUSINESS IS TO INCREASE ITS PROFITS*

By Milton Friedman†

When I hear businessmen speak eloquently about the "social responsibilities of business in a free-enterprise system," I am reminded of the wonderful line about the Frenchman who discovered at the age of 70 that he had been speaking prose all his life. The businessmen believe that they are defending free enterprise when they declaim that business is not concerned "merely" with profit but also with promoting desirable "social" ends; that business has a "social conscience" and takes seriously its responsibilities for providing employment, eliminating discrimination, avoiding pollution and whatever else may be the catchwords of the contemporary crop of reformers. In fact they are—or would be if they or anyone else took them seriously—preaching pure and unadulterated socialism. Businessmen who talk this way are unwitting puppets of the intellectual forces that have been undermining the basis of a free society these past decades.

The discussions of the "social responsibilities of business" are notable for their analytical looseness and lack of rigor. What does it mean to say that "business" has responsibilities? Only people can have responsibilities. A corporation is an artificial person and in this sense may have artificial responsibilities, but "business" as a whole cannot be said to have responsibilities, even in this vague sense. . . .

Presumably, the individuals who are to be responsible are businessmen, which means individual proprietors or corporate executives. Most of the discussion of social responsibility is directed at corporations, so in what follows I shall mostly neglect the individual proprietor and speak of corporate executives.

In a free-enterprise, private-property system, a corporate executive is an employee of the owners of the business. He has direct responsibility to his employers. That responsibility is to conduct the business in accordance with their desires, which generally will be to make as much money as possible while conforming to the basic rules of the society, both those embodied in law and those embodied

* From *The New York Times Magazine,* September 13, 1970. (Excerpts from pp. 32–33; 122 et. seq.) © 1970 by The New York Times Company. Reprinted by permission.

† The author is Professor of Economics at the University of Chicago.

in ethical custom. Of course, in some cases his employers may have a different objective. A group of persons might establish a corporation for an eleemosynary purpose—for example, a hospital or a school. The manager of such a corporation will not have money profit as his objective but the rendering of certain services.

In either case, the key point is that, in his capacity as a corporate executive, the manager is the agent of the individuals who own the corporation or establish the eleemosynary institution, and his primary responsibility is to them.

Needless to say, this does not mean that it is easy to judge how well he is performing his task. But at least the criterion of performance is straightforward, and the persons among whom a voluntary contractual arrangement exists are clearly defined.

Of course, the corporate executive is also a person in his own right. As a person, he may have many other responsibilities that he recognizes or assumes voluntarily—to his family, his conscience, his feelings of charity, his church, his clubs, his city, his country. He may feel impelled by these responsibilities to devote part of his income to causes he regards as worthy, to refuse to work for particular corporations, even to leave his job, for example, to join his country's armed forces. If we wish, we may refer to some of these responsibilities as "social responsibilities." But in these respects he is acting as a principal, not an agent; he is spending his own money or time or energy, not the money of his employers or the time or energy he has contracted to devote to their purposes. If these are "social responsibilities," they are the social responsibilities of individuals, not of business.

What does it mean to say that the corporate executive has a "social responsibility" in his capacity as businessman? If this statement is not pure rhetoric, it must mean that he is to act in some way that is not in the interest of his employers. For example, that he is to refrain from increasing the price of the product in order to contribute to the social objective of preventing inflation, even though a price increase would be in the best interest of the corporation. Or that he is to make expenditures on reducing pollution beyond the amount that is in the best interests of the corporation or that is required by law in order to contribute to the social objective of improving the environment. Or that, at the expense of corporate profits, he is to hire "hard-core" unemployed instead of better-qualified available workmen to contribute to the social objective of reducing poverty.

In each of these cases, the corporate executive would be spending someone else's money for a general social interest. Insofar as his actions in accord with his "social responsibility" reduce returns to stockholders, he is spending their money. Insofar as his actions raise the price to customers, he is spending the customers' money. Insofar as his actions lower the wages of some employees, he is spending their money.

The stockholders or the customers or the employees could separately spend their own money on the particular action if they wished to do so. The executive is exercising a distinct "social responsibility," rather than serving as an agent of the stockholders or the customers of the employees, only if he spends the money in a different way than they would have spent it.

But if he does this, he is in effect imposing taxes, on the one hand, and deciding how the tax proceeds shall be spent, on the other.

This process raises political questions on two levels: principle and consequences. On the level of political principle, the imposition of taxes and the expenditure of tax proceeds are governmental functions. We have established elaborate constitutional, parliamentary and judicial provisions to control these functions, to assure that taxes are imposed so far as possible in accordance with the preferences and desires of the public—after all, "taxation without representation" was one of the battle cries of the American Revolution. We have a system of checks and balances to separate the legislative function of imposing taxes and enacting expenditures from the executive function of collecting taxes and administering expenditure programs and from the judicial function of mediating disputes and interpreting the law.

Here the businessman—self-selected or appointed directly or indirectly by stockholders—is to be simultaneously legislator, executive and jurist. He is to decide whom to tax by how much and for what purpose and he is to spend the proceeds—all this guided only by general exhortations from on high to restrain inflation, improve the environment, fight poverty and so on and on.

* * * * *

This is the basic reason why the doctrine of "social responsibility" involves the acceptance of the socialist view that political mechanisms, not market mechanisms, are the appropriate way to determine the allocation of scarce resources to alternative uses.

* * * * *

Many a reader . . . may be tempted to remonstrate that it is all well and good to speak of government's having the responsibility to impose taxes and determine expenditures for such "social" purposes as controlling pollution or training the hard-core unemployed, but that the problems are too urgent to wait on the slow course of political processes, that the exercise of social responsibility by businessmen is a quicker and surer way to solve pressing current problems.

. . . I share Adam Smith's skepticism about the benefits that can be expected from "those who affected to trade for the public good"—this argument must be rejected on grounds of principle. What it amounts to is an assertion that those who favor the taxes and expenditures in question have failed to persuade a majority of their fellow citizens to be of like mind and that they are seeking to attain by undemocratic procedures what they cannot attain by democratic procedures. In a free society, it is hard for "good" people to do "good," but that is a small price to pay for making it hard for "evil" people to do "evil," especially since one man's good is another's evil.

* * * * *

Of course, in practice the doctrine of social responsibility is frequently a cloak for actions that are justified on other grounds rather than a reason for those actions.

To illustrate, it may well be in the long-run interest of a corporation that is a major employer in a small community to devote resources to providing amenities to that community or to improving its government. That may make it easier to attract desirable employees, it may reduce the wage bill or lessen losses from pilferage and sabotage or have other worthwhile effects. Or it may be that, given the laws about the deductibility of corporate charitable contributions, the stockholders can contribute more to charities they favor by having the corporation make the gift than by doing it themselves, since they can in that way contribute an amount that would otherwise have been paid as corporate taxes.

In each of these—and many similar—cases, there is a strong temptation to rationalize these actions as an exercise of "social responsibility." In the present climate of opinion, with its widespread aversion to "capitalism," "profits," the "soulless corporation" and so on, this is one way for a corporation to generate goodwill as a by-product of expenditures that are entirely justified in its own self-interest.

It would be inconsistent of me to call on corporate executives to refrain from this hypocritical window-dressing because it harms the foundations of a free society. That would be to call on them to exercise a "social responsibility"! If our institutions, and the attitudes of the public make it in their self-interest to cloak their actions in this way, I cannot summon much indignation to denounce them. At the same time, I can express admiration for those individual proprietors or owners of closely held corporations or stockholders of more broadly held corporations who disdain such tactics as approaching fraud.

The political principle that underlies the market mechanism is unanimity. In an ideal free market resting on private property, no individual can coerce any other, all cooperation is voluntary, all parties to such cooperation benefit or they need not participate. There are no "social" values, no "social" responsibilities in any sense other than the shared values and responsibilities of individuals. Society is a collection of individuals and of the various groups they voluntarily form.

The political principle that underlies the political mechanism is conformity. The individual must serve a more general social interest—whether that be determined by a church or a dictator or a majority. The individual may have a vote and a say in what is to be done, but if he is overruled, he must conform. It is appropriate for some to require others to contribute to a general social purpose whether they wish to or not.

Unfortunately, unanimity is not always feasible. There are some respects in which conformity appears unavoidable, so I do not see how one can avoid the use of the political mechanism altogether.

But the doctrine of "social responsibility" taken seriously would extend the scope of the political mechanism to every human activity. It does not differ in philosophy from the most explicitly collectivist doctrine. It differs only by professing to believe that collectivist ends can be attained without collectivist means. That is why, in my book "Capitalism and Freedom," I have called it a "fundamentally subversive doctrine" in a free society, and have said that in such a society, "there is one and only one social responsibility of business—to use its resources and engage in activities designed to increase its profits so long as it stays within the rules of the game, which is to say, engages in open and free competition without deception or fraud."

From

THE CAPITAL BUDGETING DECISION*

By Harold Bierman, Jr., and Seymour Smidt†

Opportunity Costs

Usually the cash outlays included in the computation of net cash flows are the outlays incurred because of the investment that would not be incurred otherwise. Outlays that would be incurred by the firm whether or not the investment is accepted should not be charged to a particular investment project. Thus the practice of allocating a share of general overhead to a new project on the basis of some arbitrary measure, such as direct labor hours or a fraction of net sales, is not recommended *unless* it is expected that general overhead will actually increase if the project is accepted.

On the other hand, in some instances an investment project may require the use of some scarce resource available to the firm, although the explicit cash outlays associated with using that resource may be nonexistent or may not adequately reflect the value of the resource to the firm. Examples are projects that require a heavy drain on the time of key executive personnel or that use valuable floor space in a plant or store already owned by the business. The costs of using such resources are called *opportunity costs,* and they are measured by estimating how much the resource (the executives' time or the floor space) would earn for the company if the investments under consideration were rejected.

It may appear that the practice of charging opportunity costs against an investment project when no corresponding cash outlay can be identified is a violation of, or exception to, the procedure of evaluating investments in terms of actual cash flows. Actually, including opportunity costs is not so much an exception to the cash flow procedure as an extension of it. The opportunity cost charged should measure net cash flows that could have been earned if the project under discussion had been rejected. Suppose one floor of a factory building owned by a business could either be rented out at $1,200 per month or used to produce a new product. After an initial outlay for equipment, the new product could produce an absolute net cash inflow of $2,000 per month after taxes but before an allowance has been made for use of the factory space. The figure of $2,000 per month overstates the benefits to be derived from the new product, because the space required could otherwise be used to earn $1,200 per month. By charging a rental opportunity cost of $1,200 per month against the new product, a more meaningful measure of its actual value to the company is obtained. An alternative procedure would be to estimate the relative cash flow from the new product compared with that produced by renting the extra space and not producing the new product.

In some instances it will be extremely difficult to estimate opportunity costs.

* Reprinted with permission of The Macmillan Company from *The Capital Budgeting Decision,* 3rd edition, by Harold Bierman, Jr., and Seymour Smidt. Copyright © 1960, 1966, 1971 by The Macmillan Company. (Excerpts from pp. 112–13.)

† Mr. Bierman is Professor of Business Administration and Mr. Smidt is Professor of Managerial Economics in the Graduate School of Business and Public Administration at Cornell University.

The temptation then is to use some other, more easily identifiable basis of charging for the use of such things as floor space or the time of key executives. This temptation must be viewed with some skepticism. The pro rata share of the costs of owning a building may be much higher or much lower than the true opportunity costs of using that space. When there is really no basis for estimating the opportunity costs associated with the use of a factor, such as the time of certain key executives, it may be preferable to note merely that the proposed project is likely to require considerably more or considerably less than the usual amount of attention from such key executives.

The only valid justification for the pro-rating of the actual costs to the proposed project would be if the actual costs are a reasonable basis for estimating the opportunity cost.

From

SIDE EFFECTS OF RESOURCE USE*

By Ralph Turvey†

Many of the problems . . . [of environmental quality] involve some sort of failure of the market mechanism as it now functions. The failure arises because decisions concerning the use of natural resources do not always take into account all the effects of that use. The neglected or side effects on the quality of the environment can, however, be very important, and thus need examination.

. . . I have endeavored to distill from it the main ideas that are relevant . . . and to present them in practical terms. Although I shall try to minimize the amount of jargon, I had better begin by stating that the technical terms used include "side-use effects," "spillovers," "externalities" or "external economies and diseconomies." These can be roughly and generally defined as the impacts of the activities of households, public agencies, or enterprises upon the activities of other households, public agencies, or enterprises which are exerted otherwise than through the market. They are, in other words, relationships other than those between buyer and seller.

To make this notion clearer it is best to proceed directly to the examples that I shall use. All seven of them are significant in practice. But it is important to note that they are used only as illustrations and that I do not pretend to deal fully with any of them.

Fisheries constitute the first example. In some kinds of fisheries, once a certain intensity of fishing is reached, the stock of fish is reduced with the result that fishing is made more difficult and costly. This means that each fisherman, by taking fish, is adding to the costs of all the other fishermen. What is more, not only the scale

---

* From *Environmental Quality in a Growing Economy: Essays from the Sixth Resources for the Future Forum*, Henry Jarrett, editor. Published for Resources for the Future, Inc. by The Johns Hopkins Press, 1966. (Excerpts from pp. 47–52.)

† The author is Chief Economist of Britain's Electricity Council.

of the activity, as measured by the weight of fish caught, but also its nature is relevant, since (in a trawl fishery) the mesh size of the nets used also affects the stock. An increase in mesh size, by raising the minimum size of fish caught, would in some fisheries ultimately result in an increase in the stock, so making fishing easier. Thus by using a smaller mesh instead of a larger one, each fisherman is raising the costs of all the other fishermen.

In this example the impact of each fisherman's activity upon that of others is reciprocal. . . .

*   *   *   *   *

Continuing, then, by enumerating real examples, my other cases are unidirectional. The [second] is the adverse effect upon households living round an airport of the noise of jets landing and taking off; the [third] is river pollution by the discharge of industrial effluents,[1] and the [fourth] is the destruction of visual amenity involved in placing overhead power transmission lines in areas of scenic beauty.

[Fifth], and last, is cattle poisoning by the emission of fluorine in the smoke from brickworks. Fluorosis causes cows' teeth to mottle and wear faster than normal. Their bones grow deformed and brittle and may break. The consequence is that milk yields and the values of the animals drop considerably; cows may even have to be slaughtered.

We can now use our examples to show that where side effects—externalities—are involved in resource use, the market mechanism, i.e., buyer-seller relationships, alone may not produce the best possible allocation of resources. Some additional mechanism may produce a better allocation of resources by causing households or firms to alter the scales or the nature of their activities.

. . . We should never aim to get rid of absolutely all external effects of one activity upon another, since the net gain from doing so would be negative. . . . The question is not one of abolishing adverse unfavorable effects, but is one of reducing them in some cases where investigation shows that on balance such a reduction is worthwhile.

Let us now list the main activity adjustments that are possible in the [five] examples. First, fishing. Here a reduction in the amount of fishing effort and an increase in mesh size will first lower the catch and then raise it and/or make possible a further reduction in the amount of fishing effort. Thus there is an initial loss, in that fewer fish are caught, followed by a continuing gain, in that the catch will rise more or fall less[2] than the number of boats and men engaged in the fishery. In either case, cost per ton of fish caught will end up lower than it was to start with.

*   *   *   *   *

[Second], aircraft noise. In unidirectional cases, such as this, there is usually scope for both the creator of the adverse external effect and the sufferer from it to adjust the scale and the nature of their activity. Thus airlines can reduce the number of night jet take-offs, modify engines to reduce noise and alter the speed

---

[1] Allen V. Kneese and Resources for the Future have provided us with such a first-rate book on water pollution, *The Economics of Regional Water Quality Management* (Baltimore: The Johns Hopkins Press, 1964), that I feel justified in treating this particular example fairly cavalierly in this paper.

[2] This is a little complicated. I have analyzed the problem and provided references to the literature in my paper "Optimization and Suboptimization in Fishery Regulation" (*American Economic Review*, March 1964).

and angle of ascent—all at a cost. The households around the airport, on the other hand, can install sound-proofing or move.

[Third], the emission of effluent into rivers. The enterprise or sewerage authority can treat the effluent before discharging it and possibly install storage facilities in order to reduce the rate of discharge at times when the river is low. In some cases an enterprise can also alter its production process in order to reduce the noxiousness of its effluent or it can even shift its location. Those enterprises or public authorities downstream can also spend money on treating the polluted river water in order to reduce the adverse consequences of the pollution and households can move.

[Fourth], power lines. These can be sited differently or put underground.

[Fifth], brickworks. Smoke filtering is possible and so is change of location—two very expensive alternatives. Farmers, on the other hand, can shift from dairy farming to poultry or arable farming.

This review of the examples shows that there are frequently several possible ways in which the nature or scale of activities can be modified in order to reduce the adverse consequences of external effects. In most actual cases, therefore, the problem is a multidimensional one: who should do what how much?

An economic criterion can be used in answering this question. It is simply that the present value of the monetray measure of all gains from modifying activities less the present value of the monetary measure of all losses from these modifications be maximized. Unfortunately, this test is rarely sufficient in itself to provide an answer, and often cannot be applied in practice.

Nobody is going to quarrel with this criterion as a principle; it is like being against sin! But it is able to give an answer only when all gains and losses can be satisfactorily measured and expressed in terms of a common denominator, dollars. Gains and losses occurring at different times are rendered comparable by using a discount rate which expresses one's evaluation of futurity to turn them into their equivalent gains and losses at a common reference date. Given satisfactory measurement, given expression in dollar terms and given an agreed discount rate, to apply the criterion is to choose the best.

The beauty of this criterion, in the eyes of some economists, is that whenever its application indicates that some course of action is desirable—gains exceed losses—the gainers can fully compensate the losers and still remain better off. Thus nobody loses on balance and at least some of the parties end up better off. What can be fairer than that?

The answer is that payment of compensation by gainers to losers is not always considered fair, so that even if it were always practicable it would not always be done. Yet the idea which lies at the root of the criterion (namely, that a course of action can be regarded unequivocally as desirable if it makes some people better off and nobody worse off) requires that compensation actually be paid.

The brickworks example can be used to illustrate this, if we take it that all that matters are brick costs and farming costs and sales, all of them measurable in monetary terms. Suppose (though it is probably not true at present) that application of the criterion showed the best course of action to be cleansing brickwork smoke.[3] This would mean that the gain to farmers from an improvement in the

---

[3] According to a report in *The Times* of London (May 5, 1965), a scheme for cleansing brickwork smoke which uses a wet scrubber and heat exchanger would put up the cost of bricks by 25 per cent.

health of any cows they keep would exceed the cost to the brickworks of cleansing the smoke, so that farmers could fully compensate the brickworks and yet remain net gainers. My point is that many people would not regard it as fair to make the farmers compensate the brickworks; on the contrary, they would claim that fairness requires the brickworks to meet the cost of cleansing the smoke since the brickworks is responsible for the damage.

Let us accept this judgment. Then the introduction of smoke cleansing will not make some people better off and nobody worse off; instead it will harm the brickworks and benefit the farmers. Thus, in deciding whether or not the smoke ought to be cleansed, we are not just comparing total gains with total losses; we are also deciding whether or not it is fair to impose a loss on the brickworks.

What this example shows, then, is that even when all gains and losses can be measured and rendered comparable by expressing them in dollar terms, the economic criterion taken by itself is not always sufficient for choosing the right course of action. Considerations of fairness may also be relevant. In a democratic country this means that the problem may have a political aspect.

When some of the gains and losses cannot be expressed in dollar terms, the choice of the right course of action always has a political aspect, for it always involves judgments about fairness as well as mere calculation. The airport example illustrates this. The cost to airlines of reducing noise and the cost to householders of soundproofing their dwellings can no doubt be calculated in monetary terms. But the gain to householders from a reduction in noise cannot. Hence deciding what measures, if any, should be taken involves:

ascertaining the cheapest way of achieving various reductions in noise levels;
choosing the reduction to aim at;
deciding who should bear the cost;

and the two latter issues, which are interdependent, both involve judgments of fairness or what I am here calling political considerations.

All this goes to show, then, that who should do what how much is often a question which cannot be decided on a purely technical basis by an economic calculation. Political considerations—judgments of what is equitable—are also required. This is the message for economists and technologists. On the other hand, there also is a message for administrators and politicians; namely, that even though an economic calculation of gains and losses is often not sufficient to reach a well based decision, it is nearly always an essential preliminary.

From

AMERICA'S EVERYDAY DREARINESS*

The most demaining evidence of American environmental failure is the sheer drabness, the routine vulgarity, and the contempt for natural beauty that characterize so much of our landscape. This general shabbiness is particularly ignoble

---

* Reprinted from the February 1970 issue of *Fortune* Magazine by special permission; © 1970 Time Inc., p. 110.

because it arises out of negligence, could easily be avoided, and even now would be readily correctable if the public awareness of it were more acute.

Dirty air and polluted water and jammed highways, after all, require complex remedies. But the depressing visage of our towns and cities—the needlessly brutal public-housing project, the jumbled resort town, the suburban terrain bulldozed beyond recognition by housing developers—is caused mainly by a lack of care and forethought. The result, a manmade landscape that is makeshift and unkempt, damages our economy. But it damages the human psyche far more.

The omnipresent ugliness and drabness cannot be blamed on a lack of money. In certain "poorer" industrial countries, cities spread across the landscape more cohesively and gracefully than they do here. Nor does the newness of our civilization explain our failures: other new countries have avoided our grosser mistakes.

Instead, our failures track back to natural wealth rather than poverty. Until recently, the supply of land has seemed inexhaustible in the U.S., even on the fringes of great cities; if a town got too messed up, plenty of virgin land remained to move to. As a result, business, government, and ordinary citizen have given little consideration to the fact that the environment can be readily destroyed by mere neglect.

The eventual improvement of our "throwaway" environment will require more than negative protest against obvious dangers like pollution. It will require a public aspiration to put something better where banality stands.

From

LANDSCAPE ESTHETICS*

By Luna B. Leopold

There are an increasing number of bills before Congress that in one way or another affect the landscape or the environment. Each of these requires seemingly endless numbers of congressional hearings, which are recorded upon endless reams of paper.

And if, for some reason, you happen to read the voluminous testimony surrounding one of these environment-affecting proposals, you will generally find a marked contrast between the volume and kind of information presented by those who are pressing for technical development—building a dam, constructing a highway, installing a nuclear power plant—and the testimony of those who either oppose the development or wish to alter it in some way. The developer usually employs numerical arguments, which tend to show that there is an economic benefit to be obtained by constructing something—whatever that something may be. The argument is usually expressed in terms of a "cost-benefit ratio." It is typically argued, for instance, that the construction cost of a given project will be repaid over a period of time and will yield a profit or a benefit in excess of the development costs by a ratio of, let us say, 1.2 to 1. The argument is further supported with great numbers of charts, graphs, tables, and additional figures.

* Reprinted with permission from *Natural History* (October 1969), p. 37. Copyright © by The American Museum of Natural History.

In marked contrast, those who favor protection of the environment against development are fewer in number, their statements are based on emotion or personal feelings, and they usually lack numerical information, quantitative data, and detailed computations. Perhaps this is the reason why this latter group seems to be continually fighting rearguard actions—losing battle after battle.

The time has come when the argument of the environmentalist might best be presented by (1) separating facts from emotions in relation to the environment, and (2) by providing him with a means of quantifying his arguments: using numbers to talk about the landscape. While to some of us this may be a little like using a computer to describe Shakespeare, it seems that society still has the right to have all aspects of any proposed development presented in a way that is as objective as possible.

22. F. A. WEBER COMPANY, INCORPORATED

Case Introduction

SYNOPSIS

The president of a medium-sized manufacturing firm is stimulated by a conference on business ethics to take a long look at the process of resource allocation in our economic system. He addresses himself to the chairman of the Business Ethics Advisory Council of the Department of Commerce in a letter which cites concrete instances of some alleged misallocations and malfunctions of the price system.

WHY THIS CASE IS INCLUDED

This case raises the issue of the adequacy of the price system in our economy in the matters of resource allocation and the satisfaction of human need through the distribution of the output of our productive system. There is opportunity to examine the working of comparative economic systems and test the applicability of conflicting conceptual schemes of economic philosophers.

DIAGNOSTIC AND PREDICTIVE QUESTIONS

The readings included with this case are marked (*). The author index at the end of this book locates the other readings.

1. From the viewpoint of economic theory, how do we account for the allocation of enough national resources for the production of over $360 million in dog food in 1961? Trace the chain of influences which determines that the average migratory farm worker receives about $200 for a summer's labor.

Read: *Weiler and Martin, *The American Economic System,* pp. 47–51, 73–77. Smith, *The Wealth of Nations,* pp. 423, 508.

(Additional reading, not in this volume: Paul A. Samuelson,

Economics [5th ed., New York: McGraw-Hill Book Co., Inc., 1961], pp. 40–44.)

2. From what you know of comparative economic systems, how would resources be allocated to dog food production under government planned or "mixed" economic systems? Compare these with the resource allocation mechanism identified in Question 1.

Read: *Loucks, *Comparative Economic Systems,* pp. 542–43. (Those interested in following up this point will want to read more extensively in Loucks and consult his bibliographic references.) Berle. *The 20th Century Capitalistic Revolution,* pp. 164–69, 171–73, 182–88. Veblen, *The Engineers and the Price System,* Chapter v. *Dimock, *Business and Government,* pp. 6, 807.

3. Looking now at the motivation of entrepreneurs, do you think the producers of Cadillac Dog Food operate their business for the same motives as Mr. Weber operates his machine tool plant?

Read: Smith, *Wealth of Nations,* pp. 423, 508. Berle, *The 20th Century Capitalistic Revolution,* pp. 164–69, 171–73, 182–88. *Coppock, *Economics of the Business Firm,* pp. 5–6, 21–22.
(Additional reading, not in this volume: Robert N. Anthony, "The Trouble with Profit Maximization," *Harvard Business Review,* December 1960.)

4. The dog food advertisement on the radio, the picture of the pampered poodle in the newspaper, and the squib from the economics textbook made Mr. Weber wonder "where our system is headed." How would you formulate Mr. Weber's concern in terms of economic philosophy? Is Mr. Weber really indicting the market system or just some businessmen who operate in the system?

Read: *Berle, "The Corporation in a Democratic Society." *von Mises, *Planning for Freedom,* pp. 7–9, 14–17, 44–17, 44–46. *Hazard, "Our National Goals—The Hard Choices." *Hayek, "The Corporation in a Democratic Society: In Whose Interest Ought It and Will It Be Run?"

POLICY QUESTIONS

5. If you were the president of the Cadillac Dog Food Company, how would you respond to Mr. Weber's inferences that resources were being wasted on pampering dogs while humans suffered for lack of food, clothes, and shelter? (See Questions 1, 3, and 4 above.)

6. Mr. Weber professes to use Article IX of the Chamber of Commerce's "Principles of Business Practices" as a guide to his policies on resource allocation: "Waste in any form—of capital, labor, services, materials or natural resources—is intolerable and constant effort will be made toward its elimination." If you were the butcher pictured in the newspaper feeding the poodle a wad of chopped beef, or if you were the president of the Cadillac Dog Food Company, would the article be a relevant guide for your policies on resource allocation? Why? Or, why not? (See Questions 1, 2, 3, 4 and the attached readings.)

7. If you were Mr. Weber, would you send the letter? If your answer

is yes, would you send it on the company letterhead and sign as company president, or not? Give your reasons.

QUESTIONS FOR ORIGINAL STUDENT WORK IN ANALYSIS AND POLICY

8. While reflecting on case facts, what additional theories from prior education give you insights as to "what is going on" in F. A. Weber Company, Inc.? As to what might be predicted to happen in the future?

9. Other than the policy questions asked by the authors, what pragmatic ways can you think of to state the practical problems faced by executives in the case?

Case Text*

Frank A. Weber is president of F. A. Weber Company, Inc., a medium-sized machine parts manufacturing firm in Westboro, New Jersey. Mr. Weber has headed the 36-year-old firm since 1951 when his father died. The bulk of Weber's $12 million sales volume comes from standard and custom-made chucks for lathes. Overseas shipments account for 16 percent of sales and 21 percent of profits.

In the late spring of 1962 Mr. Weber attended a business conference in New York City at which Mr. William C. Decker, chairman of Corning Glass Works, spoke in behalf of the Commerce Department's Business Ethics Advisory Council. The council, set up in May 1961 by Commerce Secretary Luther H. Hodges, was to explore some approaches to the development of ethical guidelines so as to renew public faith in the ethical ideal of management. Prominent businessmen, educators, clergymen, and journalists comprised the 37-member council which in 1962 was actively advising the business community. Mr. Decker's remarks and the lively discussion after the talk prompted Mr. Weber to compose the letter shown in Exhibit 1.

At the July meeting of the board Mr. Weber brought up the matter of the letter before sending it to the Commerce Department on the company stationery. Bob Doyle, insurance company vice-president, summed up the views of the board when he advised Mr. Weber to ". . . send the letter as a citizen without involving the company name. It would be unwise to do otherwise in a project or controversy which serves no useful purpose to the F. A. Weber Company." Ed Mead, president of Westboro National Bank, went further. "Frank, with all the nuts and bolts business decisions on our agenda, I honestly can't see how you can afford the time to get involved in this big picture stuff." The matter was dropped. Mr. Weber was undecided what to do about the letter.

---

* Copyright 1973 by J. J. O'Connell and Charles E. Summer.

EXHIBIT 1
F. A. Weber Company, Inc. Westboro, New Jersey

June 29, 1962

Mr. William C. Decker, Chairman
Business Ethics Advisory Council
U.S. Department of Commerce
Washington 25, D.C.

Dear Mr. Decker:

I heard you speak recently, Sir, at a business conference in New York City. At that time you explained the work of the Business Ethics Advisory Council and encouraged us to examine our own standards and performance in the light of the series of specific questions posed by the council.

Frankly, I came away from the conference disappointed that some fundamental issues of business responsibility went unnoticed. Specifically I refer to the situation, both here and overseas, where dire human want exists side by side with the production and marketing of goods which not only make scant (if any) social contribution, but also vainly sap valuable resources.

I have been unable to forget the Life *magazine story of a year ago about the 12-year-old Brazilian boy from the slums of Rio de Janeiro. You may remember this picture story of the boy, Flavio, the oldest of eight children. Here is an excerpt:*

"Jose (his father) is a nordestino, a refugee from dirt poor northeast Brazil. He was a construction worker until an accident injured his back. Now he sells kerosene and bleach in a tiny boxlike stall which he and Nair (his wife) built—as they did their tiny shack—from tin cans, broken orange crates and stolen pieces of lumber. To get $5 more to buy food, Nair, about to have her ninth child, washes clothes in the only available water—from a spigot at the foot of the hill. The children, who range from 12 years to 17 months, are penned in the shack or roam the foul pathways of the "favela" where the filth of the inhabitants is tossed out to rot. . . .

"The family's day begins at dawn. In the biggest room of the shack —it is 6 by 10 feet—12 year old Flavio gets himself up. While the rest of the family is still asleep—the parents and five children are in one bed, the other two in the crib—Flavio puts a tin of water on the fire and throws in some coffee. Sometimes there is hard bread to put in it. Sometimes not. For them all, including the baby, that is breakfast. . . .

"In the family the spark of hope and warmth and care which keeps life going comes from the boy Flavio. . . . Flavio can neither read nor write. . . . But at 12 he is already old with worry. In the tormented, closed world of the shack, assailed by the needs and complaints of his sisters and brothers who are always a little hungry, he fights a losing battle against savagery and disorder. The family has three plates. He washes these as well as the faces of the younger children. He cooks the black beans and rice which make up almost every meal. He feeds and watches over the baby, Zacarius. If his brother Mario attacks his sister

EXHIBIT 1 (*continued*)

Maria it is Flavio who breaks it up and metes out the punishment.
"It would be nice to believe that this labor of love and courage will triumph. But it won't. Disease threatens constantly in the "favela." (Last year in Rio, some 10,000 children died of dysentery alone.) And disease has touched Flavio. Wasted by bronchial asthma and malnutrition he is fighting another losing battle—against death. . . . 'I'm not afraid of death, but what will they do after?' "

*We can't sit back and be smug about such conditions and say: "That's Brazil." How about the migrant workers close by in the state of New York. Another magazine article (*Newsweek, *June 5, 1961) I saved gave some embarrassing details under the headline, "9 Cents an Hour":*

"Migratory farm laborers move restlessly over the face of the land. They neither belong to the land, nor does the land belong to them. . . . They are the children of misfortune. Today . . . a million native and foreign born children of misfortune still wander across the U.S., in bedraggled caravans, from one ill-paid job to another . . . prompting Labor Secretary Arthur J. Goldberg to call the problem 'a long festering sore in our society and in our economy.' . . . They (the migrant laborers) are protected by Federal wage and child labor laws or welfare regulations.

"Betty Jean Johnson, 52, migrated from Virginia to work 18 hours a day, six days a week, on a potato farm in Riverhead, N.Y. for $16 (a week) at the most. . . . Her crew leader charged her $3 a week for rent and $10 a week for food."

My brother-in-law, who has some apple orchards here in Jersey, showed me some data from the Monthly Labor Review *(April 1961) on migratory laborers in four counties of the Utica, New York, area. During an average stay of 11 weeks in the summer months, a worker would get an average of 48 days' work. Transportation for the families was customarily free both coming from and returning to the South. Where lodging was not provided free, the charges ran from $1.00 to $3.00 per person per week. Usually each person was charged $10 to $12 for 20 meals. Take a look at some statistics of their earnings:*

Number of Workers	1,803	Number of Workers	671
Percent	100.0	Percent	100.0
Average Daily Earnings in Dollars	%	*Total Dollar Earnings for the Summer*	%
Under 2	1.9	Under 100	6.6
2 but less than 3	11.1	100 but less than 150	17.1
3 but less than 4	25.7	150 but less than 200	22.8
4 but less than 5	24.9	200 but less than 250	20.7
5 but less than 6	16.7	250 but less than 300	11.8
6 but less than 7	8.2	300 but less than 350	10.4
7 but less than 8	5.5	350 but less than 400	3.7
8 but less than 9	2.2	400 but less than 450	3.9
9 but less than 10	1.5	450 but less than 500	1.5
10 but less than 12	1.2	500 and over	1.5
12 and over	1.1		

EXHIBIT 1 (continued)

My point, Mr. Decker, is not to grovel in sentimentality. I am concerned, knowing that such circumstances as described above actually exist, when I open the evening paper—as I did tonight—to read a headline, "Business Is Going to the Dogs; Shopkeepers Cater to Pampered Pooches." A picture accompanying the story showed a French poodle, with its front paws up on the meat case, reaching for a "wad of chopped beef" in the butcher's hand.* When I hear the radio advertisements for Cadillac Dog Food (see attached copy) I can't help wondering about where our system is headed.

Believe me, I get no assurance when I read from my son's college economic textbook: "A rich man's dog may receive the milk that a poor child needs to avoid rickets. Why? Because supply and demand are working badly? No. Because they are doing what they are designed to do—putting goods in the hands of those who can pay the most, who have the money votes."†

In our business we have tried to uphold the "Principles of Business Practices" issued years ago by the Chamber of Commerce. I respectfully submit that article IX of this code receive close consideration by the Business Ethics Advisory Council in its own deliberations and in the business conferences it conducts. Article IX reads: "Waste in any form—of capital, labor, services, materials, or natural resources—is intolerable and constant effort will be made toward its elimination."

Yours truly,
Frank A. Weber, President
F. A. Weber Company, Inc.

Enc.
Radio Advertisement for Cadillac Dog Food
Heavyweight Champ Collie Flower Was Matched with Husky Haymaker in a Fifteen-Round Dog Fight but the Fix Was in.
"The Adventures of Conway Cadillac"
(private eye dog for Cadillac beef liver for dogs)
I don't get it Conway, I don't have the old punch.

You've been training on Cadillac beef liver right?

Sure I eat liver all the time.

Not any liver, I said Cadillac liver. Others are loaded with fatty cereals and fillers. Cadillac beef liver is iron rich. Inspected nourishing beef liver rich in energy building proteins, ground and cooked right in the can sealing in the natural goodness and flavor.

With Cadillac beef liver in underdog Collie Flower's corner, Husky Haymaker went down for the count.

---

* *New York World Telegram & Sun*, June 29, 1962.

† Paul A. Samuelson, *Economics, an Introductory Analysis* (4th ed.; New York: McGraw-Hill Book Co., Inc., 1958), pp. 42.

EXHIBIT 1 (*concluded*)

For a more lustrous coat, sparkling eyes, energy to burn and no feeding problems switch to Cadillac beef liver for your dog. One of eight great varieties. It costs no more. Cadillac dog food is canned first then cooked sealing in the meaty goodness. Treat your dog to Cadillac dog food.*

* Advertisement presented on Station WNEW (New York City) 11:00 A.M., June 20, 1962.

Selected Readings

From

THE AMERICAN ECONOMIC SYSTEM*

By E. T. Weiler and W. H. Martin†

[EDITORS' NOTE: The authors explain the workings on the free, uninhibited price system in allocating resources and income.]

Although it is extremely elementary, it is also most helpful to represent such an economy by means of a diagram. In Figure 1, productive services can be thought of as moving away from the rectangle representing households and toward the rectangle representing business. And economic products can be thought of as flowing to households from business in exchange for products and also from businesses to households in exchange for productive services. Thus, economic activity is essentially a two-way circular flow. In the one direction there is a flow of productive services and products. But ours is an exchange economy—we do not trade productive services directly for products. Instead, households trade productive services for money and then trade the money for the products that they want. And so, overlying the flow of productive services and products is the flow of money payments from households to businesses and back again to households. . . .

For some purposes our diagram will be more useful if it portrays the fact that households can be conveniently classified according to the type of productive service which they supply, and businesses according to the type of product which

---

* Reprinted with permission of The Macmillan Company from *The American Economic System* by E. T. Weiler and W. H. Martin. Copyright 1955 by E. T. Weiler and W. H. Martin. (Excerpts from pp. 47–51, 73–77.)

† The authors teach economics at Purdue and Pennsylvania State Universities, respectively.

they produce. . . . Each productive service type is represented by a small letter a, b, c, . . . n. The households in each occupational group are shown by the lines clustered around each letter. . . .

FIGURE 1

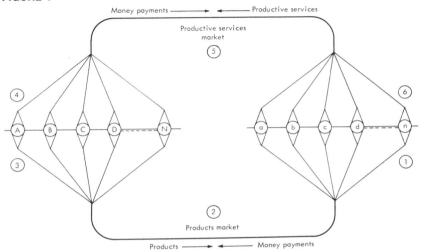

6. Households supply various quantities of the different types of productive services.
5. These productive services flow to businesses.
4. They are divided and allocated among groups of businesses, or industries, and among the separate firms comprising these groups. The productive services are then combined and converted into products.
3. Businesses supply various quantities of the different types of products.
2. These products flow to households.
1. They are distributed among different occupational groups and among individual households making up these various occupational groups.

Business firms, too, can be distinguished according to the type of product sold. . . . Each product type is indicated by the capital letters A, B, C, . . . N, and the firms in each industry are shown by the lines clustered around each letter. . . .

The Concept of the Circular Flow Is Useful in Studying the Problem of Resource Allocation. We have drawn a simplified picture of an economy to assist us in understanding the functioning of our own real-world economy. . . . Most economists would agree that the paramount problem facing any economy is how to make the most effective use of its scarce resources. We have seen that the ultimate purpose of economic activity is to provide the goods and services which contribute to the want satisfaction of the members of the community. But in a society of 49 million households, each acting individually, how are we to go about discovering what society's wants are? After this is done, how do we go about deciding which (and whose) wants are to be satisfied? These are problems because there are not enough goods and services to go around to all who want them. . . .

Closely associated with the problem of effective resource use is the problem of the distribution of income.

*   *   *   *   *

Money Payments Guide and Direct the Flow of Productive Services and Products. Our task is to see, in a preliminary fashion, how the reverse flow of money payments, starting with (1) and ending with (6), serves as a means of guiding the underlying flow of productive services and products in an enterprise economy which lacks control by central authority. This will be done by examining, at each of the numbered points on the circular-flow diagram, the nature of the exchange transactions represented and the decisions underlying these transactions.

1. Households receive money income from the sale of productive services. Households, having sold productive services and having received money payments, are now in a position to compete with other households to obtain scarce products from business firms. The distribution of money receipts among households governs the ration of products which each household is enabled to command. Those households with the largest money incomes may obtain the largest ration of products.

2. Households choose among available products. With money in hand and confronted with a variety of products available in the different product markets, households must make choices about the composition of their purchases. Their choices are registered by their offers to buy products at various prices. Consider briefly the major factors underlying these choices:
    a. Each householder's purchases are limited ultimately by the amount of his money income. Although for a time he may borrow or draw on past savings, he cannot in the long run spend more than his income.
    b. Products all have price tags on them. Money spent on one product cannot be spent on another.
    c. The householder's task is to find that combination of products which, in view of the limits on his income and the price tags on products, will bring him the greatest amount of satisfaction. He will want to substitute, as far as is feasible, some units of lower-priced products for higher-priced products. But products are imperfect substitutes for each other as bearers of satisfaction. . . .

3. Businesses respond via output decisions. In our kind of economy, business presumably react in response to profit possibilities. Businessmen, confronted with the money demands of consumers, respond in such a way as to make the best of alternative profit opportunities. They do this (a) by varying the volume of output of their products, and (b) by shifting their operations from one industry group to another, withdrawing when profit opportunities decline and entering those industries where profits seem attractive. In both cases they are guided by the behavior of the relative prices that prevail in the products market. . . .

4. Businesses obtain money from the sale of products. Businesses, in selling products and in receiving money payments therefrom, are in a position to compete with other businesses to obtain scarce productive services from households. The distribution of money receipts among businesses governs the ration of productive services which each business is enabled to command. The business groups or industries producing those goods which are most in demand by households have the largest money receipts. Consequently, they are able to obtain the largest ration of productive services with which to produce the goods wanted by households.

5. Businesses choose among available productive services. With money in

hand and confronted with a variety of productive services available throughout the markets for productive services, businesses must make choices about the composition of their purchases of productive services. They must decide what combinations of productive services to use. Their decisions are registered by their offers to buy productive services at various prices. Consider briefly the major factors underlying these decisions:

a. Each business firm's purchases are limited by the amount of its money receipts. To be sure, the business may borrow or draw on its own previously accumulated money balances. But no business is able in the long run to spend more than its gross income.

b. Productive services have price tags on them. Money spent on one productive service cannot be spent on another.

c. The businessman's task is to find that combination of productive services which will enable him to produce the largest quantity of products from a given outlay of money. His desire is to substitute the lower-priced productive services for the higher-priced productive services. But productive services are imperfect substitutes for each other. . . .

6. Households respond via occupational decisions. Householders are the owners of the scarce resources whose services are required for the production of goods and services. Confronted with business demands for productive services, householders respond by choosing the disposition of their own productive services in such a way as to make the best of their situation. Among the many things which influence their decisions are the prices that prevail in the markets for productive services, which reflect of course the productive service demands of business firms. . . . There are, of course, limits to such shifting of people among occupations. There are also limits to the shifting of nonhuman resources from one use to another. Some resources, like iron ore deposits, are not mobile; they can be used for only one purpose. In any case, these shifts have been made, new prices and quantities are established and we start again around the circular-flow diagram.

What can we learn from this brief preview of the way a money-payments economy functions?

The Two Markets in a Money-Payments Economy Are Interrelated. In the first place, it is clear that the decisions and responses occurring in both markets, the market for products on the one hand and the market for productive services on the other, are interrelated. The demands of households for products initiate certain responses on the part of business firms. An increase in the demand for a particular product will cause the business to demand more of the productive services that are required to produce that product. In other words, the demand for productive services is ultimately a reflection of the demand for products.

Conversely, the demands of businesses for productive services and the responses of households to these demands affect developments in the products market. . . . It is clear that in dealing with the problem of resource allocation in a price-directed economy, we are dealing with a set of simultaneously determined variables.

We may appreciate further the interrelation of the two markets if we recognize that business firms and households are linked to each other through both the products market and the market for productive services. The business firm is, on the one hand, a supplier of products, and on the other, a demander of productive services. The household is a supplier of productive services and a demander of products. In this way decisions of households regarding the products they consume are related intimately to the decisions they make as sellers of productive services, which contribute in turn to the supply of products. The business firm is the coordinating instrument between these two closely interrelated sets of decisions made by households.

Money Payments and Prices Serve as a Communications System Within and Between These Two Markets. In the second place, then, it is clear that money payments and prices serve as a communications system or as a means of transmitting and coordinating the decisions of thousands of economic units participating in a decentrally organized economy. Money payments and prices serve as a device by which householders, acting in their capacity as consumers, tell others about their preferences for different products and for different types of productive services. It also serves as a device by which businesses, acting in their capacity as producers of products, tell householders what productive services are wanted by the community and how much householders must give up to obtain the products that they want.

. . . We can think of householders as transmitting directions to businesses about (1) what products they want, and (2) what productive services they are prepared to supply. When these two bodies of information are coordinated by the business firms and considered in connection with the schedule of available techniques for producing products, it is possible for an economy not having a central planning board to solve the economizing problem. Prices and money payments take the place of a central authority in directing the economy, that is, in allocating scarce resources among their many alternative uses.

From

COMPARATIVE ECONOMIC SYSTEMS*

By William N. Loucks†

Economic planning in the Soviet economy neither implies a willingness to accept the totality of the results of the decisions of separate economic units and then call this a "plan," nor proceeds by projecting existing trends into the future and then developing the details of the plan around these. The former idea of planning is often held by the promulgator of economic plans in a capitalistic economy. Planners under capitalism sometimes contend that an economic bureau should estimate what the totality of the decisions of the individual and competing enterprises in the economy will be, or what it ought to be if each enterprise were to follow its profit interests. This then becomes the plan, either because it is about

* From *Comparative Economic Systems* by William N. Loucks. Copyright © 1961 by William N. Loucks. Reprinted by permission of Harper & Row, Publishers, Inc. (Excerpts from pp. 542–43.)

† At the time this book was written the author was Professor of Economics, Wharton School, University of Pennsylvania.

what *will* happen, or because some effort is made *to get it to happen* by reporting these comprehensive findings back to the individual enterprises. Clearly, this is economic forecasting, not economic planning in any real sense of the term.

Nor does Soviet planning consist of pushing trend lines into the future and then labeling them economic plans. Rather, its essence is the choosing of comprehensive goals (which are not merely projected trends) and the apportioning to the separate economic units of the specific tasks involved in achieving these goals. While it is true, of course, that the setting of comprehensive goals must be related to such things as the quantities and qualities of resources, the amounts and kinds of machinery possessed, the status of the technique of production, and the quantity and capacities of labor, Soviet planning has, nevertheless, proceeded by the periodic adoption of goals which in no sense are arbitrary projections of past trends of production. The plan becomes the substitute for markets, and relatively free movement of prices thereon, as these exist in a capitalist economy.

Although the term *economic planning* denotes a restricted scope of plans, this cannot be true in the Soviet economy. In addition to production schedules, plans for capital investment, plans for domestic and foreign trade, financial plans, taxation plans, and other strictly economic plans, the Five-Year Plans have included programs for public health, education, recreation, and a great variety of primarily noneconomic social and cultural phases of the nation's life. Hence the expression "social-economic planning" rather than merely "economic planning" is used in the Soviet Union. Since all cultural, educational, health, and similar activities both require economic goods for their prosecution and partially determine the productivity of workers, they have a double relation to economic planning. To neglect them would be to disregard sectors of the nation's life within which unplanned developments well might throw planned portions of the economy sadly out of balance. It is clear, of course, that defense facilities, space exploration projects, and scientific work all exert claims on productive resources and, so, are within the scope of economic planning.

The nature of economic planning in the Soviet Union has been summarized forcefully as follows: "In short, the Soviet economic plan is a gigantic, comprehensive blueprint that attempts to govern the economic activities and interrelationships of all persons and institutions in the USSR, as well as the economic relations of the USSR with other countries. To the extent that the plan actually controls the development of events, all the manifold activities of the Soviet economy are coordinated as if they were parts of one incredibly enormous enterprise directed from the central headquarters in Moscow."[1]

---

[1] Harry Schwartz, *Russia's Soviet Economy,* Prentice-Hall, Englewood Cliffs, N.J., 1958, p. 136.

From

BUSINESS AND GOVERNMENT*

By Marshall E. Dimock†

Can the economy remain stable and yet move forward under a democratic form of government? The liberal-democratic viewpoint asserts that this is possible but does not minimize the intelligence and good will that are required to effect the balance. Can government and the Big Three of industry, labor, and agriculture learn to concentrate on long-range as contrasted with immediate advantages, and can national economic goals be democratically attained? . . .

*   *   *   *   *

The two large questions involved in the determination of broad objectives are what to do and how to do it. The most important aspect of the matter, however, is who is to make the decisions, and the answer, of course, is that they must be made cooperatively. Society is already organized into major groupings, as has repeatedly been shown, and these are ready-made for the task at hand. Of these, business and government are the two largest and their effective collaboration is the major element involved. But the economy can also be broken down into consumers, farmers, workers, and industrialists; and each of these groups, in turn, can be still further subdivided. The problem is to secure the maximum of voluntary cooperation consonant with effective operation and continuous accomplishment.

No one segment of the economy by itself has either the right or the ability to make nationally applicable determinations. No one segment has the organization, the skill, or the representative character needed to make decisions affecting everybody. Range of vision is necessarily limited rather than comprehensive. Thus government, speaking for everybody and so far as possible reconciling every point of view, is the only agent even partially qualified for such a task. Government is best fitted to achieve the goals of the economy because it is influenced by and speaks (potentially, at least) for all members of the community, has a national and international viewpoint, and the authority and prestige to act as a catalytic agent among all groups. Nevertheless, government alone suffices only a little better than a particular economic grouping because unilateral governmental responsibility breeds a degree of authority indistinguishable from total and autocratic rule. There is no escape, therefore, from the conclusion that cooperation—difficult and cumbersome as it sometimes is—offers the desirable formula.

*   *   *   *   *

Psychologically, it seems more characteristic of people identified with power blocs to emphasize team spirit within their own group and competition with other power blocs than to seek a higher level on which national goals transcend group objectives. The situation is aggravated by the fact that as such institutional groupings become larger and more powerful, the difficulties of rising above class loyalties apparently become even more acute. Thus as shown in the chapters on

---

* Dimock, Marshall E., *Business and Government*, copyright © 1949, 1953, 1957, 1961, Holt, Rinehart & Winston, Inc. Reprinted by permission. (Excerpts from pp. 6–807.)

† At the time this book was written the author was Professor of Political Science at New York University, a former representative in a state legislature, and consultant to the federal government.

antitrust and the concentration of corporate power, both economic and political influence seem to gravitate to fewer and more powerful managers and financiers; as shown in the chapters on organized labor, industrial unions operating through national amalgams, result in class consciousness and power politics; and a similar situation appears in the agricultural segment of the economy where farmers have become well organized, class conscious, and politically highly effective. . . .

What may be in store for the nation, therefore, is a growing concentration of power in the hands of one or more of the major power blocs which comprise the economy, accompanied by a partial or perhaps even a complete eclipse of the political influence of other power blocs. For example, if the antitrust laws cannot be made more effective instruments in preventing concentration and enforcing competition, small business, which is middle class, may be progressively reduced in economic and political influence. Or present attempts to work out a peaceful accord between labor and management may prove so slow and unrewarding that one side or the other will be tempted to bypass the dilemma by consolidating its political power at the expense of its opponent, in which case the support of the farm bloc would become a prize to be sought as a major ally by both sides.

*   *   *   *   *

In any program to determine common goals, far greater difficulty is likely to be encountered in securing cooperative leadership than in devising workable methods of internal organization. Statesmanship will be required in industry, labor, and agriculture as well as in Washington, and this quality is everywhere scarce. Only in recent years have economic leaders begun to be broadly trained, and even when they are, the duties of running a business, a trade union, or a farm organization absorb so large a part of the executive's total time and energy that it is hard for him to turn his mind to matters which border on his business, much less concentrate a major part of his attention on national and international problems. This is a chief reason that no pressure group, no matter how broad its clientele, is equipped to define goals for the economy as a whole. And yet the difficulty must be overcome if America's sights are to be raised, if the Me-Firsters' approach is to give way to the All-Together slant, and if voluntary cooperation is to forestall regimentation.

In terms of the organization of business, it seems clear that leaders who will devote a large part of their time to matters of national or even international concern will have to rise into positions of authority in their respective segments of the economy.

From

ECONOMICS OF THE BUSINESS FIRM*

By Joseph D. Coppock†

. . . Sometimes it is suggested that money-making is just one of the firm's aims, even a minor one. It is contended fairly frequently that the firm is striving primarily to provide service, progress, good working conditions, the material requisites of culture, human freedom, national defense, etc.

Even though the activities of the firm may contribute importantly to these goals, it may be questioned whether in fact the firm is actually pursuing such goals. Occasional actions apparently having no immediate influence on profits can often be correctly interpreted as intended contributions toward future profits, or as lapses in the pursuit of profits. Managers and owners might be ever so philanthropic, public-spirited or religious as private citizens, but their role in the business firm would seem to be that of profit-seekers. Undoubtedly individuals are not always able, or do not wish, to keep their roles distinct. It seems correct, as a general proposition . . . that not only is the business firm *the* dominant profit-seeking organization in capitalist society but also that it is *dominantly* a profit-seeking organization.

By its drive for profits the firm plays its part in the capitalist economy. The drive for profits promotes the efficient use of resources. Profit-seeking means striving for a net income—a net revenue above costs—regardless of how the revenues or costs are calculated in particular instances. In a money-exchange economy, the effort to secure command over scarce goods and services consists, in the main, of a drive for net income, i.e., profits in the case of the business firm. Profit-seeking is the motive force, the *sine qua non,* of the free enterprise economic system. It is the counterpart of coercive power in the authoritarian economy, or of the love of one's fellow man in the utopian cooperative commonwealth. . . .

*   *   *   *   *

. . . If people's competitive instincts as well as their cooperative inclinations can be harnessed, without significant personal or social losses, so as to put things and people's efforts to uses which will cause the total of want-satisfying goods and services to be increased, people as consumers will be better off.

. . . Since it seems that many people are inclined to struggle for superiority over their fellows in one way or another, as well as to cooperate with them, it is highly important that both of these dispositions be directed into channels which are widely considered constructive rather than destructive. A combination of persuasion and compulsion seems to be required. The competitive, free enterprise economic system, which relies upon the pricing mechanism to provide rewards, and which, when combined with strong but limited government, makes the rewards generally unobtainable by unsocial means, enables those who perform highly desirable services to obtain, temporarily at least, somewhat more than average

---

* By permission from *Economics of the Business Firm,* by Joseph D. Coppock. Copyright 1959. McGraw-Hill Book Company, Inc. (Excerpts from pp. 5–6, 21–22.)

† At the time this book was written the author was Professor of Economics in Earlham College.

rewards and encourages the influx of factors into these lines. It makes extremely difficult the obtaining of higher than average rewards by those who do not render especially valuable services.

The business firm, operating within the free enterprise framework, provides very effective means for the competitive, even combative, inclinations of men to vent themselves in socially valuable ways. The legal and moral codes of a society are important influences on the forms of rivalry and determine in considerable measure the prospects of having a successful free enterprise or capitalist system.

From

THE CORPORATION IN A DEMOCRATIC SOCIETY*

By Adolf A. Berle†

. . . The conventional objections to reasonable planning (we can all recite them by heart) already have boiled down to the residual platitudinous dregs propounded for corporation presidents and chamber of commerce orators by public relations counsel.

Ineluctable fact here meets obsolete shibboleth. The fact is that the profit motive, organized through great corporations, can do many things and do them extremely well. But it does not do and apparently cannot do many things which are essential if a modern economy (and business as an essential part of it) is to progress. The profit motive, like all social devices, has certain limits. Specifically, while it can produce without apparent limit, it cannot allocate resources to certain kinds of need. . . .

. . . [T]here is one national American economic system and . . . it rises and falls as a unit. A stiff miscalculation by the automobile industry in Detroit can throw off balance as large an essential industry as steel, incidentally forcing hardships on distributors, dealers, and small suppliers literally in every village. Shifts in the technique of national defense—like the prospective change from aircraft to rockets—could make a shambles of the economic life of Long Island and Connecticut, of California and substantial parts of the Northwest. The indirect effects, though not readily calculable, could be very great, eventually impinging on a large sector of the population. In these contingencies, we think, to be sure, about "dangers to business"—but that thought will be secondary. The end of an economic system is to serve life: and life would be in travail.

In the next phase, the complaint will not be, as in 1933, that the unplanned system is financially unsound. Rather, it will be that the fluctuations of the unplanned system are unbearably inhuman. In extreme, the verdict might be still

* By permission from *Management and Corporations 1985,* by Melvin Anshen and George L. Bach. Copyright 1960. McGraw-Hill Book Company, Inc. (Excerpts from pp. 80–87.)

† At the time this book was written the author was a Professor Emeritus of Law at Columbia Law School, a corporate lawyer, corporate director, and government official.

worse: the unplanned system is inadequate. That would be the last word in damnation. The unforgivable sin of any government, economic as well as political is inability to govern.

It follows that the first brush in the evolving conception of state-corporate relations will be on the subject of planning for stability. As always, the choice will lie between taking the evolution as light—or as lightning.

The allied subject of this evolution will relate to allocation of resources. Already it is clear to economists and is dawning on financial writers that mere "production" is not an answer. Production differs in valence. Creation of a good housing development has a higher valence than production of plastic toys or electric cocktail shakers, whatever the dollar figures may be. . . . The economic cliché has always been that the public showed what it wanted by what it paid for. The fact is that it buys what it can, often taking something it wants less because it cannot get at a viable price certain goods or services it wants far more. In pleasanter theoretical terms, the unguided profit economy is showing a number of air pockets in which vivid wants go unfilled, while lesser wants are taken care of.

Third in this list will be allocation of resources to those human activities which are not, and perhaps never have been, carried on within a private profit system. Medical care, good teaching, creation of an adequate supply of public servants who are scientists, doctors, or engineers—not to mention reasonable provision of decent instead of meretricious drama and art—all fall within this field. . . .

*   *   *   *   *

Social accounting, a new subject and a new device, will be a developed and accepted tool in this future towards which we are looking. Let us suppose the case of a company transferring a plant from, say, central New York to Alabama (as General Electric might do with its Schenectady plant). This operation leaves, at best, a trail of human and community damage behind it. The operation conceivably might yield the transferring company a higher profit—indeed this calculation would have lain behind the transfer. But this does not eliminate the losses. It merely means that the social expenses are paid in some other form or by someone else. The men thrown out of work would draw from unemployment insurance. Some families would draw relief. First-rate managements endeavor to minimize these losses now—but they are never wholly avoidable. Mortgages or other debt in the area would go unpaid or only partly paid; the losses would be borne by the banks, the tradesmen, the creditors, the community tax roles, and Social Security funds. Savings of some families would be wiped out; they would thus pay part of the expense. If all the bills thus paid were added up, it might well be discovered that that transfer, whatever its impact on the financial account of the company, on balance worked out a net loss to the entire community. At this point, financial planning enters. It might literally be cheaper to work out tax relief or government orders or other form of aid than to allow the plant to move. A generation from now considerations of this kind will be adequately briefed and sufficiently calculated so that labor unions and corporations as well as local, state, and Federal government units will understand them. With understanding there should come a measure of capacity to handle forces and events with greater efficiency.

In all these and similar operations, the state necessarily enters. Meeting its own assignment—that of developing a planning mechanism insulated from conventional political influences, and of maintaining separation of the all too compulsive state from the private business mechanism—will take a good bit of doing. Yet the outlines of the problem are fairly clear even today. . . .

. . . . The economic system, not being an end in itself, must reflect the value system on which the public generally agrees.

From

PLANNING FOR FREEDOM*

By Ludwig von Mises†

. . . All those evils which the progressive interpret as evidence of the failure of capitalism are the necessary outcome of allegedly social interference with the market. . . .

It must be emphasized that we are discussing means and measures, not ends. . . . The essential problem is whether such policies can really attain the ends aimed at.

* * * * *

The market economy is an integrated system of intertwined factors that mutually condition and determine one another. The social apparatus of coercion and compulsion, i.e., the state, certainly has the might to interfere with the market. The government or agencies in which the government, either by legal privilege or by indulgence, has vested the power to apply violent pressure with impunity, are in a position to decree that certain market phenomena are illegal. But such measures do not bring about the results which the interfering power wants to attain. They not only render conditions more unsatisfactory for the interfering authority. They disintegrate the market system altogether, they paralyze its operation, they bring about chaos.

If one considers the working of the market system as unsatisfactory, one must try to substitute another system for it. This is what the socialists aim at. But socialism is not the subject matter of this meeting's discussion. I was invited to deal with interventionism, i.e., with various measures designed to improve the operation of the market system, not to abolish it altogether. And what I contend is that such measures must needs bring about results which from the point of view of their supporters are more undesirable than the previous state of affairs they wanted to alter.

* * * * *

What those allegedly planning for freedom do not comprehend is that the market with its prices is the steering mechanism of the free enterprise system. Flexibility of commodity prices, wage rates and interest rates is instrumental in adapting production to the changing conditions and needs of the consumers and in discarding backward technological methods. If these adjustments are not brought about by the interplay of the forces operating on the market, they must be enforced by government orders. This means full government control. . . .

---

* Reprinted by permission of Libertarian Press, South Holland, Ill., 1952 pp. 7–9, 14–17, 44–46).

† Professor von Mises is an Austrian economist who has taught and lectured throughout Europe, South America, and the United States (New York University).

There is no middle way. The attempts to keep commodity prices rigid, to raise wage rates and to lower interest rates ad libitum only paralyze the system. They create a state of affairs which does not satisfy anybody. They must be either abandoned by a return to freedom of the market, or they must be completed by pure and undisguised socialism.

The inequality of income and fortunes is essential in capitalism. . . . Profits and loss withdraw the material factors of production from the hands of the inefficient and convey them into the hands of the more efficient. It is their social function to make a man the more influential in the conduct of business the better he succeeds in producing commodities for which people scramble.

. . . Would the consumers be better and more cheaply supplied if the law were to prevent the most efficient entrepreneurs from expanding the sphere of their activities? The answer is clearly in the negative. If the present tax rates had been in effect from the beginning of our century, many who are millionaires today would live under more modest circumstances. But all those new branches of industry which supply the masses with articles unheard of before would operate, if at all, on a much smaller scale, and their products would be beyond the reach of the common man.

The market system makes all men in their capacity as producers responsible to the consumer. This dependence is direct with entrepreneurs, capitalists, farmers, and professional men, and indirect with people working for salaries and wages. The economic system of the division of labor, in which everybody provides for his own needs by serving other people, cannot operate if there is no factor adjusting the producers' efforts to the wishes of those for whom they produce. If the market is not allowed to steer the whole economic apparatus, the government must do it.

. . . There is no other means to attain full employment, rising real wage rates and a high standard of living for the common man than private initiative and free enterprise.

       *   *   *   *   *

As the self-styled "progressives" see things, the alternative is: "automatic forces" or "conscious planning." It is obvious, they go on saying, that to rely upon automatic processes is sheer stupidity. No reasonable man can seriously recommend doing nothing and letting things go without any interference through purposive action. A plan, by the very fact that it is a display of conscious action, is incomparably superior to the absence of any planning. Laissez faire means: let evils last and do not try to improve the lot of mankind by reasonable action.

This is utterly fallacious and deceptive talk. The argument advanced for planning is derived entirely from an inadmissible interpretation of a metaphor. It has no foundation other than the connotations implied in the term "automatic," which is customarily applied in a metaphorical sense to describe the market process. . . .

The truth is that the choice is not between a dead mechanism and a rigid automatism on the one hand and conscious planning on the other hand. The alternative is not plan or no plan. The question is: whose planning? Should each member of society plan for himself or should the paternal government alone plan for all? The issue is not *automatism versus conscious action;* it is *spontaneous action of each individual versus the exclusive action of the government.* It is *freedom versus government omnipotence.*

Laissez faire does not mean: let soulless mechanical forces operate. It means: let individuals choose how they want to cooperate in the social division of labor and let them determine what the entrepreneurs should produce. Planning means: let the government alone choose and enforce its rulings by the apparatus of coercion and compulsion.

*   *   *   *   *

Under laissez faire, says the planner, the goods produced are not those which people "really" need, but those goods from the sale of which the highest returns are expected. It is the objective of planning to direct production toward the satisfaction of "true" needs. But who should decide what "true" needs are?

From

OUR NATIONAL GOALS—THE HARD CHOICES*

By Leland Hazard†

. . . [I]f the choices I have suggested go one way, we will have more freedom; if they go the other way, more discipline. If we have more hospitals, more people, more automobiles, more education of the present undiscriminating kind, more retirement—all of these will be freedom of a sort. If we plan to utilize our resources for more theaters (symbolic of all the humanities), more living space for fewer people, more graceful urbanism . . . more culture . . . more appreciation for the skills of older persons, and more insistence that the competent young equip themselves for the changing future—if we plan for these things, then we must have more discipline.

But when I talk of discipline, what do I mean by the term? And who is to administer this discipline? Am I raising specters of "Big Brother?" If it is not that, who will make sure that they are implemented? In short, who is the somebody who must "do something" about current trends in our economy and in our culture?

Questions like these—while perfectly sound—come right out of the folk thought of America. We tend to distrust leadership. We are reluctant to place in the hands of leaders the responsibility, the obligation, and the power to make worthwhile choices.

Is this distrust something new? Not really, but leadership, once established, has usually been respected in retrospect. The colonials in America struggled over accepting one of three concepts of government—monarchy, theocracy, or democracy. Democracy won out—handsomely. And yet if we look at the strong presidents of the United States (I won't name them, but we all know who they were), we will see more identity than will usually be admitted between them and the strong men of all the ages—whatever the form of government.

---

* Reprinted by permission of *Harvard Business Review,* May–June 1963 (pp. 30, 206).

† The author is Director-Consultant of the Pittsburgh Plate Glass Company, Vice-Chairman of the National Planning Association, and Professor of Industrial Administration and Law at the Carnegie-Mellon University.

Ask yourself what the alternative is to leadership. Must we be constantly fearful of leadership? Must we believe that choices can be made only in the marketplace, only at the polls, only in the political process? If so, we then run the risk of conceding that extreme proposition about American pragmatism—*that the truth is what no one will vote against.* This, I think, can lead only to a deadly mediocrity, and then on to social failure.

The marketplace is perfectly adequate for allocating some things. It can decide styles of women's hats, the length of dresses, or whether shoes should have pointed or blunted toes. But the marketplace cannot decide spiritual questions. The marketplace cannot decide and select and choose among the truths or the untruths by which men live or die.

So who is to assert this leadership? Does business have a role to play? Is our choice that of doing nothing or of having the government take action?

My feeling is that in other societies leadership in cultural matters does come from nongovernmental sources. The European businessman, for example, is inclined to think about cultural affairs. I do suspect that the oncoming generation of American businessmen—particularly those who have been trained in the schools which are now stressing the arts—will be willing to make qualitative judgments in the fields of the arts.

But for now, government leadership is probably necessary to make the hard choices that we as a people would find difficult to make for ourselves. . . .

In itself, government leadership is not necessarily something to be afraid of. The U.S. Land-Grant Acts of 1862 and 1890 established the federal land subsidies which were the beginning of many of our great state universities. *And yet, after a hundred years, education in the land-grant colleges is as free as it is in the private institutions.*

. . . The truths by which men live have not been developed on playing fields. They have been developed in theaters, in great debates, and in the lonely struggles of lonely thinkers.

From

THE CORPORATION IN A DEMOCRATIC SOCIETY: IN WHOSE INTEREST OUGHT IT AND WILL IT BE RUN?*

By Friedrich A. Hayek†

My thesis will be that if we want effectively to limit the powers of corporations to where they are beneficial, we shall have to confine them much more than we have yet done to one specific goal, that of the profitable use of the capital en-

---

* By permission from *Management and Corporations 1985,* by Melvin Anshen and George L. Bach. Copyright 1960. McGraw-Hill Book Company, Inc. (Excerpts from pp. 100–101, 104–7, 116–17.)

† The author is Professor of Economics at the University of Chicago.

trusted to the management by the stockholders. I shall argue that it is precisely the tendency to allow and even to impel the corporations to use their resources for specific ends other than those of a long-run maximization of the return on the capital placed under their control which tends to confer upon them undesirable and socially dangerous powers and that the fashionable doctrine that their policy should be guided by "social considerations" is likely to produce most undesirable results.

*   *   *   *   *

Power, in the objectionable sense of the word, is the capacity to direct the energy and resources of others to the service of values which those others do not share. The corporation that has the sole task of putting assets to the most profitable use has no power to choose between values: It administers resources in the service of the values of others. It is perhaps only natural that management should desire to be able to pursue values which they think are important and that they need little encouragement from public opinion to indulge in these "idealistic" aims. But it is just in this that the danger rests of their acquiring real and uncontrollable power. . . . I shall maintain, therefore, that the old-fashioned conception, which regards management as the trustee of the stockholders and leaves to the individual stockholder the decision whether any of the proceeds of the activities of the corporation are to be used in the service of higher values, is the most important safeguard against the acquisition of arbitrary and politically dangerous powers by corporations.

*   *   *   *   *

There remain, then, as possible claimants for the position of the dominating interest in whose service the individual corporation ought to be conducted the owners of the equity and the public at large. . . . The traditional reconciliation of those two interests rested on the assumption that the general rules of law can be given such form that an enterprise, by aiming at long-run maximum return, will also serve the public interest best. . . .

Apart from these special instances, the general case for free enterprise and the division of labor rests on a recognition of the fact that, so long as each item of resources gets into the control of the enterprise willing to pay the highest price for it, it will, on the whole, also be used where it will make the largest contribution to the aggregate product of society. This contention is based on the assumption that each firm will in its decisions consider only such effects as will influence, directly or indirectly, the value of its assets and that it will not directly concern itself with the question of whether a particular use is "socially beneficial." I believe this is both necessary and right under a regime based on the division of labor and that the aggregation of assets brought together for the special purpose of putting them to the most productive use is not a proper source for expenditure which is thought to be generally socially desirable. Such expenditure should be defrayed either by the voluntary payment of individuals out of their income or capital or out of funds raised by taxation.

*   *   *   *   *

. . . [T]he only argument I can discover in favor of allowing corporations to devote their funds to such purposes as higher education and research—not in instances where this is likely to make it a profitable investment for their stockholders, but because this is regarded as a generally desirable purpose—is that in existing circumstances this seems to be the easiest way to raise adequate funds for what many influential people regard as important ends. This, however, seems to me not to be an adequate argument when we consider the consequences that would follow if it were to become generally recognized that managements have such power. If the large aggregations of capital which the corporations represent could, at the discretion of the management, be used for any purpose approved as morally or socially good, if the opinion of the management that a certain end was intellectually or esthetically, scientifically or artistically desirable, were to justify expenditure by the corporation for such purposes, this would turn corporations from institutions serving the expressed needs of individual men into institutions determining which ends the efforts of individual men should serve. To allow the management to be guided in the use of funds, entrusted to them for the purpose of putting them to the materially most productive use, by what they regard as their social responsibility, would create centers of uncontrollable power never intended by those who provided the capital. It seems to me, therefore, clearly not desirable that general higher education or research should be regarded as legitimate purposes of corporation expenditure because this would not only vest powers over cultural decisions in men selected for capacities in an entirely different field, but would also establish a principle which, if generally applied, would enormously enhance the actual powers of corporations.

*   *   *   *   *

. . . Unless we believe that the corporations serve the public interest best by devoting their resources to the single aim of securing the largest return in terms of long-run profits, the case for free enterprise breaks down.

I cannot better sum up what I have been trying to say than by quoting a brief statement in which my colleague Professor Milton Friedman expressed the chief contention two years ago: "If anything is certain to destroy our free society, to undermine its very foundations, it would be a wide-spread acceptance by management of social responsibilities in some sense other than to make as much money as possible. This is a fundamentally subversive doctrine."

23. POLAROID CORPORATION

Case Introduction

SYNOPSIS

Some black workers in the Massachusetts headquarters of the Polaroid Corporation demanded that Polaroid cease doing business in South Africa. A multiracial task force from all levels of Polaroid employment was established to study the matter and recommend company policy. After sending a four-man team to learn the wishes of the blacks employed by Polaroid's South African distributor, the task force recommended a one-year experiment during which amateur photographic materials as well as sunglasses would continue to be sold in South Africa while strides would be made in black wages and training. A significant portion of profits earned in South Africa were to be committed as grants for the education of black South Africans. Others doing business in South Africa were also encouraged to follow Polaroid's lead in combatting apartheid from within. Polaroid had to study the results of the year's experiment to determine policy for South Africa for the coming year.

WHY THIS CASE IS INCLUDED

The multinational corporation constantly confronts interdependencies in its worldwide system. In this case, the reader can observe how a $500 million company can have its focus and priorities shifted to a tiny distributorship 10,000 miles away from headquarters. Beyond discussing the substantive question of the "rightness" of doing business in South Africa, the reader can examine the manner in which Polaroid managed the protest and protesting employees. Comparisons can be made between Polaroid's handling of the affair and the reaction of other companies in United States and elsewhere. The reader should find it of particular interest to follow the unfolding events in the public U.S. press and also in the South African press.

DIAGNOSTIC AND PREDICTIVE QUESTIONS

The readings included with this case are marked (*). The author index at the end of this book locates the other readings.

1. Prior to October 1970, why was Polaroid doing business in South Africa? Among all the organization forms Polaroid might have used, why did it work through a distributor for cameras and film and through a licensee for sunglasses?

Read: *Kolde, *International Business Enterprise*, pp. 242–55, 260, 277–78. *Pessemier, *New Product Decisions*, pp. 8–10.

2. What would have likely happened in the camera and film business in South Africa if Polaroid had "pulled out" as demanded? What would have happened in the sunglasses business had Polaroid "pulled out"?

Read: The Kolde reading assigned in the previous question and recall what you already know about distribution from the field of marketing.

3. What options are open to an employee for effectively voicing protest about some behavior of his own firm? Compare these options with those open to an owner for effectively voicing protest (as in the General Motors case cited in the appendix).

4. Were Miss Caroline Hunter's rights violated—as she insisted—when she was dismissed from Polaroid?

Read: Evan, "Organization Man and Due Process of Law."

5. What managerial style was used by Polaroid in coping with the issue raised by the protestors?

Read: *Eells and Walton, *Conceptual Foundations of Business*, pp. 360–63. Follett, "Constructive Conflict." O'Donnell, "The Source of Managerial Authority." Newman and Summer, *The Process of Management*, pp. 439–48. Drucker, *The Future of Industrial Man*, pp. 32–38.

6. What are the essential differences between the position of Dr. Land (and the Polaroid Corporation) and Mr. Wates (and the Wates Construction Company—described in the appendix) vis-à-vis doing business in South Africa? Why do they differ?

Review carefully the January 13, 1971, advertisement by Polaroid and the June 1970 press release by Mr. Wates. Consider the status of each company vis-à-vis expansion from home country at the time each document was written.

Read: *Lilienthal, "The Multinational Corporation." Hayek, "The Corporation in a Democratic Society: In Whose Interests Ought It and Will It Be Run?"

7. In what sense might an employer in South Africa feel guilty over the results of the apartheid system even though he did everything permissable by law for his nonwhite employees?

Read: *O'Connell, "New Credentials for Moralists."

8. Why is it that Polaroid, despite its public record of social responsibility, found itself confronted on its marginal presence in South Africa?

Read: *O'Connell, "The Tactics of Creative Tension."

POLICY QUESTIONS

9. How would you have responded to the Polaroid Workers Revolutionary Movement "demands"? Recall that Polaroid insisted that it did not respond to the "demands" but rather answered the implied question: "is it right to do business in South Africa?" Review your response to Question 8 and the reading assigned with Question 8.

10. If you had been the responsible Polaroid executive, would you have dismissed Miss Hunter? Why or why not? Reread the articles assigned with Questions 3 and 4.

11. How else (in terms of managerial style and process) might Polaroid have solved the problem of doing business in South Africa? Do you agree with the Polaroid approach? (Note that the decision process at Polaroid was different from that at Wates.) How would you have managed the process? Review Question 5.

12. What other alternatives could Polaroid have considered than the one outlined in its experiment (battling apartheid from within via its distributor)? Do you agree with Polaroid's choice of tactics? If not, what would you have done? Review Questions 6 and 7. Also compare the content of the Polaroid ad in Exhibit 2 with Mr. Wates statement at the beginning of the appendix.

13. Knowing what you know at the end of the case about the results of the year-long Polaroid experiment, what would be your decision concerning doing business in South Africa? Why?

14. Under what conditions would you place a subsidiary (investments and employees) in South Africa?

QUESTIONS FOR ORIGINAL STUDENT ANALYSIS

15. While reflecting on case facts, what additional theories from prior education give you insights as to "what is going on" in the Polaroid Corporation? As to what might be predicted to happen in the future?

16. Other than the policy questions asked by the authors, what pragmatic ways can you think of to state the practical problems faced by executives in the case?

Case Text*

On October 5, 1970, signs appeared on the bulletin boards in the Polaroid Corporation's Cambridge, Massachusetts, headquarters, demanding that the company withdraw from doing business in South Africa. Two

---

* Copyright 1973 by J. J. O'Connell.

black Polaroid employees, Mr. Kenneth Williams and Miss Caroline Hunter, voiced the demands during a noisy midday demonstration outside Polaroid headquarters on October 7. They acted as spokesmen for the Polaroid Workers Revolutionary Movement (P.W.R.M.) and repeated demands for total withdrawal from South Africa even after Polaroid management had, on October 21, called a halt to all direct or indirect sales to the government of cameras or film which could be used in the apartheid-inspired passbook procedures for nonwhites in South Africa.

THE POLAROID CORPORATION

Polaroid's South African operations comprise only a small fraction of the $500 million worldwide sales in 1970—about $1.5 million. Polaroid has no investment in South Africa and, technically, none of its 10,000 employees is stationed in South Africa. Frank and Hirch, Ltd., is the distributor for Polaroid cameras and film in South Africa. The same company employs some 200 blacks producing sunglasses under license from Polaroid, with lenses imported from Polaroid's U.S. manufacturing facilities.

Polaroid has marketing subsidiaries in 13 countries and manufacturing subsidiaries in Scotland and the Netherlands. Historical patterns would seem to indicate that Polaroid transforms distributorships in foreign markets into marketing subsidiaries after about $1 million sales volume has been achieved. In 1970, two new subsidiaries were formed, one in Norway, and the other in Austria. Also in 1970, an International Division was established, combining production, marketing, and financial management of the overseas operations into a single group. Foreign subsidiaries outperformed the parent organization and its U.S. subsidiaries in 1970 in both sales growth and profitability (see the financial statements in Exhibit 1). Financial observers note that the U.S. market may be getting tougher for Polaroid in spite of its product innovation and one-step photographic technology, which is protected by a patent. The *Wall Street Journal,* on June 23, 1970, hinted that the recent Polaroid stock price slide was due to the possibility of Kodak entering the instant photo field. Earlier, *Advertising Age* (May 25, 1970) noted that Polaroid buys negatives from Kodak but, by an agreement made in December 1969, Kodak will be permitted to manufacture Polaroid-type film for sale by 1976. Though Polaroid was issued 109 new patents in 1970, increasing its total to 1,100, a number of what are thought to be key patents expire in 1984.

Almost 10 percent of Polaroid's U.S. employment is black. Fifteen percent of those applying for work at Polaroid in 1969 were black, and 22 percent of the 2,383 who were hired were black. Thirty percent of the black employees completed educational or training courses in 1969. Polaroid speaks proudly of its record of corporate citizenship, especially in the Boston area. Its community relations group participated in more than 100 projects related to urban problems in the greater Boston area. Its wholly owned Inner City training center placed 125 people in permanent jobs during 1969 and boasts of an 82 percent retention rate in those jobs—significantly higher than in any such employment orientation or preemployment training effort elsewhere. Polaroid led Boston area companies in shifting support from the United Fund to the Black United Appeal. The increase it had planned for United Fund in 1970—some $20,000—was allocated to the Black United Appeal. Polaroid's president and chairman, Edwin H. Land, insists: "Polaroid is people!"

THE SOUTH AFRICAN SETTING

Polaroid is one of some 300 American firms doing business in South Africa. U.S. investment of about $800 million in 1970 represented about 14 percent of all direct private investment in South Africa. The *Sunday Times* of London reported (on January 1, 1971) that the biggest U.S. investors are believed to be IBM, Ford, General Motors, Chrysler, Gulf, Mobil, Kodak, First National City Bank, and Chemical Bank. The U.S. share of the total has been increasing while the significantly larger (57 percent) British share is gradually diminishing. The annual net investment by U.S. corporations runs at barely 1 percent of all U.S. direct private investment abroad but the earnings from South Africa represent 2 percent of all the earnings from U.S. private investment overseas.[1] (See the table below.)

U.S. Private Direct Investment and Average Rates of Return—1960–1968

	1960	1961	1962	1963	1964	1965	1966	1967	1968
Investment in South Africa (millions of $)	− 1*	21	47	51	55	49	69	71	31
Average Rates of Return in South Africa %	17.5	19.6	19.9	20.0	18.6	19.1	20.6	19.2	17.3
Average Rates of Return Worldwide %	10.9	11.0	11.4	11.3	11.4	11.1	10.4	10.1	10.8

* Net capital outflow.

The United States received 7.1 percent of South Africa's $960 million of exports in 1969 and supplied 17.4 percent of its $1,705 million of imports.[2]

The gross domestic product of South Africa has been averaging close to a 6 percent increase in real terms over the period 1966 to 1970.

---

[1] *Foreign Investment in the Republic of South Africa,* United Nations, New York, 1970.

[2] *Quarterly Economic Review: Republic of South Africa,* Annual Supplement 1971, The Economist Intelligence Unit, London, 1971.

Trend of Gross Domestic Product*

	1966	1967	1968	1969	1970
Total Rand (millions)†					
At Current Prices	8,555	9,459	10,152	11,339	12,404
At 1963 Prices	7,799	8,391	8,712	9,326	9,807
Real Increase (%)	5.0	7.6	3.8	7.0	5.2

* *Quarterly Economic Review: Republic of South Africa,* Annual Supplement 1971, The Economist Intelligence Unit, London, 1971.

† Rand = 1.40 dollars

During the same period the consumer price index has moved as follows:

Consumer Price Index*(1963 = 100)

	1966	1967	1968	1969	1970
	109.1	112.3	113.5	115.9	119.5

* *Quarterly Economic Review: Republic of South Africa,* Annual Supplement 1971, The Economist Intelligence Unit, London, 1971.

A fact often noted about the structure of economic life in South Africa is the disparity between the wages earned by the ruling whites and the blacks who comprise almost 75 percent of total employment. The wage gap has grown in secondary industry between 1946 and 1969 so that the average black wage as a percentage of the white wage has dropped from 20.3 percent to 18.6 percent.[3] The table below gives detail by broad industry for the period 1965–70.

Wages and Employment*

	Total Wages/Year in			
	Millions of Rand		Numbers employed	
	1965	1970	1965	1970
Mining				
Whites	186.7	264.9	63,800	61,700
Coloureds	2.8	5.3	4,500	5,500
Asians			440	300
Africans	93.3	121.7	538,300	573,500
Manufacturing				
Whites	545.9	996.4	233,900	277,000
Coloureds	97.3	166.6	150,100	195,800
Asians	34.6	66.4	50,900	74,200
Africans	220.4	380.7	494,600	617,200
Construction				
Whites	83.0	226.4	36,600	59,500
Coloureds	19.7	57.5	21,500	44,600
Asians	0.9	7.8	1,100	4,500
Africans	49.3	144.9	122,300	247,000

* *Financial Times* (London), Monday, June 14, 1971, p. 16.

[3] "South Africa: The Politics of Fragmentation," Neville Curtis, *Foreign Affairs,* Vol. 50, No. 2, January 1972, p. 288.

As can be computed from the table above, the blacks (Africans) in the manufacturing sector were earning about an average of 51 rand a month in 1970. The Johannesburg Chamber of Commerce estimated that a family of five in Soweto (a black living area outside Johannesburg) required 76 rand a month for a minimum monthly budget.

It was in this economic context and in the sociopolitical environment of apartheid (separation of the races) that the challenge to Polaroid's conduct of business in South Africa was raised.

CHRONOLOGY OF THE PROTEST AT POLAROID

In 1948, Dr. Edwin H. Land, chairman of Polaroid, was offered the opportunity of significant business in South Africa at a time when Polaroid had not yet established itself as a profitable growth company. Despite the attraction of the offer, Dr. Land refused because of the racial policies of the South African Government.

During the early 60s, Polaroid established the sales distributorship through Frank and Hirsch, Ltd., and shortly thereafter established through the same company the licensed production of sunglasses with lenses imported from the United States.

In 1968, Dr. Land intervened to prevent direct sales of cameras or film by Polaroid to the South African Government. During the same year—in a seemingly unrelated episode—some Polaroid employees objected through channels to the use of Polaroid products in the passbook program implementing apartheid. These protests did not produce a top management response; top management later stated that they were not aware of indirect sales and use of Polaroid products by the government.

On October 5, 1970, the Polaroid Workers Revolutionary Movement began agitating against business in South Africa, first within Polaroid facilities, then on October 7, 1970, in the streets.

On October 21, 1970, Polaroid announced that all sales, direct and indirect, of film and cameras for use in the apartheid passbook identification program would be prohibited. Two marketing executives were dispatched to South Africa to assure compliance with the order. Polaroid's investigations showed that about 15 percent of the identification materials were Polaroid products purchased from dealers supplied by Polaroid's distributor, Frank and Hirsch, Ltd. Amateur film and cameras, as well as sunglasses, would continue to be sold as before. In announcing the decision, Dr. Land described the move as precedent setting for any U.S. company. The use of Polaroid's products in the identification program evidently had come as a surprise to Dr. Land, as had the existence of a "revolutionary" movement within the company itself. Others in top management admitted knowing about the true picture in South Africa. The sales vice president, Mr. Thomas Wyman, said: "We recognized that our film indirectly was being used in this identification program for blacks and whites and I think there was some discomfort about it, but the issue did not crystallize to a point where now we wish it had." When asked if he would condone the action of P.W.R.M. in the protest, he responded: "I think I would say so if I thought that were the issue that is on their minds." Other Polaroid executives were quick to disassociate the new policy from the P.W.R.M. demands. The senior vice president, Mr. Arthur Barnes, insisted that the new policy had nothing to do with the protests by P.W.R.M. The response to P.W.R.M was sharp. "Demands—that is not the way we operate," said Mr. Barnes.

Dr. Land emotionally reinforced the management reaction to the demands in an hour-long talk to the 14-man task force established to study the business in South Africa and to recommend company action. He decried the behavior of "a couple of revolutionaries who don't believe we mean what we say." Giving in to their demands would mean "a whole series of new demands, and there is no doubt that management would not meet them. I do not want to run a company based on demands rather than participation."

As the 14-man task force was deliberating, Mr. Kenneth Williams resigned his position at Polaroid, calling the new policy "an insult." He began organizing a coalition of blacks and white radicals to launch a boycott of Polaroid products both in the United States and overseas. Mr. Williams left behind him a career which began as a custodian and led to a creative position as design photographer.

As the task force deliberated, the idea emerged to send a racially mixed team to examine the South African situation first hand. One member of the task force, representing the Volunteers Committee (an all-black group formed in the company to process grievances from black employees) explained the task force rationale as follows: "The proposal was made that a group of four be sent to South Africa as an inspection team to review the feelings of black South Africans. The point was raised, and was well taken, that as a black in America we have had decisions made for us by people who feel that they know what we need, and I think we were repeating the same process in our initial moves here. . . . I think we should ask the black South Africans what would be the effect of total withdrawal, or of continuing our present process, to put restrictions on our methods of sale."

The task force did, in fact, send a four-man study team to South Africa for 11 days. Seemingly without government obstruction, the team (a black engineer, a black electrician, a white draftsman, and the white sales vice president) gathered data publically and privately sufficient to be convinced Polaroid should stay on in South Africa and battle apartheid from within. These views were shared with the larger task force which then fashioned a one-year experimental program which was announced in a full page ad in the *New York Times* (and other major U.S. daily newspapers plus 20 black weeklies) on January 13, 1971. Posturing itself plainly in opposition to apartheid, Polaroid launched a three-phase experiment:

1. Dramatically improve black wages and benefits within both the distributor and supplier companies in South Africa.
2. Oblige Polaroid business associates in South Africa to train nonwhites for important jobs.
3. Commit a portion of profits earned in South Africa to encourage black education (see Exhibit 2 for the full text of the ad).

Not to be overlooked is Polaroid's overt invitation to other companies operating in South Africa to follow its lead in battling apartheid from within.

Response to the Polaroid move was swift and sharp. The London *Observer*'s reporter in Cape Town headlined his story on January 17, 1971: "Polaroid move on apartheid shakes South Africa." The reaction may have been anger and alarm in official government channels but the following excerpt from the January 15 edition of the *Cape Argus* (Cape Town) shows the complexity of the issue from the optics of the opposition conservative party in South Africa:

> *American corporations investing in South Africa are today in an extremely delicate situation. They are being forced by domestic pressure to introduce socio-economic, almost political reforms in their business undertakings in this country—reforms which, while eminently sensible and desirable in themselves could force foreign investors into confrontation with the South African Government.*
>
> *Our own Government is also in a delicate position here. . . . While there is an understandable reluctance among all South Africans to allow foreigners to intervene in our domestic affairs, it must be understood that foreign investors involved in local commerce may soon have no option but to intervene or to withdraw—to succumb to the demands for effective economic boycott, in fact. . . .*
>
> *Should the Government attempt to curb any moves by Polaroid— which is now under close world scrutiny and* must *move dramatically to improve conditions for its local African staff—the damage to South Africa would be tremendous. . . .*

The announcement of the experiment, as predicted, did not still the protest at home. Mr. Williams and Miss Hunter (the only two public members of P.W.R.M.) appeared before a United Nations Sixteen Country Apartheid Committee on February 3, 1971. They characterized the Polaroid experiment a "paternalistic act of charity," a "trick," and an "insult." They reiterated their demand that Polaroid withdraw entirely and threatened to continue their four-month drive to have Polaroid products boycotted.

Another reaction came from the representatives of the United Black Appeal in Boston who had earlier welcomed Polaroid's precedent-setting gift of $20,000. Fearing that accepting the money would appear like taking a bribe to ignore the South African issue, they turned the money over to a South African revolutionary movement and to another group in Cairo, Illinois.

On February 20, 1971, Miss Hunter was suspended from her job at Polaroid without pay and was informed on February 23, 1971, that she had been dismissed "for conduct detrimental to the best interests of the company." After two and a half years as a chemist at Polaroid, Miss Hunter (a 24-year-old graduate of Xavier University) responded to her dismissal by saying: "It is just further proof of the racism that exists at Polaroid. At Polaroid they say that if my rights interfere with their profits that they can suspend those rights, as they did with mine. I intend to continue work on the boycott."

By mid-September 1971, some action was already evident within Polaroid's distributor in South Africa. Average pay of nonwhite workers was raised 22 percent and the minimum wage was raised to 70 rand from 50 rand.

On October 27, 1971, Mr. Helmut M. Hirsch, the managing director of Polaroid's distributor, labeled Polaroid's effort to counteract apartheid from within the system a "success." He said it "has done far more to bring about a civilized relaxation of prejudice than withdrawal would have done." Mr. Hirsch said in a interview with the *New York Times* that, if black employees were still being paid considerably less than some whites doing related tasks, this was due to differences in productivity and seniority. "The company fully accepts the principle of the rate for the job, but we will not artificially elevate men for the sake of improving a point." He said that his company would not contravene Government policy by appointing blacks to positions of authority over whites and that such a move would be impractical at this stage in any case. The same story was carried in the South African newspaper *STAR* on November 1, 1971, under the banner headline: "Polaroid Plan Is On Way to Success."

In November 1971, the South African Institute for Race Relations[4] published a "Report on the Polaroid Experiment" which offers the summary conclusion:

Any attempt to assess the impact of the Polaroid Corporation's experiment on other companies in South Africa is extremely difficult. Companies are usually unwilling to reveal information about wage levels and employment practices; nor is there necessarily any connection between such changes as have taken place and the publicized actions of Frank and Hirsch, Polaroid's distributors in South Africa. It is also almost impossible to discover whether whatever improvements in working conditions of Africans, Indians, and Coloured people have taken place during 1971 are on a larger scale than in previous years. The most that can be said with any degree of certainty is that the Polaroid experiment, with the attendant publicity and increased interest in South Africa in black poverty, has caused more public and press attention to be focused on black wage levels, working conditions, and employment practices. Had it not been for the initiative within Polaroid, the South African Institute of Race Relations is unlikely to have become involved at the time it did in the question of the role of foreign investment in South Africa, and the memorandum "United States Corporate Investment and Social Change in South Africa" by Dudley Horner would not have been produced. . . . This greater concern is of course a desirable development in itself, but it is no substitute for real change within individual firms. The problems

---

[4] This institute is a 40-year-old, interracial organization located in Johannesburg with 4,500 members in and outside South Africa. It opposes apartheid and works on civil rights causes with funding from membership, South African businessmen, and the Ford Foundation, with a staff of 50.

of black poverty and the increasing black/white wage gap have been with us for years, and it is doubtful whether the past year has seen any significant progress, taking a broad aggregate of statistics. This does not mean to say that some individual firms have not introduced welcome changes.

*   *   *   *   *

Mr. Wyman, a vice president of Polaroid, told Congressman Charles Diggs's Africa sub-committee that Polaroid would pull out of South Africa entirely unless the program showed solid results by 13 January 1972. He hinted strongly that the decision whether to remain in South Africa would depend in large measure upon whether other companies, particularly American companies, followed Polaroid's lead. Part of Polaroid's experiment was to promote African education and to help African cultural organizations. Several firms have followed Polaroid's example in the field of education: for example, the South African Sugar Association has voted R20,000 for African education, and one other large company has voted a similar sum, while several other firms have increased their expenditure in this field. More details are unfortunately not available.

As far as its impact on black wage levels is concerned, the Polaroid experiment may be evaluated according to different criteria:

1. If it was intended to significantly improve the wages and working conditions of black South Africans in general, it must be regarded as a failure.

2. If the intention was to create greater social concern among businessmen, it appears to have been moderately successful.

The institute report specified the climate for change by citing a research survey conducted in 1968 among American and Canadian businessmen based in South Africa. "Eighty-one percent of the businessmen —all of them top executives—believed that South Africa's racial policies represented an approach that was at least an attempt 'to develop a solution.' Eight percent considered the government's policies an 'acceptable approach,' six percent believed they were 'altogether incorrect.' Ninety-two percent believed the Republic was stable and not subject to serious jeopardy due to racial or economic unrest 'in the foreseeable future.' The survey also revealed that although businessmen based in South Africa were becoming increasingly pro-South African, many of them believed that feelings 'at home' regarding South Africa had become less tolerant than they were a year ago."

On December 3, 1971, the *Financial Mail,* a South African business periodical, went into more detail on the Polaroid experiment under the headline: "Too Early To Judge."

What is the evidence so far of success or failure?

To take F & H first. There has been evidence of fairly considerable advancement for African staff. Average African salaries have gone up 21% in a year, from R74 to R90 pm. And the minimum wage for those with one year's experience at F & H is R840 pa, or about R65 per month excluding annual bonus.

More important is the reduction in the number of those in the lower group:

F & H Salaries*

Earning group	1970	1971
R50—R70	98	39
R70—R130	49	91
R130 plus	11	21

* Including annual bonus

A surprising and disappointing feature is the R50–R70 salary group. The average salary in this income group is R58. An African F & H employee told the FM (in the presence of managing director Helmut Hirsch) that a matriculated 21-year-old had been hired only two months before at R52 per month.

This is the minimum amount F & H could legally pay him.

Hirsch argues that most untrained beginners are not worth more ("we'd pay a White the same for the same work"). He agrees they are being paid well below the Johannesburg poverty datum line of R70 per month for a family of five, but says that they are not generally sole breadwinners.

Had he checked whether they were or not? No. A couple of days after our first interview, however, he telephoned the FM and said that he had now checked and was "delighted to have had this brought to my attention." I came across a "junior" aged 44 I didn't know of before, earning R55 per month.

He has now introduced a system by which new African male employees "with proven experience" will start at a minimum of R65. Those without experience will be put on probation for three months, with clerks continuing to start at R52 and others at R55. If they prove satisfactory, their wages will then be upped immediately to R60 and R65, respectively.

All of these salaries are below the PDL level for a family of five. In any case, shouldn't these moves have been made months ago? Can the Polaroid group justify itself to its U.S. detractors when its distributor still pays some employees the minimum rate allowed by law?

On the training side of the F & H program, there are now nine African supervisors (receiving between R136 and R195 per month including annual bonuses) compared to one last year. Two African storemen have been appointed for the first time.

Hirsch says Polaroid is satisfied with the progress made by F & H so far.

Polaroid itself has played its part in the experimental program spending R45,000 on non-White bursaries, and general African educational and cultural development. This is a considerable sum, perhaps a quarter of its SA profits.

How have other firms reacted to Polaroid's lead? Have there been advances? If so, do they justify Polaroid staying here? The evidence so far is inconclusive.

Just before the end of the year of experiment, *Newsweek* (January 10, 1972) reported:

The company said its distributor, Frank & Hirsch, was giving blacks the same pay as whites for equivalent work and had raised blacks' salaries by an average of 22 per cent and provided them with pensions, educational expenses and loans. Polaroid itself has given $75,000, about half of its annual South African profit, to several black educational groups and has helped set up a black-owned distributorship in Nigeria. All of this was accomplished, the company said, without interference or pressure from the South African Government. The government, in fact, even gave its own non-white civil servants a 7 per cent pay boost.

Polaroid noted that other companies—such as Barclays Bank, Standard Bank and General Motors—have also announced equal-pay-for-equal-work policies, as had been hoped. "We think the biggest achievement," said a Polaroid executive, "has been to call attention to the fact that American, British and South African companies should not be running a double standard for employees." But at the same time, the company expressed keen disappointment that even more companies haven't liberalized their black salary scales, or are afraid to say that they have. "It is known that several of them have raised the standards of black employees," the Polaroid official declared. "It is just somewhat disappointing that more haven't stepped forward."

One reason they haven't is clearly fear of retaliation from the segregationist government. "The single most-asked question from the numerous companies that have contacted us is 'What did it cost you, how were you hurt?'" the Polaroid executive said. "The answer is there were absolutely no unfavorable results, absolutely nothing."

The wisdom of Polaroid's approach can be argued endlessly, but at least one black worker who was interviewed by the study team in 1970 is sure that the company chose the right course. "The Polaroid program has brought about great ferment in this country," he recently wrote to one of the team members. "What has happened has in fact been the thin edge of the wedge, which will—we hope—lead to a breakthrough." At home, at least, the strategy has silenced the critics; the tiny Polaroid Revolutionary Workers Movement, which began the protest in the first place, has quietly disappeared.

APPENDIX: BUSINESS RELATIONS OF OTHER COMPANIES AND INSTITUTIONS WITH SOUTH AFRICA

Immediately before and during the Polaroid protest and experiment in South Africa, many incidents commanded attention in the world press. Some of the highlights are sketched here to provide context for the Polaroid deliberations and decisions.

Wates, Ltd., one of the top six construction companies in Great Britain, was requested in January 1970 to grant a license for the use of its mechanized on-site construction methods in South Africa. Mr. Neil Wates, the managing director of the firm employing 4,447 people, earning £592,000 on a turnover of £23,312,000, refused but was persuaded not to make the decision on the basic of secondhand hostile propaganda but to visit South Africa personally. He did so at his own expense and then in June 1970 documented his reaction in a press release from which the following excerpts are drawn:

I must report prima facie South Africa is the ideal land for investment; stability is a relative term, but in the foreseeable future there can be few more stable countries than South Africa. The economic outlook is excellent. . . . Politically, the country is extremely stable— there would seem to be no prospect of ousting the present regime; the student unrest in Universities as experienced in Europe and the U.S. is completely unknown; there are no strikes and above all the non-whites are completely quiescent.

I must further report that the opportunities for a System of industrialised building, such as the Wates System—which not only saves man hours, but above all skilled man hours and eliminates wet trades —are enormous. The white dominated Unions have a virtual stranglehold on the Construction industry; the only way to cut the Gordian knot is through eliminating the wet trades and creating totally new jobs altogether, which would enable employers to open up job opportunities for non-whites without ever being accused of taking jobs away from the whites.

In this context it is only fair to say also that I met Liberal businessmen of the highest calibre who argued that economic forces were bound to bring about the downfall of apartheid—and their own system would prove a powerful weapon in the campaign.

Notwithstanding all this, I must report that the idea of doing business in South Africa is totally unacceptable; we could not be true to the basic principles on which we run our business and we should lose our integrity in the process. We should have to operate within a social climate where the colour of a man's skin is his most important attribute and where there is virtually no communication between the races; we should be locked into this system. We should have to operate within an economic climate which is designed deliberately to demoralise and to maintain an industrial helotry; we should, in turn, profit from such exploitation and ultimately end up with a vested interest in its maintenance.

We should have to operate within a legal climate where the rule of law has been abolished in favour of rule by decree, which bids fair to become a reign of terror.

The cumulative effect of all these factors in the long term must be self-defeating; within the short term it must make it impossible for ourselves individually, or as a company, to connive at anything

*which would serve to perpetuate a system which in the last analysis
has no other justification than the preservation of white supremacy
as an end in itself.*

*   *   *   *   *

*. . . The policy of reserving key jobs for whites virtually means that
3.6m whites must provide the entire management capability and key
skills for a population of over 19m.*

*   *   *   *   *

*The real scandal lies in the fact that all the real job opportunities
one can see being grasped by Africans both in supervisory management and in the area of technical skills in a country like Zambia are
totally denied to them in South Africa. It is impossible to say how
many first class minds are doing the most menial jobs and it is, of
course, impossible to measure the waste of ability.*

*The theory of separate development is plainly nonsense all the
time the whites depend on the blacks for their industrial manpower
—and of course there can be no meaningful development in the home
lands where most of the blacks are working in white areas. Only 8.7%
of employed Africans are working in the home lands—whilst over one
third "live" in the home lands, but work away from home on annual
contracts. This self-defeating policy prohibits any prospect of career
development for them, let alone the building up of any loyalty to the
company and reduces the non-white to the level of a "Labour Unit."*

*Of course we would ensure that any business we set up would be
a beacon of good employment practices, with basic principles of
equal-pay, equal-fringe benefits and working conditions. But we could
not open the career to talents in the way we strive to do in this
country and in the States through our policy of "optimising individual and the company goals"—because some goals are simply not
open to some individuals.*

*   *   *   *   *

*It is no defence to point out the undeniable truth that the black
South Africans are better off than blacks in any other country in the
world; the important factor is their relative well-being to their white
fellow citizens; the Africans constitute 68% of the population, but
their share of the National cash income is 19%—whereas the white
constitute 19% and their share of the cash income is 73%.*

*   *   *   *   *

*I will confess that I travelled South Africa hoping that I would find
good reasons for doing business there; privately I had always considered critics of South Africa to be shrill and emotional—to whom everything black was good and everything white was bad. But the parallel between Hitler's treatment of the Jews in the 1930s and South
Africa's treatment of the blacks today, became daily more obvious to
me in the course of my visit and was brought home most vividly to
me when I saw blacks being literally herded like cattle through the
Bantu Administration Courts—just as I think with hindsight it
would have been totally wrong to do anything to connive at Nazism*

in those days, so also do I think we should do nothing that would help to perpetuate apartheid.

I was frequently pressed in South Africa to say whether we were looking at it as a business or an ethical problem; there can, of course, be no difference.

On February 21, 1971, the Episcopal Church which holds 12,574 shares of General Motors stock requested the automobile company to submit a resolution to the annual shareholders' meeting requiring withdrawal from South Africa. Robert S. Potter, chairman of the Episcopal Churches Committee on Social Criteria for Investments, revealed the motivation for the move. "A pull-out by General Motors probably won't accomplish much for blacks generally, but at least then General Motors and the church wouldn't be supporting apartheid. We want to give General Motors and other companies a stick. This gives G.M. a chance to say: 'Look, we want to stay, but we're getting pressure from home. Why don't you let up a bit?'." General Motors' investment in South Africa totals some $125 million. It employs over 6,000 people in three plants. Fifty-two percent of employment is nonwhite. According to the then chairman of General Motors, Mr. James M. Roche, "G.M. South Africa does not discriminate between the races as to wages, except for a difference in starting rates which are higher for whites than for coloured or native employees." Mr. Roche replied to the demand of the Episcopal Church in a press conference on February 19 by refusing to withdraw from South Africa. He believed that the South African racial problem was slowly being solved. If the situation worsened, then, that "might pose a different problem." In a reply to the authors' inquiry on the G.M. position on the Episcopal proposal further details are revealed:

Thank you for your recent letter inquiring about General Motors' position on the stockholder proposal announced by the Episcopal Church.

General Motors operates in many countries throughout the world and is obliged to obey the law of each of these countries. We have been in South Africa since 1926, long before the current apartheid policies were instituted. Currently, G.M. employs approximately 6,000 persons in South Africa, more than half of whom are non-white. The number of non-whites employed by G.M. has been expanding steadily.

We are well aware that the policies being followed by the government in South Africa raise complex issues. The answer, however, does not lie in turning our back on these issues by eliminating our participation in that country. No matter what we as individuals may think of the political system, it is a hard fact that General Motors in South Africa is offering employment opportunities which would otherwise not be available.

We firmly believe that General Motors can best make a practical contribution to solving this problem by expanding the number of good jobs to help provide the economic prosperity and stable social climate within which reasonable and responsible people can work toward proper solutions.

Thank you for writing and giving us this opportunity to discuss this matter with you.

> Sincerely,
> Morley Warren
> Manager, Editorial Services
> Public Relations Staff

Despite the refusal to leave South Africa, General Motors agreed to place the resolution on the agenda of the May meeting of the stockholders. The new black board member, Rev. Leon Sullivan, backed this move. When the vote was taken, less than 3 percent of the shares were voted in favour of the Episcopal resolution, hence the resolution could not appear on the annual meeting agenda for three more years.

The Episcopal Church move to appeal for proxy support in the annual meeting was symptomatic of a maturing tactics of social activists. The sophistication of the approach is revealed in the following two quotes:

> *Submitting proxy proposals, and getting foundations, universities, and churches to vote their shares in favour of them is winning favour over physical action, says Alice Tepper, director of the Council on Economic Priorities. "Too often in the past," she says, "issues were lost in headlines about demonstration and disruptions."*[5]
>
> *Apart from its publicity value, the proxy route to reform has a major advantage for the corporate dissidents: management can be forced to finance most of the battle with corporate funds. A young Washington attorney, Rodney Shields, bought one share in each of 30 companies and fired off a barrage of 200 separate reform proposals for this year's proxy statements. The whole enterprise, he says, cost him $1,400. The cost to management—for fighting the proposals through the Securities and Exchange Commission and ultimately printing the 125 or so that were approved—has been estimated at $1 million or more.*[6]

Gulf Oil faced a similar resolution for its annual meeting on April 27, 1971, concerning its conduct of business in Angola and Mozambique. This time, the initiator of the proposal was the United Presbyterian Church which controlled more than 20,000 Gulf shares. Mr. Josiah H. Beeman, secretary of the Presbyterian's South African Task Force, said that when churches wanted to protest the action of a company they used to sell their stock. "I don't think this is going to be the case from now on." Just as in the G.M. situation, the resolution failed to get a 3 percent response at the annual meeting.

---

[5] *Business Week,* February 13, 1971.

[6] *Newsweek,* May 24, 1971.

A similar attempt to get a resolution on South Africa on the annual meeting agenda of Honeywell failed.

Elsewhere in the world antiapartheid critics were active as well. In early January 1971, the West German company Urangesellschaft pulled out of a major project to mine uranium jointly with Rio Tinto Zinc in South West Africa in order to avoid jeopardizing West German relations with black Africa. Also, a large Italian electrical company, SAE, and Sweden's ASEA, have withdrawn from lucrative contracts for work on the Cabora Bassa dam in Mozambique, which is being built by a South African-led consortium. In London, Sir Frederick Seebohm, chairman of Barclay's Bank, spent most of his speech at the annual general meeting in early January defending the bank's operations in South Africa where over half the bank's branches are. Protestors had objected especially to the credit given to a subcontractor in South Africa working on the Cabora Bassa dam. There had been a vigorous campaign to persuade students not to open accounts at Barclays.

Banks in the United States have been picketed as well, particularly Chase Manhattan, for its participation in a consortium providing $40 million in revolving credit to the South African government. First National City Bank reports continually receiving letters criticizing its large commitment in South Africa.

In South Africa itself, when various company representatives were asked their opinion on the protest they provided a wide range of replies. Mr. Claude G. Hall, the managing director of Champion Spark Plug, said: "Any pressures from America? They can just jump in the mud." Mr. K. A. Brooke, managing director of Timken South Africa, Ltd., said: "Attention focused on this matter can only make it worse not better. Timken S. A. does not want any more attention than is absolutely necessary." National Cash Register's managing director said: "I would not be ashamed to answer questions from the U.S. on the way we treat our non-white staff."

Public officials, including Senator Ted Kennedy and Representative Charles C. Diggs, member of the House Foreign Affairs Committee and leader of the Black Caucus, originally held opinions that U.S. investment in South Africa was not tolerable. These positions became somewhat modified during 1971 to the point that U.S. investment should cease and withdraw if there is not substantial improvement soon in the lot of the nonwhite workers in South Africa. Congressman Diggs, after a South African study trip, challenged American business firms to make more conscious effort to upgrade the pay and training of nonwhites. He was particularly critical of what he found at the NASA tracking station in South Africa where 225 white employees received a total of 100,000 rand a year whereas 61 nonwhites received only 41,320 rand a year. He found there segregated facilities and a cafeteria serving only white employees. He summarized his findings by saying he discovered at NASA "a utter lack of realization that blacks are human beings."

For some time at Princeton University both faculty and students had protested the investment of university funds in companies doing business in South Africa. The faculty-student committee appointed to exam-

EXHIBIT 1*
Polaroid Corporation and Its Domestic Subsidiaries

	1970	1969	1968	1967
Operating Results				
Sales and other income	$444,285	$465,609	$402,070	$374,354
Earnings before taxes	113,574	130,932	129,009	114,632
Income taxes	52,438	67,811	70,110	57,255
Net earnings	61,136	63,121	58,899	57,377
Earnings per share	1.86	1.94	1.86	1.81
Financial Position, End of Year				
Working capital	$301,033	$297,864	$170,917	$133,377
Net property, plant and				
equipment	172,449	125,070	95,833	80,097
Shareholders' equity	474,645	423,893	270,976	221,153
Other Statistics				
Net additions to property, plant				
and equipment	$ 63,718	$ 43,755	$ 26,099	$ 26,968
Depreciation	16,339	14,518	10,363	8,866
Occupied space (thousand sq.				
ft., end of year)	4,097	3,627	3,060	2,919
Number of employees, end of				
year	8,996	9,157	7,563	6,849
Payroll and benefits	$101,860	$100,001	$ 81,536	$ 70,402
Shares outstanding, end of				
year*	32,832	32,828	31,712	31,660
Unconsolidated Subsidiaries				
Outside the United States				
Sales and other income	$ 88,788	$ 70,459	$ 52,935	$ 52,063
Net earnings	11,008	8,547	3,551	1,082
Earnings per share				
equivalent	.34	.26	.11	.03
Shareholder's equity, end of				
year	20,293	15,041	6,696	3,406

*From the Polaroid Annual Report 1970.

ine the university investment policy found that companies in its portfolio which had investments in South Africa yielded 3 percent more than the other companies in the portfolio. To switch out of companies doing business in South Africa would entail a brokerage cost of $5 million. In their deliberations, according to chairman, Professor Marver Bernstein, they had to include consideration of "what effect any recommendation we would make would have on corporate contributions to the university, which tend to run at 10 percent of private giving."

Finally, the sensitivity of the South African government can be assessed from the story of the $2,850 gift from Israel to the Organization

EXHIBIT 1 (*continued*)

1966	1965	1964	1963	1962	1961
$316,551	$202,228	$138,077	$122,333	$102,589	$100,562
95,232	57,373	35,687	24,207	21,675	17,546
47,638	28,501	17,582	13,129	11,803	9,538
47,594	28,872	18,105	11,078	9,872	8,008
1.51	.92	.58	.35	.32	.26
$101,966	$ 86,443	$ 66,661	$ 51,656	$ 47,539	$ 41,926
61,995	37,482	30,308	27,930	22,638	18,195
170,150	125,043	97,168	79,801	70,517	60,456
$ 31,197	$ 13,087	$ 6,710	$ 9,768	$ 7,857	$ 3,877
6,684	5,587	5,234	4,379	3,400	3,742
2,305	1,659	1,646	1,321	1,216	1,118
6,705	4,947	3,570	3,864	3,536	3,109
$ 56,408	$ 40,840	$ 30,956	$ 28,512	$ 24,568	$ 19,458
31,614	31,548	31,502	31,478	31,430	31,174
$ 46,068	$ 24,335	$ 12,102	$ 9,203	$ 5,630	$ 4,751
(591)	603	645	460	360	205
(.02)	.02	.02	.01	.01	.01
1,974	2,559	1,837	1,192	732	372

of African Unity. The South African government was irked at what they
considered a subsidy for "African terrorists," a label used for black move-
ments against white rulers in Portuguese territories, Rhodesia, and
South Africa. In the words of South Africa's Prime Minister John Vorster,
"I certainly do not understand how Israel, which itself has a terrorist
problem, can justify contributions to terrorists." South Africa's finance
minister, Nico Diede Erichs, announced that the transfer of funds for
Israel would be suspended, except for small personal sums, until the
Government had obtained greater clarity about Israeli policies. For the
South African Jewish community of 120,000, this meant a freeze on the
$25 million raised in the Israeli United Appeal. It also meant a period
of turmoil in which South African Jews were arguing among themselves

on their official posture on apartheid. One representative asserted that the Jewish community "has evolved a formula of collective neutrality." A rebuttal from Mr. Gustav Sharon of the Jewish board of deputies advocated not neutrality but "collective non-intervention."[7]

EXHIBIT 2
An Experiment in South Africa*

Polaroid sells its products in South Africa as do several hundred other American companies. Our sales there are small, less than one half of one percent of our worldwide business.

Recently a group has begun to demand that American business stop selling in South Africa. They say that by its presence it is supporting the government of the country and its policies of racial separation and subjugation of the Blacks. Polaroid, in spite of its small stake in the country, has received the first attention of this group.

We did not respond to their demands. But we did react to the question. We asked ourselves, "Is it right or wrong to do business in South Africa?" We have been studying the question for about ten weeks.

The committee of Polaroid employees who undertook this study included fourteen members—both black and white—from all over the company. The first conclusion was arrived at quickly and unanimously. We abhor apartheid, *the national policy of South Africa.*

The apartheid *laws separate the races and restrict the rights, the opportunities and the movement of non-white Africans. This policy is contrary to the principles on which Polaroid was built and run. We believe in individuals. Not in "labor units" as Blacks are sometimes referred to in South Africa. We decided whatever our course should be it should oppose the course of* apartheid.

The committee talked to more than fifty prominent South Africans both black and white, as well as many South African experts. They heard from officials in Washington. They read books, papers, testimony, documents, opinion, interpretation, statistics. They heard tapes and saw films.

They addressed themselves to a single question. What should Polaroid do in South Africa? Should we register our disapproval of apartheid *by cutting off all contact with the country? Should we try to influence the system from within? We rejected the suggestion that we ignore the whole question and maintain the status quo.*

Some of the black members of the study group expressed themselves strongly at the outset. They did not want to impose on the black people of another country a course of action merely because we might feel it was correct. They felt this paternalistic attitude had prevailed too often in America when things are done "for" black people without consulting black people.

It was decided to send four of the committee members to South Africa. Since this group was to include two black and two white mem-

* *New York Times,* January 13, 1971.

---

[7] *New York Times,* May 7, 1971.

EXHIBIT 2 (*continued*)

bers, it was widely assumed they would not be granted visas. They were.

It was assumed if they ever got to South Africa they would be given a government tour. They were not.

It was assumed they would not be allowed to see the actual conditions under which many Blacks live and would be prevented from talking to any of them in private. They did see those conditions in Soweto and elsewhere. And with or without permission they met and talked to and listened to more than a hundred black people of South Africa. Factory workers, office workers, domestic servants, teachers, political leaders, people in many walks of life. They also talked to a broad spectrum of whites including members of all the major parties.

Their prime purpose in going to South Africa was to ask Africans what they thought American business should do in their country. We decided the answer that is best for the black people of South Africa would be the best answer for us.

Can you learn about a country in ten days? No. Nor in ten weeks. But our group learned one thing. What we had read and heard about apartheid was not exaggerated. It is every bit as repugnant as we had been led to believe.

The group returned with a unanimous recommendation.

In response to this recommendation and to the reports of the larger study committee, Polaroid will undertake an experimental program in relation to its business activities in South Africa.

For the time being we will continue our business relationships there (except for sales to the South African government, which our distributor is discontinuing), but on a new basis which Blacks there with whom we talked see as supportive to their hopes and plans for the future. In a year we will look closely to see if our experiment has had any effects.

First, we will take a number of steps with our distributor, as well as his suppliers, to improve dramatically the salaries and other benefits of their non-white employees. We have had indications that these companies will be willing to cooperate in this plan.

Our business associates in South Africa will also be obliged (as a condition of maintaining their relationship with Polaroid) to initiate a well-defined program to train non-white employees for important jobs within their companies.

We believe education for the Blacks, in combination with the opportunities now being afforded by the expanding economy, is a key to change in South Africa. We will commit a portion of our profits earned there to encourage black education. One avenue will be to provide funds for the permanent staff and office of the black-run Association for Education and Cultural Advancement (ASECA). A second method will be to make a gift to a foundation to underwrite educational expenses for about 500 black students at various levels of study from elementary school through university. Grants to assist

EXHIBIT 2 (*concluded*)

teachers will also be made from this gift. In addition we will support two exchange fellowships for Blacks under the U.S.-South African Leader Exchange Program.

Polaroid has no investments in South Africa and we do not intend to change this policy at present. We are, however, investigating the possibilities of creating a black-managed company in one or more of the free black African nations.

Why have we undertaken this program? To satisfy a revolutionary group? No. They will find it far from satisfactory. They feel we should close the door on South Africa, not try to push it further open.

What can we hope to accomplish there without a factory, without a company of our own, without the economic leverage of large sales? Aren't we wasting time and money trying to have an effect on a massive problem 10,000 miles from home? The answer, our answer, is that since we are doing business in South Africa and since we have looked closely at that troubled country, we feel we can continue only by opposing the apartheid *system. Black people there have advised us to do this by providing an opportunity for increased use of black talent, increased recognition of black dignity. Polaroid is a small economic force in South Africa, but we are well known and, because of our committee's visit there, highly visible. We hope other American companies will join us in this program. Even a small beginning of co-operative effort among American businesses can have a large effect in South Africa.*

How can we presume to concern ourselves with the problems of another country? Whatever the practices elsewhere, South Africa alone articulates a policy exactly contrary to everything we feel our company stands for. We cannot participate passively in such a political system. Nor can we ignore it. That is why we have undertaken this experimental program.

POLAROID CORPORATION

Selected Readings

From

INTERNATIONAL
BUSINESS ENTERPRISE*

By Endel J. Kolde†

THE STRUCTURAL SCHEME OF
INTERNATIONAL-TRADE MANAGEMENT

Multinational business organization has been changing rapidly. In the process new concepts have emerged which have greatly expanded the once rather standardized pattern. To capture the dynamics of this evolution it is necessary to start with an analytic reformulation of the international trade structure. . . . [T]he historic pattern consisted of three different business institutions: the domestic firms, including manufacturers, growers, and distributors in the country of origin; the international trade intermediaries, such as exporters, importers, and custom brokers; and the foreign firms which performed the distribution function in the country of consumption or served as sources of supply for imports.

Thus, the management of foreign trade was divided among the three institutional zones, the firms in each zone carrying out a certain part of the process and depending on firms in the other two for its completion. To visualize graphically this managerial specialization among the institutional zones, the total scope of management jobs might be viewed as a line connecting the point of production in the country of origin with the point of consumption in the country of destination as shown in Figure 1. The functions performed by each zone can then be sequestered as three successive segments in the total management process. Although interdependent, the institutions in the different zones were not integrated with those in the others through either ownership or control.

Requirements for executive capabilities varied from zone to zone. Those in the domestic zone needed, and typically only possessed, the most rudimentary acquaintance with any nondomestic aspect of the overall process. Since they functioned entirely within the jurisdiction—both legal and cultural—of the country of origin, they had minimal contact with the market overseas. For all practical purposes the domestic phase of foreign-trade management was not different from

---

* *International Business Enterprise,* Endel J. Kolde © 1968 by Prentice-Hall, Inc., Englewood Cliffs, N.J. (excerpts from pp. 242–55, 260, 277–78). Reprinted by permission.

† The author is Professor of International Business in the Graduate School of Business, University of Washington.

FIGURE 1
Managerial Phases of the Foreign-Trade Process under the Traditional Institutional Structure

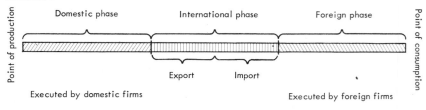

domestic business itself; the same laws, the same costs, the same courts, the same unions, the same banks, the same interest rates, and the same language applied. The transactions between the firms in the domestic zone and those in the international zone were, at least from the standpoint of managerial preparedness and competence, hardly different at all from like transactions consummated between two domestic companies. The only special capabilities required of export management on the manufacturing level were a thorough knowledge of the firms in the international zone and the ability to cultivate those relations with them which best served the foreign-trade objectives of the company.

The vitality and power in foreign-trade management lay in the international zone. The export and import intermediaries possessed the knowhow and techniques for penetrating trade barriers, reconciling incongruities among different laws and customs, and handling the commerical and financial formalities required. The expertise of the intermediaries was rated as professional competence of such high order that many countries accorded to their foreign-trade practitioners special rights and privileges similar to those granted to doctors and lawyers.[1] The process analysis in the previous chapter further elaborates the competence region of the intermediary zone.

Conceptually the foreign phase in this scheme is the mirror image of the domestic one except that pragmatic differences in business conditions and practices between the countries distorted the two in most respects. This organizational pattern evolved during the middle third of the 19th century and became accepted as the "normal" structure of international trade. However, arrangements in recent years are forcing a massive expansion of the structure and challenging the lingering on of the "normal" structure. In quantitative terms, traditional foreign-trade business has shrunk to less than a fifth of the total international business of the United States, while the business carried on under the new arrangements has increased correspondingly. The discussion here will focus on these newer arrangements.

---

[1] This notion has been revived in some foreign-trade circles, especially in Philadelphia, in the last few years, and proposals for professional accreditation of export-import executives have received considerable attention and publicity. In the light of the very basic changes in international business it seems highly unlikely that such accreditation would make any real contribution to business management.

Early Structural Models of International Industrial Companies

Deviations from the three-zone structure can be traced to the colonial companies. However, outside the colonial realm such deviations remained rather exceptional until the period between the two world wars, when extreme protectionism severely limited opportunities for international trade. Since the tariff walls were too high to climb, the only way to reach foreign markets was by being established behind them. Consequently, acquisition of foreign-based production facilities became a growing factor in international business.

Yet, both the philosophy and the organizational ideas remained embedded in the traditional concept of foreign trade. Where the choice existed, a company was interested not so much in going new ways as in gaining control of the traditional route, not so much in developing foreign production bases, except in the extractive industries, as in circumventing the international intermediaries. Accordingly the main thrust of the industrial corporation was to create its own foreign-trade organization in the image of the export and import firms it was to displace. In smaller firms the new trade organ was a foreign-trade or export department; in large ones, a foreign-trade division or *export-selling company*. The latter represented the ultimate under the foreign-trade concept. It was a wholly owned subsidiary located in the same country as the parent concern and prepared to perform all the functions previously left to the independent intermediaries. It represented a channel for direct trade and an instrument of centralized control over both the domestic and the international phases of the foreign-trade process.

When tariffs compelled direct investment in overseas facilities, the model arrangement was the so-called *allied export company*—a firm incorporated and situated abroad in which the U.S. parent held some stock but which it seldom owned outright. Although the allied export company was also engaged in manufacturing activities, its principal purpose remained export marketing, as indicated by its name. Frequently, the manufacturing operations were conceived by management as a wedge for prying market openings from within when import restrictions made markets impenetrable from without. The logic was that a company established within a country can mobilize public support and governmental interest to win special consideration and privileges in regard to foreign-trade restrictions. However, manufacturing was not purely a camouflage for the import strategy. Often the manufacturing activity outranked trade in its growth and generation of profits. But, since the top management of the parent firm was guided by an inward-looking, nationalistic perspective, exportation was generally preferred over plant and production abroad.

Both the export-selling company and the allied export company are rapidly approaching extinction. Those forms which have emerged in recent years have either absorbed them or displaced them. This process was particularly conspicuous in the 1950's.

An Overview of Alternative Organizational Arrangements

The main organizational arrangements which now exist are shown in Figure 2. The shaded areas show the international entities of the company. In a general sense, the alternatives also reflect the stages of growth from indirect exporting to a fully integrated international corporate structure. Lately, however, there has

FIGURE 2
Types of Functional Relations between Parent Organizations and Their International Entities

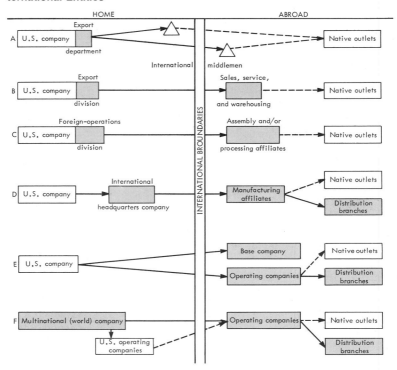

been an increasing tendency to skip the intermediate stages and to move directly from alternative *A* to *D, E,* or even *F.*

STRUCTURAL MODELS OF MULTINATIONAL COMPANIES

The most significant organizational change in the postwar period has been the replacement of foreign-trade departments or divisions with international-operations establishments. From this shift has evolved nearly all that is peculiarly characteristic of the modern multinational corporation. From this shift, also, has come an entirely new and different structural framework for international economic relations. The organizational expression of this shift can be reduced to four prototypal models: the international-headquarters company, the foreign-base company, the world company, and the transnational company. The models are not exact reproductions of a particular firm but are the conceptual expressions underlying the design of the organization. In practice such models must always be suited to the particular circumstances of a specific company.

The International-Headquarters Company (IHC Model)

The emergence of the international-headquarters company marks an important turning point in the organization of international business. Although an outgrowth of the export-selling company in older firms (but not in others), it is structurally and functionally different. Unlike the older forms, it drops all pretense of being an offshoot of the sales organization (a subordinate outlet with narrowly defined objectives) and assumes the role of an operationally autonomous enterprise whose factories, warehouses, employees, and customers are not located in its country but are scattered in different foreign areas. Production and finance are thus organic to it, and export selling is expanded to international marketing, with aspirations and capabilities of a higher order. Any need to be organized in the image of the international middlemen firms is thus eliminated and a new structural model emerges. It is shown in Figure 3.

In this prototype the top echelons of the parent company remain unaffected except for the addition of a vice-president to serve as the contact officer between the parent and the subsidiary. The latter has its own policy-making organs: board of directors, president, and staff vice-presidents for each functional area. In the chart, these latter functionaries are indicated by the oval boxes, as are their counterparts in the parent firm. The line officers, on the other hand, are indicated by rectangular boxes. The IHC board is chaired either by the contact officer or the president of the parent.

The line organization of the international-headquarters company follows the territorial principle. Divisions or subsidiary companies, set up for all appropriate world regions, carry out the actual operations of the firm. These in turn control the foreign-based affiliates—wholly owned subsidiaries, joint-venture companies, or others.

From Export Management to International Management. The underlying principle of the new model is not functional but geographic. The international-headquarters company is not limited to exporting or to any functionally delineated responsibility as such, but undertakes all functions the company carries out abroad. Its managerial jurisdiction is defined not by the nature of the job but by the geographic scope or location of the job. Accordingly, the international-headquarters company may be compared to the State Department of the U.S. government or to any ministry of foreign affairs. Its functional dimension knows no limit, but its territorial dimension is sharply defined.

The Functional Spectra. Based on this concept, the new model also creates new requirements for managerial preparedness, although the requisites for export management remain. Figure 4 shows how the spectrum of managerial functions is changed. Under the export scheme functions were limited to selling and shipping tasks; now they encompass not only a more complete multinational program but also, and more importantly, many nonmarketing responsibilities.

. In fully developed international-headquarters companies the spectrum of management functions is actually wider than that of the parent corporation itself because the former encounters problems peculiar to multinational activities: international transfer pricing, dealings with foreign governments, negotiations with supranational bodies. In addition, it must be able, on the one hand, to adapt its objectives, policies, and methods to the social and cultural conditions of each country in its territory and, on the other hand, to create sufficient uniformity and continuity for effective coordination and control of the entire multinational structure. In complexity, the skills and capabilities which the management of a multinational enterprise must possess dwarf those of the traditional foreign-trade executive. Consequently, the new scheme marks the beginning of what now is called

FIGURE 3
Structural Model of the International-Headquarters Company

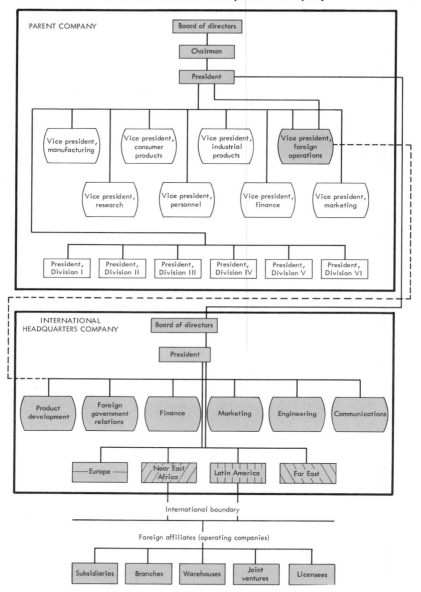

Note to Figure 3: Corporate entities with international responsibilities are shaded in the chart, and those with domestic responsibilities are not; the directors, chairman, and president of the parent have secondary responsibility in international management, as indicated by partial shading.

Source: Endel J. Kolde, "Business Enterprise in a Global Context." California Management Review, VIII, No. 4 (Summer 1966), 39.

FIGURE 4
Comparative Spectra of Functional Responsibilities: A Schematic Sketch

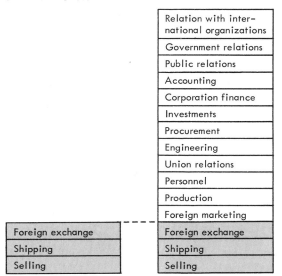

Relation with international organizations
Government relations
Public relations
Accounting
Corporation finance
Investments
Procurement
Engineering
Union relations
Personnel
Production
Foreign marketing

Foreign exchange	Foreign exchange
Shipping	Shipping
Selling	Selling

EXPORT MANAGEMENT · INTERNATIONAL MANAGEMENT

international or *multinational management* as distinct from *export* or *import management.* And, at the same time, it completely changes the concept of an international executive, together with the requirements for becoming one.

The changeover to the IHC plan reached its apex in the late 1950's, and by the early 1960's it had become the dominant organizational format for U.S. business, including both industrial and nonindustrial companies. Even service firms such as management consultants, market research agencies, and accounting firms adopted this plan.

The Base Company

The base-company format had its beginning in the search for sanctuaries where foreign-source income could be accumulated with minimum tax depletion. Wide differences in corporate income taxes among countries induced the search. The low-tax countries—especially the Bahamas, Panama, Liechtenstein, Switzerland, and Hong Kong—became the preferred locations for the *tax-haven,* or *profit-sanctuary,* subsidiaries, as the initial base companies were commonly called. Many of these were paper corporations without physical facilities or administrative capabilities. Their value derived from the fact that the U.S. internal revenue laws did not cover foreign-source income as long as it remained abroad. But, although the tax savings were real, they were not the only advantages of the foreign holding company. Many firms found it both ethically and organizationally desirable to endow them with the authority of actual management by making them the headquarters for their foreign operations.

The 1962 Revenue Act wiped out the pure tax-haven companies by making foreign-source income of U.S. firms taxable irrespective of where the funds were kept. This helped to make the base company an international-headquarters company located abroad rather than in the same country with the parent firm. In its structure the base company duplicates the international-headquarters plan with the exception of its location. The advantages that it offers over the IHC model are (a) better integration of top management and operations, (b) greater autonomy and less likelihood of interference by the parent, (c) greater financial flexibility in transferring earnings and assets from one country to another, and (d) spreading political and financial risk of the enterprise as a whole. The negative aspects are (a) complications of management—domestic routines and practices which can be employed in the IHC must be reformed; (b) loss of U.S. treaty and diplomatic protection; and (c) closer scrutiny by U.S. tax and trade authorities.

*   *   *   *   *

The World Company

Although most multinational firms now are patterned after the IHC model, the process of organizational development has not ended there. A new and still different structure has emerged. Its basic plan is shown in Figure 5. Although in the IHC model the dichotomy between domestic and international was emphasized as the fundamental criterion, the world-company model abandons this dichotomy and integrates the American and international operations by subordinating domestic to multinational affairs. The top echelons of the parent corporation, which under the IHC plan retain their inward-looking, domestic orientation, are thus reoriented to the global point of view, and the previous dualistic structure is eliminated from

FIGURE 5
Structural Model of the World Company

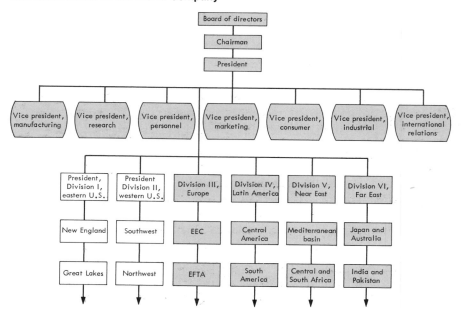

the policy-making organs. The entire headquarters staff becomes multinational in managerial responsibility and outlook.

The operating units are again organized on the territorial principle, each being defined in terms of a particular world region and thus adapted to the economic and cultural peculiarities of it. Needless to add, area expertise thus takes precedence over functional and product knowledge for general-management positions on the operational level. Some firms are now attempting to insert a product organization in the world-company framework; but, for the time being at least, no clear-cut conceptual solution has emerged. When it has been tried, the result has been a double structure utilizing both territorial and product principles.

Although the world-company plan is still in its infancy, having been first attempted in the mid 1950's, the conversion to it has been considerable, especially among companies whose product line has a relatively universal demand, such as petroleum, soft drinks, and drugs. It might be added that the model is being adopted not only by industrial giants but also by more and more smaller firms, many having skipped the IHC stage.

The Transnational Company

The transnational company originated in Europe. It differs from the world company in that both ownership and control of the corporate structure are international. Its management is polycentric; there is no parent company as such, no central source of power, no domestic market or principal domicile. Its capital is raised from whichever capital market provides the best source for a particular venture; and top management is divided among several headquarters, each in a different country, and functions as an international coalition rather than as a command hierarchy. In essence, then, the transnational company can be visualized as a group of management centers jointly administering a network of operating companies.

Although a few such polycentric multinational firms now exist (Unilever, Royal Dutch-Shell), the attitude of international executives toward this plan remains reserved. Whether it will ever reach a status comparable to that of the other plans seems doubtful at this time. However, the development of foreign-base companies with strong subsidiaries of their own resembles the transnational concept.

Contrast between the New Models and the Traditional Scheme

How basic a change these new models represent is demonstrated in the structural model of the typical industrial corporation of the foreign-trade era in Figure 6. As in the previous charts, the international organs are indicated by shading. Here the international aspects of management are limited in terms of both function and position. The operation is not well organized as a hierarchy. The chief international executive—the export manager—is subordinate to a functional department head rather than being part of general management. No top executive has his primary responsibility in the international field.

FOREIGN-BASED AFFILIATES

How the foreign entities of a company are organized is basically a matter of law. To gain entry in a particular country a company must comply with all the legal

FIGURE 6
Export (International) Department in Traditional Corporate Structure

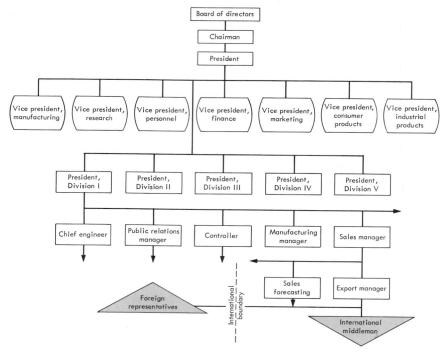

provisions applicable to it. Since the laws of no two countries are identical, the legal aspects of establishment must always be handled as special cases.

Generally speaking, visas for corporate entry into a country are subject to more restrictions than are those which apply to people, goods, or capital. To meet the requirements a company has four alternative approaches: qualify for a branch license; form a subsidiary company under the laws of the host country; create a joint venture with one or more indigenous companies; or enter into a licensing agreement with an existing firm. The last two alternatives are discussed in separate chapters; the first two are the subject of the remainder of this chapter.

Foreign Branches

From a legal standpoint a branch is not a separate juridic entity but only a physical offshoot of the parent firm. As long as both the branch and the parent are in the same country they are subject to the same national jurisdiction. The legal status of the branch is of small concern, as the parent company remains responsible for any legal action taken either by or against the branch. If, however, a branch were located in a different country, a legally intolerable situation would arise. The branch with its physical and economic powers would function as a legal nonentity over which the host country's government had no control since its juridic embodiment, the parent firm would be outside the country's jurisdiction and thus beyond the reach of the juridical organs of the government. No government can permit such immunity to law in its territory. For this reason licenses are issued for branch operations to nonresident companies only if the branch is *domesticated* by having a responsible national of the host country serve as the legal custodian of the establishment. The custodianship must be based on a formally executed power of attorney, in which the company conveys to the foreign citizen or firm involved complete jurisdiction over the branch. Since such an arrangement creates subtle problems and additional uncertainties, branches are relatively uncommon in multinational companies except as subunits of a national or regional subsidiary limited to one single country.

The foreign branch has other weaknesses also. Business licenses may be of short duration, and frequent renewals involve considerable expense; regulations and governmental surveillance may be tighter;[2] the taxable base may be so defined that the branch becomes taxable not on the basis of its own earnings or assets, but on the basis of the total profits or capitalization of the multinational corporation as a whole.

Foreign Subsidiaries

To avoid such discriminatory treatment most companies prefer to organize their affiliates as indigenous enterprises under the laws of the host country. Although the legal forms of enterprise (partnership, corporation, etc.) have over the years become relatively similar, significant differences still exist. The most significant among them is the existence of organizational forms other than the corporation which have juridic personalities separate from their owners and in which the owners' liability is limited to their investments in the enterprise. For example, German law provides for a limited-liability company (G.m.b.H.) which resembles the U.S. corporation in all features essential to management yet enjoys much greater freedom of action under law than does the German equivalent of the corporation (A/G). Thus the American term *to incorporate* is often as misleading as is the popular notion that the various national affiliates of a multinational company are corporations in form. Many are not. And many others should not be. With the growth of the multinational company, U.S. management has become more aware of the legal differences, and more sophisticated use is now being made of the various organizational opportunities which the laws of different countries provide.

To qualify for establishment in most countries, the law requires that a certain number of directorships or other key positions in the firm be occupied by local nationals. Compliance with this requirement produces a *statutory* or *de jure administration* which many companies find unsuitable for the actual management of the affiliate, so they limit the functions of these statutory executives to those prescribed by the charter: holding an annual meeting, signing necessary forms and reports, sanctioning legal contracts, etc. To safeguard itself, the parent company must fill these positions with people of unquestionable integrity, or, more commonly, counterbalance their official powers with contractual constraints such as leasing the assets to the *de jure* administration with the proviso that the officers "delegate" the operational responsibilities to individuals appointed by the lessor.

---

[2] For example, the branch may be required to patronize local suppliers, not compete with local industry, or refrain from employing nonnationals.

Another typical requirement for incorporation is that a specified portion, sometimes more than half, of the capital invested in the affiliate be controlled by local citizens. In countries where such restrictions exist, the U.S. parent company usually enters joint-venture or partial-ownership arrangements. It either buys part ownership in an existing foreign concern or induces a foreign firm to coinvest with it in a new venture. This latter practice has become popular in recent years, especially among manufacturers and distributors of technical products, for whom local facilities and technical personnel are essential for making installations and servicing their customers. To enable the foreign company to contribute the legally necessary capital, it may be permitted by the parent to turn over some existing assets such as its building, equipment, sites, production processes, and even goodwill. Monetary values can be assigned to all of them by mutual agreement, and thus the need for a cash contribution by the local concern is minimized. How far a company is willing to go in this respect depends, of course, on the alternatives available to it and the profit potential of the particular market.

*   *   *   *   *

Definition of Joint Ventures

A joint venture is sometimes defined as an overseas enterprise which is not completely owned by the parent company. This definition would embrace not only foreign-based enterprises owned by two or more different firms but also those whose stock is partially held by the general public. From a purely legal point of view a case can be made for classifying the latter enterprises as joint ventures. But from economic and administrative points of view such an extension of the joint-venture concept undermines its central idea—partnership. There can be no partnership in the pure sense of the word between a foreign corporate owner and the local or, for that matter, the international stockholders of an enterprise. Although the stockholders are entitled to exercise control over the company's activities, they do not legally share in practice in the management and direction of the firm.

Here, a joint venture is a business enterprise in which two or more economic entities from different countries participate on a permanent basis. The participation is not limited to equity capital but normally extends to control of the undertaking through manufacturing processes, patents, trademarks, managerial know-how, or other operationally essential factors. When the partners' rights stem from their equity participation, the enterprise is classified as an equity joint venture; when one or more of the partners have made no equity contribution, the enterprise is a nonequity joint venture. From a legal standpoint, the equity joint venture is a creature of company or corporation law, while the nonequity joint venture is based on contract law.

*   *   *   *   *

Foreign Licensing

Licensing makes available to a foreign firm some intangible industrial property such as a patent, a manufacturing process, or a trademark for the purpose of cultivating the foreign licensee's market. This obviates the licensor company's need for entering the foreign market through export trade or capital investment.

In return for the property rights transferred to it, the foreign firm pays royalties normally based on its output or sales of the licensed product.

The Licensing Agreement

A licensing arrangement is always formalized in a written agreement which stipulates which property rights are being transferred; the royalties or other considerations paid; where and how the rights are to be utilized; under which circumstances the rights are to revert to the licensor; and the degree of participation the licensor is to have in the licensed operations of the licensee or in the marketing of the licensed products. The contract may further cover the period of time; the size of the territory covered by the arrangement; the methods of control and payment; the applicable law in case of conflict; and the method of arbitration, if appropriate.

Besides providing an alternative to export-import trade and direct investment, licensing agreements also provide an inexpensive means for exploring and testing a company's growth potential in a particular foreign area before any irretrievable investment is made. From a risk standpoint licensing agreements entail greater risk than normal export operations but considerably less risk than direct investments. For this reason, licensing is frequently used as a transitional phase between export and foreign manufacture in a company's international expansion process and is succeeded by a more extensive commitment. So-called *royalty and stock participation agreements* are specifically designed for gradual conversion from licensing to equity operation. They provide for a low or a declining royalty plus a stock-purchase commitment in a new or existing establishment to succeed the licensing arrangement. The licensee acquires a partial ownership interest in the successor company through the stock purchases. In cases where local equity capital is not available in sufficiently large blocks to establish a joint-venture facility, the facility may initially be financed by the U.S. licensor and gradually converted into a joint enterprise under a royalty and stock-purchase agreement. Thus, such arrangements permit equity financing from the proceeds of the very product for which the equity was intended.

Licensing has sometimes been defined as exporting of know-how. However, it is also a continuous cooperative relationship between the parties for their mutual benefit. It is correct to classify licensing as a nonequity joint venture where pooling of resources among the partners is the overriding characteristic. It is not to be equated with direct investment; the industrial property rights are not sold outright but leased or loaned for a definite period, and the proceeds are royalties—not dividends or profits.

From

New Product Decisions*

By Edgar A. Pessemier†

OBJECTIVES OF NEW-PRODUCT POLICY

In the simplest terms, new-product search activities are designed to locate new products and capabilities which will yield the largest return from the firm's resources consistent with existing risk and organizational constraints. On the whole, firms lead from strength, seeking product opportunities that permit the use or extension of their special technical, production, or marketing skills, or the employment of a resource base. At times, however, the objectives may be defensive, the reduction of risk by protecting a favored position. In any of these cases, it is convenient to classify the objectives of proposed products along the two dimensions of newness suggested by Johnson and Jones.[1] The details of this classification system are contained in Table 1. As the degree of change increases along either of the newness dimensions, the higher the uncertainty and risk will tend to become and the more pronounced will be the impact of the new product on the firm's organization.

Restated in broader terms, the principal objective of a new-product policy is to direct the dynamic adjustment of the firm's resources to changing environmental conditions. Competitors' strategies and tactics, the needs of the market, the technologies with which these needs may be met, and the sociopolitical climate are continually shifting. The speed and direction of change are often difficult to assess. New, fertile areas emerge, old frontiers of growth disappear, and the productivity of mature markets declines. Not infrequently, hard-won strength in a technology, a product line, or among a class of buyers will encourage conservative, shortsighted product policy. Only when product policy is consciously developed as a *principal agent of adoption and development* will the past and present be placed in proper perspective and latent opportunity for growth be fully exploited.

In more concrete terms, it is easy to compare the product policies followed by a variety of successful organizations. At one extreme we find the very fluid, diffuse product policy followed by Textron. For an extended period, this firm expanded rapidly through acquisitions and mergers designed to take advantage of tax-loss situations. Having developed as a broad-line highly integrated producer and convertor of textiles and manufacturer of apparel, this firm became involved in a long series of unsuccessful moves designed to adapt to new conditions in the textile industry. Abandoning these efforts, textile operations were liquidated and a new series of acquisitions produced a conglomerate collection of divisions producing such diverse products as plastic boats, chain saws, and metal-can fabricating machinery. At the other extreme, we find organizations like Island Creek Coal,

---

* By permission from *New Product Decisions,* by Edgar A. Pessemier. Copyright 1966. McGraw-Hill Book Company, Inc. (Excerpts from 8–10.)

† The author is Professor of Industrial Administration at Purdue University.

[1] Samuel C. Johnson and Conrad Jones, "How to Organize for New Products," *Harvard Business Review,* May–June, 1957, p. 52.

TABLE 1
New Products Classified By Product Objective

Product Objectives		Increasing Technological Newness————————→		
		No Technological Change	Improved Technology	New Technology
Increasing Marketing Newness	No Market Change		*Reformulation* Make minor modifications in product to reduce cost and/ or improve quality.	*Replacement* Make major modifications in product to reduce cost and/ or improve quality.
	Strengthen Market	*Remerchandising* Make present products more attractive to the type of customers presently served.	*Improved product* Make present product more useful to present customers by improving present technology.	*Product-line extension* Widen the line of products offered to present customers by adopting a new technology.
	New Market	*New use* Extend sale of present products to types of customers not presently served.	*Market extension* Extend sales to types of customers not presently served by offering a modified present product.	*Diversification* Extend sales to types of customers not presently served by offering products of a new technology.

which has historically marketed a narrow product line directly tied to a stable resource base.

Along other dimensions of product policy, contrasts can be found. Some firms sell classes of products that rapidly change their physical characteristics, while other companies sell products which vary little from year to year. Firms producing data-processing equipment typify the former, and producers of salt and allied chemicals represent the latter situation. Also, the degree to which a firm possesses advanced scientific and technical skills, an established market position, and so on, may become an important influence in shaping diverse product policies. These observations underline the fact that:

1. Sound product policy is an essential ingredient of sound business management.
2. Special skills and conscious attention must be applied to the problem of maintaining an efficient product policy.
3. Effective policy must be built on a clear understanding of the dynamics of the firm's external environment and internal resources.
4. Among firms in an industry and between industries diverse product policies are common. Simple, ready-made solutions are rare.

From

CONCEPTUAL FOUNDATIONS OF BUSINESS*

By Richard Eells and Clarence Walton†

Pluralism always implies multiplicity, frequently diversity, and sometimes con-flict. It is as much the generator as the result of freedom. Pluralism is intimately associated with toleration as opposed to bigotry, with voluntarism as opposed to coercion, and with a happy blending of individualism and associationism. This reflects those differences of interests that characterize the large, modern nation-state. Indeed, James Madison's claim to immortality rests mainly on his anticipa-tion of the growth of parties and other voluntary organizations at a time when the former were unknown and the latter few in number. His prophetic observation (in No. 10 of *The Federalist*[1] that the existence of many autonomous groups makes tyranny by the majority less likely has an important place in any theory of "counter-vailing power."

Pluralism is concerned with the roles that these autonomous associations can play as a result of the power they enjoy, with the interplay of forces among these various groups as they enhance or diminish a specific group's power, and with the effect of power blocs on individual freedom and creativity.

      *   *   *   *   *

Pluralism encompasses an aim (wide diffusion of power) and a structure (volun-tary groups operating between the national government and the citizen in a man-ner that neither subordinates nor dominates the individual), but it also involves a method for evaluating results. This method does not seek to construct broad social programs on the basis of prior fixed dogma but relies on the consequences flowing from various groups' actions for the emergence of policy. Pluralism is less con-cerned with the lack among Americans of "public philosophy"—to use Lippmann's apt phrasing—than it is with the loss of a "sharp perception of consequence" by the leaders of these various private sectors in American society. . . .

      *   *   *   *   *

From a political standpoint, pluralism seeks to build a bridge connecting the traditions of liberalism and conservatism in American history. In the liberal tradition, pluralism is marked by references to problems rather than solutions, by faith in change rather than a change of faith. Whether it is Wilson's New Freedom, Roose-velt's New Deal, or Kennedy's New Frontier, this liberalism insists that transforma-tion and reformation are the natural products of a pluralistic and creative society. Pluralism's conservative lineaments show in its skepticism of state power and centralized state planning, on the one hand, and in its esteem of local responsibility and states' rights, on the other. . . .

      *   *   *   *   *

---

* Reprinted by permission of Richard D. Irwin, Inc., Homewood, Ill., 1961 (pp. 360–63).

† Dr. Walton is President of Catholic University of America. Dr. Eells is a noted author and consultant to business.

[1] James Madison, *The Federalist: A Collection of Essays* (New York: John Tiebout, 1799).

Pluralism seeks to diffuse power into many organizations and groupings and thus to prevent the development of imbalances of power and to assure the freedom of the individual from the tyranny of the one, the few, or the many. It constitutes a continuing challenge to totalitarianism of every kind, whether the rule be held by a political dictator, by a business or labor oligarchy, or by the masses themselves. It is suspicious of claims to omniscience, and omnipotence and is therefore as much opposed to the ambitious pretenses of a James Stuart (the king can do no wrong), as it is to the Rousseauian version of democracy (the collectivity can do no wrong) . . .

From

THE MULTINATIONAL CORPORATION*

By David E. Lilienthal†

Many large and even medium-sized American corporations are already operating in other countries, in one way or another. By *operating* I do not mean merely that they have a financial stake, like a portfolio investment, in business in other countries than their own; nor do I refer only to sales agencies or distributors. I have particularly in mind industrial or commercial operations abroad which directly involve corporate managerial responsibility.

Such corporations—which have their home in one country but which operate and live under the laws and customs of other countries as well—I suggest be called *multinational corporations.*

    *   *   *   *   *

RELATIONS WITH GOVERNMENTS

The most serious problems confronting the multinational corporation are those concerned in its relations with governments. These must be the everyday business of the corporate manager. If he handles them with skill and patient attention, his company should prosper; if he underestimates their importance, he fails to bring the full force of his training and resources to bear on them, then he is risking disaster.

Multiplicity of Governments

As we all know, a corporation is an artificial person, created by government. It is thus the offspring of a government. We also know how an ordinary corporation in the United States must relate to its government from its birth through its creative

---

   * By permission from *Management and Corporations 1985,* by Melvin Anshen and George L. Bach. Copyright 1960. McGraw-Hill Book Company, Inc. (Excerpts from pp. 119, 121–28, 135–36, 139–42, 146–47, 154–57.)

   † Mr. Lilienthal is Chairman of the Board and President of Development and Resources Corporation, New York, New York.

existence and ultimately to its death or dissolution. But the multinational corporation has multigovernments. It will come from the territory of one government and it will incorporate and live under the laws of another. More than that, it may incorporate and live under the laws of many governments.

* * * * *

. . . [E]ven in the simplest of examples—in which a corporation comes from country A to live and work in country B—the multiplicity of governments will be a perplexing complication. The immigrant corporation must learn to live with its new legal parent and yet honor its real parent, the government of the country of its origin. Legally, it cannot call on its true parent for protection and support, as can the traveler abroad. Yet it must be able to rely on the parent to some extent without at the same time offending its new parent. Thus one can see how delicately the relationship between the old and the new governments must be balanced.

The problem grows more complicated when the origins of the multinational corporation are multifarious. . . . Which country is the "protecting power" of such an entity? Certainly not one and one only of the several countries which have participated.

Regional Blocs

There is still a further complication for the managers of multinational corporations. They must learn to live not only with two or more different national governments, but also with regional associations, or blocs. The formation of these groups will multiply the already burdensome problems of government relations, for a regional body is essentially a kind of new government or community, though of limited powers, created by its members.

* * * * *

While this is all going on, from the period of raw newness through the growth of central power, the multinational corporations will be prominent citizens living under the developing systems. They will have to contend with both the reality and the form. The old state sovereignty will govern, the new federal authority will govern and, perhaps, contradictorily. Conflicts and contradictions must be anticipated as inescapable. Accommodating to these conflicts will become a part of the multinational corporate manager's daily tasks. . . .

Multiplicity of Regulations and Liaison

Whether the corporate manager has to deal with one foreign government or with several—perhaps including a supranational regional group—he will need the services of government, the protection of government, and an intimate knowledge of the facilities of government far more than will the man who manages a purely domestic business. Even for domestic operations, the weight of government relations has grown heavy. With the increased complexity of economic life, government regulation has naturally become intensified. Compliance with government regulations is a large and indispensable part of the corporate activity, and relations with governmental authorities are a primary duty of the corporate manager.

* * * * *

Working under Foreign Governments

But the big job of government relations for the multinational corporation will be its relations with the individual government overseas. The American business executive who thinks of his own government as ubiquitous will be surprised at how pervasive relations with governments abroad can be.

First, the multinational corporation, though it be incorporated in the country of operations, will face the problem of being a foreigner. The status of a foreigner has a very tangible significance in law and business. Emotionally, the progression of some forms of nationalism goes something like this—foreigner, alien, stranger, suspect. Legally, it is somewhat the same. There are separate laws for aliens—immigration and similar laws which govern only aliens or travelers. There are separate laws governing alien corporate registration, ownership of land and stock by foreign corporations, and always, special tax laws. Finally there are all the laws governing international business relations, financial and informational. All these require understanding, compliance, and continuing government relations. Frequent and seemingly interminable negotiations and relations with governments and their bureaucracies will be the lot of the executive in a country not his own. . . .

*   *   *   *   *

Political Activity   •

*   *   *   *   *

Should the multinational corporation go into politics? Certainly not the kind of politics which in an earlier day took the form of secretly subsidizing rebel leaders or keeping cabinets on a payroll. But can a multinational corporate management possibly avoid action—economic or business action—that has political consequences? I think not. . . .

. . . [A] corporate manager overseas must not be content simply to master the intricacies of a government's tax law. He must also study the political forces which shaped that law—and which may modify it or even strike it from the books tomorrow.

The corporate manager who is politically alert and knowledgeable will be in a position to form broad and sound judgments about the course of his firm's career. A lively awareness of politics in the broadest sense can be the key to constructive relations with governments, and these relations, in turn, have a definite bearing on the success of his business enterprise.

*   *   *   *   *

SOME LONG-RANGE EFFECTS

*   *   *   *   *

It is not out of the question that multinational corporate operations also will give us the beginnings of a world-wide system of business ethics. This system would govern business dealings between competitors, regulate sharp business practices, unfair competition, and even what we call "commerical bribery." Laws and attitudes opposed to venality in government office or to conflicts of interest by government officials, which are generallly accepted as right in the West, will come to be introduced in other areas. In the main, I would guess that in Asia, Africa, and Latin America the leaders of business will come to adopt the best of Western business ethics. In consequence, the treaties on trade practices and perhaps even the new foreign laws on commercial bribery and business expense deductions will imitate the most enlightened Western standards.

The various nations' laws—not to speak of good public relations—will generally require that there be separate corporations in the separate countries. The task will thus be to secure the benefits of centralized effort and understanding while engaged in separate ventures in the different countries. . . .

*   *   *   *   *

Multinational corporations will influence exports and imports of institutions other than those directly related to their business. They will export not only the technology of the countries of their origin, but also to a great extent the concepts of social justice of these countries.

*   *   *   *   *

There is still another significant contribution of the multinational corporation. It is patent that the multinational corporation is an exercise in international, in binational, and in multinational activity. Financiers, businessmen, managers, technicians, and laborers will work together. Governments and government officers will work together in settling the large and small problems incident to multinational corporate activities. This ferment will necessarily improve both the climate and the techniques for binational and multinational political activity. Thus with an increase in natural, functional multinational corporate activity, it is possible—perhaps inevitable—that there will be more and more likelihood that comparable efforts on the political side will be made and will succeed.

From

NEW CREDENTIALS FOR MORALISTS*

By Brian J. O'Connell, C. M.†

Men search their consciences and find no prejudice, yet thousands of black men in our ghettos work full time for $65 a week or less. The average Joe American would not assault another person, yet millions remain in deteriorated housing because only a small fraction of investment capital is being directed toward housing. Joe would not steal a nickel from another person either, yet he enjoys the fruits of the labor of migrants or Latin American miners who receive pittances for their toil.

---

* "New Credentials for Moralists," by Brian J. O'Connell, *America,* February 19, 1972. Copyright 1972 by *America.* All Rights Reserved. Excerpts from pp. 179–81. Reprinted by permission.

† The author is a priest and sociologist on leave from St. John's University for studies at Ohio State University.

Why do these built-in injustices in our institutions continue? One reason is that the responsibility for the injustice does not fall directly on any individual. This is the phenomenon that Reinhold Niebuhr described 40 years ago in *Moral Man and Immoral Society*. Joe can feel quite moral because all his face to face relationships are in order, but he shares in the benefits of a society that distributes its rewards and opportunities unjustly. The injustice may even be the product of a historical accident for which no one is responsible. . . .

Another reason for these built-in injustices is that systems or institutions have their own dynamics which resist change. Both the affluent and the poor recognize the inadequacies of the welfare system, yet the established bureaucracy with its dependent constituents continues on in unchanging patterns. Sometimes we have to stop and ask if we are compelled to serve the system or whether the system serves us. . . . The established system rolls along, gathers momentum and defies attempts to change its course.

We need a whole new ethic to confront this situation. The Second Vatican Council, for example, pointed to this new dimension of moral theology: "Profound and rapid changes make it particulary urgent that no one, ignoring the trend of events or drugged by laziness, content himself with a merely individualistic morality. It grows increasingly true that obligations of justice and love are fulfilled only if each person, contributing to the common good, according to his own abilities and the needs of others, also promotes and assists the public and private institutions dedicated to bettering the conditions of human life". . . .

. . . This stern emphasis on structural or instructional morality . . . brings up a question: for what shall the men of the late 20th century be held accountable before the judgment seat of God? We know that we will be asked what we did to aid our neighbors who were poor or hungry or in prison. The judgment on us, necessarily, will be stricter than on the Good Samaritan. His life became entwined with the victim by the side of the road because of physical proximity. But our lives are entwined with people around the globe. We may never come face to face with the Peruvian miner or the migrant, but we enjoy the fruits of his labor, and our decisions about minimum wages or import surcharges affect his life style. We can answer Christ at the judgment only if we have done something to shape our institutions to promote the common good of all men. The Good Samaritan could not be held accountable for the hungry man in India of his time. It is not so in the 1970's.

*   *   *   *   *

. . . What does it mean, for example, when the prices that Americans pay to the Third World for copper or cocoa tend to remain stationary or decline? Pope Paul is trying to make Christians aware that such issues and questions are the stuff that charity and justice are made of today.

Other men as well are calling attention to this institutional dimension. In the *Kerner Report,* the Riot Commission said in summary: "What white Americans have never fully understood—but what the Negro can never forget—is that white society is deeply implicated in the ghetto. White institutions created it, white institutions maintain it, and white society condones it."

Clearly, the cry of "institutional racism" is very threatening to a person who is charged with it but does not understand why. The great emotional responses that result can, in fact, insure that nothing is accomplished. Moral theologians, as well as social scientists, have the difficult but necessary task of explaining, therefore, how institutional imbalance and not personal prejudice is often at the heart of the racial difficulties we face today.

* * * * *

We must not expect an institutional moral code to develop in the same manner that the scholastic natural law ethic developed. There will be no absolute principles, for example, nor can we wait for unquestionable certitude. Rather, institutional morality will depend on the probable conclusions of the social scientists. These days, no one person is able to synthesize all of institutional morality in a volume of books in the manner of the scholastics. To do so, he would have to be a genius in international relations, economics, environmental science and theology, not to mention a few other social sciences. Such an animal does not and will not exist. The conclusions of institutional morality will not be valid, consequently, for any great period of time; as quickly as problems are analyzed and solved, newer and more complex issues are sure to arise.

* * * * *

Some suggestions may be helpful for those who hope to develop or communicate an institutional morality:

1. To begin with, we must anticipate the consequences of technological and social change. With the aid of social scientists, the long and short run effects, the intended as well as the unintended effects, have to be discovered.

* * * * *

2. Moralists must serve as society's conscience in its effort to be master of its destiny. The economic system should not be allowed to lead us blindly. . . .

3. Likewise, it is up to the moralist to warn those who get sidetracked from the crucial issues they have to face. In its time, romanticism, with its return to nature and the simple life, was a cop-out in the face of the Enlightenment and the Industrial Revolution. Existentialism, too, was accused by Marx of ignoring the implications of large-scale capitalism for the worker masses, while it concentrated on personal relationships and the discovery of meaning in life. Even the best of philosophies or of movements like personalism or the commune system can be evasions. Highlighting some important aspects of life, they can ignore other important values, especially in the institutional dimension. Meanwhile, as Harvey Cox says, the organization rolls on, deepening and extending its influence over men. A one-dimensional approach to life, whether it emphasizes the personal or the institutional interest, prevents us from being wholly human and facing the full reality of life in the 20th century.

4. Nor can moralists be deluded by the supposition that all power is political power. In the initial stages of social activism, politicians are often thought to have great if not exclusive power over social and economic trends. What results is wasted effort and fighting mainly strawmen and figureheads—as when people expect great changes from a new president or governor and gradually awaken to the fact that little will be changed after all. Social scientists, indeed, are becoming more aware that politicians have limited amounts of control over such aspects of the system as housing, urban development, inflation, and even the military-industrial complex. Political activism has its glamour, of course, but to influence institutional change, it may be more important to get the ear of the businessman, educator, or banker.

5. Finally, a good deal of background knowledge in the social sciences is

necessary if one is to have any real understanding of institutional morality. . . .

To sum it up, schools today must transform youth's mistrust of institutions into the realization that institutions can actually be controlled and made responsive to human need. Not only must the schools inform, they have to inspire talented young people to prepare themselves to move into the centers of power in our institutions and direct them in truly humane paths.

From

THE TACTICS OF CREATIVE TENSION*

By Jeremiah J. O'Connell

"Of course, we will support serious efforts to fight urban deterioration in our city, but under no circumstances will we tolerate the public use of our corporate name in this connection!" Making this statement was the president of a huge corporation headquartered in Megapolis. Surrounding him at a conference table were government, civic, business, ecclesiastical, and academic leaders of Megapolis. Symptoms of decay in Megapolis brought the group together for an off-the-record weekend conference. In moving from discussion to action the group was trying to marshall resources to launch renewed efforts to save the city. First to come forward with a concrete offer of support was the company president who insisted on anonymity for his organization.

Why such anonymity when so many other corporations were queuing up for corporate citizenship kudos for contributions to any and every worthy cause? Was it biblical modesty wherein the left hand was not to know the good being done by the right hand? Was it fear of back-lash from some sector(s) of corporate stakeholders who might resent support of this or that cause? Was it caution lest the corporation's good name be abused in the classic fund raiser's whip sawing technique of social blackmail? The reason offered by the president challenged some conventional wisdoms and clarified at least one page from the catechism of social activists. In paraphrase, the president's remarks follow.

Our organization publically and early backed numerous worthy causes—civil rights, minority employment, safety, consumerism, environmental management, etc. Our motivation was frankly an inextricable composite of selfishness and altruism. In a way, we believed—and still do—that "from him to whom much has been given, much will be required." In our naiveté we learned only very slowly that others had a significantly different reading of that biblical passage: "from him who has given much, much will be required." The more we gave to worthy causes and the more willing we showed ourselves to get involved, the louder became the demands to do more and commit more. We began to resent the ingratitude of those we had helped. We were hurt by having been singled out for public notoriety for what we had not done, while innumerable other organizations were left unscathed even though their record of social responsibility was insignificant or non-existent.

The "eureka" came for us when we put ourselves in the shoes of the social activist striving to coax resources from any source to achieve worthy ends. We imagined his job as a management problem of getting as much output per unit of input as possible. Why, from his perspective, push the stone up the hill with the recalcitrant and hard-headed objectors when you can preach the gospel to the already saved and trade on his demonstrated goodwill? It's a perfectly reasonable tactic from those optics—though possibly somewhat shortsighted. Cruel reality has a way of shortening the social activist's time horizon anyway.

The late Rev. Martin Luther King was fond of describing his activities as productive of "creative tension." The social activists have been creative and we've been tense. Rather than dissipate energy on a confrontation about questionable means to worthy ends, we decided to maintain a lower profile while continuing our commitment to good corporate citizenship. We have made a conscious decision to risk seeming to have adopted a posture of "benign neglect" rather than to expose our organization to the constant buffeting in the public forum. Once other corporations experience and understand the tactics of social activists, they too may discover a different cost/benefit calculus on chest thumping over their socially responsible behavior.

Indexes

INDEX OF CASES

INDEX OF AUTHORS

This book has been set in 9 point Primer and 9 point Helvetica, leaded 2 points. Part and chapter numbers are Helvetica Medium; part, chapter, and case titles are Helvetica. The size of the type page is 27 by 46½ picas.